SECRET CITY

A HISTORICAL MAP OF GAY WASHINGTON

WASHINGTON, DC

GEORGETOWN

Rock Creek

Dupont Circle

P STREET

W STREET

U STREET

S STREET

K STREET

H STREET

G STREET

E STREET

The White House

Union Station

CONSTITUTION AVE.

Lincoln Memorial

Washington Monument

U.S. Capitol

INDEPENDENCE AVE.

Potomac River

Jefferson Memorial

ARLINGTON

M STREET

L STREET

Anacostia River

CONNECTICUT AVE.

NEW HAMPSHIRE AVE.

RHODE ISLAND AVE.

FLORIDA AVE.

NEW YORK AVE.

MASSACHUSETTS AVE.

MARYLAND AVE.

PENNSYLVANIA AVE.

VIRGINIA AVE.

NORTH CAPITOL ST.

SOUTH CAPITOL ST.

16TH ST.

14TH ST.

23RD ST.

11TH ST.

8TH ST.

1ST ST.

0 Miles .5 1

0 Kilometers 1

© 2021 Jeffrey L. Ward

1 - **Chesapeake House**
(746 9th St. NW)

2 - **Cinema Follies**
(37 L St. SE)

3 - **Club Madre**
(2204 14th St. NW)

4 - **Congressional Cemetery**
(1801 E St. SE)

5 - **The Furies Collective**
(219 11th St. SE)

6 - **Gay Liberation Front House**
(1620 S St. NW)

7 - **Guild Press Warehouse**
(507 8th St. SE)

8 - **The Hay-Adams hotel**
(800 16th St. NW)

9 - **Iwo Jima Memorial**

10 - **Joe Alsop home**
(2720 Dumbarton St. NW)

11 - **Lafayette Chicken Hut**
(1720 H St. NW)

12 - **Lafayette Square**

13 - **Lambda Rising**
(1625 Connecticut Ave. NW)

14 - **Lost and Found**
(56 L St. SE)

15 - **Office of Strategic Services**
(Navy Hill, 23rd St.
and E St. NW)

16 - **P Street Beach**
(23rd St. and P St. NW)

17 - **The Power House**
(3255 Grace St. NW)

18 - **Whitman-Walker Clinic**
(2335 18th St. NW)

19 - **U.S. Department of State**
(2201 C St. NW)

20 - **YMCA**
(1736 G St. NW)

SECRET CITY

THE HIDDEN HISTORY OF GAY WASHINGTON

James Kirchick

HENRY HOLT AND COMPANY · NEW YORK

Henry Holt and Company
Publishers since 1866
120 Broadway
New York, New York 10271
www.henryholt.com

Library of Congress Cataloging-in-Publication Data

Names: Kirchick, James, author.
Title: Secret city : the hidden history of gay Washington / James Kirchick.
Description: First edition. | New York : Henry Holt and Company, 2022. |
   Includes bibliographical references and index.
Identifiers: LCCN 2021055007 (print) | LCCN 2021055008 (ebook) | ISBN 9781627792325
   (hardcover) | ISBN 9781627792332 (ebook)
Subjects: LCSH: Homophobia—Washington (D.C.)—History—20th century. | Heterosexism—
   Washington (D.C.)—History—20th century. | Gays—Washington (D.C.)—History—
   20th century.
Classification: LCC HQ76.45.U52 .W375 2022 (print) | LCC HQ76.45.U52 (ebook) |
   DDC 306.76/6097530904—dc23/eng/20220124
LC record available at https://lccn.loc.gov/2021055007
LC ebook record available at https://lccn.loc.gov/2021055008

Our books may be purchased in bulk for promotional, educational, or business use. Please contact
your local bookseller or the Macmillan Corporate and Premium Sales Department at (800) 221-7945,
extension 5442, or by e-mail at MacmillanSpecialMarkets@macmillan.com.

First Edition 2022

Map by Jeffrey L. Ward

Designed by Meryl Sussman Levavi

Printed in the United States of America

1 3 5 7 9 10 8 6 4 2

For my family
and
for all those who unburdened themselves of their secret,
so that I did not have to live with mine

A reprobate part of the human whole, but an important part, suspected where it does not exist, flaunting itself, insolent and unpunished, where its existence is never guessed; numbering its adherents everywhere, among the people, in the army, in the church, in the prison, on the throne; living, in short, at least to a great extent, in a playful and perilous intimacy with the men of the other race, provoking them, playing with them by speaking of its vice as of something alien to it; a game that is rendered easy by the blindness or duplicity of the others, a game that may be kept up for years until the day of the scandal, on which these lion-tamers are devoured; until then, obliged to make a secret of their lives . . .

—Marcel Proust, *Sodom and Gomorrah*

There are two histories: the official, lying history, which is taught in schools, history *ad usum Delphini*; and the secret history, in which the real causes of events are set forth—a shameful history.

—Honoré de Balzac, *Scenes from Provincial Life*

CONTENTS

Dramatis Personae   xiv

Introduction: Comrades   1

Franklin Delano Roosevelt

1: "No Comment"   13

2: "Worse Than a Murderer"   30

3: Senator X   43

4: Patriotic Homosexuals   58

5: "The Greatest National Scandal
   Since the Existence of the United States"   77

Harry Truman

6: The Concealed Enemy   95

7: "This Moral Leper"   110

8: Lavender Lists   120

9: "A Government Within a Government"   134

10: The Homintern   146

Dwight Eisenhower

11: "No More Bohlens!"   163

12: The Heterosexual Dictatorship   177

13: Pixies on the Potomac   189

14: "We Accuse . . ."   210

15: The Hunted   225

John F. Kennedy

16: First Friends   245

17: The Group of the Intrepid   263

18: "That Old Black Fairy"   278

Lyndon B. Johnson

19: A Long Way from Arp   297

20: "A Quite Serious Situation"   313

21: "Gone and Forgotten"   329

22: The Fruit Loop   342

23: Scandal in Sacramento   353

24: The Thrill of Treason   369

Richard Nixon

25: "Destroy Your Opponent"   381

26: Fags   395

27: "We Are Impatient"   411

28: The City of Conversation   422

Gerald Ford

29: The Ultimate Democracy   441

30: "Too Good an Opportunity"   449

Jimmy Carter

31: Out of the Closets, into the White House   459

32: Code Breakers   476

Ronald Reagan

33: "The Homosexual Thing"   491

34: The Manchurian Candidate   502

35: An Enclosed and Enchanted Garden   518

36: Sodom-on-the-Potomac   536

37: "I Don't Have It. Do You?"   553

38: "Them" Is "Us"   567

39: "Our Sebastian"   583

40: Mr. Green   594

41: The Wonderful, the Creative, and the Brave   607

George H. W. Bush

42: Naming Names   625

Bill Clinton

43: A Profoundly Important Strength   643

Conclusion: The Gay Century   651

Acknowledgments   655

Photography Credits   662

Sources   664

Notes   683

Index   803

About the Author   827

DRAMATIS PERSONAE

Franklin Delano Roosevelt

Gustave Beekman: Brooklyn brothel owner

William Christian Bullitt Jr.: Ambassador to the Soviet Union (1933–36) and France (1936–40)

Juan Francisco de Cárdenas: Spanish ambassador to the United States

William "Wild Bill" Donovan: Director, Office of Strategic Services (OSS)

Donald Downes: OSS operative

Allen Dulles: Head of OSS Bern office; director, Central Intelligence Agency (1953–61)

Morris Ernst: General counsel, American Civil Liberties Union and the *New York Post*

Lorena "Hick" Hickok: Reporter, Associated Press

J. Edgar Hoover: Director, Federal Bureau of Investigation

Cordell Hull: Secretary of state

Odessa Madre: "Female Al Capone" of Washington, DC

Eleanor Josephine Medill "Cissy" Patterson: Publisher, *Washington Times-Herald*

Carmel Offie: Aide to Ambassador William C. Bullitt; CIA officer

Drew Pearson: Syndicated columnist, Washington Merry-Go-Round

Baron Wolfgang Gans zu Putlitz: Anti-Nazi German diplomat and spy

Dorothy Schiff: Publisher, *New York Post*

Clyde Tolson: Associate director, FBI

David Walsh: Senator (D-MA)

Sumner Welles: Undersecretary of state

Harry Truman

Joe Alsop: Syndicated columnist, Matter of Fact

James Jesus Angleton: Chief of the office of special operations, CIA

Roy Blick: Director of the Morals division, Metropolitan Police Department

A. Marvin Braverman: Lawyer and "walker" of Margaret Truman

Guy Burgess: British diplomat and Soviet spy

Whittaker Chambers: Former Soviet spy; senior editor, *Time*

Francis Flanagan: Chief counsel, Senate Permanent Subcommittee on Investigations

Alger Hiss: State Department official

Clyde Hoey: Senator (D-NC)

Joe McCarthy: Senator (R-WI)

Kenneth Wherry: Senate minority leader (R-NE)

Dwight Eisenhower

Charles "Chip" Bohlen: Ambassador to the Soviet Union

Roy Cohn: Chief counsel, Senate Permanent Subcommittee on Investigations

Robert Cutler: Assistant to the president for national security affairs

John Foster Dulles: Secretary of state

Robert Gray: Appointments secretary; secretary of the cabinet

Lester Hunt: Senator (D-WY)

Franklin Kameny: President, Mattachine Society of Washington, DC

William Martin: Cryptologist, National Security Agency

R. W. Scott McLeod: Assistant secretary of state for security and consular affairs

Bernon Mitchell: Cryptologist, National Security Agency

John C. Montgomery: Finnish desk chief, State Department

Margaret Scattergood: Researcher, American Federation of Labor

G. David Schine: Consultant, Senate Permanent Subcommittee on Investigations

Florence Thorne: Director of research, American Federation of Labor

Arthur Vandenberg Jr.: Appointments secretary-designate to the president

John F. Kennedy

Kirk LeMoyne "Lem" Billings: Best friend of President Kennedy

Ben Bradlee: *Newsweek* bureau chief (1957–65); *Washington Post* executive editor (1968–91)

Eva Freund: Early member of the Mattachine Society of Washington, DC

John Nichols Sr.: Special agent, Federal Bureau of Investigation; father of Jack Nichols

John "Jack" Nichols Jr.: Cofounder, Mattachine Society of Washington, DC

Bayard Rustin: Chief organizer of the 1963 March on Washington for Jobs and Freedom

Gore Vidal: Author and playwright

Lilli Vincenz: First lesbian member of the Mattachine Society of Washington, DC

William Walton: Chairman, U.S. Commission of Fine Arts

William Wieland: Director, Office of Middle American Affairs, State Department

Herman Lynn Womack: Publisher, Guild Press

Lyndon B. Johnson

Katharine Graham: Publisher, *Washington Post*

Walter Jenkins: Special assistant to the president

Bill Moyers: Special assistant to the president

Robert Waldron: Legislative assistant to Congressman Homer Thornberry and, later, Representative J. J. Jake Pickle

Richard Nixon

Dwight Chapin: Deputy assistant to the president

Murray Chotiner: Nixon political strategist

John Ehrlichman: White House counsel

H. R. "Bob" Haldeman: White House chief of staff

Steve Martindale: Lawyer and socialite

Robert "Robbie" Merritt: FBI informant

Ray Price: Special assistant to the president and chief speechwriter

Nancy Tucker: Cofounding editor, *Gay Blade*

Gerald Ford

Oliver Sipple: Former marine

Jimmy Carter

Robert Bauman: Congressman (R-MD)

Lou Chibbaro Jr.: Senior reporter, *Washington Blade*

Margaret "Midge" Costanza: Special assistant to the president for public liaison

Jon Hinson: Congressman (R-MS)

Bobby Ray Inman: Director, National Security Agency

Jean O'Leary: Co-executive director, National Gay Task Force

Jamie Shoemaker: Cryptologist, National Security Agency

Ronald Reagan

Bill Best: California GOP activist and local television host

Lynden "Lynn" Francis Bouchey: President, Council for Inter-American Security

Dr. Cesar Caceres: Personal physician of Terry Dolan and Congressman Stewart B. McKinney

Carl "Spitz" Channell: President, National Endowment for the Preservation of Liberty (NEPL)

John Terrence "Terry" Dolan: Cofounder and chairman, National Conservative Political Action Committee (NCPAC)

Tony Dolan: Special assistant to the president and chief speechwriter

John Ford: Deputy assistant secretary for agriculture

Peter Hannaford: Advisor to former governor Ronald Reagan

Richard Kind: Proprietor, Friendly Models escort agency

Dr. Frank Lilly: Member, Commission on the HIV Epidemic

Robert Livingston: Congressman (R-LA)

Paul N. "Pete" McCloskey: Congressman (R-CA)

Stewart B. McKinney: Congressman (R-CT)

Edwin Meese: Counselor to the president (1981–85); attorney general (1985–88)

Franklyn "Lyn" Nofziger: Press secretary to Governor Reagan; assistant to the president for political affairs

Oliver North: Deputy director for political-military affairs, National Security Council

Martin Price: Publisher, president, and executive editor, *Deep Backgrounder*

Gerry Studds: Congressman (D-MA)

Leroy Williams: Congressional page

George H. W. Bush

Craig J. Spence: Lobbyist

Pete Williams: Assistant secretary of defense for public affairs

Bill Clinton

Roberta Achtenberg: Assistant secretary of housing and urban development

Bob Hattoy: Associate director, White House Office of Personnel Management

David Mixner: Friend of Bill Clinton; gay activist

SECRET CITY

COMRADES

Since its establishment by an act of Congress in 1790, Washington, DC, has attracted men and women from every segment of American society. Federalists and Anti-Federalists, Democrats and Republicans, northerners and southerners, easterners and westerners, immigrants and natives, citizens and slaves—all have come to this marble metropolis to join in the perpetual endeavor to form a more perfect union. Included among their number, though scarcely recognized then or now, has been another group of Americans, one whose obscurity was the consequence of their being forced to hide.

What linked them was a sin so vile as to be virtually unspeakable. The early Christian Church condemned these descendants of the biblical Sodom and Gomorrah as those who "exchanged natural relations for unnatural." Upon discovering his fellow passengers engaging in "dishonorable passions" aboard the ship *Talbot* sailing from London to New England in 1629, Rev. Francis Higginson expressed revulsion for a "wickedness not to bee named." In 1837, the state of North Carolina approved a law, copied almost directly from a statute adopted during the reign of King Henry VIII, mandating that anyone who performed "the abominable and detestable crime against nature, not to be named among Christians, with either mankind or beast, shall be adjudged guilty of a felony, and shall suffer death without the benefit of clergy." While the threat of capital punishment was lifted in 1869, the taboo against the unsayable "abomination" remained. In 1927, the New York State Legislature passed a theatrical "padlock bill" prohibiting any production "depicting or dealing with, the subject of sex degeneracy, or sex perversion," and on the West Coast, the Motion Picture Producers and Distributors of America released a list of guidelines banning depictions of profanity, drug trafficking, white slavery, "ridicule of the clergy," miscegenation, and "any inference of sex perversion" onscreen.

Sodomites, perverts, inverts, deviants, degenerates, queers, fairies, fruits, dykes, faggots—gay men and lesbians—these Americans were morally damned, medically pathologized, their very being legally proscribed.* Consequently, the manifestations of their likeness, and the ways they signaled it to one another, had to be disguised, insinuated, and covert. The precise color of an article of clothing, the holding of another's gaze from across a crowded room, a knowing turn of phrase, an esoteric cultural reference— such were the means by which these men and women communicated the crime of their common existence, and over time, they would develop their own vernacular, rituals, gathering places, and codes of behavior. As Washington grew both in size and significance, they would ineluctably come to populate a secret city, one hidden within the official, open one.

At first, few of those inhabiting this clandestine society understood themselves as members of a community, in the way constituents of more formal polities feel solidarity with others who speak the same language, worship the same god, or live on the same patch of land. For what united these disparate individuals, what connected them to one another as well as to generations past and future, was not a common tongue, religion, or nationality, but something that society condemned, such that what they shared was a status as pariahs. An invisible thread connecting their experiences, one of fear and fixation about same-sex desire, therefore runs through our nation's history.

The origins of this theme can be traced at least as far back as the country's War of Independence. Baron Friedrich Wilhelm Ludolf Gerhard Augustin

---

* A few words about words: the terms I employ in this book to describe gay men and lesbians will roughly correspond with those that prevailed at the time of the events I recount. During the 1940s and '50s, the media, government, medical establishment, and gay people themselves tended to use *homosexual* as a neutral epithet for gay men and lesbians, though the label often denoted gay males exclusively. By the middle of the 1960s, and especially after the Stonewall uprising of 1969, gay men and lesbians began to adopt *gay* as a self-affirming alternative to *homosexual*, which acquired a clinical connotation and fell into disfavor. For brevity's sake, *gays* and *gay people* will sometimes be used interchangeably with *gay men and lesbians*. *Queer*, which most gay (and straight) people considered pejorative during the period covered by this book, will appear in these pages only as such.

von Steuben was a veteran of the Seven Years' War and of the exclusively male court of King Frederick the Great of Prussia when Founding Father Benjamin Franklin recruited him to the American revolutionary cause in 1778. Fleeing charges that he had "taken familiarities" with young men, von Steuben arrived at Valley Forge just sixteen days after a court-martial overseen by Gen. George Washington drummed Lt. Gen. Gotthold Frederick Enslin out of the Continental Army for the same crime. Pierre L'Enfant, the French-born architect whom Washington entrusted with designing the new nation's capital, was a lifelong bachelor described as "sensitive in style and dress" and as having an "artistic and fragile temperament." Though the identity connoted by these euphemisms would not be classified as a social category until the late nineteenth century, the association of sexual and gender nonconformity with moral degeneracy is a political tactic as old as the republic itself. Before Thomas Jefferson and John Adams became great friends and political allies, a newspaper publisher supporting the former accused the latter of possessing a "hideous hermaphroditical character, which has neither the force and firmness of a man, nor the gentleness and sensibility of a woman."

Claims of homosexuality have been made upon one of our worst and one of our greatest presidents. The unmarried James Buchanan spent so much time with a fellow bachelor, Alabama senator William Rufus King, that Buchanan's critics sneered that the two must be lovers. (An academic study published in 2019 argues that they were no more than "bosom friends.") The four years that Buchanan's successor, Abraham Lincoln, spent as a young lawyer sharing a bed with another man, Joshua Speed, the passionate letters they exchanged, and the close relationship Lincoln formed with his presidential bodyguard have led some to conclude that the man whose liberation of others earned him renown as "the Great Emancipator" repressed his true self.

Lincoln might have been Walt Whitman's "captain," but Peter Doyle was his love. The self-proclaimed "bard of Democracy" was well into his fifties when he met the twenty-one-year-old horsecar conductor on the Union Line train running along Pennsylvania Avenue one wintry night in 1865. "We were familiar at once—I put my hand on his knee—we understood," Doyle recalled of their initial encounter. In a crowded city whose inhabitants frequently shared rooms and often beds, the two men would seek intimacy at a hotel on Washington Avenue after the conclusion of Doyle's shift.

Rose Cleveland, sister of President Grover Cleveland, performed the functions of first lady until her bachelor brother married two years into his administration. It was not her only unconventional relationship. "I cannot find the words to talk about it," Cleveland wrote to divorcée Evangeline Simpson Whipple of the passionate feelings she felt for her, in a disclosure as euphoric as it was apprehensive. "The right word will not be spoken." When Whipple married another man, Cleveland was heartbroken, declaring, "I will give up all to you if you will try once more to be satisfied with me. Could you not take six months for that experiment? We would go away from everyone." Following the death of Whipple's second husband, the two women reconnected and rest side by side in an Italian cemetery.

For strapping young lads passing through Progressive Era Washington, DC, the mansion at 2000 G Street shared by Archibald "Archie" Butt, President William Howard Taft's military aide, and Francis Millet, a founding member of the U.S. Commission of Fine Arts who helped design the National Mall, was a welcoming retreat. "Did you know that the kilt is worn without any drawers?" Butt mischeviously wondered in a letter to a friend, marveling at one Scottish lodger's sartorial habits, or lack thereof. In 1912, Butt and Millet sailed on the RMS *Titanic*, going down together with the doomed ship. The reason Butt remained a bachelor, a weeping President Taft explained, was "because of that love for" his mother. In recognition of Butt and Millet being the only U.S. government officials to perish in the maritime disaster, Congress appropriated funds for the construction of a monument in their honor. For over a century, the Butt–Millet Memorial Fountain in President's Park, south of the White House, has consecrated a relationship whose true nature lies with its dedicatees in a watery grave.

A member of President Warren Harding's "Ohio Gang," Jesse "Jess" Smith was a supporting player in Teapot Dome, a bribery scandal whose name was a byword for Washington corruption until Watergate surpassed it fifty years later. Smith lived in a house on K Street with his boss, Attorney General Harry Daugherty, described by one chronicler of the era as having had a "curious dependence" upon the significantly younger Smith, who served Daugherty as "a combination of son, secretary, valet, nurse and intimate friend." It was "noised about" that the men were a couple, but in accordance with the conventions of the day, the press never broached the subject. A "snappy dresser" who "showed no great interest in the girls," Smith often wore a colored handkerchief and matching tie, a coded arrangement used by gay men in the 1920s to signal their shared identity. Aristocratic women greatly valued Smith's perspective "on the cut of a skirt or the choice of a shade," most prominently First Lady Florence Harding, whom Smith regularly accompanied to social occasions. Smith was a "walker" *avant la lettre*: a man (usually, and discreetly, homosexual) who escorted the wives of powerful and busy men to parties. In what Henry James, himself a confirmed bachelor, dubbed "the city of conversation," walkers fulfilled a vital role.

An insomniac, Smith took regular evening constitutionals around the neighborhood where he and Daugherty lived, just blocks from the White House. If he ever sought company on these nocturnal rounds, he need not have traveled far. At least since the late nineteenth century, men seeking amorous connections with other men did so in Lafayette Square, the seven-acre wooded park directly north of the president's home. "Under the very shadow of the White House," Washington's chief of police reported with astonishment in 1892, officers had arrested eighteen men "*in flagrante delicto*." Soon thereafter, the U.S. Army chief of engineers, responsible for the upkeep of federally owned grounds, installed lights around the Washington Monument and other public places "in the interest of morality." The diaries of Jeb Alexander, pseudonym of a gay man who lived in Washington during the first half of the twentieth century, provide rich detail about early gay life in the nation's capital. One August evening in 1920, Alexander happened upon two "handsome, clean-looking chaps, refined and cultured," seated near a bronze statue of Baron von Steuben, beneath whose admiring eyes they "furtively engaged" in a sensual embrace "under cover of the dimness."

For those who preferred a degree of privacy the bushes and trees could not afford, the Riggs Turkish baths, located in the basement of the Belasco Theatre abutting the Square, offered alluring possibilities. Featuring a 22,000-gallon pool and sleeping cabins available to rent for the night, the bathhouse was reputed to be "the largest and best equipped south of New York." In 1911, "complaints from stars, stage managers, and players" at the Belasco, "owing to the excessive heat on the stage" from the baths underneath, forced Riggs to move around the corner, into a building opposite the Treasury Department. Alas, another type of heat sparked more serious trouble. In March 1945, responding to reports of what the *Washington Post* described as "disorderly conduct," officers from the Metropolitan Police

Department's Morals division, or vice squad, raided the baths and arrested some fifty patrons. Men of different nationalities, professions, political commitments, and social standing, they had one thing in common: citizenship in the secret city.

* * *

A DOUBLE LIFE WAS POSSIBLE FOR THESE SECRET CITIZENS, provided they exercised a requisite level of vigilance and discretion. Class, race, and sex heavily determined the degree of freedom they could enjoy—wealth, white skin, and manhood being important markers of privilege in a world where everyone was otherwise considered "degenerate." As the notion of a homosexual person, as opposed to homosexual "acts," was not widely understood until the late nineteenth century, it was unthinkable that these people might constitute a distinct identity group with its own political interests. And so, while the mainstream view held homosexuality to be sick and immoral, during the first four decades of the twentieth century, it was not considered a threat to American society, much less Western civilization.

This perception started to change with the onset of the Second World War, when the federal government began to shoulder the responsibilities of a global superpower. A culture of secrecy descended over the nation's capital, and with it, an apprehension concerning the guardians of the nation's secrets. About nobody was this apprehension greater than those who possessed, within themselves, the most damning secret of all. As America instituted a vast bureaucracy for managing sensitive information, a new priority verging on an obsession, "national security," imbued homosexuality with existential dangers. America's global preeminence transformed what had been a private vice into a public obsession as homosexuality assumed an ideological cast and treacherous, world-historical significance. In the hands of journalists and politicians, liberals and conservatives, Democrats and Republicans, presidents and Pullman car porters, the accusation of what one prominent Washingtonian would call "an offense too loathsome to mention" became the deadliest weapon in the vast arsenal of American political skullduggery.

From the Second World War until the end of the Cold War that followed, the specter of homosexuality haunted Washington. Nothing posed a more potent threat to a political career, or exerted a more fearsome grip on the nation's collective psyche, than the love expressed between people of the same sex. When America fought fascism, political and cultural leaders associated it with the nation's Nazi enemies. During the Cold War, voices from across the political spectrum linked it with communism. One of the earliest executive orders signed by President Dwight Eisenhower, a man who played a central role in the struggle against both totalitarian ideologies, prohibited those guilty of "sexual perversion" from holding any job in the federal government. For most of the twentieth century, the most terrible secret one could possibly possess—more terrible, even at the height of the Cold War, than being a Communist—was being gay.

Secret City is about the wide-ranging influence of homosexuality on the nation's capital, on the people who dwelled within it, and on the weighty matters of state they conducted. It was an influence attributable to two factors: secrecy and universality. "Secrecy is a form of power which can be used inside government," New York senator Daniel Patrick Moynihan observed in a landmark 1997 congressional study. In America's other major metropolises, New York and Los Angeles, wealth and celebrity, respectively, determine one's standing. Power is the drug to which Washingtonians have always been addicted, and it is access to secrets that establishes and augments that power. As for universality, the uniqueness of homosexuality as a trait appearing among members of every social group enhanced its spellbinding effect over the capital and the nation. Recalling the controversy over the presence of homosexuals in the federal workforce that consumed Washington in the early 1950s, Stephen Spingarn, an aide to President Harry Truman, observed that they

> live in a milieu of their own, a sort of separate world of their own which crosses all sorts of caste and cultural lines, a chauffeur and a Cabinet officer might have a homosexual affair, that sort of thing. In their own world there are no caste lines, and this is useful in espionage organizations because if you happened to know that an important Government official had that weakness, you could infiltrate a handsome young chauffeur . . .

Everywhere and nowhere, gay men and lesbians were hiding in plain sight. "The love that dare not speak its name" paradoxically assumed an awesome explanatory power as the motive force in history behind a dizzying array of complex events and phenomena. The decline and fall of ancient Rome and Greece, the collapse of the Hapsburg Empire, the failure of the Treaty of Versailles, the "loss" of China, the Cuban Revolution, the assassination of John F. Kennedy, the leak of the Pentagon Papers, the Iran-Contra scandal—these were just some of the things that leading Washingtonians attributed to the hidden machinations of this mysterious deviancy.

The secret city was as much a collection of intangible concepts (an all-pervasive sense of suspicion, webs of illusory connections, a catalogue of prejudices) as it was a topography of physical locations (sexual cruising grounds, darkened bars, sites of protest). To protect themselves within Washington's institutional order, gay men and lesbians were forced to inhabit a combination of the two, a metaphorical space within which their secrets might be safe. Preventing one's "closet" from being opened was, for many, a question of life and death. The fear of homosexuality, or even the mere accusation of it, destroyed careers, ended lives, and induced otherwise decent people to betray colleagues and friends. Yet as time wore on, a group of intrepid Washingtonians would emerge from their closets and transform the nation's capital from a city of witch hunts and recriminations into the front line of a worldwide revolution in consciousness.

The outsized role that homosexuality once occupied in the American imagination makes it a compelling framework through which to undertake a historical reassessment of Washington politics and society during the twentieth century, when a fixation with state secrecy coincided with an increase in visibility for gay men and lesbians. As is so often the case with the subject of historical homosexuality, however, much of the source material needed to tell this story is ambiguous, remains hidden, or has been destroyed. In some cases, it is gay people themselves who are responsible for this erasure, concealing their sexual orientation while they were alive and eliminating any trace of it before their deaths. In others, relatives and historians have done the obscuring. Deciphering the many ways in which homosexuality impacted Washington forced me to search in places other scholars either chose not to look or did not know existed, and to think in ways it may never have occurred to them to think. Most of all, it required that I look carefully, reading between the lines in diaries, letters, memoirs, radio and television reports, congressional hearing transcripts, depositions, and print media accounts. Writing this book often felt like holding up a mirror—one equipped with a special power to reveal once-invisible people, stories, and relationships—to the city I call home and about which I thought I knew so much.

My interest in this subject was piqued by my living in Washington, where every day I walk past the places where the events recounted in these pages occurred, and by my own identity as a gay man. How did people like me, interested in politics and public policy, survive at a time when a core aspect of their very being was considered a mortal danger to the country? What sort of choices and sacrifices did they confront? Whom could they trust? Surveying the vast literature of American political history, it became apparent how often gay people and issues have been consigned to footnotes—that is, when not expunged from the historical record altogether. Because homosexuality was (and, in some quarters, lamentably remains) a subject considered indecent if not immoral, many of the historians and institutions that have shaped our understanding of the American past have neglected to explore whole swaths of it. Due in large part to this stigma, the study of gay people and topics in history has largely been taken up by gay people themselves. Homosexuality not being a heritable trait, however, the preservation of this history lacks the natural means of continuity available to other minority groups. Stories of gay struggle and accomplishment are not passed down over dinner tables or through family heirlooms; rarely are they taught in schools. This knowledge deficit harms not only gay people, deprived of a common past and a way of understanding their place in the world, but all Americans, whose awareness of their country's history is made poorer by the large parts left unexplored.

By documenting the evolution of American politics and government secrecy through the lives of people compelled to keep a core part of themselves hidden, I hope to offer a new interpretation of our country's past. The tendency to view "gay history" as a subject separate and distinct from American history has always struck me as erroneous and constrictive. Since conceiving the idea for Secret City over a decade ago, my overriding ambition has been to integrate these two histories, to weave the invisible and visible threads together into a coherent whole, to put the central events, influential ideas, and prominent figures of an era into greater context by opening the many little (and several not-so-little) closet doors behind which so much has been secreted away. Though their stories may sometimes be hard to find, gay people have always been here, shaping the country at every level, from the lowliest of clerks to the loftiest of White House aides. In illuminating the lives of these men and women, it is my hope that this book will help them attain the place they have long been denied yet belatedly deserve in the history of the great experiment that is America.

FRANKLIN DELANO ROOSEVELT

*I HEAR it was charged against me that I sought to
    destroy institutions;*
But really I am neither for nor against institutions,
*(What indeed have I in common with them—or what
    with the destruction of them?)*
*Only I will establish in the Mannahatta, and in every
    city of these States, inland and seaboard,*
*And in the fields and woods, and above every keel
    little or large that dents the water,*
*Without edifices, or rules, or trustees, or any
    argument,*
The institution of the dear love of comrades.

—Walt Whitman, "I Hear It Was Charged Against Me"

1

"NO COMMENT"

Sumner Welles had a secret.

It was a secret that, in 1940, the forty-seven-year-old undersecretary of state had in common with thousands of other men and women across Washington, DC, a swampy southern town not yet capital of the free world—a secret that bound him to earlier generations and linked him with those not yet born. Once discovered, it was a secret that could lead to societal banishment, institutionalization, professional disrepute, and criminal prosecution. In certain parts of the country, at a certain hour of the night, this secret might elicit horrific violence or even murder. And in Welles's case, it was a secret that would set off a perilous chain of events leading to the destruction of his career, the wrecking of his marriage, and the hastening of his death, and that would, for more than half a century, leave myriad innocent victims in its wake.

By all external indicators, however, Welles had achieved nearly everything that a man of his status and vocation could have wished for. The progeny of New England blue bloods, Welles was named for his great-uncle, the abolitionist senator Charles Sumner, and he enjoyed wealth, power, and renown. As a boy of twelve, he carried the bridal train of his Groton roommate's sister, Eleanor Roosevelt, at the wedding to her cousin Franklin.

Following the same academic path as the future president he would eventually serve, Welles enrolled at Harvard, where he studied Spanish culture and history and graduated after three years. His rapid ascent up the gilded ladder of American diplomacy was guaranteed the day he scored higher than any other applicant on the Foreign Service exam, and his appointment as head of the State Department's Latin American Affairs division at the age of twenty-eight made him the youngest person ever selected to lead a regional bureau.

In 1925, Welles left his first wife for Mathilde Townsend, heiress to a railroad and coal fortune and a ravishing beauty "as well known in Paris, Philadelphia and Newport" as she was in the nation's capital. Townsend had herself been married to Sen. Peter Gerry of Rhode Island, a friend of President Calvin Coolidge. Though this was an era when the private affairs of wealthy and powerful men did not generally intrude upon their public careers, to cuckold a U.S. senator, and a close associate of the president's, no less, crossed a line. It was widely rumored that Coolidge personally ordered Welles's dismissal from the State Department as revenge.

Welles and Townsend lived luxuriantly in a French Renaissance–style mansion at the corner of Massachusetts and Florida Avenues, where they were waited upon by fifteen servants. When his old family friend Franklin Delano Roosevelt won the presidency in 1932, Welles was assured a senior State Department job, and after FDR appointed him ambassador to Cuba the following year, the *New York Times* heralded Welles as "the most-talked-of diplomat in the service of the United States." Elevated to undersecretary in 1937, he helped craft the administration's Good Neighbor policy, which sought to redress the legacy of American imperialism in the Western Hemisphere through assurances of military neutrality and reciprocal trade agreements, and authored the eponymous Welles Declaration pledging nonrecognition of the Soviet Union's brutal occupation of the three Baltic states.

FDR would have certainly chosen Welles to be secretary of state had he not been compelled to appoint the lethargic and sickly Tennessee senator Cordell Hull to placate the southern wing of his New Deal coalition. A curmudgeon with false teeth, Hull was an odd fit for the State Department, then the bastion of worldly, well-cultivated men with sophistication and class—men, in other words, like Welles, who "never walked from the State Department to the Metropolitan Club without his Malacca cane, and [who] in the summer wore an impeccable Panama" hat, as one of his administration colleagues fondly recalled. FDR's practice of dispatching personal envoys like Welles to carry out important diplomatic missions rankled Hull, who may have been genetically prediposed to holding a grudge. According to legend, Hull's father, returning home from the Civil War battlefront, got into a fight with a man who threw him into a river. Three decades later, Hull Sr. tracked the scoundrel all the way down to Alabama and shot him on his front porch.

Welles regularly found himself in the position of "acting" secretary due to the recurrent illness of his nominal superior, who frequently skipped cabinet meetings and, at those he did attend, often fell asleep. If Welles was present in Hull's stead, and the president asked him a question, "the reply would be swift, precise, and comprehensive," wrote journalist John Gunther. "FDR must have wished at least ten thousand times that Welles, not Hull, was the actual Secretary."

While FDR could always depend on him for candid assessments of the geopolitical situation, Welles was the soul of discretion. "Just to look at him can tell that the world would dissolve into its component parts if only a portion of the weighty state secrets that he carries about were divulged," Interior Secretary Harold Ickes recalled. Future secretary of state Dean Acheson, who was one year behind Welles at Groton and who worked under him in the State Department, described Welles as "not an easy man to know," citing a "manner formal to the point of stiffness." British prime minister Winston Churchill credited Welles with coining a phrase since uttered perhaps more than any other in Washington: "No comment."

Ironically, it was a secret that would be Welles's undoing.

On September 17, 1940, standing in for his titular boss, Welles accompanied the president, most of the cabinet, and some one hundred members of Congress at the funeral of former Speaker of the House William Bankhead in Jasper, Alabama. Aboard the presidential train back to Washington that night, Welles joined Vice President Henry Wallace and several other administration officials in the dining car, where he began to drink heavily. The men eventually retired to their private cabins. What happened next would assume near-mythic proportions.

At around 5 a.m., Welles pressed a buzzer, alerting the porters in the adjoining carriage. Alexander Dickson, a twenty-nine-year veteran of the Pullman Company, who had staffed the presidential train since the Harding administration, answered the call. Like every other porter, Dickson was African American.

"Come in, porter," Welles ordered. "Close and lock the door."

Dickson hesitated.

"It will be alright," Welles insisted.

Moments later, Dickson fled in distress. "You have a cocksucker up there in Compartment E," he told his colleague Samuel Mitchell. "He wanted to blow my whistle."

Welles rang the buzzer again. This time Mitchell answered. Welles, shirtless and in his pajama pants, instructed Mitchell to close the door and asked if he wanted to make twenty dollars.

"I don't quite understand what you mean," Mitchell replied.

Welles kept repeating "twenty dollars."

"No, sir, you have the wrong man," Mitchell stated firmly, leaving Welles alone.

For two hours, Welles persisted in his propositions. At one point, a porter named John Stone volunteered to answer Welles's call, telling his colleagues that he "knew how to handle that type of man." After Stone entered his compartment, Welles slipped behind him, loosened his bowtie, unbuttoned his coat, and instructed Stone to take off the rest of his clothes and get on the bed.

"You know what you are in here for, don't you?" Welles asked, his speech slurred by drink.

"To bring you coffee?" Stone answered.

Welles unfurled a roll of dollar bills. "I will give you $20, $50, or even $100; money makes no difference to me." Stone absconded.

Ten days after his return from Alabama, Welles traveled alone by train to Cleveland for a speaking engagement, again drunkenly propositioning a series of porters. "You turned down $50 to suck a nice, clean dick?" one of the men facetiously asked a colleague. The porter replied that he wouldn't accept a sum as great as $5,000 to perform such an act as "you have to work three years to become a carpenter or a bricklayer but it takes only one suck to make a cocksucker."

Word of Welles's escapades wormed its way back to Washington, consumed by debate over how the country should respond, if at all, to the growing fascist menace in Europe. Senators Burton K. Wheeler of Montana and Henrik Shipstead of Minnesota, strong opponents of FDR's policies to supply military aid to the beleaguered British, got wind of the charges and tried to persuade *Washington Times-Herald* publisher Eleanor Josephine Medill "Cissy" Patterson to expose him. One of Washington's premier "Cave Dwellers," as the coterie of fabulously wealthy families native to the city was known, Patterson lived in a thirty-room marble mansion on Dupont Circle. A vociferous opponent of the New Deal, she regularly published vitriolic front-page editorials excoriating the Roosevelt administration. Patterson felt a deep, personal loathing for the president, and the feeling was fully reciprocated. Regardless, the story about the undersecretary and the African American train porters was simply too prurient to print. The sexual habits of influential men, even morally degenerate ones whose peccadilloes transgressed the color barrier, were off-limits.

Another factor Welles had going in his favor was his assiduous cultivation of journalists—one scribe in particular. Drew Pearson began writing his nationally syndicated column, the Washington Merry-Go-Round, in 1932 for his former mother-in-law Cissy Patterson's paper. Working on a grueling daily deadline, the mustachioed and fedora-sporting Pearson provided his millions of readers across the country with a regular supply of juicy exclusives about the wheeling and dealing in the nation's capital. Pearson's prim and proper Quaker demeanor belied a professional ruthlessness, and the title of his column, evoking innocent memories of childhood frolic, disguised a transactional endeavor that rewarded Pearson's allies and punished his enemies. As a source, Welles qualified as an ally, which by extension made Hull an enemy. Thanks to information supplied by Welles, the secretary of state was a frequent target of the Washington Merry-Go-Round—such as the time Pearson reported that Hull and his "croquet clique" (named for the group of State Department "career boys" who played the lawn game every night) nearly pushed through a one-hundred-million-dollar loan to Spanish dictator Francisco Franco only to be stymied at the last minute when Welles protested directly to FDR. Hull learned to work the media as well, and when negative stories appeared in the papers about Welles, it did not require much intuition for the undersecretary to trace them back to his aggrieved boss.

There was another diplomat whom Welles suspected of trying to undermine him in the press, however, one whose privileged upbringing, aristocratic bearing, and, quite possibly, secret life closely resembled his own.

* * *

WILLIAM CHRISTIAN BULLITT WAS DESTINED TO RIVAL SUMNER WELLES. The scion of a prominent Philadelphia family, Bullitt was the grandson of one of America's ten wealthiest men and distantly related to George Washington, Patrick Henry, and Pocahontas. Voted "Most Brilliant" member of the Yale class of 1912, Bullitt became Washington bureau chief for the Philadelphia *Public Ledger*, where he developed such a talent for extracting information that rival reporters hired a private detective to tail him around the city. Bullitt's work as a roving European correspondent in the early years of World War I caught the eye of President Woodrow Wilson's State Department, which recruited him as an expert on the Central Powers and Russia's revolutionary movements.

Bullitt worked three doors down the hall from Assistant Secretary of the Navy Franklin Delano Roosevelt in the grand, French Second Empire–style building located directly next to the White House that was then home to the Departments of State, War, and the Navy. After the signing of the Armistice, Bullitt accompanied President Wilson to the Paris Peace Conference, the first international summit where modern tools of espionage, such as electronic bugging, were used. There, the twenty-seven-year-old novice diplomat headed the American delegation's Division of Current Intelligence Summaries, in which capacity he compiled a daily brief on European political developments and began to acquire a lifelong obsession with secrecy.

In March 1919, Wilson sent Bullitt on a clandestine mission to Moscow, by then under Bolshevik rule, to negotiate the removal of Allied troops deployed to Russia during its civil war. Traveling with the journalist Lincoln Steffens, Bullitt wrangled an audience with Soviet foreign minister Georgy Chicherin and Chief Commissar Vladimir Lenin, who praised the envoy as "a young man of great heart, integrity and courage." The admiration was mutual. Repeatedly declaring to Steffens, "We have seen the future, and it works!" (a quotation Steffens was to appropriate and popularize), Bullitt returned to Paris with a proposal from the Bolsheviks and admiration for their achievements. Allied leaders rejected as too lenient the peace terms Bullitt had negotiated, however, leading him to resign and angrily declare that he would go to the Riviera, "lie in the sand and watch the world go to hell." Bullitt felt especially bitter toward Wilson, who had sent him to Moscow only to sideline him afterward. He exacted revenge by testifying before the U.S. Senate against Wilson's signal foreign policy accomplishment, the Treaty of Versailles, delivering a coruscating speech that was widely credited with persuading the body to reject the compact. Breaking so publicly with Wilson put Bullitt on the outs with the Democratic Party foreign policy elite, and his diplomatic career appeared to be finished. For his public turn against the president he had once served, he was denounced as a "tattler and violator of confidence."

In 1923, Bullitt returned to Paris, where he joined the burgeoning community of American expatriates. He met and eventually married one of its brightest stars, the radical journalist Louise Bryant, widow of the Communist activist and writer John Reed. Bullitt revered Reed, author of the classic firsthand chronicle of the Russian Revolution, *Ten Days That Shook the World*. Returning to his literary roots, Bullitt published a roman à clef of Philadelphia manners and high society, *It's Not Done*, which sold more than one hundred fifty thousand copies. (*The Great Gatsby*, published the previous year, sold some twenty thousand.) He also wrote a play castigating his former boss, *The Tragedy of Woodrow Wilson*, which was never produced. When Bullitt's relationship with Bryant came under strain (allegedly due to impotence), he contacted a neurologist he had met in Vienna named Sigmund Freud. Bullitt developed such a close relationship with Freud that he was one of only three people whom the founder of psychoanalysis permitted to address him by his given name rather than the formal "Herr Doktor."

Based upon extensive correspondence between the two men, one of Bullitt's biographers speculates that the course of therapy Bullitt underwent with Freud may have centered on his sublimation of homoerotic desire for Reed, which manifested itself in his marriage to Reed's widow. Bullitt was tormented by homosexuality in other ways. When he discovered that Bryant was having an affair with the English painter and sculptor Gwen Le Gallienne, he sued for divorce and requested full custody of their daughter, so that she would no longer be exposed to Bryant's "perversity." At the divorce proceedings in Philadelphia, heard before Bullitt's friend, Judge Francis Biddle, Bullitt described with horror the time Bryant took him to a "party of homosexuals"; he insisted they leave "at once." Bullitt would express his revulsion for homosexuality more enduringly in a book he coauthored with Freud. The psychoanalyst and his patient had bonded unexpectedly over their mutual disdain for Woodrow Wilson, whom Freud blamed for the breakup of the Austro-Hungarian Empire and Bullitt for ruining his diplomatic career. Meeting in the evening hours at Freud's Vienna home, the pair hashed out a thesis as to why Wilson's presidency had been a failure. "You and I know that Wilson was a passive homosexual but we won't dare say it," Freud mischievously told Bullitt.

"Certainly we'll say it but subtly," Bullitt replied.

"That's the equivalent of not saying it at all."

Bullitt and Freud pursued their collaboration intermittently into the latter half of the 1930s, picking up in earnest after Bullitt, by then ambassador to France, spent tens of thousands of dollars of his own money to purchase passage to Paris for Freud and his family following the Nazi Anschluss of Austria. A series of editorial disagreements between the coauthors, Bullitt's political ambitions, and deference to Wilson's widow perpetually delayed publication of the book, however, and it was not released until 1967, nearly three decades after Freud's death. *Thomas Woodrow Wilson: A Psychological Study* qualifies as one of the strangest literary collaborations of the twentieth century, a "psychobiography" alleging the twenty-eighth president to have been a repressed homosexual ruled by Oedipal forces. Bullitt and Freud located Wilson's political flaws in a femininity born from hatred of his father, which led him to seek an "affectionate relationship with younger and physically smaller men, preferably blond." At Versailles, the pair wrote, Wilson "met the leaders of the Allies not with the weapons of masculinity but with the weapons of femininity: appeals, supplications, concessions, submissions." Long before armchair psychoanalysis of a sitting president became a collective national pastime, Bullitt and Freud developed a theory attributing the destabilization of interwar Europe to a former president's latent homosexual neuroses.

Like Sumner Welles, Bullitt was called back into government service after his friend FDR's election, as special assistant to Cordell Hull. The fixation with secrecy bordering on paranoia that he acquired as a young aide at Versailles had only grown more intense. At an economic conference in London, Bullitt insisted that American officials sweep all the walls, ceilings, and floors of his hotel room for recording devices—years before such precautions became standard practice for American diplomats traveling abroad. Meeting with the American ambassador at the U.S. embassy, Bul-

litt suddenly sprang up from his chair and drew back the curtain, searching vainly for a hidden microphone. When FDR established diplomatic
relations with the Soviet Union, Bullitt was the obvious choice to serve as
America's first ambassador to the revolutionary state. Immediately upon
arriving in Moscow in 1934, he visited the Kremlin to pay tribute to his
hero John Reed, whom the Bolsheviks had buried within the building's
exterior wall. Unbefitting an admirer of the Bolshevik cause, Bullitt had
a Cadillac V-12 limousine and two Pontiacs shipped to Russia at his own
expense, and he requisitioned a grand prewar mansion as his ambassadorial residence. Under Bullitt's orchestration, Spaso House became the city's
hottest social destination, once the scene of a party so lavish—replete with
a Czech jazz band, baby goats, a drunken bear, and a replica of a collective
farm—that Mikhail Bulgakov immortalized it in his novel *The Master and
Margarita*. "The best party in Moscow since the revolution," Bullitt bragged
in a cable to FDR.

Outside the embassy walls, however, the atmosphere was darkening as
Soviet leader Joseph Stalin unleashed his reign of terror. Bullitt's already
heightened sense of suspicion increased with each and every friend or
acquaintance who disappeared in the purges. One night over dinner with
his staff, Bullitt felt an unusually acute sense of unease. Looking around
the table at the men and their Soviet-born wives, he imagined himself
at the League of Nations, that ill-fated attempt at world government he
had opposed in his testimony before the Senate. The increasingly brutal
and unpredictable actions of his Soviet hosts, combined with a fear that
Soviet women were filching information from his embassy, prompted
Bullitt to recommend an executive order forbidding Foreign Service
officers from marrying foreigners without express permission from the
secretary of state. In an article about the regulation, the *Chicago Daily
Tribune* described its mastermind as a man "whose capacity for suspicion
is highly developed."

Bullitt's obsessive interest in the personal lives of his employees contrasted sharply with his public persona as a bon vivant. "Ever since resump-
tion of diplomatic relations with Russia . . . our Embassy there has had a
questionable reputation," a U.S. government official reported back to his
superiors in 1943, long after Bullitt had left. "I have visited every American Mission in Europe, the Near East, and the Americas and at almost
every post when Moscow is mentioned the discussion turns to morals."

The American legation, he elaborated, had thoroughly absorbed the values of the Soviet capital, "regarded as the city of 'free love.'" Though the report cited instances of mostly heterosexual debauchery (including a claim that the Lend-Lease program headquarters was "the scene of wild orgies" in which Gen. Omar Bradley, later to become chairman of the Joint Chiefs of Staff, participated), Embassy Moscow was also apparently home to more than its fair share of sexual deviants. Edward R. Pierce, who worked as a clerk at the embassy during Bullitt's tenure, complained about "a lot of fake marriages" among his colleagues. Bullitt, he recalled, brought with him "a weird bunch . . . straight off the Left Bank in Paris," and by the time Bullitt departed Moscow in 1936, Pierce claimed that a full third of the embassy staff was gay. When the mission was evacuated in 1941 after the German invasion of the Soviet Union, a Russian employee referred to the caravan of clerks traveling from Moscow to Vladivostok as the "pansy train."

Notwithstanding the accuracy of Pierce's estimation, the early twentieth-century U.S. Foreign Service was a uniquely attractive institution for gay men, affording them a measure of freedom and a literal world of possibilities unavailable at home. First and foremost, it offered a respectable career path for confirmed bachelors, long tours overseas obviating uncomfortable questions about the lack of a wife and family. Postings in exotic lands with more relaxed attitudes toward homosexuality also provided an escape from the repressive mores of American society. Finally, the Foreign Service was almost exclusively male. Raymond Geist, a consular official posted to Germany during the rise of the Third Reich, demonstrated how a gay man could serve as a diplomat under even the riskiest of circumstances. By day, Geist attended meetings with senior officials of a regime that herded homosexuals into concentration camps. By night, he shared his bed with a German man. Alexander Comstock Kirk, described by *Life* magazine in 1945 as "probably the outstanding career diplomat now functioning for the U.S. State Department," was a more prominent example. Heir to a Chicago soap fortune and a graduate of Yale (where he overlapped with Bullitt), Harvard Law School, and Paris's elite Sciences Po, the eccentric Kirk had a long and distinguished career. Serving at the American embassies in Moscow, Berlin, and Rome, all during periods of high diplomatic tension when Washington had withdrawn its ambassador, Kirk, a dandyish dresser who wore lavender silk tuxedos, liked to boast that he was a continual "poke in the eye" to hostile foreign governments. This ability to perform in a series of hardship posts with distinction might explain Kirk's attitude toward his gayness, which he apparently did little to conceal. A Federal Bureau of Investigation report noted that he "was commonly regarded as a homosexual," and a U.S. government official claimed that one of the reasons he entertained so lavishly was in order to buy "everyone out so that no one reports his abnormal personal conduct."

With his patrician pedigree and white, Anglo-Saxon, Protestant heritage, Kirk personified the U.S. Foreign Service, which well into the twentieth century dissuaded men lacking private incomes from even applying to join its privileged ranks. "They possessed a common background, common experience, and a common liking for old wines, proper English, and Savile Row clothing," the historian Waldo Heinrichs wrote of America's prewar diplomatic generation. "Indeed the Diplomatic Service most nearly resembled a club." The sexually unorthodox Kirk embodied the Foreign Service in another way, one likelier to raise eyebrows back home. Ruminating upon the State Department of the 1930s, it was with worldly sophisticates like Kirk in mind that one prominent historian would later ridicule it as an institution that "Americans . . . reasonably regarded as a refuge for effete and conventional men who adored countesses, pushed cookies and wore handkerchiefs in their sleeves."

* * *

IT WAS IN SEARCH OF THE FREEDOM THIS CLUB OFFERED TO MEN LIKE HIM that an ambitious son of poor Italian immigrants arrived at the gates of the U.S. embassy in Moscow on June 11, 1934. Bullitt had already exhausted two clerks when, just a few months into his stint as ambassador, he desperately cabled Washington: "Please send a secretary who can stand Moscow and me." Washington sent Carmel Offie.

Born and raised in the coalfields of Pennsylvania, Offie was a product of public schools and Cambria-Rowe Business College. This alone made him an oddity among his fellow Foreign Service officers: some three-quarters of those he served alongside in Europe had attended prestigious prep schools like Groton or St. Paul's, and of those, two-thirds had graduated from Harvard, Yale, Princeton, or one of a handful of elite foreign universities. But Offie's excellent transcription skills—"He had a mind, you know, almost like a tape recorder," one colleague recalled, enabling him to type two hundred words a minute—landed him a job with the American ambassador to Honduras, in 1931, at the age of twenty-two. Diminutive, by all accounts physically unattractive, and homosexual, Offie made up for these traits that lay beyond his control by honing a set of those he could master: charm, wit, and unflagging loyalty to his superiors. Offie's remarkable rise was evidence of his absorbing a lesson that the most successful gay Washingtonians of his generation, working across all branches of the government, learned early: to ensure your survival, become indispensable to those with power.

In Moscow, Offie made himself essential to Bullitt, taking dictation, running errands, and always available for a relaxing game of chess. "This wretched young man puts up with being at his beck and call all day and all night, for if [Bullitt] has an idea during the night he calls for his attaché to take down the draft," a British diplomat in Moscow remarked of the relationship between the American ambassador and his devoted assistant. Bullitt "gets up in the morning at any hour between five and seven and takes the unfortunate fellow for a walk with him." In 1935, Offie accompanied Bullitt on an expedition to Tokyo, where Bullitt hoped to gather intelligence for FDR on Japanese regional ambitions and the insurgency on the Chinese mainland led by the Communist leader Mao Zedong. "When Mr. Offie reached Moscow he lacked social polish and his eagerness and self-assurance often produced an appearance of 'freshness,'" Bullitt wrote the president in a report about their voyage. "However, in the course of our trip around the world he acquired the social poise he conspicuously lacked, and his 'freshness' is rapidly disappearing." Other colleagues noticed Offie's multifarious talents. A young Foreign Service officer at the Moscow embassy named George Kennan described him as "a renaissance type; earthy, extroverted, enormous energy, endless *joie de vivre*; a born 'operator.'"

When Bullitt assumed the ambassadorship to France in the fall of 1936, Offie followed. Every day at 4 a.m., the dutiful aide accompanied the embassy chef for his rounds at the Paris market stalls, helping him gather comestibles for that evening's soirée. (Bullitt earned the sobriquet "Champagne Ambassador" for his extravagant fêtes; at one party, 600 guests collectively finished off 490 bottles of Pommery 1928.) In addition to stocking the embassy pantry, Offie would occasionally acquire specialty perfumes and foie gras to send via diplomatic pouch to Marguerite "Missy" LeHand, FDR's private secretary, with whom Bullitt had initiated a romance years earlier before departing for Moscow. Keen to keep his boss in FDR's good graces, Offie wrote LeHand asking her to inform the president that Bullitt was "extremely popular here and is doing a swell job," but in order to "live up to his reputation he is kept constantly on the go from fourteen to eighteen hours a day, and it's too much." Buttering up Bullitt to the White House also paid dividends for Offie, tales of whose "social poise" (and social climbing) became a regular feature of Bullitt's witty and informative dispatches to the White House. Regularly corresponding with the president by transatlantic telephone or telegram, Bullitt displayed a phenomenal ear for gossip, a gimlet eye for detail, and an extensive assortment of connections across the Continent, his communiqués constituting what Janet Flanner, longtime Paris correspondent of the *New Yorker*, described as "a kind of extraordinary private European gazette; what interests him is the news behind the news." (FDR's nickname for Bullitt, "Bill Buddha," was as much a nod toward his oracular assessments of the international scene as it was a jibe at his bald head.) Missy LeHand lauded Bullitt's series of cables as "a confidential dispatch which reads like a most exciting novel," one in which Offie played a delightfully charming supporting role. In one telegram, Bullitt reported that Offie had become the preferred bridge partner of the Duchess of Windsor. In another, Bullitt told the president that the lover of the French politician Paul Reynaud

> summons [Offie] to her "love nest" almost daily; and he keeps her within reasonable bounds. I have less patience than he with lack of character so that more than ever, Offie is the power behind the throne . . . A few days ago, the Comtesse de Portes said to him that if the American Embassy had any difficulty with any department of the French Government or the French Army, he had only to let her know and the matter would be settled to our satisfaction at once. He tried it once and it worked!

When the twenty-year-old son of the American ambassador to Britain and his best friend, gallivanting about Europe in the summer of 1937, needed a place to stay on the Paris leg of their journey, Bullitt deputized Offie to look after the two collegians. John F. Kennedy had met Kirk LeMoyne "Lem" Billings at Choate, the tony Connecticut prep school. The boys immediately took a liking to each other, bonding over their common distaste for the institution's austere conditions and regimental ways. Billings, however, hoped there might be something more to the relationship than a shared spirit of teenage rebellion against authority, and at seventeen had expressed his sexual interest in the future president of the United States by sending him a bit of coded doggerel jotted onto a scrap of toilet paper. For the hormonal adolescents at Choate, communicating forbidden desires on bathroom tissue—easy to swallow or dispose of—was one of many traditions inherited from British boarding schools. "Please don't write to me on toilet paper anymore," Kennedy firmly responded. "I'm not that kind of boy."

Though Kennedy might not have been "that kind of boy," the depth of his platonic relationship with Billings foreshadowed how remarkably relaxed he would be around those who were. Unusual for the time, Billings's frank acknowledgment of his same-sex desires did not engender feelings of disgust or anger in the young man to whom they were addressed. On the contrary, it strengthened their friendship. Kennedy's father, Joseph Kennedy Sr., would refer to Billings as "a second son," a status that the intensely tribal family patriarch conferred upon no one outside the Kennedy clan.

When Bullitt told his counterpart in London that he had assigned Offie the task of accommodating Jack and Lem, the elder Kennedy knew they would be in good hands. Kennedy Sr. had had frequent dealings with Bullitt's aide-de-camp, sometimes calling him up to four times a day, and once even tried to hire him away as his own personal assistant. Upon the boys' arrival in Paris, Offie pulled out all the stops, ensuring that they were comfortable at the ambassadorial residence and attending to their every need. For a Mass presided over by the future Pope Pius XII at Notre Dame Cathedral, Offie secured seats near the altar, in the same row as the French president. (As tribute, the boys affectionately named the dog they bought later in their travels "Offie.") The following summer, when Jack and his eldest brother, Joe Jr., visited Paris, Offie finagled them invitations to parties at which the city's most attractive young ladies were in attendance. Offie's motives vis-à-vis the handsome future president might not have been altogether innocent; he was "always trying, *unsuccessfully*, to pour Champagne down my gullet," Kennedy complained in a letter to Billings. At the same time, in his dealings with Offie, one can already detect the blithe manner in which Kennedy used his charm, family name, and good looks to get what he wanted. "Jack came into my office," Offie recalled, "and read various things which were none of his business, but since he was who he was I didn't throw him out."

Offie, who was known to brag that his bedroom was akin to "the playing fields of Eton," did little to hide his sexual orientation. On the contrary, "he was as homosexual as you can get," his former Moscow embassy colleague Edward Pierce recalled. The epicene endearment that Bullitt, JFK, and many others used to address him, "Offlet," supports this contention, as does the testimony of countless others who worked alongside him. And Offie's frankness about his own sexuality prompted speculation about that of the ambassador he so faithfully served.

William Bullitt was a man of dramatic contradictions. Initially a starry-eyed romantic about the Bolshevik revolution who, in his enthusiasm, taught a Red Army regiment to play polo, he eventually soured on the Russians and became a militant anticommunist. An epicurean who threw wild parties with naked butlers, he once erupted at Lincoln Steffens for reading James Joyce's *Ulysses*, deemed legally "obscene" under the 1873 Comstock Act, to his young daughter. "Think of the baby!" Bullitt shouted at the muckraking journalist. "Our child—what will it turn out to be if it hears language like that?" But Bullitt's greatest contradiction may have concerned his sexuality.

Offie, according to Pierce, was "Bullitt's bedmate all over the world." Robert Joyce, a senior Foreign Service officer well acquainted with both men, recalled that Offie "made no secret of the fact that [he] had always been a homosexual and he implied, without specifically saying, that this was the basis of his relationship with Bullitt." According to an officer in the air force who met Offie in 1946, Offie claimed that "to get ahead in the State Department" one needed to "stay away from 'those dirty women' and to like men more. In this connection," Offie allegedly said that "his rapid rise in the State Department was due to Ambassador Bullitt," whom Offie "considered an eccentric individual." Offie went on to explain that "the long line theory of the State Department Foreign Service was to have male secretaries to be most completely associated to the Ambassadors and move them 'up in the organization.'" The officer also said that Offie told him that "he would rise much faster if he were to play ball with the group that Offie was associated with" and that "Offie pointed out that he had maintained homosexual tendencies since the time he had been with Ambassador

Bullitt." Offie here was less likely speaking the scandalous truth about State Department workplace culture than trying to convince a man to sleep with him. But his ability to live well beyond the means of a career Foreign Service officer did not escape notice, leading the director of one powerful government agency with extensive investigatory powers to describe "a substantial monetary gift from Bullitt" to Offie as "similar to payments bestowed upon mistresses."

Whether he harbored the same secret as Sumner Welles, Bullitt enjoyed a warm working relationship with his diplomatic colleague. Illustrative of the rapport between the two men was the telegram Bullitt sent Welles in 1939 facetiously recalling "a conversation on a subject of vital importance which you and I had" at Bullitt's ambassadorial residence in Paris on the subject of "delphinium seeds." Violating protocol by enclosing some of the precious kernels in the diplomatic pouch, Bullitt wrote that, "Within a few weeks I shall commit another crime and send you bulbs of the William C. Bullitt dahlia. I suppose we are both entitled to go to jail for carrying on such indecent transactions."

Over time, however, Bullitt grew envious of Welles's close access to FDR, and the president's decision in 1940 to send his undersecretary on a fact-finding mission to Europe, Bullitt's turf, poisoned their relationship for good. On the day Welles set sail for the Continent that February, he complained to his colleague, Assistant Secretary of State Breckinridge Long, about a series of newspaper articles that offered some rather curiously specific details concerning his ongoing feud with Cordell Hull. The source was not difficult for Welles to discern. Welles, Long wrote in his diary, "told me that the stories in the press which were so critical of him and [that] indicated that he and the Secretary had had some dispute on the subject of his mission had all emanated from the vitriolic tongue of Bill Bullitt." Meanwhile in Paris, remembered Robert Murphy, a diplomat at the American embassy, "a bitterness developed" in Bullitt as a result of the Welles mission. To avoid the indignity of having to roll out the red carpet for his State Department superior, Bullitt traveled to Florida for a vacation, making a point to stay there until after Welles had departed the French capital. Upon returning to Paris, Bullitt composed a scathing account of Welles's European tour for FDR. "I have been highly restrained in this report since certain of the remarks which have been made to me have been violent in the extreme," Bullitt wrote.

On his way back to Washington, Welles stopped briefly in Rome. He dined at the opulent Hotel Quirinale with the city's governor, who hosted Welles in his box at the Opera underneath a twenty-seven-thousand–crystal drop chandelier for a performance of Verdi's *Un ballo in maschera*. Loosely based upon the assassination of the homosexual Swedish king Gustav III at a masquerade ball, the performance uncannily foreshadowed the fate of its honored American guest, whose charmed life was about to be devastated due to the "vitriolic tongue" and "indecent transactions" of his erstwhile friend.

2

"WORSE THAN A MURDERER"

"In case I should get blown up before I see you again," William Bullitt wrote President Roosevelt on May 30, 1940, "I want you to know that it has been marvelous to work for you and that I thank you from the bottom of my heart for your friendship." For months, the American ambassador to France had promised that he had no intention of abandoning his post in the event of a German occupation of Paris. Four days after transmitting this message to the president, Bullitt met with French government officials over sherry and biscuits at the Air Ministry when an air raid siren interrupted their parley. Running for shelter, Bullitt barely escaped with his life as bombs fell all around the building, sending plaster and glass flying into the streets. "My deepest personal reason for staying in Paris," Bullitt defiantly told the president afterward, in a telegram requesting a dozen Thompson submachine guns that he offered to pay for himself, "is that whatever I have as character, good or bad, is based on the fact that since the age of four I have never run away from anything however painful or dangerous when I thought it was my duty to take a stand. If I should leave Paris now I would no longer be myself." On June 11, the day after the French cabinet fled south to Tours, Bullitt sent a telegram to Cordell Hull placing himself in the proud tradition of American ambassadors to France who remained at their posts no matter the danger to themselves. Like Gouverneur Morris, the peg-legged Founding Father who represented the new nation at the Court of Versailles throughout the Reign of Terror; Elihu Washburne, ambassador when the Germans last occupied the French capital in 1870; and Myron Herrick, envoy when the Huns threatened the city during the First World War, so, too, would Bullitt keep Old Glory flying.

As German tanks rolled down the Champs-Élysées on June 14, Bullitt held to his word, stoically assisting American citizens scrambling to escape. Carmel Offie remained by his side, "amazingly efficient" at cutting through the "interminable red tape of diplomatic procedure" and "a boon to all who were in trouble." On behalf of the exiled French government, Bullitt met with the German provisional military governor at the same hotel where his old nemesis Woodrow Wilson had held the initial talks about the formation of the League of Nations. After hectically winding down the embassy's operations, Bullitt fired off a final cable to Missy LeHand and departed south with a small entourage. When the five-car caravan reached the border of neutral Spain, a customs official inquired about one of the elegantly dressed women in the party whom the passenger manifest identified as a maid.

"She is not a maid," the officer declared.

"Of course not," Offie indignantly shot back. "Don't you understand that the ambassador has a mistress?"

Bullitt returned to the United States and, following the president's reelection in November, offered his resignation, as was tradition. Expecting to be reappointed as ambassador to the collaborationist French Vichy regime, Bullitt was incensed when FDR, on the advice of Welles, passed him over in favor of retired rear admiral William Leahy. For the first time since 1933, and at the precise moment when his diplomatic expertise was most needed, Bullitt was on the geopolitical sidelines. First in Moscow and then in Paris, this "picaresque adventurer in politics—a Tom Jones of diplomacy," in the words of historian Barbara Tuchman, had been the president's most trusted advisor on European affairs. Now, thousands of miles away from the action, he was out of the game. Bullitt blamed Welles and resolved to destroy him.

He found an ally in State Department counselor Robert Walton "Judge" Moore, who similarly resented Welles for beating him for the undersecretary job. Moore had heard about Welles's exploits on the presidential train two months prior from his friend and fellow Virginian Ernest E. Norris, president of the Southern Railway. Terminally ill, Moore urged Norris to share with Bullitt whatever information he had. On the morning of November 25, Norris visited Bullitt at his apartment in the Anchorage building on Dupont Circle accompanied by Luther Thomas, head of the Southern Railway police force. Welles, Norris revealed, "had made sexual proposals of the most indecent and immoral nature" on the trip back from Speaker Bankhead's funeral and had "behaved in a similar manner" during a journey to Cleveland, that time propositioning a Filipino club car attendant in addition to a Pullman porter.

On January 3, 1941, Maj. Gen. Edwin M. Watson, FDR's military assistant, beckoned the director of the Federal Bureau of Investigation to the White House, and on behalf of the president ordered him to investigate Welles. It was to be the first of many investigations John Edgar Hoover would launch concerning "sex perverts in government service"—an ironic role given the speculation concerning Hoover himself. Since his earliest days leading the FBI, journalists had employed code words and allusive phrases to suggest that the nation's top cop was not the model of American masculinity and traditional moral values he purported to be. In a scathing 1933 piece alleging that the FBI was beginning to constitute a "miniature American Cheka," a reference to the Bolshevik domestic security agency, the popular *Collier's* magazine mocked "Mr. Hoover and his boy detectives" for "tailing" subversives. Hoover, the magazine observed, "walks with a mincing step" and "dresses fastidiously, with Eleanor blue as the favorite color for the matched shades of tie, handkerchief and socks." (Not long after this attack, the magazine *Liberty*, which regularly featured articles under the director's byline alongside other Bureau propaganda, printed a piece observing that Hoover's "compact body, with the shoulders of a light heavyweight boxer, carries no ounce of extra weight—just 170 pounds of live, virile masculinity.") The following year, a *Washington Herald* society columnist noted that Hoover's "inner and outer sanctums are the last word in snappiness, neatness and general good looks." A single, brief paragraph at the end of a *New York Times* profile a few months later managed to squeeze in three facts about Hoover that, while unremarkable in isolation, together signaled something queer: the "unmarried" director "resides with his mother" in a home "filled with antiques," the collection of which was often presumed to connote homosexuality. To illustrate a 1936 article reporting that "Hoover walks with a rather mincing step, almost feminine," the *Chicago Tribune* chose a photo of shirtless FBI recruits performing calisthenics, captioned "Young G-men must have supple muscles."

Mirroring the enormous collection of secret files on American citizens Hoover would gradually accumulate over his decades in charge of the FBI was the encyclopedic compendium of meticulously organized index cards on various political issues and Washington personalities compiled by his primary journalistic adversary. Drew Pearson's notes and columns contain many items reflecting his long-held suspicion that the FBI director had something shameful to hide. "Shrouds himself in great secrecy," reads one note from 1933. "Offices labyrinth of doors and exits." The following year, Pearson noted that "Hoover, swarthy head of the bureau of investigation, seldom takes a day off, and when he does, devotes all his spare time to collecting antiques," that suspiciously feminine pursuit. Hoover "is different from any police official I ever knew in that he uses a distinctive and conspicuous perfume," Pearson quoted a Guatemalan diplomat telling him in 1938. "After forty-three years of bachelordom, super-sleuth J. Edgar Hoover has begun to take a fancy to the ladies," Pearson mused in an item, "Bachelor Hoover," announcing the director's sudden interest in female dining companions. "The No. 1 G-man always has preferred the company of men, and though seen almost daily in Washington restaurants, it has never been with women."

Obsessive in his accumulation of other people's secrets, Hoover was equally zealous at protecting his own.

★ ★ ★

FOR OVER TEN YEARS, the group of eight women from Cleveland and northwestern Pennsylvania had met at one another's homes for a weekly bridge match. As heated as the competition could occasionally become, never had one of their games resulted in a summons from the FBI.

This was to change one day in the summer of 1943. Apropos of seeing or hearing Hoover's name in one of the innumerable accounts of FBI gallantry that packed the pages of the popular press and filled the airwaves, one of the ladies observed that the Bureau's director was a bachelor. Not only that, another of the women interjected, he was a homosexual, one who "kept a large group of young boys around him." Unfortunately for the purveyor of this claim, the party's hostess had a nephew in the FBI, whom she promptly informed of the vile calumny that had sullied her hearth. The grateful nephew relayed this information to an assistant FBI director in Washington named Robert C. Hendon, who reported it up the food chain to his boss, J. Edgar Hoover.

Hendon didn't require instructions from the director as to what course of action he should take in response to the utterance of this slander. A protocol already existed for such cases, and Hendon followed it closely. Before he even informed the director of the incident, Hendon had already instructed Special Agent (SA) L. V. Boardman of the FBI's Cleveland field office to "vigorously" scold the woman "for her gossip." Boardman ordered the woman, whom he later described as "an old maid school teacher," to his office. He sat her down and told her that he "personally resented such a malicious and unfounded" remark and could not for the life of him comprehend why she would "make such a libelous statement concerning a man in such a responsible position as the Director who had in his hands the internal security of the country in wartime."

Terrified, the woman explained how it was that she ever got the cocka-mamie idea into her head that J. Edgar Hoover was a homosexual pedophile. Visiting Baltimore with her husband two years earlier, she had overheard a conversation at a restaurant among a group of "young men who were having a riotous time" at the adjoining table. One said that he had recently seen Hoover being driven by his chauffeur, to which another replied that the driver was "Hoover's sweetheart and that Hoover was queer." The woman lodged this observation in the back of her mind, where it sat, unbidden, until the fateful bridge party when Hoover's bachelorhood was broached and she inadvertently blurted it out. "Immediately after" uttering the disrespectful remark, the woman told Special Agent Boardman, she realized "it should not have been made," and to this day, she "could not understand" why she had made it. She emphasized that she was "deeply sorry," should "not have made" the comment, and promised Boardman that at next week's bridge match, she would "point out to each of those present that her statement was not founded on fact."

The experience of the "old maid school teacher" was far from uncommon. "Loose lips sink ships" was the slogan promoted by the U.S. government during World War II to discourage citizens from unintentionally divulging information that, in the wrong hands, might undermine the war effort. The same warning could also be applied to anyone questioning the sexuality of J. Edgar Hoover. For what unsuspecting Americans had good reason to believe was mere idle chatter about a high-profile public figure could result in an unwelcome visit by the feds and the initiation of an investigation into their own private life. The beauty salon owner who told a customer that Hoover was a "sissy" and a "queer"; the man who claimed at a party that Hoover "had a crush on a friend of theirs and made advances to him several times"; the Louisville prison inmate who alleged that Hoover had a seventeen-year-old male paramour—these were just a few of the many people whose private conversations brought the weight of the FBI down upon them. Once, the owner of a diner near FBI headquarters where many agents took their lunch told one of his customers about a ballroom dance he had attended where a fellow asked if he had "heard that the Director is a queer." When the diner owner inquired as to where his interlocutor had heard this, the man vaguely replied, "Friends from Baltimore, who are dancing teachers." Equipped with only these vague details, a crack squad of Bureau investigators soon identified the source of the rumor: a former dance instructor working as a budget examiner for the National Labor Relations Board. When the FBI informed the NLRB chairman about his underling's big mouth, the chairman apologized profusely to Hoover, expressing embarrassment over one "stupid employee's gossip."

No stone was left unturned by Hoover's G-men in their efforts to detect, hunt down, and intimidate private citizens who spoke ill of the director. "You may be assured that so long as there is a Federal Bureau of Investigation[,] those associated with you will exert every means in their power to protect you from malicious lying attacks and throw the lies down the throats of those who utter them," a special agent in Louisville wrote Hoover after pressuring one of his defamers. Almost three decades after FBI agents threatened him at his home, and nearly ten years after Hoover's death, the man who claimed at a party that Hoover coveted his friend "was still defensive and quite nervous" talking about the matter. Not even the oceans could impede Hoover's gossip-quashing apparatus. After an American citizen living in London suggested that "Hoover is a queer" to a consul at the U.S. embassy, an FBI attaché hauled him in and chewed him out as a "stoolpigeon."

Hoover's close and abiding relationship with his principal deputy, FBI associate director Clyde Tolson, fueled suspicions that the two men were lovers. Lifelong bachelors, Hoover and Tolson were inseparable, lunching regularly at the Mayflower Hotel and Harvey's Restaurant and traveling together on their vacations. Hoover left most of his estate to Tolson, and their attachment inspired the nicknames "J. Edna" and "Mother Tolson" among some agents.

Perhaps the best-known "fact" about Hoover, and one luridly connected to his alleged homosexuality, was that he was a cross-dresser. The sole source for this allegation, which first appeared in a sensationalistic 1993 biography, was a bootlegger's ex-wife, who claimed to have witnessed Hoover participating in orgies with young boys at New York City's Plaza Hotel. The FBI director, the woman averred in an interview for which she was paid, was "wearing a fluffy black dress, very fluffy, with flounces and lace stockings and high heels and a black curly wig," and he made the boys read passages from the Bible while engaging in depraved sexual acts. Hoover's reluctance to go after the Mafia, wrote the biographer who elicited these stunning allegations, derived from a fear that it would leak photographs of his homosexual encounters.

According to Athan Theoharis, a leading historian of the FBI, the contention that Hoover declined to take on the Mob due to blackmail over his participation in a homosexual orgy is "mind-boggling in its simplicity." It requires one to believe that the country's largest law enforcement organization, with thousands of agents dispersed across the country, was held in check by one man's fear of being exposed for wearing a dress. While it's certainly plausible that Hoover was gay and that Tolson was his lover, the only evidence thus far adduced has been circumstantial. That such speculation, according to the historian Claire Bond Potter, "is in part believable because perverted sex is a constant theme bordering on obsession in Hoover's own writing about criminals, Communists, and social equality movements" does not necessarily make it true. Perhaps the most accurate description of the Hoover-Tolson relationship comes from the historian Richard Gid Powers, who described it as "spousal" but not sexual, "so close, so enduring, and so affectionate that it took the place of marriage for both bachelors."

Cartha "Deke" DeLoach, who joined the FBI in 1942 and became the third most senior official after Tolson, insisted that the only person Hoover truly loved was his mother and that his "capacity to feel deeply for other human beings [was] interred with her in the Old Congressional Cemetery," where Hoover himself was buried in 1972. Three years later, Tolson was laid to rest just a few plots away. And that is where the truth about their relationship, at once blatant and inscrutable, is likely forever to remain.

* * *

A WORLD-CLASS CONNOISSEUR AND PURVEYOR OF GOSSIP, FDR was well aware of the scuttlebutt surrounding his FBI director. But according to his second son, Elliott, the president did not see any reason that it should matter, "so long as his abilities were not impaired." FDR had not always been so open-minded about the presence of homosexuals in government institutions. As assistant secretary of the navy in 1919, he was involved in the first publicized homosexual scandal to afflict the U.S. government. When reports were sent to him of homosexual activity between sailors and civilians in the vicinity of the naval base at Newport, Rhode Island, FDR wrote a letter to Attorney General A. Mitchell Palmer informing him of "conditions of vice and depravity" corrupting America's fighting men. In the ensuing investigation, FDR approved the use of sailors as sexual decoys to entrap private citizens, in effect deputizing them "perverts by official order," in the outraged words of local clergymen. For misleading a Senate subcommittee investigation, FDR and his superior, Navy Secretary Josephus Daniels, were reprimanded for showing "an utter lack of moral perspective when they allowed men in the uniform of the United States Navy . . . to publicly testify to the beastly acts that had been performed on them." Such was the ignominy with which homosexuality was imbued, however, that Americans hoping to learn what the fuss was all about would have had difficulty doing so by perusing their daily newspapers. "DETAILS ARE UNPRINTABLE" blared the *New York Times* headline over its story about the Senate report.

Like William Bullitt, abandoned by Louise Bryant for another woman, FDR had an intimate knowledge of same-sex desire in the form of his wife's passionate attachment to a female friend. Assigned to cover Eleanor Roosevelt early in her husband's presidential administration, Associated Press reporter Lorena Hickok, or "Hick," fell in love with the First Lady on an overnight train ride when Eleanor spoke candidly of the pain she felt upon discovering that her husband had consummated an affair with her own secretary, Lucy Mercer. Out of this heartfelt expression of vulnerability, Eleanor and Hick, an acknowledged lesbian, developed an intensely emotional and possibly physical bond, manifest in their many adoring letters. "I wish I could lie down beside you tonight & take you in my arms," Eleanor once wrote. "I want to put my arms around you and kiss you in the corner of your mouth," Hick declared in a missive. At one point, Eleanor advised Hick to marry a man and have children. "It would have satisfied certain cravings and given you someone in whom to lavish the love and devotion you have to keep down all the time," she urged. Responding to a complaint from Hick that she was spending too much time with other people, Eleanor replied, "Remember one thing always[:] no one is just what you are to me." (Startled to read this correspondence, Hick's biographer suggested to the director of the FDR Presidential Library that it be sealed from public view for decades.)

Whether or not Eleanor's relationship with Hick went beyond the platonic, it helped satisfy the emotional void created by her husband's infidelities. "Eleanor had so many emotions stored up inside, that when Hick came along, it was almost like a volcanic explosion," her friend Trude Lash told historian Doris Kearns Goodwin. "But does that mean that Eleanor acted on her words, that she had a lesbian relationship with Hick? I do not think so." Nonetheless, according to Eleanor's biographer Blanche Wiesen Cook, "Nobody else in [her] life filled the particular place in her heart now reserved for Hick," who also influenced Eleanor in revolutionizing the role of First Lady. It was Hick who convinced Eleanor to hold weekly press conferences for female journalists and to write the daily newspaper column that became the enormously popular My Day.

Eleanor counted several prominent lesbians among her close friends, and it was surely this exposure to gay people, in addition to her own highly charged feelings for another woman, that inclined her to sympathize with Welles as the effort to destroy him accelerated. Hull, who referred to his undersecretary as "my fairy" among associates, lamented how Eleanor worked with others in the administration to lobby her husband into retaining Welles. Hull's sentiment was shared by Hoover, who privately complained that the president did not immediately fire Welles because "that old biddy Eleanor Roosevelt protected him." Hoover was convinced that Eleanor was a lesbian, and he started a file on her that grew to become one of the largest the FBI ever compiled on a single person.

A month after receiving the order from General Watson to investigate Welles, Hoover presented the results of his work at the White House. The FBI had obtained sworn affidavits from the sleeping car porters, Hoover told the president, and their testimony was damning. Asked by FDR if he believed the accusations, Hoover replied that while "it is a common thing, unfortunately, for persons to charge men in public life with indulging in immoral acts and acts of degeneracy," all the evidence appeared to indict the undersecretary. As his behavior seemed "more of a mental condition than anything else and there could not be any assurance it would not be repeated in the future," Hoover suggested that the president assign Welles a bodyguard, albeit one of "mature" age and "not any young man who would lend credence to the stories that have already been circulated." Hoover also informed FDR that, while Bullitt was spreading news about the train incident far and wide around Washington, he was reluctant to discuss the matter with FDR himself because "anyone who took bad news to [him] 'would get his own legs cut off.'"

Luckily for Bullitt, an act of God would provide him the fortitude he needed to confront the president. A week after Hoover's meeting with FDR, Walton Moore died. Determined to pursue Welles from the grave, Moore had left behind an envelope on which was written in red pencil, "In case of death it is to be deliv'd to Wm. C. Bullitt." Inside were copies of the original affidavits collected from the train porters. Late on the morning of April 23, 1941, Bullitt met with FDR in the Oval Office. After exchanging pleasantries and political gossip, Bullitt solemnly informed the president that Moore had "sent for me on his death-bed and charged me with a duty which I could not evade, however unpleasant it was to carry out." Handing FDR an envelope containing the affidavits, Bullitt revealed that "as a dying wish," Moore had instructed him to share the enclosed information with the president.

FDR glanced at the first page. "I know about all this already," he said, tossing the sheaf of papers onto his desk. "I have had a full report on it. There is truth in the allegations." Having acknowledged Welles's behavior, the president then made light of it. "Well, he's not doing it on government time, is he?"

Bullitt was not amused. Moore, he told the president, believed that "the maintenance of Welles in public office was a menace to the country since he was subject to blackmail by foreign powers and that foreign powers had used cases of this kind to get men in their power."

FDR waved away Bullitt's concerns. No newspaper, he said, would ever publish such scandalous information about a public figure. The president had reason to be confident in this assertion. Exposing homosexuals—especially powerful, wellborn ones like Sumner Welles—was something that just wasn't done in 1941, even by the yellow press. "In the early war years," Drew Pearson was later to claim, "a former secretary of war in the Roosevelt cabinet was framed" as part of a homosexual blackmail plot in an abandoned building "opposite Lafayette Square and the White House." The unnamed war secretary allegedly paid fifty thousand dollars (an enormous sum at the time) to keep his secret hidden. While Pearson claimed to have acquired an affidavit from one of the blackmailers, he chose not to expose the compromised official. Nor did he even reveal the existence of this plot until over two decades after it allegedly occurred.

In addition to the discretion that men like Welles could expect from the fourth estate in respect to their sexual transgressions, the undersecretary also benefited from the fact that Bullitt's obsession with secrecy had yet to consume the rest of Washington. America remained officially neutral on the world stage; not for another five months would it institute a military draft. The country didn't even have a civilian intelligence agency. Illustrative of the carefree attitude to secrecy is a story told by FDR's naval aide, Capt. John L. McCrea, about the sheet of paper that flew past him one day while he was walking outside the Corcoran Gallery of Art near the White House. Crossing the street to pick it up, McCrea found, "to my amazement" that "it was stamped as originating in the Department of State and across its face there was stamped in large type, red letters and all, the word 'SECRET.' And it should have been 'secret,' too." When McCrea got to the White House, he placed the document in an envelope, inserted a brief memo explaining how he had found it, and sent the package to Sumner Welles, who wrote a thank-you note in return.

Realizing he would have to raise the stakes if he ever hoped to convince FDR of the liability Welles posed, Bullitt next told the president that Hull "considered Welles worse than a murderer." When FDR responded that he wanted Welles to remain in his position because he trusted his judgment, Bullitt declared that "since the United States was about to undergo a supreme test of character," the president "could not have around him men without character."

Whatever the president's feelings about Welles's behavior, he resented Bullitt's prying and pestering even more. That Bullitt would take such umbrage over Welles's sexual indiscretions struck the president as astoundingly hypocritical. For years, Bullitt had courted FDR's beloved personal secretary, Missy LeHand, leading her along from afar only to give her the cold shoulder after returning to the United States. Bullitt had been LeHand's one true love, and FDR never forgave him for the callous way he treated her. Bullitt had also been romantically involved with a woman the president absolutely loathed: Eleanor "Cissy" Patterson, fire-breathing editor and publisher of the right-wing *Washington Times-Herald*. As far as the president was concerned, Bullitt was the last person who should be finding fault with the sexual morals of other men.

There was also the matter of personal loyalty, a not insignificant factor in FDR's ethical calculus. "Welles was a boyhood friend of Roosevelt and Roosevelt sticks by his friends," noted Breckinridge Long. "That is one of his distinct characteristics. He has hardly a more definite trait in his entire and many-sided composition than loyalty to his friends." And he was willing to go far in reciprocating that loyalty, especially toward those who, like Welles, occasionally used alcohol to calm their nerves after a long day's work. Spruille Braden, who served in a number of senior diplomatic positions during the Roosevelt administration, recalled how "many close friends of the president" told him "that Roosevelt would forgive anything if the man were able to prove that he was drunk at the time. He had kindness in his heart for a man who had sinned under the influence of alcohol." Welles's drinking habits did not appear to hinder his work; according to his biographer (and son) Benjamin, his "ability to snap back after a night of hard drinking was phenomenal." Finally, FDR strained not to believe negative things about people he liked. According to Elliott Roosevelt, his father was initially convinced by Welles's excuse that Bullitt had bribed the train porters to proposition *him*.

The president eventually grew tired of arguing with Bullitt and pressed a button under his desk. Instantly, General Watson appeared, indicating that it was time for Bullitt to leave. Before he departed, Bullitt told FDR something that would have been rash under any circumstances, never mind coming from a man without any actual job in the government: he "would expect" an answer from the president as to what he planned to do about Welles by week's end.

Bullitt would have to wait. With Nazi Germany conquering Europe and the Japanese extending their empire across Asia, the president had far more important things to worry about than the occasional drunken escapades of his undersecretary of state, who was otherwise doing an excellent job. In July, Welles delivered a widely praised speech outlining the administration's foreign policy, for which *Time* lauded him on its cover as the "Field-Marshal in the War of Brains" against the Axis powers. The following month, he helped draft (in a process kept secret from Hull) the Atlantic Charter, the Allies' vision for postwar peace. As far as the president was concerned, there was no indication that Welles's alcohol consumption or homosexual impulses were hindering his diplomacy.

Welles, then, could assume his secret was safe, provided the most powerful man in the world was willing to protect him and that the press hewed to its long-standing practice of turning a blind eye to the sex lives of powerful men. A routine police raid in New York was about to shatter both assumptions.

3

SENATOR X

Judged solely by its exterior, 329 Pacific Street was just another Brooklyn town house. But like the men who crossed its threshold, it concealed dangerous secrets.

Located near the Brooklyn Navy Yard, the three-story brick building was rented by a fifty-five-year-old, Swedish-born naturalized citizen named Gustave Beekman. A florist by profession known as "George" to his associates, Beekman had a lucrative side hustle as "one of the best known and most popular panderers to homosexuals in the United States." No entrance fee was required at the various houses of ill repute he operated in New York City—just the purchase of a bottle of "Swedish punch," a specialty spirit "home-brewed and violent."

The house on Pacific Street, like the establishments Beekman had earlier maintained on West Forty-Third Street in Manhattan and on Warren Street in Brooklyn, was not exactly a brothel. Nor was Beekman technically a pimp. Rather, the home functioned as something akin to a social club for men seeking sex with other men, where private rooms were available to rent by the hour. Downstairs, Beekman supplied his guests with copious amounts of liquor and generous spreads of roast turkeys and hams. Upstairs could be found the "sin chamber," whose carnal activities were playfully hinted at by a Caution: Men at Work construction sign affixed to the door. Should money be exchanged inside, it was none of Beekman's business.

Beekman attracted a diverse clientele. A visit to the house on any given evening might find a Philadelphia surgeon mingling with a butler known as "Princess" or a group of sailors carousing with the composer Virgil Thomson. Many of the men went by feminine aliases, known to one another as, say, "Miss Newport," "Miss Mitzie," or "Miss Newark." The mood was festive, save for one time when Beekman evicted an impudent German by the name of Elberfeld who asserted that, with Sweden next on Chancellor Adolf Hitler's list, Beekman should not "feel so uppity-uppity." Another guest, an elderly gentleman escorted to the premises by a man known as "Madame Fox," had a "very red complexion" with almost "a booze blossom appearance," a "good size belly," "ripples of fat around his face," and a hankering for sailors. On his sporadic and unannounced visits, he would always inquire with Beekman as to the most opportune window for meeting the young seamen in their immaculate white uniforms. He would kiss, hug, and pet the sailors, "lay all over them," in Beekman's words, before escorting them upstairs to the sin chamber, paying Beekman two dollars for each hour. "You know, George, I can never tell when I can drop in," the corpulent visitor mischievously said. "I am a very busy man."

Before America declared war against Germany and Japan in December 1941, Beekman's activities occasionally landed him in trouble with law enforcement. But by the following February, with the nation's citizenry on high alert to report any form of suspicious activity (especially around military installations) to the authorities, the large numbers of sailors seen entering and exiting Beekman's home at strange hours attracted the attention of the Bureau of Naval Intelligence. Establishing themselves across the street in a room on the fifth floor of Holy Family Hospital, a team of officers initiated a round-the-clock surveillance of the house, taking down the license plate numbers of every car that deposited or collected a man at its front steps. On March 14, 1942, after six weeks of observation, a combined force of plainclothes police officers and navy intelligence agents raided the building, ripping up floorboards in search of secret compartments and arresting Beekman along with several sailors and guests. Soon, a secret too reprehensible to speak of would scandalize the Eastern Seaboard, cast a pall over the world's greatest deliberative body, and leave a legendary political career in tatters.

The first hint that the activities at 329 Pacific Street might reverberate beyond a Brooklyn courtroom appeared in the April 22 edition of the Lyons Den, the eponymous daily column penned by Leonard Lyons of the *New York Post*. "When the notorious Beekman case is prosecuted in Brooklyn's County Court next week, it will involve one of the highest ranking legislators in the country," Lyons revealed. For a columnist whose beat consisted mainly of gossip gleaned from the tables at Sardi's, the Algonquin, and other celebrity-heavy spots around the Great White Way, it was a rare political item, and one that no other reporter bothered to pursue.

Two days later, *Post* general counsel Morris Ernst included a tantalizing mention of the Beekman case in the weekly roundup of political intelligence—dubbed "tidbits"—that he sent to FDR. The president devoured Ernst's dispatches, and that week's installment of "tidbits" contained an especially delectable morsel. "Senator Walsh's name is going to appear, in secret probation officer reports, in connection with a scandalous criminal case in Brooklyn," Ernst wrote. "Unless you know about the matter, or unless you are having someone else follow it up for you, I suggest that you might want me to keep in daily touch with the situation. A shocking story will develop which may be of great help to you."

When FDR first heard that Sen. David Ignatius Walsh of Massachusetts had been implicated in a homosexual scandal, he could not have been all that surprised. According to Walsh's biographer, the senator enjoyed women as "nonromantic companions," and his unmarried status had long made him the subject of rumor. After he was elected the first Catholic governor of Massachusetts, in 1914, one of Walsh's new constituents informed him that a bachelor was "unthinkable" in the state's highest office because "the influence of a good woman" was a prerequisite. "Madam," Walsh earnestly replied, "I have been under the influence of six women all my life—my mother and five sisters." A 1929 *Time* magazine profile noted Walsh's "dandified" dress of "silk shirts in bright colors" and reported, "Ironic comments are sometimes heard on the contrast between his political representation and his social activities." Walsh's closest companion (after his sisters) was the manservant he took home with him from a visit to the Philippines, for whose aspirations of national self-determination he subsequently became a strong advocate. Around the Senate Chamber, where he was the first Democrat from Massachusetts to sit since the Civil

War, a wisecrack credited to a Boston department store owner regularly made the rounds: while a man could trust David Walsh to take his daughter sailing across the ocean on a yacht, he would be ill-advised to let him cross the Charles River with his son in a canoe. Many years after Walsh's death, the writer Gore Vidal claimed that the senator sexually propositioned Vidal's father when Vidal Sr. was a cadet at West Point.

The other salient fact about Walsh, as least as far as FDR was concerned, was that he was one of the Senate's leading noninterventionists, a bothersome circumstance that his being a member of the president's political party only exacerbated. Nearly a year to the day before the *Post* first intimated a political angle to the Brooklyn brothel story, Walsh had addressed a massive rally at the Manhattan Center sponsored by the America First Committee, the leading organization opposed to U.S. involvement in the Second World War. The event was headlined by Charles Lindbergh, the most famous opponent of FDR's policies to help Great Britain defend itself against Nazi Germany. Speaking before a crowd of thirty-five thousand people, so large that it poured into the streets, Walsh condemned as "propaganda" administration claims that the Lend-Lease program of assistance to Britain constituted "steps short of war," and he denounced the "damnation, vilification and abuse to which this great man, Colonel Lindbergh, has been subjected in this country, where free speech should be respected." That August, while the Senate debated FDR's request to extend the term of duty for draftees under the Selective Service Act, Walsh used his powerful perch as chairman of the Naval Affairs Committee to condemn the law as having been adopted under "false pretenses," part of a devious effort by the president "to lead us day by day into the war." Walsh was an irritant to FDR in other ways, opposing his effort to pack the Supreme Court and supporting a rival candidate for president at the 1940 Democratic National Convention, where FDR sought nomination for a precedent-breaking third term. Though Walsh, like most noninterventionists, abandoned his opposition to war following the attack on Pearl Harbor, he was, in the words of Attorney General Francis Biddle, "not sympathetic with" the president, "to put it mildly."

And so, while FDR felt no compunction defending his friend and ally Sumner Welles throughout his brush with homosexual scandal, he evinced less sympathy for his political adversary David Walsh, whose chairmanship of a committee dealing with military issues made him particularly vulnerable to allegations that he could be subjected to blackmail. In the armed forces, FDR supposedly told Democratic Senate majority leader Alben Barkley, the honorable course of action for a man found guilty of homosexuality was to shoot himself in the head. The news, therefore, that a prominent critic of his foreign policies was about to be exposed as a patron of an all-male brothel must have brought a smile to the president's face, at least judging by the giddy response he sent to Ernst. "Keep up the tidbits," the president wrote. "They give me a real relaxation from the high ether of naval and military strategy."

Three days later, Ernst fulfilled the president's desires by informing the FBI that Beekman "had identified a picture of Senator David I. Walsh of Massachusetts as that of an individual who had frequented" his house. Beekman made several other shocking claims. Walsh, he said, was escorted to Pacific Street by a man who used the alias "Madame Fox" and had conversed there with a German who claimed "Hitler was his god." Another German national, Beekman said, had visited the house and went by the name of Eric. The presence of these enemy aliens in a brothel soon metastasized into an extraordinary claim by unnamed sources in the district attorney's office, who alleged that "one of Hitler's chief espionage agents in this country" had visited Beekman's home for the purpose of collecting information about ship movements in and out of the Navy Yard. No longer was this a matter of a U.S. senator frolicking at a male bordello. The security of the nation was now at risk.

At least according to the media outlet that would break the story. The country's oldest continuously published daily newspaper, the *New York Post* had an illustrious history. Founded by Alexander Hamilton in 1801, it had enlisted Walt Whitman as a Civil War correspondent and courageously taken on the corrupt political bosses of Tammany Hall. At the outset of the Roosevelt administration in 1933, J. David Stern, the crusading liberal editor of the Philadelphia *Public Ledger* (Bill Bullitt's old stomping grounds), purchased the Republican-supporting *Post* at the behest of FDR, who encouraged Stern to transform it into a champion of his policies. Six years later, Stern sold the *Post* to Dorothy Schiff, granddaughter of the German-born financier Jacob Schiff, who sought to deepen the paper's New Deal bona fides by broadening its readership beyond upper-middle-class liberal professionals to the city's diverse masses. Schiff possessed two qualities advantageous to this mission: self-described "average taste" and an enthusiasm for the president that went beyond the political. "Everything about his body—except his legs—was so strong," Schiff remembered of the man with whom she carried on an affair for seven years.

Just two weeks before Leonard Lyons published his blind item predicting major political fallout from the arrest of Gustave Beekman, Schiff became the first female newspaper publisher in the history of New York City when she took over the job from her estranged husband. The *Post* was lagging far behind its rivals in circulation, and Schiff had an ambitious agenda. Declaring, "We must popularize the paper," she converted the *Post* from broadsheet to tabloid format, making it easier for working-class straphangers to read it on the subway.

One could not have concocted a more appetizing scandal for a left-wing, populist tabloid newspaper loudly supportive of the Roosevelt administration's interventionist foreign policies than that allegedly involving David Walsh. By launching a moralistic crusade against the isolationist senator, implicating him in a shocking tale abundant with squalid details seemingly designed for what the paper touted as "the story of the year," the *Post* could not only discredit one of the president's most nettlesome critics. It could also sell a massive amount of newspapers. Homosexuality, prostitution, blackmail, espionage, Nazis, and a U.S. senator—the Walsh scandal had it all.

On May 1, 1942, the *Post* splashed the sort of blunt, attention-grabbing headline for which it would soon become notorious across its newly redesigned front page. In giant white capital letters set against a pitch-black background, the paper screamed,

LINK
SENATOR
TO SPY
NEST

"A U.S. Senator was identified today as a frequenter of a 'house of degradation' in Brooklyn which was used by Nazi spies to obtain military information," the *Post* reported, identifying the culprit only as "Senator X." A large photograph of the unnamed lawmaker's face, obscured by a white silhouette, accompanied the article. "This is starting to look like pre-collapse France," Ernst merrily reported in that day's "tidbits" to FDR.

As the scandal now involved matters of national security, the FBI took an interest in the case. Elaborating upon the claims he had made to prosecutors days before, Beekman told the Bureau that in September 1940, a man named George Wilbur Fox, aka "Madame Fox," had brought a "Mr. Walsh" to the house Beekman was running at the time on Warren Street. This "Mr. Walsh" visited four times over the following three months and came to the Pacific Street house eight times. Presented with photographs of twelve different men, one of whom was Walsh, Beekman identified the senator as the man in question. When asked about statements he had made in his original affidavit concerning supposed espionage activities, however, Beekman, according to the agents who interviewed him, "was unable to furnish any definite information that such activities were, in fact, being carried on by these homosexuals."

Meanwhile in Washington, the Senate Cloakroom hummed with nervous agitation concerning the identity of "Senator X." Pro-FDR syndicated columnist Walter Winchell helpfully narrowed down the pool of suspects by revealing that the culprit was "one of four Senators with the same last initial . . . The 23rd letter in the alphabet." For almost a week, the *Post* titillated readers with a steady stream of details about the deviant doings at 329 Pacific Street, all the while withholding the identity of Senator X. Finally, on May 6, the paper declared on its front page:

SENATOR X

NAMED

as

DAVID I. WALSH

Chairman of Senate's

Naval Affairs Committee

Walsh's only consolation was that, buried deep within a story identifying him as the treasonous patron of a male brothel frequented by Nazi spies, the American sailors described him as a "very nice man."

Although there was no term for it then, this disclosure by the *Post* constituted the first "outing" in American politics. Notably, the actual word *homosexual* did not appear at all in the paper's coverage, nor in any contemporaneous media accounts. Hardly any outlet other than the *Post* even mentioned Walsh by name. Such ambiguity was characteristic of American public discourse at the time, as the term *homosexual* was rarely used outside the medical profession. Still, the media found ways of conveying just what sort of men could be found at 329 Pacific Street. "The fact that he has remained a bachelor has often caused comment," the *Post* observed of Walsh. The *Brooklyn Eagle* quoted a prosecutor who described Beekman's home as "a place of degradation operated exclusively for men," among them "certain men of some prominence" who entered under "feminine names."

Not every journalist covering the story was so indirect. Shortly after Adolf Hitler ascended to the German Chancellery in 1933, Walter Winchell wrote that the leader of the National Socialist German Workers' Party was "a homo-sexualist, or as we Broadway vulgarians say—an out and out fairy." Now, nearly a decade later, with America engaged in all-out war against Nazi Germany and the police raid of a Nazi-homosexual brothel in New York, Winchell felt vindicated. "The ad libbers are having fun with the yarn about Brooklyn's spy nest," the columnist and former vaudevillian crowed, "also known as the swastika swishery."

* * *

BY LINKING HOMOSEXUALITY WITH NAZISM, Winchell drew on a popular stereotype. Given the harsh repression that the Nazis meted out to gay men—arresting an estimated hundred thousand and murdering between five thousand and fifteen thousand over the course of their twelve-year reign—the notion that fascism was particularly attractive to homosexuals was counterintuitive, to say the least. Yet it was an idea taken quite seriously within the upper ranks of the U.S. government.

The origins of this belief predate the Third Reich, and can be traced back to the *Männerbünd*, the nationalist men's associations founded by veterans of the First World War. Inspired by the intensely emotional bonds they forged fighting in the trenches, a group of these men, according to the historian Robert Beachy, sought "to assimilate homoeroticism to a nationalist, anti-democratic politics." The most infamous figure to emerge from this scene was Ernst Röhm. A cofounder of the paramilitary Sturmabteilung (SA), the gang of right-wing ruffians known as the "Brownshirts," Röhm was unapologetic about his same-sex attraction, and he did surround himself with a number of gay men. When social-democratic activists tried to embarrass him by printing his sexually explicit letters to other men, Röhm, rather than deny authorship, attacked the "incredible prudishness" of his critics. In 1933, a massively influential Soviet propaganda booklet accused Röhm of manipulating an impressionable young homosexual prostitute into burning down the Reichstag, a crucial event in the Nazi rise to power. The celebrated Austrian writer Stefan Zweig, in his acclaimed memoir of interwar Central Europe, *The World of Yesterday*, refers portentously to "secret organizations—strongly under homosexual influence" as having conspired against the ill-fated Weimar republic.

For years, Hitler defended Röhm, dismissing the homosexual accusations with the explanation that the SA was "not an institute for the moral education of genteel young ladies, but a formation of seasoned fighters." Hitler's tolerance evaporated soon into his actual reign, however, though not because of the homosexuality of Röhm and his comrades. Perceiving the rowdy and undisciplined SA as a threat to his consolidation of power, the Führer ordered its *Stabschef* and top lieutenants executed in 1934's infamous "Night of the Long Knives." It was only after this purge that Hitler would settle upon the SA's moral depravity as the cause for its forcible dissolution. In a speech to the Reichstag, he denounced

> within the SA a sect sharing a certain, common orientation, who formed the kernel of a conspiracy not only against the moral conceptions of a healthy Volk, but also against state security. A review of promotions carried out in May led to the terrible discovery that, within certain SA-groups, men were being promoted without regard to National Socialist and SA-service, but only because they belonged to the circle of this orientation.

The myth of a Nazi-homosexual nexus would long outlive the scarfaced, barrel-chested, man-loving bully who inspired it. If Röhm constituted one homosexual stereotype (übermasculine and predatory), then Hitler embodied its opposite (effeminate and hysterical). A 1942 United Press wire service story claimed that Hitler "was psychically a marked homosexual type" who "almost invariably turns any general conversation . . . to some subject betraying his homosexual tendencies. This may consist of some observation or question or his delight in the phallic symbolism of col-umns in architecture." Hitler also "wants tall, clean-shaven, wavy-blond-haired young men around him." Though the members of Hitler's entourage "are not themselves necessarily abnormal," there is "something in Hitler" which "makes him demand this type."

Numerous U.S. government reports affirmed these journalistic impres-sions. There existed "extensive homosexuality among the upper Gestapo," John Franklin Carter, a former journalist who operated his own one-man intelligence bureau within the White House, wrote the president in a June 1941 memo, reporting on the observations of a General Motors represen-tative recently returned from a trip to Germany. Among the dozen Gestapo officials whom the GM man had met, "all gave him the impression of homo-sexual leanings . . . [I]n one instance a young officer showed him with great pride a silver ring inscribed inside with the words 'To My Darling Wilhelm from his Himmler.'" Two influential wartime studies commissioned by the federal government and published in 1943 speculated at length as to the connections between homosexuality and Nazism. *Analysis of the Personal-ity of Adolph Hitler*, by the Harvard psychologist Dr. Henry Murray, noted the "large feminine component in Hitler's physical constitution," "his initial identification with his mother," his "attraction to Röhm and other domi-neering homosexuals," and his "nightmares which, as described by several informants, are very suggestive of homosexual panic." *The Mind of Adolph Hitler*, prepared by Harvard psychoanalyst Dr. Walter C. Langer, purported to substantiate the allegation that, while living in Vienna, the future German leader stayed at a homosexual brothel. Langer's study expounded a theory as to why homosexuals, more than "normal" people, were so attracted to fascist ideology:

> The belief that Hitler is homosexual has probably arisen because he does show so many feminine characteristics and because there were so many homosexuals in the Party during the early days and many continue to occupy important positions. It does seem that Hitler feels much more at ease with homosexuals than with normal persons, but this may be because they are all fundamentally social outcasts and consequently have a community of interests that tend to make them think and feel more or less alike. In this connection it is interesting to note that homo-sexuals, too, frequently regard themselves as a special form of creation

or as chosen ones whose destiny it is to initiate a new order. The fact that underneath they feel themselves to be different and ostracized from normal social contacts usually makes them easy converts to a new social philosophy that does not discriminate against them. Being among civilization's discontents, they are always willing to take a chance on something new that holds any promise of improving their lot, even though their chances of success may be small and the risk great . . . Even today Hitler derives sexual pleasure from looking at men's bodies and associating with homosexuals. [Early Nazi Party member and later defector Otto] Strasser tells us that his personal bodyguard is almost always 100 percent homosexuals. He also derives considerable pleasure from being with his Hitler Youth, and his attitude toward them frequently tends to be more that of a woman than that of a man.

The report goes on to speculate whether Hitler's *Dolchstosslegende*, or "stab-in-the-back" myth blaming Germany's World War I loss on traitorous Jews and socialists, was a sign of latent homosexuality that "finds expression in imagery about being attacked from behind."

* * *

"IT IS A DIABOLICAL LIE, absolutely without foundation," Sen. David Walsh declared in response to the allegation that he had visited a homosexual brothel in the company of Nazi spies. "I have never in my life been to such a place." Despite the lack of solid evidence that Walsh had passed along any secrets to Nazi agents, the mere accusation that he had visited 329 Pacific Street at the same time as "one of the most dangerous Nazi spies in this country," the *Post* averred, was sufficient grounds for his permanent "banishment from public office." Furthermore, the paper threatened, "The truth is certain to come out. If it does not come out clearly, and publicly, then it will come out hazily, and privately." Over the next five days, the *Post* published no fewer than four separate editorials demanding the Senate open an investigation into Walsh.

In Boston's top political watering holes, the good money was on Walsh's imminent resignation, and attention was already turning to possible successors. The New York *Daily News* reported that the Walsh case was but one element in a much larger conspiracy, as the investigation into "Senator X" was bound to expose "a chain of houses of prostitution, throughout the coastal area, maintained especially for the purpose of obtaining war secrets, which are sent to a central clearing house for transmission to the enemy." FBI investigators, meanwhile, zeroed in on another theory: that the whole imbroglio was a case of mistaken identity. One of the witnesses who testified against Beekman had described having met a man at 329 Pacific Street who matched Walsh's profile, known to him only as "Doc." Presumably by tracing license plate numbers belonging to the men who had parked their cars outside the town house, the FBI located a Dr. Harry Stone of Connecticut, who not only matched the physical description offered by the witness but, in an interview with the Bureau, acknowledged that he had patronized Pacific Street under the name of "Doc." (At no time, he added, did he hear anything there about "Nazi Queens.") Three days later, following a punishing interrogation that began at 5:45 p.m. and lasted until midnight, and that resumed for several hours the next morning, Beekman relented and said that he had confused Sen. David Walsh with Dr. Harry Stone. With this admission in hand, the FBI promptly delivered to the president and Majority Leader Barkley a report exonerating Walsh.

Yet, before Barkley could even publicize the report, Beekman recanted his recantation. In yet *another* affidavit, containing what the *Nation* magazine termed "unprintable details," Beekman said that the statement he had given to the FBI exonerating Walsh was delivered under duress. Beekman, his lawyer declared, had been "browbeaten, persecuted, and questioned" into falsely claiming that he had mistaken the senator for another man.

On May 20, the same day that the *Post* published this retraction, eighty-four senators, including Walsh, gathered in the Senate Chamber to discuss what *Time* dubbed "one of the worst scandals that ever affected a member of the Senate." Following the opening prayer, Walsh quietly left the hall while Barkley, twenty-five-page FBI report in hand, called for a point of personal privilege. Beekman, the majority leader thundered, had been convicted of "an offense too loathsome to mention in the Senate or in any group of ladies and gentlemen." The man accusing their colleague, in other words, was a homosexual and should be discredited on that fact alone. The FBI's exculpation of Walsh contained details that were "disgusting and unprintable," Barkley continued, material that "should not be in the [Congressional] Record." As for the man misidentified by the *Post* as Walsh, "Doc" Stone, Barkley scoffed, he resembled the senator from Massachusetts no more "than I look like Haile Selassie."

Thus did it transpire that, as *Time* observed, "one of the strangest incidents in the history of the U.S. press came to general public knowledge: a major scandal had broken and, for a fortnight, only one paper had published anything about it." If propriety had prevented journalists and politicians from stating explicitly the crime "too loathsome to mention," no longer could they ignore the saga of David Walsh. Reactions fell largely along partisan lines. Missouri isolationist Democrat Bennett Clark denounced "the old hussy who runs the *New York Post*"; alleged that Morris Ernst "brought the story to Washington and went to the White House with it in an attempt to interest the highest authority in Washington in an effort to smear" Walsh; and demanded that the Senate condemn Walter Winchell, who "undertook to smear not only the senator from Massachusetts but three other members of the senate whose names happen to begin with 'W.'" Republican senator Gerald Nye of North Dakota, another FDR critic, spoke darkly of a "secret society" engaged "in an undertaking to gather such information as would permit the smearing of individual members of the Senate." The most virulent attack came from the pages of the conservative *Chicago Tribune*, owned by the rabidly right-wing Republican former army officer (and cousin of fellow Roosevelt-hater Cissy Patterson) Robert "Colonel" McCormick. A Groton classmate of FDR's and a member of the Medill media dynasty, McCormick was one of the country's most vociferous opponents of the New Deal. In a front-page story beneath the banner headline "Blast Plot to Ruin Senator," the paper detailed "one of the most despicable attempts at character assassination that could be conceived."

On the other side of the partisan divide, the *New Republic* tiptoed around the veracity of the accusations. "Whether or not the charge be true," the magazine editorialized, Walsh "would deserve defeat . . . because of his record in the Senate and as chairman of the Naval Affairs Committee," namely, his "obstruction in the war effort." Stubbornly sticking to its position was the paper that had started the whole imbroglio. In an open letter to Attorney General Biddle, *New York Post* editor Ted Thackrey declared that the FBI, "long the pride of our Democracy, has under your direction been used as though it were the counterpart of the secret police of Communist Russia or Nazi Germany." Behind the scenes, however, Dorothy Schiff was growing nervous. That summer, she hired a private investigator, Daniel A. Doran, to conduct an independent investigation into Beekman, Walsh, and the *Post* investigation thereof. Over the course of several months, Doran and his team of gumshoes fanned out across New York City, Connecticut, and Massachusetts, interviewing dozens of people and compiling their findings into an exhaustive one-hundred-fifty-page report.

At the outset, Doran faced a challenge. As deception was presumed to be an inherent feature of the secret world homosexuals inhabited, nothing they said could be taken at face value. "I never caught him in a lie and aside from the fact that he is a fag, I would believe him in anything he says," remarked a police patrolman who had questioned Beekman after a 1940 arrest. Though Doran came to the conclusion that the Swede was "unreliable and contradictory," he assured Schiff that "[i]n evaluating Mr. Beekman's credibility, I did not consider the fact that he is a panderer to homosexuals but only the obvious falsehoods and contradictions which appear from his narrative concerning the visits of Senator Walsh." As to the question of whether Walsh was himself homosexual, Doran collected a great deal of hearsay, but no proof. An official with the Coordinating Committee for Democratic Action, a pro-FDR group, recommended "reliable people" who could attest to Walsh's "meanderings in Boston." A customer of Walsh's tailor shop in New York said that the employees "all knew of Mr. Walsh's homosexual predilections," yet when an investigator paid a visit, the proprietor "froze" and "refused to even discuss" the matter. A reporter based in the DC bureau of the *New York Times* claimed that a colleague from the *New York Herald Tribune* had been the subject of "improper advances" from Walsh while traveling with the senator on the presidential train during the 1940 congressional campaign. A young woman "with a large acquaintance among homosexuals" (possessing, one of the investigators noted, a talent for recognizing men who are "that way") claimed that Walsh "put a young lawyer through Harvard College," implying that Walsh had received something more than gratitude in return. But none of this constituted evidence for what the paper had claimed.

Ultimately, Doran and his crack team of investigators did not have to travel any farther than the office of the Senate sergeant at arms to resolve the question they had been hired to answer. Walsh's attendance record—"very regular," arriving at the start of every session, staying until close, and answering every roll call vote—revealed that he could not have been in Brooklyn at the times he was alleged. The case of Senator X, Doran concluded, had been characterized by "plausible rumors or stories which by repetition had almost achieved the status of facts." While the *Post* might have "had reason to believe that Senator Walsh was a visitor to Beekman's place" at the time of its original reporting, "not a single item of legal evidence has been obtained to corroborate Mr. Beekman's statements as to the visits of Senator Walsh. On the contrary, the various leads which we pursued tended to impeach Beekman rather than corroborate him."

The *Post*, in other words, had committed an act of gross journalistic malpractice, one it never bothered to correct. Though Walsh did not speak publicly about the ordeal beyond his initial denial, "personally," he confided to a friend, it was "a tragic Gethsemane." Running for reelection in 1946, he lost to Republican Henry Cabot Lodge Jr. and died the following year a broken man.

The case of David Walsh offers a stark example of the degree to which homosexuality existed outside the realm of ordinary partisan and ideological commitments. Liberals who by contemporary standards might have been expected to defend the privacy rights of an oppressed minority group led the charge to expose and ruin one of its members. Morris Ernst, for instance, in addition to working for the *New York Post*, served as a general counsel for the American Civil Liberties Union, in which capacity he scored a major victory for the First Amendment when he successfully defended the novel *Ulysses* from obscenity charges in 1933. And yet it was Ernst and his liberal allies who used the accusation of homosexuality to destroy Walsh, while the reactionary publisher of the *Chicago Tribune* and conservative isolationist senators defended him. Homosexuality was so far removed from the traditional left–right political spectrum as to exist in a completely different universe.

Asserting that there had been "no parallel in the history of the Senate for the low-level viciousness of the attack" upon Walsh, one columnist confidently asserted that this particular "smear as a political weapon has been dealt a death blow from which it is hardly likely it can be brought back to life." It was a prediction that would prove incredibly premature.

4

PATRIOTIC HOMOSEXUALS

POSTED TO VIENNA IN 1916, THE YOUNG AMERICAN DIPLOMAT ALLEN Dulles found the capital of the Hapsburg Empire unnerved by an ominous trifecta of espionage, treason, and homosexuality. The instrument of this disturbance, an Austro-Hungarian Army colonel named Alfred Redl, had committed suicide three years earlier after being exposed as a Russian spy. Before taking his own life, Redl had been a highly decorated officer and the head of the Army's counterintelligence unit, the Evidenzbureau. According to his neighbor Stefan Zweig, Redl had an appreciation for "the pleasures of the senses," evidenced by his accumulation of a second home in Prague, four expensive automobiles, and a wine cellar stocked with more than a thousand bottles of champagne. That Redl enjoyed all these luxuries ostensibly on a colonel's salary ought to have raised suspicions among his superiors. But it was not until agents of the Evidenzbureau observed him picking up a cash-stuffed envelope at the Vienna post office in May 1913 that they discovered his treachery. Confronting Redl later in a hotel room, they obtained a confession that he had spied for the Russians, handed him a revolver, and locked the door. The following note was found after Redl pulled the trigger:

Passion and levity have destroyed me. I pay with my life
for my sins. Pray for me.

–Alfred

Almost instantly, a narrative developed conflating Redl's homosexuality with his treason. In Prague, the police who broke into his apartment reported their discovery of "a thickly perfumed homosexual pleasure cave." Hoping to alleviate the embarrassment of a mole at the very top of its counterintelligence apparatus, the military promoted the story that the Russians had blackmailed Redl into working for them on account of his sexual deviancy. Once Russia declared war on Austria-Hungary the following year, plunging the Continent into the First World War, Redl's treason began to loom larger in the public imagination as self-serving generals deflected blame for their battlefield defeats onto the dead colonel, supposedly blackmailed into passing along their battle plans to the Russians and protected while doing so by a conspiratorial "homosexual organization." So notorious was Redl's disgrace that his two surviving brothers changed their surnames.

The scandal earned a level of international infamy second only to that of the nearly contemporaneous Dreyfus affair, with which it shared one important feature. Unlike the Jewish artillery officer falsely accused of handing French military secrets to Germany, Redl was indeed guilty of treason. But as with Dreyfus, Redl's isolated example was exploited for political purposes to scapegoat an entire minority. A quarter of a century after Redl committed suicide, one of America's highest-circulation newspapers denounced him as the "Murderer of a Million Men," one who had betrayed his country "so he could buy a boyfriend a car."

Documents uncovered in Russian government archives in the early 2000s, however, suggest it was "the pleasures of the senses," *not* the pleasures of male flesh, that precipitated Redl's treason. According to an officer from the Italian intelligence service, to which he also sold secrets, Redl was so avaricious that recruiting him "required no effort." Moreover, Redl's homosexuality was apparently unknown to his Russian handler, who referred to him as "a lover of women," thereby invalidating the blackmail thesis. And even had Redl's homosexuality been exposed, it is by no means definite that this would have ruined his career. Homosexuality was quietly tolerated in some aristocratic circles of late belle époque Vienna; no less than Emperor Franz Joseph's younger brother, Archduke Ludwig Viktor, was a cross-dresser with a fondness for army officers.

These mitigating details were unknown to the twenty-three-year-old Dulles when he was present at the creation of a cultural archetype: the homosexual traitor. The future American spymaster, a grandson of one secretary of state and a nephew by marriage of another, "had never before encountered this sort of human frailty," according to his biographer Peter Grose. "Of the homosexuality he knew little and understood less. It was the betrayal of trust that brought his first shock. As the years passed, shock gave way to wonder at the impact one individual could make upon affairs of state, then to fascination that a fleeting moment of carelessness could reveal a decade of evil contrivance." Forty-five years after Redl committed suicide, Dulles included an account of the episode in an anthology he edited, *Great True Spy Stories*; elsewhere, he wrote that the Austrian colonel suffered from "two weaknesses—homosexuality and overwhelming venality." Apart from the state funeral of Emperor Franz Joseph, *l'affaire Redl* produced the only memory that Dulles retained from his time in Vienna.

Though he ascribed great significance to homosexuality in the practice of espionage, Dulles maintained a basic ignorance about it well into adulthood. In November 1942, with some fifteen years as a lawyer for the white-shoe firm of Sullivan and Cromwell under his belt, Dulles returned to Central Europe again on behalf of his government. This time, it was to the capital of Switzerland (Bern) and as a senior official in the Office of Strategic Services (OSS). FDR had established the country's first civilian-led intelligence agency that June to replace the Office of the Coordinator of Information (COI), which he had created the previous summer to facilitate information-sharing among the preexisting military intelligence outfits. To lead both organizations, FDR chose William "Wild Bill" Donovan, a Republican businessman and World War I Medal of Honor recipient who had come to his attention via the sharp-eyed analyses of the darkening international situation he had written and circulated to friends while traveling the world in the 1930s. From his base in Switzerland, Dulles was tasked with recruiting German émigrés, resistance activists, and Nazi defectors, a job to which he was well suited given his insistence, after witnessing the appalling brutalities meted out to Jews during a visit to Germany in 1935, that Sullivan and Cromwell shut down its Berlin office.

Prior to Dulles's arrival in Bern, his OSS advance man had caught wind of an "underground transnational" coterie of "upper-class" German, English, American, Swiss, and Greek homosexuals that might prove useful to the budding American intelligence network. But he ultimately withheld the information from the prim and patrician Dulles, whom he suspected "could not cope with this rather special affinity group." Such suspicion was later confirmed by Mary Bancroft, Dulles's mistress and OSS colleague in Bern. Discussing Paragraph 175, the Bismarck-era prohibition on sodomy that the Nazis were ruthlessly enforcing, Bancroft remarked that prosecutions "were unusually vicious because of the large number of homosexuals in both the SA and SS who took advantage of it to settle all manner of personal vendettas."

Dulles's curiosity was piqued. "What do those people actually do?" he asked.

"Don't you know?"

Dulles indicated that he did not.

"Do you want me to tell you?" Bancroft asked, incredulous that such a well-educated, worldly man could be so oblivious.

"If you know."

Bancroft then elucidated the mechanics of homosexual intercourse. "Those people do different things just like everyone else," she said.

"I'm glad to know," he replied with a laugh. "I've always wondered."

"Wasn't it part of my contribution to the war effort to see that this distinguished spy master was enlightened about one of life's realities of which he was apparently blissfully unaware?" Bancroft reflected some four decades later. "We had recently learned that there was a homosexual underground . . . through which information traveled even more rapidly than by the channels of the Catholic Church and various Jewish organizations. A colleague of my generation told me how essential it was for us to tap this homosexual underground by having, as he put it, 'Washington send us a guy with a pretty behind.'"

If espionage is the world's second-oldest profession and prostitution its first, then a rough combination of the two, "sexspionage," is very old indeed. The biblical character Delilah used sex to get Samson to reveal the source of his prodigious strength. The Confederate operative Isabelle "La Belle Rebelle" Boyd deployed her feminine wiles to extract battlefield maneuvers from Union soldiers. Mata Hari, a Dutch exotic dancer induced by France during the First World War to obtain information from the German officers she entertained, was executed on suspicion of being a double agent. If sex, or the promise of it, can be used to acquire clandestine information from heterosexuals, then "a guy with a pretty behind" can be an important asset, so to speak.

"The suggestion of using homosexuals in certain government work is probably a new way of serving our country that has not been brought to your attention heretofore," a special assistant to the secretary of the navy wrote to a COI official on December 24, 1941, just a few weeks after America's declaration of war against Germany and Japan. "May I confide to your judgment the letter of Alfred A. Gross, of the Committee for the Study of Sex Variants in New York City, who seeks an opportunity to serve his country along somewhat unusual lines. Merry Christmas!"

In his letter, Gross laid out a proposal concerning "homosexual men in connection with possible counter-espionage activity." The Committee for the Study of Sex Variants, he explained, had been researching male homosexuals in New York City and, "for some reason, naval personnel seem exceptionally choice objects for the interest of these individuals." Gross elaborated:

We have repeatedly come upon the ramifications of homosexual interest as transcending ordinary social restrictions, and we have seen homosexuals at home in the society of men of much more adequate social situation. . . . It is therefore entirely possible that in the subversive group with which Naval Intelligence must deal there are to be found a certain number of homosexuals. It is of more than passing interest that there is a large percentage of homosexuals among Germans. . . . It is not impossible, then, that homosexual men attempt to seduce members of the Naval forces in order to obtain vital information. It is not impossible that we could arrange to deal with such individuals through building up a force of patriotic homosexual men who were rejected from service because of the provision of the Selective Service Act excluding these men. I am thinking of men of two sorts—patriotic men who would serve through motives of national service, and the lower "stool pigeon" type of male prostitute who would probably have to be paid for services rendered.

. . . You with your long experience as an intelligence officer could easily sketch out a plan of procedure if you thought the idea were not too hare-brained and the result of having read too many detective stories.

Gross attached the résumé of his colleague Thomas Painter, a Yale- and Oxford-educated expert in the field of male prostitution, who listed under "special qualifications for this task" his

Ability to "spot" homosexuals and prostitutes on sight, not with total accuracy, but far beyond general lay or medical capacity in this line.

Knowledge of, and familiar in use of homosexual argot and ways of behavior, methods and places of assignation and resort.

Deep understanding and familiarity with both the homosexual and bisexual delinquent.

Comprehensive knowledge of the exact nature and extent of the homosexual society; of the history of past and present social and medical therapeutics; of the nature and mind set of homosexuals and delinquents toward possible therapeutics.

In what was undoubtedly a reference to David Walsh, Gross also revealed that "Painter has a man in mind right now who would bear some investigation, a Senator who is pursuing sailors."

"If it is really a serious institution, I would strongly recommend a careful study," John C. Wiley, a career diplomat recruited to run COI's Foreign Nationalities Branch, wrote his colleagues in response to Gross's proposal. The last U.S. ambassador to Latvia and Estonia before their annexation by the Soviet Union, Wiley said that America's new Russian ally had a long-standing "interest" in the espionage potential of homosexuality. A high-ranking Soviet secret police official had once told him that Dmitry Florinsky, erstwhile chief of protocol in the Soviet Foreign Ministry, had been fired on the grounds of the "political 'freemasonry' of homosexuality in Europe—namely, that Florinsky could not be trusted" due to his alleged membership in the clandestine, transnational fraternity of homosexual men. Wiley also noted the "special relationship" that had allegedly existed during the 1920s between Soviet foreign minister Georgy Chicherin and German ambassador to Moscow Count Ulrich von Brockdorf-Rantzau. Their furtive and illicit human bond emulated a diplomatic one: the secret annex to the 1922 Treaty of Rapallo allowing the German military to train on Soviet soil in contravention of the Versailles agreement. "The idea of using homosexuals for purposes of political and military intelligence," Wiley concluded, "should definitely be taken seriously." Another COI official concurred. "This should be followed up," he scribbled on an interoffice circulation memo. "I know of 2 professional sources where very complete files of all known homos in the Eastern US can be obtained."

There is no public record indicating whether the U.S. government pursued this proposal to enlist gay men in the seduction of Nazis. According to a disciple of Dr. Alfred Kinsey, whose groundbreaking study of homosexuality would have a profound impact on American society upon its publication in 1948, the sex researcher claimed personal knowledge of a male brothel that the FBI supposedly operated on MacDougal Street in Greenwich Village for the "highly successful purpose of extracting shipping information from foreign sailors" during the war. If it ever existed, this operation would have been a reverse of the gay Nazi "spy nest" supposedly used to entrap Sen. David Walsh. Though no solid evidence exists of such an establishment, "patriotic homosexual men" (and women) served the Allied cause in numerous other ways, applying their "deviant" sexuality to the fight against fascism.

* * *

WHILE THE OSS IS CHIEFLY REMEMBERED FOR BEING the predecessor to the Central Intelligence Agency, another attribute can be added to its legacy: the establishment of a culture of relative acceptance for gay people within the national security state. The reason for this tolerance, albeit brief in duration and limited in scope, was pragmatic, as gays were seen to possess qualities beneficial for espionage. For the homosexual in mid-twentieth-century America, deception and keeping secrets were matters of basic survival.

It was not until after the Second World War, when their victorious exploits were celebrated in popular films and novels, that spies would be romanticized in the American imagination. Before, espionage was widely viewed as a low and dirty business, exemplified by secretary of state Henry L. Stimson's admonition that "Gentlemen do not read each other's mail." One OSS employee observed that an agent in the organization "risked his future status as a banker or trustee or highly placed politician in identifying himself with illegality and unorthodoxy." For gay men and women, however, illegality and unorthodoxy were integral to one's existence.

The ideal OSS agent, Bill Donovan liked to say, was "a Ph.D. who can win a bar fight." To staff his ranks, he gathered a "weird collection of characters," comprising "international bankers, professors, ex-convicts, ministers, wrestlers, labor leaders, bluebloods from America's wealthiest families, explorers, confidence men." Sharing FDR's single-minded resolve to defeat Hitler, Donovan imposed no ideological litmus tests. He welcomed veterans of the Communist-aligned Abraham Lincoln Brigade who had fought against Franco's forces in the Spanish Civil War and put Marxist intellectuals like Herbert Marcuse to work in the famed OSS Research and Analysis Branch, where academics studied open-source information potentially useful to the war effort. It was a diverse band, a full third of it women, and the workplace culture was remarkably egalitarian. "I can't recall a time when your gender mattered more than your ability to contribute," recalled Marion Frieswyk, an analyst in the Mapping division. The upstart agency "had the lenient, idiosyncratic atmosphere of a small college, with the same tolerance for campus radicals, zealots and oddballs," author Jennet Conant writes in her book about one such OSS veteran, Julia Child, who worked directly under Donovan before going on to earn international fame as a culinary personality. Donovan's unorthodox approach earned the OSS its fair share of bureaucratic detractors, who ridiculed its acronym as "Oh So Social" and "Oh So Swish," the latter an intimation of one trait allegedly prevalent among its spies and spymasters.

One such individual was Cora Du Bois, a Berkeley-trained cultural anthropologist who, by war's end, was the only woman to lead an OSS branch office, on the island of Ceylon. Like many patriotic and loyal Americans with left-wing sympathies, however, Du Bois was later targeted by the FBI. According to her biographer, Susan Seymour, Du Bois's lesbianism also aroused suspicion, with FBI investigators noting her "single status" and "residence with [name redacted]," a woman whom Seymour concludes was Du Bois's lover Jeanne Taylor. Du Bois was likely aware that her relationship endangered her livelihood; upon taking a leave of absence in 1948 from her job at the State Department to teach at UC Berkeley, she and Taylor lived separately.

Before writing for newspapers such as the *Washington Daily News*, the *Baltimore Evening Sun*, *PM*, and the *New York Post*, Gordon Merrick was reputed to be "the handsomest young man on Broadway." Appearing in the original 1939 production of *The Man Who Came to Dinner*, the budding thespian lived for a time in an apartment at 17 Gay Street in Greenwich Village. In May 1944, Merrick joined OSS's counterintelligence (X-2) branch, where he was one of the earliest American spies to develop the practice of running double agents abroad. Though the tale is probably apocryphal, the daring and debonair Merrick was said to have joined the Allied landing in the South of France decked out in a white dinner jacket and black patent-leather shoes, a martini glass in hand. From the comfort of a Cannes villa replete with swimming pool, cook, and servants— his wartime experience, he later said, was "anything but grim"—Merrick supervised a French double agent code-named "Forest," an experience he fictionalized in a 1947 book, *The Strumpet Wind*. Merrick went on to earn riches and notoriety as an author of racy gay romance novels; his 1970 pulp classic *The Lord Won't Mind* earned a spot on the *New York Times* best seller list for four months.

The most consequential of the OSS's gay spies was Donald Downes. One of seven children born in 1903 to an upper-middle-class couple in suburban Baltimore, Downes discovered the meaning of the word *pervert* as a young boy, when his mother's friend burst into their home one day with the news that her husband had deserted her for a man. According to an OSS colleague, Downes formed an "exclusive association" with his Yale roommate, Robert Ullman, that was to last the better part of three decades. Neither man was closeted, or, in the words of another OSS colleague, "crypto-homosexual," their openness making them extremely unusual for their day. ("In the Yale of those years [Downes's] devotion to a Jewish roommate would hardly have improved his social standing," either, this same colleague noted.)

Following Yale, Downes spent several years bouncing around New England teaching at various boarding schools, while spending his summers in Europe perfecting his French, Spanish, and Italian. In 1940, with war brewing, he set his mind on becoming a spy after reading *The Strategy of Terror*, an exposé of German front groups (also known as fifth columns) across the Continent. "I read the book over and over," Downes recalled. "It explained all the things I had seen on my recent trips to Europe." He devised an idea for a "Sixth Column," an extensive network of sleeper cells comprised "of the U.S.'s friends throughout the countries likely to be occupied by the Germans, and probably the Japanese, in case we got into war." After both the Office of Naval Intelligence and the army's G-2 intelligence service turned him down, Downes offered his services to the British Security Co-ordination (BSC). Established secretly by that country's foreign intelligence arm, MI6, and operating out of offices on the thirty-fifth and thirty-sixth floors of Rockefeller Center in New York City, the BSC was tasked with influencing American public opinion in Britain's favor, spying on pro-Nazi groups, and foiling acts of sabotage against British interests. Leaping at the opportunity to join what he lauded as the "venerable scoundrel tradition" of the British secret service, Downes traveled undercover as an English instructor to Istanbul, which he used as a base of operations for missions across the Western Balkans gathering intelligence on the Axis powers.

When the United States finally entered the war, BSC director William Stephenson suggested that Downes legitimize his activities by joining Bill Donovan's Office of the Coordinator of Information, which the BSC had mentored into being. Alongside his lover Ullman, Downes worked in the field of counterintelligence, surveilling enemy agents spying on his country and recruiting double agents to inform on theirs. One of the couple's first assignments was to make use of an exiled anti-Nazi German diplomat, a baron named Wolfgang Gans Edler Herr zu Putlitz. An imposing man with a "face like a hooded eagle" and the heir to a twelfth-century Junker castle outside Berlin, Putlitz was working as a first secretary in Germany's London embassy during the mid-1930s when he started handing secrets over to the British. The information was extremely valuable, relating mainly to German foreign policy, the activities of Nazi Party members in Britain, and the strength of the Luftwaffe, the last of which Winston Churchill utilized in parliamentary speeches urging more funds for the Royal Air Force. According to Christopher Andrew, the leading historian of Britain's intelligence services, Putlitz was the "most important source" for Britain's domestic intelligence agency, MI5, in the years leading up to the war.

Like Downes and Ullman, Putlitz also happened to be gay. It was a trait that—the OSS-commissioned study deeming homosexuals "easy converts to a new social philosophy" like fascism notwithstanding—endowed Putlitz with a more acute grasp of the dangers Nazism posed. Putlitz had come to America thanks to the intervention of Ambassador Joseph Kennedy, who had arranged a visa for him and his "male servant," Frederick "Willy" Schneider. Before departing for New York, Putlitz was thrown what he described as a "very gay party" by a BBC journalist named Guy Burgess, whom he had met several years earlier while Burgess was an undergraduate at Cambridge University.

Almost immediately after Putlitz and Schneider disembarked in New York, the true nature of their relationship became apparent to their hosts. Concerned that the Germans might be double agents, Assistant Secretary of State Adolf Berle had asked J. Edgar Hoover to place them under surveillance. Every move the two men made, every person they met, and every establishment they visited was duly recorded by the FBI agents assigned to follow them. One night, the vigilant G-men wrote, Putlitz "was observed frequenting the darker bypaths of [Central] park which are apparently frequented by homosexuals." Another evening, Putlitz and Schneider visited a nightclub on Fifty-Second Street, which the agents following them "ascertained by personal observation and discreet inquiry of persons in the neighborhood . . . is a place catering almost exclusively to homosexuals." The following week, the couple visited the St. Nicholas Ballroom in Harlem, an establishment "frequented almost entirely by colored people" and "Lesbians and homosexuals," from which they later left "arm in arm" with "three colored men." A friend Putlitz met for lunch, the agents found, had stayed several times at the Plaza Hotel suite of one Herman Sartorius, who, according to the Plaza's manager, "is a man of good reputation with the exception that he is a homosexual." Reading these reports, one deciphers the lineaments of a hidden, radically democratic world, extending all the way from Harlem to the Plaza Hotel, in which a German aristocrat could fraternize with African Americans, all of them united in their status as sexual outlaws.

Forced to be outsiders, a disproportionate number of gays and lesbians in the twentieth century became preternaturally incisive observers. Living on society's edge, they acquired skills of perception and discernment that shone through in their work as artists, novelists, social critics, and, in the case of Downes and Putlitz, intelligence analysts. In a memo to Allen Dulles, Downes proposed that the OSS exploit Putlitz's encyclopedic knowledge of internecine Nazi bureaucratic politics—the rivalries between "the S.A., Himmler and the S.S., Goebbels and the propaganda machine, Goering and the Luftwaffe, Ribbentrop and the foreign service, the generals and the army"—in service of a propaganda strategy aimed at dividing the regime from within. Putlitz would be a valuable collaborator, Downes wrote, as he "knows the vocabulary, the attitudes, the mutual jealousies and the personalities of these very well. The proper hint, the proper innuendo, the proper suspicion might cause considerable friction between these various departments." To carry out this psychological warfare operation, Downes suggested that Putlitz issue radio broadcasts into Germany, his voice being especially valuable in that "his German is obviously the German of a Prussian aristocrat, and not, as so much of our present propaganda, rendered semi-comic by" the "Austrian and Jewish accents" of the émigrés employed by the U.S. government. Downes also had Putlitz write up a collection of brief biographical sketches of leading Nazis, several of whom the baron identified as fellow homosexuals. Meanwhile, to keep Schneider occupied, an assistant FBI director proposed to Hoover that the valet be sent to work as a bartender at the White Sulphur Springs resort in West Virginia, where German diplomats were being interned, to work as an informant for the Bureau.

The possibility of recruiting such men to work on behalf of the United States was inconceivable to J. Edgar Hoover, and not only because they were gay. Since its prewar inception as the Office of the Coordinator of Information, the OSS had constantly been in the FBI's crosshairs. Hoover, who never once traveled outside the United States in his seventy-seven years, was averse to anything even remotely foreign. The president's decision to permit intelligence agents of another country to operate on U.S. soil outraged him; that they were agents of America's closest ally made not a whit of difference. In a 1942 memo to subordinates, Hoover declared himself "disgusted with this fellow Stevenson [sic]" and "the things they have done in this country."

Another source of tension between the OSS and FBI was their widely divergent cultures, as personified by their respective leaders. Whereas Hoover was a dour dictator within the organization he founded and led, Donovan was a peripatetic champion of creativity who encouraged the men (and women) working under him in any number of daring (and occasionally futile) adventures. The historian Arthur Schlesinger Jr., one of the many academics whom Donovan recruited, later paid tribute to America's first civilian intelligence chief as "a remarkable man, a winning combination of charm, audacity, imagination, optimism and energy," constantly "coming up with ideas and initiatives and then cheerfully moving on to something else." Hoover, a natural paranoid and control freak who had begun his career at the FBI by "investigating the investigators" and who regularly dismissed agents for failure to comply with the Bureau's strict dress code, considered Donovan's hiring leftists, academics, homosexuals, and other eccentric individuals unconscionable, if not treasonous.

The prominence of a man like Donald Downes within the OSS exemplified everything Hoover hated about the organization. Downes was a product of the liberal East Coast establishment. He began his intelligence career working as the unregistered agent of a foreign government. He was politically left-wing, had lived abroad, and spoke multiple languages. Finally, and most unforgivably, there was Downes's being what his five-thousand-page FBI file described as a "sex deviate," a quality he would put to use in one of his very first missions as an OSS officer.

* * *

JUAN FRANCISCO DE CÁRDENAS was "more than merely homosexual." According to the top secret report sent by Donald Downes to Allen Dulles on March 20, 1942, the Spanish ambassador to the United States had "refinements of sexual mania, perverted with both sexes," facts "well known to his servants, to his associates, and to his wife," Lucienne. Under Cárdenas's direction, the Spanish embassy was the site of an endless bacchanal, albeit one meticulously designed to elicit valuable information for the fascist regime of Generalissimo Franco. Cárdenas's parties "usually result in excesses, alcoholic and further; guests, however, are handpicked and hand-placed, to excite romances among the various diplomatic corps that will give him an intimate insight to the private affairs of government circles." Foremost among the ambassador's American friends was none other than Sumner Welles, Downes reported, whom Cárdenas had met during his first stint in Washington as a young diplomat in the 1920s, when Welles oversaw Latin American affairs at the State Department. Welles was between the divorce from his first wife and the marriage to his second, "gossip insisting that the latter romance was Cárdenas-fostered," Downes wrote. Señora Cárdenas's explanation that her husband's biweekly trips to New York were for medical treatment, meanwhile, didn't fool anyone on the embassy staff. "One school of gossip claims he has a venereal disease, the other that these trips might easily result in a venereal disease." Reading these delightfully piquant and gossipy memos, one envisages Downes the way his friend, the playwright Tennessee Williams, would later describe him: as a man who "looks like a pleasantly depraved Roman emperor such as Tiberius and talks like a character out of Dashiell Hammett."

When Downes composed this report to Dulles in the spring of 1942, the Allies were planning for an invasion of North Africa, large parts of which had fallen under the control of the Axis powers. The geopolitical orientation of Francoist Spain was of major strategic importance. American and British military planners doubted the regime's official position of neutrality and needed to know whether Franco would remain nonaligned, allow German troops to land in Spanish-occupied Morocco, or join the Axis outright. For several years prior to America's declaration of war, the BSC had been breaking into the Washington embassies of neutral countries, Spain's included, to obtain keys for the cipher codes that were used to transmit encrypted messages to Europe. Wary of upsetting its new ally, William Stephenson asked Donovan if his men could shoulder the burden. FDR had explicitly forbidden the OSS from carrying out espionage work within the United States, however, and so Donovan devised a clever justification for the task: given that embassies technically sat on foreign territory, it would neither violate the president's edict nor intrude onto FBI jurisdiction for Americans to burgle them.

Now all Donovan had to do was choose an agent to carry out the mission. Downes was a natural fit for the job. Whenever Donovan had difficulty convincing a general of the merits of a proposed operation, one of his surefire tactics to win them over was to summon the portly former prep school teacher into the room. "Tell them about your experiences in the Mideast," Donovan instructed, at which point Downes, described by one colleague as "that strange, wild, capable fellow," would regale his inter-locutors with tales of his derring-do abroad.

To break into the embassies, Downes pioneered the use of sex as an instrument of American intelligence tradecraft. When a secretary at the mission of Vichy France demanded not only money in exchange for her cooperation as an informant but also suitors for herself and her homely daughter, Downes readily offered up two young male assistants. Pene-trating the Spanish embassy was to prove a more complex job, one for which Downes enlisted a group of Spanish anti-Franco exiles, about half of whom were Communists. Among them was twenty-six-year-old Ricardo Sicre, "the handsomest man I've ever seen," Downes recalled. Sicre went by the nom de guerre Rick Sickler, and introduced to Downes "one of the handsomest young Americans I've ever seen," an "Adonis-like" twenty-something former merchant marine who spoke flawless Spanish. Downes sent the young man to a tailor, put a wad of cash in his hand, and ordered him to seduce the secretaries at the Spanish embassy. One of those women, a "not very bright" but "good hearted" twenty-nine-year-old California-born daughter of Basque parentage, fell easily for "our Romance-on-short-notice man," Downes wrote Dulles. As his colleagues at COI headquarters—a nondescript building dubbed "the Kremlin," located on a hill overlooking the Potomac, and with an unlisted address and telephone number—toiled away at studies of German oil supply lines and the inner workings of the Japanese imperial government, Downes could often be seen "entertaining gangs of sinister young men of Hispanic appearance." Few had any inkling of the purposes, equal parts amorous and valorous, to which Downes was putting these fear-some lotharios.

Throughout the spring of 1942, Downes ordered his agents to insinu-ate themselves into the lives of the various diplomats, servants, and other hangers-on populating the expatriate "Spanish colony" of Washington, DC. Within a matter of weeks, he bragged to Dulles, Downes had amassed enough information about their stormy private lives "to prepare a docu-ment the length of a novel." Hovering like a naughty sultan at the cen-ter of this debauched milieu was Ambassador Cárdenas, whose "bizarre pleasures" were satiated through the tireless work of Paco, his sixty-one-year-old valet of nearly four decades. Paco had been Cárdenas's lover many years earlier, Downes wrote. But the debilitating effects of age, and paralysis in one leg, had reduced Paco to the role of ambassadorial pimp, "collecting young men of Washington"—or "Fairies," as Downes called them—"for trysts with his employer." Paco's responsibilities in this field extended to the employment of embassy servants, "first investigating them to be certain they are sexually 'correct.'" A recently hired Austrian butler named Karl, for instance, "shared the full confidence of both Senor and Senora Cardenas, having had sexual relations with each."

Through conversations with various embassy staff and Spanish expats, Downes learned that Paco procured young men for his priapic boss at an antiques shop on the 2400 block of Eighteenth Street. The store's owner, a Spaniard from the Canary Islands named Tomás González, was well known around Washington for his choice selection of chandeliers and his expertise in Capodimonte porcelain. As his work put him in frequent contact with embassy staff, wealthy citizens, and more than a few "fairies" around Washington, González was also a repository of valuable intelligence. After chatting with González at the shop one day, agent Sicre reported back to Downes that the antiquarian had republican sympathies and a "bigoted catholic" wife, Ascensión, whom "he fears and hates greatly," not least because she was pro-Franco. Sicre further noted González's "complicated sexual life," that "his habits must be the same as Cardenas and Paco," that he "likes to talk and comment on everything other people say and think, and he has the advantage of knowing the majority of the Spanish colony and many of the secrets of the embassy."

Downes sent another agent, Alfredo Gerassi, to cultivate González as a source. Twice, Gerassi visited the store under the pretext of purchasing some of its wares. On his third visit, Gonzalez was initially busy, but "when the conversation came to homosex," the antiques store owner "left his very urgent work and during an hour cross-examined me about all my homosexual life." Gerassi could not decipher whether González was simply curious or "playing the game to find out if I may . . . serve for the big fellow," Cárdenas. "It was pretty disgusting, but never mind." All this sex talk served a purpose, however, as Gerassi eventually discovered from González that the ambassador wanted to fire Paco, a crucial piece of information as the

Downes team now trained their sights on persuading the disgruntled valet to become an informant.

"Although there are certain differences among the friends of Cardenas," Sicre observed in a report to Downes, "they are united in their respect and friendship for him, a curious fact when one takes into consideration Spanish character and dislike for sexual degeneracies." The exception, however, was Paco. According to a series of memos Downes sent to Dulles, the valet was becoming increasingly "scared to death of being interned" as an enemy alien, and his disillusionment with the Franco regime provided a "pretty wide opening" for infiltrating the embassy. "He is very friendly with me," Downes assured Dulles. Sicre noted that Paco was "very amiable and charming" and "generally invites anyone whom he likes to visit the embassy." In a brief memorandum to Dulles enumerating "Six Sectors for Attack" on the embassy, Gerassi included "Gonzalez (Paco)—Sex Angle—Pro-American."

Ultimately, the OSS did not gain access to the embassy via the "Sex Angle," but through a secretary whom Downes had infiltrated onto its staff. One day while her boss, an attaché, was away from his desk, she broke the lock to the safe containing the cipher codes with a hammer. Downes had earlier recruited the repair man, who, while fixing the lock, made a copy of the key that Downes's team could use to open the safe and photograph the codes. The Spaniards changed their ciphers every month, however, which necessitated repeated break-ins. Though "entering a foreign embassy clandestinely and 'borrowing' code books and coding machinery was full of risks for everyone concerned," Downes did not expect that it would be an official of his own government who would foil his plans. During the October burglary, while Downes's men were inside the embassy preparing to open the safe, two FBI squad cars suddenly appeared. "A friend of ours in the Department of Justice had warned us that Edgar Hoover believed we were 'penetrating' embassies and that he was annoyed," Downes recalled, and now was his opportunity for comeuppance. The agents apprehended Downes and his operatives and brought them to FBI headquarters.

In a tense Oval Office confrontation the next day, the FBI and the OSS chieftains blamed each other for the botched operation. "I do not believe any single event in his career ever enraged him more," Downes recalled of

Donovan. Citing his earlier prohibition on the OSS engaging in domestic intelligence-gathering, FDR sided with Hoover and ordered Donovan to put a stop to the embassy break-ins. "The Abwehr [German intelligence] gets better treatment from the FBI than we do," Donovan complained. Concerned that Hoover might arrest Downes, Donovan promptly dispatched him overseas. From a base in North Africa, Downes set up a clandestine network to infiltrate Spain, which unraveled disastrously after one of his men was captured and revealed the identities of his fellow agents. After the war, Downes settled in Italy, where he wrote espionage novels and, for a time, was the lover of director Franco Zeffirelli.

For well into the twenty-first century, the relationship between the FBI and CIA was characterized by turf battles, mutual suspicion, and outright hostility. The origins of this rivalry, whose deadliest consequence resulted from the lack of intelligence sharing in the months and years leading up to the 9/11 terrorist attacks, lie with Donald Downes and his mission to break into the Spanish embassy. According to Ernest Cuneo, who had the unenviable task of working as the OSS wartime liaison officer between the White House, the FBI, and the State Department, while Downes's "burglary of the Spanish Embassy was of great value in breaking both Spanish and German codes," he was also "a Typhoid Mary contributing to the initial breaks between OSS, State Department and Justice." Downes, Cuneo said, "was offered by the FBI as prime evidence that the OSS was running amok, breaking both the criminal law and the orders of the Commander-in-Chief."

The Downes case was also the first time that homosexuality became a weapon in Washington's high-stakes bureaucratic warfare. In the wake of the Spanish embassy fiasco, Hoover and Donovan began amassing fat files full of embarrassing sexual details about each other. Hoover was widely believed to have generated the rumor that Donovan had acquired syphilis from prostitutes, while Donovan supposedly launched an investigation to prove that Hoover and Clyde Tolson were lovers. (Indeed, the pervasiveness of the latter rumor is in large part ascribable to the OSS veterans who gleefully spread it.) Unknown until now are the imaginative ways in which Donald Downes and others used their "aberrant" sexuality for patriotic purposes. "The spy must go secretly," Downes wrote in *The Scarlet Thread*, a memoir of his wartime exploits. "Society does not protect him, he is not in a stream of social duty surrounded by his peers. He is alone, furtive, and he remembers that 'dirty' is always the word coupled with spy." Though Downes was describing the realm of espionage, he could have been talking about another secret world he knew equally well: that of the midcentury American homosexual.

5

"THE GREATEST NATIONAL SCANDAL SINCE THE EXISTENCE OF THE UNITED STATES"

To the outside world, Cordell Hull and Sumner Welles were thick as thieves. "The overwhelming majority of the American people will also agree that to the list of select who have served as Secretary of State with outstanding distinction there can, with complete assurance, be added the name of Cordell Hull," Welles effused in the introduction to a 1942 biography of his boss, suggesting that the somnolent southerner deserved a place in the pantheon of American statesmen alongside Thomas Jefferson, James Madison, and John Quincy Adams. Behind closed doors, however, their relationship was rapidly deteriorating. In October 1942, after FDR took Welles's side in a dispute over whether the word *recommend* or *require* ought to be used in a communiqué, Hull summoned J. Edgar Hoover to his apartment at the stately Wardman Park building overlooking Rock Creek Parkway. As the FBI director recorded in a memo summarizing their conversation, the secretary of state complained about Welles's "headline hunting" speeches and Eleanor Roosevelt's "interference" in foreign affairs. Hull also informed Hoover that his wife, Rose, had been hearing gossip nonstop from senatorial spouses about his subordinate's behavior on the presidential train, and he asked the FBI director for a copy of the report Hoover had given the president concerning Welles's "improper actions." Hoover, not wanting FDR to suspect him of meddling, implausibly told the secretary that while he did not have a facsimile in his possession, Hull could ask the White House "to obtain access to" the one he had given the president.

On the evening of December 22, Hull invited his former special assistant Bill Bullitt to his home for dinner. As Bullitt sat quietly and listened, Hull vented about Welles for nearly two hours. FDR "was going crazy," Hull complained, describing how the president frequently bypassed him to communicate with world leaders through Welles. Hull could not accomplish anything, as he was "constantly being knifed" by underlings in his own department, Welles foremost among them.

Bullitt suggested that Hull approach FDR with an ultimatum: "You can choose between Welles and myself today and dismiss one or the other of us." FDR would "never be able to dismiss" Hull, Bullitt said, because the Tennessean "was the president's greatest political asset" in a Democratic coalition heavily dependent upon southern support.

"That man Welles has tortured us for eight years," Rose Hull said.

"It is only necessary for Cordell Hull to get one of his southern Senator friends to make one speech," Bullitt slyly suggested.

"Yes, and do you know that all of the wives of all the Senators talk to Mrs. Hull about Welles's behavior on that train?" Hull insisted.

"Indeed they do," Rose affirmed. "Why can't you handle it, Mr. Bullitt, by a little publicity?"

"I would leave that to Cordell Hull," Bullitt replied.

Two weeks later, Bullitt paid a visit to the home of Attorney General Francis Biddle, the old friend and fellow Philadelphian who had adjudicated his divorce from Louise Bryant. Biddle's wife and brother George, a social realist painter and major force behind the Federal Art Project, were also present.

"You will be amused to know, Bill," Francis Biddle began, "that the President said to me today that about ten days ago Cordell Hull said to him that he wanted to see the FBI affidavits dealing with Welles's behavior on the train coming back from Senator Bankhead's funeral." Hull, apparently, had acted on Hoover's advice by confronting the president about the evidence of Welles's indiscretions. While FDR told Hull that he was free to read the salacious document in the White House, he could not take copies with him to the State Department.

"What are the affidavits about?" asked George Biddle.

"Oh, Sumner Welles has a habit of trying to have sexual relations with negro train porters," his brother laughed. According to the attorney general, Hoover had told FDR that not only was Welles theoretically vulnerable to blackmail, but that he was *being* blackmailed, an assertion for which the FBI director did not offer any proof. At this point, the men took the conversation in a prurient direction. George Biddle, according to Bullitt's notes, "began inquiring as to the exact nature of Welles's habits, whether they were anal or [oral,] and Mrs. Biddle ended the conversation."

For months, Hull pressed FDR to rid him of his immoral, criminal undersecretary. "If my own twin brother had committed the sexual crimes that Welles had committed," he told the president, "I would not tolerate him for fifteen minutes in the American government." But the president remained unpersuaded. To Hull's insistence that Welles was a "degenerate," FDR replied that "Napoleon was a degenerate too." When Hull complained that Welles's mere presence in the State Department would make the treaty ratification process impossible because "every Senator resents having in office a man who may be subject to the worst sort of influence from a foreign country," the president "just sat back and looked miserably at the ceiling and said nothing."

Throughout this season of bitterness and frustration, Bullitt served for Hull the dual functions of sympathetic sounding board and devious instigator. The Welles matter played perfectly to Bullitt's taste for intrigue, his wounded ego, and his penchant for self-aggrandizement, the latter of which he exhibited constantly by amplifying personnel squabbles into matters of state. "Foreign affairs were, to his imaginative mind, full of lights and shadows, plots and counterplots, villains and a few heroes," remembered Raymond Morley, the leader of FDR's "Brain Trust" of advisors who had coined the term *New Deal* and who, a decade earlier, had recommended that FDR appoint Bullitt as his first ambassador to the Soviet Union. In the words of his former Moscow embassy colleague George Kennan, Bullitt was a "Midas of the spirit, in whom all the golden qualities turned to stone because he never loved anyone as much as himself." Whether the relationship was with an individual or an empire—Woodrow Wilson, the Soviet Union, and now FDR—Bullitt had a tendency to swing from adulation to loathing. When a desperate Hull asked him "what the hold was that

Welles had on the President," Bullitt intimated that FDR had had a youthful pedophiliac dalliance with his future undersecretary of state at the Roosevelt family summer estate, replying that "they had been extremely intimate when Welles was a small boy and the President was an older boy and Welles spent most of his summers at Campobello in the President's mother's house." On another occasion, when Bullitt and Hull were stewing together and strategizing how to destroy their mutual nemesis, an exasperated Rose Hull entered the room and pleaded, "Mr. Bullitt, won't you shoot that man for me?"

"Mrs. Hull," Bullitt replied, "I will buy you a pearl-handled revolver if you would like to do the job yourself."

"All you men are terrible," she replied. "You protect each other even when you commit crimes. I don't see why you or Cordell hasn't had this man put in jail or shot."

With the president showing no sign that he would so much as reprimand Welles, Bullitt took matters into his own hands by conscripting his devoted auxiliary. Since returning to Washington with his boss after the fall of France, Carmel Offie had become a bold-faced name in the city's society columns. Within a year, he had acquired (possibly through the subvention of his patron) an impressive three-story Georgetown home stocked with rare books and, according to the *Washington Post*, was renowned for serving "the best food in Washington—considering his bachelor status." As one of the city's earliest walkers, Offie fashioned a unique place for himself in a city whose centers of power were officially closed to men like him. "'What do I know about Carmel Offie?—oh, he's simply fascinating' coos just about every person, of feminine gender, one encounters," reported the *Post*'s Diplomatic Circling columnist in a piece anointing Offie "the Mystery Man" of Washington.

Bullitt ordered Offie to make copies of the incriminating affidavits and circulate them across Capitol Hill. If conspiring in the destruction of a fellow homosexual offended Offie's values, there was little he could do, short of quitting, to express it. Gays still lacked the group consciousness of other minorities, and their tenuous position as social outcasts left them vulnerable to exploitation. For Offie, loyalty to Bullitt surpassed all other considerations. With the diligence on behalf of his patron that led one government official to label him Bullitt's "slave," Offie distributed the documents among the president's senatorial critics. Upon reading the dossier, Republican senator Ralph Brewster of Maine told Hoover that unless the president fired Welles, he would have no choice but to launch an investigation, effectively threatening to go public. Less than three years earlier, Cissy Patterson had refused to print the allegations against Welles. But the smearing of David Walsh changed the rules. Having witnessed the charge of homosexuality used against one of *their* allies, the president's critics smelled blood. Welles's indiscretions were now something much more serious than a personal failing. They were a political liability.

* * *

THE SENSE OF ISOLATION EXPERIENCED BY SUMNER WELLES, Carmel Offie, Lorena Hickok, and other gay men and women was irrevocably transformed by the United States' entry into the Second World War. Up to that point, gay and lesbian subcultures scarcely existed outside major metropolitan areas. Most gay people could go through life never knowingly encountering another person like them. The drafting of millions of young people from across the country into the armed forces upended this solitary existence, inadvertently producing the largest aggregation of gay people within a single institution in American history. On the home front and across the battlefield, the intimacy of the military's exclusively male environments compelled gay recruits to confront their desires for the first time, while a similar process occurred among lesbians in the Women's Army Auxiliary Corps. The mass mobilization shattered the collective illusion that they were alone in their homosexual identity, leading to what the historian John D'Emilio has called "a nationwide coming out experience." Though the war, ironically, also occasioned the military's development of policies and procedures to exclude gays, the sheer demands of the mobilization effort—the need for every able-bodied young man to participate—meant that very few were actually barred from service. Of the eighteen million men examined by 6,400 draft boards during the war, fewer than five thousand were rejected on the grounds of homosexuality.

Washington was already a boomtown when the war began, having nearly doubled in size from 621,000 residents in 1930 to over 1 million by the declaration of war in December 1941. Many of those who swarmed into the nation's capital during the 1930s were gay men and women seeking refuge from the confines of small-town life, lured by the promise of a steady job in a large bureaucracy where they had less chance of standing out. One such transplant, who wrote under the pseudonym "Ladd Forrester," was living in a Mississippi River town of 5,000 inhabitants during the Great Depression when his father told him he could no longer afford to send him to college. Through a cousin who was a friend of their congressman, Forrester obtained a position in one of Washington's proliferating new federal agencies. "I was scared and insecure about making such a big change in my life; but I also discovered that I was Gay," he later wrote. "Subconsciously, I knew this was my opportunity to escape." He did not have to wait long before receiving confirmation that he had made the right choice, professionally and personally. Standing in line to sign up for courses at George Washington University, he met a young man who invited him to his first gay party, which took place in an old stable located between two Victorian-style homes on P Street.

When the United States entered the war, Washington became the capital of the free world overnight, transforming from a leisurely southern hamlet into a bustling center of international commerce, diplomacy, espionage, and military planning. "None of that easy-going Southern atmosphere of the past," Hazel Vandenberg, wife of the powerful Republican senator Arthur Vandenberg of Michigan, wrote in her diary at the start of the war. "Crowds in the buses and street-cars that are being used by everybody, even justices of the Supreme Court. Crowds in the restaurants where you wait interminably to be served. Crowds in the stores where the service has been equally disrupted . . . It really seems as if the world and his brother have landed here." The nationwide commitment to a life-or-death struggle abroad fueled a raucous, sybaritic social scene at home. "After government," the legendary television anchor David Brinkley wrote in *Washington Goes to War*, "socializing was Washington's second largest industry," such that on any given night, a Washingtonian could attend anywhere from fifty to one hundred cocktail parties without so much as an invitation.

This home-front hedonism had a profound effect on the lives of gay men and lesbians. In the words of one gay teenager who lived there at the time, Washington was "the ideal place to be during World War II," one where social and sexual opportunities abounded. A War Department employee recalled that he "made more new friends, had more sex, and thought less about the stigma of being queer between Pearl Harbor and V-J Day than at any time in my life." Prior to the war, Washington counted no more than a handful of establishments that catered to homosexuals, all informally. The arrival of so many young, single people from across the country sparked an increase in the number of places where gays could socialize. In addition to the bar at the Mayflower Hotel, which appealed to a mixed crowd of male and female homosexuals, the Showboat attracted mainly lesbians, who took their place at the bar on the other side of a rail dividing them from the other patrons. Carroll Tavern brought together "rough trade" (heterosexual-identifying men, often in uniform, willing to engage in sex with other men for money) and their admirers. Two waitresses, dyed-blond Rose and dark-featured Betty, kept protective watch over their clientele, which reputedly included several members of Congress as well as high-ranking officials in the Foreign Service. At the Republic Gardens, musical acts performed in the front room, and a space was unofficially reserved for homosexuals in the back. A warning system was developed for when the police entered looking to harass the clientele on trumped-up charges of disorderly conduct: the performer would stop in the middle of whatever tune she was singing and belt out the lyrics to "Alice Blue Gown," a song named for a dress worn by the daughter of President Teddy Roosevelt.

In a city where one's status can be determined by the agency, elected official, or congressional committee for which they work, it has long been a cliché that the most common question asked at any Washington cocktail party is "What do you do?" But for gays and lesbians, inquiring of somebody's place of employment was something "you didn't ask," recalled Bob Cantillion, who served as a corpsman in the physical therapy department at Bethesda Naval Hospital after the war. At gay venues, "most people were known by their first names," Cantillion recalled, or, more often, by pseudonyms. Cantillion learned the necessity of discretion one day when a passel of government security agents appeared at the hospital in advance of the visit by a VIP in need of a massage to soothe his aching body. In walked J. Edgar Hoover. "He'd go into a changing room and strip down, and get in the Hubbard tank," an immersive individual bath used for hydrotherapy. "He was always very modest," Cantillion recalled. "He was built like a barrel . . . I really struggled hard, and I couldn't move a muscle anyplace."

If Hoover ever wanted to act on a repressed sexual desire for men, this would have been the perfect opportunity. Yet not once during these regular rubdown sessions (which occurred roughly twice a week from April through August 1947) did the FBI director evince the slightest suggestion of sexual interest, Cantillion recalled. Alas, Cantillion's role as masseur ended abruptly after police raided a gay party where he was in attendance, leading to his discharge from the navy.

Though the war had elevated its global standing, Washington was still a southern city, with all the overt racial discrimination that this designation implied: segregated schools, water fountains, restrooms, dining establishments, transportation, and public accommodation. Washington "proclaimed its democratic principles on the memorial tablets of its past heroes," observed *New York Times* reporter James Reston, "but it separated its people like the colonial empires it deplored." The capital's nascent gay scene reflected this contradiction in that it, too, was racially divided, leaving Black gays burdened not only with the secrecy borne by all gay men and women at that time but the tyranny of the color bar as well.

One of the more remarkable personalities to emerge from this community was Odessa Madre. The granddaughter of a Black Civil War veteran, Odessa (or "Dess," as intimates called her) was born in 1907 to a solidly middle-class seamstress and a barbershop owner and grew up in a neighborhood of the District called Cowtown, named for the bovine creatures that sometimes meandered up and down its alleyways. Madre attended Dunbar High School, where the city's affluent Black citizens sent their children to be educated. Dark-skinned, she was often teased by her lighter-hued classmates. "There was only three Blacks at Dunbar back then—I mean Black like me," she recalled. "I had good diction, I knew the gestures, but they always made fun of me."

Madre chose not to follow her peers to nearby Howard University; nor was she much interested in a domestic life. "I just couldn't keep no whatchamacallit—a man?" she said. "I guess I was just born to give orders, not take 'em. What kind of man wants a woman like that?" Madre chose a life of crime instead, and became very successful at it, reigning for decades as "queen of the uptown underworld." In these series of life choices, she displayed an uncommon independence shaped largely by her secret. "To pursue a college education would have required Madre to join the Washington elite who had rejected her repeatedly," historian Sharon Harley writes. "Moreover, she would have found the underground world far more accepting of her homosexuality." And it was through that underground world—partly, and necessarily, gay—that she interacted with the sorts of people she would not otherwise have known.

For a nearly twenty-year period beginning in the early 1930s, Madre presided over a large swath of the city's illicit economy, becoming one of Washington's wealthiest African Americans and earning a reputation as the "female Al Capone." By 1946, she operated six brothels across the District, employed twenty women as sex workers, and ran a number of "jill joints" (dispensaries of bootleg liquor) in addition to her legitimate business, the extremely popular Club Madre, on Fourteenth Street. The crowd roared its approval whenever Madre, covered in mink furs and diamonds and trailed by a multiracial retinue of women for sale, entered the premises and sauntered over to the center table, denoted as hers by an ever-present vase holding a dozen long-stemmed roses. Billie Holiday, Duke Ellington, and Count Basie all performed at Club Madre, and the boxer Joe Louis was a regular customer. When the comedienne Moms Mabley staged her one-woman routine, she stayed at Madre's home, and though the pair became "like sisters," they were widely rumored to be much more. (In a 1953 feature about men who fall for "bad women," *Jet* magazine referred to a "one-time famous New York singer" who was "maintained" by Madre for over a decade.)

Madre was able to evade the law for so long by cultivating powerful contacts within the DC police. Many of the Irish boys she counted among her playmates growing up in Cowtown—with whom she fought side by side in the "Great Rock Chuckin' Wars" against the neighborhood's Italian and German kids—had grown up to become police sergeants, detectives, and patrolmen. "You know, I practically ran that damn police department," Madre once bragged. "I don't know how many thousands of dollars I gave [Pat] O'Shea," a police superintendent, "to stay out on the streets." Madre was allegedly the only Black woman in the city allowed to enter the swank Garfinckel's department store through its front door. Once, when she visited a shop where Black people were not welcome, she pulled out a roll of hundred-dollar bills and demanded to see the finest fur coats. When the befuddled manager showed her two minks, she snapped back, "This is nothing but crap," and walked out to her waiting chauffeured limousine. "Child, you wonder does crime pay?" Madre asked. "I'll tell you, yes. It pays a helluva lot of money." At the height of her reign, Madre reputedly earned a hundred thousand dollars a year.

Madre was more than just an ordinary madam and numbers runner. "She knew practically every big-time gangster nationwide," recalled Robert Lee, a detective with the Morals division. "She was what they call a counselor in the mob. She mediated disputes between blacks and whites, a referee. She kept a lot of people from getting hurt." And for many in the city, she was a Robin Hood figure, using her ill-gotten gains to buy toys and clothing for poor children.

Madre's fall began in 1949, with her conviction on eight separate drug counts. When the judge handed down concurrent sentences of twenty to sixty months for each of the charges, Madre quipped, "I'll need an adding machine to count that up." Three years later, she was hauled before the Senate Special Committee to Investigate Organized Crime in Interstate Commerce, also known as the Kefauver Committee, for its chairman, Tennessee senator Estes Kefauver. The body exposed Madre's payments of "ice," as bribes were called, to District cops, and she was never again able to operate her criminal syndicates with the same impunity.

From 1932 until her death from kidney failure in 1990, Madre was arrested thirty times on fifty-seven separate charges and spent a cumulative thirteen years in jail. Though she had once run a three-thousand-dollars-per-day numbers game, she died penniless in what one of her friends described as "the worst ghetto in Washington." Her corpse lay in the District morgue for over a week until a relative claimed it, and friends could muster only fifty-one dollars for funeral expenses. One of the donors was a retired police officer who had met Madre in 1942 when, as a rookie attached to the Sanitation Department, he investigated her for lacking a dog license. Instead of arresting Madre, however, he cultivated her as an informant. "I had a lot of respect for Odessa," he said.

At the funeral, a friend sang Frank Sinatra's "My Way."

* * *

His foot bandaged from an injury, William Bullitt gripped a cane and hobbled into the Oval Office on July 27, 1943. The president was waiting for him, seated behind the Resolute desk. Desperate to keep his scheming former ambassador occupied, and fully aware that no Democrat had won the Philadelphia mayoralty in more than sixty years, FDR had suggested that Bullitt return to his hometown and throw his hat into the ring. To the president's relief, Bullitt accepted the challenge. But as FDR was about to discover, Bullitt's obsession with destroying Sumner Welles was unabated.

After exchanging small talk about the campaign, Bullitt mooted the issue that had consumed him for the past two and a half years. Bullitt was dismayed, he said, to learn from a White House aide that FDR was angry with him for sharing with Cissy Patterson the affidavits taken from the Pullman train porters. Bullitt denied ever doing this, and professed himself "profoundly shocked" that FDR would even think otherwise.

"Well, we had it on the best authority," FDR replied. "We had it from that damned bitch Cissy's own lips that you had given her the affidavits."

"Any such statement made by anyone was a lie," Bullitt assured the president. Considering how Bullitt had ordered Carmel Offie to disseminate the affidavits on his behalf, his denial was a distinction without a difference.

"Well, I wouldn't have that damned bitch to dinner and you do," the president growled.

Bullitt, who had proposed marriage to Patterson during his tenure as ambassador to France (while simultaneously courting Missy LeHand), grew defensive. "She had been a friend of mine for thirty years."

"Well, if you didn't give her the affidavits, at least you let her read them."

Bullitt demurred.

"Well, if you didn't do that," the president continued, "at any rate you have talked to a lot of Senators."

This Bullitt could not deny. "When a man comes to you and says that Mr. X of the Pullman Company has given him full information about Welles's sexual advances to negroes and asks whether or not it is true, do you expect me to lie?" Bullitt asked.

"I would say nothing," the president answered. "I would refuse to discuss the matter with anybody." After a pause, he raised his voice. "You have ruined Welles's reputation and his life!"

"You have ruined him by keeping him in office," Bullitt said, "and permitting him to enunciate the policies for which you are asking our soldiers to die when you know that every one of those soldiers, if he knew what Welles was, would spit on him."

"What if he does behave that way when he has been drinking?" the president asked with annoyance. "It is cruel and un-Christian for anyone to talk about him."

"In other words, everyone should hush up and conceal his criminal behavior as you have."

FDR declined to take the bait. "Everyone says it is because you have always hated Welles."

"If you will be honest and look into your memory," Bullitt retorted, "you will recall that I attempted to have friendly relations with Welles and that repeatedly I was knifed in the back by him; that he had secret telegrams from me to you published in Drew Pearson's column and that you, yourself, on several occasions tried to stop him from knifing me in the back."

Mentioning Welles's friendship with the controversial newspaperman, a frequent thorn in the administration's side who was described as a "scavenger" by former FDR advisor and Supreme Court justice Felix Frankfurter, was a clever appeal to the president's sense of personal loyalty. Pearson had a well-deserved reputation as a scandalmonger, having once bragged about interviewing sources in sidewalk phone booths because "There are so many taps on my phone I could sell commercials." FDR, who would publicly attack Pearson as a "chronic liar," nodded his head silently in agreement with Bullitt's assessment.

"And you will remember that Judge Moore summoned me to his deathbed and handed me certain papers and told me that he could not die with an easy conscience unless he knew that you would have full knowledge of this matter," Bullitt added, depositing the final wishes of a dead man on the president's conscience.

"I would never have taken the papers from Judge Moore," FDR said.

"Balls."

"And if Judge Moore is sitting up in Heaven, where he certainly is, you can be sure he feels differently about it now. Your talking about Welles has been un-Christian. I have never attacked anyone in an un-Christian manner in my life."

"You have just called Cissy Patterson a 'damned bitch' to me twice."

"I have known you all my life and I can say anything to you. Well, having known me for so many years, you ought to know that I shoot my own meat, and if and when I decide to put Welles in jail, I will do so myself."

"In other words, you think that it is the Christian duty of an American to condone crimes of danger to the nation."

Bullitt's sanctimonious appeals to morality and "Christian duty" insulted the president's old-fashioned, aristocratic sense of honor. His patience wearing thin, FDR went in for the kill. "Bill," he said, his voice rising with anger, "if I were St. Peter and you and Sumner came before me, I would say to Sumner, 'No matter what you may have done, you have hurt no one but yourself. I recognize human frailties. Come in.' But to you I would say, 'You have not only hurt another human being, but you have deprived your country of the services of a good citizen; and for that you can go straight to Hell!'"

At this, Bullitt slowly rose himself up with his cane, turned his back to the president, and shuffled toward the door.

"Well, Bill, I hope your foot is well soon," FDR barked across the room, the sarcasm dripping from his voice. Coming from a man in a wheel-chair, the insult was especially caustic. The "impatience" that George Kennan thought Bullitt's greatest flaw had finally exacted its toll. Encountering her husband shortly after this shouting match, the First Lady observed that he could barely contain his indignation. He was "shaking with anger," Eleanor recalled. "He was white with wrath."

As much as he wanted to protect Welles and spite Bullitt, FDR faced a dilemma. Had Welles been accused of drunkenly importuning waitresses, it's highly unlikely that anyone would have tried to destroy him. It certainly would never have approached the level of Oval Office crisis. Politically powerful men in the 1940s got away with far worse than drunken lechery toward women, and they would get away with far worse for long after. A *homosexual* liaison, however, even just an attempted one, existed on an entirely different plane, and the interracial aspect only aggravated Welles's offense. With hostile senators threatening to open an investigation, FDR would be forced to defend behavior whose shades of gray, he feared, the American people would never understand.

Nine days after the president's Oval Office showdown with Bullitt, a story appeared on the front page of the *New York Times* revealing that "Rivalry between Secretary Hull and Under-Secretary Sumner Welles is common knowledge in Washington." Though the paper did not mention the train incident, word was coursing quickly across town, and it was only a matter of time before Hull threatened to resign. Also surely weighing on the president's mind was the destruction of David Walsh the previous year. That act of sexual exposure had unlocked a Pandora's box, and FDR could expect his enemies to be no less ruthless against Welles than his allies had been against "Senator X."

Two weeks later, on August 15, FDR reluctantly asked for, and promptly received, Welles's resignation.

On his last day of work at the State Department, Welles confronted Hull in his office. As his direct superior, Welles wanted to know, why had Hull gone behind his back and gotten him fired instead of doing the deed himself? "I did not speak to you," Hull replied,

> because you are the intimate friend of the President and you have been much closer to the President than I have been and I have based my request for your resignation entirely on your perverted personal habits. I even concealed this aspect of your behavior from my wife and it was brought to her attention from the wives of prominent members of the Congress. I consider that since you knew that your perverted behavior was known not only to most of the members of the Congress but also to the Soviet Government, the Free French, the British and South American countries, indeed to a large portion of the United States, you should have come to me at once . . . I have based my demands for your resignation entirely on the basis that your continuation in office would create certainly for the President and the Department of State the greatest national scandal since the existence of the United States and that you were keeping in jeopardy the President and the whole administration.

It was the last time the two men would ever speak.

Three weeks after the destruction of Sumner Welles, in which he played no small part, Carmel Offie was arrested for the same offense that was the undersecretary's undoing: soliciting a man for sex. Shortly after midnight on September 8, an undercover vice squad officer apprehended the diplomat in the vicinity of Lafayette Square. Though Offie was forced to spend the night dodging cockroaches in a jail cell reeking of urine, he never faced a court appearance, nor was he threatened with the public humiliation or loss of a job that had been Welles's fate. This was all thanks to none other than Cordell Hull, who sent one of his aides to put up Offie's bail. "I consider Mr. Offie a highly effective and loyal servant of the United States," read a note initialed by the secretary of state. "It would be unjust to penalize him for carrying out his mission." Offie, according to America's chief diplomat, had been in this notorious homosexual cruising spot at 12:40 a.m. carrying out "official business."

On the evening of September 25, the White House formally announced Welles's resignation. The reason, the president said, was a "desire to be relieved of his heavy governmental duties in view of his wife's health"—to spend more time with his family, in other words, an explanation that, like "No comment," the phrase Welles had coined, would become a cliché in Washington's political lexicon. A tone of skepticism colored the *New York Times* report, which noted that "the facts of this situation remained obscure tonight, so far as the White House statement was concerned."

The president never forgave William Bullitt for his role in ruining Sumner Welles. When Hull recommended Bullitt for a senior diplomatic post the following year, FDR sarcastically wrote back, "Why not Minister to Saudi Arabia?" And while it had been his idea that Bullitt run for the mayoralty of Philadelphia, the president told the Democratic bosses there to "cut his throat." They needn't have bothered. By then, so infamous was Bullitt's "vitriolic tongue" that Republicans in the City of Brotherly Love released a thirty-page pamphlet in which "Accused of Too Much Talk" was one of the main charges in the bill of particulars laid against him. Bullitt lost in a rout.

Cordell Hull remained obsessed with his former subordinate long after driving him out of the State Department. Meeting with Bullitt almost a year after Welles resigned, Hull complained that Welles was waging a campaign against him in the press with "that skunk, Drew Pearson." Nonetheless, Hull told Bullitt, the two men had nothing to regret. "No matter how much either of us suffer," he proclaimed, "neither of us ever did a more righteous act or a greater public service than kicking that son of a bitch into the open spaces."

After working for the State Department liaison to Allied military commanders in Italy during the final year of the war, service for which he won a Medal of Freedom, Carmel Offie served as an aide to the deputy military governor of postwar Germany, Gen. Lucius Clay. He continued to hone the skills many a gay Washingtonian would develop as consummate courtiers to the powerful, earning the nickname "Aladdin" for his ability to acquire precious goods under a regime of heavy rationing as if summoning a genie from a lamp. Once, Offie called the American legation in Budapest to demand that it obtain a special handbag produced exclusively in Hungary and send it immediately via diplomatic pouch to Clay's wife. Another time, he instructed his sister (a fellow Foreign Service officer, stationed in Paris) to amass three hundred lobsters on an airport tarmac, ready to be loaded onto an arriving army plane, which flew them to Frankfurt for a banquet Offie had organized for military and diplomatic VIPs. Offie had "more lines out than the phone company," according to one acquaintance, who expected him either to wind up becoming secretary of state or be found dead floating in the Potomac.

After his firing, Sumner Welles continued to correspond and meet privately with FDR as an informal advisor. In the months leading up to the 1945 San Francisco Conference that would establish the United Nations, the White House received scores of telegrams urging FDR's successor, Harry Truman, to appoint Welles secretary-general of the proceedings. But Welles was passed over, the job ultimately going to an up-and-coming State Department official named Alger Hiss.

When he first heard the news of Welles's sacking, Breckenridge Long took to his diary with a prediction. "The world will soon march by the little tragedy," he wrote, "and it will be smothered in the dust of rapidly succeeding events." At the time of his dismissal, Welles was a lone individual, sacrificed for the greater good of the administration he served. Washington and the world may have marched by him, but the impact of his firing would be long-lasting and profound. According to FDR biographer Ted Morgan, Welles's departure from government service "had a devastating effect on the State Department," signaling "the end of Pan-American solidarity and the Good Neighbor policy." Welles was also one of the few senior State Department officials even mildly sympathetic to the plight of Europe's Jews; had he stayed in his job, he might have persuaded FDR to accept a larger number as refugees.

In addition to these hypothetical diplomatic consequences, Welles's downfall had a tangible impact upon America's domestic politics and burgeoning national security state, as the harsh lesson of the once-powerful homosexual diplomat became an iron rule within Washington's halls of power. "There were a hell of a lot of them there," Nelson Rockefeller, who became an assistant secretary of state in 1944, recalled of the department's gay employees. "We got them out." Some of "them," to be sure, but far from all. Four years after Welles was sacked due to his homosexuality, one veteran American diplomat observed that it "was the first time in the history of this Republic that this charge was ever used to get someone out of public office." It wouldn't be the last.

HARRY TRUMAN

No one who has, even once, lived close to the making of history can ever again suppose that it is made the way history books tell it. With rare exceptions, such books are like photographs. They catch a surface image. Often as not, they distort it. The secret forces working behind and below the historical surface they seldom catch.

–Whittaker Chambers, *Witness*

6

THE CONCEALED ENEMY

THE KLIEG LIGHTS BLARED HOT IN THE PACKED HOUSE UN-AMERICAN Activities Committee (HUAC) room on August 25, 1948, as millions of Americans tuned in for the first live television broadcast of a congressional hearing. Sitting in the audience for what the newspapers dubbed "Confrontation Day" were some of the capital's most prominent citizens. "Society's attendance in town the last two weeks in August is not exactly 100 percent," *Evening Star* society columnist Betty Beale reported, "but those who are here would rather let tennis, golf, housekeeping and business, if you will, wait in favor of the unusual drama that's going on on the Hill." Across the Atlantic Ocean, the Soviets were two months into their armed blockade of war-ravaged West Berlin, brutally attempting to enshroud that part of the city behind the "Iron Curtain" former British prime minister Winston Churchill had invoked in a speech two years earlier to illustrate the expansion of Communist tyranny across the Continent. As tensions between the West and its erstwhile Soviet ally intensified, "Secrets had become secrets indeed," Harvard professor John Kenneth Galbraith later observed, "and their security was now a ruling passion in Washington."

The man whose secrets the country was transfixed upon that sweltering August day was, according to press accounts, a "sprawling, putty-faced" and "shifty-eyed" forty-seven-year-old *Time* magazine senior editor named Whittaker Chambers. Three weeks earlier, in a closed executive session hearing, Chambers had revealed his past work as a courier in the American Communist underground during the 1930s. He named nine other people as members of a clandestine cell, the "Ware Group," so called for the government agricultural expert Harold Ware, who had founded it. The most shocking name Chambers disclosed was that of the man now sitting just a few feet away in the front row of the congressional hearing room, the only man who bothered to challenge the accusation leveled against him, the man whom the committee had subpoenaed Chambers to confront: former senior State Department official Alger Hiss.

According to the endless parade of prominent men who knew and vouched for him, the well-groomed and reedy Hiss—once lauded by Chambers's own *Time* as "one of the State Department's brighter young men"—was as altruistic, patriotic, and decent a man as any of the winning young strivers conceived by his namesake, the novelist of boyhood virtue Horatio Alger. Born in Baltimore to "shabby gentility," as his contemporary Murray Kempton memorably characterized their fatherless upbringings, Hiss won a scholarship to Johns Hopkins University, where he made Phi Beta Kappa. He next studied at Harvard Law School under Felix Frankfurter, clerked for Supreme Court justice Oliver Wendell Holmes, and thereafter began a dazzling trajectory up the ranks of the State Department. As director of the Office of Special Political Affairs, Hiss sat behind President Roosevelt at the 1944 Yalta Conference, and the following year served as secretary-general at the founding of the United Nations in San Francisco. An image of Hiss holding aloft the UN Charter, evangelizing the universal brotherhood of man, was featured as "Picture of the Week" by *Life*.

In 1947, the trustees of the Carnegie Endowment for International Peace appointed Hiss president of that august institution, thereby cementing his position as an "impeccable Jeeves" of the eastern establishment. That anyone would accuse this man, one of whose responsibilities included administering the Foreign Service exam, of being a secret communist, was not just a slander against Hiss. It was an insult to the entire class of men who had selected, educated, and promoted him up the ladder that they, too, had climbed. Hiss, wrote William Manchester, "moved with the casual grace suggestive of Baltimore Cotillions or Gibson Island tennis matches, at both of which he was a familiar figure." The *Washington Post* editorialized that Hiss had been treated like "an innocent pedestrian, spattered with mud by a passing vehicle." President Harry Truman lambasted the HUAC hearings as a "red herring." To attest to his loyalty and all-around strong moral character, Hiss provided the committee with a long list of senators, congressmen, federal judges, former secretaries of state, and other distinguished personages (such as Eleanor Roosevelt) whose "labors," he said, he had supported "to build the peace."

Against these exquisite credentials, Whittaker Chambers could not compete. The son of a distant, bisexual artist father and an imperious, nerve-racked mother, the young Chambers had been a loner from birth. "I did not know that what seemed the special handicaps of my boyhood—extreme sensitivity, imaginativeness, gentleness, a need for quiet and seclusion—was the real difference between me and my fellows," he recalled of his traumatic childhood. At Columbia University, where one of his professors, the poet and critic Mark Van Doren, recalled him having a "flair for the dramatic" and a "cloak and dagger air," Chambers caused a furor by publishing a blasphemous play in a student literary magazine and was subsequently forced to withdraw from school. In 1925, feeling called by the "crisis of history," he joined the Communist Party and put his literary talents in its service as a writer for the *Daily Worker* and, later, as editor of *New Masses*. His frumpy appearance and itinerant lifestyle masked a precocious brilliance. An autodidact and master of foreign tongues, Chambers translated the Austrian children's book *Bambi*, and his reputation soon grew to the point that he was approached to translate the final volume of Marcel Proust's *Remembrance of Things Past*. Wanting to contribute more substantively to the revolutionary struggle, Chambers abandoned the life of a left-wing journalist to become a courier for Soviet military intelligence in what he would come to describe as the "big and beautiful village" of Washington, DC.

Like many young men of his generation who rushed to the banner of communism, Chambers became disillusioned with the brutalities necessary to fulfill its utopian promises and the cynicism demanded of its adherents in denying those crimes. Citing a long list of depredations, including the Soviet Union's starvation of millions of Ukrainian peasants, Stalin's refusal to cooperate with German Social Democrats against the Nazis, and the Moscow show trials, Chambers quit the party in 1938 and begged his Ware Group comrade Hiss to join him. Hiss's gentle and urbane exterior, however, concealed the soul of a hardened Communist ideologue. Stalin, Hiss had once told Chambers, "plays for keeps." At their intensely emotional last meeting, Chambers later wrote, "a molten torrent" lay between the two men. Hiss "cried when we separated," Chambers told the committee in an August 3 executive session hearing. "I was very fond of Mr. Hiss."

Just how fond the "dumpy Chambers" was of this "handsome young Galahad," to cite the description of Hiss offered by one reporter who covered the hearings, was a question lurking in many people's minds as the Republican committee chairman," J. Parnell Thomas of New Jersey, gaveled the proceedings to order. "From the very first day of the hearing it was whispered around the hearing room that he was queer," Robert Stripling, HUAC's chief investigator, said of Chambers. The whispers had been circulating for weeks. At a closed hearing in Washington on August 16, Hiss complained that the committee was colluding with Chambers by ordering him, Hiss, to reveal "details of my personal life" that Chambers could then use to embroider ever more fanciful charges against him. A testy exchange followed between Hiss and the committee's youngest member, an ambitious thirty-five-year-old freshman Republican from California elbowing his way into the role of Chambers's congressional champion. "I have seen newspaper accounts, Mr. Nixon, that you spent the weekend—whether correct or not, I do not know—at Mr. Chambers' farm in New Jersey," Hiss said, his comment laden with insinuation.

"I can say, as you did a moment ago, that I have never spent the night with Mr. Chambers," Richard Nixon shot back.

The homosexual undercurrent reemerged the following day, when Hiss and Chambers met face-to-face at another executive session hearing, in Suite 1400 of the Commodore Hotel in New York City. With both men sitting in the room, Nixon asked Hiss to state under oath whether he had ever met Chambers. Hiss inquired if he might examine his accuser's open mouth (a request that would later assume lascivious import), as the man calling himself "Whittaker Chambers," he said, vaguely resembled an old acquaintance with bad teeth. After inspecting Chambers's maw and noting the presence of "considerable dental work," Hiss acknowledged that he *had* known the man sitting beside him, though not by the name of "Whittaker Chambers." Hiss knew him as "George Crosley," a "deadbeat" freelance journalist with terrible teeth to whom Hiss had rented a room in 1935.

During his years in the Communist underground, Chambers had by his own admission employed many aliases, and it was under the name of "Crosley" that he published several obscene poems, including one that was homoerotic. Hiss's citing this particular pseudonym may have been a veiled threat—a way for Hiss to signal to Chambers that he knew something about the latter's past even more secretive and dangerous than their allegedly shared experience as Communist bedfellows.

By Confrontation Day, the possibly homoerotic nature of the Hiss-Chambers relationship had become a central, but heavily disguised, theme. After reciting his roll call of eminently worthy personal references (memorably dismissed by Nixon as a preening attempt at "innocence by association"), Hiss turned his attention toward his accuser. "His career is not, like those of *normal* men, an open book," he declared, favorably contrasting his own upstanding and seemingly transparent life with that of the surreptitious Chambers. "His operations have been furtive and concealed." Unlike the self-proclaimed penitent ex-Communist, who had spent years lurking in the shadows, Hiss had "lived a *normal*, open, public life in Washington," and he could not understand why "any *normal* person" would level such a spurious charge against him.

Next, it was Chambers's turn to testify. "Mr. Chambers," Nixon asked, "can you search your memory now to see what motive you can have for accusing Mr. Hiss of being a Communist at the present time?"

"What motive I can have?" Chambers asked.

"Yes. I mean, do you—is there any grudge that you have against Mr. Hiss over anything he has done to you?"

Chambers paused before answering,

The story has spread that in testifying against Mr. Hiss I am working out some old grudge, or motives of revenge or hatred. I do not hate Mr. Hiss. We were close friends, but we are caught in a tragedy of history. Mr. Hiss represents the concealed enemy against which we are all fighting, and I am fighting. I have testified against him with remorse and pity, but in a moment of history in which this Nation now stands, so help me God, I could not do otherwise.

To Nixon, it was "one of the most eloquent statements made in the history of" HUAC. And indeed, it was eloquent, a stirring disavowal of

E. M. Forster's aspirational confession: "If I had to choose between betraying my country and betraying my friend, I hope I should have the guts to betray my country." But there was an implicit subtext: "The story" to which Chambers alluded was the suspicion that Hiss had rebuffed his romantic advances and that, in an act of desperate, terrible vengeance, Chambers concocted a baroque fantasy involving an underground Communist cell to destroy the man he loved. In this reading, Chambers's use of the term "concealed enemy" to describe both Hiss and the totalitarian movement "against which we are all fighting, and I am fighting," contained an ulterior meaning. The suave State Department lawyer symbolized not only communism, but a force even more dangerous, the "molten torrent" of desire lurking within and between men: homosexuality.

The saga of Whittaker Chambers and Alger Hiss—which began with Chambers's HUAC testimony in the summer of 1948, continued with Hiss's conviction for perjury in 1950, and consumed partisans of both men for decades thereafter—wove matters of far-reaching historical significance with indelible evidentiary arcana. "The tragedy of history" about which Chambers rhapsodized so dramatically involved grand subjects like communism, freedom, patriotism, Christianity, and the nature of friendship. The determination of Hiss's legal guilt or innocence, meanwhile, hinged upon a series of granular details that would assume folkloric status, such as the authenticity of a Woodstock typewriter, the disposition of a Ford Roadster, the mention of a rare bird known as a "prothonotary warbler," the provenance of an old rug that Chambers gave to Hiss on behalf of "the Soviet people in gratitude for the work he had done for American Communists," and, most famously, the authenticity of a reel of microfilm hidden in a pumpkin patch. The case catapulted Richard Nixon from relative obscurity to nationwide fame, generated a groundswell of public support for a federal employee loyalty program, and paved the way for the anticommunist frenzy known as the Red Scare. For decades, where one stood on this "trial of the century" was a barometer of political commitment. By claiming that Chambers's accusations were part of a plot "to discredit recent great achievements of this country in which I was privileged to participate," Hiss opportunistically conflated his personal fate with that of the New Deal itself, attracting many of its supporters to his side. Chambers, who had evolved from Bolshevik revolutionary to conservative pessimist, also portrayed himself as a sacrificial lamb, and in near-religious terms. The "only" concern of "the man who must make the witness," he said, is "that out of his patient exposure of crime and sin, first and most mercilessly in himself, might rise the liberating truth for others." As the esteemed English journalist and veteran observer of American affairs Alistair Cooke concluded, it was not just Alger Hiss who was on trial. It was an entire generation.

Receiving barely any public scrutiny at the time, and all but forgotten today, was the subplot of homosexual passion and betrayal that many believed held the answer to this byzantine drama. In a fourteen-page "open letter" to HUAC written after Confrontation Day, Hiss referred to Chambers as a person who had lived "in the sewers" and called him "somewhat queer" four times. Chambers's former comrades at the *Daily Worker* characterized him as "a small, pudgy man with effeminate manners," and the Hiss defense team sent out investigators posing as journalists to elicit "any dirt at all that you know about Whittaker Chambers." When Hiss's lawyers obtained, courtesy of *New Yorker* writer A. J. Liebling, copies of letters Chambers had written to Mark Van Doren mentioning a romantic partner of indeterminate sex, they questioned Van Doren about the unknown paramour. Utilizing his skills as a literary scholar, Van Doren referenced a love story written by Proust in which the protagonist rhapsodizes about a woman but whose true love object is a man. Van Doren "admitted the possibility that Chambers took a bit out of Proust's book." Rumors that Chambers and Hiss had been romantically involved reached as high as the Harvard Board of Overseers and as low as the anonymously produced, palm-size pornographic comic books surreptitiously circulated and read across postwar America known as "Tijuana bibles," one edition of which, entitled "Betrayed," depicted Hiss performing oral sex on Chambers. By the end of 1948, colleagues of Chambers at *Time* were speaking of the case as a "battle between two queers."

The battle intensified on December 2, when Chambers led investigators to a pumpkin patch on his Maryland farm. From a hollowed-out gourd, he extracted five rolls of 35 mm film containing images of classified State Department documents that, he claimed, Hiss had given to him in 1938. No longer was the case merely one concerning a secret cell of Communist government officials; now it was a matter of high treason. Two days later, the FBI interviewed the former diplomat. Pressed to offer a motive as to why Chambers would falsely accuse him of espionage, Hiss told the agents that he believed Chambers to be a vengeful homosexual, citing an analysis offered by his friend, the renowned psychiatrist Dr. Carl Binger. "Homosexual behavior," Hiss told the agents, was compatible with showing "real affection and admiration for another person" while perpetrating "actions to hurt that other person." Four days later, Hiss shared with his lawyers an allegation passed along to him by another doctor, who claimed to have treated Chambers in 1937 or 1938 for "gonorrhea, frigidity, shock and persecution complex."

On December 15, a federal grand jury in Manhattan indicted Hiss on two counts of perjury—the first, for previously stating under oath that he had never given Chambers government documents, and the second for denying that he had seen Chambers after 1937. (The statute of limitations for espionage had expired.) In advance of the trial, Hiss's defense team adopted a strategy aimed at discrediting Chambers as a jilted homosexual. Private detectives hired by Hiss to collect damaging information about his accuser interviewed a raft of former associates, and tidbits of gossip and innuendo arrived over the transom. A Communist who had been a witness at Chambers's wedding told the Hiss defense team it was "common knowledge that Chambers had been a sex pervert when he was employed by the *Daily Worker*." Another former associate claimed that one night while he and Chambers were attending a 1932 convention of left-wing writers in Chicago, he awoke to find "Chambers in his bed assaulting him in a homosexual way." Syndicated newspaper columnist Joe Alsop recommended that the defense team peruse a German novel Chambers had translated two decades earlier, entitled *Class Reunion*, in which a resentful magistrate ruins his charming high school classmate in a fit of (possibly repressed homosexual) jealousy. "Chambers had a homosexual attraction toward Alger Hiss," asserted one of the defense lawyers in a memo summarizing Chambers's motive, "which caused him to identify himself with Hiss, to desire, to possess him, and to destroy him."

In between his disclosure of the "Pumpkin Papers" and the start of the perjury trial, Chambers attempted suicide. It was an act of desperation ostensibly spurred by a claim, later retracted, that the film on which Chambers had made photostatic copies of the incriminating State Department documents had been manufactured in 1945, years after Hiss had supposedly pilfered them. But Chambers had also been hearing stories about the defense team's efforts to dredge up "dirt" on his supposed homosexuality, and surely this helped drive him to the brink. It was possibly in an attempt to neutralize or preempt such smears that Chambers told HUAC in executive sessions the previous summer that "if you watch [Hiss] from behind, there is a slight mince sometimes" in his walk and that Hiss had "rather long, delicate fingers" and a "domineering" mother—all stereotypical signifiers of homosexuality.

Chambers spoke of his time in the underground as a double life, one of aliases, furtive meetings with anonymous contacts, dead letter drops, and the exchange of secrets. "I had two compartments," he told the committee, explaining his use of the pseudonym "Carl" to carry out party work. "Whittaker Chambers on the one side, which is my more or less private compartment, and 'Carl' in these groups here, and I did not want any bridge between them." But there was another dimension to this double life he had yet to share with anybody, one that the defense team's exhaustive probing would finally prompt him to unveil.

On February 15, 1949, two days before submitting himself to a pretrial deposition by Hiss's lawyers, Chambers met with the FBI for a preparatory interview. At its conclusion, he handed the agents a sealed envelope that he requested they not open until after he left the room. "We have now reached a point in my testimony where I must testify to certain facts which should be told only to a priest," the letter began:

> Alger Hiss's defense obviously intends to press the charge that I have had homosexual relations with certain individuals . . . I did not know what homosexualism meant until I was more than thirty years old. Until then, some of my friendships with men were too intense but they were completely innocent. My relations with women were slow to develop, but were normal . . . In 1933 or 4, a young fellow stopped me on the street in [New York] and asked me if I could give him a meal and lodgings for the night. I fed him and he told me about his life as a miner's son. I was footloose, so I took him to a hotel to spend the night. There he presently taught me an experience I did not know existed. At the same time he revealed to me, and unleashed, the . . . tendency of which I was still unaware. Because it had been repressed so long, it was all the more violent when once set free. For three or four years, I fought a wavering battle

against this affliction. Ten years or more ago, with God's help, I absolutely conquered it. This does not mean that I am completely immune to such stimuli. It does mean that my self-control is complete and that for years I have lived a blameless and devoted life as husband and father.

The Hiss forces, of course, will seek to prove that my weakness entered into my relations with Alger Hiss and possibly others. This is completely untrue. At no time, did I have such relations, or even the thought of such relations with Hiss or with anybody else in the Communist Party or connected with Communist work of any kind. I kept my secret as jealously from my associates in the C.P. as I did from everyone else. I tell it now only because, in this case, it has become my function to testify mercilessly against myself. I have said before that I am consciously destroying myself. This is not from love of self-destruction but because only if we are consciously prepared to destroy ourselves in the struggle can the thing we are fighting be destroyed.

Chambers added more details in a subsequent interview with the FBI. Revealing that he "actively sought out the opportunities for homosexual relationships" at the Hotel Annapolis and Hotel Pennsylvania in Washington and "the typical 'flea bag' type of hotel one finds in certain parts of Manhattan," he assured the agents that he "never had any prolonged affair with any one man" and "generally went to parks or other parts of town where these people were likely to be found." Furthermore, he had

kept this part of my life as my darkest personal secret and have never divulged these tendencies or experiences to any of my associates or friends, and particularly those in the Communist Party. I emphatically state that at no time did I even so much as hint about this to Alger Hiss or any of the people who I have been associated with either in the Communist Party, the Communist Party underground, or the Communist Party espionage apparatus from which I broke in April of 1938. I have never spoken of this to my wife or to my attorneys. As a matter of fact, my revelation of this activity has been told for the first time to anyone today . . .

It will be noted that three things of some great importance happened during the year 1938. First, my cessation of my homosexual activities;

my final break with the Communist Party, and my embracing for the first time, religion.

I do not believe that the cessation of my homosexual activities and my break with the Communist Party were in any way connected with each other. However, both of these activities on my part were more or less simultaneous with the advent of religion and God into my life.

Already at this point, the government's star witness in what was shaping up to be the most important espionage case in American history had several strikes against his credibility. He was a former Communist. He was a confessed (if remorseful) ex-spy. Now, he had revealed himself as having led a *second* clandestine life, as possibly the one thing worse than either: a homosexual. "In time," Chambers recalled, "I came to feel that the FBI knew much more about me than I knew about myself."

* * *

NINETEEN FORTY-EIGHT WAS A GROUNDBREAKING YEAR for homosexuality in America. On January 5, an Indiana entomologist named Alfred Kinsey published the doorstopper *Sexual Behavior in the Human Male*. Out of a research cohort consisting of 5,300 white men, Kinsey and his colleagues found, 37 percent reported at least one homosexual experience in their lifetime, and 10 percent were "more or less exclusively homosexual" for a period of at least three years between the ages of sixteen and fifty-five. Kinsey's tone in describing homosexuality was noteworthy for its objective detachment; same-sex attraction, he wrote, was a normal, recurring feature of humanity, and altogether harmless. "The homosexual has been a significant part of human sexual activity since the dawn of history," Kinsey wrote, "primarily because it is an expression of capacities that are basic in the human animal." The Kinsey Report, as it came to be known, was a sensation, remaining on the *New York Times* best seller list for almost seven months and selling a quarter of a million copies by summer.

Despite the best intentions of its author, however, the Kinsey study did not assuage popular anxieties over homosexuality. It inflamed them. If same-sex attraction was far more prevalent than Americans had theretofore realized, it could only mean that homosexuals were shockingly adept at concealment. For how else could so many deviants escape detection?

Kinsey's discoveries unintentionally jump-started a national effort to rip open closet doors everywhere, as the schoolteacher, the police officer, the neighbor—pretty much anyone—could be hiding inside. "Persons with homosexual histories are to be found in every age group, in every social level, in every conceivable occupation, in cities and on farms, and in the most remote areas of the country," Kinsey wrote. Homosexuals were an invisible peril. "If these figures are only approximately correct," a leading psychiatrist observed, "then the 'homosexual outlet' is the predominant national disease, overshadowing cancer, tuberculosis, heart failure, and infantile paralysis."

The very same week that Kinsey's alarming revelations struck a national chord, a young writer named Gore Vidal published his third novel, *The City and the Pillar*. With a title derived from the biblical tale of Sodom and Gomorrah, it was the first major novel to feature a gay protagonist sympathetically, though even Vidal's publisher could not help but appeal to the prejudices of mainstream readers. "Never before in American letters has there been such a revealing and frank discussion of the sexually mal-adjusted," declared E. P. Dutton, "of those of the submerged world which lives beneath the surface of normality." Though a work of fiction, *The City and the Pillar* captured a very real sense that gay men and women, long rel-egated to the shadows, had become increasingly visible in postwar Amer-ica. "There's a lot of queers here," a character observes of New York City. "They seem to be everywhere now." The need for discretion had hardly disappeared, however, and the homosexual world remained something akin to that of a secret society whose members learned, by necessity, to intuit hidden signals. "Occasionally two homosexuals might meet in either the highest or the most bourgeois society," wrote Vidal, evoking Proust, "and they would, perhaps, by a phrase, acknowledge one another's pres-ence among the enemy, but only by the slightest inflection of the voice or an understanding glance." Later that month, another novel by a precocious young homosexual, Truman Capote's *Other Voices, Other Rooms*, a gay coming-of-age story written in Southern Gothic style, made the *New York Times* best seller list, propelled in no small part by its scandalously come-hither author photograph. Nineteen forty-eight, the novelist John Cheever reflected, "was the year everybody in the United States was worried about homosexuality."

In Washington, gay visibility reached a new milestone with the opening of the Lafayette Chicken Hut, one of the city's first unofficial gay bars, at 1720 H Street. A restaurant on the first floor catered to a mostly straight crowd, while a jovial piano player named Howard, known affectionately by regulars as "Miss Hattie," entertained gay patrons on the second. (One night, when a group of out-of-town businessmen visiting for a convention asked to be seated upstairs, the waitress lied and said it had been reserved for a private meeting of the local meatpackers.) As customers alighted from the top of the staircase, Miss Hattie—accompanied on the piano bench by his lover, who turned the sheet music—welcomed them with improvised ditties. Hattie's repertoire consisted largely of popular songs with rewritten, ribald lyrics:

> Nothing could be sweeter
> than to suck a great big peter
> in the mooooorning!

"Did you hear that Ms. Blick?!" the patrons shouted whenever Hattie belted out an especially bawdy line, a reference to Lt. Roy Blick of the Metropolitan Police Department's Morals division. Soon, this taunt to the city's exorcist of homosexual iniquity entered the gay Washington vernacular, jocularly exclaimed among friends in response to the divulgence of something tantalizing, scandalous, or profane.

Such small examples of assertiveness were part of a larger postwar trend. The extensive deployment of men abroad and the enlistment of women in manual labor at home during the war years upended traditional gender roles. By placing millions of young men in single-sex environments and shipping them off to places where prostitution was freely available, employing women in factories, and dividing families, the war threatened to unleash a new era of licentiousness. "Definite changes in sexual freedom were observed in the wake of World War I, and this war, more global in character and involving many more people, is likely to bring in its wake far greater changes in sexual behavior," warned Dr. Benjamin Karpman, chief psychoanalyst at St. Elizabeths Hospital, less than two weeks after VE Day. Predicting a new era of sexual "looseness," Karpman observed that "wars tend to demoralize people and unsettle our morals and ethics in all fields of human behavior."

One way in which those morals and ethics became unsettled was the growing awareness of homosexuals, who in the popular imagination began to assume the role of social menace. Consensual sex between men had long been illegal in every state of the union; in the city where most of Chambers's surreptitious hookups occurred, New York, some fifty thousand men were arrested on homosexual charges between 1923 and 1967. In the years after the war, the term *sex deviate* came to encompass everyone from violent criminals to ordinary gay men and lesbians. Sensational media coverage of several high-profile cases involving the sexual exploitation and murder of children generated a sense, in the words of historian George Chauncey, that the country had become "overrun with murderous sex psychopaths."

As is often the case with things that the government proscribes, the criminalization of homosexuality forced it into dark and dangerous places. Gay men and women had few avenues for seeking romantic and sexual fulfillment in midcentury America. There were no lonely hearts columns in the newspapers for sex deviants, and the handful of bars that catered to them faced the constant threat of legal sanction. To meet other people like themselves, most gay men had few options other than to "cruise" public spaces like parks, restrooms, and street corners. In 1947, the *Washington Post* warned that the nation's capital "has become more or less a haven for sexual perverts and degenerates," and later that year, the U.S. Park Police initiated a "sex perversion elimination program." Increased patrols targeted Lafayette Square (where a vigilant *Post* reporter discovered a wired listening device hidden behind a bench), Dupont Circle, and some of the places Chambers had frequented a decade earlier. The following year, Congress, which governed the District of Columbia, passed a law classifying people who engaged in sodomy as "sexual psychopaths," authorizing the DC government to commit them to St. Elizabeths.

By November, an average of two men were being hauled off to court every day for committing "indecent acts" in Washington. On one especially busy night, the vice squad arrested sixty-five men in Lafayette Square alone. And whereas during the Depression it was widely assumed that those who participated in homosexual activity were vagabonds and other products of the lower classes, most of the men arrested on sex perversion charges in Washington during the late 1940s were reported as being "of above-average intelligence" and college educated. (Sometimes, the city's newspapers listed the offenders' names and addresses, ruining reputations, careers, and families.) Many of these men were apprehended by a single, strikingly handsome young rookie whom the *Post* dubbed the "one-man vice squad" for his prolific entrapments. Over a four-day period in July 1948, Pvt. Frank Manthos arrested a record seventeen men for sexual solicitation; during his first eight months on the force, he performed one hundred fifty arrests. Manthos's colleagues grew jealous of his success. The private "comes to us for advice and we give him tips and tell him how to work, then he gets all the glory," they complained.

The homosexual was a like a virus, invisible and constantly threatening to lure innocent victims (particularly children) into his dangerous netherworld. "All too often we lose sight of the fact that the homosexual is an inveterate seducer of the young of both sexes," an assistant attorney general of California warned in a 1949 text, *The Sexual Criminal*, "and that he presents a social problem because he is not content with being degenerate himself; he must have degenerate companions and is ever seeking for younger victims." Testifying before HUAC a year before Whittaker Chambers issued his charges against Alger Hiss, J. Edgar Hoover used remarkably similar language to describe the other great peril confronting America, auguring a dangerous conflation. "Communism, in reality, is not a political party," he declared. "It is a way of life—an evil and malignant way of life. It reveals a condition akin to disease that spreads like an epidemic; and like an epidemic, a quarantine is necessary to keep it from infecting the nation." And if the everyday Communist was the carrier of a disease, then the Communist spy—a "penetration agent" in espionage parlance—represented an ongoing, almost sexual violation against the country.

7

"THIS MORAL LEPER"

IN HIS OPENING ARGUMENT AT THE PERJURY TRIAL OF ALGER HISS, WHICH began on June 1, 1949, at the U.S. District Courthouse in Manhattan, Lloyd Paul Stryker demonstrated for the packed courtroom why he was the greatest criminal defense attorney since Clarence Darrow.

"I will take Alger Hiss by the hand," Stryker told the jurors, "and I will lead him before you from the date of his birth down to this hour. Even though I would go into the valley of the shadow of death I will fear no evil, because there is no blot or blemish on him." As for Hiss's accuser, Whittaker Chambers had been a "furtive, secretive, deceptive, man" even before he joined the "low-down, nefarious, filthy conspiracy . . . against the land that I love and you love" and whose blood money he accepted "for the prostitution of his soul." The "particular criminal propensities, inclinations, and activities" of Chambers "come up very naturally" for him, as he had "written a filthy, despicable play about Jesus Christ" as a college student. In summation, Stryker revealed himself to be no better a disciple of Christ's teachings than the man he had come to indict. "In the warm southern countries . . . where they have leprosy, sometimes you will hear on the streets perhaps among the lepers a man crying down the street," Stryker thundered, lifting his eyebrows for emphasis, "'Unclean! Unclean!'

at the approach of a leper." Then, gesturing toward the defendant, he made his appeal. "I say the same to you at the approach of this moral leper."

Recognizing the limits of an "innocence by association" strategy, the Hiss defense team tried to impugn Chambers as guilty by defamation. They settled on portraying him as a psychopath, strongly implying that he had turned on Hiss in outraged reaction to Hiss's rejection of his sexual advances. "The psychiatric theory has been criticized because it may be regarded as an unjustified smear of Chambers as a homosexual," one of Hiss's lawyers wrote to his colleagues in March. "Surely we intend to smear Chambers in any event. I have no objection to such smearing and hope that it will be very thoroughly and effectively done. But I see little difference between smearing Chambers as a homosexual and smearing him as a liar, a thief, and a scoundrel." And nor would any jury comprised of Hiss's peers, for whom being a homosexual was synonymous with all three. The defense may have also considered taking its case against Chambers one step farther by insinuating that he was a pedophile, a charge stemming from rumors concerning Hiss's stepson, Timothy Hobson, who was ten years old when Chambers said Hiss had passed him the State Department documents. In January, Charles Dollard, Hiss's friend and president of the Carnegie Corporation, told a defense lawyer that he had "talked about the case with various psychiatrists who all advocate the homosexual theory, sometimes involving Timothy, sometimes Alger." (According to Dollard, the psychiatrists also worried "that Alger's insistence upon [seeing] Chambers's teeth" during the HUAC executive session at the Commodore Hotel the previous August "was significant in this connection," as it could imply that the two had engaged in oral sex.) A few days after the trial began, J. Edgar Hoover reported hearing from "a confidential source" a rumor that the Hiss team planned to allege that Chambers "was in the Hiss household having relations" with Hobson while the boy's parents were away, and that this was how Chambers had gained access to the Hiss family typewriter on which he—not Hiss's wife, Priscilla, as the prosecution alleged—typed up copies of the documents, which he then hid in a pumpkin and used to frame Hiss.

According to Hobson, however, Chambers never made a move on him sexually. Indeed, Hobson was willing to testify that Chambers never visited the Hiss household in his presence, evidence, supposedly, that Chambers was lying. While Hobson would later claim that the FBI had threatened to expose his dishonorable discharge from the navy over a homosexual incident should he take the stand in his stepfather's defense, playing the homosexual card was risky for the Hiss team. Accusing Chambers of homosexuality could "boomerang" and implicate Hiss as well, unintentionally giving credence to the theory that the two men had met not under the auspices of the Communist conspiracy but the homosexual one. And were that the case, it would not be too far of a leap to surmise that maybe Hiss *had* spurned Chambers, and that Chambers, in turn, pressured Hiss into giving him the documents under threat of blackmail.

In the end, the defense team advanced a "theory of unconscious motivation." According to this hypothesis, Chambers developed an obsession with Hiss when he briefly knew him as a freelance journalist and cadger in the mid-1930s, and this obsession drove Chambers to destroy him. It was a way of spattering Chambers with mud—as the *Washington Post* had analogized in its righteous defense of Hiss the previous summer—without any of it splashing back on Hiss. In his cross-examination, Stryker entered one of the homoerotic poems Chambers had written under a pseudonym more than twenty years earlier, "Tandaradei," into evidence. Chivalrously declining to read it in front of "a mixed jury," he handed a copy to Chambers, who mumbled a few lines so incomprehensibly that Stryker snatched the document away and gave it to a court reporter, who, in the words of one journalist, recited the verse "with all the inflection of a train caller."

> As your sap drains out into me in excess,
> Like the sap from the stems of a tree that they lop

At this "especially hot passage," Judge Samuel Kaufman shielded his face with his hand. In his closing argument, Stryker denounced Chambers as nothing less than "an enemy of the republic, a blasphemer of Christ, a disbeliever in God, with no respect either for matrimony or motherhood."

After fifteen hours of deliberation, the foreman announced a hung jury. Immediately, the government declared that it would retry Hiss. With nothing left to lose, the defense amplified the homosexual component of its theory of the case. One of its key witnesses at the second perjury trial, which commenced in January 1950, was the psychiatrist Dr. Carl Binger, whose role at the first trial had been to sit silently in the witness stand for forty-five minutes as Stryker read aloud an extremely prejudicial account of Chambers's itinerant and eccentric life history, after which Stryker asked him for an assessment of Chambers's "mental condition." Before Binger could answer, the prosecution objected on the grounds that Binger had never evaluated Chambers and thus could not offer a medical diagnosis. The objection was sustained. This time, however, Judge Henry Goddard, a conservative Republican, surprised the court when he ruled that Binger's testimony would be admissible. Chambers, Binger asserted on the stand, displayed a "psychopathic personality" and an "abnormal emotionality." Overall, his behavior was "queer."

Another defense witness, Dr. Henry Murray, author of the 1943 OSS report detailing Hitler's "attraction to [Ernst] Roehm and other domineering homosexuals," tendered a similarly dubious psychological evaluation. Basing his opinion solely upon a reading of Chambers's published work, Murray concurred with Binger's assessment that Chambers had a "psychopathic personality." Murray also impeached Chambers's credibility on account of his having worked in the Communist underground. If the man had spent so many years lying and stealing on behalf of a foreign adversary, Murray said, how could he be trusted at all? By that logic, asked the prosecutor during cross-examination, could not the same be said about the thousands of patriotic Americans who had served in the OSS? Yes, Murray replied. "The whole nature of the functions of the OSS were particularly inviting to psychopathic characters," for "it involved sensation, intrigue, the idea of being a mysterious man with secret knowledge." J. Edgar Hoover could not have put it better.

The material evidence against Hiss was too strong, however, and on January 21, the jury returned a guilty verdict. The erstwhile "fair-haired boy of the State Department," as the *Star* called him, was sentenced to five years at the federal penitentiary in Lewisburg, Pennsylvania. After forty-four months, he was released, naturally, for good behavior.

* * *

THE HOMOSEXUAL SUBTEXT OF THE "TRIAL OF THE CENTURY" was not lost on close observers. But even mentioning it obliquely was considered uncouth. Summarizing the various explanations for the relationship between the celebrated former diplomat and his ex-Communist accuser, Alistair Cooke referred to "one or two other theories that went the rounds of Washington and New York which, however, so mercilessly intrude into other people's lives that the incompleteness of this report appears a small price to pay for giving anybody so slandered the benefit of a large doubt." Chambers's fellow ex-Communist Sidney Hook declared that "outrageous smears against his personal life and that of his wife surpassed in virulence anything known in recent American history." James Wechsler, a journalist who, like Chambers, had a youthful dalliance with communism in the 1930s, but unlike him, emerged from that experience a liberal, denounced "a loathsome whispering campaign," one hypocritically "encouraged with peculiarly ill grace by men who were then engaged in decrying the phenomenon of character assassination in other areas of American life." Arthur Schlesinger struck a similar note about the hypocrisy of those who denounced red-baiting while stooping to the lavender variety. Denouncing the "ugly and vicious stories invented and repeated by respectable lawyers and college professors—stories which purported to 'explain' everything, but which, when the time came, the Hiss defense never cared to bring up in court," Schlesinger pronounced that "[t]he anti-Chambers whispering campaign was one of the most repellent of modern history." What all these critiques of the Hiss team's tactics had in common, aside from righteous disgust, was a studied ambiguity: so repugnant was the accusation of homosexuality that even those condemning it could not bring themselves to identify what, exactly, they were condemning.

Chambers himself never publicly discussed this aspect of the case, but it clearly inflicted a heavy toll. As he recounted in his best-selling 1952 memoir, *Witness*, the "venomous calumnies of the Hiss forces"—which he declined to specify except for noting that they had been excreted by a "cloaca" that "fed that bilge across the land"—drove him to attempt suicide a second time. What made the act of bearing witness such a monumental burden, Chambers admitted, was not merely the risk he shouldered by standing up to international communism. It was also the possibility that what he had described to the FBI as his "darkest personal secret" would be revealed. Only a witness of "desperate integrity," one committed to "exposing the evil in himself," Chambers wrote, could "expose the evil that beset and secretly threatened other men." The concern of the witness, therefore, "must be only that out of his patient exposure of crime and sin, first and most mercilessly in himself, might rise the liberating truth for others." To the vast majority of readers, the "evil," "crime," and "sin" to which Chambers referred was communism. But there was another component to his agony, one that had to remain unsaid. In this regard, *Witness* can be read not only as the testament of one man's conversion from atheistic dialectical materialism to conservative religious faith, but also of his conversion from tortured homosexual to "devoted . . . husband and father."

Many gay men would identify with Chambers's recollection of his boyhood self, marked by "sensitivity, imaginativeness," and "gentleness." But it is his descriptions of life as a courier in the Communist underground that most echo the midcentury gay male experience. "When I try to evoke what that life was like," Chambers writes of his Communist phase, "it comes back to me as a succession of brief cases, of Washington streets at night, of a tight little world beyond the law, turning upon an axis of faith and fear." The nation's capital encompassed a secret city, "composed of trusted, clandestine people, knit invisibly by a common historical conviction in whose name they performed the rites of a common crime, and by the fact that each carried the fate of others in his hands." Chambers's description of a stealthy encounter between two Communists could be replicated, word for word, as an account of how two homosexuals signaled their secret brotherhood:

> At first, I met almost everyone in drug stores. The first man at such a meeting would buy a Coke or a pack of cigarettes, idle around the novelties or leaf through a magazine from the rack. When the second man appeared, neither would greet the other. They would saunter out on the street and greet each other only when they were satisfied that there was no surveillance.

"Communists," Chambers wrote, "were assumed to be criminals, pariahs, clandestine men who lead double lives under false names, travel on false passports, deny traditional religion, morality, the sanctity of oaths, preach violence and practice treason." Like the homosexual in post-Kinsey America, "the conspirator is indistinguishable from the man beside you." Chambers "met [his] comrades regularly, often at night, in lonely places," including once at the San Francisco YMCA, which in most cities was a popular cruising spot. Meeting a comrade for the first time, Chambers and the man "understood one another at once with a birdlike intuition in which common experience took the place of explanation." Another left Chambers a note and "meant me to read between the lines. That kind of double-talking letter, almost incredible to the rest of the world, is commonplace to underground Communists." And to members of another underground as well.

Following his release from prison in 1954 and until his death over four decades later at the age of ninety-two, Alger Hiss dedicated his very long life to winning back his reputation, a campaign in which he was joined by a small but ferocious number of dedicated acolytes. Hiss and his defenders offered a variety of alternative explanations for how copies of State Department documents in his possession wound up in the hands of a self-professed Communist agent: that the FBI forged them on a typewriter built to match Hiss's own; that Chambers had never actually left the Communist Party and falsely accused Hiss on behalf of his Soviet masters; and that Richard Nixon had fabricated the microfilm "found" in Chambers's pumpkin patch (a theory that gained traction around the time of the Watergate scandal). Underlying them all is the portrayal of Chambers as mentally ill or, as Hiss once told his son, "a nut, out for fairy vengeance."

Hiss and his defenders propounded this theme repeatedly. "My guess is that he had some obscure kind of love attachment . . . about me," Hiss told a private group of supporters in 1959, "and he came to hate my wife." After Chambers's death in 1961, the attempts to discredit him as a spurned homosexual dropped any pretense. The first major effort arrived in *Friendship and Fratricide*, a book that happened to be published the same week in January 1967 as William Bullitt and Sigmund Freud's psychobiography of Woodrow Wilson, and that demonstrated a similar obsession. Describing an "aura of homosexual conflict" surrounding Chambers from birth, author Dr. Meyer A. Zeligs noted that "though the genesis of homosexuality is infinitely varied and complex, Chambers's early background was a clear medium for its development. His father was weak, effeminate, withdrawn, or absent; his mother, cold, driven, unrealistic." Advancing the theory that Chambers himself typed the State Department documents on Hiss's typewriter, Zeligs wrote that the device was "something Chambers could secretly use in the service of both his erotic fantasies and his destructive schemes." The trial of the century had nothing to do with profound questions concerning communism and freedom, sin and redemption, or even the massive inventory of physical evidence. According to Zeligs, it all boiled down to Chambers's "childhood frustrations" and how "the fears and fantasies that filled his earliest years inexorably pre-determined his future thoughts and actions." To the charge of pedophilia involving Timothy Hobson, Zeligs added the possibility of incest, writing that "Chambers' memories of his brother reveal a homosexual attraction to him and concomitant feelings of hatred and guilt."

The 1976 release of Chambers's FBI confession, prompted by a Freedom of Information Act request, was welcomed by Hiss and his defenders as validation of his "fairy vengeance" thesis. "He never made a pass at me," Hiss snickered. Two years later, discussing why his defense team did not call forth the ex-Communist who had claimed Chambers forcibly performed fellatio on him, the ornithologically inclined Hiss remarked that "one swallow doesn't make a summer." In his 1988 memoir, *Recollections of a Life*, Hiss said that he knew as far back as the 1930s that the "short, plain-faced, and dumpy" Chambers was "a closet homosexual." Chambers, he wrote, was an "irresponsible fantasist," "a possessed man and a psychopath," and a person "whose own life had been bizarre and disordered." All this led Hiss to the conclusion that "my rebuff to him wounded him in a way that I did not realize at the time."

Hiss's campaign to exculpate himself was dealt a critical blow shortly before his death in 1996, when the U.S. government released transcripts of intercepted Soviet communications, the "Venona" decrypts, all but proving that he was a Soviet agent who operated under the code name "Ales." To be sure, many young and otherwise decent people were attracted to communism in the 1930s. What was remarkable about Hiss was his perseverance in denying he ever had been. According to the legal historian G. Edward White, for Hiss, "Denying that secret worlds existed in his life had become as natural to him as participating in those worlds." Hiss achieved "integration" in the "psychological sense of completeness, self-fulfillment, and inner peace . . . not by *being* innocent of covert espionage activity but by successfully *pretending* to be innocent." That the heterosexual Hiss, rather than the "queer" Chambers, was, in retrospect, the quintessence of what soon became the demonic cultural archetype of the Cold War homosexual—intriguing, deceitful, and treasonous—is a bitter irony. For if any character in this drama was "a possessed man and a psychopath," it wasn't Chambers. It was Hiss, who maintained a lie for nearly five decades and implicated a vast number of people, including his own family, in perpetuating it.

For both sides in this searing battle, homosexuality was a talismanic force. Among the conservative champions of Chambers, it became inextricably linked with communism. Homosexuality was something that Chambers renounced, along with *The Communist Manifesto*, when he exchanged furtive sexual encounters in "flea bag" hotels for the bourgeois domesticity of a Maryland pumpkin patch. For partisans of Hiss, Chambers's secret life not only offered a tidy alibi for their hero. It also presaged the connection they would come to make between repressed homosexuality and fervid *anti*communism. (Richard Nixon, who believed that Hiss and Chambers "were both that way," borrowed from each thesis.) Few bothered to listen to the eponymous "Witness" himself, who emphasized to the FBI that neither his embrace nor his disavowal of communism and homosexuality, though roughly simultaneous, were "in any way connected with each other." Chambers also admitted that he still felt homosexual urges, implying that someone with such a nature could still be a loyal, God-fearing patriot. Neither right nor left cared to admit the validity of mutually exclusive claims: for the former, that Chambers was (at least for a time) a homosexual, and for the latter, that Hiss was a Communist.

The Hiss-Chambers affair established a link between communism, disloyalty, and homosexuality in the minds of influential Washingtonians, broadening the incipient "Red Scare" into a lavender one. "Homosexuality has figured, off stage, in one of our traitorous operations," Sen. George Malone of Nevada declared in March 1950, the *Chicago Daily Tribune* elaborating for the benefit of its outside-the-Beltway readership that he was "apparently referring to persistent reports in Washington concerning the Hiss-Chambers case." Spotting similarities between the Communist and homosexual milieus, Arthur Schlesinger observed in his influential 1949 book, *The Vital Center*, "A curious freemasonry exists among underground workers and sympathizers. They can identify each other (and be identified by their enemies) on casual meeting by the use of certain phrases, the names of certain friends, by certain enthusiasms and certain silences." Describing the encounter of two Communist secret agents, Schlesinger referenced the French literary classic that the young Chambers had been asked to translate. "It is reminiscent of nothing so much as the famous scene in Proust where the Baron de Charlus and tailor Jupien suddenly recognize their common corruption." Communism, Schlesinger concluded, "perverts politics into something secret, sweaty and furtive like nothing so much, in the phrase of one wise observer of modern Russia, as homosexuality in a boys' school: many practicing it, but all those caught to be caned by the headmaster."

Asked about the fate of his former colleague on the day Hiss was convicted of perjury, Secretary of State Dean Acheson invoked the twenty-fifth chapter of the Gospel of Matthew, an exaltation of the Lord's infinite capacity to forgive. "I do not intend to turn my back on Alger Hiss," Acheson defiantly replied. The retort immediately drew widespread criticism in Congress, one of whose members, a relatively unknown junior senator from Wisconsin with a penchant for demagoguery and a peerless instinct for the gutter, spotted comedic potential in a comment involving the secretary of state, his backside, and a Communist spy. After denouncing Acheson's defense of Hiss as "fantastic" on the Senate floor, Senator Joe McCarthy "converted the answer into an unprintable remark which made the rounds of the Washington cocktail parties."

8

LAVENDER LISTS

Dean Acheson had more important things to do. His testimony before a Senate Appropriations subcommittee on February 28, 1950—coaxed out of him by the tribe of right-wing congressional Republicans he would come to call the "primitives"—was taking place amid a rapidly worsening international situation. Less than six months earlier, the Soviet Union had successfully detonated an atomic bomb, putting an end to the short-lived American monopoly on nuclear weapons and opening a terrifying new chapter in the Cold War. A little more than a month later, Mao Zedong's Chinese Communists declared victory over the Nationalist Army of U.S.-backed generalissimo Chiang Kai-shek, and the week after that, the Soviets established a Communist puppet government in their zone of occupied East Germany. As if this series of developments was not ominous enough, they reached an alarming climax on February 15, when China and the Soviet Union, together constituting a third of the world's population, announced a thirty-year mutual defense and assistance pact.

No more than five years after emerging on the winning side of the most destructive conflict in human history, America once again found itself confronting a very dangerous world. As secretary of state, Acheson had to manage the country's role in this complicated new geopolitical environment, a herculean task made even more difficult thanks to the administration's congressional critics, the aforementioned "primitives," who kept badgering him with their inquests and showboating. America was now a superpower, however reluctant, and its foreign policy, Acheson believed, should be crafted by highly educated men with the right credentials, not provincial solons and their "town meetings." With his elegant (if at times pretentious) locution, waxed mustache, and homburg hats, the Groton-, Yale-, and Harvard-educated Acheson cut a dashing figure on the international diplomatic circuit. Alas, the qualifications and traits that earned him respect overseas were the same ones that nettled the men who had bidden him to explain his curiously sympathetic comments about Alger Hiss.

The root of their acrimony, as Acheson saw it, was that while he recognized the greatest threats to America as originating from abroad, his senatorial inquisitors detected them at home—specifically, in his Department of State. The "surrender" of Eastern Europe to the Russians at Yalta, Moscow's acquisition of the atomic bomb, the "loss" of China—each and every demoralizing overseas reversal was inexplicable to these men as anything other than the catastrophic result of deliberate, cowardly, and borderline treasonous actions undertaken by officials operating at the highest levels of the American government. Officials like Dean Acheson, founder of what Richard Nixon, campaigning for the Senate on the strength of his reputation from the Alger Hiss case, was soon to call "Dean Acheson's cowardly college of Communist containment." Hiss's conviction for perjury did not reflect well upon the administration of the president who had initially labeled the case a "red-herring"; nor, for that matter, did the revelation the previous month that Klaus Fuchs, a member of the team that built the atom bomb at Los Alamos National Laboratory, had given sensitive material to the Soviets. "I used my Marxist philosophy to establish in my mind two separate compartments," Fuchs said in his confession, sounding very much like his former comrade in revolutionary struggle Whittaker Chambers. In the minds of a growing number of Americans, the policy of "containment" advocated by the Truman administration was at best a failure and at worst a betrayal.

This was the thrust of the speech delivered on February 9, 1950, by the senator who had made a lewd joke about Alger Hiss and Dean Acheson's posterior. Two weeks after Hiss was convicted of perjury, Joe McCarthy denounced Acheson to the Republican ladies of Wheeling, West Virginia, as "this pompous diplomat in striped pants with a phony British accent." But what made the speech infamous, what turned Washington upside down for the next four years, was McCarthy's assertion that he had in his possession a "list" of State Department employees "who would appear to be either card-carrying members or certainly loyal to the Communist Party."

The political heat generated by these accusations was still scorching when Acheson was summoned to testify before the Senate Appropriations subcommittee three weeks later. Considering his long record of public service, Acheson said, it was "fantastic" to insinuate that he "was condoning the offenses with which Mr. Hiss was charged and of which he has been convicted." Later, a senator asked Acheson to explain what sort of employee, in his view, constituted a "security risk." Acheson replied that personnel sympathetic to communism or fascism or who had "habitual or close association" with such people, those who had performed "service in the governments or armed forces of enemy countries," and the "habitual alcoholic or a person who has any other physical or moral defect which could be preyed upon or which might be used by somebody who was attempting to penetrate into the Department" all qualified for dismissal on security grounds.

"Such as homosexuality or a person with a criminal record?" New Hampshire senator Styles Bridges, the "Gray Eminence of the Republican Party," asked in clarification.

"That would be included," Acheson replied.

This exchange was pretext for the most shocking revelation to occur during the hearing, a remark made in passing by the nondescript man sitting to Acheson's right at the witness table, the deputy undersecretary of state responsible for internal security, John Peurifoy. Bridges asked Peurifoy to enumerate how many employees under investigation as security risks had resigned. "In this shady category that you referred to earlier," Peurifoy responded, checking his notes, "there are 91 cases, sir."

"What do you mean by 'shady category?'" Bridges asked.

"We are talking about people of moral weaknesses and so forth that we have gotten rid of in the Department," Peurifoy replied, desperate to avoid stating the word *homosexual* aloud.

Sen. Pat McCarran, the conservative Democratic committee chairman from Nevada, asked the deputy undersecretary to clarify.

Peurifoy finally relented. "Most of these were homosexuals, Mr. Chairman."

"You say that there were 91?" McCarran asked in disbelief.

"Yes, sir. All of them were removed."

If Joe McCarthy's Wheeling speech was the opening salvo in the "Red Scare," John Peurifoy's impromptu comments inadvertently set off a panic of a different hue: the "Lavender Scare." The former—a staple of high school history curricula, the subject of countless works of literature, its chief instigator achieving the dubious honor of having an "ism" attached to his surname—is widely recognized to have been a significant part of American history. The latter, despite having lasted far longer and claiming as many if not more victims, remains largely unknown.

The main reason for this disparity is the secrecy that shrouded the Lavender Scare's victims. By midcentury, Americans were well acquainted with communism, a century-old ideology with hefty treatises, vocal proponents, and whole nations held captive under its sway. The United States had already endured a Red Scare following the First World War, and a villainous array of party leaders, writers, and the odd celebrity could be pointed to as members of the international Communist conspiracy. The homosexual, by contrast, remained a terrifying mystery. Very few people, and certainly no public figures, were willing to identify as one. Well into the 1960s, homosexuals were administered electroshock therapies, emetics, and even lobotomies as "cures" for their affliction. "Constantly and unceasingly we carry a mask," wrote Donald Webster Cory in his pathbreaking 1951 book, *The Homosexual in America: A Subjective Approach*, "and without interruption we stand on guard lest our secret, which is our very essence, be betrayed." While homosexuality had been addressed in a handful of novels and a few arcane medical texts, *The Homosexual in America* was the first nonfiction book for a general readership to approach the subject from a sympathetic perspective. And yet even the author of this revolutionary volume was unwilling to identify himself. A transposition of *Corydon*, the bold defense of homosexuality published by French Nobel laureate André Gide, "Don Cory" was the pseudonym of a married perfume salesman named Edward Sagarin.

Like Black people and Jews, Sagarin argued, homosexuals comprised "a minority group, consisting of large numbers of people who belong, participate, and are constantly aware of something that binds them to others and separates them from the larger stream of life; yet a group without a spokesman, without a leader, without a publication, without an organization, without a philosophy of life, without an accepted justification for its own existence." The identification of homosexuals as a minority like any other was radical, to say the least. ("My God," the author Norman Mailer thought upon reading Sagarin's plea, "homosexuals are people, too.") But unlike other minorities, the very essence of what made homosexuals different was illegal. They were therefore enveloped in "a conspiracy of silence" imposed upon them by a hostile society and sustained through their own shame.

The sense that these people posed a risk to national security had been brewing for some time. "All the 'Artists' with a capital A, the parlor pinks and the soprano voiced men are banded together . . ." President Truman wrote in 1946 when explaining the firing of his pro-Soviet secretary of commerce and predecessor as vice president, Henry Wallace. "I am afraid they are a sabotage front for Uncle Joe Stalin." The following March, Truman signed Executive Order 9835, establishing a "loyalty program" across the executive branch. As the order applied only to a person's political views and associations, while leaving unaddressed those personality traits that might lead one to betray secrets unintentionally or against one's will, the threshold for what constituted "loyalty" was lower than what would be required to maintain government "security." In June 1947, concerned members of the Senate Appropriations Committee wrote a letter to Acheson's predecessor, Gen. George C. Marshall, warning of the "extensive employment in highly classified positions of admitted homosexuals, who are historically known to be security risks." In response, the department promulgated a policy authorizing the termination of those who displayed, in addition to subversive tendencies, "habitual drunkenness, sexual perversion, moral turpitude, financial irresponsibility or criminal record." Robert J. Ryan, who worked in the State Department personnel office during Marshall's tenure, recalled the first time an employee's homosexuality was discovered by investigators. "Fire the bastard," Marshall was alleged to have ordered. "And that was where the policy was inaugurated of terminating people with homosexual backgrounds," Ryan said.

The revelation that the State Department had fired nearly one hundred homosexuals, and the inference that an untold number still lurked there, was seized upon by a dedicated band of right-wing journalists and politicians, already on the hunt for saboteurs and traitors within every sphere of American society. "It is common knowledge that such persons have psychic ways of seeking one another out," the syndicated columnist Westbrook Pegler wrote, while also taking a swipe at "the Empress" Eleanor Roosevelt, whose boast on the radio that she "always had lots of queer friends" Pegler thought perversely suggestive. New York *Daily News* Washington columnist John O'Donnell claimed that "the foreign policy of the United States, even before World War II, was dominated by an all-powerful, supersecret inner circle of highly educated, socially high-placed sexual misfits, in the State Department, all easy to blackmail, all susceptible to blandishments by homosexuals in foreign nations." Of the twenty-five thousand letters sent to McCarthy's office in the weeks following his Wheeling speech and Peurifoy's testimony, only one out of four was primarily concerned with Communist infiltration of the federal government. The rest decried "sex depravity." A shrewd reader of public sentiment, McCarthy adjusted his rhetoric accordingly. The State Department, he declared in April, was riddled with "Communists and queers who have sold 400 million Asiatic people into atheistic slavery and have the American people in a hypnotic trance, headed blindly toward the same precipice." Acheson should be fired, McCarthy demanded, along with his crew of "prancing mimics of the Moscow party line in the state department." Frank Kent, sober originator of what would come to be known as "inside-the-Beltway" journalism, reported that "politicians generally agree that their constituencies have been more revolted by [Peurifoy's] voluntary disclosure than by anything else." Assessing the impact of the hearing, a professor at the University of Kansas School of Medicine wrote, "Although more than 8,000,000 Americans today are actual or potential homosexuals, it took a ballyhooed Congressional investigation to put homosexuality in the headlights, however inadequately."

Anxiety over Communist momentum abroad, growing awareness of homosexuality at home, and the increasing bureaucratization of a massively expanding federal government in Washington all converged to put gay and lesbian citizens in an extremely precarious position. Once, homosexuality had been an individualized psychiatric disorder. Now, it was gaining a fearsome relevance in national politics and in the burgeoning Cold War.

* * *

THE PROBLEM OF HOMOSEXUALS IN THE FEDERAL GOVERNMENT was one that had occupied Kenneth Wherry since the very first day he arrived in Washington as a senator from Nebraska in 1943. A chain-smoking small businessman and licensed embalmer, the Republican minority leader was quick to complain about how often the media "forget to mention that I have also been as successful a lawyer as the next one," even the legal profession apparently enjoying a better reputation than the mortuary trade. In the words of the *New York Times Magazine*, Wherry was "Washington's leading symbol and rallying point of die-hard conservatism," though he much preferred the term "fundamentalist." Infamous for "Wherryisms" like "the Chief Joints of Staff," "Indigo China," and "the senator from junior," he could swing suddenly from violent harangues resembling "wild Indian scalping yells" to the fraternal backslapping more commonly associated with the world's greatest deliberative body. According to one young Senate correspondent, Allen Drury, Wherry frequently treated the chamber as "an arena for horseplay."

Spurred by Peurifoy's testimony, Wherry and a Democratic colleague, Sen. J. Lister Hill of Alabama, formed a two-person subcommittee to investigate the homosexual infiltration of the federal government. To reveal the full scope of the problem, Wherry subpoenaed the man widely considered to be one of the country's greatest experts on the lavender menace. Lt. Roy Blick had assigned four of his officers to the pervert beat, and was by necessity familiar with the degraded lives and sordid rituals of homosexuals. The husky, graying head of the Morals division had received "a good education in the rough ways of the world" when, at thirteen, he ran away from home and sustained himself through pearl diving, potato peeling, and dishwashing. Joining the Metropolitan Police Department in 1931, Blick donned the uniform of a beat-walking cop only briefly. "I must have looked funny, because after three weeks they took me out of uniform and made me a plainclothesman," he recalled. Colleagues joked that when Blick looked at the cover of *Lady Chatterley's Lover* (the sexually explicit 1929 novel that was the subject of a watershed obscenity trial), it was Lady Chatterley's lover who averted *his* eyes. This "one-man watchdog of the city's morals" was more *Keystone Cops* than *Dragnet*, however, as evidenced by the permanent damage he sustained to his left eye after a tear gas gun accidentally went off in his face during a raid on a whorehouse. But Blick never let his ocular impairment prevent him from getting his man. When the Supreme Court freed a bookmaker whom he had arrested without a warrant in 1948, Blick patiently waited three years before leading a nine-officer team to apprehend the scofflaw in another bust. "Hi-ya Mac," Blick announced as he burst through the door. "This time I've got a warrant!"

"Then it looks like this time I'll go to jail," the bookie said with a sigh.

Decades before congressional committees conducted classified hearings in soundproof sensitive compartmented information facilities (SCIFs), Roy Blick's appearance before the Hill-Wherry subcommittee in March 1950 was reputed to be the most secretive event in the history of Congress. Though the committee produced just two transcripts of Blick's testimony, both secured in a locked vault, the information he provided was simply too sensational not to leak. Most of the hysteria over homosexuality in the post-war United States concerned gay men. But Blick warned of a sensuously sapphic danger. "A well-known espionage tactic" employed by foreign powers, Blick revealed, was to lure young, unmarried women "into the communist underground by involving them in lesbian practices." As many as forty or fifty such women—seduced from the huge pool of "government girls" who had been flocking to Washington by the tens of thousands since the early days of the New Deal—participated in these "sex orgies," which were filmed and then used to blackmail the participants. According to Richard Rovere of *The New Yorker*, another of the committee's informants revealed the existence of a plot, purportedly hatched by the Soviet Union, to bring "women employees of the State Department under their control by enticing them into a life of Lesbianism." The Communists accomplished this through "erotic demonstrations" at which the participants were "garbed in rich Oriental costumes to get into the spirit of things."

Meanwhile, in the executive branch, language depicting communism as a contagious sexual aberrancy made its way into the principal national security strategy document of the Truman administration. "Where the despot holds absolute power—the absolute power of the absolutely powerful will—all other wills must be subjugated in an act of willing submission, a degradation willed by the individual upon himself under the compulsion of a perverted faith." So affirmed "United States Objectives and Programs for National Security," better known as NSC 68, a product of the recently created National Security Council that laid down the fundamentals of American Cold War strategy. Communist society, it elaborated, was one in "which the personality of the individual is so broken and perverted that he participates affirmatively in his own degradation." Attorney General J. Howard McGrath spoke of Communists in terms interchangeable with those used to describe homosexuals; both were ubiquitous, threatening, and contagious. "There are today many Communists in America," he warned. "They are everywhere—in factories, offices, butcher shops, on street corners, in private business—and each carries with him the germs of death for society." Alfred Kinsey's statistics, J. Edgar Hoover's rhetoric, and Joe McCarthy's paranoia made for a frightful combination.

To most Americans, the notion that homosexuals were susceptible to blackmail and therefore unfit for government service made perfect sense. Homosexuals naturally lived in the shadows because the social stigma against them was deservedly strong. It was therefore axiomatic that they would go to whatever length necessary to conceal their personal secret, even if it meant divulging highly sensitive national security ones. But the theory that homosexuals were more vulnerable to blackmail—and in the absence of any actual evidence, that's all it was—was without foundation. All people have skeletons in their proverbial closets, and the average heterosexual had just as much at stake, if not more (usually in the form of a family), than his homosexual peers. An extramarital affair could serve as grounds for blackmail, and was cause for dismissal, yet nobody proposed a blanket ban on heterosexuals working in the State Department. Moreover, a homosexual was blackmailable only to the extent that their homosexuality remained a secret. Once it was discovered by his or her employer, the justification for firing them vanished. The campaign to root out and expel gay men and lesbians, then, contained within it a paradox: by threatening to fire homosexuals due to nothing other than their sexual orientation, the government was *itself* providing potential foreign blackmailers with a powerful weapon to induce treason. If that threat were revoked—if gay people were allowed to serve their country in the knowledge that their sexual orientation could not be used against them by a foreign adversary—the enemy agent would lose whatever influence he might have exerted over potential targets for recruitment. Whatever the government's theoretical rationale for denying security clearances to gays, there was no empirical justification; nor would there be. In 1991, the Department of Defense published a study analyzing the cases of 117 American citizens who had either committed or attempted to commit espionage since 1945. Only 6 were gay, and none of them had done so under the threat of blackmail.

Such nuances, alas, were lost amid the climate of fear and paranoia that pervaded the nation's capital. In May, Wherry and Hill filed an interim report. Declaring of the homosexual that "all his waking hours he is carrying out an act against detection," they urged the administration to take "expeditious action to insure that departments and agencies of our Government are cleansed of moral perverts, especially to guard and protect security secrets upon which the life of our beloved country may depend." Alarmed, the full Senate authorized Democratic senator Clyde Hoey of North Carolina, chairman of the Investigations Subcommittee of the Committee on Expenditures in the Executive Departments, to carry out a full investigation.

The following month, Francis J. Flanagan, a former FBI agent serving as chief counsel of the subcommittee, met at the White House with presidential aide Stephen Spingarn. During the Second World War, Spingarn had served alongside a gay officer who "remained just as flagrant a fairy at the end as he was at the beginning" of the conflict. Spingarn believed, however, that a man's abnormal sexual predilections did not necessarily imply that his loyalties were also suspect. "The excessively red-blooded heterosexual male, who has no discretion in such matters, and who blabs freely when he is in bed with a lady is likely to be a worse" security risk than the average homosexual, he suggested. Moreover, so grave was the mere *accusation* of homosexuality that codifying it as a ground for dismissal raised ample opportunities for abuse. "I mean, a man who may have had a wonderful career in government, just the charge of homosexuality may wreck his whole career, not to mention his family fortunes, and a whole lot of other things."

These considerations were on Spingarn's mind when Flanagan visited him at the White House to enlist the administration in purging gays and lesbians from the civil service. Flanagan wanted to amass a central index of all "suspected or known homosexuals in government," consisting of information culled from the local police, the Office of Naval Intelligence, the FBI, and the Secret Service. "I can see the homosexual as a security risk, but he's one of many," Spingarn told Flanagan. "What documentation do you have that he is a particularly bad security risk?"

"Well, it's funny," Flanagan replied. "I haven't been able to find anything in this country." The only example he *could* cite was that of Alfred Redl, the Austro-Hungarian military officer whose four-decade-old treachery still haunted Western intelligence leaders. "Flanagan seems strongly committed to the position that the homosexual is the most serious security threat of all, and he seems to regard the fact [that] there is scant documentation of this as an unfortunate accident," Spingarn wrote in a memo to colleagues summarizing the meeting. "On the basis of my experience as a counter espionage and security officer during the war, I am personally of the opinion (I believe I can cite chapter and verse to support it) that other types of security threats are more dangerous than the homosexual, although no doubt he represents one type."

Regardless of what the actual evidence indicated, the claim that homosexuals were especially choice targets for blackmailers was constantly espoused. Sometimes, it was done so in connection with a secret (and illusory) "list" of covert homosexuals from around the world. Attributed to Adolf Hitler himself, the list was supposedly discovered by the Red Army among the smoldering ruins of postwar Berlin. Speaking on the floor of the House of Representatives, Nebraska Republican Arthur L. Miller related how a "gentleman" from the Central Intelligence Agency told him

> that Mr. Goering of Germany and others had a complete list of all the homosexuals in the State Department, the Department of Commerce, and the Department of Defense and that they knew who to contact when they came over here on espionage missions. The danger of spies, the danger of blackmail, has caused those people to sabotage our Government. It was an interesting angle to me. I do know from very extensive reading the last few weeks that the Russians rather glory in the accomplishments resulting from homosexuality and they undoubtedly have the same list of homosexuals who were in key positions in Government in this country, so they knew who to contact when they came here . . .

Even a media outlet as relatively enlightened for its time as the *Washington Post*, which editorialized that there was "no reason for supposing that a person of homosexual bias is psychologically any more predisposed to the Communist ideology than a heterosexual person," gave credence to these fantastic charges. "It is known that the Gestapo kept files containing the names of persons in all parts of the world who were known or believed to have such tendencies," the paper contended, adding for good measure that "there is every reason to suppose" the Soviets now possessed the records.

Ironically, it was the American government, not its enemies, that was compiling lists of American homosexuals, demand for which was so fierce that they became a highly prized commodity in the nation's capital. The Office of Naval Intelligence told Wherry that it had spent the previous nine years accumulating the names of 7,859 sex deviants. The army, meanwhile, claimed it had a list with the identities of 5,000. Ruth Young, chief clerk of the investigations subcommittee, recalled a visit she and her colleagues paid to the Library of Congress to consult "everything they had on homosexuality. You never saw so many people reading books in your life! The whole staff was involved. Those books disappeared off my desk like that!" In their efforts to amass a catalogue of every known homosexual who had ever worked for the federal government, Young and her colleagues left no stone unturned, sending questionnaires out to fifty-three departments and agencies, including the American Battle Monuments Commission and the Philippine War Damage Commission.

The effort to compile a master list was stymied by the White House, which claimed executive privilege and refused to cooperate. "Unless the law requires that I furnish the information you desire, or higher authority instructs me to do so, I am not going to furnish it," Harry Mitchell, chairman of the U.S. Civil Service Commission, wrote to Flanagan. "Despite the mental peculiarities with which these persons are afflicted and the disgusting results of these peculiarities, they are still human and I can see no reason why they should be hounded by the government when they are no longer employed by, or asking employment from, the government." Some congressional Democrats, seeking to limit the Truman administration's exposure, tried to isolate the fuss over "homos" from the more pressing matter of Communists. Senator Millard Tydings of Maryland, the patrician chairman of the committee investigating the loyalty of State Department employees, spoke for more than a few of his colleagues when he exhaustedly implored McCarthy at one point during a debate, "Won't you stop this continued heckling about homosexuals and let us get on with the main work of finding Communists?"

Notwithstanding such partisan appeals, hardly anyone in politics, medicine, the media, or any other sector of American society was willing to challenge the underlying presumptions of the Lavender Scare. An exception was *New York Post* columnist Max Lerner. In a twelve-part series datelined from the nation's capital, "The Washington Sex Story," Lerner offered a perspective on the relationship between homosexuality and government wholly at odds with the campaign that his very own paper had waged against David Walsh less than a decade before. In articles titled "The Scientists Speak," "The Problem of Blackmail," and "Are Homosexuals Security Risks?" Lerner explored all aspects of the controversy from the perspective of an inquisitive and fair-minded observer who was tough on communism but equally stalwart in his defense of individual rights and civil liberties. Citing a fellow scribe who applied the Kinsey estimate of homosexual incidence to Congress, Lerner tabulated that some 192 members likely had a homosexual experience at some point in their lifetimes. Therefore, he cautioned, "it will be well for Congress, before waving its purge sword wildly, to ask how deep it will cut, and whether it may not cut both ways."

Everyone Lerner interviewed told him to "go see Blick," for he was the man with "the facts and figures." Lerner was most intrigued by Blick's claim, cited by Wherry in his interim report and thereafter many times in the press, that there were 5,000 homosexuals living in the District of Columbia, 3,750 of whom worked for the government. How did Blick know this? They were "my own guesses, not official figures," Blick conceded. How had he calculated them? "Well, every one of these fellows has friends," Blick explained of men arrested for sexual solicitation. "You multiply the list by a certain percentage—say three percent or four percent."

"Do you mean," Lerner asked, correcting him, "that your police list is only three or four percent of the total, and you multiply it by 25 or 30?"

"Yes," Blick answered.

"If your final estimate was 5,000, does that mean your police list was less than 200?"

"No," Blick answered. "I mean five percent."

"You mean that you multiplied your list by 20?"

"Yes," Blick replied, before, this time, correcting himself. "No. I multiply my list by five."

"You mean you started with a list of 1,000 and multiplied by five to get 5,000?"

Blick wavered. Census taking was not his specialty, never mind arithmetic. Eventually, Lerner got Blick to clarify that his estimate of the Washington homosexual population was the combined total of three different figures: the number of men arrested for solicitation, the number of names that these men (often under duress) gave to the police, and, for no reason Blick could explain, the sum of the first group multiplied by five.

"Do you think 5,000 are too many?" Blick worriedly asked the columnist.

"If you mean just any kind of homosexual, and use it loosely," Lerner replied, referring to the 10 percent figure from the Kinsey report, "I suspect you are conservative."

"That's what I keep saying," Blick responded with relief. "I'm conservative in my figures. I'm conservative about everything, Mr. Lerner."

Following this "adventure in higher mathematics," Lerner next asked Blick how he had arrived at the figure of 3,750 gays working in government.

"Oh," Blick answered. "I took the 5,000 for Washington. And I figured that three out of four of them worked for the government."

In his many interviews with various officials, Lerner did not hear of a single incident involving a government worker blackmailed over his or her sexual orientation. Blick's penchant for lists, the newspaperman wrote, was like that of Sulla, the "Great Proscriber" of ancient Rome, whose decrees arbitrarily branded citizens enemies of the state and targeted them for banishment or death. In his final column of the series, Lerner cited the dystopian novel of Communist totalitarianism recently published by a British author named George Orwell, *Nineteen Eighty-Four*. How ironic was it that, in their zealous determination to detect and eliminate every sexual deviant from U.S. government ranks, the lavender hunters had started to resemble the tyrants they purported to despise? "The impulse of the totalitarian mind," Lerner wrote, "is to stop short of nothing in its march to mastery. It treats the individual as a cipher, annihilates his personality in every area, whether political, moral, or sexual." Though Lerner agreed with the societal consensus that homosexuals were "sick people," he deemed the government's crusade to root them out "a case of the sick being pursued by the sicker."

Lerner's warnings fell on deaf ears. Just a few months later, citing his "ability" and "outstanding results," the Metropolitan Police Department promoted Lt. Roy Blick to captain.

9

"A GOVERNMENT WITHIN A GOVERNMENT"

VISITING A MOSCOW FUR MARKET "AS WELL GUARDED AS FORT KNOX," C. L. Sulzberger, the chief foreign correspondent of the *New York Times*, was startled by what he saw. "Imagine our astonishment when we were finally conducted into a large store room and there, amid a pile of furs, only his head showing, the grinning Carmel Offie," Sulzberger recorded in a 1947 diary entry. Offie was acting as if he owned the place, "heaving pelts about and saying 'I'll take this, not that, not that, this . . .' What an operator. I still don't know how he got there."

How Carmel Offie got to where he did is a subject worthy of its own book. After the war, Offie was forced out of the Foreign Service following an incident involving abuse of the diplomatic pouch. Whether it was owing to his own illicit behavior or because he took the fall for the wife of a high-ranking ambassador is unknown. If the latter, it would have been entirely consistent with his penchant for charming the wives of rich and powerful men. Either way, Offie's expulsion was but a hiccup in an extraordinary rise. On the strength of his European connections, his social networking skills, and the recommendation of a former colleague from the Moscow embassy who had risen to become a senior Foreign Service officer, Charles "Chip" Bohlen, Offie secured a job with the Office of Policy Coordination

(OPC), the covert operations wing of the CIA headed by an OSS veteran named Frank Wisner. As OPC was nominally run out of the State Department, Offie was one of the first initiates in the practice of granting diplomatic cover to CIA agents.

At OPC, Offie coordinated the agency's work with anticommunist Western European labor unions and Eastern European émigrés. He was involved in top secret missions such as "Operation Paperclip" and "National Interest," whose innocuous code names masked their morally questionable mission of recruiting former Nazi scientists and intelligence officials. Returning to Frankfurt, where he had worked during the immediate postwar period, Offie commandeered an office in a building that formerly belonged to I.G. Farben, the producer of the Zyklon B pesticide used to exterminate European Jews. Surrounding himself with a bevy of beautiful Women's Army Corps secretaries, Offie assisted in bringing to the United States figures like Nikolai Poppe, a Russian social scientist and expert on Central Asia who had worked for the Germans during the war, and Gustav Hilger, a former German diplomat and authority on the Soviet Union. In his capacity overseeing the National Committee for a Free Europe, a CIA-front group, Offie helped convince founding CIA director Allen Dulles to establish Radio Free Europe, which the agency would covertly fund for its first two decades of existence. Longtime CIA counterintelligence chief James Jesus Angleton described Offie as one of the handful of "grand masters" of early American Cold War espionage and "a world-class sophisticate who could put a stiletto in an opponent and offer him a treatise on the cognac he was serving at the same time."

In the spring of 1950, Offie's ascent ended abruptly on the floor of the Senate, when he became one of the first victims in a bureaucratic tussle between the FBI and the CIA in which the accusation of homosexuality was a potent weapon. On March 10, according to the diary of CIA legislative liaison Walter Pforzheimer, the agency received word that "Sen. McCarthy was considering charging an employee of this agency with homosexual practices in connection with the present investigation of security risks in the Government." Four days later, in a presentation before Senator Millard Tydings's committee to investigate McCarthy's charges of subversives in the State Department, the Wisconsinite declared that four people, current and former employees of the department, were poor security risks. In addition, McCarthy privately supplied the subcommittee with the name of "a man formerly in the State Department, with a record of homosexual activities" who had since been hired by the CIA.

The man who most likely leaked to McCarthy the documentation of Offie's 1943 arrest near Lafayette Square (the said "record" of his "homosexual activities") was John V. "Frenchy" Grombach. A former heavyweight boxer, decathlon athlete, and army officer who kept a black poodle under his desk, Grombach headed a semi-private intelligence network known as "the Pond." Grombach had established the Pond during World War II under the auspices of the army, and like many right-wingers working in the shadowy world of private intelligence at the time, he was deeply antagonistic toward the OSS and its successor. The CIA, Grombach and others like him were convinced, was swollen with leftists and Communists, the direct legacy of "Wild Bill" Donovan's ideological permissiveness.

Grombach's off-the-books network, consisting of former SS officers, Hungarian Arrow Cross thugs, and other dregs of European fascist movements, "effectively became the foreign espionage agency for the far right," according to the writer Christopher Simpson. But the Pond was focused mainly on enemies at home, more committed to purging U.S. government agencies of supposed "Communist dupes, homosexuals, and liberals of all stripes" than snooping on adversaries abroad. Lyman Kirkpatrick, a long-time senior CIA official, recalled that Grombach "got into a lot of garbage pails, and issued 'dirty linen' reports" on ideologically or morally suspect CIA employees. Grombach was one of several figures who comprised the "McCarthy underground," a behind-the-scenes network that supplied the Wisconsin senator and his congressional allies with intelligence about alleged "security risks." Consisting mainly of retired military officers like Grombach and far-right émigrés from Eastern Europe, the underground fed dirt to McCarthy and like-minded "countersubversives" in the FBI that could be used against rivals in the rapidly expanding national security bureaucracy. But mainly, the organization served to harass and intimidate government employees. "Within the CIA," Kirkpatrick recalled, "we had cases where individuals would be contacted by telephone and told it was known that they drank too much, or were having an affair, and that the caller would make no issue of this if they would come around and tell everything that they knew about the agency."

Homosexuals, real or suspected, were sitting ducks for such low tactics. But Offie was a unique case. He was open about his sexual orientation, sometimes outrageously so, notorious for rubbing his nipples while in conversation with other men. This meant that those who knew of his homosexuality, whether hostile foreign intelligence agencies or disgruntled right-wing critics of the CIA, did not have the power to blackmail him. "Why revoke my security clearance?" Offie asked. "I don't deny it. I'll stand up on the roof and admit it. Nobody can blackmail me." Offie's boss, Frank Wisner, was unbothered by his aide's sexual orientation. "I don't think my father could have cared less about Offie being gay," Wisner's youngest son, Graham, later said. "To him, it was all about 'are you with me in this crusade?' He wanted the most effective people who could throw off their Americanisms and be able to understand how this war was changing, so if you're gay or a woman or black, it's irrelevant. Offie was effective, and that's all that mattered." Offie was resourceful in other ways, too, finding Wisner's wife, Polly, a cook to help prepare meals for Graham and his three siblings.

Though Offie's openness invalidated the blackmail argument against him, it would have only strengthened the moral one. On April 25, McCarthy took to the Senate floor to denounce "a homosexual" who "spent his time hanging around the men's room in Lafayette Park." The political pressure to give McCarthy his scalp became too strong for the administration to resist. Democratic Senate majority leader Scott Lucas persuaded President Truman and CIA director Roscoe Hillenkoetter—who had known Offie while working as assistant naval attaché in Bill Bullitt's Paris embassy—that Offie had to go. Just half an hour after McCarthy's speech, Kenneth Wherry announced to his colleagues that he had "been informed by the head of a government agency that the man against whom the Senator from Wisconsin made a charge on the Senate floor this afternoon has finally resigned."

The exploitation of homosexuality in the torpedoing of Carmel Offie was a continuation of the battle between the FBI and the CIA that had begun in 1942, when J. Edgar Hoover sabotaged the mission of another gay intelligence agent, OSS operative Donald Downes. After the war, the FBI denied Downes a security clearance on the grounds that he was a sexual deviant. To be sure, homosexuality was just one aspect in a bureaucratic rivalry whose main flash points were conflicting institutional cultures, missions, and personalities. The FBI, disproportionately manned with blue-collar,

Catholic, "white ethnic" men from the outer boroughs of New York City and the Midwest, was responsible for domestic law enforcement and countersubversion. Its ambit, in both practical and conceptual terms, was much narrower than that of the CIA, which had the entire world as its operational playground and tilted heavily toward multilingual, Ivy League–educated WASPs.

It was just this type of person—personified by Alger Hiss—whom the increasingly assertive American right wing adjudged responsible for America's weak-kneed foreign policy. In his Wheeling speech, McCarthy had inculpated "the bright young men who are born with silver spoons in their mouths," America's ruling class, with treason. "In the era of security clearances, to be an Irish Catholic became *prima facie* evidence of loyalty," Daniel Patrick Moynihan observed in a 1963 reflection on McCarthyism. "Harvard men were to be checked; Fordham men would do the checking." And in a city where one's power was increasingly determined by access to secrets, the provision of security clearances (and the ability to deny or strip them based on homosexuality, real or presumed) was the source of enormous clout.

For the men who did the checking and their congressional allies, abnormal sexuality correlated strongly with higher socioeconomic status. As far back as the thirteenth century, the German bishop Albertus Magnus described homosexuality as an "execrable vice known to prevail more among the upper classes than the lower ones." The stereotypical homosexual was effeminate, and effeminacy was supposedly more prevalent among men of means, who never had to work with their hands. If the Soviets considered homosexuality a bourgeois decadence, many in the West viewed it to be an aristocratic one. Though "perversion is found at all levels of society," Republican congressman Arthur Miller of Nebraska asserted during a 1950 House floor debate, it is "perhaps more frequently among the higher levels where nervousness, unhappiness, and leisure time leads to vices." Almost all the forefathers of American espionage had attended elite, all-male boarding schools, where homosexuality was presumed to be tolerated, if not encouraged. Columnist Westbrook Pegler, one of the harshest press critics of the CIA, derided the agency as just a bunch of "double-dome draft-dodgers"—that is, eggheaded sissies.

Validating the perception of the CIA's covert homosexualism in the minds of its critics was its rather overt liberalism. In the early years of the Cold War, it was idealistic liberals who led and manned the CIA, a legacy later obscured by the agency's involvement in a series of Third World military coups and alliances with right-wing authoritarian forces abroad. William Colby, an OSS veteran who became CIA director under President Richard Nixon, recalled that the agency naturally attracted "politically liberal" Ivy Leaguers, as it was the "most effective place for a non-Communist liberal to do battle against the Communist menace." Before he worked alongside Carmel Offie in the CIA, covert operator Cord Meyer had been a "guru of the youthful left," a founder of the Union of World Federalists whose first marriage was officiated by liberal theologian Reinhold Niebuhr. Yale University chaplain William Sloane Coffin Jr., who became one of America's most outspoken anti–Vietnam War activists, had earlier worked for the agency recruiting anticommunist Russian refugees in West Germany. In his decade working for the CIA, one former field officer claimed that there were two kinds of people he never encountered: hitmen and Republicans. The prevalence of so many liberals aroused the ire of the pro-McCarthy right, with Pegler variously referring to the agency as a "strange spying and whispering service and goodness knows what else," a "weird system of espionage, cliques and conspiracies," and a "mischievous cabal." (Carmel Offie, he noted in one column about agency shenanigans, was William Bullitt's "intimate confidante.")

The liberal idealism of the CIA's founding generation was manifested in clandestine assistance to a wide range of initiatives and groups: the Congress for Cultural Freedom (publisher of a handful of excellent literary magazines across Europe and Latin America), the National Student Association, anticommunist trade unions, and expressionist art exhibitions. Collectively, these came to be known within the agency as the non-Communist left (NCL). By keeping its support for these efforts secret, the agency had more than just the reputations of its grantees in mind. It was also worried about the McCarthyites, who failed to appreciate the stark and important distinctions between communism, socialism, and liberalism, and who would surely see the agency's support for avant-garde art shows and erudite literary journalism as validation of their belief that the agency was a congeries of sex deviates. "It all had to be off the budget," a CIA officer who worked on the Congress for Cultural Freedom file recalled, "as none of this would ever have got through Congress. Imagine the ridiculous howlings that would've gone up: 'They're all Communists! They're homosexuals!'"

But at least as far as homosexuality was concerned, the "howlings" were not necessarily inaccurate. If, insofar as they deemed non-Communist leftists the most effective anticommunists, the early leaders of American intelligence "had few ideological constraints" in their waging the Cold War, then they had "few sexual ones" as well, writes the historian Michael Sherry. "A suspicious number" of CIA employees were "limp-wristed, if not provable homosexuals," observed the gay writer Merle Miller, a contemporary of Cord Meyer and several other early agency recruits. "At that time, homosexual activity in the agency was not a big thing—if you confessed it," recalled one early CIA veteran.

One such agent, though certainly not limp of wrist, was the doctor and anticommunist folk hero Thomas Dooley. The navy medic's 1956 memoir documenting his role in the evacuation of Catholic refugees from North Vietnam, *Deliver Us from Evil*, was instrumental in creating the ideological justification for American military intervention in that country. In the words of his biographer James Fisher, the handsome Dooley was also "an extraordinarily active gay man who was one of the great underground sex symbols of his era—a figure well-known in sophisticated gay circles as far-flung as Hollywood, Washington DC, and the capitals of Southeast Asia." Though Dooley's homosexuality got him discharged from the navy, it was of minimal concern to the CIA, which covertly enlisted him in the propaganda battle against communism in Southeast Asia. By publicizing his heroic exploits on behalf of communism's victims, the agency helped transform Dooley from a "potential sex criminal to a secular saint."

Forced to fire Offie, Wisner loaded him off onto the payroll of Jay Lovestone, a former leader of the Communist Party USA turned anti-Stalinist and CIA-funded labor union activist. Lovestone bestowed upon Offie the code name "Monk," after the famous monastery atop Offie's namesake Mount Carmel. And so Offie, ensconced in a house he had had decorated by the wife of the former Italian ambassador, stayed in the spy trade and remained a recipient of government largesse, albeit at a safe remove from congressional lavender hunters. On May 17, after the dust had settled, CIA director Roscoe Hillenkoetter wrote an apologetic letter to Offie. Expressing "great reluctance" at Offie's forced resignation, Hillenkoetter thanked him for "very loyal and competent service . . . and for . . . the industry and skill you have at all times displayed in furthering the objectives of this organization." The two men maintained a friendly correspondence for years. At one point, James Jesus Angleton, who simultaneously despised and admired Offie as a "Machiavellian" "master intriguer" and "superb bureaucratic infighter and guide"—powerful words from a man nicknamed "The Ghost"—went behind the backs of his superiors and tried to recruit Offie to infiltrate "homo circles in Europe" on behalf of the CIA. Knowing Angleton's mixed feelings about him, a skeptical Offie asked if the offer was genuine. "That's just the reason," Angleton answered. "No one would ever suspect." Offie declined.

Whatever the CIA's relative tolerance, it was highly qualified. Between 1949 and 1953, as many as three-quarters of the employees it fired, and the applicants it rejected, were dismissed on the grounds of homosexuality.

★ ★ ★

JUST TWO MONTHS AFTER THANKING CARMEL OFFIE for his services to the nation, CIA director Roscoe Hillenkoetter warned the U.S. Senate of the threat homosexuals posed to national security.

Sen. Clyde Hoey had promised to undertake his investigation into the matter of sex perverts within the federal government "on a very quiet basis." It was an issue that made him and most everyone else uncomfortable. So as not "to transgress individual rights, to subject any individual to ridicule, or to allow this investigation to become a public spectacle," Hoey decided to hold the subcommittee's hearings in executive session. In a misplaced attempt at chivalry, he tried to prohibit his own colleague, Republican Margaret Chase Smith of Maine, from entering the hearing room out of concern that the presence of a "lady" in their midst would inhibit the rest of the committee members from asking unfortunately necessary questions. Smith, a fiercely independent woman, rebuked this gesture and played an active role in the hearings, asking one witness if there was not a "quick test like an X-ray that discloses" a person's sexual orientation. As part of its standard lie detector exam, the CIA routinely asked potential recruits about any sexual abnormalities. But by the agency's own admission, this method had nabbed only one deviant. A machine designed specifically to detect homosexuals, alas, had yet to be invented.

Hillenkoetter's appearance before the subcommittee on July 14, 1950, was prompted by a phone call several weeks earlier from chief counsel Francis Flanagan to CIA congressional liaison Walter Pforzheimer. According to Pforzheimer's diary, the subcommittee wanted a senior agency official to address "whether homosexuals are considered security risks" and to provide "case examples (without names) that foreign governments have used or plan to use homosexuals for intelligence or espionage purposes." It was a conclusion in search of evidence. Though Washingtonians were alarmed by reports of government agencies "honeycombed" with gays, lists of homosexuals in the hands of Hitler and Stalin, and lesbian orgies surreptitiously filmed by Russian spies, no one had yet provided any evidence to corroborate these allegations. If anyone could, presumably it would be the director of the CIA.

Hillenkoetter devoted a full quarter of his prepared testimony to a recitation of the long-familiar Redl case, which, he told the senators, was "known all through intelligence circles." He next laid out a "general theory" as to why homosexuals should be prohibited from government service. Among the thirteen reasons Hillenkoetter offered were that "an established homosexual relationship involves emotions strong and usually stronger than a normal love relationship between man and woman" (a claim seemingly at odds with the prevailing view that gay men were congenitally promiscuous), that homosexuals are "extremely gullible," and "last, but not least," that homosexuals constitute "a government within a government."

> That is so noteworthy. One pervert brings other perverts. They belong to the lodge, the fraternity. One pervert brings other perverts into an agency, they move from position to position and advance them usually in the interest of furthering the romance of the moment.

One section of Hillenkoetter's prepared testimony was considered so sensitive that, even in executive session, it was spoken "off the record" and not transcribed by a stenographer. "I might say parenthetically as director of central intelligence that while this agency will never employ a homosexual on its rolls,"

> it might conceivably be necessary, and in the past has actually been valuable, to use known homosexual agents in the field. I am certain that if

Joseph Stalin or a member of the politbureau or a high satellite official were known to be a homosexual, no member of this committee or of the Congress would balk against our use of any technique to penetrate their operations, provided that we surrounded our agent with the proper safeguards. After all, intelligence and espionage is at best an extremely dirty business.

Hillenkoetter cited a "Soviet intelligence operation" undertaken that very year wherein "our task will be made considerably easier by the appearance in the area of a known homosexual who we think will be extremely helpful in this particular case." So, while claiming, with thirteen-point precision, that homosexuals were inherently unfit for service in the CIA, Hillenkoetter seemed to leave the door open to situations wherein their assistance "might conceivably be necessary" if not "valuable." Neither Hillenkoetter nor the senators questioning him saw fit to contemplate whether homosexuals, preternaturally skilled at keeping secrets by dint of living in a society that deemed their very nature illegal, might in fact be *better* equipped for espionage than their heterosexual peers.

A similarly implicit admission as to the fitness of homosexuals for government employment was made to the committee by Frances Perkins, the first woman to serve in a presidential cabinet (as secretary of labor in the Roosevelt administration) and a member of the Civil Service Commission. According to her biographer Kirstin Downey, while it is "probably impossible to know whether" Perkins's relationship with Junior League founder Mary Harriman Rumsey was "sexual or romantic . . . it was much more than an ordinary friendship." The two women lived, vacationed, entertained, and raised puppies together, all hallmarks of a "Boston marriage," a term used to describe the cohabitation of two, usually wealthy women during the late nineteenth and early twentieth centuries. Boston marriages, writes historian Lillian Faderman, were not uncommon among women "very involved in culture and in social betterment" for whom "these female values, which they shared with each other, formed a strong basis for their life together." Some of these women might have identified as lesbians, but Boston marriages could also be platonic. Downey writes that Perkins was "comfortable with the idea of lesbian relationships and nonjudgmental about them" and that some of her "closest friends appear to have been bisexual or exclusively lesbian." This was a side of herself, however, that

Perkins did not reveal in her testimony. While informing the senators that she was unaware of any case involving a homosexual who proved to be disloyal or the victim of blackmail by a foreign power, she stated that a ban on their employment was nonetheless justified, given that homosexuality fell under a "general prohibition of immoral or notoriously disgraceful conduct."

The summer of 1950 was the height of the McCarthy fever, the proximate start of when people in Washington began saying things like "Maybe we'd better not talk about this on the telephone." A federal government–sponsored seminar entitled "Perversion Among Government Workers" was so popular among the department personnel managers who enrolled in it that two extra sessions had to be added. Dubbed the "School for Scandal" and intended to help its students identify "the whys and wherefores of sexual aberration," the seminar caused some confusion among its participants. "All I learned was that it's supposed to be okay to keep queers on in non-sensitive jobs," one disappointed graduate of the program complained. According to another attendee, a government psychiatrist told the students that while "perverts" should be dismissed from holding sensitive positions, "inasmuch as perverts are pretty sensitive perhaps we shouldn't hurt their feelings by letting them know they're not in sensitive jobs." Prior to taking the course, this person had simply "kick[ed] perverts out wherever I found them, but now I don't know."

After holding five executive session hearings and sifting through piles of documents submitted by thirty-two government agencies, the Hoey subcommittee released its long-awaited report on December 15. Entitled *Employment of Homosexuals and Other Sex Perverts in Government*, it concluded "that those who engage in acts of homosexuality and other perverted sex activities are unsuitable for employment in the Federal Government." The report's argument was threefold. First, homosexuals could be blackmailed. "Communist and Nazi agents," the subcommittee claimed, had attempted to get "secret Government data" from federal workers "by threatening to expose their abnormal sex activities." (Still no evidence was offered for this claim.) Second, homosexuals lacked the "moral fiber" and "emotional stability" of "normal persons." And lastly, through "his tendency to gather other perverts around him" and "to entice normal individuals to engage in perverted practices," the homosexual had a loyalty to his own kind that superseded loyalty to his country. For the first time, the U.S.

Congress endorsed the contention that gay men and lesbians constituted a threat to the country's security.

"They resign voluntarily, don't they?" Kenneth Wherry had asked Max Lerner. "That's an admission of their guilt. That's all I need. My feeling is that there will be very few people hurt." From April 1, shortly after the Lavender Scare began, until publication of the Hoey Report eight months later, a total of 382 federal employees were terminated on the grounds of homosexuality. With the notion that gay men and lesbians represented a moral peril now enjoying the imprimatur of Congress, the groundwork was laid for a full-scale purge. For, as the report concluded, "One homosexual can pollute a Government office."

10

THE HOMINTERN

"If you're wondering where your wandering semi-boy is tonight," the authors of the third most popular nonfiction book of 1951 revealed, "he's probably in Washington."

An editor and a columnist, respectively, for the right-wing *New York Daily Mirror*, Jack Lait and Lee Mortimer had published moderately successful pulp paperback exposés of Chicago and New York City before setting their hard-boiled sights on the nation's capital. Though the seamy underbelly of urban America was their beat, nothing prepared these muckrakers for the depravity they would recount in *Washington Confidential*. "We think we have X-rayed the dizziest—and this will amaze you, as it did us, the dirtiest—community in America," Lait and Mortimer announced. In "this magnificent planned city of majestic proportions, the official heart of the richest and greatest and freest land in the history of mankind, we found corruption and perversion, organized and individual, that dazed a pair of hardened characters who considered themselves shock-proof after their groundwork for the books that debunked New York and deloused Chicago."

Upon its publication in February 1951, *Washington Confidential* hit its target "with the impact of an H-bomb," selling more than one hundred fifty thousand copies in its first three weeks. One Washington bookstore sold eight thousand alone. Reaching number one on the *New York Times* best seller list, *Washington Confidential* trailed only *Look Younger, Live Longer* and *Betty Crocker's Cook Book* in total sales. A reactionary, populist broadside against the capital city's "potpourri of human beings on the make," Lait and Mortimer's book portrayed a netherworld overrun with "Commies," "New Dealers," and "fags," none of them mutually exclusive.

The heart of Washington's "Garden of Pansies" (the title of the book's chapter on the homosexual demimonde) was, unsurprisingly, the State Department. "One of the queerest sights visible anywhere" in Washington, the duo revealed, was the one espied "through the window" of Dean Acheson's Georgetown home. The local YMCA, meanwhile, had apparently gone so far as to enforce an unofficial prohibition on State Department employees using its facilities, "especially the swimming pool." Nearly doubling Roy Blick's estimate of homosexuals on the federal government payroll to at least six thousand, the authors described a capital teeming with "fairies" who "recognize each other by a fifth sense immediately," "are intensely gregarious," "all know one another," and partake of a "grapevine of inter-communication as swift and sure as that in a girls' boardingschool." Though lesbians were "much less obvious" than male homosexuals, there were reportedly "twice as many Sapphic lovers as fairies" in the city, an imbalance apparently owing to the large number of government girls. While Lait and Mortimer professed grudging respect for the homosexuals they had encountered in showbiz circles, who "by a pathological compensation . . . possessed artistic traits," they found that it was "the dull, dumb deviates" who ended up in Washington. "The government is honeycombed in high places with people you wouldn't let in your garbage wagons" and who tended to be on the leftmost end of the political spectrum. "It seems that nonconformity in politics is often the handmaiden of the same proclivities in sex." (The following year, buoyed by the success of *Washington Confidential*, the sensationalistic duo published *U.S.A. Confidential*, in which they reported that the State Department, "despite denials and purges, is considerably more than 30 percent faggot.")

Washington Confidential unintentionally served a vital purpose for the "deviates" it was intended to expose. Throughout their jeremiad, Lait and Mortimer listed the names and addresses of several establishments that catered to a gay clientele—such as the Jewel Box on Sixteenth Street, the

Sand Bar in Thomas Circle, a restaurant behind the Mayflower Hotel called Mickey's, and the lobby of the Franklin Park Hotel. One night, at a spot on the second floor of a building on the 1700 block of H Street, presumably the Chicken Hut, "two Congressmen, a couple of army officers, and two young servicemen were mixing beer and gin there, and kissing each other." The authors described nearby Lafayette Square as "one of the most sordid spots in the world," where fewer than one hundred yards from the White House, "under the heroic equestrian statue of Andrew Jackson and in the shadow of the foliage of overhanging trees, there is a constant and continuous soprano symphony of homosexual twittering." Intending to outrage the average American, Lait and Mortimer had also inadvertently created a secret treasure map for gay and lesbian visitors to the nation's capital. Years before the advent of gay-friendly travel guides, *Washington Confidential* was an accidental Baedeker to the city's homosexual hangouts.

Shorn of its hyperbolic language and moralizing tone, *Washington Confidential* also offered some rather astute observations about gay life in midcentury Washington. Particularly shocking to the authors about the homosexual world was the blurring of traditional social divisions that the heterosexual one rigorously enforced. The relative egalitarianism of the modern civil service, with "no color line, no social selectivity," made it a welcoming place for "fairies and Fair Dealers," who were "unwelcome at home, pariahs afar." Meanwhile, outside the workplace, the "free crossing of racial lines among fairies and lesbians" allowed for such unusual spectacles as "aristocratic Southerners . . . hunt[ing] down Negro men for dalliance." What the authors described as "an inter-racial, inter-middle-sex mélange, with long-haired, made-up Negro and white boys simpering while females of both races mingled in unmistakable fashion," would have been unthinkable anywhere else in Washington, which was still officially segregated. Today, one can only marvel at the courage demonstrated by the "1,700 Negro men, all dressed as women" who held a party on a Potomac River cruise incongruously named the *Robert E. Lee* until it was rudely interrupted by one hundred police officers.

"Fairies are no more disloyal than the normal," Lait and Mortimer conceded. The reason they could not be trusted with the nation's secrets, however, was their increased vulnerability to blackmail as a result of being "more intense about their love life." A sensational case involving communism, treason, and homosexuality was about to nullify even that small concession.

* * *

CLICKETY CLACK CLACK CLACK. CLACK CLACK CLICKETY CLACK. So fast were the stories moving across the wire services on June 7, 1951, that the State Department secretaries had to constantly replenish the Teletype machines with paper. The news was distressing. Two British diplomats, both of whom had previously been stationed at their country's Washington embassy, had gone missing. And it wasn't a jaunt to the Caribbean that their superiors feared, but rather, a defection behind the Iron Curtain.

It was not an auspicious moment for what Winston Churchill had christened the "Special Relationship" between Britain and America. London's diplomatic recognition of the People's Republic of China in January 1950 had not gone over well in Washington, where a bipartisan policy of support for Taiwan would persist for another twenty years. Elsewhere in Asia, another rift between the two allies emerged over their divergent responses to communist North Korea's invasion of the non-communist South. And later that fall, an Italian-born British nuclear physicist who had worked on the Manhattan Project, Bruno Pontecorvo, suddenly absconded for the Soviet Union—the same place, it was feared, where Guy Francis de Moncy Burgess and Donald Duart Maclean might also be found.

At the time of their disappearance, Maclean was working as head of the American desk in Britain's Foreign Office. From 1944 to 1948, he had been a first secretary at the British embassy in Washington, where he enjoyed top level access to sensitive information about U.S. nuclear weapons policy. Burgess had started as a second secretary at the embassy the previous fall. Both men came from privileged backgrounds: Maclean's father was a minister of education, and Burgess was descended from a line of military officers. The two had met as students at Cambridge University, the site, it was later revealed, of their recruitment into the Communist conspiracy, and their enlistment in another, even fouler one.

While he occupied a lower rank than Maclean, Burgess was by far the more colorful of the pair. A blowhard and a snob, he hated everything about America except the automobile culture, and he could often be spotted driving up and down Embassy Row in a 1941 Lincoln Continental convertible. Living at the Nebraska Avenue home of his embassy colleague Kim Philby, MI6's liaison to the CIA working under the cover of a first secretary, Burgess was a rude and rambunctious drunk whose shocking behavior fast made him a notorious figure within Washington's diplomatic community. One night, what began as a pleasant dinner at the home of James Jesus Angleton came to an abrupt halt after the pickled Burgess, an amateur caricaturist, scribbled a lewd cartoon of a female guest and "precipitated a social disaster." Another soirée at Joe Alsop's home ended disagreeably when Burgess went on a tear against American policy in Korea, provoking the hawkish Alsop to kick him out.

That there might have been an element of sexual deviancy to go along with the political kind was alluded to three days after the diplomats' disappearance was first announced. "Whitehall in Queer Street," declared the headline of the *Sunday Dispatch* on June 10. During a debate in the House of Commons the next day, a member of Parliament from the opposition Labour Party asked the foreign secretary to investigate allegations of "widespread sexual perversion in the Foreign Office." Interviewed by a reporter from the British *Daily Express* at his home in Southern California, the British novelist Christopher Isherwood, who knew Burgess from London gay circles, addressed the issue euphemistically. "I have the strongest personal reasons for not wanting to go to Russia and I should think Guy Burgess would have exactly the same sort of reasons," he said. "We both happen to have exactly the same sort of tastes, and they don't meet with the approval of the Soviets. In fact, I'm told they liquidate chaps with our views—rather beastly don't you think?"

A snap FBI investigation of Burgess and Maclean offered some clarity as to those "tastes" and "views." One FBI informant, listening to an interview with a British newspaper correspondent on the radio, "received the impression from various side remarks . . . that both Maclean and Burgess were 'pansies' and were probably out together on an affair." A memo by Clyde Tolson reported another informant's contention that Maclean "was one of a ring of 12 people who were regarded as homosexuals and possibly dope addicts," were "devoted to each other," and frequently "dressed up in women's clothes." Both men, the informant said, had escaped to Buenos Aires dressed as women. "It is believed you will be interested in the fact that both individuals are reported to have been homosexuals," J. Edgar Hoover wrote the CIA's new director, Gen. Walter Bedell Smith.

Despite an assertion made to the FBI by an in-law that Maclean was homosexual, there is no evidence that he had any male sexual partners aside from a single encounter (allegedly, according to Burgess, with himself) at Cambridge. Burgess, however, was "a homosexual who boasted of it," in the words of one acquaintance interviewed by the FBI. Indeed, according to Burgess's FBI file, the overriding characteristic of "the spy who knew everyone" was that he slept with anyone. Burgess bragged about his many visits to the Everard Baths in Manhattan, where "you can get anything you desire." His regular importuning at Washington's seediest public lavatories inevitably brought him to the attention of Roy Blick, who "could state with certainty that Burgess was known to be a homosexual." So, too, could a Voice of America employee and the hitchhiker Burgess picked up on a sozzled road trip through Virginia, both of whom told the FBI that Burgess had sexually propositioned them. Blair Bolles, a former diplomatic correspondent for the *Evening Star*, told the Bureau about the handful of occasions he had met Burgess for drinks at the National Press Club bar. In addition to impressing Bolles with his ability to put back six highballs "without turning a hair," the British diplomat expressed a "general dislike for the United States Congress, in particular the attitude of some members of Congress towards homosexuals in the State Department." According to Bolles, Burgess said that he considered the ongoing investigations into homosexuals "a personal affront." Burgess's own words confirm this characterization. "Things have reached such a pitch" in Washington, he wrote a friend in England around this time, "that two members of the State Department daren't dine together in public for fear of being called homosexuals and therefore Communists." While this might have been an incisive critique of the propensity for conflating homosexuality with communism, it was an absurd one for an actual homosexual Communist like Burgess to make.

An agent from the FBI's Los Angeles field office drove to Santa Monica to interview Isherwood, who described Burgess as "a drunkard, a homosexual and an emotionally unstable person." FBI counterintelligence agent Robert Lamphere, who worked on every major Soviet espionage investigation of the early Cold War, recalled how "The names of well-known writers like [W. H.] Auden and [Stephen] Spender leaped off the page when I read the report from Los Angeles." In the view of the FBI, Burgess's association with two prominent left-wing sexual deviant poets suggested an insidious dimension to the case that Britain's intelligence services had ignored or, more worryingly, kept hidden from their American cousins. "We could not believe that the British would have allowed such people access to their diplomatic and security services," Lamphere recalled.

That the latest setback to Anglo-American relations was the work of two British Communist homosexual spies did not surprise Lamphere's boss. Burgess and Maclean were the living, breathing embodiment of the perils that J. Edgar Hoover had been warning presidents about for years. As a rule, the FBI director didn't trust foreigners, not even those who spoke English. He had suspected that the British embassy was a den of iniquity ever since Sir Archibald Clark Kerr, the kilt- (but not undergarment-) wearing lodger of Archie Butt and Francis Millet some four decades prior, darkened its door as ambassador in 1946. Described by the writer Rebecca West as "one of the most bizarre human beings ever to rise to the rank of ambassador, which is saying a great deal indeed," Kerr raised eyebrows across Washington mainly due to his curious relationship with Evgeni, his valet. Kerr would recount to anyone who would listen the marvelous story of how he had acquired the twenty-four-year-old Volga German. At the conclusion of Kerr's previous posting as ambassador to Moscow, Stalin asked the departing diplomat to choose a farewell gift. Would the Soviet leader be "willing to part with one Soviet citizen out of two hundred million?" Kerr asked. Two days later, Kerr's manservant received a rare exit visa. The presence of a Soviet citizen in the personal employ of the British ambassador scandalized Washington. So did Kerr's frequent bragging that "I have a Russian slave at the Embassy given to me by Stalin." (For this and other indiscretions, Kerr earned himself a thinly disguised mention in *Washington Confidential*, which stated outright that he "had as his lover his Russian valet.") Combined with what Kerr's former secretary recalled as a fondness for "the company and presence of good-looking young men," as well as the conspicuous appearance of strapping Iowa farm boys in the ambassadorial guesthouse, officials at the FBI started to wonder just how deep was the homosexual rot among the United States' ostensible allies.

They were hardly alone in suspecting something awfully queer about the British. Many Americans tended to associate homosexuality with Britain for the same reason they associated it with the State Department: class. The British men with whom most Americans were familiar, whether through personal interaction or merely from the movies and television shows they watched, tended to be from the upper classes. With their fancy accents, well-tailored clothes, and epicene mannerisms acquired at all-male boarding schools (notorious hotbeds of adolescent buggery), Brits were indistinguishable from the crew of "striped-pants" "cookie-pushers" at Foggy Bottom. "Until the recent purges at the State Department, there was a gag around Washington that you had to speak with a British accent, wear a Homburg hat, or have a queer quirk if you wanted to get by the guards at the door," sneered Lait and Mortimer in *Washington Confidential*. "Having spent some time during the War with British Army officers," another writer recalled, "I gave up after a while the game of guessing who was and was not an invert, for the final difference did not seem to be very great at all."

Fallout from the Burgess and Maclean defection was swift. Meeting a contrite delegation of senior MI5 officers, Hoover dressed down his British counterparts, expressing amazement that they had not instituted a loyalty program similar to the one employed by the United States. A senior MI6 officer recalled that the incident "caused a terrible rift between us and American intelligence, and at the time they simply clamped down and stopped giving us anything." On June 18, in light of Maclean's previous role as secretary of the Combined Policy Committee on Atomic Development, the U.S. National Security Council withdrew a proposal to enhance nuclear cooperation with Britain, and two days later the FBI escalated its surveillance and repression of gays through the institution of a nationwide "Sex Deviates" program. Affirming the necessity of a "uniform policy for the handling of the increasing number of reports and allegations concerning present and past employees of the United States Government who assertedly are sex deviates," Hoover ordered the creation of a central database of known homosexuals and a standardized procedure for information sharing across the federal bureaucracy to prevent their hiring.

The most profound impact of the Burgess-Maclean defection, which was to prove even more consequential than the betrayal of Colonel Redl, was on the public perception of homosexuality, communism, and treason. As the FBI quickly discovered, Burgess was the farthest thing from a covert homosexual. Indeed, tales of his outrageous sexual hijinks and louche badinage shocked American officials, who were entirely unaccustomed with the phenomenon of a blatantly open homosexual having access to sensitive government information. When an informant told the FBI that "even if this condition [homosexuality] were generally known to Burgess' friends and employers of that period it would not have made much difference since . . . homosexuality on the part of a person such as Burgess would not be considered unusual in the London of that period," it not only confirmed Bureau suspicions about high-class British homosexuality. It left open the question of motive. If Burgess was impervious to blackmail, why had he betrayed his country?

The concept of a "Homintern"—a riff on the Comintern, or Communist International—has been variously attributed to scholar Maurice Bowra, poet W. H. Auden, and critic Cyril Connolly, among others. Coined around the late 1930s as a droll reflection on the cliquishness of a particular set of interwar gay English literary figures, it attained an ominous meaning in the wake of the Burgess and Maclean defection. Like Alger Hiss, the two British diplomats had been granted every privilege that life in a Western capitalist democracy could offer, from excellent schooling, to lack of material want, to well-paying jobs at elite institutions. That they would throw it all away and become the first ideologically motivated Western spies to defect to the Soviet Union invested their treason with heightened significance. If Redl was the early twentieth-century archetype of the traitorous homosexual, who betrays his country due to fear of exposure, Burgess became the paradigmatic subversive for the Cold War age: the devious queer who exacts revenge against the society that marginalizes him by aiding its enemies.

An article published in the conservative American magazine *Human Events* the following year vividly summoned this specter. According to its author, although blackmail had long been cited as the primary justification for "the elimination of the homosexuals from all Government agencies," it was actually "a comparatively minor" factor. Far more significant to the purging of homosexuals, argued the Countess R. G. Waldeck, was the fact that "by the very nature of their vice they belong to a sinister, mysterious and efficient international." This "Homosexual International," like the Communist one with which it overlapped, constituted "a world-wide conspiracy against society"; was global in scope; "penetrates all classes; operates in armies and in prisons; has infiltrated into the press, the movies, and the cabinets; and it all but dominates the arts, literature, theater, music, and TV." Tracing the history of homosexuality back to Julius Caesar's affair with King Nicomedes IV, Waldeck noticed a recurrent pattern leading all the way up to the present. "I watched the little sodoms functioning within embassies and foreign offices," she wrote of her time as a journalist in Europe during the 1930s. "Somehow homosexuals always seemed to come by the dozen, not because they were cheaper that way but rather because a homosexual Ambassador or *chargé d'affaires* or Under Secretary of State liked to staff his 'team' with his own people." Homosexuals make "natural secret agents and natural traitors," Waldeck wrote, citing the Freudian psychoanalyst Theodor Reik's theory concerning the "fantasy of sex metamorphosis." Just as the homosexual desires to "play the role of the other sex," he seeks out "any job which gives him the chance of playing a double role." Few things can stand in the way of the awesome, invisible power that unites the members of this sinister conspiracy:

> That the Homosexual International could become dangerous should have been evident to anyone who had an opportunity to observe the mysterious manner in which homosexuals recognize each other—by a glance, a gesture, an indefinable pitch of voice—and the astonishing understanding which this recognition creates between men who seem to be socially or politically at opposite poles. True, other Internationals are better organized and more articulate. But what is the unifying force of race, of faith, of ideology as compared to the unifying force of a vice which intimately links the press tycoon to the beggar, the jailbird to the Ambassador, the General to the Pullman porter?

Or, for that matter, the Pullman porter to the undersecretary of state?

While politicians, journalists, and national security officials on both sides of the Atlantic fueled fears of a homosexual-Communist nexus, the first sustained American organization dedicated to the social advancement of homosexuals was declaring itself "unalterably opposed to Communism and Communist activity" and *expelling* Communists, its very own founder among them. Harry Hay, a budding actor and Communist Party activist in Los Angeles, was teaching a theater class in 1950 when he learned about a medieval French secret society of itinerant peasant troubadours—*les matassins*—who performed choreographed masquerades lampooning their corrupt rulers. The plight of the modern homosexual, Hay believed, was similar: he could advocate for a better society only from behind a veil of anonymity. Along with some veterans of the suggestively named group of gay men that supported Henry Wallace's 1948 presidential campaign, "Bachelors for Wallace," Hay launched the Mattachine Society of Los Angeles.

Within a few years of its formation, however, the Society decided to distance itself from Hay and other leaders with politically dicey affiliations. The purge of Communists by organized "homophiles," as Mattachine's members called themselves, was undertaken in retaliation to an earlier purge of homosexuals by the Communist Party USA. Noting how Marxist doctrine deemed homosexuality a bourgeois affliction, a writer for *ONE* magazine, the nation's first homosexual publication, marveled at "the mental convulsions" homosexual Communists "must experience in attempting to reconcile the irreconcilable contradictions in their thinking."

* * *

EVERY MORNING IN THE BRIGHT AND MAJESTIC CITY OF WASHINGTON, the gay and lesbian citizens within it awoke to join their fellow Americans who, like them, had come to play a role in forging the nation's destiny. On the gleaming marble steps of the Capitol, a congressman might greet a group of constituents visiting from some faraway corner of the country, none of them realizing that the photographs in his office of a smiling wife and family were a facade. In the basement of a departmental office building somewhere along the National Mall, an African American file clerk would sort through reams of documents, careful to disguise the sex of her spouse in conversations with coworkers. A journalist in the Senate Cloakroom would be careful never to mention the names of the bars he frequented to any of the important men he interviewed. And as these citizens of a secret city toiled away in what was now universally recognized as the capital of the free world, one of their number labored on behalf of its next leader.

The 1952 election was the first—though not the last—in which homosexuality featured as an issue. For two years, the American public had been treated to a stream of outraged congressional speeches, agitated headlines, and raunchy jokes about homosexuals overrunning the government. Exiting a taxi outside State Department headquarters, Stewart Alsop, Joe's younger brother and column-writing partner, heard the driver mutter under his breath, "Fruits and treachers [a slang term for "traitor"]. The place is full of 'em." So low had public opinion of the diplomatic corps fallen that a man standing in line for tickets to the symphony was laughed at when he remarked to the person waiting next to him that he worked for the State Department. Even to those who occupied the most high-minded precincts of American liberalism, the institution entrusted with representing the nation abroad had become a punch line. "It's true, sir, that the State Department let me go, but that was solely because of incompetence," says the man pictured applying for a job in a 1950 *New Yorker* cartoon. In the three years since John Peurifoy's testimony, far more State Department employees had been dismissed because of alleged homosexuality than disloyalty. Of the 66 people fired under the loyalty program guidelines in 1950, 54 were gay. Of the 154 dismissed in 1951, 119 were gay, as were 134 of the 204 fired in 1952, the year when prejudice against homosexuals received scientific endorsement from the American Psychiatric Association, which classified them as suffering from a "sociopathic personality disturbance," and legal sanction in form of the McCarran-Walter Act, which added those with a "psychopathic personality"—a category that included homosexuals—to the list of aliens prohibited from entering the country.

At the Republican National Convention in Chicago, where the delegates nominated Gen. Dwight Eisenhower for president and Sen. Richard Nixon as his running mate, the platform condemned "immorality" among those "entrusted with high policy-making positions." The GOP campaign pledge to "clean House" and wash away the "mess in Washington" conjured aberrant sexuality as much as Truman administration influence peddling. Communists, Senator McCarthy declared, had to be attacked by virile men, not in the "fashion of hitting them with a perfumed silk handkerchief," as those in the State Department preferred. According to McCarthy's colleague Everett Dirksen of Illinois, Democratic presidential nominee Adlai Stevenson, a former governor of Illinois and State Department official, was suspiciously close to "the lavender lads" at Foggy Bottom. Taking things one step farther, McCarthy alleged that the Democratic ticket was composed of "pinks, punks and pansies," the last, observed newspaper columnist Marquis Childs, a "public reference to the ugly whispering campaign around Stevenson's personal life." Stevenson—whose divorce, past diplomatic career, and unabashed intellectualism made him a ripe target for such innuendo—was the butt of "the foulest rumor ever circulated about a presidential candidate," in the words of one popular scandal magazine. "By phone, on planes and trains, from the racket of factory assembly lines to the quiet of hospital rooms, from the big-town sharpies to unsophisticated villagers, it burned the ears of a nation." So foul was the rumor that the magazine did not even identify it, except to say that it had been started by Stevenson's ex-wife. In truth, it was the work of J. Edgar Hoover.

Before Stevenson received his party's presidential nomination, the FBI director was accumulating information pertaining to how "Adeline" (Stevenson's alleged *nom de homosexual*) and the president of Bradley University in Peoria were the "two best known homosexuals" in Illinois. "There were a lot of us who were absolutely appalled by it," a former FBI agent remembered, "but Mr. Hoover was determined to elect Nixon and Ike, and when he made up his mind to do something there was no changing it." When Stevenson ran for president four years later, the rumors resurfaced, but with a gender-bending twist. "A vote for Adlai Stevenson," Walter Winchell announced on his radio program, "is a vote for Christine Jorgensen," a reference to the World War II veteran who made international headlines for undergoing the world's first sex-change operation.

Come Election Day, benefiting from voter exhaustion after two decades of near-uninterrupted Democratic rule and with the beloved former general who won World War II at the top of their ticket, Republicans seized control of the presidency and both chambers of Congress for the first time since the Great Depression. From his transition headquarters at New York's Commodore Hotel, and with the organizational acumen that he demonstrated in planning for the Normandy invasion, President-elect Eisenhower entertained an endless stream of foreign dignitaries, union leaders, and captains of industry, all the while overseeing the process of staffing the federal government. At his side throughout was forty-five-year-old Arthur H. Vandenberg Jr., whose selection as presidential appointments secretary the *New York Times* had announced on its front page. As J. Edgar Hoover strode into the president-elect's suite at 9:30 a.m. on December 30, 1952, it was Vandenberg's future that he wished to discuss.

The son of the recently deceased Republican senator from Michigan, whose promotion of the ideal that "politics shall stop at the water's edge" sounded, by this time, like a quaint plea from a distant era, Vandenberg was proudly hailed by his home state newspaper the *Detroit Free Press* as "the man behind" Eisenhower who "'knows everybody' in Washington." Vandenberg had become well-connected during the fifteen years spent working for his father in the Senate, where he distinguished himself from the many other senatorial relatives on the public payroll. When the *Baltimore Sun* ran a series of exposés on the family members of legislators with patronage jobs, Vandenberg was the only one whom the paper deemed actually qualified. Following his father's death in 1951, Vandenberg went to South America as an employee of Nelson Rockefeller's family business conglomerate, but soon left to lead Citizens for Eisenhower, the grassroots initiative to draft the general for the Republican nomination over the isolationist Ohio senator Robert Taft. Within five months of its creation, Citizens for Eisenhower boasted more than fifteen hundred chapters across the country. "The star of Young Arthur seems in the ascendant," enthused the *Free Press*.

In accordance with his campaign pledge to "clean up" Washington, Eisenhower mandated security background checks for all incoming White House staff and cabinet appointees. On December 20, Vandenberg paid a visit to FBI headquarters in Washington for his formal interview. Before answering the agents' questions, however, he told them that Eisenhower had expressed concern about the reporting of "unfounded rumors" and how the Bureau handled them. Assistant FBI director Lou Nichols responded that while the Bureau would not include "disproven" gossip, if stories about a person were "the subject of widespread dissemination, they had a logical place in the reports because otherwise" the officials reviewing them "would have no way of knowing whether this had been covered in the investigation if there was some future question." In other words, if enough people were discussing a rumor about someone, it would be included in that person's file, irrespective of its validity.

Though Vandenberg presented this concern as a hypothetical situation supposedly raised by the president-elect, he had a personal reason to be worried. In the course of its investigation into Vandenberg, the FBI had discovered that the presidential aide was "the subject of rumors concerning alleged homosexuality." Earlier that month, word had reached the Bureau about a young man living with Vandenberg who had been "bounced from the Navy" after being arrested in Lafayette Square on a morals charge. This man had "been advanced for some kind of job" and was "being sponsored by" Vandenberg. According to the FBI agents who conducted the interview, when they asked Vandenberg about the charges directly, "he denied these rumors but admitted association in the past with persons known to be homosexuals." Three days later, Vandenberg checked himself into a hospital, where he would remain through the New Year.

According to Senator Vandenberg's biographer, there is no evidence that the two ever discussed Art Jr.'s secret. But there is a hint that the senator might have known, and perhaps even tried, in the highly reserved manner to which men of his generation were accustomed, to signal acceptance of his son. "Just be true to yourself," he once wrote Art Jr. "I can even shorten that up. BE YOURSELF!" Vandenberg Sr. never lived to see his son's greatest professional achievement—helping elect the president of the United States—which may have been for the best. For it would have broken the older man's heart to witness what happened as a result.

At the Commodore, Hoover began his meeting with Eisenhower by informing the president-elect that CIA director Walter Bedell Smith "had inherited from OSS some elements that were not conducive to the best operations of such an agency as CIA"—Communists and queers, presumably. He then turned his focus to one such unconducive element on the president-elect's own staff. After summarizing what the FBI had discovered about Vandenberg, Hoover, according to a memo he later wrote about the meeting, "outlined briefly to the General some of the angles of the case which we were now investigating." Vandenberg, Hoover said, "had asked that we not interview the young man" living with him until after he left the hospital. Having sufficiently conveyed the unconventionality of Vandenberg's domestic arrangements, Hoover proposed a solution to spare Eisenhower embarrassment. Should Vandenberg "decide that he did not desire to continue in the position to which he had been appointed as Secretary to the President," a decision that had been all but made for him, the FBI director "could inform Vandenberg that no report would be submitted as it would then be a moot question." Vandenberg could either quit, or face a full FBI investigation and the probable leaking of it to the press.

Seven days before the inauguration, Vandenberg penned a letter to the president-elect informing him that he would not be joining his White House staff. "I realize that you have been in this thing from the very beginning and that you have given tremendously of your energies during that period," Eisenhower responded. "On that account I feel in some respects guilty." For the next four months, Vandenberg publicly maintained that he could not assume his duties at the White House due to illness. On April 14, 1953, he officially resigned, not having spent a single day in service of the president whom he had worked longer and harder than almost anyone to elect, and in whose memoirs he would rate no more than a footnote.

DWIGHT EISENHOWER

Maybe that is the only way you can tell that a certain piece of knowledge is worth anything: it has cost some blood.

—Robert Penn Warren, *All the King's Men*

11

"NO MORE BOHLENS!"

PRESIDENT EISENHOWER WASTED NO TIME IMPLEMENTING HIS PROMISE to "clean up" Washington. At his very first cabinet meeting, on January 23, 1953, he announced that "security rather than loyalty must be the test" for government workers, expanding the list of disqualifying factors far beyond "subversive" associations and beliefs. A citizen's loyalty to the United States was no guarantee against his inadvertently compromising national security, Eisenhower believed, as "many loyal Americans, by reason of instability, alcoholism, homosexuality or previous tendencies to associate with Communist-front groups, are unintentional security risks." Eisenhower also told his cabinet that he wanted the new regulations to apply to *all* employees of the federal government, not just those working with sensitive information.

Just opposite the White House, on the north side of Lafayette Square, John C. Montgomery was leading a noontime service at St. John's Episcopal Church. The forty-one-year-old head of the State Department's Finnish desk was a regular parishioner at the "church of the presidents." Rev. C. Leslie Glenn, the rector of St. John's, believed Montgomery had the qualities necessary for a man of the cloth, gained through a life of solitude and hardship. An only child left orphaned when both of his parents died,

Montgomery "wasn't accepted by the other boys" at the boarding school he attended; nor did he fit in at Princeton University, whose exclusive eating clubs passed him over for membership. At church socials, he arrived alone and departed early. But "self-sufficient, affable and dignified," Montgomery found a place for himself at St. John's. "He should have been a missionary or a minister," Reverend Glenn believed. "He was intensely earnest." Had Montgomery been born during the Middle Ages, Glenn was to say, he would have become a monk.

At the conclusion of the service, which adjourned around the same time as the president's cabinet meeting across the Square, Montgomery returned to the State Department. Though Glenn described him as "never what you would call the life of the party," Montgomery had a full social calendar that evening. Shortly before six, he departed Foggy Bottom to attend a going-away celebration for a colleague at the Chevy Chase Club, where he consumed two martinis, after which he attended a small dinner at the house of the first secretary of the Finnish Legation. Over the course of the meal, he imbibed another martini, six glasses of wine, and a glass and a half of Benedictine. Aside from awkwardly telling the same risqué story twice, his behavior was not unusual. Shortly before midnight, one of the other guests gave Montgomery a ride to the three-story Georgetown home he shared with forty-five-year-old attorney A. Marvin Braverman.

At 2 a.m., the next-door neighbor was awoken by a very loud thudding sound. Fearing it might be an intruder, she looked out her window to the Braverman-Montgomery residence. But noticing that a light was on in the other home, she retired to bed.

Two hours later, Braverman returned home from a characteristically long night of socializing. One of Washington's most eligible bachelors, he had been out with Virginia Warren, eldest daughter of California governor Earl Warren and twenty-one years his junior. Their evening had begun at a party in Georgetown hosted by a Democratic congressman, and it came to an end many hours later, at the cocktail bar of the Shoreham Hotel. Following last call, Braverman dropped Warren off at the Statler, where she was staying, and then drove home to Georgetown. He poured himself a glass of tomato juice and headed up the stairs to go to sleep.

As Braverman reached the second-floor landing, a horrifying sight stopped him in his tracks: Montgomery's nude body, a bathrobe belt tied tightly around his neck, its other end knotted to a portion of hemp rope fastened to the third-floor banister. "John! John!" Braverman cried, propelling himself backward so hard that he tumbled down the winding staircase and broke a small bone in his foot. When the police arrived, they found Montgomery's clothes folded neatly on his bed and a small memo book containing a written list of appointments for the next day. He left no suicide note. Braverman was too distraught to talk to the media.

While both bachelors were "well-known in Washington society," the Dartmouth College and Harvard Law School–educated Braverman had earned particular renown thanks to his highly public, on-again, off-again romance with President Truman's only child, the budding classical soprano Margaret. Or, at least, that is how Washington's society columnists liked to describe their curious relationship. Braverman had started escorting the First Daughter, fourteen years his junior, to social functions while serving in the White House as a military aide during the war. When Margaret received the news that President Roosevelt had died and that her father would immediately take the oath of office, it was Braverman whom she called first to cancel their date that evening. Over time, Braverman became a close friend and confidant to the First Family, as evidenced by his receiving a DC license plate with the coveted numeral "10."

Both Marvin and Margaret denied that there was anything serious between them, which did nothing to dampen press speculation that they were secretly engaged to be wed. "I never have been, I am not now, nor do I ever intend to be engaged to Mr. Braverman," Margaret once declared in a disavowal simultaneously Shermanesque and redolent of a cooperative HUAC witness. Though Braverman was "a very charming and intelligent man," she was extremely vexed by how all the public fuss over their occasional dates was spoiling her chances with other suitors. One of those suitors, another Washington lawyer named Marvin—he and Braverman competed as "friendly rivals" for Margaret's affections—labeled the engagement rumors "hokum." The denials did little to dispel the speculation. In the spring of 1952, the White House had to rebuke the assertion made by a Stanford economics professor that the reason Truman had chosen not to seek reelection that fall was due to Marvin and Margaret's impending nuptials.

As for Montgomery, though he often talked about being in love, "he never found what he frequently described as the ideal woman," and he named Braverman the executor of his substantial estate. Whether Braverman and Montgomery were lovers or simply housemates, the suicide sent ripples of fear through the secret city. Perhaps, some speculated, Montgomery was one of their own, and had been protected in his State Department job through his connection to a close friend of the First Family. Fearful that this protection would end once the Trumans left Washington, he killed himself four days into the new administration rather than face the inevitable security investigation. Braverman's nocturnal vocation as a walker of prominent young women he had no intention of marrying, along with his sharing a home with another man, aroused the curiosity of Republican congressman Fred Busbey of Illinois. Given how the State Department had been "plagued" by "poor loyalty risks," he said in a speech delivered on the House floor six days after the diplomat's suicide, Congress should "not assume that [Montgomery] was innocent of such associations" and must carry out an investigation into the circumstances of his death. "There are stories being bruited about that police have been told not to talk," Busbey thundered. "There has been protection, it is said, for Montgomery's former associates and their activities." Though "it has been hinted that Montgomery was despondent because he was lonely and unmarried," he "was a bachelor by choice." Lest the insinuation be lost on his colleagues, Busbey noted that Montgomery "shared a fashionable Georgetown home with a local attorney," and reiterated that "neither Montgomery nor the Washington attorney had ever married. This is not unusual, but it is not customary." Did Montgomery leave a note, and if he did, was it "destroyed to protect the dead, and perhaps some living?"

When a preliminary investigation by the State Department ruled Montgomery "clean as a whistle," Rep. Charles Brownson, the Republican chairman of a House subcommittee charged with investigating his suicide, lambasted its findings as "insulting to the integrity and intelligence" of Congress. At a hearing to discuss the department's internal security procedures, the army general in charge of the Selective Service told the committee that, during the war, Montgomery had received a 4-F deferment on account of his "psychoneurosis." (The designation 4-F encompassed anyone deemed "physically, morally or mentally unfit," homosexuals included.) A House report published the following year determined that while "neither the police nor the Department of State investigation found the suicide to have been related to Mr. Montgomery's official duties," the diplomat's "life, from childhood, had been one of frustration . . . [I]t seemed apparent that the crucial factor was Mr. Montgomery's reported mental and emotional instability."

Whatever the particulars of Montgomery's mental and emotional state, depression was not unusual among federal government employees in 1953, forced to endure constant, withering attacks on their loyalties and personal fitness from members of Congress and the media. Washington-area psychoanalysts reported a rise in mental illness among federal workers, many of whom were then punished for seeking therapy. When the body of a forty-two-year-old CIA stenographer was discovered in an apparent suicide that June, it marked the fifth case of a government employee engaged in classified work who had killed themselves over the previous year.

Once a boldface name in the Washington society columns, Marvin Braverman took a break from his hectic social life after the death of his fellow "bachelor by choice." By the following May, he was back to escorting Margaret Truman all over town.

* * *

JOHN FOSTER DULLES'S INTRODUCTION TO HOMOSEXUALITY was far more intense than that of his younger brother's exposure as a diplomat in late Habsburg–era Vienna. As a precocious sixteen-year-old sophomore at Princeton, Dulles developed an innocent crush on an older boy. He had never felt anything quite like that confusing mixture of emotions for another person, and the affection was reciprocated. "It was an exhilarating experience," according to Leonard Mosley, author of a group biography of the Dulles family,

> until the moment when he discovered from his adored older partner that male relationships can also have their physical side. To a young man who had, so far, only embarrassedly bussed a girl at a party, it was a devastating and shocking revelation of what he knew from his Bible to be a shame and a sin. He conveyed this sense of degradation with such effect that the fellow student walked out of his room and left the college.

The intense memory of this encounter must have occupied a prominent place in the mind of the new secretary of state as he and his brother Allen sat and listened to J. Edgar Hoover on March 17, 1953. The FBI director had come to Foster's office at the State Department to discuss President Eisenhower's nominee for ambassador to the Soviet Union. The outgoing holder of that post, George Kennan, had been declared persona non grata by the Kremlin the previous fall for stating that the atmosphere in Moscow was worse than what he had endured as an interned diplomat in Nazi Germany. When Joseph Stalin unexpectedly died a few months later, U.S.-Soviet relations entered uncharted territory, and the appointment of Kennan's replacement became even more urgent.

The man sitting across from the Dulles brothers that day possessed significantly greater bureaucratic power than the two of them combined. As the demand for more extensive internal security measures had grown, so, too, did the FBI, which increased its ranks from two thousand special agents in 1940 to more than seven thousand by the time of Eisenhower's inauguration thirteen years later. The Bureau could rely upon unquestioning support from Congress, whose members outdid one another in singing the director's praises and acceding to his budgetary requests, and it enjoyed near-universal esteem in the popular culture, where veneration of the intrepid G-man was at its most fulsome. The FBI also had the power to investigate anyone it wanted, and it was with the gravitas and authority such power conferred that Hoover arrived at Foggy Bottom bearing the fruits of his investigation into the president's ambassadorial nominee. He did not have good news.

A graduate of the exclusive St. Paul's School and Harvard, Charles "Chip" Bohlen was memorialized by Walter Isaacson and Evan Thomas as one of America's postwar foreign policy "Wise Men" in their magisterial book of that title. He began what would become his long and storied diplomatic career in 1931, at the American embassy in Prague. After studying intensive Russian, Bohlen joined William Bullitt's Moscow embassy, where he witnessed the last show trial of Communist Party officials, and he later served as President Roosevelt's interpreter at Yalta, where he sat so close to Stalin that he oversaw the Soviet leader doodling little red wolves on his notepad. (Bohlen's Russian-language skills were so impressive that he was reputed to have a better accent than the Georgian-born Soviet leader.) Widely acknowledged within the State Department as one of its sharpest analysts of Soviet affairs, Bohlen also participated in drafting the Marshall Plan. President Eisenhower had come to know the nominee and "his very charming family" in Paris after the war, when Bohlen was stationed at the American embassy and Eisenhower was serving as NATO Supreme Allied Commander. The president especially enjoyed hitting the links with Bohlen, the ultimate compliment as far as the golf-obsessed president was concerned.

In the eyes of Joe McCarthy and his growing number of admirers across the country, however, Bohlen's experience—particularly his presence at Yalta—was worse than irrelevant. It was disqualifying. The decision made there to recognize Soviet control over Eastern Europe had not been a lamentable but unavoidable acceptance of geopolitical facts on the ground. It was a deliberate betrayal, by officials within the highest reaches of the Roosevelt administration, to consign half the Continent to barbarism and slavery. And lest anyone forget: wasn't Alger Hiss at Yalta, too?

Eisenhower, whom the McCarthy wing already suspected of being insufficiently anticommunist, had formed an uneasy alliance with the senator during his presidential campaign. To the dismay of some of his strongest supporters, he had stayed quiet even as McCarthy accused his fellow war hero George Marshall of complicity in a Communist "conspiracy on a scale so immense as to dwarf any previous such venture in the history of man." As for John Foster Dulles, though he once privately likened McCarthy to Adolf Hitler, he had no desire to pick a fight with the wild man from Wisconsin. In going out of their way to avoid confrontation, the president and his secretary of state were like most of their peers in the moderate Republican establishment. Recognizing that McCarthy was a politically valuable attack dog against the Democrats and fearing a backlash from his passionate base of supporters, they let the senator and his congressional allies run riot.

When McCarthy announced his opposition to the Bohlen nomination, however, it forced the moderates to reevaluate whether this approach had been a mistake. Only two months into Eisenhower's term, McCarthy was shifting his sights away from the Democrats and onto the president from his own party. The ensuing fight was the first crisis of the Eisenhower administration, and its implications were greater than the fate of a lone ambassador. In blocking Bohlen, McCarthy threatened to undermine the executive authority of the president, aggravate U.S.-Soviet relations, and divide the Republican Party just when it had achieved dominance over the three branches of government. And by persisting in his crusade against sex deviants in the State Department, McCarthy demonstrated once again how attacks on homosexuality transcended partisan lines.

For its security investigation into Bohlen, the FBI had interviewed nearly three dozen people, including several familiar figures from Moscow. Carmel Offie, described by an FBI informant as "queer as a three dollar bill," told investigators that while he had house-sat for Bohlen and his wife and considered him an "intelligent and attractive fellow," he could not "understand the appointee's attitude of appeasement" toward Russia. Offie's former boss William Bullitt told investigators that, while there was "no question concerning [Bohlen's] loyalty to the United States or his moral character," he disagreed strongly with the nominee's views and had once called him a "cheap profiteer on American disaster" to his face.

More damaging than these mildly unfavorable assessments, however, were those that cast doubt on Bohlen's sexuality. "There is a definite shading in his conversation and in his manner of speech which indicates effeminacy," a female State Department employee observed, adding that Bohlen had a "habit of running his tongue over his lip in the manner utilized by a woman" and was "quite girlish." An ex–Foreign Service officer who had worked with Bohlen in Moscow and "freely admitted his [own] homosexual activity" volunteered to the Bureau that "in all of his forty-two years as a homosexual, he has learned to separate the 'queer' from the men." Long before the term *gaydar* was coined to describe the ability of gay people to identify one another, this man told the FBI that he possessed a "sixth sense," an ability to "spot" homosexuals "very easily" and that he "has never made a mistake in this activity." His verdict on Bohlen? He "walks, acts and talks like a homosexual."

These impressions were seemingly confirmed by other circumstantial evidence. In 1950, an anonymous source had sent a three-page letter to Iowa Republican senator Bourke Hickenlooper accusing eighteen male State Department employees (Carmel Offie among them) of homosexuality and Bohlen of being their associate. Additionally, a memo from the director of the State Department's Office of Security, a former FBI agent named John W. Ford, mentioned the existence of a tape recording in which Bohlen's brother-in-law and fellow Foreign Service officer, Charles Thayer, who had worked with Bohlen in Moscow, allegedly referred to a "high ranking official" who had "gotten into bed with him" but whom he could "under no circumstances name." Because the official had served successively in Moscow and then Paris, Ford assumed it to be Bullitt. But it also could have been Bohlen, who similarly followed Bullitt to France.

In contrast to these anonymous attacks, Bohlen received sterling recommendations from the likes of Allen Dulles, Joint Chiefs of Staff chairman Omar Bradley, and George Marshall, among many other leading statesmen and political figures. Nonetheless, when Foster Dulles asked Hoover for his personal views on Bohlen, the FBI director replied that, while the Bureau had found "no direct evidence that Bohlen had engaged in homosexual activities," it was nonetheless "a fact that several of his closest friends and intimate associates were known homosexuals" and that this, as far as Hoover was concerned, should be sufficient reason for the president to withdraw the nomination.

When John Foster Dulles accepted the position of secretary of state, a role his grandfather had performed in the administration of President Benjamin Harrison, he did not envision personnel management as being a significant part of the job. Like his predecessor, Dean Acheson, Dulles was a grand strategist. He wanted to run the world, not a bureaucracy in Washington, and to accomplish this, he would need the cooperation of the Republicans now in control on Capitol Hill. Dulles experienced a taste of what he would have to deal with after one of his first congressional hearings as secretary of state. "It must be terrible to have to work among all those homosexuals," the committee chairman said to him sympathetically. And so it was without much resistance that, as a concession to the McCarthy forces just a few weeks into the administration, Dulles accepted the appointment of Scott McLeod as assistant secretary of state in the newly established Bureau of Security and Consular Affairs. A former FBI agent and staffer for the powerful Republican Senate Appropriations Committee chairman Styles Bridges (the man who controlled Dulles's purse strings), McLeod kept an autographed photo of Joe McCarthy on his desk. ("To a great American," read the inscription.) From his fourth-floor office suite, which radiated the atmosphere of a "municipal homicide squad," McLeod acted as policeman, judge, and executioner. Annoyed at how American diplomats were adopting the "dress, accents, mannerisms, and even the thinking of foreigners," McLeod took to his job with all the enthusiasm of an exterminator in a vermin-infested cellar.

"Congress wanted heads to roll," he declared, "and I let 'em roll. Blood in the streets and all that."

In his first six weeks on the beat, McLeod presided over the firing of nineteen employees for homosexuality, or an average of one every other day, a figure that would double by June. McLeod eventually built up a staff of a thousand people, all of whom he instructed to be "completely ruthless" in their work. In a column about McLeod's "reign of terror," Drew Pearson reported that German servants at the American embassy in Berlin had been ordered to spy on their employers. ("Lots of people," McLeod admitted with pride, "think I'm an ogre.") Dulles—who, according to Richard Rovere, "cleared everything with McLeod, who cleared everything with McCarthy"—did not exactly endear himself to the men and women of the State Department by delegating the internal security portfolio to a man who took such evident pleasure in thinning their ranks.

To satiate McCarthy, Dulles agreed to allow McLeod to conduct his own security investigation of Bohlen. Questioning staff at the Paris embassy where Bohlen had previously served, McLeod's minions set off "the wildest and most damaging rumors among the puzzled Europeans," wrote the brothers Alsop. (Both were friends of Bohlen, Joe dating all the way back to their days in Harvard's elite Porcellian Club.) The nature of the rumors was alluded to in a letter by George Kennan to his sister. "No matter what you read or hear on the radio," the former holder of the job Bohlen hoped to attain wrote, "you can take it from me that Bohlen is not a homosexual, nor is he disloyal. That these things can be seriously suggested fills me with horror and foreboding."

The day before he was to testify before the Senate Foreign Relations Committee in support of Bohlen's nomination, Dulles called Bohlen into his office. "Chip, I just wanted to know whether there's anything in your past that might be damaging," the secretary of state asked. Bohlen told him there was nothing to worry about. "Well, I'm glad of that because I couldn't stand another Alger Hiss," replied Dulles, who, as chairman of the Carnegie Endowment's board of trustees, had recommended Hiss for the job of its president. For all his misgivings, Dulles served at the pleasure of President Eisenhower, who wanted Bohlen in the job even more so now that the poor man's name was being dragged through the mud. As Eisenhower wrote in a letter to his brother Edgar, Bohlen had become the victim of "completely baseless, wholly unsubstantiated rumors that he had been associated some fifteen or twenty years ago with some unsavory characters." When it came time for him to testify, Dulles expressed his support for the nomination, which the committee approved unanimously.

This expression of bipartisan support only emboldened McCarthy, however, who thrived in situations where he could pit himself against an all-powerful establishment. That afternoon, McCarthy called Hoover and asked point-blank if Bohlen was a homosexual. Hoover replied that he did not know, as it "was a very hard thing to prove and the only way you could prove it was either by admission or by arrest and forfeiture of collateral," neither of which existed in this case. That said, Hoover allowed, Bohlen "is associating with individuals of that type," "has been a very close buddy of Offie for many years," and "used very bad judgment in associating with homosexuals." In a rare and ironic moment of honesty, McCarthy admitted that "it was so easy to accuse a person of such [homosexual] acts but difficult to prove." Hoover concurred, noting "that it was often a charge used by persons who wanted to smear someone." Alas, these private acknowledgments of the manifold ways in which the charge of homosexuality could be abused had no bearing on either man's public actions.

"I know what's in Bohlen's file," McCarthy announced two days after his meeting with Hoover. Preparing to assail the nomination on the Senate floor, McCarthy sought advice from Vice President Richard Nixon. According to White House chief of staff Jerry Persons, McCarthy shared drafts of two speeches with Nixon, one "pretty rough" in its attacks on Bohlen and the other "*real* dirty." Nixon, sympathetic to the senator but ultimately loyal to his boss, advised McCarthy to go with the former. Poor Bohlen, meanwhile, was quarantined for three days after being hit with a case of German measles. "Thank goodness it was German and not Red measles," his daughter Avis recalled him joking from his sickbed.

Resentful that Dulles had disregarded his advice, McLeod, in an act of extraordinary insubordination, bypassed his boss and complained directly to the White House, at one point even threatening to resign unless it withdrew Bohlen's nomination. Concerned that McLeod might go public with his opposition if called to testify, the White House assigned him a minder to make sure he was "secure" from any place where he might be served a subpoena. When the conservative Democratic senator from Nevada, Pat McCarran, declared the Bohlen case to be the "acid test" of whether Eisenhower would live up to his promise of "cleaning up" the State Department,

Dulles countered at a press conference that it was in fact an "acid test of the orderly processes of our government," it being the role of the executive branch to nominate ambassadors and of the Senate to advise and consent on the nomination. Much more than an ambassadorship was at stake in the battle over Chip Bohlen. The ability of a president to conduct foreign policy, the apolitical status of the Foreign Service, the future of U.S.-Soviet relations, the burgeoning fight over the soul of the GOP between moderates and McCarthyites—all these highly charged questions hung in the balance. And they all hinged upon a spurious charge of homosexuality.

Having exhausted seemingly all his options, McCarthy decided to pay an unannounced visit to the man whose witness to State Department treachery had unintentionally laid the groundwork for the Wisconsin senator's crusade, an oracular figure for American conservatives who, unbeknownst to most of them, happened to possess knowledge of the homosexual underworld in addition to the Communist one. As McCarthy walked through the door of Whittaker Chambers's Maryland farmhouse on March 21, a *Washington Post* reporter called asking to speak with the senator. The paper had clearly been tipped off about McCarthy's visit, presumably by the attention-hogging legislator himself. With the press gathered outside, McCarthy tried to use Chambers as a prop, as if his host were a human incarnation of the pumpkin from which emerged the secret documents confirming Alger Hiss's treason. "Is it security or is it something else?" Chambers asked of McCarthy's evidence against Bohlen. As he later recounted to a friend, by "something else," Chambers "meant homosexualism, which I suspected was the chief difficulty." McCarthy claimed he had evidence of both, "but he was pretty vague," Chambers said. Knowing from personal experience that a homosexual nature did not necessarily predispose a man to disloyalty, Chambers was repelled by McCarthy's effort. "I must say that the Bohlen episode was a shock more educative than ten years of merely reading the Senator's remarks," he later wrote to his protégé, a young conservative Yale graduate and budding magazine editor named William F. Buckley Jr. After his meeting with McCarthy, Chambers told the assembled newsmen that he knew nothing "by direct knowledge, that bears in any way adversely or otherwise" on Bohlen.

Eager to get its nominee confirmed, the administration reached a compromise with Republican majority leader Robert Taft whereby a bipartisan group of four senators would be allowed to read Bohlen's FBI file and report back on its contents to the full Senate. Taft, one of the four, announced that there was "nothing in all the testimony to create the most remote 'guilt-by-association' accusation you could think of." McCarthy, claiming to be in possession of information so offensive that "we cannot discuss it on the floor of the Senate," stubbornly stood his ground, accusing his fellow Republicans of acceding to the creation of a "government of, by, and for Communists, crooks, and cronies." He would not be pushed aside. "We want no part of this 'Chip' off the old block of Yalta," he declared.

To ensure that Bohlen was confirmed, the administration decided to make a trade. Bohlen's brother-in-law Charles Thayer, the U.S. consul general in Munich, had also been targeted with bogus, and anonymous, accusations of homosexuality. (If Thayer was guilty of any sexual impropriety, it was for an out-of-wedlock baby produced with his secretary.) As part of a deal to secure his brother-in-law's confirmation, Thayer was forced to resign, one of many promising diplomatic careers cut pointlessly short by the Lavender Scare. "The present situation reminds me of one of those newfangled washing machines going at high speed," a former diplomatic colleague wrote Thayer after he tendered his resignation. "All I can say at the present time is 'I hope you have a big place, Charlie; you're soon going to have lots of company.'"

On March 27, the Senate voted to confirm Charles Bohlen as ambassador to the Soviet Union by a vote of 74 to 13. Of the 13 against, 11 were Republicans. It was an extremely rare instance of a president's own party supplying most of the votes against one of his nominees. At his last meeting with Dulles at the State Department before departing for Moscow, Bohlen informed the secretary that he planned to stop in Paris for a few days of consultations, where he would be joined by his family.

"Oh, don't you think it would be wise for you and your wife to travel together?" Dulles asked.

"For God's sake, why?" Bohlen responded, already knowing the answer.

"Well, you know, there are rumors in some of your files about immoral behavior and it would look better if your wife was with you," Dulles explained.

Bohlen could not believe what he was hearing. No one had produced a shred of evidence that he was anything other than a red-blooded, woman-loving, all-American man. And yet here was his boss, the country's top diplomat, telling him that he needed to prove his heterosexual bona fides by posing for a few smiling press photographs with his wife, Avis, and their children on an airport tarmac. Before he could respond to this insolent request, however, Dulles pressed further: "Why do you think Mrs. Eisenhower traveled with the President during the election campaign?" Bohlen had to summon great reserves of energy to restrain himself from punching the secretary in the face.

In securing the confirmation of his ambassador to the Soviet Union, President Eisenhower beat back the right wing of his party. But McCarthy was far from defeated. Going forward, the administration would have to consider his views to an extent it had not fully appreciated. After the bruising nomination fight had ended, Majority Leader Taft sent a message to the White House: "No more Bohlens!"

12

THE HETEROSEXUAL
DICTATORSHIP

"THE TOP SECRET KEEPER OF THE EISENHOWER REGIME," ACCORDING TO
the *St. Louis Post-Dispatch*, was a "58-Year Old Bachelor" who led a "monas-
tic life." The first person to hold the job of national security advisor, Robert
Cutler was a well-heeled Boston lawyer who had traveled with Eisenhower
aboard his whistle-stop campaign train, "the Ike Special." The *New York
Times* would later assert of Cutler that "no man in the Government, with
the possible exception of the President, knows so many of the nation's strategic secrets." But only one secret had the capacity to destroy Cutler, and it
was a secret pertaining not to national security but to love.

Cutler might have had, in the words of the *Times*, "a lifelong love affair"
with his hometown of Boston, but his affection for "the loveliest city in the
world" was certainly no secret. What was a secret, and what had to remain
so for as long as Cutler wished to work in the White House, was his infat-
uation with another man. "I hope none of you fellows will ever be such a
damn fool as to keep a diary," Eisenhower once told Cutler and a group
of staffers early in his administration. Cutler disregarded the president's
advice, and the only reason we know of his love for Skip Koons, a staffer
on the National Security Council half his age, is that the diary in which he
confessed it happened to be discovered by his great-nephew decades after

his death. Cutler surely knew that the real reason for the sudden disappearance of his colleague Arthur Vandenberg Jr. during the transition was
not due to illness but because Vandenberg's secret—Cutler's secret—had
been discovered. If the man who led Citizens for Eisenhower could be disposed of so unceremoniously, Cutler presumably concluded, then a similar
fate awaited him were *his* secret ever to become known. And so, Cutler
exercised an austere command over his emotional life, earning himself the
nickname "White House Mystery Man," and channeled his deepest desires
into a torrid record of unrequited love as heartbreaking and illustrative of
the era's soul-crushing repression of gay people as his notes of National
Security Council meetings were, in the words of the *Times*, "precise and
tidy and unmistakably clear."

Cutler lived just a few blocks away from the White House, in an apartment building next to the Chicken Hut. Though he could hear the music
of the piano and gales of laughter from the patrons every night, there is
no record of his ever having joined in the festivities. To do so would have
all but certainly meant career suicide; by the early 1950s, it was widely
assumed that the bar was under constant FBI surveillance. Never setting
foot inside the most popular gay hangout in Washington was the physical
corollary to Cutler's sequestering his personal identity as a gay man from
his professional role as national security advisor. Two incidents from early
in the administration illustrate his adherence to this rigid compartmentalization.

One day during the fight over his nomination, Chip Bohlen invited
Cutler to tea at his Georgetown home. The two had attended Harvard con-
temporaneously and both were members of the Porcellian Club. Joining
them was a fellow Porcellian man, Bohlen's neighbor and friend Joe Alsop.
Inevitably, the conversation turned to John Foster Dulles and his handling
of Bohlen's nomination. As Alsop was to write, the insinuation that Bohlen
"of all people" was homosexual was "incredible to anyone who knew him,"
for not only was Bohlen "a married man, closer to his wife than almost
any man I knew," he also enjoyed "a well-deserved reputation, before he
met Avis in Moscow, as one of the most successful ladies' men in Europe."
At one point, Cutler interjected to defend the secretary of state. That a
man with such a "well-established reputation for having what the eminent
English historian Edward Gibbon called 'incorrect tastes in love'" could be
so insouciant about the spreading of baseless homosexual rumors enraged

Bohlen. Before the visibly agitated diplomat could "remind Bobby of his own incorrect tastes," however, Avis "knocked the tea tray off its precarious perch on the coffee table," thereby averting what surely would have been an even worse disturbance.

More revealing of Cutler's sedulous ability to compartmentalize was the role he played in drafting the regulation that enabled the full-scale purge of gay men and women from the federal government. On the very day of Eisenhower's inauguration, Attorney General Herbert Brownell had sent the president a draft executive order that would have heightened internal security protocols for federal hiring, but that made no reference to sexual orientation as a prohibitive factor. Cutler advised Eisenhower to use a different template, a proposed overhaul of the internal security program developed (but never implemented) by the outgoing Truman administration that listed "sexual perversion" as cause for dismissal. Cutler's proposal won the day, which is how a gay man helped codify the most far-reaching and destructive act of federal government discrimination against gay people in American history.

On April 27, 1953, Eisenhower signed Executive Order 10450. In addition to alcoholism, drug addiction, and mental illness, it obligated *every* federal agency to investigate new and existing employees for "sexual perversion" and empowered the Civil Service Commission and the FBI to assist in the process of such investigations. With the signing of this nine-page order, the government's remit in determining suitability for employment now expanded beyond strict considerations of loyalty to the more amorphous category of "security," and this new standard applied not only to people handling classified information at agencies like the State Department and the CIA, but to curators at the Smithsonian Institution and veterinarians at the National Zoo. With 20 percent of Americans working either for the federal government or one of the myriad private contractors that flourished during the postwar economic boom, the effects of 10450 were felt far beyond Washington and its environs. "I think it is a tremendous improvement over the old method," Senator McCarthy crowed at the White House, where he had been invited to a special briefing on the order in his capacity as chairman of the Senate Government Operations Committee. "Altogether it represents a pretty darn good program. I like it. It shows that the new administration was sincere in the campaign to clean house."

As 10450 called for security checks of preexisting federal employees, a wave of dismissals soon swept across Washington as the records of those found to have been involved in past episodes of homosexual activity were dredged up and reexamined. Edwin Louis Cuckenberger had been a White House stenographer for over three years when his building pass was suddenly revoked on June 10, 1953. Six years earlier, while working at the Navy Department, he was discovered engaging in oral sex with another man in a restroom. In a panic, Cuckenberger fled down the hallway and flung himself from the second-floor window onto a concrete driveway, fracturing bones in his right leg and foot. Because of the "implication of suicide," according to a report on the incident, Cuckenberger was rushed to the psychopathic ward of a nearby hospital.

No formal disciplinary measures were leveled against him, nor was he dismissed from his job. This leniency indicates a willingness on the part of at least some government security officers to overlook homosexuality during the brief period between the end of the Second World War and the start of the twinned Red and Lavender Scares. As the 1947 incident fell under the jurisdiction of the navy, it was not reported to the FBI, Metropolitan Police Department, or Civil Service Commission. It was not even included in Cuckenberger's personnel file on record at the White House, where he began working in late 1949. Only after the implementation of 10450 did the Secret Service become aware of this episode, when a "discreet inquiry" resulted in the Office of Naval Intelligence pulling Cuckenberger's file and divulging its details. The White House fired him on the spot.

Most of the investigations and firings of homosexuals occurred within the State Department. "When in doubt, throw him out" was the unofficial mantra of the Bureau of Security and Consular Affairs under the reign of Scott McLeod. McLeod had flirted with liberal politics as a student, and according to his wife, he "was always sympathetic to the case of an employee whose file showed liberal activity in college. He believed it was normal to experiment at that age." This tolerance for youthful ideological experimentation, however, did not extend to other realms of human behavior. "Scotty had the essentially simple approach to a fairy that you will find in a cop who has never had the benefit of, let us say, courses in abnormal psychology at Yale, or some of the other things taught us of normality and abnormality," one colleague recalled. He "had a very black and white approach—and this wasn't white." At one point, McLeod appointed a former journalist for *Time* to compile a monograph for the State Department on how homosexuality had spurred the collapse of great civilizations throughout history. (The writer ultimately concluded that gays could not be blamed for the downfalls of ancient Rome and Greece. The monograph was scrapped.) When one of his investigators overheard a Foreign Service officer complain about "the apish behavior of that jumped-up gumshoe," McLeod initiated an investigation into the young man, which elicited an accusation of a homosexual episode in his distant past. Hauled before a security review committee, the officer confessed the incident and was cleared. After McLeod launched a second investigation and resubmitted the employee for review, the man admitted that there had indeed been more than one episode of homosexuality, but the committee still allowed him to remain in his position. Undeterred, McLeod had the man placed under full-time surveillance and ordered all his friends and relatives interrogated. At this point, a friend of the man recalled, "he broke down completely and told the committee: 'I was, I am, and I probably always will be a homosexual.'" He resigned forthwith.

Peter Szluk was the self-described "hatchet man" in the Bureau of Security and Consular Affairs, and he thoroughly enjoyed swinging his proverbial axe. Gays were "a pretty large percentage" of those he investigated. Szluk could be so pitiless in meting out his vision of justice that colleagues mordantly referred to him as "the social conscience of the State Department." Yet that wasn't to say he didn't occasionally have a soft spot. "The only thing I regret in my campaign to get rid the State Department of that type of individual," he recalled of his work purging gays, "was when within minutes, and sometimes maybe a week, they would commit suicide." One day, Szluk concluded a routine interrogation of an employee accused of homosexuality by telling him, "You're finished." The man promptly stood up from his chair, walked out of the building, and shot himself in the head on the corner of Twenty-First Street and Virginia Avenue.

Unlike in the American justice system, the burden of proof in State Department security cases lay with the accused, and the standards for determining whether an employee was homosexual were utterly arbitrary. "We don't have to prove a man is a duck," McLeod's staff would say. "If he waddles like a duck, quacks like a duck and associates with ducks, that's enough." The Kafkaesque atmosphere both at Foggy Bottom and American diplomatic missions abroad eerily resembled those of the godless Communist regimes the U.S. decried. Robert F. Woodward, who headed the

Foreign Service Personnel division in the early 1950s, recalled the time he successfully recruited a deputy chief of mission, the rank just below ambassador, for the U.S. embassy in Saigon. Shortly before the battle of Dien Bien Phu in 1954, the man was about to report to his new post when the Security division summoned him for an interview. According to Woodward, the criterion for determining whether someone could be dismissed on grounds of sexual perversion was whether there had been "any kind of a homosexual relationship after a date six months from his 21st birthday." Though the officer in question was in his midforties, married, and a father, "in the course of the interrogation, he admitted some kind of a homosexual incident within that narrow margin just after the cut-off date" and was summarily dismissed.

The lack of clear evidentiary standards for determining whether someone was a "sex deviant" naturally created endless opportunities for mischief. One State Department clerk reported to investigators that her female boss had a suspicious relationship with another woman who spoke with a "mannish voice." Though a male employee had just become a father, one of his coworkers alleged that he "is probably a homosexual," a conclusion she reached thanks to her "feminine intuition and the effeminate mannerisms" of the colleague in question. "These mannerisms are reflected by his walk and his 'jelly hand shake,'" she added. The scarcity of actual Communists in government jobs made homosexuals a much easier target. "There were . . . extremely few individuals (employees or applicants) who were denied security clearance due to their association with communism, or its organizations," recalled Joseph C. Walsh, a security officer within the U.S. Information Agency. "By far, the major share of the total number were those admitted homosexuals. It was a nasty business, seeking out and identifying people suspected of homosexuality. A disquieting feature to me—there were several awfully decent and intelligent people who worked within the agency whom I got to know well and enjoyed working with in the agency programs who, suddenly and peremptorily, dropped out of the picture—disappeared!" Private citizens also contributed to the effort. "We suggest that in your search for homosexuals in your Department you look very carefully into the backgrounds of the following people," read an anonymous letter sent to McLeod in April 1953, listing the names of Foreign Service officers posted at American legations from Vienna to Moscow to Tokyo. ("We know one man with whom he has had sexual relations," the informer wrote of one official. "Don't let his ardent Catholicism fool you.") Incredulously, the writer asked McLeod, "How is it you have allowed yourself to be duped by certain of the older FSO's who have gotten married since 1950 when McCarthy began his reign of terror? I think you will find a good number of deviates who are hiding behind marriage if you look closely into their backgrounds."

Around the world, McLeod's regional security officers became the eyes and ears of an international homosexual-detection force. "My informant advised that Warnecki and Stallman have just made arrangements to live together in one of the Embassy houses; that Mr. Cushing has been seen embracing a Korean boy on the streets of Pusan; and that Dilliard is always in the company of Korean males," McLeod wrote in a July 1953 memo summarizing a report on homosexuality at the American embassy in Pusan, the temporary capital of South Korea during the Korean War. An employee in the Madrid embassy was "reported to be effeminate in actions and mannerisms, to use perfume and not to go with girls. He is alleged to be a homosexual." Fired employees at overseas missions were given as little as forty-eight hours to pack their bags and leave their posts. (McLeod's men could be gentle, if necessary. "Our sympathetic and understanding treatment of homosexuals continues to pay dividends," Office of Security director John W. Ford enthused in a note to McLeod in May 1953, explaining how a former Foreign Service officer, terminated after confessing his homosexuality, "came into the office" that morning "requesting advice and offered his cooperation in ferreting out three other employees of the Department whom he had good reason to believe were homosexuals. He admitted a homosexual act with one of the three people mentioned.") As to the concern that innocent people might get swept up in the purge, it was a necessary price to pay for a State Department rid of deviants. "Grenades go off and sometimes hit a lot of people, maybe some they weren't intended to," one investigator shrugged. The conspicuousness and frequency of the expulsions created such an all-pervasive fear that, within a year of McLeod's appointment, some heterosexual employees who contemplated resigning declined to do so for fear that they would be *perceived* as homosexual by future employers. "Suppose I apply for a job in private industry," one employee postulated. "Resigned from the State Department? Why, they'd say, he must be a Commie, or at least a sexual deviate" (the 1950 *New Yorker* cartoon come to life). Overall, McLeod's performance during the Bohlen episode, and his remarkable prolificacy at expelling sex deviates, so impressed McCarthy that the senator privately suggested he consider running for president.

Unlike members of most other minority groups, whose distinguishing traits were visible and therefore difficult if not impossible to hide, gay people could try to suppress that which made them dissidents in what Christopher Isherwood called "the heterosexual dictatorship." But this capacity for concealment was a double-edged sword. While offering the benefit of self-preservation, the closet simultaneously implicated its inhabitants in their own oppression. George Tames, a photographer for the *New York Times*, sublet an apartment from one of McLeod's investigators at the height of the Lavender Scare. At work, Tames's landlord spent his hours rooting out homosexuals from the State Department. Outside the office, he lived the life of the men he surveilled, interrogated, and terminated. "I would get these mysterious phone calls from various people, and sailors knocking on my door at all hours of the night," Tames recalled. "It doesn't take an Einstein to finally realize what was going on."

Gay men, as opposed to lesbians, were the primary victims of the Lavender Scare. The main reason for this disparity was the simple fact that male federal government employees were far more likely than women to hold jobs requiring security clearances, which in turn made them more susceptible to scrutiny from government investigators. Furthermore, the ways that many gay men at the time sought sexual partners (cruising in public places) often brought them into conflict with the law. Finally, in terms of cultural disgust, media hysteria, criminalization, entrapment operations, government surveillance, medical "cures," and military discharges, antigay sentiment and persecution generally targeted male homosexuals more severely than female ones, a consequence, in part, of patriarchal attitudes privileging men over women. Men and masculinity were deemed more important than women and femininity, so, it followed that male sexual deviance was deemed a greater threat to society than lesbianism. "The government didn't even recognize lesbian women in the Foreign Service because women's role was never considered sufficiently important," recalled Barbara J. Good, who worked as a recruiter in the State Department's personnel branch in the 1960s.

All told, an estimated 7,000 to 10,000 federal employees lost their jobs owing to homosexuality in the 1950s alone, a figure that, extrapolated over time, is comparable to the estimated 14,700 people who were fired or resigned due to their political associations during the Red Scare. No statistic, however, can possibly capture the far-reaching impact that the Lavender Scare had on individual lives, public policy, and American society, just one component of which is the incalculable reserve of talent denied the country. Roger D. "Denny" Hansen was a champion swimmer, Yale graduate, and all-around young man of exceptional promise when *Life* magazine published a photo montage of him enjoying life as a Rhodes Scholar at Oxford University in 1957. Only a few years later, however, Hansen was denied a job in the Foreign Service, a rejection he came to believe was the result of someone notifying the State Department that he was gay. "The motor began to sputter right there, when the accusation to the State Department confirmed his secret fears that the life of limitless possibilities supposedly open to him could never really be," wrote Calvin Trillin in *Remembering Denny*, a reflection on the life of his Yale classmate. In 1991, after a decades-long bout with depression, Hansen locked himself in a friend's garage, turned on the ignition of his car, and sat there until the fumes took his life away.

★ ★ ★

"THERE HAVE BEEN MANY SUICIDES DUE TO THE SMEARING received either in Committee hearings or from remarks made in the United States Congress," Democratic senator Lester Hunt of Wyoming wrote a friend in October 1951. A self-described "progressive liberal, but not a radical," Hunt had earlier that year proposed a constitutional amendment to revoke the "Speech or Debate" clause that granted immunity to members of Congress for statements made on the House and Senate floors. In an article for the *New York Times Magazine* explaining the "dangers of Congressional immunity," Hunt lambasted his colleagues for exploiting their constitutional prerogative. "If situations confront the Congress in which it can no longer control its members by the rules of society, justice and fair play," he wrote, without naming any senator in particular, "then the Congress has, I feel, a moral obligation to remedy those situations."

Six months after indirectly accusing his fellow senators of driving innocent men and women to their deaths, Hunt's older brother, Clyde, shot himself in the head with a .22-caliber rifle near his ranch outside Denver, Colorado. Although unrelated, the ravages of McCarthyism and the suicide of Clyde Hunt were to become tragically linked.

The series of events leading to this terrible denouement began at around 10:15 p.m. on June 9, 1953. Lester "Buddy" Hunt Jr., Hunt's twenty-five-year-old son and the student body president at the Episcopal Theological School in Cambridge, Massachusetts, was spending the summer in Washington. Walking across Lafayette Square, he locked eyes with a man "trying to attract my attention." Buddy approached the handsome stranger and invited him back to his home for what the man, an undercover member of Roy Blick's vice squad, would later describe as the commission of "an unnatural act." With his arrest for sexual solicitation, Buddy became one of the over a thousand men apprehended annually in Washington for this crime. But his status as a first-time offender, seminary student, and son of a senator persuaded Roy Blick and the local prosecutor's office to let him go with only a warning.

This would have been the end of Buddy Hunt's troubles had not Republican senator Herman Welker, a McCarthy sycophant often referred to as "Little Joe from Idaho," got wind of his arrest. Sensing a political opportunity in the near-evenly divided chamber, Welker threatened Hunt Sr. that unless he dropped out of the 1954 Senate race, Welker would expose Buddy's incident in Lafayette Square. Hunt already faced an uphill battle for reelection. Though he was popular with Wyoming voters, his state was overwhelmingly Republican and had supported President Eisenhower by a wide margin. More concerning to Hunt about Welker's threat, however, was its heavily implied involvement of Joe McCarthy. Upon his election to the Senate in 1948, Hunt had taken an immediate dislike to his colleague from Wisconsin. It was McCarthy's reckless behavior that had inspired Hunt to put forward a constitutional amendment revoking congressional immunity, and while the amendment went nowhere, in the two years since Hunt proposed it, McCarthy had only grown stronger, acquiring what his biographer David Oshinsky describes as an "aura of political invincibility." The farthest that any of McCarthy's Republican senatorial colleagues had gone in criticizing him was Margaret Chase Smith in 1950, with her "Declaration of Conscience," an honorable rebuke to demagoguery, yet one that, like Hunt's article in the *New York Times Magazine*, did not refer to McCarthy by name. Meanwhile, McCarthy laid waste to the State Department, the CIA, and the Voice of America (among other agencies), in the process earning the distinction of becoming, in the words of Richard Rovere, "the first American ever to be actively hated and feared by foreigners in large numbers."

McCarthy could act with such impunity because of the broad support he enjoyed from Americans across the country, which he brandished by playing the role of kingmaker in several tight Senate races. In 1950, he campaigned in Maryland for the Republican candidate who unseated Millard Tydings, and two years later, he helped defeat Hunt's fellow Wyomingite Joe O'Mahoney. McCarthy flexed his muscles as a power broker through omission as well as commission. In Massachusetts, where he was extremely popular with the state's blue-collar Irish Catholics, he declined to campaign alongside his Republican colleague, Henry Cabot Lodge Jr., at the request of a friend whose son was mounting a challenge to the incumbent. McCarthy's abstention proved decisive in Congressman John F. Kennedy's upset victory.

Welker's threat weighed heavily on Hunt, but he was a man of firm principle. After discussing the matter with his wife, Nathelle, Hunt told Welker that he had no intention of withdrawing from the race. The next day, a story about Buddy Hunt's arrest appeared in the *Washington Times-Herald*, which, upon the death of Cissy Patterson in 1948, had been purchased by her cousin, the rabidly pro-McCarthy *Chicago Tribune* publisher Col. Robert McCormick. Just a little over a decade earlier, in what it termed "one of the most despicable attempts at character assassination that could be conceived," the *Tribune* condemned the smear campaign against David Walsh. But the rules of engagement had shifted fundamentally, and a tactic that one would have denounced as unconscionable when deployed against a friend was now fair game when used to destroy a foe.

With Buddy's story now public, Welker and his Republican colleague Styles Bridges used their positions as members of the Committee on the District of Columbia to put pressure on the local police and prosecutor's office to bring him to trial. Disregarding Roy Blick's insistence that normal procedures had been followed and that to prosecute a seminarian on a charge of sexual solicitation "would break down the religious foundations here in the country," Welker and Bridges handed Blick an envelope containing a typed resignation letter in his name. Unless he did as they instructed, the pair warned, they would expose corruption within his vice squad. Blick recused himself from the case, criminal charges against Buddy were subsequently filed, and a trial date was set for the fall.

As his father listened supportively in the courtroom, Buddy explained the events of June 9. "I felt he was soliciting me," he told the court about his encounter with the undercover police officer, demonstrating the subjectivity inherent to the charge of solicitation. Not only was it impossible to say who had solicited whom, but Buddy's suggestion to the officer that they retire to his private residence obviated the government's legitimate interest in prohibiting sex in public places. Buddy was not guilty of solicitation, his lawyer argued, but the victim of entrapment. The trial lasted two days, and in his explanation of the verdict, Judge John J. Malloy acknowledged the centrality of the point raised by the defense, stating that the case ultimately came down to "a question of whether Hunt solicited the officer or the officer solicited Hunt." And much hung on the answer to this question, Malloy explained, because the crime with which Buddy had been charged was "one of the most degrading that . . . [could] be made against a man."

Buddy, the judge ruled, was guilty. While the punishment was only a one-hundred-dollar fine, Buddy's name would forever be blackened with the mark of criminal sexual deviancy. Devastated by the decision, Nathelle Hunt was unable to eat for a week, and, according to Drew Pearson, Senator Hunt's hair "turned almost white."

For Senators Welker and Bridges, however, it was far too early to declare victory. They had yet to achieve their goal of pressuring Hunt Sr. into relinquishing his seat. As the two prepared their next move, their confederate McCarthy careened toward oblivion, his four-year reign of terror about to implode in a nationally televised display of hubris and corruption instigated by the homosexual lust of a young and ambitious apprentice.

13

PIXIES ON THE POTOMAC

THROUGH THE EXPLODING FLASHBULBS AND HEAVY CIGARETTE SMOKE wafting high up into the cavernous, marble-columned hearing room of the Senate Permanent Subcommittee on Investigations on April 22, 1954, one could discern the most enduring image of the spectacle that would soon captivate America: Joe McCarthy's twenty-seven-year-old chubby, raccoon-eyed chief counsel sitting next to him, whispering in his ear.

An audience of some eighty million, more than half the population of the United States, would watch at least some portion of the 187 total televised hours of what came to be called the Army-McCarthy Hearings. Department stores reported a sharp spike in the sale of television sets and a concomitant decline in daytime shopping, as people sat glued to their screens at home. One hundred twenty newspaper and magazine reporters were accredited to cover the event, and the Capitol Police estimated that 115,000 spectators attended over the course of its thirty-six days. Among the many VIPs were Teddy Roosevelt's daughter Alice Roosevelt Long-worth and the legendary socialite Perle Mesta. Usually, Mesta spent the verdant spring months hosting parties at Les Ormes, her French château–style mansion. But the hearings overshadowed the city's social life like a solar eclipse, and so Mesta declared a temporary moratorium on entertaining.

"I can't compete with this," the "hostess with the most-est" said with resignation, gesturing toward the packed committee room. At the sight of Mesta, McCarthy could barely contain his excitement. "I've never been to any of her parties, but here she is at mine," he giddily whispered to his chief counsel, whose curious ardency for another man had precipitated the hearings and attendant media frenzy.

The son of a politically well-connected New York State Supreme Court justice and a domineering heiress, Roy Marcus Cohn became fascinated with power as a young boy when the British royal abdication crisis unfolded on newspaper front pages and radio waves around the world. That a king would voluntarily relinquish his rule over a global empire owing to something so nebulous as love for another person must have made a strong impression on Cohn, for whom the ruthless accumulation of power, even at the expense of deep and meaningful relationships with other human beings, became a lifelong pursuit. Cohn's astonishing journey into the most exclusive circles of the American legal, media, and political elite began at the phase in life when most of his peers were making their awkward, fumbling first attempts at courtship with members of the opposite sex. At fifteen, he had already arranged his first kickback, connecting the father of a friend who wanted to purchase a radio station with a Federal Communications Commission lawyer happy to pull some strings. Cohn's path to the top traversed New York's exclusive Horace Mann School, where classmates described him in the yearbook as a "man behind the scenes," and Columbia University, from which he graduated with both bachelor of arts and law degrees in just three years, at the age of twenty.

Cohn had to wait a year before he was old enough to take the bar exam, and once he passed, he began to make a name for himself prosecuting Communist Party members as an assistant U.S. attorney for the Southern District of New York. The most high-profile case Cohn argued was that of Julius and Ethel Rosenberg, a married couple accused of purloining state secrets concerning the Manhattan Project and passing them along to the Soviets. The Justice Department's deliberate selection of a Jewish judge to hear the case and Jewish government attorneys like Cohn to try it reflected a well-grounded concern that the prosecution of two Communist Jews for espionage at a time of mounting Cold War tension might inflame anti-Semitism. Helping to send his fellow Jews, who had failed the ultimate test of assimilation by betraying their country, to the electric chair provided

Cohn with firsthand knowledge of where deviation from American political norms could lead for members of a minority group, a lesson even more
pertinent for those who, like him, deviated from sexual ones. And so began
a lifelong pattern by which Cohn sublimated those aspects of himself that
made him an outsider into a relentless ambition to become an insider, and
consequently pursued political power as a form of personal protection.

In September 1952, Cohn moved to Washington to become a special
assistant to Attorney General James McGranery. Bypassing his boss, who
would likely be leaving the Justice Department after the coming Republican
sweep, Cohn curried favor with the face of permanent institutional power
in Washington, J. Edgar Hoover. The FBI director appreciated the gesture,
telling Cohn that he ought to feel no compunction in circumventing the
Justice Department chain of command, because the "gossips" there were
"worse than the perverts at the CIA." It was inevitable that this whip-smart,
cunning, and ferocious anticommunist would get noticed and snatched up
by McCarthy, who hired him as chief counsel after the election. As the
committee's new chairman, McCarthy had the power to launch his own
investigations into Communist subversion, and who better to have at his
side than the young man who had sealed the fate of the Rosenbergs? Soon,
Cohn was McCarthy's closest advisor, hailed by the chairman for being "as
indispensable as I am" and trailing him everywhere, including on midnight
walks around Capitol Hill with McCarthy's Doberman pinscher. For those
who worked in proximity to Cohn, it was sometimes hard to tell the difference between the wily aide and the menacing canine. Surveying some of
his colleagues on and off the Hill, *Time* magazine identified in Cohn "a trait
that still rankles his associates: contempt of all but the top boss."

There was one glaring exception to this rule, however. When McCarthy
hired G. David Schine on Cohn's express advice in 1953, no one could have
guessed that Schine would quickly become "America's most public private,"
the man at the center of a national scandal, and the unwitting agent of Joe
McCarthy's political demise. The twenty-six-year-old, six-foot-four-inch,
blond-haired hotel chain heir did not seem to possess any qualifications
for the unpaid job of "chief consultant" that McCarthy gave him. As an
undergraduate at Harvard, Schine glided around Cambridge in a Cadillac
outfitted with a state-of-the-art (and outrageously expensive) radio phone,
and hired a personal secretary to attend classes in his stead. To be sure, he
had written a bromidic pamphlet entitled *Definition of Communism*, the

readership of which was limited to the guests at his family's lodging establishments who happened to come across it in the nightstand drawer next
to the King James Bible. But when Cohn was asked for examples of Schine's
relevant work in the field of countersubversion and answered that the hospitality scion had "written some plans for fighting communism through
psychological warfare which were used in part by the Defense Department
in the previous administration," it didn't take long for a reporter to call up
the Pentagon and discover that this wasn't true. Given the scant credentials of the committee's chief consultant, some began to question whether
Cohn's interest had an ulterior motivation, perhaps related to the fortune
of Schine's father, J. Myer Schine (who once threw a party for the Duke
and Duchess of Windsor, the couple whose dramatic love story had so
enraptured—and perplexed—the young Cohn). Or, as others suspected,
perhaps Cohn's fondness had something to do with Schine's possession of
what *Time* described as the "build and features of a junior-grade Greek
god." Whatever the reason, it had to have been compelling. For when
Schine received his draft notice, Cohn became so obsessed with pressuring the army into giving him special treatment that he unwittingly helped
destroy McCarthy's "aura of invincibility."

That aura had protected McCarthy for four whole years while he alleged
Communist subversion of the State Department, the Voice of America,
and even George Marshall. It would evaporate, however, once he decided
to target the army, a confrontation he initiated largely at Cohn's urging.
By pitting himself against a widely admired institution and the popular
president who had led it to glorious victory overseas, McCarthy signed
his own political death warrant. His blundering into this hopeless battle
was of his own doing, but his downfall was one in which the young chief
counsel whispering in his ear—the "Boy Rasputin," as Michael Straight of
the *New Republic* called Cohn—played a decisive role. The lurid backstory
to this series of events was what made a seat in Room 318 of the Senate
Office Building the hottest ticket in Washington since Whittaker Chambers and Alger Hiss appeared in that same hall for their own "Confrontation Day." And like that drama of six years before, this one also involved
allegations of Communist espionage and intimations of secret homosexual
passion.

According to Attorney General Herbert Brownell, the most noticeable
facet of Cohn and Schine was that they were "inseparable." This insepara-

bility was the most talked-about feature of the disastrous European tour they had made in April 1953, ostensibly to investigate the presence of anti-American, socialistic books on the shelves at U.S. libraries overseas. As Cohn later lamented, what had been intended as a serious effort in the crusade against international communism "turned out to be one of the most publicized trips of the decade" and "a colossal mistake." From their first stop in Paris, where they checked into the lavish Hotel de Crillon, to Munich, where Schine was spotted playfully batting Cohn over the head with a rolled-up magazine, the ten-city, eighteen-day jaunt, wrote Richard Rovere, was covered "by as many journalists as normally are assigned only to such eminences as kings, Presidents, Prime Ministers, and Rita Hayworth." Despite their expressed intention to fight the Communist infiltration of American libraries, Cohn and Schine seemed to spend the bulk of their time hassling members of the U.S. diplomatic corps, trashing hotel rooms, insulting their European hosts, and generally bringing the reputation of the United States into disrepute. "Junketeering gumshoes" was the imperishable description of the pair offered by a Bonn-based Foreign Service officer, upon whom Cohn exacted retribution by dredging up a two-decade-old play that the man had written as a college student supposedly reeking of Communistic affinities. Hauling the diplomat before McCarthy's committee, Cohn forced his resignation. "We have passed beyond the Kafka phase and are moving into Dostoievsky," Arthur Schlesinger wrote to Adlai Stevenson of this particularly egregious, and petty, abuse of power.

Cohn and Schine's trip inspired other, less literary allusions. "Keep those two pansies away from me or I'm going to ask them who buggers who" is how one deputy Treasury attaché stationed in Germany remembered his reaction to hearing that the pair planned to visit his diplomatic mission. In Paris, Drew Pearson reported, the men borrowed hundreds of dollars from an embassy official to buy "perfume." Aware of the impression their antics were creating, Cohn and Schine pretended to be in on the joke, loudly reassuring a Munich hotel clerk that they wanted separate rooms because "we don't work for the State Department."

The fun and games came to an end that summer, when Schine received his draft notice. Even before the letter arrived in the mail, Cohn had requested that the army grant his colleague a direct commission as an officer, thereby exempting him from basic training. When the army refused Cohn's entreaties, he tried his luck with the navy and air force, to no avail.

With Schine bound to report for his induction along with the three hundred thousand other young American men drafted that year, Cohn began a relentless campaign to pressure the army into granting the new private various forms of special treatment, such as abstention from kitchen duty, assignment at a base close to New York City, and extra leave so that Schine could "work on committee business." Cohn frequently enlisted McCarthy in these efforts, teaming up with the committee chairman to berate and badger army officials. Alas, the Pentagon was not the Bronx Democratic Party machine of Cohn's salad days. Nor did Cohn seem to realize the conflict of interest inherent in his pressuring the army to dispense favors for a friend while the committee for which he served as chief counsel was simultaneously investigating an army base at Fort Monmouth, New Jersey, for Communist subversion. The army refused to submit to this extraordinarily capricious abuse of the committee's oversight power, and on the order of the White House, it released a meticulously documented and dispassionately worded chronology listing forty-four episodes over a period of eight months in which Cohn or McCarthy applied pressure to secure preferment for Schine. According to the report, Cohn had used "extremely vituperative language" in his dealings with army staff (both uniformed and civilian), threatened to "wreck the Army," and told the secretary of the army that if he did not accede to Cohn's wishes, he would be "through."

The timeline also revealed something strange about the troublesome triumvirate of the senator, the chief counsel, and their consultant. Whenever McCarthy was in Cohn's presence, he was just as insistent as Cohn was in ordering the military brass to treat Schine differently from the hoi polloi. But when Cohn was absent, McCarthy referred to Schine as "a pest" who "was of no help to the committee" and was "interested in photographers and getting his pictures in the paper." McCarthy stressed, though, that he "did not want Mr. Cohn to know of these views on Mr. Schine." Indeed, McCarthy behaved as if there were nothing he could do about the situation, that even if he fired Cohn, the boy wonder "would carry on his campaign against the Army thereafter from outside Washington . . . through the medium of connections with various newspaper elements . . ."

There was something unmistakably queer about these three men. Just what was going on?

"Biggest mystery in Washington still is why the supposedly fearless McCarthy is deathly afraid of pint-sized, 27-year-old Roy Cohn," wrote

Drew Pearson, who also wanted to know what explained the "persistent attachment of Cohn for Schine." To Joe and Stewart Alsop, "The implication is clear that Cohn possessed a peculiar power over McCarthy." It was surely a "sordid" and "grossly indecent" tale, they wrote, though the exact sources of "Cohn's feverish desire to be of service to Schine" and "the strength of Cohn's apparent hold on McCarthy" remained mysteries. John Adams, Cohn's counterpart in the army, witnessed this hold most vividly during an encounter in New York City. Adams "genuinely liked Cohn. Except where Schine was concerned, I saw him as the only restraining influence on McCarthy." These roles would be reversed following a contentious lunch when Cohn offered Adams and McCarthy a ride toward Penn Station all the while "raining systematic abuse" upon the senator, his ostensible superior. At one point, Cohn grew so furious that he stopped the car and kicked Adams out onto the sidewalk. After driving three more blocks, he meted out the same punishment to McCarthy. Sen. Charles Potter, a moderate Republican on the committee, was blunt in his assessment of Cohn: "His campaign over David Schine bordered on lunacy."

McCarthy claimed that it was not he and Cohn who had acted inappropriately, but the army, which was using Schine as a "hostage" to "blackmail" his committee over its investigation. On March 14, Cohn appeared on *Meet the Press* to substantiate his boss's charge of blackmail, throwing in a bit of homosexually themed intrigue of his own. "A specific proposal was made to us that we go after an Air Force base wherein, Mr. Adams told us, there were a number of sex deviates and that that would make excellent hearings for us," Cohn told the group of journalists who composed the show's panel. The army, Cohn alleged, had offered dirt on a rival branch of the military in exchange for getting McCarthy "off the Army's back." May Craig, a correspondent for the *Portland Press Herald*, asked Cohn if an investigation ought to be held "to find out whether you have any hold on Senator McCarthy which would induce him to keep you on." Another panelist asked about Cohn's "extravagant concern for your friend Dave Schine." All these "hideous accusations and insinuations" were deeply upsetting to Westbrook Pegler, a man otherwise extremely alert to the problem of perverts in high places, but who in this case detected "a foul, dirty deal to stop the McCarthy inquiry" into communist infiltration of the army from pressing forward.

With accusations flying back and forth between McCarthy and Cohn on one side, and the army on the other, a subcommittee was formed to, in effect, investigate the investigators. The first witness to testify on April 22 was Gen. Miles Reber, who as the army's congressional liaison had been the first target of Cohn's bullying. Reber calmly told the committee how Cohn had called twice a day "urging" him to expedite the request for Schine's commission. By coincidence, Reber's brother Samuel, a twenty-seven-year Foreign Service veteran, had been acting high commissioner for Germany the previous year during the "junketeering gumshoes" jaunt. Cohn, who held Samuel responsible for the bad press he had received during the trip, forced his resignation by threatening to expose a homosexual incident in his past. When it was his turn to question General Reber, McCarthy broached this sensitive subject, one of the more blatant examples of his predilection for evidence-free guilt-by-association. "Are you aware of the fact that your brother was allowed to resign when charges that he was a bad security risk were made against him as a result of the investigations of this committee?" the senator not so much asked as announced.

The State Department had allowed Samuel Reber to resign quietly under the pretense that he had reached the voluntary retirement age of fifty. Now, before a nationwide audience of millions, he had been exposed as a homosexual to discredit testimony suggesting that the man who had accused him was also a homosexual. Fuming at this hypocrisy, but helpless to do anything about it, General Reber clenched the sides of the witness table so hard that his knuckles turned white.

* * *

"IF YOU WANT TO BE AGAINST MCCARTHY, boys, you've got to be either a communist or a cocksucker." So declared the junior senator from Wisconsin early in his campaign against both pariah groups, and in so doing made himself a target for innuendo about his own political and sexual proclivities. It would have been an inspired move on the part of the Kremlin to suborn a right-wing demagogue to discredit the cause of anticommunism, and more than a few of McCarthy's liberal anticommunist critics half-seriously suggested that it had. Similarly, the senator's public attacks on homosexuals led some to wonder if he was overcompensating for a private shame.

In May 1950, three months after McCarthy's Wheeling speech, Drew Pearson predicted on his radio program that the senator's "outcry against sex unfortunates in the State Department is about to backfire," as a member of his own staff had been arrested for homosexual solicitation. In response, McCarthy spread a rumor that Pearson had molested an African American boy. That December, an oblivious (or mischievous) hostess seated the columnist and the senator at the same table for a dinner at the elegant Sulgrave Club, a private women's association housed in a Beaux Arts–style mansion on Dupont Circle. Ever the gentleman, McCarthy told Pearson's wife that he was planning to deliver a speech on the floor of the Senate the following day that would lead her to divorce her husband. Pearson responded with a joke about McCarthy's tax returns. As reflected in the front-page *Washington Post* headline the following morning—"Sen. McCarthy Either Kicked, Slapped or Mauled Pearson"—accounts of what happened next vary. Following the meal, McCarthy and Pearson confronted each other in the coatroom, where Pearson claimed McCarthy kneed him in the groin. The altercation was broken up by Sen. Richard Nixon, but not before McCarthy got in a final slap. "That was for you, Dick," the senator said, before storming out. "I never saw a man slapped so hard," Nixon recalled. "If I hadn't pulled McCarthy away, he might have killed" Pearson.

Two days later, on the Senate floor, McCarthy delivered on his promise to Luvie Moore Pearson. "I realize the task of exposing this man, or perhaps I should say this person, will be an unpleasant, disagreeable task," he began, before labeling the columnist a "prostitute of the great profession of journalism" as well as a "degenerate liar" with a "twisted, perverted mentality." Needless to say, the Pearson marriage remained intact.

Pearson, however, refused to drop the grudge. He started a file on McCarthy filled with affidavits from men claiming sexual congress with him. Assisting Pearson was Democratic senator William Benton of Connecticut, whose staff obtained a statement, later proven to be a hoax, from an army lieutenant alleging that McCarthy had picked him up one night at the Wardman Park Hotel, plied him with liquor, and "committed sodomy" upon him. The *Milwaukee Journal Sentinel*, an anti-McCarthy paper, received reports from numerous men—none of which it ever printed—claiming they had sex with the senator. Taking McCarthy's own tactics as inspiration, one of its editors devised a creative idea for circumventing what he considered to be the paper's antiquated sense of journalistic propriety. A reporter could simply call every close friend and associate of McCarthy and ask point-blank if they thought he was a homosexual. If all of them answered in the negative, the paper would simply run a story reporting that "Thirty-five of McCarthy's closest friends deny that he is a homosexual." If, say, seven declined to answer, the headline would read, "Twenty-eight out of 35 of McCarthy's closest friends deny." Alas, the paper's top brass rejected this inspired proposal.

The most relentless propagator of the homosexual charge was Hank Greenspun, publisher of the *Las Vegas Sun*. A former publicity agent for mobster Bugsy Siegel's Flamingo Hotel who had been convicted of smuggling weapons to Israel during its war for independence, Greenspun saw in McCarthy the sort of demagogue America had defeated in the most recent world war. When McCarthy clumsily called Greenspun a "confessed ex-Communist," later admitting that he had meant to say "confessed ex-convict," during a 1952 campaign swing through Nevada, he earned the irascible publisher's undying enmity. From the perch of his daily front-page column, Where I Stand, Greenspun laid the innuendo (and sometimes a lot more than innuendo) on thick. "Joe McCarthy is a bachelor of 43 years" who "seldom dates girls and if he does, he laughingly describes it as window dressing," Greenspun wrote in response to McCarthy's attack. The senator, he charged, had "engaged in illicit acts" with a male former official in the Milwaukee County Young Republicans. Indeed, Greenspun elaborated, "It is common talk among homosexuals in Milwaukee who rendezvous at the White Horse Inn that Sen. Joe McCarthy has often engaged in homosexual activities. The persons in Nevada who listened to McCarthy's radio talk thought he had the queerest laugh. He has. He is."

As McCarthy's investigation of the army began generating headlines in the early months of 1954, Greenspun intensified his attacks both in frequency and lewdness. McCarthy, he declared, was "a sadist and a pervert" who "has been operating through a defense mechanism caused by a guilt complex." By waging a war against homosexuals in government, McCarthy hoped to "avert suspicion from himself," for "the plain unvarnished truth is that McCarthy, by his own admission is a security risk on the grounds of homosexuality." Two days later, Greenspun wrote that McCarthy walked down Senate corridors with "a gait which is a little to the left of manly"; that "in order to qualify as a member of the inner sanctum of the McCarthy cabinet, one must be a liar, a communist, a pervert, or all three"; and that "being a member of the 'Gay' set is almost a condition precedent to landing a job" on the senator's staff. Greenspun observed that there were only two things for Americans to fear about the senator. The first was that "if the person is a woman, don't get too close to McCarthy in a swimming pool." (The reason being that McCarthy "looks upon them as rivals in the game of love.") Second, "If a man, don't let him kiss you on the lips." As for McCarthy's retinue of admirers in the "extreme-right wing press" and among "some leaders of government," it "can only be compared to Hitlerian orgies . . . They are cavorting in a make-believe land, a virtual fairyland."

According to Cohn, McCarthy professed feeling a sense of validation at these attacks, which he claimed stood him in a grand American tradition. "Why should I get sore?" the senator told his chief counsel. "They called Jefferson the bastard son of an Indian woman, Lincoln a lunatic and a drunk, Roosevelt a Jew-bastard, and Grover Cleveland a lecherous old man." On September 29, 1953, McCarthy abruptly put an end to his conspicuous bachelorhood in a ceremony blessed by Pope Pius at the Cathedral of St. Matthew in Washington. Before an audience of a thousand including Vice President Nixon, White House chief of staff Sherman Adams, and a trio of Kennedys (patriarch Joe, Massachusetts senator John, and McCarthy's former assistant counsel on the investigations subcommittee, Bobby), McCarthy married his secretary, a onetime college beauty queen named Jean Kerr. The nuptials quieted much of the speculation about the senator's private life, but one man remained defiantly unpersuaded. "Even Hitler went respectable after he came to power in Germany," Greenspun wrote. "He gave up Ernst Roehm for Eva Braun and later had Roehm killed to bury his past."

A crowd of twenty-five hundred onlookers waited outside St. Matthew's for the happy couple to emerge. When the senator finally appeared on the steps with his new bride, "despite the pleadings of a horde of photographers," he declined to kiss her.

* * *

"HAVE YOU NO SENSE OF DECENCY, SIR, AT LONG LAST?" Joseph Welch, the Boston Brahmin lawyer serving pro bono as chief counsel for the army, pleaded with Joe McCarthy. "Have you left no sense of decency?"

Spoken on the thirtieth day of the hearings, these are the most famous words to have come from the hundreds of hours of testimony produced during that two-month-long media spectacle; indeed, they are some of the most famous words in the history of American politics.

McCarthy had prompted them just moments earlier, by dredging up the fact that a lawyer on Welch's team belonged to a Communist front group as a young man. What this had to do with Communist subversion of the military, or Private Schine's draft status, was a good question, and Welch seized upon McCarthy's scurrilous attack against a private citizen to illustrate, with dramatic effect, the wanton irresponsibility of his tactics. "If it were in my *power* to forgive you for your reckless cruelty, I would do so," Welch told the senator, tears forming in his eyes. "I like to think I'm a gentle man, but your forgiveness will have to come from someone other than me."

Welch is justly remembered for the pivotal role he played in turning the tide of public opinion against McCarthy. With this devastating, made-for-TV reproach that resounds into the present day, he dealt a rhetorical blow to McCarthyism from which its namesake never recovered. In January, before the hearings began, McCarthy enjoyed an approval rating of 50 percent, and practically his every utterance made national headlines. After the hearings, that figure dropped to 34 percent, and by the end of the year, the Senate formally censured him for conduct "contrary to senatorial traditions." Three years later, McCarthy drank himself to death. Welch, by contrast, became a hero of American liberalism and a national treasure. Hollywood inevitably beckoned, and he reprised his real-life role as an advocate for truth and justice by playing a judge in director Otto Preminger's 1959 courtroom drama, *Anatomy of a Murder*.

Less well remembered is Welch's own trip to the rhetorical gutter at the outset of the hearings. On April 30, Welch objected to McCarthy's introducing as evidence a photograph depicting Schine and army secretary Robert T. Stevens standing next to each other and smiling. Taken a few days after McCarthy and Cohn had, according to the army chronology, started pressuring Stevens over Schine's military service, the photo was intended to dispute this charge by showing the secretary interacting amiably with the man whose draft status was supposedly causing him so much aggravation. Welch alleged that the photo had been "doctored" so as to hide the fact that Schine and Stevens were not standing together alone, but rather, were posing as part of a larger group of people who had been cropped out of the image. Questioning a member of McCarthy's staff as to the provenance of the photograph, Welch asked in frustration if it "came from a pixie."

"Will Counsel for my benefit define—I think he might be an expert on that—what a pixie is?" McCarthy interrupted.

"Yes, I should say, Mr. Senator," Welch replied, not missing a beat, "that a pixie is a close relative of a fairy."

The room erupted in nervous laughter. It was the first time during the hearing that anyone had addressed the homosexual undercurrent so central to it. McCarthy snickered; Cohn, at whom the joke was clearly directed, displayed a nervous smile. Welch, who pursued this line of questioning with "the look of the happy leprechaun," had at long last identified, albeit in a coded way, the heart of the matter.

Two weeks later, homosexuals again served as fodder for public amusement when army counsel John Adams addressed Cohn's claim that he had offered the committee dirt on a homosexual scandal in the air force in exchange for its backing off the investigation at Fort Monmouth. Adams denied having made any such quid pro quo and added that the army was investigating its own homosexual scandal on a base located somewhere in the South. "It wasn't in Tennessee, Mr. Adams, was it?" Ray Jenkins, the committee's special counsel and a proud native of Knoxville, drawled in jest. After Adams reassured Jenkins that it was not, Sen. John McClellan of Arkansas raised a point of order.

"Let's exclude Arkansas," he said.

"I can do that sir," Adams replied.

Concerned that millions of viewers across the land might, by process of elimination, get the wrong impression of *his* state, Sen. Karl Mundt of South Dakota exercised his prerogative as chairman. "The Chair would like to raise a point of order in behalf of South Dakota, which might also be included in the South."

"I can include all of the States of the members of this committee," Adams announced to laughter.

On May 28, Jenkins asked Cohn a series of highly suggestive questions pertaining to his relationship with Schine.

JENKINS: In all fairness, Mr. Cohn, isn't it a fact that he is one of your best friends? We all have our best friends. There is no criticism of you on that account.

COHN: No, of course not, sir.

JENKINS: We have friends whom we love. I do. And the relationship between you and Dave Schine has been very close for the past two years, hasn't it?

COHN: Yes, sir. He is one of a number of good friends I am proud to have.

JENKINS: Have you known him socially?

COHN: I have.

JENKINS: Visited in his home?

COHN: Yes, sir.

JENKINS: He has visited in your home?

COHN: Yes, sir.

JENKINS: And perhaps you have had double-dated together. There is no reflection on anything about that. You are both single men as we understand it.

COHN: We have been on double dates, sir.

Later, Jenkins asked Cohn about a specific visit to Schine's apartment at the Waldorf Towers in New York City.

JENKINS: Had you spent the night there?

COHN: Had I spent the night there?

JENKINS: Yes.

COHN: No, sir.

JENKINS: You were there for breakfast.

COHN: I spent the night at my own home.

JENKINS: Mr. Cohn, you and this boy, Dave Schine, as a matter of fact, now, were almost constant companions as good, warm personal friends are, weren't you? That is the truth about it?

COHN: I am pleased to say, sir, the truth is that we were and are good friends. He is one of my many good friends. I hope you will not ask me to scale which one is a better friend. I have a lot of good friends, and I like them and I respect them all.

By June 1, Sen. Ralph Flanders had grown exasperated with all this beating around the bush. Vacationing with his wife in Australia and New Zealand the previous year, not a single day went by that the Vermont Republican was not confronted with a litany of questions from concerned antipodeans about the antics of his colleague from Wisconsin. The televised hearings were exposing McCarthy's tactics to a national audience in real time, and Flanders felt the moment was ripe to launch a full-frontal attack. In a speech to his colleagues from the well of the Senate, Flanders likened McCarthy to the popular cartoon strip character Dennis the Menace, leaving a path of destruction wherever he went. Dennis was single-handedly ruining America's image overseas, Flanders declared, distracting the nation from the real fight against international communism with his domestic witch hunts. He had accomplished the amazing feat of convincing his fellow Republicans to hunt for Communists within a Republican administration in an election year. Flanders was only getting started. "The committee has not yet dug into the real heart of the mystery," he continued.

> That mystery concerns the personal relationships of the Army private, the staff assistant, and the Senator.
>
> This hubbub centers on the Army private. What is it really all about? His usefulness as an investigator is continually asserted, but never documented. Let him also be investigated. When he is released for committee work, what does he do hour by hour? Whom does he see? What material does he analyze? What does he report? These questions are important and unanswered.
>
> Then, there is the relationship of the staff assistant to the Army private. It is natural that he should wish to retain the services of an able collaborator, but he seems to have an almost passionate anxiety to retain him. Why?
>
> And then, there is the Senator himself. At times he seems anxious to rid himself of the whole mess, and then again, at least in the presence of his assistant, he strongly supports the latter's efforts to keep the Army private's services available. Does the assistant have some hold on the Senator?

Reflecting on this speech thirteen years after he delivered it, Flanders observed, "Anybody with half an eye could see what was going on." But even then, Flanders declined to identify explicitly what was apparently so obvious.

The day after Flanders insinuated, on the floor of the U.S. Senate, a love triangle involving Cohn, McCarthy, and Schine, Cohn returned to continue his testimony. At one point, he made a passing, dismissive reference to Congressman Vito Marcantonio, a member of the left-wing American Labor Party. Marcantonio didn't hold back in reply: "I am not the type that would want anything from any character who, according to Senator Flanders, has permitted his 'almost passionate anxiety to retain Private Schine' to embarrass our national Government in the eyes of the world," Marcantonio said. "Cohn knows what I mean."

The following week, Senator McClellan joined in the attack, returning to the matter of Cohn's "friendship" with Schine.

> McCLELLAN: First, I will ask you if you have any special interest in Mr. Schine?
> COHN: I don't know what you mean by "special interest." He is a friend of mine.
> McCLELLAN: I mean in friendship or anything else which would bind you to him closer than to the ordinary friend.
> COHN: Nothing. He is one of a number of very good friends whom I have. I am fortunate to have a large number.

Three days later, Democratic senator Henry Jackson from Washington State mocked the psychological warfare plan Schine had devised for the State Department, which had as its centerpiece a so-called Deminform that would use "pictures, cartoons, humor and pinups" to advance the cause of democracy overseas. At least in name, Jackson said, this newfangled bureaucracy risked being confused with the Cominform, or Communist Information Bureau, the international alliance of Communist parties headquartered in Bucharest, Romania. No wonder the State Department rejected Schine's proposal, Jackson said. At recess, a visibly agitated Cohn approached his counterpart for the Democratic minority, Bobby Kennedy. The twenty-eight-year-old younger brother of the junior senator from Massachusetts had hated Cohn ever since Cohn bested him for the top job on the committee staff. "We'll get to Jackson on Monday and find out how he spends his spare time," Cohn threatened Kennedy about the bachelor senator.

"Don't you make any warnings to us about Democratic senators," Kennedy shot back.

"Do you want to fight right here?" Cohn dared, as onlookers interceded to separate the two young hotheads.

Lafayette Square, the capital's first gay cruising ground.

Archnemeses Cordell Hull (left) and Sumner Welles (right) arrive at the White House for a meeting with President Franklin Delano Roosevelt, 1938. Welles's sexual importuning a series of porters on the presidential train, Hull thundered, was "the greatest national scandal since the existence of the United States."

Eleanor Roosevelt (center) and Lorena Hickok (left) during a trip to Puerto Rico and the Virgin Islands in 1934. "I wish I could lie down beside you tonight & take you in my arms," Eleanor wrote her.

Drew Pearson, longtime author of the "Washington Merry-Go-Round" syndicated column and muckraker at the center of many a gay Washington scandal.

William Bullitt (at desk) and Carmel Offie. A foreign service officer who worked alongside both men claimed Offie was "Bullitt's bedmate all over the world."

Odessa Madre, Washington's "female Al Capone." One of the most powerful Black women in midcentury Washington, Madre operated a popular nightclub and was rumored to be a lover of comedienne Moms Mabley.

Massachusetts senator David Walsh, seen here reviewing a parade in 1939. Three years later, the *New York Post* accused Walsh of patronizing a male brothel in Brooklyn frequented by Nazi spies. Though the term had yet to be coined, Walsh was the first politician to be "outed" in American history.

THE SCARLET THREAD

Adventures in Wartime Espionage
DONALD DOWNES

In the spring and summer of 1942, Office of Strategic Services chief "Wild Bill" Donovan tasked gay spymaster Donald Downes with infiltrating the Spanish embassy in Washington.

Spanish ambassador Juan Francisco de Cárdenas, Downes wrote to his OSS colleague Allen Dulles, had "refinements of sexual mania" and was "perverted with both sexes," facts that were "well known to his servants, to his associates, and to his wife," Lucienne.

Federal Bureau of Investigation director J. Edgar Hoover (right) and associate director Clyde Tolson (left), circa 1939.

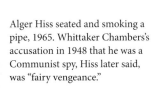

Alger Hiss seated and smoking a pipe, 1965. Whittaker Chambers's accusation in 1948 that he was a Communist spy, Hiss later said, was "fairy vengeance."

Homosexuality, Whittaker Chambers told the FBI in 1949, was his "darkest personal secret," darker, even, than his work in the Communist underground.

Republican senator Kenneth S. Wherry of Nebraska, who initiated the first congressional inquiry into federal employment of homosexuals.

Arthur Vandenberg Jr. was preparing to begin his job as President-Elect Dwight Eisenhower's White House appointments secretary when the FBI confronted him with evidence of his homosexuality just days before Christmas 1952, forcing his resignation. Three years later, *Confidential*, one of America's earliest scandal magazines, exposed Vandenberg's secret.

Charles Bohlen, standing directly behind President Harry Truman at the 1945 Potsdam Conference, was one of the State Department's most capable Soviet experts. In 1953, Senator Joseph McCarthy seized upon specious charges of homosexuality in a failed effort to torpedo his nomination as ambassador to the Soviet Union.

Roy Cohn (left) and G. David Schine (right) attend to their boss, Senator Joseph McCarthy, in 1953. Innuendo about the nature of their relationship led Lillian Hellman to call them "Bonnie, Bonnie, and Clyde."

Joe Alsop with President Lyndon Johnson. The closeted newspaper columnist partook in homosexual escapades, Johnson once said with characteristic understatement, "in practically every capital of the world."

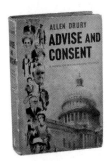

Winner of the 1959 Pulitzer Prize for Fiction and begetting the genre of the Washington political novel, *Advise and Consent* featured a closeted gay senator as its tragic hero. Author Allen Drury, who covered the U.S. Senate for the *New York Times* before writing his massive bestseller, based the plot on the suicide of Senator Lester Hunt, the Hiss-Chambers saga, and the Bohlen nomination fight.

President John F. Kennedy counted a number of gay men among his friends and associates, foremost among them his boarding school chum Lem Billings (above, with John F. Kennedy Jr. and Jackie Kennedy). At right, campaigning alongside congressional candidate Gore Vidal in 1960.

After his dismissal from the Army Map Service in 1957, Franklin Kameny became the first gay American to challenge his firing from a government job on the grounds of homosexuality. In 1971, he achieved another milestone when he became the first openly gay person to run for Congress.

H. Lynn Womack, Washington's "First King of Pornography." In a landmark 1962 decision, the Supreme Court ruled in his favor that depictions of male nudes "cannot fairly be regarded as more objectionable than many portrayals of the female nude that society tolerates."

Three weeks before the 1963 March on Washington for Jobs and Freedom, South Carolina segregationist senator Strom Thurmond exposed its chief organizer, Bayard Rustin, as a homosexual on the floor of the U.S. Senate. "The fact of the matter is, it was already known, it was nothing to hide," Rustin said. "You can't hurt the movement unless you have something to reveal."

Mattachine Society of Washington members staging one of the first demonstrations for gay equal rights outside the White House in 1965. Pickets soon followed outside the State Department, the Defense Department, and the Civil Service Commission.

Robert Waldron (above, standing at right) was an aide to Vice President Lyndon Johnson whose hopes of following his boss to the White House were dashed when a Civil Service Commission investigation conducted in the weeks after John F. Kennedy's assassination turned up evidence that he was gay.

The following year, Waldron's life would be further upended once his name surfaced amid the FBI investigation into Walter Jenkins, another Johnson aide, who was arrested for solicitation in the basement of the YMCA around the corner from the White House less than a month before the 1964 presidential election. The resulting scandal introduced the term "October Surprise" into the American political vernacular.

Watching all this transpire, and confused by what to make of it, was a seventeen-year-old congressional page named Robert Bauman. He had settled on becoming a congressman—and a Republican one at that—the day ten years prior when his aunt Louise gave him a book about Abraham Lincoln. The 1952 Eisenhower landslide gave Republicans monopoly control over the page program (a vestige of the old spoils system), and Bauman successfully applied for a position through his congressman. When the Army-McCarthy Hearings began, Bauman finagled as many SOBs (as errands to the Senate Office Building were called) from his peers as possible, sneaking into Room 318 to watch the dramatic proceedings whenever he could.

From the moment he first laid eyes on the young lawyer from New York whose "passionate anxiety" riveted the nation, Bauman detected signs—his "dress and appearance," the "slicked-back hair"—that Roy Cohn bore the same secret as he, a secret that terrified Bauman and one he lacked a language to describe. As a young boy, Bauman had a "feeling something was wrong with me and my relation to life around me," something so shameful and terrifying that it had to be "hidden, denied and fought. It was something so unique it could not be shared with anyone, not even those who loved me or that I loved." Simultaneous with this realization about his nature was his developing a fascination with politics, at which point he made "a conscious decision I was going to show a world that did not want me it would have to deal with me someday." He tried his way with girls, developing a crush on the daughter of Senator Welker, and was even interviewed on the question of "Should there be girl pages?" by a pretty young reporter from the *Washington Times-Herald*. Even at that tender young age a conservative wary of change, Bauman told Jacqueline Bouvier Kennedy that he "opposed this far too liberal departure from page tradition."

Though Bauman could not identify the sensation specifically, he felt an ineffable sense of recognition, while watching the proceedings in Room 318, that "there must have been something going on" between Roy Cohn and David Schine, something related to the "frightening force from deep within my being, an involuntary reaction to the sight, smell, and feel of other boys."

In hindsight, the role of homosexuality in the fierce interplay of the Army-McCarthy Hearings appears obvious, but it was not so widely recognized at the time. "I did not learn until somewhere around 1958 or 1959 that homosexuality had been a theme of those hearings," one otherwise alert gay observer recalled, "because it was not widely reported: the word *homosexual* was not fit to print or discuss or be heard." During the hearings, puns such as "Bedfellows make strange politics" and the parodic song lyrics "I'm gonna love you like nobody's loved you, come Cohn or come Schine," circulated around Washington and gestured toward a gay subtext too dangerous to mention. It was not until 1972 that the playwright Lillian Hellman famously described Schine, Cohn, and McCarthy as "Bonnie, Bonnie and Clyde."

The discourse around the Army-McCarthy Hearings illustrates the continued lack of any meaningful partisan or ideological divergence on the matter of homosexuality. The Joseph Welch who, with his dry wit and grandfatherly manner, became a liberal icon for driving a stake through the heart of McCarthyism was also the man who ridiculed his adversaries as "fairies" on national television. Representatives from both parties, and from both ends of the ideological spectrum, felt no moral qualms attacking gay people in furtherance of their political agendas. Whatever their differences on other issues, Democrats and Republicans, liberals and conservatives alike, whether members of the committee, observers in the press corps, or regular citizens watching the proceedings on television at home— few questioned the premise that homosexuals deserved to be objects of derision. The hearings also demonstrate once again how the charge of homosexuality could be even more dangerous than that of communism. An accusation of Communist sympathies was effective only against one side of the political spectrum; the right-wing John Birch Society became a national laughingstock after its leader alleged that President Eisenhower, of all people, was a "dedicated, conscious agent of the Communist Conspiracy." But anyone, even the top Red-hunter himself, was susceptible to the charge of sexual deviancy.

Years after the hearings, Cohn prided himself on the fan mail he received from his gentile countrymen admitting that his performance forced them to reconsider their prejudices about Jews. "One woman said candidly she had been a strong anti-Semite until she heard my testimony about my work and the fight against communism," Cohn boasted in 1968. "Now she no longer believed all Jews were Communists. Another woman wrote that she had not spoken to her son for years, ever since he had married a Jewish girl. After hearing my testimony, she said, she was welcoming the girl into her home!" As this cloying reminiscence suggests, the positive feedback Cohn received for his association with McCarthy from supposedly reformed anti-Semites instilled the same sense of satisfaction he had derived from prosecuting the Rosenbergs. Desperate to prove his worth to those in power and win acceptance from mainstream society, he considered it an honor when others distinguished him from his coreligionists. His behavior with regard to his *other* minority identity betrayed the same insecurity.

McCarthyism was ushered onto the national stage by a riveting, televised confrontation loaded with homoerotic subtext. So, too, did it come crashing down in one. Both the Hiss-Chambers affair and the Army-McCarthy Hearings featured conventionally unattractive anticommunist protagonists whose actions were attributed to their lust for another, "normal," more attractive man. The "unphotogenic young" Cohn and the "handsome, dreamy-eyed" Schine, as the reporter Jack Anderson, who covered the hearings as Drew Pearson's legman, described them, were epigones of the "short, plain-faced, and dumpy" Whittaker Chambers and the graceful, well-groomed Alger Hiss. In his 1950 series "The Washington Sex Story," Max Lerner portended "the danger of the boomerang" intrinsic to the charge of homosexuality, and McCarthy's downfall at the hands of adversaries who employed a subtler type of the smear and innuendo he did so much to popularize validated Lerner's prediction. To be sure, McCarthy did himself no favors by needlessly making so many enemies; his attack on the chief clerk of the Rules Committee, for instance, and the inflammatory accusation by his lead investigator that America's Protestant clergy were an arm of the Communist conspiracy, also helped ensure his political demise. But it was McCarthy's epic clash with the army that ultimately ended his four-year grip on the American imagination, a clash brought about by the "passionate anxiety" of his top aide, a gay man whose refusal to acknowledge this essential fact about himself and willful connivance in the destruction of other gay people would become emblematic of a special kind of Washington hypocrisy.

* * *

LESTER HUNT "APPEARED TO BE IN EXCEPTIONAL SPIRITS" as he entered the Senate Office Building shortly before 9 a.m. on June 19, commenting "pleasantly on the weather" to the young Capitol Police officer standing guard duty. The officer "thought nothing" of the .22-caliber rifle protruding from under

Hunt's jacket, as it was not unusual for members from western states to carry firearms onto Capitol grounds. Hunt took the elevator to the third floor, entered his empty office, composed four notes to members of his staff and family, and sat down in the leather swivel chair behind his desk. He then placed the barrel of the gun against his temple and pulled the trigger.

With Hunt's suicide, the first and only to occur within the Capitol complex, the ravages of McCarthyism and the death of his brother by self-inflicted gunshot wound converged in terrible synthesis. The tragedy came as a shock to the country and to Hunt's colleagues. But not to Drew Pearson. "Unfortunately I am afraid that the morals charge against his son and the experience Hunt suffered was the main factor," Pearson wrote in his diary upon hearing the news. Hunt had told Pearson that Senators Welker and Bridges had "attempted to blackmail him out of running in one of the most scandalous pressures ever exerted on any Senator." According to one Senate staffer, Sen. Bridges's administrative assistant drunkenly admitted that his boss had put pressure on Hunt to withdraw. "You sort of knew what was going on behind the scenes," he recalled. Some suspected that Roy Cohn, smarting over his humiliation in the just-concluded Army-McCarthy Hearings, might have played a backstage role in pressuring Hunt. According to a congressman who knew Bridges well, Cohn was "*extremely* tight" with the Granite Stater.

Since his son's conviction the previous October, Hunt had taken his meals in his office rather than face his colleagues in the Senate Dining Room. In December, a mysterious robbery occurred at his home. Unless Hunt quit, Welker and Bridges promised that details of Buddy's arrest "would find their way into every mailbox in Wyoming." While the majority of the state's newspapers had refrained from printing anything about the incident the previous summer, there was no way to guarantee they would maintain such discretion in the middle of a spirited election campaign. At one point, Hunt told Jack Anderson that if Buddy's troubles with the law were reported more widely, "his wife would die."

Though Hunt initially defied Welker and Bridges by announcing his intention to run for reelection in April, he reversed himself two months later, dropping out of the race and citing sickness as the cause. Yet according to the Capitol physician who examined Hunt before his suicide, there was "nothing wrong" with him. It seemed, then, that Hunt was doing everything possible to mitigate his family's agony. Removing himself from politics, he presumably believed, would remove the target on his son's back. Alas, it was apparently insufficient penance to earn him a reprieve. On June 18, McCarthy cryptically declared that he would announce imminently "very serious charges of wrongdoing" against an unnamed Democratic senator. The next day, Hunt killed himself. McCarthy never mentioned the "charges" again.

14

"WE ACCUSE..."

SEARCHING FOR A NEW LOCATION TO HOUSE HIS RAPIDLY GROWING AGENCY, Allen Dulles stayed true to the scholarly origins of its predecessor, the Office of Strategic Services. The director of central intelligence envisioned a "campus-like headquarters" for the ten thousand or so employees of the CIA—the official number, of course, was a closely guarded secret—one that would far improve upon the collection of temporary structures laid out along the Reflecting Pool of the National Mall that had been its home since its creation in 1947. These wooden, "shack-like" "tempos" were impossible to cool during the city's humid summers, nor could they long accommodate a global espionage organization with a growing staff and a need for privacy. In 1955, Dulles convinced Congress to appropriate $46 million for a "junior Pentagon" on a plot of land across the Potomac in Langley, Virginia. When the Virginia Highway Department notified Interior Secretary Stewart Udall of its plans to widen the access road leading to the future CIA facility, however, he informed it of one slight obstacle: "You'll have to go around Miss Scattergood."

Together with her former colleague, housemate, and, possibly, romantic companion, Florence Thorne, Margaret Scattergood lived in a 5,000-square-foot Georgian Revival house on a 20-acre estate abutting the future CIA headquarters. The women had purchased the property in 1933. When the Federal Highway Administration acquired the surrounding 724 acres for a research facility fifteen years later, they sold the plot to the government for $56,189 and a guarantee that it would "protect and preserve" their right to the "quiet, peaceful and uninterrupted enjoyment" of the land for the rest of their natural lives. The CIA's plans would interrupt that tranquility.

The peace that Scattergood and Thorne wished to preserve in their surroundings was an extension of the peace they sought to promote in the world. The descendant of a distinguished Quaker family, Scattergood graduated from Bryn Mawr in 1917 and worked in France after the end of World War I on a project sponsored by the American Friends Service Committee to help returning wine growers rebuild their vineyards. In 1926, she moved to Washington to take a job with the American Federation of Labor (AFL), where she met Thorne, seventeen years her senior. "She was a person who immediately inspired confidence," Scattergood remembered of their first encounter. "She was sympathetic, easy to talk to, obviously very wise and clever and had a great deal of *savoir faire*." Thorne had worked closely with AFL founder Samuel Gompers, collaborating with him on his autobiography and helping to develop the proposals that eventually became Social Security. Thorne, too, boasted a progressive lineage; her ancestor, the first Lord Baltimore, established the colony of Maryland in the seventeenth century as a haven of religious toleration. Though Thorne wore dresses with lace cuffs and ruffles and skirts that reached the floor, and had a "quiet, very turn-of-the-century way" about her, she was a "fierce partisan of the labor movement" and the strong-willed, strong men who populated it. Years before the federal government began collecting unemployment statistics, Thorne tabulated rough estimates of the jobless population by gathering data from local unions, work that contributed to her becoming the AFL's first director of research. A college graduate like Scattergood, and therefore a woman far ahead of her time, Thorne experienced significant challenges working in a field so heavily dominated by men. "It is very difficult to give these labor men advice," she complained to a friend in 1921, just a year after women earned the right to vote.

Though Scattergood and Thorne kept separate bedrooms and never acknowledged a romantic bond to others, their relationship featured all the hallmarks of a Boston marriage. The women were once listed as "partners" in a census, but the exact nature of their relationship "was always a question," according to a great-great-grandniece of "Aunt Marge." This ambiguity illustrates how it was easier for lesbians than for gay men to hide in postwar America. Such were gendered expectations of femininity that no one batted an eye when women were affectionate with each other, visited the bathroom together, or cohabitated for long periods of time—activities that invited suspicion when practiced by men. "Spinster" did not suggest homosexuality in the way "bachelor" often did. And had Scattergood and Thorne been male, it is hard to imagine this aspect not drawing scrutiny from their prying new neighbor.

Concerned by reports that the new CIA facility might encroach upon their land and thus violate the terms of their agreement with the government, the women wrote Dulles directly. "The boundaries of the proposed area to be made available for the grounds surrounding the building would not infringe on your property," deputy CIA director L. K. White told the women. "In the event it is finally decided to construct the Headquarters building at the Langley site, I should like to assure you that everything possible will be done to avoid inconvenience to you." Just a few months after construction teams broke ground in 1957, however, the state of Virginia attempted to supersede the agreement by petitioning the Circuit Court of Fairfax County to let it seize two acres from Scattergood and Thorne's front yard and cut down several hundred trees.

The halls of American justice offered a more level playing field than the Cold War's wilderness of mirrors, and achieving what no small number of determined adversaries abroad had tried and failed to do, the dowagers took on the CIA—and won. The road-widening project would have to wait.

★ ★ ★

ROBERT HARRISON WAS "QUEER FOR QUEERS." The New York advertising executive had a talent for titillating the lowest common denominator and spotted an opportunity in Jack Lait and Lee Mortimer's *Confidential* books. Harrison hatched—or, more accurately, stole—an idea: a monthly magazine that would offer readers the same potpourri of gossip, crime, reactionary populism, and hysterical scandalmongering that had made the pulp paperback series such a smashing success. In just a few years after Harrison founded it in 1952, *Confidential* magazine garnered a circulation of 3.8 million, making it one of the most popular periodicals in the country. Together with images of scantily clad women, advertisements for wonder products, and tales of celebrity romance and rejection—all written in what Harrison characterized as the magazine's "toboggan ride" prose—a regular feature of *Confidential* was the humiliation of closeted homosexuals, whose exposure the magazine touted under its motto, "Tells the facts and names the names." When no other publication would touch the rumors surrounding Adlai Stevenson, *Confidential* aired them, albeit in a circumlocutionary way, with details supplied by the FBI. Exposés alleging homosexuality against two other political figures, both printed in 1956, also bore the Bureau's fingerprints.

Though he published a best-selling book on statecraft, *The Time for Decision*, only a year into his forced retirement from the State Department, Sumner Welles continued to wrestle with his interrelated demons of alcoholism and anguished homosexuality. In the early morning hours of the day after Christmas 1948, he was discovered barely breathing on the grounds of his rural Maryland estate, a bottle of sleeping pills in his pocket and his fingers and toes frozen to the point that some required amputation. The following summer, Drew Pearson wrote in his diary, Welles had "aged ten years in ten months," and by fall, the columnist noted that Welles had "no interest in life, won't see his friends, can't sleep at night. I'm afraid he wants to die." Anxious that Welles might take his own life, Pearson considered asking *Washington Post* publisher Eugene Meyer to make Welles a "foreign affairs adviser" to the newspaper. But the idea went nowhere, and eventually Welles's lecture agency dropped him.

At the time of Welles's resignation in 1943, Cordell Hull had tried in vain to persuade the *New York Times* to reveal the true story of his professional demise. After James "Scotty" Reston wrote a dispatch lamenting the undersecretary of state's sudden departure, Hull summoned the *Times* man to Foggy Bottom. Reston was not familiar with "the facts" of the Welles case, Hull said, and Hull wanted to help him get rid of "this deficiency" in his reporting. Reaching into his desk, Hull handed Reston the FBI's full report on Welles. When Reston asked Hull if he would be willing to go on the record about its contents, Hull, full of braggadocio just moments earlier, indignantly declined. He was merely doing Reston a favor by providing him with information, he averred. Reston brought the report to his boss, *Times* Washington bureau chief Arthur Krock, who recoiled at the idea of the Gray Lady having anything to do with so repulsive a deed as publicly identifying a man as a homosexual.

Inferences to the actual reason for Welles's downfall appeared sporadically in the press over the ensuing years. After Deputy Undersecretary of State John Peurifoy revealed the existence of homosexuals in the State Department in 1950, Westbrook Pegler wrote a column describing "an old family friend of the Roosevelts whose reputation, rightly or wrongly, became notorious and who finally left apparently of his own will and in good order." (Pegler added that this person was "shown to have been put to the uses of the Communists in one conspicuous recorded case," on which he declined to elaborate.) When Welles launched an international affairs organization the following year, the right-wing syndicated columnist George Sokolsky reminded readers that "Welles's career was in the State department in the hey-day of the wild men whom Sen. Joe McCarthy has been denouncing as much for their habits as for their policies." And in *Washington Confidential*, Lait and Mortimer had referred to a "high State Department official . . . a notorious homo who preferred young Negro boys."

No matter how widespread the stories of his homosexual exploits might have been among a small coterie of Beltway journalists and politicos, it must have come as a terrible shock for the former diplomat to see the photo of himself—overlaid with the text "WE ACCUSE: SUMNER WELLES"—on the cover of the March 1956 edition of *Confidential*. Robert Harrison had dispatched private detectives to trail Welles, and had sent an investigator to Cleveland, the site of another reputedly drunken homosexual escapade. "By the time of WWII, Welles's prissiness was the butt of much pressroom humor around Washington," the article's author, a pseudonymous figure named "Truxton Decatur," wrote. "Roosevelt couldn't overlook Welles's peccadillos and the lavender stripe Welles had added to their old school tie." After misreporting the September 1941 incident aboard the presidential train to House Speaker William Bankhead's funeral in Jasper, Alabama, as having occurred in July 1937 on a train to Senate majority leader Joseph T. Robinson's funeral in Little Rock, Arkansas, Decatur rhetorically asked, "Did the flaw of Shakespearean proportions in Welles's moral character prompt him to leave his home at midnight, after imbibing liberally of Christmas cheer, for a nocturnal walk through the frozen fields of his lonely estate in search of forbidden satisfaction?" Welles spent thousands of dollars on private investigators to discover the source of the story. Naturally, he suspected William Bullitt and Carmel Offie, but he could not obtain solid evidence, "however much people knew the relationship between jackal [and] hyena."

Confidential's exposure that November of Arthur Vandenberg Jr., a man with a far lower public profile than Welles, was even more pitiless. After Hoover forced him out of his White House job, the erstwhile "man behind" the Citizens for Eisenhower Committee obtained a visiting lectureship in international affairs at the University of Miami. He stayed in friendly, intermittent touch with the president, who hosted him for coffee several times at the White House and, at Christmas, mailed him prints of portraits he had painted of his predecessors George Washington and Abraham Lincoln. In 1954, Eisenhower warmly welcomed Vandenberg's offer to brief him about his three-month fact-finding mission across Asia and the Middle East.

Though Vandenberg told a University of Miami student magazine the following year that "the political whirligig was not really what he wanted," in reading the letters he wrote to Eisenhower and his former boss Nelson Rockefeller, the interviews he gave about foreign affairs, and the occasional newspaper articles he published about the fate of the world, it's readily apparent that this was a lie. This proud son of "the man in the middle of the American century" was terribly despondent at the prospect of what his life might have been had he not lost his job due to his sexual orientation. Vandenberg's public statements to the contrary, he desperately wanted to get back into the Washington "whirligig," and the encouraging letters he received from the president indicated that he might still have a chance. And then, out of the blue, his private suffering became a public spectacle.

"The Fairy Tale the White House Never Told" was how *Confidential* headlined its exposé, and once again, the unfortunate story was left to "Truxton Decatur" to tell. "Was the hand that might have kept the President's appointment book really attached to a limp wrist, as rumored on homosexual-conscious Capitol Hill?" he asked. Quoting anonymous sources about Vandenberg's wartime military service at a base in Virginia, the magazine intimated that he had had a sexual relationship with another soldier, the unit's "swish," who "wore silk underwear and mooned over the photos of musclemen he kept in his footlocker." Unlike David Schine, Vandenberg refused a direct commission (something he could have easily acquired as the son of a powerful senator), opting instead to enlist as a buck private.

Confidential nonetheless portrayed him as an entitled brat, one who "g[o]t away with behavior that caused many another lavender lad to receive a dishonorable discharge." The magazine also published a photograph of Vandenberg's Miami home and his street address.

As he had done three years earlier when J. Edgar Hoover forced him to resign preemptively from his position as presidential appointments secretary, Vandenberg cited "ill health" and quit his job at the university, where students had just voted him one of their favorite instructors. He disconnected his phone and turned ever more inward; the occasional attempts by Eisenhower and Rockefeller to lift his spirits had little effect. Though the president could not bring himself to read the *Confidential* exposé, he was "familiar with its contents," as he explained in a letter to Rockefeller. "I am delighted that you are continuing to take a friendly interest in an individual who, regardless of anything in the past, is obviously a sensitive character, devoted to his country and well informed in the international field." When Eisenhower and his wife, Mamie, extended a personal invitation for Vandenberg to attend the second inauguration, Vandenberg could not bring himself to make the trip. "I have not been able to overcome the obstacles that stood in the way of an acceptance," he regretfully wrote the president. Devastated personally and professionally, Vandenberg never recovered from the *Confidential* story, took to drinking, and died at sixty a broken man.

Meanwhile, back in Washington, a thirty-six-year-old "handsome bachelor" assistant to the president on patronage appointments assumed the job Vandenberg had been meant to fill. Bob Gray was born in Hastings, Nebraska, a town he later recalled had "two known queers." As a child visiting his grandmother's house, Gray used to look up at the picture hanging on the a wall of the 1869 ceremony in Utah marking the completion of the Transcontinental Railroad, where a final "golden spike" was driven into the track. Of the two thousand workmen featured in the photograph, Gray was to recall, surely one hundred were gay. "Men who spent their whole lives thinking they were the only ones, thinking that they were one of nature's mistakes, misfits."

In 1952, Gray opened the first store in Hastings to sell televisions. Few families could afford the contraptions, however, and the broadcast signal from the nearest station in Omaha was spotty at best. Though the ill-timed venture ultimately failed, Gray's prescient belief in the power of television was undimmed. Shortly thereafter, he faced another disappointment when the Federal Communications Commission rejected his application for a license to start a TV station in Hastings, only to award one to the publisher of the local newspaper, a man who just happened to be a former U.S. senator and member of President Eisenhower's White House staff. Gray's rejection by a faceless government bureaucracy thousands of miles away sparked another sort of epiphany: access to powerful politicians was an important, if not obligatory, criterion for American entrepreneurial success.

And so Gray made his way to the city where the most powerful politicians dwelled. Lacking any government experience, he wrote a letter to the Eisenhower White House official who had beaten him out for the TV license and since been elevated to secretary of the interior, Fred A. Seaton, asking for advice. Impressed by the humility of a man who had every reason to resent him, Seaton helped secure Gray a position as special assistant for manpower in the Department of the Navy. But first, Gray would have to undergo a background check that took a nerve-racking six weeks. "I remember how relieved I was," Gray was to say when the approval came through. "I tried to act as nonchalant as I could, even though my heart was pounding. I was still trying to make myself straight, dating women. If I had been in any way sexually active, I would have been outed. I was an open book, working twenty-hour days. That was fulfilling enough for me." Gray's self-discipline and skills at flattery—"If I found out during an interview that your hobby was butterflies, somehow I'd find something about butterflies, an article or card or whatever, to send you," he recalled—was rewarded. In less than a year, he got a job in the White House personnel office, eventually rising to presidential appointments secretary (Vandenberg's intended role) and secretary of the cabinet.

As he ascended Washington's greasy pole, Gray was simultaneously cementing his reputation as a social butterfly, making the list of *Cosmopolitan* magazine's most eligible bachelors, and shelling out a hefty $1,000 a year (from a $12,900 salary) on clothes. He became a familiar face in the Washington beau monde, and a frequent presence at parties thrown by socialites Gwen Cafritz, Perle Mesta, and cereal heiress Marjorie Merriweather Post. "At the White House," reported *Look* magazine, "single girls have long eyed the attractive and friendly" Gray, who, alas, professed himself too busy to date. His lack of a companion, he reassured the women of Washington, was temporary. "Not forever am I going to be a bachelor," he promised when asked if he planned to marry. "That's definite."

* * *

INSIDE ITS "RICH, DARK STRAWBERRY RED" WALLS, the Kremlin was "unimaginably pretty" in winter, "the ancient churches ris[ing] to happy riots of colored and gilded domes" and the palaces "painted a bright butter yellow picked out with white." Rather than the bleak fortress of popular imagination, the seat of Soviet power more resembled a "particularly gay decoration by Bakst for one of Diaghilev's earlier ballets." At a Kremlin banquet honoring East German premier Otto Grotewohl, meanwhile, marched a "brilliantly uniformed, wonderfully smart, menacingly goose-stepping guard of honor of young Russian giants." These florid appraisals of Russian architecture and masculinity were offered by Joe Alsop in January 1957 at the start of his monthlong visit to the Soviet Union. As one of American journalism's staunchest cold warriors, Alsop had written critically about the country for years. But this was his first visit. It would also be his last.

By his own admission "an incurable homosexual since boyhood," Joseph Wright Alsop V was reared in a white, Anglo-Saxon, Protestant household where the word *homosexual* was practically unknown. The Alsop clan was unremarkable in this regard for being "a very sort of restrained family" that "didn't go in for discussing our inmost feelings," and Alsop would exist in a closet of various degrees of openness for most of his adult life. Educated at Groton and Harvard and a member in good standing of what he referred to as the "WASP ascendancy," Alsop was the sort of fellow who never went outside without a hat during his four years living in Cambridge, which wasn't very often, as he spent most of his time buried in books. Alexander Woollcott, the *New Yorker* critic and prominent member of the Algonquin Round Table, once said of the young Alsop that he was "the only young American I have ever met who is truly educated."

With his younger brother, Stewart, Alsop wrote a thrice-weekly column, Matter of Fact. Published in the *New York Herald Tribune* and syndicated nationally to some two hundred newspapers (including the *Washington Post*) with a combined readership of twenty-five million, the column stood out for its reportorial quality, and made Alsop one of the most influential journalists in the country. Alsop didn't just report the news; he made it.

His influence derived from both his distinguished lineage (his mother was a first cousin of Eleanor Roosevelt) and his determination to have the ear of those in power. Alsop was credited with convincing FDR to send World War I–era destroyers to Britain after the fall of France, a decision that played a crucial role in preventing a German invasion of the island. The Russian-British intellectual Isaiah Berlin, who got to know Alsop while working at the British embassy in Washington during the war, described him as "a fanatical Anglophile, intelligent, young, snobbish, a little pompous, and my permanent host in Washington." Alsop was indeed a terrible snob. When Harry Truman, who lacked a college degree, succeeded FDR, Alsop wrote to his cousin Eleanor that the White House had been cheapened to "the lounge of the Lions Club in Independence . . . where one is conscious chiefly of the odor of ten-cent cigars and the easy laughter evoked by the new smoking-room story." According to one acquaintance, Alsop's heavily affected Mid-Atlantic accent resembled that of "a clerk in a not-very-good London hotel trying to make people think he went to Harrow."

Pretentiousness aside, Alsop was one of the earliest and bravest critics of Sen. Joe McCarthy, whose reactionary anticommunism clashed with Alsop's internationalist brand, and whose tactics violated his traditional WASP sense of fair play. In the summer of 1950, just as the purges of sex deviants and suspected leftists were getting underway, the Alsops wrote an influential essay lambasting McCarthyism for *The Saturday Evening Post* entitled "Why Has Washington Gone Crazy?" In setting out to answer that question for the readers of America's most popular middlebrow magazine, the brothers described the paradigmatic image of the American turncoat in faintly homoerotic terms: "a handsome young man with high cheekbones, the very beau ideal of the devoted Government servant." Sen. Kenneth Wherry's crusade "to elevate the subject of homosexuality to the level of a serious political issue, on the grounds that sexual perversion presents a clear and present danger to the security of the United States," was "vulgar folly," they wrote, "examples" of which "could be extended *ad nauseam.*" McCarthyism, they concluded, had created a "miasma of fear" across Washington.

McCarthy struck back, rising before the Senate to read a letter he had sent in response to the piece. Surely, he declared, the editors of *The Saturday Evening Post* were aware that "the great Roman Empire came to an end when the ruling class became morally perverted and degenerate."

McCarthy knew some staffers at the magazine, and while he could not believe that "Senator Wherry's attempt to accomplish the long overdue task of removing perverts from our government would be considered either 'vulgar' or 'nauseating' to them," he could easily understand "why it would be considered 'vulgar' or 'nauseating' by Joe Alsop"—though not, apparently, by his coauthor Stewart. McCarthy next referenced a part of the article that referred to his office as being full of "furtive-looking characters." He could not fathom how Joe Alsop knew this, given that the only person from the magazine who had ever visited his office was a photographer who, unlike Alsop, appeared to be "a fine normal young man."

Like most gay men of his generation, Alsop tidily compartmentalized his homosexuality. After the doctors he consulted "only confirmed [his] own diagnosis" of inveterate sexual inversion, he reconciled himself to his nature, adhering to a self-fashioned code: "If I do no harm to anyone, if I am no trouble to anyone, I should not be too much troubled myself." Aside from a possible fling with a sailor named Frank Merlo—who eventually shacked up with Tennessee Williams—in the early 1940s, Alsop did not have any lasting romantic relationships with other men. Robert Rawls, a neighbor of Alsop in his later years, recalled the columnist speaking about the Riggs bathhouse near Lafayette Square, though Alsop was sufficiently vague in his recollections as to leave doubt whether he ever cruised there himself. Despite his secret, or perhaps to overcompensate for it, he had no qualms in gossiping about other people's, sometimes to a brazen extent: alerting Alger Hiss's lawyers to a German short story with homosexual themes translated by Whittaker Chambers, mocking Bobby Cutler's "incorrect tastes in love," or even chiding his relative Eleanor Roosevelt behind her back for "Sapphic tendencies."

Maintaining such a double life is a constant challenge, and Alsop's inability to do so led to what he would come to describe as an "act of very great folly" in Moscow. Soon after his arrival in the Soviet capital, he began noticing clumsy efforts—the "meaningful" stare from a young soldier on the street, the "quite obvious" homosexual with "plucked eyebrows and dyed hair" who propositioned him in the bathroom at the Sovietskaya Hotel—to compromise him, such that they amounted to "a rather continuous attempt to entrap." But the ruses were too obvious, and Alsop was too alert to their intention, for them to succeed. After scoring a huge journalistic coup (an interview with Nikita Khrushchev during which the Soviet leader behaved like "a jovial clown at a party"), he started to let his guard down. That evening, Alsop attended a dinner in honor of Chester Bowles, the former governor of Connecticut who happened to be visiting Moscow, at the Grand Hotel. There, "an athletic blonde, pleasant-faced, pleasant-mannered fellow" who gave his name as "Boris Nikolaievich" took a seat next to Alsop. Discovering that they both spoke French, the two men fell into conversation about arts in the Soviet Union, and before long, there came "a veiled confession" by the Russian that he was gay. When Alsop "did not appear shocked," Boris invited him to his room.

After they had sex, Nikolaievich suggested Alsop return the next afternoon. Reflecting on his decision to accept the invitation, Alsop could "hardly credit my own idiocy." But his "time in Russia had been so interesting, the Russians as a people had seemed to me so friendly and so vital, the presence of the police had been so little apparent, that I had just about forgotten this was a police state." Right as he and Boris were about to embrace, three men burst into the room demanding that Alsop sign a form admitting that he had committed an illegal act. Startled, Alsop replied that he could not speak Russian and therefore did not understand what the document said. Two more men, clearly KGB officers, suddenly appeared, one a chain-smoker, Alsop was to remember, "in his late forties or early fifties, moderately corpulent, of middle height," with olive-brown skin and a muskrat chapka on his head, a hooked nose, and eyes deep-set in "plump cheeks" upon which sat a pair of steel-rimmed glasses. His sidekick was an official in his early thirties, about five-ten, fat, and blond, "with a long nose and a loose-looking, rather Germanic face." Alsop, the men explained, had committed a crime, evidence for which was contained in a photograph they unveiled from a scarlet dossier. The image, Alsop realized, "was a singularly brilliant fake" in that "what it portrayed had not occurred." Yet, given the circumstances in which he found himself, it was pointless to argue.

Still, Alsop was not about to submit. Having accommodated himself to his homosexuality as a young man, he had decided many years ago that he "would much prefer any other course, however unpleasant, to paying blackmail" should he ever find himself in a compromising situation, even if it involved abandoning his journalistic career. After hours of engaging in "a most curious political discussion, about Soviet-American relations" with his dogged interlocutors, the columnist insisted he had to leave for a dinner engagement with his old friend and Georgetown neighbor, Ambassador

Charles Bohlen, at the American embassy. He arranged to meet the men the following night at the Praga restaurant.

Alsop's first instinct after the Russians left his room was to commit suicide. Ultimately rejecting this as "a cowardly alternative," he decided instead to "play the game out a bit further, to see where it would lead." To get out of the country safely, he would assent to the KGB's recruitment effort, and upon his return home make "a clean, public breast of the whole business, telling the story in detail to the whole world first as a warning and second as proof that I could not be blackmailed any longer." It would have been a profound moment in the annals of American letters, espionage, and public life—historic, even—for one of the country's most influential journalists to declare himself a homosexual in 1957 to neutralize a Soviet blackmail attempt. Doing so, Alsop believed, would go some small way toward lessening "the concealment that homosexuals must practice," even if "telling the honest truth and so ridding myself of the incubus of my folly" meant ending his career.

At their meeting the next evening over "a luxurious and enormous dinner," which Alsop warily refrained from touching, the KGB men offered the exact solution to his "problem" that he had anticipated: Would he work as an informant in Washington, speaking with a Soviet handler occasionally in "order to get advice that would assist the cause of peace"? After Alsop agreed, the senior half of the pair—neither of the men ever gave Alsop a name—generously offered him a private tour of the Hermitage's special collection as a gesture of goodwill.

The following morning, Alsop wrote down a brief account of his travails. He placed the letter in an envelope addressed to Bohlen and gave it to a friend, who took it to the American embassy. A (heterosexual) victim of the American homosexual panic and an old Russia hand under no illusions about the KGB, Bohlen was sensitive to Alsop's dilemma. Demonstrating the tact that would lead a Foreign Service colleague to describe him as "the epitome of the guy you'd most like to be like," Bohlen worked quickly to exfiltrate the columnist out of Moscow on a flight to Paris. As Alsop wrote in a statement for the CIA officers who debriefed him in the French capital, it was "an act of very great folly, unpleasant in itself," that had led to his unfortunate encounter with Soviet intelligence. As he was wont to do in his column, which routinely invested relatively minor international episodes with tremendous geopolitical significance, Alsop placed his personal ordeal within the grand strategic context of the ongoing battle between East and West. His predicament courtesy of the KGB, he wrote, was "not without interest for the light it casts upon our adversaries in the struggle for the world."

Confronted with the threat of blackmail, Alsop courageously refused to submit to the blackmailers' terms. And by divulging the secret that instigated the blackmail attempt to his own government, he did everything a homosexual in his situation was supposed to do by the lights of those who upheld the government's policy of homosexual exclusion. Discarding the self-sacrificing idea of publicly avowing his sexual orientation, Alsop entered a state of limbo: a prominent public figure, known to be a closeted homosexual by both the Soviet KGB and his own government, he would forever have to live under a sword of Damocles.

Word of Alsop's Moscow folly traveled quickly through Washington, threatening to make him a pawn in the city's internecine bureaucratic power struggles. Allen Dulles forwarded Alsop's statement to J. Edgar Hoover, who returned the favor by using it to undermine Dulles in his long-running feud with the CIA. Dulles, Hoover told Attorney General Herbert Brownell, had several years earlier allowed the Alsop brothers to use an office on the first floor of a house he was renting in Georgetown. Brownell "was shocked to hear of this particular development," Hoover wrote in an internal memo. As for Alsop himself, Hoover wasn't satisfied with his confession, expressing dismay to Dulles at the columnist's "apparent reluctance to be cooperative in that he has refused to furnish the identities of his homosexual contacts in the United States, particularly in Washington, D.C., and New York City." Hoover wanted the names of every homosexual Alsop knew and, in particular, "any which may be in Government circles." Just as he never had any intention of assisting the Soviets upon his return to Washington, Alsop refused this demand from the FBI.

For his insolence, the Bureau opened a file on Alsop. Over a year after the Moscow incident, an informant claimed that Alsop was under "heavy emotional strain," had shared a boyfriend with Guy Burgess while the British spy lived in Washington, and had "homosexual activities with several Government clerks." A few months later, a blind item appeared in *National Review* reporting that "a prominent American journalist is a target of Soviet blackmail for homosexuality. The U.S. authorities know it. His syndicate doesn't—yet." After Alsop published a series of columns criticizing the Eisenhower administration for its failure to address the so-called (and nonexistent) missile gap between the United States and the Soviet Union (a concept John F. Kennedy coined and that Alsop popularized), Brownell's successor as attorney general, William Rogers, called Hoover to report his amazement that his new cabinet colleague, Defense Secretary Neil McElroy, was unaware of Alsop's secret. As Hoover recorded in a memo for his staff, Rogers suggested that the FBI "should get together what we have on Alsop as [Rogers] believed very few people knew of this" and that he would personally inform a variety of government officials including President Eisenhower, Undersecretary of State Christian Herter, White House chief of staff Jerry Persons, and Secretary of the Cabinet Bob Gray about "Alsop's propensities." At a White House reception before a December 1959 state visit to India, Press Secretary James Hagerty angrily told one of Alsop's colleagues, "I'm taking Alsop off this trip. Did you see that piece he wrote? I'm going to lift his White House pass. He's a damn fairy. The FBI knows about him."

None of these attempts at exposing Alsop went beyond the rumor-mongering phase. His prominence in the open city, at least for the time being, would protect him from the public revelation of his citizenship in the secret one.

15

THE HUNTED

Born on the Winnebago Indian Reservation some eighty miles north of Omaha, Nebraska, Louis J. Teboe was described as a "likeable chap and a good worker" by his colleagues, and it was in some of their company that the twenty-nine-year-old accounting clerk at the Bureau of Indian Affairs went barhopping on the frigid evening of December 12, 1957. After the group split up and went their separate ways, Teboe struck out on his own for the Chicken Hut.

While Washington, unlike many other American cities, never had any ordinances on its books explicitly forbidding same-sex dancing or the sale of alcohol to homosexuals, gays and lesbians still had good reason to fear Roy Blick's vice squad. Police had the power to arrest homosexuals for committing the vague charge of "lewd, obscene or indecent acts," and they did not hesitate to abuse it. As a result, gays and lesbians learned to be on constant alert whenever they entered the premises of an establishment catering to their kind, whose owners instituted various precautions to keep their customers safe and their liquor licenses intact. At Johnnie's, a Capitol Hill bar that opened in 1949, for instance, same-sex couples knew to switch dance partners the instant they heard a loud knock at the door.

It wasn't just legal authorities whom gays had to fear, as Teboe would tragically discover that night he entered the Chicken Hut alone. Though they were hanging around a bar crawling with them, James Swearingen and Gerald Lauderdale weren't queers. They were, however, poor eighteen-year-old high school dropouts working seasonal jobs at the post office during the Christmas season rush, and they had been told that "high-class homosexuals" frequented the Chicken Hut to buy young men like them drinks in pursuit of the companionship otherwise absent in their lonely, miserable lives. If Swearingen and Lauderdale were willing to let these degenerates perform oral sex on them, they might even be able to earn some cash. "Hey Jack," one of the waitresses overheard Lauderdale say to Swearingen while the increasingly inebriated Teboe was out of earshot. "Do you want to take this guy for a ride?" The pair, described by a witness as "kind of belligerent like and mean-looking," were searching for a queer to rob, and they found their mark in the Native American accounting clerk.

At the bar, the three men struck some sort of arrangement, after which they left for Teboe's building, located at 2119 Pennsylvania Avenue. Teboe went up alone to his apartment, where he found his roommate entertaining his date for the evening. He came back downstairs, and an argument erupted in the alleyway over money Teboe had apparently promised the two young men in exchange for sex. One thing led to another, Lauderdale knocked Teboe to the ground, and Swearingen stabbed him multiple times with a stiletto knife. While a bloodied Teboe screamed for help, his killers ran away, Swearingen flinging the knife somewhere between the scene of the crime and the White House. The next morning, a sanitation worker discovered Teboe's lifeless body riddled with stab wounds on the top of his head, behind his ear, across his back, and in his heart.

Using a physical description provided by an interior decorator who had spotted him with Teboe at the Chicken Hut, the police launched a manhunt for Swearingen. After three weeks of searching, they nabbed their suspect, who under questioning implicated Lauderdale as his accomplice. At their murder trial, the pair claimed that they had unintentionally killed Teboe after he refused to hand over the money he had agreed to give them for purposes that, while unspecified by the newspaper correspondents, were not difficult to deduce. Lauderdale, his attorney, Stanley M. Dietz, argued, had acted defensively to ward off Teboe's "homosexual advances." Swearingen, meanwhile, had drawn his knife only after Teboe "grabbed at him in an indecent way," reported the *Evening Star*. "The man was like a maniac,"

Swearingen told the court. "I don't know how the knife got in my hand, but all of a sudden he was kneeling on the ground in front of me and I ran." Considering that Swearingen and Lauderdale had evidently agreed to an exchange of sex for cash with Teboe at an establishment known for serving homosexuals, this explanation lacked plausibility, and the jury returned a verdict of second-degree murder for both men. The only mitigating circumstance, according to the judge who read out their prison sentences of five to thirty years, was their age.

Swearingen and Lauderdale employed what was colloquially known as the "homosexual panic" defense, a legal strategy dating back to the 1920s whereby a criminal defendant claimed that a gay man's "indecent advances" forced him to undertake violent measures to protect himself. Like the statute prohibiting "lewd, obscene, or indecent acts," however, the definition of an "indecent advance" was so ambiguous as to encompass conduct falling far short of criminal behavior; a gentle pass or even a misinterpreted verbal come-on could suffice. Physical assault was a depressingly common feature of postwar American gay life. Because not only the way they had sex but also the mere invitation to do so was illegal, and because the places where they met one another existed on the physical margins of society, gays inhabited an outlaw social and sexual world, leaving them vulnerable to hustlers, thieves, sadists, and other criminal elements. A study conducted in the 1960s would find that 25 percent of homosexual men reported being robbed at least once in their lifetimes, usually in connection with a physical assault.

Newspapers hardly ever mentioned homosexuals in 1957, and when they did, it was usually to recount the gruesome fates of men like Louis Teboe. Even when they were murdered, the media tended to conceal the secret that led to their deaths, relying on euphemism to inform readers that the victim was a queer and that his demise, therefore, was not entirely unprovoked. No homosexual had publicly emerged to protest this dismal state of affairs; aside from the several thousand widely dispersed subscribers to *ONE* magazine and the handful of anonymous Mattachine Society members on the West Coast, there was no homosexual "community" to speak of in 1950s America. It would take a group of uncommonly courageous men and women to build one.

★ ★ ★

KAMENY MEANS "OF STONE" IN CZECH, and Franklin Kameny possessed a moral constitution as hard as a rock. Born in 1925 and raised in the Richmond Hill section of Queens, New York, Kameny was provided with a solid middle-class upbringing by his father, an immigrant from Poland, and his mother, a secretary from the Lower East Side. As a child, Kameny looked to the stars at night and settled on becoming an astronomer to uncover the secrets of the universe. His own secret would stymie those plans, but his response to adversity changed the course of history.

In September 1941, the sixteen-year-old Kameny enrolled at Queens College. Three months later, the Japanese attacked Pearl Harbor, and by 1943, Kameny was drafted into the army. After seeing frontline combat in Europe, he earned a PhD in astronomy at Harvard, and in the fall of 1956, he moved to Washington, DC, to take a teaching job at Georgetown University. Kameny's skills were in high demand. The Cold War competition with the Soviets was expanding into outer space, and the following year, he was hired by the Army Map Service, the military's cartographic agency. His passion for celestial exploration mirrored a personal process of self-discovery, as he began surveying the city's subterranean gay scene, spending most evenings at one of the handful of gay bars or at private after-hours parties. Fulfilled by his job, confident in his abilities, and increasingly comfortable in his identity as a homosexual, Kameny saw a future for himself as bright as the stars he had begun to gaze at through the starter telescope his parents gave him as a child.

And then his secret caught up with him. On October 4, 1957, the Soviets officially kicked off the space race by launching the first satellite, *Sputnik 1*, into orbit around the Earth. Kameny at the time was conducting fieldwork at an observatory twelve thousand feet above sea level, on the Big Island of Hawaii. It was an inconvenient place to be when, just a few weeks later, a letter arrived from the Civil Service Commission (CSC) ordering him back to Washington within forty-eight hours. "It is hoped that the interruption of your work will be only temporary," the message stated.

After Kameny arrived in Washington, he waited several weeks before he was summoned to a meeting at Army Map Service headquarters, in Brookmont, Maryland. Upon his arrival, a pair of investigators from the CSC were waiting. They had in their possession the record of his arrest the previous year in a San Francisco public restroom on charges of disorderly conduct. Kameny, according to the report, had solicited sex from an undercover police officer. "We have information that leads us to believe you are a homosexual," one of the investigators stated. "Do you have any comment?" All Kameny would tell them was that his sexual activity was none of their business. As far as his interrogators were concerned, this was as good as an admission of guilt. On December 20, Kameny was duly fired, and his security clearance was revoked.

"Are Homosexuals Security Risks?" *ONE* magazine had asked on the cover of its December 1955 issue. Noting that "howls of righteous indignation" had been raised when Joe McCarthy smeared George Marshall as a Communist puppet, the editorial lamented the conspicuous lack of "protest against the infamous blanket dismissal of homosexuals from government jobs *without* a public hearing." There were no civil libertarians willing to defend the due process rights of homosexuals as they did those accused of disloyalty; in January, the American Civil Liberties Union (ACLU), founded in 1920 "to defend and preserve the individual rights and liberties guaranteed to every person in this country by the Constitution and laws of the United States," had decided that it was "not within the province of the Union to evaluate the social validity of laws aimed at the suppression or elimination of homosexuals."

Prohibited from working for the federal government, Kameny applied for jobs in the private sector. But because Executive Order 10450 applied to government contractors, this Harvard-trained astronomer eager to serve his country at the height of its interstellar competition with the Soviet Union was rejected everywhere he looked. With no source of income and his savings drying up, Kameny accomodated himself to a penury that would remain a constant throughout the rest of his life. Over one particularly difficult eight-month period, he subsisted on twenty cents' worth of food a day. A pat of butter for his mashed potatoes costing five cents was a luxury he could rarely afford.

Though he had been, by his own description, "shy and retiring" as a young man, Kameny was "radicalized" by the way his government had treated him. How could his homosexual orientation possibly affect his work as an astronomer or, as he one day hoped to be, an astronaut floating hundreds of miles away from Earth's surface? On the contrary, it was the government that had wronged *him*. "I simply felt something had to be done," he recalled. And so, Kameny did what no gay man or woman in his position had yet done: he fought back.

In late 1958, after a futile year spent searching for work, Kameny contacted the ACLU. In line with its position of neutrality regarding the "suppression or elimination of homosexuals," the national organization declined to take up his case. But it referred him to its Washington, DC, chapter, where a sympathetic staff attorney acting in a personal capacity helped him file a lawsuit against the army in district court. In so doing, Kameny became the first citizen to challenge the federal government over its discrimination against homosexuals, a deed made more noteworthy by his decision to attach his name to the case rather than post it to the docket pseudonymously.

It's hard to overstate the magnitude of the cost to Kameny as an individual, or the significance of the societal changes he would achieve, by openly confronting the government over its oppression of homosexuals. Since the onset of the Lavender Scare, anonymity had characterized the purge of gay men and lesbians from the federal government. As secrecy defined their existence, so did it characterize their persecution, the many stories of personal suffering obscured by impersonal headlines like "107 Employees of State Dept. Have Been Fired This Year" or "126 Perverts Discharged." By coming out of the closet, Kameny did something that, for a homosexual in 1957, was like escaping from behind the Iron Curtain. Separated by a barrier of ignorance and fear, the secret and open cities had always existed in parallel realms of mutual suspicion. They seldom converged, and when they did, it was always in episodes of humiliation, violence, or death. The citizenship of gay men and lesbians was conditional, liable to be revoked the moment their homosexuality was discovered.

"It has been pointed out that the difference between treatment of minorities in the democracies and in totalitarian lands lies essentially in the right of those in the former countries to protest and appeal," Edward Sagarin, writing under the alias "Donald Webster Cory," had observed in *The Homosexual in America*. "The courts are free, and discriminatory action can be fought by legal means. Yet this does not hold true for the homosexual minority. The price for making the struggle is public disgrace and further economic discrimination, a price so great that society in this manner has protected itself against the possibility that its own customs will be challenged." By making the costs of disclosure so prohibitively high (between 1946 and 1961, for instance, state and municipal governments levied some one million criminal penalties against gay people for an array of offenses ranging from holding hands to dancing to sex between consenting adults), America's leading institutions had essentially trapped gay men and lesbians in a catch-22. Unlike the Red Scare, in which many of the accused were named and gained prominent defenders, only the hunters were heard from during the Lavender Scare, while, as Max Lerner wrote, "the hunted remain anonymous, unspecified, uncounted, nameless men." Thanks to Kameny, the hunted now had a name and a face.

On December 22, 1959, District Court judge Burnita Matthews granted the federal government's motion to dismiss Kameny's case against the army, and the following August, the U.S. District Court for the District of Columbia denied his appeal. To Kameny, whose determination to right the wrongs inflicted upon him would only grow stronger with each and every obstacle placed in his way, these were but temporary setbacks. Announcing his intention to continue his legal challenge, alone if necessary, the accidental activist set the tenor for what would be a decades-long campaign for equality:

> I am not a belligerent person, nor do I seek wars, but having been forced into a battle, I am determined that this thing will be fought thru to a successful conclusion, come what may, and that as long as any recourse exists, I will not be deprived of my proper rights, freedoms and liberties, as I see them, or of a career, profession, and livelihood, or of my right to live my life as I choose to live it, so long as I do not interfere with the rights of others to do likewise.

Kameny's insight was to have profound consequences, not only for his fellow gays, but for the nature of government secrecy itself. Secrecy, Kameny understood, reinforces power. Launch codes for nuclear weapons, trademarked technology, damaging information about a political rival— what advantages those privy to such information is that it is known only to a few. According to the logic that ruled Washington, because there was nothing worse than being exposed as a homosexual, an awesome power derived from the secrecy intrinsic to it. If a person's homosexuality were no longer a secret, however, this premise collapsed, along with the justification for denying him or her a job. By entering the public square as an "avowed homosexual," and by insisting that what the government deemed disqualifying because it was a secret had no reason to remain one, Kameny challenged Washington's reigning assumption that the homosexual and his country were fated to estrangement. "I decided then that I had run long enough," Kameny recalled of his decision to protest his dismissal. "All of us have to make our own compromises in life. I decided not to hide anymore." Opening the nation's closet door ever so slightly, Kameny lit a path for millions of men and women to follow him out.

* * *

"NEARLY EVERYBODY'S READING *ADVISE AND CONSENT*," the newspaper advertisement announced, together with a photograph of the two leading presidential candidates poring over what was indeed the year's hottest novel. Vice President Richard Nixon and Sen. John F. Kennedy both happened to be traveling through Chicago's Midway Airport on June 19, 1959, when a group of newsmen spotted them on the tarmac. When Kennedy, asked about the Senate's recent rejection of President Eisenhower's nominee for commerce secretary, answered, "We do have a responsibility under the Constitution to advise and consent, and we could not under this case consent," Nixon seized the book of that title which his colleague happened to be holding. Displaying the tome like a proud father, Nixon told the scrum of reporters that it was "the new one by Allen Drury," a colleague of theirs who covered the Senate for the *New York Times*. The image of Nixon and Kennedy enthusing over his novel, Drury fondly recalled, was "the greatest publicity a book has ever received."

"A Novel of Washington Politics," *Advise and Consent* was a publishing sensation. Spending a record-breaking 102 weeks on the *New York Times* best seller list, it sold more than two million copies, and for most of the period lasting from September 1959 to March 1961—a span happening to coincide with the first closely contested presidential contest in a dozen years—it was the top-selling novel in the United States. The book's commercial success was matched by its literary renown and cultural impact: winner of the 1960 Pulitzer Prize for Fiction, *Advise and Consent* birthed a popular genre, the Washington political novel.

Drury began writing his tome the same month the Soviets launched *Sputnik*, and *Advise and Consent* is very much a product of the Cold War. The novel begins when the ailing president, loosely based on FDR, nominates Robert A. Leffingwell, a left-wing bureaucrat with a "handsome, dignified face," as secretary of state. "A man so popular and with so many friends in Washington and in the press," this Alger Hiss doppelgänger is backed by an organization with the hackneyed acronym COMFORT, for "the Committee on Making Further Offers for a Russian Truce." As the Senate prepares to assume its constitutional "advise and consent" role, a figure from Leffingwell's past emerges to reveal a shocking secret. According to Herbert Gelman, a short, "stocky" man with "the appearance of one who had spent much time in libraries," Leffingwell had invited him to join an underground Communist cell two decades earlier while Gelman was a student and Leffingwell was working as an instructor at the University of Chicago. "I don't want to testify against a man who had been my friend," the stand-in for Whittaker Chambers says. In outraged response, Leffingwell accuses Gelman of being a "mentally ill individual" with no proof for his claims other than "the lurid imaginings of your own sick mind" and suggests that Gelman "go to St. Elizabeth's [sic]," repository of Washington's institutionalized homosexuals.

As was initially the case with the "tragedy of history" on which Drury based this storyline, few are inclined to accept the charges leveled by the slovenly, mysterious Gelman at the respectable, well-credentialed Leffingwell. Fortunately for Gelman, Utah senator Brigham "Brig" Anderson believes he's telling the truth. Brig, Drury writes, is "one of the few men in American politics with sufficient courage and integrity." (Nixon's enthusiasm for the book surely had something to do with this flattering portrayal of his role as Chambers's lonely champion.) Brig is also one of the few characters in a novel full of rogues, traitors, rapscallions, and lotharios who seems to be a genuinely decent person. But like Leffingwell, Brig also has a secret. Awareness of it first materialized in college, with his "underlying feelings of incompleteness, of not having found something," and developed further during his wartime service, when none of his many sexual encounters with women "made any particular impress upon him." The secret took human form with his feelings for another soldier, cascading "over and beyond his own volition" like the waves on the beaches where they met in Hawaii. Though society did not approve of what transpired between them, Brig "never tried to deny to his heart that it had, for a little while, been all-consuming." And as for the physical component of their relationship, "it was a closed book, for nothing ever again induced in him quite that combination of restlessness, uncertainty, impulse, and desire." Following the conventional path expected of a man with political ambitions, Brig married and "did his best to make [his wife] happy," and when "old memories would return like a knife . . . he put them aside ruthlessly and concentrated on his home and his career." After all, a "solid married life" was "obligatory upon most ambitious men," nowhere more so than in Washington. Yet Brig "did not regret that it happened," for "both he and society profited from it," and while his personal struggle with these emotions "had started as a weakness," they "became transmuted by a very strong character and a very decent heart into a profoundly important strength."

Drury condemned the unfairness of a city that deemed homosexuality a greater sin than communism. "The cruel irony," he wrote, is that Brig's "secret was purely personal and harmed no one else, while the nominee's went to his public philosophies and could conceivably be of great harm to his country." In a reversal of the era's political dynamics, a left-wing senator uses McCarthyite tactics against Brig by threatening to expose his homosexual affair unless he backs down and allows the Leffingwell nomination to sail through. Confronting the president, who is complicit in the blackmail plot, Brig plaintively asks, "How could people possibly be hurt, how could foreign policy possibly be affected, by what I—what I—It isn't comparable at all."

The attempt to blackmail Brig culminates in the novel's second major plot point, which Drury based on another gay-tinged Washington drama, the suicide of Lester Hunt. Terrified that his secret will become public, Brig slits his throat with a razor blade in his Senate office. "In one last moment of rigid and unflinching honesty," Drury writes, "he realized that it was not only of his family that he was thinking as he died. It was of a beach in Honolulu on a long, hot, lazy afternoon," with his beloved comrade-in-arms. Drury follows this evocation of long-suppressed homoerotic yearning with a plea for tolerance: "How could society continue if all whose hands were soiled with human living permitted themselves to be forever after paralyzed?"

This unflinching and sympathetic depiction of homosexuality within the highest temple of American representative democracy guaranteed controversy. When a well-known hostess sent a copy of *Advise and Consent* to New Mexico senator Clinton Anderson along with a facetious note—"Dear Brig: I see you are in the book"—the real Senator Anderson replied in a defensive huff. "Thank you for the book, but you have the wrong Anderson," he wrote. "I have never done such a thing in my life and, further, I have no intention of committing suicide," homosexuality a vice still too shameful to name. "The single tragedy—and here the book almost becomes a novel—of the blackmailed Senator is genuinely moving but not too moving, because the man after all really *was* a homosexual," concluded the *New Republic*, articulating what was then the enlightened liberal view of same-sex love. Reviewing the book's 1960 theatrical adaptation for the *New York Times*, Howard Taubman expressed perplexity at Drury's unusual combination of Cold War hawkishness and avant-garde sexual ethics. Noting the great "disparity" in how Drury portrays the ex-homosexual Brig and the ex-Communist Leffingwell, Taubman lamented how "'Advise and Consent' chooses to align itself with those who will never forgive political nonconformity" while condemning those who fail to tolerate the sexual kind.

Notwithstanding the author's personal views, the message *Advise and Consent* communicated to gay readers interested in public service was far from encouraging: Washington was a city where ending your life was preferable to the exposure of your secret one. So dire was its portrayal of the plight of the homosexual politician that one ambitious New Jersey high schooler resolved to keep his secret forever locked away. "If I needed any further evidence that my sexual orientation and elected office were incompatible," future congressman Barney Frank recalled of his terrified teenage self, "I received it from" *Advise and Consent*.

* * *

WASHINGTON'S "FIRST KING OF PORNOGRAPHY" was a 290-pound, bespectacled Caucasian albino homosexual former college philosophy professor with piercing pink eyes. Born in rural Mississippi to an alcoholic tenant farmer imprisoned for murdering a man over three hundred dollars, Herman Lynn Womack coped with the playground taunting that his unusual appearance inevitably elicited by burying himself in books. He developed an early antipathy toward censorship when his high school threatened to expel him for toting around a copy of Charles Darwin's *On the Origin of Species*. After obtaining bachelor's and master's degrees from George Washington University, Womack worked as a headmaster at a series of all-boys prep schools while also earning a doctorate at Johns Hopkins, alma mater of his intellectual idol John Dewey. He went on to teach philosophy at GW (where the head of the department remembered him as "the finest professor I've ever known"), Howard University, and Mary Washington College. At the age of twenty-seven, with two marriages and the birth of a daughter behind him, Womack came to the realization that he was gay. Sexually abnormal, physically anomalous, an outsider in so many ways— "Out of this might have come," one of Womack's students observed, "his determination to fight for the free exercise of his admiration and love for other men, in the pornographic arts and industry."

Womack stumbled into that industry by chance. As had been the case for Frank Kameny, the space race fundamentally changed Womack's life, albeit in dodgier fashion. "I'm going to make a lot of money," a friend declared to Womack one day after the launch of *Sputnik*. "Everything is research and development." The friend drew Womack into an arcane scheme involving phony government contracts and inflated stock transactions that ended up netting each of them half a million dollars. On a lark, Womack purchased two local printing companies with his ill-gotten gains. While most of the clients he inherited from the previous owners operated respectable businesses (manufacturers of restaurant menus and the like), one was the publisher of a small periodical entitled *Grecian Guild Pictorial*. Consisting of photographs depicting lithe young men in "posing straps" (G-strings) seductively flaunting their physiques, its contents are innocent compared to what one can find today with the click of a button. But when they flourished underground in the 1950s, "beefcake magazines" such as *Grecian Guild Pictorial* fell under the legal definition of "obscenity."

To the many men across the country who gazed at them, however, these publications played a vital social function. Memoirs, oral histories, and anecdotal evidence attest to the profound impact that beefcake magazines—read furtively at a bus station newsstand, purchased at a dirty bookstore, or ordered through the mail from publishers like Womack— had upon a generation of gay men, helping them not only come to terms with their sexuality but realize they were not alone in it. Particularly for those living in sparsely populated areas, where the sense of isolation was even more acute, beefcake mags were like dispatches from a happier, freer world.

Womack was initially hesitant to continue printing *Grecian Guild Pictorial*. But he changed his mind when he realized that the owner "paid his bills, and I saw that these type of magazines were very profitable." Womack also realized that they provided their owners with benefits beyond the pecuniary. Described by one of his photographers as "very smart, cultured," and so persuasive he could "charm the paper off the walls," Womack talked the owner into letting him arrange photo shoots with models and write editorial copy. Eventually, Womack purchased *Grecian Guild Pictorial* outright and acquired similar titles with names like *TRIM* and *MANual*. Business boomed. In 1958, Womack boasted to a colleague that *TRIM* was selling "like hotcakes," with the owner of one newsstand company telling him, "I don't think we could ever get enough of these."

While forgoing frontal nudity or the depiction of sexual acts, Womack's magazines were not subtle in appealing to their intended audience. Aside from the photographs themselves, the aesthetic of ancient Greece, known for its tolerance of same-sex relationships, served as a coded reference to homosexuality. To evade postal censors, however, the publications did not explicitly appeal to homosexuals *as* homosexuals, a strategy that also assuaged the sensitivities of a largely hidden and apprehensive readership. "Buyers like something they can stick in any pocket that won't show," one of Womack's business partners wrote concerning a redesign of *TRIM*.

Despite the ongoing societal repression of homosexuality, Womack felt confident that the government would leave him alone. A string of recent Supreme Court decisions—including a landmark 1958 case, its first to deal with homosexuality, reversing a lower court decision deeming *ONE* magazine "obscene"—had advanced the boundaries of free expression. "I am now more convinced that the [U.S. Postal Service] is going to do nothing to us for simple nudes and I feel that we can settle down and put our operations on a systemic basis," he boasted to an associate two months after the verdict. With forty thousand names, Womack's mailing list was quite possibly the largest roll of homosexuals in the country, if not the world.

For those governmental forces hard at work compiling their own such lists, however, this made Womack a target as large as his girth. The evolving standard of what the government defined as "obscene" created a legal gray area, and in response to the Supreme Court's liberal rulings, the distribution of pornographic material proliferated. Local police forces across the country, meanwhile, increased their crackdowns on publishers of risqué material. Roy Blick reacted to the efflorescence of erotica by boosting the size of his Morals division to one hundred officers, who gradually accumulated a massive collection of pornographic books, magazines, and films on the fifth floor of police headquarters large enough to rival that of any of the city's sex emporiums. It was also there that, tucked away in a four-and-a-half-foot metal safe, Blick maintained his fabled, ever-growing list of homosexuals, their names and addresses recorded on index cards, "skeletons that haunt thousands of local closets." Barely a day went by, Blick crowed, that a federal agency did not consult this unofficial census of the secret city.

On January 5, 1960, federal agents busted down the door of Womack's printing plant at 1318 Fourteenth Street. The next day, a photographer who doubled as his "technician" surrendered to U.S. Marshals, and two days after that, another one of Womack's photographers was apprehended as he went to collect his mail at the Benjamin Franklin Station Post Office on Pennsylvania Avenue. A grand jury indicted the trio on thirty-one counts related to their disseminating "obscene" material through the U.S. mail. "At first, Lynn was totally perplexed," recalled Otto Ulrich, a part-time employee and former student of Womack. "He could not fathom how the government could limit the enjoyment gay men received from looking at titillating images of other men while condoning straight men who received comparable titillation from drooling over *Playboy*." What seemed like common sense to Womack—that what was good for the heterosexual goose was good for the homosexual gander—was shared by very few. Also uncommon was his stubbornness, as Womack was not the type to turn the other cheek when confronted with what he considered to be a violation of his constitutional rights. "I live a life that is open, for I have nothing to hide in darkness nor in secret" was the credo of the Grecian Guild, the membership organization of physique enthusiasts that Womack developed out of *Grecian Guild Pictorial*. It was an ironic motto, given the indirect nature of the enterprise, which camouflaged its homoeroticism behind a patina of respectability. But Womack took it seriously. "After he thought about it for a while," Ulrich recalled, "his bewilderment turned to rage," and he decided to fight the state on free speech grounds. "There is no question that expanding the First Amendment was his central motivation," remembered Angela Grimmer, another former Womack student and employee. "He believed very strongly in the right of free expression. Everyone should have the opportunity to read what they want to read, homosexuals no less than heterosexuals." Or, as Womack was to put it, "if homosexuals want a literature, they have a right to it."

At Womack's trial, the prosecution argued that the defendant had abandoned "an honorable profession" in the academy for corrupting "impressionable young men." On March 21, the jury voted to convict Womack on twenty-nine charges of obscenity, and he was sentenced to a term of one to three years behind bars. The judge released Womack pending an appeal but vowed to imprison him if he published any more objectionable images. At the time of his arrest, Womack had denounced the government's actions as "nothing more than legal harassment . . . an attempt at illegal censorship by the Post Office." Where most others in his place would have quietly accepted defeat and returned to a life of the mind, Womack chose the route of resistance. "I intend to carry this up to the Supreme Court if I have to," he vowed.

*　*　*

SOME TWO HUNDRED REPORTERS CROWDED INTO AN AMPHITHEATER at Moscow's House of Journalists on September 6, 1960, for what the Soviet Foreign Ministry promised to be an "extraordinary news conference." Seated on the dais, behind a table on top of which stood a bouquet of microphones, were two men identified as former code clerks with the U.S. National Security Agency. Birthed in mystery in 1952, the NSA was responsible for intercepting overseas electronic communications, and its headquarters in Fort Meade, Maryland, was surrounded by an electrified, triple barbed-wire fence. The agency's very existence remained a state secret. Seven years after its creation, Congress passed a law stipulating that "nothing . . . shall be construed to require the disclosure of the organization or any function of the National Security Agency," and in high official circles, the NSA's initials were jokingly said to stand for "No Such Agency."

This precious obscurity was about to be undone, however, thanks to William Martin and Bernon Mitchell. Seven weeks earlier, the pair had departed Washington National Airport on a one-way flight to Mexico City, flown onward to Havana, where they stowed away in a fishing trawler bound for the Soviet Union. Now, prepared to address the international media, the blond, rubicund, and fastidious Martin and the dark-haired, grinning Mitchell listened quietly as a Soviet press officer announced that his government had decided to grant the pair political asylum. When it was their turn to speak, Martin cryptically refused to divulge the details of their escape because "others may want to use the same route," after which Mitchell delivered a ninety-minute harangue denouncing American foreign policy and praising the Soviet system. Fifty-three years before an NSA contractor named Edward Snowden arrived in Moscow with his own state secrets to spill, the defection of Martin and Mitchell was the biggest scandal in the history of America's most secretive government agency.

Though Martin and Mitchell were the eighth and ninth Americans to defect across the Iron Curtain within the past year alone, their sudden flight from the United States and emergence in Russia came as a shock. Nothing in either man's background seemed to indicate a propensity for Communist treason. "If any community in the United States seemed less likely to produce a defector to Communist Russia than Mitchell's hometown" of Eureka, California, one newspaper reported, "it was the hometown of Martin," Ellensburg, Washington. A furious President Eisenhower denounced the two as "self-confessed traitors," while his plainspoken predecessor, Harry Truman, suggested they "ought to be shot." The disappearance of two U.S. government employees holding security clearances, and their sudden reappearance in Moscow, invariably sparked comparisons with another pair of Western defectors, Guy Burgess and Donald Maclean—one apparent similarity in particular drawing intense interest.

On the day that Martin and Mitchell's disappearance was announced, a memo circulated within the Pentagon noting that "Havana and Mexico City"—the two legs on their journey to Moscow—"are known international gathering-places of homosexuals." After the pair surfaced in Moscow, a Hearst newspaper item claimed that "the two defecting blackmailed homosexual specialists" were part of a "love team," while the *New York Times* more soberly referred to them as "long-time bachelor friends." The following week, HUAC called Mitchell's psychiatrist to testify. Mitchell, according to his shrink, "had broken with normal moral behavior standards on several fronts, and homosexuality was not a problem of major moral significance to him."

The only evidence ever cited for Martin and Mitchell's homosexuality was a polygraph examination the latter had taken in which he admitted to sexual experimentation with animals as a boy (a revelation that evidently did not prevent him from acquiring a security clearance). From this detail, the media drew a richly detailed picture likening the duo to their infamous British predecessors in treason. "Both pairs are alleged homosexuals; in each, one is weak, the other strong," wrote Jack Anderson. "Burgess and Mitchell are the weaklings. MacLean [sic] and Martin are made of sterner though unstable stuff." Expecting such an accusation, Martin and Mitchell noted in a "Predeparture Declaration" left behind in a safe deposit box that one of their reasons for defecting was that "the talents of women are encouraged and utilized to a much greater extent in the Soviet Union than in the United States," thus "mak[ing] Soviet women more desirable as mates."

The Martin and Mitchell affair fell into the familiar pattern of episodes involving alleged homosexuality and foreign espionage, becoming a point of contention in the perpetual conflict between the FBI and the vast and growing bureaucracy known as the "intelligence community." George Sokolsky, the conservative syndicated columnist who often served as a mouthpiece for J. Edgar Hoover, used the defection to ask how it could be that "young men who have lived together for years . . . engaging in personal practices which made them subject to blackmail," had eluded security investigators at the NSA. "The Russians are notorious for taking photographs of persons who put themselves in queer and unmentionable situations," Sokolsky added, and "a growing colony of such folk has come into being in Moscow." HUAC chairman Francis Walter, presumably working off information supplied to him by a contact in the FBI, announced that the Bureau had warned the NSA that one of its men was homosexual. Two days later, Walter declared that both were known to their acquaintances as "sex deviates," information given to him, he said, "from a source in which I have great confidence."

At an October 13 session of the National Security Council, President Eisenhower asked Hoover for an update on what he knew about the defectors. "Mitchell had been found to have homosexual tendencies," Hoover said, and "Martin was noticeably unstable." Eisenhower was amazed that such men had been given security clearances, and he ordered the chairman of the Joint Chiefs of Staff to summon the officials responsible and "give them hell." Attorney General William Rogers stated that "the Soviets seem to have a list of homosexuals" and expressed concern that Martin and Mitchell were part of "an organized group of such people" embedded within the federal bureaucracy. When Treasury Secretary Robert Anderson asked if the U.S. government had such a list, Hoover replied that the FBI possessed some information on homosexuals compiled by local authorities, but by no means was it comprehensive. Rogers insisted that the federal government "needed to do something" to rectify this deficiency, even if "action in this area was so distasteful that you hated to take it." Eisenhower agreed. At the president's urging, the FBI enhanced its Sex Deviates program, in existence since 1951, into exactly what various legislators had been claiming was in the hands of the Nazis and the Soviets: a register of all known homosexuals across the United States.

Within four short months of this meeting, an NSA investigation of Martin and Mitchell, for which 450 people were interviewed, found that "no one had any knowledge of a homosexual relationship between them." On the contrary, Martin had gone on some forty dates, all paid for in cash, with a Baltimore stripper known as "Lady Zorro." Mitchell had a more pedestrian sex life, also exclusively with women. Both eventually married women in the Soviet Union, where they spent the rest of their lives stewing in alcohol-sodden resentment.

The NSA never bothered to correct the record, however, and the purge of homosexuals proceeded apace. In the wake of the Martin-Mitchell defection, according to journalist James Bamford, "any man exhibiting the slightest effeminacy became an instant suspect," and within a single year, twenty-six employees were let go on account of "sex deviation." The NSA itself, Congressman Walter charged, was a "nest of sexual deviates" so teeming and debauched that a special health clinic was necessary to set them all straight. A HUAC report faulted the NSA for loose standards; instead of simply firing anyone on mere suspicion of homosexuality, the agency had unnecessarily burdened the employment tribunal process by weighing factors such as whether "the acts are isolated instances, whether there are mitigating circumstances, whether the acts constitute a pattern, whether the Subject has a genuine perverted compulsion, as well as other facts to determine whether there is a likelihood of repetition." HUAC also lambasted the agency for not better coordinating its internal security procedures with the FBI.

Meanwhile, as the NSA purged itself of homosexual cryptographers real and imagined, an ardently heterosexual "playboy" clerk with five children was living the high life, somehow purchasing two Cadillacs, a Jaguar, and a championship racing boat on his one-hundred-dollars-a-week salary. Jack Dunlap committed suicide before the NSA discovered that he was selling secrets to Russia, the full extent and gravity of which remain unknown. A former Pentagon official hazarded a guess, describing Dunlap's treachery as "thirty to forty times as serious as the Mitchell and Martin defections."

JOHN F. KENNEDY

To state the unstated in a society seems peculiarly the task of a great leader.

—Gore Vidal to John F. Kennedy, November 14, 1960

16

FIRST FRIENDS

"I THINK YOU SHOULD KNOW THAT JOHN KENNEDY AND BOBBY KENNEDY ARE FAGS."

It was five days before the 1960 Democratic National Convention would be gaveled to order in Los Angeles, and the journalist Teddy White was on the phone with a man "very high" within Lyndon Johnson's political organization. White, who had turned down an offer to work on the Senate majority leader's undeclared presidential campaign earlier that year in order to write a book about the race, thought he had seen everything that Johnson and his allies would do to stymie his ambitious younger rival, who was heading into the convention with more delegates than any other candidate. First, Johnson tried to strong-arm the long-suffering Adlai Stevenson (Democratic sacrificial lamb against Dwight Eisenhower in 1952 and 1956) to throw his hat into the ring a third time to divert votes away from "Little Johnny" Kennedy. When that failed, Johnson threatened to withhold party funds from Democrats running for open Senate seats if they supported "the boy" from Boston. Next, he colluded with House Speaker (and fellow Texan) Sam Rayburn to pressure congressional committee chairmen to throw their support behind him. That didn't slow Kennedy's momentum, however, and so two prominent Johnson backers held a press conference alleging that the front-runner suffered from Addison's disease. "Doctors have told me he would not be alive if it were not for cortisone," one of the Johnson surrogates, former Democratic National Committee vice chair India Edwards, asserted.

As it dawned on Johnson that the job to which he had aspired since he was a teenager working on a rural Texas road-paving gang, the office he was "meant" to hold, was slipping from reach, one of his lackeys devised a final gambit: inform Teddy White that both the man the Democratic Party was about to nominate for president and his brother were "fags."

Washington had ventured west for the Democratic convention, and so did the glaring dichotomy between its open and secret realms. The Biltmore Hotel, where the delegates, media, and presidential candidates were housed, was the convention's "nerve center," White wrote. Meanwhile, observed Norman Mailer, covering the convention for *Esquire*, directly outside in Pershing Square was "the town plaza for all those lonely, respectable, small-town homosexuals who lead a family life, make children . . . the open-air convention hall for the small-town inverts who live like spies." Imagining the Kennedy brothers, of all people, as inhabitants of this shadowy and pathetic world was downright crazy, and White felt the need to say so.

"You're crazy," White replied to the man on the other end of the line. To be sure, White was well aware of Johnson's aptitude for political skullduggery. For instance, while the majority leader publicly preached the virtues of religious ecumenicism, his aides were going about telling journalists (off the record, of course) that a Catholic could never become president. Nor had Johnson ever kept his true feelings about the upstart junior senator from Massachusetts much of a secret—and don't even get him started on his "snot-nose" brother. But this ploy to tar the Kennedys as homosexuals reeked of a desperation that was egregious even by the wily Texan's notoriously ruthless standards.

"We have pictures of John Kennedy and Bobby Kennedy in women's dresses at Las Vegas this spring at a big fag party," the Johnson man told White matter-of-factly. "This should be made public."

"I'll print it if you give me the pictures," White offered.

"I'll get you the pictures in twenty-four hours," the man promised and hung up. Needless to say, White never received those photographs of the future president and attorney general of the United States decked out in women's attire at a Sin City homosexual extravaganza. And one can confidently assume that they never existed. For it is difficult to conceive of a figure from American history *less* likely to have led a secret life as a crossdressing "fag" than the thirty-fifth president. John Fitzgerald Kennedy was the first man to bring sex appeal to the White House, and it was a distinctly heterosexual appeal at that. His erotic exploits with women—embarked upon to a wanton, even compulsive degree—are today the stuff of dubious legend. A young, glamorous, and beautiful wife at his side, Marilyn Monroe sultrily crooning "Happy birthday, Mr. President" at his forty-fifth birthday party, touch football games at Hyannis Port and Hickory Hill—these are just some of the virile images associated with the "Camelot" mystique, one oozing manliness, "vigor," and raw, unbridled heterosexuality.

At the same time, Kennedy was remarkably relaxed among gay men. In this, he represented a generational shift from his predecessors. Writing from the 1960 convention where Kennedy optimistically charted America's path into the "New Frontier," James Reston of the *New York Times* observed that "to the younger men in the delegations," Kennedy represented "the new world a' comin.'" Kennedy's election indeed ushered in a new era of American politics, hastening a changing of the guard and inspiring a younger generation to public service. Concomitant with this transition, the president and his wife, Jackie, were the first presidential couple to socialize openly with gays, welcoming them into their rarefied inner circle of companions, counselors, confidants, and courtiers.

Foremost among these men was the "First Friend," Lem Billings. The secret that Billings had revealed to Kennedy when they were schoolmates at Choate was the sort of revelation over which most heterosexual men at the time would have promptly ended a friendship. And yet, not only did the fact of Billings's homosexuality fail to faze Kennedy, it brought them closer. "It's hard to describe it as just friendship; it was a complete liberation of the spirit," Kennedy's sister Eunice remembered. "I think that's what Lem did for President Kennedy. President Kennedy was a completely liberated man when he was with Lem." Before Jack wed Jackie, he left to his gay best friend the delicate task of explaining to his future wife what marriage to a man like him would entail. "Jack was thirty-five years old, had been around an awful lot all his life, had known many, many girls," Billings recalled of his prenuptial conversation with Jackie about Jack's womanizing. "She was going to have to be very understanding at the beginning, that he had never really settled down with one girl before . . . She was very understanding about it and accepted everything I said." After they were wed, Jackie told Billings that when he had gently advised her to tolerate Jack's inevitable adultery, "I thought it was a challenge."

As president, Kennedy offered Billings a choice of three jobs in his administration: director of the new international development agency known as the Peace Corps, head of the U.S. Travel Service tourism bureau, or ambassador to Denmark. Billings declined all three. "Can you imagine," Billings asked rhetorically, "my best friend becomes President of the United States and I spend his presidency *in Denmark*?" (To be sure, all three jobs required a background security check, which Billings would have had difficulty passing.) Instead, Billings continued his role as an unofficial member of the Kennedy clan. The president gave him his own room at the White House, where he took part in family rituals, presenting a pair of hamsters to three-year-old First Daughter Caroline from a young admirer in New York. He joined Kennedy frequently on his overseas travels, including the president's first trip to Europe, for a summit meeting with Nikita Khrushchev in Vienna, and his last trip, when he delivered the resounding "Ich bin ein Berliner" address to the citizens of West Berlin. At the many official White House functions Billings attended, Kennedy jokingly referred to him as "Congressman," "Senator," or "General Billings," frequently fooling guests into thinking that the lanky, unassuming man in their presence was in fact a high-ranking dignitary.

Though the Kennedys knew of his sexual orientation, Billings maintained the façade of a bachelor. "Because of him, I was never lonely," Billings recalled of the president. "He may have been the reason I never married. I mean, I could have had a wife and a family, but what the hell. Do you think I would have had a better life having been Jack Kennedy's best friend, having been with him during so many moments of his presidency . . . or having been married and settled down, and living somewhere?" For Billings, the president was clearly more than just a friend.

Jackie's enlightened attitude toward homosexuality might have had something to do with the rumored affair that her beloved father, John Vernou "Black Jack" Bouvier III, had with Cole Porter while both were Yale undergraduates. But mostly it derived from her appreciation for the contributions gay men made to so many of the fields that interested her, namely art, fashion, and literature. In 1951, while finishing her degree at George Washington University, Jackie won *Vogue* magazine's Prix de Paris contest with her essay on "People I Wish I Had Known," in which she named Baudelaire, Wilde, and Diaghilev—the first possibly bisexual, the latter two famously gay. Kennedy court historian Arthur Schlesinger Jr. once encountered Jackie reading Proust at the Kennedy compound in Hyannis Port, Massachusetts, and it was a young gay man from the provinces, a milliner named Roy Halston Frowick, who outfitted Jackie in her signature pillbox hats as First Lady.

Jackie had befriended one of the most renowned gay raconteurs of her own era, Truman Capote, in the mid-1950s, while she and Jack owned a duplex apartment on Park Avenue in New York City. With Jack in Washington or frequently on the road campaigning, Jackie spent many lonely evenings pouring her heart out to Capote over long, boozy dinners. Jack also enjoyed Capote's gift of the gab, placing calls to him that doubled as challenges to the fabled White House switchboard operators, who could reputedly locate anyone in the country at any time, even peripatetic writers with unlisted phone numbers.

Another gay writer welcomed into the Kennedy fold became one of its most famous—and disillusioned—chroniclers. Like Kennedy, Gore Vidal was preordained by his family to become president, and he sure acted like it. Vidal learned the rites and rituals of Washington that would become a running theme in his prolific literary output at the feet of the grandfather who raised him, the blind Oklahoma senator Thomas Pryor Gore. A natural-born aristocrat, Vidal attended a series of prestigious Washington-area private schools before enrolling at Phillips Exeter Academy, where he regaled classmates with stories of his "high connections in Washington." Whatever hopes that Vidal or his relations might have had for his ascending to the highest office in the land were scotched in 1948, however, when the twenty-two-year-old published his third novel, *The City and the Pillar*. Sensitively detailing a young man's coming to terms with his homosexuality, the book caused a scandal; Vidal would claim that the literary establishment, led by the *New York Times*, blacklisted him over it. From the moment he acquired the capacity for speech, Vidal had been saying he would rather become president than a writer. The hostile reaction to *The City and the Pillar*, alas, forced him to lower his ambitions.

Though he repeatedly asserted that a St. Albans classmate—Jimmie Trimble—was the one true love of his life, boasted of having slept with more than a thousand people (nearly all of them male) by the age of twenty-five, and lived with a man for fifty-three years, Vidal never accepted the label of homosexual, insisting it to be an adjective rather than a noun. "Trying to make categories is very American, very stupid, and very dangerous," he said. Fittingly, he abjured membership in, much less spokesmanship of, anything resembling a gay "community." In August 1954, a writer named James Barr Fugate solicited Vidal for a contribution to *ONE* magazine. "As the group of the intrepid grows," Fugate wrote, "this non-profit, non-political organization plans to grow with it." While supportive of homosexual equality, Vidal never contributed to the magazine; nor would he ever budge from his stubborn refusal to identify as gay.

The ambiguity that this reluctance created undoubtedly improved Vidal's prospects in the political sphere. Adlai Stevenson, the target of gay rumors unleashed by the FBI, would never have asked an "avowed homosexual" to write speeches for his presidential campaigns. But he did ask Vidal. And though Vidal positioned himself on the left side of the political spectrum, his first visit to the White House was not in service of a Democratic president but as a prospective speechwriter for Dwight Eisenhower. "The White House was as serene as a resort hotel out of season," Vidal recalled of his meeting with Chief of Staff Sherman Adams and speechwriter Bryce Harlow in the fall of 1957. President Eisenhower had recently federalized the Arkansas National Guard to thwart Governor Orval Faubus's attempt to prevent the "Little Rock Nine" from attending Central High School. While ostensibly about the scourge of racism, the speech Vidal drafted for the president attacked bigotry in such broad strokes that it could have been addressing the discrimination its author had himself experienced as a member of a sexual minority. "What is prejudice?" Vidal began.

I suppose that its origin can be found in ancient times when there was little communication between widely separated communities, when life was hard, when strangers were suspect simply because the unfamiliar was always thought to be hostile. Those were times of superstition, of dread of the unknown. Primitive man thought very simply: this man's color is not my color, his customs are not my customs. He is different. He could be dangerous. He is to be feared. Mistrust of the stranger began as a form of self defense.

Eisenhower declined to deliver the speech, a slight the notoriously thin-skinned writer never forgave. For decades thereafter, Vidal would often begin lectures by disclosing that "my mentor has always been Dwight D. Eisenhower, who always read his speeches with a great sense of discovery."

Even had Eisenhower enlisted Vidal's literary talents, it would have been a serious mismatch between president and speechwriter. The Eisenhower administration was staid, conventional, middle-class, and midwestern. Vidal was a bold, unapologetically elitist, sexual rebel reared in the institutions of the East Coast establishment. It was to be through Eisenhower's suave, handsome, ironic, and self-assured successor that Vidal would come closest to touching political power. Fortuitously, he shared a stepfather with Jackie Kennedy, and as her husband started making moves toward a presidential run, Vidal began to ingratiate himself with the couple. A few months after Vidal met at the White House with President Eisenhower's advisors, Jackie invited him for lunch in Palm Beach. Vidal brought along his friend Tennessee Williams. As Kennedy sauntered in front of them, Williams turned to Vidal and gaped, "Look at that ass."

"You can't cruise our next president," Vidal replied with mock severity.

"Don't be ridiculous," Williams replied. "The American people will never elect those two. They're far too attractive."

Told by a pair of homosexuals that they had been ogling his posterior, most any heterosexual American male in 1958 would have reacted with repulsion, if not violence. But Kennedy was a man whose best friend had sexually propositioned him in high school and suffered nothing worse than a curt reproach. When Vidal later revealed his exchange with Williams to the future president, Kennedy, clearly flattered, replied, "That's very exciting."

In 1960, the year of the Nixon-Kennedy contest, Vidal's play *The Best Man* premiered on Broadway. Set at a political convention, it follows the unscrupulous right-wing senator Joseph Cantwell and the high-minded yet philandering former secretary of state William Russell as they vie for their party's presidential nomination. Each comes into possession of embarrassing material about his opponent: Cantwell obtains Russell's medical records indicating a past nervous breakdown, while Russell is handed details of Cantwell's involvement in a homosexual incident during the war. When Cantwell publicizes the dirt on Russell's mental health, Russell, in a repudiation of the previous decade's bipartisan sport of homosexual smear and counter-smear, does the honorable thing and declines to fling mud back. With *The Best Man*, Vidal staked out a position that would become a recurring feature of his literary work and political commentary: that a boundary ought to exist between public and private lives.

The Best Man debuted amid Vidal's own foray into elective politics. Just a few days after the show's successful opening at the Morosco Theatre, where it would run for over five hundred performances, Vidal filed papers to run for Congress in New York's Twenty-Ninth District on the Democratic and Liberal Party lines. Though it encompassed Hyde Park, the ancestral estate of the Roosevelts, the Twenty-Ninth was a Republican stronghold. For this reason, Vidal downplayed his personal connection to Kennedy, a political exigency that the man at the top of the ticket understood but that infuriated his younger brother, who was also his campaign manager. Asked by Bobby Kennedy why he had chosen to distance himself from his party's presidential nominee, Vidal succinctly replied, "Because I want to win." According to Vidal, it was this exchange that sparked a long and nasty feud between him and Bobby, one of many grudges that the infamously tempestuous writer and ruthless political scion would accumulate.

Concerned that his homosexuality might become campaign fodder, Vidal sought advice from the equally promiscuous Kennedy about how to reconcile a highly active sex life with a successful political career. The boundary between a politician's public and private lives was one that the press still mostly recognized, Kennedy said, a deference to the powerful of which he was perhaps the greatest beneficiary in American history. At one point during his presidential administration, a fight nearly broke out between two journalists in the White House press room after one of the men mentioned Kennedy's philandering. "How can you say things like that about the *President*?" the other shouted. Sex had "become contagious" in the Kennedy administration, a scandalized Drew Pearson observed.

"When the president of the United States is laying every girl in sight, it sets a precedent for people around him." The prim and proper Pearson may have been disgusted with Kennedy's behavior. But it was in his diary where this expression of disgust remained.

If Vidal's opponent stooped to smearing him as a sexual deviant, Kennedy advised the political novice, then Vidal could always fire back, a bedroom adaptation of the mutually assured destruction doctrine then fashionable with theorists of nuclear weapons strategy. As it happened, Vidal's homosexuality rarely came up during the campaign, and the only reason history does not record him as the first openly gay person to run for federal office is that he refused to accept the label. Aside from oblique references, such as the *New York Times* profile depicting a decadent "bachelor . . . who lives in lovely splendor in an 1820 Greek Revival Mansion" with a cocker spaniel licking Château d'Yquem from his fingertips, the media largely avoided the issue. Asked by a reporter if being a political aspirant and a homosexual was incompatible, Vidal, noting his Republican opponent's recent marriage to his much younger secretary, replied, "If that were the case this would be the first election in American history where the electorate had its choice of perversions."

Kennedy "felt quite comfortable in the company of homosexuals," Vidal concluded, "as long as they were smart enough to hold his interest." More than any president before and arguably since, Kennedy understood what it was like to lead a secret life, the details of which would have shocked the average American, and this experience may have predisposed him to sympathize with other men who led sexually unorthodox lives. This seemed to be the conclusion reached by one such friend, who suggested that Kennedy's "flirtatiousness with men"—of the sort that he gamely displayed with Vidal and Williams that windy day in Palm Beach—was "part of his sexual drive and vanity." Dubbed "the Painting Pal of the President" by *Life*, William Walton was a craggy-faced artist and former journalist who had parachuted into France during the Normandy invasion as a correspondent for *Time*. He and Kennedy met in the late 1940s when both bachelors—Walton recently divorced, Kennedy just elected to Congress—lived next door to each other in Georgetown. Once at a party, Kennedy asked Walton how many of the women in the room he had slept with. After Walton gave him a "true count," Kennedy replied, "Wow, I envy you."

"Look, I was here earlier than you were," Walton, eight years Kennedy's senior, said.

"I'm going to catch up," Kennedy promised.

Walton, whom Kennedy affectionately called "Billy Boy," had met Jackie independently of Jack, while she was working as the Inquiring Camera Girl columnist for the *Washington Times-Herald*. This afforded him a unique place in the Kennedy entourage as someone who knew Jack and Jackie equally well. Walton was part of the small team of early Kennedy backers who canvassed West Virginia and Wisconsin in the 1960 primaries, and he oversaw the campaign's efforts in New York during the general election. He was one of the select few allowed into the room with the Kennedy family to watch the nail-bitingly close results on Election Night, and was rewarded with the job of White House arts advisor, an important role in an administration where style counted as much as substance. "I figured out later that I was a real link for both of them," Walton remembered of his relationship with the First Couple. "You can well imagine how tough that period is in anybody's life." When Jackie gave birth to John Jr. while Jack was in West Palm Beach, it was Walton who was at her side, and she leaned on Walton's discriminating and sophisticated eye for her historic restoration of the presidential mansion. (Walton, Vidal later observed, was "the only civilizing influence in that White House.")

According to the journalist Ben Bradlee, a Kennedy friend, Walton was "gay as a goose." But it was a facet of his life over which he exercised a high degree of discretion. A 1952 Betty Beale column in the *Evening Star* listed Walton alongside Carmel Offie in a "roundup" of "available men." Nancy White, the Kennedy White House social secretary, remembered Walton as "at once the most indiscreet and most discreet man alive. You could absolutely trust him. He knew with whom to be indiscreet and whom to trust. He had a lot of secrets about everyone. He knew which things to reveal." In August 1961, Walton and Vidal accompanied Jackie, disguised in a silk bandanna, for a night out in Provincetown, the popular gay summer destination on Cape Cod. The threesome caught a performance of *Mrs. Warren's Profession*, George Bernard Shaw's play about a brothel owner, and found their way to a lesbian bar, the Ace of Spades, which they left after being asked for identification. The following week Vidal "ran into Bill cruising the Atlantic House," a gay club.

A witty conversationalist and an elegant bachelor, Walton belonged to the elite caste of Washington society walkers. In addition to serving as a regular bridge partner for *Washington Post* publisher Phil Graham's wife, Katharine, and Stewart Alsop's wife, Tish, Walton's most sensitive undertaking in this field was serving as the frequent escort of Mary Pinchot Meyer. The ex-wife of CIA covert operations chief Cord Meyer and an artist like Walton, Meyer was also one of the president's many mistresses. In this sense, Meyer and Walton served as "beards" for each other: Meyer, in the classical sense of the term, concealed Walton's homosexuality, while Walton disguised Meyer's role as a presidential paramour. After Kennedy's assassination in November 1963—Meyer was herself the victim of a mysterious murder the following October—Walton reprised the role of walker for Jackie Kennedy in the early years of her post–White House life.

In 1966, Walton published *The Evidence of Washington*, a compendium of essays on the topographical, architectural, and social history of the nation's capital lavishly illustrated with photographs of its most majestic buildings and vistas. Walton chose the nineteenth-century novelist and historian Henry Adams, a grandson and great-grandson of presidents who described himself as a "stable-companion to statesmen," as the representative of a particular type of Washingtonian who, "despite his own sense of rejection," nonetheless found the city and its charms irresistible. "Adams managed to be on the edge of great events, to stay near the seat of power and to know intimately most of the great political figures of his time," Walton wrote, offering a description that could apply to himself and any number of citizens of the secret city.

* * *

WASHINGTON WAS "ALMOST A POLICE STATE" for the gay men, such as Tom Makepeace, who lived there in the 1950s and '60s, and like dissidents in a benighted foreign despotism, they learned to speak in code. Whenever the Department of the Interior employee and his gay friends at other federal agencies wished to talk to each other on the phone during work hours, they used feminine, alliterative nicknames to elude the suspicious ears of coworkers. One such friend, Byron, aka "Kitty," Kennard, recalled his first encounter with the strikingly handsome "Martha" Makepeace in an elevator at the Department of Health, Education, and Welfare building.

"Jesus Christ!" Kennard, who moved to Washington in 1959 from rural Ohio, thought to himself. "Who is that?" The two made small talk, and

Makepeace introduced the younger Kennard to his group of gay friends, whose caustic repartee came as a "revelation" to the Midwestern green-horn. "It was like I was in another civilization," Kennard recalled of his first few years in Washington's gay scene. "I can't tell you how exciting and dangerous [it was], and I think for a year I didn't say anything, because I didn't know how to talk. It was a different language," one of "witticisms and savage sexual innuendo." Makepeace, Kennard said, "should be in the Smithsonian as the last great exemplar" of a vanishing gay argot.

Adopting an effeminized pseudonym was out of the question for Joe Alsop when he called Makepeace at work one day, though he was deliber-ately vague nonetheless. "There's some Englishman on the phone," the sec-retary called out to Makepeace across the office. "He wants to talk to you." Makepeace had met Alsop the previous weekend, at the regular Sunday brunch the columnist generously hosted for handsome young men at his home in Georgetown. Winning Alsop over with his sparkling combination of physical beauty and ferocious wit, Makepeace started receiving invita-tions to dinners at classy restaurants like the Rive Gauche, where there would always be at least one other guest seated at their table to avert suspi-cion from diners who might recognize Alsop in his signature tortoiseshell frame eyeglasses. It was only a few years after his Moscow arrest, and "Joe was very, very paranoid" about being perceived as gay, Makepeace recalled. When Makepeace began visiting Alsop's house for sex dates, Alsop made him enter through the back door used by the housekeepers. Hugo Black lived across the street, and the associate justice of the Supreme Court, one of only two justices to vote against a constitutional right to privacy in the landmark case *Griswold v. Connecticut*, was a "nosy old fool."

Makepeace wasn't sexually attracted to older men, preferring "some-thing right off the street." But he was interested in interior design, and the opportunity to peruse Alsop's home stocked with fine Chinese porcelain, Japanese lacquerware, and other objets d'art collected from his extensive travels around the world (along with the free meals) made up for the oblig-atory nature of the intercourse. "I used to spend the whole evening figuring a way how to get out of" sex with Alsop, Makepeace recalled. "I wasn't mak-ing a lot of money and I dated a lot of older men." Makepeace was carrying on an ancient tradition. In his memoir of postwar gay life, *Young Man from the Provinces*, Alan Helms observed, "If you were a presentable young gay man with manners and a good suit, there wasn't anywhere you couldn't go in the worlds of art and entertainment, and those worlds easily opened up other vistas." Helms was describing Manhattan in the 1950s and the possibilities available to young men with the requisite looks and charm. "Because I was gay," he wrote, "I had much more social mobility than if I'd been straight," a unique benefit of belonging to an all-male community where sexual attraction functions as a kind of currency. Constrained by the imperatives of national security and politics, Washington did not offer gay men nearly so many professional opportunities in which they could be relaxed about their sexual orientation as New York, whose creative industries allowed for a certain degree of openness. Nonetheless, in a city ruled by men, which Washington certainly was, the ability to use sex and sexual appeal for social and career advancement provided gays with an advantage unavailable to their heterosexual male peers.

While Alsop made Makepeace and his other gay male companions use the back entrance at 2720 Dumbarton Street, he reserved the front door for Washington's most glamorous and powerful people. And none was more glamorous or powerful than the new president. Alsop had joined the Kennedy court after the war, when he met John's sister Kathleen "Kick" Kennedy in London. One night back in Washington, Kick invited Alsop to dinner at the small house that her brother, by then a freshman congressman, was sharing with their sisters not far from Alsop's home in Georgetown. At the appointed hour, the exceedingly formal Alsop appeared decked out in his "best bib and tucker" and was taken aback by the mess he found chez Kennedy, where pillows were strewn across the living room floor and unfinished hamburgers littered the mantelpiece. Whatever doubts Alsop had as to the refinement of the Kennedy family began to melt away as "one by one the occupants of the house, each more astonishingly good-looking than the last, strolled into the living room."

Alsop's skill at talent spotting applied to budding politicians as much as it did to attractive young men. The columnist was an early supporter of Kennedy's presidential aspirations, popularizing the nonexistent "missile gap" between the United States and Soviet Union that Kennedy cited relentlessly against the Republican administration during the 1960 campaign. Along with Phil Graham, he helped persuade Kennedy to choose Johnson as his running mate. Alsop played a similar role with the First Lady, advising her that, as the foremost representative of American women abroad, it was in the national interest that she purchase her maternity gowns from Bloomingdale's rather than Givenchy. Alsop also echoed Lem Billings's advice that Jackie be "understanding" about her husband's manifold infidelities. Soon, Alsop became "the only close friend who wasn't required to play touch football" with the Kennedys, a rather significant distinction within the court of Camelot.

In addition to their political allegiance, Alsop and Kennedy both used women to conceal their hidden lives, albeit in different ways. Given how both the CIA and the FBI possessed his confession about the Soviet attempt to entrap him, Alsop had to have assumed that Kennedy was also aware of the Moscow incident, as indeed Kennedy was. But now that Alsop had the ear of the most important man in the world, he also apparently believed it necessary to have a wife at home for presentation's sake, to allay any suspicion that what had transpired between him and "Boris" was in any way representative of who he was or how he lived his life. After the unexpected death of his close friend Bill Patten, a former aide to Sumner Welles, Alsop proposed marriage to Patten's widow, the socialite Susan Mary Jay. He also confessed to her that he was gay. Like Jackie Kennedy telling Lem Billings before her marriage that Jack's history of adultery was a not entirely unwelcome "challenge," Susan Mary initially treated her husband's homosexuality as a test, confidently telling her son William that she would "cure" him of it.

"Just as Jackie provided her husband with a degree of cover" for his many affairs, observed William Patten, "my mother gave Joe legitimacy as a family man, someone who would seem above reproach as a confidant to the president." Joe and Susan Mary's speedy courtship—the engagement was announced in January 1961, and the wedding took place several weeks thereafter—occurred in parallel with Kennedy's assumption of the presidency. And yet the man for whom this sham marriage was constructed could probably not have cared less about Alsop's marital arrangements or sexual habits. Indeed, it's no stretch of the imagination to assume that Kennedy was impressed by, and may have even taken some inspiration from, the columnist's courage in staring down a bunch of Soviets trying to blackmail him over a sexual indiscretion, the sort of determination Kennedy would himself have to muster in a series of tense diplomatic standoffs. Regardless, Kennedy saw through the ruse. After Alsop's wedding, according to Vidal, the new president quipped, "Now, if we can only get Bill and Gore married off."

Before his marriage to Susan Mary, Alsop had been a celebrated social host in his own right. Along with Chip Bohlen, Dean Acheson, Allen Dulles, and Phil and Katharine Graham, he was part of a close-knit group of journalists and government officials whose rotating Georgetown dinner salons in the early decades of the Cold War functioned as informal policymaking bull sessions. But now with the worldly descendant of Founding Father John Jay as his wife, a spot on the Alsops' guest list became *the* most coveted invitation in Washington. Officials like Defense Secretary Robert McNamara regularly broke bread with socialites such as Marietta Peabody Tree and Alice Roosevelt Longworth, the latter christened "Washington's Other Monument" by Joe and whose irreverence and wit ("If you don't have anything good to say about anybody, lean closer") made her something of an early gay Washington camp icon. Sunday evenings, when the servants were off, were reserved for potluck dinners, at which Alsop plied his friends and sources (usually one and the same) with liquor and mined them for information to use in his column. "The Sunday Night Drunk," he called them.

"The very oddest and most unexpected party" Alsop ever hosted was an impromptu affair in the wee hours of the morning after Kennedy's inauguration. Washington was "dazzling" and feeling "rejuvenated" in the days leading up to the event, and Alsop told friends that if the lights were on in his home after the balls had ended, then it meant the champagne would be flowing and they should feel welcome to enter. Word traveled far and fast among the inaugural revelers, and it came as a welcome surprise to Alsop when, at 2 a.m., who should appear on his doorstep but the new president himself, looking "as though he were still in his thirties" with the idling vehicles of his motorcade lined up on a snowy Dumbarton Street behind him. Jackie had collapsed into bed, the peckish Kennedy explained, and the cupboards in the White House kitchen were bare. Alas, all Alsop had to serve the recently installed leader of the free world was a bowl of terrapin. Despite these slim pickings, the president chatted up the guests for well over an hour, not returning home until nearly 4 a.m.

Two days later, Alsop visited the White House for an intimate dinner, the first of many during the Kennedy presidency, where nine people consumed ten pounds of caviar. Over the course of his administration, the president and First Lady would visit Alsop's home an average of once every six weeks, and while Kennedy generally enjoyed the company, he did complain to Alsop about the "dearth of pretty young girls."

Alsop's tastes in this regard did not match those of the president, of course, and so the guest lists would have to change. The columnist's entrée into the elite inner sanctums of Camelot, along with his simultaneous marriage to Susan Mary, put an end to his relationship with Tom Makepeace, as well as to the exclusively gay Sunday brunches where they first met. While Alsop admitted to Makepeace that his matrimony was "just for appearances," he was going to try to make it work. Besides, what would the president and First Lady, along with their distinguished retinue, think if he were to have some hunky young stud hanging around the house?

And so, the night of the inauguration, Alsop politely asked Makepeace to leave his house before the president arrived. The young man exited through the rear door, back to the secret city from which he came.

* * *

THOUGH THEY COLLECTIVELY BROKE DOWN A BARRIER, the gay friends of the Kennedys were not particularly fond of one another. "I never was a friend of Lem Billings," Walton recalled. "He was in a totally different category. He's childhood, brought along for the ride . . . I just could never bear him. He couldn't bear me." Kennedy's best friend was a "dud," in the estimation of the president's painting pal.

Most of the rancor among the gays of Camelot revolved around Vidal, for whom feuding was as serious a vocation as any among his myriad intellectual and literary pursuits. One night at the White House, Vidal was tempted to embarrass Billings—whom he derided as the president's "lifelong slave" and "principal fag at court"—in front of the First Family by mentioning how a friend of his had picked Billings up in Times Square in the 1940s, but he ultimately bit his tongue. Vidal also didn't care for Alsop, politically or personally. In *The Best Man*, the president derides the columnist as a hysterical prophet of doom. Vidal was less restrained in his 2000 novel, *The Golden Age*, likening Alsop to the lecherous homosexual from Proust's *Remembrance of Things Past*, "the Baron de Charlus of Georgetown."

For Jack and Bobby Kennedy, early personal experiences with individual gay men appeared to shape their broader attitudes about homosexuality, albeit in different directions. If Lem Billings helped Jack understand the basic humanity of gay people, the most prominent gay man Bobby knew had the opposite effect. The younger Kennedy almost got into a fistfight with Roy Cohn during the Army-McCarthy Hearings, and the two men developed a deep and abiding mutual antipathy. Bobby was a "ruthless hater," in the words of Cohn, whom he allegedly told an assistant U.S. attorney to "get" while serving as attorney general. "Where there was much fault in Cohn," Kennedy biographer Evan Thomas writes, "Kennedy's loathing may have been more personal. He would from time to time display deep homophobia, and Cohn's homosexuality was unacknowledged but obvious." Upon learning that Clyde Tolson had been rushed to the hospital for an emergency operation, Kennedy asked his aides, "What was it, a hysterectomy?" According to Vidal, not exactly the most reliable source in such matters, Bobby was known to complain about Jack's "fag friends" and the Kennedy brothers playfully argued over which one of them had come up with "Martin Luther Queen" as a sobriquet for James Baldwin. "The two people Bobby most hated," Vidal crowed, were "Jimmy Hoffa, and me," an honor for which he competed with Cohn. ("It's a toss-up between you and Jimmy Hoffa as to who's number one on [Bobby's] list," Cohn claimed the executive director of McCarthy's committee once told him.)

These resentments and animosities boiled over on November 11, 1961, at a White House dinner in honor of Lee Radziwill, Jackie's younger sister. Vidal had been writing critically about the Kennedy administration, in particular the invasive practices of the FBI, for which Bobby, as attorney general, was ultimately responsible. Early in the evening, Billings confronted Vidal over his truancy at the President's Advisory Council on the Arts, to which President Kennedy had appointed him. Milling about in the Blue Room after dinner, Vidal either (accounts differ) put his hand around Jackie's waist or rested it upon her shoulder while lowering himself to join a group of guests sitting on the floor. Spotting this trespass upon the honor of his sister-in-law, Bobby, according to the writer George Plimpton, who witnessed the incident, "quite rudely removed" Vidal's hand and stormed out of the room. A fuming Vidal marched out right after him. Accounts also differ as to what was said in the subsequent verbal exchange—abetted, in Plimpton's words, by "tankard size" drinks from the White House bar—but most feature ample utterances of the F-word. So "irritated" was Jackie with Vidal's behavior that evening, recorded Arthur Schlesinger, that she "resolved not to have him in the White House again."

The Kennedys brought art, culture, glamour, and, not coincidentally, gays to the White House. In the Washington they were creating, a certain type of gay man—literary, artistic, cultured—could be accepted, provided, of course, that he was discreet. It was an extremely exclusive station, however, accessible only to a handful of men with the right backgrounds and connections. For those lacking such privileges, Washington remained as oppressive as before.

17

THE GROUP OF THE INTREPID

BUILT IN 1928, THE HAY-ADAMS HAS LONG OFFERED GUESTS A PROXIMITY to power greater than any other hotel in Washington. Situated directly opposite the White House, on the northwest corner of Lafayette Square, it occupies the space where its namesakes, former secretary of state John Hay and writer Henry Adams, once owned adjoining Romanesque Revival–style homes. With their wives, Clara and Clover, as well as the geologist Clarence King, Hay and Adams presided over "the Five of Hearts," an intellectual salon that attracted the most esteemed literary, artistic, and political figures of the day. On the swelteringly hot evening of August 1, 1961, another group convened where the Five of Hearts once met. And while the primary purpose of that fin de siècle circle was merely the intellectual stimulation of its members, these men aimed at nothing less than changing the world.

The revolutionary potential in Room 120 of the Hay-Adams was of particular interest to the Federal Bureau of Investigation. Earlier that day, the Washington Field Office had received a call from Roy Blick reporting an anonymous tip he had received: an outfit of homosexuals calling itself the Mattachine Society would be meeting at 8 p.m. in a room at the hotel. The special agent who answered called the Hay-Adams manager Marshall

Jones and obtained the name, address, and telephone number of the person who had made the reservation, as well as a commitment from Jones to snoop on the event and report back anything he heard or saw.

The Hay-Adams gathering was the handiwork of Frank Kameny. That January, just a few days before John F. Kennedy's inauguration, Kameny had filed a petition for a writ of certiorari with the Supreme Court in the hope that it would take up his case against the army. It was the first time an openly gay person petitioned the nation's highest court to recognize the rights of homosexuals. "Our government exists to protect and assist *all* of its citizens, not, as in the case of homosexuals, to harm, to victimize, and to destroy them," Kameny, acting as his own counsel, wrote in his sixty-page brief. Solicitor General Archibald Cox articulated the government's position that it was not within the remit of the Supreme Court to arbitrate the grounds for terminating government employees, only that established procedures for termination be properly followed. The civil service regulations concerning homosexuality were clear, and the Court declined to hear Kameny's appeal on March 17. Two months later, Kameny sent a letter to President Kennedy himself, describing a predicament that touched "at least 15,000,000 Americans, and in which a 'New Frontier' approach is very badly needed." The tolerance of homosexuals at the Kennedy White House didn't extend beyond a small coterie, however, and Kameny never received a reply.

Unbowed, Kameny next wrote a letter to the chairman of the Civil Service Commission, John Macy, assailing his agency's discriminatory policies as "blatant disregard for the worth and dignity of the individual citizen." Macy replied by citing the government regulation disqualifying anyone found to have perpetrated "Criminal, infamous, dishonest, immoral, or notoriously disgraceful conduct." As such, Macy concluded, "homosexuals or sexual perverts are not suitable for federal employment." By the summer of 1961, the Supreme Court had thwarted Kameny's legal claims, the White House had shown itself indifferent to his pleas, and the federal bureaucracy had condemned him as inherently unfit. The options for fighting his "war" against government discrimination as an individual citizen exhausted, Kameny sought strength in numbers.

Friends would have to be converted into comrades. One night at a party of gay men, Kameny's distinctive voice—described by the author Edmund White as giving "the impression that he is not aware of his sympathetic listener but that he is addressing a hostile Congress or the Supreme Court or the American people"—could be heard above the din extolling the virtues of a book. "Donald Webster Cory, who wrote *The Homosexual in America*, has made an excellent case for our rights," Kameny lectured as a small group of listeners gathered around him by the window. Upon hearing this declaration, one of the partygoers, the twenty-two-year-old son of an FBI agent, leaned in closer.

"I've read *The Homosexual in America*," Jack Nichols told Kameny.

"And what did you think of it?"

"I think every gay person should read it, and that's why I came over to speak with you because I've never before met anyone discussing it in public."

Kameny and Nichols agreed to meet a few days later, and it was then that the idea for a Washington chapter of the Mattachine Society was born.

Over the course of the group's two-hour-long meeting at the Hay-Adams, Marshall Jones eavesdropped as inconspicuously as he could on the participants, who had left the door slightly ajar. As Jones related to the FBI the following day, the only words he could decipher from the mysterious gathering of sixteen "well dressed" and "very well behaved" men were "bylaws" and "resolutions." All they ordered was coffee. Roy Blick, meanwhile, had a man on the inside. Lt. Louis Fochett had spent his entire career in the Morals division, putting his good looks to societal benefit by luring homosexuals into situations where they could be charged with "indecent assault." From underneath the boughs of the deciduous trees ringing Lafayette Square to the dark staircases of downtown movie theaters, Fochett enticed men with his inviting glances and seductive murmurings. Given Fochett's prolific role in their entrapment, it was probably inevitable that at least one of the fifteen other men in the room that evening would recognize him, which is what happened when, just before the meeting was called to order, a participant pulled Kameny aside. "Do you know that that's Sergeant Louis Fochett?" he asked.

Kameny certainly knew Fochett's name from the papers, which frequently lauded the police lieutenant for his efforts, but he did not recognize his face. He moved closer to the alleged gate-crasher and spotted a gun holster bulging from his blazer. Not wanting to disrupt the meeting he had worked so hard to organize, Kameny delivered his presentation to the prospective members and waited until the question-and-answer session before confronting the intruder in their midst. "I understand that there is a member of the Metropolitan Police Department here," Kameny declared. "Could he please identify himself and tell us why he's here?" Startled, Fochett blurted out that he had received an invitation and scurried out of the room.

On November 15, 1961, the Mattachine Society of Washington was officially incorporated with Kameny as president. In its statement of purpose, the group committed itself "to secure for homosexuals the right to life, liberty, and the pursuit of happiness, as proclaimed for all men by the Declaration of Independence, and to secure for homosexuals the basic rights and liberties established by the word and the spirit of the Constitution of the United States." Over the ensuing months, Kameny, Nichols, and a small band of followers fanned out across Washington's gay bars and private parties, steadily recruiting adherents and transforming what society deemed a sexual deviancy into a political cause. One early member, Paul Kuntzler, a twenty-year-old student from Detroit, had come to Washington on a chartered train for the presidential inauguration and decided to make the capital his home. A Catholic who had endured taunts of "fish eater" for wearing a Kennedy button back home, Kuntzler was inspired by the young, "dynamic" new president. His idealistic frame of mind made him prime recruitment material for an organization like Mattachine, whose goals, in 1961, would have sounded positively utopian to most any gay or lesbian person. Visiting the Chicken Hut one evening in February 1962, Kuntzler was approached by Kameny, "the most self-confident person whom I have ever known." Kameny persuaded the newcomer to attend the next Mattachine meeting, where Kuntzler became the group's seventeenth member.

Mattachine's first lesbian member, Lilli Vincenz, was a German immigrant who came to America with her parents after the war. Visiting Provincetown in August 1961, she hesitated before entering the Ace of Spades (the lesbian bar where Jackie Kennedy had been carded only a few weeks before), contemplating the consequences of being seen by someone she knew, or of her parents discovering her secret. "But then I thought of all I'd gone through these past years and knew that I had to go," she recalled. Inside the bar, Vincenz met a group of women from New Hope, Pennsylvania, and she took encouragement from the serendipitous symbolism of that hamlet's name. From then on, Vincenz decided, her life would never be the same. "I didn't expect anything specific from this vacation: only that it would be world-shaking for me," she wrote in her diary. "And it was world-shaking!"

The following year, Vincenz joined the Women's Army Corps. Not long after being posted to Walter Reed Army Hospital as a neuropsychiatric technician, she was expelled when a fellow WAC reported her for being a lesbian. Vincenz was familiar with Kameny, having read about his legal battles with the government, and she sent him a letter requesting to join the Mattachine. Following an interview with the board—a necessary precaution to screen out potential FBI or police infiltrators—Vincenz was initiated into the fold.

Eva Freund's first brush with activism occurred in high school, when upon learning that her synagogue would lobby to have *The Merchant of Venice* removed from the local library shelves, she "requested" that the rabbi allow her to deliver a sermon against censorship. Continuing her rebellious streak, she dropped out of law school after realizing that "there's a big difference between law and justice," and joined the influx of idealistic young people who moved to Washington in 1961 heeding the new president's appeal to ask not what their country could do for them but what they could do for their country. Her first visit to the Rendezvous, a "butch" lesbian bar, was a harrowing experience. "We're getting out of here now," Freund's friend Marge ordered while grabbing her by the arm. "Put your drink down," she added, a nod to the city's blue law prohibiting patrons from standing while holding an alcoholic beverage.

Outside, Freund asked Marge what the fuss was about. "See that woman getting out of the car?" Marge asked, pointing to the parking lot next to the Rendezvous.

"Yeah," Freund replied.

"That's Stella, and she's got a knife in her French twist. And see that other woman? She just went out to her car to get her gun. Because somebody dissed somebody's woman in there."

A few years later, Freund was living with a woman in Maryland when their neighbor, a gay man named Ron, invited her to a meeting of something called the Mattachine Society.

"The what?" she asked.

"Oh, it's for gays and lesbians," Ron explained, before specifying the lopsided gender breakdown. "There are one or two women. You'll like them." Freund warily agreed to join him.

"Well, the big thrust of the day was to get the vice squad out of men's restrooms and to get the vice squad out of the Iwo Jima Memorial," Freund recalled of her first Mattachine meeting. "For the lesbians, we didn't care at all. We didn't understand why men were having sex in public." Freund also resented the group's expectation that women wear heels and makeup, be "supportive" but not take charge, and act "bright and articulate but not threatening." At one point when Freund attempted to ask a question in the middle of a meeting, Kameny shot back, "You're out of order."

On the way home, Freund asked Ron, "What is this 'Out of order'?"

"Oh, Frank is just so big on this thing called Robert's Rules."

An autodidact like Kameny, Freund went to the library and memorized parliamentary procedure. At the next meeting, she came prepared. "Point of order!" Freund exclaimed in the middle of a Kameny monologue, her hand raised to the sky.

"You can't interrupt me," Kameny replied.

"Point of order takes precedence," the novice responded. Kameny started paying attention.

Except for Kameny, the men and women of the Mattachine used pseudonyms, and for good reason: they had been under local police and FBI surveillance since the Hay-Adams meeting, before the group was even incorporated. The first time that Mattachine, whose membership peaked at one hundred, sponsored a boat ride on the Potomac, the attendees were so afraid they might be arrested that they arranged to have ACLU lawyers and a bail bondsman on standby at the dock. In 1962, an agitated man named Warren Scarberry called the FBI offering information on the group. "Angry with the homosexual element in this town" and seeking a "way of getting even with them," he had joined Mattachine and given the Bureau the name of one of its members, a Department of Commerce employee named Ronald Brass. Scarberry said he would try to obtain the group's full membership list.

Six days later, two FBI agents confronted Brass at his office. They escorted him to a private room and interrogated him about his "homosexual tendencies." When Brass told Kameny about his run-in with the FBI, the outraged Mattachine president fired off a letter to the attorney general. "We feel that American citizens have the right to band together for lawful and orderly achievement of any lawful and orderly purpose," Kameny wrote to Robert Kennedy, "however unpopular, however controversial, and however much at odds with existing official policy, without making themselves the objects of official interrogation, harassment, and intimidation, and without making themselves the objects of official inquiry, infiltration, and informants." He reminded Kennedy of the Supreme Court's unanimous 1958 decision in *NAACP v. Alabama*, which held that the African American civil rights group could not be compelled to turn over its membership rolls to the government.

As had been the case with the letter Kameny wrote to President Kennedy, the missive to his brother was ignored.

* * *

"THERE IS NO COMMUNITY THAT HAS NO HOMOSEXUALS," Stanley M. Dietz declared to the panel of robed men staring down at him on February 26, 1962. It was Dietz's first time arguing before the Supreme Court, and the small-time criminal defense attorney with the thick Brooklyn accent (and even thicker handlebar mustache) stood out like a sore thumb among the Ivy League–educated, clean-shaven lawyers and jurists seated in that august chamber. The marble-column hall was a far cry from the dingy local courthouses where Dietz normally plied his trade. And if Dietz's standard ensemble of vested suit, gaudy tie, and fedora, a toothpick perpetually dangling from his mouth, was not typical of the men who argued before the highest court in the land, nor was his area of legal expertise.

"Maybe they haven't been discovered," Dietz said of the nation's hidden homosexual minority, in the opening argument on behalf of his client, Herman Lynn Womack. "If you want to use that term. Discovered because we keep these people suppressed."

Stanley Dietz was an unlikely figure to claim the mantle of being the first lawyer to make an oral argument in favor of gay rights before the nation's highest court, and not just because he was enthusiastically heterosexual. Just two years before Womack had hired him in 1960 to defend him on obscenity charges, Dietz had stood on the other side of the barrier dividing the secret and open cities, utilizing the homosexual panic defense to try to save the skins of the two young men who had murdered Louis Teboe. Dietz had initially decided on a legal career while studying at George Washington University not out of any altruistic impulse to help the downtrodden, but because he figured it offered a faster path to getting rich than his original academic major, business administration. Determined to practice some sort of corporate law in the service of fat cats, Dietz experienced an epiphany during a taxi ride with a voluble policeman who "started telling me and my buddy how he'd shot this 'nigger' in an alley . . . I thought to myself, this is how they administer justice, I'm going to stay here for six months and defend all the Negroes that I can." Six months grew into a year, and the defense of Black people victimized by law enforcement expanded into advocacy on behalf of other marginalized groups. Eventually, Dietz earned himself "a reputation as a defender of the underdog by counseling homosexuals arrested and beaten by the police" in Lafayette Square. And through his legal partnership with Womack, he became one half of an improbable pair that helped push the secret city out into the open.

Womack was just one of many figures in the pornographic industry to whom Dietz provided his colorful legal services. To emphasize his frequent point that the very concept of "obscenity" rested in the eye of the beholder, Dietz was given to dramatic courtroom stunts like falling asleep at the defense table, snoring at full volume, while a jury watched one of his client's films. During a screening at another trial, Dietz munched on popcorn. Dietz's efforts on behalf of Womack, who had continued selling his magazines while appealing his conviction, had failed. "If a piece of cloth is bright red and the cloth is in evidence, no testimony, lay or expert, would be admissible to show the cloth is blue," the appositely named Appeals Court judge E. Barrett Prettyman ruled in January 1961, presaging the famous definition of obscenity Supreme Court justice Potter Stewart would devise a few years later, "I know it when I see it." The court sentenced Womack to four to twelve months in prison for conspiracy to send obscene materials through the mail, on top of the one-to-three-year sentence he had already earned for his earlier conviction, leading Postmaster General J. Edward Day to crow about "the toughest crackdown ever conducted" on the distribution of pornography.

Hoping to alleviate the conditions of Womack's pending prison term, Dietz argued that his client was insane and should therefore serve out his sentence in a mental institution. If, according to the American Psychiatric Association, homosexuality was a mental illness, why shouldn't Womack enjoy the amenities of St. Elizabeths Hospital? Womack, Dietz recalled, was "a genius and he knew what to say" when court-appointed doctors examined him. The pornographer was also fortunate in that, as a former student of psychology, he had friends who worked at St. Elizabeths. Dietz convinced the judge, and like a Mafia don who continues to run the family business while sitting behind bars, Womack managed his publication empire from the comfort of a private hospital room equipped with a television and a typewriter. "It was very pleasant," he later said of his time in the insane asylum. It was also very productive. Upon his release, Womack had completed a prospectus for Guild Book Service, a subscription club for readers of gay pulp fiction novels.

Womack's brush with the law radicalized him. No longer was he content with merely selling erotic literature and nudie mags. He would sue the postmaster general and fulfill the pledge he had made upon his arrest: to take his case all the way to the Supreme Court and secure a legal victory for gay equality and free speech. And where Frank Kameny had failed in convincing the justices to hear his argument against the government's anti-homosexual discrimination, Womack succeeded. In February 1962, the country's highest court heard its first case concerning the legal status of the homosexual: *MANual Enterprises v. Day*.

Dietz made a brilliant case. By singling out homosexuals and denying them the right to receive certain publications through the mail, he maintained, the government "reduces a large segment of our society to second class citizenship." It was a daring argument, utilizing a term popularized by the African American civil rights movement. Echoing the point Kameny had made in his writ of certiorari the previous year, Dietz asked the justices to recognize that homosexuals also constituted a class of citizens who were being subjected to unequal, unconstitutional treatment. "If we so-called normal people, according to our law, are entitled to have our pin-ups, then why shouldn't the second-class citizens, the homosexual group . . . why shouldn't they be allowed to have their pin-ups?" he asked.

Writing for the majority in a 6–1 decision, Justice John Marshall Harlan II stated that while he found the images in Womack's magazines to be "dismally unpleasant, uncouth and tawdry . . . these portrayals of the male nude cannot fairly be regarded as more objectionable than many portrayals of the female nude that society tolerates." However qualified by his expressions of personal distaste, Harlan's argument on behalf of the Court that erotic images created for the titillation of homosexuals were not inherently more "obscene" than those designed to arouse their heterosexual fellow citizens recognized an important principle that unwittingly laid the groundwork for gay rights legal victories to come.

Womack certainly viewed his win as having significance beyond the validation of his personal right to publish and distribute beefcake mags. "I did not fight, spend money, go to jail, come to Saint Elizabeths to spend even one moment of my life living in fear of *anything*," he triumphantly wrote in a letter to his contributing photographers following the verdict. An unsigned editorial in the July 1964 *Grecian Guild Pictorial* "Convention Issue" made an ambitious argument that its subscribers were unaccustomed to seeing (and not just because, like the subscribers to another magazine famous for publishing racy photographs, they tended not to read it for the articles). "The public view toward homosexuals and lesbians will have to change, as it has been changing in recent years," the editorial, presumably written by Womack, declared. "It will have to be more than acceptance—more like public approval. Homosexuals should be allowed to acknowledge their inclinations and be able to obtain public offices."

Emboldened by his legal victories and flush with cash from his flourishing business enterprises, Womack bought a sixteen-thousand-square-foot warehouse on Capitol Hill equipped with a state-of-the-art German printing press and expanded the size of his staff to twenty-three to handle the volume of mail from people asking to be added to the *Grecian Guild* mailing list. Around the corner, Womack purchased a town house that he decorated so exquisitely it became a stop on the annual Capitol Hill House and Garden Tour. A First Amendment pioneer in addition to the country's leading producer and distributor of gay erotica, Womack developed something of a camp following in Washington. Otto Ulrich, a Womack employee, remembered accompanying his boss to the gay bars that were then starting to pop up around Dupont Circle during the middle of the 1960s. "We would walk in the front door, and you could just see one man whispering to the next and the next and the next—there was *the* Lynn Womack, the man responsible for all of us being able to enjoy our dirty pictures," Ulrich recalled. "And on many of those occasions, more than one of these handsome young men would come over and buy Lynn a drink. It was quite a sight to see—this 300-pound man being fawned over by a cluster of comely twenty-somethings." The jovial professor, who conveniently lived just a few blocks away from the marine barracks on Eighth Street in the city's Southeast quadrant, took full advantage of his newfound celebrity. When not swarmed with society matrons marveling at his taste in antique furniture, Womack's Capitol Hill home was "full of boys," according to one guest, "and Womack was the madam."

* * *

"Never mind how many senators," a visibly nervous Otto Preminger exclaimed as he paced the aisles of the Art Deco cinema a few blocks from the White House. "I'm only interested in the Robert Kennedys."

A filibuster-proof majority had arrived at Washington's Trans-Lux Theatre for the March 20, 1962, premiere of *Advise and Consent*, the highly anticipated film adaptation of Allen Drury's best-selling novel. "There has never been a movie that has been so closely watched as this one by all the people who control public opinion," the author had written to Preminger after the legendary Austro-Hungarian-born director purchased the book's movie rights. As part of the deal, Drury relinquished editorial control over the film. But he did have some modest suggestions. "The basic purpose of the movie, as the basic purpose of the book, is to show that politicians are human," Drury explained. He understood how portraying an American president as the devious accomplice to a blackmail plot might be a bridge too far for Hollywood, just a few years removed from its complicity in the blacklist and still very much deferential to the nation's political establishment. Therefore, if "the president could be relieved of a little of his direct responsibility . . . This would, in the author's mind, weaken the situation to some degree, but would be an acceptable alternative if Hollywood proved afraid to tackle the situation as portrayed in the book." What Drury was less willing to see changed for the sake of dramatic license was his novel's controversial gay subject matter.

> The homosexual aspect of Brig's death is not imperative, providing Mr. Preminger can think of something else sufficiently grave to bring down a character of such strength. An illicit romance, even an illicit child, won't do it; Grover Cleveland fathered a bastard and went to the White House. And, any kind of financial speculation or corruption would be so utterly foreign to Brig's nature that he wouldn't be Brig any more and the whole story would be wrenched so violently out of shape that it wouldn't be ADVISE AND CONSENT any more.

The tragedy of the homosexual politician, Drury argued, was that, unlike his philandering and venal peers, what made him vulnerable to exposure and destruction was morally neutral. Society, however, viewed the matter differently, such that there was absolutely nothing, not even the fathering of an illegitimate child, that had a greater capacity to ruin a reputation and career. Drury's belief, radical for its time, was that a gay person could have a "character of such strength" as to be the hero of a Great American Novel, or, for that matter, a cinema classic.

Drury did not need to convince Preminger of the need to retain "the homosexual aspect." The director was already famous for having tackled provocative subjects like drug addiction (*The Man with the Golden Arm*) and rape (*Anatomy of a Murder*), in both cases brushing up against "the Code." Officially the "code to maintain social and community values," the Motion Picture Association of America's self-censorship guidelines dated back to a 1927 list of "Don'ts" and "Be Carefuls" that prohibited portrayals of, among other sensitive subject matter, "sex perversion." In 1953, the MPAA had withheld its seal of approval from Preminger's *The Moon Is Blue*, citing the film's "light and gay treatment of the subject of illicit sex and seduction." Preminger released the film without a rating and was vindicated when it became a commercial success. He did the same thing six years later when *Anatomy of a Murder* was denied an MPAA seal and it, too, made a fortune at the box office.

For Preminger, *Advise and Consent* offered a ripe opportunity to challenge the censors once more. Since the silent film era, exaggeratedly effeminate male characters, clearly implied to be gay, had appeared on the big screen, but thanks to the Code, Hollywood had yet to feature an "avowed" homosexual on-screen. "It was always Otto's publicity game to break the Code, and he was successful at the game," recalled Wendell Mayes, who wrote the screenplay for *Advise and Consent*. "You look at the record, and you will discover that many of the changes in the Code were a result of Otto Preminger's breaking the rules." Having depicted adultery, drug use, and other sins, Preminger was determined to surmount what *Variety* described as film's "last specific taboo" and break open Hollywood's closet door.

He wouldn't have an easy time of it. In February 1960, MPAA Code chief Geoffrey Shurlock told a House subcommittee overseeing "self-policing of the movie and publishing industry" that the gay themes in *Advise and Consent* would "have to go" from the upcoming film version. Visiting Washington for a research trip that same month, Preminger told a group of senators at a Capitol Hill luncheon that he had no intention of removing the homo-

sexual content and would handle it "like it was in the book—in good taste."
Over the next year and a half, Preminger and Shurlock negotiated the terms
of a truce: the MPAA would withdraw its prohibition on representations
of homosexuality in exchange for Preminger's agreeing not to show, in a
quick shot of a photo used to blackmail Sen. Brigham Anderson, Brig and
his wartime lover wearing military uniforms. On October 3, 1961, the
MPAA announced that it was henceforth permissible "to consider approving references in motion pictures to the subject of sex aberration," provided
they be "treated with care, discretion and restraint." *Variety* announced the
news thusly: "Discreetly the Code in Switch About Swishing."

The switch added a considerable amount of buzz to an already highly
anticipated production. Decades before the White House Correspondents' Association Dinner became an annual rite of spring for America's political and entertainment elite, the five-week, on-location shoot of
Advise and Consent was the biggest encounter yet between Washington
and Hollywood. "Capitolians Agog," declared *Variety*, as the celebrated
director transformed the nation's capital into a giant film set. At a Capitol Hill cocktail party, where actors Charles Laughton, Henry Fonda, and
Walter Pidgeon hobnobbed with the likes of Lyndon Johnson, Senator
Hubert Humphrey, and Bobby Kennedy, Drury toasted Preminger, with a
bit of foreboding, as "the only absolute dictator ever to make a film about
a democracy." The district's leading museums and philanthropists loaned
pieces of art worth a quarter of a million dollars to the film's set designers. Aiming for verisimilitude, Preminger used working journalists for a
scene where the president addresses the press corps, and he hired real-life
socialites to play themselves at a party filmed on the twenty-acre Tregaron
Estate. ("When are they going to serve us dinner?" one society doyenne
complained, while others grumbled about the dry bar.) For the dramatic
confrontation between Herbert Gelman and Robert Leffingwell that establishes the movie's conflict, Preminger chose the Old Senate Caucus Room,
site of the Army-McCarthy Hearings.

Enhancing the sense of excitement around *Advise and Consent* was
that its filming coincided with Washington's transformation from the
dreary swamp of the Eisenhower era into the enchanted kingdom known
as Camelot. "It was a wonderful moment to be in Washington," recalled
George Grizzard, who played the villainous, blackmailing senator Fred Van
Ackerman. "This was Camelot, after all, when all the bright young things

were there to build a new world." Peter Lawford, who played the rakish senator Lafe Smith (loosely based on his brother-in-law, the president), initially convinced the First Lady to let Preminger film several scenes in the White House, an offer she later rescinded. (This didn't stop her husband from calling the set to see if he could obtain an early print of the film to screen in the White House movie theater.) "*I vud haf thought zat Foshinkton vud haf been more blasé,*" Preminger enthused about the capital of his beloved adopted land. "*It isn't.*"

If Drury got his wish that the film version of *Advise and Consent* remain faithful to his novel by maintaining "the homosexual aspect," he was to be disappointed by Preminger's treatment of it. Whereas Drury portrayed his protagonist's gay affair with sensitivity and compassion, Preminger treated it with lurid sensationalism. For instance, in the novel, Brig never confronts his ex-lover, who communicates with him just once in a brief phone conversation. In the film, Brig discovers that his old flame, who is given the name of Ray, works in Greenwich Village as a prostitute whose pimp operates out of an apartment decorated in bohemian bric-a-brac. (This characterization came down from on high; as part of its agreement to approve *Advise and Consent*, the MPAA instructed Preminger that "none of the [homosexual] men in the film could be portrayed in an unduly shocking manner," and that the procurer therefore should not be a "swishy" type but more "a sort of beatnik character.") In the film's climactic scene, Brig tracks Ray down to the seedy Club 602—the first interior of a gay bar to be depicted in postwar American cinema—where men huddle together at tables illuminated by candlelights. After surveying the darkened room teeming with homosexual stereotypes, the camera zooms in on Brig's face, frozen in an expression of horror and self-revulsion. The contrast between the domestic bliss of his heterosexual Washington existence and what his life *could* have been had he followed Ray's path into homosexuality sufficiently established, Brig flees the bar and jumps into a taxi—but not before throwing his confused former squeeze into a puddle.

Preminger included this scene to show that "not only was [Brig] horrified by this life, but also attracted to it." Occurring right before Brig returns to Washington and slits his throat, it signifies a sense of shame on Brig's part nowhere to be found in Drury's source material. According to gay film historian Vito Russo, the cinematic Brig commits suicide "not because he is being blackmailed in Washington," as his literary antecedent had done, "but because he has gone to New York and found people with whom he has something in common and is so repulsed that he sees no alternative to the straight razor." By twisting what Drury poignantly described as Brig's "profoundly important strength"—the moral integrity that gay men and women acquire by virtue of living in a repressive society—into shame and self-hatred, Preminger distorted Drury's message of acceptance.

While *Advise and Consent* was nominated for the Palme d'Or at Cannes and is today considered a classic of American political cinema second only to *Mr. Smith Goes to Washington*, it was a huge disappointment to the author of the book upon which it was based. After watching the film adaptation of his runaway best seller, Allen Drury made an important announcement regarding his next novel. A thriller of high politics set at the United Nations entitled *A Shade of Difference*, it was "not available for sale to the movies."

18

"THAT OLD BLACK FAIRY"

ON THE SAME DAY THAT U.S. INTELLIGENCE ANALYSTS, STUDYING PHOTO-graphs taken by a U-2 spy plane, determined that the Soviet Union had stationed nuclear missiles in Cuba, a group of senators announced their findings regarding another threat to American security concerning the island nation ninety miles off the coast of Florida. According to the report released on October 15, 1962, by the Senate Internal Security Subcommittee, the State Department official who had once been in charge of Cuba policy was a security risk lacking "integrity and general suitability."

The case of Latin American affairs specialist William E. Wieland had been percolating for years. Appointed director of the State Department's Office of Caribbean and Mexican Affairs in September 1958, Wieland immediately recommended halting U.S. arms shipments to the Cuban military regime of Fulgencio Batista over its harsh domestic repression. When Fidel Castro and his ragtag band of revolutionaries marched into Havana four months later, and some in the United States began to ask, as they had a decade earlier about China, "Who lost Cuba?" Wieland emerged as an irresistible target for congressional conservatives. In a column entitled "Who Is He?" George Sokolsky trained his sights on Wieland's murky background, dredging up the fact that he had once been known as William

Arthur Montenegro (the surname of his father) to paint the picture of a shifty, duplicitous diplomat. The following week, Sokolsky intimated that Wieland was untrustworthy for another reason, endemic to the agency for which he worked. "What is necessary is not so much a reformulation of policy," Sokolsky declared, "as a total reorganization of the personnel of the State Department, the searching out of blackmailable homosexuals in both the State Department and the Pentagon and their elimination at any cost and the exposure of characters such as William Arthur Montenegro, by whatever name he goes."

The problem with witch hunts is that you eventually run out of witches, and by the early 1960s, the "elimination" of homosexuals from the federal government was yielding fewer and fewer of them. But the *fear* of secret homosexual plots threatening American democracy was alive and well. The Wieland case featured personalities and motifs remarkably similar to an earlier bureaucratic battle between Congress and the executive over an alleged "security risk": the nomination of Chip Bohlen as ambassador to the Soviet Union. Like Bohlen, Wieland was a debonair, multilingual diplomat whose involvement in the policymaking process at a moment of Communist advancement abroad made him a convenient scapegoat. Wieland's chief antagonist, Otto Otepka, deputy director of the State Department Office of Security and son of a Czechoslovak immigrant, reprised the role of blue-collar, white-ethnic security investigator originally played by Scott McLeod. And hovering in the background, never explicitly stated but instrumental all the same, was the specter of homosexuality.

The primary plank in the campaign against Wieland was his connection to the man whose forced resignation from the State Department nearly twenty years earlier provided the original justification for the ongoing purge of homosexuals from the federal government. Sumner Welles may have died the previous year, but congressional critics wielded his posthumous infamy to sully the reputation of a protégé. Wieland had first met Welles during the 1920s, in Cuba, where Wieland was working as a journalist and Welles was serving as ambassador, and Welles later recommended Wieland for a job at the State Department. That they met in Cuba, of all places, only made the connection more pernicious. According to one study of homosexuality on the island, "Before 1959, almost anything that was prohibited on the puritanical mainland of North America became possible in Havana," where Welles was rumored to have fulfilled his penchant for swarthy male sex partners. Internal subcommittee memos record Cuban exile informants claiming that Wieland "was a notorious homosexual with ties to another notorious homosexual," that his "morals in Cuba were very doubtful, and his entrance into and rise in the State Department was made possible by the former Ambassador to Cuba Sumner Welles, who is known to have been a homosexual." John Seigenthaler, an aide to Bobby Kennedy, recalled of the Wieland controversy that "there were all sorts of stories about orgies, and pretty gory details about him."

Called to testify, Wieland was subjected to a barrage of insinuating questions about his relationship with Welles. "Where did you see him, and how often did you see him, and under what circumstances did you see him?" demanded Sen. Thomas Dodd of Connecticut, who continued this suggestive line of questioning by asking Wieland if he had ever met with the undersecretary alone in his office. At another point in Wieland's testimony, Dodd referred to the diplomat's swim with Welles's twenty-four-year-old son Benjamin following a lunch at the Welles estate as a "swimming party." Was Wieland aware that he was known as "Sumner Welles's fair-haired boy in Havana?" inquired committee counsel J. G. Sourwine, who further prodded:

SOURWINE: Mr. Wieland, as a Government administrator, are you aware that sexual deviation, and especially homosexuality among employees, presents a very special security problem?
WIELAND: Yes, sir . . .
SOURWINE: Have you ever had to deal with this problem in any way?
WIELAND: No, sir.

Later in the hearing, Sourwine stated, "We have had testimony that you were seen with [Welles] many times, many places, that you were frequently seen together in Cuba."

As Eisenhower stuck by Bohlen, so Kennedy sided with Wieland. And he was right to do so. While Wieland might have been slow in acknowledging Castro's pro-Communist leanings, he warned as early as 1958 that if "Batista was bad medicine for everyone, Castro would be worse." Five weeks after Castro marched into Havana, Wieland advised, "We should be extremely cautious about giving any impression that we are so anxious to help Castro in the face of his anti-American statements." Otto Otepka's own report on Wieland concluded that the subject of his investigation was "not and never has been a Communist or revolutionist or a homosexual or a person who had engaged in notoriously disgraceful conduct." Yet it was not until three years after the Senate committee publicly impugned Wieland that a State Department panel cleared him of wrongdoing.

In assigning blame for complex geopolitical developments to homosexual cabals, many Cold War Washingtonians ironically emulated the Communist apparatchiks they so vehemently opposed. Both sides labored under a paranoid mindset positing history as the product of secretive machinations by mysterious cliques. "But you know the saying that there are two international conspiracies, the Cominform and the 'homo inform,'" a Kennedy advisor once riffed at a Hyannis Port bull session. "Well, Central Bankers are like homosexuals. They are not homosexuals, but they will do anything for their kind if they can get their licks in under the surface."

If there was anything considered more threatening to the American social order at this time than a homosexual Communist, it was a *Black* homosexual Communist.

* * *

SINCE HIS ELECTION IN 1930 AS THE COUNTY ATTORNEY for Edgefield, South Carolina, Strom Thurmond had devoted his political career to keeping African Americans in their place. When President Truman ordered the desegregation of the armed forces, advocated for the elimination of state poll taxes, and urged the passage of federal anti-lynching legislation all within the single year of 1948, Thurmond, then Democratic governor of the Palmetto State, launched the breakaway States' Rights Democratic Party and challenged Truman for the presidency on its ticket. Thurmond was the most prominent political figure in the country to malign the civil rights movement as Communistic; accepting Truman's racial policies, he declared, would yield "to the demands of the parlor pinks and the subversives." Nearly a decade later, preparing to torpedo the Civil Rights Act of 1957 as a U.S. senator, Thurmond took daily steam baths to dehydrate his body, thereby lessening the need to relieve himself during what would be a twenty-four-hour, eighteen-minute filibuster, the longest in history. None of these efforts had stopped the gradual advance toward equality, however, which is why on August 13, 1963, less than two weeks before the movement was set to stage the most important demonstration in its history, Thurmond strode onto the floor of the Senate clutching a document he had every reason to believe would succeed where his previous exertions at political sectarianism, cynical red-baiting, and strategic desiccation had failed.

The catalyst for Thurmond's latest maneuver against civil rights was the profile he had read two days earlier in the *Washington Post* of Bayard Rustin, chief organizer of the March on Washington for Jobs and Freedom. Scheduled for August 28 on the National Mall, the gathering promised to be the largest demonstration for civil rights in American history. The *Post* profile of Rustin, Thurmond began, was a "whitewash," and for the better part of an hour, the South Carolinian recited a litany of charges against the fifty-one-year-old Black leader. Rustin, he declared, had a "ludicrous record." He had been a member of the Young Communist League. He was a draft dodger. Most abhorrent, however, was his 1953 conviction in Pasadena, California, on what the *Post* euphemistically described as "a morals charge after being arrested with two other men." In its reprehensible attempt to take "the deplorable and disturbing record" of Rustin and make him come out "smelling like a rose and looking like a gilded lily," Thurmond fumed, the paper failed to clarify that this was in fact a case of "sex perversion." Rustin, in other words, was a homosexual. At the conclusion of his speech, Thurmond inserted into the *Congressional Record* two articles from the *Los Angeles Times* detailing the 1953 incident, as well as a copy of the original police booking slip of Rustin's arrest, which he had almost certainly obtained from the FBI.

An hour-long denunciation from the floor of the U.S. Senate by America's leading segregationist was not even close to being the harshest attack Bayard Rustin had endured over his long career advocating social change. Born in the small town of West Chester, Pennsylvania, in 1912, Rustin decided to devote himself to the cause of racial equality in high school, after he was denied service at a restaurant on account of his skin color. Though Rustin had, as Thurmond alleged, been a member of the Young Communist League for a brief spell in the late 1930s, he was quickly disillusioned by the party's attempt to hijack the African American civil rights struggle and became an ardently anticommunist social democrat. Rustin studied Gandhian tactics of nonviolence in India and was arrested more than twenty times for applying them toward the advancement of civil rights and world peace. After being arrested in North Carolina for testing the enforcement of a law prohibiting discrimination in interstate travel in 1947 (the first Freedom Ride), he spent twenty-two days on a North Carolina chain gang. Standing six feet, three inches tall and speaking with a clipped, faintly British accent picked up while studying at the London School of Economics, Rustin had a commanding presence as well as a formidable ability to motivate large numbers of people to political action. In the *Post* article, the young leader of the March, Rev. Dr. Martin Luther King Jr., praised Rustin as "a brilliant, efficient and dedicated organizer and one of the best and most persuasive interpreters of non-violence." Which is precisely why Thurmond felt it necessary to destroy him.

Thurmond's chief accusation, that Rustin had been found guilty of "sex perversion," was not inaccurate. Nor would Rustin deny that he was gay—a disposition extremely rare for men of his era and, among public figures, so exceptional as to be virtually unparalleled. (In the words of one of his closest aides, Rustin "never knew there was a closet to go into.") This caused no small amount of tension with his fellow civil rights leaders, most of them Christian clergymen who believed homosexuality to be a grave sin. Rustin's 1953 incident was not his first arrest on a homosexual charge, and at the time, he had resigned his position as an organizer with the pacifist Fellowship of Reconciliation to avoid causing the group embarrassment. According to a close colleague of Rustin's, the incident "crushed" him, and while he avoided further run-ins with the law, his status as a "sex pervert" was one that enemies of all stripes would use against him.

One of the first to do so had been a fellow Black political leader, Congressman Adam Clayton Powell Jr. In 1960, Powell threatened King that unless King called off a protest outside that summer's Democratic National Convention, he would accuse King and Rustin of being lovers. Powell had once published an article in *Ebony* magazine bemoaning how "the boys with a swish and the girls with a swagger are getting daily more numerous and more bold," and he well understood the damage that such an allegation could cause if brought to the attention of King's fellow pastors in the Southern Christian Leadership Conference (SCLC). Powell's threat reached King while the latter was vacationing in Rio de Janeiro, prompting King to call Rustin. Not wanting to discuss the details over the phone, he said that Powell, "who is very irresponsible, is threatening to do some unkind things and is going to embroil us in something unpleasant."

Rustin advised King not to back down. "Look, you know this kind of thing is first of all immoral, and second of all, if you permit a man like

Adam Powell to get away with this game, what game will he not play?" he said. "This is blackmail." According to Rustin, "My being gay was not a problem for Dr. King but a problem for the movement." Nonetheless, King could not bring himself to ask for Rustin's resignation. But upon the recommendation of other leaders within the SCLC, Rustin submitted it anyway, the second time that his sexual orientation led to his being booted from an organization.

Thurmond would attempt a trifecta. Movement leaders already feared that Rustin's homosexuality could be used to discredit their cause, and forces in the American government were ready to exploit this anxiety. In a phone conversation held shortly before the march and wiretapped by the FBI, King fretted about Rustin with an advisor.

"I hope Bayard don't take a drink before the march," King's interlocutor said.

"Yes," King replied. "And grab one little brother. 'Cause he will grab one when he has a drink."

The day before Thurmond denounced Rustin from the well of the Senate, Hoover forwarded a transcript of this discussion to Attorney General Robert Kennedy. The Kennedy brothers had an uneasy relationship with the civil rights movement, voicing general support for its goals in public but repeatedly balking at the actions necessary to make them a reality. When the question arose among march organizers as to whether President Kennedy should be invited to address the gathering, Rustin said he should not. The basic principle of a march against government inertia would be undermined, he argued, if its organizers offered a platform to the person whose inertia they were protesting. This predictably drew the ire of the attorney general. "So you're down here for that old black fairy's anti-Kennedy demonstration?" a peeved Robert Kennedy asked the socialite Marietta Tree at a Georgetown dinner party on the eve of the march.

With Rustin now the most prominent homosexual in America, the easiest course for King would have been to distance himself from his aide, just as he had done three years prior, when Adam Clayton Powell threatened to expose a nonexistent homosexual relationship between the two men. Most of his fellow civil rights leaders would have endorsed such a move. Roy Wilkins, head of the National Association for the Advancement of Colored People, had opposed Rustin's leadership role in the march long before Thurmond's speech. "I put the movement first above all things, and

I believe it is my moral obligation to go into this meeting and say that with all of your talent, I don't think you should lead this important march," Rustin recalled Wilkins telling him. On the other hand, abandoning Rustin because Thurmond had cynically seized upon a decade-old arrest record would have handed a victory to one of the movement's most vicious enemies.

What the civil rights leaders did next was unprecedented: they defended a public figure who, against his will, had been identified as a homosexual. Illustrative of their reasoning for doing so was the shift by Wilkins, who, despite having initially opposed Rustin's organizing the march, defended him in the face of Thurmond's attack. In a letter to an NAACP member outraged at the decision to retain Rustin, Wilkins praised the march organizer as "a man of exceptional ability, who has delivered an extraordinary job on a project that should have required a full three months but is being completed in two . . . It is the belief of all of us who have noted his work, regardless of our personal feelings, that . . . we could have done no better than the gentleman in question." Black trade unionist A. Philip Randolph, who had dubbed Rustin "Mr. March-on-Washington himself" just a week earlier, held an impromptu press conference at the march's headquarters in a dilapidated Harlem community center:

> I am sure I speak for the combined Negro leadership in voicing my complete confidence in Bayard Rustin's character, integrity and extraordinary ability. That Mr. Rustin was on one occasion arrested in another connection has long been a matter of public record, and not an object of concealment. I am dismayed that there are in this country men who, wrapping themselves in the mantle of Christian morality would mutilate the most elementary conceptions of human decency, privacy, and humility in order to persecute other men.

For those who might have been personally uncomfortable with his sexual orientation, which probably characterized most of the movement's leadership, Rustin explained the choice in stark terms. "The Senator is interested in attacking me because he is interested in destroying the movement," he stated. "He will not get away with this."

Up to this point, no gay person in American public life had survived a charge of homosexuality. The country was over a decade away from electing its first openly gay public official and two decades away from electing its first openly gay member of Congress. To retain Rustin was risky; that the decision to do so was undertaken by leaders of a long-oppressed racial minority, in the lead-up to the most consequential event of their struggle, makes it even more historically significant. The March on Washington was a huge success, and afterward, Rustin and Randolph appeared on the cover of *Life* magazine. According to Rustin, part of the reason King decided to stand by him was the remorse he felt for failing to do so in the face of Powell's blackmail. Given "a chance to rethink" how he had distanced himself from his aide, King gained an appreciation for how loyalty toward one's allies trumped appeasement of one's adversaries. "If I've learned anything," Rustin reflected a year and a half before his 1987 death, "it is that people, by helping others who are also in trouble, grow in strength to help themselves—that a new psychological and spiritual element is brought to bear."

Rustin, who took on a plethora of causes during his decades-long career as a human rights activist, would not align himself publicly with the gay rights movement until the end of his life. But his tribulation in the weeks leading up to the March on Washington marked an important point of convergence between the civil rights movement that had captured the nation's attention and the one then struggling just to be seen. The African American freedom struggle profoundly influenced early homophile leaders, who borrowed heavily from its nonviolent tactics and rhetorical appeals to the country's founding documents. Mattachine Society cofounder Jack Nichols recalled that he and Frank Kameny "spoke often of King's inspiring activism," and the group's "Statement of Purpose" ended with a pledge to "cooperate with other minority organizations which are striving for the realization of full civil rights and liberties for all." At a time when protesting openly against their own oppression was inconceivable, many gay people channeled their passion into fighting against the oppression of others. One gay man who participated in Washington's first picket against segregated department stores recalled that most of the male protesters that day were also gay. "Many of us who went south to work with Dr. King in the sixties were gay," said Grant Gallup, a gay priest. "A lot of gay people who could not come out for their own liberation could invest the same energies in the liberation of Black people."

Pat Hawkins was one of the many gay people who joined the March on Washington, albeit not openly so. Her awareness of racial injustice was heightened in the ninth grade, when a teacher attempted to prevent her from delivering a speech in favor of the recent Supreme Court decision striking down segregated schooling, *Brown v. Board of Education*. "Before I let that happen," the teacher vowed, foreshadowing Alabama governor George Wallace, "I'll stand in the door with a shotgun." Later, at the University of Michigan, Hawkins became romantically involved with a woman at a time when homosexuality was grounds for expulsion, an experience that made her alive to the dangerous consequences of leading an openly gay life. Hawkins was living in Washington at the time of the historic march, and there was no question she would participate. But announcing her sexual orientation on a placard was unthinkable. "A lot of gay people attended, but I wasn't attending as a gay person," she recalled. Seven members of the Mattachine Society went as a group, but they, too, declined to carry signs indicating as much. Still, they considered their mere participation an achievement. "Now we have fulfilled the last part of our Mattachine Statement of Purpose," Kameny declared, perhaps a little too triumphantly.

The Mattachine's effort to recruit Black people did not extend much beyond distributing a flyer at Black gay bars entitled *The Negro and the Homophile Movement*. Declaring that "the white homosexual has only one burden," it acknowledged that "the Negro homosexual has two. Do you know that there is someone to work with you and something to work for? *You* are invited specifically to join the homophile movement, composed of Negroes and whites, which is trying to improve the social status of the homosexual—of all homosexuals, black and white." In the end, however, hardly any Black people joined Mattachine. "I remember sitting up at the front and looking over and in a city that was roughly two-thirds black, seeing a sea of white faces, entirely so," Kameny lamented of the group's early meetings. Paul Kuntzler recalled that once, when a Black man did attend a Mattachine meeting, the other group members assumed "he was infiltrating, that he was a government agent." To some degree, this lack of Black participation was attributable to the fact that Washington's Black residents were mostly locals, whereas whites were largely transients; coming out of the closet and associating with a gay organization was significantly harder while living in the city where one's family resided.

But there was also a degree of racial obliviousness detectable among the early Mattachine activists. For instance, in a news release announcing its formation, the group declared that "the homosexual, today, is where the Negro was in the 1920s, except that the Negro has had, at worst, the mere indifference of the government, and, at best, its active assistance, whereas the homosexual has always had to contend with the active hostility of his government." Kameny was not wrong to notice that, while African Americans had been successful in gaining the support of some sectors of the federal government, homosexuals still faced opposition across the board. But Black people had suffered far worse than "mere indifference" from their government, and for Black gays still subjected to segregated public accommodations, the threat of lynching, the denial of the right to vote, and deeply ingrained economic and social inequalities—in addition to the social discrimination they faced from their white fellow homosexuals—such words must have sounded tone-deaf.

Reflecting on the time Strom Thurmond attempted to undercut the movement for racial equality with a crass appeal to homophobia, Rustin concluded that by casting off his secret, he divested it of the power to harm him. "The fact of the matter is, it was already known, it was nothing to hide," he said of his homosexuality. "You can't hurt the movement unless you have something to reveal." (Not everyone in the movement was satisfied with Rustin's performance. A few weeks after the march, Stanley Levison, a significant white funder of King's efforts with whom Rustin quarreled over Levison's Communist sympathies, described Rustin as a "shrieker" who, with James Baldwin, was "better qualified to lead a homosexual movement than a civil rights movement.") Whatever damage Thurmond hoped to inflict by publicizing Rustin's sexual orientation clearly had no impact on the movement's overall trajectory. His speech did, however, have an unintentionally positive effect on the man it was intended to harm. Thurmond had "brought out" Rustin to the nation and the world, and while Rustin was "not laughing then," he would thereafter send a red rose to Thurmond every August 28 in gratitude.

* * *

"THE WASHINGTON LANDSCAPE SEEMED TO ME TO BE LITTERED WITH MALE WIDOWS," Joe Alsop remembered of November 22, 1963, the day John F. Kennedy was assassinated. "I had no idea that I loved him," Alsop reflected in an interview several months after the murder while pacing around his Georgetown home, pulling off his glasses to wipe away the tears while his parrots squawked in the background. "I don't go in for loving men. But nothing in my life has moved me as it did, not even the death of my father." According to historian Sally Bedell Smith, "probably the saddest of the Kennedy widows"—sadder than Jackie, even—was Lem Billings. The First Friend never recovered from the murder of his schoolboy crush, descending into a pit of alcoholic despair that contributed to his own untimely death in 1981 at the age of sixty-five.

Paul Kuntzler, who had come to Washington on the wave of youthful enthusiasm for JFK, was shell-shocked at the news from Dallas. That afternoon, he called Frank Kameny to let him know that he would not be able to make the trip out to Kameny's home in the Palisades section of Washington for that evening's weekly Mattachine gathering. "Why would President Kennedy's death prevent you from attending a Mattachine Society meeting?" the unflappable activist asked.

On the day of the assassination, William Walton was scheduled to depart for Moscow, where he was set to oversee the opening of a major American art exhibition. The trip was canceled, and as the "New Frontier's artist-without-portfolio," Walton switched gears to decorate a White House in mourning. He took inspiration from an engraving of Abraham Lincoln's lying in state, which Jackie, in a tragic irony, had selected the previous year for inclusion in the first public guidebook to the White House. Walton tastefully draped the East Room windows with black curtains and borrowed a crucifix from Kennedy brother-in-law and Peace Corps founder Sargent Shriver to place in front of the martyred president's catafalque. He also advised Bobby to keep his brother's casket closed during its lying in state in the Capitol Rotunda.

In his testimony before the President's Commission on the Assassination of President Kennedy—known unofficially as the Warren Commission for its chairman, Supreme Court chief justice Earl Warren—J. Edgar Hoover discussed the investigation his Bureau had launched into the alleged assassin, an American Communist and ex-marine named Lee Harvey Oswald.

> We wanted to know whether he had been recruited by the Soviet government as an intelligence agent, which is a frequent and constant practice. There is not a year goes by but that individuals and groups of individuals, sometimes on these cultural exchanges, go through Russia and recruits

are enlisted by the Russian intelligence, usually through blackmail. The individual is threatened that if he doesn't come back to this country and work for them they will expose the fact that he is a homosexual or a degenerate or has been indiscreet.

Pictures are usually taken of individuals who become implicated in that sort of thing, so the individual is really desperate. Such blackmail has occurred year after year for some time.

Contrary to Hoover's assertion, there had not been a single example of an American homosexual blackmailed under such circumstances. Not only that, but the one attempt the Soviets *were* known to have made in this direction—on Joe Alsop in 1957—ended in failure, as Hoover well knew, considering how he had spread the story of it so widely around Washington.

The assassination of President Kennedy marked a new phase in the evolution of American paranoia, triggering the slow but steady erosion of public trust in government, media, and other institutions of establishment authority that continues to this day. Upon the release of the 888-page Warren Commission Report in September 1964, a majority of Americans said they were unpersuaded by its central finding that Oswald had acted alone, a figure that has remained steady. In the summer of 1966, a book challenging the report, *Rush to Judgment*, premiered at the top of the *New York Times* best seller list, where it stayed for twenty-nine weeks. This was the state of the nation when the district attorney for Orleans Parish, Louisiana, made a shocking announcement on February 18, 1967.

According to Jim Garrison, the assassination of President Kennedy had been the culmination of a scheme hatched in New Orleans, for which "arrests will be made." As if this was not astonishing enough, less than a week later, one of the men whom Garrison claimed he was on the verge of arresting dropped dead. A failed candidate for the Catholic priesthood, a would-be hypnotist whose apartment was littered with prescription-pill boxes, a hard-core anticommunist who wore a homemade wig and fake eyebrows to compensate for the premature hair loss he had suffered as the result of a rare skin condition, and a homosexual, David Ferrie better fit the description of eccentric bystander to history than man at the center of it. But according to Garrison, Ferrie's service alongside Oswald in the same Civil Air Patrol unit, as well as his ties to anti-Castro Cuban exile groups that Garrison believed had played a part in the assassination, made Ferrie "one of history's most important individuals."

According to the coroner, Ferrie died from a cerebral hemorrhage. Garrison, offering an early indication of the antics to follow, said he considered the death a suicide but would not rule out murder. Fortunately for Garrison, he had another, live suspect waiting in the wings: a retired businessman and pillar of New Orleans society named Clay Shaw. What connected Shaw with Ferrie and several other men whom Garrison would eventually implicate in the crime was not just their complicity in a sinister, right-wing conspiracy to kill America's beloved young leader, but their homosexuality.

Far from being the reactionary of Garrison's description, Shaw described himself as a "Wilsonian-FDR-Kennedy liberal." His connection to the plot alleged by Garrison was extremely tenuous, based entirely upon the testimony of a New Orleans attorney who claimed to have received a call the day after the assassination—a call that he later told the FBI was a "figment of his imagination"—from a "Clay Bertrand" requesting that he represent Oswald. "Clay Bertrand," Garrison alleged, was the alias Clay Shaw used in New Orleans gay society. For months, Garrison developed his conspiracy to greater and greater levels of complexity and evil. His "composite conspirator," reported *Newsweek*, "would probably be equal parts Oswald, homosexual, right-wing extremist, FBI agent, Cosa Nostra hood, CIA operative and Russian double agent." Over time, "as bread dough rises under heat," Garrison's theory of the case expanded to include "a Nazi operation whose sponsors include some of the oil-rich millionaires in Texas." In July, NBC gave Garrison a full half hour to lay out his hypothesis for the American people. "Tonight, I'm going to talk to you about truth and about fairy tales," he began.

The biggest "fairy tale," however, was Garrison's own. Although he never publicly mentioned homosexuality, Garrison expressed his belief in numerous conversations that a gay cabal had killed Kennedy. To *Newsweek* correspondent Hugh Aynesworth, Garrison introduced a witness who claimed that Oswald and the nightclub owner who fatally shot him two days after his arrest, Jack Ruby, were "gay lovers." The assassination, Garrison revealed to *Life* magazine correspondent Richard Billings, was a "sadist plot" carried out, as he told UPI's Merriman Smith, by "high-status fags." Ferrie and Shaw, Garrison explained to James Phelan of the *Saturday Evening Post*, "had the same motive as Loeb and Leopold, when they murdered Bobbie Franks in Chicago back in the twenties," a reference to the sensational 1924 kidnapping and murder of a fourteen-year-old boy by two young male lovers. "It was a homosexual thrill-killing, plus the excitement of getting away with a perfect crime," Garrison asserted. "John Kennedy was everything that Dave Ferrie was not—a successful, handsome, popular, wealthy, virile man. You can just picture the charge Ferrie got out of plotting his death."

How did Garrison know all this? "Look at the people involved," he told Phelan. "Dave Ferrie, homosexual. Clay Shaw, homosexual. Jack Ruby, homosexual." (Garrison told Phelan that he had "dug out" that Ruby's "homosexual nickname was Pinkie.") But what about the self-declared "patsy," Lee Harvey Oswald? "A switch-hitter who couldn't satisfy his wife." In addition to two "key figures" whose names Garrison claimed he could not reveal, that made "*six* homosexuals in the plot. One or maybe two, okay. But all six homosexual? How far can you stretch the arm of coincidence?" Garrison's plotters were archetypical gay villains, scheming and decadent, and homosexuality was a symbol of their corrupted souls. Shaw, the prosecutor alleged, wanted to kill "the world's most handsome man," an echo of Alger Hiss's accusation that Whittaker Chambers was motivated by "fairy vengeance." It was the return of the Homintern, albeit in extreme right-wing, rather than Communistic, guise.

Garrison devoted the full resources of the New Orleans District Attorney's Office to ruining Clay Shaw, who spent the remaining years of his life consumed in proceedings to clear his name, and his entire life savings—over $200,000—on legal defense. During the trial, a prosecutor asked Shaw and various witnesses if Shaw had ever worn "tight pants," and according to the writer James Kirkwood, who covered the case from beginning to end, the media "frequently hinted at a duality in Clay Shaw's personal life" in a way that served to signal his abnormality. "Queers know queers!" the presiding judge told Kirkwood, in justification of Garrison's tactics. "They've got a clique better than the CIA."

As intended, Garrison's charges caused an international media frenzy. Everyone from the renowned Italian journalist Oriana Fallaci to a writer for *Paris Match* to a radio correspondent from an Illinois town of just four thousand citizens descended upon the Big Easy. After nearly six weeks of testimony, and two years to the day since the defendant was arrested on conspiracy charges, the jury took less than an hour to acquit Clay Shaw. His persecution by a deranged prosecutor was a travesty of justice, "one of the most disgraceful chapters in the history of American jurisprudence," in the words of the *New York Times*. Shaw had his own explanation for why Garrison singled him out. "When death comes to the figure of a prince, as it did to Kennedy, struck down in his prime, it should come under a panoply of great tragedy with all the resulting high court intrigue—almost something out of Shakespeare—not from some poor little psychotic loser crouched with a mail-order rifle behind a stack of cardboard boxes in a warehouse." The brutal slaying of the idealistic young president was one of the most disturbing events of the twentieth century, the first collectively experienced tragedy of the modern age, and it demanded something comparably grand and sinister in meaning. Once again, homosexuality served a convenient role as scapegoat for fears about social change. Whether ascendant ideologies like fascism and communism, or shocking events such as the assassination of a president, what was strange and frightening about the modern world could reliably be imputed to this dark and secret world of sin, crime, and sickness. Assigning responsibility for a terrible national tragedy to a vast conspiracy involving the CIA, the FBI, the military-industrial complex, and a coterie of reactionary homosexuals was more comforting than acknowledging the awful, grubbier truth.

Garrison took serious umbrage at the suggestion that homophobia had anything to do with his case against Clay Shaw. "Throughout our trial, in everything I have ever written and in every public statement I have ever made—I never once made any reference to Clay Shaw's alleged homosexuality," he later insisted. "For all his faults and virtues, Shaw is dead and unable to defend himself from that kind of off the wall canard . . . a smear is still a smear." Put aside Garrison's cynicism in denying that he had ever made an issue of Clay Shaw's homosexuality. Put aside also the allegation that Garrison molested a thirteen-year-old boy in 1969. Garrison accused Shaw of complicity in a plot to kill the president of the United States. But "smear" him as a homosexual? Unconscionable.

LYNDON B. JOHNSON

One does not arrive spontaneously at that pitch
of perfection except when one meets in a
foreign country a compatriot with whom an
understanding then grows up of itself, both
parties speaking the same language, even though
they have never seen one another before.

—Marcel Proust, *Sodom and Gomorrah*

19

A LONG WAY FROM ARP

AT 7:05 A.M. THE MORNING AFTER HE SWORE THE OATH OF OFFICE in an impromptu ceremony aboard Air Force One, President Lyndon Johnson called Bob Waldron to commiserate about the colossal burden that had just been placed upon his shoulders.

A native of Arp, Texas, a town of fewer than a thousand inhabitants some 125 miles east of the city where Johnson's predecessor had just been murdered, Waldron had moved to Washington in June 1955 to work as an administrative assistant for Congressman Homer Thornberry, Johnson's successor as representative from Texas's Tenth Congressional District. By 1959, though technically still in Thornberry's employ, Waldron had for all intents and purposes become a member of Johnson's staff, one of several people "loaned" to the Senate majority leader by political allies and benefactors throughout the course of his decades-long rise from the hardscrabble Texas Hill Country to the heights of national political power. The enduring image of the thirty-sixth president involves him employing what came to be known as the "the Johnson Treatment," a physically intimidating series of maneuvers whereby he wielded his imposing six-foot-three frame over some hapless legislator in a naked attempt to get what he wanted—usually their vote. Johnson was no less persistent in accruing human resources as he was electoral ones. It was a feat he accomplished sometimes through flattery, at other moments through cajolery, and occasionally without even asking. Eventually, as if by osmosis, the quarry ended up working for Johnson even while remaining on the payroll of their ostensible employer. Such was the case with Waldron, whom Johnson initially recruited for his quick note-taking skills and who soon became something much more significant to the vice president: a combination of aide, travel companion, and personal confidant. Waldron's ubiquitous presence around the Johnson household led to, according to one friend, an "almost family relationship" with Johnson; his wife, Lady Bird; and their two daughters, Lynda Bird and Luci.

Waldron was working on Capitol Hill when word arrived that President Kennedy had been shot, and like millions of other Americans, he immediately broke down in tears. That evening, Waldron sat at home transfixed in front of his television screen, watching along with the rest of the world as Air Force One landed at Andrews Air Force Base, a hydraulic lift lowered Kennedy's casket onto the tarmac, and Lyndon Johnson, Waldron's patron, emerged for the first time as president of the United States.

Though Waldron had spent a great deal of time with Johnson during his vice presidency, hearing his voice on the phone that morning now that Johnson was the most powerful man in the world gave him "goose pimples." It was a sensation Waldron could compare to nothing else, save the feeling of "awe" that swept over him upon first meeting Johnson back in 1955. But just as Waldron was on the cusp of fulfilling a lifelong ambition to work for the president of the United States, forces beyond his control were preparing to ensure that he be prevented from doing so.

Bob Waldron was not a senior political advisor to Lyndon Johnson. Nor was he, like the other staffers Johnson took with him to the White House during those despondent and ominous final weeks of 1963, a veteran staffer who had worked for Johnson since his first election to Congress in 1937. Waldron's name appears just once in Robert Caro's magisterial multivolume biography of Johnson, the fourth part of which contains a single photograph, taken during a 1960 campaign stop in Pennsylvania, wherein Waldron can just barely be glimpsed.

And yet, for several years, Bob Waldron was for Lyndon Johnson something very close to a substitute son. Had Waldron not been burdened with the same secret that thwarted the dreams of so many other young men and women, and that eventually spelled the ruin of his own, there is no telling what he might have accomplished. His experience was hardly unique in this regard, but his proximity to Johnson illustrates how even someone unwaveringly loyal to one of the country's most skillful politicians was vulnerable to destruction.

As any gay man in American politics had to be, Waldron was protective of his secret. But he did not go to extraordinary lengths to mask or suppress his personality traits (a certain fastidiousness, a slight effeminacy, an interest in the arts) stereotypically assigned to it. "You'd have to be a blind person and deaf not to realize Bob was gay," one friend recalled. Greeting a group of Thornberry's constituents at the Capitol one day, Waldron broke the ice by announcing that he had played college football, a form of religion in the Lone Star state.

"Which school?" the visiting Texans asked incredulously.

"Vassar!" Waldron replied, to nervous laughter at his mentioning the all-female institution.

It's hard to imagine that this aspect of Waldron's identity was completely lost on Johnson, an uncannily skilled reader of men who detected profound meaning in silences and obfuscations. "The most important thing a man has to tell you is what he's not telling you," he repeatedly instructed his aides. "The most important thing he has to say is what he's trying not to say." According to Johnson's older daughter, Lynda Bird, Waldron did not acknowledge his homosexuality while working for her father; nor did her father ever discuss the subject in her presence. "[Waldron] never said, 'I am a homosexual,'" she recalled. "In those days, you would just never ask anybody about that."

Waldron gradually saw his role in the majority leader's office expand from stenographer to "body man," that term for an all-purpose gofer so particular to Washington, where some in positions of authority consider daily tasks like the insertion of contact lenses and the selection of a daily wardrobe to be beneath their dignity. According to one friend, Waldron "could say things" to Johnson "concerning his dress that no one else would dare to say," at one point making a "severe criticism" of Johnson's necktie that would have resulted in a verbal thrashing had it come from the mouth of anyone else on Johnson's staff. In time, Waldron became a fixture in Johnson's retinue outside the office, once attending dinner at the Johnson home, by his own estimate, fourteen nights in a row. Before Johnson became vice president, Waldron was part of the small group of friends and aides he took to the Shoreham Hotel every month for dinner and dancing. Both men were skilled ballroom dancers and cavorted well into the wee hours of the morning. "He was the best dancer," Lynda Bird Johnson recalled of Waldron. And not only that, but "he would dance with all the ladies, particularly the ones who were old or fat, particularly the ones who needed someone to make them feel good." Waldron was an inaugural member of the Potomac Marching Society, a dinner and dance club for Democratic bigwigs, and "so expert on his feet he is one of Lady Bird's favorite partners," marveled *Evening Star* gossip columnist Betty Beale.

Waldron described his creative employment arrangement with Johnson as the result of Thornberry being "gracious enough to 'loan me' every time Mr. Johnson wanted me to go somewhere"—which was often. As Johnson crisscrossed the country in 1959 and 1960, laying the groundwork for a presidential campaign, Waldron was often by his side, ready to hold his coat, fix his tie, or just sit and listen to his confessions of existential doubt. ("Why would anyone want to be president?" Johnson once asked Waldron in the backseat of a car. "I can't imagine why anyone would take that burden on," Waldron replied.) In Johnson's suite at the Biltmore Hotel during the Democratic National Convention in Los Angeles, Waldron sprawled out on the rug taking shorthand notes while Johnson and his chief aides wrangled over the language in a telegram challenging Kennedy to a debate. (Waldron took dictation, Lady Bird recalled, "lickety-split." Johnson's secretary Phyllis Bonanno said Waldron was "the fastest stenographer he ever had in his staff.") Before a meeting at which Robert Kennedy, whom Johnson loathed and whose loathing was more than reciprocated, begrudgingly offered Johnson a place on his brother's presidential ticket, Johnson ordered Waldron to hide in a closet and take notes. Waldron stood behind Johnson as he addressed the delegates on the second-to-last night of the convention, and on the final night, Johnson invited Waldron onto the stage with his family as they waved to the jubilant crowds under a shower of ticker tape. During the general election campaign, Waldron traveled with Johnson on the "LBJ Special" whistle-stop train tour through the South, and he was a constant presence on the campaign plane, where Anthony Lewis of the *New York Times* described him as "a man of all work."

As vice president, Johnson took Waldron along for one of his first overseas trips: a two-week, twenty-nine-thousand-mile goodwill tour of Asia.

Waldron was constantly at Johnson's side, including, as he fondly recalled, at a breakfast with President and Madame Chiang Kai-shek where he sat across the table from "a very brilliant, attractive, young Chinese" counterpart. With each city they visited and every world leader they called upon, the bond between the two small-town Texas-boys-done-good grew stronger. In particularly exotic locales or formal situations—meeting with the "very attractive young" king of Belgium, for instance—Johnson would lean his massive torso into Waldron and whisper in his ear, "It's a long way from Arp."

"Well, it's closer than Johnson City," Waldron would shoot back, Arp being three hundred miles east of the vice president's eponymous hometown. "We used to tease him about this little town," Lynda Bird Johnson recalled with a laugh. "Truly none of us had ever heard of Arp. He played out that he was this country bumpkin who came to the big city." After their audience with the Belgian king, Johnson cracked to his Secret Service detail that Waldron had curtsied before the monarch, a moment the vice president never let Waldron live down.

As a member of the Johnson retinue, Waldron was neither spared the vice president's notorious temper tantrums nor denied his equally legendary munificence. When Johnson got mad, Waldron recalled, he could subject those whose only offense was being in his presence to a "bath of fire." Yet he was also "the most generous man I've ever known." In Hong Kong, Johnson brought Waldron along to a fitting at a high-end tailor's, where he ordered several suits, shirts, and a smoking jacket for himself—and one of each item for Waldron. Every staffer on the Asia trip received a gold Patek Philippe watch with the Golden Rule—"Do unto others as you would have them do unto you"—inscribed around the face and "LBJ" above the numeral six. When Waldron applied to receive a commission in the Air Force Reserve squadron composed of various senators, congressmen, and Capitol Hill staffers led by Arizona senator (and World War II pilot) Barry Goldwater, he listed Johnson as a character reference. (Goldwater approved Waldron for promotion to the rank of major.) Once, while spending a weekend with the Johnson family at Huntland, the Virginia country estate of Houston industrialist and Johnson financial backer George Brown, Waldron mentioned in passing that he was considering buying a house near the Capitol. "[Johnson] just asked me about my financial needs, and he never said any more," Waldron remembered. At eleven o'clock on Monday morning, Waldron received a phone call from the president of the Capital National Bank in Austin, Texas, telling him that he had been preapproved for a mortgage.

An indication that Johnson was likely aware of Waldron's secret was his enlistment of Waldron as a walker for his secretary, and possible mistress, Mary Margaret Wiley. In the same way William Walton had assisted John F. Kennedy by escorting Mary Pinchot Meyer, Waldron squired Wiley on official travels, to social occasions in Washington, and for weekend trips to Huntland. Waldron may also have provided Johnson with assistance of a more intimate kind, by offering up his own living quarters as a vice presidential love nest. In 1961, Waldron lived at 2537 Queen Annes Lane in the Foggy Bottom neighborhood near George Washington University and the State Department. According to his landlord, Waldron hosted Johnson and Wiley there "many times." Visits would occur at different hours of the day, with the vice presidential limousine pulling up near the house and depositing Wiley, who "would come to the door and ask" Waldron if Johnson could enter. After Waldron moved to a town house on Capitol Hill, Johnson's visits continued, in the words of the new landlord, "on many occasions," with the DC Police preparing parking space for the vice president's motorcade in advance of his arrival.

Socially, Waldron thrived. "When Bob hit Washington," his friend (and Mary Margaret Wiley's cousin) Bill Wiley recalled, "he was at home . . . like a duck in water." At a time when the city's social whirl revolved heavily around state delegations, no crowd was livelier than the "lavish-spending" Texas State Society. Waldron's outgoing personality and proximity to the Lone Star State's most powerful political figure made him a natural fit for the group's entertainment chairman, responsible for planning parties and events. In the words of one observer, Waldron became something of "a male Perle Mesta." His boldface name appeared with regularity in the society columns, such as when he lunched with friend and fellow Texan Van Cliburn during the concert pianist's visit to Washington, or joined some three hundred "gaily-shirted Texans" for a giant barbeque. All in all, it was a great time, maybe even the best time, to be a Texan in Washington. "To come to Washington and have your state men running the nation was incredible to a Texan," Waldron later recalled. "I came for one year on my way to New York; it lasted ten. I could not have come at a more exciting moment in history, when Mr. Johnson ran the Senate, Rayburn ran the House, and with the cooperation of the Texas delegation they ran the nation."

Sam Rayburn was elected to Congress in 1912, first became Speaker of the House in 1940, and reoccupied the Speaker's chair in 1955, just a few months before Waldron came to Washington. Rayburn ultimately spent seventeen years in the speakership, the longest tenure of any Speaker in history, and was Johnson's most important political mentor and guide. Reclusive and shy around women—his marriage at the age of twenty ended after three weeks, and he remained a bachelor the rest of his life—Rayburn longed to have a son. As a man who suffered under the yoke of an abusive father and similarly desired, yet never produced, a male heir, Johnson was familiar with the feeling, and he tactfully played a filial role for Rayburn. Robert Caro has observed that Johnson "always had a gift with old men who could help him," and he employed on Rayburn the techniques of attentiveness and flattery he used on many an older man in advancement of his career.

Another figure for whom Johnson became a "professional son" was the powerful Georgia senator Richard Russell, who greased the wheels for Johnson to become Democratic floor leader in 1953, just four years into Johnson's first term. Like Rayburn, Russell was a bachelor who spent most evenings alone. Unlike Rayburn, he occasionally dated women, but he always ended the relationships when they became serious. (On the evening before his first, and last, wedding, Russell got cold feet and called the marriage off.) "Lyndon was always very smart at knowing where the seat of power was, and he recognized that at that time, in a predominantly southern Senate, Dick Russell was *the* power, and he also recognized that Russell, who was no longer so young, was a bachelor and lonely, and he started his Senate career by cultivating him, no, *courting* him—courting is the word," recalled Bobby Baker, a longtime Senate employee and Johnson ally who came to know more about the inner workings of that body, as well as the peccadilloes of its members, than almost anyone in its history. Some in Washington, Baker wrote, "snickered behind their hands at LBJ's obvious courtship" of Russell, whom Johnson "would have married" had Russell been a woman.

These relationships offered more than professional benefits for Johnson, who used them to fill the aching void in his emotional life left by his deceased father. From the time Johnson and his younger brother were little boys, Sam Ealy Johnson instilled in his sons the imperative that they not be pansies. "One of the first things I remember about my daddy," Lyndon Johnson told the historian Doris Kearns Goodwin, "was the time he cut my hair. When I was four or five, I had long curls. He hated them. 'He's a boy,' he'd say to my mother, 'and you're making a sissy of him.'" Reflecting upon his initial refusal to go to college, Johnson chalked it up to fear that filling his days reading books rather than working with his hands "would make me a sissy again and I would lose my daddy's respect." An alcoholic, Sam Johnson died just a few months after his son was first elected to Congress, and the future president mentioned him only once in his memoir. In Rayburn and Russell, Johnson sought the paternal affection denied him as a younger man, an affection he returned in kind. Sometimes, Johnson went to obsequious lengths to express it, exaggeratedly kissing Rayburn's bald dome. "How are you, my beloved?" Johnson would ask. (He took a similar approach with the conservative Democratic senator Harry Byrd, smooching the elderly Virginian's hands.) During the postwar years of Johnson's political ascent, when the country was experiencing a marriage boom and "the prevailing attitude among medical experts, social scientists and the clergy" was that "the unmarried state was unnatural and socially dysfunctional," the bachelordom of both Rayburn and Russell was a conspicuous feature of their public personas. Johnson was not above contributing to the gossip about their private lives, speculating to members of the Texas congressional delegation that Rayburn was a repressed homosexual.

While an older, unmarried man in Washington was liable to rumors of homosexuality, for a younger man, bachelorhood could be a professional asset—an asset gay men were uniquely positioned to possess. Some of the most important prerequisites for success in Washington—the ability to work long hours on a low government salary, a willingness to travel at a moment's notice, prioritizing career over family—are more easily attained by men without a wife and children to support. And in a city where government officials were often too busy to accompany their wives to parties, bachelors were, in the words of one veteran Washington society chronicler, "everybody's favorite extra man," highly in demand by hostesses who threw the parties where powerful people mingled. Recognizing the special status afforded to bachelors in Washington, foreign governments often sent single men or married men willing to leave their families behind—a disproportionate number of whom, presumably, were gay—to staff their embassies.

Asked about his prospects for marriage, Bob Waldron once told a neighbor he "had been very much in love and was almost to the point of being engaged," but that he ultimately decided against it, as he did not want to "divide his loyalty between his wife and a job." It was an excuse offered by many a Washington bachelor, and one readily accepted by legions of grateful bosses either oblivious to, or deliberately ignorant of, the double lives that their unfailingly loyal staffers led.

* * *

BY THE FALL OF 1963, Johnson had come to rely upon Waldron so much that he decided to bring him onto his White House staff. As vice president, Johnson had a limited number of positions he could fill, fewer than when he was Senate majority leader. To work around this obstacle, he decided to place Waldron on the payroll of the National Aeronautics and Space Council, the body President Eisenhower created in 1958 to coordinate government efforts on space exploration, and of which President Kennedy had appointed Johnson chairman at the outset of his administration. On October 31, Waldron filled out a formal application for the job.

Johnson left the task of coordinating this little bureaucratic sleight of hand to the man his staffers nicknamed "Mister Fixit." Born on a farm near Wichita Falls, Walter Jenkins studied for two years at the University of Texas before he could no longer afford the tuition, and in 1939, he found himself a job with then congressman Lyndon Johnson. Like Waldron a shorthand virtuoso, Jenkins suffered from high blood pressure and had a perpetually ruddy face, conditions exacerbated by the stress and strain to which Johnson subjected him for twenty-five years. Johnson spoke to Jenkins for at least an hour every day, and helpfully installed a phone in Jenkins's car so that the aide could take his calls whenever Johnson was traveling, no matter where in the country or the world. ("One of the problems" with Johnson, Waldron remembered, was that "he never realized the time difference of countries. If he wanted to call, it was done regardless of the time.") Jenkins also served as LBJ's personal accountant, a responsibility dumped into his lap when Lady Bird learned of his successful investments with government bonds. "There was a saying around the office that everything winds up on Walter's desk," the First Lady was to recall. And so it was that when Johnson wanted to add another hardworking and faithful servant to the team, he told Walter to handle it—which is precisely when Waldron's life began to unravel.

As his new job would be located within the executive branch, Waldron was required to undergo a background check. For the next several weeks, investigators from the Civil Service Commission interviewed Waldron's current and former neighbors, landlords, employers, coworkers, friends, and acquaintances, nearly all of whom provided glowing assessments. "In the time I have known Bob[,] I have never seen or heard of a thing which would raise any questions in my mind concerning his character, habits, or moral conduct," reported a man who had rented Waldron an English basement apartment. "I know of no questionable groups or organizations with which he is associated and would definitely have no reason to question his loyalty to our government," a fellow Texas State Society board member and former housemate attested.

Scattered throughout these fulsome testimonials, however, were intimations suggesting something aberrant. "He is very much interested in antique collection and is very interested in beautiful antique objects," one former landlord observed. "He struck me as being a rather odd, queer sort of fellow," remarked a schoolteacher who once lived down the street. A former roommate in Austin "considered him to be a funny bird in that he did not care anything about girls." Several of those interviewed commented on the sophistication of Waldron's clothes (and, in particular, the tightness of his pants). By all accounts, Waldron was indeed an impeccable dresser. Once, during a campaign swing through Montana, Johnson decided on the spur of the moment to visit a cattle ranch in a remote part of the state to peruse the livestock. As the pack of campaign staffers and reporters assembled to board the plane, Waldron emerged from the hotel donning spats, a Homburg hat, a chesterfield coat with a black velvet collar, and a walking stick—a foppish ensemble, CBS News correspondent Nancy Dickerson recalled, that "would have looked grand even on Fifth Avenue." Johnson, after taking one look at Waldron, deadpanned, "You're not going with me."

Two of the interviewees, Robert Best and William Carmichael, were of particular interest to investigators. Best and Carmichael—who had lived for seventeen years together "just as a married couple," according to Waldron—rented a Capitol Hill row house to Waldron for a period of twelve months in 1961 and 1962. "I would consider Bob to be 100 percent dependable in all respects," Best told the CSC investigator, adding that Waldron was the only renter to whom he and Carmichael had given a key to their home, which adjoined the one they rented out to him. Carmichael was even more effusive in his praise. "Bob is one person you will never find anything negative or derogatory about," he said, adding that Waldron was "the type of individual who would give you his life's blood" and "one of the most dedicated public servants that I have ever known." While Carmichael also said that Waldron enjoyed needlepointing and that "we often kid him about this being not too manly of a trait," he "had been very much in love and was almost to the point of being engaged." The investigator believed he had reason to doubt this last assertion, as well as the man who made it, and attempted to confirm his hunch by consulting a person he identified in his report only as "Confidential Informant A." This was a source associated with one of the "agencies in the metropolitan Washington area that maintain files on sexual perverts," presumably Roy Blick or one of his men. Waldron's name was not located in those files, but those of Best and Carmichael were recorded in the seized personal address book of a "roommate of an admitted homosexual." At least the reason for *their* esteem of Waldron was now ascertained.

Ultimately, of the more than one hundred people whom the CSC interviewed for its investigation into Waldron, about half "commented on his effeminate characteristics and many suspected homosexual tendencies." This circumstantial evidence would finally be confirmed when an investigator sat down to interview an assistant vice president of the Capital National Bank in Austin—the very same bank Johnson had persuaded to offer Waldron a mortgage. Wendal Lee Phillips first met Waldron in late 1958, when Phillips popped into Homer Thornberry's Austin district office to drop off a letter inviting the congressman to speak before the city's junior chamber of commerce. Waldron happened to be working there that week, and after making small talk, the two men became friendly. They kept in touch by mail and over the phone, and Waldron stayed at Phillips's house for two six-week periods in 1961 and 1962 while Congress was in recess.

One evening during the latter visit, Phillips recalled, he was sharing a double bed with Waldron when he "crowded me a little more closely than usual and his hands stayed in such a manner as to arouse my suspicions."

Yet nothing untoward happened, and so Phillips "more or less dismissed it as an accident."

The following May, after completing Naval Reserve duty in Norfolk, Virginia, Phillips spent a week at Waldron's home in Washington. Waldron's "friends impressed me as being strange," Phillips recalled, in that "they liked cultural events, and seemed obsessed with re-decorating their houses; they were just not very masculine." As they had in Austin the previous year, Waldron and Phillips shared a double bed. The first two nights transpired without incident. But then Waldron made a pass. Phillips thought his friend might be dreaming; indeed, he hoped this was the case.

"Bob, do you know what you are doing?" he asked.

"Yes," Waldron replied.

"I had hoped you didn't."

Waldron instantly withdrew his hand. According to Phillips, Waldron immediately grew despondent, and confessed that he "had had this problem for as long as he could remember." It was something "out of his control," "a physical ailment," and "an affliction that he had to live with." Waldron told Phillips that he had "always been attracted more by men than by women" and "had no desire ever to marry." And while it was acceptable for a "hair dresser" to be homosexual, Waldron allowed, "for a man in business or government work, it was a disgrace." He confessed that he was "worried to death" the episode would not only ruin their friendship but threaten his career, and he promised Phillips he would never make another approach. Phillips seemed to take the matter in stride, as evidenced by his decision to stay at Waldron's home, and sleep in Waldron's bed, for the rest of the week.

Maybe it was the sense of pressure conveyed by the government investigator sitting across from him, but in recounting these experiences, Phillips imbued them with a foreboding he did not seem to feel when they occurred. "Robert Waldron is a good friend of mine, but I believe that national security comes before personal friendship," he explained. "I am an officer in the local military reserve and realize the importance of maintaining strong national security. Robert Waldron has demonstrated homosexual tendencies toward me." Still, regarding the question of whether Waldron's sexual deviance affected his suitability for employment, Phillips was more sympathetic. "I believe that he is very much a loyal American citizen, and even though he has homosexual tendencies, I would still recommend him for a position involving national security on the basis of his past responsible government work and other personal characteristics."

As the CSC wound down its investigation in early December, Lyndon Johnson was barely a few weeks into his unexpected presidency, a period when Waldron was "seldom out of Johnson's sight." Two days after the Kennedy assassination, Waldron attended Sunday morning services at St. Mark's Church with the new president and First Lady and was standing nearby when a Secret Service agent brought Johnson the shocking news that Lee Harvey Oswald had been shot in Dallas. He traveled with Johnson in the presidential limousine to Kennedy's burial at Arlington National Cemetery, and for the first two weeks of the new administration, he assisted Juanita Roberts, Johnson's principal secretary, in setting up shop at the White House. But as Waldron was helping Johnson assume the responsibilities of leader of the free world, a group of men in a building just a few blocks away were compiling a report that would throw his life into disarray.

In the course of conducting its background check on the president's applicant, Space Council Executive Secretary Edward Welsh told Walter Jenkins, the CSC had discovered that he had participated in "homosexual activities." Hiring Waldron to join the White House staff, therefore, was impossible. Jenkins told Welsh that he would relay this news to the president, and Waldron's job application was formally rejected in January 1964. Waldron was further banned from the White House grounds, a development that left him, in the words of William Carmichael, "very depressed."

Waldron did not share the results of his background check with many people; nor, apparently, did Johnson. "Nobody ever said to me Bob can't work at the White House because he's gay," his daughter Lynda Bird recalled. Waldron joined the faceless masses of men and women either dismissed from their jobs or denied one in the first place due to their sexual orientation. The purge of gays and lesbians was still grinding on well into the 1960s; just a few months after Waldron was jettisoned from the White House, the State Department announced that it had separated sixty-three people as security risks the previous year, forty-five of them for being gay.

Waldron returned to his job on Capitol Hill working for Homer Thornberry's successor, a former Johnson staff man named James Jarrell "Jake" Pickle. (Thornberry had relinquished his seat after Johnson appointed him to a federal judgeship.) Though his very first encounter with Johnson had involved the future leader of the free world beckoning him while sitting on the toilet with his pajama pants around his ankles, Pickle realized early on that Johnson "had the prospects of being a . . . national figure" and that hitching his wagon to such a man "was the best way to get ahead." Waldron felt the same way. "I think we felt under the influence of this one human being," he remembered of Johnson. "When you were in his presence, and worked for him, you felt there was something going on—with a future to it. And you might have threatened to quit, but you felt, well, I'll be the loser." The wide avenues of personal and professional advancement open to Jake Pickle, however, were closed to Bob Waldron, and having experienced the singular, exhilarating life of a White House staffer for a few brief weeks, he was now back to where he started when he first moved to Washington: a lowly congressional aide.

Still, Waldron decided to make a go of it. The consummate host and epitome of Texas hospitality, he opened his home to Pickle and his family while they searched for suitable accommodation in Washington, just as he had offered Thornberry a place to stay as he transitioned from a seat in Congress to one on the federal bench. Waldron's years in the fast lane as a member of Lyndon Johnson's all-Texan clique greatly impressed his new boss, who was delighted to have such a "Washington Insider" on his staff. Pickle fondly recalled the first party he was invited to as a freshman congressman, a white-tie affair at the Finnish embassy, when he naïvely asked Waldron if he could wear a tuxedo and drive himself to the event. "Congressman, you can't park blocks from the embassy and walk down the street in white tie," Waldron gently scolded the freshman legislator. "You must have a chauffeur. I'll drive you. And protocol says you must arrive *exactly* on time." Waldron rented Pickle a white tie and tails, borrowed a chauffeur's cap, and ferried him to the party in Pickle's own 1959 Chrysler New Yorker. When they arrived at the embassy, Waldron opened Pickle's door and even bowed his head as Pickle exited the car.

Concealed by the jaunty façade, however, was a crushing despair. Once a welcome presence in Washington's most exclusive salons and a valued member of the charmed circle sitting at the apex of American political power, Waldron was now persona non grata. That May, in an envelope marked "Personal—Confidential," Waldron mailed a letter to the man in whom he had entrusted his most intimate and consequential secret.

Dear Lee,

I received your card and am glad you are able to visit the Summer White House.

Lee, I had often heard the expression "one doesn't need enemies with friends like yours." But I never knew the true meaning of that expression until last December. I am sure you well know what I mean, as you succeeded in planting the seed that would eventually completely destroy me—professionally and financially; keep me from attaining the one goal for which I had so diligently worked; and cause me to lose my commission. Then to make it more complete, your efforts will prevent me from holding any Civil Service position of any significance or any position with any firm directly connected with the Federal government, to say nothing of the final effects on my family.

It is commendable, I suppose, that you felt you "owed it to your country"—but have you ever thought—from your supposedly strong faith as a Christian—that you might owe something to a friend who might not be as strong and as perfect as you. I will give you credit for your kind remarks about what a fine person I was, but you certainly dealt the death blow with the statements that followed. I hope you would not think I would be so naïve not to find out the results of the investigation.

While I can understand that you might feel compelled to tell of your experience, I could not believe that you would betray my confidential conversation with you. I believe you will well recall your statement to me: "It is probably my fault, as I wanted to see how far you would go." And then you asked if there was anything you could do to help me. It was then that I took you into my confidence and gave you a full case history, thinking that I was talking to my *closest* friend that I could trust. Obviously I was wrong. . . .

After our close association for such a long period of time; your observations of my dedication to my work and employers and my behavior under almost every circumstance, I would think you would give me at least some benefit of the doubt that I would be loyal to the President and to my country.

Lee, the damage to me is done, but I must admonish you to be more careful in the future when a person's entire career is at stake—and yours also. As you well know, our society is great at assuming guilt by association. Just put yourself in the other person's place for a moment—as I am sure that somewhere along the line you have come so close to being there. You may rest assured that when questioned about you, I gave every assurance that you were in no way involved and the fault was all mine, even though we shared a room at various times over the last three years and that you came here to visit me.

The report has now become a permanent record and it will merely be a matter of time until the information will begin to spread. My only great concern is that it will not affect innocent friends and associates, in and out of government.

. . . Naturally, I cannot help feeling bitter about the whole thing, but I truly feel sorry for you that you have not yet come to grips with some of the true problems of life and some of the true facts of human nature. I might feel great remorse if I did not know that there are so many facing the same problem as I. Unfortunately, there is no way of solving mine now, no matter what I might do, as I will be marked by our society—which does not permit a return. Really, you might say my problem is now over, as it is now only a matter of survival in the future.

Lee, one other word of caution, if I may. Should you ever become faced with a similar problem in one of your children, I do hope you will have compassion and understanding and realize that it is quite a common problem—and one that needs the love and understanding of those close to overcome it. Your betrayal, as in my case, will merely drive the child right into the final stages as he will have no other place to go . . .

Please know that you have absolutely nothing to fear from me and I assure you that I will not contact you in the future. Should I ever again be contacted about you, you may rest assured that I can only give a good report.

Sincerely,

Bob Waldron

20

"A QUITE SERIOUS SITUATION"

RIDING IN A CAB TO UNION STATION ONE RAINY NIGHT IN THE SPRING OF 1961, Gore Vidal looked out the window as the traffic stopped in front of the YMCA on G Street around the corner from the White House. Suddenly, out of the building burst four men in trench coats and caps pushing two other men, one about sixty and the other much younger. After dragging them for several yards down the sidewalk, the trench-coated figures rained down a torrent of physical abuse on their captives, shoving the older man onto the ground and kicking him, and pounding the other one in the face "like a punching bag."

"I hate to see anybody do that to another," Vidal's elderly Black cab driver said. So did Vidal, who exited the vehicle and accosted the assailants. In response to his unbidden intervention, Vidal wrote in a piece for *Esquire*, "Threats and obscenities poured over me in one long orgiastic breath" from one of the aggressors, who revealed a police detective's badge. Determining further protest to be futile, Vidal climbed back into the cab and continued his journey to Union Station, where he rushed to a pay phone and dialed the *Washington Post*. A night editor answered, and Vidal related the horrifying display he had just seen. The editor was unfazed. The

Post "had recently run a story which had led to some arrests," he said. "The men in the light caps had been doing their duty."

The article to which the editor referred was a brief item that had appeared on April 11. In a single day, the paper reported, officers from Roy Blick's vice squad had arrested seven men on "morals charges" in the basement bathroom of the YMCA. They were anonymous participants in a silent ritual, one comprised of furtive stares and subtle gestures leading to hasty acts of sexual congress, colloquially known as the "tearoom trade," and the fetid, subterranean lair of the YMCA was reputed to be one of the busiest sites in Washington for its practice. When *Life* called homosexuality "a sad and often sordid world" in the summer of 1964, the embodiment of that world could have been this nine-by-eleven-foot dungeon, stinking of disinfectant and cheap cigar smoke, and virtually indistinguishable from thousands of other such places across the country.

"I have often thought of those two since, wondered who they were and what happened to them," Vidal wrote about the nameless victims of police abuse. "I also brooded on the curious horror of seeing our society at its most vicious two blocks from the White House." Though Vidal left readers to figure out for themselves what exactly had precipitated this paroxysm of state violence, he offered a clue, likening it to a scene from the 1952 novel *Hemlock and After* in which police brutally apprehend a male prostitute in Leicester Square. Nearly a decade after that book's publication, it was still beyond the capacities of a famous author, even one as iconoclastic as Vidal, to address plainly the harsh realities of the secret city, the rites and routines that men from all walks of life performed in this secluded place that, though lying within the shadow of the White House, was in every other respect a world away.

* * *

LESS THAN A MONTH BEFORE HIS BOSS LYNDON JOHNSON FACED THE VOTERS for the first time as president of the United States, Walter Jenkins did something extremely unusual: he left his White House office before midnight to attend a party.

It was a particularly taxing time for the forty-six-year-old father of six, who had been working a string of eighteen-hour days subsisting on little more than coffee and aspirin. Having stood for a quarter century at the side of the most demanding boss in American politics, Jenkins was used to stress. One night, back in the days when he represented Texas's Tenth Congressional District in the House of Representatives, Johnson was sharing a drink with a colleague when he summoned Jenkins into his office. "The door opened, and there was this guy—shirt rumpled, tie askew, face pale, standing in the door holding a yellow legal pad waiting for orders—like a slave," Johnson's colleague recalled. The word *slave*—used by contemporaries of Carmel Offie to characterize his relationship with William Bullitt, and which Gore Vidal chose to belittle Lem Billings's dedication to John F. Kennedy—comes up more than a few times in reminiscences of Walter Jenkins, whose devotion to Johnson was so ardent that he named one of his six children after him. When Johnson began his undeclared campaign for the presidency in 1960, it was Jenkins who organized the Johnson for President "citizen" groups across the country, much as Arthur Vandenberg had rallied grassroots support for Dwight Eisenhower. Jack Valenti, a Houston advertising executive turned Johnson staffer who married Mary Margaret Wiley after meeting her on the campaign trail, recalled that "Walter, alone among the staff members, could talk to senators and congressmen on the most important subjects without having them feel that they should talk to the president, because they knew when they talked to Walter, above all men, they were speaking to the president."

A man so devoted to the president of the United States as to be dubbed "my vice president in charge of everything" by him occasionally required a respite, and around 7 p.m. on the evening of October 7, 1964, Jenkins exited the White House grounds and walked around the corner to the new *Newsweek* headquarters at 1750 Pennsylvania Avenue. He took the elevator to the magazine's twelfth-floor offices, where its owner, *Washington Post* publisher Katharine Graham, and bureau chief, Ben Bradlee, were hosting a party. Jenkins mingled with a cast of Washington luminaries—seven cabinet members made an appearance over the course of the evening—downed three or four martinis, and waited for his wife, Marjorie, to arrive. After milling about for another half hour or so, he escorted her back downstairs to a waiting White House car, which ferried her to a dinner party. Returning to pick up his raincoat, Jenkins consumed one more drink and departed, passing Defense Secretary Robert McNamara on his way out.

Tipsy from all the alcohol he had consumed on an empty stomach, Jenkins decided to take a slight detour on his way back to the White House. He turned right at the corner, onto Seventeenth Street, and then hung another right onto G, in the direction of the YMCA. He entered the building and proceeded to make his way to the washroom downstairs.

What happened next was duly recorded by the two policemen surveilling the space through a pair of peepholes. After exchanging glances but no words, Jenkins entered a pay toilet stall with another man, a sixty-year-old army veteran named Andy Choka. When the officers recognized movements "indicating a perverted sex act was taking place," they barged into the restroom and arrested both men. At the police station, Jenkins was interrogated by Louis Fochett, the veteran Morals division officer who had infiltrated the preliminary meeting of the Mattachine Society of Washington at the Hay-Adams three years earlier. After answering Fochett's questions matter-of-factly, a shell-shocked Jenkins paid a fifty-dollar bond and went straight back to work at the White House as if nothing had happened.

On the night of October 13, *Evening Star* reporter John Barron received an anonymous tip from a man saying that he had seen Walter Jenkins's name on a police blotter the previous week in connection with an arrest for sexual solicitation at the YMCA. The next morning, Barron called the paper's police reporter, who not only confirmed the arrest but found a previous incident involving Jenkins, at the same YMCA, in 1959. Barron told *Star* managing editor Charles Seib, who called the White House seeking comment.

As Press Secretary George Reedy was in New York with the president for the Al Smith Dinner, an annual white-tie gala fund-raiser sponsored by the city's Catholic archdiocese, Liz Carpenter, Lady Bird's press secretary, took the call. A no-nonsense Texan and former reporter who covered the White House when Eleanor Roosevelt held press conferences for women journalists, Carpenter became the first female executive assistant to a vice president upon her joining Johnson's staff in 1961.

When Seib told Carpenter that Walter Jenkins had been arrested in a YMCA bathroom stall for disorderly conduct, she assumed it had to be some sort of misunderstanding. She put Seib on hold and called Jenkins, who was still at home. "Walter, I know this is not true, but tell me what to say," Carpenter said. "This must be a mistake, but this is what I've been told."

"I'll handle it," Jenkins replied. "I'll call him."

Jenkins had been dealing with journalists on a daily basis for many years, but always in relation to the affairs of his boss. He was in no state to speak with a member of the fourth estate about the mess into which he had gotten *himself*. The tragic irony, as Carpenter recalled, was that "if this had happened with another staff person, [Jenkins] would have been the first person I would have phoned to say, 'What do you do about it.'" But now Jenkins was the one in trouble, and he had no idea what to do.

Frantic, he called Abe Fortas. If anyone could get him out of this mess, it was the lawyer and Roosevelt administration veteran. While Fortas had no official job in the Johnson White House, he was the president's closest political counselor. It was Fortas who had saved Johnson's hide during his first Senate election, in 1948, by convincing Supreme Court justice Hugo Black to restore Johnson's name to the ballot after he won—or, more accurately, stole—the Democratic nomination by 87 votes. When Bobby Baker became embroiled in an influence-peddling scheme in 1963, Fortas was the first person Johnson called for advice. The following year, after President Kennedy was shot in Dallas, Fortas was also one of the first people Johnson spoke to, and the redoubtable jurisprudent was there at Andrews Air Force Base to welcome the new president back to Washington.

"I'm in terrible trouble," Jenkins said. Fortas, who was at his law office, told the distraught aide to hold himself together and meet him at his Georgetown home. When Jenkins lurched through the front door, he was barely coherent, mumbling about a party at *Newsweek*, alcoholic beverages, "another man," and an inquiry from the *Star*. Confounded, Fortas called his fellow lawyer and unofficial Johnson advisor, Clark Clifford. A special counsel to Harry Truman, Clifford had played a critical role in some of the most important Democratic Party initiatives of the previous two decades, including the Truman Doctrine, the Marshall Plan, the creation of the CIA, and the recognition of Israel. After leaving the White House, Clifford became the first of a breed, a Washington "superlawyer." Leveraging the connections he had made in government, Clifford pocketed a million dollars a year helping corporations navigate through the city's bureaucratic thickets. Though Clifford very much appreciated the pecuniary rewards of private legal practice, he retained a strong sense of civic duty and interest in public affairs. And it was in this patriotic spirit that he answered Fortas's call to undertake yet another mission that would earn him a reputation for "rescuing American presidents from disaster."

The first step would be to work the media. Washington in 1964 was a town run on gentlemen's agreements, and no agreement was more gentlemanly than the one between powerful men and the press stipulating that the latter refrain from reporting on the sexual dalliances of the former. The short, bald Fortas and the stooped, wavy-haired Clifford made a noticeable pair as they trooped from newsroom to newsroom, imploring editors not to print anything about the unfortunate episode involving the president's aide, the sexagenarian army veteran, and the YMCA restroom. Clifford and Fortas's grim procession began at the *Star*, the first recipient of the leak, where executive editor Newbold Noyes Jr. agreed to keep mum on the condition that his competitors followed suit. Editors at the *Washington Daily News*, an afternoon tabloid, were preparing an article about the arrest for their first edition when Clifford and Fortas showed up just in time pleading, "Treat it as kindly as you can and not at all if possible." *Post* editor J. Russell Wiggins was completely unaware of the Jenkins arrest until Clifford and Fortas divulged it to him, but following the lead of his fellow newspapermen, he also agreed to keep it under wraps.

Having suppressed the story, at least temporarily, Clifford rushed to the White House, while Fortas returned home to check on Jenkins, who had in the meantime suffered a nervous breakdown. After summoning a doctor, who put Jenkins under heavy sedation and checked him into George Washington University Hospital, Fortas joined Clifford in the office of Johnson aide Bill Moyers, where, at 3:56 p.m., they called Suite 35-A at the Waldorf Towers in New York, where the president had just awoken from a nap.

It would be hard to conceive of a piece of news more likely to ruin Johnson's day than what his aides were about to share with him. For months, the polls had been predicting a landslide victory for the president in his race against the Republican nominee, Barry Goldwater. The economy was booming, the GOP had been overtaken by its kamikaze right wing, and Johnson's approval rating was through the roof. Everywhere he went—except his home region of the South, indignant at his betrayal over signing the Civil Rights Act earlier that summer—he was met with huge, jubilant crowds. Johnson had every reason to be in a cheerful mood, and he was—until he answered the call from Washington and heard the flummoxed voice of Abe Fortas on the other end.

"Mr. President, this is Abe. And Clark is sitting here with me. We have had a very serious problem that came up today." Walter Jenkins had "involved himself in a quite serious situation," Fortas explained, before progressing into a long circumlocution in which "hypertension," "acute nervous exhaustion," and "doctor's orders" were mentioned. After about a minute of this hemming and hawing, Fortas asked the president, "Have I gotten this across at all to you?"

"No," Johnson replied brusquely, as Jack Valenti and George Reedy, sitting beside him, looked on with concern.

"Well, is it all right to talk on this phone?" Fortas asked.

"Yes, I think so."

Fortas proceeded to explain the "situation," beginning with Jenkins's attendance at the *Newsweek* party, his subsequent arrest on a "morals charge," and the fact that every newspaper in the city was sitting on the story. "We think we've got the situation in as good shape now as we can," Fortas concluded. "Would you like to say a word to Clark about it?"

"No, just tell me," the president said with audible tenseness. "Could this be *true*?"

Throughout the conversation, Reedy recalled, Johnson "spoke in the unusually soft voice that he always uses when some near disaster is striking, very self-contained, very composed." Valenti described the news Johnson was receiving as "an absolute blow with an axe handle to his stomach." Yet, "at no time did he give any indication, either by voice or movement or facial expression, that this terrible blow had struck him." Underneath the veneer of calm, however, Johnson was mortified. In his many retellings of the moment he first learned of Jenkins's arrest, Johnson would use a variety of analogies to describe the shock he felt: it was as if someone had told him that one of his daughters had committed treason, that Lady Bird had killed one of their daughters, or that Lady Bird had murdered the pope.

If the presidency, as Johnson would tell his successor Richard Nixon, is "like being a jackass caught in a hailstorm," then the president was now in the middle of a squall of biblical proportions. To Johnson, the most important matter at hand was not Jenkins's well-being. It was the impact that Jenkins's actions, or alleged actions, would have on the upcoming election—a factor that made Johnson suspect the entire scandal was, as he told Fortas, a "frame deal." Who was the other man arrested with Jenkins? he wanted to know. A Soviet spy? A Republican plant? The leak had likely originated with a GOP-friendly source within the Metropolitan Police Department; staffers from the Republican National Committee were already spreading word of the arrest to journalists all over town. ("I've been called by Republican headquarters," Nancy Dickerson of CBS told Carpenter when she asked the White House for comment.) Johnson always assumed the worst about his enemies, a penchant for paranoia that often led to conspiratorial thinking. The day after Kennedy's assassination, he had pointed to a photograph of South Vietnamese president Ngo Dinh Diem, who had been overthrown in a U.S.-backed military coup weeks before. "We had a hand in killing him," Johnson told Hubert Humphrey. "Now it's happening here." Was it so far-fetched to think that one of Johnson's many enemies had set Jenkins up?

"Well, you don't foresee that you can keep this lid on for three weeks, do you?" the president plaintively asked Fortas. The question was irrelevant. A little over two hours later, as Johnson was paying a courtesy call to Jackie Kennedy at her Fifth Avenue penthouse for what must have been one of the most excruciatingly restless meetings of his life, the Republican National Committee released a portentous statement to the media. "There is a report sweeping Washington," GOP chairman Dean Burch announced, "that the White House is desperately trying to suppress a major news story affecting the national security." When Johnson returned to his suite at the Waldorf, he immediately began working the phones. "It seems to me that the Presidency is at stake," he told Clifford, as United Press International moved an item over the wire breaking the story. Texas governor John Connally tried to walk the president back from the ledge. "It'll be harmful, but not appreciably so," the longtime Johnson supporter said. "Now they will be digging up the Sumner Welles thing, at least in their private conversations, you know, and talking about Communists and homos and everything else that infiltrated the government." Next, Johnson spoke with Cartha "Deke" DeLoach, deputy associate director of the FBI. As the Bureau's liaison to the White House, DeLoach interacted daily with Jenkins, a fellow Catholic and golf buddy. The two had collaborated in some of the Johnson administration's less wholesome activities, like wiretapping the African American activists who challenged Mississippi's all-white delegation at that summer's Democratic National Convention and installing a secret recording device in the Oval Office. When DeLoach first heard the news about his friend and co-congregant, he sat at his desk, dumbstruck.

"Who is supposed to have been working on who?" the president, his mind invariably drawn to the gutter, asked DeLoach.

"Walter was supposed to be the active one, Mr. President," DeLoach replied matter-of-factly, before delving into the sordid particulars. "In other words, this sixty-two-year-old man was letting Walter have it, and Walter was taking it, according to the police officer. Which is pretty hard to believe." That anything involving the human anatomy would be hard for Lyndon Johnson to believe, however, is itself hard to believe. This was a man, after all, who never exhibited the slightest compunction urinating in the congressional parking lot when he was a young member of the House of Representatives, or, later in his career as leader of the world's greatest deliberative body, conspicuously scratching the "hard-to-reach recesses of his body" on the floor of the U.S. Senate. Indeed, Johnson seemed to have an obsession with his sexual organ, which he christened "Jumbo" and proudly displayed to colleagues while standing beside them at urinals, the sort of conduct that, under slightly different circumstances, resulted in other, less powerful men like Walter Jenkins being led away in handcuffs, their reputations ruined and their careers destroyed. Not even the most feculent of basic bodily functions was considered too intimate for Johnson to perform in the presence of subordinates, as any of the aides he summoned while sitting on the toilet could attest. Yet, homosexuality? Well, that facet of the human experience was something beyond Johnson's comprehension.

The same could not be said of Johnson's host for the evening, a man who partook privately in the pleasures of the secret city while simultaneously being one of its most virulent public foes. Francis Cardinal Spellman, the Catholic archbishop of New York and a friend and political ally of Roy Cohn, declared in 1942 that Broadway "would drag the name of New York down to be synonymous with Sodom and Gomorrah." Meanwhile, that very same year, he regularly sent the archdiocesan limousine to transport the object of his affection, a dancer, from the Broadway theater where the young man performed to the Church-subsidized mansion in which Spellman lived. By the time Johnson took his seat on the dais beside Spellman in the Waldorf Astoria's Grand Ballroom, the audience of two thousand dinner guests was already buzzing about the news from Washington. As the program got underway, outside the hall, George Reedy tearfully announced to a group of reporters that Jenkins had entered the hospital, tendered his resignation, and been replaced in his duties by Bill Moyers. At 10:15, nearly an hour after he was scheduled to begin his remarks, Johnson delivered a heavily condensed version of his address in a raspy, crestfallen voice.

The next day, newspapers across the country touted the story of the White House aide arrested in the YMCA bathroom on their front pages, and the consensus among leading commentators confirmed the president's worst fear: the scandal had the potential to cost him the election. The Jenkins case was "the one thing that just might snatch a Democratic Presidential defeat from the jaws of victory," the *Wall Street Journal* declared in a representative assertion. While it was natural for voters to feel "sympathy" for a "pitiful victim of what is properly being accepted as an authentic mental disease," adjudged the "Dean of Washington newsmen," Arthur Krock of the *New York Times*, "it would be irresponsible if the American people felt no anxiety over the fact the exposure has established that a Government official to whom the most secret operations of national security were accessible, moreover the President's enforcer of security within the Administration itself, is among those unfortunates who are most readily subject to the blackmail by which security secrets are often obtained by enemy agents." Adding to the administration's embarrassment, it emerged that Jenkins had himself once circulated a memo to federal agencies endorsing stricter screening mechanisms to weed out homosexual job candidates. "It would be unfortunate if undesirable individuals were put on the payroll simply because sufficient precautions were not taken," he wrote. Johnson ordered J. Edgar Hoover to conduct a full investigation.

An exception to the generalized sense of pending political doom was *Newsweek* bureau chief Ben Bradlee. Maybe he felt guilty for supplying the alcohol that Jenkins had imbibed to loosen his inhibitions and, like so many other men, seemed to require before entering the recesses of the secret city. "The post-Jenkins atmosphere in Washington stinks to the sewer," Bradlee wrote in a memo to his staff the day the story broke. The phantasm of homosexuality, which had receded somewhat since the reign of Joe McCarthy, had returned with a vengeance, and with it, the perfervid atmosphere of charge and countercharge. "It's the day . . . of the anonymous phone call (The White House has had several), the prurient joke, and the search for scandal," Bradlee continued. "The town is alive with rumors about the morals of Barry Goldwater Jr., [Goldwater campaign speechwriter] Fulton Lewis III, key Congressional aides. Great issues wait for great men, and wait and wait."

Belying Johnson's suspicion that the scandal had been some sort of Republican dirty trick, Goldwater refused to exploit Jenkins's misfortune for political gain. To be sure, that Jenkins had served in Goldwater's Air Force Reserve squadron undetected, and that Goldwater had recommended him for promotion, essentially precluded the Republican nominee from lambasting the president for failing to spot the sex deviant in his midst. But the flinty Arizonan also adhered to an old Washington code. "Some things, like loyalty to friends or lasting principle, are more important" than winning, he later reflected of his decision not to attack Johnson over Jenkins. Not all of Goldwater's surrogates, however, emulated his honorable reticence. Speaking before a crowd of two thousand in Dayton, Ohio, GOP vice presidential candidate William Miller decried "a pitiful, sordid situation which made [Jenkins] a ready subject of blackmail and compromise as to the highest secrets of government." Former vice president Richard Nixon, campaigning in Fort Wayne, Indiana, declared that the American people would "not stand for immorality in the White House" and that the president had a duty to explain what he knew about "this sick man" in his employ. And though he refrained from public comment, privately, Goldwater could not resist joining the pile-on. "What a way to win an election," he marveled to journalists during an off-the-record conversation. "Communists and cocksuckers."

* * *

THE JENKINS SCANDAL WAS ONE OF THE EARLIEST EPISODES TO EARN THE moniker of "October surprise." And like those that followed, discussion of it was accompanied by the malignant phenomenon that surfaced whenever the specter of homosexuality arose over Washington: conspiracy theorizing. For Republicans, the arrest of the presidential aide on a morals charge summoned up all the hoary old intrigues from the previous decade involving hidden networks and foreign saboteurs. According to a memo from J. Edgar Hoover to Acting Attorney General Nicholas Katzenbach, some Goldwater staffers, tipped off to the arrest of an army lieutenant colonel in the same YMCA bathroom the day before Jenkins was detained, alleged to journalists that the officer was a "liaison" to the White House and "another Jenkins case in the offing." There was no evidence indicating that the proximity of the arrests was anything but coincidental, nor that the colonel had even visited the White House, but George Reedy nonetheless spent an entire day frenziedly batting down queries from reporters about a secret nest of executive branch homosexuals.

Johnson, meanwhile, refused to accept any explanation other than that Jenkins had been framed—the victim of a GOP dirty trick, a Soviet honey trap, or some permutation of the two. Maybe, the president mused to whomever would listen, the waiters at the *Newsweek* party were Goldwater campaign plants and had spiked Walter's drink. Or perhaps Andy Choka, the man caught with Jenkins, was a foreign agent. Or, as Johnson instructed the FBI to prove, the GOP had paid Choka to seduce Walter. "I can't begin to count the times the President asked me 'what do you think happened?'" Mildred Stegall, one of LBJ's longest-serving secretaries, recalled many years later. Campaigning with Bobby Kennedy on the last Sunday before the election, Johnson expressed fear that Goldwater would "pull something" akin to what Johnson was convinced he had already done. Considering the ruse his own campaign had tried to pull just a few days before the start of the 1960 convention with that mysterious tip to Teddy White purporting Jack and Bobby Kennedy to be "fags," Johnson's paranoia was a case of projection.

Irrespective of whatever or whoever had gotten to Walter, the president would be damned if the Republicans were to make an issue out of homosexuality in high places. No less a great American hero than Gen. Dwight David Eisenhower, Johnson reminded reporters during a campaign stop in San Diego, had "had the same type of problem" with one of *his* top staffers, a clear allusion to Arthur Vandenberg Jr. "We Democrats felt sorry for him, thought it was a sickness and a disease," Johnson said. "We didn't capitalize on a man's misfortune." Recuperating at Walter Reed Army Medical Center from bronchitis—a convenient illness with which to be stricken while studiously trying to avoid comment on your party's extremist presidential nominee or, for that matter, your decade-old dismissal of a homosexual aide—Eisenhower professed ignorance of what Johnson was jabbering about. ("It would have been better if it hadn't been said," Johnson later confessed to Nicholas Katzenbach.) Within a week, the FBI announced the results of its investigation, for which it had dispersed nearly one hundred agents across the country to interview some five hundred people. The story was tediously straightforward: Jenkins had walked into the YMCA bathroom of his own volition. There was no evidence that he posed a threat to national security. Neither the waiters at the *Newsweek* party nor Andy Choka were paid Republican (or Soviet) agents. (The exhaustive report did note, however, Jenkins's investment of nine hundred dollars in the theatrical production of *Advise and Consent*.) Dismayed that the country's chief law enforcement agency would fail to endorse their assertion that Jenkins represented a security risk, some Republicans seized upon a news report that the FBI director had sent a bouquet of flowers to the traumatized aide in the hospital. This expression of sympathy had led to "shock, disbelief, and even outrage" among Republicans, who had always considered Hoover a steadfast fellow crusader against immorality. Drew Pearson, unsurprisingly, was nonplussed; the floral arrangement was obviously tacit acknowledgment of the director's own sexual deviancy. "The Republicans, of course, don't seem to realize that Hoover has been in the same category with Jenkins for some years, only [he] has been careful not to use the YMCA," the longtime Hoover antagonist scribbled in his diary.

Most men who engaged in the tearoom trade, Jenkins included, did not identify themselves as belonging to the "category" of homosexual. Sex with other men was something they *did*; it had no bearing on who they *were*. This perspective, which explained the Jenkins incident not as the manifestation of a deeply repressed sexual and emotional identity but rather, as a momentary blunder triggered by too many martinis and too little sleep, characterized both the media coverage of the scandal and the personal reactions of those close to the man at its center. "Does Jenkins really stand 'accused as a homosexual,' as we say in the second paragraph?" *Newsweek* editor Ben Bradlee asked his reporters. "He stands accused of disorderly conduct as a participant in one of those sordid encounters that most newspapers shun reporting. He is not in fact a homosexual, in that he is not a regular practitioner of homosexual acts. It seems to us that there is a real distinction." Sarah McClendon, a White House newspaper correspondent from Texas who had known Jenkins for many years, expressed the general sentiment among Washingtonians. "There is still an air of mystery about the Jenkins incident," she reported. "Jenkins was never a man who wanted to hurt any one. He was a model husband and father of six children and served both the President and Mrs. Johnson with dedicated loyalty through decades. He loved his friends, whose souls are desolated now because of this. Why?" Most of the hundreds of his acquaintances interviewed by the FBI assumed that Jenkins had simply "cracked under the strain of eighteen-hour workdays," though why he chose to relieve himself of that pressure by seeking out sex with another man, as opposed to, say, a good nap, was a question few bothered to ponder. "I guess we've all been so tired in our lives," Johnson mused to the journalist Palmer Hoyt. "I've had a few drinks in my life and I want to call up my girlfriend." Meeting the president for dinner after a long day of work at the White House, Johnson's longtime secretary Mildred Stegall remembered that "[i]nvariably the subject of discussion was Walter. Neither of us seemed to be willing to let go of the unanswered question as to what happened and why. The truth of the matter was neither of us was willing to face up to the fact that he might have been guilty as charged." The possibility that what Jenkins did in that YMCA bathroom was an expression, however warped and unsavory, of something intrinsic to his nature was incomprehensible.

Homosexuals remained an enigma in 1960s America. They loitered in poorly lit parks and decrepit restrooms, and in the rare instances when one appeared on television or radio, it was almost always with his face concealed and his voice distorted. (Lesbians were even less visible.) "Many persons claim to be able to recognize a homosexual by sight: He is the man with an effeminate face, high lisping voice, and mincing gait," *Congressional Quarterly* reported in 1963. "But many homosexuals, perhaps the majority, are decidedly virile in appearance." (This comported with the view of the man whose job it was to eliminate gays from the federal government. "There are some people who walk kind of funny," J. Edgar Hoover explained to Johnson, who had asked him for advice on how to spot homosexuals. "That you might kind of think a little bit off or maybe queer. But there was no indication of that in the Jenkins case.") The following year, *Life* observed that "for every obvious homosexual, there are probably nine nearly impossible to detect," an observation that the *Washington Post* endorsed in its analogizing the capital's overtly gay population—whether flamboyant drag queens or conservatively dressed members of the Mattachine Society—to a "small visible layer of the iceberg of homosexuality in Washington." Over lunch with Drew Pearson, Soviet ambassador Anatoly Dobrynin asked "why there was so much homosexuality in the United States." Pearson inquired about its prevalence in Dobrynin's homeland. "Very little," he answered.

Distinguishing herself from the herd of sensationalizing newsmen, unscrupulous Republicans, and a paranoid commander in chief was the First Lady. Next to her husband, no one was more familiar with Walter Jenkins's indefatigability than Lady Bird. And no one demonstrated more levelheadedness, political savvy, or basic human decency throughout his ordeal. The morning after the Al Smith Dinner, as he sat aboard Air Force One preparing to take off from LaGuardia Airport, the president received a phone call from his wife. "I would like to do two things about Walter," she began. The first was to offer Jenkins the number two job at the television station she owned in Austin. The second was to release a statement expressing support for him and his family.

"I wouldn't say anything!" Johnson yelled over the hum of the plane's whirring engines. He had his own ideas for a statement about Jenkins, some of which he had spitballed over the phone the previous evening with Clifford and Fortas. All families have difficulties with wayward members, he had told them. "Some of us have mentally retarded brothers. Some of us have alcoholic brothers. Somebody is wrong in every family. Kind of a sympathetic statement," Johnson told them. To his wife, he instructed, "I just wouldn't be available, because it's not something for you to get involved in now." If she absolutely felt the need to say something, then run it by "Clark and Abe" first. Keep quiet, in other words, and let the men handle it. For, when it came to the unmentionable crime of which Jenkins had been accused, "The average farmer just can't understand your knowing it and approving it, or condoning it—No more than he can [Dean] Acheson not turning his back" on Alger Hiss.

If the First Lady could not persuade the president with an appeal to his basic compassion, then she would go for his political gut instincts. The previous evening, Lady Bird said, she had had a conversation with Jenkins's frazzled wife, Marjorie, whose neighbors were pitching in with the household chores and grocery shopping while she tended to her husband in the hospital. "You've ruined my life and you ruined my husband's life," she had told Lady Bird. "What am I going to tell my children?" Jenkins was a loyal soldier, the most loyal soldier of all, and to abandon him so publicly would send a terrible message to everyone Johnson depended upon to make his accidental presidency a success. Why would those who worked for Johnson continue to show him any loyalty if he hung his most loyal staffer out to dry? "I think a gesture of support on some of our part is necessary to hold our own forces together," Lady Bird said. Johnson grudgingly agreed.

That day, Lady Bird expressed her feelings to Jenkins in a letter written out in longhand.

Dear Walter:

I love you. We all love you. For 25 years you have been the best Christian I know and a good husband and father and friend.

Nothing can change that.

Now, you must take care of yourself and get well.

Devotedly,

Lady Bird

Lady Bird later summoned *Post* publisher Katharine Graham and editor J. Russell Wiggins to the White House. According to Wiggins, the First Lady entered the room "like a vessel under full sail" and dictated a statement that the paper published the following morning. "My heart is aching today for someone who has reached the end point of exhaustion in dedicated service to his country," it read. "Walter Jenkins has been carrying incredible hours and burdens since President Kennedy's murder. He is now receiving medical attention which he needs." According to Wiggins, this was "the only instance I know of where Lady Bird reacted independently . . . All other times she would have followed Lyndon to the guillotine if necessary." Too often dismissed as glorified interior decorators, covetous clotheshorses, and charming housewives, First Ladies, observes the historian Carl Anthony, "tend to have practical and human perspective on the human condition." Rarely has there been a better example of this underappreciated role than Lady Bird Johnson's intercession on behalf of Walter Jenkins.

The public and private sympathies of Lady Bird aside, Jenkins would have no future in public life. In a matter of hours, Clark Clifford was to recall, Lyndon Johnson's "faithful retainer became a nonperson," exiled from the presidential court like a servant who runs afoul of the king. Jenkins was only the most visible example of the fate that befell thousands of other men and women in Washington. But his saga has an additional, heretofore unknown, chapter. For there was another devoted Johnson man whose life would be upended on the eve of the 1964 presidential election, whose citizenship in the secret city would mark him a "nonperson" in the open one.

21

"GONE AND FORGOTTEN"

LITTLE COULD ROBERT MCNAMARA HAVE KNOWN, WHEN HE CROSSED paths with Walter Jenkins on his way into the *Newsweek* party the previous week, that the harried White House staffer was just moments away from committing an act of personal and professional self-destruction. The secretary of defense had dealt frequently with Jenkins in the year since Lyndon Johnson ascended to the presidency, and the whole sorry episode naturally made one wonder: how many other men, appearing so unflappable to the outside world, contained this dangerous secret within them?

By virtue of his status as a colonel in Maj. Gen. Barry Goldwater's 9999th Combined Air Reserve Squadron, Jenkins wasn't just a problem for the White House. He was also a problem for the military. And courtesy of air force chief of staff (and hero of the 1948 Berlin Airlift) Curtis LeMay, McNamara had a report in his hands to compound that problem: there was *another* former Lyndon Johnson aide with homosexual tendencies who had been a member of Goldwater's unit. If Bob Waldron's relationship with the president were ever revealed, it would mean that not one but *two* homosexuals had gained access to what was supposed to be the most secure building in the country, and had worked alongside the most powerful man in the world. What initially appeared to be a tragic yet isolated case might in fact be something larger—and possibly sinister.

McNamara wanted the Waldron matter disposed of quickly, and not by the Pentagon. First, he called the president and, failing to reach him, spoke with Bill Moyers. That evening, McNamara personally delivered the air force's file on Waldron to the White House aide, and the following morning, he called J. Edgar Hoover. The defense secretary was "anxious" to have the matter taken "out of the hands" of the Pentagon, Hoover wrote in a memo to subordinates, and was concerned about the possibility that "trails might lead into others in the unit." At McNamara's request, Hoover opened an investigation into Waldron. "HANDLE WITH EXPERIENCED AGENTS," Hoover ordered in a message to FBI field offices.

The Bureau's investigation of Waldron largely retraced the work done the previous year by the Civil Service Commission. An acquaintance from Chicago told the FBI that, while he did not think Waldron was homosexual when they first met, he later revised his opinion after a phone conversation in which Waldron, asked if he had gotten married, replied, "Who needs it?" (According to the man, the way Waldron said this suggested that he was "queer.") Sen. Peter Dominick of Colorado, who once traveled with Waldron on a congressional delegation inspecting air force bases overseas, said that Waldron was one of two people on the trip who were "very effeminate and queer." An air force colonel observed that Waldron "swishes" while he walks. A former congressional aide admitted that, based on "the fact that Waldron, a bachelor, was a flashy and sometimes gaudy dresser," his "first impression of Waldron was that he was quite effeminate." But once he got to know him, he "was inclined to accept him as he was."

On October 17, a pair of agents (one of whom, John Nichols Sr., happened to be the father of Mattachine Society cofounder Jack Nichols) reinterviewed two other men who were inclined to accept Waldron as he was: his former landlords Robert Best and William Carmichael. When the CSC interviewed the couple in late 1963, Carmichael said that Waldron had told him that he nearly married a woman. Now, almost a year after their friend had been cast out of the White House due to his homosexuality, and with an unannounced visit to their home by two FBI agents days after the highly publicized downfall of *another* homosexual in the Johnson administration, the pair were less restrained in revealing their attitude about the government's behavior. Waldron, Carmichael defiantly told the agents, "dates a different girl almost every night." Best told the G-men that he was "amazed at the apparent motive" of their investigation. After the interview, Nichols and his partner ran a check of military personnel records and found that Carmichael had been separated from the air force in 1944 with a "Blue" discharge "due to traits of character which rendered retention in the service undesirable—habitual homosexual." As for Best, the agents discovered that he was already known to the Bureau, having been the subject of an investigation in 1957 for failing to disclose on a government personnel security questionnaire that he had been arrested for an "attempt to perform an unnatural sex act." (At the time, "Best admitted to having been a homosexual all of his life.") Scrawled at the bottom of the FD-302 form that FBI agents use to summarize their interviews, and underlined in thick red pencil, was a single word: "HOMOSEXUAL." And with that, the men's testimony was summarily discredited.

Shortly before 4 p.m., an agitated President Johnson called Acting Attorney General Nicholas Katzenbach. According to a memo drafted by FBI assistant director Courtney Evans, with whom Katzenbach spoke immediately afterward, the president was "very much worried about the Waldron matter." In particular, Katzenbach explained, Johnson was concerned "that his relationship with Waldron will come out as a follow-up to the Jenkins story." The president told Katzenbach that the FBI had undertaken an investigation into Waldron the previous year—Johnson was mistaken; it was the CSC that had done so—in which "admissions were secured as to his homosexual difficulties" and that this "derogatory information" was given to Waldron's then boss, Congressman Homer Thornberry. The president also told Katzenbach that this investigation had uncovered a letter at the bottom of which appeared his signature as vice president, "requesting the Army to expedite Waldron's commission" in the Air Force Reserve. Walter Jenkins, the president believed, had signed this letter on his behalf.

If any of this information regarding Waldron leaked, Johnson could be in serious political trouble. Republicans would point to Waldron as proof that *multiple* sex deviants had operated under LBJ's inattentive—or, perhaps, tacitly approving—eyes. Even though Johnson had discarded Waldron as soon as the CSC turned up evidence of his homosexuality the previous year, such details would get lost in the media hysteria, and the Jenkins story would suddenly transform from an episode into a pattern.

The revelation that two of his closest aides were leading double lives aggravated Johnson's deepest insecurity. Since the assassination he had acquired an acute case of impostor syndrome, a deep and abiding fear that the public would perceive him as a devious and opportunistic usurper who owed his office to the murder of his predecessor. The exposure of Walter Jenkins (and the possible exposure of Bob Waldron) as homosexual exacerbated Johnson's anxiety that he, too, might be seen as fraudulent, as a pretender to the throne. In the eyes of the president, his relationship with Waldron was a potentially career-ending secret, the evidence of which was now in J. Edgar Hoover's hands.

Johnson was already peeved that the Bureau, due to a bureaucratic mishap, had not informed him earlier about Walter Jenkins's arrest in the same YMCA bathroom back in 1959. But he had to be careful in how he approached the matter. Since the administration of Calvin Coolidge, every president had engaged in a delicate dance with the eternal director of the Federal Bureau of Investigation. On the one hand, Hoover could be immensely valuable in dispensing damaging secrets about one's enemies. Cross him, however, and he might divulge some equally damaging secrets about oneself. Fortunately for Johnson, he had a rare bit of leverage. Earlier that year, at a surprise press conference in the Rose Garden where he lauded Hoover as "a household word, a hero to millions of decent citizens, and an anathema to evil men," the president issued an executive order indefinitely exempting the FBI director from the mandatory federal retirement age of seventy. To be sure, every president before him had renewed Hoover's mandate. But by granting him a lifetime appointment, Johnson had gone above and beyond his predecessors.

Five months after this unprecedented gesture of loyalty and three weeks before the most important political test of his life, Johnson needed the FBI to protect him from abject embarrassment and possible electoral defeat over the revelation of a *second* homosexual in his immediate circle. The president's message to the FBI director, delivered through Katzenbach, could be interpreted as follows: First, that the president expected the FBI would do everything in its power to ensure that the American people never heard the name "Robert Waldron." In the most immediate sense, this meant that the Bureau leave out any mention of him in the report it was preparing on the Jenkins incident, to be released in a matter of days. Second, that if the FBI possessed documents indicating an attempt by the president to expedite

Waldron's military commission, that those documents never see the light of day. Finally, should anybody at the FBI fall short of these standards of discretion, the president wanted it known that he also had the means of disclosing unwelcome information—in this case, the Bureau's negligence in not informing Congressman Jake Pickle about the presence of a homosexual on his staff (which happened to be a moot point given that it was the CSC, and not the FBI, that had conducted the Waldron background check in 1963). Hoover most assuredly got the message, as indicated by the handwritten note he scrawled on Evans's memo. "Keep in mind *we* are writing this report + I don't intend for it to be edited by anyone. Facts are facts + we shall confine ourselves to them."

That evening, a pair of FBI agents paid a surprise visit to Waldron at Pickle's Austin district office. They directed him to compose a statement attesting both to his homosexuality and to the nature of his relationship with Walter Jenkins. "Throughout my life I have realized that I was a latent homosexual but had completely controlled my activities until I moved to Washington, D.C.," Waldron began. That restraint lasted until 1959, "at which time I became an active homosexual, but then only limited to the privacy of my own residence." Waldron said he met Jenkins in the context of their working for members of the Texas congressional delegation, and that he had taken "many trips" with Jenkins during the 1960 campaign as well as overseas once Johnson became vice president. "I never, at any time, observed any action on his part that would in any way cause me to think that he was a homosexual or had any homosexual tendencies," Waldron wrote, adding that he knew "of no one on the staff of the President that is a homosexual nor is there anyone that I suspect of being a homosexual." When the FBI agents questioned him further on this point, Waldron confessed that he had once performed fellatio on a former roommate and colleague on Johnson's Senate staff, a man now married with a child and working for the Commerce Department. Waldron gave the agents the man's name but declined to furnish it in his signed statement, explaining that he did "not want to make it appear I am covering up any information but rather hesitate to file evidence against a close friend." And then, almost as an afterthought, Waldron revealed that the gold watch Johnson had gifted him after the May 1961 Asia trip, the one with the Golden Rule and "LBJ" inscribed on its face, had been stolen from his home sometime in early 1963.

That missing timepiece—tangible evidence of the relationship the president was desperate to conceal—had the potential to become a very serious problem for the White House. Maintaining tight control over knowledge of its existence, and the report Waldron had filed with the police at the time of its theft, was imperative. Incidentally, that same day, the FBI's liaison to the CSC received a phone call from Kimbell Johnson, the CSC's director of personnel investigations who had overseen its 1963 probe into Waldron. In the course of its investigation, Johnson said, the CSC had developed information "from a number of witnesses alluding to a close social relationship which was said to have existed over a considerable period between Waldron and Lyndon B. Johnson . . . that Johnson used to visit Waldron's Washington, DC, home often in the afternoon for cocktails, and that Johnson would be driven to Waldron's home by a female employee on Johnson's staff who would run into Waldron's home first to see if it was alright for Johnson to come in." In addition to this detail strongly implying Waldron's knowledge, and possible enablement, of an affair between the then vice president and his secretary, Mary Margaret Wiley, Kimbell Johnson added that the lead CSC investigator, Earl Haggerty, had also discovered that the vice president gave Waldron "a gold watch inscribed from Johnson to Waldron" that was subsequently stolen.

No reference to either the watch or Wiley had made it into the CSC's final report about Waldron, Kimbell Johnson assured the FBI, as it "was not considered pertinent to the issues then involved." Johnson stressed that he was supported in this assessment by his boss, CSC chairman John Macy, who agreed that any information connecting Waldron to the president "be treated on a very closely held basis." This reassurance, however, did not assuage the Bureau's concern. When the FBI asked Kimbell Johnson if he could make Haggerty available for an interview, Johnson replied that he was reluctant to do so, as it "might unnecessarily inflame the situation and possibly become a factor in the current political campaign." The following day, in what the FBI liaison described as "a most guarded manner," Johnson said Haggerty had told him that he was unsure if the local police detective who handled the watch theft had mentioned the incriminating inscription.

Determined to track down every person who knew about the watch, the FBI interviewed Haggerty on October 20. He said that he had become aware of the stolen Patek Philippe through a security officer at the Department of Commerce, William Randolph, whom the CSC had consulted in its investigation of Waldron because one of Waldron's former roommates (the one with whom he had had a sexual encounter) was employed there. When Haggerty made a check of local police files, he recalled that the complaint about the missing watch mentioned an inscription "to the effect of 'From LBJ To . . .'" but that he could not remember if it also had "the name or the initials of the person to whom it was given." That left Randolph as the last individual with knowledge about Waldron's homosexuality and the timepiece that linked him to the president of the United States. In an interview with the FBI that same day, Randolph recorded what he could remember of his investigation in a written statement, "with the exception of the inscription on the watch, which was furnished orally to the FBI as it dealt with the President of the United States." Having ascertained that the compromising nature of the missing timepiece was known only to a few, the FBI determined that the secret of Johnson's relationship with Waldron was safe. And the Bureau worked to keep it that way, carefully omitting any details regarding what it and the CSC had discovered about Waldron offering his home to Johnson and Wiley in the report it sent to Defense Secretary Robert McNamara, and making sure not to disseminate Waldron's signed statement, "which contains numerous references to the President," in any of its communications with other agencies.

On October 18, the FBI reinterviewed Waldron in Austin for two hours. They peppered him with the names of neighbors, former roommates, fellow members from the 9999th Air Reserve squadron—even "a young student given a job in the capital by Senator Lyndon B. Johnson"—and demanded to know if any of them was homosexual. Next, they pried Waldron for further details about his sex life. Waldron confessed that he had "not had more than twenty homosexual relations during his entire life," that these occurred with "no more than ten different men," two of whom were federal employees, that they were all "one time affairs," that he "avoided becoming involved for his own job protection," and "that he has had his problem under control so well that no one in the government is aware of" it. He further told the agents that he wanted to cooperate in their investigation due to his "high regard for president and Mrs. Johnson who have treated him as a son and whom he does not want to hurt." Since his dismissal from the president's employ, Waldron had remained in touch with Lady Bird, who had invited him to a party that very afternoon at the Johnson family ranch outside Austin near the town of Stonewall. Waldron cut the interview short so he could make it in time for the party's 3 p.m. start.

Shortly after receiving a report on this exchange from his agents in the field, Cartha "Deke" DeLoach called Bill Moyers at the White House. Waldron, he reported, had abruptly halted an interview with the FBI "to attend a social function" at the presidential ranch. This information must have unnerved Moyers, just three days into Jenkins's old job. He had palpable experience of the power homosexuality had to shape the course of American politics. In the summer of 1954, Moyers had been working as an intern in Johnson's Senate office when he heard a shotgun blast upstairs. It was Sen. Lester Hunt, committing suicide.

Moyers may also have had a personal motive for wanting to dispose of Waldron. Prior to his dismissal from the Johnson orbit, Waldron had been a competitor with Moyers for the president's paternal affection. "If I had a boy, I'd like him to be like this young fellow," Johnson once said of Moyers, who, at twenty-eight, became the youngest presidential appointee in history when John F. Kennedy made him deputy director of the Peace Corps in 1963. The news that Lady Bird was welcoming Waldron back into the familial fold presumably annoyed the precocious presidential aide, who, while speaking with the piety of the ordained Baptist pastor he was, also possessed a political cunning well suited to the man he served. "Whatever he does, he does with every assurance that he is carrying out the will of John the Baptist," reported one victim of Moyers's bureaucratic machinations. Eric Goldman, the Princeton University historian whom Johnson brought onto his White House staff to play the role that Arthur Schlesinger had for Jack Kennedy, described Moyers as the "classic story of the young man in a hurry," one who masked a Machiavellian temperament behind a veneer of righteous humility. Earlier that summer, Moyers had collaborated with Deke DeLoach to stymie the seating of the racially integrated Mississippi delegation at the Democratic convention, and he was also the "architect" of the infamous "Daisy" commercial likening a vote for Barry Goldwater to dropping a nuclear bomb on an angelic little girl plucking petals from a flower.

Waldron was not the only government employee suspected of homosexuality whom Moyers targeted for retribution. Days after this conversation with DeLoach, Moyers ordered the FBI to find evidence of homosexuality among members of Goldwater's Senate staff and other Johnson aides. In an October 27 phone call with the president, Deke DeLoach mentioned a "rumor" that the FBI had received concerning a possible homosexual on the White House staff. "Bill Moyers knew about it and asked me to check it out," DeLoach said. The staffer was "involved in a homosexual incident down in Houston, Texas." (DeLoach was presumably talking about Houston native Jack Valenti, whom the White House did investigate on the suspicion that he was gay.) After the election, DeLoach wrote a memo to Hoover stating that Moyers had asked the FBI to investigate two other White House colleagues for "homosexual tendencies." Asked about these events in 2009, Moyers explained that he was merely following the president's orders, and that "no harm came to a single person from any of these allegations." Furthermore, he asserted, "Nobody lost a job."

Bob Waldron's declassified FBI file reveals otherwise. After hearing that Waldron was driving to the LBJ ranch at the invitation of the First Lady, Moyers let slip a glimmer of what Eric Goldman would refer to as his "continuous and enveloping drive for power and status" and "stiletto tactics." He told DeLoach that he would "put a stop to Waldron's attending the function" and immediately call Waldron's employer, Congressman Jake Pickle, to "stop Waldron." Within the next twenty minutes, according to President Johnson's White House diary, both DeLoach and Moyers spoke with the president by phone. The next day, Jake Pickle accepted Waldron's resignation.

On October 24, at the request of the FBI, Walter Jenkins drafted a statement from his hospital bed. "Never in my years of Government service did I consciously or knowingly recommend or approve the appointment to any position of any person whom I had reason to suspect was a homosexual," he wrote. "To the contrary, in several instances, I have successfully recommended against the appointment of applicants because the file contained information providing reason to suspect that they engaged in homosexual practices." Jenkins added that he had never knowingly associated with a suspected homosexual, with one exception: Bob Waldron. After Waldron applied for a job on the National Aeronautics and Space Council, "the field investigation of Mr. Waldron came to my attention, and it contained information alleging that Mr. Waldron had engaged in homosexual acts. I did not know, and I do not know at this time, whether Mr. Waldron was or is in fact a homosexual, but I thought that the allegations were sufficient to warrant my recommending that Mr. Waldron's application should be rejected. It was rejected."

After interviewing eighty-five people in less than two weeks, the FBI concluded its investigation of Bob Waldron. "Whereas many commented on his effeminate mannerisms and characteristics, it was generally stated that they possessed no information reflecting on his moral character," the Bureau's summary report concluded. "Twenty-eight of those individuals commented on his effeminate mannerisms and suspected that he might have homosexual tendencies. Some of his associates were considered suspect due to similar effeminate characteristics. Those acquainted with his professional ability said he is a highly efficient and capable office employee and administration assistant. No question was raised concerning his loyalty to the United States."

* * *

WITHIN THREE DAYS OF THE JENKINS SCANDAL'S ERUPTION, a series of major world events overtook its place on newspaper front pages: the Soviet Politburo ousted Nikita Khrushchev, the British Labour Party won a general election for the first time in thirteen years, and the People's Republic of China detonated a nuclear bomb. According to a poll conducted the week after the story broke, 88 percent of Americans were aware of the morals charge involving the senior staff man to the president of the United States. But their reaction was not what Johnson, his Republican opponents, or the leading lights of the American media had anticipated. Fifty-nine percent did not think that the incident affected national security, a clear-cut repudiation of the federal government's rationale for prohibiting gays in government. In a hardly scientific but nonetheless revealing poll, syndicated columnists Rowland Evans and Robert Novak found that, of the 102 swing state voters whom they interviewed about the scandal, only 6 undecideds said it moved them to the Goldwater camp, 5 of whom had pulled the lever for Richard Nixon in 1960. Asked if the Jenkins affair would affect her vote, a housewife delivered a welcome dose of small-town American pragmatism. "Why should it?" she asked. "I never was going to vote for Jenkins." If letters to the president and First Lady were indicative of public opinion, the incumbent could rest assured about his reelection prospects. "The really remarkable thing was the mail that came to the White House in the aftermath, so many people saying, 'I have that problem in my family,'" remembered Liz Carpenter. "The country is really more civilized sometimes than you ever think they are." One man even mailed a five-dollar bill to the White House to assist the Jenkins family in its time of need.

Despite all the panic, catastrophizing, and conspiratorial delirium, the Jenkins scandal had no discernible effect on the election, which Johnson won with the largest landslide in modern American history. Clark Clifford, who had advised Lady Bird against issuing a supportive statement about Jenkins for fear it would tarnish the administration with the stain of homosexuality, came to believe that the collective shrug from voters illustrated how he and other Beltway insiders had underestimated the American people. "Not for the first time, the American public was well ahead of Washington in its attitude toward such matters," he observed some twenty-five years later. "The voters understood that this was a personal tragedy, not a public matter. Perhaps it marked the beginning of a new era in which the American public began to show a greater tolerance and understanding of homosexuality." Allen Drury had anticipated as much in *Advise and Consent*, when he wrote that once the "shabby double-dealing behind Brigham Anderson's death" became public knowledge, the American people, "after its first shock at the revelations concerning the Senator's private life," would "quite likely turn with a bitter contempt upon the men who used it to kill him." Drury chalked up this magnanimity to the "innate fairness" of his countrymen.

Elevated to the position of White House press secretary in 1965, Bill Moyers left the Johnson administration the following year. The reason for his departure, Moyers said, was disillusionment with the president's cutthroat tactics. "I thought I could make him more like me, but I've found in the last several months that I'm becoming more like him; so I got out."

Two years after the scandal erupted, Johnson was still privately fuming that the whole thing had been a Republican setup. He simply could not wrap his head around the possibility that his trusted friend and advisor might be a homosexual. Neither, apparently, could Jenkins, who remained married and never commented publicly on the incident. Lady Bird ultimately did not provide Jenkins with the job she had wanted to give him at her radio station. But she did offer him land on which to build a house and continued to employ him as an accountant. Toward the end of his ill-fated presidency, Johnson told an aide that the two things he most looked forward to after leaving the White House were to welcome Walter Jenkins back to his ranch and resume smoking cigarettes. He fulfilled both pledges.

Deprived of his career as a public servant, Bob Waldron enrolled at the New York School of Design to study interior decoration. He too was welcomed back into the Johnson fold after the thirty-sixth president left office and was a regular presence at the ranch from which Bill Moyers had tried to bar him, working closely with Lady Bird on its refurbishment. Perhaps, after deciding not to run for reelection and departing Washington in humiliation, Johnson acquired a heightened sensitivity to the suffering of others, and a finer ability to empathize with people, like him, rejected by the country they had committed themselves to serving. Waldron evinced no bitterness toward Johnson; on the contrary, he was effusive in his praise. "I don't think there was ever a kinder man that lived," he said in an oral history recorded five years after Johnson's death in 1973. "If I ever write anything or am ever asked to speak on Mr. Johnson, I so desperately want—if you could convince the world of what a truly human being this man was, how sensitive he was . . . When you hurt, he hurt, and when you were sad, he was sad." Asked many years later about why he left the president's employ, Waldron portrayed it as his own decision. "I went to the president and said, 'If I'm ever going back to school, this is it.'"

The tragic downfalls of the Johnson aides occurred against a backdrop of historic achievement for other minority groups also suffering the brunt of discrimination. Earlier that year, Johnson had employed the full force of his being—rhetorical, political, emotional, and physical—into passing the Civil Rights Act of 1964, a momentous piece of legislation outlawing discrimination on the basis of race, religion, sex, and national origin. Just a few months later, in connection with a Senate Internal Security Subcommittee study that called more than one hundred witnesses and generated some twenty thousand pages of testimony, a senior State Department official asserted that "homosexuality is the most disturbing security problem" the agency faced. An era of tremendous legal and moral progress for some American citizens remained a time of despair for gay and lesbian ones.

This dichotomy was present in the character of Lyndon Johnson. The president who courageously shepherded passage of the Civil Rights Act through Congress addressed his African American chauffeur as "nigger." The orator who employed soaring rhetoric in his appeals to the American people was shockingly vulgar in conversations with his aides behind closed doors. This backslapping, infectiously gregarious man could be remarkably rude toward those who dedicated their lives to him; the politician who used power to achieve far-reaching, noble ends had accumulated much of that power through ruthless and amoral means. To a degree more pronounced than any modern president, Lyndon Johnson was capable of extraordinary compassion and shocking indifference—a duality of character reflected in his treatment of Bob Waldron.

Two weeks after the 1964 election, savoring his historic victory, Johnson discussed Waldron's fate with Deke DeLoach. The Justice Department was deciding whether to prosecute Waldron for having answered "no" to the question "Have you had or have you now homosexual tendencies?" on his application to join the Air Force Reserve. While Johnson believed that his erstwhile aide, travel companion, dance buddy, body man, stenographer, and substitute son should be left alone, it ultimately did not matter to the president what happened to Bob Waldron. For he was "gone and forgotten," Johnson said. "Nobody would pay any attention to him."

22

THE FRUIT LOOP

LEROY AARONS WAS LISTENING TO THE POLICE BLOTTER ON THE AFTER-noon of April 17, 1965, when, at 4:20 p.m., the dispatcher reported something bizarre: a group of ten self-declared homosexuals was picketing the White House. The *Washington Post* journalist "thought they must be totally reckless or weird—using their names and talking to reporters for quote." But then Aarons reflected upon the broader implications of disclosing their secret—his secret—in front of the most recognizable building in the country. "My second thought was: What's that got to do with me? I had my job, I had my gay life, and I had my straight life. I had totally compartmentalized my life and I didn't like those elements of my life getting confused."

Aarons would leave it to other journalists to cover this unprecedented event outside the White House. His gay life did not extend into the *Washington Post* newsroom, where, like every other newspaper in the country, the notion of an avowedly homosexual reporter was unthinkable. This was still the case notwithstanding a clear improvement in the *Post*'s coverage of gay people under the tenure of its new publisher, Katharine Graham. Prior to her taking control of the paper following her husband's 1963 suicide, the *Post* could best be described as indifferent toward the subject of homosexuality, when it wasn't derisive. In this, it was hardly exceptional. Many states still codified homosexuality—illegal everywhere except Illinois, which decriminalized it in 1961—as "the abominable and detestable crime against nature," and news coverage of gays, which alternated between pity and disgust, reflected public antipathy. In January 1964, however, just a few months after Graham became publisher, the *Post* editorial board criticized the civil service ban on homosexuals. "Many persons who may in one degree or another feel a physical or emotional attraction to members of their own sex govern their behavior in such ways as to lead thoroughly useful, successful, and apparently normal lives," the paper argued. "To deny such persons all chance to work for their government is wholly arbitrary and unjust." Two months later, it ridiculed a congressman attempting to revoke the Mattachine Society's charitable solicitation permit as "that master of morality." Beginning in January 1965, the paper published a groundbreaking five-part series on homosexuality, whose title nonetheless demonstrated why Aarons felt the need to separate his gay and straight lives. "This series of articles would not have been written five years ago," reporter Jean M. White announced in the first installment of "Those Others," which examined homosexuality from a scientific, social, political, and legal perspective. Though White described gays as leading "furtive, lonely" lives that are "gay only in homosexual jargon," her series was praised by *The Ladder*, the first nationally distributed lesbian publication, for offering "the most astute as well as most extensive coverage so far in U.S. papers" of the subject.

While attempting to enlighten readers about the plight of homosexuals in its news pages, the *Post* refused to print any advertisement that even contained the word *homosexual*, a policy that inevitably led to some absurd editorial copy. A local experimental theater company's seasonal theme, "Focus on Homosexuality," was changed to "Focus on the Love That Dare Not Speak Its Name." The paper also refused to print meeting notices submitted by the Mattachine Society of Washington (MSW), some of whose members, after four years of obscurity, decided to seek the redress of their grievances by announcing them outside the home of the most powerful man in the world.

Inside the White House, the two aides who had tried but failed to compartmentalize their lives like Aarons were "gone and forgotten." Outside, a man who rejected that compartmentalization as false and un-American led his immaculately dressed fellow gay and lesbian citizens in adamant yet dignified protest. "If you're asking for equal employment rights," Frank Kameny had instructed them, "look employable." All seven of the men marching behind Kameny in a swift oval formation were outfitted in jackets and ties, while the three women wore blouses and skirts reaching below the knee. (It took some convincing by Eva Freund before Kameny relented and allowed the ladies to wear flat-soled shoes.) Each of the picketers held up a wooden placard on which was painted a clear proposition or demand:

**FIFTEEN MILLION U.S. HOMOSEXUALS PROTEST
FEDERAL TREATMENT**

**WE WANT: FEDERAL EMPLOYMENT; HONORABLE
DISCHARGES; SECURITY CLEARANCES**

**GOVERNOR WALLACE MET WITH NEGROES
OUR GOVERNMENT WON'T MEET WITH US**

**U.S. CLAIMS NO SECOND CLASS CITIZENS
WHAT ABOUT HOMOSEXUAL CITIZENS?**

It was a jarring sight. In the years since he decided to challenge the government's discrimination, Kameny and his followers had devoted themselves exclusively to nonconfrontational forms of protest. When the Supreme Court refused to hear his wrongful termination case in 1961, Kameny responded by initiating a letter-writing campaign to government officials—the chairman of the Civil Service Commission, every cabinet secretary, all 535 members of the House and Senate, and President Kennedy among them—calling for an end to discrimination. One of the very few people to respond was Republican congressman Charles E. Chamberlain of Michigan. "Your letter of August 28 has been received," Chamberlain wrote, "and in reply may I state unequivocally that in all my six years of service in the United States Congress I have not received such a revolting communication." In August 1963, Kameny testified before Congress—the first openly gay person to do so—in opposition to a bill nominally aimed at revoking the charitable solicitation permits of organizations deemed adverse to the "health, welfare and morals" of the city, but that singled out Mattachine. At one point during the hearing, the bill's sponsor, John Dowdy of Texas, favorably contrasted his state's handling of homosexuality—where one did not go "bragging" about it—to that endorsed by Mattachine. "This is a matter on which one doesn't brag but one doesn't have to be ashamed of something for which there is no reason to be ashamed," Kameny replied.

Excluded from all but the most menial jobs, the Harvard-trained astronomer threw himself into activism. He installed two phones in his home: one for calling a government official's office and the other for calling the same office when said official's secretary invariably put him on hold. Kameny's tactics were more provocative than those of the Mattachine affiliate in San Francisco, which mostly served the role of a social service organization, and New York, whose leaders had yet to expand their activities beyond a lecture series. As Kameny told a New York audience in the summer of 1964, "unless and until we get at and eliminate the discrimination and prejudice which underlie—and, in fact, which *are*—the homosexual's problems, we will accomplish nothing of lasting value, either, and our job will go on literally without end."

Valiant as Kameny's labors may have been, they seemed to result in little more than frequent trips to the post office and expensive phone bills. And so, by the spring of 1965, with his legal, epistolary, and testimonial avenues exhausted, Kameny set out on a more militant path.

The idea to stage a picket outside the White House was first raised by Lige Clarke, boyfriend of Mattachine cofounder Jack Nichols. The pair had met the previous summer, at the Hideaway, a basement bar catty-corner from FBI headquarters. "A soldier with a wide smile and a security clearance," Clarke worked for the Joint Chiefs of Staff editing classified documents at the Pentagon, where he also secretly distributed Mattachine leaflets informing gay soldiers of their constitutional rights. And yet it was not the U.S. government's persecution of homosexuals that inspired Clarke to action, but Fidel Castro's. On April 16, an article appeared in the *New York Times* citing a report from a Cuban state newspaper about a widespread crackdown on homosexuality, possibly to include the herding of gay men into forced labor camps. "We can't let him get away with this," Clarke implored Nichols. "The Mattachine Society should do something." The group had discussed picketing before, but Kameny was wary. A specific incident of injustice, he believed, was necessary to focus public attention. Could this imminent outrage ninety miles off the coast of Florida be the catalyst? Nichols called Kameny to find out.

"There's no Cuban embassy in Washington," Kameny replied, the United States having severed diplomatic ties with the Communist country in 1961.

"Why not the White House?" Nichols proposed. "We'd certainly be seen there."

Kameny was convinced. They would organize a picket for the next day—which is how the first demonstration for gay rights in the nation's capital was an anticommunist one as well.

"In order to make any impression on heterosexuals in power—because here we are, we are in the nation's capital—we had to look normal; we had to be rational; we had to be intelligent; we had to know what we were doing," remembered Lilli Vincenz, one of the ten Mattachine members to march that day. For an hour, in a space allocated for them by police, the picketers held their demonstration without incident. "Only a very few hostile remarks were passed by the throngs of tourists flocking and driving by," a triumphant Kameny announced in a press release. "Much interest was shown; many pictures of signs and demonstrators were taken."

Alas, only one media outlet reported on the event. "10 OPPOSE GOV'T ON HOMOSEXUALS," read the headline on page 18 of the *Washington Afro-American* the following week. Of more interest to the press that day was the much larger protest, numbering some sixteen thousand people, against the American military's bombing of North Vietnam. But to the gays and lesbians across the country who heard about it, the picket was profoundly important. "Nothing like these demonstrations has been seen before," effused an editorial in *Eastern Mattachine Magazine*. "The most hated and despised of minority groups has shown its face to the crowds, and it is plain for all to see that they are not horrible monsters. They are ordinary-looking, well-dressed human beings!" For Vincenz, the picket was "the most important day of my life" next to her marriage to her partner over two decades later.

The White House demonstration inspired further protests, each drawing more participants and press coverage than the last. Before their second White House picket in May, Mattachine members distributed flyers to local tour bus operators, ensuring for themselves a steady flow of bemused, shocked, and, one presumes, silently inspired onlookers. This time, the Associated Press, United Press International, Agence France-Presse, the *New York Times*, and the *Evening Star* all reported on the event, film of which ABC News distributed to local affiliates across the country. Later that summer, twenty-five Mattachine members picketed the Civil Service Commission to protest Chairman John Macy's continuing refusal to meet with them, and by October, forty-five people participated in a third picket outside the White House. Though the sun was not shining particularly bright that day, many of the marchers wore sunglasses to disguise their identity.

At a demonstration outside the Pentagon in July, men in civilian clothing surreptitiously took photographs of the picketers' cars. Eva Freund walked over and offered to make things easier for the snoopers by writing down the license plate numbers. She also offered to pose for a picture. Foiled by this display of prideful self-assertion, the undercover agents skulked away. Later, a two-star general came out of the Pentagon to tell the group they could not picket in the parking lot.

"Go fuck yourself," Mattachine member Otto Ulrich replied. "We're taxpayers and we're demonstrating here."

At a State Department press conference on August 27, a journalist asked Secretary of State Dean Rusk about the protest announced by "a self-declared 'minority group'" for the following day. "Well, you have been very gentle," Rusk replied sarcastically before clarifying which "minority group" the journalist had in mind. "I understand that we are being picketed by a group of homosexuals," he elaborated to peals of laughter. "The policy of the Department is that we do not employ homosexuals knowingly and that if we discover homosexuals in our department, we discharge them."

But even among those already enlisted in the cause of homosexual equality, the new militancy could be unsettling. "I see no similarity between the problems faced by the Homophile Civil Rights Movement and those faced by the Negro Civil Rights Movement and if I am not reinforced in some way in this belief, so that I might use my considerable influence with the other organizations to prevent further such demonstrations, they will surely vote to proceed," Mattachine Society of Florida president Richard Inman warned Bill Moyers in a January 1966 letter explaining his "conservative anti-public demonstration stand." If the presidential aide continued to ignore his missives, Inman continued, "demonstrations by Negros, anti-Vietnam protesters and draft card burners, will look like 'peanuts' by comparison with what you will behold in the near future by members of the Homophile Civil Rights Movement."

∗ ∗ ∗

AS A FOURTEEN-YEAR-OLD BOY growing up in the environs of Tulsa, Oklahoma, during the 1950s, Hugh Key often spent his entire, fifty-cent weekly allowance for the bus trip into town. A newsstand at the train station was the only place for miles that stocked *Physique Pictorial*, one of the early beefcake magazines of the variety H. Lynn Womack published. Should the desires aroused by the images within its pages ever become known, it would be more than enough to ruin the career in law and politics to which Key aspired, and so he kept them secret. "The first questions on the Oklahoma bar exam," he recalled, were, "'Are you a convicted felon or a homosexual?'" Key followed the path of most other men in his predicament. He married, and eventually found his way to Washington, accompanied by "a wife who looked like Jackie Kennedy and two gorgeous blond children."

Running parallel with his picture-perfect existence as a senatorial staffer and family man, however, was another life. In the spring of 1967, Key was working out at a gym near his high-rise apartment in Alexandria, Virginia, when he met a handsome young navy captain around his age named Tom Morgan. Morgan was posted as a military aide at the White House, where he could often be seen standing behind President and Mrs. Johnson at official functions. He also served on the twenty-four-man crew aboard the presidential yacht, the USS *Sequoia*. Morgan's first outing with Johnson shattered whatever illusions the young captain might have had about presidential decorum. Stationed on the deck one day, Morgan heard a buzzer beckoning him to the president's private quarters belowdecks. "Get in here!" Johnson thundered when Morgan knocked on the stateroom door. Morgan entered to find an empty bedroom. "In here!" yelled the president from the head. Morgan hesitantly opened the bathroom door and discovered the commander in chief sitting on the toilet, fumbling with the toilet roll dispenser. According to Bob Waldron, Johnson had a "hang-up on the toilet paper holder," subjecting his staff to fifteen-minute harangues accusing whoever had installed it of being a "torture expert . . . He would just go into this whole elaborate discussion that you just had to be a contortionist."

"Who is this goddamn shitter made for?" Johnson asked the startled Morgan. "A left-handed Amazonian?"

One night, Morgan invited Key to accompany him on the *Sequoia* as it sailed from Annapolis, where it had been in dry dock during the winter, through the Chesapeake Bay to its destination at a port along the Potomac River in Washington. First used by President Herbert Hoover, the 104-foot

Sequoia had been the scene of several momentous events in presidential history. It was where Harry Truman, three months after ordering the use of atomic bombs on Hiroshima and Nagasaki, first discussed the sharing of atomic technology with British prime minister Clement Attlee and Canadian prime minister Mackenzie King. President Eisenhower's Joint Chiefs of Staff used the yacht to hash out his "New Look" defense policy centered on nuclear deterrence. John F. Kennedy celebrated his forty-sixth (and final) birthday party on the vessel, in whose presidential cabin he installed a king-size bed. And it was in that very bed where Hugh Key and Capt. Tom Morgan made love.

The following year, Key served as Morgan's best man. The day of the wedding, Morgan frantically called Key asking if he had any vitamin E, an aphrodisiac.

Though the sexual revolution was dramatically transforming the rules of heterosexual courtship and intimacy, the liberating spirits of the sixties were slower to make their impact felt upon gay Americans, who by and large remained shuttered inside their closets. Furtive encounters in public lavatories, parks, or—for the more discriminating (and affluent)—hotel rooms remained the only options available for most men seeking sex with men in 1960s Washington. The restrooms at the Garfinckel's and Woodward and Lothrop department stores were popular cruising grounds during the lunch hour and afternoons; Key recalled a men's room at the Supreme Court being especially busy as it was "the cleanest bathroom in Washington." Outdoor cruising, which since the latter part of the nineteenth century had been relegated largely to the environs around Lafayette Square, began spreading northward a few blocks to Dupont Circle. Dubbed the "Fruit Loop," after the popular breakfast cereal created in 1963, it was "a prime daytime extravaganza," according to Jack Nichols, the scene of "a never-ending game of musical benches, with men moving from one to another" at all hours of the day and night. Another emerging locus of sexual adventure was the wooded area parallel to Rock Creek and adjacent to the P Street Bridge, known as "the Black Forest" for its busyness at night. For those citizens of the secret city whose power compelled more discretion, sex was an even more dangerous pursuit.

★ ★ ★

"BY REMAINING SILENT we lend credence to the view that we prefer to risk losing our freedom than to offend a questionable 'asset' to our party," Congressman Peter Frelinghuysen of New Jersey declared at a crucial moment during the Army-McCarthy Hearings when few of his Republican colleagues dared speak out against the demagoguery of its chief protagonist. A liberal who supported the Civil Rights Acts of 1957, 1960, and 1964, Frelinghuysen belonged to a political dynasty that, since the country's founding, had sent four of its sons to the Senate and two to the House of Representatives. Neither Frelinghuysen's courage nor his lineage, however, could insulate him from the dangers of his secret.

The plainclothes policeman who came to see Frelinghuysen at his office inside the Rayburn House Office Building the morning of September 15, 1965, had some awkward news. His colleagues had recently arrested a male prostitute in whose possession they discovered the congressman's wallet. The police would need Frelinghuysen to testify as a material witness against the man; but understanding how "the publicity would be most detrimental," the officer was willing to keep Frelinghuysen's name out of the papers in exchange for a modest donation to Washington's finest. How generous was Frelinghuysen willing to be?

Was two thousand dollars enough? Frelinghuysen asked.

Not nearly, the officer replied. He was thinking more in the vicinity of fifty thousand.

A descendant of Dutch bankers, Frelinghuysen was a wealthy man. But fifty thousand dollars was still an extremely large amount of money. And yet, the ruin he feared as the result of being exposed as a homosexual was apparently too ghastly to contemplate. Frelinghuysen readily agreed to pay the blackmail.

There was only one problem: between the cash in his office and his account at the Riggs National Bank downtown, he did not have sufficient funds on hand. Frelinghuysen would have to transfer money from his bank in Morristown, New Jersey, a process that would take at least several days. The police officer wanted the cash immediately, however, and persuaded Frelinghuysen to book the next available flight to Newark Airport. From a pay phone, Frelinghuysen arranged for his bank to have fifty thousand in cash ready for him by 4 p.m. He then drove with the officer to Washington National Airport, where the two boarded the 1:30 p.m. Eastern Air Lines shuttle. To avoid suspicion, the officer told Frelinghuysen to neither speak nor sit next to him on the plane.

When they finally arrived at the Morristown bank, Frelinghuysen was too nervous to count the six-inch-high stack of one-hundred-dollar bills the teller handed him. He got back into the car, gave the money to the officer, and drove to Newark Airport for the 5:30 p.m. shuttle back to Washington. When they landed, the officer handed Frelinghuysen back his wallet, and the two parted ways. Shortly before 9 p.m., Frelinghuysen returned home to Georgetown, where his anxious wife was about to call the police to report her missing husband.

If Frelinghuysen believed this payment of hush money had resolved his problem with the crooked cops, he was mistaken. Several months later, two other police officers confronted him in the congressional cafeteria and made him undertake the same ritual. Fortunately, this time they demanded only fifteen thousand dollars.

The plainclothesmen who confronted Peter Frelinghuysen were not actual police officers, but members of a nationwide blackmail ring that targeted prominent gay men. A midwestern university professor who mortgaged his home, a Boston hotel owner who shelled out more than two hundred thousand dollars—these were just some of the victims, estimated at one per day, of the extortion rings that started preying upon gay men in every major American city in the years after World War II. Entreaties by police departments that the victims of these scams come forward—to "show some guts," as one captain put it—revealed the paradoxical predicament of the homosexual, simultaneously condemned as a criminal and beseeched for his cooperation against crime. In Washington, the Mattachine Society tried to alert unsuspecting gays to the threat by distributing leaflets at gay bars with titles such as *Blackmailer at Work in Dupont Circle Area* and *How to Handle Blackmail*, advising them to request the badge numbers of the "officers" who accosted them and demand to be taken to a police station where their credentials might be confirmed.

In its 1966 bust of the ring that targeted Frelinghuysen, code-named Operation Homex (Compromise and Extortion of Homosexuals), the FBI discovered the multifarious means and lingo by which the blackmailers carried out their ruse. The Frelinghuysen scenario was a by-the-book "check play," in which a young, attractive man (known as a "chicken") would target a victim (the "baby doll"), propose a sexual assignation, and lead him to a hotel room. There, after the two engaged in sex, the chicken would steal something of value (a "poke"), which the men imitating police ("shakemen"), in possession of phony badges ("buttons"), would later present to the baby doll in exchange for cash. In a period of just two years, the ring extorted hundreds of thousands of dollars from at least seven hundred victims, including university deans, professors, businessmen, a film star, a general, and "two well-known American singers."

Frelinghuysen would go on to assume a number of high-profile assignments related to foreign affairs, including service on a bipartisan congressional delegation to the UN General Assembly and attendance at a conference in London advocating an end to white-minority rule in Africa. Yet, once the Justice Department notified congressional leaders of the blackmail money he had paid, he was quietly removed from the Armed Services Committee on the grounds that his access to classified information could pose a threat to national security.

Considering the fate that befell one of the ring's other prominent Washington victims, Frelinghuysen was lucky. A cousin of Idaho Democratic senator Frank Church and a third-generation naval officer who survived the attack on Pearl Harbor, Admiral William C. G. Church had been targeted in the same manner as Frelinghuysen after a "chicken" stole his wallet at the Astor Hotel in New York City. Later, a pair of "shakemen" posing as police officers walked straight into the Pentagon, escorted Church from his office, and extorted five thousand dollars from him on the spot. On December 15, 1965, the evening before he was scheduled to appear in New York City for questioning by police investigating the ring, Church drove to a Maryland motel and committed suicide.

"I don't think my mother believed Bill was gay," Chase Church, a son of Senator Church, recalled. "As she would say[,] he was married and that couldn't be."

23

SCANDAL IN SACRAMENTO

"My God," Ronald Reagan exclaimed, raising his eyes from the sheaf of papers he was clutching in his hands. "Has government failed?"

The governor of California was the leading spokesman of a growing political movement whose guiding principle was that the government which governed best was that which governed least. But even he was shocked by the scale of the boondoggle revealed in the report just handed to him by his senior advisors. Clad in pajamas and a bathrobe and sitting on a couch in his suite at the Hotel del Coronado in San Diego, Reagan had been recovering from a prostate operation on August 25, 1967, when not one, not two, but eleven staffers from his office up in Sacramento barged into his room. "Golly, are you quitting all at once?" the perpetually cheerful former actor quipped. Disturbed by the commotion, Reagan's vigilant wife, Nancy, emerged from the bathroom wrapped in a terry cloth robe with her hair up in a towel. Sitting next to him on the couch, she peered intently over his shoulder at the document that had delivered him such a jolt.

Its subject was Phil Battaglia, Reagan's deputy chief of staff and the man he referred to as "my strong right arm." Maybe too strong—for, less than a year into Reagan's governorship, Battaglia had already alienated most of his colleagues, earning the nickname "deputy governor" among the Sacramento press corps. The convalescence-crashing aides wanted Reagan to fire Battaglia, and their means of doing so was the dossier in the governor's hands. In vivid detail, it laid out the case that Battaglia, a scheduler named Richard "Sandy" Quinn, and a professional football player who had spent the summer off-season working in Reagan's office, Jack Kemp, were homosexuals.

Three years after the Walter Jenkins affair struck such fear into Lyndon Johnson that he worried he might lose his massive poll lead to Barry Goldwater, "men in high places were being revealed" as homosexuals, recalled one gay man who worked as an aide to California State Assembly Speaker Jesse Unruh. "It was a period of fairly high paranoia. Gay men that I knew were all sort of desperately dashing back into the closet to protect themselves."

The ringleader of the effort to fire Battaglia was Franklyn "Lyn" Nofziger, Reagan's director of communications. Rotund, gruff, perpetually disheveled, with a cigar usually protruding from his goatee-rimmed maw, Nofziger was Reagan's chief curmudgeon. Bedecked in his standard outfit of blue-checked blazer, blue oxford shirt, and, when he chose to wear one, Mickey Mouse tie knotted well below his unbuttoned collar, Nofziger made the rumpled reporters whose ranks he used to fill look dapper. Lou Cannon, the California political reporter and dean of the Reagan beat, recalled that Nofziger "dressed like a refugee who had been outfitted by a charity that didn't know his size." Whatever impression Nofziger's slovenliness might have created with the media, it undeniably made the governor look better by comparison, which is ultimately all that Nofziger cared about. He had joined Reagan's gubernatorial campaign in 1966 with the conviction that the former actor was destined for the White House. And if there was one thing capable of wrecking a politician's presidential ambitions, it was homosexuality.

A few weeks before the surprise summit at the Hotel del Coronado, Nofziger had convened "a meeting of Reagan aides we knew were heterosexual, trustworthy, and loyal to Reagan" where the decision was made to ask Art Van Court, the ex-LAPD detective in charge of Reagan's security detail, to carry out an investigation into the three suspects. From the get-go, the probe "made the Keystone Cops look good," Nogziger recalled. At one point, Van Court tried and failed to break into Quinn's apartment. The aides botched an attempt to install a bug in Battaglia's office. A private dick they subcontracted to stalk Battaglia and Kemp got lost while tailing them on a highway; another time, Battaglia and Quinn realized they were being pursued and escaped after a high-speed chase. Nofziger and his allies ultimately found no evidence of homosexuality, and much to refute it, such as hotel charges indicating that Battaglia and Kemp had booked separate, non-adjoining rooms when they traveled. Nonetheless, "We knew in our minds, though no place else for sure, that there was hanky panky; we just couldn't prove it." Undaunted, Nofziger compiled all the innuendo, gossip, and what passed for "evidence" into the memorandum Reagan had just read.

As Reagan lowered the document onto the sofa, Nofziger's hands began to shake. The last time Nofgizer had ever tried anything like this was as a boy, when he attempted to get a teacher fired over their left-wing views. But this was bare-knuckle politics, not an elementary school classroom. Nofziger's scheme to oust Battaglia was beset with risk; if Reagan reacted negatively, or the media found out, the whole plan would blow up in his face. Journeying down to San Diego over the course of the previous day, Nofziger and his accomplices staggered their departures from the State Capitol to elude the vigilant attention of journalists. Everything rode on how the governor responded.

"What do we do now?" Reagan asked. The governor had many fine qualities, but delegating authority wasn't one of them. To be sure, there was no established playbook for how a politician should handle an instance of homosexuality among his staff that was rumored but not proven. Reagan's initial response mirrored that of Johnson's. Perhaps the whole thing was a giant misunderstanding, the governor asked. No matter, the aides countered, for irreparable damage would be done to Reagan's political future if the rumors spread, and it was therefore essential that Reagan quietly let Battaglia and Quinn go. Reagan was inclined to agree with this course of action, but he was concerned that the media would find out and humiliate the men and their families. "There are innocent wives and children involved," he said. "I want to sleep on this."

Reagan's visible distress at the allegations relieved his aides. Some of them had been concerned that their boss's experience in Hollywood, where tolerance for homosexuality was substantially higher than it was in the political world, would predispose him toward ignoring the problem. But his reaction suggested they had won him over. "Those of us Reagan-ites," Nofziger recalled, "have always felt that if you let Reagan be Reagan, he would make the right decisions." After the meeting, Nofziger and his accomplices celebrated by getting drunk at the San Diego airport and drunker on the plane back to Sacramento.

Reagan hated confrontation, preferring to leave the unpleasant task of firing people to one of his minions, or to Nancy. In this case, the dirty work was given to Holmes Tuttle, a California businessman and member of Reagan's unofficial "kitchen cabinet." Tuttle summoned Battaglia to his home, and as the locks to the governor's office suite were changed, he explained that, in exchange for Battaglia's resignation, the Reaganites would keep the true story of his firing under wraps. Battaglia reluctantly agreed, and Quinn followed suit.

In its announcement of the staff changes, the governor's office explained that Battaglia and Quinn were making a long-planned return to private life. To the extent that the Sacramento press corps suspected another motive behind their abrupt departure, it was either that Battaglia was leaving to organize a Reagan presidential campaign for 1968 or that the pair had been the victims of a standard-issue intraoffice power struggle. And there the matter would likely have rested had not Battaglia reemerged so soon with a legal practice in Sacramento, bragging around the capital about his connections in the governor's office. This unseemly display offended Nancy, who had a way of signaling her desire that some concrete action be taken while maintaining a modicum of plausible deniability should said action produce unintended results. "Why doesn't someone do something about Phil?" she complained within earshot of Nofziger. Construing this as a cue to cut Battaglia down to size, Nofziger told reporters from the *Los Angeles Times*, the *San Francisco Examiner*, and CBS the real circumstances for the dismissal of the deputy chief of staff and scheduler. A few weeks later, during a meeting of the National Governors Association Conference aboard the USS *Independence*, sailing from New York to the Virgin Islands, Nofziger rubbed it in further by repeating the story to reporters from the *Washington Post*, the *Evening Star*, and *Newsweek*. His intention was not to have any of the reporters publish details about the homosexual allegations—"[W]hat I thought no reporter or columnist would do in those days," he recalled—but rather, "to destroy Battaglia's credibility as a member of the Reagan team."

Alas, it would be Reagan's credibility that Nofziger would harm with his verbosity. Shortly after the governors' conference, a blind item appeared in the "Periscope" section of *Newsweek*. "A top GOP presidential prospect has a potentially sordid scandal on his hands," the magazine revealed. "Private investigators he hired found evidence that two of his aides had committed homosexual acts. The men are no longer working for the GOP leader, but the whole story may surface any day." And surface it soon did, thanks to the journalist who had been at or near seemingly every controversy involving homosexuality and national politics since the firing of Sumner Welles a quarter century earlier. At nearly seventy years old, Drew Pearson was still publishing his daily syndicated column, the Washington Merry-Go-Round, the truthfulness of which did not always match its frequency. (Pearson's radio commentaries, his syndicate claimed tongue-in-cheek, were "82 percent accurate.") A week after the Newsweek item raised political antennae across the country, Pearson published a column entitled "Scandal in Sacramento." Coauthored with Jack Anderson, it contained a ragbag of details from Nofziger's top-secret report along with some other assertions of dubious veracity. According to the duo, Reagan had known about the existence of a "homosexual ring" operating within his office but waited "about six months" before firing the men involved, Reagan's security chief Art Van Court had obtained "a tape recording of a sex orgy" held at a Lake Tahoe cabin leased by two of the staffers, and one of the men involved was an "athletic adviser on youth activities who has since gone on leave for the fall athletic season." Pearson and Anderson didn't name any names, but in the case of Jack Kemp, they didn't have to. Then the starting quarterback for the Buffalo Bills and an aspiring public policy wonk, Kemp had spent the summer off-season working for Reagan as perhaps the most famous intern in the United States.

While the basic premise of the column was correct—Reagan had indeed fired two aides on the presumption that they were gay—the rest was almost entirely wrong. The Merry-Go-Rounders compared Reagan unfavorably to President Johnson, who had "acted immediately" to fire his aide Walter Jenkins upon hearing of his arrest. But Reagan had not known about his own alleged "ring" until August, when Nofziger and company shocked him with the news, and he promptly dismissed Battaglia and Quinn; he did not wait half a year to fire them. (And with nothing more than assertions from his staff, Reagan also lacked the sort of solid evidence that LBJ received in the form of a police report of Jenkins's arrest.) Second, there was no tape of an "orgy." And finally, while Kemp, the unnamed but obvious "athletic adviser," had indeed invested in a Lake Tahoe cabin with Battaglia, he had sold back his share. Although most of the papers in Pearson's syndicate (including the Washington Post) refused to print the column because of its salacious charges, the article had its intended effect as outlets across the country published stories *about* the column and the controversy it was creating.

Reagan had long reviled Pearson. Years earlier, when he was touring the country as spokesman for General Electric, he tussled with the columnist over the issue of compulsory medical insurance for the elderly. But now, Reagan believed, Pearson had crossed a line. The article happened to appear on the day of Reagan's weekly press conference, which Nofziger had convinced the governor, derided by critics as a dunderheaded B-movie actor, to institute so that he could show off his public policy depth and winning personality. But at his October 31 briefing, Reagan's behavior was so out of character that he might as well have been wearing a Halloween costume. The Pearson column, he roared, pounding the table in anger, was "scurrilous and ridiculous," its author denounced by "three presidents of both parties" as a liar. "I myself wonder how respectable newspapers can continue to carry this column of a man who has done what he's done, and this is about the lowest, this is just stooping to destroy human beings, innocent people, and there is just no sense in getting into that kind of contest with him," Reagan said.

A reporter asked if Nofziger had, as Pearson alleged, leaked details of the story to reporters on the USS *Independence*. "I am prepared to say that nothing like that ever happened," Reagan replied. "Want to confirm it, Lyn?"

"Confirmed," Nofziger said, shocked and sheepish.

Pearson, Reagan added for emphasis, "shouldn't be using a typewriter and papers. He's better with a pencil on out-building walls."

Pearson—the target not only of oratorical but physical assault by Joe McCarthy, also in relation to homosexual innuendo—responded to Reagan in kind. At his own hastily called press conference, the columnist challenged the governor to take a lie detector test and made a play for the moral high road by stating that while he possessed the names of the men involved in the affair, he would not print them because "there's no use hurting people who are already suffering." Asked by a dinner companion if his story violated those people's personal privacy, however, Pearson had the standard answer at the ready: San Francisco Bay was "one of the most strategic parts of the nation," and gays in the California governor's office therefore constituted an unacceptable security risk. (Pearson took comfort in the praise offered by the former diplomat and Democratic governor of

New York, Averell Harriman, who commended him for doing "a great service to the country in exposing Reagan.")

Over the next two weeks, the columnist and the governor traded barbs. Reagan, Pearson declared in a statement, "has been posing as Mr. Clean and yet tolerated homosexuals for approximately six months and did not act regarding them until he was pressured." Pearson, Reagan shot back, had better "not spit on the sidewalk" if he ever visited the Golden State. Nancy, whose offhand remark imploring "somebody" to "do something about Phil" spurred Nofziger to mount his coup, yet who had never liked her husband's unkempt communications director, was infuriated that he had leaked the story to the press, considering it a breach of privacy and damaging to her husband's image. She dispensed the silent treatment to Nofziger for six months, making him the first in a long line of Reagan aides to endure her wrath.

The homosexual scandal was still dominating the headlines at Reagan's November 14 press conference, where he finally admitted, in so many words, that both he and Nofziger had taken liberties with the truth. But they had done so, Reagan stressed, in service of a higher cause: protecting the privacy of individuals. "Now if there is a credibility gap, and I'm responsible, it is because I refuse to participate in trying to destroy human beings with no factual evidence," he insisted. Reagan retracted his threat to Pearson regarding expectoration on California pavement, and Pearson, in turn, scrapped a column he was planning to write about testing it. The verdict from political pundits, even those sympathetic to the governor, was that he had seriously erred. Reagan, according to Rowland Evans and Robert Novak, had "committed the first truly serious error of his political career" by not immediately going public with his reason for firing the staffers. "Mr. Integrity just went down the drain," one California Republican moaned. "It must inevitably raise very real doubts about his personal dedication to the truth and his fitness for the high office to which he so obviously aspires," editorialized the *Evening Star*. Reagan's concern for the welfare of the fired employees and their families, however, won plaudits from some liberal Republicans, wary of him ever since he delivered a nationally televised address, "A Time for Choosing," endorsing Barry Goldwater for president in 1964. Words of praise came in from former Kansas governor Alf Landon and from the editors of the *Ripon Forum*, the monthly publication of the liberal Republican Ripon Society. "He may be an actor," concluded John Chamberlain of the

Los Angeles Herald Examiner, "but, paradoxically, he is manifestly proving that he can rise above both Hollywood and Republican dissension by being himself."

Once the initial clamor subsided, Reagan treated the scandal with something approaching levity. After Truman Capote visited his office seeking access to death row inmates for a television documentary, Reagan joked, "Somebody call that feller back and troll him up and down a couple of times in case there's anybody else left around here." Asked during a visit to Yale University in December if gays should be barred from public office, Reagan generously allowed that they could have jobs in the "department of parks and recreation." He also referred to homosexuality as a "tragic illness" and expressed support for keeping it "illegal."

Invigorated by his role in the Reagan scandal, Pearson pursued an investigation into homosexuals on the staff of another Republican, New York City mayor John Lindsay. Word of Pearson's snooping spread fast among the city hall press corps, and a *New York Times* reporter informed his brother-in-law, City Health Services administrator Howard Brown, that he was among Pearson's suspects. Terrified that his secret would be exposed, Brown resigned the next day.

"Have you considered the possibility of adding a chapter on recent stories which have molded history, such as the Reagan piece on homosexuals on his staff?" a triumphant Pearson wrote his biographer, with characteristic humility, a few weeks after "Scandal in Sacramento" was published. "I think this has pretty well knocked Reagan out of the box as a Republican candidate and as an attempt by the far right to take over the Republican Party—and the United States—in 1968."

* * *

THE GREATEST FEAR OF THE AMERICAN MALE is that he will be homosexual. Beginning with the stern warnings he receives as a young boy about overly friendly men in public parks, through the adolescent shaming prompted by the slightest hint of effeminacy, to the suspicion provoked by an interest in artistic pursuits, he is conditioned to believe that homosexuality is incompatible with manhood. From his family to his friends, in his church and at his workplace, from the realm of the everyday experience to the popular culture surrounding him, the message is unambiguous that there is absolutely nothing worse in the world than to be a sissy, a faggot, a queer.

To be sure, Lyn Nofziger didn't have anything against homosexuals. He wasn't particularly religious, and he had a wry sense of humor that many a fellow light in the loafers could appreciate. He just didn't want his daughter marrying one, he joked, "nor my son either, if I had one."

But Nofziger saw two problems with gays serving on Reagan's staff. First, conservatives would be outraged if they knew the governor "had surrounded himself with 'queers.'" This concern was far from unusual for a politician at the time. Even most liberal Democrats were cagey about homosexuality, and it would have been extremely difficult if not impossible to find an openly gay person working on the staff of a governor anywhere in America in 1967.

But there was a more intimate reason Nofziger was concerned about the presence of homosexuals within the vicinity of his boss, one particular to Reagan's professional pedigree. The governor had spent most of his adult life working in Hollywood, "where dwell and work a significant number of homosexuals." And Nofziger, whose job it was to shape the public persona of the man whose image ranks among the most carefully cultivated in the annals of American politics, was concerned to the point of paranoia that voters might get the wrong idea. "Because he came out of the Hollywood scene, where homosexuality was almost the norm," Nofziger said, "I also feared the rumors would insinuate that he, too, was one."

This fear long predated Reagan's political career; indeed, it even predated his birth. "I had been promised a sister by my mother and father. That's all I wanted," recalled Neil Reagan about the birth of his younger brother. "I guess that shows you how early I determined not to be a queer. I was strictly a girl man." A joke, to be sure, but an unintentionally revealing one. A watchful and resentful eye was kept on the younger Reagan from the moment he left the womb. In the words of one of Neil's classmates, Reagan was a "momma's boy" who played with "sissies."

A career in the performing arts would not have diminished the suspicion that one was a sissy, a suspicion that Reagan was determined to dispel. One of his first movies, the 1939 drama *Dark Victory*, was directed by Edmund Goulding, an Englishman infamous for the bisexual orgies he planned "with the same attention he gave the directing of films," as one participant recalled. Reagan never partook in these bacchanals, and he resented what he considered Goulding's pressure to have him add a touch of lavender to his portrayal of Alec, the hard-drinking friend of the film's lead character, played by Bette Davis. As Reagan recounted in his 1965 memoir, *Where's the Rest of Me?*, published on the cusp of his foray into politics:

> I actually believe that he saw my part as a copy of his own earlier life. I was playing, he told me, the kind of young man who could dearly love Bette but at the same time the kind of fellow who could sit in the girls' dressing room dishing the dirt while they went on dressing in front of me. I had no trouble seeing him in that role, but for myself I want to think if I stroll through where the girls are short of clothes, there will be a great scurrying about and taking to cover.

When Otto Preminger asked Don Murray if he was concerned about the possible negative career consequences of portraying a homosexual senator in *Advise and Consent*, Murray responded that he had once played a cowboy. "Does that make me a cowboy?" he asked. In his abhorrence of the very suggestion of playing "a fellow who could sit in the girls' dressing room dishing the dirt while they went on dressing in front of me," Reagan displayed not only an antipathy toward the notion that a heterosexual could convincingly portray a homosexual, but also a fear that the audience might actually perceive him to *be* one.

While Reagan may have resented playing gay on the big screen, privately, according to Nofziger, he and Nancy "were tolerant of this sort of aberrant sexual behavior" in their friends. Nancy's godmother, the Russian-American Broadway actress Alla Nazimova, was a lesbian, and Nancy attended Smith College, where romantic relationships between members of the all-female student body were not uncommon. Before she met the love of her life, Nancy dated a gay man and was engaged to another. During the era when the future First Couple forged their careers in show business, from the late 1930s to the late 1950s, Hollywood was one of the most welcoming industries for gay men and lesbians in the country. "Nowhere else in America did gays have such a way of being together, of not worrying about their jobs, of just being who they were," recalled one gay dweller of the midcentury Dream Factory. Included among the Reagans' coterie was one of the city's most famous gay figures, the former silent film actor Billy Haines. In 1933, MGM head Louis Mayer had delivered Haines an ultimatum: choose a studio-arranged, sham marriage to a woman, or stay with his partner, Jimmy Shields. Haines chose Shields and abandoned Hollywood stardom for a highly successful career as an interior decorator to the rich and famous. When Reagan won the California governorship in 1966, Haines and Shields hosted a gala victory party (at which Nancy appeared radiant in a gown made by her friend, the gay fashion designer Jimmy Galanos). "There was never a problem" with her being so close to an openly gay man like Haines, she curtly told Haines's biographer.

Once Ronald Reagan ventured into politics, however, he and those responsible for maintaining his public image became extremely conscious of how such friendships and associations might be perceived, particularly among California's conservative grass roots. In 1965, activists associated with the state chapter of the far-right John Birch Society produced an affidavit from a man claiming to have had sex with liberal Republican senator Thomas Kuchel. Reagan, preparing a run for governor from the opposite ideological pole of the state GOP, denied involvement "in the despicable attempts to blacken" Kuchel's name, and the perpetrators eventually pleaded no contest to charges of libel. The experience deeply scarred Kuchel, who left politics soon thereafter.

An incident from Reagan's 1966 gubernatorial campaign illustrates the lengths to which those around him were willing to go to eliminate any hint that the Gipper was gay. Lee Houskeeper, a young folk music promoter, wanted to join the Reagan effort not out of any ideological conviction but because "all the celebrities were there," as was the girl he wanted to date. Using his music industry contacts, Houskeeper organized a concert fundraiser for Reagan at a club across the street from the Hollywood Palladium. He booked several acts, printed the tickets, and designed a poster encouraging one and all to flock to "Reagan's Camp."

A few days before the concert, Houskeeper was sitting at his desk in Reagan campaign headquarters on Wilshire Boulevard when a voice came over the public address system summoning him to the office of Jean Arthur, the actress running the campaign's celebrity bureau. When Houskeeper walked in, he found Arthur sitting at a desk covered with his "Reagan's Camp" paraphernalia. Standing behind her, glaring and with her arms folded, was Nancy. The candidate's wife was a taskmaster and micromanager, frequently calling the campaign office to offer advice on strategy and to complain about the billboard erected out front. "The color of the sign is terrible," she said. "It's ugly. It's just not Ronnie." Judging by her demeanor that day, she was similarly unhappy with the signage for Houskeeper's concert.

"Are these for your event?" Arthur asked.

"Yes," Houskeeper replied.

"You're going to have to cancel it."

"Why?"

"Because 'camp' is a gay word, and you should know that."

Houskeeper didn't know that. He was deep into the folk music scene, where "camp" was interchangeable with "festival." He was not an avid reader of the New York intellectual journal *Partisan Review*, where two years earlier a young Columbia University professor named Susan Sontag had published an essay entitled "Notes on Camp." In fifty-eight rules and observations, Sontag defined a "sensibility" characterized by "artifice and exaggeration" intended to "dethrone the serious," and of which "homosexuals, by and large, constitute the vanguard." She cited *Swan Lake*, the *National Enquirer*, Tiffany lamps, and *Flash Gordon* comic books as exemplars of the genre. "Camp was a sort of homo Esperanto," according to one of its speakers, an arcane method of communication that signaled one's membership in a secret, transnational fraternity. "At the moment the most 'in' word in the world—i.e., 'in' with the 'in' crowd, which is the only mob that swings—is 'camp,'" observed syndicated columnist Inez Robb in 1965. "All the definers agree that camp is an old word in the homosexual vocabulary, which is now the 'in' vocabulary, since no one is so 'in' in the 'in' group as the homosexual." If that was the case, then Ronald Reagan was most certainly "out."

The women grilled Houskeeper on his background and affiliations. Perhaps he was a homosexual himself, out to subvert the Reagan forces? Plastering the city with posters linking a political candidate who railed against the "sexual misconduct" of Berkeley students with a gay-themed double entendre would have been a brilliant act of high camp itself. Houskeeper was genuinely oblivious to the homosexual intimations of "camp," however, and "at some point [the two women] looked at each other and realized I was fine, that I wasn't a threat."

This anxiety about being perceived as, in Reagan's words, "that way" extended to his son Ron, whose career as a professional ballet dancer made him the subject of gay rumors. The conservative political strategist Marvin Liebman recalled a conversation with Reagan over Thanksgiving weekend at William F. Buckley Jr.'s Connecticut home in 1976 when Reagan expressed his concern about Ron dropping out of Yale to pursue his passion for dance. "Now, I don't care what the kid does so long as it's legal and makes him happy," Reagan said. "But, aren't dancers . . . aren't dancers sort of . . . funny?" Liebman, who was closeted at the time, reminded Reagan that Mikhail Baryshnikov, Gene Kelly, and Fred Astaire were all fulsomely heterosexual. "He's all man," Reagan assured the press about his son in 1980. "We made sure of that." The apprehensiveness over Ron apparently long preceded his interest in ballet. Houskeeper recalled a conversation among Nofziger and other campaign staffers where it was advocated that the candidate's then eight-year-old son not appear on the campaign trail because he appeared "limp-wristed."

To be sure, the prejudices Reagan held about gays were common to men of his generation, and they did not animate his politics in the way that anticommunism or shrinking the size of government did. According to Lou Cannon, in the 1,044 speeches Reagan wrote by hand over the course of his political career, not once did he mention homosexuality. And one of the few times he did intervene was on the side of gays. In 1978, two years after Reagan challenged President Gerald Ford for the Republican nomination and two years before he would mount another campaign for the presidency, a right-wing California state senator named John Briggs launched a ballot initiative that would have prevented gay people from teaching in public schools. A poll published two months before the vote found that 61 percent of Californians supported the initiative, a figure consistent with national sentiment. From a purely political standpoint, it made sense for Reagan to back the measure or, at the very least, stay neutral.

An enterprising gay activist saw an opportunity to persuade him otherwise. David Mixner was a leader of the anti–Vietnam War movement, a Democratic political consultant, and a strategist for the "No on 6" campaign. He had next to nothing in common with Reagan politically, but he knew two seemingly contradictory things about the former governor: that he was more familiar with gay people than the average American and that he was popular with conservatives, precisely the constituency the "No on 6" campaign needed to reach. If Mixner could finagle a meeting with Reagan, he believed, he might be able to persuade him to oppose the initiative.

Mixner called Don Livingston, a closeted gay man he knew and a former staffer in Reagan's gubernatorial administration, who put him in touch with another closeted gay man then serving as one of Reagan's closest advisors. The advisor agreed to meet with Mixner, but only on the condition that Mixner keep his identity secret. Taking every possible precaution, the advisor further insisted that they meet at a Denny's restaurant in Hispanic East Los Angeles, where few, if any, Republicans might notice them.

That advisor, a former aide in Reagan's gubernatorial office named Peter Hannaford, was at that moment one of the two most important men in Reagan's political operation. After Reagan left office in 1975, Hannaford teamed up with another former administration colleague, Michael Deaver, to set up a public relations firm whose objective was to keep Reagan in the national spotlight. Through a daily radio commentary broadcast nationwide on three hundred stations, a twice-weekly column syndicated in one hundred seventy-five newspapers, and a punishing schedule of speaking engagements across the country, Hannaford and Deaver ensured that Reagan was a constant presence in the mind of the American electorate. Yet, while Hannaford was carefully crafting Reagan's identity, he was just as studiously hiding his own. As one gay Washingtonian active in right-wing circles described the PR professional, "He was married in California; he was gay in Washington," a duality that could have described many other men at the time. "Peter played by all the rules," Mixner recalled. "The wife, the house in Pasadena. And never mixed the two at all. They were two worlds, and you occupied one and you occupied the other, and you never built a bridge to the other."

Hannaford could trust that his secret would be safe with his interlocutor. Mixner was a strict adherent of "the Code," an informal system that placed what is now an antique notion of gay brotherhood above partisan politics. Mixner knew how difficult it could be for people to come to terms with their homosexuality—as a young man, he had come close to killing himself over his own—and he "didn't want that on my hands" in relation to anybody, political adversaries included. With his lover and business partner, Peter Scott, Mixner fielded what the pair termed "coffee calls," random lunch invitations from people in the worlds of politics and entertainment who, after filling the meal with hours of ostensibly work-related conversation, would finally reveal themselves as gay by the time the coffee was ordered. "We probably had a hundred of those over time," Mixner remembered. As he earned a reputation for discretion, Mixner started to serve another function, enforcing a homosexual omertà. "Say Rock Hudson would go to orgies and then he would find out that someone in the community was talking about it," Mixner said. "And he'd have lunch with us and say, 'Is there anything you can do to help me?' And then we would go to that person and say, 'This just is not done. And as much as your ego would like you to feel powerful, you will regret that you did this. This is not smart.' Loose lips sink ships."

Mixner and Scott persuaded Hannaford to give them fifteen minutes with Reagan. When the day of the meeting arrived, Mixner recalled, Reagan "was more personable and more respectful to us and kinder than anyone I had met," putting his arm around the liberal activist as he entered the room and offering him his trademark jar of jelly beans. To convince Reagan to oppose the Briggs Initiative, Mixner recited a series of talking points sure to resonate with a former governor who had won election and reelection with a series of bracing attacks on campus radicals. If the measure passed, Mixner warned, invoking the word Reagan used to describe left-wing protesters at Berkeley, "anarchy" would be unleashed statewide as students lodged spurious charges of homosexuality against their teachers. The power of state authorities would increase over school boards as disciplinary proceedings sparked court challenges, a development that ought to raise alarm bells with any advocate of local control, as Reagan was. Finally, endless "witch hunts" against teachers would swell administrative budgets and legal fees, bugbears of every small government conservative. A seasoned political operator, Mixner had witnessed enough senators fidgeting with their paper or rearranging items on their desk to know when an interlocutor was uncomfortable or impatient. Reagan betrayed none of these telltale signs of displeasure. Instead, he "just almost grinned" as Mixner made his case, "like he was looking for an excuse not to support these people." A meeting that was supposed to last fifteen minutes ran for more than an hour.

A few days later, Mixner's gambit was vindicated. "I don't approve of teaching a so-called gay life-style in our schools, but there is already adequate legal machinery to deal with such problems if and when they arise," Reagan declared in a statement. Proposition 6 "has the potential of infringing on basic rights of privacy and perhaps even constitutional rights." And, not least for an advocate of government budget-cutting, it could be "very costly to implement." The initiative's author knew whom to blame for Reagan's surprise opposition. "I can't believe the Hollywood crowd has gotten him to take that kind of position," John Briggs grumbled. On Election Day, voters rejected Proposition 6 by a margin of 58 percent to 42 percent, a near-exact reversal of what public opinion surveys had predicted just two months before. "That one single endorsement—Ronald Reagan's—turned the polls around," Briggs said. Echoing Drew Pearson's decade-old prediction that a perceived tolerance for homosexuality would abort Reagan's presidential chances, Briggs guaranteed that *this* time, Reagan had scuttled those hopes for good. "For Ronald Reagan to march to the drums of homosexuals," he declared, "has irrevocably damaged him nationally."

24

THE THRILL OF TREASON

"Never miss a chance to have sex or appear on television," Gore Vidal used to say, and it was a credo he fulfilled with gusto. Claiming to have notched one thousand sexual encounters by the tender age of twenty-five, Vidal was also one of the first American writers to harness the power of the small screen. And while engaging in both pursuits simultaneously was inadvisable, Vidal would test the limits of mixing sex and television during the second-to-last night of the 1968 Democratic National Convention, when, before a live television audience of ten million, he showed what fury the slightest suggestion of deviancy could ignite.

To be sure, the man sitting just a few feet away from him in the ABC News studio in Chicago on the evening of August 28 was straight. As much a prescient adept of the televisual medium as Vidal, William F. Buckley Jr. had almost single-handedly enhanced the reputation of American conservatism from what Lionel Trilling described in 1950 as a set of "irritable mental gestures which seek to resemble ideas." Through his editorship of *National Review*, his spirited 1965 campaign for the New York City mayoralty, and, most famously, his hosting the public television debate program *Firing Line*, Buckley had redefined the popular image of the conservative from that of a rural troglodyte to a cosmopolitan aesthete. A prolific writer, a charming orator, and a bon vivant of seemingly superhuman energies, Buckley could punch out an editorial advocating the use of nuclear weapons in Vietnam, deliver a rousing defense of Generalissimo Franco before a gathering of midwestern businessmen, and lead a sing-along of Cole Porter standards on his harpsichord in a single day.

Buckley and Vidal were as similar in their age, aristocratic bearing, and British-inflected, Mid-Atlantic enunciation as they were different in practically every other respect, most notably their attitudes on communism abroad, "law and order" at home, and, as the nation was soon to witness, sex. Beginning with the Republican National Convention in Miami earlier that month, the two had been engaged in a series of nightly debates for what the American Broadcasting Company touted as the showpiece of its "Unconventional Convention" coverage. "Let Chet and David and Walter declare the winners," cheered the *Chicago Daily News*, in reference to the sober anchormen helming the convention broadcasts for ABC's competitors. "Bill and Gore will provide the fun." Fun was not what Buckley was expecting from his exchanges with Vidal, the one person against whom, aside from a Communist, he told ABC he would not appear when the network approached him about participating in the point-counterpoint program earlier that spring.

The reason for Buckley's distaste could be traced back twenty years earlier, to Vidal's publication of *The City and the Pillar*, whose normalization of homosexuality the staunchly Catholic Buckley detested. In 1962, Vidal lambasted Buckley on *The Jack Paar Program* for being literally more Catholic than the pope; Buckley, Vidal alleged, had "attacked" the convenor of the Second Vatican Council as "too left wing." Paar invited Buckley to defend himself, which Buckley did with aplomb. But after Buckley left the stage, Paar lampooned him for his languid manner of speaking and, the next evening, added insult to injury by inviting Vidal *back* to join in the mockery. Furious, Buckley wrote a telegram to the host.

PLEASE INFORM GORE VIDAL THAT NEITHER I NOR MY FAMILY IS DISPOSED TO RECEIVE LESSONS IN MORALITY FROM A PINK QUEER. IF HE WISHES TO CHALLENGE THAT DESIGNATION, INFORM HIM THAT I SHALL FIGHT BY THE LAWS OF THE MARQUESS OF QUEENSBERRY. HE WILL KNOW WHAT I MEAN.

Vidal certainly would have understood the reference had Buckley not thought better of his intemperance and decided against sending the telegram. The nineteenth-century Scottish nobleman John Douglas, the Ninth Marquess of Queensberry, was progenitor of the eponymous rules promoting gentlemanly conduct in boxing. He also, after discovering that the writer Oscar Wilde had had an affair with his son, levied the charge of sodomy against Wilde, which resulted in Wilde's imprisonment for two years of hard labor. Later that year, Buckley and Vidal appeared on *The David Susskind Show* in what one critic described as "an intellectual free-for-all," and two years after that, Buckley attacked Vidal's play *Romulus* for being "effeminate" in *National Review*.

A great collector and nurturer of literary feuds, Vidal leapt at the opportunity to argue opposite Buckley on live national television. In preparation, he hired a pair of researchers to pore over everything Buckley had ever written or said, and he composed a list of witty asides, wisecracks, and insults to dole out over the course of the ten tête-à-têtes. "He was like a prizefighter getting ready for a big fight," Howard Austen, Vidal's companion, recalled. From long and diligent observation, Vidal knew precisely how to get under Buckley's skin. Earlier that year, he had published an extremely controversial novel, *Myra Breckinridge*, in which the main character undergoes a sex-change operation. Vidal anticipated that Buckley would denounce the book, which Buckley did in their very first debate, calling it pornography. "If there were a contest for Mr. Myra Breckinridge, you would unquestionably win it," Vidal replied. "I based her style polemically on you—passionate but irrelevant." Later, he jibed that Buckley was "the Marie Antoinette of the right wing." All this innuendo understandably upset Buckley's wife, the regal Canadian lumber heiress and socialite Pat, who complained to the columnist Murray Kempton that "two hundred million Americans think William F. Buckley is a screaming homosexual and I've got to do something about it."

Alas for Mrs. Buckley, it only went downhill from there. By the time of their penultimate debate in Chicago, each man's patience with the other had more than run out, their mutual loathing a reflection of the battles raging inside and outside the convention hall, which were themselves microcosms of the cultural and ideological divisions roiling America in 1968. Earlier that evening, Chicago mayor Richard Daley's police had unleashed a brutal attack on anti–Vietnam War protesters in Lincoln Park, and images of bruised and bloodied young people were broadcast around the world. Meanwhile, inside the International Amphitheatre, Sen. Abraham Ribicoff of Connecticut took to the convention podium to decry "Gestapo tactics in the streets of Chicago." According to Buckley, however, it was not Chicago's finest who were acting like fascists, but the protesters, whose raising of the Viet Cong flag made them no better than the Americans who, during the Second World War, marched under the banner of Nazi Germany. At this, Vidal pounced.

"As far as I'm concerned, the only sort of pro- or crypto-Nazi I can think of is yourself. Failing that, I would only say we can't have the right of assembly if they're—"

"Let's—let's not call names," the moderator, newsman Howard K. Smith, futilely implored.

"Now listen, you queer!" Buckley shot back over Smith's hapless interjection, his lips arching into a rictus of wrath. "Stop calling me a crypto-Nazi or I'll sock you in your goddamn face and you'll stay plastered!"

The oratorical gladiators continued to trade insults while Smith tried to steer the conversation back toward something vaguely topical. But as Vidal grinned like the Cheshire cat and Buckley scowled, it was clear to both men, as well as to anyone watching, who had won.

"I've always tried to treat Buckley like the great lady he is," Vidal crowed the next day.

It was but the briefest flicker of malice from Buckley, a brutal loss of composure that he had never evinced before nor would ever display again. According to his son, Christopher, who accompanied his parents to Chicago, there were various reasons for his father's outburst. "He was wearing a clavicle brace, which *might* be the reason he didn't actually sock old Gore in the mug," Buckley fils reflected. Buckley had also served in the military during World War II (as had Vidal, though neither man saw combat) and "rightfully considered himself a patriot." There was, moreover, the not-insignificant matter of *Myra Breckinridge*, which "genuinely appalled" Buckley as a pornographic assault on traditional morality. Finally, remembered Christopher, "Vidal, being Vidal, which is to say a very nasty piece of work (and don't take my word for it) knew what buttons to push."

There is another factor, undisclosed until now, that might also explain Buckley's uncharacteristic outburst and the prejudice it revealed: the close relative who was sexually propositioned by men multiple times as a teenage boy. That homosexuality and pedophilia were interchangeable was a widely held conviction in postwar America, and Buckley's personal knowledge of one such case might have convinced him of the proposition's general validity. *National Review* prominently explored the link in one of its first issues. In "The Strange Case of Dr. Dooley," the anonymous author, over the course of seven pages, tells the harrowing story of a pediatric psychiatrist in Kent, Connecticut (twenty minutes by car from the Buckley family homestead in Sharon), who engaged in sexual relations with boys on the grounds that such practices were "therapeutic." The article suggested that Dooley was the product of a medical establishment corrupted by liberalism, the logical end point of which was tolerance of pedophilia. To the social critic Dwight Macdonald, appraising the new conservative magazine for *Commentary*, the discussion of this isolated case for "several yards of moralizing about progressive education, sexual morality, pragmatic liberalism, etc." was a straw man argument. "But even granting that Dr. Dooley's supporters were liberals—which, in fact, is likely—it seems a peculiarly indirect method of polemic," Macdonald continued. "Perverse in fact." The association of homosexuality with pedophilia would be one to which Buckley and his magazine would repeatedly return.

Despite these views, Buckley could count many "queers" among his acquaintances, beginning with the melodramatic figure who had so profoundly influenced his intellectual development. As a young man, Buckley idolized Whittaker Chambers as a martyr of American conservatism, so much so that Buckley coaxed him into joining the staff of *National Review* in 1957. Buckley would later claim to have been completely ignorant of Chambers's secret gay life. "His closest friends (I was one of them) were totally surprised by the revelation," Buckley was to profess upon the FBI's declassification, in 1976, of Chambers's confession to the FBI of his homosexual past. ("No, Whittaker Chambers Was Not Like That!" was the headline that the editors of the *Washington Star* affixed to Buckley's syndicated column.) Buckley would later reiterate his "astonishment" upon "learning that the man I had known so well had ever been a homosexual. I have probably known ten people who knew Chambers extremely well, dating back many years before the year I met him (1954), and none of them had any intimation of this chapter in Chambers' history." This is difficult to believe, and not only because the homosexual undertones of the Hiss-Chambers case were very much subjects of speculation within Buckley's conservative circles, but because those circles were themselves considerably gay.

* * *

"THE HOMOSEXUAL IS AN INDIVIDUAL, he loves his freedom too much, he is almost a rebel from conformity," Don Slater, one of the cofounders of *ONE* magazine, wrote in a 1960 editorial.

> He does not merge and jell easily with the masses, nor trust blindly like many heterosexuals in communal behavior. Why then would the homosexual want to part with that form of government which offers liberty to choose one's own way of life? If we must choose a sexual preference most likely to produce a Communist, then let it be the heterosexual who may be easily pressured in his wish to survive and conform.

This cry against conformity and paean to individualism had a particular appeal for gay people in Cold War America, whose experience was not unlike that of being a dissident in a Communist police state: both groups were heavily surveilled, vilified by society, subject to arrest, and threatened with confinement in mental institutions. For gay men, whose sexuality was policed more strictly than that of lesbians, in particular, this was a condition that drove some to view government not as a potential ally in their advancement, as did African Americans, but as an adversary. Declared enemies of the state, gays inhabited a secret world with covert habits and conspiratorial traits, and for some of these men, their immersion in this environment imparted a more acute hostility toward the machinations of another secret and conspiratorial world, that of American communism. These men knew what if felt like to live in a totalitarian state, to have their moves monitored, their liaisons scrutinized, their existences crushed; they understood better than most heterosexuals the necessity of keeping secrets—and the danger that secrets posed.

It was through this unique attraction to anticommunism and radical individualism that gay men—all of them closeted—would play such a disproportionate role in the early American conservative movement. "The liberal orthodoxy predominated for decades and I think in the back of the mind of a lot of us was [the idea] that, as being homosexual was not only frowned upon [but] was almost a kiss of death, the only way we could fight it was to embrace a philosophy that we agreed with that was revolutionary," recalled Douglas Caddy of his generation of gay conservative activists. As a Georgetown University student, Caddy had been radicalized by *The Conscience of a Conservative*, Sen. Barry Goldwater's 1960 cri de coeur (ghostwritten by Buckley's brother-in-law, L. Brent Bozell Jr.) against the postwar consensus, and he subsequently became national secretary of Youth for Goldwater for Vice President. The subconscious impulse for him and his comrades, Caddy said, was "what would it take to change the landscape of being a homosexual" in America. "If we stayed with the liberal domination of the political and social landscape, nothing would have changed."

Caddy and others like him were part of a strange development sweeping American college campuses in the early 1960s: conservative revolutionaries. Despite wearing suits and ties to class, *Time* magazine observed, these young people were "icon smashers" rebelling against the orthodoxies of their "New Deal-bred" parents. "You walk around with your Goldwater button, and you feel the thrill of treason," the president of the Conservative Club at the University of Wisconsin giddily confessed. Incongruous as it might seem today, for a student to identify as right-wing in the early 1960s—heyday of the New Frontier liberalism espoused by the youngest man ever elected president, John F. Kennedy—was akin to a similarly rebellious, if politically divergent, phenomenon: that of the gay men and lesbians "coming out" of their closets.

As a young Goldwaterite, Caddy met Marvin Liebman, another closeted homosexual and one of the most influential figures in the early American right. An ex-Communist turned anticommunist activist, Liebman pioneered the genre of "letterhead organizations," single-issue advocacy groups that attracted attention (and donations) due to the prominent personages featured on their stationery. Liebman was also a close ally and friend of Buckley. There was an "almost mystical, sort of ESP between us," Liebman was to recall of his relationship with the *National Review* founder. "We didn't have to articulate it in words, but we both knew that it was there." In September 1960, Buckley, Caddy, and Liebman organized the event that was to be the unofficial launch of the conservative movement: a conference for some one hundred fresh-faced revolutionaries at Buckley's family estate in Sharon, Connecticut, establishing Young Americans for Freedom (YAF). The group's foundational document, the Sharon Statement, endorsed the free market, personal liberty, and "victory over, rather than coexistence with," the "menace" of communism. Caddy was chosen as YAF's first national director, and Liebman, too old for membership at thirty-eight, joined its national advisory board.

An aspiring theater producer—he had tried to enlist Pat Buckley in a film adaptation of *When the Kissing Had to Stop*, an anticommunist novel featuring a traitorous, Negro-loving homosexual State Department official based on Sumner Welles—Liebman possessed a keen appreciation for the importance of drama in American politics. Surface, he understood, is as important, if not more so, than substance. "My sense of political theater and my ability to dramatize issues provided some of what was needed to translate the right wing in America from a fringe element into a historic force," he recalled. Liebman was the organizational brains behind two massive youth conclaves for Goldwater at Madison Square Garden: the 1962 red-white-and-blue-bunting-draped "Conservative Rally for World Liberation from Communism" and a similarly fervent event during the 1964 presidential campaign. A virtuoso of political exteriority, Liebman (for whom, according to the writer John Gregory Dunne, Buckley and other letterhead grandees served as "beards") had a more difficult time handling his own interiority. At a party following the 1964 Goldwater rally, Dunne wrote, Liebman "could not keep his hands off AWOL servicemen, a condition made unexpectedly poignant by the repeated droll allegations in the Garden that liberals were double-gaited, limp-wristed, and generally light on their feet." Liebman "had stashed his latest find, a youthful marine, in a back bedroom along with the attaché cases, but the marine, under the mistaken impression that he was meant to be included in the revelry, kept popping up among the aristocracy of the American right like a stripper out of a birthday cake."

Others among this category of men at Sharon included Caddy's Georgetown classmate, a former House page and District of Columbia Youth for Nixon chairman named Robert Bauman, and Jim Kolbe, a student at Northwestern University and former Goldwater Senate page. When Goldwater mounted his presidential bid four years later, one of his supporters was a Wall Street stockbroker, Harvey Milk. Fourteen years later, as an adherent of a very different political ideology, Milk would become one of the first openly gay elected officials in the country when he won election to the San Francisco Board of Supervisors. But for most mornings during the fall of 1964, Milk woke up early to pass out Goldwater leaflets with his lover in the New York subways, and he was such a passionate evangelist for the Arizonan that he convinced his otherwise apolitical ex-lover to join the effort. Goldwater's message of individualism and freedom also stirred a thirteen-year-old Ayn Rand acolyte from Aurora, Illinois, to start a YAF chapter in his hometown and volunteer for his presidential campaign. A decade later, Randy Shilts joined the influx of gay men to San Francisco, where he wrote Milk's biography. And before he earned notoriety as one of the country's most influential Republican political consultants, Arthur Finkelstein was ejected from a political science class at Queens College for his aggressive Goldwater advocacy. Extremism in the defense of liberty, Goldwater's rallying cry, would become Finkelstein's trademark; in 1970, he lost his job at NBC News when he endorsed the New York Senate candidacy of Buckley's brother James, running on the Conservative Party ticket. Gore Vidal recognized the appeal of libertarian conservatism to a certain subset of gay men in the 1960s. "All the male hustlers were supporting Goldwater for President," observes the eponymous character in *Myra Breckinridge*.

Possibly rounding out this orbit of gay men at the center of the early conservative movement was Buckley's publisher at *National Review*. "I'm not very fond of women or games," William A. Rusher, who was also a YAF cofounder, used to say. "I am entirely a political being." The line was Napoleon's, but was there a subtext? "There are loads and loads of Conservative homosexuals," Rusher told Buckley biographer Sam Tanenhaus in 2002. "I thought they just keep their mouths shut. . . . Bill seemed to have many guests who were gay that came to the house. Bill was just at the edge of homophobic." A confirmed bachelor who retired to San Francisco before his death in 2011, Rusher kept many guessing as to whether he was one such man who had just kept his mouth shut.

Neither the compatability between homosexuality and libertarianism, nor Buckley's proximity to some of the many men who embodied it, appeared to weigh upon the conscience of the conservative eminence when he lost his composure and let slip the slur that haunted him for the rest of his life. Buckley immediately regretted his rare moment of distemper. Vidal felt no such remorse over his. Their feud dragged on long after the camera lights dimmed, spilling onto the pages of *Esquire*, where it sparked a five-hundred-thousand-dollar libel suit by Buckley and a countersuit by Vidal. Though future observers would look back on their encounter with greater equanimity—acknowledging that, while what Buckley had said about Vidal, though crude, was factually true, and that what Vidal had said about Buckley, no less crude, was false—the initial verdict was that the "queer" had won the bout. For even if the target of one's opprobrium was an *avowed* sex deviant, as Vidal was, to actually call someone a "queer" on national television in 1968 was still a greater offense than to slander him as a Nazi, "crypto" or otherwise. As Buckley was to put it sarcastically in his *Esquire* essay, "faggotry is countenanced, but the imputation of it—even to faggots—is not."

It was a conclusion that America's next president, who exploited the cultural and political divisions laid bare by the Buckley-Vidal debates more skillfully than any other politician, would appreciate. To a degree surpassed by none of the men who preceded him in that high office, nor by any of those who would follow, faggotry was a subject with which Richard Nixon was positively obsessed.

RICHARD NIXON

When we have at last overthrown all existing governments, the world will enjoy not war but global orgies conducted with the utmost protocol and the most truly international spirit, for these people do transcend simple national differences. . . . Degeneracy, rather than signaling the downfall of a society, as it once did, will now signal peace for a troubled world.

—John Kennedy Toole, *A Confederacy of Dunces*

25

"DESTROY YOUR OPPONENT"

THE MOST IMPORTANT RULE OF POLITICS, ACCORDING TO MURRAY Chotiner, was "Destroy your opponent." And there was no more surefire way of doing that than to accuse him of being a queer.

From the moment he advised Richard Nixon to lambaste his Democratic adversary as a supporter of "Communist principles" during his first race for Congress in 1946, Chotiner was Nixon's tutor in the dark arts of political mudslinging. Nixon relied upon Chotiner to handle the real dirty stuff, to trawl the seamy underbelly of American politics and emerge with whatever stuck. If Nixon had a ruthless instinct for California's "culture of smear," as Lou Cannon characterized the state's rough-and-tumble political scene, then "Chotiner came along and refined it." When Nixon derided his 1950 Democratic Senate opponent, Helen Gahagan Douglas, as "pink right down to her underwear," Chotiner dreamed up the brilliant idea of printing five hundred thousand flyers on pink paper insinuating that she was a Communist. It was for the notorious "pink sheet" that Douglas bestowed upon Nixon the immortal epithet "Tricky Dick."

Two years later, when Nixon was accused of operating a slush fund while running for vice president, it was Chotiner who convinced him to reject the call from Dwight Eisenhower's advisors that he drop out. On Chotiner's advice, the hangdog candidate delivered a stirring televised address that became known as the "Checkers speech" and saved his political career. Though Chotiner was temporarily sidelined in the early years of the Eisenhower administration due to his entanglement in an influence-peddling scandal, he remained a Nixon confidant throughout Nixon's vice presidency, his 1960 presidential campaign, his failed 1962 run for California governor, the subsequent wilderness years, all the way through to his pulling off one of the most remarkable comebacks in American political history—winning the 1968 presidential election.

After two decades of loyal service, Chotiner expected a job in the new administration. He was not given one, however, a situation that left him haunting the White House, according to speechwriter William Safire, "like the ghost of Christmas Past." Chotiner attributed his misfortune to H. R. "Bob" Haldeman, Nixon's extremely disciplined and loyal chief of staff and self-appointed "s.o.b." Alongside his fellow University of California at Los Angeles alum, teetotaler, and Christian Scientist with a German-sounding surname, White House counsel John Ehrlichman, the two formed what their rivals in the administration resentfully called "the Berlin Wall" for the way they jealously guarded access to the commander in chief. Desperate to scale the Teutonic barrier, Chotiner mustered all the skills he had cultivated as Nixon's hatchet man to concoct a story guaranteed to arouse the disgust of the president, undermine his own rivals, and finally get the job he deserved.

In June 1969, Chotiner called up Jack Anderson. A year and a half earlier, Anderson and his writing partner, Drew Pearson, had caused a huge kerfuffle with their exposé of a "homosexual ring" surrounding Ronald Reagan, and Chotiner assumed the muckrakers would leap at the opportunity to report his own tantalizing tale of sexual depravity. Early in the mornings, Chotiner told Anderson, Haldeman, Ehrlichman, and a twenty-eight-year-old Nixon appointments secretary named Dwight Chapin would meet to "engage in homosexual and perverted activities," their trysts unfolding either at Haldeman's pad in the swanky new Watergate apartment and office complex—home to a bevy of administration officials, including Attorney General John Mitchell, Commerce Secretary Maurice Stans, and Nixon's doughty secretary Rose Mary Woods—or the Howard Johnson's motel across the street. Occasionally, a "notorious homosexual" naval officer, whom Chotiner claimed to have seen canoodling with Haldeman in the backseat of Ehrlichman's Mustang, would join in the fun. When they finished this morning ritual, the aides would make their separate ways to the White House, where Haldeman was the first staffer to meet with the president, utterly oblivious to the sexual debauchery occurring around him.

Unlike other journalists, who preened with their ten-dollar words and highfalutin prose, Jack Anderson took pride in the fact that a Kansas City milkman could understand his columns. If what Chotiner had told him was true—that five years after the Walter Jenkins scandal, a group of sex deviates was operating within the White House—Anderson's Everyman readers would be outraged. Anderson immediately assigned a photographer to stake out the Watergate beginning at 4 a.m. each morning, and he dispatched another to monitor the president's compound in Key Biscayne, Florida. After six weeks of round-the-clock surveillance, Anderson's shutterbugs failed to capture anything remotely sexual or suspicious on camera. Yet, according to one of Anderson's researchers, "Jack was convinced the story was true."

Frustrated at his inability to prove the existence of the White House ménage à trois, Anderson appealed to a higher authority. At 4 p.m. on June 11, the columnist showed up unannounced at FBI headquarters asking to meet with Deke DeLoach, by now the third man at the Bureau. It was an awkward request, what with Anderson and Pearson being longtime high-profile antagonists of the FBI in general and its director in particular. Cognizant of Pearson's thirty-year beef with J. Edgar Hoover, Anderson played the role of good cop, an act that came across as more than mildly irritating to the actual cop in the room. Without naming Chotiner as his source, Anderson related the allegations to DeLoach, placing them in the context of a White House "power struggle." Pearson, Anderson said, wanted to print the story, but Anderson was reluctant to do so unless he obtained more evidence, which he hoped the Bureau could help him do. DeLoach wrote up a summary of the information Anderson provided, which he characterized as "very damaging," in a memo for his boss. "There is a ring of homosexualists at the highest levels of the White House," an agitated Hoover announced to William Sullivan, his domestic intelligence chief. "I want a complete report." As his men investigated the rumors, Hoover waited until June 24, almost two weeks, before informing Attorney General John Mitchell, who duly informed the president.

That evening, Haldeman and Ehrlichman joined Vice President Spiro

Agnew and a group of Nixon staffers for dinner onboard the *Sequoia*. Mitchell gave the two aides a ride home in his limousine, and at the Watergate, he exited the car with them so that the driver would not hear what he was about to say: Jack Anderson had a source claiming that they were homosexual lovers. Though he knew the accusation was baseless, Ehrlichman was concerned. Normally, he was the one in the administration tasked with putting out fires—"Firehose speaking" was how he answered his phone—and he was damn good at it. But of all the possible charges one might level against a man, "Nothing could grab Nixon's attention faster than that allegation [of homosexuality]," he was to recall. Mitchell cautioned skepticism, suggesting that the entire affair might be an attempt by Hoover to flex his bureaucratic muscles and prove to the new administration who was boss, an explanation Ehrlichman found convincing. "I came to think that Hoover did this to show his claws, or ingratiate himself to Nixon—probably both," he recalled. "It was my early introduction to the way the game was played." To throw off the scent from his role in sparking the homo hunt, Chotiner contacted Ehrlichman and told the White House counsel that he had heard the rumor from one of Anderson's part-time stringers.

Incidentally, the Nixon aides were not the only conservative politicos in communication with the FBI director that day about a charge of homosexuality laid against them. William F. Buckley Jr. had been shocked to find his name included among "Uncle Fudge's List of Practical Homosexuals Past and Present, with Very Short Biographical Notes—a Hearsay Reference Work," on page 259 of a recently published paperback, *The Homosexual Handbook*. "Writer, professional candidate, Mr. Buckley hosts a television program and conducts it with a flourish and a zest, with such brilliant gestures and hand movement, that Gore Vidal is reported to have called him 'the Marie Antoinette of American politics,'" read Buckley's entry in what was clearly intended as a work of political satire. Either the conservative polymath's usually sharp sense of humor had failed him, or he was tetchy from his ongoing feud with Vidal. But Buckley evinced little trace of the savoir faire for which he was renowned in the fusty letter he sent to some of the other men on the list—a diverse assortment including Jack Benny, Leonard Bernstein, Robert Graves, Paul McCartney, Roddy McDowall, Archibald MacLeish, Mickey Rooney, and J. Edgar Hoover himself. "I assume that whatever your views on such related questions as censorship, the libel laws, etc., you do not believe that anyone has the right wantonly to publish untrue and defamatory material about the private lives of living people," Buckley wrote, requesting that they join him in a libel action. The book's publisher, Olympia Press, had initially agreed to issue Buckley a retraction, but later reneged, reasoning that "it cannot be held as derogatory to be called [a homosexual] anymore, professionally or socially." This was a fatuous claim, Buckley said, not least due to the analysis offered by his lawyer (also, apparently, a lover of puns) that "most jurors have not been brought up by Olympian standards." Hoover declined Buckley's invitation to join him as a co-plaintiff, noting that, from his own long experience, "those who want to believe the worst about a public figure will never be convinced of the contrary." But the director took care of the problem nonetheless, having his underlings threaten the publisher such that his name was removed from all future printings.

Meanwhile, on the streets of Greenwich Village, a turbulent situation involving proudly open homosexuals was developing revolutionary potential. Unlike gay bars in Washington—a city that, according to one gay business owner, was "the FBI's turf"—establishments serving liquor to homosexuals in New York City were largely Mafia-controlled, a circumstance owing to the New York State Liquor Authority's denial of licenses to bars that attracted the "lewd and dissolute." Though kickbacks to the NYPD allowed the bars to operate, police raids (along with the beatings, arrests, and public shaming that followed) were a common occurrence. Claiborne Pell, a Democratic senator from Rhode Island, was allegedly swept up in a sting at a Greenwich Village gay bar in 1964, extricating himself only thanks to the intervention of Tammany Hall boss Carmine DeSapio. Patrons without such esteemed connections had to accept whatever humiliations and abuse the police meted out; they were, after all, homosexuals, and that was how things had always been. Until the early morning hours of Saturday, June 28, 1969, when the police performed a routine raid on the Stonewall Inn, and a group of righteously incensed homosexuals fought back.

Over the course of the next five days and nights, hundreds of gay men, lesbians, and drag queens poured into the streets outside the Stonewall to shout, punch, and hurl projectiles at the police. Word of the uprising traveled quickly over the gay grapevine, that invisible network of gossip and occasionally lifesaving information, and hit the secret city like a lightning bolt. Though same-sex dancing was not technically illegal in Washington, gay bar owners discouraged it. At the Amber Room, which, when it opened in 1964, was one of Washington's few lesbian watering holes, same-sex dancing was permitted but only in a back room. Whenever the police made a surprise visit, the bartender in front would press a button underneath the bar and a buzzer would sound alerting the patrons in the back to split up. Four years later, the Plus One became the first gay bar in the District to break the self-imposed ban. But patrons still had to knock discreetly on the front door and pass muster with a bouncer before they were permitted to enter. On the Saturday evening of the riots, eighteen-year-old Peter Jefts was enjoying a drink there when two men excitedly entered the poorly lit space. Fresh from the rebellion in New York, they breathlessly described wild scenes of outraged homosexuals throwing cobblestones and hurling trash at police officers, shocked and bewildered by the behavior of people whom they habitually harassed and pushed around without incident. "I can remember distinctly them speaking to someone and then it very quickly spread from person to person around the bar," Jefts said of the galvanic moment when the room of Washingtonians first learned about the bravery of their brethren in New York. "I could see it traveling through the bar."

Roving street battles between cops and homosexuals were still raging on Monday morning when Dwight Chapin heard the noise of a buzzer at his desk in the White House. It was Bob Haldeman, summoning Chapin to his office. "Have a seat," Haldeman instructed the young aide as he entered the room. Already sitting there were Ehrlichman and Larry Higby, Haldeman's devoted special assistant facetiously known as "Haldeman's Haldeman."

Moments later, Mitchell entered the room. "The president has asked that we get to the bottom of this," the attorney general said, "and I am in charge of it." Mitchell told the men that he would need sworn depositions about their whereabouts and sex lives. "We're going to have to meet it head on," he declared. "We're going to get this solved. The president wants the truth."

Chapin recalled going home that night "scared to death." What he had been told was "a time bomb," and if the allegations were ever to appear in the media, it would have been "a disaster for all of us."

Next to the Oval Office, looking out onto the Rose Garden, is the Cabinet Room. It was here that, following the death of Franklin Roosevelt,

Harry Truman was solemnly administered the oath of office in a ceremony lasting less than a minute. During the Cuban Missile Crisis, John F.
Kennedy convened his legendary ExComm group of advisors around the
room's long, oval desk. Over the course of the next two days, the space
where presidents assembled the senior-most members of their administration would serve a purpose that, while perhaps not so significant as these
other events, was treated no less seriously. As President Nixon worked next
door, each one of his three aides raised his right hand, swore to tell the
truth under penalty of perjury, and declared that he was not a homosexual.

"To your knowledge do homosexual activities take place at the Watergate Inn Hotel or Apartments?" assistant FBI director Joseph J. Casper
asked Haldeman, while Erma Metcalf, Hoover's administrative assistant,
took notes.

"No," replied the chief of staff.

"Have you ever previously been accused of associating with homosexuals or perverts?"

"Never."

"Are you now or have you ever been a homosexual or have you ever
engaged in homosexual activities?"

"No."

Assistant FBI director Mark Felt interrogated Ehrlichman. "I had good
alibis for the dates alleged—I was elsewhere with other people, including
a satisfactory number of women," Ehrlichman recalled, though he "was
not sure I had convinced [Felt] of my sexual orientation." The G-man—
later to earn the pseudonym "Deep Throat" for his role in another scandal
originating at the Watergate—was "coolly noncommittal" throughout the
process.

For Chapin's interrogation, "Hoover asked all the questions." The FBI
director was determined to discover if a "gay cell" existed in the White
House, the young aide recalled. "It was just a set series of questions to try
to anchor what we were doing in Key Biscayne, and what we were involved
in, and was this an act that would be embarrassing to the President."

Once the interrogations were complete, the FBI informed Anderson
that it had investigated his charges and found them to be baseless. Readers
of the Washington Merry-Go-Round were thus never told of a homosexual ring in the highest echelons of the Nixon White House. And while the
aides were relieved at their exoneration, the episode revealed to them a

disconcerting lack of trust on the part of the president they served, one that boded ill for the future. "I felt Nixon should have taken our denials as conclusive," Ehrlichman later wrote. By that point, he and Haldeman had served Nixon for a decade. Surely, the president should have believed them when they said they were not sexual deviants. Also exacerbating the climate of suspicion within the White House was the creeping sense that Hoover had ginned up the entire affair to serve his own purposes. Hoover had earlier assured Haldeman that Anderson was "a rat of the worst type" and that Pearson "looks like a skunk and is one." But by using Anderson's scuttlebutt to justify an investigation into their private lives, the FBI director taught the aides to fear him, while simultaneously proving his utility, and ruthlessness, to Nixon. "Mitchell's conclusion was that this was an attempt by Hoover to lay a threat across our path," Haldeman recalled, "to keep us in line, remind us of his potential."

* * *

"WARNING TO DUPONT CIRCLE PEOPLE," read the third item in the leftmost column of a single-page mimeographed leaflet entitled the *Gay Blade*. "Cars seen too frequently in the Circle area are having their license numbers taken down; their owners later are being harassed and blackmailed."

Nancy Tucker was a twenty-three-year-old editorial assistant at a weekly cosmetics trade publication when the leaders of the Mattachine Society tapped her to be the founding coeditor of Washington's first gay newspaper in the fall of 1969. The *Gay Blade* was created to serve as the informal monthly bulletin of the Society, still operating clandestinely when Tucker applied to join its ranks. To ensure that Tucker was not a government informant, the group subjected her to a rigorous interview process, and its meetings, convened in a windowless room behind a furnace in a Capitol Hill church basement, resembled a scene from the hit television spy show *Get Smart*. Members gathered "like mice," Tucker recalled, adopting cloak-and-dagger methods of communication that made the late 1960s an "exciting and terrifying time to be gay."

With the help of Lilli Vincenz, Tucker assembled about fifteen Mattachine members to assist in producing the first edition of the *Blade*. The newsletter contained a dozen items, including advertisements for a blood drive, a roommate referral service, a warning not to buy a particular brand of pornography whose models "are covered head to toe in black leotards," and—for anyone seeking advice in dealing with difficulties arising out of a security clearance investigation—Frank Kameny's home telephone number. A male Mattachine member served nominally as Tucker's coeditor, but Tucker and Vincenz ended up performing most of the editorial, production, and marketing tasks. "It eventually came down to my doing all of the writing, most of the news work, some of the distribution, all of the advertising selling—and Bart did some of the distribution and let me know what news tips that he came up with," Tucker recalled. In the early evenings, she passed out copies of the *Blade* around the city's gay bars, racing to finish before 10 p.m. "There was a magic witching hour after which I just picked up the vibes" from male bar-goers that it was time to leave, Tucker remembered. "They didn't want to be disturbed by some lesbian passing out some crazy publication."

Tucker accumulated a growing number of stops along her paper route. If the Nixon White House was paranoid about homosexual infiltration, the city surrounding it was becoming more hospitable to gays and lesbians. On Capitol Hill, Mr. Henry's restaurant initially attracted three crowds: real estate brokers (its eponymous owner, Henry Yaffe, restored houses on the side), *Evening Star* reporters, and gays. Several nights a week, on the second floor, a young African American music teacher Yaffe discovered named Roberta Flack serenaded customers. On Seventeenth Street, near Dupont Circle, Annie's Paramount Steak House earned a reputation as a welcoming environment, owing largely to an incident that became well known due to word of mouth. When the eatery's namesake, bartender Annie Kaylor (known to stir drinks with her finger) saw two men sitting together while holding hands underneath the table, she walked up and reprimanded the couple. "No, no," she said, startling the men, who feared they were about to be expelled from the premises. "You hold those hands right up here on top of that table," she continued, to their relief. A new feeling of openness was palpable across the city. Asked if he was worried that visiting a gay bar might jeopardize his job at the Defense Department, a patron at the Plus One facetiously contemplated the likelihood of running into his boss. "Who's gonna see me here?" he asked. "Melvin Laird?"

While small concentrations of gay people had resided in neighborhoods like Georgetown and Capitol Hill for years, Dupont Circle became the first widely recognized Washington "gayborhood" during the late 1960s and early '70s, part of a nationwide trend of gentrification. In the aftermath of the riots sparked by the assassination of Martin Luther King Jr. in

1968, many poor Black residents were driven out of destroyed city districts, including the area east of the circle. As young, upwardly mobile gays swept into these blighted neighborhoods to purchase and restore ruined properties, "Follow the fairies" became a real estate euphemism for this pattern of urban renewal.

Located in an old factory, Washington's first gay bathhouse, the Regency, opened in 1968. Its owner, David Harris, had been institutionalized at St. Elizabeths for his homosexuality and discharged as a hopeless case after three months. (Years later, at an X-rated gay cinema, Harris encountered the doctor who had treated him.) The Regency was decorated in a kitschy, ancient Roman style, and while catering primarily to men, who wandered its labyrinthine hallways and steam rooms in pursuit of anonymous sexual encounters wearing nothing more than a towel, it held the occasional women-only night. Scrupulously adhering to city regulations did not exempt Harris from police harassment. Sometimes without notice, officers parked their squad cars outside the club during the early morning hours and trained their headlights on the front door. One evening, Harris walked out onto the curb and gave the cops a piece of his mind. "These people are not afraid of you and neither am I!" he shouted. "I don't care what you do! In fact, you should come in and enjoy yourself if you want to, it's open! Come in and take your clothes off if you want to!"

★ ★ ★

RICHARD NIXON NEVER FORGAVE JACK ANDERSON for tipping off the FBI to a nonexistent homosexual cabal in his White House, and he did not wait long to fling the charge back at him.

In the final weeks of 1971, Anderson published a pair of columns, citing leaked White House memoranda, about the administration's tilt toward Pakistan in its war with India. Nixon was outraged at what he perceived to be an assault on the president's ability to conduct foreign policy. He was determined to impugn Anderson, and he had just the group of henchmen to do it.

Earlier that year, after the *New York Times* began publishing excerpts from a confidential Defense Department history of the Vietnam War dubbed the "Pentagon Papers," Nixon authorized the creation of the White House Special Investigations Unit. Also known as the "Plumbers," for their mission of plugging leaks to the press, the team's responsibilities were wide, as was the selection of tools at its disposal. "We're up against an enemy, a conspiracy," Nixon told Haldeman at the time. "They're using any means. We are going to use any means. Is that clear?" At the behest of national security advisor Henry Kissinger, whose pro-Pakistan comments Anderson had quoted in his columns, the Plumbers narrowed down the list of possible leakers and developed a theory that a young navy yeoman serving as a stenographer on the National Security Council staff, Charles Radford, was the culprit. In their secret command post, located in the basement of the Old Executive Office Building, they affixed the columnist's name atop a growing list of White House enemies and set to work.

What was Radford's motive? In a conversation with his aides on December 22, Nixon demanded that the investigation proceed along the hypothesis that Anderson and Radford were lovers—or, as he tactfully phrased it, "sexual up the ass." This was not the first time Nixon had tried to discredit a journalistic irritant by smearing him as a homosexual. In November 1970, after Democrats gained 12 House seats in the midterm election, an aggravated Nixon ordered Haldeman to retrieve from Hoover "a run down on the homosexuals known and suspected in the Washington press corps." In a subsequent phone conversation with the FBI director, Haldeman mentioned the names of some men "rumored generally" to be gay and asked if the Bureau "had any other stuff" that might be of use to the White House. Hoover's men followed up with a report two days later, but neither its contents nor what, if anything, the White House did with it is known.

As for the navy yeoman and the columnist, there was no evidence whatsoever to indicate they were gay. Indeed, there was much to dispute it, not least the seventeen children fathered between them. None of this, however, had any impact on Nixon's conviction to prove otherwise. "I want a direct question about homosexuality asked" of Radford, the president ordered Ehrlichman and Mitchell. "You never know what you're going to find." Nixon then proceeded to rhapsodize, as he so often did, about the seminal event of his political career, the high-profile espionage case that helped set the tone for the ensuing national debate over communism and anticommunism and to which, in Nixon's mind, homosexuality held the key. "Because we got a couple on Hiss and Chambers, you know," the president told his aides. "Nobody knows that, but that's the background on how that one began. They were both that way. And relationships sometimes poison a lot of these things. Now, if Anderson, I'm just getting, but if there's any possibility of this John, that could be a key as well. If something, he may be under blackmail."

Later that day, Ehrlichman held a meeting with Adm. Robert O. Welander, Radford's superior, and David Young, a Kissinger aide who moonlighted as a White House Plumber. "One moment he would be taking bachelor Henry's dirty underwear to the laundry," Ehrlichman observed of Young, "and the next moment he would be with Henry and Chancellor Adenauer or some other world leader, taking notes." Kissinger's wasn't the only dirty laundry Young handled. Radford's "best friend" at the Pentagon, Young had discovered, was "quite effeminate." Perhaps "Anderson might have a handle on him in any way like that."

"You mean sexual deviation?" Ehrlichman asked.

"Yeah," Young answered.

"Have you seen any indication of that?" Ehrlichman asked Welander.

"Chuck is not the big manly type or anything else," Welander observed of Radford, before cautioning that this was not necessarily dispositive. "You know, high-pitched voice and he kind of prances but nine-tenths of the Navy yeomen are that way."

"Really," Ehrlichman said, surprised.

"Who else wants to be a typist?"

The next day, Young summoned Pentagon investigator Donald Stewart to the Plumbers' hideaway office and handed him an assignment. "Ensure that I found a relationship" between Anderson and Radford, regardless of whether one existed, is how Stewart remembered the order. To be sure, Stewart didn't care for Anderson. But investigating a journalist's sex life was a bridge too far, he told the Kissinger aide. "Damn it! Damn it!" Young cried. "The president is jumping up and down and he wants this and we're always telling him everything can't be done." Despite the Plumber's pleas, Stewart held his ground.

The next day, with the president breathing down his neck, Ehrlichman called Defense Secretary Melvin Laird. "John, I don't think we should go on the homosexuality thing," Laird told Ehrlichman. "We can go on everything else, but I don't think we should go on the homosexuality."

EHRLICHMAN: Why not?

LAIRD: 'Cause I don't think we have any basis to even draw up a series

of questions . . . We have no other evidence and the interrogators tell
me there is none . . . we've run so many tests on this yeoman and he's
of course . . . but there's nothing to indicate homosexuality and we
have to notify them ahead of the [polygraph] exam as to the topics
to be covered.

EHRLICHMAN: Well, that's all right. Notify them that you are going to
cover that.

LAIRD: Well . . . then he will not take . . . if he decides not to take the
test and then goes out and tells the press that that's what we're running here, I think we just get in a hell of a lot of . . . we blow the lid.

EHRLICHMAN: All right, let me explain the reason for this, aside from
the fact that the president has instructed me to go on this.

LAIRD: Did he instruct you on the homosexuality?

EHRLICHMAN: Yes sir, he certainly did. It was his idea. And here's why.
Because there is no apparent motive for this fellow turning these
papers over to Anderson.

Privately, Laird believed the president's hypothesis was "bullshit," that
Nixon had gotten "carried away" and "wanted heads to roll" and didn't
really care how they were guillotined.

With the Pentagon stonewalling their efforts, the Plumbers ordered the
FBI to establish surveillance of Anderson and Radford. Young, meanwhile,
interrogated Radford with "an obsessive line of questioning that had to do
with homosexuality," in the words of one official who read the interview
transcript, which remains classified. Still, the White House could not find
any evidence for Nixon's hypothesis.

Ultimately, the Plumbers were correct in their assessment that Radford was Anderson's source. But the connection was not, as the president
so elegantly phrased it, "sexual up the ass." Quite the opposite. Both men
were members of the same Mormon temple, and Anderson was Radford's
tutor in the faith. Undeterred by the prosaic nature of this relationship, the
White House continued searching for ways to cast doubt on the columnist's heterosexuality. Anderson's researcher, a budding young journalist
named Brit Hume, "sure looks" homosexual, Nixon special counsel Chuck
Colson blurted out in a March 1972 Oval Office meeting with Haldeman
and Nixon.

"He sure does," Haldeman concurred.

"He just has the appearance of it," Colson observed.

"He's pretty, and he's—"

"—and the way he handled his demeanor is curious."

"He acts funny."

"Well I think Anderson is," Nixon interjected. "I remember from years ago he's got a strange, strange habit of—I think Pearson was too. I think he and Anderson were . . ."

Alas, the implications of *that* enticing train of thought would have to be put on hold, as a break-in at a building across town, the place where Murray Chotiner once alleged a homosexual threesome of presidential aides, diverted the world's attention.

26

FAGS

"What starts the process, really, are laughs and slights and snubs when you are a kid," Richard Nixon once recalled of his childhood. "Sometimes it's because you're poor or Irish or Jewish or Catholic or ugly or simply that you are skinny. But if you are reasonably intelligent and if your anger is deep enough and strong enough, you can learn that you can change those attitudes by excellence, personal gut performance while those who have everything are sitting on their fat butts."

Nixon shared these personal reflections with a former aide in 1979, five years after resigning the presidency in disgrace. Reflecting on what made him tick, on what propelled him to overcome repeated setbacks and work his way up to the highest office in the land, Nixon tried to connect his experiences as an awkward child with the challenges faced by members of the very minority groups whom, during unguarded moments recorded on tape, he frequently disparaged in appalling terms. For many people, the teasing suffered during childhood becomes the source of immobilizing self-doubt. For Nixon, the manifold insecurities of his youth formed the wellspring of a relentless drive that propelled him to the summit of American politics. No amount of success, however, would ever abate his conviction that he did not fit in, that the detested cultural and political elite whose approval he still sought would never accept him.

"Richard Nixon," the historian Rick Perlstein has observed, "was a serial collector of resentments." Those resentments—against the Ivy League, the East Coast establishment, Jewish intellectuals, the Kennedys, the media, essentially anyone or anything perceived as hostile to Richard Milhous Nixon—were wide and deep, and Nixon's genius lay in the way he culti-vated the support of other Americans who shared the same antipathies. In his sweeping history of the era that birthed our contemporary political and cultural divides, *Nixonland*, Perlstein establishes this theme of mobi-lized resentment early, emblematizing it in the rivalry between two cliques at Whittier College, Nixon's alma mater. On one side of the campus were the Franklins—"well-rounded, graceful, moved smoothly, talked slickly"— and on the other were the Orthogonians—"strivers, those not to the man-ner born, commuter students like [Nixon]." The sense of grievance Nixon nurtured at Whittier laid the seeds for his most consequential political insight, one that he rode to power in 1968 and that his latter-day imita-tors invoke regularly: that there exists a "great, silent majority" of Ameri-cans, ignored and condescended to by the same stuck-up elitists who had scorned him ever since he championed a dumpy ex-Communist snitch named Whittaker Chambers against the elegant and highly credentialed State Department mandarin Alger Hiss.

Perhaps in a more enlightened era—or, more likely, an alternate history—Nixon's experiences as an outsider would have inspired him to sympathize with people who were, as he described Hiss and Chambers, "that way." The young Nixon bore more than a slight resemblance to the archetypical "best little boy in the world," Andrew Tobias's term for a cer-tain type of gay young man who diligently channels the adversity engen-dered by his secret into academic pursuits, so many of whom have made their way to Washington because of that city's peculiar appetite for the skills that secret bred. To deflect attention from their lack of interest in the opposite sex, Tobias argues, these diligent overachievers devote themselves to schoolwork, extracurricular pursuits, and pleasing those in authority. "Another important line of defense, the most important on a practical day-to-day basis, was my prodigious list of activities," Tobias writes of his high school years. "'Highly motivated; a self-starter,' the teachers would write on my character reports. Hell, yes, I was motivated! No one could expect me to be out dating on Saturday if the school paper was going to be on the stands on Tuesday. No one could expect me to be partying over Christmas vacation when I had a list of seventeen urgent projects to complete—I would be lucky to find time to open my presents, let alone go to parties or date, for crying out loud."

Born in a house hand-built by his abusive father, graduating third in his class at Duke Law School, the consummate political underdog, Nixon was a striver. He could also be the target of gay innuendo, most of it deriving either from his physical awkwardness or his close friendship with a Florida banker named Bebe Rebozo. "Somebody was asking me. Said he thought Richard Nixon was obviously homosexual," riffed Gore Vidal in a 1974 interview with the *Fag Rag*, a Boston gay alternative newspaper. "I said: 'Why do you think that?' He said: 'You know, that funny, uncoordinated way he moves.' I said: 'Yeah. Like Nureyev.'" Alexander Haig, who served as an assistant to Henry Kissinger, joked about the Rebozo rumors and mocked Nixon's "limp-wrist manner" to impress his boss.

Rather than view his own adversities and those faced by gay people as a point of commonality, however, Nixon saw homosexuality as an elitist provocation to his great silent majority, an addition to the already vast catalogue of resentments begat by "egghead" intellectuals, slippery journalists, leftist fellow travelers, uppity Blacks, disloyal Jews, bra-burning feminists, and filthy anti–Vietnam War protesters. Thanks to the ever-present recording devices Nixon installed in the White House, we know that homosexuality was something he discussed with aides on multiple occasions, and always in derogatory fashion. Nixon's attitudes were hardly unique among men of his era, and the relative frequency with which the matter arose was directly connected to the newfound prominence that the movement for gay liberation was earning in the wake of Stonewall.

Nonetheless, Nixon's fascination with homosexuality distinguishes him from every other modern American president. For most of them, homosexuality was an unfortunate fact of life, one akin to alcoholism or mental illness, and an occasional source of obscene humor. Aside from a vulnerability to blackmail, a predisposition to communism, and a disqualification for government employment, it was not something that occupied their thoughts. With the important exception of Jack Kennedy (the classic Franklin to Nixon's Orthogonian), presidents tended to confront the reality of gay existence only when it threatened their public standing, as in the cases of Bob Waldron and Lyndon Johnson, Arthur Vandenberg and Dwight Eisenhower, and Sumner Welles and Franklin Roosevelt.

For Nixon and his chief subordinates, however, homosexuality was nothing short of an obsession. It explained the collapses of ancient Greece and Rome, the disintegration of the Catholic Church, even the degradation of women's fashion. The Soviet Union and its fellow travelers, Nixon believed, promoted homosexuality as a secret weapon to destroy the United States. To be sure, these sentiments never rose above the level of Oval Office banter; they were not translated into policy. (Befitting his role as Nixon's attack dog, Vice President Spiro Agnew was the only member of the administration who made these private prejudices public, notoriously delivering speeches in which he attacked the "effete corps of impudent snobs who characterize themselves as intellectuals" and the "ideological eunuchs" whose "tantrums" were "insidiously destroying the fabric of American society.") While the federal government was still following the exclusionary policies on gay employment instituted by the Eisenhower administration, there were no exceptional Nixonian initiatives to repress or purge homosexuals. What the frequent refrain of homosexuality offers is a perspective into the psyche of Richard Nixon, perhaps our most enigmatic president.

Nixon's fixation began with the Hiss-Chambers case, an affair that loomed large over his career. It was Nixon's first turn in the national spotlight, the event that determined irrevocably the way millions of Americans felt about him. "If it had not been for the Hiss case, I think you might have been elected," a friend told Nixon after his close loss to John F. Kennedy in 1960. (To which Nixon replied, "Without the Hiss case, I would probably not have been nominated.") Nixon was of the opinion that Chambers *and* Hiss were gay, which put him in the rare spot of being convinced both of Hiss's guilt *and* that his relationship with his accuser was homoerotic. Two decades after that spellbinding confrontation helped lay the groundwork for a moral panic associating homosexuality with the State Department, Nixon was still giving voice to the stereotype that America's diplomats were light in their loafers. Delivering a pep talk to the NSC staff early in his administration, he derided "the striped-pants faggots at Foggy Bottom." Approving a series of bombing raids over Cambodia, he instructed Henry Kissinger to keep the maneuvers secret from the "impossible fags over there" at the State Department. "Typical of the group was a fellow who came through the line from California who said he was a Quaker," Nixon once remarked of a coreligionist he met in a White House receiving line. "He was an obvious, roaring fag. It was disgusting to even pass him down the line to Pat," Nixon's wife. During his last trip abroad as president, after meeting with some of the American officials seconded to the North Atlantic Treaty Organization's headquarters in Brussels, Nixon mumbled, "They're a bunch of fairies," to the U.S. ambassador, Donald Rumsfeld. "The President apparently had assumed that the NATO staff was composed of State Department people," Rumsfeld surmised.

The president sets the tone in any administration. If the tapes of the conversations recorded on secret listening devices are anything to go by, the Nixon White House had the ambiance of a high school locker room, where obsequious aides vied for the president's approval much like underclassmen jostling to impress the big man on campus. "Nixon's favor depended on the readiness to fall in with the paranoid cult of the tough guy," Kissinger recalled. "The conspiracy of the press, the hostility of the Establishment, the flatulence of the Georgetown set, were permanent features of Nixon's conversation, which one challenged only at the cost of exclusion from the inner circle." As Nixon ranted, his underlings indulged his many phobias, egging him on to pronouncements of ever greater nastiness and absurdity while trying to outdo one another with their own put-downs, invective, and macho strut. "Ehrlichman had to measure up to Bob Haldeman, Charles Colson, Henry Kissinger and Nixon himself in the show of toughness then thought necessary to the cruel job of exercising national and world leadership," former Nixon aide Len Garment remembered of the crudely competitive dynamic between the president and his underlings. An April 1971 conversation among Nixon, Haldeman, and Kissinger prompted by the resolution adopted at a National Youth Conference endorsing legal recognition of same-sex relationships is characteristic of this swaggering repartee. "Let me say something before we get off the gay thing," Nixon said.

NIXON: I don't want my views misunderstood. I am the most tolerant person on that of anybody in this shop. They have a problem. They're born that way. You know that. That's all. I think they are. Anyway, my point is, though, when I say they're born that way, the tendency is there. [But] my point is that Boy Scout leaders, YMCA leaders, and others bring them in that direction, and teachers. And if you look over the history of societies, you will find, of course, that some of the highly intelligent people . . . Oscar Wilde, Aristotle, et cetera, et cetera, et cetera, were all homosexuals. Nero, of course, was, in a public way, in with a boy in Rome.

HALDEMAN: There's a whole bunch of Roman emperors . . .

NIXON: But the point is, look at that, once a society moves in that direction, the vitality goes out of that society. Now, isn't that right, Henry?

KISSINGER: Well—

NIXON: Do you see any other change, anywhere where it doesn't fit?

KISSINGER: That's certainly been the case in antiquity. The Romans were notorious—

HALDEMAN: The Greeks.

KISSINGER: —Homosexuals . . .

NIXON: The Greeks.

KISSINGER: The Greeks.

NIXON: The Greeks. And they had plenty of it . . . By God, I am not going to have a situation where we pass along a law indicating, "Well, now, kids, just go out and be gay." They can do it. Just leave them alone. That's a lifestyle I don't want to touch . . .

KISSINGER: Well, it's one thing—

HALDEMAN: I'm afraid that's what they're doing now.

NIXON: Just leave them alone.

KISSINGER: It's one thing for people to, you know, like some people we know, who would do it discreetly, but to make that a national policy . . .

KISSINGER: But something this profoundly offensive to the majority of the population, to flaunt it as an act of public policy. That seems to me to be the issue involved here.

HALDEMAN: It's like any of those other things. You make the public policy, and then you reduce one more barrier that keeps some kids—

As it happens, one of those "kids" was Haldeman's own teenage son, Peter, struggling with his sexual orientation and contemplating suicide as his father engaged in a bull session about the evils of homosexuality with the president of the United States.

Two weeks after crediting homosexuality for the collapse of ancient civilizations, Nixon complained to Ehrlichman and Haldeman about something he had seen on television the previous night while trying to tune into a baseball game. In lieu of the national pastime, CBS had aired a "movie" with "two magnificent, handsome guys—and a stupid old fellow in it. They were glorifying homosexuality!" the president barked. (The "movie" Nixon stumbled upon was in fact a new television show, *All in the Family*.) Nixon described a character who was "obviously queer—he wears an ascot and so forth . . . but he's not offensively so." To be sure, the president acknowledged, "Allen Drury is a homosexual and so is Joe Alsop; some of our best friends are. And some of our worst enemies are. [*Washington Post* columnist Joseph] Kraft"—whose home telephone Ehrlichman had ordered bugged two years earlier—"of course is a hopeless fag."

NIXON: But the point is, I do not mind the homosexuality. I understand it . . . The point that I make is that goddammit, I do not think—that you glorify, on public television, homosexuality! The reason you don't glorify, John, any more than you glorify whores. Now we all know that people go to whores, and we all know that people just do that . . . But goddamn it what do you think that does to kids?

EHRLICHMAN: Yeah.

NIXON: What do you think that does to 11 and 12 year old boys when they see that. Why is it that the Scouts . . . we constantly had to clean up the staffs to keep the Goddamned fags out of it . . . You know there's a little tendency among them all. Well by God can I tell you it outraged me. Not for any moral reason. Most people are outraged for moral reasons, why, it outrages me because I don't want to see this country go that way. You know what happened to the Greeks. Homosexuality destroyed them. Sure, Aristotle was a homo, we all know that. So was Socrates.

EHRLICHMAN: But he never had the influence that television has.

NIXON: You know what happened to the Romans? The last six Roman emperors were fags. The last six. Nero had a public wedding to a boy . . . You know what happened to the Popes? . . . When the Catholic Church went to hell, in, I don't know, three or four centuries ago, it was homosexual. And finally it had to be cleaned out.

EHRLICHMAN: Uh-huh.

NIXON: Now, that's what's happened to Britain; it happened earlier to

France. And let's look at the strong societies. The Russians, God-damn it, they root them out, they don't let them around at all. I don't know what they do with them . . .

EHRLICHMAN: Yeah.

NIXON: Now, we are allowing this in this country when we show . . . Dope? Do you think the Russians allow dope? Hell no. Not if they can allow—not if they can catch it. They send them up. You see, homosexuality, immorality in general, these are the enemies of strong societies. That's why the Communists and the left-wingers are pushing it. They're trying to destroy us!

EHRLICHMAN: It's fatal liberality . . .

HALDEMAN: Of course, there's a big program of that now that we should be—that homosexuality should be respectable because, you know, it's just a state the way certain people are and we should respect them and all that. They're letting these people like the Gay Liberation people and the Gay May Day crowd and all the rest.

After Ehrlichman described a controversy about the recognition of a gay student caucus at the University of Southern California, the conversation drifted toward the more northernly part of Nixon's home state:

NIXON: You know what's happened to San Francisco?

EHRLICHMAN: San Francisco has just gone clear over.

NIXON: But it isn't just down in the ratty part of town.

EHRLICHMAN: No.

NIXON: But the upper class in San Francisco is that way. The Bohemian Grove that I attend from time to time—the Easterners and the others would come there—but it is the most faggy goddamned thing you could ever imagine, the San Francisco crowd that goes in there. It's just terrible. I mean, I don't even want to shake hands with anybody from San Francisco . . .

HALDEMAN: Really?

EHRLICHMAN: Well, it's a different set of values that has been induced in three or four places.

NIXON: And also in some parts of southern California.

HALDEMAN: Yeah, that's right.

NIXON: Hollywood, Pasadena. You remember when Pasadena had this thing about—many years ago, you know, where all the boys were out in the swimming pool and, well, they had to fire half the faculty of the high school, of the Pasadena high school. This was before you were born. This was a terrible, terrible thing.

HALDEMAN: And the whole decorator and sportswear manufacturer . . .

NIXON: Let me say this, I can understand that, I mean the guy probably who's putting on this [Nixon's daughter Tricia's] wedding I'm sure is a fag. Decorators. They got to do something, the rest of them. But goddamn it we don't have to glorify it.

EHRLICHMAN: That's right.

NIXON: Isn't that what it gets down to?

EHRLICHMAN: Yeah.

NIXON: You know one of the reasons that fashions have made women look so terrible is because the goddamned designers hate women. Now that's the truth. You watch . . . Some of those fellows, they have the flat-chested thing with horrible looking styles they run. That was really the designers taking it out on the women. I'm sure of that.

Over the course of several days in September 1971, Nixon and his aides discussed the gala opening-night ceremony at the Kennedy Center, the federal monument to his slain nemesis. Nixon chose not to attend, which was probably for the best, considering his apoplexy upon hearing what transpired there before and after the performance of *Mass*, Leonard Bernstein's bizarre rock-operatic interpretation of the Catholic ritual featuring a cast of two hundred singers, dancers, actors, and musicians. Listening to the tapes, one can easily imagine the disgusted expression on Nixon's face as Haldeman describes "nauseating" photos in the newspapers the following morning "of Bernstein kissing everybody he could find," including "a lot of men on the mouth including the big black guy," choreographer Alvin Ailey.

"Kissing on the mouth?!" a shocked Nixon asked.

"Yeah, right head on!" Haldeman answered.

"Absolutely sickening."

"Revolting."

The president and his aides then engaged in a brief survey of the osculatory practices of various ethnic groups, Haldeman noting that Jewish men often kiss each other on the cheek.

The following summer, gay and lesbian activists made their first organized effort to lobby the political parties at their national conventions. Commenting on Miami as the site of the Democratic gathering, Haldeman told the president, "They eliminated their law prohibiting male homosexuals from wearing female clothing, now the boys can all put on their dresses so the gay lib is going to turn out 6,000 fags." For the first time at an American political convention, gay activists addressed the hall, albeit at five o'clock in the morning. ("Quite frankly, people were terrified we were seen as radical enough as it was," Bob Shrum, an aide to that year's Democratic nominee, George McGovern, remembered.) "The Democrats were wise in limiting the official podium appearance of their homosexuals to between 4 and 5 in the morning," Dick Moore, a Nixon advisor whose waggishness earned him a perennial spot as toastmaster at his Yale reunions, wrote in a memo to Dwight Chapin. "Someone should be in charge of seeing to it that we do the same with ours. Do you have a candidate for this fulltime assignment?"

Three years after a mischievous phone call from Murray Chotiner launched a White House witch hunt, the subject of homosexuality had become a source of whimsy. But one could never be sure. Not even the most legendary of Washington's lady-killers evaded suspicion. Power, Henry Kissinger observed, "is the great aphrodisiac," and he knew of what he spoke. In between wives, a period largely coinciding with his tenure in the Nixon administration, the German-born former Harvard professor—to whom *Playboy* magazine proudly announced it had given a complimentary subscription—was Washington's most eligible bachelor, his name paired in the society columns with feminist icon Gloria Steinem, actress Jill St. John, and novelist Joanna Barnes, among several other dazzling young women. Yet before Kissinger ascended the twin heights of diplomacy and seduction, he, too, came under suspicion as a possible lavender lad. Interviewing one of his former Harvard graduate students as part of the Bureau's background check on the incoming national security advisor, a pair of FBI agents asked a series of roundabout questions pertaining to Kissinger's marital status. Failing to reap any incriminating information, one of the agents frustratedly blurted out, "Well, is he a homosexual?"

"I have no idea," the former student said. "But I do know somebody who would know."

"Yes?" the agent replied.

"Your director."

At that, the agents stood up and stormed out of the room.

The reason academic politics are so vicious, Kissinger famously observed, is because the stakes are so small. Kissinger was no shrinking violet when it came to bureaucratic infighting, as his own alleged use of the homosexual smear to undermine an administration rival demonstrates. A man of gargantuan ambition, Kissinger was not satisfied with the role of national security advisor; he wanted to be secretary of state as well. There were two small obstacles to his realizing this aspiration, however: no one had ever occupied both jobs at the same time, and, more problematically, somebody else—former Eisenhower attorney general William Rogers—already held the other one. According to the journalist Seymour Hersh, Kissinger started spreading rumors that Rogers was a "fag" who maintained a kept boy in a Georgetown love nest. Though it would ultimately be due to other factors—namely, Kissinger's frustrating habit of bypassing Rogers in his freelance diplomacy, Nixon's innate distrust of the State Department, and Rogers's deviation from the official White House line on the incipient Watergate scandal—Nixon relieved Rogers of his duties in the fall of 1973 and handed his job to Kissinger. Considering how Rogers had once suggested exposing Joe Alsop's Moscow folly as punishment for his columns criticizing the Eisenhower administration and, in the aftermath of the Martin-Mitchell defection, proposed compiling a national registry of homosexuals, there was some poetic justice in his sacking.

There was (at least) one gay man working atop the Nixon administration who evaded both the frantic inquisitions of the FBI and the pressure-cooker rumormongering of his colleagues: the president's chief speechwriter. Raymond Price was a graduate of Yale, where he followed his friend William F. Buckley Jr. into Skull and Bones, the senior secret society where weekly, ritualized confessionals provided practice in the sharing of one's innermost secrets (an association that would lead some to finger Price as "Deep Throat"). Described by his boss as "my principal idea man," Price was the lead author of Nixon's inaugural, State of the Union, and resignation addresses. He was also close to the Nixon family, spending "as much personal time with [them] as anyone in the White House," according to Garment.

But Price's greatest influence lay in his role as a shaper of the Nixon image. Once, during the early stages of the 1968 campaign, Price and several other advisors locked themselves in a CBS screening room for an entire day to analyze hours of Nixon television appearances. Price realized that while Nixon was a terrible stump speaker, sounding stilted and insincere, he performed much better in casual, one-on-one settings where he could converse with voters extemporaneously. "The greater the element of informality and spontaneity, the better [Nixon] comes across," Price wrote in a memo. The campaign, he suggested, therefore needed "to remind supporters of the candidate's strengths, and to demonstrate to nonsupporters that the Herblock images are fiction," a reference to the *Washington Post* cartoonist whose stock caricature of Nixon depicted the presidential aspirant as perpetually clammy and unshaven. "It's not the man we have to change," Price concluded, "but rather the *received impression*."

This was, as one savvy observer would write over twenty-five years later, a "revolutionary" insight for the practice of American politics. The ability to alter how others view you while maintaining some form of fidelity to one's true self is the sort of skill that a man harboring a powerful secret—a secret on the order of the one Ray Price was forced to keep—will profoundly understand. "We have to be very clear on this point: that the response is to the image, not to the man, since 99 percent of the voters have no contact with the man," Price wrote. More than anyone on the White House staff, it was Price who elicited stirrings of humanity from Nixon, drawing from the petulant and vindictive president a sympathetic quality the American public rarely saw. Trying to mine material for a speech during the 1968 presidential race while flying with Nixon on his campaign plane, Price asked his boss to share some details about his difficult childhood. As he started to wax nostalgic about his parents and the younger brother who died of tuberculosis, the usually stoic Nixon broke down in tears.

With his political moderation, rhetorical subtlety, and elite WASP pedigree, Price was a sharp contrast to another Nixon speechwriter, the right-wing, populist Catholic firebrand Pat Buchanan. Along with former public relations man William Safire, they formed what Garment called "the most celebrated writing threesome in presidential history." Whereas Price, according to Nixon biographer John Farrell, was "the most lyrical of Nixon's quite talented speechwriters and ghost writers," Buchanan embraced a more demagogic style, and a rivalry developed between the two men on the campaign trail as Price endeavored "to protect Nixon from the excesses of" Buchanan's hard-right views and penchant for inflammatory rhetoric.

"He kept trying to push the candidate into sort of Buchananism," Price recalled many years later. "But the candidate didn't want to be a Buchanan."

Once in the White House, Price and Buchanan competed constantly for the president's political and temperamental affinities. Speech drafts flew back and forth, according to Safire, with Nixon sending Price's versions to Buchanan for "toughening" and Buchanan's drafts to Price for "softening." While Buchanan penned what one former colleague described as "bang-bang-socko stuff" tailored to deliver red meat to Nixon's hard-core conservative base, Price wrote lofty homilies on aspirational themes such as "bridges to human dignity" and "black capitalism"—what Buchanan dismissively termed "blue-sky" rhetoric "full of magnanimity and hope." In their struggle for Nixon's favor, Price and Buchanan functioned as the figurative angel and devil on his shoulders, alternately stimulating the president's best and worst instincts. "The light side and the dark side are both there, and over the years these have been at constant war with one another," Price recounted. One noteworthy example of this interplay is the genesis of Nixon's famous "Silent Majority" speech. During the campaign, Price wrote a radio address for Nixon extolling "the great, quiet majority—those who pay their taxes, go to their jobs, perform their civic duties, send their children to school or college." Seventeen months later, when Nixon, as president, delivered a speech to the nation about Vietnam, the elitist intellectuals and antiwar protesters had apparently bullied the erstwhile "quiet" majority into abject muteness. Using a phrase Buchanan had coined after witnessing the bedlam of the 1968 Democratic convention, Nixon addressed "the great silent majority of my fellow Americans."

Described by the New York Times as having a "passion for anonymity," Price never discussed his sexual orientation on the record. Buchanan, asked for reminiscences of his former writing partner, replied tersely, "While Ray Price was a colleague and friend in the campaign of Richard Nixon and the White House, I have no knowledge of his private life." This assertion was doubted by Suzanne Garment, Len Garment's widow, who became friendly with Price after the Nixon administration's ignominious end. "I think his friends were aware that he was gay," she said, adding that Price benefited from "a version of 'don't ask, don't tell' that had its own species of kindness attached. It left people alone but at a cost" of becoming a nonperson should their secret be detected. According to Dwight Chapin, Price's homosexuality "made absolutely no difference with Nixon the man

I knew," who, though he might "tell a gay joke with Bebe Rebozo," did not allow his homophobia to preclude him profiting from the inspired oratory crafted by a gay man. In this sense, Nixon's close personal and professional bond with Price resembled those he enjoyed with Jewish advisors like Garment, Kissinger, and Safire—trusted confidants all, but token members of a group he privately denigrated.

* * *

As THEY HAD FOR BRIG ANDERSON, the photographs arrived in an unmarked envelope. What they exposed was a secret: a younger, naked Joe Alsop locked in a sensual embrace with another man.

In the thirteen years since the KGB ensnared him in a Moscow honey trap, Alsop had never allowed the knowledge that Soviet and U.S. officials were aware of his "act of very great folly" to inhibit him from criticizing either government. The only impact of the incident upon his work was that he had to forswear travel beyond the Iron Curtain. Still, the possibility that those who wished to harm him might publicize the episode hovered constantly. In a phone call with his defense secretary Robert McNamara a month after the Walter Jenkins affair in November 1964, President Lyndon Johnson expressed frustration with Alsop's citation of a confidential Pentagon strategy memo in his column. Johnson ordered McNamara to find the source who leaked the document and, as an aside, asked McNamara if he had read Alsop's FBI file.

"No, sir, I haven't," McNamara replied.

"Well, you better read it. You better read it," the president said, preparing for a characteristic flourish of exaggeration. "Because Walter Jenkins is just minor . . . He's been involved in practically every capital of the world. . . . I just read it the other night. Tell Bill Moyers you want to see it."

Though Alsop remained married to Susan Mary, practically everybody who knew them saw through the pretense of their relationship, which, many years later, she would describe to her grandson as akin to "living in an Edgar Allan Poe story." While Alsop's homosexuality may not have been much of a secret within these rarefied circles, the explicit photographs that circulated across Washington in 1970 startled the friends and enemies who received them. Prominent among the latter was Art Buchwald, the *Washington Post* humorist whose play mocking Alsop, *Sheep on the Runway*, had opened on Broadway earlier that year. A farce, it followed the exploits of a pretentious WASP columnist named Joseph Mayflower who invents a war in a faraway Asian country for the express purpose of writing jingoistic articles about it. The premiere created a social crisis for Washington's journalistic elite, with the decision whether to attend "a litmus test of loyalty" either to its playwright or his target. (Ben Bradlee, by now editor of the *Post*, accepted the invitation along with Lem Billings, Arthur Schlesinger, and Ethel Kennedy, while his boss, Katharine Graham, politely declined.) The long-running feud between Alsop and Buchwald was one of the city's most notorious, to the point where "every party-giver in town knew better than to put them on the same guest list," according to *Post* gossip columnist Maxine Cheshire. All the same, Buchwald did not let his strong personal and ideological aversion to Alsop override his conviction that a man's sex life was his own business. "It scared the hell out of me," Buchwald later said of the unsolicited offering. "I'm not comfortable with getting photographs of people in compromising positions in the mail."

After Alsop heard about the mysterious mailings, he asked CIA director Richard Helms for advice. Helms was more enlightened on the issue of homosexuality, and possessed a more nuanced understanding of blackmail, than his predecessors at the agency. Concerning the case of Alfred Redl, the infamous Austro-Hungarian colonel whose treachery convinced Allen Dulles and a whole generation of intelligence professionals to bar gay men and women from their spy services, Helms concluded that "homosexual activity was a criminal offense in the Austro-Hungarian Empire, but it was not necessarily at the root of his recruitment." To preempt a possible leak of the photos, Alsop asked Helms if he ought to acknowledge his homosexuality publicly, as he had contemplated doing when he was initially compromised. Helms cautioned Alsop against doing anything under duress, as that would only hand his blackmailers a victory. He said he would "quietly tell the KGB to knock it off," which he did by having one of his agents inform a Soviet contact that unless his comrades "stopped attempting to peddle this sordid story, the agency would respond in kind, and with enough data to compromise several KGB officers." Never again were indecent photographs of Joe Alsop disseminated across Washington.

At no point in his life did Alsop comment publicly on the KGB's attempt to blackmail him, which backfired in that it only intensified his already ardent anticommunism. "I have never been under the illusion that the Soviet form of government was anything but inherently aggressive and, for the most part, ferociously repressive," Alsop recalled of his first and only visit there. "This particular journey did little to change my view." Facing the threat of exposure, Alsop might have chosen to temper his Cold Warrior rhetoric so as not to antagonize his Soviet would-be blackmailers. Instead, he did the opposite, becoming hawkish to the extreme. "Walter Lippmann would read [Alsop's] columns with a sick feeling and tell friends that if Johnson went to war in Vietnam, at least 50 percent of the responsibility would be Alsop's," wrote David Halberstam in his chronicle of the war's origins, *The Best and the Brightest*. Though in his later years, Alsop would gradually come out to a small circle of friends, none ever recalled him discussing the Moscow incident, and, as many closeted gay people do, he often spoke disparagingly of other homosexuals. "I assumed that Joe was homophobic because he frequently ridiculed gays in private conversation," recalled David Satter, a protégé of Alsop's in the 1970s who went on to cover the Soviet Union as a foreign correspondent. "It was only later that I understood that that was his way of concealing his orientation and warning people off any attempt to hint at it."

In 1985, Satter penned a piece for the *Wall Street Journal* about the tactics that the Soviet intelligence services used to intimidate foreign journalists such as himself. Those who reported critically from the country, he wrote, were vulnerable to KGB "provocations," namely, the spreading of lies and innuendo designed to intimidate them. "He may not be confident that in the face of an accusation by the Soviet government of 'hooliganism,' 'espionage' or 'homosexuality,' his newspaper would be ready to believe him and not the Soviets," Satter observed. "Being honest means taking a risk."

Satter had not been in regular correspondence with Alsop for years, but the article provoked an admiring letter from his former mentor, who having found himself in just such a situation as Satter described, resolved to stand by his political convictions, his country, and his journalistic integrity and risk the revelation of his secret. "I remember reading it at the time and being convinced that I had said something that affected Joe very deeply," Satter remembered. "I wasn't sure what it was. Now I know."

27

"WE ARE IMPATIENT"

WHEN A GROUP OF MATTACHINE SOCIETY MEMBERS PROPOSED THAT A gay candidate throw his hat into the ring for the race to become Washington, DC's, first nonvoting delegate to Congress in early 1971, the question of who that candidate should be was obvious. Frank Kameny was initially skeptical of the idea that he run for public office, but the decision was made for him by a group of eager young activists who had already begun printing campaign posters and flyers emblazoned with his name. Kameny finally relented, but he was modest about his aims. "We don't expect to win, of course," he wrote a friend, "but merely to try to get enough votes to provide a show of strength in the one commodity which no politician or office-holder can ignore—Votes." To get on the ballot for the March 23 election, Kameny would have to acquire five thousand signatures, not an easy feat in a city where his natural constituency had good reason to fear affixing their names to a government document in support of an openly gay political candidate. "It was inconceivable," remembered the early Mattachine Society member Paul Kuntzler, who agreed to be Kameny's campaign manager. "I thought, gay people are so closeted. They're not going to sign."

To the welcome surprise of Kameny and his merry band of volunteers, however, a requisite number of Washingtonians were receptive to the notion of an "avowed homosexual" representing them on Capitol Hill. "We intend to remind a government and a country, which seems in many ways to have forgotten it, exactly what Americanism means," Kameny affirmed after submitting his nomination papers. "That this is a country of personal freedom and individual diversity; that Queen Victoria is dead, and the Puritans are long gone."

One of those Puritans begged to differ. "The Mattachine Society of Washington, a national organization of sexual perverts who strive for full equality as a matter of law, now announce that they have organized a political party in Washington, DC, and are fielding a candidate for the District of Columbia Delegate election," declared Democrat John R. Rarick of Louisiana in a speech from the House floor, before getting in a crack at a timeworn target. "The candidate estimates that 10 percent of the people of our Nation's Capital are homosexuals—he does not indicate whether or not he has included State Department employees in his account."

Though the campaign of the "first publicly declared homosexual to run for Congress" was a shoestring affair, it could draw on the resources of something that, while small and fledgling, could now genuinely be called a gay "community." Regency Baths owner David Harris was the largest donor to Kameny's campaign, and Lynn Womack produced its paraphernalia on his printing press for free. The ragtag Kameny team set up shop in a four-story building overlooking Pennsylvania Avenue, from which they hung a giant Kameny for Congress sign outside the windows. ("Old J. Edgar can't miss that banner," one volunteer snickered.) When the local chapter of the Legion of Decency announced that it would protest a performance of the musical *Hair* at the National Theatre nearby, Kameny's campaign released a statement supporting the celebration of hippiedom. "We are firmly convinced that if Jesus Christ were here today he would be in the National Theater approving and applauding and very probably participating as a member of the cast of *Hair*, knowing that *Hair* is a truer representation of Christianity than the dour, joyless pickets out here," it declared. During the performance that evening, the production's grateful cast carried Kameny for Congress placards onto the stage.

For the first time in Washington, gays and lesbians were receiving a steady stream of press not for threatening national security, lurking in public bathrooms, being fired from their jobs, or corrupting youth, but rather for something positive: civic engagement. In the many interviews he gave and lectures he delivered, Kameny spoke of his campaign as a patriotic effort on behalf of the nation's homosexual minority, the latest chapter in a long tradition of marginalized people claiming their place within the main-stream of American life. "The past has forced us to emerge today as homo-sexual Washington citizens, just as much was made, not long ago, of the fact that a presidential candidate was a Catholic," Kameny said, in a com-parison that probably struck most of his fellow Washingtonians as bizarre if not blasphemous. "But his very candidacy itself relegated his religion to its proper role as his own private concern alone, and he served society as a citizen, not as a Catholic, and our country was the better for his having so served. We hope that my candidacy will, in due course, relegate our private lives to matters solely of our own concern, that we too will be able to serve society fully as citizens, not as homosexuals, and that our city will be the better for it." As much as he was known around Washington as "the gay candidate," however, Kameny abjured a single-issue campaign, issuing position papers on many different subjects and accepting every speaking invitation that came his way.

Two weeks before the election, Kameny mailed a letter to one of his potential constituents asking for a meeting. "We feel, with considerable justification, that our government has declared and waged a relentless war upon us," he wrote to President Nixon.

> We are impatient with our second-class status, and are quite prepared to wage a counter-war against our government by every lawful means. That such a state of warfare should exist between our government and a large group of its citizenry who merely wish to contribute fully to society, is deplorable. The fault and the remedy both lie with *you*. It is to discuss these that I wish to meet with you.
>
> Mr. President, this country belongs to *all* of its citizens. As homosex-uals, this is *our* country, *our* society, *our* government, *our* Armed Ser-vices, and *our* government secrets, as much as those of the heterosexual majority.

Kameny proposed a meeting at the White House sometime the follow-ing week, and if that time was inconvenient, "An appointment at a later date will also be welcome."

The Kameny campaign elicited praise from influential corners. "Dr.

Franklin E. Kameny has put special emphasis on personal freedoms, running as an avowed homosexual pledged to represent all the people of the community," the *Washington Post* editorial board observed the Saturday before the election. "His contribution to discussions of civil liberties has been eloquent and erudite, and in this sense has already fulfilled his basic campaign objective." Actors Paul Newman and Joanne Woodward sent a check for five hundred dollars, which was used to buy the indigent candidate desperately needed suits for the campaign trail. On Election Day, Kameny finished fourth out of six candidates, with a total of 1,841 votes, or just 1.6 percent. Notwithstanding his disappointing result, Kameny could at least take pride in having accomplished something historic. "Kameny did not win," concluded the *New Republic*. "But he didn't lose either, for he got what he was after—serious attention to a subject in some places still regarded as taboo."

Aside from a few pranksters who egged Kameny's home, the response from the public varied from apathy to curiosity to enthusiasm. And the effect of his effort on the consciousness of gay people, both in Washington and beyond, belied his minuscule share of the vote. "It was during the Kameny campaign that the larger community and the media began to perceive gay people not as individual homosexuals, but as part of the 'gay community,'" Paul Kuntzler recalled. A volunteer from New York celebrated the sense of camaraderie the campaign fostered, building off momentum from the Stonewall uprising and offering gay people a common endeavor beyond barhopping and sex. "The fact of this cooperation demonstrates that the gay movement need not be a matter of isolated groups; that it can be rather a matter of solidarity with all varieties of cities and peoples working in common against our common oppression as homosexuals." To Eva Freund, the campaign offered "a glimmer" that "if we can get people into office, we can possibly escalate the change that's going to occur, eventually." Just the actuality of enthusiastic, proud gay people buzzing busily around a campaign office, passing out leaflets to passersby on the street, participating openly in the democratic process, and working toward a shared goal was a victory in its own right—and a welcome contrast to pseudonymous Mattachine Society members meeting secretly in a church basement. "The real meaning of the campaign," one volunteer observed, "was in its freedom, which periodically broke through the aura of fear. The campaign headquarters was a place of freedom where workers and members of the

Community felt safe. In this aspect . . . is the real meaning of what Frank Kameny did. Personal freedom was the hallmark of his campaign and this was the lesson for both straight onlooker and gay participant."

* * *

"WELCOME, DARLINGS, TO THE *GAY MILIEU OF WASHINGTON!*"

Visitors to the red stone town house occupied by the Gay Liberation Front at 1620 S Street could expect this hearty greeting, usually delivered by a bearded man in a dress wearing makeup. One of several revolutionary groups that formed in New York City following the Stonewall uprising, the GLF brought a vibrant militancy to the burgeoning gay movement. GLF members were younger, more radical, and less inhibited in their manners and appearance than the suit-and-tie- and skirt-and-blouse-clad members of Mattachine, whom they viewed as timid conservatives inordinately concerned with mainstream respectability. One of the tactics that the group pioneered was the "zap," a public confrontation with a figure deemed hostile to the advancement of gay equality, and a radical departure from Frank Kameny's orderly pickets and letter-writing campaigns.

The impetus to form a DC chapter of the group had been a letter in the June 1970 issue of the *Quicksilver Times*, an underground newspaper, written by a former Young Republican named Michael Yarr protesting the homophobic insinuation of a headline condemning Indonesia's military dictator: "Suharto Sucks." At a hastily called meeting later that month in the social hall of Georgetown's Grace Episcopal Church, a group of fifty gay men and women committed themselves to three goals:

1. To establish a sense of community among gay people
2. Self knowledge
3. Education of community at large—straights

In August, eight members of the group moved into the S Street house, establishing what came to be known as the "commune." Consistent with the era's hippie ethos, the GLFers fostered a laid-back and convivial ambiance, welcoming gay runaways evicted by their parents, antiwar protesters visiting from out of town, or anyone just questioning their sexuality. The atmosphere was one of whimsy and defiance. One flyer the group distributed, a *Questionnaire on Heterosexuality*, put readers in the shoes of gays and lesbians, constantly subjected to demeaning inquiries about their lives. "What do you think caused your heterosexuality?" "Why do heterosexuals feel compelled to seduce others into your lifestyle?" and "Why do you insist on flaunting your heterosexuality?" it asked. For Thanksgiving dinner, the commune served a turkey "stuffed with dope."

The first real test of the group's political mettle arrived unexpectedly on November 28, 1970, the weekend of the Black Panther Revolutionary People's Constitutional Convention. Heeding a call from Panther leader Huey Newton, who had written an open letter in August raising the possibility that "maybe a homosexual could be the most revolutionary," a large cohort of gay men and lesbians descended on Washington for the conclave. That evening, four gay men entered the Zephyr Bar and Restaurant on Wisconsin Avenue. "On any other night," wrote GLF member Brian Miller, "each man might have made the little behavioral adjustments that gays in 1970 automatically made when entering an overwhelmingly straight environment." But having spent the entire day being inculcated with revolutionary rhetoric, they determined that "camouflage would be a betrayal of all the visions of liberation [they] had dancing in their heads." Waiting to be served at the counter, two of the men started stroking each other's backs affectionately, and before long the Zephyr's manager told the group to leave. Unwilling to take this discrimination sitting down, the group decided to "zap the Zephyr." Back at the commune, they assembled about fifty homosexuals drawn from the ranks of the GLF and delegates to the Panther convention, some wearing makeup and female clothing, into a caravan of cars and drove back to the restaurant. Chanting Kameny's slogan, "Gay is good" (inspired by the Black Power chant "Black is beautiful"), the gaggle of gays barged into the Zephyr. Someone put a coin into the jukebox and, as patrons looked on aghast, two men started dancing together, a punch was thrown, and an all-out brawl ensued. Glasses were hurled across the room, salt and pepper shakers were torpedoed at the liquor shelves behind the bar, the front window was smashed, and fighting spilled out onto the streets. Police arrived on the scene and arrested twelve of the gays, taunting them as "fags" and "fairies" as they loaded them into paddy wagons. "There was a Stonewall equivalent, almost, in Washington," is how one participant recalled the melee. "The mood among the gay folks said, 'It's going to cost you to do what you did to us.' And it did. The place was trashed."

"The DC Twelve," as the arrestees were known, became a cause célèbre.

One of their defense lawyers, a recent law school graduate named Renee Hanover, identified an opportunity in what she believed was the first group trial of homosexuals in American legal history. During voir dire, Hanover requested permission to ask potential jurors if they felt "homosexual prejudice." Had the judge not later dismissed the case due to witness tampering on the part of the police, Hanover's line of questioning would have been the first time that the issue of antigay discrimination was raised in the jury selection process.

While women initially constituted about a quarter of the GLF's membership, the tendency of men in the group to campily call each other "queens" and "Miss," in addition to other behavior deemed chauvinistic, sparked a female exodus. "There were some women in GLF but they got tired of fighting with the enlightened men for the right to participate in the decision making as well as serving the coffee and cleaning up after meetings," Eva Freund recalled. The frustration many lesbians felt toward gay men at the time was scathingly expressed by Nancy Tucker at a June 1971 GLF meeting. Entitling her remarks, "Fuck You, 'Brothers,'" Tucker announced:

> I'm just leaving. Leaving because this organization and this movement offer me nothing. Why—they're based on (male) homosexual problems: entrapment, police harassment, blackmail, tea room assignations, venereal diseases. Christ, I can't relate to that kind of shit; it has no meaning whatsoever for me . . . I'm leaving because I'm tired of coping with massive male egos, egos which cannot comprehend how anyone could want to have nothing to do with a male-dominated movement. If you cannot understand why I wish to withdraw, then my "liberated" brother, you are part of the problem.

That fall, seeking refuge from the male-dominated gay social world, a dozen women commenced their own experiment in communal living by commandeering three adjoining town houses in the Southeast quadrant of the city, far from Dupont Circle's gay ghetto. Dubbing themselves the "Furies" (in reference to the Greek goddesses with red eyes and snakes for hair who tormented Orestes for killing his mother), they were anticapitalist, antisexist, and dedicated to dismantling the patriarchy. "The story of the Furies is the story of strong, powerful women, the Angry Ones, the avengers of matricide, the protectors of women," declared the lead article in the inaugural issue of the collective's eponymous newspaper. Sharing chores and mattresses, they learned skills traditionally claimed by men, like car repair and handiwork.

As tends to befall utopian projects, earnest affirmations of airy, revolutionary ideals were eventually undermined by eternal human shortcomings, and neither the GLF nor the Furies lasted for more than a few years. "Everything had to be a really heavy philosophical decision," remembered one frequent visitor to the GLF house, "right down to who did the dishes." Bruce Pennington, the hirsute GLF leader who often greeted guests at the town house in drag, sardonically cited the mantra "More revolutionary than thou" to illustrate the atmosphere of left-wing purity and one-upmanship that contributed to the GLF's demise. However admirable their intent, the GLFers' dedication to radical openness could sometimes veer into the naïve, as appeared to be the case with some of the suspicious characters who traipsed through their doorway. Recalling how "funny things would happen" around the house, Pennington cited the obviously heterosexual man who came in one day asking how to dress up like a drag queen. "I think he was an undercover cop," Pennington would later say. "He insisted on wearing highly polished black brogues in an attempt at being gaily fashionable."

Pennington was right to be suspicious. Like many American cities in the early 1970s, Washington, DC, was a hive of left-wing political activism. Both local and federal law enforcement agencies enlisted thousands of informants to monitor, infiltrate, and, in some cases, disrupt the many radical groups operating nationwide, one of which was the GLF. In the case of the utopian gay enclave at 1620 S Street, their primary agent provocateur was a down-on-his-luck homosexual from the West Virginia hill country named Robert Merritt. In September 1970, an undercover DC police detective and "master of disguise" named Carl Shoffler recruited Merritt after nabbing him for writing a series of bad checks totaling $225. Initially, Merritt provided Shoffler with daily reports on the local drug trade. Then, he spied on antiwar activists. Proving successful in these assignments, Merritt was ordered to expand his remit to the burgeoning gay activist scene. According to Merritt, agents in the police Intelligence division ordered him to infiltrate the GLF, collect details on the sex lives of its members ("to discredit Bruce Pennington" specifically), and obtain information about gay institutions that could be used to cause trouble with their landlords (one gay-owned print shop was put out of business due to such tactics). Working on a fifty-dollars-per-week stipend under the code name "Butch," Merritt wheedled his way into the GLF house by developing a sexual relationship with one of its members.

Merritt's interactions with law enforcement officials suggested that their attitude toward gays had barely evolved since the dark days of McCarthyism. "The gays were becoming a large and powerful movement," they told Merritt, and "gay liberation was a Communist conspiracy like the civil rights movement in the South, with the Communists trying to create turmoil and revolution." The sudden efflorescence and diversity of gay activism—ranging from the besuited, straitlaced Kameny to the cross-dressing, free-spirited GLFers—befuddled the cops. "The police were very disturbed about the fact that gay people weren't stereotyped any more," Merritt recalled. "They were very mad about it. They said they couldn't recognize them any more." Particularly concerning was Kameny, whose congressional campaign they suspected was being secretly funded by Communists.

In October 1971, per instructions communicated to him over the phone, Merritt was told to meet an FBI agent "disguised, wearing old clothes" in front of a drugstore. On the appointed day, Merritt followed the man several blocks to a station wagon in which another agent was waiting for them. The pair drove him to the waterfront Potomac Park, where they proceeded to ask him a series of questions about his sex life and what sort of men he preferred. The agents then asked him to list any prominent people who were gay or rumored to be gay, and to confirm whether anyone on a list of prominent left-wing senators and congressmen was homosexual. "The first person I named was J. Edgar," Merritt recalled. "They pretended to be insulted."

The FBI added to Merritt's responsibilities as an agent provocateur within the GLF, ordering him to spread false rumors about other gay activists being bureau informants, to place anonymous phone calls to African American gays telling them they weren't welcome at GLF meetings, and even to steal money from donation boxes. Both the police and FBI wired Merritt for sound, making him record telephone conversations with Kameny and meetings of the Gay Activists Alliance, a local group. By May 1972, Merritt had had enough, and he purposely filed a false report with his FBI handlers in the hope that the Bureau would drop him as a source.

They did, but not, according to Merritt, before issuing a threat: "We'd sure hate to have someone find you in the Potomac wearing cement galoshes."

* * *

WASHINGTON'S FIRST GAY BOOKSTORE shared space in a town house with the Defense Committee for the Black Panthers, the Youth International Party ("the Yippies"), and the *Gay Blade*. "We used to joke that the building was only held together by all the wiretaps the FBI had placed there," Deacon Maccubbin, founder and owner of Lambda Rising, recalled. Upon opening the front door to the building, one could either turn left into the bookstore, right into a head shop, or walk straight up the stairs to the offices of the Black militants and beatniks. The store's cloistered location, which allowed customers to slink in unobtrusively from the street, was deliberate, Maccubbin said, a reflection of "what the mentality was at the time" for gay people in Washington.

Lambda's creation was accidental. One day in 1969, as a National Guardsman with antiwar convictions and homosexual "tendencies," Maccubbin mustered the courage to call Frank Kameny to ask for advice on a way out. Kameny advised Maccubbin to tell his commanding officer he was gay, which Maccubbin promptly did. The confession earned Maccubbin the discharge (albeit dishonorable) he sought, and he began hawking underground comic books on the corner of Wisconsin Avenue and M Street, in Georgetown, to make ends meet. "Get your dirty comics here!" he cried to passersby. "Sex, drugs and revolution in a comic book! Mickey Mouse was never like this!" It was a surprisingly lucrative trade, the $250 he earned in one afternoon a good omen of profits to come.

Maccubbin, however, had nobler aspirations than peddling raunchy comic books off the street. Well into the 1970s, no bookseller in Washington was dedicated to selling the quality gay-themed literature and nonfiction that was then flowing from the pens of gay and lesbian writers. During these creatively fecund post-Stonewall years, the only places where one could find gay-themed material were dirty bookstores and newsstands such as the semi-open-air magazine shop on Fifteenth Street across from the U.S. Treasury. The selection was almost exclusively pornographic. "There were always men in there looking at porn and looking sideways trying to make contact," one customer recalled. "That's a block from the White House!" Walking through Greenwich Village sometime in

1973, Maccubbin experienced an epiphany when he happened upon the Oscar Wilde Memorial Bookshop, which, when it was established on Mercer Street in 1967, reputedly became the first gay bookstore in the world. He did some research and discovered that public libraries rarely collected volumes on gay subjects because they so frequently disappeared—either at the hands of moral scolds, who removed them from the shelves, or of gay readers, who, afraid to check them out, pocketed them instead. As a business proposition, opening a bookstore in Washington was a good bet in that the city was one of the most highly educated in the United States. But the ultimate reason Maccubbin decided to start Lambda Rising was civic, not pecuniary. "I want a bookstore so it will prove to other bookstores that there's a market for gay and lesbian literature," he resolved. "And eventually there won't be a need for a gay-specific bookstore because everybody will carry [it]."

With three thousand dollars of his own money and a thousand-dollar loan from a friend, Maccubbin opened Lambda Rising on June 8, 1974. Named after the letter from the Greek alphabet denoting kinetic potential that the Gay Activists Alliance in New York had chosen as its logo, the shop's initial inventory consisted of three hundred titles covering a diverse range of subjects. But Lambda's slogan, "Celebrating the Gay Experience," caused apprehension—for straights and gays alike. When Maccubbin tried to run an advertisement on a local television station, he had to make a strenuous case to its standards and practices department that it would not draw fire from the Federal Communications Commission. Meanwhile, to protect the privacy of his customers, many of them catalogue shoppers living in places far less accepting of homosexuality than the nation's capital, Maccubbin mailed books in plain brown packaging.

Despite these obstacles, Maccubbin knew his "mission" was on track when a visitor from Baltimore walked into the store one day soon after its grand opening. After turning a full 360 degrees in wonderment at the fully stocked shelves, this new customer exclaimed, "Home at last!"

28

THE CITY OF CONVERSATION

"PRECISELY BECAUSE THE OFFICIAL LIFE IS SO FORMAL," HENRY KISSINGER observed in his memoir, *White House Years*, "social life provides a mechanism for measuring intangibles and understanding nuances." According to the Nixon administration's leading grand strategist and most eligible bachelor, the Georgetown dinner party served a function greater than the quotidian enjoyment of food, drink, and gossip. Nothing less than the fate of the world hung in the balance. Around the supper table, "Moods can be gauged by newspapermen and ambassadors and senior civil servants that are not discernible at formal meetings," Kissinger wrote, bringing to bear on Washington social life the analytical discernment he usually reserved for nineteenth-century European diplomacy, nuclear weapons strategy, and the mentalities of Third World strongmen. "It is at their dinner parties and receptions that the relationships are created without which the machinery of government would soon stalemate itself."

The necessity of an impeccable guest list and proper wine pairings to the functioning of the American republic was well understood by the country's postwar generation of "Wise Men" (and women), who gathered regularly at one another's homes throughout the 1950s and '60s to devise foreign policy over martinis and canapés. It was in Joe Alsop's garden where, two days before imposing a fateful shipping quarantine on Cuba, President Kennedy interrogated his outgoing ambassador to France, Chip Bohlen, about the history of Russian responses to external military pressure. "With my little dinners," the philanthropist Gwendolyn Cafritz boasted in 1966, "I like to feel I am helping to save Western civilization."

Among the least-remembered depredations of Richard Nixon's presidency was the pall it cast over Washington social life. The president and First Lady rarely danced together at White House functions, which always ended long before midnight, a far cry from the glittering days of Camelot, when parties lasted until 4 a.m., or the hoedowns thrown by Lyndon Johnson, who, cornpone gesticulations aside, could dance anybody under the table. Just over a year into Nixon's presidency, Jack Anderson complained that a "Square Society" had been imposed on the nation's capital, which one distressed society matron described as "Dullsville-on-the-Potomac."

By virtue of necessity, the traditional Washington dinner party would undergo a dramatic, democratic transformation during the Nixon years thanks to a new breed of society host. A city of transients whose social pecking order shifts constantly with the political winds, Washington lacked a native aristocracy, a trait that distinguished it from other American cities like Atlanta, Boston, or Philadelphia where established families, private clubs, and parochial customs dominated the social whirl. "Washington is about the only town in the world where the word 'nouveau' is laudatory, where the least known people often have the greatest chance of making it," a writer for the *Washington Post* named Sally Quinn observed in 1974. Wealth, breeding, and diplomas from the right schools were never prerequisites for entry into Washington high society, a characteristic the city shared, incidentally, with gay society, wherein "a good-looking man with charm has instant status, whether or not he went to college, whatever his lineage, money, debts or office," as a then closeted federal government official once described it. "Because you are gay, you could walk into any room of gay people and find a place," Bob Witeck, who worked as an aide to Senator Bob Packwood in the 1970s, said. "You'd fit in. No matter how awkward it was, especially if you were young and attractive." There had long been a bull market in Washington for what society writer Myra MacPherson identified in 1966 as "that priceless party commodity, extra men," the demand for which gays were uniquely suited to supply. It was not until the 1970s, however, that gay men would graduate from the sidekick status of walkers—"elegant gofers," in the dismissive words of Garry Wills—to that of social gatekeepers and trendsetters.

The most visible of these men was Steve Martindale. The twenty-eight-year-old from Pocatello, Idaho, first made his mark in 1972 with a party for John Lennon and Yoko Ono. The celebrity couple were facing a celebrity problem: stymied in their effort to establish residency in the United States on account of Lennon's arrest for marijuana possession, they were desperately trying to locate Ono's eight-year-old daughter whom her ex-husband had absconded with upon joining a cult. Martindale, who had met the ex-Beatle and his Japanese artist muse at a party in New York City, offered to assist by hosting an event in Washington to which he would invite all the powerful and influential people he could muster, and where the couple could plead their case.

Washington, it has been said, is Hollywood for ugly people. The nation's political capital has its own culture of celebrity, one that ranks the city's denizens according to the power they wield rather than, as in the nation's entertainment capital, the fame they've achieved. When real star power comes to town, however, Washingtonians tend to sit up and take notice. This was especially the case during the doldrums of Richard Nixon, whom, in contrast to Jack Kennedy, Hollywood loathed. At the sparsely decorated home he shared with two other young bachelors in the tony Wesley Heights neighborhood north of Georgetown, Martindale assembled an impressive crowd for his evening with John and Yoko, including Senators Alan Cranston of California and Charles Percy of Illinois, ex-CIA officer and columnist Tom Braden, and the former chairman of the DC city council. Sporting a coat and tie and cowboy boots, Lennon contrasted his plight with that of another English rock star who had also run afoul of American law. "I'm the one who suffers because I sing 'Give Peace a Chance' and Jagger sings 'Honkytonk Woman,'" Lennon lamented as the starstruck attendees listened with rapt attention.

Martindale's was an unlikely path to Washington social renown. Raised by a pair of strict Mormon schoolteachers, he dropped out of law school at the University of Idaho to work on Nelson Rockefeller's failed campaign for the 1964 GOP presidential nomination. Later, upon Rockefeller's suggestion, Martindale dropped out of Harvard graduate school to take a job with another liberal Republican, New York senator Charles Goodell. "Steve, never has anyone so young had so much power for such a short time as you," Rockefeller once told Martindale. (At least that's what Martindale, an inveterate name-dropper, *said* Rockefeller told him.) A mere two years after throwing his party for John and Yoko, Martindale became a vice president at Hill and Knowlton, the country's oldest and most prestigious public relations firm. By day, the polished young politico held court at Washington's most exclusive restaurant, Sans Souci, with a telephone stationed at his table. By night, he was out on the town, attending parties or, almost as often, hosting them for figures ranging from Pentagon Papers leaker Daniel Ellsberg and the actress Maureen Stapleton to the cast of a Tom Stoppard play being performed at the Kennedy Center and the choreographer Martha Graham. But for Israeli prime minister Golda Meir's emergency visit to Washington a week after the Yom Kippur War, then vice president–designate Gerald Ford and his wife, Betty, would have attended that last one, Mrs. Ford having once danced in Graham's company. "Competing against Golda Meir is really something," Martindale marveled. Soon, Martindale was throwing a party nearly every week, an impressive feat for a man whose parents never entertained guests during his childhood.

It was, as George Packer writes in his biography of another, hugely ambitious and contemporaneous young Washingtonian, the diplomat Richard Holbrooke, the era of "Washington before restaurants," when an invitation to the right dinner party conferred an enviable social prestige. And Steve Martindale sent many of those invitations. He represented a new class of Washington power broker: younger, brassier, less concerned with formalities and conventions. "Anything Clark Clifford can do, I can do cheaper," proclaimed his business cards, playfully challenging one of the original Washington fixers. Although a Republican (of a decidedly liberal bent), Martindale achieved, in the words of one society columnist, the rare distinction of "nonpolitical Washingtonian" in that he would "give a party for anyone, regardless of politics." "Steve was magical. He was a great guy," his friend Dudley Cannada recalled. "Very good looking. Very gregarious and talented in so many ways. He had a wonderful voice. He could emcee and sing and do an event. Also a little in the closet." Whereas that last feature would have made a figure like Martindale inconceivable in Washington only a few years earlier—when grandes dames like Perle Mesta, Evangeline Bruce, Susan Mary Alsop, Gwen Cafritz, and Marjorie Merriweather Post ruled the roost—by the middle of the 1970s, a discreetly gay society host was not only possible, but in some ways preferable.

That's because, by the early 1970s, the gulf separating the once mutually uncomprehending worlds of gay and straight had started to narrow, part of a broader cultural shift toward the acceptance of alternative lifestyles, radical individualism, and sexual freedom. Before 1970, only one in twenty marriages ended in divorce. Ten years later, that figure had ballooned to one out of every two. Indicative of the change was the platform adopted by delegates to the 1972 Democratic National Convention, which endorsed "[t]he right to be different, to maintain a cultural or ethnic heritage or life-style, without being forced into a compelled homogeneity." Throughout the "Me Decade," as Tom Wolfe christened the 1970s, books like *Looking Out for #1* and *Open Marriage* shot to the top of best seller lists, and by the end of it, 39 percent of all Americans (and nearly 60 percent of young Americans) agreed with the statement "People should be free to look, dress, and live the way they want."

Adultery, nudism, "swinging" (Kissinger humorously referred to himself as the "Secret Swinger"), pornography, legalized abortion: all these were manifestations of an evolving ethic of sexual freedom that made homosexuality seem less alien and threatening to the heterosexual majority. Within the decade, twenty-two states repealed their sodomy laws, forty cities ratified ordinances prohibiting discrimination on the basis of sexual orientation, and more than a hundred private corporations extended antidiscrimination protections to gay employees. "Deep Throat," *Washington Post* reporter Bob Woodward's alias for his anonymous source in the emerging Watergate scandal, was the title of a 1972 pornographic film and the name of a sexual act that, while alien to most women born before World War II, was hardly unfamiliar to women born after, never mind gay men. Popular men's fashion and personal grooming habits, once typified by the loose-fitting suit, tightly collared shirt, and H. R. Haldeman buzz cut, became more body-hugging, more revealing, more blow-dried, more mustachioed, more . . . gay. In October 1969, four months after the Stonewall uprising, the *Washington Post* proclaimed that the sort of open and assertive gay world found in New York and San Francisco was "unthinkable" in the nation's capital. Just four years later, the paper announced that "for the first time since at least the advent of Christianity, the wall between the homosexual and society has begun to crack."

These sweeping, tectonic changes had a ripple effect on Washington social life as the old doyennes were supplanted by what the writer Laurence Leamer termed the "mediacracy." If the city's power elite had once been comprised of male politicians and a handful of veteran hostesses, the new establishment was a "public aristocracy of people important in the media and people who gain power through the media" and for which traditional barriers to entry no longer applied. The fall of Richard Nixon and the rise of a more adversarial press, the damage wrought to American prestige in Vietnam, the rise of the women's and gay liberation movements—such phenomena were making Washington a city less deferential to those in power and more willing to extend power to those without it. Leamer pointed to the Gridiron Club, a Washington institution dating back to 1885, as exemplifying the change. Since the Gridiron's founding, every president except Grover Cleveland had spoken at its annual dinner, an exclusive, all-male, all-white (literally up to its white-tie dress code) affair at which the most prominent journalists performed a musical revue roasting the nation's leaders. It was not until 1972 that the Gridiron welcomed syndicated columnist Carl T. Rowan as its first African American member, and in 1975 it admitted its first woman, UPI White House correspondent Helen Thomas.

Observing the Washington social scene of an earlier era, Allen Drury wrote, "Any bitch with a million bucks, a nice house, a good caterer, and the nerve of a grand larcenist can become a social success in Washington." Steve Martindale didn't have anything close to a million bucks. Nor was his bachelor pad—with its clashing furniture, broken door handle, toilet seat emblazoned with a peace symbol, and senators eating from plates positioned precariously on their laps—a candidate for *Architectural Digest*. "He had these old cable drums, wooden drums that telephone cable runs on," one close friend recalled. "Then he'd just turn them over and he'd staple a tablecloth on it. Plop candles on them. Put them in his room, turn the lights down, and boom! You had a party. And everyone came! Everyone." As for the food Martindale served, well, according to this friend, it "was just crap."

What Martindale did possess, and in abundance, was nerve, of a kind that enabled him to compile some of the most eclectic guest lists in the history of the nation's capital. The crowd at a typical Martindale affair consisted of a senator, a congressman, a prominent journalist, an administration personality like Rose Mary Woods, a local eccentric like Helen VerStandig (aka "Madame Wellington," proprietress of the costume jewelry franchise Wellington Jewels), and, if one happened to be visiting

Washington, a Hollywood star or starlet. Dennis Quaid and Michael York supped at Martindale's table, as did one of the decade's most memorable musical performers. "I was there for a dinner party with Cher," an attendee, Keith Henderson, remembered, "and she was kind of stoned out of her mind." A party for the author of a book about Jimmy Hoffa featured a posse of Teamsters, DC's mayor, Margaux Hemingway, and editors from *Playboy*, all munching on Ritz crackers with peanut butter and jelly. To fill the room, Martindale invited a few friends, and on those nights when he sprung for dining tables, he organized the seating arrangements boy, girl, boy, girl. Finally, there was "always at least one hustler there," according to Henderson, "posing as a waiter."

One party in particular earned Martindale such notoriety that Washington society would speak about it for decades with a mix of envy, loathing, and admiration. Preparing a birthday bash for a woman he barely knew but wished to impress, Martindale decided that he would have to do something drastic. A man deficient in the human quality some call shame and others call inhibition, he was the sort of person, of which there has never been a shortage in Washington, who looks over your shoulder at a party to see if someone more important is in the room. To upgrade the power quotient of his guest list, he contemplated the boldface names whose attendance guaranteed that the flower of Washington high society would follow. Among ladies, the choice was obvious. Alice Roosevelt Longworth had been living in the nation's capital since 1890 and was as much of an institution as any of the marble edifices lining the Mall. As for men, Henry Kissinger was positively brimming with social cachet. What made Washington hostesses "willing to do almost anything" to get him at their parties was his possession of "the ultimate symbol of status in Washington," at the time, a beeper.

His twin objectives in sight, Martindale endeavored to perform a feat that would either be lauded as a social coup or result in his reputational ruin. First, he dialed up Longworth. He was having a party, he would love for her to attend, and did he mention that Henry Kissinger would be there? Next, he put in a call to Kissinger's office, invited *him* to the affair, and said that Alice Roosevelt Longworth would be making an appearance. Martindale waited for the day of judgment to arrive, and when it did, so did both A-listers. The harebrained scheme succeeded, his party was a smash, and Steve Martindale solidified his status in the Washington social hierarchy.

President Richard Nixon meets in the Oval Office with Bob Haldeman, Dwight Chapin, and John Ehrlichman. Furious that he had not been selected for a White House job, Nixon confidant Murray Chotiner started a rumor that the three aides met regularly at the Watergate to "engage in homosexual and perverted activities."

The Gay Blade

October 1969   Vol. 1, No. 1
An Independent Publication Serving the Gay Community

BLOOD DRIVE LAUNCHED

The need for blood is crucial. Do help! Members and supporters of Mattachine are participating in a Red Cross blood donor program.

Give blood in the name of Mattachine (this is kept confidential). You will help the homophile movement and will make yourself, your immediate relatives and descendents (even if not related!) eligible for free blood for one year.

Join other gays in their first group donation. We'll meet in the main lobby of the Red Cross building at E St. between 20th and 21st NW between 5 and 6 pm on Mon., Oct. 13. Gay Is Good buttons will be given to all who participate.

The Homosexual Research Assn., Suite 5, 1350 N. Highland Ave., Los Angeles 90028 is advertising their porno at reduced rates. Don't buy! Models in movies and pictures are covered head to toe in black leotards.

Warning to Du Pont Circle people: Cars seen too frequently in the Circle area are having their license numbers taken down; their owners later are being harassed and blackmailed.

Is the gov't running a security check on you? Being blackmailed? Need draft counseling? Call Franklin Kameny, president of the Mattachine Society of Washington at 363-3881 for help on these and other legal complications of being gay.

New to DC bookstores will be The Same Sex, published by the United Church of Christ and containing literate articles by and about homosexuals. Should be available the third week in Oct.

Discussion group on "The Homosexual and the Medic" will be held in late Oct. Call 931-1272 for details.

Seriously looking for a roommate? Want a gay landlord? Call Gay Blade editors to register with the Blade's roommate referral service. Don't bother if you want to talk dirty. We won't listen. 234-0064 after 5 p.m.

Off-Broadway: "And Puppy Dog's Tails" is an amusing evening. Only one lament: "There's nudity -- but no passion!"

To contact the Gay Blade, call 270-2013 or 931-1272, 6-9 pm.

GAY LIBERATION FRONT

After raids on the Stonewall bar and the usual police harassment, the NYC gay community has formed the Gay Liberation Front. First to feel its influence was the Village Voice. As the result of a picket, the Voice agreed to change its ad policy and allow the word "gay" to be used, thus permitting GLF and other homophile groups to advertise. "Come Out," GLF's house organ, will appear in early Oct.

HOMOPHILE MOVEMENT AND COLLEGES -- Franklin Kameny, DC Mattachine president, spoke at American U's Kay Spiritual Center on Oct. 7 at the request of AU and Hillel. Topic was "The Homosexual Dilemma: What Every Heterosexual Should Know."

Also at AU: There's talk about having an all-college gay mixer dance in the DC area, similar to the one held last year at Columbia by its Student Homophile League.

SEE IF YOUR FAVORITE BAR CARRIES THE GAY BLADE. THE NEXT ISSUE WILL TELL YOU WHERE TO GET IT.

"Warning to Dupont Circle people," read the third item in the first issue of the *Gay Blade*, addressed to men who congregated in the park to cruise for sex. "Cars seen too frequently in the Circle area are having their license numbers taken down; their owners later are being harassed and blackmailed." The paper would be retitled the *Washington Blade* in 1980.

"Any bitch with a million bucks, a nice house, a good caterer, and the nerve of a grand larcenist can become a social success in Washington," wrote Allen Drury. What Steve Martindale lacked in money, a luxurious home, and culinary sophistication, he more than made up for in chutzpah. Here, in 1972, the twenty-eight-year-old social butterfly introduces John Lennon and Yoko Ono to Washington.

Midge Costanza (seated with back to camera) welcomes gay leaders—including her secret lover, Jean O'Leary (second from her left), and Frank Kameny (sixth from her right)—to the White House in March 1977.

Two months after the historic White House meeting, Lambda Rising bookstore celebrated the opening of its S Street location, which was unusual for a gay establishment at the time in that it had street-facing windows. "We were the de facto community center," owner Deacon Maccubbin, seen here in a white shirt smiling toward the camera, recalled. "We were the meeting place. . . . That's where [gay Washingtonians] brought their parents when they came out."

Discrimination in Washington gay bars led the city's Black gay community to start their own social organizations and nightclubs. By far the most popular was the Clubhouse, founded in 1975. Located in an abandoned car garage, the discotheque played an important role in the early development of house music.

Three months before the 1980 election, Republican congressman Jon Hinson of Mississippi announced at a press conference that he had been arrested at the Iwo Jima Memorial in 1976, and had barely escaped with his life from a fire at an X-rated Washington movie theater the following year. "I must be totally frank and tell you that both these places are frequented by some of Washington's homosexual community," he said.

Three weeks before the 1980 Republican National Convention, the *Washington Post* investigated allegations that Ronald Reagan was "in bondage" to a ring of homosexual advisors with "almost a religious zeal against communism." Among the key players in the scandal: Congressman Pete McCloskey (above), reluctantly permitting Reagan to slap a Reagan/Bush bumper sticker onto his Volkswagen.

Lynn Bouchey

Peter Hannaford

Congressman Bob Livingston (right), with Republican House minority leader John Jacob Rhodes. "I don't want to see the world run by a bunch of weirdos," Livingston told *Washington Post* reporter Bob Woodward. "If you guys ever prove it, it will be world-shaking."

All the First Lady's Men: Nancy Reagan with "first fop" Jerry Zipkin (left) and interior decorator Ted Graber (right). Zipkin, she enthused, was "a sort of modern-day Oscar Wilde."

With Rock Hudson at a state dinner for the president of Mexico in May 1984, a Kaposi's sarcoma lesion visible behind his left ear. After Hudson died from AIDS the following year, President Reagan struck the word "friend" from the draft of his and Nancy's public statement mourning the actor's death.

With fashion designer James Galanos

With hairdresser Robin Weir

With power lobbyist Bob Gray. Whenever the Reagan White House "wanted to find out if someone was loyal," one staffer recalled, it went to Gray.

THE DEEP BACKGROUNDER
Premier Issue

VOL. 1 NO. 1   MAY/JUNE

| The Washington Nobody Knows | Their Hearts Young and 'Gay' |

Homosexual Trade "In" Despite Recession

Headlines from the inaugural issue of the *Deep Backgrounder*. "No other publication," it declared, "has dared as yet to undertake such an in-depth examination with the goal of providing a complete overview of the Washington gay scene that is comprised almost totally of politicians, military personnel, lobbyists, bureaucrats, diplomats and other powerbrokers." The paper helped instigate the 1982 congressional page sex scandal.

MAY/JUNE   THE DEEP BACKGROUNDER   PAGE 3

Dial-a-Sex
'Call Boy' Ring Serving Elite Busted Up For The Moment

PAGE 4   THE DEEP BACKGROUNDER   MAY/JUNE

Homosexuals Create Problem In CIA
Deviates Among The Super Spies Threaten National Security

By Victor Marchetti

THE DEEP BACKG...

PAGE 10

Washington Nation's Homosexual Capital

Washington, D.C., the capital

One of the most important things to be kept in mind regarding the average

THE DEEP BACKGROUNDER   PAGE 9

The Homosexuals In The House

ITEM:

Craig Spence (right) at one of the many parties he hosted in his Kalorama mansion during the 1980s.

Terry Dolan, president of the National Conservative Political Action Committee. A 1987 *Washington Post* exposé about Dolan's secret gay life and death from AIDS so enraged his older brother, President Reagan's chief speechwriter, Tony Dolan, that he published a two-page advertisement in the *Washington Times* denouncing the *Post* and its editor, Ben Bradlee. "Homosexual intrigue" in the *Post* newsroom was so intense, the surviving Dolan brother wrote, that "poor Ben Bradlee has no one on whom he dares turn his back."

Carl R. "Spitz" Channell, president of the National Endowment for the Preservation of Liberty (NEPL), at one of the meetings he arranged for his pro-Contra organization's wealthy donors at the White House. The NEPL staff was "notorious in Washington" for being comprised almost entirely of gay men. "Those gay boys of Oliver North's were particularly good at going out and getting checks from rich women," one Defense Department official recalled.

The AIDS Memorial Quilt on the National Mall

This gambit was the genesis of "The Law of Twelve Which Makes Washington Whirl, and the Boy from Pocatello," a seven-thousand-word *Washington Post* feature written by Sally Quinn and published in June 1974. Occupying the entire front page of Style, the culture and society section founded in 1969 by *Post* executive editor (and Quinn's future husband) Ben Bradlee, and continuing for two full pages inside, the piece introduced readers to a man who was "bright but not brilliant, pleasant but not a wit, interested which makes him seem interesting, and, above all, attentive." Illustrated with a mock invitation announcing, "Steven A. Martindale requests the pleasure of your company," above a list of prominent figures who had attended one of his events, the article portrayed Martindale as personifying the recent disruptions to Washington's social landscape, where one's chance of success was determined by their adherence to a dozen "laws" ranging from "a very thick skin" to "an innate understanding of who's in and who's out, who to cultivate and who to stay away from." Much of the article consisted of various Washington personalities dumping on Martindale, the bulk of them anonymously. "Every town has one of these people," a "famous columnist" groaned. "You just have to put up with the Steve Martindales in Washington." One "frequent guest" confessed, "I love Steve," before proceeding to illustrate that affection in the way only a blind quote published in a major national newspaper can express: "He's such a baby. He really has nothing to offer, but in my stomach I feel sorry for him and I hate hurting people. I feel quite duped by him and yet I like him." Another ungrateful recipient of Martindale's hospitality admitted, "[H]e's everything my husband can't stand about this town but I just hate turning him down."

Surely more wounding to Martindale were the comments delivered on the record. "I don't go to his parties anymore," said the woman for whom Martindale had thrown the star-studded birthday bash, Tom Braden's wife Joan. "I haven't been for a year and a half. To tell you the truth I'm not very interested and I don't know much about him." "Who?" inquired Alice Roosevelt Longworth when asked about Martindale. "I wouldn't want to hurt his feelings. I don't want to be rude, but I just don't know who he is. He probably thinks he's very recognizable."

The most important career advice Quinn received as a budding society columnist came from a hard-boiled police reporter, who told her to cover parties "like they were crimes." Her profile of Steve Martindale read like the summary of a criminal investigation, if the suspect's offense was committing one too many social faux pas. "I would go out and think of it as a crime," Quinn recalled of her party coverage, "the hostess was the perp and the guests were the accessories." (Later, Quinn would say that discovering how Martindale achieved his social status "was like finding the cause of cancer.") Having quoted, either on or off the record, well-nigh thirty people disparaging Martindale, Quinn expressed her own judgment thusly:

> Never mind that many of the people he had invited, some for the fifth or sixth time, had turned down the invitation. Never mind that some of those who were present apologized to others for being there or made excuses. Never mind that Martindale hadn't ever been invited to many of his guests' houses himself, nor probably ever would be. From his point of view he had achieved what he wanted that evening.
>
> Steve Martindale is getting to be a controversial figure in Washington among those who make things move. To some he has emerged as the leading host in town. To others he is, well, a social climber.

"The Boy from Pocatello" was more than just a barbed profile of a Washington personality, or a commentary on the city's evolving social rites. It was also a subtle acknowledgment of gay men's ascendance into positions of prominence within Washington high society. "What baffles a lot of people around town is that nearly all the contenders for the vacated position of 'hostess with the mostest' are men," Quinn wrote of the aspiring successors to Perle Mesta, once the reigning queen of the Washington dinner party. One of Quinn's twelve rules for Washington hosts and hostesses was that they not "be a professional or sexual threat to any of his or her guests," a quality more easily attained by a discreetly gay man. And then there was the ambiguous remark from Martindale's own boss. "His entertaining is a mixed blessing for us and him at Hill and Knowlton," said the head of the firm's Washington office, former Eisenhower cabinet secretary Bob Gray. "It's fine for him to mix and be on a social basis with people who can help us. But there's a tremendous danger that he may be labeled as a male entertainer, a playboy, or that he may acquire a Perle Mesta image." Deliberately or not, Quinn captured an enduring Washington character in the Boy from Pocatello: the young and ambitious gay man from the hinterlands who, seeking to overcome the ostracism and hostility that are meant to be his fate, develops an acute social intelligence, hones it meticulously, and strikes out for the big city in pursuit of his dreams.

At the end of her profile, Quinn asked Martindale if he was planning for a career in politics, a decision that would likely mean moving back to Idaho. Martindale balked. "I guess once you've lived in Washington you can never go back to Pocatello."

* * *

THEY CAME FROM POCATELLO, Peoria, and Poughkeepsie; from Plano, Paducah, and everywhere in between. Inspired by a revolutionary change in social consciousness and a determination to seek personal fulfillment, gay men and lesbians migrated to cities in droves throughout the 1970s. Though San Francisco and New York developed the largest and most colorful urban gay subcultures, Washington was also a popular destination, and it attracted a particular type. "I think if you're smart and you have ambition, but you have this sort of huge secret, you have to find a different way to advance yourself," said Sean Strub, who moved to Washington from Iowa City in 1976 to attend Georgetown University. "You go to state capitals all over, you go to Harrisburg, you go to Des Moines, and there's a gay community in every single state capital."

As men like Steve Martindale ascended the Washington social ladder, so did some of them mimic the customs of their predecessors. During the heyday of postwar Washington social life, a friendly (and sometimes not-so-friendly) rivalry developed among the city's leading hostesses. "I think she's done very well for a woman," Gwen Cafritz once sniffed about her archrival Perle Mesta. When the hostess with the mostest publicly refused to shake Cafritz's hand, it made the newspaper, as did the photograph of their reconciliatory grip-and-grin three years later. Mesta also dueled with General Foods heiress Marjorie Merriweather Post (who divorced her fourth husband after being presented with photographs of him cavorting in the nude with young men at the oceanside pool of her Palm Beach residence, Mar-a-Lago).

A similarly competitive dynamic existed among a circle of socially prominent gay Washingtonians in the 1970s consisting of Martindale, former CIA officer and real estate magnate Bob Alfandre, Capitol Hill aide Tim Furlong, Teamsters spokesman Duke Zeller, and Bob Gray. "The gay community met at dinner tables" in the 1970s, one participant in that scene remembered. "It was the culture." Every week of the year, one could find an all-male party taking place behind the doors of a Georgetown manse, a countryside estate, or a Rehoboth Beach retreat. Some closeted men would call the host in advance for the guest list to avoid potentially awkward encounters. Robert Higdon, who came to Washington in 1979 to work for a senator, recalled "a gay world on the Hill where you went home and you had dinner with gay men, and you only socialized with gay men, but you went to work every day, and you were a straight man." Heterosexual women were often considered too great a risk to include at many of these events, ironically *because* of their tolerance. "The concept was if they are so comfortable with it, and they are in the straight world, and they don't know the boundaries and the little fences we get in between, they are much more likely in their work or whatever else to talk about who they saw at that party," remembered Dudley Cannada.

If the social currency of the postwar Washington hostess could be measured in the accumulated power of the people on her guest list, what generated esteem for their gay successors was the beauty of the boys on theirs. "There were subtle ways of one-upmanship socially that would go on in Washington, and it all involved the invitation list," remembered an habitué of the 1970s gay dinner party scene. "The prettiest boys currently working in various committees and various subcommittees up on the Hill" were a prized commodity. "If you were young and pretty, you had to know what your role was. Your role was to be eye candy, and that meant you had to wear clothing that was attractive, because you knew that as part of this entourage." One such piece of eye candy, Paul Dolinsky, was a twenty-three-year-old graduate student when a friend invited him to a Valentine's Day party at the Watergate. He had "no real understanding" of what to expect that evening when he walked into the two-story penthouse apartment, but he gradually "connected the dots that I was there as the entertainment." The apartment was filled with older men "in very powerful positions in the city," all there to celebrate the guest of honor visiting from New York: Leonard Bernstein. "I found out I was apparently the gift of the evening to Mr. Bernstein," Dolinsky said (a duty he was unable to fulfill after the maestro passed out drunk). Dolinsky had been let into the secret world of the "Chicken Ranch," an informal society composed of handsome twenty-somethings and their older admirers, most of whom worked in various branches of the Smithsonian Institution. The Ranch had loftier goals, too—namely, the social and professional advancement of its proverbial livestock. The members were "very supportive of gay young professionals and moving them into roles of leadership," Dolinsky said. "I am where I am because of the support of these individuals."

When Bob Gray first came to Washington in the 1950s, he had enough money to last for thirty days. But after serving in the Eisenhower administration and building up a client list at Hill and Knowlton whose collective economic output amounted to 16 percent of America's gross national product, he never again had to worry about the size of his bank account. With riches came a sexual confidence that, combined with the good looks of a distinguished older gentleman, was highly appealing to younger gay men. "He was the slickest character I ever met," recalled one of Gray's many sexual conquests. "He had sex with everybody. You couldn't shake his hand without having sex with him." In the words of another acquaintance, "every gay person knew Bob Gray," and Gray knew every powerful person in Washington. It was in large part due to this unique social position that he would remain closeted for the entirety of his long professional life, accumulating an impressive list of prominent women (like Rose Mary Woods) as beards. One can detect Gray's sensitivity around this subject in the title of his memoir of the Eisenhower administration, *Eighteen Acres Under Glass*, which equates the experience of working in the White House complex with having one's life placed under a microscope. "In D.C.'s top government, business, and social circles there is a division more marked and more damning than the one that separates Republicans and Democrats," Gray observed, and that was "the division of the 'ins' and the 'outs.'" It was Bob Gray's determination always to remain within the closet of power.

Though Gray's homosexuality was not much of a secret to the city's movers and shakers, the press protected him, albeit not always subtly. "No one thinks she'll marry Robert Gray," a *Washington Post* reporter mused in a profile of Woods, adding that Gray was "perfectly groomed, perfectly manicured." (The same piece described Steve Martindale as "another perfectly groomed man who works for Bob Gray . . . and has double-dated with the older couple.") In her 1978 memoir *Reporter*, Maxine Cheshire detailed "one of the oddest stories—potential stories—of my decades in Washington," the subject of which was a thinly disguised Gray. One day near the end of the Nixon administration, Cheshire wrote, a "very angry young man" called her from a pay phone to say that he was coming to the *Post* building bearing a "suitcase full of photos, letters, and canceled checks" that were "as bad as Watergate." When the man strode into Cheshire's office, he announced that he had "enough information, with documentation, to destroy the entire administration," and for over four hours, he "poured out a tale of such sordidness that it could never have been printed in the *Washington Post*." A former hairdresser who worked for a tony department store, the man claimed he was the "wife" of a "well-known Republican whose prominence in Washington dated back to the Eisenhower-Nixon years." Among the photos the young man shared with Cheshire was one in which he stood resplendent in a purple dress, wig, and white feather boa next to a "well-known lobbyist" whose "hand was inside the pants of the prominent Republican." Another photo, Cheshire alleged, was of a naked Richard Nixon in a bathtub. "His tale was a recitation of the mores and social customs of highly placed Washington 'gays,'" a world apparently consisting of "orgies, drug use, code names, blackmail, and even kangaroo divorce courts that awarded alimony." (Asked about this episode, one of Cheshire's former *Post* colleagues said that "she was a gossip columnist, so her standard for verification was that two people had heard the same rumor.")

While men like Gray locked themselves inside their closets, many others, embracing the spirit of gay liberation, took to the streets in exploration of their sexuality. Once relegated to the dimly lit grounds of Lafayette Square and Dupont Circle, the practice of cruising—"a fine art in Washington before the internet," one veteran connoisseur wistfully recalled—expanded to posher locales. "There were signals. There were ways of looking at each other; even these men at a cocktail party in Georgetown—they might all be there with their wives—they're all married," one gay attendee at many a Washington society soiree remembered. "There was a whole sort of subculture, a hieroglyphic [language] between each other, a very clear signal that said, 'I'm going to the bathroom and you should, too.'" On any given night around the intersection of Thirty-First and Dumbarton Streets in Georgetown known as "the Block," a parade of men could be found sauntering back and forth, eyeing one another in the hope of catching that flicker of mutual interest. "You would have thought you were in Grand Central Station the way things went on," recalled one frequent participant in this nocturnal ritual. Mini–traffic jams became a problem as cars rolled slowly up and down the street, their drivers surveying that evening's offerings. Henry Kissinger happened to live by the corner, and concerned by all this activity, had his security detail investigate. To their relief, the diplomatic protection agents discovered that the loiterers outside his house were interested not in Washington's most eligible bachelor but in one another. Soon, the agents and the cruisers were engaging in friendly banter.

Complaints by residents about all the libidinous young men roaming the neighborhood, however, eventually led the police to crack down. "It seriously put a damper on the cruising," Deacon Maccubbin recalled. But the cleanup operation had an unintended consequence. "Crime in that block went sky high, burglaries, assaults, everything started happening, because there wasn't anybody there on the block. The block was empty, and the crooks came in. And then the residents, the same ones who had complained before, told the police to leave them alone. They'd rather have a little bit of traffic and noise than have all the crime that came into the neighborhood."

★ ★ ★

IT ALL STARTED WITH A BREAK-IN.

Richard Nixon's political demise began not with the break-in at Democratic National Committee headquarters in the Watergate—a "third-rate burglary attempt," in the dismissive words of White House press secretary Ron Ziegler—but one on the other side of the country. On September 3, 1971, ten months before a contingent of White House Plumbers broke into the DNC, another group of presidentially sanctioned burglars trespassed into the Beverly Hills office of psychiatrist Lewis Fielding. They were searching for incriminating information about one of Fielding's patients, Daniel Ellsberg, a former defense analyst at the RAND Corporation think tank who had leaked a trove of confidential government documents about the history of American involvement in Vietnam (the so-called Pentagon Papers) to the New York Times. The leaking of these documents had inspired the creation of the Plumbers, and their effort to discredit Ellsberg—code-named "Special Project #1"—would lead to a series of illegal actions culminating in Nixon's resignation.

Beginning with the break-in at Fielding's office, homosexuality was a recurring theme over the duration of what became known as the Watergate affair. Discussing the need to discredit Ellsberg, Nixon invoked the ready-made parable of his lonely struggle amid a web of homosexual intrigue: the Hiss-Chambers affair. "I had to leak stuff all over the place," the president told Bob Haldeman and Henry Kissinger of his behind-the-scenes campaign to discredit Alger Hiss. "It was won in the papers." A similar approach was required for Ellsberg, the president believed. "You can't fight this with gentlemanly gloves." When John Ehrlichman designated a young White House aide, Egil "Bud" Krogh, to assemble the Plumbers unit, he advised him to read the chapter on the Hiss case in Nixon's book *Six Crises* so as to understand "what the president thought was at stake with Ellsberg's release of the Pentagon Papers and how the investigation should be approached." A subsequent FBI probe of Ellsberg located friends who spoke of his "latent homosexual tendencies" and "homoerotic aspects," and at one point the White House developed a theory (later shown to be baseless) that Ellsberg had been blackmailed by a male sex partner into handing over a portion of the papers, which the blackmailer gave to the Soviet embassy.

The task of burglarizing Fielding's office was assigned to E. Howard Hunt, a former CIA official who had led the abortive 1961 Bay of Pigs invasion, and G. Gordon Liddy, a Nixon aide. The goal, the duo allegedly told the Bay of Pigs veterans they recruited for the job, was to acquire embarrassing information about Ellsberg—ideally evidence of homosexuality—that would dissuade him from testifying against the administration in the same way that the FBI supposedly threatened Hiss's stepson Timothy Hobson from taking the stand in defense of his stepfather. When the Plumbers broke into Fielding's office, however, they turned up nothing incriminating about his patient, much less evidence that he was gay.

The homosexual smear was also a favored tactic of Nixon's "dirty tricksters." Donald Segretti—whose surname means "secrets" in Italian—was serving as a captain in the Judge Advocate General Corps in the spring of 1971 when his old college pal Dwight Chapin approached him with a proposal. Both men had earned their stripes in the cutthroat world of Republican student politics at the University of Southern California, where the use of sabotage against one's opponents, affectionately known as "ratfucking," was a well-honed skill. The White House, Chapin explained, needed an operative to head up a team of ratfuckers who would subvert and disrupt the campaigns of the president's Democratic rivals. One of their pranks, launched three days before the crucial Florida primary, involved mailing letters on stationery from the campaign of Democratic senator Edmund Muskie alleging that his competitor Henry "Scoop" Jackson had been arrested on a homosexual morals charge in the 1950s. Frank Mankiewicz, an aide to Sen. George McGovern, realized something fishy was going on when he saw people at rallies holding up placards for a nonexistent "Gays for McGovern" group and passing out unauthorized leaflets announcing "George McGovern supports Gay Liberation." The campaign "was so chaotic that no one put the incidents together" at the time, Mankiewicz said.

While Segretti plied his dirty tricks on the campaign trail, Charles Colson—once lauded by Nixon to Ray Price as having "the balls of a brass monkey"—masterminded operations from the White House. Early in the campaign, Colson instructed Roger Stone, a nineteen-year-old gofer in the Scheduling division of the Committee to Re-Elect the President (CREEP), to mail a two-hundred-dollar donation to the headquarters of Republican congressman Pete McCloskey (then challenging Nixon for the Republican nomination on an anti–Vietnam War platform) in the name of the Gay Liberation Front. Stone was hesitant to put his name to something that might later be used to suggest he was homosexual, and at the last minute, he listed the donation as coming from the Young Socialist Alliance instead. (Stone, who later became a protégé of Roy Cohn, would reportedly prowl gay bathhouses in New York City and place an advertisement on the internet seeking "studs for threesomes" with his wife.) A few weeks before the Democratic National Convention, an unemployed former government worker and CREEP member named Donald Disier received a phone call from a woman on behalf of Colson asking if he would be willing to attend the event and organize a demonstration of "Gay People for McGovern." Colson could offer $125 per day, and if Disier did a satisfactory job, Colson would consider him for "personal employment on the White House staff" in the second Nixon term. Disier declined. It was because of cockamamie schemes such as these that John Mitchell, asked by Price which constituency of Nixon voters Colson represented, replied, "The president's worst instincts."

The specter of homosexuality arose once more during the Watergate scandal, toward its denouement, as a means of discrediting one of the most important witnesses to Nixon's malfeasance. It was White House counsel John Dean's "boyish comeliness," wrote Star columnist Mary McGrory, that had convinced the president's senior aides to appoint him as an intermediary with hostile antiwar groups at the outset of the administration. Four years later, desperately seeking immunity in exchange for his testimony against the president, Dean allegedly invoked this same youthful visage to avoid spending time behind bars. In negotiations with prosecutors, reported Daniel Schorr on Walter Cronkite's CBS News broadcast, one of Dean's lawyers portrayed his client as terrified of going to prison because "his boyish appearance might make him a target for molestation." The former White House counsel, Joe Alsop chimed in, "is a smooth faced young man, who is reportedly obsessed by fear of going to jail because of his consciousness of his own good looks." Dean denied that he or his lawyer had ever made such an appeal, which he attributed to a White House smear operation. "How do I counter the image of an unethical, President-deceiving, fag-fearing squealer whose wife, it is rumored . . . has quietly left him because she unwittingly married the scum of the earth?" he plaintively asked his lawyer.

More than any presidential administration before or since, the Nixon White House was fixated on homosexuality. Tactically, the Nixonians weaponized the gay smear to an unprecedented degree against adversaries inside the administration and out. And on a conceptual level, Nixon's deep paranoia induced him to see hidden gay networks and schemes lurking behind the scenes. There is another, more profound way in which homosexuality intersects with the Nixon presidency, illuminating the administration and the man himself. Starting with the father of the nation—depicted in the fresco that adorns the eye of the Capitol Rotunda, *The Apotheosis of Washington*, as an angel ascending into heaven—Americans have idealized their presidents. "People identify with a President in a way they do with no other public figure," wrote Ray Price in a memo to his Nixon campaign colleagues in 1967. "Potential presidents are measured against an ideal that's a combination of leading man, God, father, hero, pope, king, with maybe just a touch of the avenging Furies thrown in." This propensity to venerate the commander in chief would be shattered forever thanks to the man Price served. Richard Nixon was the first president whose darkest personal and political secrets were unveiled while he was still in office. Before the White House tell-all—a genre that his presidency did more than any before it to popularize—became a Washington tradition, the thirty-seventh president was revealed as a man with a double identity. Prim and excessively formal in public, he was vulgar, vindictive, and criminal in private. Exposed to the world against his will, Nixon was, in a manner of speaking, the first American president to be "outed."

GERALD FORD

To grow up homosexual is to live with secrets and within secrets.

—Richard Rodriguez

29

THE ULTIMATE DEMOCRACY

"Enclosed is the Civil Service Commission's surrender document," Frank Kameny wrote in a letter to friends on July 8, 1975. "The war, which they have fought against the Gay Community since 1950, and against me personally since 1957 is over. We have won."

The government's "surrender document," a set of guidelines nullifying its prohibition on gay people from holding civil service jobs, had been promulgated five days earlier. It stipulated that gays could no longer be refused civilian employment, nor could they be fired solely on the basis of their sexual orientation. Agencies dealing with classified information were exempt, and the ban on security clearances still applied. It had only taken eighteen years, but Kameny's "litigation, cajolery, hounding, patience and perseverance" were finally beginning to show results.

But not without exacting significant personal costs for Kameny, "the constant, nagging problem of money for most of my adult life" foremost among them. From the day the Army Map Service fired him in 1957, Kameny scarcely had a full-time, decently paying job. Devoting himself to activism, he survived on meager lecture stipends, fees for representing people hauled before employment tribunals, and handouts. Correspondence over many years with Rea Kameny reveals an anxiety going far beyond that of the typical Jewish mother. "As I explained to you, your failure to file [a tax return] may cause a great deal of trouble in the future, for all of us, *financially* and *otherwise*," she wrote her forty-six-year-old son in 1972, attaching, for his edification, a collection of news clippings about people arrested for tax evasion, along with some others denoting the munificent speaking fees of various public figures. Replying to a letter from his mother urging him to invest in better optical and dental care, Kameny wrote, "No, I haven't done anything about either eyes or teeth because of lack of the two necessities—time and money, both of which are in uncomfortably short supply." After spending a few precious moments with her son at the 1973 New York Gay Pride celebration, Rea commented, "All these people I met on Sunday surely have regular incomes, while you, with all your ability, your potential, your work for everyone else, exist on crumbs, without even being able to get yourself a pair of glasses, which you need badly, and the lack of which I hope won't eventually do you harm."

The government's terms of surrender arrived two weeks late for attendees at Washington's first Gay Pride Day, officially recognized as June 22 in a resolution passed by the DC City Council. Deacon Maccubbin organized the block party outside his Lambda Rising bookstore. Every subset of the increasingly diverse gay community participated. The Eagle, a local leather bar, donated a sound system, a lesbian-feminist collective constructed the stage, and two dozen organizations set up tables distributing information about their activities. To protect the anonymity of government workers in attendance, organizers politely instructed news photographers not to take photos of participants without their explicit permission. At first, only about twenty people showed up, and Maccubbin worried that the event would be a failure. But eventually more than two thousand came.

In December, a citizen of the secret city emerged publicly from one of its most secluded corners: professional sports. Former Washington Redskins running back David Kopay was reading a series in the *Washington Star* about gay athletes when he decided that the time had finally come for him to speak openly about his experience as a closeted player in the National Football League. Upon disclosing his homosexuality in an interview with the *Star*, he became the first (retired) pro athlete to come out of the closet. Such acknowledgment from a public figure was practically unheard of in 1975 and would remain so for well into the next decade. That the most famous gay person in America would also be a former professional football player challenged the stereotype of homosexuals as weak and effeminate. The reaction to Kopay's announcement was mixed; while he inspired many with his honesty, the *Star* received a deluge of hate mail. The morning the article appeared, one particularly interested reader could be found on the floor of the House of Representatives. "Just sitting there, transfixed" at the newspaper, noted an observer from the gallery, was Kopay's former competitor, Jack Kemp.

* * *

THE FIRST TIME SEAN STRUB ENTERED THE LOST AND FOUND, it felt as if he were "crossing a threshold from which I could not return." The largest and most popular of the gay "super bars" that had started popping up inside a cluster of abandoned warehouses in the shadow of the Capitol during the early 1970s, the Lost and Found was like an oasis in the desert. Visitors traveled from as far as West Virginia and Pennsylvania to explore its three bars, two dance floors, glass-partitioned restaurant, billiard room, and floor-to-ceiling fountain, all spread out over a sleekly designed, eleven-thousand-square foot space within a building the size of an airplane hangar. On any given night, flashing laser lights covered the sprawling expanse in a hail of neon as the sultry lyrics of Donna Summer and Sylvester wafted from state-of-the-art sound systems controlled by disc jockeys in glass-enclosed booths. Meanwhile, bartenders in tight, red-white-and-blue T-shirts (and even tighter jeans) fixed drinks, and hundreds of shirtless men danced together euphorically, their natural exhilaration enhanced by the fumes from the tiny bottles of amyl nitrite they pressed against each other's nostrils.

The favorite nightspot for gay Capitol Hill staffers, the Lost and Found was the closest thing Washington ever had to New York's Studio 54. One of the distinguishing features of that world-famous discotheque was its ability to gather A-list celebrities and the most beautiful unknowns under one roof. An Iowa native augmenting his studies at Georgetown University with part-time work as a Senate elevator operator, Strub fell into the latter category. Outside, in the open city, he lacked political clout. But here inside, among his fellow citizens of the secret one, an alternate form of government reigned. "It may be the ultimate democracy," Diana McLellan, a gossip columnist for both the *Star* and the *Post*, observed of Washington's gay scene. "It transcends conventional class and race lines more than any other facet of Washington life . . . This means that beneath the ordinary web of cross connections that exist in everyday life, a totally different web of connections, social, sexual, and secret, is spun."

If the gay Washington of this era lacked the federal city's rigid hierarchies, so, too, was it missing Washington's organizing principle and chief source of division: political partisanship. Regardless of one's party affiliation or ideological camp, and despite the civil service lifting its gay ban, exposure as a homosexual could still jeopardize one's career. According to Strub, whatever political differences existed between gay men, they paled in comparison to the "enormity of the secret they shared," one whose real-life consequences meant that "to be seen anywhere within a few blocks" of the Lost and Found "indicated guilt by proximity." Entering a gay bar for the first time is a rite of passage for gay men and lesbians, and in Washington, a code of silence existed among those who made the pilgrimage. In a city defined by political conflict, this made the gay bar a highly unusual place, the functional equivalent, according to one visitor, of "neutral Switzerland," a demilitarized zone where the common feature of gayness superseded one's role in the pitched daily combat raging outside its walls. On any given evening at the Lost and Found, political consultants working for rival campaigns, lobbyists on retainer for opposing business interests, staffers from both sides of the aisle, and operatives of every ideological hue put aside their differences to share a drink (or a kiss). "I knew closeted gay people who worked for almost everybody!" Bob Witeck, a Senate aide, recalled. "You'd go to a bar, you'd run into them. You'd see them. You would be open to each other. And you were a bit flabbergasted, but at the time you realized that sort of everybody was closeted."

Strub likened the experience of visiting a gay bar in 1970s Washington to being a Marrano Jew during the Spanish Inquisition forced to convert to Christianity but practicing their religion behind closed doors. While gay men of his generation, coming to terms with their homosexuality in the immediate post-Stonewall years, were having an easier time leaving their closets, the Lavender Scare "remained fresh and frightening" in everybody's mind. In the small confines of his Senate elevator, Strub gradually learned to intuit the subtle clues—"the lingering glance, a style of dress, or conversational innuendo"—gay men have always used to signal their common identity to one another, and he developed an ability to detect in those "who were groomed more carefully than others, whose ties were tied perfectly symmetrically with a dimple in the knot," the secret they shared. Sometimes the method of intimation was more direct, like leaving a pack of matches from a gay bar on your coffee table and gauging the reaction. One night at the Lost and Found, Strub saw a man he recognized from the Senate. They had never spoken in the Capitol, but at the bar, the staffer struck up a conversation with him as if they were "old friends." A few days later, the aide stepped onto Strub's elevator with his boss. He and Strub made eye contact, and while the senator stared obliviously ahead, the staffer silently raised a finger to his lips.

Before the 1970s, Washington's handful of gay bars were poorly lit, tackily decorated dives ("high-faggot baroque" was how one patron of the Plus One described its black walls sparsely adorned with gilded empty picture frames). Just a small fraction of the city's gay and lesbian community visited them. During the "Me Decade," as larger numbers of people started coming out of the closet, the number of venues proliferated. By 1975, some four thousand gay nightlife establishments were in operation across the country, and attendance at Washington's super bars—along with the bathhouses, pornographic cinemas, and cabarets all located within a ten-block radius of the Lost and Found—rivaled those of clubs in San Francisco and New York.

It was at the Lost and Found where Strub made his first group of gay friends, "an affectionate clique of barflies who campily called each other Mary." This playful banter took some getting used to for Strub, a former altar boy at St. Mary's Church in Iowa City whose three sisters were named after the Blessed Virgin. Strub's waggish companions were representative of the clientele at Washington's gay establishments, "the only place," according to Diana McLellan, where "repartee is valued." At the Pier Nine, rotary phones installed on the numbered tables surrounding the dance floor enabled patrons to flirt telephonically, a creative workaround of the city's archaic liquor law forbidding customers to stand while holding an alcoholic beverage. The mainstream popularity of disco, a style of music pioneered by Black people and gays, meant that a healthy number of heterosexuals could always be found waiting in line to enter the super bars, a signal that yet another brick in the wall between the secret and open cities had fallen. More than a musical genre, disco was a lifestyle, and its embrace by heterosexuals was a vivid example of what the writer Frank Rich termed the "homosexualization of America," a process by which the aesthetics of gay male urban culture went mainstream. Indeed, so popular did discotheques become in the nation's capital that DC earned the nickname "Disco City."

For those used to congregating in secret, the sudden popularity of their gathering places with people who never felt the need to hide presented a new, if not entirely welcome, advance. "You bet gays are bothered when straights start invading this place," a bartender at the Pier Nine complained. "We've got the best bars in town, places where we can do what we want, and now the straights are trying to move in." Some heterosexuals even had the gall to complain that the super bars were discriminating against *them*.

While gaining a measure of acceptance from regular society, within its own confines the Washington gay community fell far short of being the "ultimate democracy" that outsiders like McLellan attributed to it. Just three days after the Lost and Found opened in October 1971, a coalition of groups dubbed the Open Gay Bars Committee protested its practice of excessively carding Black patrons. Whereas bouncers only occasionally asked whites to display identification proving they were of legal drinking age, they almost always demanded it of Black people, sometimes even asking them to provide two forms of ID. "This is a Southern City," a representative of the Lost and Found bluntly told Paul Kuntzler, who helped organize the protests. "Black people are generally poor, and besides, most of our patrons are bigots." At a protest outside the Plus One, which was accused of operating a similarly discriminatory door policy, GLF members held signs reading, "Why 2 IDs for Blacks?" while chanting "If you want only white meat, then buy Bumble Bee Tuna!"

Prejudice took form in subtler, pettier ways. Bars sometimes arbitrarily declared a "no hat" rule, caps being a particularly popular fashion accessory among Black gay men at the time. Once, a manager at the Grand Central nightclub scolded a bartender for giving a complimentary glass of water to a Black customer. "When a customer like that comes to the bar and asks for water, charge him a dollar," he told the bartender.

"A customer like that?" the bartender asked.

Pointing to a group of Black people, the manager replied, "Any of those niggers."

Such pervasive racism fostered the development of a distinct Black gay community centered around private social clubs. While white gay socialites hosted lavish dinners in their Georgetown mansions and Dupont

Circle town homes attended almost exclusively by other white gay men, organizations like the Best of Washington, the Black Diamonds, and the Associates organized their own parties, planned recreational activities, sponsored charity events, and encouraged a sense of kinship for those who, in the words of one Black gay community leader, "didn't have outlets . . . of our own . . . where we could party and meet friends and celebrate our own lives." Black-owned bars such as the Red Door, which catered to a clientele largely composed of gay federal employees, enforced house rules against behavior that could result in patrons losing their jobs (and the establishment its liquor license). "There was no kissing," recalled the owner. Customers "didn't display affection. And there were no drag queens." Housed in a one-story, L-shaped brick building in the Petworth neighborhood, the members-only Clubhouse made up for its lack of a liquor license with vats of homemade "electric" (acid-spiked) punch, to which guests contributed the ingredients and drank out of giant garbage cans. "It was a place where anyone 16 and above could go and have the House party that they couldn't have in their house, let their hair down, be themselves, and go home soaking wet," one frequent visitor fondly remembered.

Until it closed in 2004, one of the oldest gay bars in Washington was the Black-owned Nob Hill, known to many as "Snob Hill" for its jacket-and-tie dress code. Howard University student James Coleman's first visit was similar to that of many Black gay and lesbian Washingtonians, most of whom were born and raised in the city: he encountered people he knew from childhood. Coleman was the founder of a social club, "The Group," whose signature parties were the Cherry Blossom Festival and the Annual Scandal. A drag performer—appearing under the name "Juicy," bestowed upon him in high school when he handed out sticks of Juicy Fruit gum while campaigning for student body president—Coleman was a prominent fixture within the drag house scene that blossomed in Washington during the 1960s and '70s. Consisting of an older drag queen who adopted a maternal role over her brood of fellow queens (most of whom worked government day jobs), drag houses competed against each other in lip-synching and voguing contests. Some drag houses took the concept literally, with members living together in an actual home. The most famous of these was the fourteen-bedroom Hollywood House, so-called for its annual "Academy Award" dinner where little golden statues were dispensed, and over which

"Liz Taylor" reigned. One night, the queens' bawdy banter was just too loud for the middle-aged German couple living next door, who called the police to complain. "Every Saturday night, noise, noise, noise!" the husband told the responding officers. Asked for the identities of his neighbors, he wavered. It seemed that "everybody is named Mary."

30

"TOO GOOD AN OPPORTUNITY"

AT 3:30 P.M. ON SEPTEMBER 22, 1975, A GAY MAN SAVED THE LIFE OF THE president of the United States, and ruined his own.

Oliver "Billy" Sipple had fled to San Francisco two years earlier because of his secret. Part of the vast post-Stonewall migration of gays and lesbians that rolled into the City by the Bay in the early 1970s, the heavyset, thirty-three-year-old Marine Corps Vietnam veteran was not open about his sexual orientation with his family back home in Detroit, and he preferred to keep it that way. Owing to the shrapnel wound in his leg, Sipple lived on disability, and he tended to spend his days meandering around his adopted city. Which is how he happened upon a massive crowd in Union Square across the street from the entrance to the stately St. Francis Hotel.

Sipple asked one of the gawkers what they were waiting to see. "What's the matter with you, stupid?" the onlooker replied. President Gerald Ford was inside addressing a luncheon hosted by the local chapter of the World Affairs Council. The scene was somewhat tense; just three weeks prior, a member of the murderous Manson family named Lynette Alice "Squeaky" Fromme had tried to assassinate Ford outside the State Capitol in Sacramento. Working his way through the crowd to get a better view, Sipple didn't pay any attention to the gray-haired lady in the blue raincoat standing beside him. But then, just as the president emerged from the front door and strode to his waiting limousine, into Sipple's frame of vision appeared a chrome-plated .38 revolver.

Sipple, who had suffered shell shock during the war, was acutely sensitive to sudden movements and noises. Every Fourth of July, while his friends celebrated the country's independence, he spent the night at a Veterans Affairs hospital to escape the crack of fireworks. "Gun!" Sipple screamed, lunging for the woman's arm. "She's got a fucking gun!" Sipple brushed her aside just as a shot rang out. Mercifully, the bullet missed its intended target, flying into the hotel wall.

In the commotion that followed, a team of Secret Service agents rushed Sipple into the St. Francis, while another group carted off the would-be assassin, a five-time divorcée and radical political groupie named Sara Jane Moore. During his three-hour-long interrogation, Sipple shook so violently that he could neither write out a witness statement nor light himself a cigarette. It wasn't just the harrowing experience of being at the center of a barely averted national tragedy that caused Sipple anxiety; so too did the prospect of massive, unwanted media attention. Shy and reclusive, he naïvely asked the Secret Service agents not to publicize his name. But even if it had been within their power to do so, withholding the identity of the man who had prevented a madwoman's bullet from striking the president was futile—as would be the keeping of his secret.

Harvey Milk had befriended Sipple in the early 1960s, when both men were living in New York City. Milk moved to San Francisco in 1972, a year before Sipple, and opened a camera shop that doubled as the headquarters for his perpetual political campaigns in the Castro, San Francisco's gay neighborhood. Milk was one of just a tiny handful of openly gay candidates who had followed Frank Kameny's lead by running for public office in cities across America, and to him, Sipple's act of heroism was a godsend. "For once we can show that gays do heroic things," Milk said, "not just all that caca about molesting children and hanging out in bathrooms."

Milk's impulse to shout the news of Sipple's homosexuality from the rooftops was understandable. In 1972, Jack Anderson had reported that the Gay Liberation Front appeared on a Secret Service watch list of more than four hundred subversive organizations that potentially posed a threat to the president's life. Meanwhile, just three days before Sipple's act of courage, an air force administrative board recommended that Sergeant Leonard Matlovich, the first soldier to publicly declare his homosexuality for the purpose of challenging the military's gay ban and a highly decorated combat veteran, be discharged. Matlovich's face was on the cover of *Time*. Here, in the Marine Corps veteran who had saved the president's life, was another walking advertisement for the patriotism of gay people.

Unbeknownst to Sipple, Milk called up Herb Caen, whose gossip column had appeared in the *San Francisco Chronicle* since 1938. Two days after the assassination attempt, Caen published the following item:

> One of the heroes of the day, Oliver "Bill" Sipple, the ex-Marine who grabbed Sara Jane Moore's arm just as her gun was fired and thereby may have saved the President's life, was the center of midnight attention at the Red Lantern, a Golden Gate Ave. bar he favors. The Rev. Ray Broshears, head of the Helping Hands center[,] and Gay Politico Harvey Milk, who claim to be among Sipple's close friends, describe themselves as "proud—maybe this will help break the stereotype." Sipple is among the workers in Milk's campaign for Supervisor.

The mention of a gay bar as Sipple's favorite, and his association with two local gay personalities, was all that the national media needed to deem the hero's homosexuality newsworthy. "Hero in Ford Shooting Active Among S.F. Gays," blared the headline of a *Los Angeles Times* dispatch printed in newspapers around the country the following day, noting that the "husky ex-Marine" had yet to receive a call of thanks from the president. Speaking to reporters at a press conference, Sipple received more questions about the implications of his sexual orientation than the actions he had taken to save the president. "My sexuality is a part of my private life and has no bearing on my response to the act of a person seeking to take the life of another," a visibly shaken Sipple, his eyes bloodshot from insomnia, said. As to whether the president's failure to thank him had anything to do with his sexuality, Sipple demurred. "The President doesn't know about this," he said. "This is just another gimmick somebody has thought up to make a big deal out of. The President is a very busy man."

The publicization of Sipple's homosexuality exemplified a paradox that lay at the heart of the gay liberation movement: the tension between respect for personal privacy and the imperative to transform public attitudes. On the one hand, gay activists argued that gay people must have the right to determine when, how, or even if they came out of the closet. For decades, unscrupulous politicians, journalists, and other malevolent actors had weaponized the disclosure of homosexuality to end careers and devastate lives; to wield that power over gay people, even in the name of promoting their social advancement, was at the very least morally problematic. At the same time, however, the power of the accusation stemmed from its being secret, and depriving the secret of its sting required gay people to come out of their closets—as Milk and Matlovich had done. What, then, to do in the case of Billy Sipple, a gay hero who desperately wanted to keep his gayness secret?

Just as Milk's desire to advertise Sipple's homosexuality was understandable from the perspective of a gay activist determined to allay misperceptions about gay people, so did Sipple's reluctance to acknowledge it make sense from the position of a gay individual concerned about how the revelation would play back in his and Ford's home state of Michigan. While she had initially expressed pride in her son for saving the life of the president, Ethyl Sipple refused to leave her house after his sexual orientation was reported and hung up the phone when he called. "No wonder the president didn't send him a note," she told the *Detroit News*. "We were very proud of Oliver, but now I won't be able to walk down the street without somebody saying something." (As if this dismissal of her son's heroism were not enough, she then downplayed it as the by-product of his war trauma. "Oliver's quick action was probably instinct," she said. "Ever since he was in Vietnam, he's been jumpy, almost shell-shocked. I understand he still jumps for cover when he hears a truck backfire.") Sipple's father and two brothers, all assembly-line employees at a General Motors plant, endured homophobic taunts on the factory floor. Some of Sipple's former neighbors in Detroit, fortunately, were more understanding. "He could be as queer as a $9 bill but that doesn't change the fact that he helped the President of the United States," said one.

Finally, after three days of official silence, the president sent a letter to Sipple. "I want you to know how much I appreciated your selfless actions last Monday," Ford wrote.

> The events were a shock to us all, but you acted quickly and without fear for your own safety. By doing so you helped to avert danger to me and to others in the crowd. You have my heartfelt appreciation.

Five days later, the reluctant hero replied. "As you probably know, there have been a number of stories concerning my personal sexual orientation in the news media," Sipple wrote. "These stories have caused great anguish to my parents, and to the rest of my family I am sure." Sipple continued:

> My mother hung up on me when I first called her after these stories began to be published and the unexpected and glaring publicity which has been given to my private life has very seriously disrupted my family relationships. Mr. President, it is a very hard thing to have your mother, and family, not want to have any contact with you.

Sipple ended with an appeal:

> I know that your schedule is heavily occupied, but I respectfully request that you take the time to see my family or at least call my family . . . I love my family, and I do not want to be separated from their love and companionship. Your help will be gratefully appreciated.

Upon receiving this letter, White House press secretary Ron Nessen forwarded it with a brief memo to Jerry Jones, a deputy assistant to the president. Noting that "Sipple has been identified in some newspapers as an activist in the homosexual movement," Nessen determined, "I think it is more appropriate that you decided how it should be handled."

There is no indication that the president ever contacted Sipple's family. And all that Sipple would merit in Ford's memoir was the passing remark that he had been "an alert bystander."

As a result of what the former Nixon speechwriter and *New York Times* columnist William Safire described as "committing heroism in public," Sipple descended into a downward spiral. The following year, he filed a multimillion-dollar invasion-of-privacy suit against several newspapers alleging that their reporting had estranged him from his family and "exposed him to contempt and ridicule, causing him great mental anguish, embarrassment, and humiliation." (The case dragged on until 1984, when the California Supreme Court dismissed it on the grounds that Sipple's homosexuality was already "known by hundreds of people" at the time of the assassination attempt.) Sipple never reconciled with his family; when his mother died in 1979, his father forbade him from attending her funeral.

"This thing with Ford, it really fucked his mind up," Sipple's friend, Wayne Friday, recalled. "Sipple was a broken guy after that, the whole thing worked him. The publicity of it all and the fact that everyone knew he was a faggot. He said to me a couple of times, 'I went to the Marine Corps and I got hurt and now what am I known for? For being a faggot!' And I'd say, 'No you're not . . . You're known for saving the president's life.' He was just down to nothing. This thing happened, and it overcame him." Adding to his already long list of health problems, Sipple started receiving psychiatric treatment for schizophrenia and alcoholism. On February 2, 1989, amid piles of empty half-gallon bottles of bourbon and 7UP, a friend discovered Sipple's lifeless, three-hundred-pound body in his apartment, where it had been decomposing for over a week. Buried somewhere within the piles of garbage, which gave the place the aura of a "junk store gone to seed," was a framed letter from the president of the United States thanking Sipple for saving his life.

* * *

CRUISING AT THE U.S. MARINE CORPS WAR MEMORIAL, a 1972 gay travel guide warned its readers, "[r]equires great caution after 11 p.m., particularly in the woods." Located on a hill overlooking Arlington National Cemetery, the iconic bronze monument depicting six soldiers hoisting the American flag amid the Battle of Iwo Jima had recently become a popular nocturnal meeting point for men seeking sex with men. Nearly every night, the whole cross section of Washington society (colonels, diplomats, lawyers, tourists, politicians, even policemen and the occasional visitor from abroad) could be found wandering the nearby woods in search of a fleeting human connection. Whatever their station in life, these men shared a secret, the nature of which compelled them to seek anonymous encounters in darkened forests rather than deep and lasting commitments in the light of day.

The thirty-five-year-old Gentleman from Mississippi fit the standard profile of the men who visited these grounds. He had first come to Washington at seventeen to work as a congressional page, rushing messages between the legislators on the House floor and their offices across the street from the Capitol. He dreamed of returning as an elected member of the body, and after working as a House doorman, serving a stint in the Marine Corps, and now toiling as an administrative assistant for a Republican congressman, he was on his way to fulfilling that ambition. His girlfriend,

Cynthia, knew of his "problem," as they euphemistically referred to that mysterious mixture of desire and emotions that contribute to one's sexual orientation, and that drove him to places such as these, though she likely had no idea what he was doing on this particular evening. Cynthia loved him; indeed, she had never met a better man. And so, she was lucky that, when the undercover police officer locked eyes with her boyfriend by the light of the moon that September 1976 evening, and entered into the sensual pantomime that the inhabitants of this secret world performed anonymously together under cover of night, he escaped with only a one-hundred-dollar fine for the reduced charge of "creating a public nuisance." It could have been so much worse.

For, in the words of the *Washington Post*, this hallowed ground had become "a furtive rendezvous for the haunted and hunted surpassing anything Washington has ever known." The previous summer, four off-duty soldiers met a man at the memorial, lured him into a car, stripped him naked, beat him to a pulp, and left him for dead on the George Washington Parkway. (He survived, barely.) Nearby residents routinely reported hearing screams at night—whether of terror or ecstasy was often difficult to discern. The situation presented the U.S. Park Police, who exercised jurisdiction over the land, with a conundrum. When they dispatched plainclothesmen to patrol the woods, gay leaders accused them of entrapment, of dragging Washington back to the dark old days of Roy Blick. Leave the park unguarded, however, and the police were assailed for sanctioning violence against a socially marginalized population. Most of the men beaten and robbed in places such as these never came to the authorities, for reasons illustrated by a Park Police officer interviewed by the *Post*. "They are people in hiding," he said of the men, many of whom, when arrested for solicitation, wept and begged for mercy, lamenting how a record of the incident would ruin their careers and wreck their marriages. "They seem to live in fear."

Less than a month after the Gentleman from Mississippi was apprehended by law enforcement, another young man paid the ultimate price in its absence. Ronald Pettine was "one of Washington's brightest and ablest young political technicians." By the age of thirty-two, he had served as deputy secretary of state in Pennsylvania and had most recently led the advance team on Democratic congressman Morris Udall's presidential campaign. A husband and father of nine-year-old twins, Pettine led another life about which his wife and some of his colleagues were aware. "We heard periodic rumors that there was a gay cell somewhere in the campaign," Udall was to say, "but we were too busy trying to get elected to worry about everybody's sex life."

On the evening of October 1, Pettine left his home in the Virginia suburbs for the memorial. Walking its forested pathways, he was lured into a trap by three young men. After bludgeoning him with a tree limb, they tied a sock around his genitals and dragged his body to a muddy creek near the Netherlands Carillon, where they left him to die. The next morning, Pettine's battered corpse was found lying facedown, his skull crushed like a deflated beach ball.

The murder of Ronald Pettine, like the murder of Louis Teboe two decades before, was a manifestation of the secret's most awful consequence. Over the course of an eighteen-month span from 1977 to 1978, ten men would be found murdered in various locations across Washington under circumstances like Pettine's—a secluded crime scene, an absence of witnesses, the victims all having disguised their movements and identity prior to their heinous deaths. Often, the widows of the murdered men found it impossible to accept that their husbands had a separate, secret homosexual existence, and refused to cooperate in the investigations. Even in death, the victims of these "homosexual murders," as the police categorized the crimes, were rejected by their families, an indifference that illustrated why they had felt the need to live their lives in secret.

Michael Simoneau, one of the three young men charged with killing Ronald Pettine, had by his own admission visited the Iwo Jima Memorial on multiple occasions to "harass and humiliate queers," and in celebration of his sixteenth birthday, he and his pals intended only to "smack around a few" of them. Hearing other friends of Simoneau's testify about the moment the birthday boy triumphantly called them from a pay phone to boast of his killing a "faggot," and how they, in turn, casually informed others of this exciting news, unnerved a columnist for the *Washington Post*. The young men, he wrote, left "the impression that no one thought a crime had been committed."

JIMMY CARTER

The only way I can lose this election is if I'm caught in bed with either a dead girl or a live boy.

—Rep. Edwin Edwards

31

OUT OF THE CLOSETS,
INTO THE WHITE HOUSE

A FEW DAYS AFTER JIMMY CARTER'S INAUGURATION, JEAN O'LEARY looked into the face of the woman lying next to her in bed. "Midge," she said, "we're going to the White House."

Midge Costanza was better at giving orders than taking them. Beginning with the sit-down protest she staged in her parents' kitchen as a first-grader in Rochester, New York, demanding that she be sent to public rather than Catholic school, Costanza dedicated her life to the advancement of liberal causes, and she proudly adopted the mantle of "loudmouthed, pushy little broad." Two incidents during her 1972 campaign for the Rochester City Council had a profound impact on her worldview. After Costanza agreed to meet with a group of gay activists, a pair of mysterious figures picked her up in a Volkswagen, ordered her to close her eyes, and drove her to an undisclosed location where a group of gay business owners described the difficulties they faced in obtaining liquor licenses. More than the individual stories of discrimination, it was the layers upon layers of secrecy involved in just having the opportunity to hear them—the sort of precautions one might undertake if she were the interlocutor between a government and an under-ground revolutionary cell—that emphasized for Costanza the importance of public officials advocating on behalf of socially marginalized citizens. The second experience occurred right after the election, when Costanza swept ahead of four male candidates to become the first woman elected to the Rochester City Council. Traditionally, the members of the council selected the person who garnered the most votes to be mayor. But in a late-night, backroom deal, her male colleagues chose one of their own instead.

And so when a relatively unknown southern governor announced his presidential candidacy in 1975, pledging to redeem the nation's politics in the aftermath of Watergate and to never lie to the American people, Costanza was one of the first Democrats in New York State to endorse him. This early support secured her a prominent job in Jimmy Carter's White House as assistant to the president for public liaison, the first woman to hold that rank. She had been introduced to O'Leary, a former nun and co-executive director of the National Gay Task Force, by New York congress-woman Bella Abzug in the summer of 1976 when the three women tried to insert a gay rights plank into the Democratic Party platform. Though Costanza would never maintain that she was anything other than heterosexual, her political collaboration with O'Leary sparked a hidden romance that—with one partner working inside the White House and the other agitating outside it—made history.

Costanza described her role as the president's "window on the nation," and during her brief tenure, she revolutionized the position of public liaison. In less than two years, she would hold a thousand meetings, deliver on average a speech every week, and address more than a million people, all in an effort "to reach those traditionally powerless and to balance that with a continuing access for groups who've always had entrée." It would be hard to conceive of a group of Americans more politically powerless in 1977 than homosexuals, and when O'Leary told Costanza within the first week of the new administration that it was finally time for representatives of the president of the United States to hold a meeting with gay activists, Costanza agreed.

The gathering would take place on March 27, 1977, a Saturday. That the president would be visiting Camp David with his family that weekend was pure coincidence, Costanza was to say, and while she did not inform Carter of the meeting in advance, she did alert his chief of staff. The Task Force selected fourteen activists from across the country representing various constituencies of the gay community, each of whom was assigned to draft a white paper detailing the discriminatory policies of a single federal agency, ranging from the Internal Revenue Service to the Department of Defense to the Bureau of Prisons. On the night before the event, the group gathered to plot strategy in the office of Senator Alan Cranston, who had earned a reputation as the body's most supportive member after one of his aides, Gary Aldridge, became the first congressional staffer to identify publicly as gay. Aldridge was moved to do so in 1972 after witnessing the disastrous experience of vice presidential nominee Sen. Thomas Eagleton, whose past electroshock therapy treatment for clinical depression was not disclosed until over two weeks after the Democratic National Convention. The disclosure led to Eagleton's being dropped from the ticket. "Everyone was worried about hiding things," Aldridge recalled, and he decided to tell Cranston's administrative assistant his own secret. "Well, I never suspected that you weren't," she replied nonchalantly.

The morning of their meeting, the activists were overwhelmed with the sense that they were making history. "One of the biggest thrills in my life was getting into a taxi that morning and telling the driver, 'To the west gate of the White House, please,'" one member of the delegation recalled. Costanza led the group to the Roosevelt Room, where they sat around a long conference table and began their presentations. Upon no one did the significance of the moment weigh more heavily than the man who had written respectful if forthright letters to every occupant of the building in which he now sat since John F. Kennedy, not once receiving a reply. Twelve years earlier, Frank Kameny had organized the first picket for gay rights outside the White House. Now, he was advocating for equality inside it. "Frank, I'm really glad to meet you finally," Costanza said. "I'm just sorry that it has taken so long to come into a house that belongs to you as much as it belongs to anyone in this country." Three hours after the meeting began, the group triumphantly departed the White House to address a scrum of curious reporters—but not before Costanza and O'Leary sneaked into the empty Oval Office to steal a kiss.

Two months later, another milestone in gay visibility would be reached when Lambda Rising moved from its one-room shop in a town house on S Street to a larger space around the corner. It wasn't the size of the new location that was most notable, but rather its windows facing the street. Before the move, some of Deacon Maccubbin's customers had asked if he might drape the windows to protect their privacy. "I won't be able to shop there anymore," they told him. "It's too open. It's too public." Maccubbin declined, and what transpired validated his decision. "Within a few weeks of [our] opening, those same people steeled themselves and got the courage to come into the store," he remembered. "And that was part of their coming out. This wasn't one or two people. This was a lot of people. It was giving them the impetus to actually start taking these baby steps out of the closet." (Washington's first gay bar with a street-facing window, Rascals, would not open until 1979.) Lambda was becoming something bigger than just a bookshop, according to Maccubbin's lover and business partner, Jim Bennett. "We were the de facto community center. We were the meeting place. When people were going out to dinner, that's where they brought their parents [afterward] when they came out." On more than one occasion, Bennett recalled, men representing themselves as FBI agents entered the store asking to see its mailing list. They were refused.

This antagonistic encounter was illustrative of the rift between the federal government and the municipality where it was headquartered with respect to homosexuality. In 1972, the District of Columbia became the first city in the country to prohibit discrimination against gay teachers, and the following year, it extended protections to gay residents in housing, employment, and public accommodation. "Despite the predominance of the federal government," the *Washington Post* reported, "homosexuals rank Washington at or near the top among U.S. cities in terms of personal freedom." The rapid changes for the better had come about thanks in large part to a lesson that the gay community had gleaned from the Kameny campaign: progress was impossible unless you made yourself visible. When he first ran for the DC Board of Education in 1971, the African American civil rights activist Marion Barry did not even bother to return a questionnaire sent to him by the Gay Activists Alliance, earning himself a score of -15. By 1977, thanks to persistent lobbying, Barry chalked up a +20 rating from the group, and when he won the mayoralty the following year, he credited the gay community for his victory. More than three-fourths of Barry's campaign phone bankers were gay, and in twenty of the twenty-one precincts where he won a majority, gays constituted anywhere from a fifth to a third of voters. Perhaps the most dramatic example of the positive change was the trajectory of City Council member Douglas Moore. During a 1977 election debate, Moore decried "fascist faggots" and campaigned against the "three G's—gays, gambling and grass." Defeated, he ran again two years later, and not only did he abandon the hateful rhetoric, but he hired an openly gay campaign coordinator.

This newfound political influence, unthinkable only a decade earlier, helped create what *The Advocate*, a Los Angeles–based gay magazine, described as "a free-wheeling, open atmosphere for much of the capital's gay community," with the *Star* lauding Washington as the "Emerald City of live-and-let-live tolerance for homosexuals." In some neighborhoods, marveled the *Post*, "you could spend a comfortable sort of Sunday . . . without ever encountering heterosexuals." Working in the seat of the federal government nonetheless imposed its own set of demands, however, and Washington's gay community was more conservative, both in temperament and style, than those in New York and San Francisco. "We have gained this acceptance, primarily, by keeping discreet and middle-of-the-road in politics, behavior and dress—so that we don't appear to be threatening straight society," a staffer for the Gay Rights National Lobby explained. Thanks to the 1975 Civil Service Commission reform, the Carter administration was the first to offer low-level political appointments to openly gay people. One employee at a regulatory agency felt comfortable leaving his office every night to head to the gay bar across the street—not as a customer, but to moonlight as a bartender.

Midge Costanza's White House meeting helped normalize the idea of gay people as a minority group with interests like any other, and it led to a series of conversations between gay activists and federal officials. It was also the first step in Costanza's political downfall. "Homos in the White House!" a labor leader loudly complained during his own visit to the presidential mansion later that year. The perception that Costanza was too far left and that she was working on behalf of the groups lobbying the president, rather than the other way around, took hold among the all-male members of the "Georgia mafia" surrounding Carter, and it wasn't long before they were deriding Costanza anonymously to the press as a "flake," or worse. "Everyone wishes she would disappear," a White House aide sniped to *Newsweek*. Costanza had started in the administration working in an office located just a few doors down from the president's, alongside those of the vice president, chief of staff, and press secretary. By the following summer, she was exiled to a spot in the basement next to the closet where Richard Nixon once stored his secret tapes. After just twenty months on the job, she resigned.

Midge Costanza's romantic relationship with Jean O'Leary lasted the duration of her White House tenure, and the women remained close friends for the rest of their lives. Years after she departed the Carter administration, when a reporter asked if her professional interest in gay rights might be connected to her own sexuality, Costanza testily responded that her personal life was irrelevant to her political commitments, which were inspired by a long-standing belief in the equality of all people regardless of their race, sex, or sexual orientation. O'Leary held a different view of the relationship between the personal and the political. "The biggest oppression that we've always suffered has been our invisibility, our refusal to identify ourselves publicly," she said. "And we've not been able to organize because of that." Costanza and O'Leary pursued divergent paths with respect to their common secret, but those paths crossed at the right place and at the right time. While Costanza would never have been able to organize the historic first meeting of gay activists at the White House—indeed, never would have been able to get a job in the White House—had she acknowledged her lesbianism, O'Leary would never have been able to push for that meeting had she *not* acknowledged hers.

* * *

WHEN THE ANTIGAY BACKLASH CAME TO AMERICA, it was wrapped in the flag and carrying a glass of orange juice.

Anita Bryant was an ex–beauty queen, a performer of wholesome gospel standards, and the face of the Florida Citrus Commission when she rose to national prominence in 1977 by warning about the threat homosexuals posed to America's youth. Bryant was appalled by the civil rights advances won by gays, upon which Midge Costanza's White House meeting appeared to place the presidential imprimatur. "Behind the high sounding appeal against discrimination in jobs and housing—which is not a problem to the 'closet' homosexual—they are really asking to be blessed in their abnormal lifestyle by the office of the President of the United States," Bryant declared two days after the conclave. "What these people really want, hidden behind obscure legal phrases, is the legal right to propose to your children that there is an acceptable alternate way of life—that being a homosexual or lesbian is not really wrong or illegal." Under the slogan "Save Our Children," Bryant spearheaded an effort in Dade County, Florida, to repeal an ordinance protecting gays from discrimination.

Like the homosexuals she denounced, Bryant was part of a community coming out of a political closet: evangelical Christians. Estimated to number more than twenty million, these "born again" Americans had been a dormant electoral constituency, shunning political engagement on the grounds that salvation was to be found in the afterlife, not in the fallen world. This posture was to change after a series of developments—the Supreme Court's 1973 *Roe v. Wade* decision legalizing abortion, the campaign to ratify an Equal Rights Amendment (ERA) enshrining female equality in the Constitution, the federal crackdown on Christian "segregation academies," and the gay liberation movement—roused them from their slumber.

During the McCarthy era, homosexuality had been elevated from an individual medical condition to a harbinger of international communism. Twenty-five years later, it was once again being spoken of as a societal threat, this time not so much to national security as to the traditional family. Among the arguments marshaled by an Illinois housewife named Phyllis Schlafly in her crusade against the ERA was that it would pave the way to legalization of same-sex marriages. "In a healthy society, [homosexuality] will be contained, segregated, controlled, and stigmatized, carrying both a legal and social sanction," Nixon speechwriter turned syndicated columnist Pat Buchanan thundered on the morning Miamians headed to the polls to determine the fate of their city's antidiscrimination law, what Buchanan sneeringly referred to as "D-Day for the boys in lavender." In a flourish that the former president whose "dark side" he so masterfully channeled would have appreciated, Buchanan faulted homosexuals for the collapse of the Weimar Republic and the "decay of society" wherever they arose (a pronouncement even Buchanan must have recognized as hyperbole not least due to his own experience in the Nixon White House, where the moderating Tory influence of Ray Price resulted in nothing more catastrophic than a toning down of Buchanan's fire and brimstone rhetoric). Though a Catholic, Buchanan spoke for many of his evangelical Protestant coreligionists when he declared that homosexuality was "sordid and sick," and for the majority of citizens in Dade County, who followed his and Bryant's advice and voted to repeal the antidiscrimination ordinance by a margin of two-to-one. Reading this polemic and a dispiritingly high number of others like it in the conservative press, a contributor to *National Review* wondered aloud if Buchanan "has in mind all those members of

YAF whose letters turn up in the columns of" *The Advocate* while fulminating in favor of "stigmatizing, controlling, and segregating" gays.

Midge Costanza was no longer working for Jimmy Carter when he ran for reelection in 1980, but the meeting she hosted at the White House with gay activists three years earlier held an outsize place in the imaginations of Christian right leaders. Speaking at a rally in Alaska, the founder of a new political movement called the Moral Majority reenacted for his supporters a testy exchange with Carter that he claimed had transpired during a White House summit with evangelical pastors earlier that year. "Sir, why do you have known, practicing homosexuals on your senior staff here in the White House?" the Virginia televangelist Jerry Falwell said he asked the president, confusing (or distorting) a meeting with gay people with the employment of them.

"'Well, I am president of all the American people,'" Falwell said, imitating Carter, "'and I believe I should represent everyone.'"

"Why don't you have some murderers and bank robbers and so forth to represent?" Falwell said he snapped in reply, to cheers from the crowd. Upon hearing about these remarks, "angry Carter aides" produced a transcript of the White House colloquy, proving that Falwell had fabricated the entire exchange. The president, their rebuttal implied, had never defended the employment of gay people on his White House staff, much less hired any.

* * *

WHILE THE GENTLEMAN FROM MISSISSIPPI WAS AN AVID MOVIEGOER and charter member of the American Film Institute, there was no chance that the picture he had come to see at the run-down cinema in Southeast Washington on the evening of October 24, 1977, would be inducted into that august archive. *Harley's Angels*, as its name implied, was a burlesque of the hit television show *Charlie's Angels*, though instead of buxom beauties fighting crime, it featured hirsute motorcycle enthusiasts engaged in more carnal pursuits. The film was running all week at the Cinema Follies, a twenty-four-hour, X-rated gay entertainment emporium featuring a disco on the first floor and a cinema on the second. The Follies' owner, Bill Oates, dabbled as an amateur pornographic film producer and community leader, lending Frank Kameny money and running a contest for the best letter written in protest of the city's attempts to shut down his cinema.

Divine, the Baltimore drag queen and cult film icon, was a friend of Oates's projectionist and an occasional patron.

About fifteen other men were scattered throughout the theater that evening, their darkened faces made intermittently visible by the shimmering light of the projector. Should the images on the screen arouse them, alcoves on either side of the room provided semiprivate areas for sex, making the Follies a safer option for the anonymous encounters the Gentleman from Mississippi used to seek at the Iwo Jima Memorial before his unfortunate encounter with an undercover police officer the previous year. He had been coming to the Follies fairly regularly since its 1975 opening, and he thought nothing of the attendant operating a rug shampooer at the foot of the wooden staircase leading up to the screening room. Fewer things required more frequent and vigorous cleaning, after all, than the floors of a pornographic movie theater.

The Gentleman from Mississippi had been sitting in his chair for only a few minutes when he heard a voice cry out from the back, "Hey, there's a fire!" Quickly turning around, he saw clouds of dark smoke where the trail of light from the projector ought to have been. Over his many years working in state and national politics, a career filled with interminable meetings and tedious functions, he had developed the habit of immediately identifying the exits in any enclosed space he entered, and from previous visits to the Follies, he knew there was a door at the back of the theater. Struggling to make his way there through the smoke, he bumped into another man, who desperately asked him, "Is there a way out?" He grabbed the man by the collar and dragged him toward the door, which he was shocked to discover had been padlocked. As the smoke thickened, the fire grew fiercer, and the terrified screams from the other men intensified, the last thing he thought before collapsing and passing out was, "Is this the way I'm going die?"

A member of Engine Company No. 7 was lowering the flag outside the firehouse when he saw a plume of billowing black smoke across South Capitol Street. He and his fellow firefighters were already suiting up when the call came about a blaze at the Cinema Follies. A spark projected from the rug shampooer on the first floor had ignited the highly flammable homemade cleaning mixture, releasing a giant flame up the staircase. Within minutes, the entire building was engulfed, and when the firemen arrived at the scene, they found the metal front door partially melted and sealed shut. Smashing their way in through the second-floor entry, they discovered a heap of bodies piled inside. As the fire raged, a Catholic priest from a nearby church arrived and climbed a ladder to the roof, where he administered last rites to the dying men whom the firefighters had managed to extricate.

"The phones buzzed the next morning," recalled one gay Washingtonian, describing the sense of panic that swept through the secret city when the *Post* and the *Star* reported the disaster on the front pages of their early editions. The fire not only became the talk of gay Washington; it also offered a window into a milieu that, despite impressive recent advances in visibility, was still largely hidden from public view. At one downtown lunch counter, customers disparaged the sort of men who visited places like the Follies. Indeed, some went so far as to say that those who perished in the blaze deserved their fates. "What if they called and told you it was your cousin?" one woman interjected.

Each of the nine victims, of course, *was* somebody's cousin, or brother, or son, as could be said about every man killed in what the city classified as a "homosexual murder." In such cases, it took authorities longer than usual to identify the victims because they were carrying fake driver's licenses—or nothing at all. "Most of the people who go into these gay places don't take accurate IDs," explained one homicide detective. "They're afraid the place will get raided." These murky circumstances presented journalists with an ethical dilemma. While reporting the names of crime victims is standard procedure for media outlets, most of if not all the men who died in the Cinema Follies were closeted gay men, and some editors reasoned that printing their identities would cause distress and embarrassment for their families. Failing to do so, however, implied that there was something reprehensible about homosexuality, thereby exacerbating the stigma that contributed to the atmosphere of secrecy and shame so central a feature of the tragedy. The city's two major dailies responded differently to this conundrum. The *Star* revealed the identities of all nine victims and repeated their names in multiple stories. The *Post*, meanwhile, published the names of the first five victims, then backtracked and declined to identify the rest. *Post* managing editor Howard Simons said this decision was undertaken out of "compassion" for the families of the men, a sentiment indicated by the headline assertion that the tragedy left them "Doubly Shocked." It was an explanation that the paper's ombudsman, Charles B. Seib, found wanting. He could "recall no tragedy of the magnitude of the Cinema Follies fire in which a local newspaper did not publish the names of all the identified dead." By declining to do so, the paper was conceding that "homosexuality is so shameful that extraordinary steps had to be taken to protect the families of the victims."

The list of those victims read like a cross section of the city: an army major, a legislative assistant, an ex-marine, a former pastor visiting from Illinois. Charles Hamilton Beebe Jr. was a thirty-one-year-old staffer for a Democratic congressman from South Carolina and the father of a five-year-old girl. "Never in three years did he mention that place," the congressman's press secretary said. "Anybody who thinks that Charlie was defined by that place and why he died has just missed the whole point," added a teary-eyed receptionist. "He was a fantastic person." One coworker speculated that Beebe, a former journalist, was visiting the theater to research a freelance article. A colleague of the ex-pastor raised the possibility that he had just happened to be walking past the Follies when it erupted in flames and ran into the theater to save as many lives as possible. (Why the former clergyman, visiting Washington for a conference, happened to be in a remote neighborhood populated by gay discos and pornographic movie theaters was left unsaid.)

At the *Blade*, now enhanced from mimeographed bulletin to proper community newspaper, the inferno forced a more personal reckoning. Like most of his fellow volunteers, reporter Lou Chibbaro Jr. had been writing under a pseudonym since he began contributing articles to the paper. As a result of the fire, however, he decided to retire the byline "Lou Romano" and start using his real name. "It really raised the issue of being in the closet and the self-oppression that it often can cause, and I just suddenly said, 'Use my full name.'"

The Cinema Follies tragedy was a ghastly metaphor for the dangerous and even deadly consequences of the closet. Just as they were stuck inside the confines of an actual fire hazard, the men who perished in its flames were also trapped inside their self-imposed chambers of deceit. Recovering in his hospital bed, one of the four survivors recalled the specific moment when, barely able to see through the thick clouds of smoke, he realized that the exit door had been padlocked. "When I held that lock in my hand

I was very angry," the Gentleman from Mississippi said. "I cannot explain the rage that I felt at that moment." The lock on the door had been placed there by someone else. But the lock to his closet was of his own devising.

* * *

THE GENTLEMAN FROM MARYLAND NURSED HIS DRINK alone, as usual, his gaze transfixed by the barely legal boys clad in fishnet loincloths strutting along the top of the bar. Their lean, taut bodies reminded him of Michelangelo's *David*, and they could be had for a price he was all too willing to pay. Dressed conservatively in a dark suit, he came to places like this, acted on his "tendencies," only at night, when he was drunk. And this just happened to be one of those increasingly frequent occasions.

On the other side of the chintzily decorated room, a young Labor Department economist squinted through the cigarette smoke at a man who looked lonelier than anyone he had ever seen. Could it really be him? The congressman from the Eastern Shore of Maryland? The cofounder of Young Americans for Freedom and the American Conservative Union, the latter of which he had once served as chairman? If so, then the presence of the man who represented the Chesapeake Bay in Congress at a seedy gay bar called the Chesapeake House —the sort of place where, in the words of one regular, "older financiers met younger entrepreneurs"—would be the *least* ironic aspect of this situation.

The economist walked up to the bespectacled man at the bar and spoke loudly over the disco music that was fast going out of fashion. "Good evening, Mr. Bauman," he said.

Either the Gentleman from Maryland pretended not to hear or was too blitzed to respond. Though he had been living "on the edge of discovery" for decades, Bob Bauman was not yet prepared to acknowledge his secret to anyone, and certainly not here.

Bauman had come a long way from his days working as a page in the House of Representatives during the Army-McCarthy Hearings. In 1973, he finally realized his lifelong ambition when he won a special election for Maryland's First Congressional District by just 1,300 votes, becoming the first Republican page to return to the House as an elected member of the body. A dedicated legislator, he had the longest daily commute of any of his colleagues (154 miles driving round-trip from his home in Easton, Maryland), and yet every morning, he was still the first of them to enter the Republican Cloakroom. There on the wall could be found a needle-point Bauman had donated, etched with the self-deprecatory slogan that succinctly summarized his governmental, or anti-governmental, philosophy: "Anytime the U.S. Congress is in session, the American people are in danger." Bauman made good use of his time when Congress *was* in session, distinguishing himself as his party's most skilled practitioner of parliamentary procedure as well as one of its most stridently conservative spokesmen. "It's hard for me to think of anything nice to say about Bob Bauman," the usually amiable Democratic Speaker of the House Tip O'Neill confessed. Slinging arrows at Democrats did not satisfy Bauman; liberal Republicans, he scoffed, were just "Democrats in drag."

Around the same time that his aunt had inspired his journey into politics by sending him the book about Honest Abe that he would come to treasure, Bauman resolved "to construct a whole series of mental fortifications to protect and conceal the real me, not just from the external world but from myself as well." The real Bauman was one he could not accept, for to do so would have meant—by the lights of his faith, his family, and his political allies—a life of "utter depravity, sinfulness and filth." So, he repressed that part of himself and, when forced to confront the plight of those who shared his predicament, was left unmoved. Overcompensating for his secret shame, he deployed his political power against people like him, cosponsoring the Family Protection Act prohibiting the disbursement of federal funds to organizations presenting homosexuality "as an acceptable lifestyle," as well as a measure barring the federally funded Legal Services Corporation from involving itself in cases dealing with antigay discrimination.

Bauman's inability to reconcile his public duties with his private desires led him down a path fraught with risk. During the day, he thrusted and parried with Democrats on the floor of the House. At night, fortified by the alcohol he generously consumed at various conservative movement functions across the city, he drove his dark blue Lincoln Continental with congressional license plates down to the "meat rack," a one-block stretch of New York Avenue between Twelfth and Thirteenth Streets where the plethora of teenagers and young men turning tricks for forty dollars had earned Washington a reputation as "the boy-whore capital" of America. The encounters for which Bauman trawled these depths were furtive and often reckless, such as the time, late one night, the hustler he took to the office of the American Conservative Union robbed him at knifepoint.

Bauman was hardly alone in being a closeted homosexual on Capitol Hill. Even during the darkest days of the Lavender Scare, Congress was a relatively more welcoming place for gay people, as the federal order banning their employment applied only to the executive branch. Senators and congressmen had broad latitude in hiring their staffs, and except for those working with classified material, employees did not have to undergo background checks. This was how, during the 1950s, a small group of gay male congressional staffers could organize a clandestine suntanning society on the roof of the Senate Office Building. One day in the mid-1970s, Jim Graham, a closeted gay man working for Connecticut senator Abraham Ribicoff, telephoned Gary Aldridge, the openly gay Cranston staffer, on the suggestion of a friend. "Let's have lunch," Aldridge suggested.

"Where?" Graham asked, expecting Aldridge to suggest a private office or some other setting far away from the Hill where they would not be recognized.

"We'll have lunch in the Senate Cafeteria," Aldridge nonchalantly responded.

"At that moment," Graham recalled, "there was such a pause in not only my speech but in my mind." If Ribicoff discovered his sexual orientation, Graham feared, he'd be fired. "And the fact that I hesitated for a moment or two tells you just how careful and just how sensitive the situation was and how paranoid I was about it. But I said, 'Yes, of course,' and we had lunch and we got to know each other."

In a 1976 interview, Aldridge said he personally knew of at least fifty other closeted gays working on the Hill, and he suspected there were seventy to eighty more. "Most of the gay people up here sublimate everything into their professional existence," he explained. A gay staffer for Bella Abzug estimated that a full quarter of Hill staff were gay. "Sometimes I think it would be fun if we all turned purple one day," one gay federal employee mused. "Then all the unsuspecting straights out there would see how well we've worked into the system." But the secret prevalence of homosexuality on the Hill did not necessarily translate into open confidence on the part of individual gays and lesbians. "At the bar they're so friendly," the Abzug staffer remarked of his fellow gay congressional staffers. "But here you walk down the hall and they don't even look at you."

On October 14, 1979, inspired by the assassination of Harvey Milk the previous year, some seventy-five thousand people from across the country converged on the capital for the National March on Washington for Lesbian and Gay Rights. Proceeding from Judiciary Square to the Washington Monument, a panoply of groups representing the full spectrum of the gay and lesbian community joyously heeded the call Milk had made in a tape-recorded message that he instructed be released only in the event of his assassination: "If a bullet should enter my brain, let that bullet destroy every closet door." "Oh when the dykes come marching in!" a group of lesbians sang as they walked past the new FBI headquarters on Pennsylvania Avenue, a hulking structure whose brutalist architectural design was perfectly suited to its namesake, J. Edgar Hoover. "I just happened to walk down to Pennsylvania Avenue," one gay bystander recalled. "When I saw those thousands and thousands of gay people marching down the street waving banners, the tears just poured down my face." One of Bauman's colleagues, a closeted congressman from New England, changed his daily jogging route to pass by the Mall so he could at least catch a glimpse of the crowd. But he dared not join them.

Coming at the end of a decade of progress—one that had begun with the Stonewall uprising, was followed by the American Psychiatric Association's removal of homosexuality from its list of mental disorders in 1973, the federal government's reversal of its discriminatory employment policy two years later, and the historic meeting at the White House two years after that—the National March on Washington signified the high-water mark of the movement for gay legal equality. It was a stretch of good fortune, Frank Kameny was to say, "too good to last."

* * *

THE FIRST PERSON IN WASHINGTON TO BE STRUCK WITH THE STRANGE NEW DISEASE reported a loss of appetite, a severe sore throat, and difficulty breathing when he came to see his doctor at Georgetown University Hospital in July 1980. The symptoms persisted, and by September, he was suffering from consistently high fever, night sweats, headaches, and coughing. Two weeks later he was dead, the autopsy revealing that pneumonia from a rare type of bacteria known as *Pneumocystis carinii* had overtaken his lungs. He was just thirty-eight years old.

What had caused a healthy young man's immune system to collapse so rapidly that he would become the first recorded case of a person without an underlying condition to die from this type of infection since 1961?

Gestating, mutating, spreading—an invisible menace was lurking within a community still largely hidden from view, a secret embedded within a secret.

Frank Blackburn was one of Washington's first openly gay doctors, a circumstance he had once thought impossible. It was at the age of five that Blackburn came to the petrifying realization many gay people grasp before they even understand that they are gay: there was something about him, intrinsic to his being, that he would have to keep a closely guarded secret for the rest of his life. The specific moment of the epiphany arrived one day as his father regaled him with stories from his own childhood. "My father always used to tell me that one of his favorite things when he was growing up was going out and beating up gays," Blackburn remembered of the moment he understood that he himself was the sort of boy whom his father had once enjoyed bullying. An avowed homosexual becoming a doctor was unthinkable when Blackburn applied to medical school in the late 1950s, the psychiatric establishment having categorized homosexuality a mental illness, so Blackburn married, had children, and otherwise lived the life of a prosperous American family man. When he finally came out in the mid-1970s, the reaction from his colleagues was far from accepting. Told Blackburn was buying a home in Dupont Circle, one of the physicians in his medical practice asked if he might consider moving to a neighborhood that was not so notoriously gay.

As this exchange suggests, many heterosexual doctors lacked the requisite empathy for understanding the needs and sensitivities of gay patients, who, as a result, often sought out their own for medical care. Blackburn had been treating gay men for several years when one of them, the son of a former European ambassador to Washington, came to him in the summer of 1980 complaining of abdominal swelling, night sweats, and swollen glands. The young man was a relatively frequent visitor to Blackburn's office, usually to receive treatment for the various venereal diseases he contracted cruising the Greyhound bus terminal, prime spot for the "rough trade" he fancied. At most, Blackburn would administer him an antibiotic (along with avuncular instructions to abstain from sex for a few weeks), and send him on his way.

This time, however, the young man's symptoms were much more serious than the ones he normally presented; indeed, they were completely mystifying. No sexually transmitted disease of which Blackburn was aware resulted in Burkitt lymphoma, the exotic syndrome, usually found in Central Africa, with which he diagnosed his patient. Luckily, the National Institutes of Health was headquartered just a few miles north of Blackburn's practice in Bethesda, Maryland. He sent his patient up to see the doctors there.

32

CODE BREAKERS

JAMIE SHOEMAKER WAS RIDING TO WORK IN THE VANPOOL ONE MORNING when an eighty-two-year-old woman, his oldest colleague at the National Security Agency, reached down and picked up a nickel-size wooden token from the floor. Imprinted on one side of the coin was an image of a shirtless man in black pants, whip in hand, standing before a predatory bird; on the reverse the words "D.C. EAGLE" were embossed. "If you're man enough . . ." read the fine print underneath. Shoemaker hadn't realized that the souvenir coin was in his pants pocket when he got dressed that morning, and as his octogenarian coworker examined her curious discovery, he held his breath, "mortified."

"Oh, it says 'Eagle,'" the woman said nonchalantly, tossing the incriminating evidence of Shoemaker's secret back onto the van floor. Oblivious to its provenance, she had just held in her hand the means of entry to the most popular gay leather bar in the Mid-Atlantic region.

A highly skilled linguist with an equally high-level security clearance, Shoemaker was a model employee of the NSA, which by 1980 had grown to become the biggest, costliest, and most secretive organization in the national security state. While reforms undertaken in the wake of Sen. Frank Church's 1975 inquiry into intelligence agency practices had led to more transparency, the environment for gay cryptographers such as Shoemaker—still prohibited from holding security clearances—remained as oppressive as it had been in the aftermath of the 1960 Martin-Mitchell defection.

Shoemaker, however, knew that being gay had "zero effect" on his work. He had posted the highest score of anyone at the agency in the obscure language in which he specialized, and he was undergoing training in another. At the gay bars he visited, first reluctantly and then with more confidence, he occasionally encountered colleagues, detectable through "code words" picked up in casual conversation. Stating that one worked for the Department of Defense, for instance, "meant NSA." He also spotted at the bars others who shared his secret and had much more to lose. There was the faintly recognizable guy in the three-piece suit—was he a congressman?—whom Shoemaker saw every time he visited the Chesapeake House, always standing alone by himself with a drink in his hand, staring creepily at the strapping young men dancing practically naked on the bar. Shoemaker was further encouraged in his exploration of Washington's gay life by one of his fellow vanpoolers, "the biggest flaming thing you've ever seen in your life," he recalled. "If NSA didn't know he was gay," Shoemaker figured, "I was safe." The mornings after their nights out together on the town, he and his coworker adapted their cryptographic skills to the inanities of vanpool chatter—"CB," for instance, being shorthand for "cute boy."

One day in June 1980, during a language class he was taking at the Foreign Service Institute in Arlington, Shoemaker's supervisor walked into the room and tapped him on the shoulder. "You have to go down to security," he said. "They're waiting to talk to you."

Shoemaker entered a room to find two agents sitting behind a table. One of them read him the Miranda warning while the other demanded his security badge. "We understand you're leading a gay lifestyle," one of the men said.

"Well, I don't know that I was leading it," Shoemaker replied. "But I am gay."

The agents prodded Shoemaker for graphic details about his sex life, questions that he answered in a vague and roundabout way. They told him they were revoking his security clearance on the spot and sequestered him in an NSA facility near Baltimore Airport inappositely called the Friendship Annex. Shoemaker's supervisor told him that he would be fired and therefore had best resign.

Shoemaker, however, was not about to quit without a fight. "I was going to do anything to make sure that they could not fire me justly," he recalled. "I was going to go to the *New York Times*. I was going to mount a protest." The first thing he did was call Frank Kameny. The former astronomer, Mattachine Society cofounder, and congressional candidate had by this time earned a well-deserved reputation for doggedness in defending gay security clearance holders before federal government employment tribunals. An officer at the U.S. Information Agency threatened with dismissal recalled the moment he told the diplomatic security agent investigating him that he had retained Kameny as his representative. "I knew we would have problems," the diplomatic security man admitted.

"Gay is good," Kameny stated upon answering Shoemaker's call, his standard telephone greeting. ("Fuck no, it's not," one of the countless people who sought Kameny's assistance facetiously recalled of this cheery salutation. "Otherwise, I wouldn't have to be calling you.") Before Shoemaker could explain his ordeal, Kameny asked if he had answered any questions during his interrogation. When Shoemaker replied that he had, Kameny erupted. "There is simply NO—NO—excuse or reason—NONE—EVER— for providing ANY answer to ANY question on ANY subject, however harmless-seeming, when you are not accompanied by Counsel," he was to exhort gay federal employees. "I am your advisor and you do not say a word," he instructed Shoemaker. "I'll take care of it from here on." Kameny sent a letter to the NSA informing its general counsel that Shoemaker would not be resigning, and that if the agency tried to dismiss his client, it could expect a slew of bad publicity in return. As the agency contemplated what to do with its stubborn gay employee, Shoemaker was given non-classified make-work with which to bide his time. He started noticing odd happenings in his daily life, like the car that followed him into a cul-de-sac when he was driving himself home, or the strange voices talking in the background when he picked up his phone to make an outgoing call.

Fortunately for Shoemaker, the person responsible for determining his future at the agency was more forward-thinking about the nexus of homosexuality and security than his predecessors. Vaunted as "America's master spy," Bobby Ray Inman was lauded by Vice President Walter Mondale and Sen. Barry Goldwater alike as a skilled collector and interpreter of intelligence. The navy vice admiral who had led the NSA since 1977 was known for unorthodox practices, such as traveling economy class without a security detail to college campuses to speak about the world of intelligence with small groups of students and professors. When the agency's general counsel presented him with the Shoemaker case, Inman asked, "How can you make this work?" Shoemaker, Inman realized, was an excellent linguist, and as he was not susceptible to blackmail, given his openness about his sexual orientation, it made no sense for the agency to fire him and thereby lose his considerable talents. Inman devised a solution: Shoemaker could keep his job if he informed every member of his extended family that he was gay, agreed to undergo a polygraph examination annually as opposed to every five years as was normal practice for NSA employees, and, should he ever participate in a public gay activity such as a Pride parade, refrain from identifying himself as an NSA employee.

Given the potentially far-reaching implications of his decision, Inman informed the secretary of defense and the chairmen of the congressional intelligence oversight committees, all of whom gave him their support. "You made absolutely the right decision," Goldwater, chairman of the Senate Select Committee on Intelligence, told Inman. "You've protected the government's interest, the country's interest, and the rest of it is none of the government's business." On October 29, 1980, after the NSA concluded a study that they told Shoemaker cost more than what the agency spent investigating the 1968 North Korean seizure of the spy ship *Pueblo*, Kameny and Shoemaker were summoned to a meeting on the ninth floor of NSA headquarters, where the senior leadership worked. Shoemaker was presented with a document stipulating the terms of his continued employment, which he signed, thereby becoming the first openly gay person to retain a government security clearance.

To this day, Shoemaker does not know how the NSA discovered his homosexuality, though he suspects the evidence originated with a hostile foreign intelligence service. It's a plausible scenario that, if true, illustrates a fatal flaw with the entire rationale that once lay behind the prohibition on gays receiving security clearances. That policy was ostensibly designed to protect state secrets. But if a foreign adversary planted information with the NSA concerning the homosexuality of one of its employees—an employee who, like Shoemaker, did not otherwise pose any sort of security risk—then how many *other* well-qualified gays were exposed (and disposed of) in such fashion at the instigation of a hostile intelligence agency? By unnecessarily designating an entire class of its own citizens potential traitors, the U.S. government had handed its enemies a weapon, one they could exploit to target anyone (an intelligence officer, a diplomat, a politician) whom they considered an obstacle. Shoemaker's case demonstrates how it was not gay employees who constituted a national security risk but, rather, the ill-considered policy devised to drive them out.

Kameny was eager to publicize the Shoemaker decision, and the NSA initially agreed to let him do so. But after Ronald Reagan won the presidential election the following week, the agency brass reversed itself. "They had read the election returns and they felt that there would be a lot of people who would not be very happy about this," Kameny recalled. "They were concerned about a backlash from the Moral Majority." Shoemaker agreed to go along with the NSA's plea for secrecy and fulfilled his end of the bargain. On Christmas, he came out to his mother, two sisters, and five brothers, one of whom, a navy captain, already knew of Shoemaker's homosexuality from the friend and fellow officer who had consulted him about it: Bobby Ray Inman.

Five days later, Shoemaker awoke to find himself front-page, above-the-fold news. "Homosexual to Keep High-Security Job," read the headline in the *Washington Post*, which identified Shoemaker only as a "middle-level employee" of the NSA. Inman, whom the incoming administration was considering for the job of deputy director of the CIA, believed his bureaucratic adversaries had leaked the story. Soon, anonymous leaflets began appearing around NSA headquarters at Fort Meade: *NSA No Longer Has a Space Problem. They've Emptied All Their Closets.*

* * *

"THERE ARE FEW WHO FIND IT EASY TO ENGAGE IN PUBLIC DISCUSSION of that within us which strips bare our human frailty," the Gentleman from Mississippi began. Standing before a scrum of quizzical reporters at a hastily convened press conference in his Jackson district office on August 8, 1980, Jon Hinson, thirty-eight-year-old congressman and "baby-faced ex-Marine," could not have chosen a more private part of himself to strip bare than what he was about to reveal. Over a twelve-month period beginning in late 1976, Hinson "was visited with every fear and self-doubt ever conceived." These accumulated anxieties led him to take a series of risks resulting in his paying a one-hundred-dollar fine for "committing an obscene act in Arlington, Virginia," and barely escaping from a fire at a "theatre which showed X-rated films" in Washington, DC. If these revelations were not sufficiently shocking to the journalists crowded before him, what Hinson was about to say would cause some of them to question his sanity. "I must be totally frank," he said, "and tell you that both of these incidents were in areas frequented by some of Washington's homosexual community."

According to one of Hinson's staffers, "Had UFOs landed with aliens singing the Osmonds' greatest hits, the astonishment of those gathered would not have been greater." Nor was it dampened by Hinson's assurance that he had "rediscovered my basic religious values" thanks "to "Cynthia, who has been, through it all, my confidante, my friend, and now my wife."

The revelation sent shockwaves through Hinson's solidly Republican constituency, which had first sent him to Congress two years earlier by a twenty-six-point margin. Hinson had compiled a reliably conservative voting record, opposing a law to make Martin Luther King Jr.'s birthday a national holiday and achieving a 92 percent rating from the evangelical lobbying group Christian Voice. Naturally, some of these voters wondered if Hinson's presence at two of Washington's most notorious homosexual hangouts was more than simply happenstance, if their congressman was, in fact, a homosexual. Hinson provided a categorical answer the following week. "I am not, never have been, and never will be a homosexual," he promised. "I am not a homosexual. I am not a bisexual."

Hinson's denial was satisfactory for the nearly five hundred constituents who paid for a full-page newspaper advertisement pledging support for their embattled congressman. "Your hometown folks, those who know you best, are backing you all the way!" the proud citizens of Walthall, Mississippi, announced enthusiastically. (Perhaps a little *too* enthusiastically: eighteen signatories later claimed their names had appeared without their consent.) The willingness of Hinson's supporters to forgive him his moral trespasses was best explained by one of his top financial backers, who put it down to political pragmatism. "You'd think a man who had acknowledged frequenting a homosexual theater would have been run out of Mississippi," Billy Mounger, a Jackson oilman, said. "But there are folks that think they would rather have a queer conservative than a macho virile liberal in office." Hinson's father agreed. "I don't think this is going to hurt him one bit," he predicted. "Everybody's probably got a little skeleton in his closet."

Two months later, it was the turn of another conservative Republican lawmaker to address the skeleton in *his* closet. On the afternoon of October 8,

Congressman Bob Bauman strode up to the podium before a sea of reporters at the Tidewater Inn, the same Easton, Maryland, hotel where he held
his Election Night victory parties. On this occasion, however, Bauman
had nothing to celebrate. Five days earlier, he had been arraigned in DC
Superior Court for soliciting sex from a sixteen-year-old male prostitute at
the Chesapeake House. "I understand human weakness now better than
ever," said the Gentleman from Maryland, who followed Hinson's lead in
the demonstration of uxorial and ecclesiastical support by enlisting his
wife, Carol, and their parish priest to sit by his side. Also like his Mississippi colleague, Bauman denied that his actions, which he ascribed to alcoholism, signified anything essential about his nature. While admitting to
"homosexual tendencies," he assured his audience that "I do not consider
myself to be a homosexual."

Between Bauman and Hinson, the question posed by *Washingtonian*
magazine that month—"Is DC Becoming the Gay Capital of America?" —
assumed an unexpectantly mordant relevance. "It kind of makes you wonder," a customer at an Easton diner pondered aloud. "Who else?" It was a
humiliating fall especially for Bauman, who was normally so self-assured,
always on the offensive, full of fire in his belly, and primed for the deft
parliamentary maneuver or cutting rhetorical attack. "We're all a bunch of
drunks but we don't do that," a customer at the Tidewater Inn bar, over-
hearing Bauman's press conference, muttered aloud. "Many people have
learned to live with the problem of alcoholism," added a Democratic state
legislator. "People might understand that. But the sodomy is difficult to
assess." (One wag remarked that Bauman's travails would "give alcoholism
a bad name.") Still, Bauman had no intention of resigning and was buoyed
by the letters of support that poured in from across his district as well as
from the nation's most notoriously disgraced Republican, Richard Nixon.
None of these heartening missives, however, could dampen the kick in the
teeth from a treasured friend and mentor. "Robert Bauman should resign
from Congress, and resign, also, his various positions in conservative organizations, conspicuously his chairmanship of the American Conservative
Union," wrote William F. Buckley Jr. in his biweekly column, On the Right,
syndicated to 350 newspapers nationwide. Just a week earlier, he and Bauman had celebrated the twentieth anniversary of Young Americans for
Freedom at a gala dinner in Washington, where Bauman had confided to

Buckley that he had entered Alcoholics Anonymous. Buckley offered his admonishment with a heavy heart. "I never did anything that I hated more," he would later confess. But as a prominent spokesman for conservative causes, Buckley concluded in his column, Bauman had "ordained standards of conduct which he himself transgressed" and therefore had an obligation to accept "retirement from public life."

Bauman, in other words, was a hypocrite, and it was this quality that earned him a greater degree of scrutiny than his colleague Hinson, who had never positioned himself as a model of traditional family values. It did not help Bauman's case that, in his endeavor to convince the citizens of Maryland's First Congressional District that they should forgive his sexual peccadilloes, he had twice voted against measures intended to protect gays from discrimination, or that he had cultivated the public image of a moralist, or that he had been so acerbic about the foibles of his fellow legislators. For instance, once accused by Democratic congressman Wayne Hays of Ohio for lacking knowledge about foreign affairs, Bauman retorted that Hays, infamous for putting a mistress who couldn't type on his payroll, "had problems with affairs himself." Asked if he would support a conservative challenger to Maryland's liberal Republican senator Charles Mathias, Bauman took a random and gratuitous swipe at Ted Kennedy, making light of the Massachusetts senator's 1969 vehicular accident on Chappaquiddick Island that resulted in the drowning death of a young woman. "As Kennedy says, I'll cross that bridge when I come to it," Bauman cracked.

Come election day, the citizens of the Maryland First were less willing to tolerate a queer conservative than those of the Mississippi Fourth: Bauman lost 52 to 48 against his Democratic challenger and Hinson won a plurality of the vote in a four-man race. "I felt like Lazarus did when he returned from the dead," a relieved Hinson declared to supporters in Jackson. His resurrection, alas, would be short-lived.

Around 1 p.m. on February 4, 1981, Hinson tossed his coat and tie onto the chair in his office in the Cannon House Office Building, put on a sweater, and descended into the underground tunnel toward the Longworth Building. He walked up five flights of stairs and found his way to a remote restroom, where he encountered a twenty-eight-year-old Black Library of Congress clerk named Harold Moore. The two men did not know each other. What they also did not know was that Capitol Police officers were watching them engage in oral sex through a hole in the wall. Tipped off that the bathroom had become a busy cruising spot, the police had been monitoring it for the past two weeks. Before undertaking their surveillance, the chief had asked Speaker Tip O'Neill if members of Congress should be alerted in advance. O'Neill, a staunch Democrat in both the upper and lowercase sense of the word, did not think his fellow legislators were entitled to such a privilege, and told him no.

Hinson's arrest, according to a Mississippi newspaper, hit Washington "with greater force than last year's controversy about who shot J.R. Ewing," villain of the hit television series *Dallas*. At a Georgetown dinner party "teeming with some of Washington's most prominent liberals," a deeply closeted government official sat in silence as the other guests joked about men like Bob Bauman, Jon Hinson—and him. "They laughed and I laughed," the government official said. "I hated myself for laughing, and I hated my friends for laughing." Relaying the diagnosis from Hinson's physician, an aide to the congressman alerted the press that the incident was "an episode . . . termed a dissociative reaction attributed to a two-year period of intense emotional and physical exertion, which included a successful freshman term and an extremely difficult re-election campaign." No one bought it.

And not only because the "episode" seemed to fit into what was by now a clearly established pattern. Attempting to receive fellatio from a white undercover cop was something the voters of the Mississippi Fourth were willing to forgive. But performing it on a Black man, as the press accounts made clear Hinson had done, was a bridge too far. "Can you imagine walking down the main street of your hometown in southern Mississippi and knowing that everybody knows you've sucked a Black dick?" Hinson later explained to a friend. "The fact that the employee Hinson was caught with was Black added insult to injury here in Mississippi," said Leslie McLemore, a Black university professor who was one of the three candidates to challenge Hinson in his 1980 reelection race. "There are still a zillion jokes about it." Billy Mounger, the Jackson oilman who spoke for many Mississippians just a few months earlier when he said he'd rather have a queer conservative than a macho liberal representing him in Congress, theatrically tore a Hinson sticker off his wall for the local newscast. "It's all over," Mounger groused. Hinson's office was inundated with calls from constituents demanding his immediate resignation. "Roger Mudd just said oral sodomy and Mississippi in the same sentence in my living room!" one constituent screamed at a hapless receptionist. Trent Lott, the Republican whip whose congressional district bordered Hinson's, and who had rallied to his defense when all he had done was get caught cruising around the Iwo Jima Memorial and escape from a fire at a gay pornographic theater, threatened to open formal disciplinary proceedings against his fellow Mississippian unless he resigned. Both the local chapter of the Ku Klux Klan and area gay activists agreed: Hinson had to go. After five weeks, calling it "the most difficult and painful decision of my life," Hinson announced his resignation in a one-sentence letter to the governor of Mississippi.

The twin downfalls of Bauman and Hinson came at a moment when the nascent politics of homosexuality was on the cusp of becoming a partisan issue. In 1974, when Bella Abzug introduced a bill to prohibit discrimination against gays in housing, public accommodation, and private employment, it was before the emergence of the Christian right as a major voting bloc, or that of a smaller but still influential "gay vote" in cities ruled by Democratic party machines. Abzug's legislation won the support of Texas Republican senator John Tower, a conservative traditionally hostile to civil rights legislation, but not that of his fellow Texan, the Black liberal Democratic congresswoman Barbara Jordan. According to *The Advocate*, this state of affairs left gay activists "pondering a new political reality and reassessing the meaning of labels such as conservative and liberal." To be sure, very few politicians of any ideological persuasion supported gay rights at the time, but the principle of individual freedom beloved by conservatives, as much as the principle of equality championed by liberals, could be cited in their favor. The inability of traditional political labels to capture sentiment on gay rights was further underscored by far lower levels of ideological and partisan polarization. Both major parties were sufficiently capacious such that liberal Republicans and conservative Democrats were not the endangered (or extinct) species they are today. In 1976, *The Advocate* reported that "the growing number of Republican politicians who support gay rights suggests that the GOP might be fertile ground for the seeds of gay liberation," and the following year, it was a right-wing Georgia Democrat, Congressman Larry McDonald, who sponsored legislation to ban Legal Services aid to homosexuals.

The revelations, within weeks of each other, that two Republican congressmen had engaged in homosexual activity, hastened the end of this era. It was a development augured by the way in which an increasingly assertive gay left, influenced by the feminist slogan "The personal is political," came to endorse the same rationale for exposing closeted gay power brokers as Bill Buckley had offered for his friend's swift dismissal from political life: hypocrisy. For as long as it had existed, the secret city was governed by an ethic of mutually assured discretion, undergirded by a threat of mutually assured destruction: what had come to be known simply as "the Code." Like the Hollywood taboo Otto Preminger shattered with *Advise and Consent*, this tacit agreement among gays required a form of silence, obligating them to protect their common secret from outsiders. The Code transcended ideological and party divisions, personal disputes, and romantic quarrels, and it was rigorously enforced. Even while Anita Bryant was campaigning to "Save Our Children" from homosexuals, gay rights activists never disclosed that one of her own top aides was a man from whom children apparently needed saving. Straight journalists—and there was not a single openly gay journalist working in the mainstream media at this time—also respected the Code. As their coverage of Bauman and Hinson demonstrated, the media avoided reporting on the homosexuality of politicians except when it got them into legal difficulties.

The rise of a vocally antigay movement on the right, mirrored by the rise of a gay movement most of whose advocates situated themselves on the left, threatened this bipartisan convention against disclosure. In April 1980, just a few months after seventy-five thousand gays and lesbians descended upon the National Mall to advocate for societal recognition of their basic humanity, nearly three times that number of religious conservatives journeyed to the same spot to hear speakers denounce homosexuality at a "Washington for Jesus" rally. As attacks on the "homosexual agenda" became a staple of right-wing political rhetoric and action, the existence of right-wing gays presented a challenge to the inviolability of the Code. Roy Cohn's experience in the Army-McCarthy Hearings illustrated how gays could simultaneously be complicit in homophobia, as well as the target of it. Thirty years later, the involvement of not insubstantial numbers of gays in a political coalition dependent upon antigay votes would provoke a debate over the discretion due to men whose private lives contrasted with their public policies. Once the exclusive tool of those who considered homosexuality a menace, the tactic of exposure would be embraced by gays themselves to punish other gays perceived to be collaborating in their own oppression.

And so, as the Reagan Revolution rolled into town, a renewed sense of unease and suspicion descended over gay Washington. "Now, even straights are afraid to go to the gay bars they might have occasionally gone to before for fear they'll be suspect," one gay activist observed. "It really could turn into a very bloody scene in this city."

RONALD REAGAN

But I was in search of love in those days, and I went full of curiosity and the faint, unrecognized apprehension that here, at last, I should find that low door in the wall, which others, I knew, had found before me, which opened on an enclosed and enchanted garden, which was somewhere, not overlooked by any window, in the heart of that grey city.

—Evelyn Waugh, *Brideshead Revisited*

33

"THE HOMOSEXUAL THING"

It was 3:15 on the morning of June 26, 1980, and Congressman Bob Livingston was extraordinarily drunk, hiding in the Congressional Gym beneath the Rayburn House Office Building, petrified that a team of highly trained right-wing homosexual assassins working on behalf of Ronald Reagan was about to kill him.

To the extent that the Louisiana Republican is remembered today, it's for the brief but sensational role he played in America's most infamous political sex scandal. On the same day in December 1998 that Bill Clinton was impeached for lying about his affair with a White House intern, Livingston, then the House Speaker–designate, shocked the nation with his own admission of adultery. Like most of his GOP colleagues, Livingston had blasted Clinton for his relationship with Monica Lewinsky. Their moralistic outcry attracted the attention of *Hustler* magazine publisher Larry Flynt, who, sensing more than a hint of hypocrisy, put out a call for dirt on Clinton's accusers. When Livingston learned that Flynt had dredged up evidence of his past relationships with women not his wife, he decided to preempt the exposé. "I must set the example that I hope President Clinton will follow," Livingston told a stunned House Chamber and live television audience, announcing not only his refusal of the speakership, but his resignation from Congress altogether.

Nearly two decades before this bit part in the Clinton impeachment drama riveted the nation, Livingston was at the center of another scandal involving politicians and illicit sex, one that, in his own words, had the potential to be "world-shaking." The malfeasance to which he had become privy implicated the future president of the United States, Central American death squads, and a hidden circle of influence peddlers whose diabolical activities stretched all the way from the halls of power in Congress to a secluded cabin on Lake Tahoe. Most explosive about this whole terrible intrigue, and what tied it all together, was the nature of the sexual activity involved. Appropriately for something concerning an element of the human experience so widely reviled that it long existed behind a veil of secrecy, the story of Ronald Reagan, the "homosexual ring" that allegedly controlled him, and its barely averted impact on the 1980 presidential election has never been told.

The series of events that led Livingston to take refuge in the warrens of a Capitol Hill basement began innocently enough. Shortly before closing his office on the evening of June 25, 1980, Livingston's secretary received a phone call from Lynden "Lynn" Francis Bouchey, executive vice president of a small conservative foreign policy think tank called the Council for Inter-American Security. Bouchey's wife was out of town, and he was home alone facing the unsavory prospect of a TV dinner. Was Livingston free for supper? As luck would have it, Livingston's secretary said, the congressman's wife was also away, and aside from one of those utterly indistinguishable Washington drinks receptions that could fill the calendar of even the most socially unambitious denizen of the nation's capital, his evening was open. Bouchey and Livingston would meet at 7:30 at the Palm near Dupont Circle.

Bouchey drove into the city from his home in Annandale, Virginia, the pleasant suburban community where Livingston also happened to live with his family. The men had several other things in common. Both were thirty-seven years old, brothers of the Delta Kappa Epsilon fraternity, and committed conservatives. One of Bouchey's responsibilities was to enlist up-and-coming legislators in the cause of rolling back communism across Latin America, a crusade that was beginning to assume great domestic and international significance in the dawning decade of the 1980s. As the congressman representing the Port of New Orleans, Livingston had every reason to worry about this threat, and when Bouchey offered him a seat on the council's advisory board, he was happy to accept.

Bouchey was a foot soldier in an insurgent political force known as the New Right. In the four years since it alarmed the moderate GOP establishment with its backing for Ronald Reagan's surprisingly strong challenge to incumbent President Gerald Ford during the 1976 Republican primary, the New Right had built up an impressive array of think tanks, political action committees, and single-issue advocacy groups dedicated to the rollback of communism abroad and the restoration of traditional moral values at home. Populist in its grassroots appeal, powered by the novel technology of direct mail marketing, and drawing on the energies of a freshly mobilized evangelical Christian voter base, the New Right was now on the brink of extending its influence into the White House. Just weeks away from his anointment as the Republican nominee, Reagan had welcomed the New Right into the nascent conservative coalition he was constructing along the designs of a three-legged stool upheld by national security hawks, free marketeers, and religious fundamentalists.

Like many of the young men inspired by the Reagan revolution, the soft-spoken, soft-featured, sandy-haired Bouchey was a devotee of the first two groups, but he lived a secret life that placed him in the crosshairs of the third.

In 1961, as a nineteen-year-old student at the University of Washington, Bouchey took time off from his studies to join Young Americans for Freedom, spreading the gospel of individualism, free markets, and militant anticommunism on college campuses across the land. One of his earliest exploits was a campaign to discredit the rival National Student Association, a consortium of university student governments, by smearing it as a commie front. Taking a page from Murray Chotiner's playbook, Bouchey proposed that the school's YAF chapter inundate the campus with doctored NSA leaflets printed on pink paper. "We have been sold down the river once by Alger Hiss and his dandy group of subversives," one aghast parent declared. Bouchey's Oklahoma effort was a smashing success; the student body voted to split from the NSA by a whopping margin of three to one.

The tactics Bouchey honed as a conservative student activist tormenting liberals coast to coast prepared him well for his current job lobbying for the freedom fighters battling communism from the Southern Cone to the Caribbean Sea. Chaired by a former army general who had resigned in protest of Jimmy Carter's relinquishing American control over the Panama Canal, the Council for Inter-American Security had recently cosponsored the U.S. speaking tour of Salvadoran death squad leader turned politician Roberto D'Aubuisson and was running a campaign against the SALT II nuclear arms reduction treaty championed by the man Livingston derisively referred to as "that toothy Georgian peanut farmer." Bouchey's zeal was personal as well as political. Five years earlier, his wife's uncle—former "No. 2 man" in the regime of Cuban military dictator Fulgencio Batista—had been killed in a Miami car bombing likely ordered by Fidel Castro.

Settling down to dinner at the Palm three weeks before he and his fellow Republicans were to gather at the Joe Louis Arena in Detroit for their national convention, Livingston had something more urgent on his mind than the twilight struggle between capitalism and communism. For months, speculation had been mounting as to whom Reagan would choose as his running mate. In addition to former CIA director George H. W. Bush, former president Ford was being mentioned as a figure whose selection might heal the widening divide between GOP moderates and conservatives, as were Senators Howard Baker of Tennessee, Richard Lugar of Indiana, and former Treasury secretary William Simon. But it was the candidacy of a fellow House colleague that most piqued Livingston's interest— more specifically, the persistent rumor that accompanied any conversation related to his attaining higher office. After the two men dispensed with some small talk about the latest developments in Latin America and the state of his own reelection race, Livingston steered the conversation toward the Honorable Gentleman from Buffalo, Jack Kemp.

"Do you know anything about Kemp, is he AC/DC?" Livingston asked, referencing not the Australian hard rock band but the slang expression for bisexual.

"Yeah, I heard some things," Bouchey replied. "That stuff's been around."

"That stuff," or what Kemp advisor Jude Wanniski termed "the homosexual thing," had dogged the upstate New York congressman and former professional football player since the fall of 1967, when Drew Pearson connected him to a "homosexual ring" operating within then governor Reagan's Sacramento office and a timeshare in Lake Tahoe. Murmurings about the handsome young athlete spread from the political watering holes of Sacramento to the scrums of the American Football League, following him all the way to Capitol Hill, where he began a meteoric rise after winning a seat in Congress in 1970. "We used to have a saying in Sacramento in those days," former speaker of the California State Assembly Jesse Unruh joked to a group of photographers while posing for pictures with a pair of young women during his campaign against Reagan that year. "Prove you're straight and take a girl to lunch." When the rumors resurfaced at the 1976 Republican convention in Kansas City, Kemp convened an emergency dinner meeting with a group of advisors, including his wife, Wanniski, neoconservative intellectual Irving Kristol, and economist Herb Klein, where they spent an hour and a half vainly discussing a strategy to quash them. Two years later, during the congressional midterm election, senior Carter aide Hamilton Jordan told a reporter to disregard Kemp as a serious presidential contender because he was a "queer," and the chairman of the Democratic National Committee advised another journalist that a Kemp-sponsored tax bill had no chance of passing for the same reason. "There is absolutely not a shred of evidence," a fed-up Kemp complained. "There is nothing, and there was nothing." According to Evans and Novak, the "malicious and untrue gossip" about Kemp was but one of several gay rumors that "played a subterranean part in a half dozen statewide races" that election season. The "slander" and "old calumny" that the virile ex–football pro and father of four might be gay, the newspapermen thundered, was a "vicious canard," the sort of "poisonous" "garbage" one found "submerged in the political sewers" and other "gutter communications" that "not only do gross injustice to their victims but also demean and pollute democratic government."

All this was on Livingston's mind because of what he had heard the previous month at a secret meeting with members of the Republican "Wednesday Group." Founded by a dozen disgruntled liberal-to-moderate Republican congressmen just days after Barry Goldwater's landslide defeat, the Wednesday Group was formed to wrest control of the GOP away from the party's insurgent conservative wing and keep it out of their hands. At 5 p.m. every week on the club's eponymous day, some thirty to forty members would meet over pretzels and booze to talk shop and plot strategy. Livingston was not one of their number. But following the regular gathering on May 14, a colleague who was roped him into an impromptu discussion held at the office of Congressman Paul N. "Pete" McCloskey of California. Even before winning a 1967 special election to Congress from a district in the Bay Area, the dovish marine veteran of the Korean War with a jawline so sharp his staff nicknamed him "Mount Rushmore" had a tortured relationship with his party in general, and with the darling of its conservative faction in particular. McCloskey had defeated the former child movie star Shirley Temple Black, a friend of Reagan's, in an open primary, and did so while running as the only Republican in the country decisively opposed to the Vietnam War. Asked about Reagan's presidential aspirations two weeks before the election, McCloskey curtly suggested that the governor stick to finishing his term. Returning fire the following year, Reagan declared that McCloskey's refusal to endorse their party's right-wing Senate nominee amounted to a violation of the GOP's "Eleventh Commandment"—"Thou shalt not speak ill of any Republican"—as articulated by the state party chairman. "Maybe a young congressman has a little more to learn about party loyalty," Reagan cracked, putting the whippersnapper in his place.

Party loyalty, however, was a concept utterly foreign to McCloskey. In 1971, two years before the Watergate scandal broke, he said that President Nixon should be threatened with impeachment over his handling of the Vietnam War. Later that year, when McCloskey started talking about a primary challenge to Nixon, Reagan said it would not bother him a whit if the forthcoming congressional redistricting map left the mutinous Republican congressman with a constituency "the length and breadth of the San Andreas Fault." Yes, Reagan acknowledged, by attacking McCloskey it was now he who had broken the "Eleventh Commandment." But, he added, offering an amendment to a holy political decree, "There are times when a man removes himself from the umbrella of the Eleventh Commandment by his own actions." Both men would go on to challenge incumbent Republican presidents, McCloskey from the left in 1972 and Reagan from the right four years later, and so strikingly did they represent their respective ideological flanks that Lou Cannon described them as "the two most charismatic contenders for the soul of California's Republican party." When McCloskey, a cofounder of Earth Day, helped draft the Endangered Species Act, a cynic might have suggested that he had done so as a matter of self-preservation, his breed of liberal Republican fast on the path to extinction.

As Reagan progressed toward the presidency, this battle between the liberal and conservative factions of the California GOP was projected onto the national political stage. And at every step of Reagan's inexorable rise, McCloskey was there trying to stop him. In 1976, "scared to death that

Ronald Reagan was going to be the next President," McCloskey recruited fellow liberal Republicans to support Ford. At the beginning of the next election cycle, despite his preference for moderates like Congressman John Anderson and Sen. Howard Baker, McCloskey supported George Bush. "It is absolutely essential to stop Ronald Reagan from getting the Republican nomination," he declared, "and George Bush is the only candidate who can do that." Alas, Bush couldn't do it, and was now vying to be Reagan's running mate. With Reagan's nomination all but sealed, the recalcitrant ex-marine would wage one final, desperate battle for the soul of his party.

In addition to Livingston, the other congressmen huddled in McCloskey's office that evening were Jim Johnson of Colorado, Barber Conable of New York, Bill Frenzel of Minnesota, Hal Sawyer of Michigan, and Gerald Ford's former White House chief of staff, a Wyoming freshman named Richard Bruce Cheney. Kemp's possible selection as running mate, McCloskey told the group, suggested strongly to him that the "homosexual ring" around Reagan, long dismissed as rumor, might be something all too real. In recent weeks, McCloskey explained, he had been in contact with a local television news reporter named Bill Best who used to work in the Bay Area and had been active in the California chapter of Young Americans for Freedom during the late 1960s. The last time McCloskey had heard from Best was in early 1976, a few months after Reagan announced his decision to challenge Ford, when Best agitatedly told him that senior Reagan advisors had sexually propositioned him on two separate occasions. McCloskey did not hear from Best again until April 23, when Best began calling him frantically to report that "homosexual people were very close to Reagan's campaign leadership," that they were "running" Reagan's campaign, and that "the situation is absolutely out of control." It was not until a boozy lunch with a man claiming to have been a "long time Reagan associate," however, that Best found what he believed to be the "smoking gun" proving that Reagan was controlled by homosexuals. "Bill, you don't understand the problem," the man told Best. "I once engaged in a homosexual act with Reagan."

As for Jack Kemp, McCloskey had never known what to make of the rumors surrounding his colleague from New York. "The big joke on Capitol Hill," he recalled, "was that the most dangerous position in pro football is to be Jack Kemp's center." But as far as homosexuality itself was concerned, McCloskey was more progressive than the vast majority of his colleagues. As a lawyer in Palo Alto in the 1960s, he had represented men arrested for homosexual solicitation, and when Congresswoman Bella Abzug introduced the first bill in Congress prohibiting discrimination against gays, he was its only Republican sponsor. "I am heterosexual, I think," the quirky congressman told *The Advocate* in 1977. "I wonder sometimes." In the present situation, however, McCloskey's personal feelings were beside the point. He agreed with Best that a Kemp nomination would revive the 1967 "Scandal in Sacramento," possibly leading to revelations about the other homosexuals in Reagan's orbit and thereby imperiling the GOP ticket in much the same way that the release of Sen. Thomas Eagleton's medical records helped scupper George McGovern. McCloskey suggested that Best "make use of his continuing friendship with top people in the Reagan organization, both to apprise them of the dangers of a Kemp nomination in light of the Tahoe experience, and to alert Governor Reagan to move the homosexual operatives away from the leadership positions Bill said they occupied." McCloskey, meanwhile, shared Best's allegations with Republican House minority leader John Jacob Rhodes of Arizona. Like McCloskey, Rhodes was by no means antipathetic toward gays. According to a former press secretary, when one of his staffers was arrested on a homosexual offense, Rhodes kept the man in his employ and remained friends with him for the rest of his life. Rhodes was also willing to challenge powerful forces within his party, never more consequentially than in August 1974, when he accompanied his fellow Arizonan Barry Goldwater and Senate Republican minority leader Hugh Scott to an Oval Office meeting where they informed President Nixon that he faced certain impeachment, conviction, and removal by Congress if he did not step down. Nixon resigned the next day.

Like McCloskey, Rhodes also felt little affection for the man his party was on the verge of nominating for president. When Reagan challenged Rhodes's good friend and predecessor as House minority leader, Gerald Ford, in 1976, Rhodes convened a secret strategy session with Ford and Republican congressmen to discuss how to stop Reagan in his tracks. On the last night of the convention in Kansas City, over which Rhodes presided as chairman, a forty-three-minute spontaneous demonstration by Reagan supporters on the floor of the Kemper Arena left him seething at the podium. "This is the longest demonstration of my seven conventions," he complained fruitlessly. "Nothing can stop it as far as I can tell." A backer of the ERA and an opponent of a constitutional amendment banning abortion, Rhodes had come under vicious attack from his party's right wing,

Reagan included, over his endorsement of a Carter administration plan to implement Election Day voter registration. For these and other heresies, the newsletter of Citizens for the Republic, Reagan's political action committee, once featured a cartoon depicting Rhodes as having stabbed the GOP elephant. "*Et tu*, Rhode," read the caption.

Rhodes, tired of leading a rump minority caucus and preparing to step down after the election, suggested that McCloskey talk to Republican National Committee chairman Bill Brock. Before McCloskey had had a chance to do so, however, he convened the meeting with six of his colleagues at which Livingston was present. As McCloskey was to record, the group ultimately decided that "the matter should go no further; that merely to repeat the allegations, was to give credence to something that was both hearsay and possibly unfounded."

Some five weeks after this exchange, over dinner at the Palm, Livingston apparently could not get the salacious stories involving Kemp and the homosexual Reagan aides out of his mind. As he sipped white wine and Bouchey downed martinis, the subject of Kemp's sexuality "dominated" their conversation, as Bouchey was to remember. He found Livingston's "preoccupation" with whether "a colleague of his was a switch-hitter" to be curious. "He was very interested in him," Bouchey recalled. "The whole subject was raised by him. It was certainly not raised by me." At one point, however, Bouchey might have volunteered the possibility that Kemp and Reagan himself had both engaged in gay sex.

Following the meal, Livingston suggested a nightcap in Georgetown. The pair were on the verge of violating the "eleven o'clock rule," coined by Stewart Alsop two decades earlier to denote that "curious, un-American custom imposed by the fact that Washington is filled with diplomats and other protocol-conscious persons" whose professional obligations necessitate an early bedtime. But with both men's spouses out of town, the case for prolonging their time together prevailed. The two hopped into Livingston's Mustang and drove to F. Scott's, a Georgetown haunt. After a drink there, they walked a few doors down to another watering hole, the Tombs. Last round was called, and Livingston offered to give Bouchey a ride back to Capitol Hill, where Bouchey had parked his car. By this point, Bouchey remembered, both men were deep "in the cup," and he replied that he was "in no shape" to drive himself home. Livingston offered to take them both back to Annandale. Collapsing into the Mustang, the men paused for a moment, and Livingston inserted his key in the ignition. Before he could start the car, Bouchey placed his hand firmly on Livingston's knee and asked, "Are you trying to get something started with me?"

Bouchey would later insist he had intended nothing sexual by the gesture or the remark. "I guess I was drunker than he was," he conceded. It was a common justification, "a pattern with closeted men I met in those years," remembered Sean Strub. Of the ostensibly heterosexual Washingtonians who eagerly joined him in carousing the city's gay bars, Strub observed, "They could be married to women, have large families, be prominent in their churches and even advocates of anti-gay measures. When the circumstances were right, they could also be campy, sing show tunes, and be sexually adventurous—that is, as long as they could deny it the next morning and blame 'whatever happened' on alcohol."

A sexual proposition, an inebriated lark, or something in between—it was one man's hand placed upon another man's knee that set off a chain of events with the potential to rattle the Reagan campaign, upset the presidential race, and change the course of history.

Livingston panicked. "Oh hell no," he said, jerking his knee in rebuff. He quickly started the car, and an awkward silence descended over both men. Livingston's mind began to process the jumble of things he had seen and heard over the past few weeks: the long-standing rumors about Kemp; the supposed gay network encircling Reagan; McCloskey's contact who claimed that he, *too*, had been hit on by gay Reaganites; the curious recurrence of Young Americans for Freedom as a nexus of right-wing chicanery and homosexual intrigue; Bouchey's ties to various Latin American juntas and paramilitaries. None of it added up to anything good.

When Livingston reached Bouchey's home, he stopped the Mustang and unceremoniously dumped his inebriated passenger off at the curb. "Thanks for dinner," Bouchey mumbled as Livingston sped away.

Though he lived in the same town, Livingston was afraid to return home. He hightailed it back to Washington, to the safest place to which he had access: the dank subterranean chamber of the House members' gym. "When I was fifteen, someone tried to make a pass at me," he recalled. "It was the first and last time" he was so approached until that moment during the summer of 1980. "Frankly, when I was fifteen, I didn't know people were like that, and I escaped." Using a phone in the locker room, Livingston rang the Capitol Police and asked to be put through to McCloskey.

"You were absolutely right," Livingston gasped, according to a summary of their conversation later recorded by McCloskey. "I just had a terrible experience." Livingston proceeded to explain how he had just spent the night drinking with a friend and fraternity brother who "runs a security agency which furnishes support, training and weapons for Latin American governments." This person had in the past mentioned "hits" across Latin America, and the previous October, a full week before the El Salvadoran military staged a coup d'état, he predicted with chilling accuracy "precisely what was going to happen and who would be involved." He "has the capacity to 'hit' people both in Latin America and here" in the United States, and he "indicated to me during the evening that Kemp was certainly a participant in homosexual conduct and that he thought it possible Reagan was also." After making clear that he "saw nothing wrong with men enjoying each other's company sexually," this man "made a pass at me on three different occasions" over the course of the evening. Livingston was calling McCloskey from the House Gym, he explained, because he feared he might be "met by a shotgun blast at the door" of his home for having rejected the man's sexual advances. Signaling disinterest in the "AC/DC" lifestyle, apparently, constituted more than just a personal affront to an intoxicated frat brother. Apprised of a clandestine homosexual cabal with "almost a religious zeal against communism," reaching all the way from Washington to Sacramento, and from San Salvador to Santiago, Livingston had balked at its initiation rites and thus put himself in grave danger. "When he becomes sober and realizes what he has said to me, and that I refused him," Livingston said, "I think he is fully capable of violence."

"You were right," Livingston kept repeating. "There *is* a network."

34

THE MANCHURIAN CANDIDATE

WHILE THE NOTION OF A CABAL OF RIGHT-WING GAY HITMEN MIGHT SEEM
far-fetched, a tragedy involving politics, murder, and homosexuality had
occurred just three months earlier, in painful proximity to Livingston,
McCloskey, and their congressional colleagues. On the afternoon of March
14, 1980, a thirty-seven-year-old man named Dennis Sweeney walked into
the Rockefeller Center law office of former Democratic congressman Allard
K. Lowenstein. Described by the *Washington Post* as a "Pied Piper to three
generations of student activists," Lowenstein was a singularly omnipresent
and peripatetic figure of postwar American liberalism. Since his election
as president of the National Student Association in 1950, Lowenstein was
active in every great cause, present at seemingly every pivotal moment, and
had acquainted himself with every influential figure in the liberal American firmament. (And not just liberals: one of Lowenstein's most cherished
friendships was with his frequent sparring partner, William F. Buckley Jr.)
Lowenstein was most famous for organizing the "Dump Johnson" movement, formed to defeat Lyndon Johnson in the 1968 Democratic primary,
and which achieved its goal when Johnson declined to run for reelection.
This was the inspiration for McCloskey's challenge to Richard Nixon (on
whose enemies list Lowenstein earned place number seven), and after rep-

resenting Long Island for a single term in Congress from 1969 to 1971, Lowenstein worked with McCloskey on an effort to register young voters dubbed "Dump-the-War."

Sweeney was one of the thousands of young people Lowenstein had inspired during this impressive career. The two had met in the early 1960s at Stanford University, where Sweeney was a student and Lowenstein an assistant dean. Sweeney may have been a member of another, much more exclusive group of Lowenstein protégés: the invariably preppy and handsome young men with whom Lowenstein developed relationships that were intensely emotional, physical, and just at the edge of homoerotic. Though a married father of three, Lowenstein struggled with his sexuality throughout his life, and he privately discussed the possibility of his being gay or bisexual with a small number of trusted confidants. On his frequent trips abroad, Lowenstein would often abandon his traveling companion for hours at a time, leaving more than a few to wonder if he was engaged in covert action on behalf of the CIA (the thesis of a controversial book published after his death), cruising for sex, or both.

Sweeney had told at least five other people that he was the target of an unwanted sexual advance from Lowenstein in 1964, while he and Lowenstein were registering Black voters in Mississippi. Any evaluation of what transpired that night must take Sweeney's mental illness into account; according to Lowenstein, Sweeney once told him that he was having his teeth removed to make space for the CIA to implant a transmitter in his mouth. All this was prelude to the shocking encounter at Rockefeller Center, when, after entering Lowenstein's office and shaking his hand, Sweeney shot his former mentor five times with a 9 mm semiautomatic pistol, placed the weapon on a secretary's desk, and calmly smoked a cigarette while waiting for the police to arrive. Lowenstein died that night.

McCloskey, who quantified the magnitude of Lowenstein's assassination as "almost equal to that when we lost the Kennedys and Martin Luther King Jr.," delivered a eulogy at the funeral alongside Ted Kennedy and Bill Buckley. "If there was a gentle warrior in our midst," he told the mourners at New York's Central Synagogue, among whose ranks sat widows Coretta Scott King and Jacqueline Onassis, "it was Al Lowenstein." On May 12, two days before McCloskey convened the meeting with his six Republican House colleagues to discuss the allegations of a "homosexual ring" around Ronald Reagan, the *Village Voice* published an article about the relationship between Lowenstein and Sweeney. Revealing the 1964 incident, and placing it within the context of several similar ones involving other young men, the piece asserted that "there were rumors that Lowenstein and Sweeney had fallen out as a result of a lover's quarrel." After the *Washington Post* republished an abridged version of the article, McCloskey joined fifteen congressional colleagues in a letter to the editor denouncing it as "rife with unsubstantiated assertions and gratuitous innuendo," and for portraying Lowenstein as "preying on the innocence of young people."

The mysterious, quite possibly gay-related circumstances surrounding the assassination of a prominent ex-congressman were the subject of much passionate conversation and concern in Washington when, at 3:15 a.m. on the morning of June 26, Bob Livingston phoned McCloskey from the House Gym to relate his own traumatic experience involving homosexuality and (potential) homicide. In light of what Livingston had told him, McCloskey was now aware of *two* people who had "been physically and homosexually approached" by Reaganites and "feared for [their] respective lives" as a result of spurning those approaches. Combined with the long-standing Kemp rumors, McCloskey remembered, "I'm thinking back to *Advise and Consent.*"

McCloskey told his worried colleague that he could sleep on his couch. McCloskey's Georgetown bachelor pad, he said, was akin to "a rooming house" where all manner of visitors from Northern California, including the Stanford cheerleading squad, were welcome to crash while passing through the nation's capital. But Livingston preferred to stay put. They agreed to meet first thing the next day, after the Republican caucus breakfast.

That morning, McCloskey recalled, Livingston was "white as a sheet." Once the meeting ended, the two legislators marched to Livingston's office in the Cannon Building, where Livingston showed McCloskey the wallet and business card Lynn Bouchey had mistakenly left in his Mustang the previous night. McCloskey told Livingston that "it was imperative that Bouchey know that others besides him know" what had transpired between them, and that Livingston's secretary should therefore call Bouchey to inform him that the congressman had his wallet, which he should feel free to pick up anytime. And then, as McCloskey returned to his own office, a lightbulb went off in his head.

When Bill Best first told McCloskey back in 1976 about the homosexual advances made to him by the two Reagan aides, he had given McCloskey and four other people sealed envelopes containing a statement about one of those encounters. Best told his confidants not to open the letters unless something happened to him, and to destroy them if Ford won the GOP nomination, which he eventually did. McCloskey, however, held on to Best's note, storing it in the safe in the tiny lavatory adjoining his personal office. Following instructions, whether from his party leadership or a frightened former constituent entrusting him with the fate of the republic, was not McCloskey's strong suit.

McCloskey asked his legislative assistant to retrieve the sealed envelope. Written across the flap was Best's signature and, below it, the words: "To be opened only by Pete McCloskey."

Inside was a one-page statement, dated January 9, 1976:

I[,] William H. Best III, discovered, as a function of a homosexual approach being made to me on November 17th, 1975 by Peter Hannaford of the Ronald Reagan Campaign that Peter Hannaford was bisexual.

In 1967 I had indicated to the Governor's office that there were homosexuals in his office. Two were fired. From 1967 to 1975 I assumed that there were no longer any homo, or bi-sexuals associated with Ronald Reagan.

When Peter Hannaford made his advance on me in his room at the Madison Hotel on the night of November 17th, I became aware, because of the completely agressive [sic] nature of his actions toward me that my pervious [sic] assumptions were wrong.

After thinking about the matter for some time, I concluded that there was a remote possibility that Ronald Reagan might, and I repeat, might be bi-sexual. Because of the potential implications in matters of national security in the event he becomes President of the United States, I felt, since I assume I am the only person who knows, or was willing to say anything about the matter, that it was in the national interest to have a careful examination made of the possibility . . .

Deaver and Hannaford will know who "fingered" them. Therefore I placed myself in a position, possibly, of personal danger.

In the event that something happens to me, it might be possible that my actions in this matter were the cause of whatever happened. I hope and prey [*sic*] that this letter is never opened, but if it is, fight the good fight for truth, justice and honesty.

The two (seemingly Freudian) spelling errors ("pervious" and "prey") didn't fluster McCloskey. He knew what needed to be done.

Over the course of the following week, McCloskey typed up everything he knew about the intrigues concerning the presumptive Republican presidential nominee—the 1967 "homosexual ring" scandal in Sacramento, the repeated sexual importuning of Bill Best by various Reagan aides, Bob Livingston's dramatic escape from a dread squad of homosexual hitmen suborned by Latin American military juntas—into a thirteen-page, thirty-three-point confidential memorandum. The crux of the document, which could also serve as the synopsis for a 1970s paranoid conspiracy thriller entitled *Three Days of the Boys in the Band*, was encapsulated in point thirty-two: "Bill [Best] expressed extreme concern about the danger of a former Hollywood actor in fact being the 'Manchurian candidate' and spoke at length on the nature of the Hollywood movie industry and the fact that an actor is in the hands and under the manipulation of studios, producers, directors, etc., and that he *must* carry out orders in order to survive. He felt that Reagan had been manipulated all of his life, and that he was essentially 'in bondage' to those around him." Ronald Reagan as the ventriloquized pawn of shadowy and sinister forces—his "kitchen cabinet" of California millionaires, his wife Nancy, Nancy's astrologers, the Mafia—has long been a motif in assessments of the fortieth president, and what McCloskey's contribution to the genre might have lacked in plausibility, it more than made up for with originality. Controlling Reagan in *this* scenario was a "network" of homosexuals who "shared an almost religious zeal against communism and in behalf of right-wing causes."

McCloskey had to act fast. He was scheduled to depart with his girlfriend-cum-press-secretary on July 3 for a backpacking trip to Yellowstone National Park, where they would stay until the twelfth, just two days before the start of the Republican convention. This left precious little time to avert a *Manchurian Candidate*-style catastrophe at the Joe Louis Arena. And so, demonstrating a flash of the spontaneity that some dismissed as "quixotic" and other, more sympathetic, observers admired as the passion of a man who "navigates by his own special compass," McCloskey sprang into action. It was the sort of impulsiveness that, when he was young, prompted him to lie to the father of his fiancée that she was pregnant to obtain his permission to marry her. Or, after they had wed, had induced him to stand up suddenly in the middle of a meal with some buddies in the Bay Area, announce to the table that he missed his wife, and drive three hundred miles south to Los Angeles to visit her.

Taking his concerns to the FBI was a nonstarter. The Bureau was overly bureaucratic, its reputation still tarnished by the legacy of Hoover's abuses. This left McCloskey with only one option: he would play the role of Deep Throat. After midnight on July 3, he put a copy of his confidential memo and Bill Best's 1976 statement into a manila folder, walked a few blocks to a home near Dupont Circle, and knocked on the door. Answering in his slippers and a bathrobe was the editor who had become legendary for his role in helping to bring down the last Republican president, Ben Bradlee of the *Washington Post*. McCloskey quickly summarized the matter and handed him the documents. Intrigued, Bradlee said he would put his best reporters on the story and update McCloskey on their progress at the Republican convention.

At *Post* headquarters the next day, Bradlee assembled a group of journalists—assistant managing editor Bob Woodward and reporters Scott Armstrong, Lou Cannon, Ted Gup, and Patrick Tyler—in his office. According to Armstrong, Bradlee spoke of the story related to him by McCloskey as if it had the potential to be what he was fond of calling a "holy shit" exclusive. "The brass ring is up there, boys," Bradlee said, offering one of his favorite metaphors for a huge journalistic scoop. "We just got to reach up and grab it!" As to the story's newsworthiness, "the focus was that there could be a circle of people trying to control Reagan and there may be a commonality of gay-ness," Tyler recalled. "We weren't investigating whether there were gay people around [Reagan]," per se. Bradlee was determined to find out more, and like every great newspaper editor, he was determined to beat the competition and find it out before anyone else. "He didn't know where the story was in this, but he felt that there was a story in there and we better be the first to get it," Tyler said.

Reinforcing Bradlee's hunch, according to Armstrong, Gup, and Tyler, was that Sen. Barry Goldwater had also urged the *Post* to investigate the matter. But how did Goldwater know about it? McCloskey says he never divulged the details to Goldwater, which narrows the possibilities down to one of the handful of congressmen he had informed. A process of deduction strongly suggests it was Goldwater's fellow Arizonan, close friend, and onetime Reagan adversary: Republican House minority leader John Rhodes. On June 19, Reagan had visited Capitol Hill to solidify his support among the congressional rank and file. Rhodes had yet to endorse Reagan, and he held a private meeting with the candidate in his office. According to Reagan's congressional steering committee chairman, Tom Evans of Delaware, the only other man present at the meeting, Rhodes discussed "rumors about people on Reagan's staff that were gay." Reagan, Evans recalled, said "he didn't know that he had any gay people on his staff," but he nonetheless promised to "look into it." Rhodes announced his endorsement the same day.

If Goldwater had urged Bradlee to investigate the "homosexual ring" allegations, his participation in a shambolic effort to stop Reagan's nomination would have been yet another episode in a long-simmering rivalry dating back to his 1964 presidential defeat. Goldwater had taken it personally when Reagan, running for governor two years later and wary of being associated with a loser, rejected Goldwater's offer to campaign for him. The decisive rift would not arrive until 1976, however, when Reagan, having spurned Goldwater's aid ten years earlier but now running for president on the back of a movement that had recast the 1964 rout as a heroic martyrdom, asked for Goldwater's endorsement. Goldwater declined. The following month, making much the same argument against Reagan that his old nemesis LBJ had made against him, Goldwater criticized Reagan's position on retaining control over the Panama Canal by force as reflective of "a surprisingly dangerous state of mind" that "could needlessly lead this country into open military conflict." The two men would not speak for over a year.

Bradlee had personal reasons for taking Goldwater's judgment seriously. The Arizonan was an important source for the *Post* during Watergate, and the friendship between the two men deepened once Goldwater began dating Bradlee's mother-in-law. When Bradlee and Sally Quinn moved into a Georgetown mansion, it was "Goldy," as Bradlee called him, who installed the hi-fi stereo sound system. Goldwater admiringly dubbed Bradlee's paper the "*Post*-mortem," because "if you manage to survive everything else in Washington, Bradlee and the *Post* will eventually get you." Now, at the instigation of a motley crew of Republicans from the party's ideological poles, the *Post* was coming to get Ronald Reagan.

The team of reporters scrambled. Scott Armstrong traveled to Phoenix, where Bill Best was working as a reporter for KTVK, a local news station. Best told Armstrong that his ordeal began in 1966, when, while running for a seat in the California State Assembly, he had dinner with a political consultant, Fred Haffner, whose firm was running Reagan's campaign. As he drove an inebriated Haffner back to his car, Haffner put his hand on Best's leg. "He propositioned me," Best told Armstrong. "He indicated to me that it would be very much in my interest to cooperate, and he indicated to me who else had benefited. It included a lot of people I knew, but I took it with a grain of salt. I was skeptical, but the implication was that Haffner protégés slept with him and then became successful." Haffner also advised Best that "you should go sleep with [Michael] Deaver, it would do you a lot of good."

Fast-forward nine years, to November 1975, and Best was visiting Washington in hopes of landing a job with Reagan's presidential campaign. Best crashed at McCloskey's house in Georgetown, and through the recommendation of Deaver, he set up a meeting with Peter Hannaford in his room at the Madison Hotel. The two depleted the minibar, and as Best got up to leave at around 1 a.m., Hannaford abruptly asked, "Are you ready to go to bed?"

"What?" Best replied.

"Are you ready to go to bed?"

"What are you talking about?"

"If you didn't come over here to go to bed, why did you come over here?"

"To discuss a job with the campaign."

"We did, so now it's time to go to bed," Hannaford replied.

Best fled the room, stumbling down five flights of stairs to his car. Speeding back to McCloskey's, he was pulled over by a cop, who asked him why he was in "the ghetto," before helpfully giving him directions to his destination.

Best told Armstrong that he had informed a few other Republican activist types about these incidents and was confounded by their nonchalance. "Big Deal," was the reaction of Egil "Bud" Krogh, head of the Nixon Plumbers unit. "There were lots of gays in the Nixon administration too." At one point, Best confronted Deaver over lunch about Hannaford's proposition. "It's your partner and you ought to know," Best told him.

"Who else knows?" Deaver asked.

"I told two groups," Best replied. "Those I needed to talk to and those I needed to protect me."

Deaver evinced no reaction as he continued eating his lunch. "You could probably keep eating if I told you that World War III had started," Best remarked, adding that Kemp as the VP pick would be a "giant mistake," an assertion with which Deaver apparently agreed.

Best also told Armstrong about the man, a then seventeen-year-old volunteer on Reagan's first gubernatorial campaign named William Seals Jr., who claimed to have had sex with Reagan. According to Seals, the encounter took place on the night of Reagan's first inauguration in Sacramento. Reagan, wearing nothing but a bathrobe, had invited Seals into his hotel suite. "If Reagan is elected president," Seals boasted to Best, "I could be First Lady." Seals further asserted that he had participated in the alleged Lake Tahoe orgy and had "gone to bed" with Kemp. Despite his best efforts, Armstrong was unable to track down this elusive figure.

The essence of Best's allegations, Armstrong wrote in a memo to his colleagues, was that submission to the sexual demands of an influential circle of gay men was "the sine qua non of success in the Reagan organization." Best, he wrote, was "sane, sober, careful and restrained," not "flaky or kooky." In appearance, he was "sort of Calif. Preppy (Woodward as beach-boy)" and "probably jail bait when he was in his early 20's." But Best also struck Armstrong "as a man who has seen a flying saucer on two separate occasions and can't get anyone to believe him," which left the reporter with the feeling that the story lacked legs. "Count me out until someone on this list [of alleged homosexuals] is actually serving in a presidential administration with access to national security information or until a more current pattern of some group is evident," Armstrong concluded.

Ted Gup tracked down Lynn Bouchey in a depressed suburb outside Dallas, where the think tank director was with his wife and children visiting his father-in-law at his mobile home. Bouchey was "shocked" that a *Post* reporter would come all the way to interview him, Gup later wrote in a memo, but he agreed to speak outside, in the 112-degree heat, away from his family. As Bouchey described the events of June 25 and 26, he reenacted for Gup the moment that sent Livingston fleeing to the basement of the Rayburn Building, grabbing Gup's "knee and thigh firmly" in a "quick unexpected action." ("His hands were strong," Gup recounted. "I thought, 'my God, if he grabbed Livingston that way, no wonder the guy spent the night in the gym.'") As for ordering "hits," Bouchey unreservedly denied that "any of his contacts were terrorists or violent," and he expressed bewilderment that Livingston had felt fearful for his safety. He was less surprised, however, about the existence of a "gay network" surrounding Reagan. "He didn't laugh at the idea," Gup wrote. "He took it seriously. He did not question the legitimacy of a reporter inquiring into it."

Bob Woodward interviewed Livingston, whom McCloskey had apparently not bothered to consult before relating their conversations to the *Post*. "I'm petrified and paranoid about this," Livingston said, according to notes taken by Woodward, who wrote that there was "lots of pushing necessary to get him to talk." Livingston disputed McCloskey's characterization of his early morning phone call from the House Gym, specifically that he told McCloskey that Bouchey had alluded to assassinations. "McCloskey's imagination went wild," Livingston said. That grumble aside, Livingston was concerned about the hidden gay network. A group of men Bouchey periodically assembled over dinner at Capitol Hill restaurants to discuss Latin America, some of whose confabs Livingston had attended, disturbed him. Livingston refused to divulge the names of the people in this group; all he would allow was that it "may tie into [North Carolina Republican senator] Jesse Helms" and that "the inner circle of 1960s YAFers are the key to this." Livingston further told Woodward that it would "take us months to do this story right," but that he hoped the *Post* would pursue it because "I don't want to see the world run by a bunch of weirdos." While Livingston allowed for the possibility that what he took as a sexual advance on the part of Bouchey might have been a mere drunken misunderstanding, "I would never base a story on just what happened to me. If you guys ever prove it, it will be world-shaking."

A few days before the Republican convention in Detroit, the *Post* team regrouped in Washington. Undoubtedly, gay men had played prominent roles in Reagan's political career. But with the important possible exception of Peter Hannaford, none were expected to hold a job in a potential Reagan administration requiring a security clearance. As a rule, Bradlee was hesitant to report on the private lives of public officials unless it had a tangible, direct impact on their work. In 1976, explaining his decision to spike a Jack Anderson column divulging details of congressional adultery, Bradlee wrote, "Public persons' private lives tend to be their own business unless their personal conduct is alleged to violate the law or interfere with performance of the public job." And just a few months before McCloskey showed up on his doorstep urging him to investigate a homosexual ring around Reagan, he had been approached by another congressman, Democrat William Moorhead of Pittsburgh, whose escapades with a transsexual prostitute the *Post* was in the midst of investigating. A rattled Moorhead "went to Bradlee and pleaded with him not to print the story," a British journalist working at the *Post* recalled. "Bradlee suppressed it, saying, rightly, that a man's private sexual entanglements were his own affair." While gay sex might still have been illegal in most American states at the time, it was hard to see how any of the alleged activity involving the Reagan aides threatened the public trust. "In the end, I can't remember anyone postulating a lede that made sense of this," remembered Patrick Tyler. There was smoke but no fire, as Bradlee would tell McCloskey when he saw him at the Republican convention.

The rumors about Jack Kemp, however, still overshadowed his effort to become Reagan's running mate. On the first day of the gathering, Lyn Nofziger told Bob Novak that the New York congressman was a strong contender for the veep nomination. This surprised the columnist, considering how Nofziger had never been a fan of Kemp; indeed, it was Nofziger who had fomented the gay rumors about him. After Reagan selected George Bush, Novak asked Nofziger what had dashed Kemp's chances. "It was that homosexual thing," Nofziger conceded, repeating Kemp advisor Jude Wanniski's phrase. "The governor finally said, 'We just can't do this to Jack.'"

* * *

"LET'S HEAR IT FOR GAY POWER!" It was a few weeks after the convention, and Pete McCloskey was enjoying a homemade Bloody Mary with his girlfriend Helen at the P Street Beach when they heard a voice ring out through a bullhorn. Looking across the field, the couple saw a group of men—"not fragile guys," as McCloskey was to describe them—running sprints, lifting weights, and performing calisthenic exercises around a tent with a sign identifying them as gay ex-marines. "You'd never know they were gay," McCloskey remembered thinking to himself.

Meanwhile, not far from where McCloskey went to work each morning, a gay bar named Equus had recently opened its doors on Pennsylvania Avenue, around the corner from the marine barracks on Eighth Street. No one could say exactly what it was that had ignited the antipathy between the soldiers at the base and the patrons of the bar—the gays who whistled at the marines as they jogged past, the marines who resented the gays for cruising around their memorial, the "cult of Manhood" that the Marine Corps drilled into its young recruits—but in the four months since the bar's grand opening, there had already been six confrontations, part of a broader climate of hostility. In May, two marines had been arrested and charged with assaulting a man near the memorial, and the previous October, another had allegedly thrown a tear gas bomb into a lesbian bar. It also did not help that the building that housed Equus had previously been a topless joint where, the ever-salty McCloskey said, "Marines were accustomed to go meet their future wives."

Whatever lay at the root of their tempestuous relationship, the tensions between the marines and the gays boiled over shortly after midnight on August 16, when a crowd of one hundred fifty stick-wielding leathernecks marched out of their barracks and onto Pennsylvania Avenue shouting Marine Corps chants interspersed with homophobic taunts. When they reached Equus, a group of five split from the mass and burst into the bar, sparking a minor riot. A gay ex-marine who happened to be inside the bar barked orders at the intruders while warding them off with a pool cue; other patrons hurled beer mugs and made a run for the back door. Punches were thrown, trash cans were overturned, windows were smashed, and two marines were taken into custody. A co-owner of Equus, whose lover was injured in the fracas, said the attack might arouse Washington's gay community to righteous anger not unlike Anita Bryant's campaign had motivated gays nationwide just a few years before.

Seeking an interlocutor respected by both parties, an editor from the *Washington Blade* called the congressman who was both an ex-marine and a rare Republican supporter of gay rights. It was entirely by coincidence that, just a few days earlier, McCloskey had had his own encounter with gays and marines—except, in his case, they were one and the same. When the editor asked McCloskey if he might serve as a mediator, McCloskey recalled, "Helen and I have just seen these guys lifting weights, and we think, 'Oh Christ.'" Immediately, McCloskey phoned the commanding officer at the barracks and told him, "If you don't pay for those damages, 200 gay ex-Marines are going to come and raise holy hell." A week later, the money was raised. And within a year, the marines were running "courtesy patrols" around the Southeast neighborhood they shared with Equus, entrusted with the authority to arrest any of their comrades should they give the gays any (unwanted) attitude.

The arbitrator in a public homosexual drama, McCloskey remained a protagonist in another covert one. By September, the maverick congressman was still withholding his endorsement of Reagan. The presence of a closeted homosexual, Peter Hannaford, in a potential Reagan administration could pose a threat to national security, McCloskey believed, and so he took his concerns directly to Reagan's longtime advisor and campaign chief of staff, Edwin Meese. "United States cryptographers and British scientists have defected to the Soviet Union, reportedly in part because of the threat of exposure of homosexual conduct," McCloskey wrote Meese. "With the growing numbers and political involvement of the homosexual communities across the nation," a development McCloskey welcomed, "it would be my judgment that there will be very few secrets about who has and who has not engaged in homosexual conduct. You may have noted the recent case of a Republican Member of Congress arrested for such conduct [a reference to Jon Hinson] and the confrontation between Washington's growing gay activist community and the Marines stationed at the 8th and I Street barracks." McCloskey suggested that Meese ask "any persons against whom *reputable* citizens have raised contentions of homosexual conduct to step aside from positions of responsibility in the Reagan team at the earliest possible date. I make this suggestion solely in the interest of trying to give Governor Reagan the best possible chance of being the kind of President the country desperately needs at this time."

On September 4, Meese met with McCloskey at the congressman's Capitol Hill office. In a letter to Bill Best recapitulating the hour-long conversation, McCloskey wrote that while Meese "accepted Pete Hannaford's absolute denial of your allegations . . . he does not expect to allow Hannaford to be in a job which would embarrass the Governor if others come forward to raise the issue." Meese disputed this account. While he did not "specifically" recall the meeting with McCloskey, "the implication that Pete [Hannaford] had anything to do with homosexuality is absolutely false, and the reason, if I said [he was not joining the administration] at the time was that there was no point in going into it because Pete wasn't going into the administration anyway."

Whatever the nature of their discussion, McCloskey endorsed Reagan two weeks later, sealing the deal by letting the candidate slap a "Reagan/ Bush" bumper sticker on his beat-up 1971 Volkswagen convertible.

As the Reagan campaign dealt gingerly with the presence of gays within its ranks, it also had to formulate a position on the emergent political issue of homosexuality. In an interview with the *Los Angeles Times* published earlier that year, Reagan had criticized the gay rights movement for demanding "recognition and acceptance of an alternative lifestyle which I do not believe society can condone, nor can I," elaborating "that in the Bible it says that in the eyes of the Lord, this is an abomination." Two weeks before the election, that same paper published a side-by-side comparison of the three major candidates' views on a variety of issues. Under "homosexual rights," Reagan's position was described thusly:

> Believes all citizens, regardless of sexual preference, have equal rights before the law. Says the government should not interfere with the private lives of Americans. However, does not advocate gay lifestyle. Declares that hiring should be based on who can do the best job and that one's private life, so long as it does not interfere with job performance, should have no bearing on hiring. Says employers should not be subject to laws compelling them to hire a person because of that person's sexual preference.

Except for its reference to nonexistent proposals "compelling" employers to hire people on the sole basis of their "sexual preference," and the use of the pejorative phrase "gay lifestyle," Reagan's position was comparable to that of his opponents. It also happened to be written by the man whom others would try to blacklist from holding a job in a potential Reagan administration on account of his homosexuality. "I was pleasantly surprised to see that RR's position on the issue noted seems to have come from the pro forma statement I drafted last spring for handling letter inquiries," Peter Hannaford wrote, alongside a clipping of the *Times* feature, in a letter to the gay journalist Larry Bush.

As Meese promised McCloskey, Hannaford did not join the Reagan administration. But was the decision to remain at the public relations firm he had founded with Mike Deaver (who became White House deputy chief of staff) Hannaford's own, or had it been made for him? In 1983, Hannaford published a hagiography of the First Couple, *The Reagans: A Political*

Portrait. Its jacket copy describes the author as "probably the man 'most inside'" the Reagan campaign who nonetheless "made a deliberate decision to stay in business rather than take a job in the Reagan administration." To enter the White House would have required this "most inside" man to remain inside his closet, something that was highly unlikely given what had become known about him during the campaign, and it's hard to read this description today, both with the perspective offered by time and in the full knowledge of the facts now established, and not feel at least some inkling that there is more to the story.

Had the whole farrago of rumor and innuendo about the gay Reagan conspiracy come to light during the campaign, it's difficult to say what effect it would have had on the election. Reagan's landslide victory over Carter—he won the popular vote 51 percent to 41 percent and took all but six states and the District of Columbia—obscures how close the race was during the final stretch. In June, just as the *Post* investigation was about to unfold, Carter led Reagan 35 percent to 33 percent in a national Gallup poll, and few predicted anything near the landslide Reagan ultimately won. If the muted public reaction to the Walter Jenkins affair is any indication, perhaps voters would have shrugged at the charges against Reagan. But the allegations handed to the *Post* purported something more nefarious and extensive than the arrest of one aide for "disorderly conduct" in a YMCA restroom. Moreover, while the Jenkins episode seemed to fit within a pattern of "immorality" and corruption inside the Johnson administration that most voters were content to overlook in the wake of the Kennedy assassination, a booming economy, and a GOP lurch to the hard right, Reagan was projecting an image of moral rectitude that would have been seriously undermined by the revelation of yet another "homosexual ring" operating under his nose. Of all the voters most likely to be troubled by such charges, it would have been the evangelicals whose support Reagan was courting so assiduously.

As for Best and McCloskey, the passage of time validated the *Post* team's intuition that the instigators of this wild goose chase might not have been the most credible sources. Best came to regret the role he played in denying Hannaford a job in the White House, phoning McCloskey at one point in the mid-1980s to complain that the Reagan administration was "going to hell in a handbasket" and that "the worst thing I ever did was get rid of Hannaford. He was the smartest guy of all. Nancy's running it with an astrologer in San Francisco," a reference to Joan Quigley, the oracle whom the First Lady began consulting after the 1981 assassination attempt on her husband. McCloskey gave up his House seat in 1982 to run for the Senate, losing in the Republican primary after campaigning against "the Jewish lobby." In 2000, he emerged briefly from obscurity to deliver a speech at a Holocaust denial conference. In light of this record, his last-ditch effort to torpedo Ronald Reagan with a tale portraying him as the dupe of a right-wing homosexual conspiracy looks like just another episode in a career spent tilting at windmills—his unlikely friend John Ehrlichman described him as "a latter-day Don Quixote"—though one much less honorable than challenging Richard Nixon for the presidency. And yet, for all its seeming absurdity, the story McCloskey and Best offered the *Post* eerily presaged a real-life saga involving gays, guns, and *golpistas* that would materialize toward the end of the Reagan administration.

Long after it prompted the destruction of Sumner Welles, purges in the State Department, and Nixon's White House witch hunts, the secret of homosexuality continued to captivate Washington, its power stemming from a capacity to explain otherwise mystifying episodes and phenomena. When the nation was gripped by an anxiety over communism, red hunters invoked an omnipotent "Homintern" to link the sexually and politically deviant. Now, with conservatism in the ascendant, a similar mindset took hold to explain an increasingly influential force on the right. An irony, one that was to prove both trenchant and tragic, was that for all the Reaganites' efforts to distance their icon from the slightest whiff of homosexuality, his would be the gayest of any presidential administration yet.

35

AN ENCLOSED AND ENCHANTED
GARDEN

THE INAUGURATION OF RONALD REAGAN, ACCORDING TO THE MAN charged with organizing its every detail, would be "snappy, flashy, yet dignified." Bob Gray, co-chairman of the 1981 Inaugural Committee, was describing what was to be the most expensive such ceremony in history. But the words he used to envisage it applied equally to himself.

Gray's event would be unlike anything Washington had ever seen, and a most welcome departure from the inauguration that preceded it. Four years earlier, when a young man with a banjo ambled into Jimmy Carter's inauguration committee headquarters and offered up his services, the overworked staff gave him a gig at one of the balls. Forgoing the pomp and circumstance customary to the quadrennial ceremony, Carter spurned formal wear for a business suit and ditched the presidential limousine for a walk along the mile stretch of Pennsylvania Avenue connecting the Capitol to the White House. Practically any Tom, Dick, or Harry was free to march along with him, cheered on by crowds of awestruck Georgians who had ridden up to Washington on an eighteen-car train christened "the Peanut Special." The highest-priced ticket to an inaugural event was a mere twenty-five dollars.

Befitting the actor-turned-president whom it was to honor, Gray planned a Hollywood-style extravaganza that would set the tone for the decade of glamour and excess to come. The Reagan inaugural cost four times as much (albeit, Gray hastened to add, in heavily inflated "Carter dollars") as what the outgoing administration had dubbed its "Y'all come, people's celebration." Nearly one hundred parties—including a disco-themed dance for Reagan youth—would be held over the course of four days, and guests could purchase seats to the five-hundred-dollars-a-plate dinner at the Kennedy Center to gawk at Dean Martin, Ethel Merman, Jimmy Stewart, Charlton Heston, Bob Hope, Frank Sinatra, and the Reagans' many other celebrity friends. Where Carter became the first president to walk from his investiture at the Capitol to his new digs at the White House, Reagan would be the first to deliver an inaugural speech on the Capitol Building's west side, facing the majesty of the National Mall and declaiming into its natural amphitheater. As for the parade, "only the cream of the crop," Gray promised, would march. And along with the rest of the six hundred VIPs, Jimmy Carter would wear formal attire.

To an extent matched by few men of his era, Gray understood the importance of image in politics, and he harnessed the power of television to amplify it. "We're concentrating entirely on television," he said. "Every event has a TV mode to make sure it will get across to the country. It's all geared to television." A seasoned public relations man with decades of experience working at the nexus of Capitol Hill and Madison Avenue, Gray applied the conventions of advertising to the realm of politics with impeccable finesse. Live coverage of the inauguration (including, for the first time, the post-ceremony lunch in the Capitol Rotunda) was to be beamed to eighty-five "satellite balls" across the nation via closed-circuit camera. "This is the first administration to have a premiere," cracked Johnny Carson, host of ABC's *All-Star Inaugural Gala* telecast, produced by the same man who did the Academy Awards. When Inauguration Day finally arrived, viewers were treated to a made-for-Hollywood ending that not even a man of Gray's prodigious talents could devise. Just moments after Reagan concluded his inaugural address, while 41.8 million viewers watched at home, the American hostages who had been held captive for 444 days by the revolutionary regime in Iran were set free. Not bad for a failed TV salesman from Hastings, Nebraska.

Only one detail escaped Gray's painstaking command. Back in November, Gray had announced that military units marching in the parade would carry American flags in place of rifles. "It would seem out of place to have tanks or missile launchers in the parade and the governor believes the same is true about sidearms," he said. "We are a patriotic nation, not a militaristic one." Alas, this idea did not go down so well with the men of the armed forces, one of whom reportedly told Gray that "marching in the parade without our guns is like walking down the street with your fly open." Upon reading this exchange in the paper, some of the incoming president's flock of gay supporters reacted with naughty amusement. Did not the men in the Pentagon realize that soldiers marching with their pants unzipped was exactly what Bob Gray—"Reagan's Capote," as some snickered behind his back—wished to see?

Not since Camelot had Washington been so glamorous, glitzy, or star-studded. And never had it been so gay.

According to Charles Brydon, a Democrat who served as coexecutive director of the National Gay Task Force in the late 1970s, the incoming Reagan administration had more gays serving on its White House staff than the departing Carter team. One of the most high-ranking members of this group was John Ford. A president of the Young Republicans and Young Americans for Freedom chapters at the University of Texas during the 1960s, Ford had the requisite charisma and ambition for a career in electoral politics. But as that option was foreclosed to him due to his sexual orientation, he set his sights on the highest government position attainable for a gay Republican in 1981, which meant a job that did not require an FBI background check. For Ford, that was deputy assistant secretary of agriculture. In the years since the Civil Service Commission lifted its ban on homosexual employment, Ford said, Washington became for gays something akin to what the North was for Black people during the Great Migration: a place of relative tolerance and opportunity. Ford attested to "a vast gay presence" throughout the Reagan administration, which he estimated at about one thousand of its fifty-five hundred total political appointees.

This "vast gay presence," however, was not accompanied by a similar degree of openness. During the Reagan years, "gays got in the government and then kept in the closet," Ford recalled. Larry Reynolds, who worked in the Labor Department during the early 1980s, "was told from the very beginning, coached by older gay men, to be very quiet, to dress conservatively," and to avoid doing anything that might generate awkward questions about his personal life. The circumspect workplace habits adopted by an earlier generation of gay federal employees as a survival mechanism were handed down to a new generation. When discussing friends and romantic partners over the phone, Reynolds remembered, it was necessary "to change my pronouns"—as in "I had such a great time with *her* last night"—so as not to attract the suspicion of one's cubicle mates. As a gay person, "the way you were successful was to ask *other* people what they did on the weekend. Don't talk about what *you* did on the weekend."

The Reagans arrived in Washington on a wave of support from evangelical Christians determined to reverse the social and political advances achieved by gay people over the preceding decade. The president, and especially his wife, however, counted numerous gay men among their friends and associates, a not insignificant number of whom played important roles in Reagan's political career. From the ethical quandaries of a new phenomenon known as "outage" to the devastation wrought by a deadly epidemic, an irresolvable tension coursed through Reagan-era Washington between the powerful electoral constituency whose support the president needed and his loyal cadre of gay foot soldiers whom that constituency condemned.

No member of this secret fraternity was more loyal, or more attuned to the vulnerability of his privileged position, than Bob Gray. One of the most emblematic figures of Reagan-era Washington, Gray had a thirst for power, and the obsessive determination to remain closeted essential to its pursuit, that were symbols of the age. His attitude toward public relations, described by one writer as "the theory that if a story did not appear on television, the problem did not exist," pertained as much to the arts of media manipulation he had mastered on behalf of an array of powerful clients as it did to his own carefully managed existence as a closeted homosexual. A tidy encapsulation of the double life Gray and other men like him led is revealed by an anecdote from a young man who encountered him twice during the same evening: first, at a dinner party attended exclusively by other gay men, and then, an hour later, in the lobby of a chic condo complex on his way to a function at the home of a wealthy Republican widow.

The afternoon of the inauguration, Gray quit his job as director of Hill and Knowlton's Washington office and founded his own public relations shop, Gray & Company. He dubbed the new firm's headquarters, an imposing nineteenth-century brick building that had previously contained the power generator for Georgetown's cable car system, "the Power House" (which, thanks to his pulling some strings with the postmaster general, became its official address). He decorated his office with the "Early Reagan" style of exposed brick, antique oak furniture, and oriental rugs. Gray's longtime status as a leading walker of Washington society women became especially useful as he went from squiring to hiring the wives of rich and powerful men, an effective if ethically questionable way to win friends and influence people on behalf of a long list of clients ranging from the Conference of Catholic Bishops to the Teamsters to the Church of Scientology and the scandal-plagued Bank of Credit and Commerce International. "He knows everyone in town," said Liz Carpenter, the former LBJ staffer and one of several prominent Democrats ensconced at the Power House. "And he's probably danced with his wife."

Gray was Reagan-era Washington's premier social host and political fixer, a lofty status signified by the second tuxedo he began wearing out every year, up from his usual one. "He's turned into the poor man's Perle Mesta," joked Nevada senator Paul Laxalt, Reagan's "first friend" on Capitol Hill and a cosponsor of the Family Protection Act, for whom Gray threw a gala party under a massive circus tent on the Mall six months into the administration. "What always fascinates me is how cleverly he walks through this city," marveled Gray's former employee and rival on the Washington social circuit, Steve Martindale, whom Gray had himself once compared to Washington's original hostess with the mostest. "'I've never seen him make a mistake."

Gray was meticulous at designing façades: for his clients, for political allies, and, most of all, for himself. During the Eisenhower administration, Gray would often have his secretary interrupt his meetings to announce a fake call from the president to impress his guest. He was "very fastidious, perfectly coiffed, almost like Jack Valenti," recalled Gahl Hodges Burt, who served as White House social secretary from 1983 to 1985. Media profiles of Gray frequently commented on his dapper appearance, the prominent women he escorted to parties, and his bachelor status, while coyly avoiding, and sometimes even obfuscating, the subject of his sexual orientation. Rule number seven in a 1983 *Washington Post* guide to "the Tippy Top" of society, "If you're a single man, stay that way," listed Steve Martindale and Bob Gray as among the city's most eligible bachelors and advised single women to "get married—preferably to one of the above." And yet, even if never acknowledged by the media, Gray's homosexuality was hardly a secret. Gray & Company was known around Washington as "Gay & Company," both for its proprietor and the throng of handsome young men he employed. According to one acquaintance, Gray was "always surrounded by this bevy of pretty, pretty boys." "Half of Gray and Company was [at the Eagle] on Friday and Saturday night," recalled Robert Higdon, a Yale dropout and former model who worked for Gray. When Gray hired the former Robert Kennedy aide Frank Mankiewicz, the subject of Gray's sexual orientation awkwardly came up in conversation. "I guess when I hired you, you didn't know that about me," Gray said.

"Bob, when you hired me, that was the only thing I knew about you," Mankiewicz replied.

Nonetheless, Gray feared that if his open secret became an acknowledged one, it would threaten his privileged status with an administration where forces hostile to homosexuality were leveraging their power. Gray allegedly spent over a million dollars in legal fees and settlements to keep former sexual partners from revealing that he was gay. And while he lived an active gay social life behind the doors of his homes in Arlington and Rehoboth Beach, and was a regular at the private parties and social occasions hosted by other wealthy conservative gay men, he was extremely cagey about his sexual orientation in public. W. Scott Thompson, a gay Republican foreign policy hand who served on the board of the U.S. Institute of Peace during the Reagan administration, once introduced a man as his "lover" to Gray at a party in the presence of heterosexuals. Gray immediately walked away. He wasn't "so stupid as to be *open* about his homosexuality," Thompson observed, "because such a person would have no staying power in the federal city." When the Marxist government of Angola hired Gray & Company at the same time the CIA was funding an insurgency to overthrow it, an anonymous letter attacking the firm's owner circulated around the White House. "Don't help pay for the pink Cadillac Gray will buy with his contract money—a car that will match his morality," the missive read, sounding oddly like a line ripped from a Pat Buchanan column, which would make sense considering that the memo was rumored to have originated from the White House Communications Office that Buchanan was hired to lead in 1985.

That the administration figure with whom Gray was closest, Ed Meese, was also the White House's conduit to the religious right surely intensified Gray's preoccupation with secrecy. If Gray's homosexuality ever became the subject of public speculation, it would have embarrassed Meese and imperiled Gray's direct line to the White House (not to mention his role as a walker for Ursula, Meese's wife). The prevalence of men like Gray through-out and adjacent to an administration so heavily dependent upon evan-gelical Christian voters (and evangelical Christian staffers) confronted the Reaganites with a conundrum—to which they responded with an attitude described as "closet tolerance." It was a posture illustrated by no one better than Meese, who was either spectacularly ignorant of, or willingly oblivi-ous to, the fact that both he and the president he served were practically surrounded by gay men. Hal Gordon, a Meese speechwriter, remembered perusing the stacks at Lambda Rising one afternoon when he bumped into one of his colleagues. "We were both kind of amused by the whole thing because poor Ed Meese never knew he had *two* gay speechwriters," Gordon recalled. In 1983, Meese asked Roy Cohn, at that point a high-powered New York attorney, if Cohn could get him tickets to the Broadway open-ing of *La Cage aux Folles*, a musical comedy about a gay couple (one of them a drag queen) managing a cabaret on the French Riviera. Alarmed that Meese suspected he might have a personal interest in the show, Cohn insisted he could not obtain the tickets and offered Meese seats to a "third rate" musical instead.

Gray was adept at ingratiating himself with members of the presidential court, where obsequiousness served as a sort of insurance policy against the risk of exposure. Though he had no official role in the administra-tion, his efforts on behalf of its senior figures were so wide-ranging that he earned the reputation of "First Flack." According to Gahl Hodges Burt, if the White House "wanted to find out if someone was loyal, Republican or Democrat," they went to Gray, "one of the handful of people I would call to get the skinny." Gray developed a particularly close relationship with Nancy Reagan, who had come to Washington with few social con-tacts there and subsequently felt besieged by a hostile media and political establishment. Portrayed as a domineering and acquisitive shrew, the First Lady was deeply suspicious of anyone outside her trusted circle and grew to depend on Gray for professional and emotional support. "Is he or she with us or against us?" Nancy would often ask him, Burt recalled.

In 1988, when Nancy was criticized for "borrowing" high-priced designer clothing and diamond jewelry worth hundreds of thousands of dollars, Gray rushed to her defense. Over the course of her husband's eight years in office, he noted in a letter to the editor of the *New York Times* enti-tled "What It Takes to Dress Like a First Lady," Nancy had attended some one hundred official luncheons and state dinners, delivered eighty-nine speeches, and made twenty overseas visits. "When in public, no First Lady dresses for herself, but for all 243 million Americans," Gray wrote. "So, she showed the world the works of our best designers. Who's complaining?"

This ringing defense of her right to look fabulous was but one of countless benefactions furnished upon Nancy Reagan by the myriad gay men in her life, a coterie of friends and courtiers so large that it led some waspish observers to anoint her "First Fag Hag." "Scratch the surface and what do you get?" asked Way Bandy, the two-thousand-dollars-a-day makeup artist to the stars who "designed" Nancy's face. "More surface." To a much greater extent than that of her husband, whose public image was carefully crafted by the likes of Peter Hannaford and Bob Gray, Nancy's was almost entirely the work of gay men. Her jewelry was crafted by Kenneth Jay Lane. Her inaugural outfits, both gubernatorial and presidential, were designed by Jimmy Galanos. Her hair was done by Robin Weir, her Washington stylist, and colored by Julius Bengtsson, her California one. Her astrological reading (and that of her husband) was provided by Carroll Righter. According to the Washington Post, the dress code for a White House dinner honoring Prince Charles (at which the legendary cabaret singer Bobby Short entertained on piano) could "better be described as Bill Blass and Adolfo." Nancy met the "first decorator," Ted Graber, back in California, where he had been a business partner of her close friend, the gay silent film star turned interior designer Billy Haines. Graber, who flew to Washington for the inaugural with the Reagans aboard Air Force One, spent most of the first year of the administration living in the White House to oversee an ambitious remodeling. On Nancy's sixtieth birthday, Graber and his "live-in friend," as the Washington Post referred to his partner, Archie Case, became the first same-sex couple to stay overnight at the White House.

When Nancy visited New York, real estate heir and "first fop" Jerry Zipkin escorted her to society events, and when she was in Washington, he delivered her a daily "river of small, hilarious defamations" while yakking over the phone. (Nancy was a "compulsive user of the telephone," according to Michael Deaver, and two of her favorite interlocutors were Truman Capote and Merv Griffin.) "Zipkin either has no love life, it seems, or is impressively discreet about it," hinted the New York Daily News, while Nancy knowingly enthused that he was "a sort of modern-day Oscar Wilde." It was Zipkin who convinced Nancy to pose for the cover of the

December 1981 issue of *Interview* magazine, for which she was photographed by the gay camp icon Cris Alexander and subjected to a hilariously awkward parley with its taciturn editor in chief, Andy Warhol. Nancy outsourced the management of her social world to Zipkin, who, in accepting and rejecting would-be members of the Reagan camarilla, behaved as if he were Saint Peter at the pearly gates. Two weeks before a deranged loner vying for the affections of actress Jodie Foster tried to assassinate President Reagan outside the Washington Hilton, the writer Bob Colacello spent a festive evening at Le Cirque, then the chicest of New York's haute cuisine restaurants, with the First Couple and their entourage, one replete with "male and female homosexuals of varying degrees of closetedness." It was a characterization that would have suited the Reagan milieu at practically any point since Ronald and Nancy became an item in 1949, including their White House staff. One employee for a labor union remembered the senior Reagan aide—so close to the First Lady that he "literally held Nancy's pocketbook"—who used to cruise for sex across the street from his office in Lafayette Square. "We'd sit out there and he would pick me up and we'd go bang our brains out for an hour" at a nearby hotel, he recalled. When Scott Thompson revealed himself as gay to Reagan, not for nothing did the president jokingly reply that so were "half of my friends and all of Nancy's."

With a "vast gay presence" throughout an administration at best lukewarm to it, early Reagan-era Washington contained a paradox. Still, the "antagonistic divide between straight and gay" of earlier eras continued to dissipate, recalled Alan Zuschlag, who traveled in gay conservative circles while attending college and graduate school in Washington during the late 1970s and early 1980s. To earn extra cash, Zuschlag worked as a waiter for the Reaganites' caterer of choice, Glorious Food of New York City. Glorious "only hired very, very handsome gay young men," Zuschlag said, "one handsomer than the next." ("I don't know how they hired me," he humbly professed.) At one party, an opening at the National Gallery of Art done to "over-the-top Reagan excess," Zuschlag overheard one big-haired Republican socialite whisper to another, "I can't believe they're all gay!"

"They're all gay?" the other woman asked in nervous excitement, as if she were being let in on a naughty secret. The women had fallen victim to what Jerry Zipkin termed a "staff infection," a sudden loss of one's senses brought about by the mere presence of Glorious Food waiters. Robin Weir's salon, where clients munched on Republican-themed candies like chocolate elephants and red, white, and blue jelly beans, was one of the trendiest places in Reaganite Washington. A constant stream of Republican women filed in and out to have their hair done and to share confidences with Weir, who visited Nancy at the White House for appointments twice a week.

Given the extreme sensitivity bordering on paranoia she displayed at the mere mention of the word when her husband ran for governor in 1966, it's ironic how Nancy emerged as a camp icon, her pop culture notoriety owing in large part to her myriad gay friends and courtiers and the stereotype associating homosexuality with decadence. In the fall of 1981, the hottest seller at a Georgetown gift shop was a postcard entitled "Queen Nancy," depicting the First Lady in a brocade dress, ermine cape, and bejeweled golden crown. Robert Higdon, who worked for Nancy in several capacities, including as a fund-raiser for her husband's post-presidential foundation, described the complex allure she held for many gay men, even those who despised the Reagans' politics. "How can you work for them?" they would proclaim in disgust, before lowering their voice to ask, "Does she really wear Chanel?" The contradictory impulse was one that Nancy could well appreciate. Throughout her lifetime and well after her death, the phrase "fiercely protective" was so overused to describe how she attempted to control her husband's public image that it became a cliché, and one of the images she worked to protect him from was that of gayness. Meanwhile, more so than that of any First Lady, her own persona is inescapably, irrepressibly gay, embodied by the retinue that designed, dressed, escorted, entertained, flattered, housed, humored, pampered, styled, and titillated her.

* * *

"GRAB ONE OF THOSE HALSTON NUMBERS—the black one, I think—and come on down for my dinner on Saturday," Craig Spence ordered his friend Liz Trotta over the phone. "Everyone's coming, and I'll need a hostess."

Spence was "a man for the eighties," Trotta remembered, "smart, ruthless, and on the make." And whenever he invited her to the nation's capital during those heady early years of the Reagan administration, she usually dropped whatever she was doing and booked the next shuttle to Washington. Trotta and Spence had first met in 1966 as rival reporters attending a packed press conference at Leonard Bernstein's Upper East Side penthouse. Bernstein's wife was releasing a collection of anti–Vietnam War Christmas cards, and Spence and Trotta became entangled in the scrum of journalists vying for an interview. They started shouting at each other and did not stop until Spence offered his version of a surrender: "I will desist because I'm the gentleman and not because you are a lady."

Over-the-top declarations (and even more melodramatic behavior) were Craig Spence's specialty. Only a few months after this testy exchange at Bernstein's apartment, Trotta reconnected with Spence in Vietnam, where the two worked as competing television network news correspondents. Spence was "the only man I ever knew who wore a Cartier dress watch in combat," Trotta recalled, and he smoked a corncob pipe in honor of his hero, Douglas MacArthur. When Spence was stripped of his press credentials and forced to leave the country, some speculated it was due to his pitiless treatment of the "boy majors" he peppered with questions at the daily U.S. military press briefings in Saigon, dubbed the "Five O'Clock Follies" for their ever-more-fanciful projections of inevitable American victory. Others claimed that Spence's expulsion had something to do with his trading on the Saigon black market or smuggling gold. The reason was never made clear, but then, nothing about Craig Spence was as it seemed.

One of the most colorful of the many and varied "best little boys in the world" who made their way to Washington during the latter half of the twentieth century, Craig Spence had a preternatural capacity to dissimulate. Like a politician trying to stay current, or the decade's hottest pop star, Madonna, he "constantly reinvented himself," as one friend put it. One of three children raised by a widowed nurse in Kingston, New York, a hamlet some one hundred miles north of New York City, Spence would tell New Yorkers he was a Boston Brahmin and Bostonians that he was a New York aristocrat. The usual pursuits of the rebellious American teenager held little interest for Spence, who took pleasure in pleasing authority; according to one high school classmate, he was "the type of guy who carried a briefcase to school." While his peers might have spent their weekends chugging beer and chasing girls, Spence enlisted himself in the town pastor's crusade against underage drinking by visiting local taverns undercover and asking to be served alcohol. "He was a loner so I can't tell you really of a single friend he had," the pastor's wife recalled. "Because he was brilliant, he didn't mix well with other boys his age." In the early 1960s, Spence studied at Boston University and lived a hippie existence, riding a Vespa and listening to folk music in coffeehouses. For two years, he tricked his classmates into thinking he was an exchange student from Australia.

After his eviction from Vietnam, Spence spent most of the 1970s working as a journalist and consultant in Japan, an experience that suited him well for his move to Washington in 1979, as the Land of the Rising Sun was rapidly approaching a zenith thanks to its booming, technology-driven economy. Working on behalf of an opaque consortium of Japanese companies and government ministries, Spence ensconced himself in a mansion right in the heart of the tony Embassy Row section of Kalorama, which he hired a former *Vogue* editor to decorate. The house became the nerve center for what Spence called "Operation Sunshine," a bimonthly salon dinner series bringing senior U.S. government officials, journalists, and business tycoons together with their Japanese counterparts and that soon ranked among the most exclusive, and mysterious, social gatherings in Washington.

"Not since Ethel Kennedy used to give her famous Hickory Hill seminars for great minds of our times during the days of Camelot has anyone staged seminars successfully on a continuing social basis in Washington," raved Maxine Cheshire in the *Washington Post*. Though the shindig Spence had invited her to cover was ostensibly in honor of CBS News anchor Eric Sevareid, it was, she wrote, effectively a "coming-out party" for its host.

"Coming out," of course, in the old-fashioned sense, for to "come out" in the more recent understanding of the term would have threatened Spence's social advancement. The following April, just three months into the new Reagan administration, Spence teamed up with former Nixon attorney general John Mitchell to throw a surprise going-away party at the Four Seasons for the president's ambassador-designate to Saudi Arabia. "If anybody can dance between OPEC and AWACS, you can do it," Spence joked upon his presentation of a Waterford Crystal jar full of "the new national candy, jelly beans," to the guest of honor. The following day, a photograph of a beaming, tuxedo-clad Spence appeared on the front page of the *Post*'s Style section, the holy grail of press coverage for aspiring Washington social climbers.

Spence owed a considerable debt to the previous decade's most ambitious male society host. "Craig would make it very clear, 'I'm just having a very, very, very small, very exclusive gathering, of course, you'll be there and Eric [Sevareid] will be there,' and then he would run off a bunch of names and that's how he would entice people to come to these little events," recalled ABC News anchor Ted Koppel, effectively describing the party planning trick that put Steve Martindale on the map. Koppel was first charmed by Spence's theatricality at the Hong Kong Mandarin Hotel, where, after failing to attract the waiter's attention over lunch one day, Spence "very ostentatiously got up," walked to the serving station, picked up the pitcher, and poured himself a glass of water while loudly announcing, "No, you're much too busy to take care of things like this" as the maître d' protested helplessly. "He loved the show," Koppel said. "He was an extraordinary showman," one who consciously styled himself after William F. Buckley Jr., adopting his patrician accent and mannerisms. (Another role model was Jay Gatsby, comparisons to whom Spence encouraged.) In addition to Koppel, Spence would attract an array of boldface names—Vice President Bush, Rock Hudson, *New York Times* columnist William Safire, diplomat Richard Holbrooke, CIA director William Casey, FDR-era power broker Tommy "the Cork" Corcoran, the commandant of the Marine Corps—over the course of his tenure as one of Washington's top party-givers.

Spence wasn't humble about the company he kept or the connections he made. Richard Nixon, he was sure to tell you, was a "friend," Sen. John Glenn "a good friend," and Eric Sevareid "an old, dear friend." In a 1982 profile anointing Spence a "mystery man," the same title conferred upon other Washington bachelors like Carmel Offie and Robert Cutler, the *New York Times* trumpeted Spence's "ability to master the social and political chemistry of" Washington, his "personal phone book and party guest lists constitut[ing] a 'Who's Who' in Congress, government and journalism." With his outsider status and shameless ability to "network" (a noun then coming into usage as a verb), Spence symbolized the continuing evolution of the Washington socialite, whose erstwhile creed of noblesse oblige was being supplanted by ostentatious displays of wealth and status seeking.

To the many recipients of his hospitality, however, it was never entirely clear just what Spence was trying to accomplish. Ostensibly, "Operation Sunshine" was intended to provide a relaxed setting for Japanese and American leaders to understand each other better. Some guests to 2445 Kalorama grew suspicious about the role Spence played in the Japanese "vacuum cleaner" approach to information gathering. Summoned to Kalorama one day for lunch, a magazine writer found it odd when Spence's white-gloved butler led her into the dining room and seated her opposite

Spence at the end of a very long table. Only later did she realize that this awkward arrangement might have been orchestrated to make her speak loudly, such that a listening device could record what she said. (As for the food, it was of "decidedly Stouffer's quality.")

Another seminar attendee, a Pentagon official who worked on missile defense research, remembered meeting Spence at a gay disco where, "dripping with pretension" and "dressed to the nines" in a dark suit and monogrammed French-cuff shirt, Spence introduced himself by name-dropping Phyllis Schlafly—what must surely rank as one of the strangest icebreakers uttered within the confines of a gay bar. Intrigued nonetheless, the official accepted Spence's invitation to a seminar. After the first round of cognac was served, however, he grew wary when four Japanese men suddenly appeared and started peppering him with questions about the Strategic Defense Initiative. At that point, he said, "I got the hell out of there."

Wrapped up in the Spence mystique—along with the pipe, the chauffeur-driven limousine, the black cape, the wide-brimmed Panama hat, the silk handkerchiefs, the Maltese dog named Winston, the retired African American army sergeant and head of household whom he berated in front of guests, and the off-duty soldiers he recruited to work "security" at his parties—was what Trotta described as the "remote presence of his homosexuality." Fittingly, Spence's favorite book was Thomas Mann's *Death in Venice*, in which the homoeroticism of the protagonist's fatal obsession with a beautiful teenage boy is palpable but never explicit. "He knew I knew, I knew he knew I knew, that kind of thing," was how Trotta characterized their mutually assumed comprehension of his sexuality.

Mark Falcoff was only a few months into his job as a Latin America analyst at the conservative American Enterprise Institute when he received a phone call from Spence at the end of 1981, offering him five hundred dollars to show up and say a few words at a party honoring the ambassador-designate to Chile. When Falcoff arrived, a woman answered the door. "Mrs. Spence," Falcoff said in appreciation as she graciously accepted his garment and scurried off without bothering to correct him. The guests that evening were mainly Japanese government officials and entrepreneurs as well as women wearing kimonos. "Afterward, Craig had rather a lot to drink, and he made a little speech which was so campy, I thought, 'What's going on here?'" Falcoff said. "'Is this guy gay or what?'" Falcoff's question was answered a few weeks later, when, as a sign of appreciation, he took

Spence out for dinner. After imbibing a few drinks—Spence "had a very low resistance to alcohol"—he drunkenly made a pass at the valet parking attendant. "I mean he was pretty damn flamboyant," Falcoff said. "He was a good actor. He could put on the straight role very easily and play that, but when he had a little to drink . . ."

Occasionally, Spence made exceptions to the strict bifurcation of his secretive professional life and his even more secretive gay one, such as the dinner party where the guest sitting next to a female journalist leaned over and asked, "Have you noticed you're the only woman here?" Or the birthday party for Roy Cohn attended by CIA director Bill Casey. On some evenings, when the policy seminar had concluded "and after everybody left, a certain group of people stayed behind and—you know," one of the relatively few witnesses to both of Spence's double lives recalled. "There was never any sex," at least none that he saw, though there was a lot of heavily inebriated carousing, with the host coaxing members of his "personal honor guard" to take off their shirts. Mark Falcoff speculated that most of if not all the soldiers in Spence's retinue were "straight men who nonetheless were willing to accommodate him, and he would give them Rolex watches and this sort of thing" to show his gratitude. From his days wading through the rice paddies and jungles of Vietnam with a Cartier fastened around his wrist, Spence knew the value of a proper timepiece. When National Security Advisor Richard Allen was ousted from his job in 1982, partly over his acceptance from a Japanese businessman of two Seiko watches valued at $340, Spence scoffed at Allen's naïveté. He, too, had been given cheap wristwatches as gifts, "but I always gave them to my butler."

A man for the eighties, indeed. As one of his associates reflected, "With Craig, you never knew what was true and what was not."

* * *

IT WAS AN EXHILARATING TIME TO BE GAY IN WASHINGTON, especially if you were a white Republican man. "Dynasty and Dallas were your TV shows, and it was all about white people being rich," remembered Robert Higdon. When Alan Zuschlag departed for a junior year abroad at the tail end of the Carter administration, he left a country mired in double-digit inflation, humiliated by the Iranian hostage crisis, and racked by an omnipresent sense of decline. He returned the following year to "Morning in America," "a completely different world," one characterized by "a certain brightness, a certain quickening of things, a certain sense of malaise being lifted." Part of the brightening, at least for him and others of this soigné set, was "an acceptance of gay people, at least unofficially," observable in the boldness of the homoerotic imagery suddenly pervasive across pop culture. In 1982, tourists in Times Square were startled to see a forty-five-by-forty-eight-foot billboard featuring a young male model, his hands placed sensually on his thighs, clad only in Calvin Klein briefs. This overt sexualization of the male body, designed to appeal to gay men as much as to heterosexual women, reached audiences beyond the island of Manhattan the following year, when the movie *Risky Business* hit multiplexes across the country. In its most famous scene, the teenage protagonist (played by a young actor named Tom Cruise) struts around the living room in his tighty-whities. Three years later, a strange synthesis of Reaganism and homoeroticism would be reached when *Saturday Night Live* guest host Ron Reagan opened the show dancing across a deserted White House in *his* tighty-whities, a skit occasioned by Cruise's appearance in *Top Gun*, described by Frank Rich as "a promotional film for defense spending and hawkish foreign policy propelled by male bodies and disco music" whose box office success proved that "gay eroticism" had been "assimilated into the highest grossing, most patriotically pro-establishment movie of the year."

A gay Reaganite social milieu developed in Washington—one composed of wealthy gay white men that existed in parallel, and occasionally intersected with, the rest of Republican Washington. Some of these men, in a nod to their devotion to supply-side economics, referred to themselves as "laissez-fairies," while another group dubbed itself the RPQs, short for "rich and powerful queens." There were never more than a dozen RPQs at any one time (opportunities for membership arising only when a reigning queen died or abdicated), and aspiring members were required to have a sufficiently large dining room and corresponding sets of china, crystal, and sterling to host the group's opulent dinner parties. Others joined the blossoming number of gay social groups with playful acronyms like BLOW (Bachelor Lawyers of Washington) and GATT (Gays Assembled to Talk Trade).

Zuschlag's own introduction to this world came by way of the gym. Like many cultural trends, the fitness craze that had swept America in recent years was pioneered by gay men. For a certain subset of the urban gay male community, gyms served multiple functions: part athletic studio, community center, and sexual cruising ground, they were as integral to the 1980s gay social scene as the "super bars" had been to that of the previous decade. Exercising on a weightlifting machine one day, Zuschlag and the man using the adjoining device caught each other's eye, subtle hints were dropped, and an invitation was extended to join a group of friends meeting later that night at Kramerbooks, a bookstore and café on Dupont Circle that also served as a pre-barhopping rendezvous point for the neighborhood's growing gay community. Entering that dazzling realm of dance clubs, private parties, and Rehoboth Beach weekends was like discovering a "whole secret world that you had no idea existed, which was even more fabulous and glamorous than everything else on the outside," Zuschlag recalled, similar to the moment in the *Wizard of Oz* when the picture suddenly transforms "from black and white to Technicolor."

Zuschlag offered another literary metaphor to evoke this experience of wondrous discovery. If there was a contemporaneous cultural artifact that most captured the halcyon days of young gay Reaganite abandon, it was the 1982 television serialization of *Brideshead Revisited*. Set at Oxford during the interwar period, Evelyn Waugh's semiautobiographical 1945 bildungsroman depicts the "romantic friendship" between a budding historian named Charles Ryder (Jeremy Irons in his breakout role) and Sebastian Flyte, the troubled scion of a wealthy English Catholic family and an epicene, dissolute dandy of "arresting" and "magical" beauty whose homosexuality is all but acknowledged. Coming on the heels of the previous summer's royal wedding (at which Nancy, her hairstylist Julius Bengtsson in tow, represented the United States), the series kicked off an Anglomania not seen since the Beatles played Shea Stadium. Every Monday night for eleven straight weeks, an estimated five million Americans switched on PBS to feast their eyes upon scenes of verdant English landscapes, sumptuous eighteenth-century manor homes, and the most unabashedly homoerotic relationship yet portrayed on mainstream television—a delicious irony given the conservative Catholicism of both the novel's author and the man who introduced each episode, William F. Buckley Jr. Charles and Sebastian languorously quaff champagne beneath a tree, sunbathe nude on the roof of the Flyte family manor, and traipse arm in arm through the narrow streets of Venice, the smoldering sexual tension between them palpable but never explicitly addressed. "One might think such a theme would be off-putting to some viewers," wrote *Washington Post* television critic Tom Shales, "but there is no such sign." In homage to Sebastian and the stuffed animal, Aloysius, he faithfully carries around the Oxford campus, grown men began showing up at Washington parties decked out in Sebastian's signature white linen suit clutching teddy bears.

Brideshead Revisited enthralled a generation of gay men, a cohort of Republican and Tory ones especially. Airing at a moment of maximum conservative political dominance on both sides of the Atlantic—embodied in the rapport between Reagan and British prime minister Margaret Thatcher, the "Iron Lady" herself on her way to becoming something of a right-wing gay icon—the show's lavish evocation of a refined yet repressed aristocratic homosexuality uncannily mirrored the gay conservative demimonde of 1980s Washington, an "enchanted garden . . . in the heart of that grey city" not unlike Charles Ryder's Oxfordian Arcadia.

Alas, all good things must come to an end.

36

SODOM-ON-THE-POTOMAC

SUMMER IS "SILLY SEASON" IN WASHINGTON, A TIME OF FRIVOLOUS POLIT-
ical initiatives and trivial journalistic pursuits. But for the denizens of the
secret city, the summer of 1982 was anything but amusing.

A taste of the trouble to come was betokened by the boisterous, twelve-
page tabloid that appeared on newsstand kiosks across the city on May
14, 1982. "It is the *Deep Backgrounder*'s purpose in this first edition to
expose one of the most politically sensitive and potentially explosive issues
in Washington today," the new publication declared. "This is the issue of
homosexuality within the federal government and its effects on how our
government operates in both the domestic and international arenas."

Not much was known about Martin Price, the fifty-two-year-old publisher, president, and executive editor of the *Deep Backgrounder*, except
that he had formerly served as chief investigative reporter for *Spotlight*, the
weekly newspaper of the extreme right-wing, anti-Semitic Liberty Lobby.
Price's sidekick was more of a known quantity, ironic given his fourteen-
year career at the CIA. Not long after Victor Marchetti quit his position
as executive assistant to the deputy director in 1969, a former colleague
suggested he be assassinated for starting work on a roman à clef about the
agency, a proposal that its then-director, Richard Helms, vetoed. Or, at

least, that's what Marchetti *believed* had happened. He also believed that NSA cryptographers William Martin and Bernon Mitchell were "secret lovers," and that E. Howard Hunt had helped orchestrate the Kennedy assassination, a theory whose baroque particulars he expounded upon in an article for *Spotlight* (based, he would later admit, almost entirely upon rumors retailed to him by a columnist for *Penthouse*). Sustained by copious amounts of alcohol and lunging between bouts of literary inspiration and paranoid delusion, Marchetti spent his days in the basement recreation room of his Virginia home obsessing over the many enemies out to get him and hammering away at his typewriter. He kept a locked and loaded .45 pistol on his desk, not only for the inevitable moment when the boys at the Company tried to kill him again, but also for more mundane nuisances, like the plumber who improperly installed a water heater. "I'll blow your belly all over the floor if you don't do what I told you and do it right," Marchetti ordered as he pointed his weapon at the poor sap's stomach.

That can-do attitude was one Marchetti and Price took to their practice of journalism, a profession full of sycophants unwilling to investigate the sinister forces manipulating the nation from behind closed (closet) doors. "To our knowledge no other publication has dared as yet to undertake such an in depth examination with the goal of providing a complete overview of the Washington gay scene that is comprised almost totally of politicians, military personnel, lobbyists, bureaucrats, diplomats and other powerbrokers," they declared in the *Deep Backgrounder*'s mission statement. "Unlike [in] San Francisco, Houston, and other major cities with large and vocal homosexual communities, Washington's gay community is composed of individuals whose work-a-day actions can, and for the most part do, effect [*sic*] the lives of every American." Equipped with little more than some well-placed sources, a flair for bombastic prose, and a total lack of journalistic scruple, this cantankerous and conspiratorial duo helped spark a media frenzy involving callboys, congressmen, congressional pages, foreign spies, and lists of high-class homosexuals that made the summer of 1982 a miasma of fear and suspicion not seen since the Lavender Scare.

The proximate origins of that season of scandal can be traced to an event three years earlier. On August 14, 1979, a twenty-four-year-old navy yeoman working at the Pentagon, Lee Eugene Madsen, stuffed a file containing confidential documents down his pants, walked past the guards on duty, and attempted to sell the purloined material to an undercover FBI officer for two hundred dollars. According to his roommate, Madsen had often talked about wanting more money to buy expensive things like a car, an indication that, like most other spies at this late stage in the Cold War, it was not ideology but greed that motivated him. Other details, however, obtruded on this straightforward analysis: the report that Madsen occasionally moonlighted as a bartender at the Chesapeake House, that a list of Pentagon employees with "homosexual proclivities" had been found among the documents he stole, and that Madsen's personal address book contained the names of an alleged "gay ring" inside the Department of Defense.

It would take two years, however, before anyone made a connection between this seemingly isolated incident and something more nefarious. On November 24, 1981, after conducting what it claimed had been months of research, NBC News aired a shocking report on its national evening broadcast: foreign intelligence operatives were attempting to infiltrate Washington homosexual "outcall" prostitution services with the aim of blackmailing their influential clients into handing over classified information. NBC's sole source for these allegations was an anonymous male prostitute, who issued his sensational claims from behind a darkened silhouette. The callboy—who boasted of a congressman, a diplomat, and several military officers among his clients—told NBC that he had met with a "Soviet colonel" and a "Soviet agent" to discuss homosexuals in the American government and military. Buttressing the young man's claims, reporter Brian Ross averred, was that a "known KGB agent" had been stopped earlier in the year by DC Police after picking up a male prostitute off the street and that "suspected foreign agents" had been spotted at the Chesapeake House, the den of iniquity where Lee Madsen had worked nights and where Bob Bauman's political career met its humiliating denouement. As Ross recited these alarming details, a montage flashed across the screen featuring images of a go-go boy gyrating atop a bar, participants at the 1979 National March on Washington for Lesbian and Gay Rights, and a group of preppily dressed young men exiting a Georgetown home identified as the headquarters of a prostitution ring. "For people in the intelligence community," Ross intoned, "what's happening in Washington after dark with callboy services, military men, and suspected agents in gay bars is a national security nightmare."

The nation's capital had changed a great deal for the better since the antigay witch hunts of the 1950s and '60s cast their pall. Yet Washington's buttoned-down culture compelled most gay federal workers to remain closeted in their professional lives, a trend that NBC's sensational broadcast seemed designed to reinforce. Five months after one of the country's top media outlets labeled the Washington gay community "a national security nightmare," Legal Services Corporation director Dan Bradley became the highest-ranking government official to come out of the closet in a profile published by the *New York Times*. The significance of Bradley's achievement was matched only by its brevity, however, as the publication of the article coincided with the day of his resignation. "I was ready to come out a year ago, but I knew that it probably would be used by the enemies of legal services in their effort to abolish the corporation," he explained. To the quintessentially New York gay activist and playwright Larry Kramer, who grew up in Washington and loathed its conservatism and conformity, the capital's closet was disproportionately large and absurdly overprotected, a function of Washington being a single-industry town whose industry still regarded homosexuality as the worst of all taboos. "Homosexual 'smears' appear to be of interest today mainly in Washington, which more and more is sounding like the last provincial town in America," Kramer scoffed.

Exacerbating this dynamic was Washington's place as a site of increasing scandal and exposure. Beginning with the Vietnam War and progressing through Watergate, the Church Committee investigation, Koreagate, Abscam, and a spate of (gay and straight) congressional sex scandals, the 1970s was one long succession of shocks to public confidence in government. By the time the first issue of the *Deep Backgrounder* hit newsstands in the spring of 1982, twenty-five members of Congress had been convicted of criminal charges in just the past decade. With good reason, the American public had grown more skeptical of their political elites, and a rising generation of investigative journalists, proudly rejecting the deference shown to authority figures by their predecessors, was eager to feed this skepticism. The *Deep Backgrounder* was an entrant into the riotous world of the American alternative press, an ideologically diverse media subculture where an instinctive opposition to authority (whether greedy corporate polluters or secretive homosexual cliques) was the common thread. Urging readers to "venture further behind Washington's closed doors into the secret world of power and politics where deals are struck, reputations made and broken," the *Deep Backgrounder* spoke to a readership amenable to its dark narratives of morally corrupted, power-mad elites.

With their hardboiled, feverishly sensationalistic style lifted straight from the pages of *Washington Confidential*, Price and Marchetti were the latter-day Jack Lait and Lee Mortimer, updating the pulp best seller's heady brew of red-baiting, populism, and moral clamor for a capital reverting to an atmosphere of superpower tension. By the summer of 1982, the Cold War was entering a new and more dangerous phase, marked by increasingly combative rhetoric and military brinksmanship. Addressing the British Parliament in June, President Reagan boldly declared that Marxism-Leninism would wind up "on the ash-heap of history," while on the Continent, the Soviet Union was threatening the balance of power through the deployment of nuclear missiles in Eastern Europe. The ripple effects of this growing confrontation were felt far beyond high-stakes diplomatic negotiations and abstruse theorizing about nuclear throw weights, yields, and decapitation strikes. According to one gay man who worked in the Pentagon at the time, the Soviets were "sending over these young, dapper, well-trained, westernized types"—men and women—"that were trying to infiltrate the social circles of the administration and government people and Capitol Hill people. We were regularly getting FBI briefings on that kind of stuff." In this agitated environment, the notion that the KGB and other foreign intelligence agencies might try to use male prostitution rings to gather information did not seem so far-fetched.

Regardless, neither NBC nor any other media outlet followed up on the November 1981 report, which relied upon the testimony of a single, anonymous source. It would take another series of accusers for the story to catch fire, accusers who were the only thing that could make a tale involving homosexual prostitution rings, congressmen, and Russian spies even more sensational than it already was: teenage boys.

* * *

"PAGES AS A RULE IMITATE THE MEN WHOM THEY SERVE in chewing tobacco, smoking cigars and cigarettes, playing the races, and drinking beer," the newspaperman and explorer Walter Wellman reported upon a visit to Congress in 1890. "If the pages of the Capitol were to tell all they know[,] what a commotion there would be in the big building and out of it!"

The presence of a messenger corps in American legislative bodies dates back to the Continental Congress. The House of Representatives instituted a formal page program in the late 1820s. Reflecting upon the "magnificent grandeur" of representative government in an 1832 diary entry composed during his first term as a member of Congress, John Quincy Adams likened pages to "tripping Mercuries" scurrying about the chamber, copies of bills and written messages in hand. Over time, and like the government it served, the page program became more bureaucratized, such that by the early twentieth century, pages attended their own school, rising before dawn every day the House was in session to take a full slate of classes beginning at 6:10 a.m. After several hours of study, it was off to work at the Capitol, toiling in the service of democracy from the moment the House was gaveled to order until its adjournment late at night.

While the page system evolved significantly over the course of its long history—admitting its first full-time girl in 1973—some things are resistant to change. The system of patronage that dominated the page appointment process in its early days, while significantly attenuated, remained largely in effect by the early 1980s, with page positions often going to the sons and daughters of the wealthy and well connected. But more important to understanding the events that transpired over the summer of 1982 is the fact that boys have never stopped being boys, one of life's eternal verities that, as Walter Wellman noted nearly a century earlier, often resulted in "bumptiousness and disaster."

Leroy Williams did not fit the profile of the typical page when he arrived in Washington on June 29, 1981. The seventeen-year-old African American from North Little Rock, Arkansas, was the fifth of six children from a dysfunctional family, attended a fundamentalist Christian church, and hid his homosexuality from everyone he knew. Living and working away from home among children of great privilege, Williams coped with the resultant insecurities by spinning tall tales. He told his fellow pages that his father was a heart surgeon and that his mother was an opera singer, that they lived on a spacious ranch and made annual pilgrimages to Europe, that his whole family attended cotillions every Christmas, and that he had a girlfriend back home named Nancy. Whereas, in Arkansas, he consumed alcohol no more than once a month, in Washington he became "literally an alcoholic," a vice to which he added heavy use of the decade's most fashionably illicit accessory: cocaine.

A week into Williams's Washington odyssey, a curious item appeared on the first page of the *Morbidity and Mortality Weekly Report*, a publication of the Centers for Disease Control in Atlanta. Over the past two and

half years, the journal noted in dry, scientific language, a rare skin cancer usually seen in elderly Mediterranean males with impaired immune
systems, Kaposi's sarcoma, had been diagnosed in twenty-six homosexual
men and had killed eight of them. Some in the gay community speculated
that the victims had become ill by inhaling amyl nitrite, a drug known as
"poppers" popular in gay clubs; others believed it was all a hoax, a justification for the government to repress gay men's hard-won sexual freedom.
Maybe Williams read the short article summarizing the CDC finding on
the front page of the *Blade*, whose editors had allotted it space below the
fold, beneath a story about an effort to repeal the District's antiquated sodomy law. If so, it did not appear to have much effect on his sexual activity.

As any hormonal teenager living largely free from adult supervision
could be expected to do, Williams started to explore his sexuality, with the
added condition that his sexuality was one that, while enjoying a degree of
visibility and acceptance greater than ever before, remained highly stigmatized, especially in parts of the country like the one from which he hailed.
And so, despite his extravagant claims to the contrary, Williams didn't
engage in the romantic or sexual relationships with girls that his heterosexual peers pursued. Instead, he secretly sought male partners at the bars,
bookstores, and the bathhouse he surreptitiously read about in the back
pages of the *Blade*. Williams did not know the men with whom he slept
(of which there were an average of three per week) on anything more than
a first-name basis, and besides the Government Printing Office employee
and the Georgetown hairdresser, he never saw any of them again. Except,
perhaps, in those inadvertent moments around the Capitol Building when,
either entering a congressman's office or walking through the underground
passageways, he unexpectedly crossed paths with one of his fleeting intimates, and the burden of his secret became ever so slightly less difficult to
bear.

Williams also found companions in the directory from Friendly Models, an escort agency that offered its discriminating customers an array of
alluring Adonises starting at fifty dollars a pop. Williams became a regular
customer, and soon his seven-hundred-dollars-per-month page stipend
was no longer enough to satisfy his alcohol, cocaine, and callboy habits.
He stopped paying the rent and started writing bad checks. The parties
he hosted in his apartment, attended by other pages, became louder and
longer. There is only so much dissolution that those who administer the

page program were willing to tolerate, and eventually, Williams's drinking and drugging and carousing, along with his failing grades, led the House Clerk's Office to dismiss him and two other pages in January 1982.

Just as Williams and his classmates were departing Washington amid swirling rumors of drug- and alcohol-fueled debauchery, a sixteen-year-old from Denver, Colorado, named Jeffrey Opp arrived to take up his page duties. Described by one of his nominal supervisors in the House Door-keeper's Office as "someone who believed his goal in life was to change the system," Opp refused to open a checking account because to do so would violate his strongly held beliefs against banking. According to the congressional staffer who provided him temporary housing, Opp had a "super-hyper imagination" that manifested itself in the expression of outrageous claims. His fellow pages said he tended to "blow things way out of proportion."

As spring turned to summer, it was these two troubled young men whose testimonies would petrify the secret city.

★ ★ ★

SITTING AT A DESK WITH SIX PHONE LINES, "just blocks from the stately homes that house some of Washington's best-known politicians, pundits and old-money elite" in Georgetown, a slim thirty-eight-year-old man named Richard Kind labored to fulfill the sexual desires of the capital's closeted gay power brokers. Friendly Models was the oldest and largest gay escort service in the Washington area, and its proprietor had earned the trust of his eminent clients through guarantees of quality and discretion. Kind distributed to all his escorts a twenty-page manual instructing them in the finer arts of entertaining distinguished older gentlemen, along with a beeper to ensure that he could reach them at a moment's notice. From 6 p.m. until 3 a.m. every night at the Georgetown house that served as Friendly Models' headquarters, a group of well-groomed and well-built young men would gather around a pool table or play video games while waiting for Kind to dispatch them to one of the city's finer hotels, a private home, or, occasionally, an ambassadorial residence. (Kind employed escorts who spoke French, Spanish, German, and Italian.) Once booked, the escort was driven by a Friendly Models chauffeur in a Continental Mark IV to the agreed-upon place of assignation, where the customer had the option of paying by Visa or MasterCard and received a receipt discreetly stamped "RSK Associates." Every week, Kind incentivized superior service by awarding twenty-five-dollar bonuses to those escorts who had racked up six outcalls and a color television to the most popular.

Martin Price was convinced that behind the dignified Georgetown home and the trappings of respectability, Friendly Models was more than just an elite prostitution service. Relying mostly on a sometime hustler named David Schauer as a source, Price would later claim that, prior to every assignation, Kind gave his escorts strict instructions to "conduct an informal surveillance of the client's home or hotel room to ascertain as much as possible about" him. Afterward, the escort was driven back to Georgetown for a "debriefing." With 10 percent of his clientele coming from the military, Price alleged, Kind maintained a "sophisticated coding system" corresponding to rank, through which he paired the most desirable young men with the senior-most officers. Friendly Models, Price was convinced, had all the signs of being an elaborate foreign honey trap operation.

In March, Price introduced Schauer to Carl Shoffler, the local police detective who ran Robbie Merritt as an undercover informant inside the early 1970s gay liberation scene and who had been the first officer to arrive at the Watergate break-in. Shoffler's colleagues in nearby Arlington, Virginia, had been investigating Friendly Models for several months, and had pressured two escorts into working as informants. On the evening of Saturday, March 18, a team of officers from the Arlington and DC police departments, accompanied by an FBI agent, raided the Friendly Models house in Georgetown. They did not find Kind, who had skipped town before the raid. But in the thirteen boxes of business records carted out of his home, they discovered something far more valuable than, in the words of a Chesapeake House go-go boy who once hooked for him, "a white, pasty-faced pimp": a list with the names of five hundred to a thousand "preferred customers."

Not since the days of Roy Blick and his apocryphal list of five thousand homosexuals had such terror swept through the capital's community of gay men. The first thing Blade editor Steven Martz felt when he read about the Friendly Models raid in the Post was a sharp pang of dread that a string of suicides would follow. Among reporters, the "List of One Thousand Names" assumed a near-mythical sheen, an elusive treasure trove that had the awesome potential to break a thousand stories and as many lives. When it appeared on newsstands two months later, the inaugural issue of the Deep Backgrounder, which claimed credit for the raid on Friendly

Models, contained an article about another Washington homosexual out-call service, the Stables. The proprietors of this concern, the paper alleged, had gone to the police and FBI with an ultimatum: shut us down, and we'll release "customer names, occupations, sexual proclivities, etc." to the press, disclosures that would cause "a number of high government officials, members of Congress and even White House staff members" a great deal of embarrassment. "That such a threat might even have been made by oper-ators of what is unquestionably a house of prostitution is almost beyond belief," the *Deep Backgrounder* inveighed. "Yet in the nation's capital, where police are ever mindful of VIP reputations, it is perhaps not so surprising after all." Less than a week later, surely goaded by the *Deep Backgrounder*'s insinuation that it was in thrall to homosexual panderers, police raided the Stables, sparking fears that another list of prominent homosexuals would find its way into the hands of the highest bidder. Speculation as to whose names appeared on these rapidly proliferating registers of sexual deviants consumed Washingtonians, gay and straight. Shortly after a dinner party at which the host discussed a congressman who had hired a private detective to investigate whether his opponent was gay, the names of both the host and the congressman were added to different lists of alleged homosexuals being passed around by journalists and law enforcement authorities.

In the meantime, the scandals of the pages and the prostitutes, which until then had been developing in parallel, were about to intersect in the person of Leroy Williams. Following Williams's tumultuous departure from Washington earlier that year, the Capitol Police launched an investi-gation into drug and alcohol use by pages. Capitol Hill being, in the words of one veteran, "the rumor capitol of the world," it was only a matter of time before stories involving pages, drugs, and—despite Williams's best efforts to conceal it—homosexuality began to spread all over Washington, and beyond. In March, Williams sat for an interview with the Independent News Network, a syndicated television show, during which he made a few nebulous allegations about congressional staffers propositioning pages that were so vague the producers declined to air it.

On June 9, Jeffrey Opp received a phone call at his apartment from an unidentified man who said he had an important party invitation to deliver and thus needed Opp's address. Opp readily gave it, and within five min-utes, CBS News reporter John Ferrugia knocked on his apartment door. Ferrugia proceeded to share with Opp a series of disturbing allegations he was investigating: that there was a "homosexual ring" involving twenty-five to fifty congressmen for whom pages were procured by a House employee, that members of Congress frequented the "red light" district populated with boy prostitutes, and that there was a congressman who liked eight-year-olds, another who was "after little kids," and yet a third who was "an avid coke fiend." Ferrugia told Opp that he had heard he had a reputation among his peers for being a perceptive young man who was most certainly not an "air head," and that he might know something about the charges. Flattered, and in what he would later characterize as the actions of "a 16 year old kid satisfying his ego," Opp described for Ferrugia a series of past conversations with three congressmen as "homosexual approaches."

The next day, Opp related his encounter with Ferrugia to two congressional aides, adding, for dramatic effect, that he had been working undercover for CBS the past two weeks on a planned exposé of young homosexual prostitutes working along New York Avenue. Aghast that the Tiffany Network had conscripted one of their charges in such a mission, the aides called Ferrugia to complain. Ferrugia replied that the matter was too sensitive to discuss over the phone, and he asked the aides to meet him at a rendezvous point outside the East Wing of the National Gallery of Art. When they met, the reporter displayed a hand-drawn diagram featuring the U.S. Capitol at the center, with various lines sticking out of it like bicycle spokes leading to the Departments of Justice and State as well as the General Accounting Office. This was the visual representation, Ferrugia said, of "a widespread, organized homosexual ring" involving congressmen, members of the executive branch, and various other senior government officials.

On June 30 and July 1, tens of millions of Americans tuned into the *CBS Evening News with Dan Rather* to hear two young men explicitly detail their moral corruption by homosexuals in the halls of Congress. Cast in silhouette, Jeffrey Opp repeated the stories he had told Ferrugia about being preyed upon by congressmen. But it was the testimony of Leroy Williams that was the most shocking. Similarly shadowed and wearing a large hat to further obscure his identity, Williams spoke of graver debasements: that he had procured a male prostitute for a congressional aide, that he himself had had sex with three different congressmen (one of them on three separate occasions; twice at his office and once at the Watergate), and that the experience of being a page was essentially one of submission to the carnal needs of powerful men. "You know, the way the Hill works is that you climb the ladder, and so one favor, you know, deserves another," he explained.

Washington descended into panic. The House Committee on Standards of Official Conduct, informally known as the Ethics Committee, announced an investigation, led by the congressman who had chaired the body's inquiry into the assassinations of John F. Kennedy and Martin Luther King Jr. In its segment about the scandal, the flagship ABC program *Nightline*, hosted by Ted Koppel, displayed a graphic featuring a gigantic congressman grabbing a tiny page by the shoulders. "Why don't congressmen like to use bookmarks?" went the setup to a joke that made the rounds of Capitol Hill. "They'd rather turn over the page." Inevitably, the names of certain congressmen were mentioned behind closed committee-room doors and whispered over hushed lunchtime conversations, but only one man chose to come forward and defend himself. "When all else fails, persons who are unmarried by choice or circumstance have always been the subject of innuendos, gossip and false accusations," declared Larry Craig, Republican of Idaho and a bachelor. "This is despicable." That Craig felt the need to preemptively deny the charge of homosexuality, reported NBC News, illustrated "the sheer panic that reigns in certain quarters of Congress." And that he represented Boise, scene of one of the twentieth century's most infamous antigay witch hunts, added a harrowing wrinkle to the suspicion that perhaps the congressman doth protest too much.

On June 27, the Ethics Committee announced its retention of Democratic bigwig Joseph Califano as special counsel, an assignment the Johnson and Carter administration veteran accepted "with the greatest reluctance." That evening, a report on *ABC World News Tonight* produced another reason for Califano to lament his involvement. Bringing the number of silhouetted figures alleging homosexual depravity to four, a male prostitute identified only as "Fred" declared that it was "common practice for foreign agents to hire male hustlers to obtain U.S. government secrets" in Washington and that the Soviet, British, Israeli, and West German intelligence agencies were all players in this sensuous and treacherous game. Though ABC offered no proof for this claim, it earned the status of conventional wisdom among local law enforcement, the FBI, and the media. A DC homicide detective told *Blade* reporter Lou Chibbaro that, based on "extremely reliable sources," he was "absolutely certain" KGB agents were trying to compromise "closet queens" in the city. "You have to realize that the closeted homosexual, the married man with kids, who may have a top secret job, is in a very vulnerable position," he said. "The KGB know this and they go after this type of person. I can tell you for sure that this has happened." An FBI official told the *Washington Post* that "[w]e do know that Soviet intelligence officials have been known to frequent gay bars and that sort of thing in an effort to identity defense and other [officials] who are homosexuals." A story for the Knight Ridder news service, appearing in major newspapers across the country, declared that "Soviet Spies May Have Snooped on Homosexuals in D.C.," and anonymous sources confirmed to the *Post* that the State Department had fired a midlevel employee whose name appeared on a list of alleged clients of a male prostitution service seized by police earlier that year.

On August 1, the *Deep Backgrounder* lived up to its promise to "name names." Citing Leroy Williams's lawyer as its source, the paper identified the three congressmen with whom the former page said he had sex, and a senator for whom he claimed to have procured a male prostitute. No other media outlet followed suit, and to complaints that it was impugning potentially innocent men, the *Backgrounder* replied that it was actually doing Congress *a service* by removing the cloud of suspicion from the 531 members who "may wrongfully be suspected by constituents or others of being possibly enmeshed in this latest scandal." Elsewhere in the issue, Price identified two of the city's most influential "Washington Insiders"—true to his nonpartisan promise, one Democrat and one Republican—as gay drug abusers. First was Alan Baron, a slovenly yet brilliant thirty-nine-year-old former executive director of the Democratic National Committee and publisher of his own political newsletter, the *Baron Report*. Despite his left-wing politics and labor union roots, "the Baron," as he was affectionately known, could often be found holding court at the Palm, a giant bottle of Tab soda always on the table as he collected tidbits for his monthly digest. Baron's homosexuality was not a particularly well-guarded secret, as it hovered rather thickly about the freewheeling political salon he had established in his ramshackle Capitol Hill town house. Sean Strub, who learned the ropes of political communication at Baron's side, attributed to his mentor the creation of "a safe, intellectually, as well as sexually stimulating environment for all the boys from all across the country who wanted to grow up and be president and were in varying stages of getting there, either as a page in the Congress or as a member of Congress." The *Deep Backgrounder*, alas, was

more inclined to see Baron as presiding over a harem. The newsletter proprietor, it alleged, was "very active in the capital's homosexual community
where he is known to pay male hustlers between $100 and $500 a night and
to provide them with generous amounts of cocaine." He was, furthermore,
"a masochistic type of homosexual with a penchant for abuse and humiliation . . . described by our sources as being in the midst of 'a very sick
scene.'" According to Strub, Baron was convinced that the source of these
allegations was a rival (and closeted) political newsletter publisher seeking
to gain market dominance by embarrassing his chief competitor. Where
better to settle the score than through a shadowy right-wing rag willing to
go where no other publication dared to tread?

"Reagan Inaugural Co-Chairman Powerful 'Closet Homosexual?'" was
the headline, hardly in need of a question mark, above the adjoining *Deep
Backgrounder* item about Bob Gray, whose sexuality the paper labeled "the
worst kept secret in Washington today." So poorly kept was it that "if Mr.
Reagan does not know of Gray's sexual inclinations, he is unquestionably the
only member of the capital's establishment who remains unaware of this."
Gray, the *Deep Backgrounder* claimed, was "infamous for his alleged sex
and drug parties that are held primarily at his summer home in Rehoboth
Beach," a detail that would surely have upset Ed and Ursula Meese. (Only a
week earlier, the Meeses' son had died in a car crash, and Gray offered his
house to the grieving couple.) According to one close acquaintance, Gray
became convinced around this time that the FBI was tapping his phones.

From Congress to the White House, and from the NSA to the *Washington Blade*, the saga of the pages, prostitutes, congressmen, and Soviet agents
gripped Washington. Jamie Shoemaker, by now a year and a half into his
tenure as the NSA's first openly gay employee, suddenly found himself with
a new asset to offer his employer on top of his exceptional language skills.
One day during the height of the scandal, Shoemaker's superior called him
into his office and displayed a photograph, taken surreptitiously at the
Chesapeake House, of a man whom American intelligence officials suspected of being a Soviet spy. "Have you ever seen him there, ever talked to
him?" the superior asked.

"No," Shoemaker replied. "To be honest with you, he looks like a lot of
guys I've seen there."

Meanwhile at the *Blade*, staffers were puzzled by the random man who
showed up at their offices one day asking for child pornography and by

another who called asking to be set up with a "15-year-old." Attendance at gay bars, usually hopping in Washington's humid summer months, plummeted as rumors of FBI surveillance spread across the gay grapevine. "Business is way off," the manager of one establishment complained. "A lot of people are downright frightened. Twenty years ago, to get into a place like this, you had to be screened at the door through a peephole and buzzed in. I think we're headed back to those days."

* * *

DISCREPANCIES IN THE PAGES' STORIES had been apparent almost immediately after CBS aired its initial report. Realizing it had spoken with the same silhouetted young man in the large hat just a few months earlier, the Independent News Network broadcast the interview with Leroy Williams it never aired in which he omitted any mention of sex with congressmen. A few days later, the *Washington Post* published a front-page story, based on ten hours of interviews with Williams, detailing numerous inconsistencies in the various accounts he had provided to the media and authorities, ranging from the number of congressmen he claimed to have slept with to the locations where the assignations allegedly transpired. "You associate congressmen with big things; the Watergate's something big in D.C. any way you look at it," he said, explaining why he had asserted the apartment complex was the site of his purported deflowering by a member of Congress. "And so, I guess it was just . . . the evil part of me saying, hey, here's something that sounds good, you know . . ." The *New York Times*, meanwhile, interviewed dozens of pages, none of whom could corroborate anything alleged by their erstwhile peers.

Two weeks before Labor Day, just in time to mark the official end of the Washington silly season, the story collapsed. On the evening of August 22, Leroy Williams was arrested in Little Rock for public intoxication at a midnight screening of *The Rocky Horror Picture Show*. Five days later, he told a news conference that everything he had said about having sexual relations with congressmen was a lie, an assertion he repeated the next day under oath before a closed session of the Ethics Committee. The liaisons he claimed to have set up between prostitutes and others, he admitted, had been for himself. An interim committee report released in December 1982 revealed the cynically circular role of the television media in promoting what one critic later called "Trial by Silhouette." It was reporter John

Ferrugia's sharing of lurid allegations with Jeffrey Opp that had persuaded the impressionable sixteen-year-old to retail a series of embellishments to congressional staffers, who introduced Opp to Justice Department officials, whose opening up of an investigation into claims originating *with Ferrugia* provided CBS with the pretext it needed to air a baseless story that it had essentially ginned up, thereby setting off a homosexual panic. The final report, for which a team of investigators traveled 100,000 miles, held 700 interviews, conducted 125 depositions, issued 111 subpoenas, and compelled testimony from twelve people through grants of immunity, concluded that "allegations and rumors of misconduct were the product of gossip or even out-and-out fabrication."

As for the charges of male prostitution services infiltrated by foreign spies, it was later revealed that the callboys who had made these claims were working simultaneously as informants for the FBI and DC Police. Their charges, far from being based on any personal knowledge of espionage, had been fed to them by law enforcement in the hope that generating a media firestorm would pressure other gays to inform. Only one Soviet agent was ever identified as a possible patron of the Chesapeake House, and it was unclear if his visits had anything to do with spying. According to Jack Anderson, in the early morning hours of February 24, 1981, a cultural attaché at the Soviet embassy named Yuriy Igorevich Osipov departed a diplomatic reception and walked to Meridian Hill Park, where he drunkenly started importuning another man for sex. A pair of muggers approached, but before they could rob the diplomat, a nineteen-year-old Black man named Sammie Smith, who happened to be crossing the park after visiting his girlfriend, talked the men out of it. Osipov gratefully offered Smith a ride home, and in the car, according to Smith, "tried to grab my privates." When Smith resisted, Osipov parked the vehicle and attempted to strangle the Good Samaritan. "The white man was choking the brother," one witness said. Osipov never had an opportunity to tell his side of the story, as his comrades put him on the first plane back to Moscow. "It turned out that guy was just a Russian having fun like everybody else," Jamie Shoemaker's boss told him when Shoemaker asked about the fate of the suspected Russian spy whose photograph he had been shown.

Martin Price and Victor Marchetti knew from the beginning that taking on the homosexual conspiracy controlling Washington would be an uphill battle. By their second issue, attempts to place advertisements for the

Deep Backgrounder in more mainstream outlets—even reliably right-wing ones like *Conservative Digest* and *Human Events*—had been "consistently stymied" by sinister, unnamed forces. And on Capitol Hill, Price alleged, the leadership of both parties had "deliberately blocked" distribution of his paper. (Not so, countered the House Postmaster, pointing to a 1972 prohibition on the delivery of periodicals to congressional offices unless specifically requested.) Hoping to amplify (and monetize) his crusade to expose "a life-style that right now is threatening the very existence of civilization," Price broke into the burgeoning field of single-issue advocacy, founding an outfit called the Truth About Gays Political Action Committee (TAG-PAC) in 1983.

Ironically, in its condemnations of influential covert homosexuals, the *Deep Backgrounder* anticipated the rhetoric of some gay activists on the opposite side of the political spectrum, who had concluded that the biggest impediment to their progress was not the prejudicial straight power broker but the closeted gay one. Asked by the *Blade* how he justified revealing the homosexuality of people who did not hold security clearances and therefore could not be construed as security risks, Price said that one of the men he identified had evinced a "holier than thou" attitude while the other, though not a government official, "exerts tremendous influence" and was "hypocritical." Recognizing an insidious link between the closets of power and their own persecution, gay activists would use strikingly similar language to describe individuals who, by their silence, not only sacrificed their personal integrity but sustained an oppressive system.

Price would not live to witness his adversaries adopt the tactics he had deployed to such chilling effect, dying unexpectedly in October 1983. The *Deep Backgrounder* expired soon thereafter. His erstwhile associate Marchetti remained a prominent figure within the conspiracy theorist subculture, writing for Holocaust denial journals until the more prosaic form of dementia overtook him a few years prior to his death in 2018. The *Deep Backgrounder* may have faded from Washington's collective memory almost as suddenly as it appeared. But the fear it instilled among the citizens of "Sodom-on-the-Potomac" remained potent as a force of nature beyond anyone's imagination threatened to push their secrets out into the open.

37

"I DON'T HAVE IT. DO YOU?"

"Larry," Lester Kinsolving interjected, as Acting White House Press Secretary Larry Speakes finished answering a question about the Producer Price Index on October 15, 1982. "Does the President have any reaction to the announcement—the Centers for Disease Control in Atlanta, that A-I-D-S is now an epidemic in over 600 cases?"

It was an unusually topical question from Kinsolving, a fifty-four-year-old, six-foot-one, 220-pound former Episcopal priest and gadfly journalist who, prior to his defrocking, donned a clerical collar to White House press briefings. Until a dispute with a potential publisher led him to choose "death before dishonor" and fold it entirely, Kinsolving's *Washington Weekly* was a fixture in the universe of right-wing periodicals where the *Deep Backgrounder* had made such a splash the previous summer, and Kinsolving retained his membership in the fourth estate as a syndicated newspaper columnist and radio correspondent. His questions usually ranged from the slightly off-kilter to the downright bizarre, their effect heightened by Kinsolving's resolute determination to never break character as a just-the-facts newsman from a bygone era. "What are the president's views on nude swimming in the White House pool?" was a memorable example from the

Kinsolving oeuvre, as was the earnest inquiry, inspired by the 1976 Captain & Tennille hit, "What does the president think about muskrat love?"

Every now and then, however, in the manner of, but hardly so frequently as, a stopped clock, Kinsolving asked a question about an important issue ignored by his oh-so-sophisticated colleagues in the mainstream media, whose nickname for Kinsolving, "the Mad Monk," illustrated the contempt in which they held him. "Lester, by his mannerisms, can be an irritant," recalled Gerald Ford's press secretary Ron Nessen, who once tried to counter a hostile Kinsolving interrogatory by quoting scripture back at him. "But in my experience he often asked important questions on important issues long before other people realized they were important." And so it was that, well over a year after the condition that the CDC had just begun calling acquired immunodeficiency syndrome (AIDS) was first identified in more than two dozen gay men, it was left to the Mad Monk to pose a question nobody in the White House press corps cared to ask.

"A-I-D-S?" Speakes responded quizzically, searching through his pile of briefing papers at the podium. "I haven't got anything on it."

"Over a third of them have died," Kinsolving explained. "It's known as 'gay plague.'"

The room erupted in laughter. *There goes old Lester again.*

"No, it is," Kinsolving continued, a trace of indignation perceptible in his voice. "I mean it's a pretty serious thing that one in every three people that get this have died. And I wondered if the president is aware of it?"

Perhaps this was just another of Lester's ruses. He was certainly not known for caring about the plight of homosexuals—or, as he referred to them, the "militant sodomy lobby." Speakes, a former press secretary for segregationist senator James Eastland, had earned a moniker in Washington, "the Mississippi Catfish," for his tendency to sting when attacked. If the Mad Monk was pulling his leg, then two could play at this game.

"I don't have it," Speakes asserted. "Do you?"

As the image of prudish old Lester Kinsolving contracting a "gay plague" sank in, the journalists in the room let out another peal of laughter.

"No, I don't," Kinsolving answered tersely.

"You didn't answer my question."

"Well, I just wondered, does the President—"

"How do you know?" Speakes pressed. He wasn't letting up. Rarely did the man standing at the Briefing Room lectern expend so much effort to get a laugh at the Mad Monk's expense, and judging by the response from Kinsolving's colleagues, Speakes was on a roll.

"In other words, the White House looks on this as a great joke?" Kinsolving asked.

"No, I don't know anything about it, Lester."

"Does the President, does anybody in the White House, know about this epidemic, Larry?

"I don't think so. I don't think there's been any—"

"Nobody knows?"

"There has been no personal experience here, Lester."

"No, I mean, I thought you were keeping—"

"I checked thoroughly with [White House physician] Dr. Ruge this morning and he's had no patients suffering from A-I-D-S or whatever it is."

"The President doesn't have gay plague, is that what you're saying or what?"

"No, I didn't say that."

"*Didn't* say that?"

"I thought I heard you on the State Department over there," an exasperated Speakes said in reference to Kinsolving's former beat, cracks about the lavender lads at Foggy Bottom apparently still good for a laugh nearly thirty years after the purge of homosexuals reached its height. "Why didn't you stay there?"

Resigning himself to the futility of trying to get a serious answer from the president's press secretary about AIDS, Kinsolving threw in the towel. "Because I love you, Larry, that's why."

"Oh, I see," Speakes said, relishing the victory. "Just don't put it in those terms, Lester."

"Oh, I retract that."

"I hope so."

Larry Speakes was hardly alone in dismissing the significance of the strange new disease afflicting gay men, as his carefree colloquy before the White House press corps—none of whose members bothered to report it— attests. "White House reporters can be as isolated from America as the president," Larry Bush, the Washington correspondent of *The Advocate*, observed. "At papers like the *Washington Post* and the *New York Times*, editors would sit down with the reporters before press conferences—they had so few of them—and work out what questions to ask. AIDS wasn't on anybody's agenda; just putting it on the agenda was what the gay movement was about. But there was this attitude that to write a story was to put it on the news agenda and to pander to gays. It got very bizarre." At the *Wall Street Journal*, it was not until a reporter, after lobbying his editors for months to let him write about AIDS, pitched an article concerning the disease's emergence among heterosexuals that the paper deigned to print its first piece on the subject. Published in February 1982, the article appeared under the revealing headline "New, Often-Fatal Illness in Homosexuals Turns Up in Women, Heterosexual Males."

While Speakes and Kinsolving were engaging in their White House pas de deux over "A-I-D-S," the country was freaking out about an ostensibly more urgent public health crisis. Every day for the entire month of October, and on twenty-three days after that, the *New York Times* published a story about the discovery of cyanide in a handful of Tylenol bottles in the Chicago area. Immediately, the Food and Drug Administration took drastic action, ordering the removal of every single Tylenol capsule from store shelves across the country. Within five weeks, the Department of Health and Human Services promulgated new regulations governing tamper-proof packaging to prevent future incidents of what ended up being an isolated event that, while unnerving, killed just seven people.

"The bitter truth was that AIDS did not just happen to America, it was allowed to happen by an array of institutions, all of which failed to perform their appropriate tasks to safeguard the public health," wrote Randy Shilts in his history of the epidemic's early years, *And the Band Played On.* As the swift and comprehensive reaction to a few poisoned pain reliever tablets demonstrated, neither the U.S. government nor the mainstream media lacked zeal in confronting what they perceived to be a public health emergency. But it would take years before either treated AIDS as a national priority, and the two-minute exchange in the White House Briefing Room between the president's spokesman and a gadfly reporter is a stunning reminder of a major reason why: the primary victims were homosexuals.

* * *

"WHAT THE HECK IS THE UNITED STATES GOVERNMENT getting in the business of dealing with VD?" the slim, mustachioed, puckishly handsome political operative asked. "If their past record of dealing with interstate commerce is anything, they'll wind up giving it to everybody."

John Terrence "Terry" Dolan's conservative political philosophy could be inferred from his ideal federal budget: "99 percent for defense—keep America strong—and 1 percent on delivering the mail. That's it. Leave us alone." His tactical philosophy in dealing with liberal opponents was that of a marine drill sergeant. "Make them angry," "stir up hostilities," "the shriller you are," he liked to say, the better. "That's the nature of our beast." Dolan didn't care for the Republican Party, viewing it as nothing more than a temporarily useful vehicle for advancing his aggressively anti-Communist, radically small government ideology. Chairman Bill Brock should have been "fired long ago," Dolan declared. The party itself was a "fraud" and "a social club where the rich people go to pick their noses."

Many wondered how a man not yet thirty years of age could speak with such bravado about people older and more experienced than he. But Dolan's confidence, if not his attitude, was well earned. In just a few short years, he had revolutionized American politics. As chairman of the National Conservative Political Action Committee (NCPAC, pronounced "NICK-pack"), Dolan led one of the first groups to take advantage of the campaign finance loopholes created by the post-Watergate electoral reforms. Until the mid-1970s, the funding of American political campaigns was an opaque business rife with corruption; in 1972, for instance, just 153 people donated twenty million dollars to Richard Nixon's Committee to Re-Elect the President. A 1974 amendment to the Federal Election Campaign Act capping the amount an individual could contribute to a campaign, combined with a Supreme Court decision two years later removing the limit on funds independent groups could raise and spend during an election, inadvertently shifted money and influence from candidates to political entrepreneurs.

Dubbed the "fourth horseman of the apocalyptic right" by the *Washington Post* alongside Conservative Caucus founder Howard Phillips, direct mail impresario Richard Viguerie, and Heritage Foundation cofounder Paul Weyrich, Terry Dolan was the most aggressive of this new breed of ideological warriors. And NCPAC was the most powerful organization in the New Right, spoken of with reverence and dread around Washington and in political circles across the country for its ability to raise huge sums of money and to deploy them against candidates who crossed its hard-right agenda. NCPAC exerted its influence primarily through the medium of the fifteen- and thirty-second television attack ad, which Dolan pioneered and made into a staple of American political campaigns. "A group like ours," Dolan once bragged, "could lie through its teeth, and the candidate it helps stays clean."

By 1980, NCPAC was one of the country's richest "independent expenditure" outfits and Dolan one of its most effective political operatives. In addition to spending two million dollars on Reagan's election, NCPAC was widely credited with claiming the scalps of four leading liberal Democratic senators (including the party's 1972 presidential nominee, George McGovern, whom it memorably denounced as a "baby killer"), helping the GOP recapture control of the body for the first time since Dwight Eisenhower's 1952 sweep. Adding to the Dolan mystique was the fact that he was one half of a political power tandem: as Terry advanced the banner of conservatism outside the White House, his older brother, Tony, a Pulitzer Prize–winning former journalist, furthered the cause from within as President Reagan's chief speechwriter. Where Terry was vociferous in his views and unrestrained in throwing punches, Tony (who performed conservative folk songs at Yale and required any girl he dated to take out a subscription to *National Review*) preferred to place his fillips in the mouths of others. "Speech writers should be seen and not heard" was his credo. Not since Jack and Bobby Kennedy had two brothers exercised more political influence in Washington.

Born and raised in southern Connecticut by working-class Catholic Democrats, Terry Dolan acquired a taste for politics in 1960 while working as a nine-year-old volunteer on Richard Nixon's presidential campaign against John F. Kennedy. Endeavoring to defeat the coreligionist who became America's first Catholic president presaged a life full of provocations. Four years later, Dolan was so wowed by Ronald Reagan's speech endorsing Barry Goldwater for president, "A Time for Choosing," that he purchased an LP record of it, which he listened to regularly well into adulthood. As a student at Georgetown, Dolan joined Young Americans for Freedom and came to the realization that Nixon was "the most liberal president we've ever had." His political identity drifted from that of loyal Republican Party man to conservative movement insurrectionary. "I used to be a Republican," Dolan confessed to the *Washington Post* in 1980. "I used to be a political hack, but then in 1972, it was like a sexual awakening. I couldn't understand these strange urgings to do conservative things."

It was an ironic comparison for Dolan to draw, considering how his actual sexual awakening would come to overshadow his political one. Of all the many gay men working in the Reagan administration and conservative movement during the 1980s, none more vividly exposed the punishing contradictions of their precarious existence than Terry Dolan. By day, he attended Catholic Mass and delivered speeches containing assertions like "I can think of virtually nothing that I do not endorse on the agenda of the Christian right." By night, he frequented the Eagle and cruised the steam room at a Capitol Hill gym. Dolan spent a lot of time at these temples of bodily self-perfection (three hours in the weight room every morning and sometimes a quick cardio exercise during lunch) to maintain his footing in the "aristocracy of beauty" that defined the 1980s urban gay male subculture. Though Dolan was careful never to acknowledge his homosexuality outside the environs of that world, he was not exactly a model of discretion. One evening, after addressing a business trade association at a Denver hotel, Dolan descended into the lobby for a night of prowling the local leather bar scene decked out in the era's "gay clone" uniform (tight jeans, leather cowboy boots, flannel shirt, and studded leather wristband), the attendees to whom, just moments earlier, he had served up a generous helping of right-wing rhetorical red meat none the wiser. Dolan's organization, meanwhile, sent out fund-raising letters like the one signed by far-right Republican congressman Dan Crane, declaring, "Our nation's moral fiber is being weakened by the growing homosexual movement and the fanatical ERA pushers (many of whom publicly brag they are lesbians)."

Dolan, whose favorite movie was *The Producers*, exuded mischief. At NCPAC headquarters, he regularly leavened the office drudgery with squirt gun fights and played pranks on the young staff involving a litter of hamsters, his favorite a "sexually active male named Susan." The rascally exterior, however, masked a conflicted soul. "He was very private about his life," remembered Mike Murphy, who started his career at NCPAC before going on to advise leading Republican politicians including Sen. John McCain and Governors Jeb Bush and Arnold Schwarzenegger. "His sexual orientation never was discussed, at least between him and I or any staffer there that I know of that I ever spoke to . . . I did feel for him; that if he was gay and I thought the odds were that he was, it must have [been] very tough to exist in the larger conservative movement that was overtly hostile to gay rights."

The day after Reagan's landslide, the wry and wiry Dolan appeared alongside his fellow horseman of the apocalyptic right, the dour and rotund Paul Weyrich, not to celebrate their candidate's victory, but to read him the riot act. The expected ascension of the moderate Tennessean Howard Baker (whom Weyrich denounced as "a roll-over-and-play-dead senator") to the position of Senate majority leader was unacceptable, the two men declared, and if incoming vice president George H. W. Bush did not immediately rectify his less-than-enthusiastic embrace of the conservative agenda, he, too, could expect to face political retribution. Bush, Dolan later threatened, better "mind his p's and q's or he'll find himself out of a job." Maureen Reagan, the president's daughter from his first marriage to the actress Jane Wyman, and a 1982 Republican Senate candidate who supported abortion rights and the ERA, was "the type of person who, in the middle of a war, would go out and shoot our wounded." Not even Reagan was immune from criticism. Once, he called Dolan to offer his appreciation for a supportive film NCPAC had produced about him. After summarily thanking the president, Dolan proceeded "to give him hell" over his appointing New Right bête noire Henry Kissinger to a commission on Central America.

. Dolan's apparent hypocrisy in the way he conducted his public and private lives—sidling up to the likes of Jerry Falwell while maintaining an active presence on Washington's gay social circuit—presented a serious test case for the Code. "Why should we protect you?" Larry Kramer once snapped at Dolan during a gay dinner party, as Dolan's lover sat by his side. "Because you have more to gain by letting me fight for you from the inside," Dolan shot back. Dolan occasionally made good on this pledge. In February 1982, he wrote a letter to Ed Meese offering his "unsolicited advice" on the Family Protection Act, which he labeled "a contradiction in terms." Dolan criticized the law on federalism grounds, asserting, "To deny funds to a school district which 'denigrates the traditional role of women' is just as bad as denying funds because a school district doesn't have bilingual education." If the Reagan administration were to support the law, he warned, "our adversaries in the 1982 election will attack us for invading the bedroom." Acknowledging that "I might be putting myself at odds with some of my friends in the movement on this subject," Dolan concluded that "the long-range development of our cause requires us to be consistent with our philosophy." He sent copies of the letter to his three fellow horsemen, and to Falwell.

The following month, Dolan gave an interview to Larry Bush of *The Advocate* in which he spoke out against the federal government discriminating against homosexuals and apologized for the antigay language that had previously appeared in NCPAC paraphernalia. "I truly regret that we ever put into print anything questioning the morality or patriotism of any person," Dolan said. "That's totally inappropriate." Speaking from personal belief, he added that, "sexual preference is irrelevant to political philosophy." That Dolan would even talk to such a publication outraged Weyrich. "I told Terry that I thought he used poor judgement," Weyrich said, adding that *The Advocate* "is not a pleasant magazine." By contrast, Weyrich's Free Congress Foundation was publisher of *The Homosexual Network: Private Lives and Public Policy*, a dense, conspiratorial, 680-page tome penned by a Catholic priest assailing the gay rights movement. At a press conference to distribute the text in his hometown of Kenosha, Wisconsin, Weyrich excoriated a bill being debated in the state legislature that would outlaw discrimination against gays. "I think it is an insult to blacks and Hispanics and other people who have been given some kind of special status whom I support," he said. "I mean, if you are going to do it for homosexuals, why not rapists."

Despite Dolan's denials, sightings of him at the Eagle and other dens of homosexual iniquity kept finding their way to Weyrich. The suspenders-clad, teetotaling "Robespierre of the New Right" had coined the term "Moral Majority," and he took care to mention that Wrigley's Doublemint gum was his only vice. He had been the first conservative activist to demand Bob Bauman's resignation in 1980, and his guide for dealing with those who strayed from the straight-and-narrow path was the book of Matthew:

> If your brother does something wrong, go and have it out with him alone, between yourselves. If he listens to you, you have won back your brother. If he does not listen, take one or two others with you. But if he refuses to listen to these, report it to the community; and if he refuses to listen to the community, treat him like a pagan or a tax collector.

Weyrich sent an "emissary" to ask Dolan about the rumors floating around town that he was a homosexual. "How dare you question me?" Dolan responded. He realized, however, that he had gone too far in his interview with *The Advocate*, and that some damage control was necessary.

"I do not, nor have I ever, endorsed gay rights," Dolan declared in a letter to NCPAC donors. "I have also discussed this matter with Jerry Falwell and other leaders of the Christian right. While we may and do disagree on a few issues, we all support the same conservative goals."

Dolan's place in the closet all but guaranteed the precarious situation in which he found himself. Any effort to disavow the open homophobia of his New Right allies lent credence, in their eyes, to rumors that he was gay, while any attempt to distance himself from the increasingly assertive gay rights movement frustrated activists who knew he was living a lie. While reporters at mainstream media outlets refused to broach the matter of Dolan's homosexuality, there was one publication that lacked such inhibitions. "Thus Dolan, who heads what is generally considered the wealthiest and most conservative political action group in the country, frequents a bar filled with motorcycle club members and tough-talking jocks who dress in country-western and avant-garde leather attire usually associated with certain aspects of the homosexual scene," railed the *Deep Backgrounder*, in an item leaving little to the imagination about Dolan's frequent patronage of the Eagle. A more consequential revelation appeared later that year in *God's Bullies: Power, Politics and Religious Tyranny*, an exposé of the religious right. For a chapter on gays in the conservative movement, author Perry Deane Young profiled Dolan, and published an affidavit from a male federal government employee who claimed to have had sex with Dolan after meeting him at the Eagle. The *Blade* printed an excerpt from the book on its front page, and Dolan's face appeared on the cover of *Christopher Street*, a New York City–based gay magazine. Photocopies of the chapter were passed like samizdat throughout the White House, including Tony Dolan's speechwriting shop.

Ever since the *New York Post* identified David Walsh as "Senator X" in 1942, the charge of homosexuality had been the atomic bomb of political weaponry. And like the doctrine of mutually assured destruction that evolved to maintain peace between the nuclear superpowers, so was "the Code" designed to protect gays on either side of the political aisle. But as one flank became more tolerant of homosexuality and the other less so, the equilibrium on which the system depended began to falter. A rising generation of openly gay activists, journalists, and political operatives started to embrace a new tactic initially known as "outage." According to an article by a pseudonymous author in the *Blade*, the unprecedented exposure of a gay public figure by a gay publication had an intimidating effect on Washington's "sizeable community of conservative and moderate Gays and Lesbians," and threatened "to end a decade-long experiment which encouraged hundreds of these individuals to enjoy limited exposure in the city's once protective Gay social circles." The writer noted a "decline in the size and number of openly Gay parties which traditionally fill Washington's fall season," as those who normally attended them steered clear of events where one's presence might insinuate homosexuality by association. And it wasn't just liberals who could play the "outage" card. An administrative assistant on the staff of a far-right senator warned of revenge against closeted liberals who had dealings with "super straight" labor unions. "Thank God, I don't have a family and kids; I'm ready for them," a gay coal industry executive said of the gay journalists Larry Bush and Perry Deane Young. "But if either of them comes after me, I'm taking [a senator with presidential ambitions] down with me. I've got a few friends in the press, too."

Dolan denied the one-night stand recounted in *God's Bullies*, and whatever problems the episode might have created for him among his adversaries within the New Right or on the gay left, it did not hurt his standing with the most important constituency, the Reagan administration. Just a few months after the book was released, White House chief of staff James Baker welcomed a group of NCPAC donors to the executive mansion for a day of private briefings with the president and his senior aides. In May 1983, Baker personally escorted Dolan to an Oval Office photo session with the president, and the following week, he served as co-chairman of a $125-a-plate dinner honoring Dolan in the Riverview Room at the Watergate, where two hundred of the city's most powerful conservative luminaries roasted the young activist. "Terry Dolan is our kind of moderate," cracked Utah Republican senator Orrin Hatch, one of the first men to benefit from Dolan's political wizardry in 1976. Republican senator Steve Symms of Idaho blessed the honoree for the assistance NCPAC had lent his campaign to "separate Church and state," a reference to Symms's upset victory over Frank Church in 1980. For his services to the cause, Dolan was awarded an antique plaque adorned with an apt quote from Teddy Roosevelt: "Aggressive fighting for the right is the noblest sport the world affords."

A guest from outside the Beltway would never have guessed that the toast of conservative Washington had been exposed just a few months earlier as a homosexual. Such calculated ambiguity was important first and foremost to right-wing gays, who needed it to preserve their status in a political movement increasingly hostile to them. But the ruse also served the purposes of their straight patrons, who profited from the talents of their gay advisors while opposing the "homosexual agenda" that aimed to make them full and equal citizens. This minuet of mutual hypocrisy and deceit left Dolan and others like him serving the role of modern-day eunuchs, reliable servants to the powerful whose public denial of a personal life— according to one of his employees, Dolan took "10 to 15 pounds of polling" data home to analyze every night—and vulnerability to exposure guaranteed their steadfast loyalty.

The Dolan dinner ended as did any conservative outing in Reaganite Washington, with a word of thanks to the men and women in uniform abroad and a prayer for grace from the Lord above. "John Terrence Dolan is a patriot," Hatch declared. "He's an exemplary leader. God bless him and keep him."

* * *

GERRY STUDDS HAD NEVER MET AN OPENLY GAY PERSON when he came to Washington in 1973 as a thirty-five-year-old congressman representing the Cape Cod and Islands region of Massachusetts. When the first national rally for gay rights took place on the National Mall six years later, Studds felt so personally conflicted about attending that his compromise solution was to alter his daily jogging route to within a block of the Washington Monument, where he gazed longingly at those who had the courage to unburden themselves of the secret they shared. Occasionally, Studds would sneak into Lambda Rising, which had become the largest gay bookstore in the world. (Such was the shop's reputation that, in 1980, the Republican congressman and presidential candidate John Anderson dropped in to ask owner Deacon Maccubbin "what I [would] need to talk about" if the subject of gay rights were to arise at an upcoming debate.) These and other cautious forays into the gay world earned Studds a mention, alongside his Bay State colleague Barney Frank, in the first issue of the *Deep Backgrounder*, both men "reportedly seen frequenting gay bars here and in Boston."

Soon after arriving in Washington, Studds initiated a sexual relationship with a seventeen-year-old male congressional page. Though the young man would later describe Studds as "an intelligent, gentle man" who "did nothing to me which I would consider destructive or painful," the relationship was clearly inappropriate. It became public in the summer of 1983 as an inadvertent byproduct of Special Counsel Joseph Califano's investigation into the sex and drugs scandal that had rocked Capitol Hill the previous summer. While the investigation refuted the charges of Leroy Williams and Jeffrey Opp, Califano's team yielded discoveries of two *past* instances of sexual relationships between congressmen and pages dating to the 1970s. The first concerned Republican Dan Crane of Illinois—whose signature had graced the prior year's NCPAC letter decrying the homosexual threat to the nation's "moral fabric"—and a seventeen-year-old girl. The second involved Studds.

Facing a censure motion from his colleagues, precedent dictated Studds resign. That was the path trod by his predecessors in public homosexual disgrace, Robert Bauman and Jon Hinson. But Studds decided at the outset that he would not follow their lead. There would be no reaching for alcoholism as an excuse or vague references to "human frailty" and "self-doubt," followed by resolute denial that he was gay or sheepish admissions that he merely suffered from "homosexual tendencies." On July 14, 1983, Studds delivered a speech on the House floor unprecedented in the extent of its disclosure. "All Members of Congress must cope with the challenge of initiating and maintaining a career in public office without destroying entirely the ability to lead a meaningful and emotionally fulfilling private life," he began. "It is not a simple task for any of us to meet adequately the obligations of either public or private life, let alone both. But these challenges are made substantially more complex when one is, as am I, both an elected public official and gay." At that moment, Gerry Studds became the first openly gay member of Congress.

In the five days between Studds's groundbreaking speech and the determination of his fate by the House, the mail and phone calls to Studds's office tilted nine to one in his favor. For hours at a time, he sat and read letters from people across the country, many of them tormented by their own secret. "If at times you find it difficult to rest," a gay man from Oregon wrote, "please remember that, although you are in pain, there are millions of gay people who are prouder of themselves because of the way you have chosen to publicly respond to the realities of your life." On July 20, clutching a folder full of these missives, Studds made his way to the well of the

House. Facing Speaker Tip O'Neill, he held his head high as the vote for censure was read, 420–3.

Studds's homosexuality, long rumored but now official, inevitably became a topic of contention during his reelection campaign the following year, when he again made history as the first openly gay person to win a congressional race. That he did so from a district that simultaneously voted 55 percent to 45 percent to keep Ronald Reagan in the White House and, prior to his first election in 1973, had not elected a Democrat to represent it in Congress for half a century, earned Studds praise from an unlikely quarter. "I don't know many men who could have done it," said Stewart McKinney, Republican from Connecticut. "To march in those parades in those small New England towns as an openly gay man took courage. If anyone wanted me to say gays are sissies, I'd point to Gerry Studds" to refute it.

38

"THEM" IS "US"

"A LOT OF GREAT POLITICAL MOVEMENTS START IN UNDERGROUND BUN-kers," Bob Bauman announced to the one hundred or so gay Reaganites gathered in Peter Hannaford's basement on the evening of May 14, 1984.

"And end in one!" Hal Gordon, Ed Meese's speechwriter, interjected to laughs.

Bauman's tragic inability to reconcile his public and private lives had served as an object lesson for gay conservatives. After failing to recapture his old congressional seat in 1982, an effort through which he publicly maintained his heterosexuality, Bauman came out of the closet the follow-ing summer in a speech to the American Bar Association urging the group to endorse laws prohibiting discrimination against citizens like him. It was an issue that affected Bauman personally. In the three years since his down-fall, he had been unable to find steady work. "I desperately need your talent in this agency," one senior government official told him, "but I do not have the courage to appoint you to any post." Bauman fared even worse among his ideological confrères in the conservative movement, some of whom tried to evict him from the board of the American Conservative Union, an organization he cofounded. (Terry Dolan, who called the attempted ouster a "not-so-subtle fag-bashing," led a successful behind-the-scenes effort to stymie the coup.) Neither this vindictive treatment by his erstwhile friends and allies, nor his acknowledgment that coming out of the closet had fostered a greater appreciation for what he termed "the human factor" of politics, altered Bauman's worldview. He remained a conservative, and he yearned to make it possible for these two parts of his identity to coexist.

As the crowd in Hannaford's basement attested, Bauman was not alone in this ambition. The group, which included people "representing positions from the White House staff, to offices of the most conservative Republican senators and congressmen, the Republican National Committee, and all parts of the Reagan administration," had gathered under the auspices of Concerned Americans for Individual Rights (CAIR), a recently formed organization whose mission was to make the Republican Party a more hospitable place for gays and lesbians. The idea for such an effort had been hatched in the summer of 1981 at a resort on the Russian River, a gay vacation community in Northern California, by Dolan and Bruce Decker, the latter an aide to Republican governor George Deukmejian. Decker, who mischievously called himself "Deukmejian's house fairy," tapped Leonard Matlovich, the gay former air force officer who had appeared on the cover of *Time* in 1975, as the group's figurehead. "God, the power in this room is incredible," Matlovich thought to himself as he surveyed the attendees.

The members of CAIR faced a massive obstacle, however, in exercising their potential influence: the secret they shared and of which they were unwilling to let go. "How do you form a gay political organization with a Board of Directors of twenty or thirty people when only two are willing to put their names on anything?" Matlovich asked, in reference to Bauman and himself. Despite coming up with the idea for the group, Dolan would have nothing to do with it; nor would Hannaford publicly associate himself in any way. (A story in the *Washington Post* about the event referred only to "a private home in the Washington area.") The collective silence of those involved with CAIR was a reflection of the president they supported, who had yet to mention the disease that had by now taken the lives of more than sixteen hundred Americans, most of them gay men. Just a few hours before CAIR's inaugural meeting, Reagan had appeared on the South Lawn of the White House to make a highly publicized statement about another public health crisis. "Michael, you've made it possible for us to warn millions of young Americans about the dangers of drinking and driving," the president told the twenty-five-year-old pop star bedecked in a blue military-style tunic with gold epaulets, a single, white sequined glove on his right hand. Michael Jackson, the "King of Pop," had earned the Presidential Public Safety Communications Award for giving the U.S. Department of Transportation permission to use his hit song "Beat It" in a public service announcement warning young people about the dangers of drunk driving. "If Americans follow his example, then we can face up to the problem of drinking and driving, and we can, in Michael's words, beat it," Reagan cheerily declared, while Nancy, upon whose initiative the ceremony had been organized, smiled by his side.

The next evening brought more star power to the White House when actor Rock Hudson, an old friend of the Reagans, attended a state dinner for the president of Mexico. Hudson's homosexuality was long an open secret in Hollywood. In 1955, he barely avoided exposure in *Confidential* when his agent sacrificed another gay actor he represented, matinee idol Tab Hunter, in exchange for the magazine's promise not to reveal the truth about his biggest star. Ten years later, an item in *Variety* reporting that Hudson would play an FBI agent in an upcoming film caused consternation at the Bureau because, according to an internal memo, "it is general common knowledge in the motion picture industry that Hudson is suspected of having homosexual tendencies." After inquiring with a movie industry source, a special agent in the Los Angeles Field Office reassured Hoover that, while Hudson's character would be "associated with the U.S. Embassy in Rome," he would not be "identified as representing any agency of the U.S. Government." Larry Kramer, who had worked as a Hollywood screenwriter in the 1960s, was well aware of Hudson's secret, with which he happily taunted the First Couple. "Mrs. Reagan, your best friend is gay!" he had shouted the previous spring in a speech following a Madison Square Garden fundraiser for Gay Men's Health Crisis, a charity he had cofounded. "Mrs. Reagan, while you wear your Adolfo and your Calvin Klein and your Bill Blass and your James Galanos and your Geoffrey Beene and your Perry Ellis," he continued, reading out a list of the First Lady's favorite gay fashion designers, "don't you think you could get your husband off his Levi 501s to help the dying brothers of your best friend?"

At the state dinner, Hudson sat at the same table as Nancy. "You're too thin," she told him. "Fatten up."

"You're thin, also," Hudson replied jokingly, adding that he had lost the weight while working hard on a film.

After the meal, Hudson attended a gay cocktail party before heading out for a night on the town in a rented limousine. When he walked into Badlands, a recently opened gay club across from the P Street Beach, the crowd on the dance floor made way for the star as if it were the "Red Sea parting," remembered one man in Hudson's entourage.

The following week, White House social secretary Gahl Burt mailed out the pictures taken of the receiving line at the state dinner. She did not notice, in the photo of Hudson shaking Nancy's hand, the small purple lesion behind his left ear. Examining the photograph in his Los Angeles home, Hudson was startled by what he saw. He had thought the year-old growth was just a pimple, but it looked larger than it felt. Hudson did not know that less than two weeks before the state dinner, a casual sex partner of his in San Francisco had visited the doctor worried about a similar-looking purple spot.

"Rock, you've gotta do something about that pimple on your neck," Hudson's personal assistant told him. The actor visited a dermatologist, who took a biopsy and called him with the results a few days later. "Are you sitting down?" she asked.

"No," Hudson replied.

"I think you'd better sit down. It's Kaposi's sarcoma."

Immediately, Hudson sent anonymous letters to three people with whom he'd had sex in the previous months, including a twenty-two-year-old man he had met at the White House dinner, informing them of his diagnosis.

In August, CAIR made its official debut at the Republican National Convention in Dallas with a reception at a gay-owned restaurant. Though the convention organizers chose not to include the event in the official daily schedule (which did list the Longhorn Breeders Association cattle drive), two hundred fifty Republicans gathered in a room festooned with red, white, and blue balloons. Terry Dolan briefly dropped by, but he could not stay long, as he had to preside over the NCPAC bash at billionaire oilman Nelson Bunker Hunt's twenty-five-hundred-acre ranch. Purposely scheduled to overlap with the speech delivered by the previous Republican president, the squishy moderate Gerald Ford, the party brought eighteen hundred guests under a massive, air-conditioned tent to hear a Benediction from Jerry Falwell and a comedy routine by Bob Hope. In a dispatch from the convention, a correspondent for the *New Republic* described Dolan's "short hair, manicured moustache, tight knit shirt, stacked-heel boots, and tight jeans, a pair of aviator frame sunglasses inserted neatly into his back pocket." For readers who missed this thorough description of the 1980s "gay clone" aesthetic, the writer's further mentioning of how Dolan "pranced up to the microphone" drove the point home.

Two nights later, as the hour of Reagan's acceptance speech approached, the era's decadence and hypocrisy converged in scenes that played out across the bathrooms of the Dallas Convention Center. The stalls "were absolutely mobbed as people were snorting coke so they would have a high on during the speech," recalled John Ford. "You could hear people snorting" over the music and the cheering inside the auditorium, oblivious to Nancy's trademark admonition, "Just Say No."

AIDS went unaddressed at both party conventions that summer. Dr. W. A. Criswell, the former president of the Southern Baptist Convention who delivered the Benediction at the Republican gathering, saw fit to mention the disease a few days later, however, during a sermon at his First Baptist Church of Dallas. "In our lifetime we are scoffing at the word of God . . . and opening up society and culture to the lesbian and sodomite and homosexual . . . and now we have this disastrous judgment . . . the disease and sin of AIDS," he declared. At the tony Cosmos Club in Washington (housed in the mansion where Sumner Welles once lived), a twenty-six-year-old man who had worked as a waiter for five years was informed that his services were no longer needed after he recovered from a bout of pneumonia. "Nobody said to him, 'You can't work because you have AIDS,'" the chairman of the club's legal affairs committee explained. "But if you went into your favorite restaurant and your waiter was known to have AIDS . . . would you stay? Until medical science says to my satisfaction that you can't get AIDS that way, then I'll say there wasn't any job for him." Fearful that the disease could be spread through saliva, bartenders at gay bars started putting straws in glasses.

Nobody, it seemed, wanted anything to do with these men and their illness, and the stigma associated with the disease was so intense that many who contracted it suffered alone. "They'd quietly go away," remembered a gay congressional staffer of the colleagues who stopped showing up for work one day, only to die a few months later. The Whitman-Walker Clinic, a gay health center, kept the location of a five-bedroom convalescent home for AIDS sufferers a closely guarded secret for fear that neighbors would demand its closure. Not even in death were AIDS victims spared the shame associated with their malady. In August 1985, an editor at the *Wall Street Journal* announced that he could identify "130 recent deaths for which strong circumstantial evidence exists that AIDS was involved" among a year's worth of *New York Times* obituaries, only four of which, however, mentioned the disease. "Decoding the *Times* obituaries for cause of death has become a somber breakfast acrostic," the newly installed editor of *Vanity Fair*, a young British transplant named Tina Brown, noted in her diary. For gay men, checking the *Blade*'s new Obituary section—created expressly to memorialize the recurring waves of AIDS victims, "box scores of homosexual life and death"—was less a puzzle than a social obligation. Whereas gay men of an earlier generation once scoured the newspapers to discover if any of their friends had been arrested in stings by the vice squad the previous night, now they searched them to learn the grim results of that week's culling. Once, in a single day, John Ford lost three friends, and Deacon Maccubbin attended three funerals. David Mixner estimated that he delivered ninety eulogies over a two-year span, roughly one per week. "We would have Saturday morning funerals and Saturday night disco to just forget about it.'"

The growing divide between gays who had abandoned the closet and those who remained burrowed deep inside complicated efforts to fight the disease. When the real estate developer Bob Alfandre was raising money for a hospice care center that would come to be named after his lover, who eventually succumbed to AIDS, he had to threaten his friend Bob Gray to contribute. "There needs to be a big check from you, and it needs to come soon," Alfandre told him. If there was a silver lining to all the suffering and death, it was that the relationship between gay men and lesbians, uneasy from the time of those first Mattachine Society meetings, improved as the latter heroically stepped up to advocate and care for their gay brethren. "To me, one of the most profound things that happened was that gay men and women came back together again," recalled Nancy Tucker, the *Blade* cofounder who had famously denounced gay male misogyny in her

1971 "Fuck You, Brothers" speech. "I was really glad for that because I had hated the fact that we were separate."

* * *

"COMMANDING GENERAL OF PERCY HOSPITAL HAS TURNED DOWN ROCK HUDSON AS A PATIENT BECAUSE HE IS NOT FRENCH," read the July 24, 1985, telegram from Dale Olson, Hudson's publicist, to the White House. "DOCTOR DORMONT IN PARIS BELIEVES A REQUEST FROM THE WHITE HOUSE OR A HIGH AMERICAN OFFICIAL WOULD CHANGE HIS MIND."

Twelve thousand Americans were either dead or dying from AIDS when Rock Hudson flew to France in hopes of securing access to a rare treatment being tested at a military hospital outside Paris. Olson, who happened to have been the first self-identified homosexual to appear on television (albeit with his face blurred and using a pseudonym) when he was interviewed in his capacity as national secretary of the Mattachine Society of Los Angeles in 1954, hoped that pressure from the Reagan administration might help.

An assistant press secretary brought the request to the First Lady. Nancy Reagan, he wrote in a memo to an official on the National Security Council, "did not feel this was something the White House should get into." Instead, the president called Hudson to express his and Nancy's best wishes. "We never knew him too well but did know him & thought under the circumstances I might be a reassurance," Reagan noted in his diary. "Now I learn from TV there is question as to his illness & rumors he is there for treatment of AIDS."

The following day, the rumors were confirmed when a French spokeswoman announced to the world that "Mr. Hudson has AIDS." It was the first time that a public figure acknowledged he had the disease. Before Hudson's revelation, wrote Randy Shilts, AIDS "had seemed a comfortably distant threat to most of those who had heard of it before, the misfortune of people who fit into rather distinct classes of outcasts and social pariahs." After Hudson's announcement, "the AIDS epidemic became palpable and the threat loomed everywhere." Visits to the Whitman-Walker Clinic increased to capacity as a procession of nervous and frightened young men passed through its doors seeking tests for the human immunodeficiency virus (HIV) that caused AIDS. One of the president's children believed that it took the illness of a friend to focus his mind. "My father has the sort of psychology where he grasps on to the single anecdote better than the broad wash of a problem," said Ron Reagan, who would later film a safe-sex PSA cheekily urging viewers to "write to your congressman—or to someone higher up" to support more government action to fight the disease. "So when it's a particular name he knows, suddenly the problem crystallizes." On September 17, during a press conference in the East Room, Reagan finally uttered the word *AIDS* publicly for the first time, in response to a question from a reporter about federal research efforts. "This is a top priority with us," Reagan said, citing the half-billion dollars the federal government had spent over the previous four years. "Yes, there's no question about the seriousness of this and the need to find an answer." It was his thirtieth news briefing since the CDC announced the emergence of AIDS.

Two weeks later, after abandoning his efforts to gain admission to the French hospital, Hudson died at his home in Los Angeles. When her refusal to intercede on his behalf was made public in 2015, Nancy was lambasted as coldhearted, yet it's just as easy to imagine her being attacked for favoritism had she used her influence to obtain special treatment for a celebrity friend. (A concern for fairness was absent the summer after Hudson died with respect to another high-profile AIDS patient, Roy Cohn, who, the *Wall Street Journal* reported, had "moved ahead of other potential candidates for an experimental AIDS drug after the White House intervened" with the National Institutes of Health.) More revealing about the Reagans was the statement they released upon Hudson's death, the multiple drafts of which, with the president's handwritten edits, can be found buried deep

---

Nancy and I are ~~profoundly~~ saddened by the news of Rock Hudson's death. He will always be remembered for his dynamic impact on the film industry and fans all over the world will certainly mourn his loss. ~~Our memories will also be of~~ his humanity, his sympathetic spirit and well-deserved reputation for kindness. ~~He was our friend and we will miss him greatly.~~ May God rest his soul.

He will be remembered for his—

RR changed

in the archives at the Ronald Reagan Presidential Library and Museum in Simi Valley, California.

In his public statement about the most famous figure in the world to die from AIDS, the president purged all references to the nature of their decades-long friendship, turning an expression of personal grief into one of anodyne regret.

The shadow of AIDS descended over the White House again in August 1986, when Way Bandy, the best-selling author and makeup artist who counted Elizabeth Taylor, Catherine Deneuve, Barbra Streisand, Lee Radziwill, Cher, and Nancy Reagan among his many celebrity clients, succumbed to the disease. Just a few months earlier, Bandy had flown down from New York to spend several hours with the First Lady at the White House, preparing her for a photo shoot that would appear in the "10 Most Beautiful Women" issue of *Harper's Bazaar*. The night Bandy died, the White House sent a photograph of him and Nancy to his hospital room. Though Bandy had kept his illness a secret, he was adamant that his obituary list the cause of death; not for him the posthumous denial of another gay fashion icon, the designer Perry Ellis, widely assumed to have been felled by AIDS but whose spokesmen insisted the cause was viral encephalitis.

This time, the White House response to news that AIDS had taken the life of someone in its midst was even more estranging than the one it had released after Hudson's death. "Maybe he was with her 15 minutes," Nancy's press secretary said, and besides, "She uses very little makeup." The First Lady "had seen the obit in the paper and was surprised and sorry," the spokeswoman continued. "She knows there was nothing more than a handshake. And we've all been told by the medical community that you can't contract the disease that way." On another occasion, after Nancy took a sip of water from her hairstylist Robin Weir's glass, she paid an anxious visit to the White House physician.

Homosexuality and AIDS were occasional sources of humor in the Reagan White House. Larry Speakes fondly recalled the impersonations that Reagan, after his weekly shampoo, used to do of a stereotypically effeminate homosexual. "I washed my hair last night and I just can't do a thing about it," the former actor would lisp while flicking his hand. "If those fellows don't leave me alone, I'll just slap them on the wrist." During a meeting with his top national security officials to discuss a psychological warfare operation against Libyan strongman Muammar Gaddafi, Reagan allegedly made a joke about his garish wardrobe. "Why not invite Gadhafi to San Francisco, he likes to dress up so much," the president said.

"Why don't we give him AIDS!" Secretary of State George Shultz interjected. "Others at the table laughed," according to a report by Bob Woodward in the *Washington Post*.

What explains the yawning gap between the Reagans' private acceptance of gay men and their public indifference, bordering on callousness, to their plight? "They lived most of their lives in the entertainment community," Ron Reagan explained when *People* magazine asked him about his parents' views on homosexuality. "Their attitude toward people's sexuality is it's everyone's private business." But a belief that gay people have a right to privacy—the laudable impulse that drove Reagan to dissemble about the alleged homosexual ring in his gubernatorial office and to oppose the Briggs Initiative a decade later—does not necessarily imply acceptance of those private lives. For all their many gay friends, the Reagans had a basic discomfort with homosexuality. It stemmed, in part, from a general prudishness about sex—the president often bragged about making movies in the days when "you could do an entire love scene with your clothes on," Michael Deaver recalled—and a predisposition to define gay people by the kind of sex they had, a kind of sex that happened to be the means by which the disease that was killing them was transmitted. Deaver remembered the time he recommended that the First Couple watch *Kiss of the Spider Woman*, a film about two inmates in the jail of an unidentified Latin American military junta. One of the prisoners, portrayed by William Hurt, is a flamboyant, cross-dressing homosexual. Taking Deaver up on his suggestion, the president had a print of the movie delivered to Camp David.

"Mike," Nancy reproached Deaver afterward. "How could you recommend that film? It was dreadful. We turned it off halfway through the reel."

"Once you get past the subject," Deaver replied, "it was an incredible picture."

"How can you get past that?" she responded.

Politics, of course, also played a factor, particularly during the early years of the epidemic when fear and ignorance of the disease often crossed over into hysteria. On the first day of school in the fall of 1985, between the announcement of Rock Hudson's AIDS diagnosis and his death two months later, 944 out of the 1,100 students enrolled at P.S. 63 in Queens stayed home after it was revealed that a single second-grader at an undisclosed public school in New York City had tested positive for HIV. In Washington, a child with the virus was taught alone in a separate room. Following Hudson's death, a *Los Angeles Times* poll reported that more than half of American adults supported quarantining AIDS patients, and a conservative pollster found that a third of the public supported quarantining all male homosexuals, a distinction, apparently in the minds of many, without a difference. The antipathy was particularly strong among evangelicals, 78 percent of whom voted for Reagan in 1984. "It justifies their prejudices against homosexuals, and it gets Africans, too," the pollster explained. "If it would only strike at the Soviets, it'd be perfect."

It also did not help the predicament of AIDS sufferers that their very public agony contrasted so sharply with the sunny, buoyant image that the movie star president and his glamorous wife wished to project. "To be pro-life," observed V. S. Naipaul among the Republicans in Dallas, was not just to be antiabortion, but "to be vigorous, joyful, and optimistic; it was to turn away from the gloom and misery of the other side, who talked of problems and taxes." The Reagans had a tendency to gloss over or airbrush things that interfered with that optimism, and homosexual men wasting away on hospital gurneys, their emaciated bodies enveloped in pustulating lesions, belied the cheerful declaration that it was "Morning in America," the Reagan reelection advertisement featuring young newlyweds, hardworking citizens on their way to work, and other touching scenes of wholesome Americana. The things these dying men had created—their clothes, their jewelry, their interior designs, their films, their speeches, their political strategies, their friendship, Nancy's face—were allowed to be part of that picture. But not their love, and certainly not their suffering and death. When Reagan published his post-presidential memoirs in 1990, the AIDS crisis did not even appear in it.

Another element not to be underestimated in any appreciation of the Reagans' record on AIDS was their emotional reserve. Nancy was notoriously icy, and the couple did not have a conventionally close relationship with any of their children. It wasn't a homosexual cabal that surrounded Ronald but, in the words of one close associate, "sort of a celluloid barrier." Edmund Morris, Ronald Reagan's authorized biographer, found his subject so inscrutable that he ended up partly fictionalizing him in his book *Dutch*. "Nobody around him understood him," Morris said. "I, every person I interviewed, almost without exception, eventually would say, 'You know,

I could never really figure him out.'" When the California businessman Holmes Tuttle, who led Reagan's gubernatorial "kitchen cabinet," fell seriously ill during Reagan's governorship, never once did Reagan call him at the hospital. Even the woman closest to Reagan found herself at a remove. "There's a wall around him," Nancy wrote in her memoir, *My Turn*. "He lets me come closer than anyone else, but there are times even I feel that barrier." Assessing his record in Sacramento, a pair of journalists wrote that Reagan had governed as he had acted, "waiting for direction." Yet there was nobody close to Reagan willing to provide direction for how to tackle AIDS.

Not that he always followed direction. A final, and possibly the most significant, factor in Reagan's indifference can be traced all the way back to that moment in 1939, when a young movie actor bristled at the suggestion, given to him by a bisexual filmmaker, that he play "the kind of fellow who could sit in the girls' dressing room dishing the dirt while they went on dressing in front of me." This fear of the homosexual aura would resurface nearly three decades later, when Reagan was running for governor and his top image maker worried that a Hollywood background left him vulnerable to the suspicion that he was himself just such a "kind of fellow." It was reinforced the following year, when a newspaper columnist alleged a "homosexual ring" in Reagan's gubernatorial office. The fear intensified in the days leading up to his nomination for president in 1980, when the *Washington Post* investigated the charge that he was the "Manchurian candidate" for a shadowy gay cabal. And it continued to linger well into his presidency, glimpsed in his retrospective distancing from a friend, the most famous victim to die from a disease whose spread was exacerbated by this very fear.

* * *

"IF IT'S 2 PERCENT," Bill Buckley would say about the size of the gay population, "I know them all personally."

By the middle of the 1980s, Buckley was not nearly so oblivious to homosexuality or homosexuals as he had been just a decade earlier, when the public release of Whittaker Chambers's confession of "homosexualism" left him "totally surprised." Since then, the conservative luminary had witnessed the public disgrace of his friend Bob Bauman, and in 1985, he testified as a character witness for another friend, Roy Cohn, at his disbarment proceedings. Writing a syndicated twice-weekly newspaper column, hosting a weekly television show, and editing a fortnightly magazine—in

addition to constant travel across the country for speaking engagements—
Buckley relied upon a large pool of gay men to serve as walkers for his
wife, Pat, one of New York's reigning society hostesses and a prodigious
fund-raiser for AIDS charities. Indeed, in her accumulation of gay male
companions (among them the designers Bill Blass and Valentino Garavani, jeweler Kenneth Jay Lane, actor Peter Glenville, Truman Capote,
and the ubiquitous Jerry Zipkin), Pat Buckley rivaled Nancy Reagan. ("In
Mum's case, it seemed to have more to do with laughter than moisturizers,"
observed her son, Christopher.)

All this is to say that Bill Buckley had come to know a fair number of
homosexuals by the time he suggested, in the pages of the *New York Times*,
that AIDS victims be permanently branded. "Everyone detected with AIDS
should be tattooed in the upper forearm, to protect common-needle users,
and on the buttocks, to prevent the victimization of other homosexuals,"
Buckley wrote on March 18, 1986. Reactions to the column were among
the most impassioned for anything he had written. "Did it start out as 'A
Modest Proposal?'" Buckley's friend Robert K. Massie asked in disbelief.
Given how Buckley's "proposals could only be enforced on a free population
by the kind of government which I thought you had devoted your life to
opposing," the Swiftian context was the only one in which Massie, coauthor
of the best-selling book about the last tsar of Russia and his family, *Nicholas
and Alexandra*, could comprehend it. "I don't recognize William F. Buckley
Jr. in this essay." (As Massie noted in a letter published in the *Times*, he had
a "personal stake in this issue," in that his son was a hemophiliac, the inspiration for Massie and his wife's interest in the Romanovs, whose son, Alexei,
also suffered from the disease.) "WILLIAM BUCKLEY'S FINAL SOLU-
TION," declared the *New York Native* in a banner front-page headline above
a photograph of a naked man bent over, his posterior facing the camera.

The most poignant response to the column was a private one mailed to
the author by three of his fellow "Pats" (short for 'patriarch,' the honorific
used among Skull and Bones alums) from the Yale College class of 1972.
One had AIDS; all had "lost friends or lovers to AIDS and all of us suffer
from the anxiety surrounding this tragic disease." But the worse tragedy,
the men wrote,

is the potential for legitimized bigotry that your proposal in the New York
Times invites. It is an "us against them" attitude that we feel is divisive. We

wanted you to consider that in the community of the Bones, as well as in the larger community, "them" is "us." In fact, this is a disease that affects everyone and must be approached with the compassion of communality.

One assumes that you can't really mean that people who test positive for the AIDS antibody should be tattooed but that you are overstating the case to spark dialogue. . . . If you did, in fact, actually mean what you wrote about tattooing, we must ask you how you intend to enforce such a Draconic idea and then ask why not use a pink triangle or a yellow star. If you did mean what you wrote, then your America must be closer to the reality of an America we can only imagine in our worst nightmares.

. . . Your proposal reflects values contrary to the humanism that a liberal education, at Yale, for instance, helps to foster. One would have hoped that at Yale, or even in the Bones, you would have come into contact with men whose backgrounds, points of view and, perhaps, sexual orientation were different from yours and that you benefitted from coming into contact with their humanity and their differences.

We would venture to guess that there are other Bones men who are homosexuals; we cannot speak for them but can only suggest to you that Bones, an institution created for the purpose of debate and the sharing of personal histories among men of disparate and perhaps antagonistic backgrounds, [the sharing of which might produce greater understanding], is a group that reflects the larger family. "Us" is "Them." We would hope that you would choose not to look down on groups on the ground but to look behind you, right behind you, in our common Ivory Tower and see that there are human beings in our family—your family—who are at risk, who have lost loved ones through AIDS or who are suffering from it now. They should not be tattooed, Mr. Buckley; they should be loved and helped and given the benefit of a well educated populace that will understand the problem and of a medical establishment that is well funded to do everything possible to find a cure for AIDS.

Within three years of sending this letter, all its authors would be dead from the disease.

Like the secret shared by so many of its victims, AIDS transcended all human categories. "One of the things that I've heard said is that the one good thing that you could say about HIV is that it's a leveler," observed James "Juicy" Coleman, a leader in Washington's African American gay community, who estimated that he had lost 75 percent of his friends to the disease. "And when I say that I mean that it brought all of the particular populations, the professionals, along with the hoodlum on the corner, along with the drag queen, all to the table for once because it didn't discriminate across those barriers." It also brought down a great athlete. When he retired from the Washington Redskins in 1978, Jerry Smith held the NFL record for most career touchdowns by a tight end. In August 1986, Smith entered the history books for a more sorrowful reason when he became the first professional athlete to declare, in a front-page interview with the *Washington Post*, that he had AIDS. Smith didn't come out of the closet, but he didn't need to. According to David Mixner, Smith's homosexuality was "the worst kept secret in the gay community, the best kept secret in the straight community." Two weeks after Smith's death that fall, the Redskins inducted him into its Hall of Stars. As Smith's mother walked out onto the field at RFK Stadium for the ceremony, a crowd of fifty thousand fans rose to their feet with applause.

Though the disease crossed all sorts of divisions, within Washington's gay community it also exacerbated them: between the infected and the uninfected, the open and the closeted, the Democrat and the Republican. For years beginning sometime in the 1970s, a men-only sex party was held every Friday night after six o'clock in the back room of a furniture repair shop on the 1400 block of Church Street; "I'm here to see Rick" was the pass phrase. One evening during the height of a congressional budget battle over funding for AIDS research, the participants angrily kicked out a Republican operative—the first time anyone could remember such a thing happening (at least over politics).

For those working within the closets of power, the epidemic forced a reckoning. John Ford had managed to keep his sexual orientation a secret from his boss, Agriculture Secretary John Block, for the first term of the Reagan presidency. But it was becoming a difficult burden to bear by the second. "I was giving speeches across the land about integrity, while I was lying to the most important people in my life about who I was," Ford remembered. One day, a political appointee who was part of an evangelical morning prayer group barged into Ford's office, furious that Ford had passed him over for a promotion overseas. "You know, it's just really a shame some of the rumors that are going around the department about you," the man told Ford.

"What are those rumors?" Ford asked.

"Well, that you're a homosexual."

"Really?"

"I don't want to throw my weight around here," the appointee threatened, "but if I don't get this job to Brussels, I'm just going to have to tell the secretary about you."

"Well, let's don't wait," Ford said, picking up his phone and dialing Block's assistant. "Let's do it right now." Ford wagered that he had developed a close enough working relationship with Block to risk the consequences of coming out. "There's a gentleman here who needs to see the secretary right away," Ford told the assistant, who replied that Block was available to meet.

Ford escorted the man into Block's office. "Mr. Secretary, this gentleman has just threatened that if I don't give him a job in Brussels, he's going to tell you that I'm homosexual."

Block stared at the man. "So, is this correct?"

"Oh, well, no, Mr. Secretary," the man stammered. "I was just trying to warn John that there were rumors going on. I never threatened him."

"Well, we have a lot to do in this administration," Block said. "I don't have time for crap like this and I suggest you get back to work."

Ford resigned in December 1985, partly over disagreements with the administration's agriculture policy, but also in protest of its sluggish response to AIDS, with which he had recently been diagnosed. Demonstrating the same candor that he had shown in dealing with the political appointee who threatened to expose him, Ford would go on to become an outspoken critic of the administration, discarding the silence required of gays who remained working within it. Both the power and the peril that Washington associated with homosexuality derived from the closet, which provided a veneer of respectability to those who wished to slip between the open and secret cities, albeit at the price of losing at least some part of their integrity. This had long been the compromise that most gays, given little choice, were willing to accept. But it was a compromise that AIDS, by casting its victims out into the open, was rendering obsolete.

What one gay federal employee described as the "massive, disease-driven outing" was about to strike uncomfortably close to the White House, as the plague yanked a high-profile victim from his gilded Reaganite closet.

39

"OUR SEBASTIAN"

ONCE AGAIN, THE CREAM OF CONSERVATIVE WASHINGTON CONVENED TO celebrate Terry Dolan. But whereas, less than four years earlier, the purpose had been to praise him, on January 8, 1987, it was to bury him.

Dolan had been hospitalized the previous summer, according to his colleagues at NCPAC, for a combination of anemia and diabetes. But the signs that his malady was of a different nature were difficult to ignore. At one of his last public appearances, a celebration of NCPAC's tenth anniversary held aboard a Potomac River cruise, the thirty-six-year-old activist looked conspicuously lethargic and gaunt, his face heavily covered in makeup to disguise the lesions that had sprung up across it. Dolan's debilitated condition mirrored the state of the organization he had founded, which in the weeks leading up to the 1986 midterm elections was $3.9 million in debt, enmeshed in a dispute with its direct mail consultant, and listless without its once-fiery captain at the helm. The subsequent election, in which the Republicans lost eight Senate seats along with control of the body, marked a humiliating fall for NCPAC, and the furious refusal by the man who replaced Dolan as leader to acknowledge this sobering fact revealed yet another similarity between the group and its pugnacious former president: denial. In a letter to the *Post* challenging a story about NCPAC's financial woes and atrophied political muscle, L. Brent Bozell III asked if the paper had not grown "tired of writing biennial obituaries about NCPAC and other conservative groups," answering his own rhetorical question with the statement that "expecting the Post to be consistent is like expecting the Democrats to cut wasteful spending." Published less than two months before Dolan's eventual demise on December 28, the headline over Bozell's missive was morbidly ironic: "NCPAC's Death Has Been, Well, Exaggerated."

During his short but energetic life as a guerrilla warrior in the conservative movement, Dolan had regularly attacked the Post as a liberal rag, gleefully distributing "I Don't Believe the Post" bumper stickers. So, it would no doubt have infuriated him that the paper essentially revealed his secret in the obituary it published on New Year's Eve. "Widely recognized as one of the New Right's most articulate spokesmen" and one of the leading figures to "devise and promote negative political advertising," Dolan died of congestive heart failure at his home in Washington, the Post reported, from complications due to AIDS. Confirmation for the cause of death, the paper's obituary editor would later say, came "from a very reliable source, on deep, deep background," though he did offer a piece of circumstantial evidence: when Dolan was called to testify before an Alexandria courtroom a few months before his death, his lawyers told the judge that their client would be unable to do so because of an illness the details of which "would be embarrassing to his family."

Across town, what Dolan used to call "the best newspaper in America" was telling a different story about the circumstances of his passing. Founded in 1982 with financial backing from the South Korean business tycoon and Unification Church leader Sun Myung Moon, the Washington Times had quickly earned a reputation as "the internal newsletter of the conservative movement." In its editorial and news sections, the boundary between which was frequently blurred, the Times pushed the stridently anticommunist and socially conservative views of its benefactor, and its front-page obituary of Dolan honored both ideological commitments by highlighting the deceased's political bona fides while making no mention of the disease that had killed him. And in a piece elaborating on Dolan's legacy a few days later, the paper quoted his physician denying AIDS had been the cause. "I have no data to indicate that," said Dr. Cesar A. Caceres, who instead cited "a cardio-myopathy, an enlargement of the heart which is due to a variety of reasons, none of which can be determined." Caceres had rather unorthodox views on AIDS. Two years earlier, in an interview with *Christopher Street*, he had traced the syndrome to drug use, smoking, alcohol, "travelers' disease," and poppers. ("You Think That Sex Causes AIDS?" asked the magazine on its cover. "You've Been Had.") Scott Thompson, who had met Caceres at a soiree hosted by Craig Spence, recalled the time the doctor delivered him an HIV-positive test result "with a whimsical chuckle" and advice not to worry because "there was no such thing as AIDS." A year and a half later, when Thompson applied to enter an NIH trial for a new HIV drug, he received a phone call from the director of the National Institute of Allergy and Infectious Diseases himself, Dr. Anthony Fauci. "You're not HIV-positive, so we can't use you," Fauci told Thompson, who was so overcome with emotion that he processed the second clause of the sentence before the first. In early 1986, a group of Washington physicians sent a letter to the city's public health commissioner complaining that Caceres "promotes dangerous messages" about the origins of AIDS and its transmission. The scientifically aberrant views of Dr. Caceres, however, were what Dolan's confederates in the conservative movement preferred to hear. That the *Post* would claim their colleague had contracted a disease associated with homosexuals, Bozell sneered, amounted to "gutter journalism."

At the Catholic monastery where Dolan's evening memorial service was held a few days after his burial, the controversy over his alleged AIDS diagnosis presented the hundreds of friends and political allies in attendance with an uncomfortable realization: here was the conservative movement's most effective strategist reportedly struck down by a plague many of them considered divine punishment for an immoral lifestyle. Perhaps the most incongruous of the mourners at the Dominican House of Studies was White House communications director Pat Buchanan. "The poor homosexuals," Buchanan had written with mock sympathy in his syndicated column four years earlier. "They have declared war upon nature, and now nature is exacting an awful retribution." Vicious as those words might have been, the casualty of nature's awful retribution whose life was being commemorated that evening had been willing to overlook them. "Terry held a deep affection for you and asked that you be invited," Bozell wrote in the Mailgram invitation sent to Buchanan at the White House. Paul Weyrich, who had once tried to interest the *Washington Times* in publishing an exposé of Dolan's secret gay life and AIDS diagnosis, was also in the pews. So, too, was New Hampshire senator Gordon Humphrey, who credited Dolan with playing a "pivotal" role in his 1978 election and who, the following year, attended a "Clean Up America" rally on the steps of the Capitol Building alongside Jerry Falwell. "You can tell the boys from the girls without a medical examination," the preacher declared while looking proudly over the crowd of eight thousand gender-conforming supporters.

Dolan's secret gay life was an even more uncomfortable subject for the man delivering his eulogy. Homosexuality was a touchy issue in the White House speechwriting office Tony Dolan led, something best not mentioned, even obliquely. Once, after a young speechwriter named Peggy Noonan, instructed to stop using the word *happy* in her drafts, started inserting variations of *gay* instead, a member of the president's advance team called her in a panic. There was a problem, he explained, with the appearance of *gaiety* in an upcoming speech congratulating the U.S. Olympic swimming team.

"I think you better strike that," the advance man told her.

"Why?" Noonan asked.

"It sounds like he's calling them gay."

"No one will think, no one would ever think, that the president of the United States would hail our Olympic heroes by accusing them of being homosexual," Noonan responded. "I promise you this."

The word, alas, was removed.

Tony Dolan was used to writing speeches, not delivering them, and he began his remarks with a warning. "We are not, as they say in some parts of the government (though not in Presidential Speechwriting, I can assure you) in a 'risk-free environment.'" Should the depths of his grief overwhelm his ability to speak, Tony continued, "please do not be embarrassed if I just sit down and send along to you later in the mail what I wanted to say— which is just to thank you for being here tonight and for praying for Terry and us." He then proceeded to share a series of touching reminiscences about his younger brother, whom he had visited regularly during his illness on his way to and from work at the White House. Terry had worn an alarm watch around his weakened and withered wrist that reminded him to pray every hour, Tony said, and on the last night of his life, barely able to move, he sipped some milk "just to humor me I am certain." At one point before

Terry's death, the brothers discussed the case of Father Charles Curran, a theologian who had recently been fired from a teaching position at Catholic University over his questioning Church doctrine on homosexuality and other matters pertaining to sexual ethics. "Terry was usually just dismissive of those he thought in the wrong," Tony emphasized, "but he considered the theologian gravely in error and this time Terry was solemn; it was the first occasion I could remember him so." On his deathbed, Tony implied, Terry had renounced his homosexuality.

Tony saved the most vivid symbolism for the end. It was a flourish one might have expected from the pen of a Pulitzer Prize–winning journalist and presidential wordsmith responsible for such an indelible turn of phrase as "freedom and democracy will leave Marxism and Leninism on the ash heap of history" and the description of the Soviet Union as an "evil empire." Invoking another, albeit fictional, Catholic family, Tony told the bereaved that the Dolans were suffering their own "fierce little human tragedy," Evelyn Waugh's description of the sorrows inflicted upon the Flyte clan in *Brideshead Revisited* by their wayward son, Sebastian. Terry, he continued, "was our Sebastian, through his suffering, showing us God's goodness and mercy, leading us to deeper things and holy moments." It was a striking association, likening the torment of his younger brother who had just died of AIDS to this literary archetype of dissolute and aristocratic homosexuality. In Waugh's novel, Sebastian leaves the family homestead to shack up with a German deserter from the French Foreign Legion in Tangier—a destination popular with generations of gay European men in search of sexual freedom—where he nearly dies of pneumonia, which happened to be the leading opportunistic infection among AIDS victims. When the visual image of the gray and withered Sebastian, his face almost entirely drained of its once-enchanting beauty, flashed across millions of American television screens in 1982, it had been a chilling premonition of the disease that would soon kill Terry Dolan, along with so many other young men.

A character from a forty-two-year-old novel was not the only allusion Tony Dolan made to homosexuality by referring to his brother as "our Sebastian." In saying that Terry's "suffering" had guided those around him "to deeper things and holy moments," Tony was also invoking the Catholic saint Sebastian, a member of the third-century Roman emperor Diocletian's Praetorian Guard. Like Terry, Sebastian had a secret—Christian faith—and its discovery led to his execution by arrows. The martyrdom of the young saint, his taut and muscular torso penetrated with sharpened projectiles, has inspired centuries of homoerotic art, from Caravaggio to the Japanese author Yukio Mishima, and the British filmmaker Derek Jarman.

Two days later, a delegation from the secret city where Terry Dolan dwelled congregated at the Cathedral of St. Matthew on Rhode Island Avenue, the cavernous Catholic church that hosted Joe McCarthy's wedding and John F. Kennedy's funeral. About fifty gay men and women, most of them involved with the conservative movement, gathered to remember their fallen brother. In addition to Bob Bauman, some of the other founding members of CAIR were present, though by this point the group was defunct, as much a victim of the AIDS crisis as the man who had helped plot its creation at a Russian River resort just a few years earlier. Presiding over the Mass was Rev. John Gigrich, a closeted gay priest (and World War II spy) who was the diocese's unofficial minister to people with AIDS, Dolan included. Whereas the first memorial service, attended by Dolan's family and political allies, was held in the open, the one at St. Matthew's was conducted in secret. Still, despite all the precautions undertaken by its organizers to keep the event from leaking to the press, some of those who had been invited stayed home. Afraid the media would hear about the ceremony and stake out the church, they, like the man they had been invited to memorialize, were desperate to protect their secret.

Terry Dolan was a public figure, and the dilemma symbolized by his dueling memorial services intrigued *Washington Post* editor Ben Bradlee. Under his leadership, the paper's coverage of gay issues had steadily improved. Yet it still had a long way to go, especially concerning AIDS. During the early years of the epidemic, according to Randy Shilts, the *Post* had done "a singularly deplorable job in covering federal AIDS policy," an area that ought to have been a strong suit given the paper's unparalleled resources in reporting on the machinations of the byzantine federal bureaucracy. But the *Post* lacked a basic familiarity with gay people, and in this deficiency, it was hardly an outlier. Shilts was the first openly gay reporter at a major American newspaper when he started at the *San Francisco Chronicle* in 1981, and by the time of Terry Dolan's death five years later, there were only a handful of openly gay journalists working at the *Post* or in any other American newsroom of comparable size. The

Post also resembled the rest of the mainstream media in its conservative institutional culture, which tended to treat the subject of homosexuality with a tone alternating between squeamish and voyeuristic. In 1984, after a reporter interviewed an AIDS victim at their home, she returned to the newsroom to find her colleagues aghast. "Why didn't you just interview her by phone?" a fellow reporter, the child of a physician, asked. "Are you sure you're OK?" inquired another. While the paper had no trouble reporting the details of President Reagan's colon and prostate exams, or his wife's mastectomy, it was much more circumspect when it came to describing the sexual practices most liable to transmit HIV. Once, when a reporter complained to an editor that the paper was putting its own readers at risk by avoiding such frank discussions, the editor replied that the *Post* was a "family newspaper" that avoided use of the words "anal sex." (As an internal *Post* memorandum on the paper's gay coverage would later explain, it was not just openly gay readers who were harmed by the paper's silence on such matters, but also closeted married ones, who did not go out of their way to seek safe-sex information distributed at gay health clinics or advertised in venues like the *Blade*.)

The paper was also conservative, indeed cruel, in its refusal to list the same-sex partners of AIDS victims in their obituaries. When the father of a twenty-nine-year-old photographer who died of the disease called the *Post* to ask that his son's partner be mentioned as one of the "immediate survivors," the paper flatly refused. "There is something fundamentally wrong here," said Jim Graham, administrator of the Whitman-Walker Clinic. "In the midst of an epidemic, when 90% of the local AIDS cases are gay or bisexual males, the city's major newspaper continues to ignore the existence, status, and importance of the primary relationship in the gay community." A survey of AIDS victim obituaries found that the most common phrase was "survived by his mother."

Another, more personal factor influenced Bradlee's decision to pursue the Dolan story. Like Tony Dolan, Bradlee had a gay brother. But unlike Dolan, Bradlee accepted his sibling's sexual orientation—though not at first. In his memoir, Ben described his early relationship with his older brother Freddy as "a pitched battle for the first thirteen years of my life." It was a dynamic familiar to many gay-straight sibling relationships—Ben's world being that of "tennis, butterflies, chopping wood, girls" and Freddy's one of "imagination, actors and actresses, theater." Ben "scorned [Freddy's] world, because I didn't understand it. He ignored mine, because it bored him." But as Ben grew older, he came to appreciate his brother more. A great mimic who performed spot-on impersonations of family members as well as of Eleanor Roosevelt, Tallulah Bankhead, and Katharine Hepburn, Freddy dropped out of Harvard after two months and got a role on Broadway at the age of nineteen. According to Ben's wife, Sally Quinn, Ben "loved, adored Freddy" and "totally accepted him as gay."

Bradlee's relationship with his gay brother gave him a sensitive and empathetic perspective on homosexuality unusual among men of his generation. "I'm sure he made some limp-wristed jokes along the way, he's a creature of his time," remembered Ted Gup, one of the reporters Bradlee assigned to the 1980 Reagan "homosexual ring" story. "But if anybody discriminated against somebody who was gay, I would not want to be in his shoes." One time, Gup recalled, a *Post* employee used the word *queer* at an editorial meeting. "'We don't use that word around here," Bradlee announced. "I was so struck that a guy who came out of World War II, from his generation, would snap in a meeting of senior people and tell someone directly" not to denigrate gays, Gup said.

The day after Terry Dolan died, an editor on the *Post* assignment desk told a reporter in the Style section, Elizabeth Kastor, to start gathering research materials for a possible story about the life and death of a closeted gay conservative activist in the age of AIDS. Kastor read through old newspaper clippings about Dolan, interviewed friends and associates, and finished a four-thousand-word draft by the end of January. On February 9, Kastor wrote a letter addressed to Tony Dolan requesting an interview; her colleague, White House correspondent David Hoffman, hand-delivered it to Dolan's office. In a tense meeting at the Hay-Adams, Dolan attempted to persuade Kastor to abandon the profile. Kastor said she would "keep an open mind," and over the course of the next three months, as the *Post* wrestled over what to do with her piece, Dolan repeatedly implored the paper's top editors to heed the wishes of his family and spike it. "Dear Ben, We've suffered enough," Dolan pleaded in a handwritten note to Bradlee. "Please. There is no journalistic good that possibly authorizes the grief you will cause."

It would take more than emotional blackmail from a presidential speechwriter and former fellow journalist, even one as gifted with language as Dolan, to intimidate the man who successfully stood up to the

Nixon administration over the Pentagon Papers and Watergate. Dolan and Bradlee's disagreement over the newsworthiness of Terry's secret life boiled down to a set of issues—the boundary between the public and the private, the role of hypocrisy in politics, the devastating effects of an epidemic—all stemming from the increasing visibility of homosexuality. "We've just got to get over that," Bradlee had told a reporter from the *Los Angeles Times* the previous fall when asked about the propriety of listing AIDS as a cause of death in media accounts. "AIDS has the potential of a scourge, and to deny that people are dropping like flies from it is putting your head in the sand. It's clearly news and clearly justified." The same went for the sexual orientation of the deceased. "If you are a public figure and seek to be a public figure and thrive on being a public figure, the public has a right to know about you." Terry Dolan fit Bradlee's criteria perfectly.

As Tony Dolan tried to thwart the *Post* investigation into his brother, the disease that killed Terry continued to cut a wide swath across Washington. On April 1, President Reagan delivered his first major address about AIDS, telling the Philadelphia College of Physicians that it constituted "public health enemy No. 1." Meanwhile, a thirty-three-year-old Federal Trade Commission paralegal and performance poet named Chasen Gaver was diagnosed with the disease and momentarily rendered speechless. One of the most prolific figures on the local arts scene—he had delivered spoken-word poetry performances at more than one hundred locations across the Washington area, earning himself an invitation to the White House in 1978 from Midge Costanza—Gaver decided to stop keeping his daily diary, and destroyed most of his completed ones to make room for all the various medicines he now had to fit into his tiny apartment. "I didn't want to 'hide' in writing—and I know how easy it is for me to create a 'better reality' through words," he would recall. And on April 22, the *Washington Times* published a story about a very different sort of journal, a medical logbook allegedly containing the AIDS antibody test results "of numerous professionals and some politicians" that had gone missing from the DC Department of Human Services. City officials, reporter Jerry Seper wrote, feared that the logbook had "fallen into the hands of blackmailers."

The same evening that the *Times* raised the perennial specter of a secret homosexual list haunting the corridors of power, more than two thousand members of the city's media and political elite packed into the spacious ballroom of the Washington Hilton for the annual White

House Correspondents' Association Dinner. Since its inception in 1921, the black-tie event had been a dull affair, primarily an opportunity for reporters to ingratiate themselves with government sources by inviting them to a shindig at which the president delivered some stale remarks. All this would change in 1987, when a young reporter for the *Baltimore Sun*, Michael Kelly, snagged a former secretary at the National Security Council, Fawn Hall, as his date. The twenty-seven-year-old strawberry blonde bombshell had become a household name in recent months for her part in a developing scandal known as Iran-Contra, a covert operation in which Reagan administration officials authorized the sale of weapons to the Islamic regime in Iran, the proceeds from which they used to purchase arms for anticommunist revolutionaries fighting the Marxist Sandinista government in Nicaragua. Hall had worked for the point man behind the effort, a U.S. Marine lieutenant colonel and former NSC staffer named Oliver North, on whose orders she shredded a raft of incriminating documents. Kelly's escorting Hall to a rubber chicken dinner theretofore the preserve of midlevel bureaucrats was to prove a momentous event in the history of Washington social life, and every spring from that point forward, media outlets would compete against one another in wooing celebrities to the event. Soon, the Correspondents' Dinner became a spectacle, the night when America's three metropolitan power centers (Washington, New York, and Los Angeles) converged, and a major accelerant to the blurring of the line between politics and entertainment.

Few could foresee this development on the evening of April 22, 1987, and while a procession of "hard bitten newsmen" lined up to beseech the paper-shredding administrative assistant for an autograph, the president's chief speechwriter stormed through the Hilton's arcing hallways to the pre-dinner cocktail party hosted by the *Washington Post*. Spotting Bob Woodward, Tony Dolan asked for an introduction to Leonard Downie, the *Post*'s managing editor, with whom Dolan had spoken on the phone in one of his many futile attempts at convincing the paper to call off its exposé. In that conversation, Downie had reproved Dolan for "the edge" in his voice, and after Woodward introduced the two men, Dolan opted for a softer touch. Publication of the piece, Dolan said, would "deeply affect my parents," to the point that "it might well shorten their lives."

Downie was unmoved. "I thought that AIDS was a terribly under-covered story and not understood at all," he explained more than three decades after this exchange. "Terry was very much a public figure . . . involved in aspects of gay life and politics, and so there's no doubt he was newsworthy."

Dolan asked if "a former Congressman and a deeply committed parti-san of homosexuality had had a role in this story."

"Listen, Bauman has had nothing to do with this story, absolutely noth-ing," Downie answered. Dolan didn't believe it. He had heard rumors that Bauman was behind the "counter-memorial service" at St. Matthew's.

Dolan next tried something guaranteed to generate a reaction—though not necessarily the one he needed if his goal was to get the *Post* to accede to his wishes. Were the paper to publish the story it had prepared on Terry, Dolan avowed, it would be viewed "as a far greater mistake than the Janet Cooke episode," a reference to the *Post* reporter who had written a heart-wrenching story about an eight-year-old heroin addict in 1980, only to have it exposed as fraudulent two days after winning a Pulitzer Prize. Bradlee was forced to return the award on the paper's behalf.

"If you think the way to get somewhere with Ben Bradlee is to wave around Janet Cooke," Downie said, Dolan was mistaken.

On his way out of the reception, Dolan crossed paths again with Wood-ward. "So, did you get me fired?" the reporter asked.

"I'm working on it."

The following week, as the *Post* exposé of Terry Dolan languished in the paper's production queue, a protégé of the late conservative activist was made to answer for his dodgy dealings with Oliver North. It was a saga involving guns, gays, and Central American death squads. And this time, it was for real.

40

MR. GREEN

Lt. Col. Oliver North's specialty was slide shows, and Carl "Spitz" Channell *hated* slide shows. The founder of the National Endowment for the Preservation of Liberty (NEPL), the leading group behind the Reagan administration's secret plan to privately arm the Nicaraguan counterrevolutionaries, or Contras, Channell had sat through a series of "horrible, boring" presentations by administration bureaucrats. And so, when the White House offered to host a briefing for NEPL donors with the National Security Council's deputy director for political-military affairs on June 27, 1985, Channell had little reason to believe it would be anything other than a "disaster." There were other bad omens that day: it rained heavily, and Channell, escorting one of his benefactors, a wheelchair-bound elderly woman, arrived late at the wrong entrance to the Old Executive Office Building. By the time they reached the conference room, North was already halfway finished.

Listening to the tall, broad-shouldered marine with salt-and-pepper hair explain the state of play between the Soviet-backed Sandinista regime and the Contra rebels, Channell was unimpressed. Though North "was pretty good," Channell remembered, he was "not nearly as good as I would think you should be." Channell was prepared to give up on North until he looked around the table at his donors, their faces illuminated by the slide projector's light. They were transfixed, Channell realized, "all excited to death" as North regaled them with tales of Contra bravery. Suddenly, as the projector clicked for the last time and the final image of a wooden cross pitched atop the grave of a Nicaraguan freedom fighter flashed across the screen, Channell felt a revelatory frisson. At that precise moment, he was to recall, North "became so powerfully emotive it was just like his whole spirit exploded. He took you beautifully through the whole situation and prepared you for this very powerful emotional climax." When the lights came up, "everyone was just riveted," and it was then and there that Spitz Channell grasped what the rest of America would soon discover: Ollie North was a star.

The Iran-Contra scandal had all the elements of a Hollywood plot: mustache-twirling anti-American villains; courageous, plucky revolutionaries; a beautiful young ingénue; and at its center, a roguish hero who defied the will of Congress to serve what he believed to be a greater cause. Unlike any previous Washington scandal, Iran-Contra produced bona fide celebrities, owing in no small part to the Reaganite glamour of its key players. When the plans unraveled in full public view, Ollie North became a champion to conservatives—and a political sex symbol to boot. And he was "discovered," as it were, by a gay man.

Spitz Channell had been inspired to join the pro-Contra cause in 1985, after hearing Reagan speak at a fund-raiser for Nicaraguan refugees. "We cannot have the United States walk away from one of the greatest moral challenges in postwar history," Reagan told the crowd of six hundred guests at the five-hundred-dollars-a-ticket dinner at the JW Marriott around the corner from the White House, a message he emphasized by holding up an adorable little refugee girl and planting a kiss on her cheek. Reagan's performance, Channell was to recall, "set me on fire" in a way akin to "lightning and dry timber." The president's address was "probably one of the finest speeches for freedom he has ever made, and I was electrified by that speech . . . I felt more convinced than I ever had that I could raise support for the freedom fighters."

If there was one thing Spitz Channell was good at, it was generating cash for the cause of freedom. He had started his career as a fund-raiser for

NCPAC, whose handsome young president, Terry Dolan, shared the same secret (and style of mustache) as he. "You know, Terry hasn't paid himself a salary in three months, because we are so broke" went a typical Channell solicitation, delivered by phone to a donor well past dinnertime to create the impression that Channell was burning the midnight oil back in Washington. "And here you are sitting in your $400,000 home and Terry is out there fighting your fight and you're not doing a thing. Now I want you to send me a check for $2,500 right now." He proved remarkably adept at the fine art of doing well by doing good, growing NCPAC's base of major donors over fifteenfold in six years. While Dolan's passion lay in revolutionizing the mechanics of domestic American politicking, Channell had bigger ambitions. Determined to put his fund-raising skills to use in the cause of rolling back the Red Menace, he enlisted the animal spirits of American capitalism in the twilight struggle against international communism and struck out on his own.

At first, Channell struggled. In the Capitol Hill town house that initially served as headquarters for the Channell Corporation, his office was a shambles, furnished with an antique desk, a Chinese vase, a dead plant in the corner, and curtainless windows. Belying his modest digs, Channell dressed like the consummate DC power broker he longed to be, sporting French-cuffed monogrammed shirts and tailored suits. Bob Bauman recalled once visiting Channell's ramshackle digs. Hanging on one wall, Bauman noticed, was a chalkboard with the names of some well-known conservative donors written on it, and he ultimately came away with the impression that Channell "seemed to know everybody's grandchildren and what kind of car" they drove.

At the end of 1984, the ideal opportunity to combine his political passions, fund-raising prowess, and taste for the finer things fell into Channell's lap when the Democratic Congress passed the Boland Amendment prohibiting military assistance to the Contras. Operating under a novel interpretation of the law, the Reagan administration turned to wealthy private citizens to underwrite the rebels, and a raft of "contrapreneurs" emerged to raise the funds that Congress had withheld. By the summer of 1985, nearly two dozen such efforts had sprung up, including ones backed by Colorado beer magnate Joseph Coors, *Soldier of Fortune* magazine, and retired army general John Singlaub, whom Jimmy Carter had relieved from duty in 1978 for insubordination after Singlaub publicly criticized the president's plans to withdraw troops from South Korea.

Channell's contribution to the private Contra supply network, the tax-exempt NEPL, was distinguished from the other contrapreneur groups by a pair of innovations learned at the feet of Terry Dolan. "I had unlocked several facts that had heretofore not been appreciated in American politics," Channell was to recall with characteristic humility about his work with the NCPAC founder. First, he "discovered there was so much money ready for conservative organizations in the United States that we needed ways to spend that money." The way to build the conservative coalition, Channell realized, was through highly charged appeals on behalf of single-issue advocacy organizations devoted to hot-button issues, whether abortion, the Panama Canal Treaty, school prayer, or the homosexual menace. Channell's second intuition came from watching the spectacular rise of his mentor, around whom he formulated a "philosophy of fundraising alien to political action groups" that took advantage of a distinctive "personality." Channell once tried to convince Dolan that he "could become as powerful a personal leader in America as any Senator or congressman, but we would focus, we had to focus, on Terry Dolan as a leader." Ultimately, Channell argued, NCPAC's goal should be to "create a personal leader who could meet with people, talk with people as a senator or congressman could and evoke the same type of long-term loyalty and financial sacrifice that the congressmen and senators do." Channell proposed inviting small groups of wealthy donors to Washington for exclusive "briefings" with Dolan during which the NCPAC president would "listen to their concerns about America and listen for their interest in what they would like to do for America."

In the plight of the Contra rebels coldly abandoned by the Democratic Congress, Channell had an emotional issue guaranteed to tug at conservative heart (and purse) strings. Now all he needed was a charismatic leader like Terry Dolan to sell it. Enter Oliver North.

From the moment they met that rainy afternoon at the Old Executive Office Building, this unlikely pair of right-wing gay money-spinner and ramrod-straight military aide developed what would later be described as an extremely effective "one-two punch" for convincing wealthy patriots to fund the Nicaraguan resistance. Over the years, Channell found that some of the most generous contributors to his mini-empire of important-sounding initiatives and causes (the American Conservative Trust, the Anti-Terrorism American Committee, the Grow Washington Political Action Committee, the American Space Frontier Committee, etc.) were dowagers. These senior citizens were imbued with a strong sense of civic duty, were susceptible to the charms of younger men, and had vanishingly little time left to enjoy their fortunes. Channell traveled far and wide to cultivate his "blue-rinse brigade," flying to Europe at least once, according to an associate, "to raise money from rich German widows." One NEPL employee likened Channell's technique of courting old ladies (to whom he sent roses on their birthday) as an exercise in seduction, using "this soft-spoken, mellifluous voice, drawing her in, wooing."

From the second his donors arrived in Washington, Channell tended to their every need. A limousine met them at the airport and ferried them straight to the Hay-Adams, where Channell arranged for chocolates to be placed in their rooms. Then, Channell escorted them across the street to the White House for the first "punch": a North briefing, during which the NSC staffer occasionally divulged information he characterized as "secret." Channell and North developed a coded language to describe the donors, with "no little girls" implying that North should skip any discussion of humanitarian issues and "tigers" referring to "arch-conservative" patrons who "preferred blood and guts." Because North, as a government official, was prohibited from soliciting money from private citizens, the second "punch" was not delivered until after his presentation, when the group trooped back across Lafayette Square to the Hay-Adams, where Channell wined and dined them before making his pitch.

Ostensibly, the money Channell raised through his interlocking web of nonprofit foundations and political action committees was to support humanitarian aid for the Contras. ("Are we getting this money through the Spitz channel?" one State Department wag was moved to ask.) Due to a law prohibiting U.S. citizens from soliciting funds for the export of weapons abroad, the contrapreneurs could only supply "non-lethal" aid and matériel, such as the sixty-five-thousand-dollar medical evacuation helicopter Singlaub christened "Lady Ellen" after the octogenarian Texas cotton heiress who paid for it, Ellen Garwood. As illustrated by the reaction of one Contra leader upon receiving a State Department shipment of seventeen hundred miles of dental floss—"We're guerrillas. We don't floss our teeth"—what the freedom fighters in Nicaragua needed most in their battle against the Sandinistas, however, was guns.

NEPL helped fill the void. At one Hay-Adams dinner, Channell led Garwood into a room next to the cocktail lounge, where he presented her with another, far more expensive menu: an à la carte list of items that included bullets, cartridge belts, hand grenades, and "possibly surface-to-air missiles." The daughter of a Truman State Department official who had played a central role in crafting the Marshall Plan, Garwood was an especially enthusiastic donor. "When you have a Congress that doesn't do its duty, it's like when your house is burning down and the fire department doesn't come," she said. "The private citizen has to act." Within days of Channell's solicitation, Garwood acted, transferring more than $1 million in stock to NEPL and wiring an additional $470,000 a few days later. Channell deposited these and other funds for "weapons and ammunition" into an account listed "Toys."

"Ollie had a well-oiled machine to grind out money, and Spitz made sure it paid off," marveled one attendee of several North briefings. But Channell wanted more. At the end of 1985, he started paying Reagan's former body man twenty thousand dollars per month to help arrange briefings with the president himself, reportedly once offering a donor a private meeting for a modest donation of three hundred thousand dollars. Reagan signed a letter to Channell heartily endorsing NEPL's work, and soon Channell was addressing his donors as if the president had personally requested their financial support. "The president has asked us to undertake this effort; the president asked me to contact you" were the sort of intimacies with which Channell peppered his conversations, while bragging to a reporter that he could raise "$40,000 before lunch" and describing himself as the administration's "point man" on Contra aid. His benefactors enjoyed the intrigue. "I got the impression that she was talking to me on the telephone underneath her bed, about the fun she was having," Channell said of his conversations with Garwood. After receiving especially large checks, Channel giddily called North and told him, "[Y]ou won't believe what we have received."

Assisting Channell in this flurry of activity—coordinating the travel arrangements, guaranteeing that meetings ran smoothly, and most important, making sure the checks earmarked for "Toys" arrived on time—was the NEPL staff of about thirty people, "notorious in Washington" for being composed almost exclusively of gay men. "Those gay boys of Oliver North's were particularly good at going out and getting checks from rich women," a gay official working at the Pentagon at the time remembers of Channell and company. According to Alan Carrier, a gay media consultant who worked with the group, some of the staffers gushed about how "sexy" and "very handsome" North was, lamenting how he was straight and probably having an affair with Fawn Hall. To maintain operational security, Channell instructed his staff to refer to North by an alias denoting his ability to reel in the dough: "Mr. Green." North's briefings at the White House were termed "Green Meetings," and the relationship between the marine lieutenant colonel and the swooning NEPL staffers came to resemble that of a movie star and his management team. If the stalwart, conservative North was ever uncomfortable collaborating with a passel of gay men in their shared battle against the Sandinistas, he didn't show it. His office at the NSC was a welcoming place; Hall "thought nothing of" bringing gay friends there. According to Carrier, North "would have to be blind not to know almost everybody was gay" within the organization, Channell especially. Like Dolan a regular patron of the Eagle, he was often accompanied by his lover, Eric Olson, at NEPL events. At one point, a rumor spread about a videotape of a gay orgy organized by Channell supposedly showing North sitting on the floor in his underwear drinking a beer; the tape seems to have existed only in the imagination of the embittered Contra leader who concocted it after falling out with North.

In a city where loyalty is valued so highly because it is so rare, the gay aide (whether an appointments secretary, chief counsel, best friend, walker, speechwriter, gofer, chief of staff, inauguration planner, bare-knuckle activist, or back-channel fund-raiser) was a highly prized commodity. Perhaps it was the gravity of the secret these men shared, and the vulnerability it created, that drove them to go over and above the call of duty. While gay men on both sides of the partisan divide possessed this trait, it was particularly pronounced among conservatives, a dynamic that paradoxically intensified the more hostile to homosexuality was the politician for whom they worked. "Just about every Republican campaign I've worked on had a sizable gay contingent of staffers," observed Stuart Stevens, a longtime GOP strategist, one of whose first employers was Congressman Jon Hinson. "The more conservative the candidate, the greater seemed the percentage of gay staffers." The prevalence of so many gay men on the hard right might have also been attributable to a twisted sense of elitism—working for a politician or movement whose leaders considered one degenerate providing its own strange rewards. "It's a perverse kind of self-esteem," remarked one gay observer of this coterie. "Like you're so much smarter than the guy you're working for."

By the time Terry Dolan entered the hospital in the summer of 1986, his protégé was reputed to be the leading conservative fund-raiser in Washington, generating nearly ten million dollars for the Contra cause from what he claimed was "the best conservative list of corporate high-rollers." Flush with cash, Channell shifted his operations from the drab Capitol Hill town house to a well-appointed office suite two blocks from the White House. He also started living larger, purchasing a three-hundred-thousand-dollar condominium (stuffed with antiques and expensive artwork) overlooking Rock Creek Park in Kalorama, where a liveried Lincoln Town Car picked him up every day. Amid the luxury, it became increasingly difficult to discern where the genuine anticommunist fervor ended and the grifting began. Channell would start talking about "commies under the bed," one acquaintance recalled, "and we all just rolled our eyes." Publicly, Channell lauded his donors in martial terms. They were "warriors," he said, valiant fighters for liberty who were "somewhat ill at ease at a time of peace." He would later describe his relationship with them as a "cross between the camaraderie of combat soldiers and the emotional bonds binding a dispersed but close family," their "commitment to each other . . . only exceeded by our commitment to The Cause."

Channell's laudations to the gallantry of his donors contrasted sharply with how he spoke about them behind their backs. "Dog Face" and "Ham Hocks" were the nicknames Channell conceived for two of his most generous patrons; "Mrs. Malleable" for another. "I don't care if they have to mortgage their homes or sell their children," Channell barked to his staff. "What we are doing is more important." In order to teach them how to raise "big money," former colleagues said, Channell recorded his telephone conversations with donors and "used to play them back and laugh. It was degrading." (Channell wasn't so contemptuous of *all* his donors. "Didn't I tell you he'd be gorgeous?" he once mused to an aide following a meeting with a young Republican real estate executive.) "I never saw an operator quite like Spitz," one associate recalled. "He would develop personal relationships with people, and he was a master at playing them."

On the other side of the Potomac, another elderly heiress was intervening in the struggle for Central America, albeit on the other side of the blue-rinse brigade. After her companion, Florence Thorne, died in 1973, Margaret Scattergood started a daily routine that began with the writing of her memoirs in the morning, followed by intensive study of international relations in the afternoon. "I'm particularly interested now in avoiding World War III," the octogenarian corresponding clerk of the Langley Hill Friends Meeting said. "I think it's possible." Having spent decades as a researcher for the nation's leading union, she was convinced that the processes of labor arbitration could be applied successfully to the realm of geopolitical conflict resolution. "I'm hoping to find ways I can help in developing negotiations between nations to replace war," she said. "Collective bargaining between nations is really the only thing that makes sense." Scattergood gave to pacifist organizations a significant chunk of the $125,000 she derived annually from the trust fund established by her father. "She lived a simple life, she and Miss Thorne," Scattergood's grand-niece recalled. "So, she gave away between a third and a half of her money each year."

Scattergood also resumed the confrontation—nonviolently, of course—with her nosy neighbor. The CIA had grown exponentially in the three decades since it relocated to the patch of land adjoining Scattergood's property, and as a gesture of concern, the agency's deputy director for administration sent a security patrol to check on her every day. This didn't stop Scattergood from writing letters to congressional leaders advocating cuts to the CIA's budget, or from offering space in her large house to Central American refugees fleeing conflicts in which it was embroiled. Sometimes, searching for the entrance to Scattergood's estate, weary Sandinista sympathizers would get lost and mistakenly show up at the CIA's front gate.

"Agency's dear neighbor, Miss Scattergood," read the note to CIA director Bill Casey from one of his subordinates in June 1984. "Perhaps I can persuade her to invite you for tea! She's quite a peace-monger." A few months later, Casey extended an olive branch, inviting Scattergood and her niece to lunch in his private dining room. Over sherry, the three discussed the book Casey had published about the American Revolution. "My relatives were in jail at the time," Scattergood remarked.

"What do you mean?" Casey asked.

"They were Quakers and were doing civil disobedience," she explained. "They don't believe in war and don't believe in killing other people and would rather go to jail and lose everything rather than participate in war."

Scattergood passed away in 1986, at the age of ninety-two. As per the agreement reached in 1947 with the federal government when it purchased the property on which she and Thorne lived, control of the land reverted to the CIA upon her death. The agency has since converted the house where the women shared their lives into a conference center where "employees seek refuge from the demands of the Headquarters environment to meet in seclusion and tranquility."

* * *

FAWN HALL WAS GROWING TIRED OF SPITZ CHANNELL. He was "a very aggressive, persistent person," calling her constantly and demanding to speak to her boss. Ollie North was also growing "frustrated" with the heavy volume of requests for NEPL donor meetings, so Hall sometimes told Channell that North was unavailable. Nonetheless, on the night of the 1986 midterm election, North returned the admiration his comrade so clearly felt for him by presenting Channell with a "Freedom Fighter" award at a black-tie dinner at the Willard InterContinental Hotel.

Three weeks later, it was for his own freedom that North would have to fight when the Justice Department announced that he had orchestrated the diversion of thirty million dollars in proceeds from the shipment of weaponry to Iran toward the purchase of arms for the Contras. President Reagan fired North, and in March, investigators discovered that the tax-deductible contributions to the NEPL "Toys" account had not subsidized Christmas gifts for the children of Nicaraguan rebels but, via a circuitous path through a few Swiss bank accounts and Cayman Islands shell companies, the purchase of guns and ammo.

That their donations had been used in possible violation of the Neutrality Act did not much upset Channell's donors; most of them knew what they were getting into. But then investigators discovered that of the ten million dollars Channell ultimately raised on behalf of the Contras, he had sent them only four million, with the rest going to salaries, overhead, and expenses, including Channell's credit card bills and house cleaner. More curious was the $17,500 that had gone to Eric Olson, described in the press as Channell's "roommate," and the $56,000 disbursed to a San Francisco consulting firm whose president had a similar cohabitational relationship with NEPL's executive director. This rerouting of suspect monies to same-sex lovers within the broader diversion of profits to the Contras—what North described as his "secret within a secret"—added yet another layer of intrigue to an already rococo international political drama. John Singlaub derided Channell and his associates as a "gang of crooks whom the intelligence community disparaged as 'the Fruit Loop.'" These interlopers, the retired two-star general alleged, "skillfully exploited Ollie" with their homosexual wiles to raise money that "went directly into the silk-lined pockets of Channell and his colleagues." It could only have distressed NEPL's donors, Singlaub said, to hear "disturbing reports that a lot of the money they were raising did not end up buying ponchos and jungle boots for the Contras, but supported an extravagant life-style for Channell and his dubious band of patriots."

On April 29, Channell became the first person charged with a crime in the burgeoning Iran-Contra affair when he pleaded guilty to conspiring to defraud the government by using a tax-exempt entity to fund the Contras. Asked by the judge if he wished to name any coconspirators, Channell clenched his hands and, in a voice rising barely above a whisper, spoke the name of the U.S. Marine lieutenant colonel and former NSC staffer whose charisma earned him the moniker "Mr. Green" among Channell's charmed associates. "Oh, the heartbreak I saw in his face on TV," said one NEPL donor, who in spite of it all wished she had contributed more than the sixty thousand dollars she already gave Channell. "Did you ever see such sad eyes in your life? Jiminy Cricket, he's usually so full of life." Another benefactor, an eighty-seven-year-old woman who donated just a few hundred dollars from her meager savings, vowed that "if it would help our country I would go sit in jail with him. I would." Not all of Channell's donors, however, were so sympathetic. A Texas oilman and friend of Ellen Garwood's, Bert Hurlbut, expressed displeasure upon hearing that Channell was gay, as communism was not the only menace whose advance he opposed. "I certainly don't approve of the homosexual lifestyle expanding in this country," he said, adding that he had actually started an organization "to oppose the homosexual expansion" whose mission had since been obviated by nature. "If AIDS had not come along to more or less do it for us, we would have been readily in the middle of a vigorous opposition to what homosexuals were doing to the moral structure of this country." As a token gesture, Channell had donated a thousand dollars to Hurlbut's group.

To Ben Bradlee, contemplating how his paper ought to cover the life and death of Terry Dolan, the revelation of a secret gay network within the secret Contra supply network was further evidence of an "important link between important parts of the conservative movement and homosexuals," as he wrote in a memo to *Post* colleagues. Channell and Richard Miller, a public relations consultant whom Channell had enlisted in his fund-raising schemes, "have both pleaded guilty to conspiracy to defraud the government. Both are gay, I am told." (According to a source interviewed by a *Post* journalist at the time, Miller was actually believed to be the only man in the Channell operation who was straight. "Maybe this will show 'em I'm not gay," Miller defiantly told a reporter from the *Baltimore Sun* as he posed with his wife for a photograph.) Though the *Post* had allegedly obtained credit card receipts indicating the use of NEPL funds to purchase men's silk underpants, Bradlee ultimately decided against pursuing the gay aspect of Iran-Contra, in contrast to the decision he had made seven years earlier concerning another circle of right-wing gay anticommunist gunrunners supposedly manipulating Ronald Reagan.

What makes Channell more than a footnote to the biggest political scandal of the 1980s was the way he embodied some of the decade's dominant themes—greed, ambition, the centrality of image in politics—each of which resonated with his identity as a closeted gay conservative. In Channell, a picture developed of a man whose fraudulence as a political grifter was entwined with his double life as a covert homosexual, a con man who had exploited elderly American widows and anticommunist freedom fighters to bankroll his lover, a harem of gay collaborators, and their decadent lifestyles. Adept at presenting a facade, men like Marvin Liebman, Bob Gray, Terry Dolan, Craig Spence, and Spitz Channell developed an acute appreciation for the power of artifice in politics, one to which the president could intimately relate. Often chided for blurring the line between reality and fantasy, Ronald Reagan saw his background in the entertainment industry as an *asset* to his political career. Indeed, he did not understand how one could successfully perform the job of president "without being an actor." An actor's "whole life," he said, "is devoted to pleasing and serving the people who are going to buy tickets to see you," a necessity for the commander in chief, as well as for the closeted political homosexual, forced to play one role at work while leading another offstage.

In Oliver North, Channell presciently recognized the intrinsic appeal of an American archetype: the tragic hero, sometimes (if not usually) a soldier, who bends the rules in the name of serving a cause greater than himself. When North appeared before the congressional committees investigating Iran-Contra in the summer of 1987, hundreds of people lined up outside the Capitol for hours in the sweltering July heat, and millions more flocked to their television screens to watch his riveting testimony. "Olliemania" swept the country, as a New York deli named a sandwich after him (a hero, natch), a San Francisco businessman created a Ken doll in his likeness, and talk of a presidential candidacy inevitably arose. At one point during the hearings, Republicans insisted that North be permitted to display the slide show that had so aroused Spitz Channell during that rainy day in June 1985. Due to security reasons, Democratic Senate committee chairman Daniel K. Inouye decided that the bright television lights inside the Caucus Room could not be dimmed, and so North could deliver his presentation at night in another location. Republicans objected. Moving North to prime time, they argued, would force him to compete against *Jeopardy!* and the All-Star baseball game.

41

THE WONDERFUL, THE CREATIVE, AND THE BRAVE

STEWART B. MCKINNEY WAS A MAN OF SHARP CONTRASTS. A REPUBLICAN representing southwestern Connecticut in the House of Representatives, he was an economic moderate and self-described "screaming social liberal." A Yale-educated son of privilege who represented one of the country's wealthiest congressional districts, he was an outspoken champion of the poor. And a married father of five whose family lived in Westport, Connecticut, he led a secret life in Washington, comprised of gay dinner parties at his Capitol Hill home and sexual liaisons with other men.

A regular attendee at those parties, Richard Mangan, recalled the time he met McKinney while flying back to Washington from Fort Lauderdale sometime during the late 1970s. The man sitting next to him on the plane struck up a chat, and because "if two gay people are talking, it doesn't take long for each of them to figure [it out]," the conversation eventually turned to the subject of Washington's gay bars. Mangan asked his interlocutor if he had ever visited the Hideaway or Mr. Henry's. "In my job, I can't really risk that," the man replied.

"Can I ask you what you do?" Mangan asked.

"I'm a member of Congress."

Another contradiction in Stewart McKinney's life would materialize after his May 1987 death, when he became the first congressman to die of AIDS. The news came as a shock to Washington, where a fifty-six-year-old, mild-mannered, blue-blooded Republican family man was considered to be an unlikely victim of the disease. According to his doctor, McKinney "wanted the cause of his death known after he passed away, in hopes that this information might help others to deal with what is becoming a national crisis." What Cesar Caceres, who had wrongly attributed the demise of his patient Terry Dolan to an enlarged heart, also made sure to say was that McKinney had contracted AIDS not through gay sex, but via blood transfusions administered to him in 1979 while undergoing heart bypass surgery. In a story citing "knowledgeable sources on Capitol Hill and in the gay community," however, the *Washington Post* shed doubt on this claim, reporting that "McKinney had had homosexual relationships."

Though he displayed an honesty in death that eluded him in life, McKinney refrained from leaving behind any acknowledgment of his secret gay existence to avoid causing any further pain to his wife of thirty-seven years. It was just the sort of well-intentioned ambiguity one would have expected from this "affable facilitator," but it became a source of strain between his family, his colleagues, the media, and the gay community. "Stewart and I had long communications before he died and knew that his death would be used by certain people," Lucie McKinney told the *Post*. Some of McKinney's colleagues were less diplomatic. "Here's another example of a person whose contribution won't be remembered," complained Connecticut senator Christopher Dodd. "He'll be defined by what a couple of reporters decided to write about what they had to go out and discover from some undisclosed sources in town." But it wasn't prurience that drove the *Post* to report on McKinney's sexual history. To treat the subject of homosexuality as a source of shame, as the paper had done by refraining to print the names of the victims of the Cinema Follies fire ten years earlier and would have done again had it pretended that McKinney never engaged in gay sex, would only reinforce the stigma that fused homosexuality and secrecy together in a tortuous synthesis. Furthermore, as managing editor Len Downie said in defense of his paper's decision to acknowledge McKinney's sexuality, had the *Post* let stand Caceres's specious claim—the chances of a blood transfusion recipient contracting AIDS in 1979 being ten thousand to one—it would have sparked unwarranted panic over the safety of the nation's blood supply.

Three weeks before he entered the hospital on April 22, McKinney penned a letter that was sent to every member of the Connecticut General Assembly, a body in which he had once served, urging them to approve a bill outlawing discrimination against gays and lesbians. "I do not believe people should be discriminated against for their sexual preference any more than for their skin color or religious affiliation," he wrote. "There are 20 million homosexual men and women in the United States. And like most Americans, they work hard and contribute to society." McKinney ultimately did not have the wherewithal to designate himself in that group of citizens. But he would not allow this reticence to inhibit his empathy for others. The same, alas, could not be said for the Assembly, which, just a week after McKinney died and following a debate in which the member from McKinney's party representing Greenwich referred to gays as "sick" and "perverts," rejected the bill.

"It is a fantastic tribute to this man's courage and compassion that he insisted on making known the cause of his death," said the reverend who presided over McKinney's funeral, attended by an overflow crowd that included Vice President Bush and forty House members. Gerry Studds, whose controversial and historic coming out of the closet McKinney had praised back in 1983, moved into his fallen colleague's office in the Cannon Building, and another Massachusetts congressman, Barney Frank, would cite McKinney's death as the incident that finally moved him to come out of the closet three weeks later in an interview with the *Boston Globe*.

The death of a Republican congressman from AIDS, coupled with the exposure of the gay conservative network assisting Oliver North, convinced Ben Bradlee that the *Post* could no longer wait to publish its feature on Terry Dolan. He had far exceeded his professional obligations to the subject's surviving brother, going so far as to send him a final version of reporter Elizabeth Kastor's article for him to review. Such courtesy was an extremely unusual departure from journalistic convention, but if Bradlee thought that extending it to Tony Dolan might bring the president's chief speechwriter to reason, he was sorely mistaken. At one point, Dolan called *Post* publisher Don Graham and, portentously inverting the words John Dean had uttered to an increasingly paranoid Richard Nixon, warned, "There is a cancer on your newspaper." Ignoring these threats, Bradlee scheduled the story for the May 11 edition. On the evening of May 10, Kastor tried one final time to get in touch with Dolan to solicit a comment for the record. She called his home phone and then, not receiving any answer, rang his office at the White House. Forty-five minutes later, she called the White House switchboard, where the operator told her she would page Dolan. Kastor left her home phone number, but Dolan never called back.

The next day, the entire front page of the *Post* Style section was taken up with the image of a half-open door, above which appeared the headline, "The Cautious Closet of the Gay Conservative." The piece recounted Dolan's astonishingly fast rise within the conservative movement, the life he led as a closeted gay man, and the conflicts these dual identities created. Kastor quoted conservatives praising Dolan as a passionate visionary, gay activists assailing him as a self-loathing hypocrite, and others who, like the subject of the article, straddled the perilous space between the secret and open cities. Sen. Gordon Humphrey of New Hampshire, the New Right favorite whom Dolan helped elect in 1978 and a mourner at his funeral, gave voice to a view held by many of the late activist's ideological allies. "At one time he was one of the bright stars in the conservative movement, and I think because of these rumors some of the luster wore away," Humphrey said. The claim that Dolan was gay disturbed Humphrey, "because if it was true, it would be a great personal tragedy. It is tragic when anyone embraces an unhealthy personal life style, whether it's alcoholism, drug abuse, homosexuality, venality . . ."

Early that morning, an enraged Tony Dolan called Ben Bradlee. Both he and the paper he edited, Dolan fumed, stank of corruption. The *Post* may have brought down one president, Dolan allowed, "and thank God for that, but this was too much." Bradlee, he said, "didn't have the guts to listen to my sister sob." He suspected that Len Downie was the man pulling the strings, that he was a "Prussian" who wanted Bradlee's job and that Bradlee "should look out." That afternoon, Margaret Dolan, the seventy-one-year-old family matriarch, called Bradlee. She related to him how she had "lived through hell" nursing two sons and a husband with polio in addition to a senile mother. Though she was "absolutely devastated" by the story in that morning's paper—the author of which, she hoped, would "never have a day's love"—she was comforted by the fact that "Terry died in God's Hand." Through tears, she said that she felt "terribly sorry" for Bradlee and the paper, and she asked him to pass that message along to his staff.

Bradlee reassured his team that they had done everything by the book. "This is one of these cutting edge pieces, which are far more easily left unwritten, but when written sensitively, shed light on an important area of our society," he wrote in an all-staff memo. But Tony Dolan was far from finished with Ben Bradlee and the *Post*. Somehow, amid his heavy duties as chief speechwriter to the president of the United States, he found the time over the course of the following week to dash off an eight-thousand-word essay, comprised mostly of a painstaking rehash of his interactions with various *Post* staffers and a diatribe about the pernicious place of homosexuality in journalism and public life. The finished manuscript occupied twenty-nine double-spaced pages, and Dolan demanded that the *Post* publish it, in its entirety, as a correction. When the paper asked Dolan to trim it to seven hundred fifty words, the length of an op-ed, he sent it to the *Washington Times*.

Bumping into *Times* managing editor Wesley Pruden at a Georgetown cocktail party, Bradlee asked what he planned to do with the Dolan doorstopper.

"Probably print some of it, if he'll cut it," Pruden replied.

"Aw, come on, you guys will print it all," Bradlee ribbed.

"Are you kidding?" Pruden said. In addition to "prudenizing," his penchant for injecting a right-wing slant into any and all copy that crossed his desk, Pruden was also notorious for demanding that no story run over fifteen column inches. "That manuscript runs to 28 double-spaced typewritten pages," Pruden said.

"Twenty-nine," Bradlee corrected. "We told him that if he cut it back to 750 words, we would consider running it."

"We might go more than that," Pruden replied. "But not the whole thing."

"You're going to run the whole thing," Bradlee taunted. "I know you are."

"No, not at that length," Pruden assured him. "Stories of paralyzing length is what *you* guys do."

Bradlee was right. After Dolan declined to cut his treatise by a word, the paper offered a compromise: it would print the piece in its entirety, but only as a paid advertisement. The sprawling essay would require two full pages, a rarely afforded chunk of newspaper real estate known in the industry as a "double-truck," and it set Dolan back five thousand dollars. On May 22, *Washington Times* readers—the most prominent of whom, editor Arnaud de Borchgrave boasted, was the president of the United States—happened upon an extremely unusual tableau in their morning paper positioned between the roundup of political news and the box scores. There, on pages 8 and 9, the tiny letters spelling "ADVERTISEMENT" inside a very thin banner along the top the only indication that it was not an editorial feature of massive significance, was a work unprecedented in the annals of presidential speechwriting, an exclusive guild wherein anonymity is a sacred code. As Dolan himself had said at the outset of his tenure working for Ronald Reagan, "Speech writers should be seen and not heard." On this day, Tony Dolan would be heard.

Reading "What the Washington Post Doesn't Tell Its Readers" was like rubbernecking at a car crash, if the accident site were the pages of a national newspaper and its victim the president's chief speechwriter. In publishing an exposé of his brother, Dolan declared, the *Washington Post* had been "disrespectful of the public's right to know; incapable of self-examination or introspection; self-righteous; arrogant and heartless in the relentless pursuit of those on its own enemy's [*sic*] list." He further charged that "homosexual intrigue" in the *Post* newsroom was so intense that "poor Ben Bradlee has no one on whom he dares turn his back" and that the paper "subordinates its public and journalistic responsibilities to its role as a political and ideological power-center promoting an anti-conservative, pro-gay agenda." Pushing that agenda was "a special interest who wanted to claim my brother as well as other prominent people as one of their own," an ultimately futile endeavor because, as he lay dying, "my brother had a deeply religious conversion and had completely rejected homosexuality." To leave out any mention of this deathbed metanoia put Dolan in mind of the tortured soul who preceded his brother as a great anticommunist ex-homosexual, and whose participation in, and subsequent witness against, a depraved and immoral enterprise might be likened to Terry's "heroic struggle for life." This man, Dolan had incidentally told the *Post* just two months before Terry's passing, was "a crucial figure to a lot of people in the administration," as indicated by Reagan's posthumous bestowal of a Medal of Honor upon him in 1984. "You cannot write a story about Augustine of Hippo and not note that he became a Christian," Dolan wrote, just as "you cannot write an account of Whittaker Chambers and leave out the part about his crusade for Western values and freedom."

Dolan also alluded to something that helped explain the massive gulf between him and Bradlee concerning the controversy at hand: their gay brothers. "Mr. Bradlee has repeated often and in writing his view that there is nothing wrong with homosexuality," Dolan asserted. "This feeling runs very deep in him and he has told me why. It does not concern his personal sexuality but it is a private matter. I leave it to Mr. Bradlee to decide whether he will fully discuss this with the public." Dolan ended on a note of Christian charity, telling conservatives that the best way to honor the legacy of his late brother, who had died "a courageous, holy—and I use the word advisedly—glorious death," was to "reform" the *Post*. "But remember: your ultimate duty to Terry Dolan is a duty to Ben Bradlee, Len Downie, and all those who have a part in this terrible moment. Forgive them. Help them make a change, if you can. But forgive them."

This fusillade against his newspaper by the president's chief speechwriter prompted *Post* publisher Don Graham to ask ombudsman Joseph Laitin to review the process by which the profile of Terry Dolan had been published. "Anthony Dolan's niagara of words, his 10,000 word diatribe against . . . the *Post*, should have been a catharsis for him—the long bitter letter most of us would have written at least once, and were smart enough not to mail," Laitin wrote. "My reading of that missive is that it is tormented, it is sick, it is threatening, it is unreasonable and should be ignored. One doesn't have to be a psychiatrist or a psychologist to speculate that the real target of Anthony Dolan's venom and hatred is his own brother for having humiliated him and his family." The only possible error in judgment on the part of the *Post* that Laitin could conceive of was that, in waiting two months to publish its story in deference to Dolan, the paper had been overly *solicitous* toward the man now accusing it of high journalistic crimes.

"As an irrelevant postscript," Laitin added, "I shudder to think that the author of that document also puts words into the mouth of the President."

Back at the White House, the words being put into the mouth of the president, though not by Dolan, were about AIDS. On May 31, at a Georgetown restaurant overlooking the Potomac, Reagan addressed a benefit dinner for the American Foundation for AIDS Research (amfAR) organized by his friend Elizabeth Taylor. Perhaps rattled by Dolan's very public intervention on the subject, Nancy ensured that her husband's remarks were drafted far outside the White House speechwriting office. She called one of its alumni, Landon Parvin, who had joined the administration at its outset upon the recommendation of his boss at the time, Bob Gray, to write the address. "She didn't want the speech to be taken off to the far right, and she thought that the first time the president really spoke about this that it should be something that was more moderate than perhaps what would come out of the White House itself," Parvin recalled.

The First Lady had reason to worry. A draft of Parvin's speech with the handwritten edits of associate director of the Office of Public Liaison Mildred Webber, found at the Reagan Presidential Library, reveals the heated internal disagreements that raged in the Reagan administration over AIDS policy. Webber demanded that a line Parvin had written praising Surgeon General C. Everett Koop, a supporter of safe sex education, as "an honest man, a good scientist, and an advocate for the public health," be removed as it "would enrage the conservative community and it is not necessary." Webber had a similar opinion of the president's avowing, "I don't blame those who were out marching and protesting to get the AIDS drugs released before the t's were crossed and the i's were dotted," jotting "This is terrible!!!" in the margin of the text, and, "If I had AIDS, I'd feel the same frustration," a sentiment she labeled "dumb." She further suggested that the mention of "young men" in a sentence listing the groups most at risk for contracting the disease be qualified with the word *homosexual*, that a sentence asserting "Passing moral judgments is up to God" be excised ("This is why we have this disease in the first place," she scribbled. "No moral control."), and that an entire paragraph calling on Americans not to discriminate against people with AIDS be struck. Aside from deleting the line putting the president in an AIDS victim's shoes (ultimately changed to "I sympathize with them, and we'll supply help and hope as quickly as we can"), Webber's recommendations were rejected.

Over veal and asparagus, the six-hundred-person audience including actor George Hamilton; Washington, DC, mayor Marion Barry; closeted magazine publisher Malcolm Forbes; and polio vaccine inventor Jonas Salk listened as the president mentioned hemophiliacs but not the main group at risk for AIDS and the one that had borne the brunt of discrimination because of it: gay men. On top of this omission, Reagan's statement that "innocent people are being infected by this virus" seemed to designate gays as a category of AIDS victims who were culpable for their misfortune. Nonetheless, elsewhere Reagan called for "compassion, not blame" and spoke out against the idea that people with AIDS "wear a scarlet A." At the end of the evening, Taylor pulled from her bosom a million-dollar check signed by a Japanese philanthropist, while outside the party tent, a crowd of three hundred people stood vigil holding candles above their heads.

The following day was so hot at the sit-in outside the White House that Deacon Maccubbin brought carpet sample squares so that he and others would not burn their behinds on the pavement. When police arrived to haul the protesters away into paddy wagons wearing disposable yellow rubber gloves—an unnecessary precaution given that HIV, as the president himself had acknowledged the previous evening, could not be transmitted casually—one of the demonstrators let out a spontaneous war cry, a mixture of camp and pithiness so perfect that the entire group joined in unison: "Your gloves don't match your shoes! They'll see it on the news!"

On June 2, Tony Dolan called Joseph Laitin from the White House in a rage. "There is no chance of satisfying him in this dispute, short of turning over the Post to him," the ombudsman wrote in a memo to Don Graham. Dolan, he went on, "is belligerent, wild, and borders on the irrational on the subject of his brother." He harped on Terry's deathbed "spiritual conversion," assailed the Post for its "total lack of ethical behavior in general," and repeatedly made "historical allusions as though his brother had achieved sainthood." In life, Terry Dolan was unable to reconcile his public persona as a New Right firebrand with his private existence as a gay man. In death, the behavior of his older brother—lashing out at anyone who had the temerity to acknowledge this tension—suggested why. "He wants his pound and a half of flesh," Laitin concluded; "he wants the Post to crawl publicly and nothing less will do." Dolan ended his diatribe after fifteen minutes, informing Laitin that he had to get to the airport for the president's trip to Europe. The tour included stops in Vienna for a G-8 summit, Rome for an audience with Pope John Paul II, and West Berlin, where Reagan, standing before the seemingly impenetrable edifice John F. Kennedy had condemned as an "offense against humanity," an oppressive barrier dividing an open city from a secret one and separating "a people who wish to be joined together," would speak the words Dolan put into his mouth and urge his Soviet counterpart to "tear down this wall."

*　*　*

"I DO NOT KNOW HOW COMMITTED YOU MAY OR MAY NOT BE to the idea of a gay person on the coming AIDS National Board," New York Daily News gossip columnist Liz Smith wrote her frequent phone buddy Nancy Reagan on July 15, 1987. "May I put in my oar and recommend Larry Kramer as the person." Smith, who for most of her decades-long career dishing about the private lives of America's most famous people kept her own bisexuality a closely guarded secret, was writing the First Lady about a report that had recently appeared in the rival *New York Post* claiming that she was pushing her husband to appoint a gay man to the commission he had created the previous month to devise a national strategy for combating AIDS. "Mrs. Reagan is just a tigress," one senior administration official was quoted telling the *Post*. "When she gets her teeth into something, she just doesn't let go."

However strong her determination to see a gay man appointed to the President's Commission on the Human Immunodeficiency Virus Epidemic, as the body was formally to be called, it would be hard to imagine anyone, gay or straight, *less* likely to earn Nancy's endorsement than the novelist, playwright, and rabble-rousing AIDS activist who had been assailing the First Couple for years over their indifference to the disease killing so many of his friends. Kramer's 1985 play, *The Normal Heart*, one of the first dramatic works to tackle AIDS, was a howl against apathy, and just a few months before the commission was announced, Kramer had excoriated the president in the pages of the *New York Times*. The following year, Kramer would put on *Just Say No*, "a play about a farce" based in the fictional country of New Columbia, wherein everyone calls the president "Daddy," the First Lady is a harridan named "Mrs. Potentate," and the couple's ballet dancer son pines for his Secret Service detail. ("Does the play indulge in poor taste?" asked the *Times* theater critic. "Imagine the worst possible taste, then take it several steps further.")

Since President Reagan's announcement of the commission in June, recommendations for potential members had poured into the White House from across the political spectrum. Sen. Strom Thurmond suggested Paul Cameron, a Nebraska-based psychologist (expelled from the American Psychological Association) who advocated a "rolling quarantine" of homosexuals. A member of the West Hollywood City Council sent a list of openly gay elected officials. Congressman Dick Cheney of Wyoming called to recommend Stephen Herbits, a gay executive with the Seagram's liquor conglomerate alongside whom he had worked in the Ford White House. Bob Bauman recommended himself. The president's Domestic Policy Council, meanwhile, presented a "mixture of medical experts and public-spirited citizens," including the philanthropist Eunice

Kennedy Shriver, former congresswoman Barbara Jordan, a virologist at the Walter Reed Army Institute of Research named Robert Redfield, and William F. Buckley Jr.

Though his recommendation of the man whose signal contribution to the national conversation about AIDS had been a proposal to tattoo the buttocks of its victims was ultimately rejected, Gary Bauer was determined to make *his* mark upon AIDS policy. An evangelical Christian who had previously served as undersecretary of education, the White House domestic policy advisor was on the record with his opposition to an openly gay panelist. "I don't want people who have axes to grind," he said in May. "I don't feel that we have to have an IV drug user on the commission. Therefore it doesn't follow that we have to have a homosexual." He stressed this view privately to the president as well. "Millions of Americans try to raise their children to believe that homosexuality is immoral," Bauer wrote Reagan in a June 30 memo. "For you to appoint a known homosexual to a Presidential Commission will give homosexuality a stamp of acceptability. It will drive a wedge between us and many of our socially conservative supporters." In conclusion, Bauer wrote the president, "If you feel we must appoint a homosexual, I would recommend a 'reformed' homosexual— that is, someone not currently living a gay life style."

Under pressure from his wife, the president ignored his domestic policy advisor. "As far as I know I am probably among the first openly gay persons to have been appointed to a significant position in any U.S. administration," Dr. Frank Lilly, chairman of the genetics department at Albert Einstein Medical Center, said upon his appointment to the AIDS commission, adding a pledge "to forcefully represent the gay community as well as the biomedical community." Lilly had been recommended by Dr. Richard Davis, Nancy's stepbrother, and according to one administration official, he was appointed "because the first lady said so." This came as no surprise to the far-right columnist Joseph Sobran. "So Ronald Reagan becomes the first President to give legitimacy to homosexual conduct. Why?" he asked. "Well, Nancy Reagan's court is said to have included a number of the breed over the years."

Lilly understood that many administration critics viewed the commission as a fig leaf. But the doctor, who had come out of the closet late in life after marrying and raising a family, was an institutionalist, not an activist, and he committed himself to working within the system. At the press conference announcing the panel's formation, he chatted amiably with fellow commission member Cardinal John O'Connor, the Catholic archbishop of New York who had repeatedly denounced homosexuality from the pulpit. The appointment of an openly gay man was the newsiest aspect of the commission's creation; immediately after the event, Lilly was swarmed by a throng of journalists and television cameras that left him "shell-shocked" and "scared to death." Despite his political inexperience, Lilly seized the opportunity to influence the president and other elected officials as an openly gay man. When Sen. Jesse Helms led an effort to revoke funding for AIDS education initiatives that "promote, encourage or condone" gay sex, Lilly fired off an angry letter. "Do you really hate [gays] so much that, instead of trying to stop the spread of HIV-infection, you want to facilitate it among them?" he asked. Following the release of an interagency study suggesting that the federal government withhold support from efforts granting gays the right to adopt children, Lilly sent an impassioned letter to the man who had appointed him. "It is not clear to me that you recognize that homosexual people are, on the whole, neither better nor worse citizens than are heterosexuals," he wrote President Reagan. "The sooner this nation joins with much of the advanced world in rejecting homophobia, just as we reject racism and religious discrimination, the sooner we will be on the road to eliminating a serious source of friction and injustice in our society." The letter was routed to Gary Bauer from the White House director of correspondence with a sarcastic note attached: "Your friend."

Bauer's extensive correspondence about AIDS (with random citizens, White House colleagues, and the president himself) reveals the animus toward homosexuality that existed at the highest levels of the Reagan administration and with which Lilly had to contend. For instance, while Bauer grandiosely referred to the disease as "the worst threat our nation has ever known" in a letter to a political supporter, six months later he flippantly told a more critical citizen that "the people dying with AIDS constitute a very small percentage of our population." In reply to a letter "concerning public reaction to homosexuals since AIDS has become a national threat," Bauer made sure to note that "innocent people have fallen victim to AIDS because of contaminated blood supplies," reinforcing the moral distinction between those who contracted the disease through transfusions and the homosexuals who acquired it via sexual contact. "While many members of the homosexual community have shown exemplary bedside compassion for patients with AIDS," Bauer wrote in the first draft of a letter responding to a writer upset about Bauer's opposition to the appointment of a gay commissioner, "homosexuals as a class have a less spectacular record regarding the spread of the disease." (Bauer, or a colleague, thought better of this remark and deleted it before mailing out his reply.)

In August, three weeks after Reagan unveiled his commission, the General Accounting Office released a report stating that the administration's proposed $790 million appropriation for AIDS research and prevention was nearly $400 million short of what medical experts believed was necessary and that its overall strategy was "uncoordinated and insufficient." By contrast, in Great Britain, the government of Reagan's conservative ally Margaret Thatcher implemented a robustly funded public health awareness campaign, and the incidence of HIV infection was one-tenth that of the United States. A comparison between the memberships of the AIDS panel and a contemporaneous presidentially appointed body, the commission to investigate the 1986 *Challenger* space shuttle disaster, illuminates the administration's priorities. Among other relevant experts, the *Challenger* group included a leading authority on rocket engines, a Nobel Prize–winning physicist, several astronauts, and an air force general who had overseen the military's space programs. The AIDS commission, by contrast, included a chairman who, while a medical doctor and CEO of the Mayo Clinic, confessed upon his appointment, "I'm no AIDS expert"; a sex therapist who endorsed the unfounded hypothesis that the disease could be transmitted via toilet seats and insects; and a Reagan campaign donor. Even Lilly was a geneticist who had never treated an AIDS patient. While the *Challenger* commission boasted a staff of nearly fifty people and a three-million-dollar operating budget, the AIDS panel had only six staffers and a budget of less than a million. This lack of resources, combined with various factional struggles, came to a head on October 8, when the commission's chairman, vice chairman, and single medical staff officer resigned.

Three days later, hundreds of thousands of people from across the country descended upon the capital for the Second National March on Washington for Lesbian and Gay Rights. It was a more somber procession than the one that preceded it in 1979, eclipsed by an epidemic that, by this point, had taken an estimated twenty-five thousand lives. Visitors who picked up a copy of that morning's *Washington Post* found a map of the march route, which began at the Ellipse, proceeded past the White House, and culminated with a rally on the west side of the Capitol Building. ("For the first time in my memory," a lesbian reporter for the paper observed, "we did something specifically for our gay readers.") The day's most emotional moment had transpired hours before, at the sunrise unveiling of the AIDS Memorial Quilt, a massive tapestry composed of 1,920 panels, each dedicated to an individual victim of the plague. For three hours, as volunteers unfurled the three-and-a-half-ton tableau across a two-block-long expanse of the Mall, the only sound that could be heard above the mournful silence was the weeping of friends and family who had come to commemorate their loved ones. Gerry Studds joined a group of mourners in reading the names, as did a new colleague who had won a special election to the House that summer from San Francisco, Nancy Pelosi. The gathering was the largest civil rights demonstration since Martin Luther King Jr. and Bayard Rustin's 1963 March on Washington for Jobs and Freedom, and at an estimated two hundred fifty thousand participants, it constituted the biggest gathering of gay people in history. "Walking around, I was just bloody-eyed I had been crying so much," recalled John Ford. His feelings of grief were exacerbated when "the President's helicopter flew over the quilt, landed at the White House, the ignoring of it. He had been invited to show up, he just flew over it in his big fucking helicopter."

Chasen Gaver, the Federal Trade Commission paralegal and performance poet whose AIDS diagnosis earlier that year had impelled him to quit keeping his diary, was inspired by the march to resume writing it. "History was made on Sunday (so many people *risking* a public appearance for *ideas*), and I must document my own personal history at this time of AIDS," Gaver wrote on October 13, 1987, the maiden entry of his "Fever Journal," a daily chronicle of his life with the disease, for which he recorded his temperature, symptoms, and ruminations both quotidian and profound. Gaver stopped working at the FTC just two days later, the early "retirement" of a thirty-four-year-old man one of the plague's most gruesomely common auguries of the hundreds of thousands of individual tragedies to come.

On January 13, 1988, experiencing "raging fevers" of 104 degrees ("It climbs and my forehead burns and I see a deep red light around my head— even with my eyes closed"), Gaver wrote that "AIDS has made everything so 'do or die' that people are taking more risks. This may mean that, politically, Gay people will take more risks in the public sphere to 'save ourselves.'" The following month, recording his weight at 106 pounds and sleeping eighteen hours per day, Gaver penned a letter to family and friends:

At times I try to see myself in a future month (when I was diagnosed, I "visualized" myself in Michigan at Christmas, and felt I'd make it). The furthest I've been able to go in my mind now is my birthday (August 7, 1988—when I'll be 35); but that image sometimes blurs. The doctors cannot predict much, so we just keep plugging along, but I am getting much thinner, weaker, and in many ways am ready to pass on. My goal has never been to live a long life (even before I was sick), my goal was to live a productive, full, free life—and I've met my goal. I have thought of very few things I would do over. I'm glad I was born a writer. I'm glad I was born Gay. And I'm glad the people around me taught me compassion for others. I'm glad I moved to Washington, traveled to Greece, Morocco, the Caribbean, and elsewhere. I'm glad I never voted for Ronald Reagan (and never trusted Nancy any further than I could see her with that fake smile pasted over her lips).

Gaver ended on a darkly humorous note. "Don't fight over my ashes," he instructed his survivors. "You don't get much from a cremation, you get other people's ashes mixed in (if it's a busy day), and I've instructed Craig [the executor of his will] to dispense cigarette ashes to pests. He will do the best he can with what he has."

Gaver's correspondence over the course of the succeeding months documents a steady decline toward the inevitable, all undertaken with remarkable dignity and good cheer. Accepting that the end was near, Gaver had begun sketching a design for his own panel in the AIDS Memorial Quilt, based on a theme from the 1939 New York World's Fair. That December, he sent a copy of the design to the NAMES Project, the San Francisco–based organization that administered the quilt. The following month, Gaver mailed a brief journal entry—illustrated with a black-and-white photograph of Jackie Kennedy at her husband's state funeral—to close family and friends, informing them that he had only four to five months left. "One thing to keep in mind," he wrote in closing, "this is a relatively painless way to die—so I won't be in a lot of pain (I hope)." A few weeks later, Gaver sent a polite but firm letter to the Washington Better Business Bureau complaining about the rude service he had encountered at the pharmacy where he picked up his medications. The half-page typewritten letter took him forty-five minutes to compose.

On March 11, 1989, Chasen Gaver died at home. At his memorial service, held in a Quaker meetinghouse on Florida Avenue, a friend, dressed in drag as Diana Ross, performed the national anthem and "Ain't No Mountain High Enough." A tape recording was played of Gaver discussing the role of various women in his life, and the Reagan appointee for whom he had worked at the FTC read aloud one of his poems. (Public officials delivering eulogies for their AIDS-afflicted staffers were a regular occurrence in late 1980s Washington. After Texas Democratic senator Lloyd Bentsen, fresh from losing his campaign for the vice presidency in 1988, concluded a tribute to his former staffer Tim Furlong, "I don't think anybody that was at that funeral who went in a Republican, left a Republican," one attendee recalled.) Gaver's work as an art critic for the *Blade* prompted one of his longtime detractors to compose a letter to the editor assessing his legacy. "I have been angered by Chasen Gaver's reviews and articles on arts for as long as I've been reading the *Blade*," the long-suffering reader began. But over time, she had come to develop an appreciation for the late artist's discerning eye and cultivated taste. "I'm a better reader, reviewer, and probably a better dyke because of his influence."

In 1991, students at Gaver's alma mater, the College of Wooster, finished the panel he had begun before sickness intervened, thereby fulfilling his dying wish to be included "among the wonderful, creative and brave people in the Quilt."

GEORGE H. W. BUSH

There is only one thing in the world worse than being talked about, and that is not being talked about.

—Oscar Wilde

42

NAMING NAMES

THE DECLINE OF CRAIG SPENCE, HIS FRIENDS WOULD LATER SAY, BEGAN around the summer of 1988. His work for Japan had dried up the previous year, and "the more often you came to Craig's house," Scott Thompson remarked of the declining quality of the guest list at 2445 Wyoming Avenue, "the more likely you were a misfit." Long gone were the days when a gathering chez Spence merited comparisons to those legendary meetings of the minds presided over by Ethel Kennedy and Arthur Schlesinger at Hickory Hill. "The more you were a real catch," Thompson said, "the less likely you were to come back."

Spence's associates began noticing strange behavior, stranger than what they had amusedly grown accustomed to during his reign at the pinnacle of Washington social life. Spence frequently alluded to working for the CIA; according to one friend, he once claimed "the Company" might "double cross" him by killing him and making it "look like a suicide." A growing phalanx of bodyguards, apparently off-duty GIs, would circulate throughout the crowd at Spence's parties, communicating by cuff mics and plastic earphones, and they followed him everywhere he went. At John Mitchell's funeral in St. Alban's Episcopal Church, Spence arrived with two limousines and an entourage of six muscular young men who, he bragged, were more efficient than Richard Nixon's Secret Service detail for extracting him out of the building first.

Unable to live within his means, Spence decided to downsize by selling his Kalorama house. Before relocating to a condo, he invited friends from around the world to Washington for a final bash on Fourth of July weekend, promising them a specially arranged tour of the White House. On the evening of July 3, as guests including a Catholic law professor, the son of a Chinese military officer, and a retired Italian opera singer milled about his entry hall, the fading forty-seven-year-old doyen of Washington society suddenly made a grand entrance atop the staircase, like Norma Desmond in *Sunset Boulevard*. "Ah, well, here we are," he announced. "Old friends on the nation's birthday." After the party wound down, a group left for the White House, where they asked for the uniformed Secret Service officer named Reggie, who, Spence had told them, would lead their special tour. At the end of their visit, which included a stop for pictures in the White House barber shop, Reggie handed an eight-by-twelve-by-six-inch sealed white box containing "something that rolled around" to one of the participants, with instructions that it be given to Spence.

On June 29, 1989, nearly a year to the day after this nocturnal excursion to the presidential mansion, a double-deck banner headline atop the front page of the *Washington Times* heralded the scandal that would dominate the remaining months of the capital's silly season, one with more than a passing resemblance to another summer-long uproar from the not-so-distant past. "Homosexual Prostitution Inquiry Ensnares VIPs with Reagan, Bush," the paper declared over a story that had the potential to become a major headache for Reagan's successor, George H. W. Bush. The shocking tale began with a February raid by several law enforcement agencies, including the Secret Service, of a home in Chevy Chase, Maryland, that had served as a dispatch hub for a network of male prostitution companies operating under the innocuous name "Professional Services Inc." Many of the escort service's clients had used credit cards for payment, and reports of unauthorized purchases made with those card numbers led to the identification of a merchant account associated with the Chevy Chase address. An enterprising *Times* reporter named Paul M. Rodriguez discovered that Professional Services was a subsidiary of Chambers Funeral Home, one of the leading mortuary chains in the Washington area, and that its off-the-books bookkeeper was one Robert Chambers, fourth of the owner's eight children. To mask its true purpose, the escort service listed sexual services as various mortuary products ("cremation urn, $150"), giving a whole new meaning to the French expression for orgasm, *la petite mort.*

Rodriguez appeared at the Chambers Funeral Home headquarters asking to see the family's black sheep. "He was nervous," Rodriguez recalled of Chambers. "Very effeminate. I told him I could help them get law enforcement off their backs if he could provide us names of high-profile clients." At this offer of assistance, the desperate Chambers led Rodriguez to a back room where there were several cabinets filled with credit card receipts. The mortician and would-be pimp gave the reporter a blue women's Samsonite cosmetic case and told him to take as many receipts as he could stuff into it. Like a pirate finding buried treasure, Rodriguez greedily filled the bag that he and his *Times* colleagues would call "the football," a reference to the briefcase carried by the president's military aide containing nuclear launch codes.

It was an apt moniker, for judged solely by the amount of ink the *Times* devoted to the "White House call boy scandal" over the ensuing five months, the paper expected the fallout to be the political equivalent of a nuclear strike on Washington. As Rodriguez and his coauthor on the initial June 29 piece, George Archibald, breathlessly wrote, the clientele of Professional Services—comprising "key officials of the Reagan and Bush administrations, military officers, congressional aides and U.S. and foreign businessmen with close social ties to Washington's political elite"—was so "well-connected" that one client had been able to arrange a "middle-of-the-night tour of the White House" for several friends and "two male prostitutes." According to "a former top-level Pentagon officer," the revelations were extremely concerning to senior U.S. intelligence officials, already ridden with anxiety thanks to "a nest of homosexuals at top levels of the Reagan administration" that "may have been penetrated by Soviet backed espionage agents."

Though the *Times* said it would "only print the names of those found to be in sensitive government posts or positions of influence," none of the men it identified as clients could be described as such. Paul Balach, a low-ranking staffer in the Labor Department, shamefacedly confessed to the paper that "loneliness and laziness" had led him into the arms of a male prostitute who returned his affections by charging tens of thousands of dollars to his credit card. Ironically, it was Balach's complaint about this theft that had spurred the police investigation leading to his public humiliation and professional downfall. The day the *Times* story appeared, Balach's boss informed him that he could resign or be fired. "Somebody else is going to clean out my office," he told the paper. "They didn't want me to come back into my office."

Charles Dutcher, a former associate director of presidential personnel in the Reagan administration and, before that, an aide to Congressman Bob Bauman, told the *Times* he was "bisexual," had patronized the service due to "stress," had used it just once for thirty-five minutes, and that the sex "was safe—extremely . . . I've had friends who died of AIDS." He also said that the Reagan administration was "very tolerant towards gays" and that "Nancy Reagan, half her friends were gay." Nonetheless, Dutcher assured the paper, in all his time working at the White House, he had never knowingly put a homosexual in a government job.

"I am innocent," the third man named by the paper, Todd A. Blodgett, declared. A lowly opposition researcher at the Republican National Committee, and, thus, like the other men named by the *Times*, hardly a person in a "position of influence," Blodgett said it was a gay friend who had charged $325 to his American Express card for a male escort. Depending on whether Blodgett was telling the truth, that friend, a Boston antiques dealer named Benedict J. Hastings, was either a world-class scrounger or a remarkably selfless fall guy. In a meeting at the paper's offices, Hastings explained that he had decided to throw a party in Blodgett's apartment at the last minute and was in urgent need of a bartender—but not just any bartender. "I needed . . . someone who would wear just a black bow tie and [under]shorts," he said, and he therefore used his friend's credit card to hire one.

By revealing the involvement of three anonymous bureaucrats in "crimes" that the police had no intention of pursuing (on the contrary, it was their status as *victims* of credit card fraud that drew the interest of law enforcement, including the Secret Service, which investigates such cases), the *Times* caused these men needless embarrassment. But in its reckless determination to name names, the paper also embarrassed itself. According to managing editor Wesley Pruden, when Rodriguez opened the "football" and dumped the hundreds of credit card vouchers onto a desk, "just about the first one that tumbled out was our own man." In a farcical demonstration of the "boomerang" effect that Max Lerner had identified nearly four decades earlier, it turned out that an assistant managing editor who had previously worked in the White House Office of Personnel Management was himself a client of Professional Services. The editor admitted to contacting the agency, not to hire male escorts, but to interview two *female* escorts for the purposes of an "investigation" he was conducting into prostitution. Alas, this assignment was news to his superiors, who promptly asked for, and received, his resignation. That their "own man" would have been among the clients ought hardly have come as a shock to *Times* management. According to *Washington City Paper* editor Jack Shafer, like virtually every other establishment in Washington, the conservative daily had a "near-Kinseyian percentage of gays and lesbians" on its staff.

The most prominent person the *Times* would ever name was the man whose rapid ascent up the Washington social ladder at the start of the decade had so dazzled the city's elites, and whose just-as-precipitous fall from grace the paper would cover as a story of world historical significance. "Power Broker Served Drugs, Sex at Parties Bugged for Blackmail," read the headline over another blockbuster *Times* exclusive, the first of more than sixty items it published about Spence that year. The lobbyist, wrote reporters Michael Hedges and Jerry Seper, had spent tens of thousands of dollars on male escorts from Professional Services, two of whom participated in a midnight White House tour Spence had arranged the previous July, one of four tours he organized for friends and business associates. The paper interviewed numerous attendees at Spence's "glittery parties for key officials of the Reagan and Bush administrations," one of whom recounted the time Spence dispatched a limousine to pick him up. Over the course of the evening, he met several suspiciously friendly young men. "I didn't bite, it's not my inclination," the guest said. "But he used his homosexual network for all it was worth." A parade of "current and former friends" attested to a gamut of disreputable behavior, ranging from Spence's heavy cocaine use to the "tall, handsome, stalwart young men" whom "he liked to surround himself with [as] decorations" and the eight-foot-long two-way mirror hanging over his library that many suspected was used to entrap guests in compromising sexual encounters. Many of the city's boldfaced names, who had happily partaken of Spence's hospitality, rushed to defend themselves. "I think it's quite clear that perfectly innocent people can be inadvertently used by someone who is leading a double life," former U.S. attorney Joseph diGenova, who had accompanied Spence on a trip to Japan, told the *Washington Post*. "I am, of course, appalled," said former ambassador to Saudi Arabia Robert Neumann, for whom Spence had thrown a going-away party at the Four Seasons in 1981. The two men were mere acquaintances, Neumann emphasized, but "that's how Washington works." The depredations of Spence's cohost for that party, John Mitchell, who was convicted on multiple counts of conspiracy, obstruction of justice, and perjury related to his role in Watergate, and who had arranged for his wife to be held captive to keep her from speaking to the press, were apparently not so appalling.

Spence's "trump card" as a Washington power broker, the South Korean–owned newspaper averred, was the "access to high-ranking orientals" he provided to American government officials and business leaders, and the appearance of his name on the client list of a male outcall service was therefore a matter with serious national security implications. "We have known for many, many years that there is a department of the KGB whose job it is to prey on sexual deviants," a former head of the Defense Intelligence Agency, Lt. Gen. Daniel Graham, told the *Times*, adding that "we have always in intelligence tried very hard not to be giving classified information to known homosexuals." And yet, somehow this knowledge, accrued from "many, many years" of service atop the American intelligence apparatus, had failed to inhibit Graham from accepting an all-expenses-paid trip to Japan from, and speaking at an exclusive policy seminar hosted by, none other than Craig Spence—a seemingly relevant relationship that the *Times* curiously overlooked in its voluminous coverage of coke, corruption, and callboys.

Immediately after the story hit newsstands, Spence's friend Liz Trotta recalled, "Almost everyone who knew him turned on their answering machines." Spence skipped town, and one of the last sightings of him was by a friend who entered his apartment only to find him hanging upside down from a metal bar affixed to a doorframe like the actor Michael Keaton in the titular role of that summer's blockbuster film *Batman*. Some associates reported Spence speaking cryptically about his impending death at the hands of a shadowy intelligence service. There were also rumors concerning his health, though none of his friends could say what had caused his apparent sickness. "I can unhappily confirm that," one acquaintance told the *Times* when asked about Spence's poor physical state. "He has been in ill health. I am not truly aware of what it is that is wrong with him."

Over at *Times* headquarters, a brick behemoth whose remote location on the Maryland border the paper's partisans cited as evidence of its independence from the liberal Beltway elite, editor in chief Arnaud de Borchgrave was giddy. "One of the most powerful guys in the city told me 'If you guys don't get the Pulitzer for this one, then there is no justice,'" he crowed. A former Belgian count who renounced his title to become an American citizen, de Borchgrave rivaled Spence for eccentricity, and nearly matched him for delusions of grandeur. At any moment during the day or night, *Times* reporters might experience a downfall of "yellow rain," a flurry of lemon-colored index cards with news tips scrawled on them that de Borchgrave, donning blue silk pajamas, would shower over the newsroom from the balcony outside his second-floor office. Under his direction, the scrappy conservative paper covered the Spence story as if it were the biggest Washington scandal since the one famously exposed by its downtown competitor. "This story is going to be much like Watergate," de Borchgrave confidently predicted. "It will go on for months; each time you shake the tree, something else falls out of it." Public demand for wall-to-wall coverage of the man whom the *Times* described as "the elusive Mr. Spence" was so high, de Borchgrave claimed, that he increased the paper's daily print run by ten thousand copies. He specially dispatched a group of *Times* newsboys to hawk papers on the sidewalk directly outside the *Post's* office on Fifteenth Street.

Central to the paper's coverage of the Spence story was an aspect of his identity that Trotta had described as "a remote presence," but that the *Times* treated as the clarifying essence of his persona. "Just as the nocturnal tourists are now 'in,' so the tour leader seems on the way 'out,'" taunted an unsigned item. "Another of the cognoscenti was heard to declare, 'That Craig Spence! Compared to him, Spitz Channell is Mr. Cordiality.'" Managing editor Wesley Pruden mocked the *Post* for its hesitance to report on "the dandy little Craig" and his "sordid after-hours life on Wyoming Avenue, where no self-respecting AIDS virus would have dared tread." While Washington's corrupt and perverted elites failed to recognize him as the moral degenerate he was, Spence "would have been seen early on as a phony by any Texarkana Toyota mechanic or Waukesha waste-management tycoon." Echoing Tony Dolan's "advertisements for his brother" in the *Times* two years earlier, Pruden gestured toward a shadowy, sexually aberrant influence over the *Post*. "Katharine Graham doesn't want to embarrass her dinner-party A-list, which was, of course, Craig Spence's dinner-party A-list," he wrote, passing over the inconvenient fact that his own editor, de Borchgrave, had once been on said A-list, and not the *Post* publisher.

The *Times*'s flogging of the Spence story was consistent with its fear-mongering coverage of homosexuality. In 1983, seventy-one *Times* staffers signed a letter protesting a cartoon that the paper published mocking AIDS patients, to which editors replied that homosexual behavior was responsible for the disease and that federal AIDS funding research was too high. (When gay activists subsequently met with the *Times* leadership to complain, they gestured toward the editors' cigarette packs on the table and asked if they believed funding for cancer research was similarly excessive.) *Times* reporters who strove for objectivity bristled when the managing editor invariably "prudenized" their copy to disparage gays, and the paper's institutional bias against homosexuality grew so extreme that it "became the subject of concerned interoffice messaging among the closeted gays at the paper," according to one gay staffer who worked at the *Times* in the late 1980s. In an editorial published amid the paper's crusade against Spence entitled "Frisco on the Potomac?" the *Times* urged its readers to attend a public meeting of a DC commission studying the feasibility of a proposal, modeled on a measure adopted in San Francisco, to provide benefits to the same-sex partners of municipal employees. Gay relationships, the paper inveighed, were akin to "a good old boy's relationship with his hunting dog, or an elderly lady's with her pet parakeet." Alas, just one reader took up the charge.

As had been the case the last time a scandal involving male prostitutes and men in high places roiled an otherwise lazy Washington summer, the 1989 White House callboy story fizzled once most of its shocking allegations failed to pan out. Craig Spence was indeed a frequent customer of Professional Services Inc., but none of its stable of "Dream Boys" or "Jack's Jocks" had received a White House tour. ("The thing you never knew about the people he had at his house," one Spence friend recalled, "was which ones were rent boys and which ones were the actual Marines.") Spence's worst offense, it appeared, was his apparent trading of an eight-thousand-dollar Rolex watch for a piece of White House china from the Truman collection ("this little 'dish,' as Rosalynn Carter would say"), stolen for him by the Secret Service officer who led the tour. "To this day, I still believe that Craig is still an American hero," the guard said, making clear that "the guy never hit on me."

* * *

WHILE IT FELL FAR SHORT OF BEING ANOTHER WATERGATE, the *Times* crusade to expose "high level" homosexuals honeycombed throughout the government inspired a reassessment of the previous Republican president. According to an advisor close to RNC chairman Lee Atwater, a struggle for power was being waged at the time within the GOP between "those who want to clean out homosexuals from government" and "more pragmatic types" willing to tolerate gays so long as they stayed in the closet. The *Times* series brought these "subsurface tensions" to the fore, giving social conservatives a scapegoat to blame for the perceived failures of the Reagan administration in advancing their agenda. Perhaps, they speculated, the reason President Reagan had failed to implement prayer in public schools or pass a constitutional amendment banning abortion was because of the gays who had permeated his administration. "That's not surprising because the Reagans, after all, were Hollywood folks," one former Reagan official observed. "Even their straight friends were a little odd, and Nancy Reagan's hairdresser and his [male] lover stayed in the White House." (It was actually her interior designer.) Paul Weyrich speculated that the paper's revelations "would explain a certain resistance to pro-family policies on the part of the Reagan administration which were popular and in the interest of the administration."

Invariably, the latest iteration of the homosexual panic involved that highly coveted Washington bounty: the list of covert homosexuals. "What are they saying, that you should have sexual-preference checks on people that come into the White House?" an exasperated White House press secretary Marlin Fitzwater asked in response to queries about whether his boss, in the words of the *Times*, "considered it appropriate for male prostitutes to be touring the White House at 1 a.m." As one Democratic consultant put it, "right-wing Republicans might like to use it against other Republicans they don't like, but they don't have the top names yet." In the absence of top Republicans, a top Democrat would have to suffice.

As the Spence scandal unraveled, congressional Democrats were ousting their party's Speaker of the House, Jim Wright, whom an ethics investigation had faulted for taking bribes. Among Wright's allies, word spread of a mysterious FBI report containing "wild and ridiculous accusations" against his probable successor, Representative Tom Foley of Washington State. Eventually, the rumors crossed the aisle, where they mutated and took on sickening new form. "We hear it's little boys," an aide to House Republican whip Newt Gingrich told a handful of reporters, performing the Washington equivalent of pouring gasoline on a fire by adding that their journalistic competitors were already investigating the charges. On June 5, the day before Foley assumed the speakership, RNC communications director Mark Goodin distributed a memo to state GOP leaders entitled, "Tom Foley: Out of the Liberal Closet." Lest there be any doubt as to his aim with this insinuation, Goodin included a side-by-side comparison of Foley's voting record with that of a colleague who just happened to be one of only two openly gay members of Congress, Barney Frank of Massachusetts. Republican Senate leader Bob Dole called the memo "garbage" and President Bush said it was "disgusting." But in their vehemence, these outraged Republican reactions illustrated the problematic premise of the controversy, or any controversy involving an accusation of homosexuality, which is the assumption that it constitutes an insult. (Goodin's "appeal to mindless bigotry," wrote Hendrik Hertzberg in the *New Republic*, was "combined with a groundless imputation of the quality on which the bigotry battens.") What ultimately foiled the smear campaign against Foley was not Republican professions of outrage from the president on down, but Frank's threat to start naming names in retaliation. "I think if they don't cut the crap, something might happen and I'm going to happen it," the legendarily blunt Democrat warned his Republican colleagues. "The right to privacy and the right to hypocrisy do not coexist." Frank's exception to the Code—that the revelation of a public figure's homosexuality is justified if they use their political power to harm homosexuals—would come to be known as the "Frank rule."

"Where in the world is Craig Spence?" was the most popular parlor game in the summer of 1989, with sightings (or imaginings) of him reported at a Georgetown disco (sans cape), reading his favorite novel of unrequited love while lounging within a gondola along a Venice canal, kicking back a few with his favorite bartender at the Tokyo Hilton, visiting his old haunts in his "hometown" of Boston, yapping away in the greenroom of his friend

Ted Koppel's show *Nightline*, sitting morosely on the seat of a Washington, DC, city bus, or engaged in one final mission for the CIA, which, he claimed, was using the prostitution service whose models he so fancied as a front to blackmail foreign intelligence officials and diplomats. Friends reported hang-up calls at random hours, a "classic" Spence tactic to express displeasure, while others described him saying things like "Casey's boys are out to get me," a reference to his erstwhile dinner companion, former CIA director William Casey, who had died two years earlier.

At 9 a.m. on July 31, officers from the New York City Police Department arrested Spence with a twenty-two-year-old prostitute after finding cocaine, a crack pipe, and an unloaded 9 mm pistol in Spence's room at the Barbizon Hotel. Upon his release on personal recognizance, Spence gave a rambling interview to a pair of *New York Times* reporters who had tracked him down to a friend's apartment on the Upper East Side. Over the course of several hours, Spence delivered a scattershot disquisition about his varied life, imminent death, and the shameless hypocrisy of the VIPs who gravitated toward him when he had access to power only to wash their hands of him the second he lost it. "How do you think a little faggot like me moved in the circles I did?" he boasted. "It's because I had contacts at the highest levels of this government. They'll deny it. But how do they make me go away, when so many of them have been at my house, at my parties and at my side?"

The most unsettling revelation Spence made was one that neither the reporters recording it for posterity nor the Washingtonians voyeuristically watching his epic downfall appreciated at the time. "Mr. Spence said the discovery in 1986 that he had AIDS triggered his descent into using call boys and crack," reporters Michael Hedges and Jerry Seper revealed in a piece published on the front page of the *Times*. Aside from a brief sentence containing Spence's claim that the only thing he had left behind in his Washington apartment were vials of the anti-AIDS medicine AZT, the *Times* reporters did not address this topic again until the very last sentence of the story, where they quoted Spence saying that he had learned he had the disease "about three years ago," after his doctor advised him to take a test at Johns Hopkins Medical Center. Judging by the press coverage of Spence up to that moment, replete with hair-raising disclosures from "current and former friends," there had to have been very few people in whom

636 | JAMES KIRCHICK

Spence confided his diagnosis. After all the posturing, the sensationalism and the intrigue, the drama and the mystery, the grubby truth that no one wanted to confront much less discuss was that, like the ailing men whose lugubrious presence inside the windowed patio at Annie's Paramount Steak House earned it the morbid nickname of the "glass coffin"—Craig Spence was just another victim of the plague.

"Rumors of my death have been greatly exaggerated," Spence told a small group of friends three months later over a black-tie dinner at his favorite haunt in Washington, where the staff was so delighted to see their former customer in fighting trim that they presented him with a one-hundred-thirty-year-old bottle of brandy. Spence had adopted a droll perspective about his pummeling in the media, expressing frustration at how another scandal involving the *Washington Times*, male prostitution, and a gay public figure (Barney Frank, embroiled in a House Ethics Committee investigation over his relationship with Professional Services Inc's most indiscreet former employee, Steven Gobie, with whom Spence also happened to be acquainted) was surpassing his own in notoriety. A few days later, Spence checked into Room 429 at the Ritz-Carlton in Boston, whose obliging staff would remember him as by turns flagrantly rude and inexplicably generous, demanding chocolate truffles and flowers at random hours while doling out two-hundred-dollar tips. In the early afternoon of November 10, a caller to the hotel switchboard reported that he had just spoken to a guest named Craig Spence, who was in need of urgent help. No one with that name was registered at the hotel, however, and it took some time before the staff at the front desk surmised that the tempestuous lodger in 429, known to the staff as "C. S. Kane" (a reference to Charles Foster Kane, the eponymous newspaper baron of Orson Welles's 1941 film *Citizen Kane*), might be the elusive Mr. Spence. By the time they broke through the barricaded door to his room, it was too late. Lying on the bed wearing a black tuxedo with white suspenders and a white bow tie, his black shoes freshly polished and three dollars in his pocket, was Craig Spence. A Walkman headset playing Mozart's *A Little Night Music* was dangling from his neck, and a recent newspaper clipping about the CIA's attempt to protect the identities of its operatives lay by his side.

He had overdosed on pills. Written on the mirror in black felt-tip marker was a note:

Chief,

Consider this my resignation, effective immediately. As you always said, you can't ask others to make a sacrifice if you are not ready to do the same. Life is duty. God bless America.

To the Ritz, please forgive this inconvenience.

Today, Craig Spence is largely forgotten. In the madcap, highly publicized final months of his life, and in the wake of his no-less-bizarre death, he was portrayed as one of the great Washington mountebanks, a fraud and a con man who lied and flattered his way into the good graces of the city's A-listers. In this sense, he served as a useful foil for a variety of Washington players and agendas. He was the target of moralistic denunciation by a right-wing newspaper determined to turn his life into a cautionary tale for other closeted gay conservatives, earnest lectures from more respectable precincts about the unseemly world of Beltway influence-peddling, and plain ridicule from nearly everyone else. But as much as Spence's ten-year odyssey across Washington stands as a testament to his personal cunning, so, too, did it expose a certain pretense among the capital's most socially prominent citizens, whose susceptibility to the fraudulence and flattery they claimed to detest Spence unwittingly revealed.

Hypocrisy its lifeblood, Washington was simultaneously the gayest and most antigay city in America, a place where Phyllis Schlafly could inveigh against the homosexual menace during the day and attend a party at the home of its most prolific connoisseur of male prostitutes that same night. Like many people who come to Washington, Spence had reinvented himself, lying about his humble origins and boasting about his work for various intelligence services. And in that sense, his glamorous ascendance fueled by these deceptions, his swift decline as the contradictions became too great, and his ultimate demise due to AIDS can be seen as a metaphor for the decade-long trajectory of a particular gay conservative Washington milieu.

"I've had the world at my house and now they don't know who I am," Spence said three months before his suicide. "But they did come, didn't they?"

★ ★ ★

"SINCE PERSECUTION IS NOT AN OPTION IN A CIVILIZED SOCIETY, why not coax gays into traditional values rather than rail incoherently against them?" So asked a twenty-six-year-old gay, English-born, Irish Catholic former president of the Oxford Union named Andrew Sullivan in the August 28, 1989, edition of the *New Republic*. The liberal journal of politics and the arts could stake a serious claim to covering homosexuality with more depth and sophistication than any other general interest periodical in America, publishing work by Martin Duberman, John Boswell, and George Chauncey, three of the leading scholars in the emerging field of gay history. Despite this pedigree and the magazine's well-earned reputation for contrarianism, "Here Comes the Groom: A (Conservative) Case for Gay Marriage," left most readers—and staffers—perplexed.

Sullivan had pitched his idea on a lark during one of the magazine's freewheeling weekly editorial meetings. Citing a recent decision by a New York court to grant a gay man the right to stay in his deceased partner's rent-controlled apartment, Sullivan proposed that gays be given the same right to civil marriage as heterosexuals. Most of Sullivan's colleagues around the table scoffed. Not necessarily because they were homophobic but because the idea was so outlandish, not least among gays, many of whom viewed marriage as emblematic of the patriarchal system under which they suffered and against which they rebelled.

Crucially, one of the few people in the meeting not to sneer was the magazine's brilliant editor, Michael Kinsley, whose advice to young writers—"If you think you've gone too far, you haven't gone far enough," and "write it now, because you won't want to when you're older"—had initially attracted Sullivan to work at the magazine. Long after its publication, "Here Comes the Groom" stands as one of the most influential articles in the magazine's century-plus-long history. In 1988, the first year that the General Social Survey polled the American public on the subject, only 11.6 percent of respondents said gay couples should have the right to marry. Thirty years later, that share grew to 68 percent. In terms of the speed and the degree of the shift in public opinion, the campaign for same-sex marriage might be considered the most successful social movement in American history.

Sullivan became editor of the *New Republic* in 1991. Under his leadership, the magazine continued its bracing coverage of homosexuality, including one subject that became a major cultural and political question of the 1990s: outing. Since the *New York Post*'s campaign against Sen.

David Walsh in 1942, the tactic of disclosing the homosexuality of a public figure had been employed many times. But the phenomenon would not earn the designation of "outing" until 1990, when *Time* published an article about a bundle of controversies regarding the naming of gay names. The major difference between the earlier spates of exposure and more recent ones concerned the people doing the exposing. Whereas before the outers had been almost exclusively straight, now many of them were gay. The most high-profile case concerned Defense Department spokesman Pete Williams, who had emerged as the public face of the Gulf War, the first armed conflict to be televised in real time around the world. Himself a former TV reporter, Williams was naturally suited for the role of on-air talent, so much so that he developed a fan club among female news junkies. "It would be nice to find him a wife," said Williams's assistant, Carole Manlove, whose unimprovable surname hinted at why he had yet to find one. The *New York Times* reported that Williams was "showered" with marriage proposals from smitten women across the country, but that "marriage, or even a social life, does not seem to be part of his agenda at the moment." Williams was not exactly closeted in Washington. But his senior position within an institution that discriminated against gays was cited as evidence of hypocrisy by the group Queer Nation, one of whose leaders, Michael Petrelis, had declared open season on people like Williams the previous spring when he stood on the steps of the Capitol before a pack of reporters and identified three senators, five congresspeople, two governors, an official of a northeastern city, and an entertainment industry icon as gay.

With Williams, Queer Nation took its confrontational tactics to another level, plastering two hundred and fifty posters around Washington with a photo of his face beneath the words "Absolutely Queer." When Jack Anderson heard that Williams was considering resigning, he disclosed Williams's homosexuality in his syndicated column, to which some eight hundred newspapers, including six in Williams's home state of Wyoming, subscribed. When Wyoming newspapers had printed a sensitive story concerning homosexuality nearly forty years earlier in the case of Sen. Lester Hunt, it ended in tragedy. This time, after Secretary of Defense Dick Cheney told Barney Frank during a congressional hearing that the military policy deeming gay people security risks was "a bit of an old chestnut," and further stated on ABC News that he had no intention of asking Williams to quit, much of Washington shrugged.

Cheney was a rare figure of tolerance on the right, however, and for gays who didn't enjoy the allegiance of a politically powerful patron, the threat of being outed was a constant worry. Michael Hess, a lawyer for the Republican National Committee, once snatched a camera out of the hands of a man who had used it to take a photograph of him standing with a group of friends at a Chicago leather bar and, according to one of those present, "broke it into pieces." Visiting a gay bar after the last night of the 1988 Republican convention in New Orleans, a young lawyer for the Bush campaign named Trevor Potter recalled encountering a shocked Hess.

"What are you doing here?" Hess asked Potter. The two men had sat in meetings together at RNC headquarters in Washington, but neither knew the other was gay.

"Well, I came out for a drink," Potter replied.

"Someone's going to see you," Hess said incredulously.

"Well, somebody might see you, Michael."

BILL CLINTON

He said a little prayer of thankfulness, sitting there at his desk in the United States Senate, to all the men and women back over the centuries who by their dreaming and their striving and their working and their dying had made it possible for their heirs to take with them into so dark and fearful a future so great and wonderful a gift and so strong and invincible an armor.

—Allen Drury, *Advise and Consent*

43

A PROFOUNDLY
IMPORTANT STRENGTH

"I HAVE A VISION, AND YOU ARE A PART OF IT." WITH THOSE TEN WORDS, uttered in Los Angeles on May 18, 1992, Bill Clinton did something that no candidate who went on to become the presidential nominee of a major party had yet done: make an explicit appeal to gay people for their support. The event at which he did so raised a hundred thousand dollars for his campaign, but something far greater was produced inside the Palace Theatre that evening: the glimmer of recognition that gay people ought to be treated as equal citizens.

The divide between the leading presidential candidates on this question was stark. At the Democratic National Convention in New York City, a gay Clinton campaign staffer with AIDS, Bob Hattoy, delivered a moving speech in prime time. At the Republican gathering in Houston, Pat Buchanan, who had mounted a surprisingly strong primary challenge to President Bush from the right under the slogan "America First," spoke ominously of a "culture war" and elicited boos from the crowd when he mentioned that a "militant leader of the homosexual rights movement" had praised the Democrats as "the most pro-lesbian and pro-gay ticket in history." First Lady Barbara Bush, who had written a letter two years earlier to the president of the Parents and Friends of Lesbians and Gays stating that "we cannot tolerate discrimination against any individuals or groups in our country," wore a red AIDS ribbon on her lapel throughout the RNC convention. Yet she took it off before joining her husband onstage.

A Gallup poll conducted after the conventions found that over a quarter of voters believed the Republicans had overdone it in their attacks on gays. With 43 percent of Americans now reporting that they knew a gay person (double the number from just seven years earlier), the palpably different approaches by the two parties to the matter of how America ought to treat its gay citizens contributed to a broader perception that the incumbent was a man of the past and his challenger a man of the future. At Clinton's inauguration, the gay activist David Mixner, who had known the new president since their days as anti–Vietnam War activists, struggled with a dilemma unknown and unfathomable to the gay men and women who had come before him: whether to dance with his male date at an inaugural ball. After a great deal of arguing the pros and cons with himself and his friends, Mixner decided to do it. As a space cleared around the two men on the dance floor, Mixner's heart momentarily sank . . . until an older, straight couple sidled up next to them and said, "We always like to dance next to the best dancers."

Clinton was the first president to recruit gay people to work in his administration. In November 1993, the Office of Personnel Management (formerly the Civil Service Commission, and therefore the bureaucratic legatee of the federal government's historic effort to expel gay workers) recognized a chapter of the Gay, Lesbian or Bisexual Employees (GLOBE), kicking off a cascade of other agencies and cabinet departments doing the same. Conversing with his colleagues in the office, one gay OPM employee breathed a sigh of relief that there was no longer any need for the "pronoun playing" of the past to disguise the identity of his partner.

"This is the thing of the 90s," enthused lesbian Democratic Party activist Hilary Rosen, and there was no better barometer of the zeitgeist than the magazine in which her declaration appeared, *Vanity Fair*. Its article about the waves of change emanating out of Washington, "The Gay Nineties," heralded a seismic shift in public perception. One unforeseen aspect of the new gay visibility was its impact on the conversation about powerful women political figures. Never had so many women occupied positions of influence and power in Washington, jobs requiring attributes (determination, decisiveness, ruthless pragmatism) that lesbians were assumed to possess in abundance over their heterosexual peers. Starting with First Lady Hillary Clinton, who had famously dispelled the notion during the campaign that she would "bake cookies" or be "standing by my man like Tammy Wynette" as a presidential spouse, several other high-profile women in the Clinton administration faced charges of lesbianism. "Have I lived an alternative lifestyle?" Health and Human Services secretary Donna Shalala asked in response to the accusation from Queer Nation that she was gay. "The answer is no." Attorney General Janet Reno, like Shalala also unmarried, had earlier denied gay rumors while running for office in Florida. "I'm attracted to strong, brave, rational and intelligent men," she said when a right-wing group recirculated the charges in advance of her confirmation hearings. "The White House satisfied itself that Reno is not gay," reported National Public Radio, though how it came to that conclusion, or why it mattered, was not divulged. As for the first openly gay person to receive Senate confirmation for a cabinet department position, Assistant Secretary for Housing and Urban Development Roberta Achtenberg, to Jesse Helms she was nothing more than "a damn lesbian."

Less than three months into the new administration, on April 25, 1993, some three hundred thousand people converged on the National Mall for the March on Washington for Lesbian, Gay, and Bi Equal Rights and Liberation. Their demands echoed those that had been issued at the first such march, in 1979, along with those newly added at the second, in 1987: passage of antidiscrimination legislation, repeal of sodomy laws, the right to serve openly in the military, and increased funding to combat HIV/AIDS. President Clinton sent a five-paragraph letter of support, read aloud by Congresswoman Nancy Pelosi. Clinton's compromise position on the issue of gays in the military, a policy that would allow them to serve but not openly, encapsulated as "Don't Ask, Don't Tell, Don't Harass, Don't Pursue," was one of his first missteps as president, engendering feelings of betrayal from gay activists and a backlash from congressional Republicans. When one of their leaders, GOP House whip Newt Gingrich, had resisted President Bush's tax increases in 1990, it was a character from Allen Drury's *Advise and Consent* who had inspired him. Four years later, as he led Republicans to their first House majority since Eisenhower, Gingrich assigned the novel to his caucus as homework. Drury's message on homosexuality, alas, was lost on the new Speaker. Defending three of his colleagues who had said that they would not hire gay staffers, Gingrich stated that homosexuality was an orientation "like alcoholism is an orientation."

On August 2, 1995, Clinton partly made up for his blunder on gays in the military by signing an executive order rescinding homosexuality as a cause for denying a security clearance. Executive Order 12968 effectively overturned his predecessor Dwight Eisenhower's Executive Order 10450, reversing a more than forty-year-old policy of exclusion. The move by no means marked the end of the struggle for gay legal equality, bookended as it was by the implementation of "Don't Ask, Don't Tell" the year prior and Clinton's signing the Defense of Marriage Act, which prohibited the federal government from recognizing same-sex marriages, the year after. Both measures would be repealed during the presidency of Clinton's Democratic successor, Barack Obama, who lit up the north face of the White House in the rainbow colors of the Gay Pride flag when the Supreme Court recognized the right of same-sex couples to wed in 2015.

* * *

WHEN THE WHITMAN-WALKER CLINIC OPENED its Elizabeth Taylor Medical Center on Fourteenth Street in 1993, it installed frosted glass windows to protect the anonymity of its patients. Twelve thousand Washingtonians had died of AIDS by that year, though the lesbian doctor Pat Hawkins stopped entering the names of victims she knew into her "death book" once she reached five hundred. "I couldn't cope anymore," she recalled. "I just couldn't write another name in that book." The introduction of lifesaving drug therapies in the middle of the decade brought a welcome change to the composition of the *Blade*, which, according to one reader, "once fat with obituaries, shrunk when the cocktails came." At conventions of the Log Cabin Republicans, a gay GOP group, President Rich Tafel had to ensure that the hotel rooms were stocked with refrigerators because so many of his attendees needed them to store their medications.

It was too late for some. "His IQ is lower than my T-cell count," John Ford would joke with his sister about this or that handsome young man lacking in the smarts department. Over the course of his illness, the six-foot-one former deputy assistant agriculture secretary was reduced from 175 to 118 pounds. Wheelchair-bound, he delivered a speech in 1993 at a meeting of the American Corn Growers Association calling for national unity in finding a cure for AIDS. In a room full of farmers hardened by drought, tornadoes, and the natural elements, "there was not a dry eye in the audience," according to the group's president. Ford's partner, Doug Colagerakis, also contracted the disease, and they spent their final days lying in gentle repose in the same bed, surrounded by family. Together for seventeen years, they died within seventeen hours of each other on April 3, 1993.

Ford was part of the wave of AIDS fatalities that peaked in the early 1990s, a grim toll during a period otherwise remembered for an economic boom at home and a peace dividend abroad. Steve Martindale succumbed in 1990, and while his old friend Madame Wellington delivered a eulogy at his memorial service, the event was not the star-studded affair one might have expected given his fifteen-year run as one of Washington's most active socialites. "Noticeably absent from the list" of speakers, observed the *Washington Post* society scribe in whose columns the "ubiquitous host" had frequently appeared, were "all those socially prominent and politically powerful friends who attended so many Martindale parties or attended other parties with him."

Jon Hinson broke his promise to the voters of Mississippi's Fourth Congressional District that he would "never" be homosexual. After resigning from Congress, he accepted his identity as a gay man and helped found a gay rights organization in Alexandria, Virginia, where he settled down with a Black lover. He, too, was felled by AIDS in 1995.

Bob Waldron flourished in his post-political life as one of Washington's most in-demand interior designers, counting the Johnsons, a diplomatic register full of ambassadors, the Organization of American States, and numerous other prominent Washingtonians and storied institutions as his clients. In the Kalorama section of the city where he lived, he fed the neighborhood cats from porcelain plates, and "his house was a wonderful clutter of stuff he had assembled from auctions," remembered his friend Dana Westring. "It was a great house with a big dining room where he held court at very glamorous dinners. Always crowded with interesting people—political players, musicians, actors and old ladies with good jewelry. If you complimented him on some object in the house he ALWAYS would say the same thing—drawled in his East Texas best. 'I can have it delivered tomorrow, it's all for sale.'"

Waldron's terminal AIDS diagnosis didn't dampen his sense of humor. Lynda Bird Johnson recalled attending a dinner at Waldron's home and being told not to wipe her lipstick on the linen napkins—he had left them in his will for *another* friend. In early December 1995, Waldron entered the Washington Home, a hospice center for AIDS patients, where Johnson visited him to administer a final shave. "I know he wanted to meet his maker looking very, very good," she recalled. "And he was in a bed and couldn't do it for himself. So, with another friend of his, I just went over and we cleaned him up. Because that's the kind of thing you do for someone that you care about. You want them to look their best. And Bob knew his Bible—you know that growing up in that part of the world, meeting your maker with reverence and looking as swell as you can." Five days after Waldron was admitted, he passed away at the age of sixty-eight.

The following summer, Lady Bird Johnson dedicated a memorial plaque honoring Waldron in the hospice's Barbara Bush Garden, named after the First Lady who had volunteered there for twenty years. "When I see Barbara Bush, which I do from time to time, I will have great pleasure in telling her how pretty her garden is," Lady Bird said. "And thank you for doing this for Bob."

* * *

LESS THAN TWENTY YARDS FROM WHERE J. EDGAR HOOVER and Clyde Tolson lie buried, Leonard Matlovich's tombstone explains the essence of the cause to which he devoted the final thirteen years of his life. Engraved into the black slab, the gilded letters read:

A GAY VIETNAM VETERAN

WHEN I WAS IN THE MILITARY
THEY GAVE ME A MEDAL FOR KILLING TWO MEN
AND A DISCHARGE FOR LOVING ONE

The Purple Heart and Bronze Star recipient had earned the right to be interred alongside his fellow veterans at Arlington National Cemetery. But one day in the early 1980s, while walking through his neighborhood in Southeast DC, Matlovich happened upon Congressional Cemetery. Passing through the rows of graves where more than seventy representatives, a Supreme Court justice, a vice president, one FBI director and his associate director are buried, Matlovich was overwhelmed. "He loved the history," the cemetery's former administrator remembered of Matlovich. "He was one of the most patriotic men I ever met."

Inspired by a recent visit to Père Lachaise Cemetery in Paris, the final resting place of Oscar Wilde, Gertrude Stein, and Stein's lover, Alice B. Toklas, Matlovich realized that there was no place in America for gay people to gather and remember their forebears. On November 26, 1984, he purchased two burial plots—one for himself and one, he hoped, for a partner—for eight hundred dollars. "The public is never told that a famous figure is lesbian or gay unless an attempt is made to discredit the individual, or the individual has been diagnosed with AIDS," Matlovich lamented in a 1987 article for *The Advocate*. He did not know at that point how soon his own life would end, cut short by a disease whose effect on the gay population would be more devastating, in terms of lives lost, than the war in which he fought. Matlovich died the following year and was buried with full military honors.

That Matlovich's grave would be so close to that of the man who did more than possibly any other single figure in American history to ruin the lives of gay people, and who might very well have been gay himself, was intentional. Matlovich "couldn't resist the last laugh," according to his friend Michael Bedwell. What Matlovich did not expect was that his grave site would inspire a posthumous gay community. In the decades since his death, over a dozen gay men and women have bought burial plots around Matlovich's headstone, the citizens of a once-secret city proudly, and eternally, declaring their place in the open one. Today, Congressional Cemetery boasts of having a "gay corner," believed to be the only such designated burial ground in the world, a fitting distinction considering how Congressional welcomed the remains of AIDS victims when even the corpses of those stricken with the disease were rejected. Today, some of Matlovich's neighbors include Frank Kameny (who was cremated and is commemorated by a headstone), the lesbian activist Barbara Gittings, a grandson of the founder of the Boy Scouts, the man who designed the Main Street Electrical Parade at Disneyland, the founder of a teleprompter company, a couple who met at the Chicken Hut while students at Catholic University in the 1950s, and Alain Locke, the Howard University philosophy professor considered the father of the Harlem Renaissance.

Entombed in the northwest corner lies Peter Doyle, the love of American democracy's greatest poet, whose "Song of the Open Road" endures as a paean to the promise of freedom and of lives lived in truth.

> Camerado, I give you my hand!
> I give you my love more precious than money,
> I give you myself before preaching or law;
> Will you give me yourself? will you come travel
> with me?
>
> Shall we stick by each other as long as we live?

THE GAY CENTURY

Everything secret degenerates, even the administration
of justice; nothing is safe that does not show how it can
bear discussion and publicity.

—Lord Acton

FOR NEARLY HALF A CENTURY, NO GRAVER SIN EXISTED in the black
book of American politics than homosexuality. Sumner Welles's indiscretions on the presidential train were the "greatest national scandal since the
existence of the United States." The crime of which David Walsh was accused
constituted an offense "too loathsome to mention." In the anguished letter
he composed to the man who outed him, Bob Waldron explained that,
once identified, homosexuals were "marked by our society—which does
not permit a return." Even at the height of the Cold War, it was safer to
be a Communist than a homosexual. A Communist could break with
the party. A homosexual was forever tainted. Whittaker Chambers could
share his story of redemption earned through struggle against the "concealed enemy" as represented by Alger Hiss. His "wavering battle" against
the *other* concealed enemy, on the other hand, was the sort of thing that
"should be told only to a priest." (And, in his case, to the FBI.)

It was the specter of homosexuality that provoked the first and only suicide by a member of Congress in his Capitol Hill office, caused Lyndon Johnson to fret that he would lose the presidency, and seized the paranoid mind of Richard Nixon second only to the plots of his ever-expanding list of enemies. It drove the man who saved Gerald Ford's life into a depression from which he never recovered, and it inhibited Ronald Reagan from mentioning the disease that was killing thousands of Americans (the brother of his chief speechwriter among them). The farcically corrupt Louisiana governor Edwin Edwards might have been joking when he quipped that the only way he could lose an election "is if I'm caught in bed with a dead girl or a live boy." But he was also telling an important truth. For there was only one offense that rivaled murdering a member of the opposite sex and that was loving a member of the same one.

To assess the full scale of the damage that the fear of homosexuality wrought on the American political landscape, one must take into account not only the careers ruined and the lives cut short, but something vaster and unquantifiable: the possibilities thwarted. "The President and I were born three days apart," David Mixner wrote about his friend Bill Clinton. "We both dreamed of serving our country. There was one difference. He could pursue his dreams while I felt I could not. Bill Clinton was born straight and I was born gay." For Sean Strub, the realization that he was gay coincided with another epiphany, that "one of the most sort of salient truths that I embraced . . . was that I couldn't run for office." Not long before he died, John Ford wrote a letter to his niece encouraging her never to take for granted the opportunity, denied to men and women such as he, to pursue her dreams. "If I had not been gay, Carrie, I would have entered elective politics, and I would have been successful." How many other patriotic Americans declined to run for public office, withheld their mastery of a foreign language, refrained from applying their hard-earned scientific knowledge, or forwent serving their country in myriad other ways solely because of its hostility to the way they loved other people?

To the extent that Americans have rejected this hostility, it's thanks in large part to a small yet diverse group of intrepid individuals who lived in its capital city, where they laid the groundwork for a revolution in consciousness. Most narratives of the movement for gay equality exalt an uprising by the patrons at a New York City bar, the martyrdom of a San Francisco city councilor, and the activism against an orange juice spokeswoman in

Miami. All of these played a significant role. But the spark for the revolution was lit, and its flame was tended, in Washington, DC, by a motley procession of once-secret people beginning with a stubborn astronomer who fought back against government discrimination by appealing to the country's founding documents; an obese albino pornographer who won for his fellow gay men the same freedom to read that their heterosexual countrymen enjoyed; the African American civil rights leader who refused to let a powerful segregationist dictate the terms of his citizenship as a man who was both Black *and* gay; the lesbian presidential aide so deeply closeted that she never came out yet who organized the first meeting of gay activists at the White House; and the thousands of clerks, managers, secretaries, legislative directors, technology specialists, cryptologists, speechwriters, legal counsels, librarians, and other ordinary people who chose to live their lives honestly. Like the tormented young senator in the classic novel of Washington politics whose love for another man society had condemned, "What had started as a weakness" within these citizens "became transmuted by a very strong character and a very decent heart into a profoundly important strength."

The story of the secret city—of the slow but inexorable increase in acceptance, the expansion of opportunity, and the extension of rights and responsibilities to citizens unjustly excluded from their promise— mirrors that of the country at large. As America emerged from the ashes of World War II a global superpower, gay people collectively "came out" as a minority population. The 1950s was characterized by the rise of the national security state, an obsession with secrecy, and oppressive political conformity, a toxic brew that whipped up a social panic whose archetypical enemy was the traitorous, secretive, sexual nonconformist. The 1960s was the era of civil rights (driven by African Americans) and sexual revolution (driven by the feminist movement), echoed in the formation of the Mattachine Society and the Stonewall uprising. The 1970s was a time of self-actualization, personal fulfillment, and gay liberation. Conservative backlash to these trends, homosexuality prominent among them, arrived in the 1980s, accompanied by an epidemic whose primary victims were gay men. And the 1990s saw American victory over an evil empire abroad and the welcoming of gay people into the halls of power for the first time at home.

The story of the secret city is also the story of a nation overcoming one of its deepest fears. The collective realization by millions of people that their homosexuality was something about which they need not feel ashamed constituted more than a series of individual acts of personal liberation. Through their willingness to challenge the dogmas of the medical, religious, and political establishments, these people helped liberate America, moving our country out from under a dark shadow of fear and ignorance. Though belated and unfinished, the inclusion of gay people in all aspects of society—like the more long-standing yet similarly incomplete endeavor to include women and people of color—has been a salutary development for all Americans, regardless of sexual orientation.

The story of the secret city is the story of openness triumphing over concealment. Across the broad sweep of American history, no minority group has witnessed a more rapid transformation in its status, in the eyes of the law and of their fellow citizens, than gay people during the second half of the twentieth century. This is a magnificent accomplishment of the liberal society, enabled by the fundamentally American concepts of free expression, pluralism, and open inquiry. When homosexuality was a crime "not to bee named," it was fodder for wild conspiracy theories, and gay people were the targets of vicious hatred and calumny. At a time when most homosexuals lived a lie, hardly any American could claim to know one (though many, of course, unknowingly did). Only when gay men and lesbians started living their lives openly did the hysteria start to become plain for what it was.

Finally, the story of the secret city is quintessentially American in its egalitarianism. What so many once cited as homosexuality's greatest peril— its existence within every stratum of society—was and remains its most promising attribute. In its transcending "caste lines"; in the presence of "its adherents everywhere, among the people, in the army, in the church, in the prison, on the throne"; in the "unifying force" of what Walt Whitman called the "dear love of comrades" are the seeds for a more harmonious world. If the secret city was as much a mental landscape of repressive ideas as it was a physical one of secluded places, its story ends with a revolution in public attitudes and material reality. Fear and discrimination no longer define the gay experience, nor are gay people condemned to the fringes of society. In many respects, but this one most of all, Washington today is a city that very few of the men and women whose lives are recounted in this book would recognize. For the secret that haunted the capital, transfixed the country, and upended so many lives, is secret no more.

ACKNOWLEDGMENTS

This book would not have been possible without the inspiration, encouragement, and constructive criticism provided by a long list of people. I will do my best to acknowledge them here.

The idea for writing a narrative history about the intersection of homosexuality and political power in twentieth-century Washington, DC, can be traced back to a Yale College seminar I took in the spring of 2005, "The Art of Biography," taught by John Lewis Gaddis. Professor Gaddis was at work on what would become his Pulitzer Prize–winning life of George Kennan, and the opportunity to study the writing of biography with such an esteemed practitioner was a highlight of my undergraduate education. Every week, my classmates and I read and discussed a biography (the definition of which was sufficiently expansive to include fictional works like Virginia Woolf's *Orlando* and Colm Tóibín's *The Master*), in preparation for our final assignment: a fifty-page biography of an individual, living or deceased, whose personal papers resided in the Yale archives.

As my subject, I chose the novelist, playwright, and AIDS activist Larry Kramer, who had recently donated hundreds of boxes containing the artifacts of his considerable epistolary and literary legacy to Yale. Although I did not realize it at the time, this improbable duo of sober Cold War historian and strident political rabble-rouser were preparing me to write this book. In addition to being one of the first researchers to utilize his voluminous collection, I interviewed Larry at his Greenwich Village apartment, a historical landmark in its own right for being the site where Gay Men's Health Crisis was founded at the dawn of the AIDS epidemic in 1981. I remained in touch with Larry after graduating and moving to Washington, and during our occasional lunches when I visited New York, he would pepper me with questions about the presumed homosexuality of this or that contemporary or historic political figure. Even if his suppositions occasionally strayed from the realm of rigorous exactitude, Larry's curiosity was not the prurience of the gossipy gay. He believed that homosexuality— both the bonds it created and the fear it engendered—was a major historical phenomenon worthy of serious intellectual inquiry.

My appreciation for the history of gay Washington, and the urgency of its telling, was deepened through my friendship with another, only somewhat less cantankerous gay elder, Frank Kameny. I had also met Frank while at Yale, albeit on a train platform as he was arriving in New Haven and I was departing, and I saw him with some regularity once I settled in Washington. In 2009, I was fortunate to witness a deeply moving ceremony presided over by First Lady Michelle Obama at the headquarters of the Office of Personnel Management (OPM), successor to the Civil Service Commission, the agency responsible for terminating Frank's employment with the Army Map Service in 1957. At its conclusion, OPM Director John Berry—himself an openly gay man—issued a formal apology to Frank, which Frank cheerfully accepted. A conversation in New York City with Adam Bellow several months earlier had helped me formulate the concept for a book exploring the themes of power, secrecy, and homosexuality in Cold War Washington, and witnessing such a dramatic historical arc in the life of a single man was epiphanous. It is one of my greatest professional regrets that Larry and Frank were not able to enjoy the fruits of my labors.

Having a general idea for a book is very different from convincing a publisher to pay you to write it, and several individuals were crucial toward my accomplishing the latter feat. I was astounded to learn that more than a dozen publishing houses rejected Randy Shilts's *And the Band Played On* and that eighteen turned down Vito Russo's *The Celluloid Closet*, both seminal works of history that were influential in the writing of my own. That these books, now rightly considered classics, eventually saw the light of day is due not only to the determination of the authors—both of whom were lost to AIDS—but of visionary agents and editors willing to take a risk on subject matter that the publishing industry deemed unmarketable. Over thirty years later, that industry has changed a great deal with respect to its interest in gay voices and stories, but shepherding a book proposal (no matter how compelling) into the actual tome you find on store shelves remains an arduous task, and it is in large part thanks to the persistence of my agent Keith Urbahn that *Secret City* exists. Keith knew of my interest in pursuing the themes explored in this book since our college days, and it's to his credit that I abandoned an increasingly dissolute life in Berlin for one in Washington finally putting words to paper. Along with Matt Latimer and the rest of the Javelin team, he has my deep appreciation. At Henry Holt, Paul Golob needed little convincing as to the significance and commercial viability of this project, and was a constant source of advice and encouragement. James Melia picked up the editorial baton at the outset of a global pandemic and handled my obsessive nitpicking with patience and aplomb. Lori Kusatzky ensured that the many elaborate pieces required to create a book fit together smoothly (and on time), and her colleagues Janel Brown, Hannah Campbell, Eva Diaz, Jenna Dolan, Meryl Levavi, Carolyn O'Keefe, Caitlin O'Shaugnessy, Pauline Post, Maggie Richards, Jason Reigel, Kenn Russell, Maia Sacca-Schaeffer, and Christopher Sergio all contributed mightily to the effort.

My passion for the process of archival research that produced so much of the information contained within these pages also began at Yale, where I worked as a part-time research assistant for Sam Tanenhaus on his forthcoming biography of William F. Buckley Jr. I don't think there is a single individual as knowledgeable about twentieth-century American politics as Sam; I recall one three-hours-long phone conversation at the outset of my writing process as being particularly revelatory as to what *Secret City* might accomplish. Sam's exhortation to "master your material" was probably the best advice I received in undertaking this project. Sam and his wife Kathy were most hospitable in providing me with a place to sleep during a research visit to my alma mater, as were Shmully and Toby Hecht. Carol Blue was similarly generous with her home when I visited the Hoover Institution archives at Stanford.

Susan Ford Wiltshire, who sent me several hours of interviews she conducted with her brother John as he died of AIDS, is the sort of person everyone should want in a sibling. Enclosed within the package containing the CD-ROMs onto which Susan had helpfully transferred the original tape recordings was a handwritten note, which I affixed to a corkboard above my writing desk: "Jamie—The book you are writing is very important and you are the person to write it. Onward, Susan." Whenever I felt overwhelmed by the task at hand—too many archives to visit, too many declassification requests to file, too many books to read, too many leads to follow—I had only to glance at Susan's frank but reassuring missive to remind me of the necessity that I continue.

Charles Francis and Pate Felts of the reconstituted Mattachine Society of Washington, DC, have been doing yeoman's work unearthing the documentary record of the federal government's animus against gay people. It was Charles who alerted me to the existence of Robert Waldron, and who therefore deserves much of the credit for my ability to share his painful story for the first time. Skip Moskey also provided me with many helpful hints and clues along the way, and both he and Jana Fuhrmann saved me the chore of transcribing hundreds of hours of interviews and oral histories.

I am extremely fortunate to count so many discerning readers among my colleagues, friends, and mentors, who so graciously agreed to offer feedback on my manuscript. Michael Barone, Paul Berman, Bob Bookman, Dale Carpenter, Ash Carter, Christian Caryl, Mark Falcoff, John Gaddis, Eric Garber, Judy Goldstein, Jeffrey Herf, Hussein Ibish, Bruce Jones, Geoffrey Kabaservice, Robert Kagan, Christopher Kerns, Chuck Lane, Tod Lindberg, Thomas Mallon, Doyle McManus, Edward Mogul, Michael O'Hanlon, Walter Olson, Peter Pomerantzev, Jonathan Rauch, Billy Ray, Frank Rich, Yossi Siegel, and George Stephanopoulos all took the time to help me transform an unwieldy document into a book that people might actually want to purchase.

I could not have chosen a better intellectual home at which to complete this project than the Brookings Institution, an opportunity for which I primarily have Bruce Jones, Tom Wright, and Robert Kagan to thank. Andy Moffat, the team at the Center on the United States and Europe, and the rest of the scholars within the Foreign Policy program all helped make Brookings a wonderful environment in which to work. Special thanks go to the indefatigable Brookings librarian Laura Mooney, who never failed to answer my frequent requests for obscure books and articles with alacrity and good cheer, along with her colleagues David Bair, Cy Behroozi, Sarah

Chilton, and Elif Ecer. At *Tablet*, Alana Newhouse and David Samuels have nurtured my writing and intellectual growth.

This book benefited enormously from the archivists and librarians who are the unsung heroes of preserving our nation's history. At the National Archives and Research Administration, Archivist of the United States David Ferriero more than lives up to the grandeur of his title. David reached out to me upon reading an article I had published on the fiftieth anniversary of the Stonewall uprising and helped me acquire Robert Waldron's FBI file. Also at NARA, I was assisted by Richard Peuser, Eric Van Slander, Megan Dwyre, David Fort, Noah Shankin, Abiola Neptune, David Langbart, Adam Berenbak, and Cary McStay. The Library of Congress is a national treasure, not only for its collections but its staff, and I am particularly thankful to Ryan Reft, Megan Metcalf, Amber Paranick, Megan Halsband, and the enormously patient men and women of the Manuscript and Newspaper and Current Periodical Reading Rooms. The Rainbow History Project is a model in the growing movement of volunteer-based community history preservation, and I thank Vincent Slatt for introducing me to its wonderful oral history collection, and Rob Berger for helping me secure access to a photograph of the Clubhouse. I was assisted by numerous archivsts at our presidential libraries, namely Kirstin Carter and Sarah Navins of the FDR Library, Randy Sowell and Lisa A. Sullivan (Truman), Valoise Armstrong, Michelle Kopfer, and Timothy Rives (Eisenhower), Abigail Malangone (JFK), Brian McNerney and Samantha Stone (LBJ), Ryan Pettigrew (Nixon), John J. O'Connell (Ford), and Michael Pinckney and Ray Wilson (Reagan). Other librarians and archivists who aided my research were Stephen Ross and Christine Weideman (Yale Manuscripts and Archives), Andrea Mohr (Special Collections and University Archives at the University of Oregon), Caitlin Donnelly and Kathy Lafferty (Kenneth Spencer Research Library at Kansas University), Tal Nadan (New York Public Library), Elizabeth Garver (Harry Ransom Center at the University of Texas), Christine Jacobson (Harvard Houghton Library), Brenda J. Marston (Rare and Manuscript Collections at Cornell University), Kanisha Greaves (Rockefeller Archive Center), Anne McDonough and Jessica Smith (Historical Society of Washington, D.C.), and the staffs of the Washingtoniana Room at the Martin Luther King Jr. Memorial Library in Washington, DC, and the Special Collections Research Center of the George Washington University Gelman Library. To help defray the costs associated with traveling to these archives, I received financial support in the form of a Martin Duberman Visiting Fellowship from the New York Public Library, a Phil Zwickler Memorial Research Grant from the Cornell University Library's Division of Rare and Manuscript Collections, a Truman Library Research Grant, an LBJ Library Moody Research Grant, and two D.C. Commission on the Arts and Humanities fellowships.

Christopher Buckley grasped the importance of this project and generously allowed me to peruse his father's papers. Todd Purdum shared his Princeton undergraduate thesis on Scott McLeod. At National Public Radio, Annie Mitchell, Jenna Meade, and April Fehling helped me track down Frank Browning's 1987 series on Spitz Channell and the NEPL crew. Answering queries or assisting me in other ways were Sara Lichterman and Chelsea Robinson of the Central Intelligence Agency, Hillary Hoffman and Gabrielle Barr of the National Institutes of Health, and Yolanda Davis of the *Journal of the American Medical Association*. So, too, must I acknowledge Jonathan Adler, Carl Anthony, Anne Applebaum, Peter Baker, Alex Bartlett, Michael Bedwell, Rob Bernstein, John Berresford, Frank Bruni, Eric Chenoweth, Gary Cohen, Harry Cohen, Jeff Cook-McCormac, Francesca Craig, Simon Doonan, Jack Farrell, David Friend, Jeff Gedmin, Susan Glasser, Paul Glastris, Bill Goldstein, Mark Hosenball, William Inboden, Ben Jacobs, Terry Kassel, Gregory King, Irena Lasota, Fred Litwin, Dan Loeb, Dave Marash, John Marble, Ned Martel, Shawn McCreesh, Hank Meijer, Judy Miller, Kevin Naff, Adam Nagourney, Tom Neale, Lauren Noble, Jay Nordlinger, Sam Patten, Marty Peretz, Arch Puddington, Ronald Radosh, Roxane Roberts, Bob Roehr, Dan Senor, Jack Shafer, Gary Shapiro, Roger Sharpe, Eric Shorr, Doug Silverman, Paul Singer, Sam Smith, Daniel Sperling, BJ Stiles, Strobe Talbott, Ben Terris, Evan Thomas, Ryan Trapani, Douglas Waller, Leon Wieseltier, Lucas Wittman, and Ben Yagoda.

I mentioned *And the Band Played On* at the outset of these acknowledgments, and every gay person who aspires to a career in journalism owes Randy Shilts a posthumous debt for paving the way. Christopher Hitchens provided early encouragement and advice, and his words will always remain a guide. And then there are the innumerable men and women—many unknown to us—who suffered grievously due to the attitudes and policies recounted in this book. Even when it seemed that America had given up on them, they never gave up on America. Their resilience under such oppressive conditions stands as a collective exemplar of Václav Havel's exhortation to live in truth.

Finally, to this book's other set of dedicatees: my parents William and Carol, my brother Jeff, and my partner Josef. I may be a man of many (frequently too many) words, but words cannot convey the depth of my love for you.

PHOTOGRAPHY CREDITS

1. View of Lafayette Square: Library of Congress, Prints & Photographs Division, HABS DC, WASH,613—3
2. Cordell Hull and Sumner Welles: Library of Congress, Prints & Photographs Division, photograph by Harris & Ewing, LC-DIG-hec-25086
3. Eleanor Roosevelt and Lorena Hickok: Courtesy of the FDR Presidential Library
4. William Bullitt and Carmel Offie: United States Holocaust Memorial Museum, courtesy of National Archives & Records Administration
5. Drew Pearson: Photo by: Yoichi Okamotò / Courtesy of the Lyndon B. Johnson Presidential Library
6. Odessa Madre: Reprinted with permission of the DC Public Library, Star Collection © *Washington Post*
7. Loving a Parade: Library of Congress, Prints & Photographs Division, photograph by Harris & Ewing, LC-DIG-hec-25829
8. Donald Downes: Image from interior of Robin W. Winks, *Cloak and Gown: Scholars in the Secret War, 1939–1961* (New York: William Morrow, 1987)
9. Juan Francisco de Cárdenas: Library of Congress, Prints & Photographs Division, photograph by Harris & Ewing, LC-DIG-hec-26476
10. J. Edgar Hoover and Clyde Tolson: uclalat_1387_b16_20733-1, Los Angeles Daily News Negatives (Collection 1387). Library Special Collections, Charles E. Young Research Library, UCLA
11. Alger Hiss: Alger Hiss seated and smoking a pipe, 1965, Los Angeles Times Photographic Archive (Collection 1429). Library Special Collections, Charles E. Young Research Library, UCLA
12. Whittaker Chambers: Library of Congress, Prints and Photographs Division, NYWT&S Collection, LC-USZ62-114739
13. Kenneth S. Wherry: Library of Congress, Prints & Photographs Division, photograph by Harris & Ewing, LC-H22-D-8718
14. & 15. *Confidential* magazine: Courtesy of The Library of Congress
16. 1945 Potsdam Conference: United States Army Signal Corps, Harry S. Truman Library & Museum
17. Joseph McCarthy, Roy Cohn, and G. David Schine: uclalat_1429_b185_82805-2, Los Angeles Times Photographic Archive (Collection 1429). Library Special Collections, Charles E. Young Research Library, UCLA

18. Joe Alsop and Lyndon Johnson: Alsop, Joseph, 1910–, Biographical info page, LBJ Presidential Library, accessed July 13, 2021, https://www.discoverlbj.org/item/alsopj

19. *Advise and Consent*: First edition cover image of Allen Drury, *Advise and Consent* (New York: Doubleday, 1959)

20. John F. Kennedy and Lem Billings: Cecil Stoughton. White House Photographs. John F. Kennedy Presidential Library and Museum, Boston

21. John F. Kennedy and Gore Vidal: AP Photo

22. Franklin Kameny: Photo by Kay Tobin ©Manuscripts and Archives Division, The New York Public Library

23. H. Lynn Womack: H. Lynn Womack papers, #7441. Division of Rare and Manuscript Collections, Cornell University Library

24. Bayard Rustin: Library of Congress, Prints and Photographs Division, Washington, D.C. 20540, USA LC-DIG-ppmsc-01272

25. Mattachine Society members: Photo by Kay Tobin ©Manuscripts and Archives Division, The New York Public Library

26. Robert Waldron and Lyndon Johnson: Frank Muto. Pre-Presidential Photo Collection, LBJ Presidential Library

27. Walter Jenkins: Yoichi Okamoto. White House Photo Office Collection, LBJ Presidential Library

28. Richard Nixon meeting: From the holdings of the Richard Nixon Presidential Library and Museum

29. *Washington Blade*: Republished with permission, *Washington Blade*

30. Steve Martindale: *The Washington Post* / Contributor

31. Midge Costanza at the White House: Courtesy of Jimmy Carter Presidential Library

32. Lambda Rising bookstore: Courtesy of Deacon Maccubbin

33. Clubhouse: Courtesy of the Rainbow History Project

34. Jon Hinson: *Congressional Pictorial Directory*, 96th US Congress, p. 75

35. Pete McCloskey: AP Photo/Harrity

36. Lynn Bouchey: Courtesy of the C-SPAN Archives

37. Peter Hannaford: Courtesy of the Ronald Reagan Presidential Library & Museum

38. Bob Livingston: *Times-Picayune*, June 21, 1977, Capital City Press/Georges Media Group, and Baton Rouge, LA

39. Nancy Reagan, Jerry Zipkin, and Ted Graber: Courtesy of the Ronald Reagan Presidential Library & Museum

40. Nancy Reagan and Rock Hudson: Courtesy of the Ronald Reagan Presidential Library & Museum

41. Nancy Reagan and James Galanos: Courtesy of the Ronald Reagan Presidential Library & Museum

42. Nancy Reagan and Robin Weir: Courtesy of the Ronald Reagan Presidential Library & Museum

43. Nancy Reagan and Bob Gray: Courtesy of the Ronald Reagan Presidential Library & Museum

44. 45, 46, 47, & 48. *Deep Backgrounder* 1–5: Division of Special Collections and University Archives, University of Oregon Libraries

49. Craig Spence: Courtesy of Mark Falcoff

50. Terry Dolan: Courtesy of the Ronald Reagan Presidential Library & Museum

51. Carl R. "Spitz" Channell: Courtesy of the Ronald Reagan Presidential Library & Museum

52. AIDS Memorial Quilt: Courtesy of the National Institutes of Health

SOURCES

ARCHIVAL COLLECTIONS

Boston University; Boston, Massachusetts
    James McCargar Papers
Cornell University, Division of Rare and Manuscript Collections; Ithaca, New York
    Larry Bush Papers
    Chasen Gaver Papers
    National Gay and Lesbian Task Force Records
    H. Lynn Womack Papers
Dwight D. Eisenhower Presidential Library; Abilene, Kansas
    Presidential Papers of Dwight D. Eisenhower
    Sherman Adams Papers
    Eli Ginzberg Papers
Franklin Delano Roosevelt Presidential Library; Hyde Park, New York
    President's Secretary's File
George Washington University, Special Collections Research Center; Washington, DC
    Jack Anderson Papers
    Lou Chibbaro Jr. Papers
    Jim Graham Papers
Gerald R. Ford Presidential Library; Grand Rapids, Michigan
    Ron Nessen Papers
    White House Press Releases
    Sheila Weidenfeld Files
Hagley Museum and Library; Wilmington, Delaware
    Sophie du Pont May Papers
Harry Ransom Center, The University of Texas at Austin; Austin, Texas
    Benjamin C. Bradlee Papers
Harry Truman Presidential Library; Independence, Missouri
    George Elsey Papers

Records of the U.S. Secret Service, Personal Investigation Files
Stephen J. Spingarn Papers
Charles Thayer Papers
White House Central Files
Harvard University; Cambridge, Massachusetts
Gore Vidal Papers
Historical Society of Washington, DC
David Aiken Papers
Gay Liberation Front Collection
Rainbow History Project Collection
Hoover Institution; Palo Alto, California
Allen Drury Papers
Thomas Byrne Edsall Papers
Peter Hannaford Papers
Paul N. McCloskey Papers
Robert D. Murphy Papers
John F. Kennedy Presidential Library; Boston, Massachusetts
White House Central Name File
Pre-Presidential Papers
Lyndon Baines Johnson Presidential Library; Austin, Texas
Aides Files of Mildred Stegall
Drew Pearson Papers
Presidential Papers
Library of Congress; Washington, DC
Franklin E. Kameny Papers
Paul Kuntzler Papers
Breckenridge Long Papers
Bayard Rustin Papers
Lawrence E. Spivak Papers
Lilli Vincenz Papers
Paul M. Weyrich Scrapbooks
National Archives and Records Administration
Washington, DC
U.S. Senate Internal Security Subcommittee Files
College Park, Maryland
Department of State Central Files, RG 59
Records of the Federal Bureau of Investigation, RG 65
Records of the War Department General Staff (Army), RG 165
Records of the Central Intelligence Agency, RG 263
Records of the Office of Strategic Services, RG 266
Records of the Watergate Special Prosecution Force, RG 460
National Archives of the United Kingdom
Foreign and Commonwealth Office Files
New York Public Library, Manuscripts and Archives Division; New York, New York
Barbara Gittings and Kay Tobin Lahusen gay history papers and photographs
Dorothy Schiff Papers
Mattachine Society of New York Papers
ONE LGBT Archive, University of Southern California; Los Angeles, California Concerned Americans
for Individual Rights (CAIR) Records ONE Inc. Records
Paul "Pete" McCloskey Personal Papers
Ronald Reagan Presidential Library; Simi Valley, California
Howard Baker Files
Gary Bauer Files
Kenneth T. Cribb Files
Kenneth M. Duberstein Files

Robert Sweet Files
White House Office of Records Management (WHORM) Alpha File
WHORM Subject File
Tamiment Library, New York University; New York, New York
John Lowenthal Papers
William A. Reuben Papers
University of North Carolina at Chapel Hill, Wilson Library; Chapel Hill, North Carolina
Perry Deane Young Papers
University of Virginia, Albert and Shirley Small Special Collections Library; Charlottesville, Virginia
Papers of Edwin M. Watson and of Frances Nash Watson
Wisconsin Historical Society; Madison, Wisconsin
Clark Mollenhoff Papers
Yale University Library; New Haven, Connecticut
Manuscripts and Archives
William F. Buckley Jr. Papers
William C. Bullitt Papers
Donald C. Downes Papers
Max Lerner Papers
Robin Winks Papers
Beinecke Rare Book and Manuscript Library; New Haven, Connecticut
Larry Kramer Papers

JOURNAL ARTICLES

Barrett, David M. "Secrecy, Security, and Sex: The NSA, Congress, and the Martin-Mitchell Defections." *International Journal of Intelligence and Counterintelligence* 22, no. 4 (2009): 699–729.

Baxter, Randolph W. "'Homo-Hunting' in the Early Cold War: Senator Kenneth Wherry and the Homophobic Side of McCarthyism." *Nebraska History* 84 (2003): 119–32.

Bergler, Edmund. "The Myth of a New National Disease." *Psychiatric Quarterly* 22 (January1948): 66–88.

Bresler, R. J. "Hoover and Donovan: The Politics of Bureaucratic Empire Building." *International Journal of Public Administration* 16, no. 1 (1993): 67–105.

Campbell, J. F. "'To Bury Freud on Wilson': Uncovering *Thomas Woodrow Wilson, A Psychological Study*, by Sigmund Freud and William C. Bullitt." *Modern Austrian Literature* 41, no. 2 (2008): 41–56.

Carew, Anthony. "The American Labor Movement in Fizzland: The Free Trade Union Committee and the CIA." *Labor History* 39, no. 1 (1998): 25–42.

Chauncey Jr., George. "From Sexual Inversion to Homosexuality: Medicine and the Changing Conceptualization of Female Deviance." *Salmagundi* 58/59 (Fall 1982–Winter 1983): 114–46.

Comstock, Gary David. "Dismantling the Homosexual Panic Defense." *Law and Sexuality: A Review of Lesbian and Gay Legal Issues* 2 (1992): 81–102.

Costigliola, Frank. "'Unceasing Pressure for Penetration': Gender, Pathology, and Emotion in George Kennan's Formation of the Cold War." *Journal of American History* 83, no. 4 (March 1997): 1309–39.

Critchlow, Donald T. "Rethinking American Conservatism: Toward a New Narrative." *Journal of American History* 98, no. 3 (December 2011): 752–55.

Epstein, Barbara. "Anti-Communism, Homophobia, and the Construction of Masculinity in the Postwar U.S." *Critical Sociology* 20, no. 3 (1994): 21–44.

Ewig, Rick. "The Ordeal of Senator Lester Hunt." *Annals of Wyoming* 55, no. 1 (Spring 1983): 9–21.

Frank, Gillian. "Discophobia: Antigay Prejudice and the 1979 Backlash Against Disco." *Journal of the History of Sexuality* 16, no. 2 (May 2007): 276–306.

Forstie, Clare, and Gary Alan Fine. "Signaling Perversion: Senator David Walsh and the Politics of Euphemism and Dysphemism." *Sexualities* 20, no. 7 (2017): 772–92.

Freedman, Estelle B. "'Uncontrolled Desires': The Response to the Sexual Psychopath, 1920–1960." *Journal of American History* 74, no. 1 (June 1987): 83–106.

Friedman, Andrea. "The Smearing of Joe McCarthy: The Lavender Scare, Gossip, and Cold War Politics." *American Quarterly* 57, no. 4 (December 2005): 1105–29.

Hatton, Jackie. "The Pornography Empire of H. Lynn Womack: Gay Political Discourse and Popular Culture 1955–1970." *Thresholds: Viewing Culture* 7 (Spring 1993): 9–32.

Mattingly, Doreen J., and Ashley Boyd. "Bringing Gay and Lesbian Activism to the White House: Midge Costanza and the National Gay Task Force Meeting." *Journal of Lesbian Studies* 17 (2013): 365–79.

Murphy, Lawrence R. "The House on Pacific Street: Homosexuality, Intrigue, and Politics During World War II." *Journal of Homosexuality* 12, no. 1 (1985): 27–49.

Ortiz, Joseph M. "The World Won't Mind: The Accidental Success of Gordon Merrick." *Princeton University Library Chronicle* 67, no. 3 (Spring 2006): 611–26.

Peacock, Kent W. "Race, the Homosexual, and the Mattachine Society of Washington, 1961–1970." *Journal of the History of Sexuality* 25, no. 2 (2016): 267–96.

Potter, Claire Bond. "Queer Hoover: Sex, Lies and Political History." *Journal of the History of Sexuality* 15, no. 3 (September 2006): 355–81.

Roorda, Eric Paul. "McCarthyite in Camelot: The 'Loss' of Cuba, Homophobia, and the Otto Otepka Scandal in the Kennedy State Department." *Diplomatic History* 31, no. 4 (September 2007): 723–54.

Russell, Thaddeus. "The Color of Discipline: Civil Rights and Black Sexuality." *American Quarterly* 60, no. 1 (March 2008): 101–28.

Schindler, John R. "Redl—Spy of the Century?" *International Journal of Intelligence and Counterintelligence* 18, no. 3 (2005): 483–507.

Smith, Geoffrey S. "National Security and Personal Isolation: Sex, Gender, and Disease in the Cold-War United States." *International History Review* 14, no. 2 (May 1992): 307–37.

Solms, Mark. "'Freud' and Bullitt: An Unknown Manuscript." *Journal of the American Psychoanalytic Association* 54, no. 4 (Fall 2006): 1263–98.

Streitmatter, Rodger, and John C. Watson. "Herman Lynn Womack: Pornographer as First Amendment Pioneer." *Journalism History* 28, no. 2 (Summer 2002): 56–66.

GOVERNMENT REPORTS AND PUBLICATIONS

Congressional Record

Federal Bureau of Investigation Records
Bohlen, Charles E.
Chambers, Whittaker
Compromise and Extortion of Homosexuals (HOMEX)
Frelinghuysen Jr., Peter
Hudson, Rock
Jenkins, Walter
Mattachine Society of Washington, DC
Offie, Carmel
Philby, Kim, Guy Burgess, and Donald Maclean
Thayer, Charles W.
Waldron, Robert Earl
    J. Edgar Hoover, Official and Confidential Files
        16: Adlai Stevenson
        26: Joseph Wright Alsop Jr.
        88: Cordell Hull
        119: Richard Nixon—Homosexuals in Government
        153: David Walsh
        157: Sumner Welles

Foreign Relations of the United States
U.S. House of Representatives. Hearings Regarding Communist Espionage in the United States Government, Special Subcommittee on Un-American Activities, August 1948.

U.S. Senate. Committee on Expenditures in the Executive Department. *Employment of Homosexuals and Other Sex Perverts in Government: Interim Report Submitted to the Committee on Expenditures in the Executive Department.* 81st Cong., 2nd Sess., S. Doc. 241. Washington, DC: U.S. Government Printing Office, 1950.

U.S. Senate. Committee on Expenditures in the Executive Department, Investigations Subcommittee. Hearings Pursuant to S. Res. 280, Executive Session Transcripts. 81st Cong., 2nd Sess., July 14–September 8, 1950. Washington, DC: U.S. Government Printing Office, 1950.

U.S. Senate. Committee on Secret Military Assistance to Iran and the Nicaraguan Opposition. *Report of the Congressional Committees Investigating the Iran-Contra Affair,* 100th Cong., 1st Sess., S. Rept. No. 100–216. Washington, DC: U.S. Government Printing Office, 1987.

U.S. Senate. Special Subcommittee on Investigations of the Committee on Government Operations. *Special Senate Investigation on Charges and Countercharges Involving: Secretary of the Army Robert T. Stevens, John G. Adams, H. Struve Hensel and Senator Joe McCarthy, Roy Cohn and Francis P. Carr.* 83rd Cong., 2nd Sess., May 25, 1954. (Army-McCarthy Hearings).

U.S. Senate. Subcommittee Appointed by the Subcommittee on Appropriations for the District of Columbia, on the Infiltration of Subversives and Moral Perverts in the Executive Branch of the United States Government. *Report of the Investigations on the Junior Senator of Nebraska,* S. Doc. 4179. 81st Cong., 2nd Sess., May 1950. Washington, DC: U.S. Government Printing Office, 1950. (Wherry Report).

U.S. Congress. Warren Commission. *Investigation of the Assassination of President John F. Kennedy: Hearings Before the President's Commission on the Assassination of President Kennedy.* Washington, DC: U.S. Government Printing Office, 1964.

United States of America v. Alger Hiss. United States District Court, Southern District of New York. 1949.

United States of America v. Alger Hiss. United States Court of Appeals, Second Circuit. 1949–1950.

Oral Histories and Recordings

Association for Diplomatic Studies and Training Foreign Affairs Oral History Project
-Charles Anthony Gillespie, Barbara J. Good, Parke D. Massey, James McCargar, Edward R. Pierce, Robert J. Ryan, Peter J. Skoufis, Joseph C. Walsh, Robert F. Woodward
California State Archives, State Government Oral History Program
-Leland L. Nichols
Columbia Center for Oral History, Columbia University
-Spruille Braden, Ralph Flanders, Bruce Voeller, Henry Agard Wallace
Miller Center of Public Affairs
-Presidential Recordings Project
-Ronald Reagan Oral History Project
-Peter Hannaford, Lyn Nofziger, Stu Spencer, Peter Wallison
United States Senate Oral History Project
-Leonard H. Ballard, Roy Elson, George Tames, Ruth Young Watt
Rainbow History Project
-David Harris, Pat Hawkins, Peter Jefts, Nancy Tucker, Otto Ulrich, Lilli Vincenz, Allen Young
Presidential Libraries
Franklin Delano Roosevelt Presidential Library
-John L. McCrea
Harry Truman Presidential Library
-George Elsey, Stephen Spingarn, George Tames, Robert K. Walsh
John F. Kennedy Presidential Library
-Joseph W. Alsop, Kirk LeMoyne Billings, Roy Cohn, John F. English, Laura Bergquist Knebel, Frank Mankiewicz, Eugene H. Nickerson, Robert Pierpoint, Pierre Salinger, John Seigenthaler
Lyndon Baines Johnson Presidential Library
-Phyllis Bonnano, Cartha D. "Deke" DeLoach, Nancy Dickerson, Lady Bird Johnson, George E. Reedy, Bayard Rustin, Robert Waldron

Richard Nixon Presidential Library
   -White House Tapes: Sound Recordings of Meetings and Telephone Conversations of the
      Nixon Administration
University of California at Los Angeles, Oral History Program
   -Neil Reagan
Washington, DC, Public Library, Special Collections, March on Washington Oral History Project
   -Paul Kuntzler

NEWSPAPERS AND PERIODICALS

Advocate
Arizona Daily Sun
Arizona Republic
Arkansas Democrat-Gazette
Atlantic Monthly
Austin-American Statesman
Baltimore Afro-American
Baltimore News-American
Baltimore Sun
Bay Area Reporter
Blueboy
Boston
Boston Globe
Boston Herald-Traveler
Brooklyn Eagle
Brooklyn Times-Union
Bush Report
Chicago Daily Tribune
Christian Science Monitor
Christopher Street
Clarion-Ledger
Collier's
Columbia Journalism Review
Commentary
Confidential
Coronet
Cosmopolitan
Deep Backgrounder
Des Moines Register
Detroit Free Press
Eastern Mattachine Magazine
Editor & Publisher
Esquire
Fag Rag
The Furies
Gay Blade
Gay Forum
Gay and Lesbian Review
Gay Sunshine
Grand Street
Grecian Guild Pictorial
Harper's
Hartford Courant
Human Events
Idaho State Journal

In These Times
Jet
Journal of American Medicine
Ladder
Las Vegas Sun
Life
Los Angeles Herald-Examiner
Los Angeles Times
Miami Herald
Minneapolis Star-Tribune
Morbidity and Mortality Weekly Report
Nation
National Journal
National Review
New Republic
New York
New York Daily Mirror
New York Daily News
New York Post
New York Review of Books
New York Times
New Yorker
Newsday
Newsweek
ONE
Partisan Review
People
Philadelphia Inquirer
Pittsburgh Press
Pittsburgh Tribune-Review
Policy Review
Raleigh News & Observer
The Reporter
Roll Call
Rolling Stone
Sacramento Bee
St. Louis Post-Dispatch
San Francisco Chronicle
San Francisco Examiner
Santa Fe New Mexican
Saturday Evening Post
Smithsonian
Studies in Intelligence
The Tablet
Time

Times Literary Supplement
U.S. News & World Report
Vanity Fair
Variety
Village Voice
Wall Street Journal
Washington Afro-American
Washington Blade
Washington City Paper
Washington Daily News

Washington Dossier
Washington Evening Star
Washington Herald
Washington Post
Washington Times (1894–1939)
Washington Times (1982–)
Washington Times-Herald
Washingtonian
Whisper
Wisconsin State Journal

UNPUBLISHED SOURCES

Dolinsky, Rebecca C. "Lesbian and Gay DC: Identity, Emotion and Experience in Washington, DC's Social and Activist Communities (1961–1986)." PhD diss., University of California, Santa Cruz, 2010.

Gambino, Matthew Joseph. "Mental Health and Ideals of Citizenship: Patient Care at St. Elizabeths Hospital in Washington, D.C., 1903–1962." PhD diss., University of Illinois at Urbana-Champaign, 2010.

Purdum, Todd S. "The Politics of Security: The Eisenhower State Department and Scott McLeod." Undergraduate thesis, Princeton University, 1982.

BOOKS

Acheson, Dean. Present at the Creation: My Years at the State Department. New York: W. W. Norton, 1969.

Adams, John G. Without Precedent: The Story of the Death of McCarthyism. New York: W. W. Norton, 1983.

Adelman, Bob. Tijuana Bibles: Art and Wit in America's Forbidden Funnies, 1930s–1950s. New York: Simon and Schuster Editions, 1997.

Adler, Ken. The Lie Detectors: The History of an American Obsession. New York: Free Press, 2007.

Allara, Pamela. Pictures of People: Alice Neel's American Portrait Gallery. Hanover, NH: Brandeis University Press, 1998.

Allen, Gay Wilson. The Solitary Singer: A Critical Biography of Walt Whitman. New York: New York University Press, 1955.

Alsop, Joseph W., with Adam Platt. "I've Seen the Best of It": Memoirs. New York: W. W. Norton, 1992.

Alsop, Stewart. The Center: The Anatomy of Power in Washington. New York: Harper and Row, 1968.

Alwood, Edward. Straight News: Gays, Lesbians and the News Media. New York: Columbia University Press, 1996.

Andersen, Kurt. Fantasyland: How America Went Haywire: A 500-Year History. New York: Random House, 2017.

Anderson, Jack, with Daryl Gibson. Peace, War, and Politics: An Eyewitness Account. New York: Forge, 1999.

Anderson, Scott. The Quiet Americans: Four CIA Spies at the Dawn of the Cold War—A Tragedy in Three Acts. New York: Doubleday, 2020.

Andrew, Christopher. Defend the Realm: The Authorized History of MI5. New York: Vintage, 2009.

Andrew, Christopher, and Vasili Mitrokhin. The Sword and the Shield: The Mitrokhin Archive and the Secret History of the KGB. New York: Basic Books, 1999.

Andrew III, John A. The Other Side of the Sixties: Young Americans for Freedom and the Rise of Conservative Politics. New Brunswick, NJ: Rutgers University Press, 1997.

Andriote, John-Manuel. Victory Deferred. Chicago: University of Chicago Press, 1999.

Anthony, Carl Sferrazza. First Ladies. Vol. 2, The Saga of the Presidents' Wives and Their Power, 1961–1990. New York: William Morrow, 1991.

Archibald, George. Journalism Is War: Stories of Power Politics, Sexual Dalliance and Corruption in the Nation's Capital. Crane, MO: Anomalos Publishing House, 2009.

Bach, Steven. *Dazzler: The Life and Times of Moss Hart*. New York: Alfred A. Knopf, 2001.

Balcerski, Thomas J. *Bosom Friends: The Intimate World of James Buchanan and William Rufus King*. New York: Oxford University Press, 2019.

Bamford, James. *The Puzzle Palace: A Report on America's Most Secret Agency*. Boston: Houghton Mifflin, 1982.

Bancroft, Mary. *Autobiography of a Spy*. New York: William Morrow, 1983.

Barbas, Samantha. *Confidential Confidential: The Inside Story of Hollywood's Notorious Scandal Magazine*. Chicago: Chicago Review Press, 2018.

Barrett, David M. *The CIA and Congress: The Untold Story from Truman to Kennedy*. Lawrence: University Press of Kansas, 2005.

Bauman, Robert. *The Gentleman from Maryland: The Conscience of a Gay Conservative*. New York: Arbor House, 1986.

Bayer, Ronald. *Homosexuality and American Psychiatry: The Politics of Diagnosis*. Princeton, NJ: Princeton University Press, 1987.

Beachy, Robert. *Gay Berlin: Birthplace of a Modern Identity*. New York: Vintage, 2015.

Beemyn, Genny. *A Queer Capital: A History of Gay Life in Washington, D.C.* New York: Routledge, 2015.

Beisner, Robert L. *Dean Acheson: A Life in the Cold War*. Oxford: Oxford University Press, 2006.

Berlin, Isaiah. *Flourishing: Letters 1928–1946*. Edited by Henry Hardy. London: Chatto and Windus, 2004.

Bérubé, Allan. *Coming Out Under Fire: The History of Gay Men and Women in World War Two*. New York: Free Press, 1990.

Beschloss, Michael R. *Reaching for Glory: Lyndon Johnson's Secret White House Tapes, 1964–1965*. New York: Simon and Schuster, 2001.

Biddle, Francis. *In Brief Authority*. New York: Doubleday, 1962.

Bissell, Richard M., with Jonathan E. Lewis and Francis T. Pudlo. *Reflections of a Cold Warrior: From Yalta to the Bay of Pigs*. New Haven, CT: Yale University Press, 1996.

Bohlen, Charles E. *Witness to History: 1929–1969*. New York: W. W. Norton, 1973.

Boswell, John. *Christianity, Social Tolerance, and Homosexuality: Gay People in Western Europe from the Beginning of the Christian Era to the Fourteenth Century*. Chicago: University of Chicago Press, 1980.

Bower, Tom. *The Perfect English Spy: Sir Dick White and the Secret War, 1935–1990*. London: Heinemann, 1995.

Bradlee, Ben. *A Good Life: Newspapering and Other Adventures*. New York: Simon and Schuster, 1995.

Branch, Taylor. *Parting the Waters: America in the King Years, 1954–1963*. New York: Simon and Schuster, 1988.

Breitman, Richard. *The Berlin Mission: The American Who Resisted Nazi Germany from Within*. New York: PublicAffairs, 2019.

Breuer, William B. *Hoodwinking Hitler: The Normandy Deception*. Westport, CT: Praeger, 1993.

Brinkley, David. *Washington Goes to War*. New York: Alfred A. Knopf, 1988.

Brinkley, Douglas, and Luke Nichter, eds. *The Nixon Tapes: 1971—1972*. Boston: Houghton Mifflin Harcourt, 2014.

Broder, David S. *Changing of the Guard: Power and Leadership in America*. New York: Simon and Schuster, 1980.

Brown, Howard J. *Familiar Faces, Hidden Lives: The Story of Homosexual Men in America Today*. New York: Harcourt Brace Jovanovich, 1976.

Brown, Tina. *The Vanity Fair Diaries: 1983–1992*. New York: Henry Holt, 2017.

Brownell, Herbert. *Advising Ike: The Memoirs of Attorney General Herbert Brownell*. Lawrence: University Press of Kansas, 1993.

Brownell, Will, and Richard N. Billings. *So Close to Greatness: A Biography of William C. Bullitt*. New York: Macmillan, 1987.

Buckley, Christopher. *Losing Mum and Pup: A Memoir*. New York: Twelve, 2009.

Buckley Jr., William F. *Overdrive: A Personal Documentary*. Garden City, NY: Doubleday, 1983.

Bullitt, Orville H., ed. *For the President: Personal and Secret: Correspondence Between Franklin D. Roosevelt and William C. Bullitt*. Boston: Houghton Mifflin, 1972.

Burns, James MacGregor. *Roosevelt: The Soldier of Freedom, 1940–1945*. New York: Harcourt Brace Jovanovich, 1970.

Burns, John Horne. *The Gallery*. New York: Harper, 1947.

Caddy, Douglas. *Being There: Eyewitness to History*. Walterville, OR: Trine Day, 2018.

Califano, Joseph A. *Inside: A Public and Private Life*. New York: PublicAffairs, 2004.

——. *The Triumph and Tragedy of Lyndon Johnson*. New York: Simon and Schuster, 1991.

Canaday, Margot. *The Straight State: Sexuality and Citizenship in Twentieth-Century America*. Princeton, NJ: Princeton University Press, 2009.

Cannon, Lou. *Governor Reagan: His Rise to Power*. New York: PublicAffairs, 2003.

——. *The McCloskey Challenge*. New York: E.P. Dutton, 1972.

——. *President Reagan: The Role of a Lifetime*. New York: Simon and Schuster, 1991.

——. *Ronnie & Jesse: A Political Odyssey*. Garden City, NY: Doubleday, 1969.

Carlston, Erin. *Double Agents: Espionage, Literature, and Liminal Citizens*. New York: Columbia University Press, 2013.

Caro, Robert A. *The Years of Lyndon Johnson*. Vol. 1, *The Path to Power*. New York: Alfred A. Knopf, 1982.

——. *The Years of Lyndon Johnson*. Vol. 2, *Means of Ascent*. New York: Alfred A. Knopf, 1991.

——. *The Years of Lyndon Johnson*. Vol. 3, *Master of the Senate*. New York: Alfred A. Knopf, 2002.

——. *The Years of Lyndon Johnson*. Vol. 4, *The Passage of Power*. New York: Alfred A. Knopf, 2012.

Caroli, Betty Boyd. *Lady Bird and Lyndon: The Hidden Story of a Marriage That Made a President*. New York: Simon and Schuster, 2015.

Carpenter, Donald H. *Man of a Million Fragments: The True Story of Clay Shaw*. Nashville: Donald H. Carpenter, 2014.

Caute, David. *The Great Fear: The Anti-Communist Purge Under Truman and Eisenhower*. New York: Simon and Schuster, 1978.

Cecil, Matthew. *Hoover's FBI and the Fourth Estate: The Campaign to Control the Press and the Bureau's Image*. Lawrence: University of Kansas Press, 2014.

Chafe, William. *Never Stop Running: Allard Lowenstein and the Struggle to Save American Liberalism*. New York: Basic Books, 1993.

Chambers, Whittaker. *Odyssey of a Friend: Whittaker Chambers Letters to William F. Buckley, Jr., 1954–1961*. Edited by William F. Buckley Jr. Washington, DC: Regnery, 1987.

——. *Witness*. New York: Random House, 1952.

Charles, Douglas M. *Hoover's War on Gays: Exposing the FBI's "Sex Deviates" Program*. Lawrence: University Press of Kansas, 2015.

Chauncey, George. *Gay New York: Gender, Urban Culture, and the Making of the Gay Male*. New York: Basic Books, 1994.

Cheever, John. *The Journals of John Cheever*. New York: Alfred A. Knopf, 1991.

Cheshire, Maxine, with John Greenya. *Maxine Cheshire, Reporter*. Boston: Houghton Mifflin, 1978.

Clarke, Gerald. *Capote: A Biography*. New York: Simon and Schuster, 1988.

Clarke, Lige, and Jack Nichols. *I Have More Fun with You Than Anybody*. New York: St. Martin's Press, 1972.

Clendinen, Dudley, and Adam Nagourney. *Out for Good: The Struggle to Build a Gay Rights Movement in America*. New York: Simon and Schuster, 1999.

Clifford, Clark, with Richard Holbrooke. *Counsel to the President: A Memoir*. New York: Random House, 1991.

Cline, Ray S. *Secrets, Spies, and Scholars: Blueprint of the Essential CIA*. Washington, DC: Acropolis Books, 1976.

Cohn, Roy. *McCarthy*. New York: New American Library, 1968.

Colacello, Bob. *Ronnie and Nancy: Their Path to the White House, 1911 to 1980*. New York: Warner Books, 2004.

Colby, William, and Peter Forbath. *Honorable Men: My Life in the CIA*. New York: Simon and Schuster, 1978.

Cook, Blanche Wiesen. *Eleanor Roosevelt*. Vol. 2, *1933–1938*. New York: Viking, 1999.

Cooke, Alistair. *A Generation on Trial: U.S.A. vs. Alger Hiss*. New York: Alfred A. Knopf, 1950.

Cordery, Stacy A. *Alice: Alice Roosevelt Longworth, from White House Princess to Washington Power Broker*. New York: Viking, 2007.

Cory, Donald Webster. *The Homosexual in America: A Subjective Approach*. New York: Greenberg, 1951.

Costello, John. *Mask of Treachery*. New York: William Morrow, 1988.

Costigliola, Frank. *Roosevelt's Lost Alliances: How Personal Politics Helped Start the Cold War*. Princeton, NJ: Princeton University Press, 2012.

Croall, Jonathan. *John Gielgud: Matinee Idol to Movie Star*. London: Methuen Drama, 2012.

Cummings, Richard. *The Pied Piper: Allard K. Lowenstein and the Liberal Dream*. New York: Grove Press, 1985.

Cuordileone, K. A. *Manhood and American Political Culture in the Cold War*. New York: Routledge, 2005.

Cutler, Robert. *No Time for Rest*. Boston: Little, Brown, 1966.

Dallek, Robert. *Flawed Giant: Lyndon Johnson and His Times, 1961–1973*. New York: Oxford University Press, 1998.

——. *Franklin D. Roosevelt and American Foreign Policy, 1932–1945*. Oxford: Oxford University Press, 1979.

——. *Lyndon B. Johnson: Portrait of a President*. Oxford: Oxford University Press, 2004.

——. *An Unfinished Life: John F. Kennedy, 1917–1963*. New York: Back Bay Books, 2003.

Davenport-Hines, Richard. *Enemies Within: Communists, the Cambridge Spies and the Making of Modern Britain*. London: William Collins, 2018.

Dean, Robert D. *Imperial Brotherhood: Gender and the Making of Cold War Foreign Policy*. Amherst: University of Massachusetts Press, 2001.

Dearborn, Mary V. *Queen of Bohemia: The Life of Louise Bryant*. Boston: Houghton Mifflin, 1996.

Deaver, Michael K. *Behind the Scenes: In Which the Author Talks About Ronald and Nancy Reagan . . . and Himself*. New York: William Morrow, 1987.

DeLoach, Cartha "Deke." *Hoover's FBI: The Inside Story by Hoover's Trusted Lieutenant*. Washington, DC: Regnery, 1995.

de Margerie, Caroline. *American Lady: The Life of Susan Mary Alsop*. Translated by Christopher Murray. New York: Viking, 2011.

Demaris, Ovid. *The Director: An Oral Biography of J. Edgar Hoover*. New York: Harper's Magazine Press, 1975.

D'Emilio, John. *Lost Prophet: The Life and Times of Bayard Rustin*. Chicago: University of Chicago Press, 2003.

——. *Sexual Politics, Sexual Communities: The Making of a Homosexual Minority in the United States, 1940–1970*. Chicago: University of Chicago Press, 1983.

——. *The World Turned: Essays on Gay History, Politics, and Culture*. Durham, NC: Duke University Press, 2002.

Doherty, Thomas. *Cold War, Cool Medium: Television, McCarthyism, and American Culture*. New York: Columbia University Press, 2003.

Donner, Frank J. *The Age of Surveillance: The Aims and Methods of America's Political Intelligence System*. New York: Alfred A. Knopf, 1980.

Downes, Donald. *The Scarlet Thread: Adventures in Wartime Espionage*. London: Derek Verschoyle, 1953.

Downey, Kirstin. *The Woman Behind the New Deal: The Life of and Legacy of Frances Perkins, Social Security, Unemployment Insurance, and the Minimum Wage*. New York: Anchor Books, 2010.

Driberg, Tom. *Guy Burgess: A Portrait with Background*. London: Weidenfeld and Nicolson, 1956.

Drury, Allen. *Advise and Consent*. Garden City, NY: Doubleday, 1959.

Dulles, Allen. *The Craft of Intelligence*. New York: Harper and Row, 1963.

——, ed. *Great True Spy Stories*. New York: Harper and Row, 1968.

Dunlop, Richard. *Donovan: America's Master Spy*. Chicago: Rand McNally, 1982.

Dunne, John Gregory. *Quintana and Friends*. New York: E.P. Dutton, 1978.

Dynes, Wane R. *Encyclopedia of Homosexuality*. Vol. 1, A–L. New York: Garland, 1990.

Ehrenstein, David. *Open Secret: Gay Hollywood, 1928–1998*. New York: William Morrow, 1998.

Ehrlichman, John. *Witness to Power: The Nixon Years*. New York: Simon and Schuster, 1982.

Eisenhower, Dwight D. *Mandate for Change, 1953–1956*. Garden City, NY: Doubleday, 1963.

Epstein, Daniel Mark. *Lincoln and Whitman: Parallel Lives in Civil War Washington*. New York: Random House, 2004.

Eskridge Jr., William N. *Dishonorable Passions: Sodomy Laws in America, 1861–2003*. New York: Viking, 2008.

———. *Gaylaw: Challenging the Apartheid of the Closet*. Cambridge, MA: Harvard University Press, 1999.

Etkind, Alexander. *Roads Not Taken: An Intellectual Biography of William C. Bullitt*. Pittsburgh: University of Pittsburgh Press, 2017.

Faber, Doris. *The Life of Lorena Hickok: E.R.'s Friend*. New York: William Morrow, 1980.

Faderman, Lillian. *The Gay Revolution: The Story of the Struggle*. New York: Simon and Schuster, 2015.

———. *Odd Girls and Twilight Lovers: A History of Lesbian Life in Twentieth-Century America*. New York: Penguin, 1991.

Fariello, Griffin. *Red Scare: Memories of the American Inquisition*. New York: Avon Books, 1995.

Farnsworth, Beatrice. *William C. Bullitt and the Soviet Union*. Bloomington: Indiana University Press, 1967.

Farrell, John. *Richard Nixon: The Life*. New York: Doubleday, 2017.

Feldstein, Mark. *Poisoning the Press: Richard Nixon, Jack Anderson, and the Rise of Washington's Scandal Culture*. New York: Farrar, Straus and Giroux, 2010.

Fisher, James T. *Dr. America: The Lives of Thomas A. Dooley, 1927–1961*. Amherst: University of Massachusetts Press, 1997.

Fite, Gilbert C. *Richard B. Russell, Jr.: Senator from Georgia*. Chapel Hill: University of North Carolina Press, 1991.

Fleming, John V. *The Anti-Communist Manifestos*. New York: W. W. Norton, 2009.

Ford, Corey, and Alastair MacBain. *Cloak and Dagger: The Secret Story of the OSS*. New York: Random House, 1945.

Ford, Gerald. *A Time to Heal: The Autobiography of Gerald R. Ford*. New York: Harper and Row, 1979.

France, David. *How to Survive a Plague: The Inside Story of How Citizens and Science Tamed AIDS*. New York: Alfred A. Knopf, 2016.

Frank, Barney. *Frank: A Life in Politics from the Great Society to Same-Sex Marriage*. New York: Farrar, Straus and Giroux, 2015.

Freud, Sigmund, and William C. Bullitt. *Thomas Woodrow Wilson: A Psychological Study*. Boston: Houghton Mifflin, 1966.

Friedman, Mack. *Strapped for Cash: A History of American Hustler Culture*. Los Angeles: Alyson Books, 2003.

Friend, David. *The Naughty Nineties*. New York: Hachette, 2017.

Fromkin, David. *In the Time of the Americans: FDR, Truman, Eisenhower, Marshall, MacArthur—The Generation That Changed America's Role in the World*. New York: Alfred A. Knopf, 1995.

Fullilove, Michael. *Rendezvous with Destiny: How Franklin D. Roosevelt and Five Extraordinary Men Took America into the War and into the World*. New York: Penguin, 2013.

Fursenko, Alexander, and Timothy Naftali. *One Hell of a Gamble: Khrushchev, Castro, and Kennedy, 1958–1964*. New York: W. W. Norton, 1997.

Gardner, Virginia. *"Friend and Lover": The Life of Louise Bryant*. New York: Horizon Press, 1982.

Garment, Leonard. *Crazy Rhythm: My Journey from Brooklyn, Jazz, and Wall Street to Nixon's White House, Watergate, and Beyond*. New York: Times Books, 1997.

Garrow, David J. *Bearing the Cross: Martin Luther King, Jr., and the Southern Christian Leadership Conference*. New York: Vintage, 1986.

Gellman, Irwin. *Secret Affairs: Franklin Roosevelt, Cordell Hull, and Sumner Welles*. Baltimore: Johns Hopkins University Press, 1995.

Gentry, Curt. *J. Edgar Hoover: The Man and the Secrets*. New York: W. W. Norton, 1991.

Giles, Frank. *Sundry Times: Autobiography*. London: John Murray, 1986.

Gillette, Michael L. *Lady Bird Johnson: An Oral History*. Oxford: Oxford University Press, 2012.

Goldman, Eric Frederick. *The Tragedy of Lyndon Johnson*. New York: Alfred A. Knopf, 1969.

Goldwater, Barry M. *With No Apologies: The Personal and Political Memoir of United States Senator Barry M. Goldwater*. New York: William Morrow, 1979.

Goldwater, Barry M., with Jack Casserly. *Goldwater*. New York: Doubleday, 1988.

Goodwin, Doris Kearns. *Lyndon Johnson and the American Dream*. New York: St. Martin's Press, 1976.

———. *No Ordinary Time: Franklin & Eleanor Roosevelt: The Home Front in World War II*. New York: Simon and Schuster, 1994.

Graham, Katharine. *Personal History*. New York: Alfred A. Knopf, 1997.

Gray, Robert Keith. *Eighteen Acres Under Glass*. Garden City, NY: Doubleday, 1962.

Griffin, Mark. *All That Heaven Allows: A Biography of Rock Hudson*. New York: HarperCollins, 2018.

Grose, Peter. *Gentleman Spy: The Life of Allen Dulles*. Boston: Houghton Mifflin, 1994.

———. *Operation Rollback: America's Secret War Behind the Iron Curtain*. Boston: Houghton Mifflin, 2000.

Gunther, John. *Roosevelt in Retrospect: A Profile in History*. New York: Harper, 1950.

Halberstam, David. *The Fifties*. New York: Villard Books, 1993.

Haldeman, H. R. *The Haldeman Diaries: Inside the Nixon White House*. New York: G.P. Putnam's Sons, 1994.

Hamilton, Charles V. *Adam Clayton Powell, Jr.: The Political Biography of an American Dilemma*. New York: Atheneum, 1991.

Hamilton, Nigel. *J.F.K.: Reckless Youth*. New York: Random House, 1992.

Haskins, Faye. *The Evening Star: The Rise and Fall of a Great Washington Newspaper*. Lanham, MD: Rowman and Littlefield, 2019.

Haygood, Wil. *King of the Cats: The Life and Times of Adam Clayton Powell, Jr.* New York: Houghton Mifflin, 1993.

Heinrichs Jr., Waldo H. *American Ambassador: Joseph C. Grew and the Development of the United States Diplomatic Tradition*. Boston: Little, Brown, 1966.

Helms, Alan. *Young Man from the Provinces: A Gay Life Before Stonewall*. Boston: Faber and Faber, 1995.

Helms, Richard, with William Hood. *A Look over My Shoulder: A Life in the Central Intelligence Agency*. New York: Presidio Press, 2003.

Henry, Lauren Luther. *Presidential Transitions*. Washington, DC: Brookings Institution, 1960.

Herken, Gregg. *The Georgetown Set: Friends and Rivals in Cold War Washington*. New York: Alfred A. Knopf, 2014.

Hersh, Burton. *The Old Boys: The American Elite and the Origins of the CIA*. New York: Charles Scribner's Sons, 1992.

Hersh, Seymour M. *The Price of Power: Kissinger in the Nixon White House*. New York: Summit Books, 1983.

Heymann, David C. *The Georgetown Ladies Social Club: Power, Passion, and Politics in the Nation's Capital*. New York: Atria, 2003.

Himmelman, Jeff. *Yours in Truth: A Personal Portrait of Ben Bradlee*. New York: Random House, 2012.

Hinton, Harold B. *Cordell Hull: A Biography*. Garden City, NY: Doubleday, Doran, 1942.

Hippler, Mike. *Matlovich: The Good Soldier*. Boston: Alyson, 1989.

Hirsch, Foster. *Otto Preminger: The Man Who Would Be King*. New York: Alfred A. Knopf, 2007.

Hiss, Alger. *Recollections of a Life*. New York: Seaver Books, 1988.

Hiss, Tony. *Laughing Last*. New York: Houghton Mifflin, 1977.

———. *The View from Alger's Window*. New York: Alfred A. Knopf, 1999.

Hitchcock, William I. *The Age of Eisenhower: America and the World in the 1950s*. New York: Simon and Schuster, 2018.

Hodges, Andrew. *Alan Turing: The Enigma*. London: Burnett, 1983.

Horne, Alistair. *But What Do You Actually Do? A Literary Vagabondage*. London: Weidenfeld and Nicolson, 2011.

Howard, John. *Men Like That: A Southern Queer History*. Chicago: University of Chicago Press, 1999.

Hunter, John Francis. *The Gay Insider*. New York: Stonehill Publishing, 1972.

Ibson, John. *Men Without Maps: Some Gay Males of the Generation Before Stonewall*. Chicago: University of Chicago Press, 2019.

Ickes, Harold. *The Secret Diary of Harold Ickes: The Inside Struggle*. New York: Simon and Schuster, 1954.

Isaacson, Walter, and Evan Thomas. *The Wise Men: Six Friends and the World They Made*. New York: Simon and Schuster, 1986.

James, Henry. *The American Scene*. London: Chapman and Hall, 1907.

Johnson, David K. *Buying Gay: How Physique Entrepreneurs Sparked a Movement*. New York: Columbia University Press, 2019.

———. *The Lavender Scare: The Cold War Persecution of Gays and Lesbians in the Federal Government*. Chicago: University of Chicago Press, 2004.

Johnson, Lady Bird. *A White House Diary*. New York: Holt, Rinehart and Winston, 1970.

Judis, John B. *William F. Buckley, Jr.: Patron Saint of the Conservatives*. New York: Simon and Schuster, 1988.

Kabaservice, Geoffrey. *Rule and Ruin: The Downfall of Moderation and the Destruction of the Republican Party, from Eisenhower to the Tea Party*. Oxford: Oxford University Press, 2012.

Kaiser, Charles. *The Gay Metropolis: The Landmark History of Gay Life in America*. New York: Grove Press, 1997.

Kalman, Laura. *Abe Fortas: A Biography*. New Haven, CT: Yale University Press, 1990.

Kaplan, Fred. *Gore Vidal: A Biography*. New York: Doubleday, 1999.

Katz, Jonathan Ned. *Gay American History: Lesbians and Gay Men in the U.S.A*. New York: Thomas Crowell, 1976.

Kelley, Kitty. *Nancy Reagan: The Unauthorized Biography*. New York: Simon and Schuster, 1991.

Kessler, Ronald. *Inside the CIA: Revealing the Secrets of the World's Most Powerful Spy Agency*. New York: Atria, 1992.

Kimmage, Michael. *The Conservative Turn*. Cambridge, MA: Harvard University Press, 2009.

Kinsey, Alfred, Wardell B. Pomeroy, and Clyde E. Martin. *Sexual Behavior in the Human Male*. Bloomington: University of Indiana Press, 1948.

Kirkendall, Richard S., ed. *Civil Liberties and the Legacy of Harry S. Truman*. Kirksville, MO: Truman State University Press, 2013.

Kirkwood, James. *American Grotesque: An Account of the Clay Shaw–Jim Garrison Affair in the City of New Orleans*. New York: Simon and Schuster, 1970.

Kissinger, Henry. *White House Years*. Boston: Little, Brown, 1979.

———. *Years of Upheaval*. Boston: Little, Brown, 1982.

Klurfeld, Herman. *Behind the Lines: The World of Drew Pearson*. Englewood Cliffs, NJ: Prentice-Hall, 1968.

Knightley, Phillip. *The Second Oldest Profession: Spies and Spying in the Twentieth Century*. New York: W. W. Norton, 1987.

Knowles, John. *A Separate Peace*. New York: Macmillan, 1960.

Kondracke, Morton, and Fred Barnes. *Jack Kemp: The Bleeding-Heart Conservative*. New York: Sentinel, 2015.

Kornitzer, Bela. *The Real Nixon: An Intimate Biography*. New York: Rand McNally, 1960.

Lait, Jack, and Lee Mortimer. *U.S.A. Confidential*. New York: Crown, 1952.

———. *Washington Confidential*. New York: Crown, 1951.

Lakoff, Sanford. *Max Lerner: Pilgrim in the Promised Land*. Chicago: University of Chicago Press, 1998.

Langer, Walter C. *The Mind of Adolph [sic] Hitler: The Secret Wartime Report*. New York: Basic Books, 1972.

Lash, Joseph P. *Love, Eleanor: Eleanor Roosevelt and Her Friends*. New York: Doubleday, 1982.

Latham, Earl. *The Communist Controversy in Washington*. Cambridge, MA: Harvard University Press, 1966.

Leavitt, David. *The Man Who Knew Too Much: Alan Turing and the Invention of the Computer*. New York: W. W. Norton, 2006.

Lewis, Wyndham. *The Hitler Cult*. London: Dent, 1939.

Liebman, Marvin. *Coming Out Conservative: An Autobiography*. San Francisco: Chronicle Books, 1992.

Lipsey, Roger. *Hammarskjöld: A Life*. Ann Arbor: University of Michigan Press, 2016.

Litwin, Fred. *I Was a Teenage JFK Conspiracy Freak*. Ottawa: NorthernBlues Books, 2018.

Livingston, Bob. *The Windmill Chaser: Triumphs and Less in American Politics*. Lafayette: University of Louisiana at Lafayette Press, 2018.

Long, Michael G. *Martin Luther King, Jr., Homosexuality, and the Early Gay Rights Movement: Keeping the Dream Straight?* New York: Palgrave Macmillan, 2012.

Loughery, John. *The Other Side of Silence: Men's Lives and Gay Identities: A Twentieth-Century History.* New York: Henry Holt, 1998.

Lownie, Andrew. *Stalin's Englishman: Guy Burgess, the Cold War, and the Cambridge Spy Ring.* New York: St. Martin's Press, 2015.

Lukacs, John. *Philadelphia: Patricians and Philistines, 1900–1950.* Philadelphia: ISHI Publications, 1980.

———, ed. *Through the History of the Cold War: The Correspondence of George F. Kennan and John Lukacs.* Philadelphia: University of Pennsylvania Press, 2010.

Lumsden, Ian. *Machos, Maricones, and Gays: Cuba and Homosexuality.* Philadelphia: Temple University Press, 1996.

Mann, William J. *Behind the Screen: How Gays and Lesbians Shaped Hollywood, 1910–1969.* New York: Viking, 2001.

———. *Wisecracker: The Life and Times of William Haines, Hollywood's First Openly Gay Star.* New York: Viking, 1998.

Marcus, Eric. *Making History: The Struggle for Gay and Lesbian Equal Rights, 1945–1990.* New York: Harper Perennial, 1992.

Markmann, Charles Lam. *The Buckleys: A Family Examined.* New York: William Morrow, 1973.

Marotta, Toby. *The Politics of Homosexuality.* Boston: Houghton Mifflin, 1981.

Martin, Ralph G. *Cissy: The Extraordinary Life of Eleanor Medill Patterson.* New York: Simon and Schuster, 1979.

Marton, Kati. *Hidden Power: Presidential Marriages That Shaped Our Recent History.* New York: Pantheon, 2001.

Mattingly, Doreen. *A Feminist in the White House: Midge Costanza, the Carter Years, and America's Culture Wars.* New York: Oxford University Press, 2016.

McCubbin, Lisa. *Betty Ford: First Lady, Women's Advocate, Survivor, Trailblazer.* New York: Gallery Books, 2018.

McGinnis, Joe. *The Selling of the President, 1968.* New York: Trident Press, 1969.

McIntosh, Elizabeth P. *Sisterhood of Spies: The Women of the OSS.* New York: Dell, 1998.

McManus, Doyle, and Jane Mayer. *Landslide: The Unmaking of the President, 1984–1988.* Boston: Houghton Mifflin, 1988.

Meijer, Hendrik. *Arthur Vandenberg: The Man in the Middle of the American Century.* Chicago: University of Chicago Press, 2017.

Merrick, Gordon. *The Lord Won't Mind.* New York: Avon, 1970.

———. *The Strumpet Wind.* New York: William Morrow, 1947.

Merry, Robert W. *Taking On the World: Joseph and Stewart Alsop, Guardians of the American Century.* New York: Viking, 1996.

Meyer, Cord. *Facing Reality: From World Federalism to the CIA.* Latham, MD: University Press of America, 1980.

Michaelis, David. *The Best of Friends: Profiles of Extraordinary Friendships.* New York: William Morrow, 1983.

Miller, Brian. *Here Because We're Queer: Inside the Gay Liberation Front of Washington, D.C., 1970–72.* Washington, DC: IngramSpark, 2020.

Miller, Merle. *Lyndon: An Oral Biography.* New York: G.P. Putnam's Sons, 1980.

Miller, Nathan. *FDR: An Intimate History.* New York: Doubleday, 1983.

Miller, William "Fishbait," as told to Frances Spatz Leighton. *Fishbait: The Memoirs of the Congressional Doorkeeper.* Englewood Cliffs, NJ: Prentice-Hall, 1977.

Mixner, David. *Stranger Among Friends.* New York: Bantam Books, 1996.

Monette, Paul. *Becoming a Man: Half a Life Story.* New York: Harcourt, 1992.

Morgan, Ted. *A Covert Life: Jay Lovestone, Communist, Anti-Communist, and Spymaster.* New York: Random House, 1999.

———. *FDR: A Biography.* New York: Simon and Schuster, 1985.

———. *Reds: McCarthyism in Twentieth-Century America.* New York: Random House, 2003.

Morley, Raymond. *After Seven Years.* New York: Harper and Brothers, 1939.

Morris, Roger. *Richard Milhous Nixon: The Rise of an American Politician.* New York: Henry Holt, 1991.

Mosley, Leonard. *Dulles: A Biography of Eleanor, Allen, and John Foster Dulles and Their Family Network.* New York: Dial Press, 1978.

Murdoch, Joyce, and Deb Price. *Courting Justice: Gay Men and Lesbians v. the Supreme Court*. New York: Basic Books, 2001.

Murphy, Lawrence R. *Perverts by Official Order: The Campaign Against Homosexuals by the United States Navy*. New York: Harrington Park Press, 1988.

Murphy, Robert. *Diplomat Among Warriors*. New York: Doubleday, 1964.

Muzzy, Frank. *Gay and Lesbian Washington, D.C.* Charleston, SC: Arcadia, 2005.

Newton, Verne W. *The Cambridge Spies: The Untold Story of Maclean, Philby, and Burgess in America*. Lanham, MD: Madison Books, 1991.

Nichols, David A. *Ike and McCarthy: Dwight Eisenhower's Secret Campaign Against Joseph McCarthy*. New York: Simon and Schuster, 2017.

Nichols, Jack. *The Tomcat Chronicles: Erotic Adventures of a Gay Liberation Pioneer*. New York: Harrington Park Press, 2004.

Nissenson, Marilyn. *The Lady Upstairs: Dorothy Schiff and the* New York Post. New York: St. Martin's Press, 2007.

Nixon, Richard. *RN: The Memoirs of Richard Nixon*. New York: Grosset and Dunlap, 1978.

———. *Six Crises*. New York: Doubleday, 1962.

Nofziger, Lyn. *Nofziger*. Washington, DC: Regnery Gateway, 1992.

Noonan, Peggy. *What I Saw at the Revolution: A Political Life in the Reagan Era*. New York: Random House, 1990.

Novak, Robert. *The Prince of Darkness: 50 Years Reporting in Washington*. New York: Crown Forum, 2007.

O'Donnell, Patrick K. *Operatives, Spies, and Saboteurs: The Unknown Story of the Men and Women of World War II's OSS*. New York: Free Press, 2004.

Oppenheimer, Jerry. *RFK Jr.: Robert F. Kennedy Jr. and the Dark Side of the Dream*. New York: St. Martin's Press, 2015.

Oshinsky, David. *A Conspiracy So Immense: The World of Joe McCarthy*. New York: Free Press, 1983.

O'Sullivan, Christopher D. *Sumner Welles, Postwar Planning, and the Quest for a New World Order, 1937–1943*. New York: Columbia University Press, 2008.

Parini, Jay. *Empire of Self: A Life of Gore Vidal*. New York: Doubleday, 2015.

Parker, Robert, with Richard Rashke. *Capitol Hill in Black and White*. New York: Dodd, Mead, 1986.

Patten, Bill. *My Three Fathers: And the Elegant Deceptions of My Mother, Susan Mary Alsop*. New York: PublicAffairs, 2008.

Pearson, Drew. *Drew Pearson Diaries: 1949–1959*. Edited by Tyler Abell. New York: Holt, Rinehart, and Winston, 1974.

———. *Washington Merry-Go-Round: The Drew Pearson Diaries, 1960–1969*. Edited by Peter Hannaford. Lincoln: University of Nebraska Press, 2015.

Penner, James. *Pinks, Pansies, and Punks: The Rhetoric of Masculinity in American Literary Culture*. Bloomington: Indiana University Press, 2011.

Perlstein, Rick. *Before the Storm: Barry Goldwater and the Unmaking of the American Consensus*. New York: Hill and Wang, 2001.

———. *Nixonland: The Rise of a President and the Fracturing of America*. New York: Charles Scribner's Sons, 2008.

Perret, Geoffrey. *Jack: A Life Like No Other*. New York: Random House, 2001.

Persico, Joseph E. *Roosevelt's Secret War: FDR and World War II Espionage*. New York: Random House, 2001.

Phelan, James. *Scandals, Scamps, and Scoundrels: The Casebook of an Investigative Reporter*. New York: Random House, 1982.

Philipps, Roland. *A Spy Named Orphan: The Enigma of Donald Maclean*. London: The Bodley Head, 2018.

Pilat, Oliver. *Drew Pearson: An Authorized Biography*. New York: Harper's Magazine Press, 1973.

Pitts, David. *Jack and Lem: John F. Kennedy and Lem Billings: The Untold Story of an Extraordinary Friendship*. New York: Carroll and Graf, 2007.

Plant, Richard. *The Pink Triangle: The Nazi War Against Homosexuals*. New York: Henry Holt, 1986.

Plimpton, George. *Truman Capote: In Which Various Friends, Enemies, Acquaintances, and Detractors Recall His Turbulent Career*. New York: Nan A. Talese/Doubleday, 1997.

Polchin, James. *Indecent Advances: A Hidden History of True Crime and Prejudice Before Stonewall*. Berkeley, CA: Counterpoint, 2019.

Potter, Jeffrey. *Men, Money, and Magic: The Story of Dorothy Schiff*. New York: Coward, McCann and Geoghegan, 1976.

Powers, Richard Gid. *Broken: The Troubled Past and Uncertain Future of the FBI*. New York: Free Press, 2004.

———. *Not Without Honor: The History of American Anti-Communism*. New York: Free Press, 1995.

———. *Secrecy and Power: The Life of J. Edgar Hoover*. New York: Free Press, 1987.

Prados, John. *Safe for Democracy: The Secret Wars of the CIA*. Chicago: Ivan R. Dee, 2006.

Purvis, Stewart, and Jeff Hulbert. *Guy Burgess: The Spy Who Knew Everyone*. London: Biteback, 2016.

Quinn, Sally. *The Party: A Guide to Adventurous Entertaining*. New York: Fireside, 1997.

Quinn, Susan. *Eleanor and Hick: The Love Affair That Shaped a First Lady*. New York: Penguin, 2016.

Radosh, Ronald, and Joyce Milton: *The Rosenberg File: A Search for the Truth*. New York: Holt, Rinehart and Winston, 1983.

Reagan, Nancy. *My Turn: The Memoirs of Nancy Reagan*. New York: Random House, 1989.

Reagan, Ronald. *An American Life*. New York: Simon and Schuster, 1990.

Rees, Goronwy. *A Chapter of Accidents*. London: Chatto and Windus, 1972.

Reeves, Richard. *President Nixon: Alone in the White House*. New York: Simon and Schuster, 2001.

Reeves, Thomas C. *The Life and Times of Joe McCarthy*. New York: Stein and Day, 1982.

Reston, James. *Deadline*. New York: Random House, 1991.

Riebling, Mark. *Wedge: From Pearl Harbor to 9/11: How the Secret War Between the FBI and CIA Has Endangered National Security*. New York: Touchstone, 1994.

Ritchie, Donald A. *The Columnist: Leaks, Lies, and Libel in Drew Pearson's Washington*. Oxford: Oxford University Press, 2021.

Robinson, Forrest G. *Love's Story Told: A Life of Henry A. Murray*. Cambridge, MA: Harvard University Press, 1992.

Roosevelt, Eleanor. *This I Remember*. New York: Harper, 1949.

Roosevelt, Elliott. *A Rendezvous with Destiny*. New York: Putnam, 1975.

Rosenau, James. *The Nomination of "Chip" Bohlen*. New York: Henry Holt, 1958.

Rosenfeld, Seth. *Subversives: The FBI's War on Student Radicals, and Reagan's Rise to Power*. New York: Farrar, Straus and Giroux, 2012.

Rosswurm, Steve. *The FBI and the Catholic Church, 1935–1962*. Amherst: University of Massachusetts Press, 2009.

Roudinesco, Élizabeth. *Freud: In His Time and Ours*. Cambridge, MA: Harvard University Press, 2016.

Rovere, Richard H. *Senator Joe McCarthy*. New York: Harcourt, Brace, 1959.

Rowan, Richard Wilmer. Excerpt of *The Story of the Secret Service*. In *Great True Spy Stories*, edited by Allen Dulles. New York: Harper and Row, 1968.

Ruddy, T. Michael. *The Cautious Diplomat: Charles E. Bohlen and the Soviet Union, 1929–1969*. Kent, OH: Kent State University Press, 1986.

Rueda, Enrique. *The Homosexual Network: Private Lives and Public Policy*. Old Greenwich, CT: Devin Adair, 1982.

Rumsfeld, Donald. *Known and Unknown*. New York: Sentinel, 2011.

Russell, Ina, ed. *Jeb and Dash: A Diary of Gay Life, 1918–1945*. Boston: Faber and Faber, 1993.

Russell, Jan Jarboe. *Lady Bird: A Biography of Mrs. Johnson*. New York: Scribner, 1999.

Russo, Vito. *The Celluloid Closet: Homosexuality in the Movies*. New York: Harper and Row, 1981.

Saunders, Frances Stonor. *The Cultural Cold War: The CIA and the World of Arts and Letters*. New York: The New Press, 1999.

Schlesinger Jr., Arthur M. *A Life in the Twentieth Century: Innocent Beginnings, 1917–1950*. Boston: Houghton Mifflin, 2000.

———. *Journals: 1952–2000*. New York: Penguin, 2007.

———. *Robert Kennedy and His Times*. New York: Ballantine Books, 1978.

———. *The Vital Center: The Politics of Freedom*. Boston: Houghton Mifflin, 1949.

Schmidgall, Gary. *Walt Whitman: A Gay Life*. New York: Penguin, 1997.

Schoultz, Lars. *That Infernal Little Cuban Republic: The United States and the Cuban Revolution*. Chapel Hill: University of North Carolina Press, 2009.

Schroeder, Richard E. *The Foundation of the CIA: Harry Truman, the Missouri Gang, and the Origins of the Cold War*. Columbia: University of Missouri Press, 2017.

Schulman, Bruce J., and Julian E. Zelizer, eds. *Rightward Bound: Making America Conservative in the 1970s*. Cambridge, MA: Harvard University Press, 2008.

Schuparra, Kurt. *Triumph of the Right: The Rise of the California Conservative Movement, 1945–1966*. London: Routledge, 1998.

Scott, Henry E. *Shocking True Story: The Rise and Fall of Confidential, "America's Most Scandalous Scandal Magazine."* New York: Pantheon, 2010.

Seymour, Craig. *All I Could Bare: My Life in the Strip Clubs of Gay Washington, D.C.* New York: Atria, 2008.

Seymour, Susan C. *Cora Du Bois: Anthropologist, Diplomat, Agent*. Lincoln: University of Nebraska Press, 2015.

Sherry, Michael S. *Gay Artists in Modern American Culture: An Imagined Conspiracy*. Chapel Hill: University of North Carolina Press, 2007.

Shesol, Jeff. *Mutual Contempt: Lyndon Johnson, Robert Kennedy, and the Feud That Defined a Decade*. New York: W. W. Norton, 1997.

Shilts, Randy. *And the Band Played On: Politics, People, and the AIDS Epidemic*. New York: St. Martin's Press, 1987.

———. *Conduct Unbecoming: Gays and Lesbians in the U.S. Military*. New York: St. Martin's Press, 1993.

———. *The Mayor of Castro Street: The Life and Times of Harvey Milk*. New York: St. Martin's Press, 1982.

Shinkle, Peter. *Ike's Mystery Man: The Secret Lives of Robert Cutler*. Hanover, NH: Steerforth Press, 2018.

Shirer, William L. *The Rise and Fall of the Third Reich*. New York: Simon and Schuster, 1960.

Shogan, Robert. *No Sense of Decency: The Army-McCarthy Hearings: A Demagogue Falls and Television Takes Charge of American Politics*. Chicago: Ivan R. Dee, 2009.

Signorile, Michelangelo. *Queer in America*. New York: Random House, 1993.

Simpson, Christopher. *Blowback: America's Recruitment of Nazis and Its Effects on the Cold War*. New York: Weidenfeld and Nicolson, 1988.

Singlaub, John, with Malcolm McConnell. *Hazardous Duty: An America Soldier in the Twentieth Century*. New York: Summit Books, 1991.

Sister Circle: Black Women and Work. Edited by Sharon Harley and the Black Women and Work Collective. New Brunswick, NJ: Rutgers University Press, 2002.

Smant, Kevin J. *How Great the Triumph: James Burnham, Anticommunism, and the Conservative Movement*. Lanham, MD: University Press of America, 1992.

Smith, Jean Edward. *Eisenhower in War and Peace*. New York: Random House, 2012.

———. *FDR*. New York: Random House, 2007.

Smith, John Chabot. *Alger Hiss: The True Story*. New York: Holt, Rinehart and Winston, 1976.

Smith, Kathryn. *The Gatekeeper: Missy LeHand, FDR, and the Untold Story of the Partnership That Defined a Presidency*. New York: Touchstone, 2016.

Smith, R. Harris. *OSS: The Secret History of America's First Central Intelligence Agency*. Berkeley: University of California Press, 1972.

Smith, Sally Bedell. *Grace and Power: The Private World of the Kennedy White House*. New York: Random House, 2004.

Speakes, Larry, with Robert Pack. *Speaking Out: The Reagan Presidency from Inside the White House*. New York: Charles Scribner's Sons, 1988.

Spring, Justin. *Secret Historian: The Life and Times of Samuel Steward, Professor, Tattoo Artist, and Sexual Renegade*. New York: Farrar, Straus and Giroux, 2010.

Srodes, James. *On Dupont Circle: Franklin and Eleanor Roosevelt and the Progressives Who Shaped Our World*. Berkeley, CA: Counterpoint, 2012.

Stadiem, William. *Too Rich: The High Life and Tragic Death of King Farouk*. New York: Carroll and Graf, 1991.

Steel, Johannes. *Hitler as Frankenstein*. London: Wishart, 1933.

Stimson, Henry L., and McGeorge Bundy. *On Active Service in Peace and War*. New York: Harper, 1948.

Streitmatter, Rodger, ed. *Empty Without You: The Intimate Letters of Eleanor Roosevelt and Lorena Hickok*. New York: Free Press, 1998.

———. *Unspeakable: The Rise of the Gay and Lesbian Press in America*. Boston: Faber and Faber, 1995.

Strub, Sean. *Body Counts: A Memoir of Politics, Sex, AIDS, and Survival*. New York: Scribner, 2014.

Sullivan, William C. *The Bureau: My Thirty Years in Hoover's FBI*. New York: W. W. Norton, 1979.

Sulzberger, C. L. *A Long Row of Candles: Memoirs and Diaries, 1934–1954*. New York: Macmillan, 1969.

Summers, Anthony. *Official and Confidential: The Secret Life of J. Edgar Hoover*. New York: G.P. Putnam's Sons, 1993.

Talbot, David. *Brothers: The Hidden History of the Kennedy Years*. New York: Free Press, 2007.

Tanenhaus, Sam. *Whittaker Chambers: A Biography*. New York: Random House, 1997.

Teeman, Tim. *In Bed with Gore Vidal: Hustlers, Hollywood, and the Private World of an American Master*. Bronx, NY: Magnus Books, 2013.

Terry, Jennifer. *An American Obsession: Science, Medicine, and Homosexuality in Modern Society*. Chicago: University of Chicago Press, 1999.

Theoharis, Athan. *Chasing Spies: How the FBI Failed in Counterintelligence but Promoted the Politics of McCarthyism in the Cold War Years*. Chicago: Ivan R. Dee, 2002.

———. *From the Secret Files of J. Edgar Hoover*. Chicago: Ivan R. Dee, 1991.

———. *J. Edgar Hoover, Sex, and Crime: An Historical Antidote*. Chicago: Ivan R. Dee, 1995.

Theoharis, Athan, and John Stuart Cox. *The Boss: J. Edgar Hoover and the Great American Inquisition*. Philadelphia: Temple University Press, 1988.

Theoharis, Athan, and Robert Griffith, eds. *The Specter: Original Essays on the Cold War and the Origins of McCarthyism*. New York: New Viewpoints, 1974.

Thomas, Bob. *Winchell*. New York: Berkley Medallion, 1971.

Thomas, Evan. *Robert Kennedy: His Life*. New York: Simon and Schuster, 2000.

———. *The Very Best Men: The Daring Early Years of the CIA*. New York: Simon and Schuster, 1995.

Thompson, Scott W. *The Price of Achievement: Coming Out in Reagan Days*. London: Cassell, 1995.

Timmons, Stewart. *The Trouble with Harry Hay: Founder of the Modern Gay Movement*. Boston: Alyson, 1990.

Tobias, Andrew. *The Best Little Boy in the World*. New York: Ballantine Books, 1973.

Tommasini, Anthony. *Virgil Thomson: Composer on the Aisle*. New York: W. W. Norton, 1997.

Trento, Joseph J. *The Secret History of the CIA*. New York: Random House, 2001.

Trento, Susan B. *The Power House: Robert Keith Gray and the Selling of Access and Influence in Washington*. New York: St. Martin's Press, 1992.

Trillin, Calvin. *Remembering Denny*. New York: Farrar, Straus and Giroux, 1993.

Trilling, Lionel. *The Middle of the Journey*. New York: Charles Scribner's Sons, 1947.

Tripp, C. A. *The Homosexual Matrix*. New York: McGraw-Hill, 1975.

Trotta, Liz. *Fighting for Air: In the Trenches with Television News*. New York: Simon and Schuster, 1991.

Trout, Charles H. *Boston, the Great Depression, and the New Deal*. Oxford: Oxford University Press, 1977.

Truman, Margaret. *Harry S. Truman*. New York: Avon, 1972.

Tumulty, Karen. *The Triumph of Nancy Reagan*. New York: Simon and Schuster, 2021.

Valentine, Steven R. *Each Time a Man: Family Roots and a Young Life in Politics*. Richmond, IN: Friends United Press, 1978.

Vidal, Gore. *The City and the Pillar*. New York: E.P. Dutton, 1948; rev. ed., 1965.

———. *The Golden Age*. New York: Doubleday, 2000.

———. *Myra Breckinridge*. Boston: Little, Brown, 1968.

———. *Palimpsest*. New York: Random House, 1995.

von Hoffman, Nicholas. *Citizen Cohn*. New York: Doubleday, 1988.

Wackerfuss, Andrew. *Stormtrooper Families: Homosexuality and Community in the Early Nazi Movement*. New York: Harrington Park Press, 2015.

Wallace, Henry A. *The Price of Vision: The Diary of Henry A. Wallace, 1942–1946*. Edited by John Morton Blum. Boston: Houghton Mifflin, 1973.

Waller, Douglas. *Disciples: The World War II Missions of the CIA Directors Who Fought for Wild Bill Donovan*. New York: Simon and Schuster, 2015.

——. *Wild Bill Donovan: The Spymaster Who Created the OSS and Modern American Espionage*. New York: Free Press, 2011.

Waugh, Evelyn. *Brideshead Revisited*. London: Chapman and Hall, 1945.

Wayman, Dorothy G. *David I. Walsh: Citizen-Patriot*. Milwaukee: Bruce Publishing, 1952.

Wechsler, James. *The Age of Suspicion*. New York: Random House, 1953.

Weeks, Jeffrey. *Coming Out: Homosexual Politics in Britain from the Nineteenth Century to the Present*. London: Quartet, 1977.

Weil, Martin. *A Pretty Good Club: The Founding Fathers of the U.S. Foreign Service*. New York: W. W. Norton, 1978.

Weiner, Tim. *Enemies: A History of the FBI*. New York: Random House, 2012.

——. *Legacy of Ashes: The History of the CIA*. New York: Random House, 2008.

Weinstein, Allen. *Perjury: The Hiss-Chambers Case*. New York: Alfred A. Knopf, 1978.

Welles, Benjamin. *Sumner Welles: FDR's Global Strategist*. New York: St. Martin's Press, 1997.

Wells, Tom. *Wild Man: The Life and Times of Daniel Ellsberg*. New York: Palgrave, 2001.

West, Nigel. *Historical Dictionary of Sexspionage*. New York: Scarecrow Press, 2009.

West, Rebecca. *The New Meaning of Treason*. New York: Viking, 1964.

White, Theodore H. *The Making of the President 1964*. New York: Atheneum, 1965.

White, William S. *The Taft Story*. New York: Harper and Row, 1954.

Wicker, Randy, and Kay Tobin. *The Gay Crusaders*. New York: Arno Press, 1972.

Wicker, Tom. *One of Us: Richard Nixon and the American Dream*. New York: Random House, 1991.

Wildeblood, Peter. *Against the Law*. New York: Julian Messner, 1959.

Wilentz, Sean. *The Age of Reagan: A History, 1974–2008*. New York: Harper, 2008.

Wilford, Hugh. *The Mighty Wurlitzer: How the CIA Played America*. Cambridge, MA: Harvard University Press, 2008.

Williams, Robert Chadwell. *Klaus Fuchs: Atom Spy*. Cambridge, MA: Harvard University Press, 1987.

Wills, Garry. *The Kennedy Imprisonment: A Meditation on Power*. Boston: Houghton Mifflin, 1981.

——. *Nixon Agonistes: The Crisis of the Self-Made Man*. Boston: Houghton Mifflin, 1970.

——. *Reagan's America: Innocents at Home*. Garden City, NY: Doubleday, 1987.

Wiltshire, Susan Ford. *Seasons of Grief and Grace: A Sister's Story of AIDS*. Nashville: Vanderbilt University Press, 1994.

Winks, Robin. *Cloak and Gown: Scholars in the Secret War, 1939–1961*. New York: William Morrow, 1987; 2nd ed., New Haven, CT: Yale University Press, 1996.

Woods, Gregory. *Homintern: How Gay Culture Liberated the Modern World*. New Haven, CT: Yale University Press, 2016.

Woods, Randall B. *LBJ: Architect of American Ambition*. New York: Free Press, 2006.

Woodward, Bob, and Carl Bernstein. *The Final Days*. New York: Simon and Schuster, 1976.

Yoder Jr., Edwin M. *Joe Alsop's Cold War: A Study of Journalistic Influence and Intrigue*. Chapel Hill: University of North Carolina Press, 1995.

Young, Perry Deane. *God's Bullies: Native Reflections on Preachers and Politics*. New York: Holt, Rinehart and Winston, 1982.

Zeligs, Meyer A. *Friendship and Fratricide: An Analysis of Whittaker Chambers and Alger Hiss*. New York: Viking, 1967.

Zion, Sidney. *The Autobiography of Roy Cohn*. Secaucus, NJ: Lyle Stuart, 1988.

zu Putlitz, Wolfgang. *The Putlitz Dossier*. London: Allan Wingate, 1957.

Zweig, Stefan. *The World of Yesterday*. Translated by Anthea Bell. London: Pushkin Press, 2009.

——. *The World of Yesterday*. New York: Viking, 1943.

Ephemera

"Chambers and Hiss in BETRAYED."

"Who is William C. Bullitt," Philadelphia: Republican Central Campaign Committee, Circa 1943.

NOTES

Introduction

1 **"exchanged natural relations for unnatural":** Romans 1:26.

1 **Rev. Francis Higginson expressed revulsion:** Jonathan Ned Katz, *Gay American History: Lesbians and Gay Men in the U.S.A.* (New York: Thomas Crowell, 1976), 20.

1 **Carolina approved a law:** Perkins v. State of North Carolina (1964).

1 **In 1927, the New York State Legislature passed a theatrical "padlock bill":** Katz, *Gay American History*, 90–91.

1 **the Motion Picture Producers and Distributors of America released a list:** Joel Spring, *Images of American Life: A History of Ideological Management in Schools, Movies, Radio, and Television*, (Albany: State University of New York Press, 1992), 86.

3 **"taken familiarities":** Randy Shilts, *Conduct Unbecoming: Gays and Lesbians in the U.S. Military* (New York: St. Martin's Press, 1993), 7–12.

3 **Pierre L'Enfant:** Frank Muzzy, *Gay and Lesbian Washington, D.C.* (Charleston, SC: Arcadia, 2005), 9.

3 **"hideous hermaphroditical character":** Fawn McKay Brodie, *Thomas Jefferson: An Intimate History* (New York: W. W. Norton, 1974), 321. The man who leveled this charge, pamphleteer James T. Callender, was later accused of sodomy. Ron Chernow, *Alexander Hamilton* (New York: Penguin, 2005), 664.

3 **An academic study:** Thomas J. Balcerski, *Bosom Friends: The Intimate World of James Buchanan and William Rufus King* (New York: Oxford University Press, 2019).

3 **The four years that:** C. A. Tripp, *The Intimate World of Abraham Lincoln*, ed. Lewis Gannett (New York: Free Press, 2005).

3 **"We were familiar at once":** *The Complete Prose Works of Walt Whitman*, ed. Richard Maurice Bucke, Thomas Biggs Harned, and Horace Traubel (New York: G.P. Putnam's Sons, 1902), 8:5.

3 **In a crowded:** Daniel Mark Epstein, *Lincoln and Whitman: Parallel Lives in Civil War Washington* (New York: Random House, 2004), 245–50.

4 **"I cannot find the words":** *Precious and Adored: The Love Letters of Rose Cleveland and Evangeline Simpson Whipple*, ed. Lizzie Ehrenhalt and Tilly Laskey (St. Paul: Minnesota Historical Society Press, 2019).

4 **"Did you know"**: Archibald W. Butt, *Taft and Roosevelt: The Intimate Letters of Archie Butt, Military Aide* (Garden City, NY: Doubleday, Doran, 1930), 2:686.

4 **The reason Butt**: "President Weeps as He Eulogizes His Former Aide," *Washington Times*, May 2, 1912, 1.

4 **In recognition of**: "Butt-Millett Memorial Fountain," National Park Service, https://www.nps.gov /places/000/butt-millet-memorial-fountain.htm.

4 **described by one chronicler**: Mark Sullivan, *Our Times, 1900–1925*, vol. 6, *The Twenties* (New York: Charles Scribner's Sons, 1935), 24–25.

4 **"noised about"**: Carl Sferrazza Anthony, *Florence Harding: The First Lady, the Jazz Age, and the Death of America's Most Scandalous President* (New York: William Morrow, 1998), 293.

4 **"snappy dresser"**: Francis Russell, *The Shadow of Blooming Grove: Warren G. Harding in His Times* (New York: McGraw-Hill, 1968), 336.

4 **Smith often wore**: Anthony, *Florence Harding*, 293–94.

4 **a coded arrangement**: *Before Stonewall*, directed by Greta Schiller and Robert Rosenberg (First Run Features, 1984).

5 **Aristocratic women**: Samuel Hopkins Adams, *Incredible Era: The Life and Times of Warren Gamaliel Harding* (Boston: Houghton Mifflin, 1939), 42.

5 **"the city of conversation"**: Henry James, *The American Scene* (London: Chapman and Hall, 1907), 342.

5 **"Under the very shadow"**: Irving C. Ross, "Sexual Hypochondria and Perversion of the Genetic Instinct," *Journal of Nervous and Mental Disease* 17, no. 11 (November 1892), quoted in Katz, *Gay American History*, 42.

5 **"in the interest"**: Genny Beemyn, *A Queer Capital: A History of Gay Life in Washington, D.C.* (New York: Routledge, 2015), 22.

5 **One August evening**: Jeb Alexander diary entry, August 21, 1920, from Ina Russell, ed., *Jeb and Dash: A Diary of Gay Life, 1918–1945* (Boston: Faber and Faber, 1993), 30.

5 **the Riggs Turkish baths . . . was reputed to be**: "The Lafayette Turkish and Russian Bath House," *Washington Post*, August 14, 1903, 8.

5 **"complaints from stars"**: "Baths Leave the Belasco," *Washington Post*, March 19, 1911, SM3.

5 **"disorderly conduct"**: "30 of 50 Seized at Bath Forfeit Collateral of $25," *Evening Star*, March 26, 1945, 19. The police raided the baths at least once before, in 1921, at the height of Prohibition, absconding with three gallons of wine and a quart of whisky. "Arrested in Bath Raid," *Washington Post*, October 31, 1921, 2.

7 **"Secrecy is a form"**: *Hearing of the Senate Governmental Affairs Committee, Subject: Government Secrecy*, 105th Cong. 13 (May 7, 1997).

7 **"live in a milieu"**: Stephen J. Spingarn, interviewed by Jerry N. Hess, March 24, 1967, Harry S. Truman Library, Independence, MO (hereafter cited as "Truman Library"), https://www.trumanlibrary.gov /library/oral-histories/sping5.

1: "No Comment"

13 **named for his great-uncle**: Harold B. Hinton, "Welles: Our Man of the Hour in Cuba," *New York Times*, August 20, 1933, 3.

13 **As a boy of twelve**: Christopher D. O'Sullivan, *Sumner Welles, Postwar Planning, and the Quest for a New World Order, 1937–1943* (New York: Columbia University Press, 2008), 2.

14 **graduated after three years**: "Speaking of Pictures . . . ," *Life*, April 26, 1943, 7.

14 **scored higher**: Irwin Gellman, *Secret Affairs: Franklin Roosevelt, Cordell Hull, and Sumner Welles* (Baltimore: Johns Hopkins University Press, 1995), 60.

14 **"as well known"**: "Mrs. P. G. Gerry Weds Diplomat," *New York Times*, June 29, 1925, 17.

14 **Coolidge personally ordered**: James B. Reston, "Acting Secretary," *New York Times*, August 3, 1941, 9.

14 **fifteen servants**: Ted Morgan, *FDR: A Biography* (New York: Simon and Schuster, 1985), 678.

14 **"the most-talked-of diplomat"**: Hinton, "Welles."

14 **"never walked"**: Francis Biddle, *In Brief Authority* (New York: Doubleday, 1962), 180.

15 **According to legend**: Drew Pearson, "The Washington Merry-Go-Round," Bell-McClure Syndicate, January 1, 1949.

15 **Welles regularly:** John L. McCrea, interviewed by W. W. Moss, March 19, 1973, transcript FDR Map Room Papers, Franklin D. Roosevelt Presidential Library and Museum, Hyde Park, NY (hereafter cited as "FDR Library"), https://www.fdrlibrary.org/documents/356632/390886/mccrea+maproom.pdf/e10e4efe-e2cf-4b81-a5b4-06dc2eac74a7.

15 **"the reply would be":** John Gunther, *Roosevelt in Retrospect: A Profile in History* (New York: Harper, 1950), 131–32.

15 **"Just to look at him":** Harold L. Ickes, *The Secret Diary of Harold L. Ickes*, vol. 2, *The Inside Struggle* (New York: Simon and Schuster, 1954), 351.

15 **"not an easy man":** Reston, "Acting Secretary."

15 **"manner formal":** Dean Acheson, *Present at the Creation: My Years at the State Department* (New York: W. W. Norton, 1969), 12.

15 **British prime minister:** "No Comment," Associated Press, February 12, 1946.

15 **one hundred members:** "Roosevelt Attends Bankhead Funeral," *Stevens Point Journal*, September 19, 1940, 3.

15 **Welles accompanied the president:** Benjamin Welles, *Sumner Welles: FDR's Global Strategist* (New York: St. Martin's Press, 1997), 1.

15 **he began to drink:** Henry A. Wallace, *The Price of Vision: The Diary of Henry A. Wallace: 1942–1946*, ed. John Morton Blum (Boston: Houghton Mifflin, 1973), 68.

15 **At around 5 a.m.:** Statement of Alexander Dickson, January 9, 1941 (p. 80), J. Edgar Hoover Official and Confidential File (hereafter cited as "Hoover O&C"), Folder 157: "Sumner Welles, Under Secretary of State, Investigative File, January 23, 1941–September 14, 1943," Papers of Edwin M. Watson and of Frances Nash Watson, Accession no. 9786, Special Collections, University of Virginia Library, Charlottesville, VA (hereafter cited as "Folder 157: 'Sumner Welles'").

16 **"You have a cocksucker":** Memorandum from Dwight Brantley to J. Edgar Hoover, January 23, 1941, Hoover O&C, Folder 157: "Sumner Welles."

16 **Welles unfurled:** Statement by William F. Kusch, January 12, 1941, Hoover O&C, Folder 157: "Sumner Welles."

16 **Senators Burton K. Wheeler:** Welles, *Sumner Welles*, 272.

17 **"Cave Dwellers":** Barbara Gamarekian, "The Lives of the Cave Dwellers," *New York Times*, March 26, 1985, 20.

17 **Patterson lived:** David Brinkley, *Washington Goes to War* (New York: Alfred A. Knopf, 1988), 279.

17 **Drew Pearson:** Alden Whitman, "Watchdog of Virtue," *New York Times*, September 2, 1969, 44.

17 **"croquet clique":** Drew Pearson and Robert S. Allen, "The Washington Merry-Go-Round," United Feature Syndicate, December 19, 1940.

18 **ten wealthiest:** Janet Flanner, "Mr. Ambassador—I," *New Yorker*, December 10, 1938, 32.

18 **related to George Washington, Patrick Henry, and Pocahontas:** Sam Roberts, "Paris Saved by a Bullitt," *Foreign Affairs*, June 2, 2015.

18 **"Most Brilliant":** John Lukacs, *Philadelphia: Patricians and Philistines, 1900–1950* (Philadelphia: ISHI Publications, 1980), 151.

18 **Bullitt became:** Alden Whitman, "Energetic Diplomat; William C. Bullitt, First U.S. Envoy to Soviet, Dies," *New York Times*, February 16, 1967, 1.

18 **rival reporters:** Beatrice Farnsworth, *William C. Bullitt and the Soviet Union* (Bloomington: Indiana University Press, 1967), 8.

18 **Bullitt worked:** David Fromkin, *In the Time of the Americans: FDR, Truman, Eisenhower, Marshall, MacArthur—The Generation That Changed America's Role in the World* (New York: Alfred A. Knopf, 1995), 352.

18 **the first international summit:** Alexander Etkind, *Roads Not Taken: An Intellectual Biography of William C. Bullitt* (Pittsburgh: University of Pittsburgh Press, 2017), 30.

18 **daily brief on European political developments:** Whitman, "Energetic Diplomat."

18 **"a young man":** Walter Duranty, "The American Flag Flies Again in Moscow as Cordial Welcome Is Given to Our Envoy," *New York Times*, December 12, 1933, 1.

18 **"We have seen":** Will Brownell and Richard N. Billings, *So Close to Greatness: A Biography of William C. Bullitt* (New York: Macmillan, 1987), 86.

19 **"lie in the sand":** Edwin L. James, "Saw Lenin's Hand in Bullitt's Plan," *New York Times*, September 23, 1919, 17.

19 **He exacted:** Roberts, "Paris Saved by a Bullitt."

19 **"tattler and violator":** *Wilmington News Journal*, September 16, 1919, 4.

19 **one hundred fifty thousand:** Kathryn Smith, *The Gatekeeper: Missy LeHand, FDR, and the Untold Story of the Partnership That Defined a Presidency* (New York: Touchstone, 2016), 143.

19 **allegedly due to impotence:** Virginia Gardner, *"Friend and Lover": The Life of Louise Bryant* (New York: Horizon Press, 1982), 256.

19 **one of only three people:** Ben Yagoda, "What Drove Sigmund Freud to Write a Scandalous Biography of Woodrow Wilson?," *Smithsonian*, September 2018, 60–62.

19 **Based upon extensive:** Etkind, *Roads Not Taken*, 74–75.

19 **"perversity":** Mary V. Dearborn, *Queen of Bohemia: The Life of Louise Bryant* (Boston: Houghton Mifflin, 1996), 3.

19 **"party of homosexuals":** Gardner, *"Friend and Lover,"* 271.

19 **book he coauthored:** Sigmund Freud and William C. Bullitt, *Thomas Woodrow Wilson, Twenty-Eighth President of the United States: A Psychological Study* (Boston: Houghton Mifflin, 1966).

20 **"You and I know":** Yagoda, "What Drove Sigmund Freud to Write a Scandalous Biography," 64.

20 **spent tens of thousands:** Élizabeth Roudinesco, *Freud: In His Time and Ours*, trans. Catherine Potter (Cambridge, MA: Harvard University Press, 2016), 396.

20 **"affectionate relationship":** Freud and Bullitt, *Thomas Woodrow Wilson*, 94.

20 **"met the leaders":** Freud and Bullitt, *Thomas Woodrow Wilson*, 269. A manuscript prepared by Freud for the book but ultimately suppressed by Bullitt prior to publication suggests that the hostility to homosexuality evident in the final product was more the influence of the latter contributor than the former. In the manuscript, which was not published until 2005, Freud argues that by transcending class, race, and nationality, homosexuality had the capacity to reconcile mankind. "It is homosexuality—although not in its manifest form but rather in its sublimations—that ensures the continuation of a community of men and that will perhaps succeed one day in uniting all races of humanity in one great brotherhood." Upon its release, *Thomas Woodrow Wilson* caused a minor scandal, drawing a critical reception that the *Times Literary Supplement* characterized as "a practical unanimity of condemnation that has had few parallels in recent historical controversy." The eminent psychologist Erik Erikson declared it "Freudulence" in the *New York Review of Books*. "The publication of this book has been long delayed, but not, in my opinion, long enough," wrote the historian Richard Hofstadter, who dismissed it as "a vendetta carried out in the name of science," while his colleague Barbara Tuchman wrote that the psychoanalytic community received the book "as if it were something between a forged First Folio and the Protocols of Zion." See Mark Solms, "'Freud' and Bullitt: An Unknown Manuscript," *Journal of the American Psychoanalytic Association* 54, no. 4 (Fall 2006): 1295; Denis William Brogan, "President on the Couch," *Times Literary Supplement*, June 22, 1967, 551; Erik H. Erikson, "The Strange Case of Freud, Bullitt, and Woodrow Wilson: I," *New York Review of Books*, February 9, 1967, 3; Richard Hofstadter, "The Strange Case: II," *New York Review of Books*, February 9, 1967, 6; and Barbara Tuchman, "Can History Use Freud? The Case of Woodrow Wilson," *The Atlantic Monthly*, February 1967, 39.

20 **At an economic conference:** "Bar Envoys from Marriage Without State Dept. O.K.," *Chicago Daily Tribune*, December 7, 1936, 6.

21 **Bullitt had a Cadillac:** Paul Roazen, "Oedipus at Versailles," *Times Literary Supplement*, April 22, 2005, 12.

21 **"The best party":** Bullitt to Roosevelt, May 1, 1935, in Orville H. Bullitt, ed., *For the President: Personal and Secret; Correspondence Between Franklin D. Roosevelt and William C. Bullitt* (Boston: Houghton Mifflin, 1972), 117.

21 **"whose capacity":** "Bar Envoys from Marriage Without State Dept. O.K.," 6.

21 **"our Embassy there has had a questionable reputation":** "Brigadier General Philip R. Faymonville Morals Charge," September 29, 1943, Papers of Edwin M. Watson and of Frances Nash Watson, Accession no. 9786, Special Collections, University of Virginia Library, Charlottesville, VA.

22 **"a lot of fake marriages"**: Edward R. Pierce, interviewed by Charles Stuart Kennedy, August 12, 1997, Association for Diplomatic Studies and Training, Foreign Affairs Oral History Project, Library of Congress, Washington, DC.

22 **"a weird bunch"**: Edward R. Pierce, interviewed by Charles Stuart Kennedy.

22 **full third:** Edward R. Pierce, interviewed by Charles Stuart Kennedy.

22 **"pansy train"**: "Brigadier General Philip R. Faymonville Morals Charge."

22 **Raymond Geist:** Geist's remarkable story is told by Richard Breitman in *The Berlin Mission: The American Who Resisted Nazi Germany from Within* (New York: PublicAffairs, 2019).

22 **"probably the outstanding"**: Noel F. Busch, "Ambassador Kirk," *Life*, August 13, 1945, 81.

22 **Heir to a Chicago soap fortune:** Margaret B. Downing, "Tales of Well Known Folk in Social and Official Life," *Washington Sunday Star*, September 18, 1927, 10.

22 **lavender silk tuxedoes:** William Stadiem, *Too Rich: The High Life and Tragic Death of King Farouk* (New York: Carroll and Graf, 1991), 216.

22 **"poke in the eye"**: James McCargar, interviewed by Charles Stuart Kennedy, May 1995, Association for Diplomatic Studies and Training, Foreign Affairs Oral History Project, Library of Congress, Washington, DC.

23 **"was commonly regarded"**: Douglas M. Charles, *Hoover's War on Gays: Exposing the FBI's "Sex Deviates" Program* (Lawrence: University Press of Kansas, 2015), 53. While ambassador to Egypt, Kirk kept a shrine to his late mother, after whom he christened a water buffalo. He drank its milk every day. Stadiem, *Too Rich*, 216.

23 **"everyone out"**: "Brigadier General Philip R. Faymonville Morals Charge."

23 **dissuaded men:** Martin Weil, *A Pretty Good Club: The Founding Fathers of the U.S. Foreign Service* (New York: W. W. Norton, 1978), 46.

23 **"the Diplomatic Service most nearly resembled"**: Waldo H. Heinrichs Jr., *American Ambassador: Joseph C. Grew and the Development of the United States Diplomatic Tradition* (New York: Little, Brown, 1966), 98.

23 **"Americans . . . reasonably"**: Arthur M. Schlesinger Jr., *The Vital Center: The Politics of Freedom* (Boston: Houghton Mifflin, 1949), 166.

23 **"Please send"**: Janet Flanner, "Mr. Ambassador—II," *New Yorker*, December 17, 1938, 27.

23 **Born and raised:** Ted Morgan, *A Covert Life: Jay Lovestone, Communist, Anti-Communist, and Spymaster* (New York: Random House, 1999), 210.

23 **product of public schools:** J. Edgar Hoover to Sherman Adams, "CARMEL OFFIE," February 11, 1953, Eisenhower Library.

23 **some three-quarters of those:** Weil, *A Pretty Good Club*, 46.

23 **"He had a mind"**: Burton Hersh, *The Old Boys: The American Elite and the Origins of the CIA* (New York: Charles Scribner's Sons, 1992), 65.

23 **type two hundred words a minute:** Robert Joyce, notes from interview with Benjamin Welles, March 26, 1974, James McCargar Papers, Howard Gotlieb Archival Research Center, Boston University.

23 **landed him a job:** "Carmel Offie, Victim in Jet Crash," *Washington Post*, June 20, 1972, C5.

24 **"This wretched young"**: Bullitt, *For the President*, 135.

24 **"When Mr. Offie"**: Hersh, *Old Boys*, 44.

24 **"a renaissance type"**: George Kennan to John Lukacs, August 15, 1978, from John Lukacs, ed., *Through the History of the Cold War: The Correspondence of George F. Kennan and John Lukacs* (Philadelphia: University of Pennsylvania Press, 2010), 71.

24 **"Champagne Ambassador"**: Whitman, "Energetic Diplomat."

24 **initiated a romance:** Smith, *Gatekeeper*, 145–46.

25 **"extremely popular"**: Brownell and Billings, *So Close to Greatness*, 211.

25 **corresponding with the president:** Robert Murphy, *Diplomat Among Warriors* (New York: Doubleday, 1964), 33.

25 **"a kind of extraordinary"**: Flanner, "Mr. Ambassador—I."

25 **"Bill Buddha"**: Bullitt, *For the President*, 114.

25 **"a confidential dispatch"**: Etkind, *Roads Not Taken*, 107.

25 **Offie had become:** Bullitt to FDR, November 24, 1937, Folder 1794, Box 71, Series 1, William C. Bullitt Papers, Manuscripts and Archives, Yale University Library, New Haven, CT (hereafter cited as "Bullitt Papers").

25 **"summons [Offie]":** Bullitt to FDR, June 6, 1940, Folder 1811, Box 72, Series 1, Bullitt Papers.

26 **"Please don't write":** David Pitts, *Jack and Lem: John F. Kennedy and Lem Billings: The Untold Story of an Extraordinary Friendship* (New York: Carroll and Graf, 2007), 22.

26 **"a second son":** Pitts, *Jack and Lem*, 36.

26 **tried to hire him away:** A. H. Belmont to D. M. Ladd, "CARMEL OFFIE," July 22, 1953, FBI file no. 65–32871–194.

26 **For a Mass:** John Ibson, *Men Without Maps: Some Gay Males of the Generation Before Stonewall* (Chicago: University of Chicago Press, 2019), 70.

26 **named the dog:** Nigel Hamilton, *JFK: Reckless Youth* (New York: Random House, 1992), 193.

26 **"always trying, *unsuccessfully*, to pour Champagne":** Michael R. Beschloss, *The Crisis Years: Kennedy and Khrushchev, 1960–1963* (New York: HarperCollins, 1991), 17.

26 **"Jack came into":** Morgan, *A Covert Life*, 210.

27 **"the playing fields of Eton":** Morgan, *A Covert Life*, 212.

27 **"he was as homosexual":** Edward R. Pierce, interviewed by Charles Stuart Kennedy.

27 **The epicene endearment:** William C. Bullitt to Carmel Offie, May 5, 1944, Folder 1532, Box 63, Series 1, Bullitt Papers; Robert D. Murphy to Carmel Offie, August 21, 1952, Folder 4, Box 90, Robert D. Murphy Papers, Hoover Institution Archives, Stanford, CA; Hamilton, *JFK*, 258.

27 **"Think of the baby":** Whitman, "Energetic Diplomat."

27 **"Bullitt's bedmate":** Edward R. Pierce, interviewed by Charles Stuart Kennedy.

27 **"made no secret":** Robert Joyce, notes from interview with Benjamin Welles, March 26, 1974.

27 **"to get ahead":** J. Edgar Hoover to James E. Hatcher, "Alleged Sex Deviates in Department of State," July 8, 1953, Folder: "Checks on Security Risks," Box 12, RG 59, National Archives and Records Administration, College Park, MD (hereafter cited as "NARA").

28 **"a substantial monetary gift":** Hoover to Adams, "CARMEL OFFIE."

28 **"a conversation":** Bullitt to Welles, October 9, 1939, Folder 2264, Box 88, Series 1, Bullitt Papers.

28 **"told me that":** Breckinridge Long diary, February 17, 1940, Box 5, Breckinridge Long Papers, Manuscript Division, Library of Congress, Washington, DC (hereafter cited as "Breckinridge Long diary").

28 **"a bitterness developed':** Murphy, *Diplomat Among Warriors*, 35.

28 **"I have been highly restrained":** Michael Fullilove, *Rendezvous with Destiny: How Franklin D. Roosevelt and Five Extraordinary Men Took America into the War and into the World* (New York: Penguin, 2013), 31, 50.

29 **He dined:** Walter Trohan, "Welles' Aplomb Upset as Hitler Sees Mussolini," *Chicago Daily Tribune*, March 19, 1940, 8.

29 **twenty-seven-thousand–crystal drop chandelier:** Caroline Elderfield, "Bringing Opera Back to Rome with The Barber of Seville," *Daily Telegraph*, June 29, 2016.

2: "Worse Than a Murderer"

30 **"In case I should get blown up":** Bullitt, *For the President*, 441.

30 **Four days after:** Bullitt, *For the President*, 449.

30 **"My deepest personal reason":** Bullitt, *For the President*, 466

30 **a dozen Thompson submachine guns:** Bullitt, *For the President*, 455.

30 **fled South to Tours:** "French Ministries Moved Southward," *New York Times*, June 11, 1940, 1.

31 **Like Gouverneur Morris:** Bullitt, *For the President*, 468.

31 **"amazingly efficient":** Carolyn Bell, "Offie, the Mystery Man, to Take London Job," *Washington Post*, October 12, 1941, S5.

31 **Bullitt met:** "French Prisoners Herded into Paris," *New York Times*, June 18, 1940, 6.

31 **Bullitt fired off:** Smith, *Gatekeeper*, 223.

31 **When the five-car caravan:** Brownell and Billings, *So Close to Greatness*, 262.

31 **on the advice of Welles:** Bullitt, *For the President*, 505–6; "Sending of Leahy Encourages Vichy," *New York Times*, November 24, 1940, 19.

31 **"picaresque adventurer":** Barbara W. Tuchman, "Woodrow Wilson on Freud's Couch," in *Practicing History: Selected Essays* (New York: Alfred A. Knopf, 1981).

31 **Moore had heard:** Welles, *Sumner Welles*, 272.

32 **"had made sexual proposals":** Bullitt memorandum, November 25, 1940, Folder 217, Box 210, Group 112, Series VI, Bullitt Papers.

32 **On January 3:** Memorandum from J. Edgar Hoover, January 3, 1941, Hoover O&C, Folder 157: "Sumner Welles."

32 **"miniature American Cheka":** Ray Tucker, "Hist! Who's That?," *Collier's*, August 19, 1933, 15 and 49.

32 **"compact body":** Richard Harwood, "J. Edgar Hoover: A Librarian with a Lifetime Lease," *Washington Post*, February 25, 1968, D4.

32 **"inner and outer sanctums":** Mabelle Jennings, "Along the Rialto," *Washington Herald*, March 8, 1934.

32 **The "unmarried" director:** Rex Collier, "Why Uncle Sam's Agents Get Their Men," *New York Times*, August 19, 1934, 4.

32 **"Hoover walks":** Walter Trohan, "Chief of the G-Men—Record of His Career," *Chicago Sunday Tribune*, June 21, 1936, 72.

33 **notes and columns:** The Washington Merry-Go-Round card index is contained within the Jack Anderson Papers, Gelman Library, George Washington University, Washington, DC (hereafter cited as "Gelman Library").

33 **"Shrouds himself":** Notecard, October 12, 1933, Box 176, Series 2, Jack Anderson Papers, Gelman Library.

33 **"Hoover, swarthy head":** Drew Pearson and Robert S. Allen, "The Daily Washington Merry-Go-Round," Bell-McClure Syndicate, September 22, 1934.

33 **"is different from":** Drew Pearson and Robert S. Allen, "The Washington Merry-Go-Round," Bell-McClure Syndicate, January 19, 1938.

33 **"After forty-three years":** Drew Pearson and Robert S. Allen, "The Washington Merry-Go-Round," Bell-McClure Syndicate, April 5, 1938.

33 **"kept a large group":** Robert C. Hendon to Clyde Tolson, June 30, 1943, FBI memorandum, Official and Confidential Files of Louis B. Nichols (hereafter cited as "Nichols O&C"), NARA.

35 **"sissy":** FBI Assistant Director Louis Nichols to Clyde Tolson, June 20, 1951, FBI memorandum, found in Athan Theoharis, ed., *From the Secret Files of J. Edgar Hoover* (Chicago: Ivan R. Dee, 1991), 353–54.

35 **"had a crush":** L. B. Nichols to Clyde Tolson, June 1, 1955, FBI memorandum, Joseph Bryan folder, Nichols O&C, NARA.

35 **Louisville prison inmate:** SAC [Special Agent in Charge] Louisville M. W. McFarlin to J. Edgar Hoover, July 14, 1944, FBI memorandum, found in Theoharis, *From the Secret Files*, 355–56.

35 **"heard that":** D. M. Ladd to Hoover, March 24, 1952, FBI file no. 67–561–279.

35 **one "stupid employee's gossip":** D. M. Ladd to Hoover, April 1, 1953, FBI file no. 67–561–280.

35 **"You may be assured":** SAC Louisville M. W. McFarlin to J. Edgar Hoover, July 14, 1944, FBI memorandum, in Theoharis, *From the Secret Files of J. Edgar Hoover*, 356.

35 **"was still defensive":** Athan Theoharis, *J. Edgar Hoover, Sex, and Crime: An Historical Antidote* (Chicago: Ivan R. Dee, 1995), 52.

35 **"Hoover is a queer":** William Reimbold to Drew Pearson, n.d., Folder 25, Box 285, Drew Pearson Papers, LBJ Presidential Library, Austin, TX (hereafter "LBJ Library").

36 **"J. Edna":** Ovid Demaris, *The Director: An Oral Biography of J. Edgar Hoover* (New York: Harper's Magazine Press, 1975), 30.

36 **"wearing a fluffy black dress":** Anthony Summers, *Official and Confidential: The Secret Life of J. Edgar Hoover* (New York: G.P. Putnam's Sons, 1993), 253–58. Despite their flimsiness, Summers's charges were treated seriously at the time, and are widely believed to this day. His book became the basis for a PBS *Frontline* documentary and was the subject of significant national media coverage and public commentary. Discussing his search for a new FBI director at a Washington dinner gala in 1993, President Bill Clinton joked that it would "be hard to fill J. Edgar Hoover's pumps," while Republican Senate minority leader Bob Dole observed that Helen Thomas, then the dean of the White House press corps, was wearing a "lovely dress . . . from the new J. Edgar Hoover collection." Almost two decades later, Clint Eastwood's biopic *J. Edgar* lent further validation to the cross-dressing myth. Leonardo DiCaprio, in the titular role, mournfully attires himself in his late moth-

er's clothes and jewelry before a mirror and attempts to wrestle a kiss from Armie Hammer's Tolson. Karen de Witt, "Bipartisan Barbs Served at Gridiron Dinner," *New York Times*, March 29, 1993A13; Paul Houston and William J. Eaton, "Least Wanted G-Man?," *Los Angeles Times*, April 5, 1993, 5.

36 **"mind-boggling":** Theoharis, *J. Edgar Hoover, Sex, and Crime*, 17.

36 **"is in part believable":** Claire Bond Potter, "Queer Hoover: Sex, Lies, and Political History," *Journal of the History of Sexuality* 15, no. 3 (September 2006): 364.

36 **"spousal" but not sexual:** Richard Gid Powers, *Secrecy and Power: The Life of J. Edgar Hoover* (New York: Free Press, 1987), 171.

36 **Cartha "Deke" DeLoach:** Bruce Weber, "Cartha D. DeLoach, No. 3 in the F.B.I., Is Dead at 92," *New York Times*, March 16, 2013, A22.

36 **"capacity to feel":** Cartha D. "Deke" DeLoach, *Hoover's FBI: The Inside Story by Hoover's Trusted Lieutenant* (Washington, DC: Regnery, 1995), 65.

37 **"so long as his abilities":** Ronald Kessler, *The Bureau: The Secret History of the FBI* (New York: St. Martin's Press, 2002), 47.

37 **"conditions of vice":** Morgan, *FDR: A Biography*, 235.

37 **"perverts by official"** Lawrence R. Murphy, *Perverts by Official Order: The Campaign Against Homosexuals by the United States Navy* (New York: Harrington Park Press, 1988).

37 **"an utter lack":** "Alleged Immoral Conditions at Newport Naval Training Station," Report of the Committee on Naval Affairs, United States Senate, 67th Cong., 1st Sess., Relative to Alleged Immoral Conditions and Practices at the Naval Training Station, Newport, RI, 1921.

37 **"DETAILS ARE UNPRINTABLE":** "Lay Navy Scandal to F.D. Roosevelt," *New York Times*, July 20, 1921, 4.

37 **"I wish I could":** Doris Faber, *The Life of Lorena Hickok: E.R.'s Friend* (New York: William Morrow, 1980), 176.

38 **"I want to put":** Faber, *Life of Lorena Hickok*, 160.

38 **"It would have satisfied":** Blanche Wiesen Cook, *Eleanor Roosevelt*, vol. 2, *The Defining Years: 1933–1938* (New York: Viking, 1999), 253.

38 **"Remember one thing":** Eleanor Roosevelt to Lorena Hickok, March 10, 1933, from Joseph P. Lash, *Love, Eleanor: Eleanor Roosevelt and Her Friends* (New York: Doubleday, 1982), 140.

38 **Startled to read:** Faber, *Life of Lorena Hickok*, 329–32.

38 **Whether or not:** Kati Marton, *Hidden Power: Presidential Marriages That Shaped Our Recent History* (New York: Pantheon, 2001), 52–53.

38 **"Eleanor had so many emotions":** Doris Kearns Goodwin, *No Ordinary Time: Franklin and Eleanor Roosevelt; The Home Front in World War II* (New York: Simon and Schuster, 1994), 221.

38 **"Nobody else":** Cook, *Eleanor Roosevelt*, 2:42.

38 **Eleanor counted:** Susan Quinn, *Eleanor and Hick: The Love Affair That Shaped a First Lady* (New York: Penguin, 2016), 73–74.

38 **"my fairy":** Morgan, *FDR: A Biography*, 679.

38 **lamented how Eleanor:** William C. Bullitt, memorandum, December 19, 1943, Folder 219, Box 210, Series VI, Bullitt Papers.

38 **"that old biddy":** Curt Gentry, *J. Edgar Hoover: The Man and the Secrets* (New York: W. W. Norton, 1991), 310.

38 **Hoover was convinced:** Gentry, *J. Edgar Hoover*, 302.

38 **started a file:** Eleanor Roosevelt's FBI File, Franklin Delano Roosevelt Presidential Library and Museum, http://www.fdrlibraryvirtualtour.org/page09-08.asp.

38 **Hoover presented the results of his work:** Memorandum by J. Edgar Hoover, January 30, 1941, Folder 157, "Sumner Welles."

39 **Moore had left:** William C. Bullitt, memorandum, undated, Folder 218, Box 210, Series VI, Bullitt Papers.

39 **"sent for me":** William C. Bullitt, "Memo of Conversation with the President," April 23, 1941, Folder 217, Box 210, Series VI, Bullitt Papers.

39 **"I know about":** Bullitt, *For the President*, 513.

39 **"Well, he's not":** Gentry, *J. Edgar Hoover*, 309.

39 **"the maintenance of Welles in public office":** Bullitt, "Memo of Conversation with the President."

40 **part of a homosexual blackmail plot:** Drew Pearson, "The Washington Merry-Go-Round," Bell-McClure Syndicate, October 19, 1964. The official may have been Henry Woodring, who served as secretary of war from 1936 to 1940, before Henry Stimson, the only other man to serve as war secretary in the Roosevelt administration. In his 1964 column, Pearson mentions that Henry Grunwald, a political fixer whom he dubbed the "Mystery Man" of Washington, was "a friend of the cabinet member involved" and had paid the blackmailers fifty thousand dollars in hush money. Pearson had earlier identified Grunwald as using a suite at the Washington Hotel, registered in Woodring's name, for some of his shady dealings. Drew Pearson, "The Washington Merry-Go-Round," Bell-McClure Syndicate, May 2, 1953.

40 **"to my amazement":** John L. McCrea, "Setting Up Map Room in White House and Other Incidents in Connection with Service There," interviewed by W. W. Moss, March 13, 1973, Box 178, FDR Map Room Papers, FDR Library.

40 **"considered Welles":** Bullitt, "Memo of Conversation with the President."

41 **FDR never forgave:** Nathan Miller, *FDR: An Intimate History* (New York: Doubleday, 1983), 213.

41 **Bullitt had also been:** Ralph G. Martin, *Cissy: The Extraordinary Life of Eleanor Medill Patterson* (New York: Simon and Schuster, 1979), 217, 350–51. Following a press conference in which he denounced ultra-rich "parasites" for refusing to let the government requisition their mansions for public use, FDR whispered "I hope Cissy won't take that personally" to his press secretary. After a brief pause, he reconsidered. "I hope she will" (Brinkley, *Washington Goes to War*, 141).

41 **"Welles was a boyhood":** Breckinridge Long diary, August 29, 1943.

41 **how "many close friends":** Spruille Braden, Columbia Oral History Collection, Columbia University, New York, p. 619.

41 **"ability to snap":** Welles, *Sumner Welles*, 274.

41 **According to Elliott Roosevelt:** Elliott Roosevelt and James Brough, *A Rendezvous with Destiny: The Roosevelts of the White House* (New York: G.P. Putnam's Sons, 1975), 263.

41 **something that would have been rash under any circumstances:** Bullitt, "Memo of Conversation with the President."

42 **"Field-Marshal":** "Foreign Relations: Diplomat's Diplomat," *Time*, August 11, 1941.

3: Senator X

43 **Located near the Brooklyn Navy Yard:** Memorandum, "Re: William Elberfeld, with aliases; Espionage—G; Alien Enemy Control," June 27, 1942, Folder 153: "David I. Walsh," Hoover O&C.

43 **"one of the best known":** Report of Leon Pearle, "Interview with Pat. Latwin" (p. 67), from Daniel A. Doran, "Confidential Report to Mr. Ted O. Thackrey," Box 207: "Confidential Report to Ted Thackrey, Relative, to the Investigation of Senator David Walsh, 1943," Dorothy Schiff Papers, Manuscripts and Archives Division, New York Public Library (hereafter cited as "Doran Report").

43 **"Swedish punch":** Mack Friedman, *Strapped for Cash: A History of American Hustler Culture* (Los Angeles: Alyson Books, 2003), 79.

43 **Beekman supplied his guests with copious amounts of liquor:** "U.S. Probes Link of Spies to Senator," *New York Post*, May 2, 1942, 3.

43 **"sin chamber":** The People of the State of New York v. Gustave Beekman, Supreme Court of the State of New York, Appellate Division—Second Department, Respondent's Brief, November 17, 1942.

44 **Philadelphia surgeon:** "Senator X's Name to Be Told Soon," *New York Post*, May 4, 1942, 3.

44 **butler known as "Princess":** Gustave Beekman affidavit (p. 55), April 30, 1942, Folder 153: "David I. Walsh," Hoover O&C.

44 **a group of sailors:** Anthony Tommasini, *Virgil Thomson: Composer on the Aisle* (New York: W. W. Norton, 1997), 356.

44 **"feel so uppity-uppity":** Doran Report, 33.

44 **"Madame Fox":** "Walsh Named as 'Sen. X', Linked to Nazi Spy Nest," *New York Post*, May 6, 1942, 3.

44 **kiss, hug, and pet:** Beekman affidavit, April 30, 1942, 53.

44 **"You know, George":** Gustave Beekman affidavit (p. 57), May 4, 1942, Folder 153: "David I. Walsh," Hoover O&C.

44 **Establishing themselves:** "Senator X's Name to Be Told Soon," 3.

44 **On March 14:** Doran Report, 62.

45 **"When the notorious":** Leonard Lyons, "The Lyons Den," *New York Post*, April 22, 1942, 30.

45 **For a columnist:** John L. Hess, "Lyons Drops His Broadway Column After 40 Years," *New York Times*, May 21, 1974, 43.

45 **Two days later:** Morris Ernst to Franklin Delano Roosevelt, April 24, 1942, President's Secretary's File, Box 146: "Ernst, Morris L.," FDR Library.

45 **"nonromantic companions":** Dorothy G. Wayman, *David I. Walsh: Citizen-Patriot* (Milwaukee: Bruce Publishing, 1952), 56.

45 **"unthinkable":** "First Hint of Walsh in the Post Apr. 22," *New York Post*, May 6, 1942, 4.

45 **"dandified":** "Massachusetts' Walsh," *Time*, November 25, 1929.

45 **closest companion:** Wayman, *David I. Walsh*, 95.

46 **first Democrat:** "Scandal Scotched," *Newsweek*, June 1, 1942, 30.

46 **a wisecrack:** William "Fishbait" Miller, as told to Frances Spatz Leighton, *Fishbait: The Memoirs of the Congressional Doorkeeper* (Englewood Cliffs, NJ: Prentice-Hall, 1977), 181.

46 **senator sexually propositioned:** Gore Vidal, "Gore Vidal: The Fag Rag Interview," *Fag Rag*, Winter/Spring 1974, reprinted in Richard Peabody and Lucinda Ebersole, eds., *Conversations with Gore Vidal* (Jackson: University Press of Mississippi, 2005), 16.

46 **Walsh had addressed:** "British Seek Another A.E.F., Lindbergh Tells 10,000 Here," *New York Times*, April 24, 1941, 1.

46 **"false pretenses":** "Selective Service Act Deception Is Charged," United Press, August 3, 1941.

46 **opposing his effort:** "Tribune Personality Sketch: Hard Going Not New to Sen. Walsh," *Minneapolis Star-Tribune*, May 21, 1942, 2.

46 **supporting a rival candidate:** Charles H. Trout, *Boston, the Great Depression, and the New Deal* (Oxford: Oxford University Press, 1977), 292–93.

46 **"not sympathetic":** Biddle, *In Brief Authority*, 202.

47 **In the armed forces:** Morgan, *FDR: A Biography*, 684.

47 **"Keep up the tidbits":** Franklin Delano Roosevelt to Morris Ernst, April 27, 1942, President's Secretary's File, Box 146: "Ernst, Morris L.," FDR Library.

47 **"had identified a picture":** Blind Memorandum, "Re: William Elberfeld, with aliases; Espionage—G; Alien Enemy Control," June 27, 1942, Folder 153: "David I. Walsh," Hoover O&C.

47 **Another German national:** Beekman affidavit, April 30, 1942, 54

47 **"one of Hitler's chief espionage agents":** "Senator Linked to Spy Nest Which Lured Service Men," *New York Post*, May 1, 1942.

47 **J. David Stern, the crusading liberal editor:** "J. David Stern, Publisher, Dies. Signed First Pact with Guild," *New York Times*, October 11, 1971, 38.

47 **encouraged Stern to transform:** Alex S. Jones, "The Post: 187-Year Fight to Survive Wildly Political and Violent Heritage," *New York Times*, February 9, 1988, B3.

48 **"average taste":** "Woman to Guide Oldest Paper Here," *New York Times*, April 5, 1942.

48 **"Everything about his body":** Jeffrey Potter, *Men, Money and Magic: The Story of Dorothy Schiff* (New York: Coward, McCann and Geoghegan, 1976), 184; Nan Robertson, "Dorothy Schiff Tells of Relationship with Roosevelt," *New York Times*, May 27, 1976, 1.

48 **lagging far behind:** Marilyn Nissenson, *The Lady Upstairs: Dorothy Schiff and the New York Post* (New York: St. Martin's Press, 2007), 56.

48 **"We must popularize":** Gail Sheehy, "The Life of the Most Powerful Woman in New York," *New York*, December 10, 1973, 58.

48 **"the story of the year":** "Senator Linked to Spy Nest Which Lured Service Men."

49 **"This is starting":** Morris Ernst to Franklin Delano Roosevelt, May 1, 1942, President's Secretary's File, Box 146: "Ernst, Morris L.," FDR Library.

49 **Beekman told the Bureau:** Blind Memorandum, "Re: William Elberfeld, with aliases."

49 **"one of four Senators":** Walter Winchell, "On Broadway," *New York Daily Mirror*, May 4, 1942.

49 **a "very nice man":** "Walsh Named as 'Sen. X,'" 3.

50 **the term *homosexual* was rarely used:** Clare Forstie and Gary Alan Fine, "Signaling Perversion: Senator David Walsh and the Politics of Euphemism and Dysphemism," *Sexualities* 20, no. 7 (2017): 778.

50 **"The fact that he":** "Sen. Walsh Powerful Chief of Naval Affairs Committee," *New York Post*, May 6, 4.

50 **"place of degradation"**: "Service Men Lured to 'Den' Called Spy Nest," *Brooklyn Eagle*, April 10, 1942, 1.

50 **"homo-sexualist"**: Walter Winchell, "On Broadway," *New York Daily Mirror*, February 2, 1933.

50 **"The ad libbers"**: Walter Winchell, "On Broadway," *New York Daily Mirror,* May 14, 1942.

50 **arresting an estimated**: United States Holocaust Memorial Museum, "Gay Men Under the Nazi Regime," https://encyclopedia.ushmm.org/content/en/article/persecution-of-homosexuals-in-the-third-reich.

50 **murdering between**: Richard Plant, *The Pink Triangle: The Nazi War Against Homosexuals* (New York: Henry Holt, 1986), 154.

50 **"assimilate homoeroticism"**: Robert Beachy, *Gay Berlin: Birthplace of a Modern Identity* (New York: Vintage, 2015), 243. For more on the association between homosexuality and fascism, see James Kirchick, "A Thing for Men in Uniforms," *NYR Daily* (blog), *The New York Review of Books*, May 14, 2018, https://www.nybooks.com/daily/2018/05/14/a-thing-for-men-in-uniforms/.

50 **"Brownshirts"**: In a letter to FDR written soon after arriving in Moscow, William Bullitt noted that "the most fantastic thing which has happened" in Germany was "the christening of the new military academy" after Ernst Röhm. "In view of the revelations about Roehm," Bullitt observed, "the English equivalent would be for the renaming of Sandhurst 'Oscar Wilde Institute.'" Bullitt to FDR, January 1, 1934, Folder 1780, Box 70, Bullitt Papers.

51 **"incredible prudishness"**: Plant, *Pink Triangle*, 60.

51 **accused Röhm**: *The Brown Book of the Hitler Terror and the Burning of the Reichstag* (New York: Alfred A. Knopf, 1933), 45–53. Germany's Social Democrats frequently lobbed charges of homosexuality at their Nazi enemies, with one sympathetic journalist warning that "lustful perverts" in the SA threatened German youth. "The conclusion is," declared the Social Democratic Party newspaper *Vorwärts*, "Röhm, who lauds the youth of the Black Reichswehr as his sexual delicacy, can and is allowed with his orientation to remain Highest leader of the similarly oriented Hitler army." Harry Oosterhuis, "The 'Jews' of the Anti-fascist Left: Homosexuality and Socialist Resistance to Nazism," in, *Gay Men and the Sexual History of the Political Left*, ed. Gert Hekma, Harry Oosterhuis, and James Steakley (New York: Harrington Park Press, 1995), 231.

51 **"secret organizations"**: Stefan Zweig, *The World of Yesterday* (New York: Viking, 1943), 310.

51 **"not an institute"**: Hans Peter Bleuel, *Sex and Society in Nazi Germany* (Philadelphia: Lippincott, 1973), 97–98.

51 **"within the SA"**: *Hamburger Tageblatt*, July 13, 1934, cited in Andrew Wackerfuss, *Stormtrooper Families: Homosexuality and Community in the Early Nazi Movement* (New York: Harrington Park Press, 2015), 302.

51 **A 1942 United Press wire service story**: Frederick C. Oechsner, "War Stopped Hitler's Wedding," *Wisconsin State Journal*, June 9, 1942. In his magisterial *The Rise and Fall of the Third Reich*, published in 1960, William L. Shirer writes that Röhm was "a tough, ruthless, driving man—albeit, like so many of the early Nazis, a homosexual" and that "many of [the SA's] top leaders . . . were notorious homosexual perverts." Nearly a decade later, *Time* declared with breezy confidence that "Sexual deviance of every variety was common during the Nazis' virulent and corrupt rule of Germany." (William L. Shirer, *The Rise and Fall of the Third Reich* [New York: Simon and Schuster, 1960], 38, 120); "The Homosexual: Newly Visible, Newly Understood," *Time*, October 31, 1969, 56.

52 **"extensive homosexuality"**: John F. Carter to Franklin D. Roosevelt, "Memorandum of Interview with Mr. W. H. Thoresen, Norwegian and German Representative of General Motors (Returned from Germany last of May), June 25, 1941," President's Secretary's File: "Carter, John F., March—October 1941," FDR Library.

52 **commissioned by the federal government**: Forrest G. Robinson, *Love's Story Told: A Life of Henry A. Murray* (Cambridge, MA: Harvard University Press, 1992), 276–78.

52 **"large feminine component"**: Henry A. Murray, "Analysis of the Personality of Adolph [*sic*] Hitler: With Predictions of His Future Behavior and Suggestions for Dealing with Him Now and After Germany's Surrender," Office of Strategic Services, 1943, 19, http://lawcollections.library.cornell.edu/nuremberg/catalog/nur:01134.

52 **homosexual brothel**: Walter C. Langer, *The Mind of Adolph [sic] Hitler: The Secret Wartime Report* (New York: Basic Books, 1972), 124.

52 **"The belief that Hitler"**: Langer, *Mind of Adolph Hitler*, 178–79.

53 **"finds expression"**: Langer, *Mind of Adolph Hitler*, 179.

53 **"It is a diabolical lie"**: "Walsh Named As 'Sen. X,'" 3.

53 **"The truth is certain"**: "The Name Is Walsh," *New York Post*, May 6, 1942, 33.

53 **four separate editorials**: "Break the Walsh Case Open," *New York Post*, May 12, 1942, 25; "Break the Walsh Case Open," *New York Post*, May 13, 1942, 29; "Break the Walsh Case Open," *New York Post*, May 14, 1942, 29; "Break the Walsh Case Open," *New York Post*, May 16, 1942, 23.

53 **Boston's top political watering holes**: "'Fixing' of Walsh's Accuser Is Foiled," *New York Post*, May 7, 1942, 2.

53 **"a chain of houses"**: Danton Walker, "Broadway," *New York Daily News*, May 5, 1942, 36.

54 **One of the witnesses**: Affidavit of Dr. Harry Russell Stone, May 13, 1942, Blind Memorandum, "Re: William Elberfeld, with aliases."

54 **"unprintable details"**: "The Walsh Case," *The Nation*, May 30, 1942, 617.

54 **delivered under duress**: "FBI Whitewashes Walsh After 'Sweating' Witness—Beekman Repeats the Charge," *New York Post*, May 20, 1942, 3.

54 **"browbeaten, persecuted, and questioned"**: "Persecuted, Says Walsh's Accuser," *New York Post*, May 19, 1942.

54 **"one of the worst scandals"**: "The Press: The Case of Senator X," *Time*, June 1, 1942, 48.

54 **"an offense too loathsome"**: 77 Cong. Rec. S4375 (May 20, 1942) (statement of Sen. Barkley).

55 **"one of the strangest"**: "Case of Senator X," 48.

55 **"the old hussy"**: 77 Cong. Rec. S4376 (May 20, 1942) (statement of Sen. Clark).

55 **"secret society"**: 77 Cong. Rec. S4378 (May 20, 1942) (statement of Sen. Nye).

55 **Groton classmate**: "McCormick Crusades Built the Tribune," *Washington Post*, April 2, 1955, 24.

55 **most vociferous opponents**: "Col. McCormick Warns of Rising Red Tide In U.S.," *Chicago Tribune*, July 31, 1945, 5.

55 **"Whether or not"**: "Who Are the Smearers?," *New Republic*, June 8, 1942, 784.

55 **"long the pride"**: Ted O. Thackrey, "An Open Letter to the U.S. Attorney General," *New York Post*, May 21, 1942, 5.

56 **"I never caught him"**: Doran Report, 62–63.

56 **"unreliable and contradictory"**: Doran Report, 8

56 **"[i]n evaluating Mr. Beekman's credibility"**: Doran Report, 8.

56 **"reliable people"**: Doran Report, 60.

56 **"all knew of"**: Doran Report, 58–59.

56 **"improper advances"**: Dolan Report, 79.

56 **"with a large acquaintance"**: Doran Report, 77–78. Interviewed in his suite at the Knickerbocker hotel, the fashion designer Max von Waldeck told investigators that the *Post* series had been "the cause of many discussions among people in the theatrical profession" in New York and in "the costuming and designing business and other allied industries" heavily populated with homosexuals. That "very many people who are famous in their professions or in business have serious sexual eccentricities and indulge in conduct which is not normal is a matter that a newspaper should not publish and divulge," he asserted. This formality out of the way, von Waldeck proceeded to dish. That the secretly homosexual actor Monty Woolley—whose distinctive facial hair earned him the doubly apposite nickname "the Beard"—"receives extreme delight and pleasure in having someone urinate on his" whiskers, or that Woolley's chum "Cole Porter is a frequenter of houses of male prostitution," ought to have been no one else's business. As for Walsh, while "the Senator has been famous for his proclivities for many years," von Waldeck revealed that said proclivities involved not young sailors but "colored men of a size over 250 lbs." Waldeck also speculated that the *Post* series prompted Schiff's business competitor and political rival, Cissy Patterson, to retaliate and "show her friendship for Sen. Walsh" by publishing an item in the *Times-Herald* revealing Schiff's affair with another man. Schiff sued and won an apology. Doran Report, 129–134; Martin, *Cissy*, 442.

56 **Walsh's attendance record**: Doran Report, 48.

56 **"plausible rumors"**: Doran Report, 139

57 **"had reason to believe"**: Doran Report, 141.

57 **"not a single item"**: Doran Report, 138.

57 **"tragic Gethsemane"**: Wayman, *David I. Walsh: Citizen-Patriot*, 317.

57 **Running for reelection:** "Ex-Senator Walsh Dead at 74; Was Wartime Navy Chairman," *Washington Post*, June 12, 1947, 12.

57 **general counsel for the American Civil Liberties Union:** Alden Whitman, "Morris Ernst, 'Ulysses' Case Lawyer, Dies," *New York Times*, May 23, 1976, 40. It was not until after his death that Ernst was exposed as having informed on his ACLU colleagues for the FBI. Frank J. Donner, *The Age of Surveillance: The Aims and Methods of America's Political Intelligence System* (New York: Alfred A. Knopf, 1980), 147.

57 **"no parallel":** George Rothwell Brown, "The Political Parade," *San Francisco Examiner*, May 26, 1942, 12.

4: Patriotic Homosexuals

58 **Posted to Vienna:** Peter Grose, *Gentleman Spy: The Life of Allen Dulles* (Boston: Houghton Mifflin, 1994), 4.

58 **highly decorated officer:** Richard Grenier, "Colonel Redl: The Man Behind the Screen Myth," *New York Times*, October 13, 1985, A13.

58 **"the pleasurers of the senses":** Stefan Zweig, *The World of Yesterday*, trans. Anthea Bell (London: Pushkin Press, 2009), 228.

58 **a second home:** Phillip Knightley, *The Second Oldest Profession: Spies and Spying in the Twentieth Century* (New York: W. W. Norton, 1987), 50.

58 **Confronting Redl:** It was likely this episode that FDR had in mind when he told Alben Barkley, in a discussion concerning the fate of Sen. David Walsh, that the honorable thing for a man to do once exposed as a homosexual was commit suicide. Another doomed homosexual whose fate might have inspired FDR's admonition was Ernst Röhm, whom Hitler allegedly instructed be given a pistol upon his capture during the Night of the Long Knives. "If I am to be killed, let Adolf do it himself," Röhm reportedly said. Shirer, *The Rise and Fall of the Third Reich*, 221.

59 **"a thickly perfumed":** Frederic Morton, "The Empire He Served Was Not His Own," *New York Times Book Review*, May 24, 1959, 7.

59 **"homosexual organization":** John R. Schindler, "Redl—Spy of the Century?," *International Journal of Intelligence and CounterIntelligence* 18, no. 3 (2005): 498.

59 **two surviving brothers:** Grenier, "Colonel Redl."

59 **"Murderer of a Million Men":** Peter Levins, "When Justice Triumphed," *New York Daily News*, April 28, 1940, C11. "Among Redl's contemporaries," a writer for the *New York Times* claimed in 1959, "only Rasputin at the court of Nicholas II cast so gothic a shadow," and in symbolizing "the twilight of an empire," Redl amounted to nothing less than a "one-man Goetterdaemmerung."

59 **"required no effort":** Schindler, "Redl—Spy of the Century?," 492.

59 **"a lover of women":** Schindler, "Redl—Spy of the Century?," 489–90.

60 **"had never before encountered":** Grose, *Gentleman Spy*, 4.

60 **Dulles included an account:** The excerpt is "The Archtraitor," from the book *The Story of the Secret Service*, by Richard Wilmer Rowan, from Allen Dulles, ed., *Great True Spy Stories* (New York: Harper and Row, 1968), 353–63. The Redl story has inspired dramatizations in print (Robert Asprey's *The Panther's Feast*), film (Istvan Szabo's *Colonel Redl*), and on the stage (John Osborne's *A Patriot for Me*). The last was censored by the British government in 1965. Karl E. Meyer, "Lords Debate Easing of Homosexual Curbs," *Washington Post*, May 13, 1965, D5.)

60 **"two weaknesses":** Allen Dulles, *The Craft of Intelligence* (New York: Harper and Row, 1963), 119. Three years before Dulles published his study of espionage, and while he was still serving as CIA director, the agency's in-house journal, *Studies in Intelligence*, published a review of a fictionalized book about the Redl affair, which it referred to as "this famous espionage case long cited, without detailed or adequate study, as a classic instance of the recruitment of a homosexual under threat of exposure" (Anonymous, book review of *The Panther's Feast* by Robert Asprey, *Studies in Intelligence* 4, no. 2 [Spring 1960]: A43–A47).

60 **the only memory:** Grose, *Gentleman Spy*, 25.

60 **Dulles was tasked with recruiting:** Grose, *Gentleman Spy*, 121–22.

61 **"underground transnational":** Grose, *Gentleman Spy*, 153–54.

61 **"were unusually vicious":** Mary Bancroft, *Autobiography of a Spy* (New York: William Morrow, 1983), 132–33.

61 **"sexspionage":** Nigel West, *Historical Dictionary of Sexspionage* (New York: Scarecrow Press, 2009).

62 **The Confederate operative:** Karen Abbott, *Liar, Temptress, Soldier, Spy: Four Women Undercover in the Civil War* (New York: Harper Perennial, 2014).

62 **"The suggestion of using homosexuals":** Frank E. Mason to Wallace Phillips, December 24, 1941, Entry 92, Folder 14, Box 580, RG 226, NARA.

62 **"homosexual men":** Alfred A. Gross to Frank E. Mason, December 19, 1941, Entry 92, Folder 14, Box 580, RG 226, NARA.

63 **"special qualifications":** "Outline for Thomas Painter," Entry 92, Folder 14, Box 580, RG 226, NARA. This letter was written three months before the police raid on George Beekman's establishment at 329 Pacific Street.

63 **"If it is really":** John C. Wiley to Wallace B. Phillips, Interoffice Memo, Coordinator of Information, January 15, 1942, Entry 92, Folder 14, Box 580, RG 226, NARA.

63 **last U.S. ambassador:** Christof Mauch, *The Shadow War Against Hitler: The Covert Operations of America's Wartime Secret Intelligence Service*, trans. Jeremiah M. Riemer (New York: Columbia University Press, 2003), 44.

64 **"This should be followed up":** Robert Cresswell to David Williamson, March 14, 1942, Entry 92, Folder 14, Box 580, RG 226, NARA.

64 **a male brothel that the FBI supposedly operated:** C. A. Tripp, a Kinsey disciple, claims that Kinsey told him this: see Tripp's *The Homosexual Matrix* (New York: McGraw-Hill, 1975), 204.

65 **"Gentlemen do not read":** Henry L. Stimson and McGeorge Bundy, *On Active Service in Peace and War* (New York: Harper, 1948), 188.

65 **"risked his future":** R. Harris Smith, *OSS: The Secret History of America's First Central Intelligence Agency* (Berkeley: University of California Press, 1972), 7.

65 **"weird collection":** Ford and MacBain, *Cloak and Dagger*, 5–6.

65 **imposed no ideological litmus tests:** R. J. Bresler, "Hoover and Donovan: The Politics of Bureaucratic Empire Building," *International Journal of Public Administration* 16, no. 1 (1993): 92–93.

65 **"I can't recall":** Marion A. Frieswyk, as told to Katie Sanders, "The Women Whose Secret Work Helped Win World War II," *New York Times Magazine*, March 6, 2019.

65 **"had the lenient":** Jennet Conant, *A Covert Affair: Julia Child and Paul Child in the OSS* (New York: Simon and Schuster, 2011), 45.

65 **"Oh So Social":** Robin W. Winks, *Cloak and Gown: Scholars in the Secret War, 1939–1961,* 2nd ed. (New Haven, CT: Yale University Press, 1996), 58.

65 **Berkeley-trained:** Susan C. Seymour, *Cora Du Bois: Anthropologist, Diplomat, Agent* (Lincoln: University of Nebraska Press, 2015), 169.

65 **island of Ceylon:** Theater Service Record, September 15, 1945, Box 201, RG 226, Cora DuBois OSS File, NARA.

65 **targeted by the FBI:** Cora Du Bois, June 7, 1948, FBI file no. 121–8038.

66 **"the handsomest young man":** Steven Bach, *Dazzler: The Life and Times of Moss Hart* (New York: Alfred A. Knopf, 2001), 158.

66 **17 Gay Street:** Application for Employment and Personal History Statement, Part 2, p. 34, Box 519, RG 226, Gordon Merrick OSS File, NARA.

66 **In May 1944:** Theater Service Record, July 21, 1945, Part 1, p. 3, Box 519, RG 226, Gordon Merrick OSS File.

66 **joined the Allied landing:** R. Hunter Garcia, "Gordon Merrick's Groundbreaking Gay Novels," *Princeton Alumni Weekly*, January 28, 1998, 16.

66 **"anything but grim":** "Author Gordon Merrick Hops Atlantic to Exotic Locales," *Daily Independent Journal*, April 26, 1958, 28.

66 **Merrick supervised:** C. V. Terry, "The Passive Fascist," *New York Times*, March 2, 1947, 202.

66 **author of racy:** "Gordon Merrick, 71, Reporter and Novelist," *New York Times*, April 23, 1988. Commenting on the book's title, taken from a character's remark, "I say if it's love, the Lord won't mind," one critic groaned, "Maybe the Lord won't, but the reader will" (Bobby Mather, "Plastic Surgery: It's in for the 70's," *Detroit Free Press*, May 10, 1970, 25).

66 **discovered the meaning:** Winks, *Cloak and Gown*, 156.

66 **"exclusive association":** Gordon Browne to Robin Winks, April 25, 1985, Folder 10, Box 18, Winks Papers, Yale University Manuscripts and Archives, New Haven, CT (hereafter cited as "Winks Papers").

66 **"crypto-homosexual":** David Seiferheld to Robin Winks, June 19, 1985, Folder 2, Box 22, Winks Papers.

67 **"I read the book":** U.S. Department of Justice, Registration Statement, Folder 40, Box 3, Downes Papers, NARA (hereafter cited as "Downes Papers")

67 **"venerable scoundrel tradition":** Winks, *Cloak and Gown*, 160.

67 **"face like a hooded eagle":** Claud Cockburn, *A Discord of Trumpets: An Autobiography of Claud Cockburn* (New York: Simon and Schuster, 1956), 109.

67 **information was extremely valuable:** Chapman Pincher, *Traitors: The Anatomy of Treason* (New York: St. Martin's Press, 1987), 109–110.

67 **"most important source":** Christopher Andrew, *Defend the Realm: The Authorized History of MI5* (New York: Vintage, 2009), 213.

68 **thanks to the intervention:** Personal and Strictly Confidential telegram from Johnson (U.S. Embassy London) to Dunn (State Department), May 29, 1940, 1437, Decimal File 1940–1944, Box 3188: "Alleged Subversive Activities in US of Wolfgang Putlitz," RG 59, NARA.

68 **"very gay party":** Wolfgang zu Putlitz, *The Putlitz Dossier* (London: Allan Wingate, 1957), 247–49.

68 **had asked J. Edgar Hoover:** Adolf Berle to J. Edgar Hoover, June 14, 1940, Decimal File 1940–1944, Box 3188: "Alleged Subversive Activities in US of Wolfgang Putlitz," RG 59, NARA.

68 **"was observed frequenting":** B. Stern, FBI NY file no. 65–3961, July 9, 1940, Decimal File 1940–1944, Box 3188: "Alleged Subversive Activities in US of Wolfgang Putlitz," RG 59, NARA.

68 **"ascertained by personal observation":** B. Stern, FBI NY file no. 65–3961, July 9, 1940, Decimal File 1940–1944, Box 3188: "Alleged Subversive Activities in US of Wolfgang Putlitz," RG 59, NARA.

68 **"frequented almost entirely":** J. D. Milenky, FBI NY file no. 65–3961, July 16, 1940, Decimal File 1940–1944, Box 3188, "Alleged subversive activities in US of Wolfgang Putlitz," RG 59, NARA.

69 **"knows the vocabulary":** Donald Downes to Allen Dulles, "Memorandum for A.D., Subject: Baron Putlitz," April 13, 1942, Entry 136A, Folder: "Germany," Box 4, RG 226, Downes Papers.

69 **brief biographical sketches:** "Nazi Officials Profiles by Baron Putlitz March 1942," Entry 92, Folder 37, Box 7, RG 226, NARA.

69 **to keep Schneider occupied:** P. E. Foxworth to J. Edgar Hoover, FBI memorandum, March 12, 1942, FBI file no. 65–41748, Folder 41748, Box 201, RG 65, NARA. Putlitz returned alone in 1944 to London, where he allegedly became the lover of Guy Burgess's friend, a fellow Cambridge graduate, art historian, and MI5 officer named Anthony Blunt, who was himself exposed as a Soviet spy in 1979. Peter Wright, *Spycatcher: The Candid Autobiography of a Senior Intelligence Officer* (New York: Penguin, 1987), 257.

69 **never once traveled:** "Biography of John Edgar Hoover," J. Edgar Hoover Foundation, http://www.jedgarhooverfoundation.org/hoover-bio.asp.

69 **"disgusted with"** Hoover Memorandum, February 13, 1942, Folder 41748, Box 201, RG 65, NARA.

70 **"a remarkable man":** Arthur M. Schlesinger Jr., *A Life in the Twentieth Century: Innocent Beginnings, 1917–1950* (Boston: Houghton Mifflin, 2000), 305.

70 **"investigating the investigators":** Collier, "Why Uncle Sam's Agents Get Their Men," 4.

70 **five-thousand-page:** Email from FBI FOIPA Negotiation Team, FOIA Request 1432191, August 6, 2019.

70 **"more than merely homosexual":** Donald Downes to Allen Dulles, March 20, 1942, Entry 136A, Folder: "Gerassi," Box 4, RG 226, NARA.

71 **"looks like a pleasantly depraved":** Tennessee Williams, *Notebooks*, ed. Margaret Bradham Thornton (New Haven, CT: Yale University Press, 2006), 472.

71 **FDR had explicitly forbidden:** Joseph E. Persico, *Roosevelt's Secret War: FDR and World War II Espionage* (New York: Random House, 2001), 197.

72 **"Tell them about":** Richard Dunlop, *Donovan: America's Master Spy* (Chicago: Rand McNally and Co., 1982), 348–49.

72 **"that strange"**: *Wartime Washington: The Secret OSS Journal of James Grafton Rogers, 1942–1943*, ed. Thomas F. Troy (Frederick, MD: University Publications of America, 1987), 162.

72 **secretary at the mission of Vichy France**: Donald Downes, *The Scarlet Thread: Adventures in Wartime Espionage* (London: Derek Verschoyle, 1953), 88.

72 **enlisted a group**: Dilys Winn, "Notes on March/April 1977 Interview with Donald Chase Downes by American Journalist," Folder 13, Box 29, Winks Papers.

72 **twenty-six-year-old**: Ricardo Sicre, "No. 2," April 5, 1942, Entry 136A, Folder: "Gerassi," Box 4, RG 226, NARA.

72 **"the handsomest man"**: Patrick K. O'Donnell, *Operatives, Spies, and Saboteurs: The Unknown Story of the Men and Women of World War II's OSS* (New York: Free Press, 2004), 27.

72 **Rick Sickler**: Elizabeth P. McIntosh, *Sisterhood of Spies: The Women of the OSS* (New York: Dell, 1998), 191.

72 **"one of the handsomest young Americans"**: Robin Winks, *Cloak and Gown*, 172.

72 **sent the young man**: Winn, "Notes on March/April 1977 Interview with Donald Chase Downes."

72 **"not very bright"**: Downes to Dulles, March 20, 1942.

72 **"the Kremlin"**: Ford and MacBain, *Cloak and Dagger*, 24.

72 **"entertaining gangs"**: David Seiferheld to Robin Winks, June 19, 1985, Winks papers, Box 22, Folder 2, Yale University Manuscripts & Archives.

72 **"to prepare a document"**: Donald Downes to Allen Dulles, "Memorandum for A.D.," April 9, 1942, Entry 136A, Folder: Gerassi," RG 226, NARA.

73 **"collecting young men"**: Donald Downes, "On Rivero and Cuba," April 25, 1942, Entry 136A, Folder: "Gerassi," Box 4, RG 226, NARA.

73 **2400 block**: "Tomas Gonzalez, 75, Owned Antique Store," *Washington Post*, July 20, 1964, B2.

73 **"bigoted catholic"**: Sicre, "No. 2."

73 **"when the conversation"**: Alfred Gerassi, "Notes on Gonzalez," n.d., from "G-S-H Work in Washington," April 9, 1942, Entry 136A, Folder: "Gerassi," Box 4, RG 226, NARA.

74 **"Although there are"**: Sicre, "No. 2."

74 **"scared to death"**: Downes, "On Rivero and Cuba."

74 **"pretty wide opening"**: Donald Downes to Allen Dulles, "G-S-H Work in Washington."

74 **"He is very friendly"**: Downes, "On Rivero and Cuba."

74 **"very amiable"**: Ricardo Sicre, "No. 1."

74 **"Six Sectors"**: Downes to Dulles, "G-S-H Work in Washington."

74 **"entering a foreign embassy"**: Downes, *Scarlet Thread*, 93.

74 **"A friend of ours"**: Downes, *Scarlet Thread*, 94.

74 **The agents apprehended**: Anthony Cave Brown, *The Last Hero: Wild Bill Donovan* (New York: Random House, 1982), 229.

74 **"I do not believe"**: Downes, *Scarlet Thread*, 95.

75 **"The Abwehr"**: David C. Martin, "OSS into CIA," *Grand Street* 2, no. 2 (Winter 1983): 180.

75 **Concerned that Hoover**: Douglas Waller, *Wild Bill Donovan: The Spymaster Who Created the OSS and Modern American Espionage* (New York: Free Press, 2011), 127.

75 **was the lover**: Williams, *Notebooks*, 472.

75 **"burglary of the Spanish Embassy"**: Ernest Cuneo to Robin Winks, July 28, 1987, Folder 3, Box 19, Winks Papers.

75 **"was offered by the FBI"**: Cuneo to Winks, September 10, 1985.

75 **The Downes case**: According to David Seiferheld, "it was alleged that when [Donovan] was finally convinced of Donald's homosexuality he wept." Seiferheld doubted the accuracy of this story himself, however, noting that "the story of Donovan's tears sounds improbable." Robert Ullman was allegedly forced out of the OSS after soliciting a sailor at a bar on Forty-Second Street in Manhattan. He would remain Downes's "perennial roommate" until his death in an auto accident in the 1970s. David Seiferheld to Robin Winks, June 19, 1985, Folder 2, Box 22, Winks Papers.

75 **Hoover and Donovan began amassing**: Waller, *Wild Bill Donovan*, 127–28.

75 **generated the rumor**: Mark Riebling, *Wedge: From Pearl Harbor to 9/11: How the Secret War Between the FBI and CIA Has Endangered National Security* (New York: Touchstone, 1994), 131.

75 **launched an investigation:** Persico, *Roosevelt's Secret War*, 198.

75 **"The spy must go":** Downes, *Scarlet Thread*, 174.

5: "The Greatest National Scandal Since the Existence of the United States"

77 **"The overwhelming majority":** Sumner Welles, foreword to Harold B. Hinton, *Cordell Hull: A Biography* (Garden City, NY: Doubleday, Doran, 1942), vi.

77 *recommend* **or** *require:* Morgan, *FDR: A Biography*, 682.

77 **"headline hunting":** J. Edgar Hoover Memo (second of two), October 29, 1942, File 88: "Cordell Hull," Hoover O&C.

78 **"to obtain access":** J. Edgar Hoover Memo (first of two), October 29, 1942, File 88: "Cordell Hull," Hoover O&C.

78 **On the evening of December 22:** William C. Bullitt, Memorandum, December 22, 1942, Folder 946, Box 40, Series I, Group 112, Bullitt Papers.

78 **Two weeks later:** William C. Bullitt, Memorandum, January 5, 1943, Folder 217, Box 210, Series VI, Bullitt Papers. In Bullitt's memo recording this conversation, he writes of "aural" copulation, which is presumably a typo.

79 **"If my own twin":** William C. Bullitt, Memorandum, April 25, 1943, Folder 219, Box 210, Series VI, Bullitt Papers.

79 **"degenerate":** William C. Bullitt, Memorandum, January 15, 1943, Folder 218, Box 210, Series VI, Bullitt Papers.

79 **"every Senator resents":** William C. Bullitt, Memorandum, June 2, 1943, Folder 219, Box 210, Series VI, Bullitt Papers.

79 **"Foreign affairs were":** Raymond Moley, *After Seven Years* (New York: Harper and Brothers, 1939), 136.

79 **"Midas of the spirit":** George F. Kennan to John Lukacs, December 11, 1976, from Lukacs, *Through the History of the Cold War*, 63.

79 **"what the hold was":** Bullitt, Memorandum, January 15, 1943.

80 **On another occasion:** Bullitt, Memorandum, April 25, 1943.

80 **bold-faced name:** Sally Swift, "Capital Whirl," *Washington Post*, October 4, 1940, 22; Sally Swift, "Capital Whirl," *Washington Post*, October 11, 1940, 18; "Wileys Honored at Cocktails," *Washington Post*, November 1, 1940, X18; Sally Swift, "Capital Whirl," *Washington Post*, February 17, 1941, 10.

80 **"the best food":** Bell, "Offie, the Mystery Man," S5.

80 **"What do I know about Carmel Offie?":** Bell, "Offie, the Mystery Man," S5.

80 **Bullitt ordered:** James McCargar, interviewed by Charles Stuart Kennedy, 86.

80 **Bullitt's "slave":** Rogers and Troy, *Wartime Washington*, 91.

81 **Ralph Brewster:** Morgan, *A Covert Life*, 210; Memorandum by J. Edgar Hoover, May 3, 1943, Folder 157: "Sumner Welles."

81 **The drafting of millions:** Charles Kaiser, *The Gay Metropolis: The Landmark History of Gay Life in America* (New York: Grove Press, 1997), xiv.

81 **exclusively male environments:** Allan Bérubé, *Coming Out Under Fire: The History of Gay Men and Women in World War Two* (New York: Free Press, 1990) 36.

81 **Women's Army Auxiliary Corps:** Lillian Faderman, *Odd Girls and Twilight Lovers: A History of Lesbian Life in Twentieth-Century America* (New York: Penguin, 1991), 125.

81 **"nationwide coming out":** John D'Emilio, *Sexual Politics, Sexual Communities: The Making of a Homosexual Minority in the United States, 1940–1970* (Chicago: University of Chicago Press, 1983), 24.

81 **exclude gays:** Bérubé, *Coming Out Under Fire*, 2.

81 **Of the eighteen million:** John Loughery, *The Other Side of Silence: Men's Lives and Gay Identities: A Twentieth-Century History* (New York: Henry Holt, 1998), 138.

81 **having nearly doubled in size:** Brinkley, *Washington Goes to War*, 107.

82 **"I was scared":** Ladd Forrester, "Washington in the 1930s: An Opportunity to Escape," *Washington Blade*, August 1, 1986, 1.

82 **"None of that":** Hendrik Meijer, *Arthur Vandenberg: The Man in the Middle of the American Century* (Chicago: University of Chicago Press, 2017), 180.

82 **"After government":** Brinkley, *Washington Goes to War*, 142.

82 **"the ideal place"**: Loughery, *Other Side of Silence*, 151.

83 **Mayflower Hotel:** Haviland Ferris, "Has Gay life Changed Much in Fifty Years?," *Washington Blade*, October 1, 1982, 18.

83 **Carroll Tavern:** Haviland Ferris, "An Extract from Washington Gay History," *Washington Blade*, September 11, 1980. A-5.

83 **At the Republic Gardens:** Ladd Forrester, "D.C. Bars in the 1930s: From Poetry to Parody," *Washington Blade*, September 5, 1986, 11.

83 **"you didn't ask":** Bob Cantillion, author interview, October 2014, Washington, DC. Cantillion also said that he met Clyde Tolson at a brunch attended exclusively by gay men, in Arlington, Virginia, sometime in the 1950s.

84 **"proclaimed its democratic principles":** James Reston, *Deadline* (New York: Random House, 1991), 101.

84 **The granddaughter:** Courtland Milloy, "The Odessa File," *The Washington Post Magazine*, September 28, 1980,

84 **"I just couldn't keep":** Milloy, "Odessa File," 17.

84 **"queen of the uptown underworld":** Al Sweeney, "She Ran Business," *Baltimore Afro-American*, March 22, 1952, 18.

84 **"To pursue":** Sharon Harley, "'Working for Nothing but for a Living': Black Women in the Underground Economy," in *Sister Circle: Black Women and Work*, ed. Sharon Harley and the Black Women and Work Collective (New Brunswick, NJ: Rutgers University Press, 2002), 49.

85 **"female Al Capone":** Thomas Bell, "Once the 'Queen' of Washington's Underworld, Odessa Madre Dies Penniless," *Washington Post*, March 8, 1990, 11.

85 **The crowd roared:** Thaddeus Russell, "The Color of Discipline: Civil Rights and Black Sexuality," *American Quarterly* 60, no. 1 (March 2008): 109.

85 **"like sisters":** Milloy, "Odessa File."

85 **"bad women":** Dale Wright, "Whey Men Love Bad Women," *Jet*, July 2, 1953.

85 **only Black woman:** Patrice Gaines-Carter, "Club to Reopen Door to Stardust Memories," *Washington Post*, March 5, 1989, D8.

85 **visited a shop:** Milloy, "Odessa File," 18.

86 **"She knew practically":** Milloy, "Odessa File," 20.

86 **buy toys and clothing:** Courtland Milloy, "A Detective and an 'Underworld Queen,'" *Washington Post*, March 27, 1990, B3.

86 **"I'll need an adding machine":** "Dope Queen Put Out of Circulation 8 Years," *Baltimore Afro-American*, November 12, 1949, 13.

86 **From 1932:** Milloy, "A Detective and an 'Underworld Queen'", B3

86 **Her corpse:** Bell, "Once the 'Queen' of Washington's Underworld, 11.

86 **"I had a lot of respect':** Milloy, "A Detective and an 'Underworld Queen,'" B3.

86 **a friend sang:** Bell, "Once the 'Queen' of Washington's Underworld," 11.

86 **Desperate to keep:** Lukacs, *Philadelphia*, 194.

87 **Bullitt mooted:** This conversation is reconstructed from Bullitt memorandum, July 27, 1943, Folder 219, Box 210, Series VI, Bullitt Papers; James MacGregor Burns, *Roosevelt: The Soldier of Freedom* (New York: Harcourt Brace Jovanovich, 1970), 350; and Eleanor Roosevelt, *This I Remember* (New York: Harper, 1949), 63.

87 **proposed marriage:** Martin, *Cissy*, 371, 446–47.

88 **"scavenger":** "The World of Felix Frankfurter," *Washington Post*, August 10, 1975, B1.

88 **"There are so many taps":** Brinkley, *Washington Goes to War*, 186–87.

88 **"chronic liar":** "Roosevelt Calls Pearson a Liar," Associated Press, August 31, 1943.

89 **"impatience":** George F. Kennan, *Memoirs: 1925–1950* (Boston: Little, Brown, 1967), 79.

89 **Nine days after:** John H. Crider, "Conflicts Impair State Department, President Is Told," *New York Times*, August 4, 1943, 1.

90 **Two weeks later:** Gellman, *Secret Affairs*, 317; Cordell Hull, *The Memoirs of Cordell Hull* (New York: Macmillan, 1948), 2:1230–31.

90 **"I did not speak":** Bullitt memorandum, December 19, 1943, Folder 218, Box 210, Series VI, Bullitt Papers.

90 **Three weeks after:** September 9, 1943, FBI file no. 65–32871–2.

90 **"I consider Mr. Offie":** Morgan, *Covert Life*, 211.

91 **On the evening of September 25:** "Stettinius Named for Welles Post; Crowley Shifted," *New York Times*, September 26, 1943, 1.

91 **"Why not Minister to Saudi Arabia?":** Michael Casella-Blackburn, *The Donkey, The Carrot, and the Club: William C. Bullitt and Soviet-American Relations, 1917–1948* (Westport, CT: Praeger, 2004), 218.

91 **"Accused of Too Much Talk":** *Who Is William C. Bullitt?* (Philadelphia: Republican Central Campaign Committee, c. 1943).

91 **"No matter how much":** Bullitt was careful to preserve for history that he had performed a literal transcription of Hull's comment, noting, "I wrote down the exact wording of this above quotation immediately on leaving Hull's inner office and going to his outer office." Bullitt memorandum, June 21, 1944, Folder 219, Box 210, Series VI, Bullitt Papers.

91 **Medal of Freedom:** Department of State Appropriation Bill for 1948, *Hearings on March 3, 1947, Before the Subcommittee of the House Committee on Appropriations*, 80th Cong., 1st Sess., 225; Belmont to Ladd, "CARMEL OFFIE." This was a decoration established by Harry Truman to recognize civilians who assisted in the war effort, not to be confused with the Presidential Medal of Freedom instituted by President John F. Kennedy in 1963.

91 **earning the nickname:** Mary Van Rensselaer Thayer, "Bullitt's Walls Are Bulging with Murphys," *Washington Post*, October 19, 1947, S1.

91 **Offie called:** Hersh, *Old Boys*, 153.

91 **he instructed his sister:** Belmont to Ladd, "CARMEL OFFIE."

92 **"more lines out":** Gregg Herken, *The Georgetown Set: Friends and Rivals in Cold War Washington* (New York: Alfred A. Knopf, 2014), 107.

92 **White House received:** O'Sullivan, *Sumner Welles, Postwar Planning, and the Quest for a New World Order, 1937–1943*, 229.

92 **the job ultimately going:** James B. Reston, "U.S. Retains Right to Alter Oaks Plan," *New York Times*, April 7, 1945, 7.

92 **"The world will soon march by":** Breckinridge Long diary, August 29, 1943.

92 **"had a devastating effect":** Morgan, *FDR: A Biography*, 684.

92 **"We got them out":** Gellman, *Secret Affairs*, 373.

92 **"was the first time":** James McCargar, interviewed by Charles Stuart Kennedy, 86.

6: The Concealed Enemy

95 **first live television:** Fox Butterfield, "TV Plays the Hiss Case Down the Middle," *New York Times*, May 6, 1984, B1.

95 **"Confrontation Day":** C. P. Trussell, "Alger Hiss to Face Chambers Aug. 25," *New York Times*, August 17, 1948, 1; Howard Norton, "Probers Call 3 Who Knew Hiss, Accuser," *Baltimore Sun*, August 19, 1948, 1.

95 **"Society's attendance":** Betty Beale, "Capitalites Crowd Caucus Room to Hear Alger Hiss Testify," *Evening Star*, August 26, 1948, B3.

95 **"Secrets had become":** John Kenneth Galbraith, "Alger Hiss and Liberal Anxiety," *Atlantic Monthly*, May 1978, 303.

96 **"sprawling, putty-faced":** Merle Miller, "The Second Hiss Trial," *New Republic*, February 6, 1950, 11.

96 **"shifty-eyed":** John V. Fleming, *The Anti-Communist Manifestos: Four Books that Shaped the Cold War* (New York: W. W. Norton, 2009), 296.

96 **courier in the American Communiust underground:** One of Chambers's operational bases during his underground years was an apartment located at 17 Gay Street in Greenwich Village, the same address where the future OSS operative Gordon Merrick would live while working as an actor on Broadway. Sam Tanenhaus, *Whittaker Chambers: A Biography* (New York: Random House, 1997), 85; Whittaker Chambers, *Witness* (New York: Random House, 1952), 299.

96 **He named nine:** "State Department Official Linked to Red Underground," Associated Press, August 3, 1948.

96 **The most shocking name:** The men had encountered each other two weeks earlier, at a hastily arranged executive session at New York's Commodore Hotel. The August 25 HUAC hearing was their first public confrontation.

96 **"one of the State Department's":** "Conferences: Chief Clerk," *Time*, April 16, 1945.

96 **his namesake:** Miller, "The Second Hiss Trial," 11.

96 **"shabby gentility":** Murray Kempton, *Part of Our Time: Some Monuments and Ruins of the Thirties* (New York: Simon and Schuster, 1955), 16.

96 **won a scholarship:** Megan Rosenfeld, "Alger Hiss: Pleading His Cause—Still," *Washington Post*, November 9, 1980, L1.

96 **studied at Harvard:** William Fitzgibbon "Hiss Had Fulfilled 'Success' Prophecy," *New York Times*, January 22, 1950, 51.

96 **sat behind President Roosevelt:** Edward R. Stettinius Jr., *Roosevelt and the Russians: The Yalta Conference* (Garden City, NY: Doubleday, 1949), 103.

96 **"Picture of the Week":** *Life*, July 16, 1945, 23.

96 **"impeccable Jeeves":** Garry Wills, "The Honor of Alger Hiss," *New York Review of Books*, April 20, 1978, 29.

96 **administering the Foreign Service exam:** Weil, *A Pretty Good Club*, 47.

96 **"moved with the casual grace":** William Manchester, *The Glory and the Dream: A Narrative History of America, 1932–1972* (Boston: Little, Brown, 1973), 503–4.

97 **"an innocent pedestrian":** "Thanks for Nothing," *Washington Post*, August 14, 1948, 4.

97 **"red herring":** C.P. Trussell, "President is Blunt," *New York Times*, August 6, 1948, 1.

97 **"to build the peace":** *Hearings Regarding Communist Espionage in the United States Government, Before the Committee on Un-American Activities*, House of Representatives, 80th Cong. (hereafter cited as "HUAC Hearings") 1162–64 (August 25, 1948).

97 **"I did not know":** Chambers, *Witness*, 115.

97 **"flair for the dramatic":** *The Autobiography of Mark Van Doren* (New York: Harcourt, Brace, 1958), 307.

97 **blasphemous play:** Tanenhaus, *Whittaker Chambers*, 31–33.

97 **"crisis of history":** Chambers, *Witness*, 192, 193, 410, 627, 763.

97 **joined the Communist Party:** Tanenhaus, *Whittaker Chambers*, 45.

97 *Remembrance of Things Past*: Tanenhaus, *Whittaker Chambers*, 68.

97 **"big and beautiful village":** Chambers, *Witness*, 427–28.

98 **"plays for keeps":** Chambers, *Witness*, 248.

98 **"a molten torrent":** Chambers, *Witness*, 72–73.

98 **"cried when we separated":** HUAC Hearings, 572 (August 3, 1948).

98 **"dumpy Chambers":** Robert K. Walsh, interviewed by Jerry N. Hess, October 12, 1970, Truman Library.

98 **"From the very first day":** Email from John Berresford, October 3, 2019.

98 **"details of my personal life":** HUAC Hearings, 945 (August 16, 1948).

98 **"considerable dental work":** HUAC Hearings, 979 (August 17, 1948).

98 **"deadbeat":** HUAC Hearings, 957 (August 16, 1948).

99 **under the name of "Crosley":** Tanenhaus, *Whittaker Chambers*, 250; Meyer A. Zeligs, *Friendship and Fratricide: An Analysis of Whittaker Chambers and Alger Hiss* (New York: Viking, 1967), 203, 213–14.

99 **"innocence by association":** Richard M. Nixon, *Six Crises* (Garden City, NY: Doubleday, 1962), 46.

99 **"His career":** HUAC Hearings, 1165 (August 25, 1948).

99 **"lived a *normal*":** HUAC Hearings, 1173 (August 25, 1948).

99 **Next, it was Chambers's:** HUAC Hearings, 1191 (August 25, 1948).

99 **"one of the most eloquent":** Nixon, *Six Crises*, 46.

100 **"If I had to choose":** E. M. Forster, "Living Philosophies I: Two Cheers for Democracy," *The Nation*, July 16, 1938, 66.

100 **"the Soviet people":** Edwin A. Lahey, "Hiss Trial Produces Dramatic Spy Story," *Detroit Free Press*, June 3, 1949, 16.

100 **where one stood:** Diana Trilling, *The Beginning of the Journey: The Marriage of Diana and Lionel Trilling* (New York: Harcourt, Brace, 1993), 358–59.

100 **"to discredit recent":** HUAC Hearings, 1162 (August 25, 1948).

101 **"only" concern:** Chambers, *Witness*, 762.

101 **As the esteemed:** Alistair Cooke, *A Generation on Trial: U.S.A. v. Alger Hiss* (New York: Alfred A. Knopf, 1950).

101 **fourteen-page "open letter":** Allen Weinstein, *Perjury: The Hiss-Chambers Case* (New York: Alfred A. Knopf, 1978), 69.

101 **"a small, pudgy man":** Weinstein, *Perjury*, 283.

101 **"any dirt":** Chambers, *Witness*, 474. Meyer Schapiro, an undergraduate contemporary of Chambers, was one of many such people approached by the Hiss defense team. Before the perjury trial began, he wrote, one of Hiss's lawyers "came to see me then, fishing for information to support this idea" that Chambers was a resentful homosexual. Meyer Schapiro, "Dangerous Acquaintances," *New York Review of Books*, February 23, 1967, 6.

101 **"admitted the possibility":** Weinstein, *Perjury*, 166–7.

101 **Harvard Board of Overseers:** In October 1948, a friend of Hiss, Charles Wyzanski, described to Hiss lawyer William Marbury a conversation with his fellow Harvard trustee, the newspaper publisher John Cowles. According to Cowles, "the working newspaper men . . . are inclined to believe that Alger is shielding [his wife,] Priscilla. Others have the notion that Alger had a homosexual relationship with Chambers" (Weinstein, *Perjury*, 383).

101 **pornographic comic books:** Bob Adelman, *Tijuana Bibles: Art and Wit in America's Forbidden Funnies, 1930s–1950s* (New York: Simon and Schuster, 1997). The earliest public insinuation as to the case's homosexual subtext was made a year before Chambers's HUAC testimony. In his 1947 novel, *The Middle of the Journey*, Columbia University professor Lionel Trilling depicted an ex-Communist writer, Gifford Maxim, who has found religion and tries to convince his former comrades to abandon their secular faith. In passing, Trilling mentions that Maxim—whom he later admitted was based on his college classmate Whittaker Chambers—had published an essay on Herman Melville's *Billy Budd*, a novella with strong homoerotic themes. Lionel Trilling, *The Middle of the Journey* (New York: Charles Scribner's Sons, 1947), 153–57; Lionel Trilling, "Whittaker Chambers and 'The Middle of the Journey,'" *New York Review of Books*, April 17, 1975, 18–24. On homosexual themes in *Billy Budd*, see W. D. Redfern, "Between the Lines of *Billy Budd*," *Journal of American Studies* 17, no. 3 (December 1983): 357–65.

101 **"battle between two queers":** Tanenhaus, *Whittaker Chambers*, 579. It is worthwhile to note that the gaybaiting of Chambers did not extend to the Truman administration, which had every reason to want to see him discredited. In a "strictly confidential" memo sent to White House counsel Clark Clifford, his assistant George Elsey wrote that "an inquiry of local officials and persons" in Chambers's hometown of Lynbrook, Long Island, found that Chambers "and family keep much to themselves and are regarded by some as queer, and eccentric." Handwritten on the side of the memo, presumably in Clifford's handwriting, was "'Discrediting of [Elizabeth] Bentley + Chambers' *only* their stories *not* their personalities" (George Elsey to Clark Clifford, "Strictly Confidential Memo for Clark Clifford Alone," August 9, 1948, Folder 1, Box 57: "Internal Security—Congressional Loyalty Investigations," George Elsey Papers, Truman Library).

101 **classified State Department documents:** Included among the documents Hiss stole were diplomatic cables marked "strictly confidential" sent by William Bullitt to Cordell Hull (Tanenhaus, *Whittaker Chambers*, 293–94) and a memo sent by Sumner Welles to the German ambassador (Tanenhaus, *Whittaker Chambers*, 305). Chambers also tasked a member of his cell, a friend of Bullitt, to rummage through Bullitt's home office desk (Weinstein, *Perjury*, 124).

102 **"Homosexual behavior":** Weinstein, *Perjury*, 270.

102 **"gonorrhea":** Dictated by Alger Hiss, "Hiss Personal 2395," December 8, 1948, Folder 40, Box 4, William A. Rueben Papers, Tamiment Library, New York University.

102 **On December 15:** Associated Press, "Not Guilty Plea Offered by Hiss; $5,000 Bail Set," *Evening Star*, December 16, 1948, 1.

102 **Private detectives:** Weinstein, *Perjury*, 165–66.

102 **"common knowledge":** Weinstein, *Perjury*, 381.

102 **"Chambers in his bed":** "Hiss Personal 2395," February 8, 1949, Folder 30, Box 6, John Lowenthal Papers, Tamiment Library, New York University; Zeligs, *Friendship and Fratricide*, 216–17; Weinstein, *Perjury*, 382–83.

102 **Syndicated newspaper columnist:** Weinstein, *Perjury*, 182. The plot of *Class Reunion* is similar to that of the 1959 American novel *A Separate Peace*, which charts the tumultuous friendship of two students at an all-male New England boarding school, one of whom covets and kills the other. Though the author, John Knowles, denied that his book had any homoerotic undertones, generations of gay readers have passionately disagreed. Chauncey Mabe, "Now Thirty Years After He Wrote 'A Separate Peace,' John Knowles Is Coming to South Florida to Teach Creative Writing—Even Though He Says, 'Everybody Knows You Can't Teach Anyone to Write,'" *South Florida Sun Sentinel*, March 15, 1987.

102 **"Chambers had a homosexual attraction":** Weinstein, *Perjury*, 183.

102 **Chambers attempted suicide:** Chambers, *Witness*, 773–75; Tanenhaus, *Whittaker Chambers*, 577n7.

102 **ostensibly spurred by a claim:** Tanenhaus, *Whittaker Chambers*, 308.

102 **later retracted:** Tanenhaus, *Whittaker Chambers*, 309.

103 **Chambers had also:** Tanenhaus, *Whittaker Chambers*, 343

103 **"if you watch":** HUAC Hearings, 667, 669 (August 7, 1948). Twelve years after Chambers made these observations, a writer for *Esquire* interviewed Hiss for a profile, describing him as "a tall man in a summer straw, with certainly no mince to his energetic walk" (Brock Bower, "The Problems of Alger Hiss," *Esquire*, December 1960, 145).

103 **"domineering" mother:** HUAC Hearings, 669 (August 7, 1948). In his 1952 memoir, *Witness*, Chambers recounts the moment Hiss instructed him to obtain admittedly necessary dental work: "I saw that I had touched something very important—his fastidiousness," Chambers wrote, using the same suggestive word *Collier's* had chosen to describe a young J. Edgar Hoover back in 1933. Chambers, *Witness*, 363.

103 **"I had two compartments":** Testimony at HUAC Hearings, 1263 (August 27, 1948).

103 **On February 15:** FBI file no. 74–1333–2237, February 15, 1949; Edith Tiger, ed., *In Re Alger Hiss: Petition for a Writ of Error Coram Nobis* (New York: Farrar, Straus and Giroux, 1979), 259–66, 430–31.

104 **Chambers added more details:** FBI file no. 74–1333–2152, February 18, 1949.

105 **"In time":** Chambers, *Witness*, 788.

105 **On January 5:** Paul F. Ellis, "Scientists Study Petting Customs," United Press International, January 5, 1948.

105 **"The homosexual":** Alfred C. Kinsey, Wardell B. Pomeroy, and Clyde E. Martin, *Sexual Behavior in the Human Male* (Bloomington: University of Indiana Press, 1948), 666.

105 *New York Times* **best seller list:** Geoffrey S. Smith, "National Security and Personal Isolation: Sex, Gender, and Disease in the Cold-War United States," *The International History Review* 14, no. 2 (May 1992): 325.

105 **quarter of a million:** "There Is a Mrs. Kinsey: She Supports His Views," *The Gazette* (Montreal), July 2, 1948, 5.

106 **"Persons with homosexual histories":** Kinsey, Pomeroy, and Martin, *Sexual Behavior in the Human Male*, 627.

106 **"If these figures":** Edmund Bergler, "The Myth of a New National Disease," *Psychiatric Quarterly* 22 (January 1948): 86.

106 **The very same week:** Vidal's *The City and the Pillar* was published on January 10, 1948.

106 **"Never before":** Kaiser, *Gay Metropolis*, 60.

106 **"There's a lot of queers":** Gore Vidal, *The City and the Pillar* (New York: E. P. Dutton, 1948), 185.

106 **"Occasionally two homosexuals":** Vidal, *City and the Pillar*, 149. Accentuating the clandestine aspect in the 1965 revised edition, Vidal described the homosexual demimonde as "a form of freemasonry" (Vidal, *City and the Pillar*, 156).

106 **Later that month:** Luca Prono, *Encyclopedia of Gay and Lesbian Popular Culture* (Westport, CT: Greenwood Press, 2008), 57.

106 **"was the year":** *The Journals of John Cheever*, ed. Robert Gottlieb (New York: Alfred A. Knopf, 1991), 157.

107 **"Miss Hattie":** David Harris, interviewed by Mark Meinke, March 23, 2002, Rainbow History Project, Washington, DC.

107 **a group of out-of-town businessmen:** Cantillion, author interview.

107 **his lover, who turned:** Forrester, "D.C. Bars in the 1930s," 1.

107 **"Nothing could be sweeter"**: Byron Kennard, author interview, February 15, 2014, Washington, DC. Howard died at the piano sometime in the 1960s.

107 **"Did you hear"**: Harris, interviewed by Meinke.

107 **The extensive deployment**: Estelle B. Freedman, "'Uncontrolled Desires': The Response to the Sexual Psychopath, 1920–1960," *Journal of American History* 74, no. 1 (June 1987): 89–90.

107 **"Definite changes"**: United Press, "Era of Sexual Looseness Is Predicted," *Washington Post*, September 17, 1945, 1.

108 **some fifty thousand men**: George Chauncey, "A Gay World, Vibrant and Forgotten," *New York Times*, June 26, 1994, 17.

108 **the term *sex deviate***: George Chauncey Jr., "The Postwar Sex Crime Panic," in William Graebner, ed., *True Stories from the American Past* (New York: McGraw-Hill, 1993), 170.

108 **"overrun with murderous"**: Chauncey, "Postwar Sex Crime Panic," 164.

108 **"has become more or less"**: "Sex Crimes," *Washington Post*, August 27, 1947.

108 **"sex perversion elimination program"**: *Hearings Before a Special Subcommittee of the Committee on the District of Columbia, on H. R. 340*, House of Representatives, 81st Cong. 622–623.

108 **vigilant *Post* reporter**: "Bench in Park Is Tattle-Tale," *Washington Post*, November 11, 1947, 1.

108 **places Chambers had frequented**: *Hearings Before the Judiciary Subcommittee of the Committee on the District of Columbia, on H.R. 28, H.R. 2505, H.R. 4981, and S. 1527*, House of Representatives, 81st Cong. 622, 631.

108 **passed a law**: An Act to Provide for the Treatment of Sexual Psychopaths in the District of Columbia and for Other Purposes, H.R. 6017, 80th Cong. (1948); Matthew Joseph Gambino, "Mental Health and Ideals of Citizenship: Patient Care at St. Elizabeths Hospital in Washington, D.C., 1903–1962" (PhD diss., University of Illinois at Urbana-Champaign, 2010), 226–38.

108 **By November**: Joseph Paull, "Male Pervert Arrests Rise in District," *Washington Post*, November 7, 1948, M19.

108 **On one especially**: Max Lerner, "'Scandal' in the State Department: VIII—Blick of the Vice Squad," *New York Post*, July 18, 1950, 26.

108 **during the Depression**: Margot Canaday, *The Straight State: Sexuality and Citizenship in Twentieth-Century America* (Princeton, NJ: Princeton University Press, 2009), 99.

108 **most of the men**: Paull, "Male Pervert Arrests Rise in District," M19.

109 **"one-man vice squad"**: "Told How to Testify, Policeman Informs ABC," *Washington Post*, November 10, 1948, 1.

109 **Over a four-day period**: "Vice Squad of One Has 17 Arrests," *Washington Post*, July 13, 1948, 1.

109 **during his first eight months**: "Pvt. Manthos Resigns from Police Force," *Washington Post*, July 12, 1952, 21.

109 **"comes to us"**: John London, "Probe Is Ordered into 'Frame' Charge," *Washington Post*, November 11, 1948, 20.

109 **"All too often"**: Eugene D. Williams, introduction to J. Paul de River, *The Sexual Criminal: A Psychoanalytic Study* (Springfield, IL: Charles C. Thomas, 1949), xii.

109 **"Communism, in reality"**: *Investigation of Un-American Activities in the United States: Hearings Before the Committee on Un-American Activities on H.R. 1884 and H.R. 2122, Bills to Curb or Outlaw the Communist Party of the United States*, House of Representatives, 80th Cong., 1st Sess., 44 (March 24, 1947).

109 **"penetration agent"**: W. Thomas Smith Jr., *Encyclopedia of the Central Intelligence Agency* (New York: Facts on File, 2003), 171.

7: "This Moral Leper"

110 **greatest criminal defense attorney**: "Lloyd Stryker, Attorney, Dead," *New York Times*, June 22, 1955, 29.

110 **"I will take"**: United States District Court, Southern District of New York, United States of America v. Alger Hiss, Stenographer's Minutes, June 1, 1949, 38 (hereafter cited as "United States of America v. Alger Hiss").

110 **"furtive, secretive"**: United States of America v. Alger Hiss, 39.

110 **"low-down"**: United States of America v. Alger Hiss, 41.

110 **"particular criminal propensities"**: United States of America v. Alger Hiss, 41–42.

110 **"In the warm southern countries"**: United States of America v. Alger Hiss, 54.

110 **lifting his eyebrows**: Cooke, *Generation on Trial*, 118.

111 **"The psychiatric theory"**: Weinstein, *Perjury*, 379.

111 **"talked about the case'**: Weinstein, *Perjury*, 384.

111 **FBI had threatened:** Timothy Hobson, "Eyewitness to the Alger Hiss Case," *Gay & Lesbian Review Worldwide*, January/February. 2018, 19–21.

112 **"boomerang":** Weinstein, *Perjury*, 380

112 **"theory of unconscious motivation":** Tanenhaus, *Whittaker Chambers*, 360.

112 **handed a copy:** United States v. Alger Hiss, June 6, 1949, 422–24.

112 **"with all the inflection":** Grace Robinson and James Desmond, "Defense Opens Attack on Chambers' Sanity," *New York Daily News,* June 7, 1949, 36.

112 **"with no respect":** Tanenhaus, *Whittaker Chambers*, 400.

112 **government declared:** Tanenhaus, *Whittaker Chambers*, 411.

113 **"psychopathic personality":** United States District Court, Southern District of New York, United States of America v. Alger Hiss, Stenographer's Minutes, January 5, 1950, 3650 (hereafter cited as "United States of America v. Alger Hiss II).

113 **"abnormal emotionality":** United States of America v. Alger Hiss II, 3689.

113 **Overall, his behavior was "queer":** United States of America v. Alger Hiss II, 3680.

113 **Murray concurred:** United States of America v. Alger Hiss II, 4135.

113 **Murray also impeached:** Cooke, *Generation on Trial*, 310.

113 **on January 21:** Newbold Noyes Jr., "Hiss, Found Guilty of Perjury, Will Be Sentenced Wednesday; Up to 10-Year Penalty Possible," *Evening Star*, January 22, 1950, 1.

113 **sentenced to five years:** Garnett D. Horner, "Refusal of Acheson to Desert Hiss Stirs Republican Wrath," *Evening Star*, January 26, 1950, 2.

113 **After forty-four months:** United Press, "Hiss Leaves Prison Vowing Fight to 'Dispel Deception,' Clear Name," *Washington Post*, November 28, 1954, M1.

113 **"One or two other theories":** Cooke, *Generation on Trial*, 354.

114 **"outrageous smears":** Sidney Hook, "The Faiths of Whittaker Chambers," *New York Times Book Review*, May 25, 1952, 1.

114 **"a loathsome":** James Wechsler, *The Age of Suspicion* (New York: Random House, 1953), 235.

114 **"ugly and vicious":** Arthur Schlesinger Jr., "Whittaker Chambers and His 'Witness,'" *Saturday Review*, May 24, 1952, 9.

114 **"venomous calumnies":** Chambers, *Witness*, 20.

114 **"cloaca":** Chambers, *Witness*, 789.

114 **"desperate integrity":** Chambers, *Witness*, 762.

115 **"When I try":** Chambers, *Witness*, 441.

115 **"At first":** Chambers, *Witness*, 428.

115 **"Communists," Chambers wrote:** Chambers, *Witness*, 9.

115 **"the conspirator":** Chambers, *Witness*, 34.

115 **"met [his] comrades":** Chambers, *Witness*, 37.

115 **San Francisco YMCA:** Chambers, *Witness*, 369.

115 **popular cruising spot:** John Donald Gustav-Wrathall, *Take the Young Stranger by the Hand: Same-Sex Relations and the YMCA* (Chicago: University of Chicago Press, 1998).

115 **"understood one another":** Chambers, *Witness*, 391. One detects echoes of the first encounter between Walt Whitman and Peter Doyle. "We were familiar at once—I put my hand on his knee—we understood."

115 **"meant me to read":** Chambers, *Witness*, 401.

116 **"a nut":** Tony Hiss, *Laughing Last: Alger Hiss* (Boston: Houghton Mifflin, 1977), 133.

116 **"My guess":** Weinstein, *Perjury*, 627.

116 **death in 1961:** William Fitzgibbon, "Chambers Is Dead; Hiss Case Witness," *New York Times*, July 12, 1961, 1.

116 **the same week:** Eliot Fremont-Smith, "Red Flags and Psychopaths, Psychoanalysis and History," *New York Times*, January 23, 1967, 41.

116 **"aura of homosexual conflict":** Zeligs, *Friendship and Fratricide*, 213.

116 **"something Chambers":** Zelig, *Friendship and Fratricide*, 374.

116 **"childhood frustrations":** Zelig, *Friendship and Fratricide*, 432.

117 **"Chambers' memories":** Zelig, *Friendship and Fratricide*, 213.

117 **"He never made":** Associated Press, April 8, 1976.

117 **"one swallow":** Joseph P. Ippolito, Herbert Travers, and Charles P. Kindregan, "An Interview with Alger Hiss: November 2, 1978," *The Advocate* (Suffolk University Law School Journal) 10, no. 1 (Fall 1978): 7.

117 **"short, plain-faced, and dumpy":** Alger Hiss, *Recollections of a Life* (New York: Seaver Books, 1988), 208.

117 **"a closet homosexual":** Hiss, *Recollections of a Life*, 210.

117 **"a possessed man":** Hiss, *Recollections of a Life*, 207.

117 **"bizarre and disordered':** Hiss, *Recollections of a Life*, 209.

117 **"my rebuff to him":** Hiss, *Recollections of a Life*, 208. The spurned homosexual theme is a favorite among Hiss's most ardent defenders. In an unpublished manuscript entitled "The Dream of Whittaker Chambers," William A. Reuben, a friend of Hiss who considered him "an American saint," located a sign of the forthcoming "fairy vengeance" in a bookplate that Chambers's father, Jay, a professional illustrator, designed for his one-year-old son. "In a burst of artistic creation that seems astonishingly prophetic," Reuben writes, the elder Chambers emblazoned his son's coat of arms upon the breastplate of a page boy waving what one author described as a "flamboyant banner" while standing amid a "charming fairy land." Reuben quoted the mother of a childhood classmate who remembered that Chambers "seemed to prefer staying at home reading and was termed a sissy by the neighborhood children" and "retained his effeminate mannerisms as he grew into manhood." His seventh-grade teacher remembered Chambers "as being a sissified student" whose only friend was "a little girl named Vermilea." In high school, "many of his classmates believed he had a touch of lavender in him." John Lowenthal, the producer of a 1980 documentary that attempted to exonerate Hiss, alleged in his own unfinished book that Chambers's denial to the FBI that he had ever "even thought of such [homosexual] relations with Hiss may be taken with a grain of salt, given Chambers's active homosexual life at the time of their acquaintance (the mid-1930s) and in light of his love/hate words and deeds concerning Hiss." And as late as 2018, Timothy Hobson, by that point a ninety-one-year-old retired surgeon who had settled into a same-sex relationship following a four-decade-long marriage to a woman, was claiming that Chambers "had fallen in love with Hiss . . . but then was rebuffed by Hiss and became pathologically hateful towards him." William A. Reuben, "The Dream of Whittaker Chambers," Folder 18, Box 3, William A. Reuben Papers, Tamiment Library, New York University; Wilbur Macey Stone, *Jay Chambers: His Book-Plates* (New York: Randolph R. Beam, 1902); John Lowenthal, "Hiss Manuscript (JL): Whittaker Chambers's Homosexuality," Folder 12, Box 14, John Lowenthal Papers, Tamiment Library, New York University; Lynn Duke, "Stepping Out of the Shadows," *Washington Post*, April 5, 2007; and Hobson, "Eyewitness to the Alger Hiss Case."

117 **Hiss's campaign:** Daniel Patrick Moynihan, chairman, *Report of the Commission on Protecting and Reducing Government Secrecy*, March 3, 1997, xlii, A34–37; John Earl Haynes, Harvey Klehr, and Alexander Vassiliev, *Spies: The Rise and Fall of the KGB in America* (New Haven, CT: Yale University Press, 2009), 1–31.

117 **"Denying that secret":** G. Edward White, *Alger Hiss's Looking-Glass Wars: The Covert Life of a Soviet Spy* (New York: Oxford University Press, 2004), 245.

117 **"integration":** White, *Alger Hiss's Looking-Glass Wars*, 247.

118 **presaged the connection:** See Sidney Blumenthal, "The Cold War and the Closet," *New Yorker*, March 17, 1997, 112–17; Hobson, "Eyewitness to the Alger Hiss Case," 19–21; David Harley Serlin, "Christine Jorgensen and the Cold War Closet," *Radical History Review* 62 (1995): 136–65. Tony Hiss, Alger Hiss's, speculates that "perhaps [Chambers's] stories about underground communist activities were basically a metaphor" for his "underground sexual experiences" (Tony Hiss, *The View from Alger's Window* [New York: Alfred A. Knopf, 1999], 202).

118 **Hiss and Chambers "were both that way":** OVAL 640–5, December 22, 1971, White House Tapes, Richard Nixon Presidential Library and Museum, Yorba Linda, CA (hereafter "Nixon Library").

118 **"Homosexuality has figured':** Willard Edwards, "Senators Told of Immorality in Washington," *Chicago Daily Tribune*, March 30, 1950, 2.

118 **"A curious freemasonry":** Schlesinger, *Vital Center*, 127.

118 **"perverts politics"**: Schlesinger, *Vital Center*, 151. This was the same book in which Schlesinger decried the 1930's State Department as a haven of "effete and conventional men who adored countesses, pushed cookies and wore handkerchiefs in their sleeves." Ironically, in this very same passage, Schlesinger favorably contrasts the "highly able" Sumner Welles to the coterie of limp-wristed cookie-pushers, ruefully noting how "The mountaineer vindictiveness of Mr. Hull hampered Welles's efforts and eventually drove him from the Department." Schlesinger, *Vital Center*, 166–7.

119 **"I do not intend"**: Marshall Andrews, "Secretary Cites Principles Stated on Mount of Olives; Senators Hit Stand," *Washington Post*, January 26, 1950, 1.

119 **After denouncing**: Horner, "Refusal of Acheson to Desert Hiss Stirs Republican Wrath," 2.

119 **"converted the answer"**: Oliver Pilat, *Drew Pearson: An Unauthorized Biography* (New York: Harper's Magazine Press, 1973), 214. "We tried the experiment of examining the conduct of both on the assumption that what Chambers had said was true, and then on the assumption that it was false," Acheson recalled. "On neither assumption was their conduct explicable on any reasonable basis. Some parts of the puzzle seemed to be missing." More than two decades after Chambers first leveled his charges, Acheson concluded that "The mystery remained, as it does today" (Acheson, *Present at the Creation*, 252).

8: Lavender Lists

120 **"primitives"**: Acheson, *Present at the Creation* 12, 334–70.

120 **detonated an atomic bomb**: William L. Laurence, "Soviet Achievement Ahead of Predictions by 3 Years," *New York Times*, September 24, 1949, 1.

120 **declared victory**: Walter Sullivan, "Reds Proclaim a Republic in China; Chou Is Premier," *New York Times*, October 2, 1949, 1.

120 **Soviets established**: "Reds Promise End of Reich Occupation," *Washington Post*, October 6, 1949, 4.

120 **third of the world's population**: John Patrick Diggins, *The Proud Decades: America in War and Peace, 1941–1960* (New York: W. W. Norton, 1988), 86.

120 **defense and assistance pact**: Associated Press, "Red China and Russia Sign 30-Year Alliance," *Baltimore Sun*, February 15, 1950, 1.

121 **"town meetings"**: Roy Jenkins, "To Better Order the Universe: Recalling Dean Acheson," *Foreign Affairs*, September/October 1998, 137.

121 **waxed mustache**: Robert L. Beisner, *Dean Acheson: A Life in the Cold War* (Oxford: Oxford University Press, 2006), 88–89.

121 **"surrender"**: Walter Trohan, "Busbey Blasts Chinese Policy of Democrats," *Chicago Daily Tribune*, August 7, 1948, 7.

121 **Moscow's acquisition**: Willard Edwards, "Truman's 'Red Herring' Turns into Booby Trap," *Chicago Daily Tribune*, August 17, 1950, 14.

121 **"loss" of China**: "'China Lobby,' Once Powerful Factor in U.S. Politics, Appears Victim of Lack of Interest," *New York Times*, April 26, 1970, 14.

121 **"cowardly college"**: Associated Press, "Nixon Calls Stevenson Appeaser of Communism," *Los Angeles Times*, October 17, 1952, 22.

121 **"I used my"**: Robert Chadwell Williams, *Klaus Fuchs: Atom Spy* (Cambridge, MA: Harvard University Press, 1987), 184.

122 **"pompous diplomat"**: David M. Oshinsky, *A Conspiracy So Immense: The World of Joe McCarthy* (New York: Free Press, 1983), 108–9; *Major Speeches and Debates of Senator Joe McCarthy Delivered in the United States Senate, 1950–1951* (Washington, DC: U.S. Government Printing Office, 1952), 14.

122 **"fantastic"**: "Text of Acheson's Statement on Hiss," *New York Times*, March 1, 1950, 2.

122 **senator asked Acheson**: U.S. Congress, Senate Subcommittee of the Committee on Appropriations, Departments of State, Justice, Commerce, and the Judiciary Appropriations for 1951, 81st Cong., 2nd Sess. (hereafter cited as "U.S. Congress, Subcommittee on Appropriations") 596–98 (February 28, 1950). And yet, in the case of Sumner Welles, Acheson was inclined to be more forgiving. "For some time rumors of a personal nature about Welles had been circulating in Washington, assiduously furthered by his malign enemy, William Christian Bullitt, a singularly ironic middle name," Acheson wrote in his 1969 memoir. Bullitt orchestrated a coup that achieved bureaucratic "peace through human sacrifice" (Acheson, *Present at the Creation*, 46).

122 **"Gray Eminence"**: "Styles Bridges Is Dead at 63; Republicans' Senior Senator," *New York Times*, November 27, 1961, 1.

122 **"In this shady category"**: U.S. Congress, Subcommittee on Appropriations, 601–3 (February 25, 1950).

123 **"Lavender Scare"**: The definitive book on this subject is David K. Johnson's *The Lavender Scare: The Cold War Persecution of Gays and Lesbians in the Federal Government* (Chicago: University of Chicago Press, 2004).

123 **electroshock therapies:** Jennifer Terry, *An American Obsession: Science, Medicine, and Homosexuality in Modern Society* (Chicago: University of Chicago Press, 1999), 470.

123 **emetics:** Katz, *Gay American History*, 170–201.

123 **"Constantly and unceasingly"**: Donald Webster Cory, *The Homosexual in America: A Subjective Approach* (New York: Greenberg, 1951), 10.

123 **transposition of *Corydon*:** Martin Duberman, "Dr. Sagarin and Mr. Cory: The 'Father,' of the Homophile Movement," *Gay and Lesbian Review* 4 (Fall 1997): 9.

123 **"a minority group"**: Cory, *Homosexual in America*, 5–6.

124 **"My God"**: Norman Mailer, "The Homosexual Villain," *One*, January 1955, 10.

124 **"conspiracy of silence"**: Cory, *Homosexual in America*, 45.

124 **"All the 'Artists'"**: Robert Griffith, "Harry S Truman and the Burden of Modernity," *Reviews in American History* 9, no. 3 (September 1981): 291.

124 **"extensive employment"**: The June 10, 1947, letter is cited in 97 Cong. Rec. (1951), Part 5, p. 6599.

124 **"habitual drunkenness"**: "Security Principles and Hearing Procedures of the Personnel Security Board," October 7, 1947, *The Department of State Bulletin* XVII, no. 431, Publication 2931 (October 5, 1947): 780.

124 **"Fire the bastard':** Robert J. Ryan Sr., interviewed by Charles Stuart Kennedy, Association for Diplomatic Studies and Training, Foreign Affairs Oral History Project, November 7, 1991.

124 **"It is common knowledge"**: Westbrook Pegler, "Peurifoy's Amazing Disclosure," King Features Syndicate, March 24, 1950.

125 **"Communists and queers"**: United Press, "McCarthy Labels Marshall 'Unfit,'" *New York Times*, April 21, 1950, 3.

125 **"prancing mimics"**: Associated Press, "Fire Acheson, McCarthy Repeats," May 16, 1950.

125 **"inside-the-Beltway"**: Theo Lippman Jr., "First One 'Inside the Beltway,'" *Baltimore Sun*, April 16, 1997, 2.

125 **"politicians generally agree"**: Frank R. Kent, "McCarthy's Charges Express Public View," *Evening Star*, April 2, 1950, 51.

125 **"Although more than 8,000,000"**: Ralph H. Major Jr. "New Moral Menace to Our Youth," *Coronet*, September 1950, 101.

125 **Increasing bureaucratization:** Canaday, *Straight State*, 2–4.

125 **The problem of homosexuals:** Max Lerner, "'Scandal' in the State Department: VII—Sen. Wherry's Crusade," *New York Post*, July 17, 1950, 2.

125 **chain-smoking:** Randolph W. Baxter, "'Homo-Hunting' in the Early Cold War: Senator Kenneth Wherry and the Homophobic Side of McCarthyism," *Nebraska History* 84 (2003): 119.

126 **"forget to mention"**: William S. White, "Senator Wherry Dies at 59; Republicans' Floor Leader," *New York Times*, November 30, 1951, 24.

126 **"Washington's leading symbol"**: William S. White, "Portrait of a 'Fundamentalist,'" *New York Times Magazine*, January 15, 1950, 14.

126 **"Wherryisms"**: Robert C. Albright, "Ike's Lips Could Be Opened," *Washington Post*, August 5, 1951, B5.

126 **"wild Indian scalping"**: Max Lerner, 'Scandal' in the State Department: XI—Sex and Politics," *New York Post*, July 21, 1950, 2.

126 **"an arena"**: Allen Drury, *A Senate Journal: 1943–1945* (New York: McGraw-Hill, 1963), 180.

126 **Wherry subpoenaed:** Don S. Warren, "Senators Defer Meeting on D.C. Subversive Curb," *Evening Star*, March 24, 1950, B1.

126 **"a good education"**: Jean R. Hailey, "Roy Blick, Ex-Police Official, Dies at 72," *Washington Post*, June 19, 1972, C4.

126 **Colleagues joked:** Alfred E. Lewis and Harry Gabbett, "It's D.C.'s Sex File but Blick's Key," *Washington Post*, September 29, 1963, E2.

126 **"one-man watchdog":** "Roy E. Blick, 72, Dies; Ex-Vice Squad Chief," *Evening Star*, June 19, 1972, 39.

126 **freed a bookmaker:** "Police Peek in Gambling Case Upheld," *Washington Post*, February 17, 1948, 9; McDonald et al. v. United States, 69 S. Ct. 191 (1948).

127 **"Hi-ya Mac":** "Numbers Raiders, with Warrant, Net 6," *Washington Post*, February 18, 1951, M9.

127 **just two transcripts:** "Congress Quiz Bares Vice Arrests, 'Fixes,'" *San Francisco Examiner*, March 25, 1950, 2.

127 **"A well-known espionage tactic":** Willard Edwards, "Senators Told of Immorality in Washington," *Chicago Daily Tribune*, March 30, 1950, 1.

127 **"government girls":** Joseph A. Fox, "City Has Acute Problem Caring for Government Girls Arriving 100 a Day," *Evening Star*, February 8, 1942, B5; William J. Moyer, "Government Girls: Past, Present and Future," *Sunday Star Pictorial Magazine*, May 6, 1951, 10–11. The classified pages of the *Evening Star* regularly featured housing advertisements for "government girls."

127 **"women employees":** Richard Rovere, "Letter from Washington," *New Yorker*, April 22, 1950, 105–6.

127 **"Where the despot holds":** "A Report to the National Security Council—NSC 68," April 7, 1950, President's Secretary's Files: "Ideological Foundations of the Cold War," Truman Library.

128 **"There are today":** William R. Tanner and Robert Griffith, "Legislative Politics and 'McCarthyism': The Internal Security Act of 1950," in *The Specter: Original Essays on the Cold War and the Origins of McCarthyism*, ed. Robert Griffith and Athan Theoharis (New York: New Viewpoints, 1974), 179.

128 **theory that homosexuals:** The fallacies inherent in the argument that homosexuals posed a uniquely serious security risk are laid out eloquently in Marlin Prentiss, "Are Homosexuals Security Risks?," *ONE*, December 1955, 4–6.

128 **117 American citizens:** Theodore R. Sarbin, *Homosexuality and Personnel Security*, PERS-TR-91–008 (Monterey, CA: Defense Personnel Security and Research Education Center, 1991), 30.

129 **"all his waking hours":** U.S. Congress, Senate Committee on Appropriations, "Report of the Investigations of the Junior Senator of Nebraska, a Member of the Subcommittee Appointed by the Subcommittee on Appropriations for the District of Columbia on the Infiltration of Subversives and Moral Perverts into the Executive Branch of the United States Government," 81st Cong., 2nd Sess. (hereafter cited as "Wherry Report"), 11 (May 1950).

129 **"expeditious action":** Wherry Report, 15.

129 **former FBI agent:** "F. Flanagan Dies; Official at Grace & Co.," *Washington Post*, April 5, 1999, B5.

129 **"remained just as flagrant:"** Stephen J. Spingarn, interviewed by Jerry N. Hess, March 24, 1967, Truman Library.

129 **"The excessively":** Spingarn, interviewed by Hess.

129 **"I mean":** Spingarn, interviewed by Hess.

129 **"suspected or known":** Francis Flanagan, "Files Desired by Investigations Subcommittee in Conduct of Investigations, June 27, 1950, Box 26: "Sex Perversion," White House Central Files, Harry S. Truman Papers, Truman Library.

129 **"the homosexual as a security risk":** Spingarn, interviewed by Hess.

129 **"Flanagan seems":** Stephen J. Spingarn, "Memorandum for the Hoey Subcommittee Sex Pervert Investigation File," July 10, 1950, Box 28, Stephen J. Spingarn Papers, Truman Library.

130 **Attributed to Adolf Hitler:** "Hitler is said to have amassed the names of homosexuals around the world, chiefly in capitals of countries on his now-destroyed timetable for subjugation," Wherry and Hill wrote in their interim report. "The Hitler list is rumored to have been acquired by Russia when the Hitler regime crashed to defeat and unconditional surrender" (Wherry Report, 11).

130 **Nebraska Republican:** 96 Cong. Rec. 5402, 5403 (April 19, 1950).

130 **"no reason":** "The Aberrants," *Washington Post*, March 17, 1950, 22. The specter of a comprehensive, international register of homosexuals was first raised in 1918 by Noel Pemberton Billing, an inventor and member of the British Parliament. In an article entitled "The Forty-Seven Thousand," published in the weekly journal he founded and edited, *The Imperialist*, Pemberton claimed the existence of a "Black Book" containing the names of English lesbians and homosexuals, compiled by agents of the German intelligence service "so vile and spreading such debauchery and such

lasciviousness as only German minds can conceive and only German bodies execute." Included among the indicted were "Privy Councillors, wives of Cabinet Ministers, even Cabinet Ministers themselves, diplomats, poets, bankers, editors, newspapers proprietors, and members of His Majesty's Household" (Gregory Woods, *Homintern: How Gay Culture Liberated the Modern World* [New Haven, CT: Yale University Press, 2016], 44).

131 **Office of Naval Intelligence:** "Senator Hill Proposes Complete Inquiry into Hiring of Undesirables," *Evening Star*, May 20, 1950, 35.

131 **"everything they had":** Ruth Young Watt, interviewed by Donald A. Ritchie, U.S. Senate Oral History Project, September 7, 1978, https://www.senate.gov/artandhistory/history/resources/pdf/watt_interview_2.pdf.

131 **sending questionnaires:** Judith Adkins, "'These People Are Frightened to Death': Congressional Investigations and the Lavender Scare," *Prologue* 48, no. 2 (Summer 2016).

131 **"Unless the law":** Harry B. Mitchell to Homer Ferguson, May 18, 1950, Subject File, Folder: "Sex Perversion [Investigations of Federal Employees]," Box 26, Confidential File, White House Central Files, Truman Papers, Truman Library.

131 **"Won't you stop"** William S. White, "M'Carthy Asserts Budenz Named Red in Acheson Office," *New York Times*, April 26, 1950, 3.

132 **Lerner tabulated:** Max Lerner, "'Scandal' in the State Department: IV—Kinsey in Washington," *New York Post*, July 13, 1950, 26.

132 **"go see Blick":** Lerner, "'Scandal' in the State Department: VIII," 2, 26.

133 **In his many interviews:** Max Lerner, "'Scandal' in the State Department: V—The Problem of Blackmail," *New York Post*, July 14, 1950, 2.

133 **"The impulse":** Max Lerner, "'Scandal' in the State Department: XII—What Can We Do About It?," *New York Post*, July 22, 1950, 2.

133 **citing his "ability" and "outstanding results":** "Roy Blick Promoted to Police Captaincy," *Washington Post*, November 17, 1950, B1.

9: "A Government Within a Government"

134 **"as well guarded":** C. L. Sulzberger, *A Long Row of Candles: Memoirs and Diaries, 1934–1954* (New York: Macmillan, 1969), 346–47.

134 **forced out of:** Benjamin Welles notes from interviews with Robert Joyce, March 26, 1974, and James Jesus Angleton, December 25, 1975, James McCargar Papers, Boston University.

134 **recommendation of a former colleague:** Hersh, *Old Boys*, 252.

134 **Office of Policy Coordination:** "National Security Council Directive on Office of Special Projects," NSC 10/2, June 18, 1948.

135 **nominally run out:** Anthony Carew, "The American Labor Movement in Fizzland: The Free Trade Union Committee and the CIA," *Labor History* 39, no. 1 (1998): 26; "Office of Policy Coordination, 1948–1952," *Studies in Intelligence* 17, no. 2-S (Summer 1973).

135 **Returning to Frankfurt:** Joseph J. Trento, *The Secret History of the CIA* (New York: Random House, 2001), 51–52.

135 **Offie assisted** Kevin Conley Ruffner, *Eagle and Swastika; CIA and Nazi War Criminals and Collaborators*, Draft Working Paper, April 2003, History Staff, Central Intelligence Agency, Washington, DC, chap. 7, 6–15.

135 **helped convince:** Trento, *Secret History of the CIA*, 47.

135 **"grand masters":** Trento, *Secret History of the CIA*, 479.

135 **"a world-class sophisticate":** Trento, *Secret History of the CIA*, 48.

135 **"Sen. McCarthy was":** David M. Barrett, *The CIA and Congress: The Untold Story from Truman to Kennedy* (Lawrence: University Press of Kansas, 2005), 8.

135 **"a man formerly":** "Persons Listed by McCarthy Now Total 9," *Washington Post*, March 15, 1950, 1.

136 **The man who:** Hersh, *Old Boys*, 512; Christopher Simpson, *Blowback: America's Recruitment of Nazis and Its Effects on the Cold War* (New York: Weidenfeld and Nicolson, 1988), 237; Mark Stout, "The Pond: Running Agents for State, War, and the CIA," *Studies in Intelligence* 48, no. 3 (2004): 69–82.

136 **A former heavyweight:** Simpson, *Blowback*, 57.

136 **black poodle:** Christian Salazar and Randy Herschaft, "Before the CIA, There Was the Pond," Associated Press, July 29, 2010.

136 **"effectively became"**: Simpson, *Blowback*, 273.

136 **Lyman Kirkpatrick**: Richard Pearson, "Lyman Kirkpatrick Jr. Dies," *Washington Post*, March 5, 1995, B6.

136 **"got into a lot of garbage pails"**: Simpson, *Blowback*, 236–37

136 **Consisting mainly of retired military officers**: Oshinsky, *Conspiracy So Immense*, 323.

136 **"Within the CIA"**: Lyman B. Kirkpatrick Jr., *The Real CIA* (New York: Macmillan, 1968), 136.

137 **rubbing his nipples**: Herken, *Georgetown Set*, 107.

137 **"Why revoke'**: Thomas Powers, *The Man Who Kept the Secrets: Richard Helms and the CIA* (New York: Macmillan, 1969), 75.

137 **"I don't think my father"**: Scott Anderson, *The Quiet Americans: Four CIA Spies at the Dawn of the Cold War—A Tragedy in Three Acts* (New York: Doubleday, 2020), 234. CIA congressional liaison Walter Pforzheimer remembered another instance of Wisner's efforts on behalf of a gay employee, "a guy that some of us thought was homosexual[,] and some of us were involved in trying to get him out. He was one of Frank's pets. He was fired from the CIA, but I heard that he was given a job in Latin America and that Frank arranged that" (Barrett, *CIA and Congress*, 75).

137 **Offie was resourceful**: Trento, *Secret History of the CIA*, 48.

137 **On April 25**: 96 Cong. Rec. 5703 (April 25, 1950).

137 **persuaded President Truman**: Barrett, *CIA and Congress*, 76.

137 **"been informed"**: 96 Cong. Rec. 5712 (April 25, 1950).

137 **the FBI denied**: Riebling, *Wedge*, 117.

137 **blue-collar, Catholic**: On the heavily Catholic composition of the FBI, see Tim Weiner, *Enemies: A History of the FBI* (New York: Random House, 2012), 147; Athan Theoharis and John Stuart Cox, *The Boss: J. Edgar Hoover and the Great American Inquisition* (Philadelphia: Temple University Press, 1988), 201–3; Steve Rosswurm, *The FBI and the Catholic Church, 1935–1962* (Amherst: University of Massachusetts Press, 2009), 2, 41–42; Gentry, *J. Edgar Hoover*, 347; William Overend, "Richard T. Bretzing: FBI's L.A. Boss Passes Hardest Test," *Los Angeles Times*, January 11, 1987, 1. The Catholic reach extended into the CIA's own internal security office, where, according to one State Department security officer, the majority, "if not all," were "graduates of Notre Dame, Villanova, or other Catholic universities, and had been in the Marine Corps more often than not . . . If you looked carefully, you would find a lot of Irish-American Catholics" (Charles Anthony Gillespie, interviewed by Charles Stuart Kennedy, September 19, 1995, Association for Diplomatic Studies and Training, Foreign Affairs Oral History Project).

138 **"In the era"**: Daniel Patrick Moynihan, "A 'Commentary' Report: The Irish of New York," *Commentary*, August 1963, 102.

138 **determined by access to secrets**: McCarthyism's long-term effect on the intelligence community was to produce a "change in the social composition of the services," John C. Sutherland, an analyst in the Army Security Agency, recalled. "Lower middle class graduates of second and third rank colleges, many of them Roman Catholic or Protestant fundamentalist in their religious views, came to dominate the structure of the intelligence services" (John C. Sutherland to Robin Winks, February 8, 1988, Folder 2, Box 22, Winks Papers).

138 **"execrable vice"**: John Boswell, *Christianity, Social Tolerance, and Homosexuality: Gay People in Western Europe from the Beginning of the Christian Era to the Fourteenth Century* (Chicago: University of Chicago Press, 1980), 316.

138 **"perversion is found"**: 96 Cong. Rec. (May 15, 1950), Part 15, Appendix, A3661.

138 **"double-dome"**: Westbrook Pegler, "Fair Enough," King Features Syndicate, January 28, 1953. The term *egghead* was coined in 1952 by Stewart Alsop, Joe's younger brother and column-writing partner, to describe the intellectual supporters of Adlai Stevenson, who was bald. Joseph and Stewart Alsop, *The Reporter's Trade* (New York: Reynal, 1958), 188.

139 **"politically liberal"**: William Colby and Peter Forbath, *Honorable Men: My Life in the CIA* (New York: Simon and Schuster, 1978), 77.

139 **"most effective"**: Colby and Forbath, *Honorable Men*, 80.

139 **"guru"**: Merle Miller, "One Man's Long Journey—From a One-World Crusade to the 'Department of Dirty Tricks,'" *New York Times Magazine*, January 7, 1973, 54.

139 **worked for the CIA:** Marc D. Charney, "Rev. William Sloane Coffin Dies at 81; Fought for Civil Rights and Against a War," *New York Times*, April 13, 2006; A21.

139 **two kinds of people:** Jean M. White, "Espionage—But No Escape: The Spy Thriller as Metaphor," *Washington Post*, June 26, 1977, F1.

139 **"strange spying":** Westbrook Pegler, "Fair Enough," King Features Syndicate, December 30, 1952.

139 **"weird system":** Westbrook Pegler, "Fair Enough," King Features Syndicate, January 31, 1953.

139 **"mischievous cabal":** Westbrook Pegler, "Fair Enough," King Features Syndicate, March 4, 1953.

139 **"intimate confidante":** Westbrook Pegler, "Fair Enough," King Features Syndicate, May 19, 1960.

139 **non-Communist left:** On the CIA's support for the non-Communist left, see Frances Stonor Saunders, *The Cultural Cold War: The CIA and the World of Arts and Letters* (New York: New Press, 1999); and Hugh Wilford, *The Mighty Wurlitzer: How the CIA Played America* (Cambridge, MA: Harvard University Press, 2008).

139 **"It all had to be off the budget":** Saunders, *Cultural Cold War*, 197.

140 **"few ideological constraints":** Michael S. Sherry, *Gay Artists in Modern American Culture: An Imagined Conspiracy* (Chapel Hill: University of North Carolina Press, 2007), 39.

140 **"suspicious number":** Miller, "One Man's Long Journey."

140 **"At that time":** "Memorandum for the Record, Subject: Interview with [Redacted]," June 14, 1989, Approved for Release January 15, 2020, C06619080.

140 **"an extraordinarily active":** James T. Fisher, *Dr. America: The Lives of Thomas A. Dooley, 1927–1961* (Amherst: University of Massachusetts Press, 1997), 83.

140 **"potential sex criminal":** Fisher, *Dr. America*, 96.

140 **Forced to fire:** Morgan, *Covert Life*, 213.

140 **decorated by the wife:** Betty Beale, "Exclusively Yours," *Evening Star*, September 8, 1950, B3.

140 **On May 17:** Richard E. Schroeder, *The Foundation of the CIA: Harry Truman, the Missouri Gang, and the Origins of the Cold War* (Columbia: University of Missouri Press, 2017), 131.

141 **friendly correspondence:** Carew, "The American Labor Movement in Fizzland," 36n55.

141 **"Machiavellian":** Benjamin Welles notes from interview with James Jesus Angleton, December 25, 1975, James McCargar Papers, Boston University.

141 **"the Ghost":** Jefferson Morley, *The Ghost: The Secret Life of CIA Spymaster James Jesus Angleton* (New York: St. Martin's Press, 2017).

141 **"That's just the reason":** Benjamin Welles notes from interview with James Jesus Angleton, November 11, 1977, James McCargar Papers, Boston University.

141 **Between 1949 and 1953:** "The 20th Anniversary of ANGLE," Agency Network of Gay and Lesbian Employees, https://web.archive.org/web/20201016160302/https://www.cia.gov/news-information/featured-story-archive/2016-featured-story-archive/images/angle/ANGLE_TimelineDisplay.pdf.

141 **"on a very quiet basis":** Associated Press, "McCarthy Is Accused by State Department of 'Crude Misquotation,'" *Evening Star*, May 21, 1950, 4.

141 **"to transgress":** "'Unspectacular' Pervert Probe Promised by Hoey Committee," *Washington Post*, June 15, 1950, 1.

141 **the presence of a "lady" in their midst:** Johnson, *Lavender Scare*, 102–3.

141 **"quick test like":** Ken Adler, *The Lie Detectors: The History of an American Obsession* (New York: Free Press, 2007), 224. Smith's question might have had a personal dimension. After assuming her husband's seat in Congress upon his death in 1940, Smith developed an extremely close, and platonic, relationship with her top aide, a retired air force brigadier general named Bill Lewis. "The man behind the woman," in Smith's words, Lewis lived with Smith throughout her decades in Congress and afterward into retirement. He remained a bachelor throughout. "I don't know what I would have done without him," Smith told a reporter in 1975. "He has devoted his life to me" (Ann Blackman, Associated Press, September 11, 1975).

141 **only one deviant:** Bert Wissman, "Federal Agency Spots Perverts by Lie-Detector," *Washington Times-Herald*, May 21, 1950.

142 **"whether homosexuals are":** Director of Central Intelligence phone log, Walter Pforzheimer to Roscoe Hillenkoetter, June 27, 1950.

142 **"known all through":** *Hearings Pursuant to S. Res. 280 Before the Senate Committee on Expenditures in the Executive Departments, Investigations Subcommittee*, 81st Cong., 2nd Sess. [Executive

Session] (hereafter cited as "Hoey Committee Hearings") 2093 (July 14, 1950) (testimony of Roscoe Hillenkoetter).

142 **"an established homosexual relationship"**: Hoey Committee Hearings, 2094.

142 **"extremely gullible"**: Hoey Committee Hearings, 2099.

142 **"I might say parenthetically"**: Hillenkoetter prepared testimony, Hoey Committee Hearings, 19.

143 **"probably impossible"**: Kristin Downey, *The Woman Behind the New Deal: The Life and Legacy of Frances Perkins—Social Security, Unemployment Insurance, and the Minimum Wage* (New York: Anchor Books, 2010), 165–69.

143 **"very involved"**: Lillian Faderman, *Surpassing the Love of Men: Romantic Friendship and Love Between Women from the Renaissance to the Present* (New York: William Morrow, 1981), 190–203.

144 **While informing**: U.S. Senate, Investigations Subcommittee, Committee on Expenditures in the Executive Departments, Executive Session, September 8, 1950, 2752, 2754, 2728.

144 **"Maybe we'd better"**: Joseph Alsop and Stewart Alsop, "Why Has Washington Gone Crazy?," *The Saturday Evening Post*, July 29, 1950, 21.

144 **"Perversion Among Government Workers"**: "School Dealing with Perversion Opened by U.S.," *Washington Times-Herald*, June 24, 1950, 4.

144 **After holding five executive session hearings:** "Hoey Readies Measure on Homosexuals," *Washington Post*, September 24, 1950, M13.

144 **"those who engage in acts of homosexuality"**: *Employment of Homosexuals and Other Sex Perverts in Government, Interim Report Submitted to the Committee on Expenditures in the Executive Departments, Subcommittee on Investigations Pursuant to S. Res 280*, Senate Doc. 241, 81st Cong., 2nd Sess. (December 15, 1950) (hereafter cited as "Hoey Report"), 19.

144 **"Communist and Nazi agents"**: Hoey Report, 6.

145 **"They resign"**: Lerner, "'Scandal' in the State Department: VII," 20.

145 **From April 1**: Hoey Report, 8.

145 **"One homosexual"**: Hoey Report. In 1933, the German journalist Johannes Steele used imagery similarly redolent of pollution to describe the proliferation of homosexuals among the Nazi leadership. "The moral baseness of the Hitler Movement is clearly illuminated by the type of men Hitler has collected around him . . . one lunatic in office gives another lunatic a post; one murderer, who is a Police Chief, makes another murderer a Captain of Police; one homosexual 'youth regenerator' makes another homosexual his [aide de camp]." Johannes Steel, *Hitler as Frankenstein* (London: Wishart and Co., 1933), 147.

10: The Homintern

146 **"If you're wondering"**: Jack Lait and Lee Mortimer, *Washington Confidential* (New York: Crown, 1951), 116.

146 **editor and a columnist:** "Jack Lait, 71, Dies; Editor of Mirror," *New York Times*, April 2, 1954, 27.

146 **"We think we"**: Lait and Mortimer, *Washington Confidential*, 11–12.

146 **"with the impact"**: Harvey Breit, "Talk with Lait and Mortimer," *New York Times Book Review*, April 15, 1951, 23.

147 **trailed only:** Daniel S. Burt, ed., *The Chronology of American Literature: America's Literary Achievements from the Colonial Era to Modern Times* (Boston: Houghton Mifflin, 2004), 492.

147 **"potpourri"**: Lait and Mortimer, *Washington Confidential*, 20.

147 **"One of the queerest"**: Lait and Mortimer, *Washington Confidential*, 25.

147 **"especially the swimming pool"**: Lait and Mortimer, *Washington Confidential*, 124–25.

147 **"fairies"**: Lait and Mortimer, *Washington Confidential*, 116

147 **"much less obvious"**: Lait and Mortimer, *Washington Confidential*, 121.

147 **"pathological compensation"**: Lait and Mortimer, *Washington Confidential*, 117.

147 **"The government is honeycombed"**: Lait and Mortimer, *Washington Confidential*, 125.

147 **"It seems that nonconformity"**: Lait and Mortimer, *Washington Confidential*, 26.

147 **"despite denials"**: Jack Lait and Lee Mortimer, *U.S.A. Confidential* (New York: Crown, 1952), 44.

148 **"two Congressmen"**: Lait and Mortimer, *Washington Confidential*, 120.

148 **"one of the most sordid"**: Lait and Mortimer, *Washington Confidential*, 35.

148 **"no color line"**: Lait and Mortimer, *Washington Confidential*, 117.

148 **"fairies and Fair Dealers"**: Lait and Mortimer, *Washington Confidential*, 21.

148 **"free crossing"**: Lait and Mortimer, *Washington Confidential*, 120–21.

148 **"Fairies are no"**: Lait and Mortimer, *Washington Confidential*, 122–23.

149 **constantly replenish**: Verne W. Newton, *The Cambridge Spies: The Untold Story of Maclean, Philby, and Burgess in America* (Latham, MD: Madison Books, 1991), 325.

149 **Two British diplomats**: "'Yard' Now Thinks 2 Diplomats Are Behind 'Curtain,'" *Washington Post*, June 14, 1951, 1.

149 **"Special Relationship"**: Winston Churchill, "The Sinews of Peace" (speech), March 5, 1946, Fulto, MO.

149 **London's diplomatic recognition**: Clifton Daniel, "British Fear Split with U.S. on China," *New York Times*, January 3, 1950, 1; Raymond Daniell, "U.S.-British Relations Are Under New Strains," *New York Times*, January 8, 1950, E5.

149 **rift between the two allies**: M. L. Dockrill, "The Foreign Office, Anglo-American Relations and the Korean War, June 1950–June 1951," *International Affairs* 62, no. 3 (Summer 1986): 459–76.

149 **Bruno Pontecorvo**: "British 'Sure' Atomic Scientist Is in Russia," *Washington Post*, November 7, 1950, 15.

149 **Both men came**: "British Hunt 2 Missing Diplomats Ranked as High and Trusted Aides," *New York Times*, June 8, 1951, 1.

149 **often be spotted**: Newton, *Cambridge Spies*, 275.

150 **"precipitated a social disaster"**: David Martin, *Wilderness of Mirrors: Intrigue, Deception, and the Secrets That Destroyed Two of the Cold War's Most Important Agents* (New York: HarperCollins, 1980), 53.

150 **Another soirée**: Newton, *Cambridge Spies*, 312; Tom Driberg, *Guy Burgess: A Portrait with Background* (London: Weidenfeld and Nicolson, 1956), 87.

150 **"Whitehall in Queer Street"**: Alastair Forbes, "Whitehall in Queer Street," *Sunday Dispatch*, June 10, 1951, 4.

150 **"widespread sexual perversion"**: House of Commons Debate, June 11, 1951, Hansard Debate (or HC Deb), vol. 488, col. 1672.

150 **"I have the strongest"**: "Great Britain: Infection from the Enemy," *Time*, June 25, 1951, 29.

150 **"received the impression"**: New York to Director, FBI Teletype, June 11, 1951, FBI 100–374183.

150 **"was one of a ring"**: L. B. Nichols to Clyde Tolson, FBI Memo, Subject: DONALD MCLEAN, GUY BURGESS, June 30, 1951, FBI 100–374183.

150 **"It is believed'**: J. Edgar Hoover to Director, Central Intelligence Agency, FBI Memo, June 16, 1951, FBI 100–374183.

151 **Despite an assertion**: "Summary Brief: Donald Duart Maclean; Guy Francis De Moncy Burgess; Harold Adrian Russell Philby," FBI Memo, November 8, 1955, FBI 100–374183 (hereafter cited as "Summary Brief").

151 **there is no evidence**: Roland Philipps, *A Spy Named Orphan: The Enigma of Donald Maclean* (London: The Bodley Head, 2018), 270–71.

151 **"a homosexual who boasted"**: SAC New York to Director, FBI Memo, "Subject: DONALD MCLEAN; GUY BURGESS; ESPIONAGE—R," August 15, 1951, FBI 100–374183.

151 **"the spy who knew"**: Stewart Purvis and Jeff Hulbert, *Guy Burgess: The Spy Who Knew Everyone* (London: Biteback, 2016).

151 **"you can get"**: SAC New York to Director, FBI Memo, "Subject: DONALD MCLEAN."

151 **"could state with certainty"**: "Summary Brief," 13–14.

151 **Blair Bolles**: "E. Blair Bolles, 78, A Retired Journalist and Colt Executive," *New York Times*, January 29, 1990, B7.

151 **"without turning"**: SAC Washington Field Office (WFO) to Director, FBI Memo, "Subject: DONALD MCLEAN; GUY BURGESS; ESPIONAGE—R," July 14, 1951; "Summary Brief," 16.

151 **"Things have reached"**: Goronwy Rees, *A Chapter of Accidents* (London: Chatto and Windus, 1972), 190–191. Burgess, who did not publicly resurface until a 1956 Moscow press conference alongside Maclean, was apparently asked by his Soviet patrons for a list of gay British ambassadors abroad, presumably for blackmail purposes. He refused, declaring "himself anxious to harm no one, except J. Edgar Hoover" (Purvis and Hulbert, *Guy Burgess*, 352).

151 **"a drunkard":** "Summary Brief," 17.

151 **Robert Lamphere:** Douglas Martin, "Robert J. Lamphere, 83, Spy Chaser for the F.B.I., Dies," *New York Times*, February 11, 2002, A25.

151 **"The names of":** John Costello, *Mask of Treachery: Spies, Lies, Buggery and Betrayal* (New York: William Morrow, 1988), 289.

152 **living, breathing embodiment:** Tom Bower, *The Perfect English Spy: Sir Dick White and the Secret War, 1935–1990* (London: Heinemann, 1995), 121.

152 **"one of the most bizarre":** Rebecca West, *The New Meaning of Treason* (New York: Viking, 1964), 227.

152 **At the conclusion:** Frank Giles, *Sundry Times* (London: J. Murray, 1986), 52.

152 **The presence of:** Costello, *Mask of Treachery*, 291.

152 **"I have a Russian":** Giles, *Sundry Times*, 60.

152 **"had as his lover":** Lait and Mortimer, *Washington Confidential*, 185.

152 **"the company and presence of good-looking young men":** Giles, *Sundry Times*, 50.

153 **"Until the recent purges":** Lait and Mortimer, *Washington Confidential*, 124.

153 **"Having spent":** William Barrett, "New Innocents Abroad," *Partisan Review*, March 1953, 291.

153 **"caused a terrible":** Andrew Lownie, *Stalin's Englishman: Guy Burgess, the Cold War, and the Cambridge Spy Ring* (New York: St. Martin's Press, 2016), 256.

153 **previous role:** Wolfgang Saxon, "Maclean, an Upper-Class Briton Lured by Marxism," *New York Times*, May 12, 1983, 1.

153 **withdrew a proposal:** Gordon Dean to William Foster, November 27, 1951, in *Foreign Relations of the United States 1951, National Security Affairs; Foreign Economic Policy, Volume I*, ed. Neal H. Petersen et al. (Washington, DC: Government Printing Office, 1979), 787.

153 **"uniform policy":** J. Edgar Hoover, "RE: Sex Deviates in Government Service," FBI memo, June 20, 1951.

153 **farthest thing from a covert homosexual:** Purvis and Hulbert, *Guy Burgess*, 20–21.

154 **"even if this condition":** SAC Los Angeles to Director, FBI Memo, "Subject: DONALD MCLEAN; GUY BURGESS; ESPIONAGE—R," July 18, 1951.

154 **variously attributed:** Woods, *Homintern*, 6.

154 **first ideologically motivated:** Sheila Kerr, "NATO's First Spies: The Case of the Disappearing Diplomats—Guy Burgess and Donald Maclean," in *Securing Peace in Europe, 1945–1962: Thoughts for the Post–Cold War Era*, ed. Beatrice Heuser and Robert O'Neill (New York: Palgrave Macmillan, 1992), 293.

154 **exacts revenge:** In reporting his "Washington Sex Story" series for the *New York Post*, Max Lerner interviewed a doctor named Lawrence Kubie, who thought Lerner too quick to dismiss the purported relationship between communism and homosexuality. In his work with homosexual patients, Kubie wrote, he had "analyzed some who were very naïve in their economic theorizing, and in whom the unconscious fantasy underlying the drive to make everybody have the same of everything had a specific reference to genital differences between men and women. In other words, the unconscious fantasies which make some people homosexuals and the unconscious fantasies which make some people very literal-minded Communists can overlap." Kubie also called attention to the "minority group identifications among homosexuals," which, he wrote, resulted in a "tendency to develop a special solidarity of their own with a weakening of their identifications with groups which are predominantly heterosexual" (Lawrence S. Kubie to Max Lerner, August 1, 1950, Max Lerner Papers, MS 322, Folder 9, Box 1, Series 1, Manuscripts and Archives, Yale University Library).

154 **"the elimination of":** R. G. Waldeck, "The Homosexual International," *Human Events*, April 16, 1952, 1. Released the same year that the "The Homosexual International" was published, the film *My Son John* insinuated a link between communism and homosexuality. Starring Robert Walker, fresh off his appearance as a homoerotic killer in Alfred Hitchcock's *Strangers on a Train*, the movie features an effeminate government worker who moonlights as a Communist agent. "The parents' reaction upon learning of their son's Communist activities is exactly the same as if they had discovered their child's homosexuality," observed the gay film historian Vito Russo. Vito Russo, *The Celluloid Closet: Homosexuality in the Movies* (New York: Harper and Row, 1981), 99.

155 **"unalterably opposed":** D'Emilio, *Sexual Politics, Sexual Communities*, 84.

155 **Harry Hay:** Mary Rourke, "Harry Hay, 90; Gay Liberation Pioneer, Communist," *Los Angeles Times*, October 25, 2002, 31; Stuart Timmons, *The Trouble with Harry Hay: Founder of the Modern Gay Movement* (Boston: Alyson, 1990), 174–78; Julia Sutton et al., "Matachins," in *The International Encyclopedia of Dance*, ed. Selma Jeanne Cohen (Oxford: Oxford University Press, 1998).

156 **"the mental convulsions":** Harry Johnson, "And a Red Too . . ." *One*, September 1953, 2.

156 **"Fruits and treachers":** Stewart Alsop, *The Center: People and Power in Political Washington* (New York: Harper and Row, 1968), 101.

157 **standing in line:** "Witch-Hunts Won't Work," *Washington Post*, May 22, 1950, 10.

157 **"It's true, sir":** Alan Dunn, *New Yorker*, June 17, 1950.

157 **people fired under the loyalty program guidelines:** "107 U.S. Aides Ousted on Morals, Security," *New York Times*, July 3, 1953, 6.

157 **American Psychiatric Association:** *Diagnostic and Statistical Manual of Mental Disorders* (Washington, DC: American Psychiatric Association, 1952).

157 **"psychopathic personality":** H.R. 5678, June 27, 1952, "An Act to Revise the Laws Relating to Immigration, Naturalization, and Nationality; and for Other Purposes."

157 **"immorality":** 1952 Republican Platform, adopted by the Republican National Convention, July 11, 1952.

157 **"fashion of hitting":** Ruth Montgomery, "Hail M'Carthy Blast at Red Links," *New York Daily News*, June 10, 1952, 2.

157 **"lavender lads":** "Name Calling Begins Early and Bitterly," *Des Moines Register*, August 5, 1952, 1.

157 **"pinks, punks and pansies":** Marquis Childs, *Witness to Power* (New York: McGraw-Hill, 1975), 67.

157 **"foulest rumor":** Joseph M. Porter, "How That Stevenson Rumor Started," *Confidential*, August 1953, 41.

158 **In truth:** Athan Theoharis, "How the F.B.I. Gaybaited Stevenson," *The Nation*, May 7, 1990, 1.

158 **Before Stevenson received:** Theoharis, "How the F.B.I. Gaybaited Stevenson."

158 **"There were a lot":** Gentry, *J. Edgar Hoover*, 402.

158 **"A vote for":** Bob Thomas, *Winchell* (New York: Berkeley Medallion, 1971), 259. Following her gender transition, Jorgensen became an entertainer, and her 1953 performance at a Washington, DC, nightclub—which billed her as "The World's Most Talked About Personality"—provoked the ire of Capt. Roy Blick. Prior to the show, Blick warned Jorgensen that if she tried to use the ladies' bathroom, he would arrest her for disorderly conduct. When Jorgensen remonstrated that a Michigan police chief had once made her honorary chief-for-a-day and invited her over to his home for dinner, Blick demurred. "Did it ever occur to you that a lot of damn fools like to look at freaks?" On the evening of her performance, according to the nightclub owner, Jorgensen "didn't go into either of our rest rooms all the while she was here" (Lewis and Gabbett, "It's D.C.'s Sex File but Blick's Key," E2).

158 **transition headquarters:** Lauren Luther Henry, *Presidential Transitions* (Washington, DC: Brookings Institution, 1960), 489.

158 **announced on its front page:** Russell Porter, "Vandenberg Jr. Is Selected as Eisenhower's Secretary," *New York Times*, November 27, 1952, 1.

158 **"the man behind":** John Griffith, "Where to, Young Van?," *Roto Magazine* (*Detroit Free Press*), August 10, 1952, 5.

158 **" 'knows everybody' ":** James M. Haswell, "Vandenberg Key Aide of Ike at Convention," *Detroit Free Press*, July 11, 1952, 1.

159 **deemed actually qualified:** Martin S. Hayden, "Arthur Vandenberg Will Be 'Man to See' if Audience Is Desired with Eisenhower," North American Newspaper Alliance/*Birmingham News*, November 28, 1952, 7.

159 **fifteen hundred chapters:** Haswell, "Vandenberg Key Aide at Convention," 1.

159 **On December 20:** Lou Nichols to Director, FBI Memo, December 23, 1952, Dwight David Eisenhower Folder, Nichols O&C.

159 **"the subject of rumors":** Lou Nichols to Clyde Tolson, FBI memo, December 9, 1952, Dwight David Eisenhower Folder, Nichols O&C.

159 **"he denied":** Rosen to Ladd, FBI memo, "Eisenhower Special Inquiries," December 28, 1952, FBI file no. 62–81742–49.

160 **there is no evidence:** Meijer, *Arthur Vandenberg*, 345.

160 **At the Commodore:** J. Edgar Hoover to Tolson, Nichols, and Ladd, FBI Memo, January 5, 1953, FBI file no. 62–81942–51.

160 **"I realize":** Dwight Eisenhower to Arthur H. Vandenberg Jr., January 17, 1953, Vandenberg Family Papers, Bentley Historical Library, University of Michigan (hereafter "Vandenberg Family Papers").

160 **officially resigned:** Associated Press, April 14, 1953.

160 **no more than a footnote:** Dwight D. Eisenhower, *Mandate for Change, 1953–1956: The White House Years* (Garden City, NY: Doubleday, 1963), 28.

11: "No More Bohlens!"

163 **At his very first:** Presidential Appointment Book for January 23, 1953, Eisenhower Library, https://www.eisenhowerlibrary.gov/sites/default/files/research/online-documents/presidential-appointment-books/1953/january-1953.pdf.

163 **"many loyal Americans":** Eisenhower, *Mandate for Change,* 309.

163 **Just opposite:** "Death of a Diplomat," *Newsweek,* February 9, 1953, 29.

163 **Rev. C. Leslie Glenn:** "The Montgomery Case," *Washington Sunday Star,* February 15, 1953, 1.

164 **eldest daughter:** "Virginia Warren Daly: 1928–2009; Socialite, Daughter of Justice," *Chicago Tribune,* March 5, 2009, 23.

165 **When the police:** "State Dept. Expert Handled Secret Data; Mystery Veils Death," *Boston Globe,* January 24, 1953, 1.

165 **"well-known":** "State Dept. Aide Found Hanged Here," *Washington Post,* January 25, 1953, M1.

165 **highly public:** Marie McNair and Elizabeth Maguire, "First Family Starts Some Talk," *Washington Post,* November 1, 1950, C1; Elizabeth Maguire, "This Time She's No. 1 Guest," *Washington Post,* November 13, 1950, B3; Walter Winchell, "Man About Town," *Washington Post,* April 21, 1952, B9.

165 **Braverman had started:** International News Service, November 15, 1950.

165 **When Margaret received:** In her biography of her father, Margaret Truman refers just once to Braverman, and as her "boyfriend," in connection with this episode. Margaret Truman, *Harry S. Truman* (New York: Avon, 1972), 210.

165 **DC license plate:** *Indianapolis News,* March 19, 1953, 29.

165 **"I never have":** Elizabeth Maguire, "Romance Rumors Play Havoc with Her Other Dates, Says Margaret," *Washington Post,* December 5, 1950, B5.

165 **"friendly rivals":** Elizabeth Maguire, "The Two Marvins Keep Right on Denying," *Washington Post,* April 20, 1952, S2.

165 **"hokum":** Elizabeth Maguire, "Is Margaret Engaged? If So, the White House Isn't Saying," *Washington Post,* November 15, 19509, B5.

165 **had to rebuke:** "Margaret Truman Denies Fall Wedding Planned," United Press, April 8, 1952.

165 **"he never found":** "Montgomery Leaves $54,000 to Home," *Evening Star,* April 9, 1953, 24.

166 **sent ripples:** Nicholas von Hoffman, *Citizen Cohn* (New York: Doubleday, 1988), 128.

166 **"plagued":** 99 Cong. Rec. 653 (January 29, 1953).

166 **"clean as a whistle":** "Death of a Diplomat," 29.

166 **"insulting":** "House Group Rejects State Dept. Report on Montgomery Suicide," *Evening Star,* February 10, 1953, 1.

166 **"psychoneurosis":** *Security and Personnel Practices and Procedures of the Department of State, Hearings before the House Subcommittee on International Operations,* 83rd Cong., 1st Sess., 4 (April 29, 1953).

166 **"physically, morally":** Lewis B. Hershey, *Selective Service as the Tide of War Turns: The Third Report of the Director of Selective Service, 1943–1944* (Washington, DC: Government Printing Office, 1945), 63.

166 **"neither the police":** *Security and Personnel Practices and Procedures of the Department of State, Submitted by the Subcommittee on International Operations,* Report 1334, March 9, 1954.

167 **Washington-area psychoanalysts:** David Caute, *The Great Fear: The Anti-Communist Purge Under Truman and Eisenhower* (New York: Simon and Schuster, 1978), 275.

167 **When the body:** "Mystery Death of CIA Aide," *Long Beach Independent,* June 30, 1953, 1.

167 **By the following:** George Dixon, "Washington Scene," *Washington Post,* May 11, 1954, 46. As promised, Margaret did not wed Braverman, marrying *New York Times* reporter Clifton Daniel in

1956. See Edith Evans Asbury, "Miss Truman Wed to Clifton Daniel," *New York Times*, April 22, 1956, 1. Braverman married in 1968, at the age of sixty, and died childless twelve years later. See *Cedar Rapids Gazette*, November 2, 1982, 2A.

167 **"It was an exhilarating":** Leonard Mosley, *Dulles: A Biography of Eleanor, Allen, and John Foster Dulles and Their Family Network* (New York: Dial Press, 1978), 24.

168 **persona non grata:** Walter H. Waggoner, "Kremlin Demands U. S. Recall Kennan, Charging Slander," *New York Times*, October 4, 1952, 1.

168 **increased its ranks:** David M. Oshinsky, "The Senior G-Man," *New York Times Book Review*, September 15, 1991, 3.

168 **"Wise Men":** Walter Isaacson and Evan Thomas, *The Wise Men: Six Friends and the World They Made* (New York: Simon and Schuster, 1986).

168 **his long and storied diplomatic career:** Robert H. Phelps, "Charles Bohlen, Diplomat, 69, Dies," *New York Times*, January 2, 1974, 1.

168 **Russian-language skills:** Marilyn Berger, "Former Diplomat Charles E. Bohlen Dies at 69," *Washington Post*, January 2, 1974, B7.

168 **"very charming family":** Edward T. Folliard, "Aide Held Best Fitted for Difficult Moscow Post," *Washington Post*, March 27, 1953, 1; Eisenhower, *Mandate for Change*, 212–13.

169 **"conspiracy on a scale so immense":** Murrey Marder, "Hoffman Calls McCarthy's Charges False," *Washington Post*, August 20, 1952, 1; Gerald Griffin, "Ike Praised by McCarthy," *Baltimore Sun*, October 9, 1952, 1.

169 **privately likened:** Republican senator Ralph Flanders, who would later initiate the Senate's censure motion against McCarthy, recalled being in the presence of Dulles while a McCarthy speech played on the radio. "Did you ever hear that kind of a speech before?" Flanders asked. "Yes—in the early 1930s," Dulles replied. Ralph Flanders, interviewed by Ed Edwin, February 4, 1967, *New York Times* Oral History Program, Oral History Collection, Columbia University.

170 **"three dollar bill":** "Charles Eustis Bohlen," March 16, 1953, Folder 38, Hoover O&C.

170 **In 1950:** Todd S. Purdum, "The Politics of Security: The Eisenhower State Department and Scott McLeod" (undergraduate thesis, Princeton University, 1982), 19–20.

171 **"no direct evidence":** L. B. Nichols to J. Edgar Hoover, "Director's Conferences Regarding Charles E. Bohlen, Ambassador to Russia," March 16, 1954, Hoover O&C no. 38.

171 **his grandfather:** "Dulles Formulated and Conducted U.S. Foreign Policy for More than Six Years," *New York Times*, May 25, 1959, 10.

171 **"It must be":** Peter Edson, "Capitol Ideas," *Pensacola News Journal*, July 2, 1953, 4.

171 **Dulles accepted:** Ferdinand Kuhn, "State Dept. Cut Promised by Dulles," *Washington Post*, February 28, 1953, 1; Charlotte Knight, "What Price Security?," *Collier's*, July 9, 1954, 59.

171 **"To a great American":** Isaacson and Thomas, *Wise Men*, 567.

171 **"municipal homicide squad":** William Harlan Hale, "'Big Brother' in Foggy Bottom," *The Reporter*, August 17, 1954, 10.

171 **"dress, accents, mannerisms":** Clark Mollenhoff, "State Department Security Chief Once a Reporter in Iowa," *Des Moines Register*, March 15, 1953, 16.

172 **"Congress wanted heads":** Knight, "What Price Security?," 59.

172 **McLeod presided over:** Associated Press, "19 Lose U. S. Posts on Morals Charge," *New York Times*, April 21, 1953, 32.

172 **every other day:** "Fires Five Each Week," United Press, April 21, 1953.

172 **double by June:** Edson, "Capitol Ideas," 4.

172 **thousand people:** Hale, "'Big Brother' in Foggy Bottom," 12.

172 **"reign of terror":** Drew Pearson, "Dulles Ducks Morale for Money," *Washington Post*, June 7, 1953.

172 **"cleared everything":** Richard H. Rovere, *Senator Joe McCarthy* (New York: Harcourt, Brace, 1959), 23.

172 **"the wildest":** Joseph and Stewart Alsop, "Is Dulles a Good Security Risk?," *Washington Post*, May 27, 1953, 15.

172 **"No matter what":** Isaacson and Thomas, *Wise Men*, 568.

172 **The day before:** James Reston, "Dulles Facing Test Today in Testimony About Bohlen," *New York Times*, March 18, 1953, 20.

172 **"Well, I'm glad"**: Charles E. Bohlen, *Witness to History: 1929–1969* (New York: W. W. Norton, 1973), 322.

172 **had recommended Hiss**: Murrey Marder, "Dulles Backed Hiss for Job, Davis Asserts," *Washington Post*, December 1, 1952, 2.

172 **"completely baseless"**: William I. Hitchcock, *The Age of Eisenhower: America and the World in the 1950s* (New York: Simon and Schuster, 2018), 128.

173 **That afternoon**: J. Edgar Hoover to Tolson, Ladd, and Nichols, March 18, 1953, "Joseph McCarthy," no. 105, Hoover O&C.

173 **"I know what's"**: Clark Mollenhoff, "Denies Charge He Overruled Security Aide," *Des Moines Register*, March 21, 1953, 8.

173 **"pretty rough"**: Emmett John Hughes, *The Ordeal of Power: A Political Memoir of the Eisenhower Years* (New York: Dell, 1962), 94.

173 **"Thank goodness"**: Avis Bohlen, author interview, January 28, 2020, Washington, DC.

173 **threatening to resign**: "Bohlen Report Builds Up Feud in State Dept.," *Chicago Daily Tribune*, March 20, 1953, 3.

173 **assigned him a minder**: Hughes, *Ordeal of Power*, 85

173 **"acid test"**: 99 Cong. Rec. 2157 (March 20, 1953).

174 **Dulles countered**: State Department Press Release 151, March 20, 1953, *Department of State Bulletin* XXVIII, no. 719 (April 6, 1953): 519.

174 **a *Washington Post* reporter**: Whittaker Chambers to Ralph de Toledano, *Notes from the Underground: The Whittaker Chambers–Ralph de Toledano Letters 1949–1960* (Washington, DC: Regnery, 1997), 115–16; Edward F. Ryan, "Senator's Trip Not Linked with Fight on Envoy Choice, He Says," *Washington Post*, March 22, 1953, M1.

174 **"Is it security"**: Weinstein, *Perjury*, 537.

174 **"I must say"**: Whittaker Chambers to William F. Buckley Jr., February 7, 1954, from William F. Buckley Jr., ed., *Odyssey of a Friend: Whittaker Chambers Letters to William F. Buckley, Jr., 1954–1961* (Washington, DC: Regnery, 1987), 28.

174 **"by direct knowledge"**: "Chambers Denies Knowing Bohlen," *Baltimore Sun*, March 24, 1952, 2.

175 **"nothing in all"**: 99 Cong. Rec. 2278 (March 25, 1953).

175 **"we cannot discuss"**: 99 Cong. Rec. 2192 (March 23, 1953).

175 **"Communists, crooks, and cronies"**: 99 Cong. Rec. 2291 (March 25, 1953).

175 **"We want no"**: 99 Cong. Rec. 2295 (March 25, 1953).

175 **out-of-wedlock**: Robert D. Dean, *Imperial Brotherhood: Gender and the Making of Cold War Foreign Policy* (Amherst: University of Massachusetts Press, 2001), 101.

175 **Thayer was forced to resign**: Dean, *Imperial Brotherhood,* 130. Ironically, in a diary entry from his time in Moscow, Thayer expressed the sort of disgust toward homosexuals common at the time, and an admiration for Russia's perceived lack of them. "After the theatre I went to Metropole for a bite to eat and while at the bar was joined by elderly Englishman. With whom I eventually sat down to dinner. He turned out just what one would expect but I didn't discover it till I had sat down at the table with him. He was extremely amusing in his misery in Russia (where there is said to be practically no homosexuality). He had been here for three days and was furious with everyone and everything—it spoke rather well for Russia I thought" (Charles Thayer diary, October 27, 1933, Folder "Moscow—September 20, 1933—February 17, 1934," Box 6, Charles W. Thayer Papers, Truman Library).

175 **"The present situation"**: Glenn G. Wolfe to Charles Thayer, May 12, 1953, Alpha Correspondence File, Box 4: "State Department, correspondence re. Thayer's resignation—1953," Charles W. Thayer Papers, Truman Library.

175 **the Senate voted**: William S. White, "Bohlen Confirmed as Envoy, 74 to 13," *New York Times*, March 28, 1953, 1.

175 **At his last**: Bohlen, *Witness to History*, 335.

176 **Bohlen had to summon**: Oshinsky, *Conspiracy So Immense*, 293.

176 **Taft sent a message**: William S. White, *The Taft Story* (New York: Harper and Row, 1954), 239.

12: The Heterosexual Dictatorship

177 **"The Top Secret"**: Raymond P. Brandt, "White House Mystery Man Is the Top Secret Keeper of Eisenhower Regime," *St. Louis Post-Dispatch*, March 7, 1954, 1C.

177 **"the Ike Special":** Earl Banner, "Boston Banker Works 16-Hour Day with Ike," *Boston Globe*, September 26, 1952, 18.

177 **"no man":** "Puritan—Up to a Point," *New York Times*, May 24, 1957, 6.

177 **"I hope none":** Robert Cutler, *No Time for Rest* (Boston: Little, Brown, 1966). 4.

177 **the diary in which he confessed:** Peter Shinkle, *Ike's Mystery Man: The Secret Lives of Robert Cutler* (Hanover, NH: Steerforth Press, 2018).

178 **"White House Mystery Man":** In addition to the *Post-Dispatch*, Cutler also earned this sobriquet from *The Saturday Evening Post*. Samuel Lubell, "Mystery Man of the White House," *The Saturday Evening Post*, February 6, 1954, 27.

178 **"precise and tidy":** This resolute self-control, however, did not relieve Cutler from suspicion. In 1956, the charge of homosexuality was lobbed at him by William Bullitt, who told a Senate investigator that Cutler "was engaged in a homosexual incident at Harvard University in his young days" and that "several hundred people know of Cutler's sex deviation activities" (Shinkle, *Ike's Mystery Man*, 211).

178 **Cutler lived:** Shinkle, *Ike's Mystery Man*, 76, 162.

178 **FBI surveillance:** Shinkle, *Ike's Mystery Man*, 162.

178 **One day during:** Joseph W. Alsop with Adam Platt, *"I've Seen the Best of It": Memoirs* (New York: W. W. Norton, 1992), 349–50.

179 **Cutler advised:** Shinkle, *Ike's Mystery Man*, 116–17; Joseph Young, "U. S. Procedures on Dismissals to Be Unified," *Evening Star*, August 9, 1952, 1; "Partial Text of Recommendations on Employee Security Program," *Evening Star*, August 9, 1952, 5.

179 **"sexual perversion":** Exec. Order No. 10,450, 18 Fed. Reg. 2489 (Apr. 27, 1953).

179 **With 20 percent:** Rick Perlstein, *Before the Storm: Barry Goldwater and the Unmaking of the American Consensus* (New York: Hill and Wang, 2001), 490.

179 **"I think it is":** Anthony Leviero, "New Security Plan Issued; Thousands Face Re-Inquiry," *New York Times*, April 28, 1953, 1.

180 **Edwin Louis Cuckenberger:** SA Andrew P. O'Malley, Memorandum, U.S. Secret Service, Treasury Department, June 5, 1953; Chief's Office, Protective Research Section to SAIC Beary, "Edwin L. Cuckenberger, White House Employee," June 23, 1953; Stanley B. Phillips to U. E. Baugham, "Re: Edwin Louis Cuckenberger," September 6, 1949—all in Records of the U.S. Secret Service: Personnel Investigation Files (RG87), Box 33: "5-P-3716, Edwin Cuckenberger," Truman Library.

180 **"When in doubt":** Hale, "'Big Brother' in Foggy Bottom," 12.

180 **"was always sympathetic":** Purdum, "Politics of Security," 43.

180 **"Scotty had":** Mosley, *Dulles*, 313.

180 **McLeod appointed:** Drew Pearson, "The Washington Merry-Go-Round," Bell-McClure Syndicate, April 30, 1957.

181 **"apish behavior":** Mosley, *Dulles*, 313–14.

181 **"hatchet man":** Peter Szluk, interviewed by Griffin Fariello, in *Red Scare: Memories of the American Inquisition* (New York: Avon Books, 1995), 122–24.

181 **"the social conscience":** Peter J. Skoufis, interviewed by Thomas Stern, January 27, 1992, Association for Diplomatic Studies and Training, Foreign Affairs Oral History Project.

181 **"We don't have":** Knight, "What Price Security?," 64.

181 **Robert F. Woodward:** Robert F. Woodward, interviewed by Charles Stuart Kennedy, May 5, 1987, Association for Diplomatic Studies and Training, Foreign Affairs Oral History Project.

182 **"mannish voice":** Michael J. Ambrose to C. M. Dulin, "Allegations of Lesbianism, Homosexuality and Disloyalty," April 16, 1953, Bureau of Security and Consular Affairs, Decimal File, Box 12, RG 59, NARA.

182 **"is probably a homosexual":** M. J. Ambrose and James E. Place to C. M. Dulin, "Allegations of Lesbianism, Homosexuality and Disloyalty—Interview with Miss Blanche Cleo Blevins," April 20, 1953, Bureau of Security and Consular Affairs, Decimal File, Box 12, RG 59, NARA.

182 **"few individuals . . . denied security clearance":** Joseph C. Walsh, interviewed by G. Lewis Schmidt, April 25, 1989, Information Series, Association for Diplomatic Studies and Training, Foreign Affairs Oral History Project.

182 **"your search for homosexuals in your Department":** Anonymous to Scott McLeod, April 21, 1953, Decimal File Box 12, RG 59, NARA. Like their peers in the FBI, McLeod's team tilted heavily

Catholic. Charles Stuart Kennedy, a former Foreign Service officer and oral historian of American diplomats, observed that "a considerable number of the people" in McLeod's office "had a middle initial of X," indicating "they came from a solid Catholic background" (Charles Anthony Gillespie, interviewed by Charles Stuart Kennedy, September 19, 1995, Information Series, Association for Diplomatic Studies and Training, Foreign Affairs Oral History Project, 48).

183 **"My informant"**: Scott McLeod to John W. Ford, "Suspected Homosexuals," July 29, 1953, Decimal File, Box 12, RG 59, NARA.

183 **"reported to be"**: State Department document marked "Confidential," Decimal Files 1953–60, Folder: "Security Risks—Other," Box 15, RG 59, NARA.

183 **Fired employees:** Nancy Davis, interviewed by Mark Meinke, April 21, 2001, transcript, Rainbow History Project, Washington, DC.

183 **"Our sympathetic":** John W. Ford to W. Scott McLeod, "Informant Development Among Dismissed Homosexuals," May 26, 1953, Decimal Files "1953–1960, Bureau of Security and Consular Affairs," Box 12, RG 59, NARA.

183 **"Grenades go off":** Knight, "What Price Security?," 69.

183 **"Suppose I apply":** Knight, "What Price Security?," 61.

184 **privately suggested:** Purdum, "Politics of Security," 39.

184 **"heterosexual dictatorship":** Christopher Isherwood, *Kathleen and Frank: The Autobiography of a Family* (New York: Simon and Schuster, 1971), 380.

184 **"I would get these mysterious phone calls":** George Tames, interviewed by Donald A. Ritchie, January 13, 1988, Transcript, Truman Library, https://www.trumanlibrary.gov/library/oral-histories /tamesg2a.

184 **"The government didn't even recognize":** Barbara J. Good, interviewed by Charles Stuart Kennedy, May 25, 1993, Association for Diplomatic Studies and Training, Foreign Affairs Oral History Project.

184 **an estimated 7,000 to 10,000:** Baxter, "Homo-Hunting' in the Early Cold War," 128.

185 **14,700 people:** Landon R. Y. Storrs, "Revisiting Truman's Federal Employee Loyalty Program," in *Civil Liberties and the Legacy of Harry S. Truman,* ed. Richard S. Kirkendall (Kirksville, MO: Truman State University Press, 2013), 70.

185 **"Denny" Hansen:** "Man of Eli at Oxford," *Life,* December 2, 1957, 81.

185 **"The motor began":** Calvin Trillin, *Remembering Denny* (New York: Farrar, Straus and Giroux, 1993), 194–95.

185 **locked himself in a friend's garage:** W. Scott Thompson, *The Price of Achievement: Coming Out in Reagan Days* (London: Cassell, 1995), 14.

185 **"There have been many suicides":** Rick Ewig, "The Ordeal of Senator Lester Hunt," *Annals of Wyoming* 55, no. 1 (Spring 1983): 13.

185 **"progressive liberal":** "Hunt Saw Himself as a Progressive," *New York Times,* June 20, 1954, 72.

185 **proposed a constitutional amendment:** "Congress Slander Actionable in Bill," *New York Times,* January 30, 1951, 18.

185 **"If situations confront":** Lester C. Hunt, "Dangers in Congressional Immunity," *New York Times Magazine,* June 24, 1951, 14.

185 **Hunt's older brother:** Associated Press, "Rites for Hunt Brother Set in Denver Saturday," *Casper (WY) Star-Tribune,* April 10, 1952, 1.

186 **"trying to attract":** "Senator's Son Convicted on Morals Charge," *Washington Post,* October 7, 1953, 11.

186 **over a thousand:** D'Emilio, *Sexual Politics, Sexual Communities,* 49.

186 **"Little Joe":** LeRoy Ashby and Rod Gramer, *Fighting the Odds: The Life of Senator Frank Church* (Pullman: Washington State University Press, 1994), 60–61.

186 **Welker threatened:** Ewig, "Ordeal of Senator Lester Hunt," 14.

186 **"aura of political invincibility":** Oshinsky, *Conspiracy So Immense,* 178.

186 **"Declaration of Conscience":** William S. White, "Seven G.O.P. Senators Decry 'Smear' Tactics of McCarthy," *New York Times,* June 2, 1950, 1.

186 **"the first American":** Rovere, *Senator Joe McCarthy,* 10.

187 **campaigned in Maryland:** Oshinsky, *Conspiracy So Immense,* 174–78,

187 **In Massachusetts:** Oshinsky, *Conspiracy So Immense,* 239–42.

187 **Hunt told Welker:** Ewig, "Ordeal of Senator Lester Hunt," 14; Drew Pearson, "The Washington-Merry-Go-Round," Bell-McClure Syndicate, June 21, 1954.

187 **death of Cissy Patterson:** "Mrs. Eleanor (Cissy) Patterson Dies at 63 of Heart Attack," *Washington Post*, July 25, 1948, M1.

187 **purchased by her cousin:** "McCormick Paid 4.5 Million in Cash for the Times-Herald," *Washington Post*, August 16, 1949, 1.

187 **"would break down":** Rodger McDaniel, *Dying for Joe McCarthy's Sins: The Suicide of Wyoming Senator Lester Hunt* (Cody, WY: WordsWorth, 2013), 285–87.

187 **"I felt":** "Theological Student Convicted in Morals Case, Is Fined $100," *Evening Star*, October 7, 1953, 22.

188 **lasted two days:** "Senator's Son Convicted on Morals Charge," *Washington Post*, October 7, 1953, 11.

188 **"whether Hunt solicited the officer":** "Theological Student Convicted in Morals Case," *Evening Star*.

188 **"one of the most degrading":** "Sen. Hunt's Son Found Guilty on Sex Charge," *Washington Times-Herald*, October 7, 1953, 5.

188 **Nathelle Hunt:** Drew Pearson, "The Washington-Merry-Go-Round," Bell-McClure Syndicate, June 21, 1954.

13: Pixies on the Potomac

189 **eighty million:** Oshinsky, *Conspiracy So Immense*, 416–17.

189 **One hundred twenty:** Lawrence Van Gelder, "Crash Kills G. David Schine, 69, McCarthy-Era Figure," *New York Times*, June 21, 1996, 25.

189 **Alice Roosevelt Longworth:** Thomas Doherty, *Cold War, Cool Medium: Television, McCarthyism, and American Culture* (New York: Columbia University Press, 2003), 196–97.

190 **"I can't compete":** John D. Morris, "Hearings Remain a Top Attraction," *New York Times*, May 7, 1954, 13.

190 **"I've never been":** Roy Cohn, "Believe Me, This Is the Truth About the Army-McCarthy Hearings. Honest," *Esquire*, February 1968, 122.

190 **fascinated with power:** von Hoffman, *Citizen Cohn*, 67.

190 **At fifteen:** The friend was Generoso Pope Jr., founder of the *National Enquirer*. Sidney Zion, *The Autobiography of Roy Cohn* (Secaucus, NJ: Lyle Stuart, 1988), 61–62; von Hoffman, *Citizen Cohn*, 71–72.

190 **"man behind':** Thomas B. Morgan, "The Pleasures of Roy Cohn," *Esquire*, December 1960, 149.

190 **Julius and Ethel Rosenberg:** Zion, *Autobiography of Roy Cohn*, 76–79.

190 **a Jewish judge:** Ronald Radosh and Joyce Milton, *The Rosenberg File: A Search for the Truth* (New York: Holt, Rinehart, and Winston, 1983), 351–55.

191 **In September 1952:** "National Affairs: The Self-Inflated Target," *Time*, March 3, 1954, 23.

191 **"gossips":** von Hoffman, *Citizen Cohn*, 124.

191 **"as indispensable":** "Self-Inflated Target," 23.

191 **"America's most public private":** Saul Pett, "Army's 'Best-Known Private' Wanted to Be Someone Special," Associated Press, May 3, 1954.

191 **hired a personal secretary:** Drew Pearson, "The Washington Merry-Go-Round," Bell-McClure Syndicate, May 4, 1954.

192 **"written some plans":** Pett, "Army's 'Best-Known Private.'"

192 **"build and features":** "Self-Inflated Target," 26.

192 **"Boy Rasputin":** Michael Straight, "Trial by Television V: The Two Roy Cohns," *New Republic*, June 14, 1954, 11.

192 **"inseparable":** Herbert Brownell with John P. Burke, *Advising Ike: The Memoirs of Attorney General Herbert Brownell* (Lawrence: University Press of Kansas, 1993), 257.

193 **"turned out":** Roy Cohn, *McCarthy* (New York: New American Library, 1968), 81.

193 **playfully batting:** Drew Pearson, "The Washington Merry-Go-Round," Bell-McClure Syndicate, April 22, 1953. The widely reported story stung. Schine disputed it in 1971. G. David Schine, interviewed by Mary Jane Pew, January 13, 1971, Eisenhower Administration Project, Oral History Research Office, Columbia University.

193 **"by as many journalists as":** Richard H. Rovere, "The Adventures of Cohn and Schine," *The Reporter*, July 21, 1953, 15.

193 **"Junketeering gumshoes":** C. P. Trussell, "Kaghan Tells McCarthy Unit He Has Fought Reds Decade," *New York Times*, April 30, 1953, 1.

193 **Cohn forced:** W. H. Lawrence, "U.S. Public Affairs Officer in Germany Was Target of McCarthy Inquiry," *New York Times*, May 12, 1953, 1.

193 **"We have passed':** Dean, *Imperial Brotherhood*, 141.

193 **"Keep those two":** Parke D. Massey, interviewed by Morris Weisz, March 19, 1992, Labor Series, Association for Diplomatic Studies and Training, Foreign Affairs Oral History Project.

193 **borrowed hundreds:** Drew Pearson, "The Washington Merry-Go-Round," Bell-McClure Syndicate, June 5, 1954.

193 **"we don't work":** Rovere, "Adventures of Cohn and Schine," 15.

193 **Even before the letter arrived in the mail:** "Stevens-Adams Chronology," Exhibit No. 1, U.S. Senate, Special Subcommittee on Investigations of the Committee on Government Operations, 83rd Cong., 2nd Sess., Part 3, 136, 138, 140, 141 (April 23, 1954).

194 **"Biggest mystery":** Drew Pearson, "The Washington Merry-Go-Round," Bell-McClure Syndicate, April 1, 1954.

195 **"persistent attachment":** Drew Pearson, "The Washington Merry-Go-Round," Bell-McClure Syndicate, March 17, 1954.

195 **"The implication":** Joseph and Stewart Alsop, "McCarthy-Cohn-Schine Tale Was Half Told," *Washington Post*, March 15, 1954, 11.

195 **"genuinely liked":** John G. Adams, *Without Precedent: The Story of the Death of McCarthyism* (New York: W. W. Norton, 1983), 104.

195 **These roles:** Adams, *Without Precedent*, 85–86.

195 **"His campaign":** Charles E. Potter, *Days of Shame* (New York: Coward-McCann, 1965), 42.

195 **McCarthy claimed:** W. H. Lawrence, "M'Carthy Charges Army 'Blackmail,' Says Stevens Sought Deal with Him; 'Utterly Untrue,' Secretary Replies," *New York Times*, March 13, 1954, 1.

195 **"A specific proposal":** *Meet the Press*, March 14, 1954, Box 209, Lawrence E. Spivak Papers, Manuscript Division, Library of Congress, Washington, DC.

195 **"hideous accusations and insinuations":** Westbrook Pegler, "A Foul, Dirty Deal to Stop McCarthy," *Cincinnati Enquirer*, March 22, 1954, 4.

196 **Reber calmly told:** United States Senate Special Subcommittee on Investigations of the Committee on Government Operations, *Special Senate Investigation on Charges and Countercharges Involving: Secretary of the Army Robert T. Stevens, John G. Adams, H. Struve Hensel and Senator Joe McCarthy, Roy Cohn and Francis P. Carr*, 83rd Cong., 2nd Sess. (hereafter "Army-McCarthy Hearings") 40 (April 22, 1954).

196 **twenty-seven-year:** "Samuel Reber to Retire," *New York Times*, May 30, 1953, 13.

196 **threatening to expose:** von Hoffman, *Citizen Cohn*, 184.

196 **"Are you aware":** Army-McCarthy Hearings, 70 (April 22, 1954).

196 **clenched the sides:** "Investigations: The First Day," *Time*, May 3, 1954, 17.

196 **"If you want":** David Halberstam, *The Fifties* (New York: Villard Books, 1993), 54.

196 **"outcry against":** "Pearson Says McCarthy Probe to Be Exposed as Great Fraud," *Capital Times*, May 1, 1950, 1.

197 **spread a rumor:** Andrea Friedman, "The Smearing of Joe McCarthy: The Lavender Scare, Gossip, and Cold War Politics," *American Quarterly* 57, no. 4 (December 2005): 1111.

197 **McCarthy told:** Pilat, *Drew Pearson*, 26–27.

197 **Pearson responded:** "That Sulgrave Club Battle Marked by Two Encounters," *Washington Post*, December 15, 1950, 1.

197 **front-page *Washington Post* headline:** "Sen. McCarthy Either Kicked, Slapped or Mauled Pearson," *Washington Post*, December 14, 1950, 1.

197 **Pearson claimed:** "Contradictory Accounts Mark McCarthy-Pearson Fracas," *Evening Star*, December 14, 1950, 5.

197 **broken up:** Herman Klurfeld, *Behind the Lines: The World of Drew Pearson* (Englewood Cliffs, NJ: Prentice-Hall, 1968), 180–81.

197 **"That was for":** Richard Nixon, *RN: The Memoirs of Richard Nixon* (New York: Grosset and Dunlap, 1978), 169–70.

197 **"I never saw":** Ralph de Toledano, *Nixon* (New York: Henry Holt, 1956), 167–68.

197 **"I realize the task"**: 96 Cong. Rec. 16634–41 (December 15, 1950).

197 **"committed sodomy"**: Oshinsky, *A Conspiracy So Immense*, 222–23; Drew Pearson, *Diaries: 1949–1959*, ed. Tyler Abell (New York: Holt, Reinhart and Winston, 1974), 190, 192.

198 **"Thirty-five of "**: Edwin R. Bayley, *Joe McCarthy and the Press* (Madison: University of Wisconsin Press, 1981), 134. Harry Truman, one of McCarthy's chief targets, similarly demurred when presented with the opportunity to deploy the homosexual smear against him. As reported by the writer John Hersey, who was given unprecedented access to the president in the early part of 1951 for a multipart *New Yorker* profile, the following exchange occurred during an evening bull session between Truman and his top advisors. After the president asked what should be done about the rampaging senator from Wisconsin, someone suggested that a "thick and devastating dossier" containing the details of "hotel rooms in which Joseph McCarthy had stayed and the names of the Senator's bedmates in all those rooms"—presumably the file amassed by Pearson and Benton—be leaked to the press. Several other men in the room voiced support, and it was at this that "the flat of [Truman's] hand came sharply down on the table," putting an end to the conversation. John Hersey, "The Truman Way," *New York Times*, August 3, 1973, 31.

198 **publisher of the *Las Vegas Sun***: Tracy Wood, "Hank Greenspun, Fiery Publisher of Las Vegas Sun, Dies," *Los Angeles Times*, July 23, 1989, 3.

198 **convicted of smuggling weapons**: Ari L. Goldman, "Hank Greenspun, 79, Publisher," *New York Times*, July 24, 1989, D11.

198 **"confessed ex-Communist"**: "Red Charge Lie Greenspun Says, Wires Candidate," *Reno Evening Gazette*, October 15, 1952, 1.

198 **"Joe McCarthy is a bachelor"**: Hank Greenspun, "Where I Stand," *Las Vegas Sun*, October 25, 1952, 2.

198 **"sadist and a pervert"**: Hank Greenspun, "Where I Stand," *Las Vegas Sun*, February 1, 1954, 1.

198 **"a gait"**: Hank Greenspun, "Where I Stand," *Las Vegas Sun*, February 3, 1954, 2.

199 **"if the person"**: Hank Greenspun, "Where I Stand," *Las Vegas Sun*, February 5, 1954, 1–2.

199 **"Why should I"**: Cohn, *McCarthy*, 245.

199 **"He gave up"**: Greenspun, "Where I Stand," February 5, 1954, 2.

199 **"despite the pleadings"**: "McCarthy Weds Jean Kerr; Couple Gets Pope's Blessing," *Washington Evening Star*, September 29, 1953.

199 **"Have you no sense"**: Army-McCarthy Hearings, 2429 (June 9, 1954).

200 **an approval rating**: George Gallup, "Group of Those Undecided About McCarthy Up by 6%," *Washington Post*, November 12, 1954, 29.

200 **"contrary to senatorial traditions"**: Senate Resolution 301, December 2, 1954, SEN 83A-B4, Records of the United States Senate, RG46, NARA.

200 **"came from a pixie?"** Army-McCarthy Hearings, 543 (April 30, 1954).

201 **"the look of "**: Associated Press, "Joseph N. Welch, Army Counsel in McCarthy Hearings, Is Dead," *New York Times*, October 7, 1960, 1.

201 **"It wasn't in Tennessee"**: Army-McCarthy Hearing, 1118–19 (May 13, 1954).

201 **"In all fairness"**: Army-McCarthy Hearings, 1664–65 (May 28, 1954).

202 **"Had you spent"**: Army-McCarthy Hearings, 1680 (May 28, 1954).

202 **Vacationing with his wife**: Ralph Flanders, *Senator from Vermont* (Boston: Little, Brown, 1961), 253–54.

203 **"The committee has not"**: 100 Cong. Rec. 7389–90 (June 1, 1954).

203 **"Anybody with half "**: Ralph Flanders, interviewed by Ed Edwin, New York Times Oral History Program, Columbia University Oral History Collection, Eisenhower Administration Project, February 4, 1967.

204 **"I am not"**: "Cohn and Marcantonio Swap Non-Pleasantries," *New York Times*, June 3, 1954, 13.

204 **"First, I will ask"**: Army-McCarthy Hearings, 2300 (June 8, 1954).

204 **"We'll get to"**: Philip Potter and William Knighton Jr., "Kennedy and McCarthy Counsel Clash at End of Quiz On Schine Plan," *Baltimore Sun*, June 12, 1954, 1.

204 **"Do you want to fight"**: W. H. Lawrence, "Cohn Threatens to 'Get' Senator for Gibe at Schine," *New York Times*, June 12, 1954, 1.

205 **Watching all this**: Bob Bauman, author interview, March 4, 2019, Wilton Manors, FL.

205 **"dress and appearance"**: Bob Bauman email to author, November 26, 2020.

205 **"feeling something"**: Robert Bauman, *The Gentleman from Maryland: The Conscience of a Gay Conservative* (New York: Arbor House, 1986), 155.

205 **"hidden, denied and fought"**: Bauman, *Gentleman from Maryland*, 155–56.

205 **"a conscious decision"**: Bauman, *Gentleman from Maryland*, 164.

205 **"opposed this"**: Bauman, *Gentleman from Maryland*, 172.

205 **"there must have"**: Bob Bauman, email to author, November 26, 2020.

205 **"frightening force"**: Bauman, *Gentleman from Maryland*, 163.

205 **"I did not learn"**: Franklin Kameny, interviewed by Eric Marcus, in *Making History: The Struggle for Gay and Lesbian Equal Rights, 1945–1990* (New York: Harper Perennial, 1992), 97.

206 **"Bedfellows make"**: Robert Shogan, *No Sense of Decency: The Army-McCarthy Hearings; A Demagogue Falls and Television Takes Charge of American Politics* (Chicago: Ivan R. Dee, 2009), 121.

206 **"Bonnie, Bonnie and Clyde"**: Lillian Hellman, *Scoundrel Time* (Boston: Little, Brown, 1976), 150–51.

206 **"dedicated, conscious agent"**: James E. Clayton, "John Birch 'Antis' Point Unwelcome Spotlight: Conservative Complaints," *Washington Post*, March 26, 1961, E1.

206 **"One woman"**: Cohn, "Believe Me, This Is the Truth," 130.

207 **crashing down**: Earl Latham, *The Communist Controversy in Washington: From the New Deal to McCarthy* (Cambridge, MA: Harvard University Press, 1966), 10.

207 **"unphotogenic young"**: Jack Anderson, *Confessions of a Muckraker: The Inside Story of Life in Washington During the Truman, Eisenhower, Kennedy and Johnson Years* (New York: Random House, 1979), 262.

207 **his attack on:** Robert Dallek, *Lone Star Rising*, vol. 1, *Lyndon Johnson and His Times, 1908–1960* (Oxford: Oxford University Press, 1991), 453; Oshinsky, *A Conspiracy So Immense*, 319–23.

207 **"appeared to be"**: Leonard Ballard, interviewed by Richard A. Baker, August 18, 1983, Oral History Project, United States Senate Historical Office.

208 **Hunt took the elevator:** "Hunt Takes Life in Senate Office," *New York Times*, June 20, 1954, 1.

208 **"Unfortunately I am"**: Pearson, diary entry, June 9, 1954, *Diaries: 1949–1959*, 321.

208 **"You sort of knew"**: Roy Elson, interviewed by Donald A. Ritchie, May 10, 1990, U.S. Senate Oral History Project.

208 **"*extremely* tight"**: von Hoffman, *Citizen Cohn*, 232.

208 **had taken his meals:** Drew Pearson, "The Washington Merry-Go-Round," Bell-McClure Syndicate, June 21, 1954.

208 **"would find their way"**: Marquis Childs, "Smears and Tears Plague the Senate," *Washington Post*, June 30, 1954, 12.

208 **state's newspapers:** Ewig, "Ordeal of Senator Lester Hunt," 16.

208 **"his wife would die"**: Pearson, diary entry, June 19, 1954, *Diaries: 1949–1959*, 323.

208 **dropping out:** Associated Press, "Senator Hunt Retiring," *New York Times*, June 9, 1954, 23.

14: "We Accuse . . ."

210 **"campus-like headquarters"**: "Langley CIA Site Asked by Dulles," *Washington Post*, November 5, 1955, 21.

210 **"shack-like"**: Robert C. Albrook, "U.S. Building Master Plan Is Approved," *Washington Post*, December 16, 1955, 16.

210 **"tempos"**: Robert C. Albrook, "Intelligence Agency Studies 3 Areas; GSA Backs Plan to Replace Tempos," *Washington Post*, April 15, 1955, 25.

210 **Dulles convinced Congress:** "$46 Million Set for New Home of CIA," *Washington Post*, July 7, 1955, 26.

210 **"You'll have to"**: "CIA Campus Chronicles: The History of the Scattergood-Thorne Property," CIA, August 29, 2011.

211 **"She was a person"**: Margaret Scattergood, interviewed by Alice Hoffman, "The Reminiscences of Margaret Scattergood," December 3, 1976, Oral History Research Office, Columbia University.

211 **"fierce partisan"**: J. Y. Smith, "Florence Calvert Thorne, Early Labor Researcher," *Washington Post*, March 17, 1973, E3.

211 **Years before:** "Florence Thorne of A.F.L. Is Dead," *New York Times*, March 17, 1973.

211 **"It is very difficult"**: Elizabeth Fones-Wolf, "Florence Thorne," in *Notable American Women: The Modern Period*, ed. Barbara Sicherman and Carol Hurd Green (Cambridge, MA: Belknap Press, 1980), 689.

211 **listed as "partners"**: Jessica Contrera and Gillian Brockell, "In 1933, Two Rebellious Women Bought a Home in Virginia's Woods. Then the CIA Moved In," *Washington Post*, February 14, 2020, https://www.washingtonpost.com/history/2020/02/14/cia-women-neighbors-langley/.

212 **Concerned by reports:** Robert C. Albrook, "CIA Officials Hear Offers for Site of New Quarters at Open Meeting," *Washington Post*, September 22, 1955, 21.

212 **"The boundaries":** L. K. White to Florence Thorne and Margaret Scattergood, September 23, 1955, CIA-RDP63T00245R000100170054–3.

212 **broke ground:** Jack B. Pfeiffer, "The Construction of the Original Headquarters Building," in *Central Intelligence: Fifty Years of the CIA*, ed. Michael Warner and Scott A. Koch (Washington, DC: Central Intelligence Agency, 1997), 133–34.

212 **attempted to supersede:** "2 Langley Women Block Widening of CIA Route," *Evening Star*, February 11, 1958, 1.

212 **would have to wait:** "History of the Scattergood-Thorne Property," September 29, 1989, CIA-RDP91–00280R000300370011–9.

212 **"queer for queers":** Henry E. Scott, *Shocking True Story: The Rise and Fall of "Confidential," "America's Most Scandalous Scandal Magazine"* (New York: Pantheon, 2010), 80.

212 **Harrison hatched:** Samantha Barbas, *Confidential Confidential: The Inside Story of Hollywood's Notorious Scandal Magazine* (Chicago: Chicago Review Press, 2018), 23.

212 **circulation of 3.8 million:** Barbara Epstein, "Anti-Communism, Homophobia, and the Construction of Masculinity in the Postwar U.S.," *Critical Sociology* 20, no. 3 (1994): 23.

213 **"toboggan ride":** J. Howard Rutledge, "Rise of the Exposé Magazines," *Kansas City Times*, August 10, 1955, 30.

213 **best-selling book:** Robert McParland, *Bestseller: A Century of America's Favorite Books* (Lanham, MD: Rowman and Littlefield, 2019), 33.

213 **In the early morning:** Associated Press, "Sumner Welles Found Lying Dazed in Field," *Baltimore Sun*, December 27, 1948, 1.

213 **"aged ten years":** Pearson, diary entry, July 1, 1949, *Diaries: 1949–1959*, 61.

213 **"no interest in life":** Pearson, diary entry, September 19, 1949, *Diaries: 1949–1959*, 76.

213 **lecture agency:** Morgan, *FDR: A Biography*, 685.

213 **dispatch lamenting:** James B. Reston, "Russia Is Forcing Issues as We Delay Post-War Plan," *New York Times*, September 27, 1943.

213 **Hull summoned:** Reston, *Deadline*, 102–3.

214 **"an old family friend":** Pegler, "Peurifoy's Amazing Disclosure."

214 **"Welles's career":** George Sokolsky, "New Organization Formed by Sumner Welles," *Argus-Leader* (Sioux Falls, SD), March, 17, 1951, 4.

214 **"high State Department":** Lait and Mortimer, *Washington Confidential*, 124.

214 **Harrison had dispatched:** Barbas, *Confidential Confidential*, 207.

214 **"By the time":** Truxton Decatur, "We Accuse . . . Sumner Welles," *Confidential*, March 1956, 12.

215 **"however much":** Welles, *Sumner Welles*, 371–72. In a 1976 excerpt from what was to become his unfinished, posthumously published novel, *Answered Prayers*, Truman Capote detailed a chance sighting of the deteriorating Welles, seen dining in the company of "Mr. Wallace," a thinly disguised Tennessee Williams. "It was after midnight in Paris in the bar of the Boeuf-sur-le-Toit," Capote wrote, "when [Williams] was sitting at a pink-clothed table with three men, two of them expensive tarts, Corsican pirates in British flannel, and the third none other than Sumner Welles—fans of *Confidential Magazine* will remember the patrician Mr. Welles, former undersecretary of State, great and good friend of the Brotherhood of Sleeping Car Porters" (Truman Capote, "Unspoiled Monsters," *Esquire*, May 1976, 122).

215 **hosted him:** Dwight D. Eisenhower Presidential Appointment Book, December 6, 1954, and August 11, 1955, Eisenhower Library.

215 **predecessors George Washinton and Abraham Lincoln:** Dwight Eisenhower to Arthur H. Vandenberg Jr., December 22, 1954, Vandenberg Family Papers; Dwight Eisenhower to Arthur H. Vandenberg Jr., January 7, 1954, Vandenberg Family Papers.

215 **warmly welcomed:** Dwight D. Eisenhower to Arthur H. Vandenberg Jr., August 20, 1954, Vandenberg Family Papers. Arthur H. Vandenberg Jr. to Ann Whitman, August 18, 1954, Papers as President: Ann Whitman File, Administration Series, Eisenhower Library.

215 **"the political whirligig":** Kevin Doyle, "UM's Arthur Vandenberg," *Tempo*, March 1955, 17.

215 **interviews he gave:** Marshall Shapo, "West Must Spike Red Lies in Orient, Vandenberg Says," *Miami Herald*, March 20, 1955, A20.

215 **headlined its exposé:** Truxton Decatur, "The Fairy Tale the White House Never Told," November 1956, *Confidential*, 21–25, 56. That the FBI likely fed *Confidential* information about Vandenberg is attested to by Dudley Clendinen, Vandenberg's godson. Dudley Clendinen, "J. Edgar Hoover, 'Sex Deviates,' and My Godfather," *New York Times*, November 27, 2011, SR7.

215 **Vandenberg refused:** Associated Press, "Arthur H. Vandenberg Jr. Dies; Led '52 Citizens for Eisenhower," *New York Times*, January 19, 1968, 47.

216 **"ill health:"** United Press, "Vandenberg Resigns Post," *Orlando Evening Star*, September 25, 1956.

216 **students had just voted:** Barton Hickman, "Vandenberg Resigns from UM Faculty," *Miami Herald*, September 25, 1956, 1.

216 **disconnected his phone:** Clendinen, "J. Edgar Hoover, 'Sex Deviates,' and My Godfather," SR7.

216 **he was "familiar with its contents":** Dwight D. Eisenhower to Nelson Rockefeller, February 23, 1957, Folder: "Rockefeller, Nelson, 1956–57," Papers as President: Ann Whitman File, Administration Series, Presidential Papers of Dwight D. Eisenhower, Eisenhower Library.

216 **"I have not been able to overcome the obstacles":** Arthur H. Vandenberg Jr. to Dwight Eisenhower, January 8, 1957, Vandenberg Family Papers, Bentley Historical Library, University of Michigan.

216 **"handsome bachelor":** Associated Press, "Patronage Aide Due to Advance," *Spokesman-Review*, December 13, 1957.

216 **"two known queers":** Bob Gray, interviewed by Charles Francis, Mattachine Society of Washington, DC, April 25, 2014, https://mattachinesocietywashingtondc.org/2014/04/25/bob-gray-1923-2014-you-cannot-conceive/.

216 **Gray opened:** Susan B. Trento, *The Power House: Robert Keith Gray and the Selling of Access and Influence in Washington* (New York: St. Martin's Press, 1992), 12–13.

217 **"I remember":** Gray, interviewed by Francis.

217 **"If I found out":** Megan Rosenfeld, "Inaugural Insider," *Washington Post*, December 15, 1980, B1.

217 **making the list:** Jack Scott, "The Life of a Bachelor in Washington," *Cosmopolitan*, May 1958, 45.

217 **He became a familiar face:** Robert Keith Gray, *Eighteen Acres Under Glass* (Garden City, NY: Doubleday, 1962), 244–49.

217 **"single girls":** Sue Seay, "Washington Party Crasher—To Meet the Elite . . . All You Need Is Gall," *Look*, April 26, 1960, 46.

217 **"Not forever":** Marvin L. Arrowsmith, "New Cabinet Secretary Answered Summons by Eisenhower's Dog," Associated Press, *Tallahassee Democrat*, May 2, 1958.

218 **"rich, dark strawberry":** Joseph Alsop, "Coziness at the Kremlin," *Washington Post*, January 16, 1957, A11.

218 **"an incurable homosexual":** Allen Dulles to J. Edgar Hoover, "Subject: Joseph Alsop," April 1, 1957, Folder 26: "Joseph Alsop," Hoover O&C.

218 **where the word *homosexual*:** Brendan Gill, *A New York Life of Friends and Others* (New York: Poseidon Press, 1990), 17.

218 **"WASP ascendancy":** Joseph W. Alsop and Adam Platt, "The WASP Ascendancy," *New York Review of Books*, November 9, 1989, 48.

218 **"the only young American":** Merle Miller, "Washington, the World, and Joseph Alsop," *Harper's*, June 1968, 48.

219 **credited with convincing:** Caroline de Margerie, *American Lady: The Life of Susan Mary Alsop*, trans. Christopher Murray (New York: Viking, 2011), 112.

219 **"a fanatical Anglophile":** Letter from Isaiah Berlin to Marie and Mendel Berlin, May 17, 1941, in Isaiah Berlin, *Flourishing: Letters 1928–1946*, ed. Henry Hardy (London: Chatto and Windus, 2004), 372.

219 **"the lounge of":** Miller, "Washington, the World, and Joseph Alsop," 54,

219 **"a clerk"** Miller, "Washington, the World, and Joseph Alsop," 49.

219 **an influential essay:** Alsop and Alsop, "Why Has Washington Gone Crazy?," 20–21, 59–61.

219 **"the great Roman"**: 96 Cong. Rec. 11979 (August 8, 1950).

220 **"only confirmed"**: Allen Dulles to J. Edgar Hoover, "Subject: Joseph Alsop."

220 **possible fling:** C. David Heymann, *The Georgetown Ladies' Social Club: Power, Passion, and Politics in the Nation's Capital* (New York: Atria, 2003), 45.

220 **recalled the columnist:** Robert Rawls, author interview, October 3, 2019, phone.

220 **"Sapphic tendencies"**: Gore Vidal, *Palimpsest* (New York: Random House, 1995), 339.

220 **"act of very great folly"**: This account of Alsop's Moscow incident comes from his written recollection, found in Allen Dulles to J. Edgar Hoover, "Subject: Joseph Alsop," April 1, 1957, Folder 26: "Joseph Alsop," Hoover O&C.

221 **"jovial clown"**: Alsop and Platt, *"I've Seen the Best of It,"* 401.

222 **"epitome of the guy"**: Marilyn Berger, "Former Ambassador Charles E. Bohlen Dies at 69," *Washington Post*, January 2, 1974. B7.

223 **"was shocked"**: J. Edgar Hoover memo, April 2, 1957, Hoover O&C, 26.

223 **"apparent reluctance"**: J. Edgar Hoover to Allen W. Dulles, April 19, 1957, Hoover O&C, 26.

223 **"heavy emotional strain"**: G. H. Scatterday to A. H. Belmont, October 28, 1958, Subject: Joseph Alsop, Hoover O&C, 26.

223 **"a prominent American journalist"**: "For the Record," *National Review*, January 3, 1959.

223 **criticizing the Eisenhower administration:** Joseph Alsop, "The Smug Risk Takers," *Washington Post*, March 4, 1959, A13; Joseph Alsop, "Russian Roulette, ICBM Version," *Washington Post*, March 22, 1959, E5.

224 **Alsop popularized:** See, among many others, "SAC's End in Sight," *Washington Post*, February 5, 1958, A11; "Eisenhower Gauges the Gap," November 12, 1958, A15; "The Theory of the Deterrent," November 14, 1958, A19.

224 **"should get together"**: J. Edgar Hoover to files, April 14, 1959, Hoover O&C, 26.

224 **"I'm taking Alsop"**: David Wise, *Molehunt: The Secret Search for Traitors That Shattered the CIA* (New York: Random House, 1992), 77.

15: The Hunted

225 **"likeable chap"**: "U.S. Accountant Slain After Night Spot Tour," *Evening Star*, December 13, 1957, 6.

225 **Police had the power to arrest homosexuals:** B. D. Colen, "How Police Interpret Indecent Acts Related," *Washington Post*, January 21, 1972, A13.

225 **At Johnnie's:** Bobby Miller, author interview, August 28, 2020, Provincetown, MA.

226 **"high-class homosexuals"**: "Youth Denies He Stabbed Interior Aide," *Washington Post*, April 24, 1958, A3.

226 **"Hey Jack"**: "Officers Tell of Trying to Stop Teboe Stabbing," *Washington Post*, April 23, 1958, B9.

226 **"kind of belligerent"**: "2 Men Sought in Slaying of U.S. Worker," *Evening Star*, December 15, 1957, 29.

226 **At the bar:** Alfred E. Lewis and Albon B. Hailey, "Youths Lay Slaying to Money Row," *Washington Post*, January 4, 1958, A1.

226 **Using a physical:** "Youths Charged with Murder in Teboe Killing," *Evening Star*, January 3, 1958, 1.

226 **"homosexual advances"**: "2 Youths Go on Trial," *Washington Post*, April 22, 1958, A3.

226 **"grabbed at him"**: "'Must Have' Stabbed Clerk, Youth Tells Jury," *Evening Star*, April 24, 1958, 59.

226 **"The man was"**: "'Must Have' Stabbed Clerk, Youth Tells Jury," 59.

227 **The only mitigating:** "Youths Get 5–30 Years for Slaying," *Washington Post*, May 30, 1958, B16.

227 **"homosexual panic"**: Gary David Comstock, "Dismantling the Homosexual Panic Defense," *Law and Sexuality: A Review of Lesbian and Gay Legal Issues* 2 (1992): 81–102.

227 **"indecent advances"**: James Polchin, *Indecent Advances: A Hidden History of True Crime and Prejudice Before Stonewall* (Berkeley, CA: Counterpoint Press, 2019).

227 **25 percent:** "The Homosexual: Newly Visible, Newly Understood," 56

228 **Kameny was provided:** Eric Cervini, *The Deviant's War: The Homosexual vs. the United States of America* (New York: Farrar, Straus and Giroux, 2020), 9–10.

228 **surveying the city's:** Franklin Kameny, author interview, June 6, 2010, Washington, DC.

228 **On October 4, 1957:** William J. Jorden, "Soviet Fires Earth Satellite into Space; It Is Circling the Globe at 18,000 M.P.H.; Sphere Tracked in 4 Crossings Over U.S.," *New York Times*, October 5, 1957, 1.

228 **"It is hoped"**: "Memo Routing Slip," October 24, 1957, Folder 12, Box 43, Franklin Edward Kameny Papers, Library of Congress, Washington, DC (hereafter cited as "Kameny Papers").

228 **a pair of investigators**: Cervini, *Deviant's War*, 26.

229 **"howls of righteous"**: Prentiss, "Are Homosexuals Security Risks?," 5.

229 **"not within the province"**: William N. Eskridge Jr., *Dishonorable Passions: Sodomy Laws in America, 1861–2003* (New York: Viking, 2008), 152.

229 **twenty cents'**: Marcus, *Making History*, 94.

229 **"shy and retiring"**: Joyce Murdoch and Deb Price, *Courting Justice: Gay Men and Lesbians v. the Supreme Court* (New York: Basic Books, 2001), 52.

229 **"radicalized"**: Kameny, in Marcus, *Making History*, 96.

230 **impersonal headlines**: Associated Press, "107 Employees of State Dept. Have Been Fired This Year," *Washington Post*, July 3, 1953, 11; United Press, "126 Perverts Discharged," *New York Times*, March 26, 1952, 25.

230 **"It has been pointed"**: Cory, *Homosexual in America*, 45.

230 **between 1946 and 1961**: William N. Eskridge Jr., *Gaylaw: Challenging the Apartheid of the Closet* (Cambridge, MA: Harvard University Press, 1999), 60.

231 **"the hunted remain"**: Max Lerner, "The Washington Sex Story: No. 1—Panic on the Potomac," *New York Post*, July 10, 1950, 4.

231 **On December 22, 1959**: Cervini, *Deviant's War*, 57–59.

231 **"I am not"**: Franklin E. Kameny to One, August 27, 1960, Box 29: One Inc. Records, One Archives, Los Angeles, CA.

232 **"I decided then"**: Jean M. White, "Those Others: A Report on Homosexuality," *Washington Post*, January 31, 1965, E3. Though this article identifies the speaker only as a "former Government astronomer with a doctor's degree from Harvard" who "lost his Government job because of a report he was a homosexual," it is clearly Kameny.

232 **"Nearly Everybody's Reading"** Margo Hammond, "The Inside Outsider of Washington," *Tampa Bay Times*, September 6, 1998, 6D.

232 **"We do have"**: "1960: Nixon & Kennedy at Chicago's Midway Airport," F.2012–03–0632, Frank Koza Collection, Chicago Film Archives, http://www.chicagofilmarchives.org/collections/index .php/Detail/Object/Show/object_id/12230.

232 **"the greatest publicity"**: Hammond, "Inside Outsider of Washington."

232 **102 weeks**: Tom Kemme, *Political Fiction, The Spirit of the Age, and Allen Drury* (Bowling Green, OH: Bowling Green State University Popular Press, 1987), 242.

232 **"handsome, dignified"**: Allen Drury, *Advise and Consent* (Garden City, NY: Doubleday, 1959), 210. In a speech to the National Press Club, Drury listed the Charles Bohlen controversy as one of several contentious nomination battles that inspired him to write the book. "The Story That the Correspondent Told," *New York Times Book Review*, September 6, 1959, 7.

232 **"A man so popular"**: Drury, *Advise and Consent*, 233.

233 **COMFORT**: Drury, *Advise and Consent*, 28.

233 **"much time in libraries"**: Drury, *Advise and Consent*, 229. Chambers had been dismissed from his job at the New York Public Library for stealing dozens of books. Weinstein, *Perjury*, 106.

233 **"I don't want"**: Drury, *Advise and Consent*, 235.

233 **"mentally ill individual"**: Drury, *Advise and Consent*, 246.

233 **"the lurid imaginings"**: Drury, *Advise and Consent*, 248.

233 **"go to St. Elizabeth's"**: Drury, *Advise and Consent*, 250.

233 **"one of the few men"**: Drury, *Advise and Consent*, 356.

233 **"underlying feelings"**: Drury, *Advise and Consent*, 286.

233 **"made any particular"**: Drury, *Advise and Consent*, 286

233 **"over and beyond"**: Drury, *Advise and Consent*, 445.

233 **"never tried"**: Drury, *Advise and Consent*, 288.

233 **"a closed book"**: Drury, *Advise and Consent*, 294.

233 **"did his best"**: Drury, *Advise and Consent*, 290.

234 **"solid married life'**: Drury, *Advise and Consent*, 292.

234 **"did not regret"**: Drury, *Advise and Consent*, 295.

234 **"became transmuted"**: Drury, *Advise and Consent*, 294–95.

234 **"The cruel irony"**: Drury, *Advise and Consent*, 433.

234 **"How could people"**: Drury, *Advise and Consent*, 445.

234 **"In one last moment"**: Drury, *Advise and Consent*, 447.

234 **"How could society"**: Drury, *Advise and Consent*, 446.

234 **sent a copy**: "Homosexual Senator Stays—Prem," *Variety*, February 23, 1960, 7.

235 **"The single tragedy"**: Patrick O'Donovan, "The Current National Myth," *New Republic*, September 14, 1959, 19.

235 **"disparity"**: Howard Taubman, "Truth on Its Head," *New York Times*, November 27, 1960, X1. In the play's national touring production, the role of Brig was played by the gay actor Farley Granger, who also portrayed sexually ambiguous characters in the Alfred Hitchcock films *Rope* and *Strangers on a Train*.

235 **"If I needed"**: Barney Frank, *Frank: A Life in Politics from the Great Society to Same-Sex Marriage* (New York: Farrar, Straus and Giroux, 2015), 13–14. *Advise and Consent* described the yearnings of the closeted homosexual with such feeling, empathy, and—at least to many gay readers— accuracy that some questioned whether its author, who remained a bachelor until his death in 1998, possessed firsthand knowledge of the tribulations through which he put his tortured protagonist. Drury was "a very complex and very private man who never explained himself to anyone," remembers his nephew and co-literary executor Kevin Killiany. "This made him difficult to know and, to many, a blank canvas on which to project their own assumptions." Kevin's brother Kenneth said that "All indications were that he liked women and was very serious about several. However, he had something that made it hard for him to connect with others, and he was very private." At a time when gay characters in fiction were almost always criminal or crazy, *Advise and Consent* was revolutionary. A number of subsequent Drury novels contained gay themes and characters, all treated with the humanity shown in his debut effort. On Drury's rumored homosexuality, see Thomas Mallon, "'Advise and Consent' at 50," *New York Times Book Review*, June 25, 2009, 23; email to author from Kevin Killiany, September 22, 2018; email to author from Kenneth Killiany, September 22, 2018; see *The Throne of Saturn*, *Toward What Bright Glory*, *Into What Far Harbor?*, and *Public Men*, the last of which also features homosexual characters driven to suicide.

235 **"First King of Pornography"**: James Lardner, "A Pornographer's Rise, Fall," *Washington Post*, January 12, 1978, A1.

235 **Born in rural Mississippi**: James Griffin, "Dr. Womack and the Nudie Magazines," *Washington Daily News*, April 30, 1970, 5.

235 **"the finest professor"**: Peter Osnos, "Womack Arrested Again as Obscenity Publisher," *Washington Post*, April 25, 1970, B2.

236 **"Out of this"**: Ken Hodges, "The Womack School: An Education of Sorts," 2003, no. 7716, H. Lynn Womack Papers, Division of Rare and Manuscript Collections, Cornell University Library, Ithaca, NY (hereafter cited as "Womack Papers").

236 **"I'm going to make"**: Lardner, "A Pornographer's Rise, Fall," A1.

236 **vital social function**: For more on the role of beefcake magazines in developing gay social consciousness, see David K. Johnson, *Buying Gay: How Physique Entrepreneurs Sparked a Movement* (New York: Columbia University Press, 2019).

236 **"very smart, cultured"**: Johnson, *Buying Gay*, 161.

237 **"like hotcakes"**: Lynn Womack to Randy Benson, March 29, 1958, Folder 6, Box 1, Womack Papers.

237 **"Buyers like"**: Randy Benson to Lynn Womack, March 27, 1958, Folder 6, Box 1, Womack Papers no. 7441.

237 **landmark 1958 case**: *One, Inc. v. Olesen*, 355 U.S. 371 (1958).

237 **"I am now"**: Lynn Womack to Randy Benson, March 29, 1958, Folder 6, Box 1, Womack Papers.

237 **forty thousand names**: "Educator Convicted of Sending Obscene Literature Through Mail," *Washington Post*, March 22, 1960, A3.

237 **Roy Blick reacted**: Lewis and Gabbett, "It's D.C.'s Sex File but Blick's Key," E2.

238 **On January 5, 1960**: "Mailing Lewd Pictures Charged to Two Here," *Washington Post*, January 7, 1960, D5.

238 **two days after**: "Lewd Ring Is Reported Smashed," *Evening Star*, January 9, 1960, 3.

238 **A grand jury**: "Lewd Mail Indicts Two," *Evening Star*, January 14, 1960, D4; "3 Indicted on Lewd Mail Charge," *Washington Post*, January 14, 1960, A15.

238 **"At first"**: Rodger Streitmatter and John C. Watson, "Herman Lynn Womack: Pornographer as First Amendment Pioneer," *Journalism History* 28, no. 2 (Summer 2002): 59.

238 **"I live a life"**: "I Am a Grecian," *Grecian Guild Pictorial* 2, no. 1 (January 1957): 15.

238 **"There is no question"**: Streitmatter and Watson, "Herman Lynn Womack: Pornographer as First Amendment Pioneer," 59.

238 **"if homosexuals want"**: Griffin, "Dr. Womack and the Nudie Magazines," 5.

238 **jury voted to convict**: "Educator Convicted of Sending Obscene Literature Through Mail," *Washington Post*, March 22, 1960, A3.

239 **"nothing more than"**: "Mailing Lewd Pictures Charged to Two Here."

239 **"extraordinary news conference"**: "Moscow Stages a Lavish Scene for U.S. Defectors' Appearance," *New York Times*, September 7, 1960, 1.

239 **headquarters in Fort Meade**: "Intelligence: Security Risks," *Time*, August 15, 1960, 18.

239 **Congress passed**: An Act to Provide Certain Administrative Authorities for the National Agency, and for Other Purposes (National Security Agency Act of 1959), H. R. 4599, 86th Cong., 1st Sess. (1959).

239 **"No Such Agency"**: George Lardner Jr., "National Security Agency: Turning On and Tuning In," *Washington Post*, March 18, 1990, 1.

239 **"others may want'**: "Moscow Stages a Lavish Scene for U.S. Defectors' Appearance," 1.

240 **eighth and ninth**: "Defections Recall Case of 2 Britons," *New York Times*, September 7, 1960, 8.

240 **"If any community"**: Wayne G. Barker and Rodney E. Coffman, *The Anatomy of Two Traitors: The Defection of Bernon F. Mitchell and William H. Martin* (Laguna Hills, CA: Aegean Park Press, 1981), 19.

240 **"self-confessed traitors"**: Jack Raymond, "President Calls Pair Traitorous," *New York Times*, September 7, 1960, 1.

240 **"Havana and Mexico City"**: Brig. Gen. Lansdale to Deputy Secretary Douglas, Office of the Secretary of Defense, August 1, 1960, U.S. Declassified Documents Online.

240 **"the two defecting blackmailed homosexual specialists"**: David Sentner, "U. S. Will Probe Sex Deviates in Key Jobs," *San Francisco Examiner*, September 11, 1960, 16.

240 **"long-time bachelor"**: "Moscow Stages a Lavish Scene for U.S. Defectors' Appearance," 1.

240 **HUAC called Mitchell's psychiatrist**: Eve Edstrom, "Defector's Psychiatrist Got No Hint of Treason," *Washington Post*, September 15, 1960, A1.

240 **"Both pairs"**: Jack Anderson, "What Happens to American Traitors?," *Parade*, December 4, 1960, 8.

241 **safe deposit box**: Associated Press, "White House Assails Defectors Following Moscow Appearance," *Baltimore Sun*, September 7, 1960, 1.

241 **"the talents of women"**: "Predeparture Declaration," *New York Times*, September 7, 1960, 10.

241 **mouthpiece for J. Edgar Hoover**: von Hoffman, *Citizen Cohn*, 106. For more on Sokolsky's relationship with the FBI, see Matthew Cecil, *Hoover's FBI and the Fourth Estate: The Campaign to Control the Press and the Bureau's Image* (Lawrence: University Press of Kansas, 2014), 235–37.

241 **"young men who"**: George Sokolsky, "These Days," September 14, 1960.

241 **the Bureau had warned**: Associated Press, "One Mentally Ill, Other Confused," *San Francisco Examiner*, September 7, 1960, 18.

241 **"from a source"**: Jack Raymond, "House Units Map Defector Studies," *New York Times*, September 9, 1960, 9.

241 **"Mitchell had been found"**: "Discussion at the 463rd Meeting of the National Security Council, Thursday, October 13, 1960," October 18, 1960, Box 13, NSC Series, Papers of the President of the U.S., 1953–1961, Ann Whitman Files, Eisenhower Library.

241 **At the president's urging**: Weiner, *Enemies*, 213–15.

242 **"no one had any knowledge of a homosexual relationship"**: Rick Anderson, "The Worst Internal Scandal in NSA History Was Blamed on Cold War Defectors Homosexuality," *Seattle Weekly*, July 17, 2007, https://www.seattleweekly.com/news/the-worst-internal-scandal-in-nsa-history-was-blamed-on-cold-war-defectors%C2%92-homosexuality/.

242 **exclusively with women**: "The Security Program of AFSA and NSA 1949–1962," October 1963, Office of Central Reference, NSA Historian, Released by NSA on January 29, 2007, FOIA case no. 17515.

242 **eventually married women**: Andrew and Mitrokhin, *Sword and the Shield*, 179. And yet, as late as 1985, the *Washington Post* claimed that "investigators later established that they were homosexuals." "Mitchell and Martin," *Washington Post*, July 21, 1985, A28.

242 **"any man exhibiting the slightest effeminacy":** James Bamford, *The Puzzle Palace: A Report on America's Most Secret Agency* (Boston: Houghton Mifflin, 1982), 149.

242 **twenty-six employees:** *Security Practices in the National Security Agency (Defection of Bernon F. Mitchell and William H. Martin)*, Committee on Un-American Activities, 87th Cong., 2nd Sess., 15–16 (August 13, 1962).

242 **"nest of sexual deviates":** United Press International, "U.S. Security Unit Ousts 26 Deviates," *New York Times*, July 29, 1961, 13.

242 **ardently heterosexual "playboy":** Don Oberdorfer, "The Playboy Sergeant Who Spied for Russia," *The Saturday Evening Post*, March 7, 1964, 40, 44–45.

242 **"thirty to forty":** Bamford, *Puzzle Palace*, 149–53.

16: First Friends

243 **"To state the unstated":** Gore Vidal to John F. Kennedy, November 14, 1960, Item 2610, Houghton Library, Harvard College Library, Cambridge, MA.

245 **"I think you should":** Pierre Salinger, interviewed by Theodore H. White, July 19, 1965, transcript, John F. Kennedy Library Oral History Program, John F. Kennedy Presidential Library and Museum, Boston, MA (hereafter cited as "JFK Library").

245 **turned down:** Robert A. Caro, *The Years of Lyndon Johnson: The Passage of Power* (New York: Alfred A. Knopf, 2012), 71–72.

245 **more delegates:** John D. Morris, "Johnson Enters Race Officially; Sees 500 Votes," *New York Times*, July 5, 1960, 1.

245 **"Little Johnny":** Caro, *Passage of Power*, 93–95.

245 **he colluded:** James Reston, "Decision on Session Is Campaign Move," *New York Times*, June 30, 1960, 1; Russell Baker, "Long Agenda Cited—Some Protest Effects on the Campaign," *New York Times*, June 20, 1960, 1.

246 **"Doctors have told":** W. H. Lawrence, "Johnson Backers Urge Health Test," *New York Times*, July 5, 1960, 19.

246 **since he was a teenager:** Caro, *Passage of Power*, 3.

246 **"nerve center":** Theodore H. White, *The Making of the President 1960* (New York: Atheneum, 1961), 151.

246 **"town plaza":** Norman Mailer, "Superman Comes to the Supermart," *Esquire*, November 1960, 121.

246 **religious ecumenicism:** John D. Morris, "Johnson Strives to Halt Kennedy," *New York Times*, July 13, 1960, 1.

246 **telling journalists:** White, *Making of the President, 1960*, 134.

246 **"snot-nose":** Caro, *Passage of Power*, 66.

246 **"We have pictures":** Salinger, interviewed by White.

247 **"to the younger men":** James Reston, "New Political Trends at Convention," *New York Times*, July 10, 1960, E10.

247 **"It's hard to describe":** Pitts, *Jack and Lem*, xv.

247 **Billings recalled of his prenuptial conversation:** Kirk LeMoyne Billings, interviewed by Walter D. Sohier, July 7, 1964, JFK Library Oral History Program.

238 **"Can you imagine":** David Michaelis, *The Best of Friends: Profiles of Extraordinary Friendships* (New York: William Morrow, 1983), 172.

248 **pair of hamsters:** UPI, "Caroline's 2 Hamsters Hunted in White House," *New York Times*, March 5, 1961, 95.

248 **Kennedy jokingly referred:** Michaelis, *Best of Friends*, 175.

248 **"Because of him":** Michaelis, *Best of Friends*, 181.

248 **rumored affair:** Charles Schwartz, *Cole Porter: A Biography* (New York: Da Capo, 1977), 176.

249 **her appreciation for the contributions gay men made:** Robert D. McFadden, "Jacqueline Kennedy Onassis Dies of Cancer at 64," *New York Times*, May 20, 1994, 1.

249 **Jackie reading Proust:** Arthur M. Schlesinger Jr., diary entry, July 19, 1959, from *Journals: 1952– 2000* (New York: Penguin, 2007), 56.

249 **a milliner named Roy Halson Frowick:** Bernadine Morris, "Halston, Symbol of Fashion in America in 70's, Dies at 57," *New York Times*, March 28, 1990, A1.

249 **Jackie had befriended:** Gerald Clarke, *Capote: A Biography* (New York: Simon and Schuster, 1988), 271–72.

249 **Vidal attended:** Jay Parini, *Empire of Self: A Life of Gore Vidal* (New York: Doubleday, 2015), 15.

249 **"high connections":** Parini, *Empire of Self*, 29.

249 **blacklisted him:** Gore Vidal, interviewed by Jon Wiener, from Richard Peabody and Lucinda Ebersole, eds., *Conversations with Gore Vidal* (Jackson: University Press of Mississippi, 2005), 106–107.

249 **rather become president:** Richard H. Rovere, "Vidal," *New Yorker*, April 23, 1960, 39.

250 **Jimmie Trimble:** Vidal, *Palimpsest*, 23–40.

250 **a thousand people:** Vidal, *Palimpsest*, 121.

250 **fifty-three years:** Charles McGrath, "Gore Vidal Dies at 86; Prolific, Elegant, Acerbic Writer," *New York Times*, August 1, 2012, 1.

250 **"Trying to make":** Tim Teeman, *In Bed with Gore Vidal: Hustlers, Hollywood, and the Private World of an American Master* (Bronx, NY: Magnus Books, 2013), 89.

250 **"As the group":** James (Barr) Fugate to Gore Vidal, August 20, 1954, MS Am 2350, Folder 1793, Gore Vidal Papers, 1875–2008, Houghton Library, Harvard University, Cambridge, MA.

250 **did ask Vidal:** Hugh A. Mulligan, "Meet Gore Vidal, One of Season's Most Unusual Political Candidates," *Daily Oklahoman* (Oklahoma City), August 28, 1960.

250 **"The White House":** Gore Vidal, "President Kennedy," *Sunday Telegraph* (London), April 9, 1961, from *United States: Essays, 1952–1992* (New York: Random House, 1993), 797. Vidal met with Adams and Harlow on October 4, 1957, and solely with Adams on October 21, 1957. "Vidal, Gore V.," Box 42, Sherman Adams Papers, Eisenhower Library.

250 **"What is prejudice?":** Gore Vidal, "Speech for / Eisenhower / Oct. '57 / re: Little Rock / integration," 1957, Box 75, Gore Vidal Papers, Houghton Library, Harvard University, Cambridge, MA.

251 **"my mentor":** In later iterations of the joke, Vidal replaced "Eisenhower" with "Ronald Reagan." Michael Glover, "All-Amnesiac Hero," *Independent*, October 7, 1997, 4; Parini, *Empire of Self*, 319.

251 **"Look at that ass":** Vidal, *Palimpsest*, 335–36.

251 ***The Best Man:*** Gore Vidal, *The Best Man* (New York: Dramatists Play Service, 1960). A B-movie actor and budding conservative political activist named Ronald Reagan auditioned for the role of Russell in the play's original run. "Nobody thought he was credible as a presidential figure," Vidal recalled. Henry Fonda, who played Robert Leffingwell in the 1962 film version of *Advise and Consent*, played Russell in the 1964 film adaption of Vidal's play. Parini, *Empire of Self*, 137.

252 **over five hundred performances:** Fred Kaplan, *Gore Vidal: A Biography* (New York: Doubleday, 1999), 474.

252 **"Because I want":** Kaplan, *Gore Vidal*, 475. A former aide to Bobby Kennedy, John F. English, remembers the details of this conversation differently. When Bobby confronted Vidal on the campaign trail, Bobby "didn't know who he was, and Vidal got very uptight about it. And Kennedy was embarrassed because he [Vidal] was related to Jackie and so forth, and he [RFK] was really on himself for not having a better memory." John F. English, interviewed by Robert Greene, November 3, 1969, Robert F. Kennedy Oral History Program, JFK Library.

252 **Vidal sought advice:** Prior to the Broadway debut of *The Best Man*, Vidal sent a copy of the script to Kennedy. "Is Gore writing about me?" the senator asked his wife in reference to the adulterous Russell character. According to Vidal, Russell was based mostly on Adlai Stevenson, but Kennedy wasn't paranoid to suspect he had been the inspiration. According to Allen Drury, whose *Advise and Consent* was published just seven months earlier, the character of the tomcatting junior senator from Rhode Island, Lafe Smith, so upset JFK that the author was barred from the Kennedy White House. Kaplan, *Gore Vidal*, 471; Margo Howard, "The Inside Outsider of Washington," *Tampa Bay Times*, September 6, 1998, D6.

252 **"How can you say":** Marton, *Hidden Power*, 111.

252 **had "become contagious":** Drew Pearson, *Washington Merry-Go-Round: The Drew Pearson Diaries, 1960–1969*, ed. Peter Hannaford (Lincoln: University of Nebraska Press, 2015), 163. Robert Pierpoint, a CBS White House correspondent during the Kennedy administration, was representative of his colleagues when he said, "I knew about John Kennedy's, some of his sexual endeavors outside of his marriage, and I didn't report it . . . And I had eyewitness information, so it didn't

have to be second-hand" (Robert Pierpoint Oral History, interviewed by Sheldon Stern, November 18, 1982, John F. Kennedy Oral History Program, JFK Library).

253 **Kennedy advised:** Kaplan, *Gore Vidal*, 464–65.

253 **decadent "bachelor":** Ira Henry Freeman, "The Playwright, the Lawyer and the Voters," *New York Times*, September 15, 1960, 20.

253 **"If that were":** Parini, *Empire of Self*, 139–40.

253 **"felt quite comfortable":** Pitts, *Jack and Lem*, 201.

253 **"flirtatiousness with men":** Vidal, *Palimpsest*, 379.

253 **William Walton:** "The Painting Pal of the President," *Life*, March 17, 1961, 149.

253 **Once at a party:** Robert Dallek, *An Unfinished Life: John F. Kennedy, 1917–1963* (New York: Back Bay Books, 2003), 49.

254 **"Billy Boy":** David Talbot, *Brothers: The Hidden History of the Kennedy Years* (New York: Free Press, 2007), 25.

254 **"I figured out":** Talbot, *Brothers*, 27.

254 **When Jackie gave birth:** Sally Bedell Smith, *Grace and Power: The Private World of the Kennedy White House* (New York: Random House, 2004), 18–19.

254 **"the only civilizing":** Talbot, *Brothers*, 27.

254 **"gay as a goose":** Smith, *Grace and Power*, 136.

254 **"roundup":** Betty Beale, "Exclusively Yours," *Evening Star*, January 6, 1952, 55. "The United States Government is the biggest business in the world and it draws men of all ages and interests to the Capital," Beale wrote. "That it also draws a lot more women is, shall we say, simply revolting, but all the more reason why you should get busy now." By all accounts, the dating situation for single women in Washington has not changed in the interceding seventy years.

254 **"at once the most indiscreet and most discreet man alive":** Smith, *Grace and Power*, 136.

254 **"ran into Bill":** Vidal, *Palimpsest*, 379.

255 **regular bridge partner:** Smith, *Grace and Power*, 136.

255 **The ex-wife:** Nina Burleigh, *A Very Private Woman: The Life and Unsolved Murder of Presidential Mistress Mary Meyer* (New York: Bantam, 1998), 21, 195, 21; Barbara Leaming, *Mrs. Kennedy: The Missing History of the Kennedy Years* (New York: Simon and Schuster, 2001), 209, 228, 240.

255 **"despite his own":** William Walton, *The Evidence of Washington* (New York: Harper and Row, 1966), 25–26. A portrait of Walton by the painter Alice Neel held by the National Gallery of Art features the subject with rolled-up sleeves and a large watchband, what one art historian describes as "coded signals" of homosexuality. Pamela Allara, *Pictures of People: Alice Neel's American Portrait Gallery* (Hanover, NH: Brandeis University Press, 1998), 295.

255 **"almost a police state":** Tom Makepeace, author interview, March 18, 2014, Arlington, VA.

255 **talk to each other:** Byron Kennard, author interview.

256 **one of only two justices:** Griswold v. Connecticut, 381 U.S. 479 (1965).

256 **"If you were a presentable":** Alan Helms, *Young Man from the Provinces: A Gay Life Before Stonewall* (Boston: Faber and Faber, 1995), 78.

257 **"best bib":** Alsop and Platt, *"I've Seen the Best of It,"* 407–10.

257 **he helped persuade:** Katharine Graham, *Personal History* (New York: Alfred A. Knopf, 1997), 261–62.

258 **maternity gowns:** Herken, *Georgetown Set*, 249.

258 **"understanding" about her husband's manifold infidelities:** William S. Patten, *My Three Fathers: And the Elegant Deceptions of My Mother, Susan Mary Alsop* (New York: PublicAffairs, 2008), 182–83.

258 **"the only close friend":** Miller, "Washington, the World, and Joseph Alsop," 55.

238 **Kennedy was also aware:** David Streitfeld, "The Hawk and the Vultures," *Washington Post*, April 13, 1995, C1.

258 **former aide to Sumner Welles:** De Margerie, *American Lady*, 17.

258 **He also confessed:** Patten, *My Three Fathers*, 185.

258 **"cure":** Patten, *My Three Fathers*, 185.

258 **"Just as Jackie":** Patten, *My Three Fathers*, 183.

258 **wedding took place:** "Mrs. William S. Patten—Joseph W. Alsop," *Washington Post*, February 17, 1961, C3.

259 **"Now, if we can"**: Vidal, *Palimpsest*, 360. "Joe is a fag," the playwright Lillian Hellman once told a friend. "There's no reason for my liking him except that he was very good during the McCarthy period." Rosemary Mahoney, *A Likely Story: One Summer with Lillian Hellman* (New York: Anchor Books, 1998), 250.

259 **"Washington's Other Monument"**: Miller, "Washington, the World, and Joseph Alsop," 45.

259 **camp icon:** Stacy A. Cordery, *Alice: Alice Roosevelt Longworth, from White House Princess to Washington Power Broker* (New York: Viking, 2007), 464.

259 **"The very oddest"**: Alsop and Platt, *"I've Seen the Best of It,"* 433–35.

259 **not returning home:** President's Appointments, January 21, 1961, President's daily diary, January 1961–August 1962, Personal Secretary's Files, Schedules, Papers of John F. Kennedy, JFK Library.

259 **intimate dinner:** De Margerie, *American Lady*, 120.

260 **once every six weeks:** Alsop and Platt, *"I've Seen the Best of It,"* 440.

260 **"dearth of pretty young girls"**: Alsop and Platt, *"I've Seen the Best of It,"* 411.

260 **"just for appearances"**: Tom Makepeace, author interview.

260 **"I never was"**: Pitts, *Jack and Lem*, 195.

260 **"dud"**: Smith, *Grace and Power*, 10

260 **tempted to embarrass:** Vidal, *Palimpsest*, 380.

260 **"lifelong slave"**: Vidal, *Palimpsest*, 380.

260 **"principal fag"**: Vidal, *Palimpsest*, 392.

260 **president derides:** Vidal, *The Best Man*, 24.

260 **"Baron de Charlus"**: Gore Vidal, *The Golden Age* (Doubleday: New York, 2000), 321.

261 **"ruthless hater"**: Roy Cohn, interviewed by James A. Oesterle, March 24, 1971, Robert F. Kennedy Oral History Project of the John F. Kennedy Library Oral History Program, John F. Kennedy Library.

261 **told an assistant U.S. attorney:** Tom Goldstein, "Was an Assistant U.S. Attorney Told to 'Get' Roy Cohn?," *New York Times*, December 13, 1976, 46.

261 **"Where there was"**: Evan Thomas, *Robert Kennedy: His Life* (New York: Simon and Schuster, 2000), 65.

261 **"What was it"**: Taylor Branch, *Parting the Waters: America in the King Years, 1954–1963* (New York: Simon and Schuster, 1988), 402.

261 **"fag friends"**: Vidal, *Palimpsest*, 360.

261 **"Martin Luther Queen"**: Vidal, *Palimpsest*, 360.

261 **"The two people"**: Vidal, *Palimpsest*, 350.

261 **"It's a toss-up"**: Roy Cohn, interviewed by James A. Oesterle. To be sure, despite his personal comfort around gay people, JFK was hardly immune to the prejudices of the age. "What's really wrong with the State Department?" Kennedy once asked Stewart Alsop. In a group of a thousand identically dressed people, the president explained, you could spot the twenty Foreign Service officers easily. "There's something about them," he remarked. Discussing a roster of diplomatic assignments with his advisors in the summer of 1962, Kennedy complained that "I just see an awful lot of fellows who, I think . . . don't seem to have *cojones*," and mentioned one in particular who didn't "present a very virile figure." Following a visit with Dwight Eisenhower, Kennedy told Arthur Schlesinger, "You know what he said to me? We were talking about Laos. Eisenhower said, 'A State Department man told me—*and it was odd coming from him*—that Laos is a nation of homosexuals.'" Kennedy, Schlesinger noted, "repeated the phrase I have italicized with a kind of wonder." Alsop, *Center*, 18; "Meeting on Europe and General Diplomatic Matters," July 30, 1962, Presidential Recordings, Digital Edition, Miller Center, University of Virginia; Schlesinger, diary entry, March 31, 1962, *Journals, 1959–2000*, 152.

261 **Billings confronted Vidal:** Vidal, *Palimpsest*, 392.

261 **"quite rudely removed"**: George Plimpton, *Truman Capote: In Which Various Friends, Enemies, Acquaintances, and Detractors Recall His Turbulent Career* (New York: Nan A. Talese/Doubleday, 1997), 378–79.

262 **"irritated"**: Kaplan, *Gore Vidal*, 499.

262 **"resolved not to have him"**: Arthur M. Schlesinger Jr., *Robert Kennedy and His Times* (New York: Ballantine Books, 1978), 595.

17: The Group of the Intrepid

263 **"Five of Hearts":** Patricia O'Toole, *The Five of Hearts: An Intimate Portrait of Henry Adams and His Friends, 1880–1918* (New York: Clarkson Potter, 1990).

263 **Earlier that day:** SAC, WFO to Director, FBI, August 8, 1961, FBI file no. 100–403320–87.

264 **"Our government exists":** Franklin Edward Kameny v. Wilbur M. Brucker, Secretary of the Army et al., Respondents, Petition for Writ of Certiorari, no. 676, U.S. Supreme Court, Argued: May 18, 1960, 49.

264 **the government's position:** Murdoch and Price, *Courting Justice*, 57–60.

264 **"at least 15,000,000":** Franklin E. Kameny to John F. Kennedy, May 15, 1961, John F. Kennedy Presidential Papers, White House Central Name File: "Kameny, Franklin E.," JFKWHCNF-1418–002, JFK Library.

264 **"blatant disregard":** Franklin E. Kameny to John Macy Jr., June 5, 1961, Folder 12, Box 41, Kameny Papers.

264 **"Criminal, infamous, dishonest":** John Macy Jr. to Franklin E. Kameny, June 22, 1961, Folder 12, Box 41, Kameny Papers.

264 **"the impression":** Edmund White, *States of Desire: Travels in Gay America* (New York: Plume, 1980), 328.

265 **"Donald Webster Cory":** James T. Sears, Foreword to Jack Nichols, *The Tomcat Chronicles: Erotic Adventures of a Gay Liberation Pioneer* (New York: Harrington Park Press, 2004), i.

265 **"I've read":** James T. Sears, "Jack Nichols," in *Before Stonewall: Activists for Gay and Lesbian Rights in Historical Context*, ed. Vern L. Bullough (New York: Harrington Park Press, 2002), 224–25.

265 **"well dressed":** SAC, WFO to Director, FBI, August 8, 1961.

265 **Lt. Louis Fochett:** Morrey Dunie, "Court Warns Police on Methods of Getting Evidence in Morals Cases," *Washington Post*, September 28, 1956, 32; "District Judge Dismisses Indecent-Action Charge," *Evening Star*, November 26, 1956, 3.

265 **"Do you know":** Marcus, *Making History*, 97.

266 **Fochett blurted:** Johnson, *Lavender Scare*, 183.

266 **"to secure for homosexuals":** "Statement of Purpose," Folder 5, Box 85, Kameny Papers.

266 **One early member:** Paul Kuntzler, "Frank Kameny Remembrance," Folder 7, Box 2, Paul Kuntzler Papers, Manuscript Division, Library of Congress, Washington, DC.

266 **seventeenth member:** Paul Kuntzler, interviewed by Kelly Navies, July 11, 2013, March on Washington Oral History Project, Special Collections, Public Library, Washington, DC.

266 **"But then I thought":** Lilli Vincenz journal entry, August 27, 1961, Folder 2, Box 1, Lilli Vincenz Papers, Manuscript Division, Library of Congress, Washington, DC (hereafter "Vincenz Papers").

266 **"I didn't expect":** Lilli Vincenz, journal entry, September 3, 1961, Vincenz Papers.

267 **sent him a letter:** Lilli Vincenz to Franklin E. Kameny, August 30, 1963, Folder 5, Box 18, Vincenz Papers.

267 **she "requested":** Eva Freund, "A Lesbian in the Early Gay Movement," undated, Rainbow History Project, Washington, DC.

267 **"We're getting out":** Eva Freund, author interview, January 29, 2014, Washington, DC.

268 **membership peaked:** Kameny, in Marcus, *Making History*, 102.

268 **sponsored a boat ride:** Freund, "Lesbian in the Early Gay Movement."

268 **"Angry with":** [Redacted] Clerk to SAC, WFO, May 27, 1962, FBI file no. 100–33796–24; Cervini, *Deviant's War*, 90–92.

268 **"We feel that"** Franklin E. Kameny to Robert F. Kennedy, June 28, 1962, Folder "K," Box 82, Kameny Papers.

269 **"There is no community":** Manual Enterprises v. Day, oral argument by Stanley M. Dietz, February 26, 1962.

269 **Dietz's standard ensemble:** Judith Valente, "Making a Living Defending the Pornographers," *Washington Post*, January 11, 1978, A1.

270 **"a reputation":** Jerry Oppenheimer, "Smut Merchants Go Establishment," *Washington Daily News*, December 7, 1970, 6.

270 **dramatic courtroom stunts:** Valente, "Making a Living Defending the Pornographers," A1.

270 **"If a piece":** "Ex-Professor Loses Lewd Photo Appeal," *Washington Post*, January 13, 1961, B3.

270 **"I know it":** Jacobellis v. Ohio, 378 U.S. 184, (1964), Justice Stewart concurrence.

270 **"the toughest crackdown":** "Womack Jailed Anew in Obscenity Crackdown," *Washington Post*, January 28, 1961, B2.

270 **"a genius":** Lardner, "A Pornographer's Rise, Fall," A1.

271 **"dismally unpleasant":** Manual Enterprises v. Day, 370 U.S. 478, (1962), Justice Harlan ruling. Justices Felix Frankfurter, who had suffered a stroke, and Byron White, who was not confirmed to the Court until after oral arguments had taken place, abstained.

272 **"I did not":** Johnson, *Buying Gay*, 169.

272 **An unsigned editorial:** "Less Taxes for Bachelors!," *Grecian Guild Pictorial* no. 45 (July 1964).

272 **sixteen-thousand-square-foot warehouse:** Johnson, *Buying Gay*, 154.

272 **volume of mail:** Sarah McClendon, "8 Periodicals Feature Photos of Young Males," *Honolulu Advertiser*, December 27, 1964, 55.

272 **House and Garden Tour:** "Capitol Hill Tour Set Sunday, May 14," *Evening Star*, April 23, 1967, 54.

272 **"We would walk":** Streitmatter and Watson, "Herman Lynn Womack," 63.

273 **"full of boys":** Johnson, *Buying Gay*, 188.

273 **"Never mind":** Maxine Cheshire, "'Consent' Lacks Consensus," *Washington Post*, March 22, 1962, D1.

273 **"There has never":** Allen Drury to Otto Preminger, November 21, 1959, "Basic Factors Involved in Maintaining Integrity of 'Advise and Consent' in Movie Form," Folder 15, Box 25, Allen Drury Papers, Hoover Institution.

273 **movie rights:** Philip K. Scheuer, "Bartlett's 'Men' Odd Cross Section," *Los Angeles Times*, November 12, 1959, IV 13.

274 **1927 list:** Jon Lewis, *Hollywood v. Hard Core: How the Struggle over Censorship Saved the Modern Film Industry* (New York: NYU Press, 2002), 301–2.

274 **"light and gay":** Kenneth Turan, "The Man with the Golden Touch," *Los Angeles Times*, February 23, 2005, E1.

274 **"It was always":** Russo, *Celluloid Closet*, 121.

274 **"last specific taboo":** "Homosexuality Theme Now Okay," *Variety*, September 27, 1961, 1.

274 **Geoffrey Shurlock:** "Homosexual Senator Stays—Prem," 7.

275 **"to consider approving":** Murray Schumach, "Film Code Change Vexes Producers," *New York Times*, October 23, 1961, 22.

275 *Variety* **announced:** "Discreetly the Code in Switch About Swishing," *Variety*, October 4, 1961, 7.

275 **"Capitolians Agog":** Les Carpenter, "Capitolians Agog, Seek Bit Parts, as 'Advise & Consent' Rolls There September 1," *Variety*, July 19, 1961, 1.

275 **pieces of art:** "HOLLYWOOD: Advise and Consent," *Time*, September 29, 1961, 69.

275 **"When are they":** Associated Press, "Movie Version of Washington Party Is Dull," September 23, 1961.

275 **dramatic confrontation:** Eugene Archer, "Cinema Congress," *New York Times*, October 1, 1961, X7.

275 **"It was a wonderful":** Foster Hirsch, *Otto Preminger: The Man Who Would Be King* (New York: Alfred A. Knopf, 2007), 354–55.

276 **initially convinced:** James Spada, *Peter Lawford: The Man Who Kept the Secrets* (New York: Bantam, 1992), 309.

276 **later rescinded:** Hirsch, *Otto Preminger*, 354.

276 **calling the set:** Garry Wills, *The Kennedy Imprisonment: A Meditation on Power* (Boston: Houghton Mifflin, 1981), 22.

276 **"I vud haf":** "Hollywood: Advise und Consent," *Time*, September 29, 1961, 29.

276 **the MPAA instructed:** G. Tom Poe, "Secrets, Lies and Cold War Politics: 'Making Sense' of Otto Preminger's 'Advise and Consent,'" *Film History* 10, no. 3 (1998): 339–40.

275 **Preminger included:** "Preminger in the Middle," *New York Herald Tribune*, June 3, 1962, Section 4, 4.

275 **The cinematic Brig:** Russo, *Celluloid Closet*, 142.

277 **"not available":** "A Patriotic Movie . . . or Not," *Life*, July 6, 1962, 74.

18: "That Old Black Fairy"

278 **stationed nuclear missiles:** "Cuban Crisis: A Step-by-Step Review," *New York Times*, November 3, 1962, 1.

278 **"integrity"**: Cabell Phillips, "Officer Whom Kennedy Upheld Is Impugned by Senate Group," *New York Times*, October 16, 1962, 15; U.S. Congress, *The Case of William Wieland: Report of the Subcommittee to the Investigate the Administration of the Internal Security Act and Other Internal Security Laws of the Committee on the Judiciary* (Washington, DC: U.S. Government Printing Office, 1962), 2.

278 **When Fidel Castro:** Wieland was appointed to the position on September 7, 1958, and Castro entered Havana on January 8, 1959. *The Biographic Register* (Washington, DC: Department of State, 1960), 776; R. Hart Phillips, "Havana Welcomes Castro at End of Triumphal Trip," *New York Times*, January 9, 1959, 1.

278 **"Who Is He?":** George Sokolsky, "Who Is He?," *Washington Post*, December 22, 1960, A15.

279 **"What is necessary":** Interestingly, in the version of this column published on its op-ed page, the *Washington Post* excised these lines about homosexuals. Earlier that week, the paper's own editorial board reprimanded Sokolsky for his "mean innuendoes" about Wieland. For original column, see George Sokolsky, "House Cleaning Needed at State Department," *Tampa Times*, December 30, 1960, 8; George Sokolsky, "Each Year Its Own," *Washington Post*, December 30, 1960, A13; George Sokolsky, "Scapegoat for Castro?," *Washington Post*, December 24, 1960, A8.

279 **have died:** "Sumner Welles, 69, Diplomat, Is Dead," *New York Times*, September 25, 1961, 1.

279 **"Before 1959":** Ian Lumsden, *Machos, Maricones, and Gays: Cuba and Homosexuality* (Philadelphia: Temple University Press, 1996), 33.

280 **"was a notorious":** Benjamin Mandel to J. G. Sourwine, December 27, 1960, Box 117, Wieland SISS File, NARA Washington, DC.

280 **"morals in Cuba":** Eric Paul Roorda, "McCarthyite in Camelot: The 'Loss' of Cuba, Homophobia, and the Otto Otepka Scandal in the Kennedy State Department," *Diplomatic History* 31, no. 4 (September 2007): 739

280 **"there were all sorts":** John Seigenthaler, interviewed by Ronald J. Grele, February 23, 1966, John F. Kennedy Library Oral History Program, JFK Library.

280 **"Where did you see":** Questioning about Welles at 492–93, "Fair-haired boy" at 565, exchange about homosexuality at 609, and "seen with him" at 619 of *Subcommittee to Investigate the Administration of the Internal Security Act and Other Internal Security Laws of the Committee on the Judiciary*, 87th Cong., 1st Sess., February 8, 1961.

280 **Kennedy sided:** News conference, January 24, 1962, State Department Auditorium, Washington, DC; Phillips, "Officer Whom Kennedy Upheld Is Impugned by Senate Group," 15.

280 **"Batista was bad":** Halberstam, *The Fifties*, 717.

280 **"We should be":** Lars Schoultz, *That Infernal Little Cuban Republic: The United States and the Cuban Revolution* (Chapel Hill: University of North Carolina Press, 2009), 133–34.

281 **"not and never has been":** Roorda, "McCarthyite in Camelot," 742.

281 **cleared him:** Richard Eder, "U.S. Cuban Expert Restored to Duty," *New York Times*, July 19, 1965, 6.

281 **"But you know":** "Hyannis Economic Conference," Press Secretary's Subject File 1960, Speeches and the Press, Presidential Campaign Files 1960, Pre-Presidential Papers of John F. Kennedy, JFK Library.

281 **"demands of the parlor pinks":** "Thurmond Says Foes Yield to 'the Pinks,'" *New York Times*, October 14, 1948, 23.

281 **daily steam baths:** Adam Clymer, "Strom Thurmond, Foe of Integration, Dies at 100," *New York Times*, June 27, 2003, A1.

282 **chief organizer:** Susanna McBee, "Organizer of D.C. March Is Devoted to Non-Violence," *Washington Post*, August 11, 1963, A6.

282 **"whitewash":** 109 Cong. Rec. 14836–44 (August 13, 1963); William Moore, "Calls Rustin Convicted Pervert," *Chicago Tribune*, August 15, 1963; "Lecturer Sentenced to Jail on Morals Charge," *Los Angeles Times*, January 23, 1953.

282 **West Chester, Pennsylvania:** Eric Pace, "Bayard Rustin Is Dead at 75; Pacifist and a Rights Activist," *New York Times*, August 25, 1987, 1.

282 **arrested in North Carolina:** J. Y. Smith, "Bayard Rustin Dies; Civil Rights Theorist, Activist, Was 75," *Washington Post*, August 25, 1987, B7.

283 **"never knew":** Rachelle Horowitz interview, https://www.cnn.com/videos/politics/2013/08/22/preview-bayard-rustin-documentary.cnn.

283 **"crushed":** Arch Puddington, author interview, July 26, 2017, New York, NY.

283 **"the boys with":** Michael G. Long, *Martin Luther King Jr., Homosexuality, and the Early Gay Rights Movement: Keeping the Dream Straight?* (New York: Palgrave Macmillan, 2012), 43.

283 **"who is very irresponsible":** Bayard Rustin, interviewed by T. H. Baker, June 17, 1969, Oral Histories, LBJ Library; David J. Garrow, *Bearing the Cross: Martin Luther King, Jr., and the Southern Christian Leadership Conference* (New York: Vintage, 1986), 139–40; Branch, *Parting the Waters*, 314–18.

284 **"My being gay":** "An Interview with Bayard Rustin," in Redvers Jeanmarie, *Other Countries: Black Gay Voices* (New York: Other Countries, 1988), 5; Wil Haygood, *King of the Cats: The Life and Times of Adam Clayton Powell, Jr.* (New York: Houghton Mifflin, 1993), 265, and Charles V. Hamilton, *Adam Clayton Powell, Jr.: The Political Biography of an American Dilemma* (New York: Atheneum, 1991), 336.

284 **Rustin submitted:** Long, *Martin Luther King, Jr.*, 75.

284 **"I hope Bayard":** Branch, *Parting the Waters*, 841–42.

284 **When the question:** Jacqueline Trescott, "The March, the Dream," *Washington Post*, August 21, 1983, H1.

284 **"So you're down":** Thomas, *Robert Kennedy*, 263.

285 **"I put the movement":** "An Interview with Bayard Rustin," in Jeanmarie, *Other Countries*, 5; Branch, *Parting the Waters*, 846–47.

285 **"a man of exceptional":** Jervis Anderson, *Bayard Rustin: Troubles I've Seen* (New York: HarperCollins, 1997), 251.

285 **"Mr. March-on-Washington":** McBee, "Organizer of D.C. March Is Devoted to Non-Violence," A6.

285 **"I am sure":** Associated Press, "Membership in Red Front Admitted by Top Marcher," *Montgomery Advertiser*, August 16, 1963.

285 **"The Senator is interested":** Newsreel footage from *Brother Outsider*, directed by Nancy D. Kates and Bennett Singer (Independent Television Service, 2003).

286 **Rustin and Randolph appeared on the cover:** *Life*, September 6, 1963.

286 **"chance to rethink":** Rustin, interviewed by Baker.

286 **"If I've learned":** Bayard Rustin, interviewed by Peg Byron, February 5, 1986, *Making Gay History: The Podcast*, https://makinggayhistory.com/podcast/bayard-rustin/.

286 **"spoke often":** Chap. 2 in *Memoirs of Jack Nichols: Unfinished and Unedited*, Jack Nichols Photographs and Papers, Rainbow History Project, Washington, DC.

286 **"cooperate with other":** "Statement of Purpose."

286 **most of the male protestors:** Forrester, "D.C. Bars in the 1930s," 11.

286 **"Many of us":** *Before Stonewall* (film).

287 **"Before I let":** Pat Hawkins, interviewed by Mark Meinke, May 22, 2009, transcript, Oral History Program, Rainbow History Project, Washington, DC.

287 **"Now we have fulfilled':** Nichols, *Tomcat Chronicles*, 196.

287 **"the white homosexual":** *The Negro and the Homophile Movement*, flyer, n.d., Folder 3, Box 85, Kameny Papers.

287 **"I remember sitting":** Rebecca C. Dolinsky, "Lesbian and Gay DC: Identity, Emotion, and Experience in Washington, DC's Social and Activist Communities (1961–1986)" (PhD diss., University of California, Santa Cruz, 2010), 103.

287 **"he was infiltrating":** Kent W. Peacock, "Race, the Homosexual, and the Mattachine Society of Washington, 1961–1970," *Journal of the History of Sexuality* 25, no. 2 (2016): 269.

288 **"the homosexual, today":** "News Release from the Mattachine Society of Washington," August 28, 1962, Barbara Gittings and Kay Tobin Lahusen papers and photographs, box 68, folder 5, Manuscripts and Archives division, New York Public Library.

288 **"The fact of the matter":** "Time on Two Crosses: An Interview with George Chauncey, Jr.," in Devon W. Carbado and Donald Weise, eds., *Time on Two Crosses: The Collected Writings of Bayard Rustin* (San Francisco: Cleis Press, 2003), 299.

288 **"shrieker":** John D'Emilio, *Lost Prophet: The Life and Times of Bayard Rustin* (Chicago: University of Chicago Press, 2003), 372.

288 **"brought out":** Doug Hinckle, "'I Wasn't Laughing Then' Says Rustin," *Washington Blade*, October 18, 1985, 1.

288 **red rose:** Matt Brosius, "Notes on Bayard Rustin Keynote Speech to BMWT/DC Anniversary Weekend," October 12, 1985, Bayard Rustin Papers, Manuscript Division, Library of Congress, Washington, DC.

288 **"The Washington landscape":** Alsop and Platt, *"I've Seen the Best of It,"* 464.

288 **"I had no idea":** Joseph W. Alsop, interviewed by Elspeth Rostow, June 18, 1964, Oral History Program, JFK Library.

289 **"probably the saddest":** Smith, *Grace and Power,* 465.

289 **alcoholic despair:** Pitts, *Jack and Lem,* 293–294.

289 **"Why would President Kennedy's":** Kuntzler, "Frank Kameny Remembrance."

289 **"New Frontier's artist-without-portfolio":** William Manchester, *The Death of a President: November 20–November 25, 1963* (New York: Harper and Row, 1967), 436–38.

289 **advised Bobby:** Schlesinger, *Robert Kennedy and His Times,* 658.

289 **"We wanted":** *Investigation of the Assassination of President John F. Kennedy: Hearings Before the President's Commission on the Assassination of President Kennedy* (Washington, DC: U.S. Government Printing Office, 1964), 112.

290 **American paranoia:** Kurt Andersen, *Fantasyland: How America Went Haywire: A 500-Year History* (New York: Random House, 2017), 215.

290 **majority of Americans:** Art Swift, "Majority in U.S. Still Believe JFK Killed in a Conspiracy," Gallup, November 15, 2013.

290 **premiered at the top:** Keith Schneider, "Mark Lane, Early Kennedy Assassination Conspiracy Theorist, Dies at 89," *New York Times,* May 12, 2016, B14.

290 **shocking announcement:** Gene Roberts, "The Case of Jim Garrison and Lee Oswald," *New York Times Magazine,* May 21, 1967, 32.

290 **"arrests will":** Gene Roberts, "Death of Ferrie Called Natural," *New York Times,* February 24, 1967, 21.

290 **A failed candidate:** Gene Roberts, "Figure in Oswald Inquiry Is Dead in New Orleans," *New York Times,* February 23, 1967, 22.

291 **"one of history's":** Associated Press, "New Oswald Clue Reported Found," *New York Times,* February 19, 1967, 43.

291 **considered the death:** Associated Press, "Death of Ferrie Stymies JFK Probe," *Fort Worth Star-Telegram,* February 23, 1967, 2A.

291 **"Wilsonian-FDR-Kennedy":** James Kirkwood, *American Grotesque: An Account of the Clay Shaw–Jim Garrison Affair in the City of New Orleans* (New York: Simon and Schuster, 1970), 17.

291 **"composite conspirator":** Hugh Aynesworth, "The JFK 'Conspiracy,'" *Newsweek,* May 15, 1967, 40.

291 **"as bread dough":** Martin Waldron, "Some Say It's Garrison Who's in Wonderland," *New York Times,* May 14, 1967, E5.

291 **"a Nazi operation":** United Press International, September 22, 1967.

292 **"gay lovers":** Hugh Aynesworth, *November 22, 1963: Witness to History* (Dallas: Brown Books, 2013), 193.

292 **"sadist plot":** Dave Reitzes, "Assassination a Homosexual Thrill Killing," http://mcadams.posc.mu.edu/jimloon5.htm.

292 **"high-status fags":** Donald H. Carpenter, *Man of a Million Fragments: The True Story of Clay Shaw* (Nashville, TN: self-pub., 2014), 317.

292 **"had the same motive":** James Phelan, *Scandals, Scamps, and Scoundrels: The Casebook of an Investigative Reporter* (New York: Random House, 1982), 150–51.

292 **kill "the world's":** Carpenter, *Man of a Million Fragments,* 313.

292 **"tight pants":** Testimony of Clay Shaw, State of Louisiana v. Clay L. Shaw, February 27, 1969, Criminal District Court, Parish of Orleans, State of Louisiana.

292 **"frequently hinted":** Kirkwood, *American Grotesque,* 26.

292 **"Queers know queers!":** Kirkwood, *American Grotesque,* 637.

293 **Everyone . . . descended upon the Big Easy:** Phelan, *Scandals, Scamps, and Scoundrels,* 139.

293 **less than an hour:** "Clay Shaw Acquitted of Conspiracy," *Washington Post,* March 1, 1969, A1.

293 **"one of the most disgraceful":** "Justice in New Orleans," *New York Times,* March 2, 1969, 12E.

293 **"When death comes":** Kirkwood, *American Grotesque,* 28.

293 **vast conspiracy:** Garrison died in 1992. But his "homosexual thrill killing" thesis lives on thanks to the conspiracy-obsessed director Oliver Stone, who made it the centerpiece of his 1991 feature film *JFK*. The premise of that movie is encapsulated in a line uttered by a gay prostitute, a composite of several real-life figures whom Garrison accused of involvement in the assassination. "You a goddamn liberal, Mr. Garrison," Kevin Bacon's rent boy tells the protagonist, played by Kevin Costner. "You don't know shit because you never been fucked in the ass." (Forget the Warren Commission report; according to Stone, receptive male anal sex is the Rosetta Stone by which the most shocking American political event of the twentieth century can be understood.) Defending his film from accusations of homophobia, Stone said it was "Not about being gay; it's about the connections that being gay makes," which he depicted as a group of demented homosexual criminal masterminds plotting to murder the thirty-fifth president of the United States while partaking in a drug-fueled, sadomasochistic orgy. Critically panned, *JFK* earned $195 million at the box office, was nominated for eight Academy Awards, and won two. Jeff Yarbrough, "Heart of Stone," *The Advocate*, April 7, 1992, 44–49; "Political Dramas at the Box Office," *Hollywood Reporter*, December 2, 2011, 16.

293 **"Throughout our trial":** Fred Litwin, *I Was a Teenage JFK Conspiracy Freak* (Ottawa: Northern-Blues Books, 2018), 99.

293 **Garrison molested:** Jack Anderson, "The Washington Merry-Go-Round," January 23, 1970.

19: A Long Way from Arp

297 **At 7:05 a.m.:** Bob Waldron, interviewed by Michael L. Gillette, February 1, 1976, Oral Histories, LBJ Library. This is confirmed by Johnson's daily diary, which records a phone call at 7:05 a.m. placed to Homer Thornberry, who was living with Waldron at the time. Lyndon B. Johnson's Daily Diary Collection, November 23, 1963, LBJ Library, http://www.lbjlibrary.net/collections/daily -diary.html.

297 **accruing human resources:** Robert A. Caro, *The Years of Lyndon Johnson: Master of the Senate* (New York: Alfred A. Knopf, 2002), 311–14; Caro, *Passage of Power*, 172, 181–82; George Bristol, *On Politics and Parks* (College Station: Texas A&M University Press, 2012), 109–10; Douglas Martin, "W. Marvin Watson, Johnson's Unofficial Chief of Staff, Dies at 93," *New York Times*, November 29, 2017, B13.

298 **"almost family relationship":** Bill Wiley, author interview, June 25, 2019, phone.

298 **broke down:** Bristol, *On Politics and Parks*, 94.

298 **"goose pimples":** Waldron, interviewed by Gillette, February 1, 1976.

298 **appears just once:** Caro, *Passage of Power*, 106.

298 **single photograph:** Caro, *Passage of Power*, photo insert II, page 10, bottom.

299 **"You'd have to be":** Bill Wiley, author interview.

299 **Greeting a group:** Bristol, *On Politics and Parks*, 87–88, 109.

299 **"The most important":** Caro, *Master of the Senate*, 136.

299 **"[Waldron] never said":** Lynda Bird Johnson Robb, author interview, November 30, 2020, phone.

299 **insertion of contact lenses:** SAs J. Richard Nichols and John A. Van Wagenen, October 17, 1964, FBI file no. 161-HQ-2854, WFO 161–2404.

299 **"say things" to Johnson:** SAs James E. Ritter and John R. Ale, October 18, 1964, FBI file no. 161-HQ-2854.

299 **attending dinner:** Waldron, interviewed by Gillette, February 1, 1976.

300 **"He was the best dancer":** Robb, author interview.

300 **"so expert":** Betty Beale, "First Lady Duties Assessed; Moreira Salles Visit Here," *Evening Star*, March 22, 1961, C4.

300 **"Why would anyone":** Bob Waldron, interviewed by Michael L. Gillette, January 28, 1976, Oral Histories, LBJ Library.

300 **In Johnson's suite:** Waldron, interviewed by Gillette, January 28, 1976.

300 **"lickety split":** Lady Bird Johnson, interviewed by Harry Middleton, August 1994, Oral Histories, LBJ Library.

300 **"the fastest stenographer":** Phyllis Bonanno, interviewed by Michael L. Gillette, May 9, 1983, Oral Histories, LBJ Library.

300 **hide in a closet:** George E. Reedy, interviewed by Michael L. Gillette, September 13, 1984, Oral Histories, LBJ Library. The actual number of meetings between RFK and LBJ, and who was present at them, remains a matter of historical uncertainty. Caro, *Passage of Power*, 129–34.

300 **stood behind Johnson:** Associated Press photo ID: 343068047715, July 14, 1960.

300 **"man of all work":** Anthony Lewis, "Johnson Upsets Plans," *New York Times*, October 10, 1964, 14.

300 **twenty-nine-thousand-mile:** "No Troops Asked, Says Johnson," *Washington Post*, May 25, 1961, A1.

301 **"a very brilliant":** Waldron, interviewed by Gillette, January 28, 1976.

301 **"It's a long way":** Waldron, interviewed by Gillette, January 28, 1976.

301 **"We used to tease":** Robb, author interview.

301 **"bath of fire":** Waldron, interviewed by Gillette, January 28, 1976.

301 **Every staffer:** SAs Clyde B. Johnson and George W. H. Carlson, October 17, 1964, FBI file no. SA 161–173; SAC WFO to Director, October 20, 1964, FBI file no. 161–2854–133. The FBI agent who wrote this report on Waldron misquoted the inscription as "Do Unto Others as They Would Do Unto You." In fairness, it is not hard to imagine Johnson dispensing this pearl of wisdom.

301 **Goldwater approved:** Air Force Form 1085, September 1, 1962, FBI file no. 161-HQ-2854.

301 **"just asked me":** Waldron, interviewed by Gillette, January 28, 1976.

302 **Waldron as a walker:** Waldron, interviewed by Gillette, January 28, 1976.

302 **possible mistress:** Randall B. Woods, *LBJ: Architect of American Ambition* (New York: Free Press, 2006), 405–6.

302 **assistance of a more intimate:** SAC WFO to Director, October 20, 1964.

302 **"on many occasions":** SAs Nichols and Van Wagenen, October 17, 1964.

302 **"When Bob hit Washington":** Bill Wiley, author interview.

302 **"lavish-spending":** Mary V. R. Thayer, "Why So 'Quiet' for Van?," *Washington Post*, May 26, 1958, B4.

302 **entertainment chairman:** Texas State Society History, https://www.texasstatesociety.org/about-the-tss/tss-history/1950-1969/.

302 **"male Perle Mesta":** Jackson to Director, Atlanta, Chicago, Washington, October 22, 1964, FBI file no. 161–2854–165.

302 **society columns:** "Party Celebrates Adjournment of Congress," *Evening Star*, September 2, 1957, 32; Thayer, "Why So 'Quiet' for Van?," B4; Muriel Brown, "Gaily-Shirted Texans Dine on Barbecued Chicken, Pork," *Washington Post*, July 22, 1957, B4.

302 **"To come to Washington":** Merle Miller, *Lyndon: An Oral Biography* (New York: Putnam, 1980), 204.

303 **Sam Rayburn:** United Press International, "Rayburn Is Dead; Served 17 Years as House Speaker," *New York Times*, November 17, 1961, 1.

303 **longed to have:** Robert A. Caro, *The Years of Lyndon Johnson: The Path to Power* (New York: Alfred A. Knopf, 1982), 333.

303 **abusive father:** Dallek, *Lone Star Rising*, 38–40.

303 **"always had a gift":** Caro, *Master of the Senate*, 154. See also Caro, *Path to Power*, chaps. 8, 11, and 16.

303 **"professional son":** Caro, *Master of the Senate*, 158.

303 **greased the wheels:** Caro, *Master of the Senate*, 475.

303 **always ended:** Caro, *Master of the Senate*, 173.

303 **got cold feet:** Gilbert C. Fite, *Richard B. Russell, Jr.: Senator from Georgia* (Chapel Hill: University of North Carolina Press, 1991), 171–72.

303 **"Lyndon was always":** Miller, *Lyndon*, 142.

303 **Senate employee:** Neil Genzlinger, "Bobby Baker, String-Puller Snared in Senate Scandal, Dies at 89," *New York Times*, November 17, 2017, D6.

303 **"snickered behind":** Bobby Baker, with Larry L. King, *Wheeling and Dealing: Confessions of a Capitol Hill Operator* (New York: W. W. Norton, 1978), 42.

303 **"would have married":** *The American Experience: LBJ*, directed by David Grubin (PBS Home Video, 1997).

304 **"One of the first":** Doris Kearns Goodwin, *Lyndon Johnson and the American Dream* (New York: St. Martin's Press, 1976), 24.

304 **"would make me":** Goodwin, *Lyndon Johnson*, 43.

304 **mentioned him only once:** Lyndon Baines Johnson, *The Vantage Point: Perspectives of the Presidency, 1963–1969* (New York: Holt, Rinehart and Winston, 1971), 567.

304 **kissing Rayburn's bald dome:** Caro, *Master of the Senate*, 402.

304 **Harry Byrd:** Caro, *Passage of Power*, 473.

304 **"the prevailing attitude":** Howard P. Chudacoff, *The Age of the Bachelor: Creating an American Subculture* (Princeton, NJ: Princeton University Press, 1999), 255.

304 **speculating to members:** Richard E. Farley, *Wall Street Wars: The Epic Battles with Washington that Created the Modern Financial System* (New York: Regan Arts, 2015), 247.

304 **"everybody's favorite":** Sally Quinn, author interview, October 17, 2018, Washington, DC.

304 **foreign governments:** Winzola McLendon, "Playboys of Power," *Washington Star-News*, March 25, 1973, D1.

305 **"had been very much in love":** Earl D. Haggerty, Report of Investigation, Civil Service Commission, November 30, December 2, 3, 4, 1963, CSC Case Serial No. 2.23.64.2133, from FBI file no. 161-HQ-2854.

305 **limited number:** Caro, *Passage of Power*, 169.

305 **place Waldron:** SA Joseph W. Speicher, October 17, 1964, FBI file no. 161-HQ-2854.

305 **President Eisenhower created:** "President Hails New Space Board," *New York Times*, July 30, 1958, 10.

305 **"Mister Fixit":** Jan Jarboe Russell, *Lady Bird: A Biography of Mrs. Johnson* (New York: Scribner, 1999), 245.

305 **Born on a farm:** Woods, *LBJ*, 430.

305 **shorthand virtuoso:** Theodore H. White, *The Making of the President, 1964* (New York: Atheneum, 1965), 348.

305 **high blood pressure:** Harry McPherson, interviewed by T. H. Baker, March 24, 1969, Oral Histories, LBJ Library.

305 **ruddy face:** Russell, *Lady Bird*, 1999), 245.

305 **hour every day:** Lewis, "Johnson Upsets Plans," 14.

305 **installed a phone:** Jonathan Darman, *Landslide: LBJ and Ronald Reagan at the Dawn of a New America* (New York: Random House, 2014), 193.

305 **"he never realized":** Waldron, interviewed by Gillette, January 28, 1976.

305 **LBJ's personal accountant:** Russell, *Lady Bird*, 245.

305 **"There was a saying":** Michael L. Gillette, *Lady Bird Johnson: An Oral History* (Oxford: Oxford University Press, 2012), 284.

306 **"In the time I have known Bob":** Haggerty, Report of Investigation.

306 **"He is very much":** Joe H. Jackson, Report of Investigation, United States Civil Service Commission, November 19–21, 1963, FBI file no. 161-HQ-2854.

306 **during a campaign swing:** Nancy Dickerson, interviewed by Joe B. Frantz, August 11, 1972, Oral Histories, LBJ Library.

306 **"just as a married couple":** Clyde B. Johnson, FD-204, October 18, 1964, FBI file no. 161–2854–103.

306 **"I would consider":** Haggerty, Report of Investigation.

307 **about half:** W. V. Cleveland to Rowland Evans, October 23, 1964, FBI file no. 161–2854–175.

307 **Wendal Lee Philips:** Jackson, Report of Investigation.

308 **The following May:** SAs Joseph E. Jones and Matthew B. Boyhan, October 17, 1964, FBI file no. 161-HQ-2854; Jackson, Report of Investigation.

308 **"Robert Waldron is":** Report of Investigation, November 19, 20, and 21, 1963, U.S. Civil Service Commission, FBI file no. 161-HQ-2854.

309 **"seldom out of":** SAs Nichols and Van Wagenen, October 17, 1964.

309 **Sunday morning services:** Waldron, interviewed by Gillette, February 1, 1976.

309 **"homosexual activities":** SA Speicher, October 17, 1964.

309 **formally rejected:** Walter Jenkins Statement, undated, Aides Files of Mildred Stegall, Box 29B, LBJ Library (hereafter "Stegall Files").

309 **"very depressed":** SAs Nichols and Wagenen, October 17, 1964.

309 **"Nobody ever said":** Robb, author interview.

309 **State Department announced:** Willard Edwards, "63 Security Risks Quit in State Department," *Chicago Tribune*, April 25, 1964, 16.

309 **Though his very first:** Chuck Lindell, "The People's Politician," *Austin-American Statesman*, June 19, 2005, 1.

309 **"had the prospects":** Caro, *Master of the Senate*, 126.

310 **"I think we felt":** Miller, *Lyndon*, 215.

310 **"Washington Insider":** Jake Pickle and Peggy Pickle, *Jake* (Austin: University of Texas Press, 1997), 109–10.

310 **persona non grata:** A search of the Johnson presidential diary denotes a long gap in Waldron's theretofore frequent encounters with Johnson lasting from December 2, 1963 to September 4, 1964. Lyndon B. Johnson's Daily Diary Collection, LBJ Library.

310 **"Dear Lee":** Bob Waldron to W. Lee Phillips, May 15, 1964, FBI file no. 161-HQ-2854, 161–73.

20: "A Quite Serious Situation"

313 **Riding in a cab:** Gore Vidal, "The Race into Grace, or the Civilization Gap," *Esquire*, August 1961, 120–23.

314 **Roy Blick's vice squad had arrested seven men:** "Vice Squad Nabs Seven on Sex Counts at YMCA," *Washington Post*, April 11, 1961, B8.

314 **"tearoom trade":** Laud Humphreys, *Tearoom Trade: Impersonal Sex in Public Places* (London: Duckworth, 1970).

314 **"sad and often sordid":** "Homosexuality in America," *Life*, June 26, 1964, 66.

314 **cheap cigar smoke:** "Nation: The Senior Staff Man," *Time*, October 23, 1964, 21.

315 **The word *slave*:** Caro, *Master of the Senate*, 129; Caro, *The Path to Power*, 495–96; Cartha D. "Deke" DeLoach, interviewed by Michael L. Gillette, January 11, 1991, Oral Histories, LBJ Library.

315 **Jenkins who organized:** Caro, *Passage of Power*, 71.

315 **married Mary Margaret Wiley:** Betty Boyd Caroli, *Lady Bird and Lyndon: The Hidden Story of a Marriage That Made a President* (New York: Simon and Schuster, 2015), 327; David M. Halbfinger, "Jack Valenti, 85, Confidant of a President and Stars, Dies," *New York Times*, April 27, 2007, C10.

315 **"Walter, alone among":** Jack Valenti, interviewed by Joe B. Frantz, February 19, 1971, Oral Histories, LBJ Library.

315 **"my vice president":** Bart Barnes, "LBJ Aide Walter Jenkins Dies," *Washington Post*, November 26, 1985, C4.

315 **seven cabinet members:** White, *Making of the President, 1964*, 367.

315 **Tipsy from all:** Report on Walter Wilson Jenkins, October 1964, FBI file no. 61–2848–960.

316 **October 13:** Faye Haskins, *The Evening Star: The Rise and Fall of a Great Washington Newspaper* (Lanham, MD: Rowman and Littlefield, 2019), 204–5.

316 **Reedy was in New York:** Liz Carpenter, interviewed by Joe B. Frantz, August 27, 1969, Oral Histories, LBJ Library.

316 **covered the White House:** Enid Nemy, "Liz Carpenter, Journalist, Feminist and Johnson Aide, Dies at 89," *New York Times*, March 20, 2010, A22.

316 **"Walter, I know":** Carpenter, interviewed by Frantz.

317 **saved Johnson's hide:** Lewis Wood, "Texas Ballot Writ Is Stayed by Black," *New York Times*, September 29, 1948, 22.

317 **stole—the Democratic nomination:** Robert A. Caro, *The Years of Lyndon Johnson*, vol. 2, *Means of Ascent* (New York: Alfred A. Knopf, 1991), 303–17.

317 **When Bobby Baker:** Caro, *Passage of Power*, 277–78.

317 **one of the first people:** Linda Greenhouse, "Ex-Justice Abe Fortas Dies at 71; Shaped Historic Rulings on Rights," *New York Times*, April 7, 1982, A1.

317 **"I'm in terrible trouble":** David Wise, "'O, No, Not Walter!'—LBJ," *Boston Globe*, October 18, 1964, 1.

317 **Jenkins lurched:** Clark Clifford, with Richard Holbrooke, *Counsel to the President: A Memoir* (New York: Random House, 1991), 399.

317 **special counsel:** Marilyn Berger, "Clark Clifford, a Major Adviser to Four Presidents, Is Dead at 91," *New York Times*, October 11, 1998, 1.

317 **"rescuing American presidents":** James Reston, "Pray Silence for Mr. Clark Clifford," *New York Times*, June 20, 1969, 40.

318 **grim procession:** Clifford and Holbrooke, *Counsel to the President*, 399.

318 **"Treat it":** Russell Freeburg, "Reveal FBI Told Jenkins Facts," *Chicago Tribune*, October 17, 1964, 7.

318 **After calling:** Michael Beschloss, ed., *Reaching for Glory: Lyndon Johnson's Secret White House Tapes, 1964–1965* (New York: Simon and Schuster, 2001), 54.

318 **"Mr. President, this is Abe":** Lyndon Johnson and Abe Fortas, 3:56 p.m., October 14, 1964, Citation no. 5876, Presidential Recordings Project, LBJ Recordings, Miller Center, Charlottesville, VA (hereafter "LBJ Recordings").

319 **"spoke in the":** George Reedy, interviewed by T. H. Baker, December 20, 1968, Oral Histories, LBJ Library.

319 **"an absolute blow":** Valenti, interviewed by Frantz, February 19, 1971.

319 **variety of analogies:** Beschloss, *Reaching for Glory*, 81; United Press International, "LBJ's Views of Jenkins, Baker Cases," *San Francisco Examiner*, October 25, 1964, 1; Goodwin, *Lyndon Johnson*, 208.

319 **"like being a jackass":** Leo Janos, "The Last Days of the President," *The Atlantic Monthly*, July 1973, 40.

319 **"frame deal":** Johnson and Fortas, 3:56 p.m., October 14, 1964, LBJ Recordings.

319 **"I've been called by Republican headquarters":** Carpenter, interviewed by Frantz, 33.

320 **"We had a hand in killing":** Robert Shesol, *Mutual Contempt: Lyndon Johnson, Robert Kennedy, and the Feud That Defined a Decade* (New York: W. W. Norton, 1997), 131.

320 **"Well, you don't foresee,"** Johnson and Fortas, 3:56 p.m., October 14, 1964, LBJ Recordings.

320 **as Johnson was paying a courtesy call:** As Johnson would later recall in a phone conversation with the former First Lady, it was difficult for him to converse with her while "all the time my mind was down there about who was going to jail that night." Lyndon Johnson and Jacqueline Kennedy, 4:56 p.m., March 26, 1965, Citation no. 7158, LBJ Recordings.

320 **"There is a report sweeping Washington":** Max Frankel, "President's Aide Quits on Report of Morals Case," *New York Times*, October 15, 1964, 1.

320 **"the Presidency is at stake":** Lyndon Johnson and Clark Clifford, 8:02 p.m., October 14, 1964, Citation no. 5886, LBJ Recordings.

320 **"It'll be harmful":** Lyndon Johnson and John Connally, 8:45 p.m., October 14, 1964, Citation no. 5882, LBJ Recordings.

320 **DeLoach interacted daily:** DeLoach, interviewed by Gillette, January 11, 1991.

320 **wiretapping the African American activists:** David J. Garrow, *The FBI and Martin Luther King, Jr.: From "Solo" to Memphis* (New York: W. W. Norton, 1981), 119.

320 **installing a secret recording device:** DeLoach, *Hoover's FBI*, 380–81,

320 **"Who is supposed to have been":** Lyndon Johnson and Cartha "Deke" DeLoach, October 14, 1964, 9:00 p.m., Citation no. 5884, LBJ Recordings.

321 **urinating in the congressional parking lot:** Caro, *Master of the Senate*, 586.

321 **"Jumbo":** Caro, *Master of the Senate*, 122.

321 **"would drag the name":** John Cooney, *The American Pope: The Life and Times of Francis Cardinal Spellman* (New York: Times Books, 1984), 109.

321 **the object of his affection:** Loughery, *Other Side of Silence*, 152.

321 **Reedy tearfully announced:** Mary McGrory, "Johnson Shaken by Events," *Evening Star*, October 15, 1964, 13; Clifford and Holbrooke, *Counselor to the President*, 400–401; White, *Making of the President, 1964*, 369.

321 **nearly an hour after:** Pearson, *Diaries: 1960–1969*, 257.

321 **raspy, crestfallen voice:** Woods, *LBJ*, 548.

322 **"the one thing that just might snatch":** Henry Gemmill, "The Jenkins Affair," *Wall Street Journal*, October 16, 1964, 1.

322 **While it was natural:** Arthur Krock, "The Jenkins Case," *New York Times*, October 18, 1964, E11.

322 **"It would be unfortunate":** Ben A. Franklin, "Ex-Homosexual Got U.S. Job Back," *New York Times*, October 18, 1964, 54.

322 **"The post-Jenkins atmosphere in Washington":** Bradlee to Nation, Bernstein, Martin, October 14, 1964, Folder 4, Box 6, Benjamin C. Bradlee Papers, Harry Ransom Center, University of Texas at Austin (hereafter "Bradlee Papers").

323 **"Some things, like loyalty to friends"**: Barry M. Goldwater, with Jack Casserly, *Goldwater* (New York: Doubleday, 1988), 204.

323 **"a pitiful, sordid situation"**: Associated Press, "White House Cloud Darker, Miller Holds," *Chicago Tribune*, October 22, 1964, 8.

323 **"not stand for immorality"**: United Press International, "Jenkins Report Sought by Nixon," *New York Times*, October 16, 1964, 25.

323 **"What a way to win"**: Robert Dallek, *Flawed Giant: Lyndon Johnson and His Times, 1961–1973* (New York: Oxford University Press, 1998), 181.

323 **memo from J. Edgar Hoover to Acting Attorney General:** Director to Acting Attorney General, October 28, 1964, FBI file no. 62–109747–1.

323 **Reedy nonetheless spent an entire day:** George Reedy, interviewed by T. H. Baker, December 20, 1968, Oral Histories, LBJ Library.

324 **waiters at the *Newsweek* party:** Goodwin, *Lyndon Johnson*, 269. Drew Pearson fed this paranoia, telling the president that a Republican operative named Lou Guylay had come to Washington to entrap Jenkins. Pearson's legman, Jack Anderson, obtained an affidavit from the boyfriend of Guylay's daughter claiming this, but the young man later claimed to be joking. Pearson, *Diaries, 1960–1969*, 264–66.

324 **perhaps Andy Choka:** Beschloss, *Reaching for Glory*, 79.

324 **Johnson instructed the FBI to prove:** William C. Sullivan, with Bill Brown, *The Bureau: My Thirty Years in Hoover's FBI* (New York: W. W. Norton, 1979), 68.

324 **"I can't begin to count"**: Mildred Stegall, "LBJ as I Knew Him," 1996, Stegall Files.

324 **"pull something"**: Shesol, *Mutual Contempt*, 245. It was only a matter of time before Walter Jenkins found his his way into Jim Garrison's intricate fairy tale. One night over dinner with his mother and a journalist, Garrison marveled at the publicity his case would receive were he to name Jenkins as a participant in the plot, thereby establishing a link between the murderous homosexual conspiracy that assassinated Kennedy and his devious successor. "Oh, do do that Jim," Garrison's mother goaded. "I think that would be a wonderful idea" (Thomas Bethell, diary entry, October 26, 1967, at "Inside the Garrison Investigation: The Thomas Bethel Diary," http://mcadams.posc.mu.edu/bethell3.htm).

324 **"had the same type of problem"**: Rowland Evans and Robert Novak, *Lyndon B. Johnson: The Exercise of Power* (New York: New American Library, 1966), 505.

324 **"We Democrats felt sorry"**: United Press International, "Ike Says He Knows of No Case Similar to Jenkins's in His Terms," *Washington Post*, October 30, 1964, A2.

324 **"It would have been better"**: Lyndon Johnson and Nicholas Katzenbach, 7:52 a.m., October 29, 1964, LBJ Recordings.

324 **dispersed nearly one hundred agents:** Tom Wicker, "Jenkins Cleared of Security Slip in F.B.I. Report," *New York Times*, October 22, 1964, 1.

324 **Jenkins had walked:** Report on Walter Wilson Jenkins, October 1964.

325 **FBI director had sent a bouquet:** Ben A. Franklin, "Hoover Assailed on Jenkins Case," *New York Times*, October 28, 1964, 34.

325 **"The Republicans, of course"**: Pearson, *Diaries: 1960–1969*, 262.

325 **Most men who engaged:** Humphreys, *Tearoom Trade*, 104–30.

325 **"Does Jenkins really stand"**: Bradlee to Bernstein, Elliott, "N 17 Violin," Folder 4, Container 6, Bradlee Papers.

325 **"There is still an air"**: Sarah McClendon, "Remarks Indicate Baker Knew About Aide's Past," *Houston Tribune*, October 22, 1964, 12.

325 **"cracked under the strain"**: Robert Dallek, *Lyndon B. Johnson: Portrait of a President* (Oxford: Oxford University Press, 2004), 188.

325 **"I guess we've all been so tired"**: Lyndon Johnson and Palmer Hoyt on 16 October 1964, Conversation 5900, LBJ Recordings.

326 **"[i]nvariably the subject of discussion"**: Stegall, "LBJ as I Knew Him."

326 **"Many persons claim to be"**: Richard L. Worsnop, "Homosexuality: Morals and Security," *Editorial Research Reports 1963*, vol. 2 (Washington, DC: CQ Press, 1963).

326 **"There are some people who walk"**: President Johnson and J. Edgar Hoover, October 31, 1964, 10:35 a.m., from Beschloss, *Reaching for Glory*, 101. To Johnson's recounting of this advice from

Hoover, Robert Kennedy joked, "Well, what does that mean, that you'll watch the cabinet carefully as they walk into the cabinet meeting?" The idea of the commander in chief warily evaluating the gait of his cabinet secretaries for signs of latent homosexuality elicited peals of laughter from both men, usually locked in a state of unrelenting animosity. "One thing I can assure you of, Mr. President, it isn't me," Kennedy promised the president. Eugene H. Nickerson, interviewed by Roberta Greene, May 2, 1972, Robert F. Kennedy Oral History Program, JFK Library, 14.

326 **"for every obvious homosexual"**: "Homosexuality in America," 66.

326 **"small visible layer"**: White, "Those Others," E3.

326 **"why there was so much homosexuality"**: Pearson, *Diaries: 1960–1969*, 267.

327 **"I would like to do"**: President Johnson and Lady Bird Johnson, 9:12 a.m., October 15, 1964, Citation no. 5895, LBJ Recordings.

327 **"Some of us have mentally retarded"**: Beschloss, *Reaching for Glory*, 63.

327 **whose neighbors were pitching**: "Neighbors Offer Services to Assist Walter Jenkins," *Washington Post*, October 25, 1964, A8.

327 **"I think a gesture of support"**: President Johnson and Lady Bird Johnson, 9:12 a.m., October 15, 1964.

328 **"Dear Walter"**: Lady Bird Johnson to Walter Jenkins, October 15, 2020, Alpha File, Box 1022, White House Social Files, LBJ Library.

328 **"like a vessel under"**: Miller, *Lyndon*, 400.

328 **"My heart is aching today"**: Lawrence Stern, "LBJ Orders FBI Probe on Jenkins," *Washington Post*, October 16, 1964, A1.

328 **"tend to have practical"**: Carl Sferrazza Anthony, author interview, April 17, 2019, Los Angeles.

328 **"faithful retainer became a nonperson"**: Clifford and Holbrooke, *Counsel to the President*, 402.

21: "Gone and Forgotten"

330 **"anxious" to have the matter**: Hoover to staff, October 16, 1964, FBI file no. 161–2854–1.

330 **"HANDLE WITH EXPERIENCED AGENTS"**: Director, FBI to SAC, San Antonio, October 16, 1964, FBI file no. 161–2854–3.

330 **"Who needs it?"**: SAs Maurice F. Dean and Lewis E. Ross, October 17, 1964, FBI file no. 161-HQ-2854.

330 **"very effeminate and queer"**: SAC, WFO to Director and SAC Minneapolis, October 17, 1964, FBI file no. 161–2854–57.

330 **"swishes" while he walks**: SAs Robert J. Perry and Albert N. Nencioni, October 18, 1964, FBI file no. 161-HQ-2854.

330 **"first impression of Waldron"**: SAs Coleman Mabray and Ronald E. Brinkley, October 21, 1964, FBI file no. 161-HQ-2854

330 **"dates a different girl"**: SAs Nichols and Van Wagenen, October 17, 1964. For more on John Richard Nichols Sr., see Douglas M. Charles, "'A Source of Great Embarrassment to the Bureau': Gay Activist Jack Nichols, His FBI Agent Father, and the Mattachine Society of Washington," *Historian* 79, no. 3 (Fall 2017): 504–22.

331 **ran a check of military personnel records**: SAs Nichols and Van Wagenen, October 17, 1964.

331 **"very much worried"**: C. A. Evans to A. H. Belmont, October 17, 1964, FBI file no. 161–2854–66. According to a letter from the air force general who recommended Waldron for his commission, dated July 13, 1961, "[t]he Vice President has expressed personal interest" in the matter "and it was at his request that expeditious action was taken" to effectuate it. F. L. Vidal, "Appointments in the Air Force Under Paragraph 6c, AFM 36–5," July 13, 1961, FBI file no. 161-HQ-2854.

332 **"a household word"**: Homer Bigart, "J. Edgar Hoover: 40 Years the No. 1 Policeman," *New York Times*, May 10, 1964, 58.

333 **"Keep in mind"**: Evans to Belmont, October 17, 1964.

333 **"Throughout my life"**: San Antonio to Director, October 17, 1964, FBI file no. 161–2854–53.

333 **When the FBI agents questioned him**: SAs Johnson and Carlson, October 17, 1964, SA FBI file no. 161-HQ-2854. The next day, a pair of FBI agents interviewed the former Johnson staffer in a parked car several blocks away from his house, out of earshot of his family. "Terribly shocked," the man adamantly denied Waldron's charge. He then demonstrated for the agents Waldron's manner-

isms by swinging his hands "excessively in such a manner that these actions would be construed as effeminate." While confessing that he did "not know the gauge for masculinity," he did find Waldron's voice to be "funny" (October 18, 1964, FBI file no. 161-HQ-2854).

334 **Incidentally, that same day:** D. J. Brennan to Sullivan, October 18, 1964, FBI file no. 161-2854-105.

334 **"might unnecessarily inflame the situation":** Brennan to Sullivan, October 18, 1964.

334 **"most guarded manner":** W. V. Cleveland to Rowland Evans, FBI memo, October 19, 1964, FBI file no. 161-2854-130.

335 **"with the exception of the inscription":** SAC, WFO to Director, FBI, Airtel, October 20, 1964, FBI file no. 161-2854-133.

335 **omitting any details regarding:** Cleveland to Evans, October 23, 1964.

335 **"which contains numerous references":** W. V. Cleveland to Mr. Gale, January 27, 1965, FBI file no. 161-2854-187.

335 **On October 18, the FBI reinterviewed Waldron:** San Antonio to Director, October 18, 1964, FBI file no. 161-2854-20.

336 **Waldron cut the interview short:** W. V. Cleveland to Rowland Evans, October 19, 1964, FBI file no. 161-2854-15.

336 **In the summer of 1954:** Bill Moyers, "No, I Wasn't a Party to J. Edgar Hoover's Exploits," *Wall Street Journal*, February 26, 2009, A12.

336 **"If I had a boy":** Eric Frederick Goldman, *The Tragedy of Lyndon Johnson* (New York: Alfred A. Knopf, 1969), 108.

336 **youngest presidential appointee in history:** Don Oberdorfer, "The Man Who Speaks for LBJ," *The Saturday Evening Post*, October 23, 1965, 33.

336 **"Whatever he does":** Goldman, *Tragedy of Lyndon Johnson*, 109.

336 **Johnson brought onto his White House staff:** Tom Wicker, "Princeton Historian Named 'Idea Man' at the White House," *New York Times*, February 4, 1961, 1.

336 **"classic story of the young man in a hurry":** Goldman, *Tragedy of Lyndon Johnson*, 108.

336 **Moyers had collaborated with Deke DeLoach:** Garrow, *FBI and Martin Luther King, Jr.*, 119.

336 **"architect" of the infamous "Daisy" commercial:** Patrick Anderson, *The Presidents' Men: White House Assistants of Franklin D. Roosevelt, Harry S. Truman, Dwight D. Eisenhower, John F. Kennedy and Lyndon B. Johnson* (Garden City, NY: Doubleday, 1968), 321.

336 **homosexuality among members of Goldwater's Senate staff:** William Sullivan to John Dean, January 31, 1975, in *Select Committee to Study Governmental Operations with Respect to Intelligence Activities, Hearings*, 94th Cong., 1st Sess., vol. 6 (Washington, DC: US Government Printing Office, 1976), 539, exhibit 52. The Moyers request was first reported in 1975 when Attorney General Edward H. Levi revealed the existence of J. Edgar Hoover's "official and confidential" files, a vast compendium, spanning decades, of derogatory information about public figures. Testifying before the House Judiciary Committee, Levi said the files indicated "misuse of the resources" of the FBI, one instance of which was "a check of FBI files on the staff of a campaign opponent" undertaken during the Johnson administration. After Deputy Attorney General Laurence Silberman identified Moyers as the Johnson aide who had made the request, an "outraged" Moyers called Silberman charging that the memo was a forgery concocted by the CIA. When Silberman offered to launch an investigation into the memo's provenance, Moyers backed down. "I was very young," he pleaded. "How will I explain this to my children?" In 2005, Silberman clarified that the damaging information Moyers sought was "evidence of homosexual activity." Nicholas M. Horrock, "Levi Details Wide Scope of Hoover's Secret Files," *New York Times*, February 28, 1975, 1; Lawrence Meyer, "Hoover Kept Secret Files on 17 Hill Figures," *Washington Post*, February 28, 1975, A1; Laurence H. Silberman, "Hoover's Institution," *Wall Street Journal*, July 20, 2005, A12.

337 **"Bill Moyers knew about it":** Beschloss, *Reaching for Glory*, 97.

337 **investigate on the suspicion that he was gay:** Joe Stephens, "Valenti's Sexuality Was Topic for FBI," *Washington Post*, February 19, 2009, A1.

337 **Moyers had asked the FBI:** C. D. DeLoach to J. Edgar Hoover, November 27, 1964, FBI file no. 161-2641.

337 **"No harm came to a single person":** Bill Moyers, "Moyers Responds to Slate," *Slate*, February 24, 2009.

337 **"continuous and enveloping drive for power and status":** Goldman, *Tragedy of Lyndon Johnson*, 109.

337 **Within the next twenty minutes:** President Lyndon B. Johnson's Daily Diary, October 18, 1964, LBJ Library.

337 **Pickle accepted Waldron's resignation:** San Antonio to Director, October 19, 1964, FBI file no. 161–2854–112.

337 **Jenkins drafted a statement:** Walter Jenkins, undated version of final document dated October 24, 1964, Folder: "Jenkins Investigation," Box 29A, Stegall Files, LBJ Library. Jenkins was released from the hospital November 9. "Jenkins Rests at Home After Hospital Release," Herald Tribune Service, November 11, 1964.

338 **investigation of Bob Waldron:** J. Edgar Hoover to William D. Moyers, "Robert Earl Waldron," October 27, 1964, FBI file no. 161–2854–180. Though the threat that Bob Waldron posed to Lyndon Johnson's reelection seemed to be contained, Moyers did not leave anything to chance. Four days before Election Day, he instructed the FBI to hold off on sending a copy of its report to the Defense Department as there "were too many mentions of President Johnson's name in this investigation" and Moyers feared it would be leaked. The day after the election, a relieved Moyers had his assistant authorize the FBI to release the report to Secretary McNamara. Moyers was far less restrained about airing the sexual secrets of his political adversaries. Just a few weeks after this episode, he authorized the extensive, government-wide dissemination of FBI surveillance concerning the sex life of Rev. Dr. Martin Luther King Jr. C. D. DeLoach to Mohr, October 30, 1964, FBI file no. 161–2854–177; W. V. Cleveland to Rowland Evans, November 6, 1964, FBI file no. 161–2854–179; Garrow, *FBI and Martin Luther King, Jr.*, 131.

338 **Within three days:** Austin C. Wehrwein, "Global Events Seen Overshadowing Jenkins Case in Midwest," *New York Times*, October 19, 1964, 19.

338 **88 percent of Americans were aware:** Louis Harris, "Introducing Today: Lou Harris Survey," *Sioux City (IA) Journal*, October 23, 1964, 1.

338 **Fifty-nine percent:** Harris, "Introducing Today: Lou Harris Survey," 1.

338 **102 swing state voters:** Rowland Evans and Robert Novak, "Reaction to Jenkins Is Small," *Washington Post*, October 19, 1964, A17.

338 **"Why should it?":** Evans and Novak, *Lyndon B. Johnson*, 515.

338 **"The really remarkable thing":** Carpenter, interviewed by Frantz, August 27, 1969.

339 **five-dollar bill:** H. N. Pankey to George Reedy, October 15, 1964, White House Central Files, FG 11–8–1, Box 88, LBJ Library.

339 **"Not for the first time":** Clifford and Holbrooke, *Counsel to the President*, 402.

339 **"shabby double-dealing":** Drury, *Advise and Consent*, 456.

339 **"I thought I could make him more like me":** Frank Mankiewicz, interviewed by Larry J. Hackman, August 12, 1969, Oral History Program, JFK Library.

339 **Johnson was still privately fuming:** Goldman, *Tragedy of Lyndon Johnson*, 250.

339 **two things he most looked forward to:** Joseph A. Califano Jr., *The Triumph and Tragedy of Lyndon Johnson: The White House Years* (New York: Simon and Schuster, 1991), 281.

339 **fulfilled both pledges:** Janos, "Last Days of the President," 40; Mark E. Feeney, "The Triumph and Tragedy of Walter Jenkins, LBJ's Alter Ego," *Hartford Courant*, December 22, 1999, 44. Along with the Martin-Mitchell defection, the Jenkins saga inspired a major plot point in a popular 1968 novel, *Vanished*, wherein the president's chief advisor, "in a mixture of sexual aberration and warped ideology," absconds with his male lover "to a Communist country where, in due time, they would be paraded before TV cameras as examples of Western decadence." The book was adapted into a 1971 television miniseries. Fletcher Knebel, *Vanished* (New York: Avon, 1968), 212–13.

340 **enrolled at the New York School of Design:** "R. F. Waldron, Johnson Aide, Designer, Dies," *Washington Post*, December 10, 1995, B8. In January 1965, the FBI contacted Waldron to see if he would testify against the former colleague then working at the Commerce Department with whom he had had sex and against whom removal procedures had been initiated. Waldron refused, saying he was "appalled to learn that in handling the investigation relative to himself in Washington, D.C., the FBI had divulged information furnished by him in confidence to various friends in this area." He said he had "lost faith" in the Bureau, would not "furnish any information to representatives of the FBI regarding any matter,"

and intended to "express his feelings" to J. Edgar Hoover himself. The next month, Senate Rules Committee ranking Republican Carl Curtis of Nebraska released a list of questions he wanted Walter Jenkins to answer, one of which pertained to whether he had ever worked with the army colonel arrested for solicitation in the YMCA bathroom the day before his own arrest, and another to his associations with Waldron. Presumably, the names of the colonel and Waldron were leaked to Curtis by the FBI. SAC WFO to Director, January 11, 1965, FBI file no. 161–2854–185; Clark Mollenhoff, "Curtis Bares Questions in Jenkins Case," *Des Moines Register*, February 27, 1965, 1.

340 **"I don't think there was ever a kinder man"**: Waldron, interviewed by Gillette, January 28, 1976.

340 **"I went to the president and said"**: Jura Koncius and Patricia Dane Rogers, "Recalling the Waldron Style," *Washington Post*, January 4, 1996, 9.

340 **"homosexuality is the most disturbing security problem"**: Robert S. Allen and Paul Scott, "Allen-Scott Report," *Las Vegas Sun*, November 2, 1964.

340 **addressed his African American chauffer as "nigger"**: Robert Parker, with Richard Rashke, *Capitol Hill in Black and White* (New York: Dodd, Mead, 1986), v.

341 **"gone and forgotten"**: C. D. DeLoach memo, November 18, 1964, FBI file no. 161–2854–19.

22: The Fruit Loop

342 **"thought they must be totally reckless"**: Edward Alwood, *Straight News: Gays, Lesbians, and the News Media* (New York: Columbia University Press, 1996), 13.

343 **illegal everywhere except Illinois;** Eskridge, *Dishonorable Passions*, 124–27.

343 **"Many persons who may in one degree"**: "Misplaced Morality," *Washington Post*, January 21, 1964, A12.

343 **"that master of morality"**: "Piety by Fiat," *Washington Post*, March 9, 1964, A14.

343 **"This series of articles"**: White, "Those Others," E1.

343 **"the most astute"**: "Cross-Currents," *The Ladder*, April 1965, 19.

343 **"Focus on Homosexuality"**: Tony Jackubosky, "Washington File," *The Advocate*, March 31–April 13, 1971, 4; see *Washington Post* on August 22, 1970, C9.

344 **"If you're asking for"**: Chap. 7 in *Memoirs of Jack Nichols*.

344 **convincing by Eva Freund:** Lou Chibbaro Jr., "Our Fighting Founders," *Washington Blade*, November 21, 1986, 13.

344 **FIFTEEN MILLION U.S. HOMOSEXUALS:** "News Bulletin," Folder 14, Box 85, Kameny Papers.

344 **"Your letter of August 28"**: Charles E. Chamberlain to Franklin Edward Kameny August 30, 1962, Folder 5, Box 85, Kameny Papers.

344 **"This is a matter on which"**: *Committee on the District of Columbia, Subcommittee No. 4, Amending District of Columbia Charitable Solicitation Act*, 88th Cong., 1st Sess. (August 8, 1963) (hereafter cited as "Dowdy Hearings"), 28. At a conference of regional homophile groups held in October 1964 at Washington's Sheraton Park hotel (chosen after four other hotels refused to host the event), the organizers presented a citation in absentia to Dowdy, who had "caused more attention to be called to the homosexual problem than anyone else" (Jean White, "Homophile Groups Argue Civil Liberties," *Washington Post*, October 11, 1964, B10).

345 **He installed two phones:** Kuntzler, "Frank Kameny Remembrance."

345 **"unless and until"**: "Civil Liberties: A Progress Report," *New York Mattachine Newsletter* 10 (January 1965): 7–22.

345 **"A soldier with a wide smile"**: Jack Nichols, "Lige Clarke (1942–1975)," from *Before Stonewall*, 233–36.

345 **inspired Clarke to action:** Chap. 7 in *Memoirs of Jack Nichols*.

345 **an article appeared in the *New York Times*:** Paul Hofmann, "Cuban Government Is Alarmed by Increase in Homosexuality," *New York Times*, April 16, 1965, 2.

345 **"We can't let him get away"**: *Memoirs of Jack Nichols*.

345 **severed diplomatic ties with the Communist country:** E. W. Kenworthy, "Regime Is Scored," *New York Times*, January 4, 1961, 1.

346 **"In order to make any impression"**: Lilli Vincenz, interviewed by Mark Meinke, April 21, 2001, transcript, Rainbow History Project, Washington, DC.

346 **"Only a very few hostile remarks"**: "News Bulletin," Folder 14, Box 85, Kameny Papers.

346 **only one media outlet:** "10 Oppose Gov't on Homosexuals," *Washington Afro-American*, April 20, 1965, 18.

346 **the much larger protest:** "Viet-Nam War Protest Is Staged by 16,000," *Washington Post*, April 18, 1965, A1.

346 **"Nothing like these demonstrations":** "'We're on the Move Now . . . ,'" *Eastern Mattachine Magazine* 10, no. 5, June 1965, 4.

346 **"the most important day of my life":** Dolinsky, "Lesbian and Gay DC," 95–96.

346 **distributed flyers to local tour bus operators:** "Information Bulletin," Mattachine Society of New York, Reel 18, Mattachine Society, Inc. of New York Records, Manuscripts and Archives Division, New York Public Library.

346 **a steady flow:** Eva Freund, author interview.

346 **This time, the Associated Press:** Alwood, *Straight News*, 54.

346 **twenty-five Mattachine members:** "Information Bulletin," June 26, 1965, Folder 13, Box 85, Kameny Papers.

347 **by October, forty-five:** "Information Bulletin," October 23, 1965, Box 102, Folder 14, Barbara Gittings and Kay Tobin Lahusen Gay History Papers and Photographs, Manuscripts and Archives Division, New York Public Library (hereafter "Gittings Papers").

347 **men in civilian clothing:** Freund, "Lesbian in the Early Gay Movement."

347 **"Go fuck yourself":** Otto Ulrich, interviewed by Mark Meinke, July 27, 2001, transcript, Rainbow History Project, Washington, DC.

347 **"a self-declared 'minority group'":** "Secretary Rusk's News Conference of August 27," *Department of State Bulletin* LIII, no. 1369 (September 20, 1965).

347 **"I see no similarity":** Richard A. Inman to Bill Moyers, January 26, 1966, Name File M, Box 167, White House Central Files, LBJ Library.

348 **As a fourteen-year-old boy:** Hugh Key, author interview, March 1, 2019, Key West, FL.

348 **twenty-four-man crew:** Marie Smith, "Sequoia Décor to Get LBJ Brand," *Washington Post*, February 28, 1964, C3.

348 **"hang-up on the toilet paper holder":** Waldron, interviewed by Gillette, February 1, 1976.

348 **First used by President Herbert Hoover:** Ken W. Sayers, *Uncommon Warriors: 200 Years of the Most Unusual Naval Vessels* (Annapolis, MD: Naval Institute Press, 2012), 16.

349 **first discussed the sharing of atomic technology:** J. A. Fox, "Truman Seeks Foreign Policy Unchanged by Political Ties," *Evening Star*, November 11, 1945, 1.

349 **used the yacht to hash out:** Geoffrey C. De Tingo, *Eisenhower's Pursuit of Strategy: The Importance of Understanding the Influence of Leadership Styles on Strategic Decision Makers* (Fort Leavenworth, KS: School of Advanced Military Studies, United States Army Command and General Staff College, 2013), 33–34

349 **celebrated his forty-sixth:** Associated Press, "Kennedy at 46: Busy, Cheerful 'Father of the Year,'" *New York Times*, May 30, 1963, 1.

349 **installed a king-size bed:** "Nonprofit Trust Rescues Presidential Yacht," *Los Angeles Times*, June 19, 1986, 2.

349 **served as Morgan's best man:** "Lt. Cmdr. Morgan, Sandra Spurgeon Wed in Virginia," *Bridgeport Post*, July 14, 1968, 30.

349 **restrooms at the . . . department stores:** Guy Ross, author interview, March 1, 2019, Key West, FL.

349 **created in 1963:** Zlati Meyer, "Cereal Makers Hope to Charm Millennials, Not Just Youngsters," *Des Moines Register*, June 17, 2017, B4.

349 **"a prime daytime extravaganza":** Nichols, *Tomcat Chronicles*, 196.

350 **"By remaining silent":** United Press, "Flanders Supported," *New York Times*, May 13, 1954, 8.

350 **A liberal who supported:** Joseph P. Fried, "Peter Frelinghuysen Jr., 95, Former Congressman, Dies," *New York Times*, May 23, 2011, B17.

350 **The plainclothes policeman:** SAs David W. Bowers and Eugene C. Gles, May 12, 1966, FBI file no. WFO 166–590.

351 **"show some guts":** Lloyd Wendt, "The Vilest of Rackets," *Esquire*, April 1950, 53, 140–42. Ironically, by the mid-1960's Washington was one of the few places where the police had adopted a more enlightened attitude toward combatting the scourge of homosexual blackmail. In 1964, the MSW secretary penned a letter to the *Washington Post* to "commend" Roy Blick and Louis Fochett for their

cooperation in a case involving a gay blackmail victim. "Without condoning violations of the law thereby, we have stated, publicly, that in those rare instances in which homosexuals find themselves subjected to attempted blackmail or extortion, they need not fear going to the Police Department for assistance" (Bruce Schuyler, "Commendation," *Washington Post*, January 20, 1964, A12).

351 **distributing leaflets at gay bars:** *Blackmailer at Work in Dupont Circle Area* and *How to Handle Blackmail*, 1969, Folder 4, Box 80, Kameny Papers.

351 **"check play":** SAs Robert T. Tolan and Redacted, June 6, 1966, FBI file no. 166-1818-40.

352 **extorted hundreds of thousands of dollars:** "Extortionist Gets Maximum Five Years," *New York Times*, July 12, 1967, 31.

352 **university deans, professors, businessmen:** Jack Roth, "Blackmail Paid by Congressman," *New York Times*, May 17, 1967, 1.

352 **high-profile assigments:** "U.S. Lists Ten U.N. Delegates," *Washington Post*, September 23, 1965, A25; Louis B. Fleming, "A Congressman Goes International," *Washington Post*, December 26, 1965, E4; "Africa Shift Urged by Congress Group," *New York Times*, May 2, 1966, 74.

352 **he was quietly removed:** William McGowan, "The Chickens and the Bulls," *Slate*, July 11, 2012.

352 **targeted in the same manner:** McGowan, "Chickens and the Bulls."

352 **drove to a Maryland motel:** "Suicide Ruled in Death of Adm. William Church," *Evening Star*, December 16, 1965, 36.

352 **"I don't think my mother":** Chase Church, email to author, November 13, 2019.

23: Scandal in Sacramento

353 **"My God":** Lou Cannon, *Ronnie and Jesse: A Political Odyssey* (Garden City, NY: Doubleday, 1969), 183.

353 **"Golly, are you quitting all at once":** Lyn Nofziger, *Nofziger* (Washington, DC: Regnery Gateway, 1992), 77–78.

353 **"my strong right arm":** Lou Cannon, *Governor Reagan: His Rise to Power* (New York: PublicAffairs, 2003), 239.

353 **"deputy governor":** Cannon, *Governor Reagan*, 240.

354 **"men in high places":** Leland L. Nichols, interviewed by Donald B. Seney, State Government Oral History Program, Office of the Secretary of State, California State Archives.

354 **his standard outfit:** Lee Lescaze, "Reagan's Press Secretary Takes His Leave," *Washington Post*, December 1, 1980, A7; John Gizzi, "Lyn Nofziger, Loyal Reaganite," *Human Events* 62, no. 12 (2006): 20.

354 **"dressed like a refugee":** Lou Cannon, "Lyn Nofziger, R.I.P.," *National Review*, April 24, 2006, 58.

354 **"a meeting of Reagan aides"** Nofziger, *Nofziger*, 77.

355 **"We knew in our minds":** Nofziger, *Nofziger*, 77.

355 **Nofziger compiled all the innuendo:** Cannon, *Governor Reagan*, 243.

355 **Nofziger's hands began to shake:** Cannon, *Governor Reagan*, 244.

355 **"What do we do now?"** Nofziger, *Nofziger*, 78.

355 **"There are innocent wives and children":** Cannon, *Ronnie and Jessie*, 186.

355 **"I want to sleep on this":** Cannon, *Governor Reagan*, 244.

355 **"Those of us Reaganites":** Lyn Nofziger, interviewed by Stephen F. Knott and Russell Riley, March 6, 2003, Ronald Reagan Oral History Project, Presidential Oral History Program, Miller Center.

356 **"kitchen cabinet":** Constance L. Hays, "Holmes Tuttle, 83, of Reagan's 'Kitchen Cabinet,'" *New York Times*, June 18, 1989, A30.

356 **suspected another motive behind their abrupt departure:** Bill Boyarsky, "Battaglia's Departure Remains a Mystery," Associated Press, September 11, 1967.

356 **"Why doesn't someone do something about Phil?":** Cannon, *Governor Reagan*, 247.

356 **Nofziger told reporters:** Tom Wicker, "Reagan Rebutted on Aides' Ouster," *New York Times*, November 5, 1967, 1.

356 **"[W]hat I thought no reporter or columnist":** Nofziger, *Nofziger*, 94.

356 **a blind item appeared:** "A Scandal at the Top," *Newsweek*, October 30, 1967, 15.

357 **"82 percent accurate":** William V. Shannon, "The Sol Hurok of the Washington Press Corps," *New York Times Book Review*, April 29, 1973, 4.

357 **"Scandal in Sacramento":** Drew Pearson and Jack Anderson, "Scandal in Sacramento," *New York Post*, October 31, 1967.

357 **Kemp had spent the summer off-season:** Bill Stall, "Pro QB Jackie Kemp Learns Politics Is a Rough Game," *Santa Cruz Sentinel*, July 11, 1967. This Associated Press story appeared in dozens of newspapers.

357 **Although most of the papers in Pearson's syndicate:** Donald A. Ritchie, *The Columnist: Leaks, Lies, and Libel in Drew Pearson's Washington* (Oxford: Oxford University Press, 2021), 264.

358 **tussled with the columnist:** Drew Pearson, "The Washington Merry-Go-Round," Bell-McClure Syndicate, June 17, 1961.

358 **pounding the table in anger:** Martin Smith, "Reagan Blasts Report of Homosexual Aides," *Sacramento Bee*, October 31, 1967, 1.

358 **A reporter asked if Nofziger:** Press Conference, October 31, 1967, Box P01, Reagan, Ronald: Gubernatorial Papers, 1966–1974: Press Unit, Ronald Reagan Presidential Library, Simi Valley, CA (hereafter "Reagan Library").

358 **"there's no use hurting people":** Pearson, *Diaries: 1960–1969*, 509.

358 **"one of the most strategic parts of the nation":** Pearson, *Diaries: 1960–1969*, 511.

359 **"a great service to the country":** Pearson, *Diaries: 1960–1969*, 511.

359 **"has been posing as Mr. Clean":** Associated Press, "'Perversion Ring' Denied by Reagan," *Fort Worth Star-Telegram*, November 1, 1967, 2A.

359 **"not spit on the sidewalk":** "Grim Governor Snaps at Sex Ring Queries," *Sacramento Bee*, November 14, 1967, B1.

359 **considering it a breach of privacy:** Carl Sferrazza Anthony, *First Ladies*, vol. 2, *The Saga of the Presidents' Wives and Their Power, 1961–1990* (New York: William Morrow, 1991), 146.

359 **She dispensed the silent treatment:** Cannon, *Governor Reagan*, 250.

359 **"Now if there is a credibility gap":** Press Conference, November 14, 1967, Box P01, Reagan, Ronald: Gubernatorial Papers, 1966–1974: Press Unit, Reagan Library.

359 **scrapped a column:** Pearson, *Diaries: 1960–1969*, 516.

359 **"committed the first truly serious error":** Rowland Evans and Robert Novak, "Reagan's Denial of Staff Problem Seen as First Serious Political Error," *Washington Post*, November 6, 1967, A21.

359 **"It must inevitably raise very real doubts":** "The Fallen Knight," *Evening Star*, November 7, 1967, 10.

359 **Words of praise came in:** John Chamberlain, "Reagan Rolls On," *Los Angeles Herald Examiner*, January 11, 1968, B-10.

360 **"Somebody call that feller back":** William F. Buckley Jr., *The Reagan I Knew* (New York: Basic Books, 2008), 30.

360 **"department of parks and recreation":** "Reagan Finds Key to Yale," *Arizona Republic*, December 5, 1967, 4.

360 **"tragic illness":** William Borders, "Reagan in New Role: Yale Lecturer on History," *New York Times*, December 5, 1967, 49.

360 **Brown resigned the next day:** Howard J. Brown, *Familiar Faces, Hidden Lives: The Story of Homosexual Men in America Today* (New York: Harcourt Brace Jovanovich, 1976), 15; Martin Tolchin, "Dr. Brown Quits Post as City Health Chief," *New York Times*, December 6, 1967, 1. Brown came out very publicly in a 1973 front-page interview with the *New York Times*. Marcia Chambers, "Ex-City Official Says He's Homosexual," *New York Times*, October 3, 1973, 1.

360 **"Have you considered":** Klurfeld, *Behind the Lines*, 265.

361 **He just didn't want his daughter:** Nofziger, *Nofziger*, 90.

361 **conservatives would be outraged:** Nofziger, *Nofziger*, 76.

361 **"where dwell and work a significant number":** Nofziger, *Nofziger*, 74.

361 **"Because he came out of the Hollywood scene":** Nofziger, *Nofziger*, 76–77.

361 **"I had been promised a sister":** Neil Reagan, interviewed by Stephen Stern, transcript, June 25, 1981, UCLA Oral History Program.

361 **Reagan was a "momma's boy":** Garry Wills, *Reagan's America: Innocents at Home* (Garden City, NY: Doubleday, 1987), 27.

361 **"with the same attention he gave":** David Ehrenstein, *Open Secret: Gay Hollywood, 1928–1998* (New York: William Morrow, 1998), 88–90.

362 **"I actually believe"**: Ronald Reagan, with Richard G. Hubler, *Where's the Rest of Me?: The Ronald Reagan Story* (New York: Duell, Sloan and Pearce, 1965), 118–19.

362 **"Does that make me a cowboy?"**: Hirsch, *Otto Preminger*, 351.

362 **"were tolerant of this sort"**: Nofziger, *Nofziger*, 74.

362 **Nancy's godmother:** Gavin Lambert, *Nazimova: A Biography* (New York: Alfred A. Knopf, 1997).

362 **romantic relationships between members of the all-female:** Kitty Kelley, *Nancy Reagan: The Unauthorized Biography* (New York: Simon and Schuster, 1991), 31–32.

362 **Nancy dated a gay man and was engaged to another:** Bob Colacello, *Ronnie and Nancy: Their Path to the White House, 1911 to 1980* (New York: Warner Books, 2004), 185, 147.

362 **"Nowhere else in America did gays"**: William J. Mann, *Behind the Screen: How Gays and Lesbians Shaped Hollywood, 1910–1969* (New York: Viking, 2001), ix–x.

362 **Included among the Reagans' coterie:** William J. Mann, *Wisecracker: The Life and Times of William Haines, Hollywood's First Openly Gay Star* (New York: Viking, 1998), xiv.

363 **her friend, the gay fashion designer:** Vincent Boucher, "The Washington Legacy of James Galanos," *New York Times*, November 2, 2016, D6.

363 **"There was never a problem"**: Mann, *Wisecracker*, 345–46.

363 **produced an affidavit:** Richard Corrigan, "A Lie That Had to Be Nailed," *Washington Post*, March 14, 1965, E1.

363 **"in the despicable attempts to blacken"**: Kurt Schuparra, *Triumph of the Right: The Rise of the California Conservative Movement, 1945–1966* (London: Routledge, 1998), 125.

363 **deeply scarred Kuchel:** Kenneth Reich, "Ex-Sen. Kuchel Dies; Last of State's GOP Progressives," *Los Angeles Times*, November 23, 1994, 1.

363 **incident from Reagan's 1966 gubernatorial campaign:** Lee Houskeeper, author interview, October 16, 2019, Guinda, CA.

364 **"The color of the sign is terrible"**: Jules Witcover and Richard M. Cohen, "Where's the Rest of Ronald Reagan?" *Esquire*, March 1976, 90.

364 **Susan Sontag had published:** Susan Sontag, "Notes on 'Camp,'" *Partisan Review* 31, no. 4 (Fall 1964): 515–30.

364 **"Camp was a sort of homo Esperanto"**: Brian Miller, *Here Because We're Queer: Inside the Gay Liberation Front of Washington, D.C., 1970–72* (Washington, DC: self-pub., 2020), 18.

364 **"At the moment the most 'in' word"**: Inez Robb, "Un-Camp Writer Switched Off in Charisma Age," *Miami Herald*, August 16, 1965, 2-B.

364 **"sexual misconduct"**: Seth Rosenfeld, *Subversives: The FBI's War on Student Radicals, and Reagan's Rise to Power* (New York: Farrar, Straus and Giroux, 2012), 323–24.

364 **"that way"**: Lou Cannon, *Reagan* (New York: G.P. Putnam's Sons, 1982), 132.

365 **"Now, I don't care what the kid does"**: Liebman, *Coming Out Conservative*, 16.

365 **"He's all man"**: William Scobie, "Can Reagan Run America?," *Maclean's*, July 21, 1980, 17.

365 **in the 1,044 speeches Reagan wrote:** Cannon, *Governor Reagan*, 242.

365 **a ballot initiative that would have prevented gay people:** "Calif. Move to Bar Gays as Teachers Qualifies for Ballot," *Washington Post*, June 1, 1978, A6.

365 **A poll published two months before the vote:** Associated Press, "Backing Slips for Prop. 6, Poll Reveals," *Sacramento Bee*, October 6, 1978, A7.

365 **consistent with national sentiment:** Donia Mills, "Homosexuals and Their Professions," *Evening Star, November 1, 1977*, B1.

365 **An enterprising gay activist:** David Mixner, author interview, February 11, 2019, New York, NY.

366 **a closeted gay man:** Livingston died of AIDS in 1991. "Donald Livingston; Aide to Gov. Reagan," *Los Angeles Times*, July 24, 1991, 16.

366 **Through a daily radio commentary:** Colacello, *Ronnie and Nancy*, 431–32; Cannon, *Reagan*, 196.

366 **"He was married in California; he was gay in Washington"**: Author interview with conservative political activist.

366 **"Peter played by all the rules"**: David Mixner, author interview.

367 **"anarchy"**: Ronald Reagan, "The Morality Gap at Berkeley," Speech at Cow Palace, Daly City, CA, May 12, 1966.

367 **"I don't approve of teaching"**: Richard West, "Prop. 6 Dangerous, Reagan Believes," *Los Angeles Times*, September 23, 1978, 26.

368 **"I can't believe the Hollywood crowd":** Bill Boyarsky, *Ronald Reagan: His Life and Rise to the Presidency* (New York: Random House, 1981), 181.

368 **"That one single endorsement":** Doyle McManus, "Briggs to Try Antigay Move Again in 1980," *Los Angeles Times*, November 9, 1978, 21.

24: The Thrill of Treason

369 **"Never miss a chance":** Gore Vidal, *Point to Point Navigation: A Memoir, 1964–2006* (New York: Doubleday, 2006), 249–251.

369 **one thousand sexual encounters:** Vidal, *Palimpsest*, 121.

369 **television audience of ten million:** Parini, *Empire of Self*, 186.

369 **"irritable mental gestures which seek to resemble ideas":** Lionel Trilling, *The Liberal Imagination: Essays on Literature and Society* (New York: Viking, 1950), ix.

370 **advocating the use of nuclear weapons:** William F. Buckley Jr., "On the Right," February 25, 1968.

370 **sing-along of Cole Porter standards:** "Playboy Interview: William F. Buckley, Jr.," *Playboy*, May 1970, 76.

370 **"Let Chet and David and Walter":** Dean Gysel, "ABC to Pair Buckley and Vidal," *Washington Post*, July 22, 1968, C11.

370 **"Vidal lambasted Buckley":** John B. Judis, *William F. Buckley, Jr.: Patron Saint of the Conservatives* (New York: Simon and Schuster, 1988), 203–4.

370 **"Please inform Gore Vidal":** William F. Buckley Jr., "On Experiencing Gore Vidal," *Esquire*, August 1, 1969, 109.

371 **"an intellectual free-for-all":** Kaplan, *Gore Vidal*, 555.

371 **"He was like a prizefighter":** Parini, *Empire of Self*, 185.

371 **"two hundred million Americans think":** Judis, *William F. Buckley, Jr.*, 1988), 291.

372 **"Gestapo tactics in the streets of Chicago":** J. Anthony Lukas, "Police Battle Demonstrators in Streets," *New York Times*, August 29, 1968, 1.

372 **"He was wearing a clavicle brace,"** Christopher Buckley, email to author, October 30, 2020.

372 **the close relative:** Buckley detailed these episodes in a letter that I located within his paper collection at Yale University. Those papers are closed to the public, and I have refrained from publishing the relative's identity out of respect for his privacy.

373 **"The Strange Case of Dr. Dooley":** "The Strange Case of Dr. Dooley," *National Review*, December 7, 1955, 9.

373 **"several yards of moralizing":** Dwight Macdonald, "On the Horizon: Scrambled Eggheads on the Right," *Commentary*, April 1956, 367.

373 **his magazine would repeatedly return:** Jere Real, "Minority Report: Mad About the Boys," *National Review*, March 17, 1978, 344.

373 **coaxed him into joining the staff:** Tanenhaus, *Whittaker Chambers*, 500.

373 **"His closest friends":** William F. Buckley Jr., "No, Whittaker Chambers Was Not Like That!" *Washington Star*, June 28, 1978.

373 **"astonishment":** William F. Buckley Jr., *Overdrive: A Personal Documentary* (Garden City, NY: Doubleday, 1983), 37.

374 **"The homosexual is an individual":** Don Slater, "Editorial," *One*, October 1960, 4–5.

374 **"The liberal orthodoxy predominated':** Douglas Caddy, author interview, February 20, 2020, phone.

375 **ghostwritten by Buckley's brother-in-law:** Claudia Levy, "L. Brent Bozell Dies at 71; Conservative Writer, Editor," *Washington Post*, April 19, 1997, B4.

375 **national secretary of Youth for Goldwater:** John A. Andrew III, *The Other Side of the Sixties: Young Americans for Freedom and the Rise of Conservative Politics* (New Brunswick, NJ: Rutgers University Press, 1997), 27; Marvin Liebman, *Coming Out Conservative: An Autobiography* (San Francisco, CA: Chronicle Books, 1992), 145.

375 **"icon smashers":** "Education: Campus Conservatives," *Time*, February 10, 1961, 34, 37.

375 **"coming out":** One of the earliest published mentions of the "coming out" process appeared in a 1965 article by Evelyn Hooker, "Male Homosexuals and Their 'Worlds,'" in *Sexual Inversion: The Multiple Roots of Homosexuality*, ed. Judd Marmor (New York: Basic Books, 1965), 98–99.

375 **Caddy met:** Liebman, *Coming Out Conservative*, 145.

375 **an "almost mystical, sort of ESP between us"**: Liebman, *Coming Out Conservative*, 144–45.

376 **"victory over, rather than coexistence with"**: The Sharon Statement, September 11, 1960, https://www.yaf.org/news/the-sharon-statement/.

376 **Liebman, too old for membership**: Andrew, *Other Side of the Sixties*, 65.

376 **he had tried to enlist**: John Gregory Dunne, *Quintana and Friends* (New York: E.P. Dutton, 1978), 73.

376 **"My sense of political theater"**: Liebman, *Coming Out Conservative*, 14.

376 **Liebman was the organizational brains behind**: Peter Kihss, "18,000 Rightists Rally at Garden," *New York Times*, March 8, 1962, 1; Thomas P. Ronan, "Campaign Funds Bloom in Spring," *New York Times*, May 17, 1964, 74.

376 **"could not keep his hands off"**: John Gregory Dunne, "Happy Days Are Here Again," *New York Review of Books*, October 13, 1983, 20.

376 **Caddy's Georgetown classmate**: Andrew, *Other Side of the Sixties*, 67.

376 **When Goldwater mounted his presidential bid**: Randy Shilts, *The Mayor of Castro Street: The Life and Times of Harvey Milk* (New York: St. Martin's Press, 1982), 33.

377 **stirred a thirteen-year-old**: Andrew E. Stoner, *The Journalist of Castro Street: The Life of Randy Shilts* (Urbana: University of Illinois Press, 2019), 13.

377 **Arthur Finkelstein was ejected**: Stephen Rodrick, "Puppetmaster: The Secret Life of Arthur J. Finkelstein," *Boston Magazine*, October 1996, 57.

377 **"All the male hustlers"**: Gore Vidal, *Myra Breckinridge* (Boston: Little, Brown, 1968), 43.

377 **"I'm not very fond of women"**: David B. Frisk, *If Not Us, Who? William Rusher, "National Review," and the Conservative Movement* (Wilmington, DE: ISI Books, 2012), 18.

377 **YAF cofounder**: Andrew, *Other Side of the Sixties*, 64.

377 **"There are loads"**: William Rusher, interviewed by Sam Tanenhaus, April 9, 2002, author's collection.

377 **five-hundred-thousand-dollar libel suit**: "Vidal Is Sued by Buckley," *New York Times*, May 7, 1969, 44; "Buckley Drops Vidal Suit, Settles With Esquire," *New York Times*, September 26, 1972, 40.

378 **the initial verdict was that the "queer" had won**: Hendrik Hertzberg, "Buckley, Vidal, and the 'Queer' Question," *New Yorker*, July 31, 2015, https://www.newyorker.com/news/daily-comment/buckley-vidal-and-the-queer-question.

378 **"faggotry is countenanced"**: Buckley, "On Experiencing Gore Vidal," 132.

25: "Destroy Your Opponent"

381 **"The most important rule of politics"**: Bela Kornitzer, *The Real Nixon: An Intimate Biography* (New York: Rand McNally, 1960), 184.

381 **advised Richard Nixon to lambaste**: Christopher Lydon, "Murray Chotiner, Nixon Mentor, Dies," *New York Times*, January 31, 1974, 36.

381 **"culture of smear"**: Lou Cannon, interviewed by Timothy J. Naftali and Greg Cumming, February 21, 2008, Richard Nixon Oral History Project, Nixon Library.

381 **"pink right down to her underwear"**: Tom Wicker, *One of Us: Richard Nixon and the American Dream* (New York: Random House, 1991), 76.

381 **five hundred thousand flyers**: Earl Mazo, *Nixon: A Political and Personal Portrait* (New York: Harper and Brothers, 1959), 81.

381 **"pink sheet"**: Wicker, *One of Us*, 79.

381 **Chotiner who convinced him**: Nixon, *Six Crises*, 138–39.

381 **On Chotiner's advice**: Wicker, *One of Us*, 86–102.

382 **"like the ghost of Christmas Past"**: William Safire, *Before the Fall: An Inside View of the Pre-Watergate White House* (New York: Belmont Tower, 1975), 320.

382 **Chotiner attributed his misfortune**: Rowland Evans Jr. and Robert D. Novak, *Nixon in the White House: The Frustration of Power* (New York: Random House, 1971),70–74.

382 **self-appointed "s.o.b."**: R. W. Apple Jr., "Haldeman the Fierce, Haldeman the Faithful, Haldeman the Fallen," *New York Times Magazine*, May 6, 1973, 39.

382 **fellow University of California at Los Angeles alum**: Sally Quinn, "Haldeman: No-Nonsense Guardian of Keys to the Kingdom," *Washington Post*, October 27, 1972, B1.

382 **"the Berlin Wall":** Martin Schram, "A Man Who Knew a High Crime or Two," *Newsday*, February 17, 1999, A41.

382 **Chotiner called up Jack Anderson:** Mark Feldstein, *Poisoning the Press: Richard Nixon, Jack Anderson, and the Rise of Washington's Scandal Culture* (New York: Farrar, Straus and Giroux, 2010), 107–8.

382 **"engage in homosexual and perverted activities":** C. D. DeLoach to Clyde Tolson, "Richard Nixon—Homosexuals in Government," June 11, 1969, Hoover O&C 119.

382 **home to a bevy of administration officials:** Maxine Cheshire, "VIP: Magnificent Penthouse," *Washington Post*, January 17, 1969, B1.

383 **Anderson took pride in the fact:** Douglas Martin, "Jack Anderson, Investigative Journalist Who Angered the Powerful, Dies at 83," *New York Times*, December 18, 2005, 58.

383 **"Jack was convinced":** Feldstein, *Poisoning the Press*, 107–8.

383 **"There is a ring of homosexuals":** Gentry, *J. Edgar Hoover*, 624.

383 **Hoover waited until June 24:** J. Edgar Hoover, "Memorandum for Official-Confidential," July 3, 1969, Hoover O&C 119.

383 **Haldeman and Ehrlichman joined:** H. R. Haldeman, *The Haldeman Diaries: Inside the Nixon White House* (New York: G.P. Putnam's Sons, 1994), 66.

384 **"Firehose speaking":** Robert B. Semple Jr., "Nixon's Inner Circle Meets," *New York Times Magazine*, August 3, 1969, 6.

384 **"Nothing could grab Nixon's attention":** John Ehrlichman, *Witness to Power: The Nixon Years* (New York: Simon and Schuster, 1982), 159.

384 **"I came to think that Hoover":** Summers, *Official and Confidential*, 375–76.

384 **"Writer, professional candidate":** Angelo d'Arcangelo, *The Homosexual Handbook* (New York: Ophelia Press, 1968), 262, 270.

384 **"I assume that whatever":** Wm. F. Buckley Jr. to Leonard Bernstein, Robert Graves, J. Edgar Hoover, Paul McCartney, Roddy McDowell, Archibald MacLeish, and Mickey Rooney, June 24, 1968, FBI file no. 94–42995–29.

385 **"it cannot be held as derogatory":** Maurice Girodias to C. Dickerman Williams Esq., May 21, 1969, FBI file no. 94–42995–29.

385 **Hoover declined:** J. Edgar Hoover to William F. Buckley Jr., July 2, 1969, FBI file no. 94–42995–29.

385 **having his underlings threaten:** Ian Young, "How Gay Paperbacks Changed America," *Gay & Lesbian Review Worldwide* 8, no. 6 (November/December 2001): 14.

385 **"the FBI's turf":** Harris, interviewed by Meinke.

385 **"lewd and dissolute":** David Carter, *Stonewall: The Riots That Sparked the Gay Revolution* (New York: St. Martin's Press, 2004), 17–18.

385 **Claiborne Pell:** Robert N. Winter-Berger, *The Washington Pay-Off: An Insider's View of Corruption in Government* (Secaucus, NJ: Lyle Stuart, 1972), 86–88.

386 **At the Amber Room**, Hawkins, interviewed by Meinke.

386 **first gay bar in the District to break:** Lou Chibbaro Jr., "In 1969, D.C.'s Gay Life Was Already Thriving," *Washington Blade*, October 7, 1994, 12.

386 **"I can remember distinctly":** Peter Jefts, interviewed by Allen Young, April 24, 2012, Rainbow History Project, Washington, DC.

386 **heard the noise of a buzzer:** Dwight Chapin, interviewed by Timothy J. Naftali, April 2, 2007, Richard Nixon Oral History Project, Nixon Library.

386 **"Haldeman's Haldeman":** John Saar, "'Haldeman's Haldeman' in Changed Status at White House," *Washington Post*, September 30, 1973, A4.

387 **Truman was solemnly administered the oath of office:** C. P. Trussell, "Truman Is Sworn in the White House," *New York Times*, April 13, 1945, 1.

387 **"To your knowledge do homosexual activities":** Deposition of H. R. Haldeman, July 1, 1969, J. Edgar Hoover O&C 119.

387 **"I had good alibis":** Ehrlichman, *Witness to Power*, 159–60.

387 **"Hoover asked all the questions":** Chapin, interviewed by Naftali.

388 **"I felt Nixon":** Ehrlichman, *Witness to Power*, 160.

388 **"a rat of the worst type":** J. Edgar Hoover, "Memorandum for Personal Files," July 1, 1969, 9:09 a.m., Hoover O&C 119.

388 **"Mitchell's conclusion":** Summers, *Official and Confidential*, 376.

388 **"Warning to Dupont Circle people":** *Gay Blade*, October 1969.

388 **a twenty-three-year-old editorial assistant:** Nancy Tucker, "Gay Power to Gay People: The Gay Liberation Front DC Public Panel Discussion," June 7, 2014, Washington, DC.

389 **"It eventually came down":** Lou Chibbaro Jr., "Blade's 50-Year History Reflects Struggles, Advances of LGBT community," *Washington Blade*, October 18, 2019, 38.

389 **"There was a magic witching hour":** Nancy Tucker, interviewed by Mark Meinke, August 1, 2009, Rainbow History Project.

389 **"They didn't want to be disturbed":** Sheila Walsh, "Born in a Basement, the *Blade* Has Come a Long Way," *Washington Blade*, October 7, 1994, 15.

389 **Mr. Henry's restaurant:** David Braaten, "Drinking: Success Hasn't Ruined Mr. Henry's," *Washington Star*, January 30, 1977; G25; Raphaella Baek, "Did Washington's Gay Bars Open as Gay Bars?" *Washington City Paper*, January 24, 2014.

389 **known to stir drinks with her finger:** Tom Makepeace, author interview.

389 **"No, no" she said:** Lou Chibbaro Jr., "Annie Kaylor of Annie's Paramount Steakhouse Dies at 86," *Washington Blade*, July 25, 2013.

389 **"Who's gonna see me here?":** Richard Lee, "The Gay Life," *Washingtonian*, February 1970, 44.

390 **"Follow the fairies":** J. Anthony Lukas, *Common Ground: A Turbulent Decade in the Lives of Three American Families* (New York: Vintage, 1986), 168.

390 **officers parked their squad cars:** Nancy Tucker, "Washington File," *The Advocate*, July 8–21, 1970, 24.

390 **"These people are not afraid of you":** Harris, interviewed by Meinke.

390 **Anderson published a pair of columns:** Jack Anderson, "Pearson Foresaw U.N. Failures," *Washington Post*, December 13, 1971, C23; Jack Anderson, "U.S., Soviet Vessels in Bay of Bengal," *Washington Post*, December 14, 1971, B15.

391 **"We're up against an enemy":** Richard Reeves, *President Nixon: Alone in the White House* (New York: Simon and Schuster, 2001), 339.

391 **At the behest of national security advisor:** Ehrlichman, *Witness to Power*, 302.

391 **In their secret command post:** Jack Anderson and Les Whitten, "Nixon's 'Anderson Conspiracies,'" *Washington Post*, November 11, 1975, B26.

391 **"sexual up the ass":** Conversation 640–5, December 22, 1971, nixontapes.org.

391 **Democrats gained 12 House seats:** *Statistics of the Congressional Election of November 3, 1970* (Washington, DC: U.S. Government Printing Office, 1971).

391 **"a run down on the homosexuals":** Hoover to Tolson, Sullivan, Bishop, Brennan, and Rosen, FBI Memo, November 25, 1970, Clyde Tolson FBI file.

391 **seventeen children:** Feldstein, *Poisoning the Press*, 183.

391 **"I want a direct question about homosexuality":** Conversation 640–5, December 22, 1971.

392 **"One moment he would be taking bachelor Henry's":** Ehrlichman, *Witness to Power*, 302–3.

392 **Radford's "best friend" at the Pentagon:** Memorandum for the Record, Transcription of Tape-recorded Interview, December 22, 1971, 1:00–2:12 p.m., Folder: "Young Report [1 of 2]," Box 55, Staff Member and Office Files: "J. Fred Buzhardt," White House Central Files, Nixon Library.

392 **"Ensure that I found a relationship":** Jack Anderson, with Daryl Gibson, *Peace, War, and Politics: An Eyewitness Account* (New York: Forge, 1999), 225.

392 **"John, I don't think":** John Ehrlichman and Melvin Laird phone call, December 23, 1971, 10 a.m., U.S. Declassified Documents Online.

393 **"bullshit":** Feldstein, *Poisoning the Press*, 210.

393 **"an obsessive line of questioning":** Feldstein, *Poisoning the Press*, 185–86.

393 **correct in their assessment:** Feldstein, *Poisoning the Press*, 200.

393 **"sure looks":** Conversation 692–7C, March 23, 1972, nixontapes.org.

26: Fags

395 **"What starts the process":** Ken W. Clawson, "5 Years Later: A Loyalist Relives the Nixon Resignation," *Washington Post*, August 9, 1979.

396 **"serial collector of resentments":** Rick Perlstein, *Nixonland: The Rise of a President and the Fracturing of America* (New York: Scribner, 2008), 21.

396 **"well-rounded, graceful":** Perlstein, *Nixonland*, 22.

396 **"great, silent majority":** "Text of President Nixon's Address to Nation on U.S. Policy in the War in Vietnam," *New York Times*, November 4, 1969, 16.

396 **"best little boy in the world":** Andrew Tobias, *The Best Little Boy in the World* (New York: Ballantine Books, 1973), 39.

397 **graduating third in his class:** John Herbers, "The 37th President; in Three Decades, Nixon Tasted Crisis and Defeat, Victory, Ruin and Revival," *New York Times*, April 24, 1994.

397 **target of gay innuendo:** "There were rumors of even homosexual affairs, which I didn't believe and don't believe, but there were rumors," remembered Robert Pierpoint, a White House correspondent for CBS News from 1957 to 1980. "I had two or three people claim that Richard Nixon had a homosexual relationship with one of his close friends" (Robert Pierpoint, interviewed by Sheldon Stern, November 18, 1982, Oral History Program, JFK Library).

397 **"Somebody was asking me":** Vidal, "Gore Vidal: The Fag Rag Interview."

397 **"limp-wrist manner":** Bob Woodward and Carl Bernstein, *The Final Days* (New York: Simon and Schuster, 1976), 197.

398 **"effete corps of impudent snobs":** Marjorie Hunter, "Agnew Says 'Effete Snobs' Incited War Moratorium," *New York Times*, October 20, 1969, 1.

398 **"ideological eunuchs":** Sherry, *Gay Artists in Modern American Culture*, 217.

398 **"If it had not been for the Hiss case":** Richard Nixon, "Lessons of the Alger Hiss Case," *New York Times*, January 8, 1986, A23.

398 **"the striped-pants faggots at Foggy Bottom":** Jack Anderson, "Kissinger: 1-Man State Department," *Washington Post*, October 18, 1974, D19.

398 **"impossible fags over there":** Reeves, *President Nixon: Alone in the White House*, 181.

398 **"Typical of the group":** Reeves, *President Nixon: Alone in the White House*, 322.

399 **"They're a bunch of fairies":** Donald Rumsfeld, *Known and Unknown* (New York: Sentinel, 2011), 156.

399 **"Nixon's favor depended":** Henry Kissinger, *Years of Upheaval* (New York: Little, Brown, 1982), 94.

399 **"Ehrlichman had to measure":** Leonard Garment, "John Ehrlichman's Other Legacy," *New York Times*, February 17, 1999, 15.

399 **"Let me say something":** Transcript, April 28, 1971, 9:28 a.m., Conversation 489–35/491–1, in Douglas Brinkley and Luke A. Nichter, eds., *The Nixon Tapes, 1971–1972* (Boston: Houghton Mifflin Harcourt, 2014), 111–12, http://nixontapeaudio.org/chron1/rmn_e489d.mp3.

400 **own teenage son:** Peter Haldeman, "Growing Up a Haldeman," *New York Times Magazine*, April 3, 1994, 30.

401 **CBS had aired a "movie":** Conversation No. 498–5, May 13, 1971, Nixon Library.

401 **"Ehrlichman had ordered bugged":** Seymour M. Hersh, "Spying Missions and 2 Wiretaps Laid to Ehrlichman by Officials," *New York Times*, June 6, 1973, 1.

403 **"the designers taking it out on the women":** Here Nixon was channeling what the psychoanalyst Edmund Bergler described in his 1953 *Fashion and the Unconscious* as "a fashion hoax, unconsciously perpetrated by homosexuals" (Sherry, *Gay Artists in Modern American Culture*, 6).

403 **rock-operatic interpretation:** Paul Hume, "Bernstein's Mass: 'A Reaffirmation of Faith,'" *Washington Post*, September 9, 1971, A1.

403 **"nauseating":** Conversation 571–1, September 13,1971, Nixon Library.

404 **"They eliminated their law":** Conversation 741-2, 10:04 a.m., June 23, 1972.

404 **five o'clock in the morning:** Dudley Clendinen and Adam Nagourney, *Out for Good: The Struggle to Build a Gay Rights Movement in America* (New York: Simon and Schuster, 1999), 133–34.

404 **"Quite frankly":** Bob Shrum, author interview, May 17, 2019, Los Angeles, CA.

404 **"The Democrats were wise":** Dick Moore to Dwight Chapin, "Democratic Convention Second Night," July 12, 1972, Folder 22, Box 45, Contested Materials Collection, Nixon Library. The presence of gays on the dais of the Miami Beach Convention Center elicited rebukes from within the party as well. "We heard from the people who looked like Jacks, acted like Jills and had the odor of Johns about them" was how the gruff president of the AFL-CIO, George Meany, described the event. According to Maurice Isserman and Jack Newfield, the author of these words was the anticommunist labor activist Tom Kahn, a former lover of Bayard Rustin's. However, Rachelle Horowitz, who had worked as an aide to Rustin and later with Kahn, said it was "inconceivable"

that he had written the speech. Her sentiment was endorsed by another colleague of Kahn, Arch Puddington. Asserting that Kahn wrote the speech "assumes that because Kahn was not publicly gay he had to be a gay basher. He never was." Jerome Cahill, "Capitol Stuff," *New York Daily News*, September 22, 1972, 4; Maurice Isserman, *The Other American: The Life of Michael Harrington* (New York: PublicAffairs, 2000), 298; Jack Newfield, *Somebody's Gotta Tell It: A Journalist's Life on the Lines* (New York: St. Martin's Press, 2002), 66; Rachelle Horowitz, "Tom Kahn and the Fight for Democracy: A Political Portrait and Personal Recollection," *Democratiya* (Winter 2007).

404 **earned him a perennial spot:** "Nixon Aide and Friend," *New York Times*, July 13, 1973, 16.

404 **complimentary subscription:** Maxine Cheshire, "VIP," *Washington Post*, January 15, 1970, C1.

404 **his name paired:** Hedrick Smith, "Foreign Policy: Kissinger at Hub," *New York Times*, January 19, 1971, 1.

404 **Interviewing one of his former Harvard graduate students:** Stephen Herbits, author interview, March 19, 2019, phone.

405 **Kissinger started spreading rumors:** Seymour M. Hersh, *The Price of Power: Kissinger in the Nixon White House* (New York: Summit Books, 1983), 108.

405 **Nixon relieved Rogers of his duties:** David Stout, "William P. Rogers, Who Served as Nixon's Secretary of State, Is Dead at 87," *New York Times*, January 4, 2001, B7.

405 **followed his friend William F. Buckley Jr.:** Ron Rosenbaum, "The Last Secrets of Skull and Bones," *Esquire*, September, 1977, 88.

405 **"my principal idea man":** Nixon, *Memoirs*, 1:345.

405 **"as much personal time":** Leonard Garment, *Crazy Rhythm: My Journey from Brooklyn, Jazz, and Wall Street to Nixon's White House, Watergate, and Beyond* (New York: Times Books, 1997), 298.

406 **"The greater the element of informality":** Joe McGinniss, *The Selling of the President, 1968* (New York: Trident Press, 1969), 194.

406 **stock caricature of Nixon:** David Von Drehle, "Herblock, Drawing on Principle," *Washington Post*, October 9, 2001, C1.

406 **"It's not the man":** McGinniss, *Selling of the President*, 194.

406 **a "revolutionary" insight:** Michael Kelly, "David Gergen, Master of the Game," *New York Times Magazine*, October 31, 1993, 64. "The Democrats had never really advanced past the press-agentry techniques of inflating accomplishments and hiding flaws—maintaining a tenuous connection to reality," Kelly wrote. "Price postulated that a new political reality need not correspond at all to objective reality, that a new image could override both the known facts and the previous image of a candidate to become the only reality that mattered."

406 **"We have to be very clear":** McGinniss, *Selling of the President*, 193.

406 **Trying to mine material:** Chapin, interviewed by Naftali.

406 **"the most celebrated writing threesome":** Garment, *Crazy Rhythm*, 106.

406 **"the most lyrical of Nixon's":** John Farrell, email to author, February 8, 2020.

406 **"protect Nixon from the excesses":** Raymond Price, interviewed by David Greenberg, Timothy Naftali, and Paul Musgrave, April 6, 2007, Oral History Program, Nixon Library, 73.

407 **"toughening":** Safire, *Before the Fall*, 100.

407 **"bang-bang-socko stuff":** Jonathan Schell, "The Time of Illusion," *New Yorker*, June 2, 1975, 48.

407 **"bridges to human dignity":** Patrick J. Buchanan, *Nixon's White House Wars: The Battles That Made and Broke a President and Divided America Forever* (New York: Crown Forum, 2017), 118.

407 **"blue-sky":** Buchanan, *Nixon's White House Wars*, 22.

407 **"The light side and the dark side":** Raymond Price, *With Nixon* (New York: Viking, 1977), 29.

407 **"the great, quiet majority":** William H. Honan, "The Men Behind Nixon's Speeches," *New York Times Magazine*, January 19, 1969, 21.

407 **Using a phrase Buchanan had coined:** Buchanan, *Nixon's White House Wars*, 66.

407 **"the great silent majority":** Richard M. Nixon, "Address to the Nation on the War in Vietnam," November 3, 1969, *Public Papers of the Presidents of the United States: Richard M. Nixon, 1969* (Washington, DC: Government Printing Office, 1971), 909.

407 **"passion for anonymity":** Douglas Martin, "Raymond K. Price Jr., 88, a Key Nixon Speechwriter, Is Dead," *New York Times*, February 14, 2019, A24.

407 **"While Ray Price was a colleague":** Patrick J. Buchanan, email to author, February 26, 2020.

407 **"I think his friends were aware":** Suzanne Garment, author interview, March 7, 2020, phone.

407 **"made absolutely no difference":** Dwight Chapin, author interview, June 23, 2020, phone.

408 **the photographs arrived:** Herken, *Georgetown Set*, 340.

408 **The only impact of the incident:** Edwin M. Yoder Jr., *Joe Alsop's Cold War: A Study of Journalistic Influence and Intrigue* (Chapel Hill: University of North Carolina Press, 1995), 156–58.

408 **expressed frustration:** Lyndon Johnson and Robert McNamara, November 23, 1964, Conversation WH6411–23–6459, LBJ Recordings.

408 **"living in an Edgar Allan Poe story":** Sam Patten, author interview, July 15, 2014, Washington, DC. In her memoir, the usually perspicacious Katharine Graham describes Susan Mary as "the perfect wife for" Joe, an assertion that one might charitably attribute to Graham's sense of grace overruling her commitment to accuracy. Graham, *Personal History*, 286.

409 **"a litmus test of loyalty":** Maxine Cheshire, "VIP," *Washington Post*, January 15, 1970, C1.

409 **Bradlee . . . accepted the invitation:** Art Buchwald, "My Broadway Journal, Or: How I Got 'Sheep' Off the Runway," *New York*, September 21, 1970, 37; Sally Quinn, author interview.

409 **"every party-giver in town":** Maxine Cheshire, "VIP," November 7, 1972, B1.

409 **"It scared the hell out of me":** Streitfeld, "Hawk and the Vultures," C1.

409 **"homosexual activity was a criminal offense":** Richard Helms, with William Hood, *A Look over My Shoulder: A Life in the Central Intelligence Agency* (New York: Presidio Press, 2003), 79.

409 **"quietly tell the KGB":** Helms and Hood, *Look over My Shoulder*, 151. As the Nixon administration implemented a strategy of "détente" aimed at reducing tensions with Moscow, the Soviets made a concerted effort to smear as a homosexual one of the policy's strongest American critics, Democratic senator Henry "Scoop" Jackson. "Jackson's strong point is the fact that, during his nearly thirty-five years in Congress, he has never been involved in any sort of political or personal scandal," the top KGB agent in New York reported back to his superiors in Moscow. Therefore, "It is necessary to find some stains on the Senator's biography and use them to carry out an active measure which will compromise him." And if no stains could be found, the KGB would happily invent them. Jackson's marriage at the age of forty-nine, according to his KGB file, "amazed many of his colleagues, who had considered him a confirmed bachelor." When Jackson ran for the Democratic presidential nomination in 1976, the KGB disseminated fabricated government documents alleging he was gay. In one fake FBI memo mailed to the *Chicago Tribune*, the *Los Angeles Times*, the *Topeka Capital*, and rival Jimmy Carter's campaign headquarters, J. Edgar Hoover claims Jackson is a homosexual. After Jackson got into a televised row with gay activists at a campaign event, the KGB sent forged documents to Sen. Edward Kennedy, Jack Anderson, *Playboy*, and *Penthouse* purporting to show that he and his national security aide, Richard Perle, were members of a gay sex club. The "active measures" continued after Jackson dropped out of the race. In 1977, the KGB sent a counterfeit FBI document to the magazine *Gay Times* indicating that Jackson had led a secret homosexual life during his tenure as a local prosecutor in Washington State. The Soviets also sent letters to newspaper editors, supposedly written by members of the Ku Klux Klan, alleging that Hoover promoted homosexuals within the FBI in exchange for sexual favors, thereby transforming the Bureau into a "den of faggots." The letters furthermore accused Hoover of conspiring to fill the ranks of the CIA and State Department with gays, a ludicrous charge considering the ample documentation indicating the precise opposite to be true. Andrew and Mitrokhin, *Sword and the Shield*, 239–40.

409 **"I have never been under the illusion":** Alsop and Platt, *"I've Seen the Best of It,"* 400.

410 **"Walter Lippmann would read":** David Halberstam, *The Best and the Brightest* (New York: Random House, 1972), 500.

410 **often spoke disparagingly of other homosexuals:** Patten, *My Three Fathers*, 202.

410 **"I assumed that Joe was homophobic":** David Satter, email to author, January 13, 2017.

410 **Satter penned a piece:** David Satter, "Moscow Feeds a Lap-Dog Foreign Press," *Wall Street Journal*, October 22, 1985.

410 **"I remember reading it":** David Satter, email to author.

27: "We Are Impatient"

411 **Kameny was initially skeptical:** Bart Barnes, "Kameny Stresses Personal Freedom," *Washington Post*, March 13, 1971, B1.

411 **group of eager young activists:** John Fialka, "Kameny Pegs Campaign on Honesty," *Evening Star*, March 16, 1971, B4.

411 **"We don't expect to win":** FEK to Thomas W. Parker, January 26, 1971, Folder 6, Box 8, Kameny Papers.

411 **"It was inconceivable":** Cynthia Gorney, "District's Gays Gain Power After Shedding Secrecy," *Washington Post*, May 23, 1977, C1.

412 **"We intend to remind a government":** David R. Boldt, "Homosexual Files Delegate Papers: Number of Contestants Is Now Eight," *Washington Post*, February 23, 1971, A17.

412 **"The Mattachine Society of Washington":** John R. Rarick, "Homosexuality—The Holy Bible versus the Washington Post," 92nd Cong., 1st Sess., 117 Cong. Rec. 1831 (February 3, 1971). While Kameny was citing the famous Kinsey figure of men who identify as primarily homosexual for at least a period of time during their adult lifespan, his estimate was remarkably prescient. In 2013, Gallup found that 10 percent of adults living in the District of Columbia identify as lesbian, gay, bisexual, or transgender, making it the gayest state per capita in the country—by a factor of two. Gary J. Gates and Frank Newport, "LGBT Percentage Highest in D.C., Lowest in North Dakota," Gallup, February 15, 2013, https://news.gallup.com/poll/160517/lgbt-percentage-highest-lowest-north-dakota.aspx.

412 **"first publicly declared homosexual":** Boldt, "Homosexual Files Delegate Papers," A17.

412 **four-story building:** Nancy Tucker, "Campaign Center Opened by Kameny," *The Advocate*, March 31–April 13, 1971, 3.

412 **"Old J. Edgar":** Lige Clark and Jack Nichols, *I Have More Fun with You than Anybody* (New York: St. Martin's Press, 1972), 115.

413 **"The past has forced us":** "Statement by Dr. Franklin E. Kameny at the Opening of the Kameny for Congress Campaign Headquarters," March 6, 1973, Folder 6, Box 9, Gittings Papers.

413 **"We feel":** Kameny to Nixon, March 13, 1971, Folder 4, Box 125, Kameny Papers.

414 **"Franklin E. Kameny has put":** "Tuesday's Vote," *Washington Post*, March 21, 1971, B6.

414 **On Election Day:** David R. Boldt, "Fauntroy Sweeps Delegate Race," *Washington Post*, A1.

414 **"Kameny did not win":** "Also Ran," *New Republic*, April 3, 1971, 10.

414 **"It was during the Kameny campaign":** Kuntzler, "Frank Kameny Remembrance."

414 **"The fact of this cooperation":** Jim Owles, n.d., Folder 25, Box 1, Rainbow History Project Collection, Bruce Pennington Papers, Historical Society of Washington, DC.

414 **"a glimmer":** Eva Freund, author interview.

414 **"The real meaning of the campaign":** John Francis Hunter, *The Gay Insider* (New York: Stonehill Publishing, 1972), 312.

415 **"Welcome, Darlings":** Dolinsky, "Lesbian and Gay DC," 126.

415 **At a hastily called meeting:** "Proposals for Organization of Gay Liberation Front," July 14, 1970, Rainbow History Project Collection, Series XVII: DC Gay Liberation Front (GLF) Collection, Historical Society of Washington, DC.

415 **One flyer the group distributed:** *Questionnaire on Heterosexuality*, flyer, n.d., Rainbow History Project Collection, Series XVII: DC Gay Liberation Front (GLF) Collection, Historical Society of Washington, DC.

416 **turkey "stuffed with dope":** Bruce Pennington, interviewed by Brian Miller, December 29, 1994, Folder 20, Box 1, Series IV: Bruce Pennington Collection, Rainbow History Project Collection, Historical Society of Washington, DC.

416 **"maybe a homosexual could be the most revolutionary":** Huey Newton, "A Letter from Huey to the Revolutionary Brothers and Sisters About the Women's Liberation and Gay Liberation Movements," *Black Panther*, August 15, 1970, 15.

416 **"On any other night":** Miller, *Here Because We're Queer*, 73–75.

416 **makeup and female clothing:** Miller, *Here Because We're Queer*, 82.

416 **"Gay is good":** Long, *Martin Luther King, Jr.*, 126.

416 **caravan of cars:** Ned Scharf, "The New Radicals: Homosexuals Join Activist Ranks, Seek Legal, Social Changes," *Evening Star*, January 24, 1971, D1.

416 **"There was a Stonewall equivalent":** Bruce Pennington, interview, March 3, 2001, Folder 20, Box 1, Rainbow History Project Collection, Series IV: Bruce Pennington Collection, Historical Society of Washington, DC.

417 **Had the judge not later dismissed:** Maurine Beasley, "4 Homosexuals Freed, Witnesses Doubted," *Washington Post*, February 19, 1971.

417 **women initially constituted about a quarter:** Brian Miller and Steve Behrens, "Ideology and Action in a Young Movement: The Gay Liberation Front, Washington, D.C., 1970–1972," 2017, Rainbow History Project, Washington, DC.

417 **"There were some women":** Freund, "Lesbian in the Early Gay Movement."

417 **"I'm just leaving":** Nancy Tucker, "'Fuck You, 'Brothers'! or Yet Another Woman Leaves the Gay Liberation Movement," n.d., Folder 5, Container 1, Rainbow History Project Collection, Series XVII, Historical Society of Washington, DC.

417 **"The story of the Furies":** Ginny Berson, untitled essay, *Furies* 1, no. 1 (January 1972), 1.

418 **learned skills:** Lillian Faderman, *The Gay Revolution: The Story of the Struggle* (New York: Simon and Schuster, 2015), 238–39.

418 **"Everything had to be":** Penningtoni, interviewed by Miller.

418 **down-on-his-luck homosexual:** Sasha Gregory-Lewis, "Revelations of a Gay Informant: Part 1," *The Advocate*, February 23, 1977, 12–15.

418 **"master of disguise":** Lawrence Meyer, "Watergate Defendant Claims 'Bugs' Legal," *Washington Post*, January 17, 1973, A1.

418 **"discredit Bruce Pennington":** Gregory-Lewis, "Revelations of a Gay Informant: Part 1," 14.

419 **code name "Butch":** Paul W. Valentine, "Informant's Data Mostly Irrelevant," *Washington Post*, March 28, 1975, C1.

419 **"The gays were becoming,"** Gregory-Lewis, "Revelations of a Gay Informant: Part 1," 13.

419 **"The police were very disturbed":** Gregory-Lewis, "Revelations of a Gay Informant: Part 1," 14.

419 **"disguised, wearing old clothes":** Sasha Gregory-Lewis, "Revelations of a Gay Informant: Part 2," *The Advocate*, March 9, 1977, 14.

419 **wired Merritt for sound:** Gregory-Lewis, "Revelations of a Gay Informant: Part 1," 15.

420 **"We'd sure hate to have someone":** Jared Stout and Toni House, "Informers Spied on D.C. Activists," *Washington Star-News*, October 7, 1973, 1.

420 **"We used to joke that":** Liz Highleyman, "What Is the History of Gay Bookstores," *Bay Area Reporter*, February 13, 2003, 8.

420 **"what the mentality was":** Deacon Maccubbin, author interview, November 3, 2014, Washington, DC.

420 **"There were always men in there":** Skip Moskey, email to author, October 7, 2014.

421 **the first gay bookstore in the world:** Larry Fish, "World's First Gay Bookstore to Close," Knight-Ridder News Service, January 20, 2003.

421 **"I want a bookstore":** Maccubbin, author interview.

421 **Named after the letter:** Wayne R. Dynes, ed., "Lambda," in *Encyclopedia of Homosexuality*, vol. 1, *A–L* (New York: Garland Publishing, 1990).

28: The City of Conversation

422 **"Precisely because the official life":** Henry Kissinger, *White House Years* (Boston: Little, Brown, 1979), 20.

422 **It was in Joe Alsop's garden:** Lynn Rosellini, "A Capital Game of Power," *New York Times Magazine*, January 4, 1981, 5.

423 **"With my little dinners":** Myra MacPherson, "Hostess Guide Wards Off Fete Worse than Death," *New York Times*, November 27, 1966, 108.

423 **"Square Society":** Thomas Meehan, "Washington Society Isn't Exactly Swinging," *New York Times Magazine*, March 8, 1970, 30.

423 **"Washington is about the only town":** Sally Quinn, "The Law of Twelve Which Makes Washington Whirl, and the Boy from Pocatello," *Washington Post*, June 23, 1974, L1.

423 **"a good-looking man with charm":** Thompson, *Price of Achievement*, 175.

423 **"Because you are gay":** Bob Witeck, author interview, July 17, 2014, Washington, DC.

423 **"that priceless party commodity":** MacPherson, "Hostess Guide Wards Off Fete Worse than Death," 108.

424 **"elegant gofers":** Wills, *The Kennedy Imprisonment*, 112.

424 **first made his mark:** Sally Quinn, "Party of Parties," *Washington Post*, May 10, 1972, C1.

424 **dropped out of law school:** Rod Gramer, "Idaho Man Professional Party-Giver," *Reno Gazette-Journal*, May 31, 1978, 49.

424 **"Steve, never has anyone":** "Steve Martindale, Pocatello Success Story at Age 26," *Idaho State Journal*, January 3, 1971, B6.

425 **Maureen Stapleton:** McLendon, "Playboys of Power," D1.

425 **"Competing against Golda Meir":** Ymelda Dixon, "Panama's Pan-Am Carnival," *Washington Star-News*, November 5, 1973, C2.

425 **"Washington before restaurants":** George Packer, *Our Man: Richard Holbrooke and the End of the American Century* (New York: Alfred A. Knopf, 2019), 117.

425 **"Anything Clark Clifford can do":** Phyllis Theroux, "Great Washington Charmers," *Washington Post Magazine*, June 20, 1982, 8.

425 **"nonpolitical Washingtonian":** Ymelda Dixon, "Awards Are Being Given All over the Town," *Washington Star*, January 15, 1976, C3.

425 **"Steve was magical":** Dudley Cannada, author interview, October 14, 2014, Washington, DC.

426 **one in twenty marriages ended in divorce:** David Frum, *How We Got Here: The 70s, the Decade That Brought You Modern Life—For Better or Worse* (New York: Basic Books, 2000), 73.

426 **[t]he right to be different":** "New Directions: 1972–1976," July 11, 1972, The American Presidency Project, University of California at Santa Barbara, https://www.presidency.ucsb.edu/documents /1972-democratic-party-platform.

426 **Tom Wolfe christened:** Tom Wolfe, "The 'Me' Decade and the Third Great Awakening," *New York*, August 23, 1976, 26–45.

426 **shot to the top of best seller lists:** Frum, *How We Got Here*, 58.

426 **39 percent of all Americans:** Daniel Yankelovich, *New Rules: Searching for Self-Fulfillment in a World Turned Upside Down* (New York: Random House, 1981), 21.

426 **"Secret Swinger":** Sally Quinn, "Salon for Gloria Steinem—'American Folk Hero,'" *Washington Post*, October 10, 1969, B1.

426 **Within the decade:** Frum, *How We Got Here*, 206.

426 **"unthinkable":** Nancy L. Ross, "Homosexual Revolution," *Washington Post*, October 25, 1969, C1.

426 **"for the first time since":** Robert Mott, "Life Becomes Somewhat Easier for D.C. Homosexuals," *Washington Post*, April 23, 1973, C1.

427 **"mediacracy":** Laurence Leamer, "The Birth of the Mediacracy," *Washingtonian*, April 1975, 77–83.

427 **first African American member:** "Names in the News," *Asbury Park Press*, November 11, 1972, 2.

427 **admitted its first woman:** Charles B. Seib, "Gridiron: Mixed Review," *Washington Post*, March 30, 1979, A23.

427 **"Any bitch with a million bucks":** Drury, *Advise and Consent*, 44.

427 **"He had these old cable drums":** Friend of Steve Martindale, author interview.

428 **"I was there for a dinner party":** Keith Henderson, author interview, October 9, 2014, Washington, DC.

428 **featured a posse of Teamsters:** Rita Kempley, "Steve Martindale's Can-Do Cancan," *Washington Dossier*, June 1979, 22.

428 **"always at least one hustler":** Henderson, author interview.

428 **looks over your shoulder at a party:** Ann McFeatters, "Outsider Captivates Washington Society," *Pittsburgh Press*, May 12, 1978, 25.

428 **"willing to do almost anything":** Meehan, "Washington Society Isn't Exactly Swinging," 30.

428 **First, he dialed up Longworth:** Sally Quinn, *The Party: A Guide to Adventurous Entertaining* (New York: Fireside, 1997), 22.

429 **This gambit was the genesis:** Quinn, "Law of Twelve Which Makes Washington Whirl," L1.

429 **"like they were crimes":** Roxanne Roberts, "No Matter the Era, Washington's Boldface Names Know Where to Find a Good Time," *Washington Post*, June 5, 2002, L30.

430 **"was like finding the cause of cancer":** Tom Kelly, *The Imperial Post: The Meyers, The Grahams, and the Paper That Rules Washington* (New York: William Morrow, 1983), 161.

430 **"It's fine for him to mix":** Reflecting on Quinn's profile of Martindale many years later, Gray said the reporter "slashed him to pieces. It was a ruthless piece . . . I'm still surprised he didn't just pack his bags after that and leave town." Heymann, *Georgetown Ladies' Social Club*, 223.

431 **migrated to cities in droves:** Frances Fitzgerald, *Cities on a Hill: A Journey Through Contemporary American Cultures* (New York: Simon and Schuster, 1987), 42.

431 **"I think if you're smart":** Sean Strub, author interview, May 22, 2019, New York, NY.

431 **"I think she's done very well":** "Gwen Airs Views on Hostess-ing," *Washington Post*, May 14, 1957, B3.

431 **refused to shake Cafritz's hand:** Maryland McCormick, "Rival Hostesses Just Don't Meet," *Washington Post*, April 18, 1954, S8.

431 **reconciliatory grip-and-grin:** Bart Barnes, "D.C. Hostess Gwendolyn Cafritz Dies," *Washington Post*, November 30, 1988, D4.

431 **divorced her fourth husband:** Nancy Rubin, *American Empress: The Life and Times of Marjorie Merriweather Post* (New York: Villard Books, 1995), 350–53.

431 **"The gay community met at dinner tables":** Herbits, author interview.

432 **"a gay world on the Hill":** Robert Higdon, author interview, June 16, 2015, Washington, DC.

432 **"The concept was":** Cannada, author interview.

432 **"There were subtle":** Ross, author interview.

432 **"no real understanding":** Dolinsky, author interview, October 22, 2019, phone.

433 **enough money to last:** "Bob Gray (1923–2014): 'You Cannot Conceive.'"

433 **16 percent of America's gross national product:** Trento, *Power House*, 107.

433 **"He was the slickest character":** Glenn Pinder, author interview, February 14, 2014, Washington, DC.

433 **"every gay person knew Bob Gray":** Herbits, author interview.

433 **"In D.C.'s top government":** Gray, *Eighteen Acres Under Glass*, 94.

433 **"No one thinks she'll marry":** Judy Bachrach, "Rose Mary Woods: Facing Her Two Crises," *Washington Post*, July 7, 1974, H1.

433 **"one of the oddest stories":** Maxine Cheshire, with John Greenya, *Maxine Cheshire, Reporter* (Boston: Houghton Mifflin, 1978), 197–98. That Gray was the person alluded to in Cheshire's book was confirmed by a former *Washington Post* reporter to whom Cheshire told the story.

434 **"There were signals":** Ross, author interview.

434 **"You would have thought":** Joel Martin, interviewed by Mark Meinke, August 2, 2001, Rainbow History Project, Washington, DC.

434 **Kissinger happened to live by the corner:** Ulrich, interviewed by Meinke; Edmund White, *States of Desire Revisited: Travels in Gay America* (Madison: University of Wisconsin Press, 2014), 324.

435 **agents and the cruisers:** Lenny Giteck, "Gay Power on the Potomac," *The Advocate*, November 29, 1979, 15.

435 **"It seriously put a damper":** Maccubbin, author interview.

435 **"a third-rate burglary attempt":** Tad Szulc, "Ex-GOP Aide Linked to Political Raid," *New York Times*, June, 20, 1972, 1.

435 **On September 3, 1971:** Associated Press, "Break-in Charges Returned," *Baltimore Sun*, September 5, 1973, A1.

435 **"I had to leak stuff":** Stanley I. Kutler, *Abuse of Power: The New Nixon Tapes* (New York: Free Press, 1997), 7–9.

436 **"what the president thought was at stake":** Egil "Bud" Krogh, with Matthew Krogh, *Integrity: Good People, Bad Choices, and Life Lessons from the White House* (New York: PublicAffairs, 2007), 22.

436 **"latent homosexual tendencies":** Tom Wells, *Wild Man: The Life and Times of Daniel Ellsberg* (New York: Palgrave Macmillan, 2001), 476.

436 **a theory (later shown to be baseless):** Gerald S. Strober and Deborah H. Strober, *Nixon: An Oral History of His Presidency* (New York: HarperCollins, 1994), 234–35.

436 **allegedly told the Bay of Pigs veterans:** Daniel Ellsberg, interviewed by Timothy Naftali, May 20, 2008, Oral History Program, Nixon Library.

436 **turned up nothing incriminating:** Egil Krogh, "The Break-In That History Forgot," *New York Times*, June 30, 2007, A17.

436 **was serving as a captain:** "Dirty Tricks," *New York Times Magazine*, July 22, 1973, 22.

436 **One of their pranks:** Martin Waldron, "Segretti Indicted in Mailing of Bogus Muskie Letter," *New York Times*, May 5, 1973, 1. Jackson could be proud that both the Soviets and the Nixonians tried using the same, sleazy tactic against him and that, in both cases, it didn't work.

437 **realized something fishy:** George Mendenhall, "Watergate: Were Gays 'Used' in GOP Plot?," *The Advocate*, June 6, 1973, 8.

437 **"the balls of a brass monkey":** Jonathan Aitken, *Nixon: A Life* (Washington, DC: Regnery, 1993), 414.

437 **Colson instructed Roger Stone:** "Dirty Tricks," 22.

437 **reportedly prowl gay bathhouses:** Sean Strub, *Body Counts: A Memoir of Politics, Sex, AIDS and Survival* (New York: Scribner, 2014), 57; "Roger Stone: Calls X-Rated Story a 'Dirty Trick,'" *National Journal*, "The Hotline," September 12, 1996.

437 **unemployed former government worker:** "James Walter McCord Jr., et al., Burglary, Democratic National Committee Headquarters, Washington, D.C., June 12, 1972, Interception of Communications," June 12, 1973, "Colson's Recruitment of Homosexuals," Entry A1 103: "Investigations of Other Illegal Activities," Box 15, RG460: "Records of the Watergate Special Prosecution Force," NARA.

437 **"the president's worst instincts":** Price, interviewed by Greenberg.

437 **"boyish comeliness":** Mary McGrory, "'Truth . . . Won't Hurt My Hide,'" *Washington Star-News*, May 15, 1973,

438 **"his boyish appearance":** Daniel Schorr, *Clearing the Air* (Boston: Houghton Mifflin Harcourt, 1977), 79.

438 **"is a smooth faced young man":** Joseph Alsop, "Dealing with Dean and the Dollar," *Washington Post*, June 6, 1973, A19.

438 **"How do I counter the image":** John W. Dean III, *Blind Ambition: The White House Years* (New York: Simon and Schuster, 1976), 285.

438 **"People identify with a President":** McGinniss, *Selling of the President 1968*, 194.

29: The Ultimate Democracy

441 **"Enclosed is the Civil Service":** Frank Kameny to Barbara Gittings and Kay Tobin, July 8, 1975, Folder 1, Box 90, Gittings Papers, Manuscripts and Archives Division, New York Public Library (hereafter "Gittings Papers").

441 **promulgated five days earlier:** Stephen Green, "Homosexuals Win Job Right," *Washington Post*, July 4, 1975, A1.

441 **"litigation, cajolery, hounding":** Donia Mills, "Washington Called the Gay Capital," *Washington Star*, October 30, 1977, D19.

441 **"the constant, nagging problem":** Marcus, *Making History*, 103.

442 **"As I explained to you":** Rae Kameny to Franklin Kameny, January 13, 1972, Folder 3, Box 1, Kameny Papers.

442 **"No, I haven't done":** Franklin Kameny to Rae Kameny, n.d., Folder 3, Box 1, Kameny Papers.

442 **"All these people I met":** Rae Kameny to Franklin Kameny, June 26, 1973, Folder 3, Box 1, Kameny Papers.

442 **donated a sound system:** "D.C. Observes Gay Pride Day '75," *Gay Blade*, July 1975, 1.

442 **In December:** Lynn Rosellini, "Dave Kopay—Out in the Open," *Washington Star*, December 11, 1975, C1.

443 **a deluge of hate mail:** David Kopay, interviewed by Marcus in *Making History*, 276.

443 **"Just sitting there, transfixed":** Key, author interview.

443 **"crossing a threshold from which I could not return":** Strub, *Body Counts*, 33.

443 **as far as West Virginia and Pennsylvania:** Mills, "Washington Called the Gay Capital," D19.

443 **three bars, two dance floors:** Cade Ware, "Here's Gay Washington," *Blueboy* 1, no. 1 (1974): 7.

443 **"It may be":** Diana McLellan, *Ear on Washington* (New York: Arbor House, 1982), 54.

444 **"enormity of the secret":** Strub, *Body Counts*, 55.

444 **"neutral Switzerland":** Clendinen and Nagourney, *Out for Good*, 431.

444 **"I knew closeted gay people":** Witeck, author interview.

444 **Strub likened the experience:** Strub, *Body Counts*, 34.

444 **"remained fresh and frightening":** Strub, *Body Counts*, 54.

444 **"the lingering glance":** Strub, *Body Counts*, 15.

445 **leaving a pack of matches:** Miller, *Here Because We're Queer*, 18.

445 **One night at the Lost and Found:** Strub, *Body Counts*, 33.

445 **"high-faggot baroque":** Jefts, interviewed by Young.

445 **some four thousand:** "Homosexuality: Gays on the March," *Time*, September 8, 1975.

445 **rivaled those of clubs:** Mary Anne Dolan, "Washington's New Super Bars," *Washington Star*, October 7, 1975, C1.

445 **"an affectionate clique":** Strub, *Body Counts*, 34.

445 **"the only place":** McLellan, *Ear on Washington*, 279.

445 **At the Pier Nine:** "More Bars in D.C.," *Gay Blade*, May 1970, 2.

445 **"homosexualization of America":** Frank Rich, "The Gay Decades," *Esquire*, November 1987, 88.

446 **"Disco City":** Bruce Pennington, "Washington D.C.," *The Advocate*, April 7, 1976, 40.

446 **"You bet gays":** Tom Zito, "Anything's Cool at the Discos," *Washington Post*, October 17, 1974, E1.

446 **Open Gay Bars Committee:** Robert Mott, "Homosexual Lives as Varied as Those of Any Other Group," *Washington Post*, April 24, 1973, C2.

446 **Whereas bouncers only occasionally:** "Gay People: Have We Come This Far Only to Leave Behind Some of Us," October 23, 1971, Folder 16, Box 2, Series 2, David Aiken Papers, Rainbow History Project Collection, Historical Society of Washington, DC.

446 **"This is a Southern City":** Nancy Tucker, "Washington File," *The Advocate*, February 17–March 2, 1971, 9. As part of his assignment to "creat[e] racial dissension" within the local gay activist community, Robert Merritt claimed that one of his duties was to support these protests. Gregory-Lewis, "Revelations of a Gay Informant: Part 1," 15.

446 **a particularly popular fashion accessory:** Otis T. "Buddy" Sutson, interviewed by Mark Meinke, January 22, 2001, Rainbow History Project, Washington, DC.

446 **a manager at the Grand Central:** David Aiken, "Subtle or Blatant, Discrimination Exists in the Gay Community," *The Advocate*, March 23, 1977, 7.

447 **"didn't have outlets":** Dolinsky, "Lesbian and Gay DC," 6.

447 **"There was no kissing":** Chibbaro, "In 1969, D.C.'s Gay Life Was Already Thriving," 12.

447 **"electric" (acid-spiked) punch:** Christopher Prince, interviewed by Mark Meinke, September 8, 2001, Rainbow History Project, Washington, DC.

447 **drank out of giant garbage cans:** Michael Sainte-Andress, interviewed by Mark Meinke, 2001, Rainbow History Project, Washington, DC.

447 **"It was a place where":** "Clubhouse Trailer," SmallWonderMedia, https://www.youtube.com/watch?v=cXwkWwJ77FQ&feature=youtu.be.

447 **one of the oldest gay bars:** Justin Moyer, "On the Hill," *Washington City Paper*, January 26, 2001.

447 **Coleman's first visit:** James Coleman, interviewed by Mark Meinke, August 20, 2001, Rainbow History Project, Washington, DC.

447 **Consisting of an older drag queen:** White, "Those Others," E1.

447 **most of whom worked government day jobs:** Mott, "Homosexual Lives as Varied as Those of Any Other Group," C2.

448 **"Every Saturday night":** Harris, interviewed by Meinke.

30: "Too Good an Opportunity"

449 **he happened upon a massive crowd:** "Security: Protecting the President," *Time*, October 6, 1975, 6.

450 **"Gun!":** Daniel Luzer, "The Gay Man Who Saved Ford's Life," *Gay and Lesbian Review Worldwide* 16, no. 4 (July/August 2009): 23–26.

450 **In the commotion that followed:** "The Assailant: Making of a Misfit," *Time*, October 6, 1975, 18.

450 **shook so violently:** "The Nation: The Man Who Grabbed the Gun," *Time*, October 6, 1975, 20.

450 **Harvey Milk had befriended:** Shilts, *Mayor of Castro Street*, 121–23.

450 **Secret Service watch list:** Jack Anderson, "U.S. Watches Joiners, Not Loners," *Washington Post*, May 27, 1972, B11.

451 **an air force administrative board:** Jay Mathews, "Matlovich Verdict: General Dischrage," *Washington Post*, September 20, 1975, A1; *Time*, September 8, 1975.

451 **"One of the heroes":** Herb Caen, "In This Corner," *San Francisco Chronicle*, September 24, 1975.

451 **blared the headline:** Daryl Lembke, "Hero in Ford Shooting Active Among S.F. Gays," *Los Angeles Times*, September 25, 1975, 3. Lembke's story appeared in, among many others, the *Honolulu Advertiser*, the *Tucson Daily Citizen*, and the *Boston Globe*.

451 **"My sexuality is a part"**: Daryl Lembke, "Ford to Thank S.F. Man Who Deflected Gun," *Los Angeles Times*, September 26, 1975, 3.

451 **"This is just another gimmick"**: Associated Press, "Ex-Marine Who Deflected Gun Delighted Ford Sending Thanks," *Indianapolis Star*, September 26, 1975, 18.

452 **"No wonder the president"**: Pat Murphy, "Ford Hero's Mother Has Misgivings," *Detroit News*, September 26, 1975, 1

452 **Sipple's father and two brothers**: Lynne Duke, "Caught in Fate's Trajectory, Along with Gerald Ford," *Washington Post*, December 31, 2006, D1.

452 **"He could be as queer"**: Murphy, "Ford Hero's Mother Has Misgivings."

452 **"I want you to know"**: Gerald Ford to Oliver Sipple, September 25, 1975, Folder: "Sipple, Oliver," Box 2932, White House Central Files, Gerald R. Ford Presidential Library and Museum, Grand Rapids, MI (hereafter cited as "Ford Library").

453 **"As you probably know"**: Oliver Sipple to Gerald Ford, September 30, 1975, Folder: "Sipple, Oliver," Box 2932, White House Central Files, Ford Library.

453 **"Sipple has been identified"**: Ron Nessen to Jerry Jones, October 4, 1975, Folder: "Jones, Jerry," Box 130, Ron Nessen Papers, Ford Library.

453 **There is no indication**: John J. O'Connell, archives technician at Ford Library, email correspondence with author, April 30, 2019.

453 **merit in Ford's memoir**: *A Time to Heal: The Autobiography of Gerald R. Ford* (New York: Harper and Row, 1979), 302–3.

453 **"committing heroism in public"**: William Safire, "Big Week for Gays," *New York Times*, September 29, 1975, 31.

453 **"exposed him to contempt and ridicule"**: United Press International, "Homosexuality Bared, Brings $9 Million Suit," *Pittsburgh Press*, September 23, 1976, 3.

453 **"known by hundreds of people"**: Associated Press, "Homosexual Is Rebuffed in Suit of Newspaper," *New York Times*, June 23, 1984, 6.

453 **father forbade him**: Duke, "Caught in Fate's Trajectory."

454 **"This thing with Ford"**: "Oliver Sipple," reported by Latif Nasser and Tracie Hunte, produced by Matt Kielty, Annie McEwen, Latif Nasser, and Tracie Hunte, *Radio Lab*, WNYC Studios, September 21, 2017.

454 **started receiving psychiatric treatment**: Jesus Rangel, "O. W. Sipple, 47, Who Blocked an Attempt to Kill Ford in 1975," *New York Times*, February 4, 1989, 32.

454 **"junk store gone to seed"**: Dan Morain, "Sorrow Trailed a Veteran Who Saved a President and Then Was Cast in an Unwanted Spotlight," *Los Angeles Times*, February 13, 1989, V1.

454 **"[r]equires great caution"**: Hunter, *The Gay Insider*, 325.

454 **He dreamed**: Johanna Neuman, "'Dream' Job Provides Its Nightmares," *Clarion-Ledger* (Jackson, MS), December 23, 1979, 3A.

454 **working as a House doorman**: Cliff Treyens, "Hinson's Political Odyssey Began Before College Ended," *Clarion-Ledger* (Jackson, MS), February 6, 1981, 5C.

455 **knew of his "problem"**: Jeannette Smyth, "Attempting to Deal with the Pressures," *Washington Star*, May 31, 1981, 17.

455 **September 1976 evening**: Willard P. Rose, "Despite Revelations, Hinson Still Favored to Win," *Clarion-Ledger* (Jackson, MS), October 12, 1980, 1.

455 **"creating a public nuisance"**: David Bates, "Revelations from Jon Hinson Could Alter Congressional Race," *Clarion-Ledger* (Jackson, MS), August 9, 1980, 1.

455 **"a furtive rendezvous"**: Ken Ringle, "Iwo Jima Monument Grounds Have a Darker Attraction," *Washington Post*, October 7, 1976, C1.

455 **"one of Washington's brightest"**: Ken Ringle, "'A Passion for Politics,'" *Washington Post*, October 14, 1976, 1.

455 **father of nine-year-old twins**: Calvin Zon, "A Landmark Turns Tough at Night," *Washington Star*, October 6, 1976,

456 **which his wife**: Adrienne Washington, "Memorial Slaying Defense: 'Caught in Macho Syndrome,'" *Washington Star*, June 6, 1978, B1.

456 **bludgeoning him with a tree limb**: Richard Cohen, "The Puzzle of People Who Hate Homosexuals," *Washington Post*, June 8, 1978, C1.

456 **eighteen-month span:** Larry Van Dyne, "Is DC Becoming the Gay Capital of America?," *Washingtonian*, October 1980, 96.

456 **widows of the murdered men:** Keith B. Richburg and Alfred E. Lewis, "8 Killings Tied to 'Strip' Chill Homosexuals," *Washington Post*, August 17, 1978, C1.

456 **"harass and humiliate queers":** Adrienne Washington, "Teen on Trial for Gay's Murder Tells His Side," *Washington Star*, June 9, 1978, 28.

456 **"smack around a few":** Jane Seaberry and Neil Henry, "Jury Finds Man Guilty of Murder in Pettine Killing," *Washington Post*, June 9, 1978, C1.

456 **"the impression that no one":** Cohen, "Puzzle of People Who Hate Homosexuals," C1. Simoneau was convicted of first-degree murder and attempted robbery and sentenced to thirty-five years in prison. A twenty-two-year-old accomplice was sentenced to forty years, and a twenty-four-year-old who suffered from birth defects was convicted of involuntary manslaughter, handed a year-long prison term, and made to pay a thousand-dollar fine. Jane Seaberry, "Youth, 17, Gets 35 Years for Slaying of Udall Aide," *Washington Post*, July 22, 1978, C2; "Second Man Sentenced in Bludgeoning," *Washington Post*, August 9, 1978, C2; Madeline Lewis, "3rd Defendant Given Suspended Sentence, Fine in Pettine Slaying," *Washington Post*, June 8, 1979, C5.

31: Out of the Closets, into the White House

459 **Jean O'Leary looked:** Jean O'Leary, interview with Eric Marcus, *Making Gay History: The Podcast*, https://makinggayhistory.com/podcast/episode-15-jean-oleary-part-2/.

459 **sit-down protest:** Karen De Witt, "Midge Costanza: The President's 'Window on the Nation,'" *Washington Post*, April 26, 1977, B1.

459 **"loudmouthed, pushy little broad":** Doreen J. Mattingly, *A Feminist in the White House: Midge Costanza, the Carter Years, and America's Culture Wars* (New York: Oxford University Press, 2016), 89.

459 **a group of gay activists:** Doreen J. Mattingly and Ashley Boyd, "Bringing Gay and Lesbian Activism to the White House: Midge Costanza and the National Gay Task Force Meeting," *Journal of Lesbian Studies* 17, no. 3/4 (2013): 372.

460 **The second experience:** Mattingly and Boyd, "Bringing Gay and Lesbian Activism to the White House," 374.

460 **"window on the nation":** De Witt, "Midge Costanza," B1.

460 **address more than a million people:** "Midge Costanza," *People*, December 26, 1977, 40.

460 **"to reach those traditionally powerless":** James T. Wooten, "Midge Costanza: Enduring a New Life in a Niche in the White House Cellar," *Washington Post*, July 4, 1978, 22.

460 **the president would be visiting Camp David:** Clendinen and Nagourney, *Out for Good*, 287.

461 **first congressional staffer to come out of the closet:** Bill Rushton, "A Stage Set for the Great American Movie," *The Advocate*, March 10, 1976, 24; Donia Mills, "Homosexuals and Their Professions," *Washington Star*, November 1, 1977, B1.

461 **"One of the biggest thrills":** Michael Bedwell, "The Secret Lesbian Couple Behind a Historic Meeting at the White House," LGBTQ Nation, October 25, 2019, https://www.lgbtqnation.com/2019/10/secret-lesbian-couple-behind-historic-meeting-white-house/.

461 **"Frank, I'm really glad":** "Commemorating the 30th Anniversary of First-Ever Meeting Between White House and Gay and Lesbian Leaders," press release, March 26, 2007, National Gay and Lesbian Taskforce.

461 **sneaked into the empty Oval Office:** O'Leary, interview with Marcus.

461 **Before the move:** Maccubbin, author interview.

462 **"We were the de facto community center":** Jim Bennett, author interview, November 3, 2014, Washington, DC.

462 **first city in the country:** Gorney, "District's Gays Gain Power After Shedding Secrecy," C3; Kirk Scharfenberg, "City Council Passes Bias Ban," *Washington Post*, August 8, 1973, A1.

462 **"Despite the predominance":** Mott, "Life Becomes Somewhat Easier for D.C. Homosexuals," C3.

462 **DC Board of Education:** "GAA Final Report on Attitudes of School Board Candidates About Gay Issues in the November 2 Election," Folder 3, Box 14, Kameny Papers.

462 **Barry chalked up a +20 rating:** Donia Mills, "Gay Political Experience in Washington," *Evening Star*, October 31, 1977, 1.

462 **More than three-fourths:** Milton Coleman, "Washington's Gay Vote," *Washington Post*, April 21, 1979, A1.

462 **"fascist faggots":** Milton Coleman, "Moore Not Always a Gay Rights Foe," *Washington Post*, September 22, 1977, D1.

463 **hired an openly gay campaign coordinator:** Coleman, "Washington's Gay Vote," A1.

463 **"a free-wheeling":** Giteck, "Gay Power on the Potomac," 15.

463 **"Emerald City":** Mills, "Washington Called the Gay Capital," 1.

463 **"you could spend a comfortable":** Gorney, "District's Gays Gain Power After Shedding Secrecy," C3.

463 **"We have gained this acceptance":** Mills, "Washington Called the Gay Capital," 1.

463 **One employee at a regulatory agency:** Mills, "Homosexuals and Their Professions," B2.

463 **"Homos in the White House!":** Tom Mathews, with Eleanor Clift and Thomas M. De Frank, "The Trouble with Midge," *Newsweek*, November, 7, 1977, 9.

463 **Costanza had started in the administration:** Fred Barbash, "Midge Costanza Resigns," *Washington Post*, August 2, 1978, A1.

464 **when a reporter asked:** Mattingly and Boyd, "Bringing Gay and Lesbian Activism to the White House," 365–79.

464 **"The biggest oppression":** David S. Broder, *Changing of the Guard: Power and Leadership in America* (New York: Simon and Schuster, 1980), 146.

464 **"What these people really want":** United Press International, "Anita Bryant Scores White House Talk with Homosexuals," March 28, 1977, 56.

465 **Estimated to number:** "Preachers in Politics: Decisive Force in '80?" *U.S. News and World Report*, September 15, 1980, 24.

465 **spoken of as a societal threat:** Matthew D. Lassiter, "Inventing Family Values," in *Rightward Bound: Making America Conservative in the 1970s*, ed. Bruce J. Schulman and Julian E. Zelizer (Cambridge, MA: Harvard University Press, 2008), 23.

465 **legalization of same-sex marriages:** Jules Witcover, "Women on Both Sides of Equal Rights Amendment Argument," *Washington Post*, February 8, 1975, A7.

465 **"In a healthy society":** Patrick J. Buchanan, "Gay Day," *New York Daily News*, June 7, 1977, 12C.

465 **margin of two-to-one:** B. Drummond Ayres Jr., "Miami Votes 2 to 1 to Repeal Law Barring Bias Against Homosexuals," *New York Times*, June 8, 1977, 1.

465 **"has in mind all those members":** Real, "Minority Report," 344.

466 **Speaking at a rally:** Dudley Clendinen, "White House Says Minister Misquoted Carter Remarks," *New York Times*, August 8, 1980, A16.

466 **charter member:** Johanna Neuman, "Hinson Was Regular Visitor at Theatre, Deposition Reveals," *Clarion-Ledger* (Jackson, MS), August 28, 1980, 18.

466 *Harley's Angels:* Alfred E. Lewis and Martin Weit, "At Least 5 Die in Fire at Film Club," *Washington Post*, October 25, 1977, A1.

466 **lending Frank Kameny money:** Franklin E. Kameny to William Oates, Folder 3, Box 121, Kameny Papers.

466 **running a contest:** Undated flyer, Folder 3, Box 121, Kameny Papers.

467 **About fifteen other men:** Phil McCombs and Alfred E. Lewis, "Club Fire Toll Is 8; Regulations Held Too Lax," *Washington Post*, October 26, 1977, C1.

467 **"Hey, there's a fire!":** Neuman, "Hinson Was Regular Visitor at Theatre," 1A.

467 **"Is there a way":** Donia Mills, "Hinson, Grateful to Be Alive, Told About His Past After Follies Fire," *Washington Star*, April 7, 1981, 6.

467 **A member of Engine Company No. 7:** McCombs and Lewis, "Club Fire Toll Is 8," C1.

467 **A spark projected:** Joseph D. Whitaker, "Theater Head Fined $650 in Fatal Blaze," *Washington Post*, March 20, 1979, C3.

468 **a heap of bodies:** Kenneth Walker, "6 Dead in Gay Movie Blaze," *Washington Star*, October 25, 1977, A1.

468 **"The phones buzzed":** Tom Regan, author interview, May 29, 2014, Washington, DC.

468 **"What if they called":** Phil McCombs, "Fire Victims' Families Doubly Shocked," *Washington Post*, October 27, 1977, A1.

468 **"Most of the people":** Walker, "6 Dead in Gay Movie Blaze," A1.

468 **The *Star* revealed:** The last victim died two weeks after the fire. "9th Fire Victim Dies," *Evening Star*, November 7, 1977, 17.

469 **"recall no tragedy":** Charles B. Seib, "How the Papers Covered the Cinema Follies Fire," *Washington Post*, October 30, 1977, C7. Two years earlier, the *Post* had published, to great controversy, a ghastly photograph on its front page of a young woman jumping to her death from a fire in Boston. The image elicited "the largest reaction to a published item" in Seib's tenure as ombudsman, almost all of it negative. By refusing to identify the victims of the Cinema Follies fire, the *Post* implied that printing the mere name of a deceased homosexual was a greater violation of privacy and journalistic ethics than printing a photograph of "the stuff of which nightmares are made," in Seib's words. Charles Seib, "'Impact Photographs and Reader Sensibilities,'" *Washington Post*, August 3, 1975, C6.

469 **Charles Hamilton Beebe Jr.:** Kenneth Walker, "Aide to Congressman Identified as Victim of Cinema Follies Blaze," *Washington Star*, October 26, 1977, B1.

469 **research a freelance article:** McCombs, "Fire Victims' Families Doubly Shocked," A1.

469 ***Blade*:** The *Gay Blade* changed its name to the *Blade* in June 1975, and to the *Washington Blade* in October 1980.

469 **Like most of his fellow volunteers:** Lou Chibbaro Jr., interviewed by Mark Meinke, August 26, 2009, Rainbow History Project, Washington, DC. Chibbaro would go on to become the *Blade*'s longest-serving full staffer, working there for over thirty-five years.

469 **"When I held that lock":** McCombs and Lewis, "Club Fire Toll Is 8," C1.

470 **barely legal boys clad in fishnet:** John Aloysius Farrell et al., "The Two Worlds of Robert Bauman," *Baltimore News American*, October 26, 1980, 1A; Bauman, *Gentleman from Maryland*, 37.

470 **"older financiers met younger entrepreneurs":** Craig Seymour, *All I Could Bare: My Life in the Strip Clubs of Gay Washington, D.C.* (New York: Atria, 2008), 53.

470 **"on the edge of discovery":** Robert E. Bauman, "A Former Congressman, Once a Staunch Foe of Gay Rights, Confronts His Own Homosexuality," *People*, September 19, 1983, 61.

470 **first Republican page to return:** Jack Kneece, "Page Becomes a Congressman," *Washington Star-News*, August 26, 1973, B1.

470 **longest daily commute:** Donald P. Baker, "Maryland Conservative Is Watchdog of the House," *Washington Post*, December 18, 1977, B1.

471 **There on the wall:** Johanna Neuman, "A Day in the Life," *Clarion-Ledger* (Jackson, MS), December 23, 1979, 3.

471 **"It's hard for me to think":** Baker, "Maryland Conservative Is Watchdog of the House," B1.

471 **"to construct a whole series":** Bauman, *Gentleman from Maryland*, 163–64.

471 **"utter depravity":** Bauman, *Gentleman from Maryland*, 162.

471 **turning tricks for forty dollars:** Joann Stevens, "The Boy-Whore World," *Washington Post*, October 7, 1980, A1.

471 **robbed him at knifepoint:** Bauman, *Gentleman from Maryland*, 189.

472 **clandestine suntanning society:** von Hoffman, *Citizen Cohn*, 187–88.

472 **telephoned Gary Aldridge:** Jim Graham, author interview, March 3, 2016, Washington, DC.

472 **1976 interview:** Rushton, "Stage Set for the Great American Movie," 24.

472 **"Sometimes I think it would be fun":** Mills, "Washington Called the Gay Capital," D19.

472 **"At the bar they're so friendly":** Rushton, "Stage Set for the Great American Movie," 24.

472 **On October 14, 1979:** Jo Thomas, "75,000 March in Capital in Drive to Support Homosexual Rights," *New York Times*, October 15, 1979, 14.

473 **"If a bullet should enter":** Shilts, *Mayor of Castro Street*, 184.

473 **"Oh when the dykes":** Giteck, "Gay Power on the Potomac," 15.

473 **"I just happened":** Ruth Sheehan, "We are your neighbors," *News and Observer*, April 25, 1993, E1.

473 **One of Bauman's colleagues:** Frank, *Frank*, 157.

473 **"too good to last":** Franklin Kameny, interviewed by Dori Friend, Oral History Collection, Gay, Lesbian, Bisexual, Transgender Historical Society, San Francisco, 1994.

473 **The first person in Washington:** Alma Guillermoprieto, "Epidemic of Fear: D.C. Homosexuals Face AIDS," *Washington Post*, June 5, 1983, A1.

473 **reported a loss of appetite:** Richard E. Waldhorn, Edward Tsou, and Donald M. Kerwin, "Pneumocystis carinii Pneumonia in a Previously Healthy Adult." *Journal of American Medicine*, 247, no. 13 (1982): 1860–61.

474 **one of Washington's first openly gay doctors:** Frank Blackburn, interviewed by Jerry Wei, September 20, 2015, Rainbow History Project, Washington, DC.

32: Code Breakers

476 **riding to work in the vanpool:** Jamie Shoemaker, author interview, December 12, 2014, Washington, DC.

478 **"I knew we would have problems":** Jan Krc, author interview, November 13, 2019, Washington, DC.

478 **"Fuck no, it's not":** Ross, author interview.

478 **"There is simply NO":** Franklin E. Kameny, "Shut Up and Don't Resign," *Washington Blade*, January 23, 1981, A19. That Kameny, who was not a lawyer, represented so many gay people in employment tribunals throughout the 1970's and 80's testifies to the dearth of legal professionals who were willing to help them.

478 **"America's master spy":** Philip Taubman, "Nominee for Deputy Director of C.I.A. an Electronic-Age Intelligence Expert," *New York Times*, February 2, 1981, A14.

479 **"How can you make this work?":** Bobby Ray Inman, interviewed by Timothy J. Naftali, author collection.

480 **"They had read the election returns":** Bamford, *Puzzle Palace*, 84.

489 **headline in the *Washington Post*:** Michael Getler, "Homosexual to Keep High-Security Job," *Washington Post*, December 30, 1980, A1.

480 **believed his bureaucratic adversaries:** Inman, interviewed by Naftali.

480 **"There are few who find it":** Bates, "Revelations from Jon Hinson," 1.

480 **"baby-faced ex-Marine":** Rose, "Despite Revelations, Hinson Still Favored to Win," 1.

481 **"Had UFOs landed":** Stuart P. Stevens, "School for Scandal," *Washingtonian*, March 1981, 134.

481 **twenty-six-point:** Felicity Barringer and Sandra G. Boodman, "Congressman's Revelation," *Washington Post*, A1.

481 **reliably conservative voting record:** Rose, "Despite Revelations, Hinson Still Favored to Win," 1.

481 **"I am not, never have been":** David Bates, "Hinson: I Was Sick and Tired of Worrying," *Clarion-Ledger* (Jackson, MS), August 16, 1980, 3.

481 **"Your hometown folks":** "Hinson Gives New Statement on '76 Arrest," *Clarion-Ledger* (Jackson, MS), October 2, 1980, 21.

481 **"You'd think a man":** Cliff Treyens, "Hinson Didn't Give Up Without a Stout Battle," *Clarion-Ledger* (Jackson, MS), June 24, 1981, 3B.

481 **"I don't think this is going to hurt":** Barringer and Boodman, "Congressman's Revelation," A1.

482 **Election Night victory parties:** Bauman, *Gentleman from Maryland*, 62.

482 **"I understand human weakness":** Donald P. Baker and Jackson Diehl, "'Compulsions' Admitted by Rep. Bauman," *Washington Post*, October 9, 1980, A1.

482 **the question posed by *Washingtonian* magazine:** Van Dyne, "Is DC Becoming the Gay Capital of America," 96.

482 **"It kind of makes you wonder":** Dale Russakoff and Jackson Diehl, "Reaction in Easton," *Washington Post*, October 4, 1980, A1.

482 **"We're all a bunch of drunks":** Patrick Owens, "'Family Man' in a Fix," *Newsday*, October 20, 1980, 3.

482 **"Many people have learned":** Russakoff and Diehl, "Reaction in Easton," A1.

482 **letters of support:** John Aloysius Farrell, "Bauman: 'It Can Never Be the Same,'" *Baltimore News American*, October 26, 1980, 1A.

482 **"Robert Bauman should resign":** William F. Buckley Jr., "A Congressman's Duty: Bauman Should Resign," *Washington Star*, October 9, 1980, A15. Privately, Buckley was more supportive, sending Carol Bauman a check for twenty thousand dollars to help the family through its financial difficulties. Bauman, *Gentleman from Maryland*, 124.

483 **"I never did anything that I hated"**: William F. Buckley Jr. to Paul Weyrich, October 23, 1980, Folder: "Robert Bauman," Box 6, Series III, William F. Buckley Jr. Papers, Yale University, New Haven, CT (hereafter "Buckley Papers").

483 **"had problems with affairs himself"**: "PostScript," *Washington Post*, February 12, 1979, A3.

483 **"As Kennedy says"**: Donald P. Baker, "Conservative from Shore Won't Challenge Mathias," *Washington Post*, January 29, 1980, 1.

483 **"I felt like Lazarus did"**: "Hinson Overcomes Charge to Win Election," Associated Press, November 5, 1980.

483 **Around 1 p.m.**: Johanna Neuman, "The Hinson Drama: Shattering, Ironic, Improbable," *Clarion-Ledger* (Jackson, MS), March 15, 1981, 1.

484 **"with greater force"**: Johanna Neuman, "Hinson Arrest Is the Talk of Washington," *Clarion-Ledger* (Jackson, MS), February 6 1981, 1.

484 **"teeming with some of Washington's"**: Donia Mills and Phil Gailey, "Official Pursues Double Life in Halls of Power, Seedy Bars," *Washington Star*, April 8, 1981, 1.

484 **"an episode"**: Michael Vitez, "Hinson Pleads Innocent, Enters Hospital," *Washington Star*, February 8, 1981, 8.

484 **performing it on a Black man:** Johanna Neuman, "Wednesday Arrest Rocks Hinson Staff," *Clarion-Ledger* (Jackson, MS), February 8, 1961, 1.

484 **"Can you imagine"**: Jerry Anderson, author interview, May 16, 2019, Los Angeles.

484 **"The fact that the employee"**: Art Harris and Cliff Treyens, "Hinson's Memory Haunts His Mississippi District," *Washington Post*, A7.

484 **tore a Hinson sticker off:** Neuman, "Hinson Drama," 1.

485 **Both the local chapter:** John Howard, *Men Like That: A Southern Queer History* (Chicago: University of Chicago Press, 1999), 274.

485 **"the most difficult and painful decision"**: Johanna Neuman, "Hinson Resigns Effective April 13," *Clarion-Ledger* (Jackson, MS), March 14, 1981, 1.

485 **"pondering a new political reality"**: Hugh Crell, "Politics Texas Style: Two Views on Gay Rights," *The Advocate*, April 7, 1976, 6.

485 **"the growing number of Republican politicians"**: Sasha Gregory-Lewis, "The Republicans: Embracing Homophobes and Gay Rights Backers," *The Advocate*, October 6, 1976, 7.

486 **never disclosed that one of her own top aides:** Larry Bush, "Naming Gay Names," *Village Voice*, April 27, 1982, 22.

486 **nearly three times that number:** Paul W. Valentine and Marjorie Hyer, "Vast and Joyous Crowd," *Washington Post*, April 30, 1980, A1.

487 **"Now, even straights are afraid"**: Donia Mills and Phil Gailey, "Politics Forces Many Gays to Wear Elaborate Masks," *Washington Star*, April 7, 1981, 4.

487 **"It really could turn"**: Donia Mills, "Gays Find D.C. Area Good Place to Live," *Evening Star*, April 6, 1981, 12.

33: "The Homosexual Thing"

491 **3:15 on the morning:** This reconstruction of the events of June 25 and 26, 1980 is based upon interviews with the surviving participants, documents found in Folder 15 ("Reagan, Ronald, allegations about, 1967–1980, undated,") Box 168 of the Benjamin C. Bradlee Papers at the University of Texas at Austin, and papers from the personal collection of Paul N. "Pete" McCloskey.

491 **same day in December 1998:** Guy Gugliotta and Juliet Eilperin, "House Embraces Livingston," *Washington Post*, November 19, 1998, A1.

491 **"I must set the example"**: Eric Pianin, "Livingston Quits as Designated House Speaker," *Washington Post*, December 20, 1998, A1.

492 **"world-shaking"**: Bob Woodward, "Woodward Phone Interview with Bob Livingston," July 5, 1980, Folder 15, Box 168, Bradlee Papers.

492 **Shortly before closing his office:** Ted Gup to Bob Woodward, "Memo Re: L. Francis Bouchey," July 6, 1980, Folder 15, Box 168, Bradlee Papers.

492 **Livingston also happened to live:** Bob Livingston, *The Windmill Chaser: Triumphs and Less in American Politics* (Lafayette: University of Louisiana at Lafayette Press, 2018), 105.

493 **as a nineteen-year-old student:** "Conservatism Pushed in Southland Colleges," *Los Angeles Times*, December 7, 1961, iv–16.

493 **"We have been sold down the river":** Nan Robertson, "Struggle on the Campus: How a Liberal Group Lost at the University of Oklahoma," *New York Times*, May 15, 1962, 43. As for the NSA's patriotic bona fides, not only was it not communist, it was secretly funded by the Central Intelligence Agency. Neil Sheehan, "A Student Group Concedes It Took Funds from C.I.A.," *New York Times*, February 14, 1967, 1.

494 **Chaired by a former army general:** Barbara Crossette, "A Team at State Is Key to El Salvador Policy," *New York Times*, February 24, 1982, A16; Mary Russell, "White House Seeks Showdown on Implementing Canal Pacts," *Washington Post*, June 8, 1979, A5.

494 **"that toothy Georgian peanut farmer":** Livingston, *Windmill Chaser*, 83.

494 **"No. 2 man":** "Hearings Set for Masferrer," *Miami Herald*, April 16, 1959, 2.

494 **killed in a Miami car bombing:** "Ex-Batista Aide Killed by Bomb as He Starts His Auto in Miami," *New York Times*, November 1, 1975, 30.

494 **Ford was being mentioned:** Carl P. Leubsdorf, "Several Conservatives Eyed for Reagan Ticket," *Baltimore Sun*, June 1, 1980, A8.

494 **as were Senators Howard Baker:** Lou Cannon, "Reagan Campaign Looks to Running Mate," *Washington Post*, May 13, 1980, A4; Judith Miller, "Reagan's Quarterback," *New York Times*, June 8, 1980, F1; John McLaughlin, "If Reagan's No. 1, Who's on Second?" *New York Daily News*, June 1, 1980, 46.

494 **"Do you know anything about Kemp":** Gup, "Memo Re: L. Francis Bouchey."

494 **"the homosexual thing":** Martin Tolchin, "Jack Kemp's Bootleg Run to the Right," *Esquire*, October 24, 1978, 67.

495 **"We used to have a saying":** Lou Cannon, "The Sluggers: Closeup View of Bitterest Political Fight in California," *Independent Press-Telegram*, November 1, 1970, 9.

495 **Jordan told a reporter to disregard Kemp:** Robert D. Novak, *The Prince of Darkness: 50 Years Reporting in Washington* (New York: Crown Forum, 2007), 354.

495 **"There is absolutely not a shred":** Tolchin, "Jack Kemp's Bootleg Run to the Right," 67. Though the author of this profile, *New York Times* reporter Martin Tolchin, concluded with respect to the rumors of Kemp's homosexuality that "Everyone who has looked into the case has come to the same conclusion" that they were false, he also noted, in reference to his subject's charisma, that "Jack Kemp turns people on—and not just women" (Tolchin, "Jack Kemp's Bootleg Run to the Right," 67, 59).

495 **"played a subterranean part":** Rowland Evans and Robert Novak, "Ugly Political Rumors," *Washington Post*, December 29, 1978, A15.

495 **dozen disgruntled liberal-to-moderate:** Robert C. Albright, "Barry Says Burch Did Good Job, Urges GOP Leaders to Keep Him," *Washington Post*, November 7, 1964, A1; Marjorie Hunter, "Capitol Hill Clubs Have Many Roles," *New York Times*, December 26, 1975, 33.

495 **some thirty to forty members:** "The House Wednesday Group," April 1979, Box 188: "Wednesday Group," Paul N. McCloskey Papers, Hoover Institution Archives, Palo Alto, CA.

496 **jawline so sharp:** R. W. Apple Jr., "Is McCloskey the McCarthy of '72?," *New York Times Magazine*, April 18, 1971, 29.

496 **McCloskey had defeated:** "McCloskey Victor in San Mateo Vote," *Los Angeles Times*, December 13, 1967, 1.

496 **only Republican in the country:** Geoffrey Kabaservice, *Rule and Ruin: The Downfall of Moderation and the Destruction of the Republican Party, from Eisenhower to the Tea Party* (Oxford: Oxford University Press, 2012), 218.

496 **stick to finishing his term:** Baxter Omohundro, "GOP Victor Over Shirley Temple Tells Reagan to Stick to Governor Job," *Long Beach Independent*, November 30, 1967, A23.

496 **"Maybe a young congressman":** UPI, "Reagan Hits M'Closkey's Loyalty," *Press Democrat* (Santa Rosa, CA), July 17, 1968, 14.

496 **threatened with impeachment:** "Impeach Nixon, G.O.P. Foe Urges," *New York Times*, February 17, 1971, 9; Richard L. Lyons and Spencer Rich, "House Democrats Press End-War Act," *Washington Post*, May 11, 1972, A1.

496 **talking about a primary challenge:** Apple, "Is McCloskey the McCarthy of '72?," 28.

496 **Reagan said it would not bother him:** David Kraslow, "Apologize to President, Reagan Tells Kennedy," *Los Angeles Times*, June 16, 1971, 9.

496 **"There are times when a man removes himself":** Lou Cannon, *The McCloskey Challenge* (New York: E. P. Dutton, 1972), 215.

496 **"the two most charismatic contenders":** Cannon, *The McCloskey Challenge*, 214.

496 **cofounder of Earth Day:** Beverly Beyette, "Earth Observance: The Day Politics Stood Still," *Los Angeles Times*, May 23, 1985, V1.

496 **"scared to death":** David B. Goodstein, "Our Outspoken Republican Support," *The Advocate*, April 20, 1977, 43.

497 **recruited fellow liberal Republicans:** Rowland Evans and Robert Novak, ". . . and Reagan Prepares for His 'Last Stand,'" *Washington Post*, February 26, 1976, A19.

497 **"It is absolutely essential":** Benjamin Taylor, "Moderates, Liberals and Bush," *Boston Globe*, February 2, 1980, 11.

497 **other congressmen:** Pete McCloskey, author interview.

497 **In recent weeks:** Pete McCloskey to File, "Bill Best/Ronald Reagan," June 26, 1980, Personal Papers of Pete McCloskey (hereafter, "McCloskey Papers").

497 **"The big joke on Capitol Hill":** McCloskey, author interview.

498 **only Republican sponsor:** Associated Press, "Bill Would Uphold Homosexual Rights," *Tampa Tribune*, March 26, 1975, 9A.

498 **"I am heterosexual, I think":** Goodstein, "Our Outspoken Republican Support," 9.

498 **one of his staffers was arrested:** J. Brian Smith, *John J. Rhodes: Man of the House* (Phoenix, AZ: Primer, 2005), 70.

498 **accompanied his fellow Arizonan:** Bart Barnes, "John J. Rhodes Dies; Led GOP in House During Watergate," *Washington Post*, August 26, 2003, B4; Ben Bradlee, *A Good Life: Newspapering and Other Adventures* (New York: Simon and Schuster, 1995), 373; *With No Apologies: The Personal and Political Memoir of United States Senator Barry M. Goldwater* (New York: William Morrow, 1979), 265–66.

498 **Rhodes convened a secret strategy session:** Jack Anderson and Les Whitten, "Ford Strategy Huddle," *Washington Post*, May 28, 1976, D15.

498 **forty-three-minute spontaneous demonstration:** James T. Wooten, "Reagan's Backers Stage Noisy Last-Ditch Parade," *New York Times*, August 19, 1976, 1.

498 **backer of the ERA:** Jack W. Germond and Jules Witcover, "GOP Right in House Takes Aim at Rhodes," *Baltimore Sun*, April 13, 1977, A15.

499 **newsletter of Citizens for the Republic:** Lou Cannon, "Rhodes Withdraws Support to Register Voters Election Day," *Washington Post*, May 17, 1977, A15.

499 **preparing to step down:** Carl P. Leubsdorf, "Michel to Be GOP Floor Leader in Detroit," *Baltimore Sun*, May 18, 1980, A3.

499 **"the matter should go no further":** Pete McCloskey to File, "Bill Best/Ronald Reagan," June 26, 1980, McCloskey Papers.

499 **subject of Kemp's sexuality "dominated":** Gup, "Memo Re: L. Francis Bouchey."

499 **Bouchey might have volunteered the possibility:** McCloskey, "RE: Bill Best/Ronald Reagan."

499 **"eleven o'clock rule":** Alsop, *Center*, 2.

500 **"a pattern with closeted men":** Strub, *Body Counts*, 61.

500 **"Oh hell no":** Gup, "Memo Re: L. Francis Bouchey."

500 **"When I was fifteen":** Bob Livingston, author interview, September 25, 2019, Washington, DC.

501 **"You were absolutely right":** McCloskey, "RE: Bill Best/Ronald Reagan."

501 **staged a coup d'état:** "President Ousted by Army Units in El Salvador," *Washington Post*, October 16, 1979, A1.

34: The Manchurian Candidate

502 **"Pied Piper to three generations":** Robert G. Kaiser et al., "Ex-Rep. Lowenstein Fatally Shot by Gunman in N.Y. Law Office," *Washington Post*, March 15, 1980, A1.

503 **Lowenstein worked with McCloskey:** Flora Lewis, "Coalition Concentrates on Registering Young Voters," *New York Times*, June 18, 1971, A26.

503 **had met in the early 1960s:** "Ex.-Rep Lowenstein Killed by a Gunman," *New York Times*, March 15, 1980, 1.

503 **privately discussed the possibility:** Bruce Voeller, interviewed by William Chafe, December 12, 1989, Lowenstein Oral History Project, Columbia University, New York. See further William Chafe, *Never Stop Running: Allard Lowenstein and the Struggle to Save American Liberalism* (New York: Basic Books, 1993), 216–27, 409–10, 445–54.

503 **thesis of a controversial book:** Richard Cummings, *The Pied Piper: Allard K. Lowenstein and the Liberal Dream* (New York: Grove Press, 1985).

503 **cruising for sex:** Andrew Kopkind, "Neglect of the Left: Allard Lowenstein," *Grand Street* 5, no. 3 (Spring 1986): 230–40.

503 **told at least five other people:** David Harris, *Dreams Die Hard: Three Men's Journey Through the Sixties* (New York: St. Martin's Press, 1982), 329.

503 **after entering Lowenstein's office:** Kaiser et al., "Ex-Rep. Lowenstein Fatally Shot."

503 **"almost equal to that":** Pete McCloskey, email to author, December 1, 2020.

503 **delivered a eulogy:** Michael Daly, "Writing a Eulogy for 'a Gentle Warrior in Our Midst,'" *New York Daily News*, March 18, 1980, 7.

504 **"there were rumors that Lowenstein":** In the wake of Lowenstein's death, a number of his influential friends made strenuous efforts to suppress revelations about his sexuality. According to David Harris, a Lowenstein protégé whom the *New York Times Magazine* commissioned to write a piece about his relationship with the former congressman, within days of his filing the article (which detailed Sweeney's allegations), the magazine received calls from a prominent newspaper columnist, a member of the New York City Council, and a former member of the American delegation to the United Nations all stressing that any insinuation Lowenstein was gay was "unfounded." The *Village Voice* article was one in a three-part series that earned its author, Teresa Carpenter, the 1981 Pulitzer Prize for Feature Writing. Harris, *Dreams Die Hard*, 329–31; Teresa Carpenter, "From Heroism to Madness: The Odyssey of the Man Who Shot Al Lowenstein," *Village Voice*, May 12, 1980, 1. (The piece was reprinted, in shorter form, in the *Washington Post* as "Long Journey into Darkness," May 18, 1980, H1.) The letter McCloskey cosigned appeared as "Gratuitous Innuendo," *Washington Post*, June 22, 1980, D6.

504 **"been physically and homosexually approached":** Paul N. McCloskey Jr. to Pete Best, July 2, 1980, Box 168, Folder 15, Bradlee Papers.

504 **"I'm thinking back to *Advise and Consent*":** McCloskey, author interview.

504 **"it was imperative":** McCloskey, "RE: Bill Best/Ronald Reagan."

505 **"I[,] William H. Best III, discovered":** William H. Best III, "Exhibit A," January 9, 1976, Box 168, Folder 15, Bradlee Papers.

506 **the Mafia:** Dan E. Moldea, *Dark Victory: Ronald Reagan, MCA, and the Mob* (New York: Viking, 1986).

506 **a "network" of homosexuals:** McCloskey, "RE: Bill Best, Ronald Reagan."

506 **"quixotic":** Apple, "Is McCloskey the McCarthy of '72?," 29.

507 **only one option:** Pete McCloskey, email to author, October 20, 2019.

507 **After midnight on July 3:** Amber Scholtz to File, Memorandum, July 10, 1980, McCloskey Papers.

507 **"holy shit" exclusive:** Mike Sager, "The Fabulist Who Changed Journalism," *Columbia Journalism Review* (Spring 2016).

507 **"the focus was that there":** Patrick Tyler, author interview, September 15, 2019, phone.

507 **Goldwater had also urged:** Ted Gup alluded to Goldwater's involvement—albeit mistaking his role with that of McCloskey—in an appreciation of Bradlee published after the legendary newspaperman's 2014 death. "A Republican senator had gone to Ben's house in the middle of the night, Ben said, alleging that the candidate Ronald Reagan had a number of gay staffers" (Ted Gup, "The Ben Bradlee Who Hired Me—Finally," *New York Times*, October 22, 2014).

508 **"rumors about people on Reagan's staff":** Tom Evans, author interview, December 8, 2020, phone.

508 **Rhodes announced his endorsement:** "Reagan Undecided on Running Mate," *Arizona Republic*, June 20, 1980, 5; Terence Hunt, "Reagan Seeks to Broaden Congressional Base," Associated Press, June 18, 1980.

508 **rejected Goldwater's offer to campaign:** Associated Press, "Reagan Shuns Goldwater Aid," *Washington Post*, June 23, 1966, B4.

508 **"a surprisingly dangerous state of mind"**: Bill McAllister and Don Oberdorfer, "Goldwater, Reagan at War over Canal," *Washington Post*, May 5, 1976, A1.

508 **not speak for over a year**: Donald T. Critchlow, "Rethinking American Conservatism: Toward a New Narrative," *Journal of American History* 98, no. 3 (December 2011): 755.

508 **began dating Bradlee's mother-in-law**: James Hohmann, "Watergate's 'Last Chapter,'" *Politico*, April 19, 2011.

508 **"Goldy"**: Bradlee, *Good Life*, 378.

508 **installed the hi-fi stereo**: Scott Armstrong, author interview.

508 **"*Post*-mortem"**: Goldwater and Casserly, *Goldwater*, 81.

509 **Best told Armstrong**: Scott Armstrong to All, "Re: Bill Best Interview July 4 and Other Info," Box 168, Folder 15, Benjamin C. Bradlee Papers, Harry Ransom Center, University of Texas at Austin.

510 **tracked down Lynn Bouchey**: Gup, "Memo Re: L. Francis Bouchey."

511 **Woodward interviewed Livingston**: Woodward, "Woodward Phone Interview with Bob Livingston."

511 **"Public persons' private lives"**: Benjamin C. Bradlee, "Why the Post Killed That Anderson Column," *Washington Post*, June 21, 1976, A23.

512 **been approached by another congressman**: J. R. Freeman, "Post Suppressed Story on Moorhead Scandal," *Pittsburgh Tribune-Review*, December 22, 1981, A2.

512 **"went to Bradlee and pleaded"**: David Leigh, "A Fleet Streeter Looks at the Washington Post," *Columbia Journalism Review* (March/April 1981): 54.

512 **"In the end"**: Tyler, author interview.

512 **On the first day of the gathering**: Novak, *Prince of Darkness*, 353–54.

512 **"Let's hear it for gay power!"**: McCloskey, author interview.

513 **a crowd of one hundred fifty**: Lou Chibbaro Jr., "Officials Condemn Equus Attack," *Washington Blade*, August 21, 1980, 1.

513 **Punches were thrown**: Thomas Morgan, "The Battle of Capitol Hill: Gays vs. the Leathernecks," *Washington Post*, August 24, 1980, B1.

513 **said the attack might arouse**: "Marines Probe Assault on Gay Bar in D.C.," *Washington Star*, August 18, 1980, B3.

513 **"courtesy patrols"**: Pete Earley, "Marines Patrol SE Area to Halt Confrontations," *Washington Post*, August 21, 1981, B4.

514 **"United States cryptographers"**: Pete McCloskey to Edwin Meese, n.d., McCloskey Papers.

514 **"accepted Pete Hannaford's absolute denial"**: Pete McCloskey to William Best, September 9, 1980, McCloskey Papers.

514 **Meese disputed**: Edwin Meese, author interview, January 22, 2020, phone.

514 **McCloskey endorsed Reagan**: Associated Press, "McCloskey Endorses Reagan Despite Feuds in the Past," *Santa Cruz Sentinel*, September 26, 1980, 6.

515 **demanding "recognition"**: Robert Scheer, "Reagan Views Issues at Home, Abroad," *Los Angeles Times*, March 6, 1980, 8.

515 **side-by-side comparison**: Ronald L. Soble, "The Issues: How the Candidates Compare," *Los Angeles Times*, October 23, 1980, 11.

515 **"I was pleasantly surprised"**: Peter Hannaford to Larry Bush, Folder 16, no. 7316, Box 4, Larry Bush Papers, Division of Rare and Manuscript Collections, Cornell University Library, Ithaca, NY (hereafter cited as "Larry Bush Papers").

516 **"probably the man 'most inside'"**: Peter D. Hannaford, *The Reagans: A Political Portrait* (New York: Coward-McCann, 1983). In his later years as a political consultant, what David Mixner described as Hannaford's "two worlds," homosexuality and right-wing politics, bizarrely intersected when Hannaford took on as a client the far-right Austrian Freedom Party. Its closeted führer, Jörg Haider, died in a drunk-driving accident after leaving a gay bar in 2008. In another irony, Hannaford was the editor of Drew Pearson's second volume of diaries, which cover the columnist's breaking the 1967 "homosexual ring" story.

516 **Carter led Reagan**: "Gallup Presidential Election Trial-Heat Trends, 1936–2008," Gallup, n.d., https://news.gallup.com/poll/110548/gallup-presidential-election-trialheat-trends-19362004.aspx#4.

517 **Joan Quigley:** David Colker, "Joan Quigley, 1927–2014; Astrologer Who Advised Reagans," *Los Angeles Times*, October 26, 2014, A32.

517 **gave up his House seat:** John Maclean, "Israel Loses the Glitter of a Shining Star," *Chicago Tribune*, September 26, 1982, 18; Bill Boyarsky and Jerry Gillam, "Stand on Mideast Draws $30,000 to McCloskey's Effort," *Los Angeles Times*, May 23, 1982, 25; Kim Murphy, "'Holocaust Denier' Launches U.S. Tour," *Los Angeles Times*, May 30, 2000, A5.

517 **"a latter-day Don Quixote":** Dave Kiesel, "Mellowed but Unbowed," *Press Democrat*, April 21, 1981, 13.

35: An Enclosed and Enchanted Garden

518 **"snappy, flashy, yet dignified":** Pete Earley, "A Snappy Inauguration," *Washington Post*, November 30, 1980, A1.

518 **most expensive such ceremony in history:** Pete Earley, "Reagan Inauguration Most Expensive Ever," *Washington Post*, January 16, 1981, A1.

518 **"the Peanut Special":** B. Drummond Ayres Jr., "Special Train Bears Joyous Carter Neighbors North," *New York Times*, January 20, 1977, 32.

519 **"Carter dollars":** Carter's inaugural cost $3.5 million; the price tag on Reagan's was $16 million. Earley, "A Snappy Inauguration," A1; Phil Gailey, "Capital Begins Its Celebration of Reagan's 2d Inauguration," *New York Times*, January 19, 1985, 1.

519 **Nearly one hundred parties:** Marie Brenner, "Social Notes from Reagan's Washington," *New York*, February 15, 1982, 39.

519 **Carter would wear formal attire:** "Carter Plans to Wear Formal Attire Jan. 20," *New York Times*, January 3, 1981, 9.

519 **"We're concentrating entirely on television":** Lynn Rosellini, "A Preview of the Reagan Inauguration," *New York Times*, December 10, 1980, D22.

519 **Live coverage of the inauguration:** Pete Earley, "Eight Invitation-Only Inaugural Balls On Reagan's List, but Not Disco Party," *Washington Post*, December 10, 1980, C1.

519 **"This is the first administration":** Megan Rosenfeld and Joseph McClellan, "Inaugural Gala," *Washington Post*, January 20, 1981, B1.

520 **"It would seem out of place":** Pete Earley, "Inaugural Panel Drops Plans for Military Parade with Flags Only," *Washington Post*, December 5, 1980, A3.

520 **"Reagan's Capote":** In his 1982 book, *God's Bullies*, Perry Deane Young identifies "Reagan's Capote" only as a "friend" of Reagan who suggested the "flamboyant idea of having the military units in the inaugural parade march with American flags instead of rifles" (Perry Deane Young, *God's Bullies: Native Reflections on Preachers and Politics* [New York: Holt, Rinehart and Winston, 1982], 133).

520 **more gays serving on its White House staff:** Charlie Brydon, interviewed by Eric Marcus, in *Making History*, 312. Toward the end of the Reagan administration, White House counsel Peter Wallison would recall, "In most cases I said we're not going to raise any question about" a job applicant's sexual orientation. "If it had been a case involving a person in a national security position, it would have been a closer case. I probably would have brought it up higher and talked to [Chief of Staff Don] Regan about it, just to get another judgment, but in all the cases that I can recall where that came up, when I talked about it with the staff, the principle was that Reagan would not discriminate against people on the basis of homosexuality, so we should not raise that as an issue, because we believed that he was quite open-minded about that sort of thing" (Peter Wallison, interviewed by Jeff Chidester and Christine Nemacheck, October 28, 2003, Ronald Reagan Oral History Project, Miller Center).

520 **A president of the Young Republicans:** Susan Ford Wiltshire, *Seasons of Grief and Grace: A Sister's Story of AIDS* (Nashville: Vanderbilt University Press, 1994), 20–23.

520 **"a vast gay presence":** John Ford, interviewed by Susan Ford Wiltshire, July 31, 1992, author's collection.

520 **estimated at about one thousand:** John Ford, "Cocktails at Six: An Overview of the Story," author's collection.

520 **"was told from the very beginning":** Larry Reynolds, author interview, May 29, 2014, Washington, DC.

521 **"the theory that if a story":** Trento, *Power House*, 138.

521 **tidy encapsulation:** Jim Lardner, author interview, July 8, 2019, Washington, DC.

521 **"'Early Reagan" style:** Lynn Rosellini, "Bob Gray: Public Relations Man to the Powerful," *New York Times*, February 26, 1982, A18.

522 **"He knows everyone":** Rosenfeld, "Inaugural Insider," B1.

522 **"He's turned into":** Barbara Gamarekian, "Bob Gray, Man About Capital, Has a Party," *New York Times*, July 10, 1981, B4.

522 **Reagan's "first friend":** Steven V. Roberts, "Reagan's 'First Friend,'" *New York Times Magazine*, March 21, 1982, 26.

522 **cosponsor of the Family Protection Act:** Family Protection Act S. 1808, 96th Cong (1979).

522 **"What always fascinates me":** Rosellini "Bob Gray," A18.

522 **have his secretary interrupt his meetings:** Trento, *Power House*, 167.

522 **"very fastidious, perfectly coiffed":** Gahl Hodges Burt, author interview, September 16, 2019, New York, NY.

522 **"the Tippy Top":** Stephanie Mansfield, "You Are What You Pretend to Be," *Washington Post Magazine*, January 2, 1983, 7.

522 **"Gay & Company":** Lardner, author interview.

523 **"always surrounded by this bevy":** Graham, author interview.

523 **"Half of Gray and Company":** Robert Higdon, author interview, June 16, 2015, Washington, DC.

523 **"I guess when I hired you":** Witeck, author interview.

523 **spent over a million dollars:** Trento, *Power House*, 188.

523 **first openly gay person to hold:** Thompson, *Price of Achievement*, 161.

523 **"so stupid as to be *open*":** Thompson, *Price of Achievement*, 170.

523 **Marxist government of Angola:** Trento, *Power House*, 315–16.

524 **evangelical Christian staffers:** Daniel K. Williams, "Reagan's Religious Right: The Unlikely Alliance Between Southern Evangelicals and a California Conservative," in *Ronald Reagan and the 1980s: Perceptions, Policies, Legacies,* ed. Cheryl Hudson and Gareth Davies (New York: Palgrave Macmillan, 2008), 142.

524 **"closet tolerance":** Robert G. Kaiser, "This Puffed-Up Piety Is Perfectly Preposterous," *Washington Post*, March 18, 1984, C1; Larry Bush, "Republican Gays Set to Emerge as 84 GOP Force," *The Bush Report*, April–May 1984, 1.

524 **"We were both kind of amused":** Hal Gordon, author interview, January 18, 2019, phone.

524 **Meese asked Roy Cohn:** Von Hoffman, *Citizen Cohn*, 418–19.

524 **"First Flack":** "The Ear," *Washington Post*, December 30, 1981, B1.

524 **"wanted to find out if someone":** Burt, author interview.

524 **he noted in a letter:** Robert Keith Gray, "What It Takes to Dress Like a First Lady," *New York Times*, October 30, 1988, E24.

525 **"Scratch the surface":** Dick Polman, "Private Life; Public Death," *Palm Beach Post*, January 17, 1987, 1F.

525 **Kenneth Jay Lane:** Nina Hyde, "Red, White & Nancy," *Washington Post*, January, 14, 1985, C1.

525 **Jimmy Galanos:** Guy Trebay, "James Galanos, Fashion Designer for the Elite, Dies at 92," *New York Times*, October 31, 2016, D8.

525 **Carroll Righter:** Lou Cannon, "Astrologers Used by First Lady, Regan Book Says," *Washington Post*, May 3, 1988, A1.

525 **"better be described as Bill Blass":** Elisabeth Bumiller, "A Cozy Little Dinner, Fit for a Prince," *Washington Post*, May 4, 1981, B1.

525 **Ted Graber:** Enid Nemy, "Ted Graber, 80, Decorator for Reagans, Dies," *New York Times*, June 12, 2000, B6.

525 **"live-in friend":** Elisabeth Bumiller and Donnie Radcliffe, "Nancy Reagan: The First Two Years," *Washington Post*, January 23, 1983, G1.

525 **"first fop":** Blythe Babyak, "First Fop," *The Washington Monthly*, December 1981, 50.

525 **"river of small, hilarious defamations":** Tina Brown, *The Vanity Fair Diaries, 1983–1992* (New York: Henry Holt, 2017), 144.

525 **"compulsive user of the telephone":** Michael K. Deaver, *Behind the Scenes: In Which the Author Talks About Ronald and Nancy Reagan . . . and Himself* (New York: William Morrow, 1987), 106.

525 **"Zipkin either has no love life":** Jennifer Allen, "The Other Man in Nancy's Life," *New York Daily News*, November 25, 1980.

525 **"a sort of modern-day Oscar Wilde":** Babyak, "First Fop," 52.

525 **Zipkin who convinced Nancy:** Colacello, *Ronnie and Nancy*, 6.
526 **behaved as if he were Saint Peter:** Beth Landman, "The Last of New York City's 'Walkers: 'They Knew Everyone's Secrets'" *Hollywood Reporter*, April 17, 2019.
526 **"male and female homosexuals":** Colacello, *Ronnie and Nancy*, 4.
526 **"literally held Nancy's pocketbook":** Author interview with former labor union employee.
526 **"half of my friends":** Mark Falcoff, author interview, February 23, 2015, Washington, DC.
526 **"antagonistic divide":** Alan Zuschlag, author interview, July 8, 2014, Washington, DC.
526 **"staff infection":** William Norwich, "Sean Driscoll," *Air Mail*, May 8, 2021, https://airmail.news/issues/2021-5-8/sean-driscoll.
526 **Robin Weir's salon:** Barbara Gamarekian, "Hairdos and Champagne Before the Ceremony," *New York Times*, January 21, 1985, A18.
527 **one of the trendiest places:** Martin Weil, "Robin Weir Dies at 45," *Washington Post*, September 4, 1993, D1; "Robin Weir Dies at 45; Cut First Lady's Hair," *New York Times*, September 5, 1993, 26.
527 **hottest seller at a Georgetown gift shop:** Lynn Rosellini, "First Lady Tells Critics: 'I Am Just Being Myself,'" *New York Times*, October 13, 1981, A20.
527 **"How can you work for them?"** Higdon, author interview.
527 **"Grab one of those Halston numbers":** Liz Trotta, *Fighting for Air: In the Trenches with Television News* (New York: Simon and Schuster, 1991), 302.
527 **press conference at Leonard Bernstein's:** Liz Trotta, *Booknotes*, C-SPAN, August 18, 1991.
528 **"the only man I ever knew":** Trotta, *Fighting for Air*, 91–92.
528 **"constantly reinvented himself":** Frank Greve and Nelson Schwartz, "Party's Over," *Philadelphia Inquirer*, July 29, 1989, 29.
528 **"He was a loner":** Judy Mathewson, Untitled, States News Service, July 21, 1989.
529 **tricked his classmates:** Jerry Seper and Michael Hedges, "Spence Elusive, Said to Be Everywhere but Isn't," *Washington Times*, August 3, 1989, A1.
529 **"Not since Ethel Kennedy":** Maxine Cheshire, "VIP: Gilded Trail of a Man About Town," *Washington Post*, May 9, 1980, E1.
529 **"If anybody can dance":** Donnie Radcliffe, "The Saudi Hot Spot," *Washington Post*, April 28, 1981, B1.
529 **"Craig would make it very clear":** Ted Koppel, author interview, November 8, 2018, phone.
530 **Another role model:** Seper and Hedges, "Spence Elusive," A1.
530 **boldface names:** Michael Hedges, "White House Access Probed," *Washington Times*, July 3, 1989, 1; Koppel, author interview.
530 **"mystery man":** Phil Gailey, "Have Names, Will Open Right Doors," *New York Times*, January 18, 1982, A14.
531 **"decidedly Stouffer's quality":** Charlotte Hays, "Shocking Revelation: I Was Dropped by Craig Spence," *Washington Times*, July 11, 1989, E1.
531 **"dripping with pretension":** Author interview with former Pentagon official.
531 **the "remote presence":** Trotta, *Fighting for Air*, 303.
531 **Spence's favorite book:** Seper and Hedges, "Spence Elusive," A1.
531 **"He knew I knew":** Trotta, *Booknotes*, C-SPAN, August 18, 1991.
531 **received a phone call:** Falcoff, author interview.
532 **"Have you noticed":** Hays, "Shocking Revelation."
532 **birthday party for Roy Cohn:** Michael Hedges and Jerry Seper, "Power Broker Served Drugs, Sex at Parties Bugged for Blackmail," *Washington Times*, June 30, 1989, A1.
532 **"and after everybody left":** Author interview with attendee at Craig Spence parties, February 27, 2015, Miami, FL.
532 **two Seiko watches valued at $340:** Lee Lescaze and Patrick E. Tyler, "Japanese Presented 2 Watches to Allen," *Washington Post*, November 21, 1981, A1; Michael Isikoff, "Richard Allen's Ties to Japan Now Formal," *Washington Post*, April 11, 1983, A9.
532 **"With Craig, you never knew":** Author interview with attendee at Craig Spence parties.
533 **"Morning in America":** Zuschlag, author interview.
533 **tourists in Times Square:** Rich, "Gay Decades," 88.
533 **"laissez-fairies":** David Brock, *Blinded by the Right: The Conscience of an Ex-Conservative* (New York: Three Rivers Press, 2002), 40.

533 **RPQs:** Young, *God's Bullies*, 132; Lardner, author interview.

533 **BLOW:** Taylor Branch, "Closets of Power," *Harper's*, October 1982, 44.

534 **"One might think such a theme":** Tom Shales, "America's Fascination with 'Brideshead,'" *Washington Post*, February 15, 1982, B1.

535 **In homage to Sebastian:** Two years after the show first aired, the British writer and Washington resident Christopher Hitchens happened to be walking home in a white suit while carrying a teddy bear for his newborn son. He was routinely accosted by pedestrians shouting, "Hi, Sebastian!" Christopher Hitchens, "It's All on Account of the War," *Guardian Review*, September 27, 2008, 2.

36: Sodom-on-the-Potomac

536 **"It is the *Deep Backgrounder*'s purpose":** "Statement of Purpose: The Great Untold Story," *Deep Backgrounder*, May/June 1982, 2.

536 **chief investigative reporter for *Spotlight*:** Steve Martz, "Right-Wing Tabloid Called 'Scurrilous,'" *Washington Blade*, May 28, 1982, 3.

536 **Not long after Victor Marchetti quit:** Phil McCombs, "Former Spy Victor Marchetti: 11 Years of Truth and Fantasy," *Washington Post*, December 15, 1980, A1. The agency did take Marchetti to court in an unsuccessful attempt to suppress his next book, a purportedly nonfiction exposé. Victor Marchetti and John D. Marks, *The CIA and the Cult of Intelligence* (New York: Alfred A. Knopf, 1974).

537 **"secret lovers":** Victor Marchetti, "Homosexuals Create Problem in CIA," *Deep Backgrounder*, May/June 1982, 4.

537 **Hunt had helped orchestrate the Kennedy assassination:** Stephen K. Doig, "Ex-CIA Agent Admits He Used JFK 'Rumors,'" *Miami Herald*, February 2, 1985, 2B.

537 **"I'll blow your belly":** McCombs, "Former Spy Victor Marchetti."

537 **On August 14, 1979:** Robert Meyers, "Espionage Is Admitted by Sailor," *Washington Post*, September 26, 1979, C1.

538 **According to his roommate:** Stephanie Mansfield, "Sailor Accused of Espionage Wanted to 'Buy Things,'" *Washington Post*, August 16, 1979, A2.

538 **most other spies at this late stage:** Scott Shane, "A Spy's Motivation: For Love of Another Country," *New York Times*, April 20, 2008, WK3.

538 **"homosexual proclivities":** Charles R. Babcock and Stephanie Mansfield, "File on Pentagon Homosexuals Seized in Spy Case," August 22, 1979, A1.

538 **"gay ring":** Lisa M. Keen et al., "Do These People a Witch Hunt Make?" *Washington Blade*, August 6, 1982, 11–12.

538 **NBC News:** Steve Martz, "Television News Reports Draw Rebuttals," *Washington Blade*, December 4, 1981, A3.

538 **"For people in the intelligence community":** "The Media Coverage: Four Excerpts," *Washington Blade*, August 20, 1982, SR-12.

539 **Legal Services Corporation director Dan Bradley:** Phil Gailey, "Homosexual Takes Leave of a Job and of an Agony," *New York Times*, March 31, 1982, A24.

539 **"Homosexual 'smears' appear to be":** Larry Kramer, "Terry Dolan and the Homosexual's Dilemma," n.d., YCAL MSS 722, Box 1: "1981/1982," Larry Kramer Papers, Beinecke Rare Book and Manuscript Library, Yale University, New Haven, CT (hereafter "Larry Kramer Papers").

539 **twenty-five members of Congress:** Richard Pienciak, "The Rise and Fall of a Washington Sex Scandal," Associated Press, September 18, 1982.

539 **American alternative press:** For more on the political ecosystem of right-wing newsletters that flourished in the 1970s and '80s, see James Kirchick, "Angry White Man: The Bigoted Past of Ron Paul," *New Republic*, January 1, 2008, 20–24.

539 **"venture further behind Washington's closed doors":** "Continue Your Journey Through the World of *Deep Backgrounder*," *Deep Backgrounder*, May/June 1982, 12.

540 **"on the ash-heap of history":** Lou Cannon, "President Calls for 'Crusade,'" *Washington Post*, June 9, 1982, A1.

540 **"sending over these young":** Former Pentagon official, author interview, February 19, 2015, Arlington, VA.

540 **"Pages as a rule":** Walter Wellman, "Smart Boys Are They," *Fall River (MA) Globe*, July 18, 1890, 7.

540 **messenger corps in American legislative bodies:** *History of the House Page Program* (Washington, DC: Office of the Historian and Office of the Clerk, U.S. House of Representatives, 2014), 2.

540 **"magnificent grandeur":** *The Diary of John Quincy Adams, 1794–1845: American Diplomacy and Political, Social, and Intellectual Life, from Washington to Polk*, ed. Allan Nevins, New York: Charles Scribner's Sons, 1951), 430.

541 **first full-time girl:** *House Page Program*, 18.

541 **fifth of six children:** *Report of the Committee on Standards of Official Conduct "On the Inquiry Under House Resolution 12 into certain Narcotics Investigations by the United States Capitol Police,"* Report No. 98–205, 98th Cong., 1st Sess. (May 18, 1983). Hereafter "House Page Report."

541 **item appeared:** "Kaposi's Sarcoma and Pneumocystis Pneumonia Among Homosexual Men— New York City and California," *Morbidity and Mortality Weekly Report* 30, no. 25 (July 3, 1981), 1.

542 **front page of the *Blade*:** Janis Kelly, "Rare, Fatal Pneumonia Hits Gay Men," *Washington Blade*, July 10, 1981, 1; Jim Marks, "Council Skirts Snag on Sex Law Reform," *Washington Blade*, July 10, 1981, 1.

542 **sought male partners:** House Page Report, 35.

543 **"someone who believed":** House Page Report, 12.

543 **six phone lines:** "Dial-a-Sex," *Deep Backgrounder*, May/June 1982, 3.

544 **"conduct an informal surveillance":** "Dial-a-Sex," 3. The tabloid claimed credit for the raid. "Probe Prompts Crackdown," *Deep Backgrounder*, May/June 1982, 2.

544 **Price introduced Schauer:** Keen et. al., "Do These People a Witch Hunt Make?"

544 **thirteen boxes of business records:** Superior Court of the District of Columbia, Search Warrant, March 18, 1982.

544 **"a white, pasty-faced pimp":** "Interviews at Chesapeake House—April 30, about 12:30 a.m.," Folder 5, Box 39, *Washington Blade* Lou Chibbaro senior reporter files, Special Collections Research Center, George Washington University, Washington, DC (hereafter "Chibbaro Papers").

544 **five hundred to a thousand:** Ed Burke, "Male Modeling Service in Georgetown Raided," *Washington Post*, March 20, 1982, B2.

544 **pang of dread:** Larry Bush, "Naming Gay Names," Folder 6, Box 7, Larry Bush Papers.

544 **"List of One Thousand Names":** William Greider, "Trial by Silhouette," *Rolling Stone*, February 17, 1983, 7.

545 **"customer names, occupations, sexual proclivities, etc.":** "How the Stables Stays in Business," *Deep Backgrounder*, May/June 1982, 5.

545 **police raided the Stables:** "Dial-a-Sex Services Come Under Close Scrutiny," *Deep Backgrounder*, July/August 1982, 9.

545 **Shortly after a dinner party:** Larry Bush, "Anatomy of a Scandal," *Advocate*, October 14, 1982, 21.

545 **"the rumor capitol of the world":** House Page Report, 29.

545 **On June 9:** House Page Report, 30.

546 **"a 16 year old kid":** House Page Report, 45.

546 **"a widespread, organized homosexual ring":** House Page Report 31.

546 **On June 30 and July 1:** Pienciak, "The Rise and Fall of a Washington Sex Scandal."

546 **spoke of graver debasements:** House Page Report 33, 38.

547 **"You know, the way the Hill works":** "Pages claim sexual abuse in Congress," *Miami Herald*, July 2, 1982, 4A.

547 **"Why don't congressmen like to use bookmarks?":** Nicholas von Hoffman, "Prelude to a Scandal," *Spectator*, August 14, 1982, 7.

547 **"When all else fails":** Robert Pear, "Authorities Meet on Capitol Sex and Drug Inquiry," *New York Times*, July 8, 1982, B9.

547 **"the sheer panic that reigns":** Lisa Myers, NBC News, July 2, 1982.

547 **antigay witch hunts:** John Gerassi, *The Boys of Boise: Furor, Vice, and Folly in an American City* (New York: Macmillan, 1966). Twenty-five years after denying a charge of homosexuality no one had made against him, Craig was arrested in a Minneapolis-St. Paul International Airport men's room for tapping his foot beneath a toilet stall partition in a manner suggestive of sexual solicitation. "I'm a fairly wide guy," then senator Craig said in his defense, explaining how his foot wound up in the neighboring stall of an undercover police officer. The lawyer who represented Leroy Williams in 1982 used this occasion to confirm that Craig was one of the congressmen with whom

his client claimed to have had sex, something he had already told Martin Price at the time. William Yardley and Duff Wilson, "Tape Shows a Senator Protesting After Arrest," *New York Times*, August 31, 2007, A17; Andy Davis, "NLR Teen's Allegations Surface in Light of Craig Arrest," *Arkansas Democrat-Gazette*, August 31, 2007.

547 **"with the greatest reluctance":** Martin Tolchin, "With 'Reluctance,' Califano Steps into Sex-Drug Inquiry," *New York Times*, July 28, 1981, A18.

547 **"common practice for foreign agents":** "Capitol Hill Investigation," *World News Tonight*, ABC, July 27, 1982.

547 **"extremely reliable sources":** "Interview with Homicide Det. Mike Helwig," July 28, 1982, Folder 4, Box 73, Chibbaro Papers.

548 **"[w]e do know that Soviet intelligence":** Joe Pichirallo, "Sale of Male Sex Client Lists Unconfirmed, Ex-Investigator Says," *Washington Post*, July 28, 1982, A13.

548 **story for the Knight Ridder:** Frank Greve, "Soviet Spies May Have Snooped on Homosexuals in D.C.," *Miami Herald*, July 16, 1982, 1A.

548 **State Department had fired:** Walter Pincus, "State Department Checks Alleged Gay Client Lists," *Washington Post*, August 4, 1982, A13.

548 **"name names":** "We Are First!" *Deep Backgrounder*, July/August 1982, 1.

548 **Citing Leroy Williams's lawyer:** Martin Price, "Three Congressmen, Senator Named in Homosexual Probe," *Deep Backgrounder*, July/August 1982, 1.

548 **No other media outlet:** United Press International, August 6, 1982.

548 **Elsewhere in the issue:** "Danger: Insiders at Large," *Deep Backgrounder*, July/August 1982, 6.

548 **"the Baron":** Jane Mayer, "Politics '84—Report on 'The Baron': Political Guru Finds Opinions Pay," *Wall Street Journal*, June 27, 1984, 1.

548 **a giant bottle of Tab:** "Suspicions," *Washington Post Sunday Magazine*, December 9, 1979, 5.

548 **"stimulating environment":** Sean Strub, interviewed by Dudley Clendinen, December 6, 1993, transcript provided by Adam Nagourney.

549 **"very active in the capital's homosexual community":** "Democratic Insider Alleged to Deal in Cocaine," *Deep Backgrounder*, July/August 1982, 6–7. Baron's 1979 arrest on cocaine possession had made the front page of the *Washington Post*. Tom Sherwood and Alfred E. Lewis, "Newsletter Editor Arrested in SE on Drug Charge," *Washington Post*, August 22, 1979, A1.

549 **Baron was convinced:** Strub, interviewed by Clendinen.

549 **"the worst kept secret in Washington":** "Reagan Inaugural Co-Chairman Powerful 'Closet Homosexual?'" *Deep Backgrounder*, July/August 1982, 6–7. While different in practically every respect, the unkempt, leftist, louche Baron (whose table manners were so "atrocious," remembered Robert Novak, that he often "emit[ted] a fine spray of food while eating") and the dapper, conservative, discreet Gray actually did know each other, albeit not through their membership in a nefarious and secret sexual conspiracy alluded to so ominously by the *Deep Backgrounder*. "He and Alan weren't chummy," Strub recalled of Baron's relationship with Gray; "they didn't call each other up. But there was sort of that acknowledgment of each other in their own spheres and they knew each other was gay and they were each sort of power players, and sort of a kind of protection, even though they're ideologically very different and so on." Strub observed how "the strength of that affinity was more relevant to their lives than whether they were Republicans or Democrats or whatever" (Novak, *Prince of Darkness*, 284; Strub, interviewed by Clendinen).

549 **son had died in a car crash:** Celestine Bohlen and Patricia E. Bauer, "Crash Kills Son of Adviser to President," *Washington Post*, July 24, 1982, B1; Witeck, author interview.

549 **Gray became convinced:** Anderson, author interview.

549 **"Have you ever seen him":** Shoemaker, author interview.

549 **staffers were puzzled:** Keen et al., "Do These People a Witch Hunt Make?" 15.

550 **"Business is way off":** Courtland Milloy, "Gay Community Worried in Wake of Sex Probes," *Washington Post*, August 16, 1982, B1.

550 **"You associate congressmen":** Joe Pichirallo and Walter Pincus, "Ex-Page Fails Part of FBI Lie Test," *Washington Post*, July 10, 1982, A1.

550 **interviewed dozens of pages:** Tony Schwartz, "Story of Scandal in Congress Raises Basic Problems in Treatment of News," *New York Times*, September 8, 1982, A22.

550 **On the evening of August 22:** Pienciak, "The Rise and Fall of a Washington Sex Scandal."

550 **repeated the next day:** "Ex-Page Swears Charges Were Lies," *New York Times*, August 29, 1982, 28.

550 **"Trial by Silhouette":** Greider, "Trial by Silhouette," 7.

551 **"allegations and rumors":** *Report of the Committee on Standards of Official Conduct on the Inquiry Under House Resolution 12.*

551 **working simultaneously as informants:** Bush, "Anatomy of a Scandal," 21.

551 **in the early morning hours:** Jack Anderson, "Soviet Diplomat Abruptly Sent Home," *Washington Post*, April 21, 1981, B8.

552 **"consistently stymied":** "House Leaders Suppress Deep Backgrounder," *Deep Backgrounder*, July/August 1982, 8–9.

552 **House Postmaster:** United Press International, August 6, 1982.

552 **Truth About Gays Political Action Committee:** "We Cannot Protect 'Gay' Life-style," *Deep Backgrounder*, March/April 1983, 10.

552 **"holier than thou":** Martz, "Right-Wing Tabloid Called 'Scurrilous.'"

552 **dying unexpectedly:** Editors to Jim Corbett, November 28, 1983, Wilcox Collection of Contemporary Political Movements, "Deep Backgrounder Publications," Kenneth Spencer Research Library, Lawrence, KS.

552 **dementia overtook him:** Katharine Q. Seelye, "Victor Marchetti, 88, Who Exposed Workings of a Covert C.I.A., Dies," *New York Times*, November 1, 2018, B15.

552 **"Sodom-on-the-Potomac":** Martin Price form letter, May 1983, Wilcox Collection of Contemporary Political Movements, "Deep Backgrounder Publications," Kenneth Spencer Research Library, Lawrence, KS.

37: "I Don't Have It. Do You?"

553 **"Larry":** White House Press Briefing by Larry Speakes, October 15, 1982, 12:45 p.m., #481, Box 12, Series II: Press Briefings, White House Office Of the Press Secretary, Reagan Library.

553 **six-foot-one, 220-pound:** Bill McAllister, "Priest as Gadfly: Kinsolving Irks Nessen," *Washington Post*, July 6, 1975, B1.

553 **former Episcopal priest:** Chip Brown, "Lester Kinsolving: Raising Cain in the Press Corps," *Washington Post*, November 17, 1981, C1.

554 **"Lester, by his mannerisms":** Brown, "Lester Kinsolving," C1.

554 **acquired immunodeficiency syndrome:** The September 24, 1982, edition of the *Morbidity and Mortality Weekly Report* was the first in which the acronym AIDS appeared.

554 **"militant sodomy lobby":** William Thompson, "Lester Kinsolving: Opinionated Commentator Is Quick with a Barb," *Baltimore Evening Sun*, February 4, 1987, B1.

554 **"Mississippi Catfish":** Bernard Weinraub, "The Mississippi Catfish Is Finally Smiling," *New York Times*, February 14, 1985, B10.

555 **"White House reporters can be":** Alwood, *Straight News*, 234.

556 **It was not until a reporter:** Randy Shilts, *And the Band Played On: Politics, People, and the AIDS Epidemic* (New York: St. Martin's Press, 1987), 126.

556 **Every day for the entire month:** Shilts, *And the Band Played On*, 191.

556 **"What the heck":** Larry Bush, "Interview with John T. (Terry) Dolan," transcript, n.d., Folder 44, Box 1, Larry Bush Papers.

557 **"99 percent for defense":** Myra MacPherson, "The New Right Brigade," *Washington Post*, August 10, 1980, F1.

557 **"Make them angry":** Alan Crawford, *Thunder on the Right: The "New Right" and the Politics of Resentment* (New York: Pantheon, 1980), 51.

558 **"A group like ours":** MacPherson, "The New Right Brigade."

558 **required any girl he dated:** "Tony Dolan Reacts with Folk Songs," *Baltimore Sun*, April 13, 1969, 3.

558 **"Speech writers should be seen":** Carol Giacomo, "The Dolan Boys," *The Hartford (CT) Courant Magazine*, October 18, 1981, 9.

558 **so wowed by Ronald Reagan's speech:** Young, *God's Bullies*, 142.

558 **"the most liberal president":** Young, *God's Bullies*, 141.

558 **"I used to be a Republican":** MacPherson, "The New Right Brigade," F1.

559 **frequented the Eagle:** Steve Endean, *Bringing Lesbian and Gay Rights into the Mainstream: Twenty Years of Progress*, ed. Vicki L. Eaklor (New York: Harrington Park Press, 2006), 269.

559 **cruised the steam room:** Bob Kabel, author interview, January 30, 2019, Washington, DC.

559 **"aristocracy of beauty":** Shilts, *And the Band Played On*, 149.

559 **business trade association at a Denver hotel:** Dolan acquaintance, author interview.

559 **"Our nation's moral fiber":** Bill Peterson, "NCPAC's Dolan Quoted as Endorsing Gay Rights," *Washington Post*, March 18, 1982, A2.

559 **"sexually active male":** Ellen Hume, "Fear and Self-Loathing on the Far Right," *Regardie's*, March 1988, 89.

559 **"He was very private":** Mike Murphy, email to author, April 30, 2019.

559 **The day after Reagan's landslide:** David Nyhan, "New Right Warn Reagan," *Boston Globe*, November 7, 1980, 10.

560 **"mind his p's and q's":** Peter Baker, "Terry Dolan, Vocal Leader of NCPAC, Dead at 36," *Washington Times*, December 30, 1986, 1A.

560 **Once, he called Dolan:** Elizabeth Kastor, "The Cautious Closet of the Gay Conservative," *Washington Post*, May 11, 1987, B1.

560 **"Why should we protect you?":** Kramer, "Terry Dolan and the Homosexual's Dilemma."

560 **wrote a letter to Ed Meese:** John T. Dolan to Ed Meese, February 10, 1982, Alpha File: "Dolan, John," White House Office of Records Management (hereafter "WHORM"), Reagan Library.

561 **Dolan gave an interview:** Larry Bush, "New Right Leader Terry Dolan," *The Advocate*, April 15, 1982, 15.

561 **"I told Terry":** "Terry Dolan's Gay-Rights Problem," *New York*, April 19, 1982, 10.

561 **"I think it is an insult":** Frederick L. Berns, "State Shows 'Gay Strength,'" *Kenosha (WI) News*, December 31, 1982, 7.

561 **"Robespierre of the New Right":** James Conaway, "Righting Reagan's Revolution," *Washington Post*, March 22, 1983, D1.

561 **first conservative activist to demand:** Paul Weyrich to William F. Buckley Jr., October 9, 1980, Folder: "Robert Bauman," Box 6, Series III, Buckley Papers.

561 **"If your brother does something wrong:"** Paul Weyrich, "The Scarlet Letter," *Policy Review* (Spring 1988): 26.

561 **"How dare you question me?"** George Archibald, "Dolan's Role as Political Leader Praised by Hundreds at Service," *Washington Times*, January 9, 1987, 5A.

562 **"I do not, nor have I ever":** John T. Dolan, March 29, 1982, Folder 44, Box 1, Larry Bush Papers,

562 **"Thus Dolan, who heads":** "'Conservative' Roustabout Defends Homosexuals," *Deep Backgrounder*, May/June 1982, 10.

562 **on its front page:** "Out of the Closet—and into Print," *Washington Blade*, October 1, 1982, 1; *Christopher Street*, August 1982.

562 **Photocopies of the chapter:** "Diana Hears," *Washington Times*, October 12, 1982, 1B.

563 **"sizeable community of conservative and moderate":** John Gilbert, "'Hatchet Job' on Dolan: A Victory? For Whom?" *Washington Blade*, October 22, 1982, 22.

563 **White House chief of staff James Baker:** Fred Barnes, "Unlikely Allies: White House Chief of Staff and New Right Leader," *Baltimore Sun*, May 19, 1983, 16.

563 **$125-a-plate dinner:** Ann L. Treboe, "The Roasters from the Right," *Washington Post*, May 19, 1983, C1; Tom Carter, "Terry Dolan Honored as 'Our Kind of Moderate,'" *Washington Times*, May 20, 1983, B3.

564 **"10 to 15 pounds of polling" data:** Deposition of Carl R. Channell, September 1, 1987, Appendix B of Senate Report No. 216, *Iran-Contra Investigation*, vol. 4, *Depositions* (Washington, DC: U.S. Government Printing Office, 1989), 24.

564 **"John Terrence Dolan is a patriot":** Treboe, "Roasters from the Right."

564 **never met an openly gay person:** Larry Bush, "Electing to Speak Out: Congressman Gerry Studds," *The Advocate*, September 15, 1983, 15.

564 **alter his daily jogging route:** Damien Cave, "Gerry Studds Dies at 69; First Openly Gay Congressman," *New York Times*, October 15, 2006, 41.

564 **largest gay bookstore in the world:** Michele Siung, "Book Report," *Washington Post Book World*, June 19, 1983, 15.

564 **John Anderson dropped in:** Maccubbin, author interview. Four years later, through a friend of former vice president Walter Mondale's wife, Maccubbin convinced the Democratic presidential nominee to replace the clinical-sounding "homosexual" with "gay" in his public statements. That same year, the store moved from S Street to a bigger and more prominent location on Connecticut Avenue, where it remained until its closure in 2010.

564 **"reportedly seen frequenting gay bars":** "Men in High Places Found in Low Places," *Deep Backgrounder*, May/June 1983, 11.

565 **"an intelligent, gentle man":** *Report of the Committee on Standards of Official Conduct on the Inquiry Under House Resolution 12*, Report No. 98–297, 98th Cong., 1st Sess. 39 (July 14, 1983).

565 **"All Members of Congress must cope":** "Statement by Studds," *Boston Globe*, July 15, 1983, 6.

565 **tilted nine to one in his favor:** Dana Hornig, "Studds," *City Paper*, August 19–25, 1983, 1.

565 **"if at times you find it difficult":** Larry Bush, "Personal Thoughts on Coming Out," *Advocate*, September 29, 1983, 19.

566 **vote for censure:** David Rogers, "US House Censures Studds, Crane," *Boston Globe*, July 23, 1983, 1.

566 **first openly gay person to win:** Mark Robert Schneider, *Gerry Studds: America's First Openly Gay Congressman* (Amherst: University of Massachusetts Press, 2017), 134–46.

566 **"I don't know many men":** Associated Press, "Congressman at Ease with His Homosexuality," November 11, 1985.

38: "Them" Is "Us"

567 **"A lot of great political movements":** Hal Gordon, email to author, January 10, 2019.

567 **failing to recapture his old congressional seat:** Sandra Saperstein, "Bauman Bows Out of Race, Citing 'Scurrilous Attacks,'" *Washington Post*, July 30, 1982, A1.

567 **"I desperately need your talent":** Fred Barbash, "'Yes, I Am Gay,'" *Washington Post*, August 3, 1983, A7.

567 **"not-so-subtle fag-bashing":** John Feinstein, "Bauman's Gay Rights Bill Condemned by Conservatives," *Washington Post*, November 8, 1983, B5; Evans Witt, "Admitted Homosexual Retains Membership in Conservative Group," Associated Press, November 8, 1983.

568 **"the human factor":** Bauman, "Former Congressman," 61.

568 **"representing positions from the White House staff":** Bauman, *Gentleman from Maryland*, 261.

568 **had been hatched in the summer:** Lou Chibbaro Jr., "Dolan Was Hidden Backer of Gay Republican Group," *Washington Blade*, January 2, 1987, 1; Concerned Americans for Individual Rights, "Year-End Report," December 15, 1984, Folder 1, Box 1, Concerned Americans for Individual Rights Records, ONE National Gay and Lesbian Archives, Los Angeles, CA.

568 **"Deukmejian's house fairy":** David W. Dunlap, "Bruce B. Decker, 45, Outspoken Advocate for AIDS Patients," *New York Times*, November 16, 1995, B16.

568 **"God, the power in this room":** Mike Hippler, *Matlovich, the Good Soldier* (Boston: Alyson, 1989), 126.

568 **"a private home":** Carlyle Murphy, "Republican Homosexuals Form Gay Rights Group," *Washington Post*, May 19, 1984, B8.

568 **taken the lives of more than sixteen hundred:** Loretta McLaughlin, "Rate of AIDS Cases Rising; Related Disease New Concern," *Boston Globe*, March 11, 1984, 1.

568 **"Michael, you've made it":** Benjamin Taylor, "Michael Jackson Goes to Washington," *Boston Globe*, May 15, 1984, 1.

569 **barely avoided exposure:** Mark Griffin, *All That Heaven Allows: A Biography of Rock Hudson* (New York: HarperCollins, 2018), 114–15.

569 **item in *Variety*:** "Rock Hudson and Claudia Cardinale 'The Quiet Couple," *Variety*, September 5, 1967, 1; SAC Los Angeles to J. Edgar Hoover, airtel, September 8, 1967, FBI 94–63352–1.

569 **"it is general common knowledge":** [Redacted] to W. C. Sullivan, memo, June 2, 196, FBI: The Vault, Rock Hudson FBI File.

569 **After inquiring with a movie industry source:** SAC Los Angeles to J. Edgar Hoover, airtel, September 8, 1967, FBI 94–63352–1.

569 **"associated with the U.S. Embassy in Rome":** SAC Los Angeles to J. Edgar Hoover, airtel, October 5, 1967, FBI 94–63352–2.

569 **"Mrs. Reagan, your best friend is gay!":** Untitled speech, April 30, 1983, Box 60, Larry Kramer Papers.

569 **"You're too thin":** Rock Hudson and Sara Davidson, *Rock Hudson: His Story* (New York: William Morrow, 1986), 239.

570 **he had lost the weight:** Nancy Reagan, with William Novak, *My Turn: The Memoirs of Nancy Reagan* (New York: Random House, 1989), 281.

570 **Gahl Burt mailed:** Burt, author interview.

570 **a casual sex partner of his:** Shilts, *And the Band Played On*, 453.

570 **"Rock, you've gotta do":** Hudson and Davidson, *Rock Hudson*, 239–40.

570 **sent anonymous letters:** Hudson and Davison, *Rock Hudson*, 252.

570 **CAIR made its official debut:** Peter Freiberg, "Gays Muster a Presence at GOP Convention," *The Advocate*, October 2, 1984, 9.

570 **Terry Dolan briefly dropped by:** Shilts, *And the Band Played On*, 473.

570 **eighteen hundred guests:** Elizabeth Kastor et al., "Ford Fanfare and Celebrating at Circle T," *New York Times*, August 21, 1984, B6.

571 **"short hair, manicured moustache":** Sidney Blumenthal, "The G.O.P. 'Me Decade,'" *New Republic*, September 17, 1984, 12.

571 **"were absolutely mobbed":** John Ford, interviewed by Susan Ford Wiltshire, author's collection.

571 **"In our lifetime we are scoffing":** V. S. Naipaul, "Among the Republicans," *New York Review of Books*, October 25, 1984, 5.

571 **"Nobody said to him":** Sandra G. Boodman, "AIDS Patients Fight Pain and Misconceptions," *Washington Post*, December 2, 1984, A1.

571 **Fearful that the disease:** Richard Araujo, author interview, February 27, 2015, Miami, FL.

571 **"They'd quietly go away":** Witeck, author interview.

572 **location of a five-bedroom convalescent home:** Michael Specter, "'Secret' House Provides Financial Refuge for AIDS Victims," *Washington Post*, August 31, 1985, C1.

572 **"130 recent deaths":** David Sanford, "Need We Guess Why Young Men Are Dying?" *Wall Street Journal*, August 29, 1985, 20. Sanford later learned that he, too, had become infected with the virus. He would be one of the very few people who contracted the disease early to survive. David Sanford, "Back to a Future: One Man's AIDS Tale Shows How Quickly Epidemic Has Turned," *Wall Street Journal*, November 8, 1996, 1.

572 **"Decoding the *Times* obituaries":** Brown, *Vanity Fair Diaries*, 210.

572 **created expressly to memorialize:** Don Michaels, interviewed by Mark Meinke, July 28, 2007, Rainbow History Project.

572 **"box scores of homosexual life and death":** Jeffrey Schmalz, "Gay Politics Goes Mainstream," *New York Times Magazine*, October 11, 1992, 18.

572 **social obligation:** Bob Kabel, *Inside and Out: The Odyssey of a Gay Conservative* (Pennsauken Township, NJ: self-pub. 2020), 185.

572 **Ford lost three friends:** Wiltshire, *Seasons of Grief and Grace*, 44.

572 **"We would have Saturday morning funerals":** Mixner, author interview.

572 **"a big check":** Cannada, author interview.

572 **"To me, one of the most profound":** Tucker, interviewed by Meinke.

573 **"Commanding General of Percy Hospital":** Dale Olson, July 24, 1985, 2:07 p.m., ID no. 336565, Subject File: HE 005, WHORM, Reagan Library.

573 **first self-identified homosexual to appear on television:** Elaine Woo, "Dale Olson Dies at 78; Publicity Agent for Rock Hudson, Other Stars," *Los Angeles Times*, August 10, 2012, A6.

573 **"did not feel this was something":** Mark Weinberg to Bill Martin, July 24, 1985, ID no. 336565, Subject File: HE 005, WHORM, Reagan Library.

573 **the president called Hudson:** United Press International, "Reagan Calls Rock Hudson," July 25, 1985.

573 **"We never knew him too well":** Ronald Reagan, diary entry, July 24, 1985, from *The Reagan Diaries*, ed. Douglas Brinkley (New York: HarperCollins, 2007), 345.

573 **AIDS "had seemed":** Shilts, *And the Band Played On*, xxi.

573 **Visits to the Whitman-Walker Clinic:** Paul Berg, "To Know You've Been Exposed," *Washington Post*, September 4, 1985, H11.

573 **"My father has the sort of psychology":** Scot Haller, "If Papa Won't Preach It, Young Ron Reagan Will, with a TV Pitch Promoting Safe Sex," *People*, July 13, 1987, 40.

574 **"This is a top priority":** "The President's News Conference," September 17, 1985, Reagan Library, https://www.reaganlibrary.gov/research/speeches/91785c; Philip Boffey, "Reagan Defends Financing for AIDS," *New York Times*, September 18, 1985, B7.

574 **thirtieth news briefing:** David France, *How to Survive a Plague: The Inside Story of How Citizens and Science Tamed AIDS* (New York: Alfred A. Knopf, 2016), 191.

574 **Two weeks later:** Carla Hall, "Rock Hudson Dead at 59 of AIDS Complications," *Washington Post*, October 3, 1985, A1.

574 **lambasted as coldhearted:** Chris Geidner, "Nancy Reagan Turned Down Rock Hudson's Plea for Help Nine Weeks Before He Died," Buzzfeed News, February 2, 2015.

574 **"moved ahead of other potential candidates":** Marilyn Chase, "Cohn Is Said to Get White House Assist on AIDS Drug Test," *Wall Street Journal*, August 1, 1986, 1.

575 **counted Elizabeth Taylor:** "Way Bandy, Makeup Artist and Best-Selling Writer, Dies," *New York Times*, August 15, 1986, D15.

575 **Though Bandy had kept his illness a secret:** Polman, "Private Life; Public Death," 1F; Nina Hyde, "Fashion Designer Perry Ellis Dies," *Washington Post*, May 31, 1986, B6.

575 **"Maybe he was with her 15 minutes":** Ann L. Trebbe, "Death and the AIDS Disclosure," *Washington Post*, August 19, 1986, C1.

575 **On another occasion:** Karen Tumulty, *The Triumph of Nancy Reagan* (New York: Simon and Schuster, 2021), 414.

575 **"I washed my hair last night":** Larry Speakes, with Robert Pack, *Speaking Out: The Reagan Presidency from Inside the White House* (New York: Charles Scribner's Sons, 1988), 103.

576 **"Why not invite Gadhafi":** Bob Woodward, "Gadhafi Target of Secret U.S. Deception Plan," *Washington Post*, October 2, 1986, A1. The State Department refused to comment on Shultz's "private remarks," while all Reagan would say was "I don't want Gadhafi anywhere in the United States" (Peg Byron, "Joke Between Reagan, Shultz About AIDS 'Shameful,'" United Press International, October 3, 1986; "Report of AIDS Joke Roils San Franciscans," Associated Press, October 3, 1986).

576 **"They lived most of their lives":** Haller, "If Papa Won't Preach It, Young Ron Reagan Will," 40.

576 **"you could do an entire love scene":** Deaver, *Behind the Scenes*, 101–2.

576 **944 out of the 1,100 students:** Evan Thomas, "The New Untouchables," *Time*, September 23, 1985, 24.

577 **more than half of American adults:** John Balzar, "The Times Poll: Tough New Government Action on AIDS Backed," *Los Angeles Times*, December 19, 1985, 1.

577 **78 percent of whom voted for Reagan:** *New York Times*/CBS News poll, 1988.

577 **"It justifies their prejudices":** Fred Barnes, "The Politics of AIDS: A New Issue for the Right Wing," *New Republic*, November 4, 1985, 11.

577 **"To be pro-life":** Naipaul, "Among the Republicans," 5.

577 **post-presidential memoirs:** Ronald Reagan, *An American Life* (New York: Simon and Schuster, 1990).

577 **"sort of a celluloid barrier":** Witcover and Cohen, "Where's the Rest of Ronald Reagan?" 93

577 **"Nobody around him understood him":** David Stout, "Edmund Morris, Reagan Biographer Who Upset Conventions, Dies at 78," *New York Times*, May 28, 2019, A25.

578 **never once did Reagan call him:** Witcover and Cohen, "Where's the Rest of Ronald Reagan?" 90.

578 **"There's a wall around him":** Reagan, *My Turn*, 106.

578 **"waiting for direction":** Witcover and Cohen, "Where's the Rest of Ronald Reagan?" 150.

578 **"If it's 2 percent":** Rich Lowry and Jay Nordlinger, emails to author, February 9, 2020.

578 **"totally surprised":** Buckley, "No, Whittaker Chambers Was Not Like That!," A19.

578 **public disgrace of his friend:** Asked by Bauman to write the foreword to his memoir, Buckley composed an exegesis doubting the book's ability to be "the instrument by which traditionalists will be disenthralled from superstitions respecting the diverse sexual appetites of the homosexual." Bauman's publisher, unsurprisingly, rejected it. William F. Buckley Jr., "The Problem of Unruly Sex," *National Review*, August 29, 1986, 40.

578 **testified as a character witness:** David Margolick, "Cohn, Ill and Weak, Reflects on His Latest Battles," *New York Times*, November 17, 1985, 42.

579 **"In Mum's case":** Christopher Buckley, *Losing Mum and Pup: A Memoir* (New York: Twelve, 2009), 66–67.

579 **"Everyone detected with AIDS":** William F. Buckley Jr. "Crucial Steps in Combating the AIDS Epidemic: Identify All the Carriers," *New York Times*, March 18, 1986, A27.

579 **"Did it start out":** Robert K. Massie to William F. Buckley Jr., March 18, 1986, Folder: Folder "AIDS," Box 3, Series III, Buckley Papers.

579 **"personal stake":** Robert K. Massie, "AIDS Needs Medical, Not Emotional, Solutions," *New York Times*, March 27, 1986, A26.

579 **banner front-page headline:** "William Buckley's Final Solution," *New York Native*, April 7, 1986, 1.

579 **The most poignant response:** Peter Evans, Stan Ziegler, and Robert Walden to William F. Buckley Jr., April 24, 1986, Folder: "AIDS," Box 3, Series III, Buckley Papers.

580 **Within three years of sending this letter:** "Actor Peter Evans Dies at Age 38," Associated Press, May 22, 1989; Yale AIDS Memorial Project profile, Stan Ziegler, http://yamp.org/Profiles/StanZiegler; Yale AIDS Memorial Project profile, Robert Walden, http://yamp.org/Profiles/RobertWalden.

580 **"One of the things that I've heard":** Coleman, interviewed by Meinke.

581 **first professional athlete to declare:** George Solomon, "Ex-Redskin Jerry Smith Says He's Battling AIDS," *Washington Post*, August 26, 1986, A1.

581 **"the worst kept secret":** "A Football Life: Jerry Smith," National Football League, 2014, https://gamepass.nfl.com/video/a-football-life-jerry-smith.

581 **men-only sex party:** B. J. Stiles, author interview, February 17, 2014.

581 **"I was giving speeches":** Wiltshire, *Seasons of Grief and Grace*, 58.

579 **One day, a political appointee:** Ford, interviewed by Wiltshire. Recounted, somewhat differently, in Wiltshire, *Seasons of Grief and Grace*, 136–37.

582 **Ford resigned:** "2 Key Aides Leave USDA," *Washington Post*, December 23, 1985, A11.

582 **"massive, disease-driven outing":** Larry Reynolds, author interview, May 29, 2014, Washington, DC.

39: "Our Sebastian"

583 **one of his last public appearances:** George Archibald, *Journalism Is War: Stories of Power Politics, Sexual Dalliance and Corruption in the Nation's Capital* (Crane, MO: Anomalos, 2009), 126.

583 **$3.9 million in debt:** Thomas B. Edsall, "Financial Woes, Legal Fights Weaken Conservative PACs," *Washington Post*, October 29, 1986, A1.

584 **"tired of writing biennial obituaries":** L. Brent Bozell III, "NCPAC's Death Has Been, Well, Exaggerated," *Washington Post*, November 8, 1986, A21.

584 **gleefully distributing:** Jack Shafer, "Advertisements for His Brother," *Washington City Paper*, April 8, 1988, 6.

584 **"Widely recognized":** Bart Barnes, "Cofounder of NCPAC John (Terry) Dolan Dies," *Washington Post*, December 31, 1986, B6.

584 **"from a very reliable source":** Jon Cohen and Jack Shafer, "Press After Death," *Washington City Paper*, January 9, 1987, 5.

584 **"the best newspaper in America":** Ellen Hume, "Times of Washington Is Attaining Credibility But Not Profitability," *Wall Street Journal*, December 17, 1985, 1.

584 **front-page obituary:** Baker, "Terry Dolan, Vocal Leader of NCPAC, Dead at 36," 1A.

584 **"I have no data to indicate that":** George Archibald, "Party Leaders Credit Terry Dolan for GOP's Big Senate Win in '80," *Washington Times*, December 31, 1986, page 3A.

585 **traced the syndrome:** Ann Giudici Fettner, "Bringing Scientists to Their Senses: Cesar Caceres vs. Selective Blindness," *Christopher Street*, April 1985, 15–18.

585 **"with a whimsical chuckle":** Thompson, *Price of Achievement*, 130–32.

585 **"promotes dangerous messages":** David Lightman and Lou Fintor, "Questions Raised on Report by McKinney's Physician," *Hartford (CT) Courant*, May 16, 1987, 1.

585 **"gutter journalism":** Cohen and Shafer, "Press After Death," 5. Bozell was a nephew of Bill Buckley, who was a mentor and friend of Tony Dolan. "On which buttocks should we place his tattoo?"

read the note from one angry correspondent to Buckley, underneath a clipping of Dolan's obituary. David Perrin to William F. Buckley Jr., December 31, 1986, Box 1, Series III, Buckley Papers.

585 **hundreds of friends and political allies:** Archibald, "Dolan's Role as Political Leader."

585 **"The poor homosexuals":** Patrick J. Buchanan, "AIDS Disease: It's Nature Striking Back," *New York Post*, May 24, 1983, 31.

585 **"Terry held a deep affection for you":** L. Brent Bozell III to Pat Buchanan, December 29, 1986, PA002, Case File 427435, WHORM, Reagan Library.

585 **Paul Weyrich:** Archibald, *Journalism Is War*, 126–27.

586 **credited Dolan with playing a "pivotal" role:** Kastor, "Cautious Closet of the Gay Conservative," B1.

586 **attended a "Clean Up America" rally:** Stephanie Mansfield, "'Clean Up America' Rally at Capitol," *Washington Post*, April 28, 1979, C1.

586 **instructed to stop using the word** *happy*: Peggy Noonan, *What I Saw at the Revolution: A Political Life in the Reagan Era* (New York: Random House, 1990), 230–31.

586 **"We are not, as they say":** Anthony R. Dolan, "John Terrence Dolan, 1950–1986," Alpha File: "Dolan, John," WHORM, Reagan Library.

587 **been fired from a teaching position:** Lois Romano, "The Convictions of Father Curran," *Washington Post*, September 4, 1986, B1.

587 **responsible for such an indelible turn of phrase:** Mike Allen, "Reagan Veterans Bring Back the '80s," *Washington Post*, June 11, 2004, A31.

588 **inspired centuries of homoerotic art:** "My dear, I should like to stick you full of barbed arrows like a p-p-pin-cushion," the explicitly gay dandy Anthony Blanche tells Sebastian Flyte in *Brideshead Revisited*, merging these two homoerotic allusions into one. Following his release from Reading Gaol on charges of buggery, Oscar Wilde adopted the pseudonym "Sebastian Melmoth" in his French exile. In his 1949 autobiographical novel, *Confessions of a Mask*, Mishima attributed his sexual awakening to the moment he first laid eyes upon Guido Reni's depiction of the "remarkably handsome youth" of "white and matchless nudity," and in his 1976 Latin-language film *Sebastiane*, Derek Jarman retold the story of Sebastian's life and death as an X-rated homosexual romp. When the gay journalist David Brock announced his split from the conservative movement in a 1997 article for *Esquire*, he was photographed in a Sebastian-esque pose, tied to a tree, his shirt unbuttoned to the navel. Evelyn Waugh, *Brideshead Revisited* (London: Chapman and Hall, 1945), 33; Richard Ellmann, *Oscar Wilde* (New York: Alfred A. Knopf, 1988), 523; Yukio Mishima, *Confessions of a Mask*, trans. Meredith Weatherby (New York: New Directions, 1958), 38–39; David Brock, "Confessions of a Right-Wing Hit Man," *Esquire*, July 1997, 53.

588 **Two days later:** Kastor, "Cautious Closet of the Gay Conservative," B1.

588 **closeted gay priest:** Stephen Martz, "Remembering Fr. Paul Murray," *Washington Blade*, February 13, 2009.

588 **World War II spy:** "Ex-spies, Out of the Cold," *New York Daily News*, October 2, 1982, 55. Gigrich, who served in World War II and spent twenty years in the Defense Department before entering the priesthood, read the invocation at a 1982 meeting of the Association of Retired Intelligence Officers, where he was introduced as a "former member of intelligence."

588 **unofficial minister to people with AIDS:** Naina Ayya, "Rev. John P. Gigrich, a Friend of the Gay Community, Dies at 69," *Washington Blade*, November 30, 1990, 19.

588 **"a singularly deplorable job":** Shilts, *And the Band Played On*, 601.

589 **after a reporter interviewed an AIDS victim:** Sandra G. Boodman, "Covering the AIDS Beat: Fear, Compassion, Duty," *Washington Post*, August 14, 1988, B1.

589 **an internal** *Post* **memorandum on the paper's gay coverage:** Joyce Murdoch, "An Examination of the Washington Post's Approach to Gay News; A Prescription for Improving Our Coverage," April 22, 1988, Folder 1, Box 23, Bradlee Papers.

589 **twenty-nine-year-old photographer:** "Jeffrey David Clopper," *Washington Post*, May 4, 1987, B10.

589 **"There is something fundamentally wrong here":** Jim Graham, "What's with the Post?!" *Washington Blade*, July 3, 1987, 25.

589 **"survived by his mother":** Murdoch, "Examination of the Washington Post's Approach to Gay News." This exhaustive internal report on the *Post*'s coverage of gay issues faulted the paper on many

fronts, citing, among other blind spots, a reliance on photos of drag queens and men dressed in leather to illustrate stories about homosexuality, an editorial attitude that "lesbians don't exist," and a sense that "Many of our reporters now seem to approach gay people as if they were from Mars." A memo by the ombudsman the following year found that the paper was usually "tongue-tied or mute" in its coverage of gay issues. "It seems reasonable for the paper, from time to time, to take a rather broad look at this segment of our society so that our 'future historians' will have some clue as to the fact that it existed in Washington and in the United States in the last years of the 20th Century" (Richard Harwood to Ben Bradlee, Meg Greenfield, Staff, Etc., Ombudsman's Memo, June 9, 1989, Folder 1, Box 23, Bradlee Papers).

589 **"a pitched battle":** Bradlee, *Good Life*, 24–25.

590 **A great mimic:** Bradlee, *Good Life*, 44.

590 **"loved, adored Freddy":** Quinn, author interview.

590 **"I'm sure he made":** Ted Gup, author interview, January 30, 2020, phone.

590 **The day after Terry Dolan died:** "Proof of Story CHRONOLOGY," May 11, 1987, Folder 8, Box 20, Bradlee Papers.

590 **Dolan repeatedly implored:** Benjamin C. Bradlee, Memorandum for the Record, May 11, 1987, Folder 8, Box 20, Bradlee Papers.

590 **"Dear Ben":** Notecard from Tony Dolan to Ben Bradlee, n.d., Folder 8, Box 20, Bradlee Papers.

591 **"We've just got to get over that":** David Shaw, "Journalistic Ethics: AIDS Rumors—Do They Belong in News Stories?" *Los Angeles Times*, September 3, 1986, 1.

591 **"public health enemy No. 1":** James R. Dickenson, "Reagan: AIDS Is 'Health Enemy No. 1,'" *Washington Post*, April 2, 1987, A4.

591 **more than one hundred locations:** "C. R. Gaver, 'Performance, Poet Dies," *Washington Post*, March 15, 1989, C7.

591 **earning himself an invitation:** Chasen Gaver, "Who's Who/What's What," Folder 22, Box 1, Chasen Gaver Papers, Division of Rare and Manuscript Collections, Cornell University Library, Ithaca, NY (hereafter "Gaver Papers").

591 **"I didn't want to 'hide'":** Chasen Gaver, October 13, 1987, Folder 22, Box 1, Gaver Papers.

591 **"of numerous professionals and some politicians":** Jerry Seper, "Officials Fear Blackmailers Stole District AIDS Test List," *Washington Times*, April 22, 1987, 1A. Two days later, the *Blade* put a damper on these sensationalist fears, quoting a local official who said it was "extremely unlikely" that a politician or prominent public figure would have entered the public drug treatment program from which the logbook had been stolen. Rick Harding, "Blackmail Unlikely in Logbook Theft, Says City," *Washington Blade*, April 24, 1987, 3.

592 **"hard bitten newsmen":** Betty Cuniberti, "A Reporter Pulls Off Social Coup," *Los Angeles Times*, April 24, 1987, V2.

592 **"deeply affect my parents":** Anthony R. Dolan, "What the Washington Post Doesn't Tell Its Readers," *Washington Times*, May 22, 1987, 8A.

592 **"I thought that AIDS":** Len Downie, author interview, November 11, 2019, phone.

593 **heart-wrenching story:** Janet Cooke, "Jimmy's World," *Washington Post*, September 28, 1980, A1; Robert Reinhold, "Washington Post Gives Up Pulitzer, Calling Article on Addict, 8, Fiction," *New York Times*, April 16, 1981, A1.

40: Mr. Green

594 *hated* **slide shows:** Deposition of Carl R. Channell, September 1, 1987, Appendix B of Senate Report No. 216, *Iran-Contra Investigation*, vol. 4, *Depositions* (Washington, DC: U.S. Government Printing Office, 1989), 88–89.

595 **"We cannot have the United States":** Bernard Weinraub, "Reagan Campaigns for Latin Package," *New York Times*, April 16, 1985, A1.

595 **"set me on fire":** Deposition of Carl R. Channell, September 2, 1987, 167.

596 **"You know, Terry hasn't paid":** Michael Kelly and Robert Timberg, "Style, Connections Made Channell Leader of PACs," *Baltimore Sun*, March 8, 1987, 1.

596 **growing NCPAC's base:** Deposition of Carl R. Channell, September 1, 1987, 23.

596 **his office was a shambles:** Untitled notes, February 2, 1987, Folder 16, Box 8, Thomas Byrne Edsall Papers (hereafter "Edsall Papers").

596 **"contrapreneurs":** David Ignatius, "The Contrapreneurs: Skirting Congress and the Law for Years," *Washington Post*, December 7, 1986, D1.

596 **nearly two dozen:** George D. Moffett III, "Private Groups Channel Aid to 'Contras,'" *Christian Science Monitor*, June 5, 1985, 3.

596 **including ones backed by:** Doyle McManus, "Contras to Seek More Private Donations," *Los Angeles Times*, September 11, 1985, 12.

597 **"I had unlocked several facts":** Deposition of Carl R. Channell, September 1, 1987, 20–24.

597 **"one-two punch":** Nancy J. Schwerzler, "North Said to Ply Donors with Tales of 'Secret Plan,'" *Baltimore Sun*, May 22, 1987, 1A.

598 **the American Conservative Trust:** R. W. Apple Jr., "Lobbyist Said to Have Several Ties to White House," *New York Times*, December 16, 1986, A1.

598 **"blue-rinse brigade":** George Hackett, with David Newell and Robert Parry, "Putting the Arm on Rich, Right-Wing Widows," *Newsweek*, April 20, 1987, 30.

598 **"to raise money from rich German widows":** Ben Bradlee Jr., *Guts and Glory: The Rise and Fall of Oliver North* (New York: Donald I. Fine, 1988), 227.

598 **"this soft-spoken, mellifluous voice":** Kelly and Timberg, "Style, Connections," 1.

598 **A limousine met them:** Richard L. Berke, "Enigmatic Fund-Raiser Is Focus of 3 Inquiries," *New York Times*, April 26, 1987, A32.

598 **"no little girls":** U.S. House of Representatives, Select Committee to Investigate Covert Arms Transactions with Iran, Deposition of Richard Roderick Miller, September 15, 1987, 544.

598 **"Are we getting this money":** Former State Department official, author interview, March 25, 2021.

598 **medical evacuation helicopter:** "A Copter Called Lady Ellen," *New York Times*, August 13, 1985, A10.

598 **"We're guerrillas":** Christopher Drew and William Gaines, "Profit Fever Fueled Drive for Contra Aid," *Chicago Tribune*, May 5, 1987, 1.

599 **"possibly surface-to-air missiles":** Dan Morgan and Walter Pincus, "North Gave Pitch; Channell Collected, Contributors Testify," *Washington Post*, May 22, 1987, A1.

599 **"When you have a Congress":** Howard LaFranchi, "Feisty Texan, Who Sees Congress as Soft on Communists, Aids 'Contras' with Hard Cash," *Christian Science Monitor*, August 22, 1985, 1.

599 **transferring more than $1 million:** Alison Mitchell, "Raising Cash, and His Profile," *Newsday*, April 30, 1987, 2.

599 **"Ollie had a well-oiled machine":** William C. Rempel, "Channell Used White House as Bait for Fundraising," *Los Angeles Times*, May 12, 1987, 16.

599 **started paying Reagan's former body man:** George Lardner Jr., "Contras Backer Pleads Guilty to Tax Fraud on Weapons," *Washington Post*, May 7, 1987, A1; Karen Hosler, "Conservative Fund-Raiser Linked to Diversions Adopts Low Profile," *Baltimore Sun*, December 17, 1986, 15A.

599 **modest donation of three hundred thousand dollars:** Rita Beamish, "Beleaguered Fund-Raiser Channell Eager to Return to Aiding Contras," Associated Press, July 27, 1987, A4.

599 **Reagan signed a letter:** Ronald Reagan to Spitz Channell, February 11, 1986, Folder 1, Box 11: "JGR/Contra Aid," John G. Robert Collection, Reagan Library.

599 **"The president has asked us":** Jane Mayer and Doyle McManus, *Landslide: The Unmaking of the President, 1984–1988* (Boston: Houghton Mifflin, 1988), 157.

599 **"$40,000 before lunch":** Richard L. Berke with Kenneth B. Noble, "Lobbying and Contributions by Conservative Fund-Raiser Evoke Questions," *New York Times*, January 9, 1987, A10.

599 **"I got the impression":** Deposition of Carl R. Channell, September 1, 1987, 382.

599 **"[Y]ou won't believe":** Deposition of Carl R. Channell, September 1, 1987, 106.

599 **staff of about thirty people:** Lou Chibbaro Jr., "North Worked with Gay Men Behind the Scenes," *Washington Blade*, May 13, 1994, 1.

599 **"notorious in Washington":** Christopher Hitchens, "It Dare Not Speak Its Name," *Harper's*, August 1987, 70; Frank Browning, "Channell Contra Fundraising Run by Gays," *All Things Considered*, National Public Radio, April 8, 1987.

600 **"Those gay boys of Oliver North's":** Former Pentagon official, author interview.

600 **gushed about how "sexy":** Chibbaro, "North Worked with Gay Men Behind the Scenes," 12.

600 **"Mr. Green":** Robert Pear, "North Described as Central Figure in a Contra Fund," *New York Times*, February 26, 1987, 1.

600 **"thought nothing of"**: Fawn Hall, author interview, July 24, 2014, Los Angeles, CA.

600 **"would have to be blind"**: Chibbaro, "North Worked with Gay Men Behind the Scenes," 10.

600 **videotape of a gay orgy**: Steve Chapple and David Talbot, *Burning Desires: Sex in America; A Report from the Field* (New York: Doubleday, 1989), 157.

600 **"Just about every Republican campaign"**: Stuart Stevens, *It Was All a Lie: How the Republican Party Became Donald Trump* (New York: Borzoi, 2020), 15.

601 **"It's a perverse kind of self-esteem"**: Megan Rosenfeld, "Pink Elephants," *Washington Post*, October 18, 1995, B1.

601 **leading conservative fund-raiser**: Richard L. Berke, "Iran-Contra Figure Besieged by Debt," *New York Times*, August 7, 1987, A18.

601 **"the best conservative list"**: Alfonso Chardy and Sam Dillon, "North Aimed Ads at Contra Aid Foes," *Miami Herald*, December 14, 1986, 1.

601 **well-appointed office suite**: Hosler, "Conservative Fund-Raiser Linked to Diversions Adopts Low Profile," 15A.

601 **"commies under the bed"**: Cannada, author interview.

601 **"warriors"**: Deposition of Carl R. Channell, September 1, 1987, 49.

601 **"cross between the camaraderie"**: Carl R. (Spitz) Channell, "Betrayed by a President, Yet Vindicated" *Los Angeles Times*, March 22, 1990, B7.

601 **"Dog Face"**: "Fund-Raiser for Contra Aid: Conservative with a Cause," *New York Times*, February 26, 1987, A10.

601 **"used to play them back and laugh"**: Hackett with Newell and Parry, "Putting the Arm on Rich, Right-Wing Widows," 30.

601 **"Didn't I tell you he'd be gorgeous?"**: Mayer and McManus, *Landslide*, 154.

602 **"I'm particularly interested now"**: Sally Ann Stewart, "I Wanted to Give My Life to Help Humanity Advance," *Arlington (VA) Journal*, December 29, 1981, A3.

602 **"She lived a simple life"**: Ronald Kessler, *Inside the CIA: Revealing the Secrets of the World's Most Powerful Spy Agency* (New York: Atria, 1992), 179.

602 **"Agency's dear neighbor"**: CIA Memo, June 4, 1984, CIA-RDP86M00886R000200080006–9.

602 **inviting Scattergood and her niece**: CIA-RDP93–00415R000200200009–9.

602 **Over sherry**: Kessler, *Inside the CIA*, 179–80.

603 **"employees seek refuge"**: "CIA Campus Chronicles."

603 **"a very aggressive, persistent person"**: Testimony of Fawn Hall in *Joint Hearings Before the Senate Select Committee on Secret Military Assistance to Iran and The Nicaraguan Opposition and the House Select Committee To Investigate Covert Arms Transactions With Iran*, 100th Cong., 1st Sess. 563 (June 9, 1987).

603 **"Freedom Fighter" award**: Ted Gup and Thomas B. Edsall, "Fund-Raisers for Contras Capitalized on Access," *Washington Post*, March 25, 1987, A1.

603 **few Swiss bank accounts**: Thomas B. Edsall and Ted Gup, "The Crisis of the Reagan Presidency; The Lake Resources Account; $1.7 Million Funneled to North; Documents Show Rout of Funds to Swiss Account Used by NSC Aide," *Washington Post*, March 7, 1987, A1; Ted Gup, "Donor Intended to Buy Contra Arms," *Washington Post*, March 12, 1987, A26.

603 **of the ten million dollars**: Michael Wines, "Carl Channell, 44, Fund-Raiser for Conservatives, Dies of Injuries," *New York Times*, May 9, 1990, D31.

603 **$17,500**: Browning, "Channell Contra Fundraising Run by Gays."

604 **"secret within a secret"**: Oliver North, with William Novak, *Under Fire: An American Story* (New York: HarperCollins, 1991), 265.

604 **"gang of crooks"**: John K. Singlaub, with Malcolm McConnell, *Hazardous Duty: An American Soldier in the Twentieth Century* (New York: Summit Books, 1991), 19.

604 **"disturbing reports"**: Singlaub, *Hazardous Duty*, 478.

604 **On April 29**: Rita Ciolli, "Contra Fund Raiser Guilty in Conspiracy," *Newsday*, April 30, 1987, 2.

604 **"Oh, the heartbreak"**: Richard L. Berke, "Channell Backers Sad and Dismayed," *New York Times*, May 3, 1987, A18.

604 **Another benefactor**: Berke, "Enigmatic Fund-Raiser Is Focus of 3 Inquiries," A32.

604 **friend of Ellen Garwood's**: Suzanne Gamboa, "Ellen Garwood, Philanthropist Known for Contra Aid, Dies at 89," *Austin American-Statesman*, March 21, 1993, 1.

604 **"I certainly don't approve":** Browning, "Channell Contra Fundraising Run by Gays."

605 **"important link between":** Bradlee, Memorandum for the Record, May 11, 1987.

605 **only man in the Channell operation who was straight:** Untitled notes, February 18, 1987, Folder 16, Box 8, Edsall Papers.

605 **"Maybe this will show 'em":** Michael Kelly, "Two Men Who Helped North Still Support the Cause," *Baltimore Sun*, August 9, 1987, 1A.

605 **obtained credit card receipts:** Joel Bleifuss, "Contragate Fund-Raising for Guns and Lovers," *In These Times*, April 22, 1987, 4. The first outlet to report the existence of a gay "network" tied to Iran-Contra appeared was *Executive Intelligence Review*, mouthpiece of the late political cult leader Lyndon LaRouche. Citing "high-level intelligence sources," *EIR* alleged that "the 'gay' network within the GOP—its libertarian wing—is not only the party's Achilles' heel, but may have also compromised the National Security Council . . . since the Soviet KGB uses homosexuality for blackmail purposes, the fact that the NSC's top domestic fundraiser supporting the 'Reagan Doctrine' came out of a homosexual network, gave the Soviets a window into the U.S. strategic fiascos in Iran and Central America." *EIR* tied Channell, through Terry Dolan and CAIR, to Bruce Decker, who served as finance director of the committee formed to oppose a 1986 LaRouche-backed ballot initiative to quarantine AIDS victims. It also speculated that the gay Contra network was behind the federal law enforcement raid carried out on LaRouche's Leesburg, Virginia, offices the previous year. The LaRouche organization had surprisingly extensive contacts within the Reagan administration, including on the NSC, and *EIR* published interviews with a variety of high-ranking officials, including agriculture secretary John Block and undersecretaries at the Departments of Defense and Commerce. In the 1980s, one of the stranger claims pushed by the group—which purports that the Queen of England is one of the world's most powerful drug smugglers—was that Henry Kissinger was a "faggot." In 1982, a LaRouche disciple approached the former secretary of state and his wife, Nancy, at Newark International Airport and asked, "Is it true that you sleep with young boys at the Carlyle Hotel?" Herbert Quinde, "Disturbing Role of GOP 'Gaypatriots,'" *Executive Intelligence Review*, February 27, 1987, 59; John Mintz, "Some Officials Find Intelligence Network 'Useful,'" *Washington Post*, January 15, 1985, A1; John Mintz, "The Lash of LaRouche," *Washington Post*, April 7, 1986, A1; Robin Toner and Joel Brinkley, "LaRouche Savors Fame that May Ruin Him," *New York Times*, April 4, 1986, A1.

605 **"without being an actor":** Lou Cannon, "The 8 Decades of Ronald Reagan," *Washington Post*, February 7, 1991, B1.

606 **New York deli:** "North Souvenirs Draw Few Takers," *New York Times*, September 13, 1987, 42.

606 **talk of a presidential candidacy:** Jon Margolis, "Truth and Consequences: A Second Look at 'Olliemania' as Hype Fades," *Chicago Tribune*, July 19, 1987, Section 4, 1. North ultimately opted to run for the Senate in 1994, unsuccessfully challenging incumbent Chuck Robb, Lynda Bird Johnson's husband.

606 **display the slide show:** "North Does Slide Show Without Slides," Associated Press, July 15, 1987.

41: The Wonderful, the Creative, and the Brave

607 **"screaming social liberal":** Charles F. J. Morse, "McKinney's Gusto for Public Service Never Waned," *Hartford (CT) Courant*, May 8, 1987, A16.

607 **the time he met McKinney:** Richard Mangan, author interview, January 22, 2018, phone.

608 **"wanted the cause of his death":** Clifford D. May, "McKinney Dies of Illness Tied to AIDS," *New York Times*, May 6, 1987, B1.

608 **"knowledgeable sources on Capitol Hill":** Michael Specter and Richard Pearson, "Rep. Stewart B. McKinney Dies of AIDS Complications," *Washington Post*, May 8, 1987, A1.

608 **"affable facilitator":** Morse, "McKinney's Gusto for Public Service Never Waned," A16.

608 **"Stewart and I had long communications":** Specter and Pearson, "Rep. Stewart B. McKinney Dies of AIDS Complications."

608 **"Here's another example of a person":** Death of Congressman Stewart B. McKinney, 100th Cong., 1st Sess., 133 Cong. Rec. S6198 (May 8, 1987).

608 **Downie said in defense:** Associated Press, "Friends Hope AIDS Won't Obscure McKinney Legacy," *Boston Globe*, May 11, 1987, 3.

609 **"I do not believe people"**: Barbara T. Roessner, "The Ignorance of the Straight and Narrow," *Hartford (CT) Courant*, May 19, 1987, 21.

609 **"It is a fantastic tribute"**: Richard L. Madden, "McKinney Recalled as Fighter for the Poor," *New York Times*, May 15, 1987, B1.

609 **moved into his fallen colleague's office**: Sandra Bodovitz, "McKinney's Aides Pursuing His Policies," *New York Times*, June 7, 1987, CN1.

609 **come out of the closet**: John Robinson, "Frank Discusses Being Gay," *Boston Globe*, May 30, 1987, 1; Claudia Dreifus, "And Then There Was Frank," *New York Times Magazine*, February 4, 1996, 23.

609 **send him a final version**: Bradlee, Memorandum for the Record, May 11, 1987.

609 **"There is a cancer"**: Dolan, "What the Washington Post Doesn't Tell Its Readers," 8A.

610 **entire front page**: Kastor, "Cautious Closet of the Gay Conservative," B1.

610 **"This is one of these cutting edge pieces"**: Bradlee, Memorandum for the Record, May 11, 1987.

611 **paper asked Dolan to trim**: Andrew Radolf, "$5,000 Ad Challenges Washington Post Story," *Editor and Publisher*, June 6, 1987, 18.

611 **Bumping into:** John Elvin, "Inside the Beltway," *Washington Times*, May 22, 1987, 3A.

612 **"disrespectful of the public's right"**: Dolan, "What the Washington Post Doesn't Tell Its Readers," 8A.

612 **"a crucial figure"**: David Remnick, "Alger Hiss Goes Ungently into That Good Night," *Washington Post Magazine*, October 12, 1986, 23.

612 **posthumous bestowal**: Lou Cannon, "Reagan Honors Whittaker Chambers," *Washington Post*, March 27, 1984, A7.

613 **"Anthony Dolan's niagara of words"**: Joseph Laitin to Donald Graham, May 28, 1987, Folder 8, Box 20, Bradlee Papers. Laitin did not mention what was perhaps the most conspicuous gaffe in Tony Dolan's jeremiad about journalistic inaccuracy: his repeated misspelling of Elizabeth Kastor's surname as "Castor." The following year, after a local Washington magazine published its own exposé on Terry Dolan, Tony issued yet another *Washington Times* double-truck, once again decrying the perfidy of the media. The article about Terry, he wrote, was a "hate piece," "a political-attack piece," and a "Screwtape-inversion of the truth." Dolan called upon people to boycott the magazine's advertisers. Anthony R. Dolan, "Regardie's Journalism and the New Bigotry," *Washington Times*, March 30, 1988, A6–7.

613 **upon the recommendation of his boss**: Donnie Radcliffe, "Landon Parvin, Speaking Easy," *Washington Post*, May 31, 1987, F1.

613 **"She didn't want the speech"**: Landon Parvin, "The Age of AIDS," *Frontline*, PBS, 2006.

614 **A draft of Parvin's speech**: Mildred Webber to Mari Maseng, Memorandum for Mari Maseng, May 28, 1987, AIDS Folder 5, OA 15172, Series 1, Rebecca G. Range Files, Reagan Library.

614 **Webber's recommendations were rejected**: "Remarks at the American Foundation for AIDS Research Awards Dinner," May 31, 1987, Reagan Library, https://www.reaganlibrary.gov/archives/speech/remarks-american-foundation-aids-research-awards-dinner.

614 **pulled from her bosom**: Elizabeth Kastor and Sandra G. Boodman, "The Flap at the AIDS Fundraiser," *Washington Post*, June 1, 1987, B1.

615 **day was so hot**: Maccubbin, author interview.

615 **"There is no chance"**: Joseph Laitin to Donald Graham, June 2, 1987, Folder 8, Box 20, Bradlee Papers.

615 **"I do not know how committed"**: Liz Smith to Nancy Reagan, July 15, 1987, Folder: "Letters Circa 1987–1988," Box 63, Larry Kramer Papers.

615 **frequent phone buddy**: Donnie Radcliffe, "Why Nancy Reagan Just Said No," *Washington Post*, February 6, 1990, C2.

616 **kept her own bisexuality**: Jonah Engle Bromwich, "Liz Smith's Complicated Relationship with the Closet," *New York Times*, November 16, 2017, D5.

616 **pushing her husband to appoint a gay man**: Rachel Flick and Ransdell Pierson, "Storm as Nancy Urges Prez: Put a Gay on the AIDS Panel," *New York Post*, July 6, 1987.

616 **created the previous month**: Exec. Order No. 12,601 (1987).

616 **excoriated the president**: Larry Kramer, "The F.D.A.'s Callous Response to AIDS," *New York Times*, March 23, 1987, 19.

616 **"a play about a farce"**: Larry Kramer, *Just Say No: A Play About a Farce* (New York: St. Martin's Press, 1989).

616 **"Does the play indulge"**: Mel Gussow, "Skewers for the Political in Kramer's 'Just Say No,'" *New York Times*, October 21, 1988, C3.

616 **Sen. Strom Thurmond suggested**: "Candidates for the Commission on AIDS 5/22/87," Box 1, Kenneth T. Cribb Jr. Files, Reagan Library.

616 **"rolling quarantine"**: Marlene Cimons, "Dannemeyer Hires AIDS Quarantine Advocate," *Los Angeles Times*, August 20, 1985, 4.

616 **member of the West Hollywood City Council**: John Heilman to the President, June 26, 1987, FG466, Box 1, Reagan Library.

616 **Cheney of Wyoming called to recommend**: Memo, Gina Kormanik to Bob Tuttle, May 6, 1987, "Subject: Cong. Cheney Call," OA 11308, Box 1, Kenneth T. Cribb Jr. Files, Reagan Library.

616 **Bauman recommended**: Robert E. Bauman to the President of the United States, May 19, 1987, OA 14572, Carl Anderson Files, Reagan Library.

616 **"mixture of medical experts and public-spirited citizens"**: Gary L. Bauer to the President, "Recommendations for Your Advisory Commission on AIDS," May 22, 1987, OA 11308, Box 1, Gary L. Bauer Files (hereafter "Bauer Files"), Reagan Library.

617 **"I don't want people"**: Saul Friedman, "Backstage Battle over AIDS Panel," *Newsday*, May 14, 1987, 4.

617 **"Millions of Americans try to raise"**: Gary L. Bauer to the President, Memorandum, June 30, 1987, OA11308, Box 2, Bauer Files, Series I. Presumably, Bauer had in mind people like the White House drug policy advisor, who had suggested that marijuana made youths more susceptible to homosexuality—and, therefore, to AIDS—as well as a subordinate on the Domestic Policy Council, who, in a memo entitled "Recommended Actions to Stop THE SPREAD OF THE DEADLY AIDS VIRUS IN AMERICA," suggested that state governments "outlaw sodomy." Terry E. Johnson, Margaret Garrard Warner and George Raine, "Reagan Aide: Pot Can Make You Gay," *Newsweek*, October 27, 1986, 95; "Recommended Actions to Stop THE SPREAD OF THE DEADLY AIDS VIRUS IN AMERICA," Box 1, Robert Sweet Files, Reagan Library.

617 **"someone not currently living a gay life style"**: In a 1988 speech to the Association of Christian Schools International, Bauer approvingly quoted University of Chicago professor Allan Bloom, whose book criticizing postmodernism and other faddish academic trends, *The Closing of the American Mind*, became a surprise best seller upon its publication and was embraced by conservatives for its spirited defense of the Western canon against the forces of academic postmodernism and deconstruction. Bloom was gay and died of AIDS in 1992. Jack Klenk to Gary Bauer, February 12, 1988, Box 2, Robert Sweet Files, Reagan Library; Dinitia Smith, "A Bellow Novel Eulogizes a Friendship," *New York Times*, January 27, 2000, E1.

617 **Under pressure from his wife**: Lou Cannon, "Writing Reagan's Final Scenes," July 27, 1987, A1; Randy Shilts, *And the Band Played On*, 2nd ed. (New York: St. Martin's Press, 1988), 610.

617 **"As far as I know"**: Philip M. Boffey, "Reagan Names 12 to Panel on AIDS," *New York Times*, July 24, 1987, A12.

617 **recommended by Dr. Richard Davis**: Carl Anthony, author interview; Ronald Reagan, diary entry, July 23, 1987, in Brinkley, *Reagan Diaries*.

617 **"because the first lady said so"**: Julie Johnson, "Strong Opinions with No Apologies," *New York Times*, May 25, 1988, A22.

617 **"So Ronald Reagan becomes"**: Joseph Sobran, "The AIDS Commission," *Wanderer*, August 6, 1987.

617 **At the press conference**: Boffey, "Reagan Names 12 to Panel on AIDS," A12.

618 **"promote, encourage or condone"**: Jill Lawrence, "Helms Wins Bid to Limit Material in AIDS Teaching," *Boston Globe*, October 15, 1987, 3.

618 **"Do you really hate [gays] so much"**: Frank Lilly to Senator Jesse Helms, November 2, 1987, OA 11308, Box 2, Bauer Files.

618 **"It is not clear to me"**: Frank Lilly to President Ronald Reagan, December 9, 1987, OA 11308, Box 2, Bauer Files.

618 **"the worst threat our nation has ever known"**: Gary L. Bauer to William E. Melby, July 7, 1987, and Gary L Bauer to Tim Taylor, January 13, 1988, OA 11308, Box 4, Bauer Files.

618 **"concerning public reaction to homosexuals"**: Gary L. Bauer to W. B. Hurd, May 14, 1987, OA 11308, Box 4, Bauer Files.

618 **"While many members of the homosexual community":** Gary L. Bauer to Chuck Angeluca, June 25, 1987, OA 11308, Box 4, Bauer Files; Gary L. Bauer to Chuck Angeluca, June 29, 1987, OA 11308, Box 4, Series I, Bauer Files.

619 **General Accounting Office released a report:** David S. Hilzenrath, "Government's Response to AIDS Epidemic Hit," *Washington Post*, August 13, 1987, A13.

619 **incidence of HIV infection was one-tenth:** Sean Wilentz, *The Age of Reagan: A History, 1974–2008* (New York: Harper, 2008), 186.

619 **the *Challenger* commission:** Philip M. Boffey, "Can the AIDS Panel Now 'Pull It Together?,'" *New York Times*, October 16, 1987, A16.

619 **came to a head on October 8:** Philip M. Boffey, "Leaders of AIDS Panel Quit Amid Feuds and Criticism," October 8, 1987, A18.

619 **hundreds of thousands of people:** Karlyn Barker and Linda Wheeler, "Hundreds of Thousands March for Gay Rights," *Washington Post*, October 12, 1987, A1.

619 **a map of the march route:** "National March on Washington for Lesbian and Gay Rights," *Washington Post*, October 11, 1987, B1.

619 **"For the first time in my memory":** Murdoch, "Examination of the Washington Post's Approach to Gay News."

620 **the only sound that could be heard:** Sandra G. Boodman, "A Somber Crowd Dedicates AIDS Quilt to AIDS Victims," *Washington Post*, October 12, 1987, C1.

620 **new colleague:** Associated Press, "Democrat Elected in San Francisco," *New York Times*, June 3, 1987, A20.

620 **biggest gathering of gay people in history:** France, *How to Survive a Plague*, 296.

620 **"Walking around":** Ford, interviewed by Wiltshire.

620 **"History was made":** Chasen Gaver, "Fever Journal," October 13, 1987, Folder 22, Box 1, Gaver Papers.

620 **"raging fevers":** Chasen Gaver, "Fever Journal," January 13, 1988, Gaver Papers.

621 **"At times I try to see myself":** Chasen Gaver, February 19, 1988, Folder 23, Box 1, Gaver Papers.

621 **sent a copy of the design:** Chasen Gaver to the Names Project, December 15, 1988, Box 12, Gaver Papers.

621 **mailed a brief journal entry:** Chasen Gaver, "Journal Entry," January 27, 1989, Folder 26, Box 2, Bruce Pennington Papers, Rainbow History Project.

621 **sent a polite but firm letter:** Charles R. Gaver to Better Business Bureau, February 25, 1989, Folder 12, Box 1, Gaver Papers.

621 **On March 11, 1989:** "C. R. Gaver, 'Performance' Poet, Dies," C7.

621 **At his memorial service:** Chasen Gaver Memorial Service Program, March 24, 1989, Folder 6, Box 1, Gaver Papers.

622 **"I don't think anybody":** Cannada, author interview.

622 **"I have been angered by":** Janelle Lavelle, "Chasen's Challenge," *Washington Blade*, April 14, 1989, 33.

622 **Students at Gaver's alma mater:** Judy Nichols, "McGaw Displays AIDS Memorial Quilt," *Wooster (OH) Voice*, September 20, 1991, 6.

622 **"among the wonderful, creative, and brave":** Chasen Gaver to the Names Project, December 15, 1988.

42: Naming Names

625 **work for Japan had dried up:** Joan Mower, "Lobbyist at Center of Capital Vice Cases," Associated Press, July 15, 1989.

625 **"The more often you came to Craig's house":** Greve and Schwartz, "Party's Over," 29.

625 **"the Company":** Hedges and Seper, "Power Broker Served Drugs, Sex at Parties."

626 **Fourth of July weekend:** Trotta, *Fighting for Air*, 367.

626 **asked for the uniformed Secret Service officer:** Jerry Seper and Michael Hedges, "Spence Tourist Left with Package; White House Items Vanish," *Washington Times*, July 19, 1989, A1.

626 **a double-deck banner headline:** Paul M. Rodriguez and George Archibald, "Homosexual Prostitution Inquiry Ensnares VIPs with Reagan, Bush," *Washington Times*, June 29, 1989, A1.

627 **"He was nervous":** Archibald, *Journalism Is War*, 131–33.

627 **"key officials of the Reagan and Bush administrations"**: Rodriguez and Archibald, "Homosexual Prostitution Inquiry Ensnares VIPs."

627 **Balach's complaint:** Archibald, *Journalism Is War*, 136.

628 **Balach's boss informed him:** George Archibald and Paul M. Rodriguez, "RNC Calls Scandal a 'Tragic Situation,'" *Washington Times*, June 30, 1989, A1.

628 **"just about the first one that tumbled out"**: James M. Perry, "Washington Times and Post Do Battle in Scandal Involving 'Call Boys,' Fraud and Social Climbing," *Wall Street Journal*, July 28, 1989, A12.

629 **"near-Kinseyian percentage"**: Jack Shafer, "News Bites," *City Paper*, June 7, 1991, 12.

629 **the first of more than sixty items:** Hedges and Seper, "Power Broker Served Drugs, Sex at Parties."

629 **"I think it's quite clear"**: John Mintz, Martha Sherrill, and Elsa Walsh, "The Shadow World of Craig Spence," *Washington Post*, July 18, 1989, D1.

630 **convicted on multiple counts:** "John N. Mitchell Dies at 75," *New York Times*, November 10, 1988, A1; UPI, "McCord Declares That Mrs. Mitchell Was Forcibly Held," *New York Times*, February 19, 1975, 18.

630 **"We have known for many"**: Rodriguez and Archibald, "Homosexual Prostitution Inquiry Ensnares VIPs."

630 **all-expenses-paid trip to Japan:** David Osborne, "Lobbying for Japan Inc.," *New York Times Magazine*, December 4, 1983, 133.

630 **speaking at an exclusive policy seminar:** J. S. Porth, "The End-Run, Quantum Leap Strategy," *Defense and Foreign Affairs*, May 1981, 36.

630 **"Almost everyone who knew him"**: Trotta, *Fighting for Air*, 368.

630 **one of the last sightings:** Thomas Neale, author interview, August 1, 2019, Washington, DC.

631 **"One of the most powerful guys"**: Eleanor Randolph, "The Bombshell That Didn't Explode," *Washington Post*, August 1, 1989, D1.

631 **A former Belgian count:** Sam Roberts, "Arnaud de Borchgrave, Journalist Whose Life Was a Tale Itself, Dies at 88," *New York Times*, February 17, 2015, A16.

631 **"the elusive Mr. Spence"**: Michael Hedges and Jerry Seper, "Once Host to Powerful Reduced to Begging, Sleeping in Park," *Washington Times*, August 9, 1989, A1.

631 **specially dispatched:** Larry J. Sabato, *Feeding Frenzy: How Attack Journalism Has Transformed American Politics* (New York: Free Press, 1991), 56.

631 **"Just as the nocturnal tourists"**: "The In-Crowd," *Washington Times*, July 4, 1989.

631 **"the dandy little Craig"**: Pruden, "Craig J. Spence and the A-list," A4.

631 **"advertisement for his brother"**: Shafer, "Advertisements for His Brother," 6.

632 **had once been on said A-list:** Hedges and Seper, "Once Host to Powerful Reduced to Begging."

632 **seventy-one *Times* staffers:** Larry Bush, "The Right Side," *The Bush Report*, July 1983, 7.

632 **"prudenized"**: Lou Chibbaro Jr., "Anti-Gay Columnist to Head *Washington Times*," May 24, 1991, 3.

632 **"became the subject of concerned interoffice messaging"**: Brock, *Blinded by the Right*, 57.

632 **"a good old boy's relationship"**: "Frisco on the Potomac?" *Washington Times*, July 11, 1989, F2.

632 **just one reader:** Lisa M. Keen, "Washington Times' Call for Action Rallies One Reader," *Washington Blade*, July 14, 1989, 7.

632 **"The thing you never knew"**: Author interview with Spence friend.

632 **apparent trading:** "Former Secret Service Officer Sentenced," Associated Press, November 13, 1990.

632 **"this little 'dish'"**: Hedges and Seper, "Once Host to Powerful Reduced to Begging."

632 **"To this day"**: Paul M. Rodriguez and George Archibald, "U.S. Expands Probe of 'Call Boy' Ring," *Washington Times*, July 6, 1989, A1.

633 **"those who want to clean out homosexuals"**: Ralph Z. Hallow, "Scandal No Use to Democrats," *Washington Times*, July 7, 1989, A1.

633 **"a certain resistance to pro-family policies"**: Archibald and Rodriguez, "RNC Calls Scandal."

633 **"What are they saying"**: Frank J. Murray, "White House Mute on 'Call Boy' Probe," *Washington Times*, July 7, 1989, A1.

633 **As one Democratic consultant put it:** Hallow, "Scandal No Use to Democrats," A1.

634 **"wild and ridiculous"**: Gloria Borger, "Anatomy of a Smear," *U.S. News and World Report*, June 19, 1989, 40.

634 **"We hear it's little boys"**: Lars-Erik Nelson, "Newt Tastes Blood and Has Feeding Frenzy," *New York Daily News*, June 5, 1989, 27.

634 **distributed a memo to state GOP leaders:** Hendrik Hertzberg, "Atwatergate," *New Republic*, July 3, 1989, 4. When Oliver North ran for Senate from Virginia in 1994, Mark Goodin's talent for gay-baiting made him a fine choice for campaign manager. "Homosexual groups are pouring money into my Democrat opponent's campaign coffers," North wrote in a letter to supporters. Sen. Chuck Robb, claimed the man who had earned the nickname "Mr. Green" from the gay clique that helped him raise millions of dollars for the contras, "picks up the phone and calls some radical homosexual or feminist special interest and . . . boom . . . $1,000 or $5,000 is on his desk the next day" (Donald P. Baker and Kent Jenkins Jr., "Coleman, Wilder Eye Senate Race," *Washington Post*, April 16, 1994, A1; Lars-Erik Nelson, "A Hilarious Outing by Ollie North," *Newsday*, November 3, 1994, A17).

634 **"I think if they don't cut the crap":** Joseph Mianowany, "Democrats Say GOP Attack on Foley Is 'Abominable,'" United Press International, June 7, 1989.

634 **"Frank rule":** Barney Frank, "My Life as a Gay Congressman," *Politico*, March 12, 2015.

634 **"Where in the world":** Seper and Hedges, "Spence Elusive," A1.

635 **"Casey's boys are out":** Michael Hedges and Jerry Seper, "In Death, Spence Stayed True to Form," *Washington Times*, November 13, 1989, A1.

635 **At 9 a.m. on July 31:** Bill Dedman and Marianne Yen, "Spence Faces Drug, Weapon Charges After Being Found in New York Hotel," *Washington Post*, August 9, 1989, B1.

635 **rambling interview:** Hedges and Seper, "Once Host to Powerful Reduced to Begging."

636 **the "glass coffin":** Mark Hunker, author interview.

636 **"Rumors of my death":** Charlotte Hays, "Charlotte's Web," *Washington Times*, November 8, 1989, E1.

636 **adopted a droll perspective:** Trotta, *Fighting for Air*, 370.

636 **Spence checked into Room 429:** Matthew Brelis, "Lobbyist in Call-Boy Investigation Found in Dead in Boston Hotel Room," *Boston Globe*, November 12, 1989, 31.

636 **Written on the mirror:** Hedges and Seper, "In Death, Spence Stayed True to Form," A1.

637 **"I've had the world":** Hedges and Seper, "Once Host to Powerful Reduced to Begging."

638 **"Since persecution is not an option":** Andrew Sullivan, "Here Comes the Groom," *New Republic*, August 28, 1989, 20.

638 **Sullivan had pitched his idea:** Andrew Sullivan, author interview, November 23, 2020, Washington, DC.

638 **In 1988:** Shankar Vedantam, et al., "Radically Normal: How Gay Rights Activists Changed the Minds of Their Opponents," *Hidden Brain*, National Public Radio, April 8, 2019.

639 **"outing":** William A. Henry III, "Ethics: Forcing Gays Out of the Closet," *Time*, January 29, 1990, 67.

639 **"It would be nice to find him":** Elaine Sciolino, "Voice of Pentagon Delivers Press Curbs with a Deftness Honed on TV," *New York Times*, February 8, 1991, A1.

639 **stood on the steps of the Capitol:** Glenn R. Simpson and Craig Winneker, "What to Do When Members Are Cited as Homosexuals," *Roll Call*, June 4, 1990, 14.

639 **plastering two hundred fifty posters:** Jack Anderson, "Pete Williams Targeted by Queer Nation," United Features Syndicate, August 5, 1991.

639 **some eight hundred newspapers:** Alwood, *Straight News*, 280.

639 **"a bit of an old chestnut":** Barton Gellman, "Cheney Rejects Idea That Gays Are Security Risk," *Washington Post*, August 1, 1991, A33.

640 **"broke it into pieces":** Henderson, author interview. Hess, whose unwed eighteen-year-old Irish mother was forced to give him up for adoption, was raised by an American Catholic family in St. Louis. The story of her search for him was told in the 2013 film *Philomena*.

640 **Visiting a gay bar:** Trevor Potter, author interview, May 28, 2019, Washington, DC.

43: A Profoundly Important Strength

643 **"I have a vision":** Bill Clinton, "Let Us Rise to the Challenge," (speech), Palace Theatre, May 18, 1992, Los Angeles, CA.

643 **raised a hundred thousand dollars:** David Maraniss, "Clinton Finds New Voice of Emotion," *Washington Post*, May 20, 1992, A1.

643 **Pat Buchanan:** E. J. Dionne Jr., "Buchanan Challenges Bush with 'America First' Call," *Washington Post*, December 11, 1991, A1.

644 **"we cannot tolerate"**: Paulette Goodman, "My Correspondence with Mrs. Bush," *Washington Post*, June 2, 1990, A17.

644 **took it off**: Schmalz, "Gay Politics Goes Mainstream," 18.

644 **At Clinton's inauguration**: David Mixner, *Stranger Among Friends* (New York: Bantam Books, 1996), 280.

644 **first president to recruit gay people**: Adam Nagourney, "Homophiliac," *New Republic*, January 4, 1993, 16.

644 **recognized a chapter**: Lou Chibbaro Jr., "OPM Grants Formal Status to Gay Group," *Washington Blade*, November 26, 1993, 1; Lou Chibbaro Jr., "Federal Workers Make Inroads at Interior, Transportation," *Washington Blade*, February 4, 1994, 1; Lou Chibbaro Jr., "Shalala Issues Strong Pro-Gay Policy at HHS," *Washington Blade*, December 17, 1993, 21; Lou Chibbaro Jr., "State Department Says Gay Workers Are Protected," *Washington Blade*, August 27, 1993, 17.

644 **"pronoun playing"**: Hunker, author interview.

644 **"This is the thing of the 90s,"** Luisita Lopez Torregrosa, "The Gay Nineties," *Vanity Fair*, May 1993, 122.

645 **"bake cookies"**: Alessandra Stanley, "A Softer Image for Hillary Clinton," *New York Times*, July 13, 1992, B1.

645 **"Have I lived an alternative lifestyle?"**: Associated Press, "Clinton Appointee Denies Group's Claim that She's a Lesbian," December 30, 1992.

645 **"I'm attracted to strong, brave"**: Nina Totenberg, "Search for Attorney General Finally Final," *Morning Edition*, National Public Radio, February 12, 1993.

645 **"a damn lesbian"**: Al Kamen, "Helms on Nominee: 'She's a Damn Lesbian,'" *Washington Post*, May 7, 1993, A21.

645 **some three hundred thousand**: Jeffrey Schmalz, "Gay Marchers Throng Capital in Appeal for Rights," *New York Times*, April 26, 1993, 1.

645 **it was a character from Allen Drury's *Advise and Consent***: David S. Broder, "Loyalty, Ideology, Ambition—and Newt Gingrich," *Washington Post*, October 7, 1990, D7.

645 **assigned the novel to his caucus**: Margo Hammond, "Reading Gingrich," *St. Petersburg Times*, March 12, 1995, D1.

646 **"like alcoholism is an orientation"**: Kim I. Mills, "Gingrich Calls on GOP to Tolerate Gays," Associated Press, November 24, 1994.

646 **Clinton's signing the Defense of Marriage Act**: Peter Baker, "President Quielty Signs Law Aimed at Gay Marriages," *Washington Post*, September 22, 1996, A21.

646 **lit up the north face of the White House**: Robert Barnes, "A Deeply Divided Supreme Court on Friday Delivered a Historic Victory," *Washington Post*, June 27, 2015, A1.

646 **Twelve thousand Washingtonians**: Hawkins, interviewed by Meinke.

646 **"once fat with obituaries"**: Brad McKee, author interview, August 14, 2014, Washington, DC.

646 **At conventions of the Log Cabin Republicans**: Rich Tafel, author interview, May 30, 2019, Washington, DC.

646 **"His IQ is lower than my T-cell count"**: Wiltshire, *Seasons of Grief and Grace*, 74.

647 **"there was not a dry eye"**: Sarah McClendon, John Edward Ford obituary, author's collection.

647 **spent their final days**: Keith Easthouse, "By Choice or by Chance, They Died as They Lived—Together," *New Mexican*, Sunday April 11, 1993, E1.

647 **wave of AIDS fatalities**: "HIV and AIDS—United States, 1981–2000," *Morbidity and Mortality Weekly Report* 50, no. 21 (June 1, 2001): 430–34.

647 **"Noticeably absent from the list"**: Chuck Conconi, "Personalities," *Washington Post*, July 10, 1990, C3.

647 **"ubiquitous host"**: Chuck Conconi, "Personalities," *Washington Post*, December 23, 1983, D3.

647 **settled down with a Black lover**: Anderson, author interview.

647 **felled by AIDS in 1995**: Louie Estrada, "Jon C. Hinson Dies at 53," *Washington Post*, July 26, 1995, B4.

647 **"his house was a wonderful clutter"**: Dana Westring, email to author, February 25, 2016.

647 **attending a dinner at Waldron's home**: Robb, author interview.

648 **Five days after Waldron was admitted**: Jura Koncius, "Lady Bird Johnson Joins in Memorializing Designer Bob Waldron," *Washington Post*, June 20, 1996, 5.

648 **volunteered there for twenty years:** Patricia Dane Rogers, "First Lady's Garden," *Washington Post*, April 25, 1991, 5.

648 **"When I see Barbara Bush":** Koncius, "Lady Bird Johnson Joins in Memorializing."

649 **"He loved the history:** "Services for L. Matlovich; Gay Vet Who Was Discharged by Air Force," *Los Angeles Times*, July 3, 1988, 32.

649 **purchased two burial plots:** "Sale of Lots," Association for the Preservation of Historic Congressional Cemetery, November 26, 1984, author's collection.

649 **"The public is never told":** Leonard Matlovich, "Monumental Dreams: Remembering Our Lesbian and Gay Heroes," *The Advocate*, June 23, 1987, 9.

649 **Matlovich died the following year:** Associated Press, "Gay Activist Matlovich Buried with Military Honors," *Baltimore Sun*, July 3, 1988, 3A.

649 **"couldn't resist the last laugh":** Michael Bedwell, "Story of His Stone," http://www.leonardmatlovich.com/storyofhisstone.html.

649 **believed to be the only such designated burial ground:** "LGBT Community," Association for the Preservation of Historic Congressional Cemetery, author's collection.

650 **Camerado, I give you my hand!:** Walt Whitman's poem "Song of the Open Road" in his collection *Leaves of Grass*.

Conclusion: The Gay Century

652 **"caught in bed with a dead girl or a live boy":** A variation on this maxim was offered by Tip O'Neill to Joseph Califano upon the latter's submission of his report concerning the 1982 page sex scandal. "I always knew you got the luck of the Irish from your mother," the Boston pol said. "Only someone with a shamrock could end a House sex investigation by nailing a conservative Republican with a girl and a liberal Democrat with boys!" (Joseph A. Califano Jr., *Inside: A Public and Private Life* [New York: PublicAffairs, 2004], 410).

652 **"The President and I were born":** Mixner, *Stranger Among Friends*, xiii.

652 **"one of the most sort of salient truths":** Strub, interviewed by Clendinen.

652 **"If I had not been gay":** Wiltshire, *Seasons of Grief and Grace*, 61.

653 **"What had started":** Drury, *Advise and Consent*, 295.

INDEX

Entries in italics refer to maps.

Aarons, Leroy, 342–43
ABC News, 346, 369–70, 530, 639
ABC World News Tonight, 547
abortion, 465, 560
Abraham Lincoln Brigade, 65
Abscam, 539
Abwher (German intelligence), 75
Abzug, Bella, 460, 472, 485, 498
Ace of Spades bar, 254, 266
Acheson, Dean, 15, 119–22, 124–25, 147, 171, 258, 327
Achtenberg, Roberta, xxi, 645
Acton, Lord, 651
Adams, Clover, 263
Adams, Henry, 255, 263
Adams, John (Army counsel), 195
Adams, John (president), 3
Adams, John Quincy, 77, 541
Adams, Sherman, 199, 250
Adenauer, Konrad, 392
Adolfo, 525, 569
Advise and Consent (Drury), 232–35, 273, 339, 504, 641, 645; film, 273–77, 362, 486; theater production; 325
Advocate, 463, 466, 485, 498, 555, 561, 649

African Americans, 16–17, 68, 84–86, 123, 148, 269–71, 281–88, 320, 340, 374, 390, 427, 446–48, 462, 483–84, 503, 541, 653
Agence France-Presse, 346
Agnew, Spiro, 383–84, 398
Agriculture Department, xx, 581, 582
AIDS, 473–74, 553–56, 571–93, 604, 608–9, 613–21, 628, 631–32, 635, 637, 643–49
AIDS Memorial Quilt, 620–22
Ailey, Alvin, 403
Air Force Reserve, 301, 323, 329, 331, 335, 341
Albert Einstein Medical Center, 617
Alcoholics Anonymous, 483
Aldridge, Gary, 461, 472
Alexander, Cris, 526
Alexander, Jeb (pseudonym), 5
Alfandre, Bob, 431, 572
Alger, Horatio, 96
Algonquin Round Table, 45, 218
Allen, Richard, 532
All in the Family (TV show), 401
All-Star Inaugural Gala (1981), 519
All the King's Men (Warren), 161
Alsop, Joseph Wright, *v*, xviii, 102, 150, 156, 172, 178, 195, 218–24, 256–60, 288–90, 401, 405, 408–10, 422–23, 438
Alsop, Stewart, 156, 172, 195, 218, 220, 254, 499
Alsop, Susan Mary Jay, 258–50, 408, 425

Alsop, Tish, 254
Amber Room bar, 386
America First, 643
America First Committee, 46
American Bar Association, 567
American Battle Monuments Commission, 131
American Civil Liberties Union (ACLU), xvii, 57, 229–30, 268
American Conservative Trust, 598
American Conservative Union, 470, 471, 482, 567
American Corn Growers Association, 646–47
American Enterprise Institute, 531
American Federation of Labor (AFL), xviii, 211
American Film Institute, 466
American Football League, 495
American Foundation for AIDS Research (amfAR), 613
American Friends Service Committee, 211
American Labor Party, 204
American Psychiatric Association, 157, 270, 473
American Psychological Association, 616
American Space Frontier Committee, 598
Analysis of the Personality of Adolph Hitler (Murray), 52
Anatomy of a Murder (film), 200, 274
Anderson, Clinton, 234–35
Anderson, Jack, 207–8, 240, 357, 382–84, 387–94, 423, 450, 511–12, 551, 639
Anderson, John, 497, 564
Anderson, Robert, 241
Andrew, Christopher, 67
And the Band Played On (Shilts), 556
Angleton, James Jesus, xviii, 135, 141
Angola, 523
Annie's Paramount Steak House, 389
Annual Scandal, 447
Anschluss, 20
Anthony, Carl, 328
anticommunism, 27, 109, 118, 122, 125, 127–28, 131, 135, 139–40, 147, 196, 374–76, 409–10, 557
antidiscrimination laws, 464–65, 485, 498, 561, 567
anti-lynching legislation, 281
anti-Semitism, 190, 206–7
Anti-Terrorism American Committee, 598
anti-Vietnam War movement, 139, 365, 372, 420, 437, 644
Archibald, George, 627
Aristotle, 400, 401
Arkansas National Guard, 250
Arlington National Cemetery, 454
Armistice, 18
Armstrong, Scott, 507, 509–10

Army-McCarthy Hearings, xviii, 189–208, 261, 275, 350, 470, 486
Arthur, Jean, 363, 364
Associated Press (AP), 346
Associates, The, 447
Astaire, Fred, 365
Astor Hotel, 352
Atlantic Charter, 42
Atlantic House bar, 254
Attlee, Clement, 349
Atwater, Lee, 633
Auden, W. H., 151, 154
Austen, Howard, 371
Austria, 20
Austro-Hungarian Empire, 20, 58–60, 129, 409
Axis Powers, 42, 67, 71
Aynesworth, Hugh, 291–92
AZT, 635

Badlands club, 570
Baker, Bobby, 303, 317, 560
Baker, Howard, 494, 497
Baker, James, 563
Bakst, Leon, 218
Balach, Paul, 627–28
Baldwin, James, 261, 288
Balkans, 67
Baltic states, 14
Baltimore, first Lord, 211
Baltimore Sun, 66, 159, 592
Bambi (Salten), 97
Bamford, James, 242
Bancroft, Mary, 61
Bandy, Way, 525, 575
Bankhead, Tallulah, 590
Bankhead, William, 15, 32, 78, 214
Bank of Credit and Commerce International (BCCI), 522
Barkley, Alben, 47, 54
Barnes, Joanna, 404
Baron, Alan, 548–49
Baron Report, 548
Barron, John, 316
Barry, Marion, 462, 614
Baryshnikov, Mikhail, 365
Basie, Count, 85
Batista, Fulgencio, 494
Batman (film), 630
Battaglia, Phil, 353–57
Bauer, Gary, 617–19
Bauman, Louise, 205
Bauman, Robert (Gentleman from Maryland), xx, 205, 376, 470–73, 482–86, 538, 561, 565, 567–68, 578, 588, 593, 596, 616, 628
Bay of Pigs invasion, 436

BBC, 68
Beachy, Robert, 50
Beale, Betty, 254, 300
Bedwell, Michael, 649
Beebe, Charles Hamilton, Jr., 469
Beekman, Gustave "George," xvii, 43–45, 47–49, 54–57
Beene, Geoffrey, 569
Belasco Theatre, 5
Belgium, King of, 301
Bengtsson, Julius, 525, 534
Bennett, Jim, 462
Benny, Jack, 384
Benton, William, 197
Bentsen, Lloyd, 622
Berle, Adolf, 68
Berlin, 248; Airlift, 329; blockade, 95; U.S. embassy, 22, 172
Berlin, Isaiah, 219
Bern, Switzerland, 60–61
Bernstein, Leonard, 384, 432, 527–28; *Mass*, 403
Best, Robert, 306–7, 330–31
Best, William H., III, xx, 497–98, 504–7, 509–10, 516–17
Best and the Brightest, The (Halberstam), 410
Best Man, The (Vidal), 251–52, 260
Best of Washington, 447
Bethesda Naval Hospital, 83
Betty Crocker's Cook Book, 147
Biddle, Francis, 19, 46, 55, 78–79
Biddle, George, 78–79
Billings, Kirk LeMoyne "Lem," xix, 25–26, 247–48, 257–58, 260–61, 289, 315, 409
Billings, Richard, 292
Binger, Dr. Carl, 102, 112–13
Bismarck, Otto von, 61
Black, Hugo, 256, 317
Black, Shirley Temple, 496
Blackburn, Frank, 474–75
Black Diamonds, 447
"Black Forest," 349
blackmail, 137, 144, 148, 154
Black Panthers: Defense Committee, 420; Revolutionary People's Constitutional Convention, 416
Black Power, 416
Blass, Bill, 569, 579
Blick, Roy, xviii, 107, 126–27, 132–33, 147, 151, 186–87, 225, 237–38, 263–65, 307, 314, 455, 544
Block, John, 581–82
Blodgett, Todd A., 628
BLOW (Bachelor Lawyers of Washington), 533
Boardman, L. V., 34
Bohemian Grove, 402

Bohlen, Avis, 173, 176, 178–79
Bohlen, Charles "Chip," 134, 168–76, 178–79, 184, 222, 258, 279–80, 423
Boland Amendment, 596
Bolles, Blair, 151
Bolsheviks, 18–19, 21, 27, 32, 100
Bonanno, Phyllis, 300
Borchgrave, Arnaud de, 611–12, 631
Boston Globe, 609
Boston marriage, 143, 211–12
Boston University, 528
Boswell, John, 638
Bouchey, Lynden Francis "Lynn," xx, 492–94, 499–500, 504, 510–11
Bouvier, John Vernou, III, 248–49
Bowles, Chester, 221
Bowra, Maurice, 154
Boyd, Isabell "La Belle Rebelle," 62
Bozell, L. Brent, III, 584–85
Bozell, L. Brent, Jr., 375
Braden, Joan, 429
Braden, Spruille, 41
Braden, Tom, 424, 429
Bradlee, Ben, xix, 254, 315, 322, 325, 409, 429, 507–8, 511–12, 588–91, 593, 605, 609–13
Bradlee, Freddy, 589–90
Bradley, Dan, 539
Bradley, Omar, 22, 171
Bradley University, 158
Brain Trust, 79
Brass, Ronald, 268
Braun, Eva, 199
Braverman, A. Marvin, xviii, 164–67
Brewster, Ralph, 81
Brideshead Revisited (Waugh), 489, 534, 587; TV show, 534–35, 587
Bridges, Styles, 122, 171, 187–88, 208
Briggs, John, 365, 368
Briggs Initiative, 576
Brinkley, David, 82
Britain, 17, 46, 67–68, 149, 153–55
British *Daily Express*, 150
British embassy, 149–52, 219
British Foreign Office, 149–55
British intelligence, 67, 152, 547
British Labour Party, 150, 338
British Parliament, 150, 540
British Royal Air Force, 67
British Security Co-ordination (BSC), 67, 71
Brock, Bill, 499, 557
Brockdorf-Rantzau, Count Ulrich von, 64
Brooklyn County Court, 45
Brooklyn Eagle, 50
Brooklyn Navy Yard, 47
Broshears, Ray, 451

Brown, George, 301
Brown, Howard, 360
Brown, Tina, 572
Brownell, Herbert, 179, 192–93, 223–24
Brownson, Charles, 166
Brown v. Board of Education, 287
Bruce, Evangeline, 425
Bryant, Anita, 464–66, 486, 513
Bryant, Louise, 19, 37, 78
Brydon, Charles, 520
Bryn Mawr College, 211
Buchanan, James, 3
Buchanan, Pat, 406–7, 465–66, 523, 585, 643
Buchwald, Art, 408–9
Buckley, Christopher, 372, 579
Buckley, James, 377
Buckley, Pat, 371, 376, 579
Buckley, William F., Jr., 174, 365, 369–78,
    384–85, 405, 482–83, 486, 502–3, 530, 534,
    578–80, 617
Bulgakov, Mikhail, 21
Bullitt, William Christian, Jr., xvii, 18–32, 37,
    39–42, 47, 78–81, 86–89, 91, 116, 137, 139,
    168, 170–71, 214, 315
Burch, Dean, 320
Bureau of Indian Affairs, 225
Bureau of Naval Intelligence, 44
Bureau of Prisons, 461
Burgess, Guy Francis de Moncy, xviii, 68,
    149–54, 223, 240
Burt, Gahl Hodges, 522, 524, 570
Busbey, Fred, 166
Bush, Barbara, 643, 648
Bush, George H. W., xxi, 494, 497, 512, 530, 560,
    609, 623, 626, 634, 640, 645
Bush, Jeb, 559
Bush, Larry, 515, 555, 561, 563
Butt, Archibald, 4, 152
Butt-Millet Memorial Fountain, 4
Byrd, Harry, 304

Caceres, Dr. Cesar, xx, 584–85, 608
Caddy, Douglas, 375–76
Caen, Herb, 451
Caesar, Julius, 155
Cafritz, Gwen, 217
Cafritz, Gwendolyn, 423, 425, 431
Califano, Joseph, 547, 565
California: Proposition 6, 365–68; State
    Assembly, 509; Supreme Court, 453
Cambodia, 398
Cambria-Rowe Business College, 23
Cambridge University, 68, 149, 151
Cameron, Paul, 616
Cannada, Dudley, 425, 432

Cannon, Lou, 354, 365, 381, 496, 507
Cantillion, Bob, 83–84
Capital National Bank, 302, 307
Capitol Hill House and Garden Tour, 272
Capitol Police, 189, 207–8, 483–84, 545
Capote, Truman, 106, 249, 360, 525, 579
Caravaggio, 588
Cárdenas, Juan Francisco de, xvii, 70–74
Cárdenas, Lucienne, 70–71, 73
Carmichael, William, 306–7, 309, 330–31
Carnegie Corporation, 111
Carnegie Endowment for International Peace,
    96, 172
Caro, Robert, 298, 303
Carpenter, Liz, 316–17, 320, 338–39, 522
Carrier, Alan, 600
Carroll Tavern, 83
Carson, Johnny, 519
Carter, Jimmy, xx, 459–61, 463–64, 466, 494–95,
    499, 516, 518–20, 532, 547, 596–97
Carter, John Franklin, 52
Carter, Rosalynn, 632
Case, Archie, 525
Casey, William, 530, 532, 602–3, 635
Casper, Joseph J., 387
Castro, Fidel, 278, 280, 345, 494
Cathedral of St. Matthew, 588
Catholic Church, 61, 370, 401, 403
Catholic University, 587
Cave Dwellers, 17
CBS News, 306, 320, 356, 401, 438, 545–46,
    550–51, 546
Centers for Disease Control (CDC), 541–42,
    553–54, 574
Central America, 560, 602
Central Intelligence Agency (CIA), xvii, xviii,
    64, 75, 130, 135–43, 150–51, 160, 167, 179,
    186, 191, 210–12, 222–23, 255, 258, 291,
    293, 317, 409, 436, 480, 494, 503, 523, 530,
    532, 536, 602–3, 625, 635; Langley facility,
    210–12
Central Powers, 18
Ceylon, 65
Challenger shuttle disaster, 619
Chamberlain, Charles E., 344
Chamberlain, John, 359–60
Chambers, Robert, 626–27
Chambers, Whittaker, xviii, 93, 96–105, 108–19,
    121, 174, 207, 220, 233, 292, 373, 391, 396,
    398, 435, 578, 612, 651
Chambers Funeral Home, 626
Channell, Carl "Spitz," xx, 594–606, 631
Chapin, Dwight, xix, 382, 386–87, 404, 407–8,
    436
Chappaquiddick incident, 483

Charles, Prince of Wales, 525
Charlie's Angels (TV show), 466
Chauncey, George, 108, 638
Checkers speech, 382
Cheever, John, 106
Cheney, Richard B., 497, 616, 639–40
Cher, 428, 575
Cherry Blossom Festival, 447
Chesapeake House bar, *v*, 477, 482, 538, 544, 549, 551
Cheshire, Maxine, 409, 433–34, 529
Chevy Chase Club, 164
Chiang Kai-shek, 120, 301
Chiang Kai-shek, Madame, 301
Chibbaro, Lou, Jr. (Lou Romano), xx, 469, 547
Chicago Daily News, 370
Chicago Tribune, 21, 33, 55, 57, 118, 187
Chicherin, Georgy, 18, 64
Chicken Ranch, 432–33
Child, Julia, 65
Childs, Marquis, 157
Chile, 531
China, Communist, 8, 24, 120–21, 149; nuclear bomb and, 338; Soviet mutual defense pact, 120
China, Republic of (Taiwan), 149
Chinese Nationalists, 120
Choate, 25–26, 247
Choka, Andy, 316, 324
Chotiner, Murray, xix, 381–84, 394, 404, 493
Christian right, 562
Christians, evangelical 465–66, 481, 485, 493, 516, 521, 524, 617
Christian Voice, 481
Christopher Street, 562, 585
Church, Chase, 352
Church, Frank, 352, 476–77, 563
Church, William C. G., 352
Church Committee, 539
Churchill, Winston, 15, 67, 95, 149
Church of Scientology, 522
Cinema Follies fire, *v*, 466–70, 480–81, 485, 608
Circuit Court of Fairfax County, 212
Citizen Kane (film), 636
Citizens for Eisenhower, 159, 178, 215
Citizens for the Republic, 499
City and the Pillar, The (Vidal), 106, 249, 370
Civil Air Patrol, 291
Civil Rights Act: (1957), 281, 350; (1960), 350; (1964), 318, 340, 350
civil rights movement, 271, 281–88, 419
civil service, 129, 148
Civil Service Commission (CSC; *later* Office of Personnel Management), 131, 143, 179,

228–31, 264, 306–9, 311, 333–35, 344, 346–47, 441, 644; reform of 1975, 463, 520
Civil War, 15, 47, 62, 84
Clark, Bennett, 55
Clarke, Lige, 345
Class Reunion (Werfel), 102
Clay, Lucius, 91
Cleveland, Grover, 4, 199, 427
Cleveland, Rose, 4
Cliburn, Van, 302
Clifford, Clark, 317–20, 327–28, 339, 425
Clinton, Bill, xxi, 491–92, 641, 643–46, 652
Clinton, Hillary, 645
Clubhouse bar, 447
Club Madre, *v*, 85
Code, the, 366, 486, 560, 562, 634
Coffin, William Sloane, Jr., 139
Cohn, Roy M., xviii, 190–96, 199–208, 261, 321, 437, 486, 524, 532, 574, 578
Colacello, Bob, 526
Colagerakis, Doug, 647
Colby, William, 139
Cold War, 6–7, 117, 120, 125, 127, 135, 139–40, 151, 154, 190, 212, 219, 228, 235, 259, 281, 374, 410, 540
Coleman, James "Juicy," 447–48, 580–81
College of Wooster, 622
Collier's, 32
Colson, Chuck, 393–94, 399, 437
Columbia University, 97, 190, 364
Combined Policy Committee on Atomic Development, 153
Cominform (Communist Information Bureau), 204, 281
Comintern (Communist International), 154
Commentary, 373
Commerce Department, 130, 268, 333, 334
Committee for the Study of Sex Variants, 62
Committee to Re-Elect the President (CREEP), 437, 557
communism, 7, 19, 95, 125, 127, 131, 132, 133, 139, 140, 149–50, 151, 153, 155, 157, 169, 374–376, 419
Communist Manifesto, The (Marx and Engels), 118
Communist Party U.S.A, 96–105, 109, 112–19, 122, 125, 140, 155, 156, 190
Comstock Act (1873), 27
Conable, Barber, 497
Conant, Jennet, 65
concentration camps, 22
Concerned Americans for Individual Rights (CAIR), 568–70, 588
Confederacy, 62
Confederacy of Dunces (Toole), 379

Conference of Catholic Bishops, 522
Confidential, 212–16, 569
Confrontation Day, 99, 101
Congress for Cultural Freedom, 139–40
Congressional Cemetery, *v*, 649
Congressional Quarterly, 326
Congressional Record, 282
Connally, John, 320
Connecticut General Assembly, 609
Connolly, Cyril, 154
Conscience of a Conservative, The (Goldwater/
    Bozell), 375
Conservative Caucus, 557
Conservative Digest, 552
Conservative Party, 377
conservatives, 206, 485
containment policy, 121
Continental Army, 3
Continental Congress, 540
Cook, Blanche Wiesen, 38
Cooke, Alistair, 101, 113–14
Cooke, Janet, 593
Coolidge, Calvin, 14, 332
Coordinating Committee for Democratic
    Action, 56
Coors, Joseph, 596
Corcoran, Tommy, 530
Cory, Donald Webster (Edward Sagarin), 123,
    230, 265
Corydon (Gide), 123
Cosa Nostra, 291
Cosmopolitan, 217
Cosmos Club, 571
Costanza, Margaret "Midge," xx, 459–61,
    463–64, 466, 591
Council for Inter-American Security, xx,
    492–94
Cox, Archibald, 264
Craig, Larry, 547
Craig, May, 195
Crane, Dan, 559, 565
Cranston, Alan, 424, 461, 472
Criswell, Dr. W. A., 571
Cronkite, Walter, 438
Cruise, Tom, 533
cruising, 8, 90–91, 108, 115, 184, 220, 251, 254,
    349, 434–35, 454–55, 474, 484–85, 503, 513,
    534, 559
Cuba, 14, 279–80, 345–46, 423; Missile Crisis,
    278, 387, 423; Revolution, 8, 278, 280
Cuban exiles, 280, 291
Cuckenberger, Edwin Louis, 180
Cuneo, Ernest, 75
Curran, Father Charles, 587
Cutler, Robert, xviii, 177–79, 220, 530

Daily Worker, 97, 101–2
Daley, Richard, 371–72
Dallas (TV show), 484, 532
Daniels, Josephus, 37
Dark Victory (film), 361
Dartmouth College, 165
Darwin, Charles, 235
D'Aubuisson, Roberto, 494
Daugherty, Harry, 4–5
David Susskind Show, The, 371
Davis, Bette, 361
Davis, Dr. Richard, 617
Day, J. Edward, 270
DC Twelve, 416–17
Dean, John, 437–38, 609
Death in Venice (Mann), 531
Deaver, Michael, 366, 505, 509–10, 515, 525, 576
"Decator, Truxton" (pseudonym), 214–15
Decker, Bruce, 568
"Declaration of Conscience" (Smith), 186
Deep Backgrounder, xxi, 536–37, 539, 544–45,
    548–49, 552–53, 562, 564
Deep Throat (film), 426
Defense Department (Pentagon), 128, 130, 192,
    224, 259, 330, 345, 347, 352, 389–90, 392–
    93, 408, 461, 477, 537–38, 540, 600, 639
Defense Intelligence Agency, 630
Defense of Marriage Act (1996), 646
Definition of Communism (Schine), 191–92
Deliver Us from Evil (Dooley), 140
DeLoach, Cartha "Deke," 36, 320–21, 336–37,
    341, 383
D'Emilio, John, 81
Democratic National Committee, 246, 435–36,
    495, 548
Democratic National Convention: (1940), 46;
    (1960), 245, 283, 300; (1964), 320, 336;
    (1968), 369, 371–72; (1972), 404, 426, 437,
    461; (1976), 460; (1992), 643
Democratic Party, 19, 55, 91, 122, 126, 131, 137,
    157, 169, 185, 197, 204, 206, 303, 361, 365,
    391, 460, 484–85, 634, 644
Deneuve, Catherine, 575
Denmark, 248
Depression, 82, 108, 158
DeSapio, Carmine, 385
desegregation, 250, 281
Detroit Free Press, 158–59
Detroit News, 452
Deukmejian, George, 568
Dewey, John, 235
Diaghilev, Sergei, 218
Dickerson, Nancy, 306, 320
Dickson, Alexander, 15–16
Dien Bien Phu, Battle of, 182

Dietz, Stanley M., 226, 269–71
diGenova, Joseph, 629–30
Diocletian, Emperor of Rome, 587
Dirkson, Everett, 157
Disier, Donald, 437
District of Columbia Youth for Nixon, 376
Divine, 467
Division of Current Intelligence Summaries, 18
Dobrynin, Anatoly, 326
Dodd, Christopher, 608
Dodd, Thomas, 280
Dolan, John Terrence "Terry," xx, 557–64, 567–71, 583–93, 596–97, 600–601, 605, 608–13, 615
Dolan, Margaret, 610
Dolan, Tony, xx, 558, 562, 586–93, 609–13, 615, 631
Dole, Bob, 634
Dolinsky, Paul, 432–33
Dollard, Charles, 111
Domestic Policy Council, 616
Dominick, Peter, 330
Donovan, William "Wild Bill," xvii, 60, 65, 67, 70–72, 75, 136
Don't Ask, Don't Tell, 646
"Dooley, Dr.," 373
Dooley, Thomas, 140
Doran, Daniel A., 55–56
Douglas, Helen Gahagan, 381
Downes, Donald, xvii, 66–76, 137
Downey, Kirstin, 143–44
Downie, Leonard, 592–93, 608, 610, 613
Doyle, Peter, 3, 650
Dreyfus affair, 59
Drury, Allen, 126, 232–35, 273–77, 339, 401, 427, 641, 645
Duberman, Martin, 638
Du Bois, Cora, 65–66
Duke Law School, 397
Dulles, Allen, xvii, 58, 60–61, 69–72, 74, 135, 167–68, 171, 210, 212, 223, 258–59, 409
Dulles, John Foster, xviii, 167–76, 178
Dunbar High School, 84
Dunlap, Jack, 242
Dunne, John Gregory, 376
Dupont Circle, v, 108, 272, 349, 388–90, 434, 447, 534
Dutcher, Charles, 628
Dutch (Morris), 577–78
Dynasty (TV show), 532

Eagle bar, 442, 476, 561, 562, 600
Eagleton, Thomas, 461, 498
Earth Day, 496
Eastern Europe, 121, 135–36

Eastern Mattachine Magazine, 346
East Germany, 120
Eastland, James, 554
Ebony, 283
Edwards, Edwin, 457, 652
Edwards, India, 246
Ehrlichman, John, xix, 382–84, 386–88, 391–93, 399–403, 436, 517
Eighteen Acres Under Glass (Gray), 433
Eisenhower, Dwight, xviii, 7, 157–60, 163, 168–69, 172–77, 179, 186, 205–6, 215–17, 224, 232, 240–41, 245, 250–51, 275, 280, 305, 315, 324, 349, 381–82, 398, 405, 430, 433–34, 522, 558
Eisenhower, Edgar, 172
Eisenhower, Mamie, 216
elections: (1912), 303; (1946), 381; (1948), 186, 281, 317; (1950), 187, 381; (1952), 156–58, 191, 198, 205, 245, 381–82; (1954), 186; (1956), 245; (1960), 245, 254, 257, 300, 382, 558; (1962), 382; (1964), 322–25, 328, 332, 336, 338–39, 341, 359, 376, 508; (1968), 356, 382, 502; (1970), 391; (1971), 411–14; (1972), 558, 460; (1976), 460, 493, 498, 508; (1978), 586; (1980), 466, 484, 492, 515–16, 558–59; (1982), 517, 560; (1986), 583, 603; (1990), 645
Elizabeth Taylor Medical Center, 646
Ellington, Duke, 85
Ellis, Perry, 569, 575
Ellsberg, Daniel, 425, 435–36
El Salvador, 501
Employment of Homosexuals and Other Sex Perverts in Government (Hoey report), 144–45
Endangered Species Act (1973), 496
Engine Company No. 7, 467
Enslin, Gotthold Frederick, 3
Episcopal Theological School, 186
Equal Rights Amendment (ERA), 465, 499, 559–60
Equus bar, 512–14
"Eric" (Beekman house visitor), 47
Ernst, Morris, xvii, 45, 47, 49, 55, 57
Esquire, 246, 313, 377–78
Evans, Courtney, 331, 333
Evans, Rowland, 338, 359, 495
Evans, Tom, 508
Everard Baths, 151
Evidence of Washington, The (Walton), 255
Evidenzbureau (Austro-Hungarian counterintelligence unit), 58–59
ExComm group, 387
Executive Order: (9835, loyalty program), 124; (10450), 179–80, 229, 646; (12968), 646

Faderman, Lillian, 143
Fag Rag, 397
Falcoff, Mark, 531–32
Fallaci, Oriana, 293
Falwell, Jerry, 466, 560, 562, 571, 586
Family Protection Act (proposed, 1981), 471, 522, 560
Farrell, John, 406
fascism, 52–53, 64, 68, 136
Faubus, Orval, 250
Fauci, Dr. Anthony, 585
Federal Bureau of Investigation (FBI), xvii, xix, 23, 32–39, 47, 49, 54–55, 64–65, 68–71, 74–78, 84, 102–5, 111–18, 129, 135–38, 150–54, 158–60, 168, 170–71, 174–75, 178–80, 191, 213, 223–24, 241–42, 250, 258, 261–68, 282, 284, 289, 291, 293, 320, 324–25, 330–38, 345, 351–52, 373, 383–84, 387–91, 393, 404–5, 408, 419–20, 436, 462, 473, 507, 520, 537, 540, 544–51, 569, 634, 651
Federal Communications Commission (FCC), 190, 217, 421
Federal Election Campaign Act (1974 amendment), 557
Federal Highway Administration, 211
Federal Trade Commission (FTC), 591, 620–622
Fellowship of Reconciliation, 283
Felt, Mark, 387
Ferrie, David, 291, 292
Ferrugia, John, 545–46, 550–51
"Fever Journal" (Gaver), 620
Fielding, Lewis, 435–36
Finkelstein, Arthur, 377
Finnish embassy, 310
Finnish Legation, 164
Firing Line (TV show), 369
First Amendment, 57, 238, 272
Fisher, James, 140
Fitzwater, Marlin, 633
Five of Hearts salon, 263
Flack, Roberta, 389
Flanagan, Francis J., xviii, 129–31, 142
Flanders, Ralph, 202–4
Flanner, Janet, 25
Flash Gordon comic books, 364
Florida Citrus Commission, 464
Florinsky, Dmitry, 63
Flynt, Larry, 491
Fochett, Louis, 265–66, 316
Foley, Tom, 634
Fonda, Henry, 275
Food and Drug Administration (FDA), 556
Forbes, Malcolm, 614
Ford, Betty, 425

Ford, Gerald, xx, 365, 425, 439, 449–54, 493–94, 497–98, 505, 554, 570–71, 616, 652
Ford, John W., 170–71, 520, 571–72, 581–82, 620, 646–47, 652
Fordham University, 138
Foreign Service, 21–24, 27–29, 83, 92, 96, 134, 170, 174, 181–85, 193, 196; Personnel division, 182, 183
Foreign Service Institute, 477
"Forrester, Ladd" (pseudonym), 82
Forster, E. M., 100
Fortas, Abe, 317–20, 327
Fort Meade, 239
Fort Monmouth, 194, 201
Foster, Jodie, 526
Fox, George Wilbur, 44, 49
France, xvii, 24, 31, 62, 66, 219; Revolution, 314; Vichy, 31, 72
Franco, Francisco, 17, 65, 70–71, 73, 370
Frank, Barney, 235, 564, 609, 634, 636, 639
Frankfurter, Felix, 88, 96
Franklin, Benjamin, 3
Franklin Park Hotel, 148
Franks, Bobbie, 292
Franz Joseph, Emperor of Austria-Hungary, 60
Frederick the Great, King of Prussia, 3
Free Congress Foundation, 561
Freedom of Information Act, 117
Freedom Rides, 283
Frelinghuysen, Peter, 350–52
French Air Ministry, 30
Frenzel, Bill, 497
Freud, Sigmund, 19–20, 116, 155
Freund, Eva, xix, 267–68, 344, 347, 414, 417
Friday, Wayne, 454
Friendly Models, xx, 542–45
Friendship and Fratricide (Zeligs), 116
Frieswyk, Marion, 65
Fromme, Lynette Alice "Squeaky," 449
Frowick, Roy Halston, 249
F. Scott's bar, 499
Fuchs, Klaus, 121
Fugate, James Barr, 250
Furies, *v*, 417–18
Furlong, Tim, 431, 622

G-2 Intelligence Service, 67
Gaddafi, Muammar, 575
Galanos, Jimmy, 363, 525, 569
Galbraith, John Kenneth, 95
Gallup, Grant, 286
Garavani, Valentino, 579
Garfinckel's department store, 85, 349
Garment, Len, 399, 406–8
Garment, Suzanne, 407

Garrison, Jim, 290–93
Garwood, Ellen, 598, 599, 604
GATT (Gays Assembled to Talk Trade), 533
Gaver, Chasen, 591, 620–22
Gay, Lesbian or Bisexual Employees (GLOBE), 644
Gay Activists Alliance, 419, 421, 462
Gay Blade (later *Washington Blade*), xix, 388–89, 420, 469
gay liberation, *v*, 427, 451–52, 465
Gay Liberation Front (GLF), 415–20, 437, 446, 450–51
Gay Men's Health Crisis, 569
Gay Pride Day, 442
Gay Rights National Lobby, 463
Geist, Raymond, 22
General Accounting Office, 546, 619
General Electric, 358
General Motors, 52, 452
General Social Survey, 638
Georgetown University, 228, 375, 431, 443, 558; Hospital, 473
George Washington University, 82, 235, 269; Hospital, 318
Gerassi, Alfredo, 73, 74
German Americans, 67, 85
German Chancellery, 50
Germany, xvii, 97; Nazi, 7, 20, 22, 31, 41, 44, 46, 49–55, 60–62, 64, 67–69, 130, 135, 168, 219;; WW I and, 62. *See also* West Germany
Gerry, Peter, 14
Gestapo, 52, 130
Gibbon, Edward, 178
Gide, André, 123
Gigrich, Rev. John, 588
Gingrich, Newt, 634, 645–46
Gittings, Barbara, 649
Glenn, John, 530
Glenn, Rev. C. Leslie, 163–64
Glenville, Peter, 579
Glorious Food, 526
Gobie, Steven, 636
Goddard, Henry, 113
God's Bullies (Young), 562–63
Goebbels, Joseph, 69
Goering, Hermann, 69, 130
Golden Age, The (Vidal), 260
Goldman, Eric, 336–37
Goldwater, Barry, 301, 318, 322–24, 329, 336–38, 354, 359, 375–77, 478–79, 495, 498, 507–8, 558
Gompers, Samuel, 211
González, Ascensión, 73
González, Tomás, 73–74
Good, Barbara J., 184

Goodell, Charles, 424–25
Goodin, Mark, 634
Good Neighbor policy, 14, 92
Goodwin, Doris Kearns, 38, 304
Gordon, Hal, 524, 567
Gore, Thomas Pryor, 249
Goulding, Edmund, 361
Government Printing Office, 542
Graber, Ted, 525
Grace Episcopal Church, 415
Graham, Daniel, 630
Graham, Don, 609, 613, 615
Graham, Jim, 472, 589
Graham, Katharine, xix, 254, 259, 315, 328, 342–43, 409, 631–32
Graham, Martha, 425
Graham, Phil, 254, 257, 259
Grand Central nightclub, 446
Grand Hotel (Moscow), 221
Graves, Robert, 384
Gray, Robert, xviii, 216–18, 224, 430–34, 518–25, 549, 572, 605, 613
Gray & Company, 521–23
Great Gatsby, The (Fitzgerald), 19
Great True Spy Stories (Dulles), 60
Grecian Guild, 238
Grecian Guild Pictorial, 236–38, 272
Greece, ancient, 8, 181, 237, 400–401, 417
Greenspun, Hank, 198–99
Greenwich Village, 64, 385
Gridiron Club, 427
Griffin, Merv, 525
Griswold v. Connecticut, 256
Grizzard, George, 275
Grombach, John V. "Frenchy," 136
Gross, Alfred A., 62–63
Grotewohl, Otto, 218
Groton, 15, 23, 55, 121, 218
Group, the, 447
Grow Washington Political Action Committee, 598
Guild Book Service, 271
Guild Press, *v*, xix
Gulf War, 639
Gunther, John, 15
Gup, Ted, 507, 510–11, 590
Gustav III, King of Sweden, 29

Haffner, Fred, 509
Hagerty, James, 224
Haig, Alexander, 397
Haines, Billy, 362–63, 525
Hair (musical), 412
Halberstam, David, 410

Haldeman, H. R. "Bob," xix, 382–88, 391, 393–94, 399–403, 436
Haldeman, Peter, 400
Hall, Fawn, 592, 600, 603
Hamilton, Alexander, 47
Hamilton, George, 614
Hannaford, Peter, xx, 366–67, 505, 509, 511, 514–16, 525, 567–68
Hanover, Renee, 417
Hansen, Roger D. "Denny," 185
Hapsburg Empire, 8, 58
Harding, Florence, 5
Harding, Warren, 4, 15–16
Harlan, John Marshall, II, 271
Harley, Sharon, 84
Harley's Angels (film), 466
Harlow, Bryce, 250
Harper's Bazaar, 575
Harriman, Averell, 359
Harris, David, 390, 412
Harrison, Benjamin, 171
Harrison, Robert, 212–14
Harvard Board of Overseers, 101
Harvard University, 14, 23, 121, 138, 168, 172, 178, 191, 218, 228, 404, 424; Law School, 22, 96, 165
Hastings, Benedict J., 628
Hatch, Orrin, 563–64
Hattoy, Bob, xxi, 643
Hawkins, Pat, 287, 646
Hay, Clara, 263
Hay, Harry, 155–56
Hay, John, 263
Hay-Adams Hotel, v, 263–65, 268
Hays, Wayne, 483
Health, Education, and Welfare Department, 255
Health and Human Services Department, 556, 645
Hedges, Michael, 629, 635
Heinrichs, Waldo, 23
Helms, Alan, 256–57
Helms, Jesse, 511, 618, 645
Helms, Richard, 409, 536
Hemingway, Margaux, 428
Hemlock and After (Wilson), 314
Henderson, Keith, 428
Hendon, Robert C., 34
Henry, Patrick, 18
Henry VIII, King of England, 1
Hepburn, Katharine, 590
Herbits, Stephen, 616
Herblock, 406
Heritage Foundation, 557
Herrick, Myron, 31

Hersh, Seymour, 405
Herter, Christian, 224
Hertzberg, Hendrik, 634
Hess, Michael, 640
Heston, Charlton, 519
Hickenlooper, Bourke, 170
Hickok, Lorena "Hick," xvii, 37–38, 81
Hideaway bar, 345, 607
Higby, Larry, 386
Higdon, Robert, 432, 523, 527, 532–33
Higginson, Rev. Francis, 1
Hilger, Gustav, 135
Hill, J. Lister, 126–27, 129
Hill and Knowlton, 425, 430, 433, 521
Hillenkoetter, Roscoe, 137, 140–43
Himmler, Heinrich, 52, 69
Hinson, Cynthia, 481
Hinson, Jon ("Gentleman from Mississippi"), xx, 454–56, 466–67, 470, 480–86, 514, 565, 600, 647
Hiroshima and Nagasaki, 349
Hiss, Alger, xviii, 92, 96–105, 109–14, 116–19, 121–22, 138, 154, 172, 174, 207, 220, 233, 292, 327, 373–74, 391, 396, 398, 435–36, 493, 651
Hiss, Priscilla, 111
Hitler, Adolf, 44, 47, 50–53, 65, 113, 130, 142, 169, 199
Hitler Youth, 53
Hobson, Timothy, 111–12, 117, 436
Hoey, Clyde, xviii, 129, 141, 144
Hoey Report, 144–45
Hoffa, Jimmy, 261, 428
Hoffman, David, 590
Holbrooke, Richard, 425, 530
Holiday, Billie, 85
Holmes, Oliver Wendell, 96
Holy Family Hospital, 44
"Homintern," 154–55, 292, 517
Homosexual Handbook, The (d'Arcangelo), 384
Homosexual in America, The (Cory), 123, 230, 265
Homosexual Network, The (Rueda), 561
"homosexual panic" defense, 227, 269
Honduras, 24
Hook, Sidney, 114
Hoover, Herbert, 348
Hoover, J. Edgar, xvii, 32–39, 68–70, 74–84, 109, 111, 113, 128, 137, 151–53, 158, 160, 167–68, 171, 173, 191, 215–16, 223–24, 241, 284, 289–90, 322–26, 330, 332–33, 337, 383–88, 391, 412, 419, 473, 507, 569, 648
Hope, Bob, 519, 571
Horace Mann School, 190

House Un-American Activities Committee (HUAC), 95–103, 109, 111, 165, 240, 241, 242

Housing and Urban Development Department (HUD), 645

Houskeeper, Lee, 363, 364, 365

Howard "Miss Hattie" (piano player), 107

Howard University, 84, 235, 447, 649

Hoyt, Palmer, 326

Hudson, Rock, 367, 530, 569–70, 573–77

Hull, Cordell, Jr., xvii, 14–15, 17, 20, 28, 30–31, 38, 40, 42, 77–80, 90–91, 213

Hull, Cordell, Sr., 15

Hull, Rose, 77–78, 80

Human Events, 154, 552

Hume, Brit, 393

Humphrey, Gordon, 586, 610

Humphrey, Hubert, 275, 320

Hungarian Arrow Cross, 136

Hunt, Clyde, 185, 208

Hunt, E. Howard, 436, 537

Hunt, Lester, Jr. "Buddy," 186–88, 208–9

Hunt, Lester, Sr., xviii, 185–88, 207–9, 234, 336, 639

Hunt, Nathelle, 187–88, 208

Hunt, Nelson Bunker, 570

Hunter, Tab, 569

Hurlbut, Bert, 604

Hurt, William, 576

Hustler, 491

Ickes, Harold, 15

I.G. Farben, 135

Independence, USS, 356, 358

Independent News Network, 545, 550

India, 390

Indonesia, 415

Inman, Bobby Ray, xx, 478–80

Inman, Richard, 347

Inouye, Daniel K., 606

Inquiring Camera Girl (Jackie Kennedy), 254

Interior Department, 210, 217, 225, 255

Internal Revenue Service (IRS), 461

Interview, 526

Iran-Contra scandal, 7, 592–96, 603–6

Iron Curtain, 95, 149, 240, 408

Irons, Jeremy, 534

Isaacson, Walter, 168

Isherwood, Christopher, 150–51, 184

Israel, 317, 425

Israeli intelligence, 547

Istanbul, 67

Italian intelligence service, 59

It's Not Done (Bullitt), 19

Iwo Jima Memorial, *v*, 268, 513, 454, 456, 467, 485

Jack Paar Program, The (TV show), 370

Jackson, Andrew, statue, 148

Jackson, Henry, 204

Jackson, Michael, 569

Jackson, Henry "Scoop," 436–37

James, Henry, 5

Japan, 24, 41, 44, 62, 67, 228, 529, 630

Jarman, Derek, 588

Jay, John, 259

Jay, Susan Mary, 258–59

Jefferson, Thomas, 3, 77, 199

Jefts, Peter, 386

Jenkins, Marjorie, 315, 327

Jenkins, Ray, 201–2

Jenkins, Walter, xix, 305–6, 309, 314–29, 331–33, 337–40, 354, 357, 383, 408, 516

Jet, 85

Jewel Box, 147

Jews, 123, 190–91, 206–7; Nazi Germany and, 53, 60–61, 92, 135

Jill joints, 85

John Birch Society, 206, 363

Johnnie's bar, 225

John Paul II, Pope, 615

Johns Hopkins University, 96, 235; Medical Center, 635

Johnson, Jim, 497

Johnson, Kimbell, 334

Johnson, Lady Bird, 298, 300, 305, 316, 319, 326–28, 335–40, 348, 648

Johnson, Luci, 298

Johnson, Lynda Bird, 298–301, 309, 647–48

Johnson, Lyndon B., xix, 245–46, 257, 275, 297–311, 314–41, 348, 354, 357, 398, 408, 410, 423, 502, 508, 516, 547, 652

Johnson, Sam Ealy, 304

Joint Chiefs of Staff, 22, 171, 241, 345, 349

Jones, Jerry, 453

Jones, Marshall, 263–65

Jordan, Barbara, 485, 617

Jordan, Hamilton, 495

Jorgensen, Christine, 158

Joyce, James, 27

Joyce, Robert, 27

Judge Advocate General Corps, 436

Junior League, 143

Justice Department, 74–75, 190, 191, 341, 352, 546, 551, 603

Just Say No (Kramer), 616

Kameny, Franklin, xviii, 228–3, 236–69, 271, 286–87, 289, 344–46, 389, 411–16, 419–20, 441–42, 450, 461–62, 466, 473, 478–80, 649
Kameny, Rea, 442
Kaposi's sarcoma, 542, 570
Karpman, Dr. Benjamin, 107
Kastor, Elizabeth, 590, 609–10
Katzenbach, Nicholas, 323–24, 331–32
Kaufman, Samuel, 112
Kaylor, Annie, 389
Keaton, Michael, 630
Kerr, Jean, 199
Kefauver, Estes, 86
Kelly, Gene, 365
Kelly, Michael, 592, 605
Kemp, Jack, 354–55, 357, 443, 494–501, 504, 510, 512
Kempton, Murray, 96, 371
Kennan, George, 24, 79, 89, 168, 172
Kennard, Byron 255–56
Kennedy, Caroline, 248
Kennedy, Ethel, 409, 529, 625
Kennedy, Jacqueline Bouvier, 205, 247–49, 251, 253–62, 266, 276, 289, 320, 348, 503, 621
Kennedy, John F., xix, 25–27, 187, 199, 224, 232, 243, 245–61, 264, 266, 269, 276, 280–81, 284, 300, 302, 305, 315, 324, 336, 344, 349, 375, 387, 397–98, 403, 423–24, 461, 558, 615; assassination of, 7, 255, 288–93, 298, 309, 317, 320, 328, 332, 503, 537, 547, 588
Kennedy, John F., Jr., 254
Kennedy, Joseph, Jr., 26
Kennedy, Joseph, Sr., 26, 68, 199
Kennedy, Kathleen "Kick," 257
Kennedy, Robert F. "Bobby," 199, 204, 245–47, 252, 260–62, 268–69, 273, 275, 280, 284, 289, 300, 324, 503
Kennedy, Ted, 483, 503
Kent, Frank, 125
Kerr, Sir Archibald Clark, 152
Key, Hugh, 348–49
KGB, 221–23, 408–10, 538, 540, 547–48, 630
Khrushchev, Nikita, 220–21, 248, 338
Kind, Richard, xx, 543–44
King, Clarence, 263
King, Coretta Scott, 503
King, Mackenzie, 349
King, Rev. Martin Luther, Jr., 283–86, 288, 389, 481, 503, 547, 620
King, William Rufus, 3
Kinsey, Dr. Alfred, 64, 105–6, 128, 132
Kinsley, Michael, 638
Kinsolving, Lester "Larry," 553–56
Kirk, Alexander Comstock, 22–23
Kirkpatrick, Lyman, 136

Kirkwood, James, 292
Kissinger, Henry, 391–92, 397–400, 404–5, 408, 422, 426, 428, 434–36, 560
Kiss of the Spider Woman (film), 576
Klein, Calvin, 569
Klein, Herb, 495
Knight Ridder, 548
Kolbe, Jim, 376
Koons, Skip, 177
Koop, C. Everett, 614
Kopay, David, 442–43
Koppel, Ted, 530, 547, 634–35
Koreagate, 539
Korean War, 149–50, 183
Kraft, Joseph, 401
Kramer, Larry, 539, 560, 569, 616
Kramerbooks, 534
Kristol, Irving, 495
Krock, Arthur, 213, 322
Krogh, Egil "Bud," 436, 509
KTVK, 509
Kuchel, Thomas, 363
Ku Klux Klan, 485
Kuntzler, Paul, 266, 287, 289, 411, 414, 446

Labor Department, 470, 520, 627
La Cage aux Folles (musical), 524
Ladder, 343
Lady Chatterley's Lover (Lawrence), 126
"Lady Zorro" (stripper), 242
Lafayette Chicken Hut, v, 107, 148, 178, 225–26, 266
Lafayette Square, v, 5, 90, 108, 136–37, 159, 186, 263, 265, 270, 349, 434, 526
Laird, Melvin, 389, 392–93
Lait, Jack, 146–49, 153, 212, 214, 540
Laitin, Joseph, 613, 615
Lambda Rising, v, 420–21, 442, 461–62, 524, 564
Lamphere, Robert, 151–52
Landon, Alf, 359
Lane, Kenneth Jay, 525, 579
Langer, Dr. Walter C., 52
Lash, Trude, 38
Las Vegas Sun, 198
Lauderdale, Gerald, 226–27
Laughton, Charles, 275
Lavender Scare, 123–45, 175, 180, 184–85, 230–31, 444, 472
Lawford, Peter, 275–76
Laxalt, Paul, 522
League of Nations, 21, 31
Leahy, William, 31
Leamer, Laurence, 427
Lee, Robert, 86
Le Gallienne, Gwen, 19

Legal Services Corporation, 471, 485, 539
Legion of Decency, 412
LeHand, Marguerite "Missy," 24–25, 31, 41, 87
LeMay, Curtis, 329
Lend-Lease program, 22, 46
L'Enfant, Pierre, 3
Lenin, Vladimir, 18
Lennon, John, 424–25
Lerner, Max, 131–33, 145, 207, 231, 628–29
Levison, Stanley, 288
Lewinsky, Monica, 491
Lewis, Anthony, 300
Lewis, Fulton, III, 322
liberals, 139, 157, 185, 200, 206, 375, 485, 502
libertarians, 377
Liberty, 32
Liberty Lobby, 536
Library of Congress, 131
Liddy, G. Gordon, 436
Liebling, A. J., 101
Liebman, Marvin, 364–65, 375–76, 605
Life, 22, 96, 185, 253, 286, 292, 314, 326
Lilly, Dr. Frank, xx, 617–19
Lincoln, Abraham, 3, 199, 205, 289
Lindbergh, Charles, 46
Lindsay, John, 360
Lippmann, Walter, 410
Little Rock Central High School, 250
Livingston, Don, 365–66
Livingston, Robert, xx, 491–97, 499–501, 504,
    506, 510–11
Locke, Alain, 649
Lodge, Henry Cabot, Jr., 57, 187
Leopold, Nathan and Loeb, Richard, 292
Log Cabin Republicans, 646
London, U.S. embassy, 35
London School of Economics, 283
Long, Breckinridge, 28, 41, 92
Longhorn Breeders Association, 570
Longworth, Alice Roosevelt, 83, 259, 428–29
Look, 217
Looking Out for #1 (Ringer), 426
Look Younger, Live Longer (Hauser), 147
Lord Won't Mind, The (Merrick), 66
Los Alamos National Laboratory, 121
Los Angeles, 7
Los Angeles Herald-Examiner, 359–60
Los Angeles Police Department (LAPD), 354
Los Angeles Times, 282, 356, 451, 515, 577, 591
Lost and Found bar, v, 443–46
Lott, Trent, 485
Louis, Joe, 85
Lovestone, Jay, 140
Lowenstein, Allard K., 502–4
Lucas, Scott, 137

Ludwig Viktor, Archduke of Austria-Hungary,
    60
Luftwaffe, 67, 69
Lugar, Richard, 494
Lyons, Leonard, 45, 48

Mabley, Moms, 85
MacArthur, Douglas, 528
Maccubbin, Deacon, 420–21, 435, 442, 461–62,
    564, 572, 615
Macdonald, Dwight, 373
Maclean, Donald Duart, 149–54, 240
MacLeish, Archibald, 384
MacPherson, Myra, 423
Macy, John, 264, 334, 346–47
Madison, James, 77
Madonna, 528
Madre, Odessa, xvii, 84–86
Madsen, Lee Eugene, 537–38
Mafia, 36, 385, 506
Magnus, Bishop Albertus, 138
Mailer, Norman, 124, 246
Makepeace, Tom, 255–57, 260
Malloy, John J., 188
Malone, George, 118
Mangan, Richard, 607
Manhattan Project, 149, 190
Mankiewicz, Frank, 437, 523
Manlove, Carole, 639
Mann, Thomas, 531
Männerbünd, 50
Manson family, 449
Manthos, Frank, 109
MANual Enterprises v. Day, 271
MANual magazine, 237
Man Who Came to Dinner, The (Kaufman and
    Hart), 66
Man with the Golden Arm, The (film), 274
Mao Zedong, 24, 120
Marcantonio, Vito, 204
Marchetti, Victor, 536–37, 540, 551–52
March on Washington for Jobs and Freedom
    (1963), xix, 282, 285–87, 620
March on Washington for Lesbian, Gay, and Bi
    Equal Rights, and Liberation (1993), 645
Marcuse, Herbert, 65
Marshall, George C., 124, 169, 171, 192, 229, 599
Marshall Plan, 168, 317
Martin, Dean, 519
Martin, William, xviii, 239–42, 405, 537
Martindale, Steve, xix, 424–31, 433, 522, 530,
    647
Martz, Steven, 544
Marxism, 65, 156
Maryland, 211

Mary Washington College, 235–36
Massie, Robert K., 579
Master and Margarita, The (Bulgakov), 21
Mata Hari, 62
Mathias, Charles, 483
Matlovich, Leonard, 451–52, 568, 648–49
Mattachine Society of Florida, 347
Mattachine Society of Washington (MSW), xviii,
    xix, 156, 227, 263–69, 286–89, 316, 326,
    330, 343–47, 351, 388–89, 411–12, 414–15,
    478, 572–73, 653
Matter of Fact (Alsop column), xviii, 218–19
Matthews, Burnita, 231
Mayer, Louis, 362–63
Mayes, Wendell, 274
Mayflower Hotel, 83
Mayo Clinic, 619
McCain, John, 559
McCarran, Pat, 122–23, 173
McCarran-Walter Act (1952), 157
McCarthy, Joe, xviii, 119, 121–23, 125, 128, 131,
    135–39, 144, 157, 169–76, 179, 185–92,
    194–204, 206–8, 214, 219–20, 229, 234, 261,
    322, 358, 419, 588
McCartney, Paul, 384
McClellan, John, 201, 204
McClendon, Sarah, 325
McCloskey, Paul N. "Pete," xx, 437, 496–507,
    509, 511–17
McCormick, Robert "Colonel," 55, 187
McCrea, John L., 40
McDonald, Larry, 485
McDowall, Roddy, 384
McElroy, Neil, 224
McGovern, George, 404, 437, 498, 558
McGranery, James, 191
McGrath, J. Howard, 127–28
McGrory, Mary, 437
McKinney, Lucie, 608
McKinney, Stewart B., xx, 566, 607–9
McLellan, Diana, 443–44, 445, 446
McLemore, Leslie, 484
McLeod, R. W. Scott, 171–73, 180–84, 279
McNamara, Robert, 259, 315, 329–30, 335, 408
Meese, Edwin, xx, 514–15, 523–24, 549, 560, 567
Meese, Ursula, 524, 549
Meet the Press (TV show), 195
Meir, Golda, 425
Mercer, Lucy, 37
Merchant of Venice, The (Shakespeare), 267
Merlo, Frank, 220
Merman, Ethel, 519
Merrick, Gordon, 66
Merritt, Robert, xix, 418–20, 544
Mesta, Perle, 189–90, 217, 425, 430–31

Metcalf, Erma, 387
Metropolitan Club, 14
Metropolitan Police Department (MPD), 5,
    85–86, 133, 180, 187–88, 319, 342, 350–51,
    418, 538, 544, 551; Intelligence division,
    418; Morals (vice) division, xviii, 5–6,
    86, 90, 107–8, 126, 237–38, 265–66, 268,
    313–14, 316
Meyer, Cord, 139–40, 255
Meyer, Eugene, 213
Meyer, Mary Pinchot, 254–55, 302
MI5 (British domestic intelligence), 68, 153
MI6 (British foreign intelligence), 67, 150, 153
Mickey's restaurant, 148
Milk, Harvey, 376–77, 450–52, 472–73
Miller, Arthur L., 130, 138
Miller, Brian, 416
Miller, Merle, 140
Miller, Richard, 605
Miller, William, 323
Millet, Francis, 4, 152
Milwaukee County Young Republicans, 198
Milwaukee Journal Sentinel, 197
Mind of Adolph Hitler, The (Langer), 52
Mishima, Yukio, 588
Mississippi Democratic Party, 320, 336
Mississippi voter registration drive, 503
Mitchell, Bernon, 239–42, 537
Mitchell, John, 382–84, 386, 388, 391, 437, 529,
    625, 630
Mitchell, Samuel, 16
Mitchell, Harry, 131
"Mitzie, Miss," 44
Mixner, David, xxi, 365–67, 572, 581, 644, 652
Mondale, Walter, 478
Monroe, Marilyn, 247
Montenegro, William Arthur. *See* Wieland,
    William E.
Montgomery, John C., xviii, 163–67
Moon, Sun Myung, 584
Moon Is Blue, The (film), 274
Moore, Dick, 404
Moore, Douglas, 462–63
Moore, Harold, 483–84
Moore, Robert Walton "Judge," 31–32, 39, 88
Moore, Sara Jane, 450–51
Moorhead, William, 512
Moral Majority, 466, 480, 561
Morbidity and Mortality Weekly Report, 541
Morgan, Ted, 92
Morgan, Tom, 348–49
Morley, Raymond, 79
Mormons, 393
Morocco, 71
Morris, Edmund, 577–78

Morris, Gouverneur, 31

Mortimer, Lee, 146–49, 153, 212, 214, 540

Moscow: British embassy, 152; show trials, 97, 168; U.S. embassy, 21–24, 168–71, 175, 222

Mosley, Leonard, 167

Motion Picture Association of America (MPAA) Code, 274–76

Motion Picture Producers and Distributers of America, 1

Mounger, Billy, 481, 484

Moyers, Bill, xix, 318, 321, 330, 336–37, 339–40, 347, 408

Moynihan, Daniel Patrick, 7, 138

Mr. Henry's restaurant, 389, 607

Mr. Smith Goes to Washington (film), 277

Mrs. Warren's Profession (Shaw), 254

Mudd, Roger, 484–85

Mundt, Karl, 201

Munich, U.S. consul, 175

Murphy, Mike, 559

Murphy, Robert, 28

Murray, Don, 362

Murray, Dr. Henry, 52, 113

Muskie, Edmund, 436–37

"My Day" (Eleanor Roosevelt), 38

Myra Breckinridge (Vidal), 371–72, 377

My Turn (Reagan), 578

NAACP v. Alabama, 269

Naipaul, V. S., 577

NAMES Project, 621

Napoleon Bonaparte, 79, 377

National Aeronautics and Space Council (NASC), 305, 309, 337

National Association for the Advancement of Colored People (NAACP), 269, 284–85

National Committee for a Free Europe, 135

National Conservative Political Action Committee (NCPAC), xx, 557–63, 565, 570, 583–84, 596–97

National Endowment for the Preservation of Liberty (NEPL), xx, 594, 597–600, 603–5

National Enquirer, 364

National Football League (NFL), 442, 581

National Gay Task Force, xx, 460–61, 520

National Governors Association Conference, 356

National Guards, 420

National Institute of Allergy and Infections Diseases, 585

National Institutes of Health (NIH), 475, 574, 585

"National Interest," Operation, 135

National Labor Relations Board (NLRB), 35

National March on Washington for Lesbian, and Gay Rights: (1979), 473, 486, 538; (1987), 619

National Press Club, 151

National Public Radio, 645

National Review, 223, 369, 371, 373, 375, 377, 465–66, 558

National Security Agency (NSA), xviii, xx, 239–42, 476–80, 537, 549

National Security Council (NSC), xxi, 31, 127, 153, 177–78, 241–42, 391, 398, 573, 592, 594, 598, 600; NSC 68, 127

National Socialist German Workers' (Nazi) Party, 50, 97, 242. See also Germany, Nazi

National Student Association, 139, 493, 502

National Theatre, 412

National Youth Conference, 399

National Zoo, 179

Navy Department, 18, 37, 180, 217

Nazimova, Alla, 362

Nazi Party (Britain), 67

Nazi SA (Sturmabteilung), 50–51, 69

Nazi SS (Schutzstaffel), 61, 69, 136

NBC News, 291, 377, 538–40, 547

Negro and the Homophile Movement, The (flyer), 287

Nero, Emperor of Rome, 400

Nessen, Ron, 453, 554

Neumann, Robert, 630

Neutrality Act (1794), 603

"Newark, Miss," 44

New Deal, 14, 17, 47, 55, 79, 100, 127, 147

New Frontier, 264, 375

New Look policy, 349

Newman, Paul, 414

New Masses, 97

"Newport, Miss," 44

New Republic, 55, 192, 235, 414, 571, 634, 638

New Right, 493, 557, 560, 562–63, 584, 610, 615

Newsweek, xix, 291, 315, 317, 319, 322, 324–25, 356–57

Newton, Huey, 416

New York City, 7, 108, 385–86

New York Daily Mirror, 146

New York Daily News, 53, 125, 525, 615–16

New Yorker, 25, 101, 127, 157, 183, 218

New York Gay Pride celebration, 442

New York Herald Tribune, 56, 218

New York Native, 579

New York Police Department (NYPD), 385, 635

New York Post, xvii, 45–48, 50, 53–57, 66, 131, 562, 616, 638–39

New York School of Design, 340

New York State Legislature, 1

New York State Liquor Authority, 385

New York State "padlock bill" (1927), 1
New York State Supreme Court, 190
New York Times, 14, 32, 37, 56, 66, 84, 89, 91, 105–6, 134, 147, 158, 177–78, 184, 213, 232, 235, 240, 247, 249, 253, 290, 293, 300, 322, 345–46, 360, 390, 407, 435, 453, 478, 524, 530, 539, 550, 555–56, 572, 579, 591, 616, 639; *Magazine*, 126, 185–86
New York World's Fair (1939), 621
Ngo Dinh Diem, 320
Nicaraguan Contras, 594–601, 603–4
Nicaraguan Sandinistas, 592, 594, 599–600, 602
Nicholas and Alexandra (Massie), 579
Nichols, John, Jr. "Jack," xix, 265–66, 286, 330, 345–46, 349
Nichols, John, Sr., xix, 330–31
Nichols, Lou, 159
Nicomedes IV, King of Bithynia, 155
Niebuhr, Reinhold, 139
Nightline (TV show), 547, 634
Night of the Long Knives, 51
"Nikolaievich, Boris," 221, 258
Nineteen Eighty-Four (Orwell), 133
Nixon, Pat, 399
Nixon, Richard, xix, 98–100, 116, 118, 121, 139, 157–58, 173, 197, 199, 232–33, 319, 323, 338, 378, 381–408, 413, 422–24, 427, 433–38, 453, 463, 465, 482, 496, 498, 502, 509, 517, 529–30, 557–58, 591, 609, 626, 652
Nixonland (Perlstein), 396
Nob Hill bar, 447
Nofziger, Franklyn "Lyn," xxi, 354–62, 365, 512
non-Communist left (NCL), 139–40
Noonan, Peggy, 586
Normal Heart, The (Kramer), 616
Norris, Ernest E., 31–32
North, Oliver ("Mr. Green"), xxi, 592–600, 603–4, 606, 609
North Africa, 71, 75
North Atlantic Treaty Organization (NATO), 169, 399
North Carolina law against "abomination" (1837), 1
North Korea, 149, 479
North Vietnam, 140, 346
Northwestern University, 376
"Notes on Camp" (Sontag), 364
Notre Dame Cathedral, 26
Novak, Robert, 338, 359, 495, 512
Noyes, Newbold, Jr., 318
nuclear weapons, 120–21, 149, 153, 338, 349, 494, 540
Nureyev, Rudolf, 397
Nye, Gerald, 55

Oates, Bill, 466, 467
Obama, Barack, 646
obscenity laws, 126, 236–38, 269–71
O'Connor, Cardinal John, 618
O'Donnell, John, 125
Office of Naval Intelligence, 67, 129, 131, 135, 180
Office of Personnel Management (OPM; *formerly* Civil Service Commission), 629, 644
Office of Policy Coordination (OPC), 134–35
Office of Pubic Liaison, 614
Office of Strategic Services (OSS), *v*, xvii, 60–61, 64–71, 74–75, 113, 135–37, 139, 160, 210; Mapping division, 65; Research and Analysis Branch, 65
Office of the Coordinator of Information (COI), 60, 62–64, 67, 69, 72; Foreign Nationalities Branch, 63
Offie, Carmel, xvii, 23–28, 31, 80–81, 87, 90–92, 134–41, 170, 214, 254, 315, 530
O'Leary, Jean, xx, 459–61, 463–64
Olson, Dale, 573
Olson, Eric, 600, 603
Olympia Press, 385
O'Mahoney, Joe, 187
Onassis, Jacqueline, 503. *See also* Kennedy, Jacqueline Bouvier
O'Neill, Tip, 471, 484, 566
ONE magazine, 156, 227, 229, 237, 250, 374
Ono, Yoko, 424–25
On the Origin of Species (Darwin), 235
On the Right (Buckley column), 482
OPEC, 529
Open Gay Bars Committee, 446
Open Marriage (O'Neill), 426
Operation Homex, 351
Opp, Jeffrey, 543, 545–46, 551, 565
Organization of American States, 647
Orwell, George, 133
Oscar Wilde Memorial Bookshop, 421
O'Shea, Pat, 85
Oshinsky, David, 186
Osipov, Yuriy Igorevich, 551
Oswald, Lee Harvey, 289–92, 309
Otepka, Otto, 279, 280–81
Other Voices, Other Rooms (Capote), 106
Oxford University, 63, 185

Paar, Jack, 370
Packer, George, 425
Packwood, Bob, 423
Paco (valet), 72–74
Painter, Thomas, 63
Pakistan, 390

Palmer, A. Mitchell, 37
Panama Canal, 494, 508
Panama Canal Treaty, 597
Paperclip, Operation, 135
Paragraph 175, 61
Parents and Friends of Lesbians and Gays, 643
Paris, U.S. embassy in, 24–26, 28, 30–31, 137, 169, 171, 193
Paris Match, 293
Paris Peace Conference (1918–19), 18
Partisan Review, 364
Parvin, Landon, 613–14
Patten, William, Jr., 258
Patten, William, Sr. "Bill," 258
Patterson, Eleanor Josephine Medill "Cissy," xvii, 17, 41, 81, 87–88, 187
Peace Corps, 248, 289, 336
Pearl Harbor attacks, 46, 228, 352
Pearson, Drew 17, 33, 40, 88, 91, 172, 188, 193, 195–97, 207–8, 213, 252, 325–26, 357–60, 368, 382–83, 388, 394, 494
Pearson, Luvie Moore, 197
Pegler, Westbrook, 124–25, 138–39, 195, 214
Pell, Claiborne, 385
Pelosi, Nancy, 620, 645
Pennington, Bruce, 418
Pentagon Papers, 8, 390–91, 425, 435–36, 591
Penthouse, 537
People, 576
Percy, Charles, 424
Perkins, Frances, 143–44
Perlstein, Rick, 396
Persons, Jerry, 173, 224
"Perversion Among Government Workers" (seminar), 144
Petrelis, Michael, 639
Pettine, Ronald, 455–56
Peurifoy, John, 122–23, 125–26, 157, 214
Pforzheimer, Walter, 135, 142
Phelan, James, 292
Philadelphia, 91
Philadelphia College of Physicians, 591
Philadelphia *Public Ledger*, 18, 47
Philby, Kim, 150
Philippines, 45
Philippine War Damage Commission, 131
Phillips, Howard, 557
Phillips, Wendal Lee, 307–8
Phillips Exeter Academy, 249
Physique Pictorial, 348
Pickle, James Jarrell "Jake," xix, 309–10, 333, 337
Pidgeon, Walter, 275
Pierce, Edward R., 22, 27
Pier Nine bar, 445, 446
Pius XII, Pope, 26, 199

Playboy, 238, 404, 428
Plaza Hotel, 68
Plimpton, George, 261
Plus One bar, 386, 389, 445–46
PM, 66
Pocahontas, 18
Poe, Edgar Allan, 408
poll taxes, 281
"Pond, the" (intelligence network), 136
Poppe, Nikolai, 135
Porcellian Club, 172, 178
pornography, 237, 270, 426
Porter, Cole, 249, 370
Portes, Comtesse de, 25
Portland Press Herald, 195
Post, Marjorie Merriweather, 217, 425, 431
Potomac Marching Society, 300
Potter, Charles, 195
Potter, Claire Bond, 36
Potter, Trevor, 640
Powell, Adam Clayton, Jr., 283–84, 286
Power House, *v*, 521–22
Powers, Richard Gid, 36
Prague, U.S. embassy, 168
Preminger, Otto, 200, 273–77, 362, 486
President's Advisory Council on the Arts, 261
President's Commission on the Assassination of President Kennedy (Warren Commission), 289
President's Commission on the Human Immunodeficiency Virus Epidemic (AIDS commission), xx, 615–19
President's Park, 4
Prettyman, E. Barrett, 270
Price, Martin, xxi, 536–37, 540, 544, 551–52
Price, Raymond, xix, 405–8, 437–38, 465
Princeton University, 23, 164, 167
Producers, The (film), 559
Professional Services, 626–29, 632, 636
Progressive Era, 4
Proust, Marcel, 97, 101, 118, 249, 260, 295
Pruden, Wesley, 611, 628, 631–32
P.S. 63 (Queens), 576
Pueblo incident, 479
Pullman porters, 15–17, 32, 39, 79, 87, 155
"Pumpkin Papers," 102, 116, 118
Pusan, South Korea, U.S. embassy, 183
Putlitz, Baron Wolfgang Gans E. H. zu, 67–69

Quaid, Dennis, 428
Queensberry, Ninth Marquess of, 371
Queens College, 228, 377
Queer Nation, 639, 645
Questionnaire on Heterosexuality, 415–16
Quicksilver Times, 415

Quigley, Joan, 517
Quinn, Richard "Sandy," 354–57
Quinn, Sally, 423, 429–31, 508, 590

racial discrimination, 84, 283, 446–47
racial segregation, 84, 148, 282
Radford, Charles, 391–93
Radio Free Europe, 135
Radziwill, Lee, 261, 575
Rand, Ayn, 377
RAND Corporation, 435
Randolph, A. Philip, 285–86
Randolph, William, 334–35
Rapallo, Treaty of (1922), 64
Rarick, John R., 412
Rascals bar, 462
Rather, Dan, 546
Rawls, Robert, 220
Rayburn, Sam, 245, 303–4
Reagan, Maureen, 560
Reagan, Nancy, 353, 356, 359, 362–64, 506,
    516–17, 524–27, 534, 569–79, 613–17, 628,
    633
Reagan, Neil, 361
Reagan, Ronald, xx, xxi, 353–68, 382, 480, 487,
    491–527, 529, 535, 540, 549, 558–60, 563,
    566, 568–69, 571, 573–78, 581, 589–91,
    594–95, 599, 603, 605–6, 612–19, 622, 626,
    628, 633, 652
Reagan, Ron (son), 364–65, 533, 574, 576
Reagans, The (Hannaford), 515–16
Reber, Miles, 196
Reber, Samuel, 196
Rebozo, Bebe, 397, 408
Recollections of a Life (Hiss), 117
Red Army, 27, 130
Red Door bar, 447
Redfield, Robert, 617
Redl, Alfred, 58–60, 129, 142, 153,
    409
Red Lantern bar, 451
Red Scare, 100, 118, 123, 180, 185, 231
Reed, John, 19, 21
Reedy, George, 316, 319, 321, 323
Regency Baths, 390, 412
Reichstag, burning of, 51
Reik, Theodor, 155
Remembering Denny (Trillin), 185
Remembrance of Things Past (Proust), 97,
    260
Rendezvous bar, 267
Reno, Janet, 645
Reporter (Cheshire), 433
Republican National Committee, 319–20, 499,
    568, 628, 633–34, 640, 644

Republican National Convention: (1952), 157;
    (1968), 370; (1972), 404; (1976), 495,
    498–99; (1980), 506–12; (1984), 570–71
Republican Party, 47, 55, 98, 113, 120–22, 126,
    130, 139, 158, 166, 169–70, 175, 186–87,
    191, 195, 203, 205–6, 252, 257, 318, 323,
    325, 331, 339, 350, 360, 363, 365, 437,
    470–71, 481–86, 495–99, 505–14, 557, 568,
    583, 600–601, 606, 633–34, 645–46
Republican Ripon Society, 359
Republican Wednesday Group, 495–96
Republic Gardens, 83
Reston, James "Scotty," 84, 213, 247
Reynaud, Paul, 25
Reynolds, Larry, 520–21
Rhodes, John Jacob, 498–99, 508
Ribbentrop, Joachim von, 69
Ribicoff, Abraham, 372, 472
Rich, Frank, 445, 533
Riggs National Bank, 350
Riggs Turkish baths, 5, 220
Righter, Carroll, 525
Ripon Forum, 359
Risky Business (film), 533
Rive Gauche restaurant, 256
Robb, Inez, 364
Robert E. Lee (river boat), 148
Roberts, Juanita, 309
Robinson, Joseph T., 214
Rochester City Council, 459–460
Rockefeller, Nelson, 92, 159, 215–16, 424–25
Rodriguez, Paul M., 626–28
Rodriguez, Richard, 439
Roe v. Wade, 465
Rogers, William, 224, 241, 405
Röhm, Ernst, 50–52, 113, 199
Romanov, Alexei, 579
Rome, ancient, 8, 133, 181, 400–401
Rome, U.S. embassy, 22
Romulus (Vidal), 371
Rooney, Mickey, 384
Roosevelt, Eleanor, 13, 37–38, 77, 89, 97, 124–25,
    219–20, 316, 590
Roosevelt, Elliott, 37, 41
Roosevelt, Franklin D., 11, 13–18, 20–21, 24–25,
    28, 30–32, 37–41, 45–49, 52, 54–55, 60, 65,
    71, 75, 77–81, 86–92, 96, 143, 165, 168, 199,
    214, 219, 232–33, 386, 398
Roosevelt, Teddy, 83, 189, 563
Roosevelt family, 214, 252
Rosen, Hilary, 644
Rosenberg, Ethel, 190–91, 207
Rosenberg, Julius, 190–91, 207
Ross, Brian, 538
Rovere, Richard, 127, 172, 186

Rowan, Carl T., 427
RPQs, 533
RSK Associates, 543
Ruby, Jack, 292
Ruge, Dr. Daniel, 555
Rumsey, Mary Harriman, 143
Rumsfeld, Donald, 399
Rusher, William A., 377
Rush to Judgment (Lane), 290
Rusk, Dean, 347
Russell, Richard, 303–4
Russia: post-Soviet archives, 58–59; pre-Soviet, 18, 59; Revolution, 18–19. *See also* Soviet Union
Russo, Vito, 276–77
Rustin, Bayard, xix, 282–88, 620
Ryan, Robert J., 124

Safire, William, 382, 406–8, 453, 530
Sagarin, Edward (Donald Webster Cory), 123–24, 230, 265
Saigon, U.S. embassy, 182
Salk, Jonas, 614
SALT II, 494
Salvadoran death squads, 494
same-sex marriage, 638–39
Sand Bar, 148
San Francisco Chronicle, 451, 588
San Francisco Conference (1945), 92, 96
San Francisco Examiner, 356
Sanitation Department, 86
Sans Souci, 425
Sardi's, 45
Sartorius, Herman, 68
Satter, David, 410
Saturday Evening Post, 219, 292
Saturday Night Live (TV show), 533
Saudi Arabia, 529
Save Our Children, 464, 486
Sawyer, Hal, 497
Scarberry, Warren, 268
Scarlet Thread, The (Downes), 75
Scattergood, Margaret, xviii, 210–12, 602–3
Schauer, David, 544
Schiff, Dorothy, xvii, 47–48, 55–56, 215
Schine, G. David, xviii, 191–96, 200–207
Schine, J. Myer, 192
Schlafly, Phyllis, 465, 531, 637
Schlesinger, Arthur, Jr., 70, 114, 118–19, 193, 261, 336, 409, 625
Schneider, Frederick "Willy," 68–69
Schorr, Daniel, 438
Schwarzenegger, Arnold, 559
Sciences Po (Paris), 22
Scott, Hugh, 498

Scott, Peter, 366–67
Seals, William, Jr., 510
Seaton, Fred A., 217
Sebastian, Saint, 587–88
Secret Service, 129, 180, 301, 309, 450–51, 626, 628, 632–33
Segretti, Donald, 436–37
Seib, Charles B., 316, 469
Seigenthaler, John, 280
Selective Service, 166
Selective Service Act, 46, 62
Seper, Jerry, 591, 629, 635
September 11, 2001 attacks, 75
Sequoia, USS (presidential yacht), 348–49, 384
Sevareid, Eric, 529–30
Seven Years' War, 3
sex-change operations, 158
sex deviate, as term, 108
"Sex Deviates" program, 153, 241
sexspionage, 61–62
Sexual Behavior in the Human Male (Kinsey), 105–6
Sexual Criminal, The (de River), 109
Seymour, Susan, 65
Shade of Difference, A (Drury), 277
Shafer, Jack, 629
Shalala, Donna, 645
Shales, Tom, 535
Sharon Statement, 375–76
Shaw, Clay, 291–93
Shaw, George Bernard, 254
Sheep on the Runway (Buchwald), 408–9
Sherry, Michael, 140
Shields, Jimmy, 363
Shilts, Randy, 377, 556, 573, 588
Shipstead, Henrik, 16–17
Shoemaker, Jamie, xx, 476–80, 549, 551
Shoffler, Carl, 418, 544
Shoreham Hotel, 300
Short, Bobby, 525
Showboat, 83
Shriver, Eunice Kennedy, 247, 616–17
Shriver, Sargent, 289
Shrum, Bob, 404
Shultz, George, 576
Shurlock, Geoffrey, 274–75
Sicre, Ricardo "Rick Sickler," 72–74
Siegel, Bugsy, 198
Simon, William, 494
Simoneau, Michael, 456
Simons, Howard, 468
Simpson, Christopher, 136
Sinatra, Frank, 86, 276, 519
Singlaub, John, 596–98, 604
Sipple, Ethyl, 452–54

Sipple, Oliver "Billy," xx, 449–54
Six Crises (Nixon), 436
"Six Sectors for Attack" (Gerassi), 74
Skull and Bones, 405, 579–80
Slater, Don, 374
Smith, Howard K., 372
Smith, Jerry, 581
Smith, Jesse "Jess," 4–5
Smith, Liz, 615–16
Smith, Margaret Chase, 141, 186
Smith, Merriman, 292
Smith, Sally Bedell, 289
Smith, Sammie, 551
Smith, Walter Bedell, 151, 160
Smith College, 362
Smithsonian Institution, 179, 432
Snowden, Edward, 239–40
Sobran, Joseph, 617
Social Democrats (Germany), 97
socialism, 53, 139
Social Security, 211
Socrates, 401
Sodom and Gomorrah, 1
Sodom and Gomorrah (Proust), xi, 295
sodomy laws, repeal of, 426
Sokolsky, George, 214, 241, 278–79
Soldier of Fortune magazine, 596
Sontag, Susan, 364
Sourwine, J. G., 280
Southeast Asia, 140
Southern Baptist Convention, 571
Southern Christian Leadership Conference (SCLC), 283–84
Southern District of New York, 190
Southern Railway, 32
South Korea, 149, 183, 597, 630
South Vietnam, 320
Soviet Communist Party, 168
Soviet embassy, 551
Soviet Foreign Ministry, 63–64, 239
Soviet intelligence, 97, 143, 547–48, 551. *See also* KGB
Soviet Politburo, 338
Sovietskaya Hotel, 220
Soviet Union, xvii–xviii, 14, 21–22, 51, 55, 63, 79, 95, 117, 120–21, 127, 130, 138–39, 149–54, 168–69, 218, 220–24, 228–29, 242, 257–58, 278, 290, 408–10, 423, 514, 540, 587. *See also* Russia
Spain, xvii, 70–71, 75; Civil War, 65
Spanish embassy, 70, 74, 75
Speakes, Larry, 553–56, 575
Speed, Joshua, 3
Spellman, Francis Cardinal, 321

Spence, Craig J., xxi, 527–32, 585, 605, 625–26, 629–37
Spender, Stephen, 151
Spingarn, Stephen, 7, 129–30
Spotlight, 536–37
Sputnik 1 (satellite), 228, 232, 236
Stables, 545
St. Albans, 249
Stalin, Joseph, 21, 97–98, 124, 142–43, 152, 168
Stanford University, 503–4
Stans, Maurice, 382
Stapleton, Maureen, 425
State Department, v, xviii, 14–18, 22–23, 27–28, 31–32, 40, 66, 75, 78–79, 90–92, 96, 100–103, 111, 113, 116, 121–31, 135–36, 147, 149, 151, 153, 156–57, 164–74, 179–86, 192, 196–97, 204, 214, 224, 278–81, 309, 340, 347, 376, 396, 398–99, 405, 412, 517, 546, 548, 555, 598; Bureau of Security and Consular Affairs, 171–72, 180–84; Caribbean and Mexican Affairs, 278; Finish desk, xviii, 163; Latin American Affairs, 14, 71, 278; Middle American Affairs, xix; Office of Security, 170–71, 279; Office of Special Political Affairs, 96; OPC and, 135
States' Rights Democratic Party, 281
Steffens, Lincoln, 18, 27
Stegall, Mildred, 324, 326
Stein, Gertrude, 649
Steinem, Gloria, 404
St. Elizabeths Hospital, 108, 270, 272, 390
Stephenson, William, 67, 71
Stern, J. David, 47
Steuben, Baron Friedrich von, 2–3, 5
Stevens, Robert T., 200
Stevens, Stuart, 600
Stevenson, Adlai, 157–58, 193, 213, 245, 250
Stewart, Donald, 392
Stewart, Jimmy, 519
Stewart, Potter, 270
Stimson, Henry L., 65
St. John, Jill, 404
St. John's Episcopal Church, 163–64
St. Louis Post-Dispatch, 177
St. Nicholas Ballroom, 68
Stone, Dr. Harry "Doc," 54
Stone, John, 16
Stone, Roger, 437
Stonewall uprising, 2n, 385–86, 414–15, 426, 473, 653
Stoppard, Tom, 425
St. Paul's, 23, 168
Straight, Michael, 192
"Strange Case of Dr. Dooley, The," 373
Strasser, Otto, 53

Strategy of Terror, The (Taylor), 67
Streisand, Barbra, 575
Stripling, Robert, 98
Strub, Sean, 431, 443–45, 500, 548–49, 652
Strumpet Wind, The (Merrick), 66
Stryker, Lloyd Paul, 110, 112
Studds, Gerry, xxi, 564–66, 609, 620
Studio 54, 443
Suharto, 415
Sulgrave Club, 197
Sulla, Roman dictator, 133
Sullivan, Andrew, 638–39
Sullivan, William, 383
Sullivan and Cromwell, 60–61
Sulzberger, C. L., 134
Summer, Donna, 443
Sumner, Charles, 13
Sunday Dispatch, 150
Swan Lake (ballet), 364
Swearingen, James, 226–27
Sweden, 44
Sweeney, Dennis, 502–4
Switzerland, 60
Sylvester, 443
Symms, Steve, 563
Szluk, Peter, 181

Tafel, Rich, 646
Taft, Robert, 159, 174–76
Taft, William Howard, 4
Taiwan, 149
Talbot (ship), 1
Tames, George, 184
Tammany Hall, 47
"Tandaradei" (Chambers), 112
Tanenhaus, Sam, 377
Taubman, Howard, 235
Taylor, Elizabeth, 575, 613–15
Taylor, Jeanne, 65–66
Teamsters, 428, 431, 522
Teapot Dome scandal, 4
Teboe, Louis J., 225–27, 269, 456
Ten Days that Shook the World (Reed), 19
Texas State Society, 306
Thackrey, Ted, 55
Thatcher, Margaret, 535, 619
Thayer, Charles, 170–71, 175
The Wise Men (Isaacson and Thomas), 168
Theoharis, Athan, 36
Thomas, Evan, 168, 261
Thomas, Helen, 427
Thomas, J. Parnell, 98
Thomas, Luther, 32
Thomas Woodrow Wilson (Bullitt and Freud), 20
Thompson, W. Scott, 523, 526, 585, 625

Thomson, Virgil, 44
Thornberry, Homer, xix, 297, 299–300, 307, 309–10, 331
Thorne, Florence, xviii, 210–12, 602–3
Thurmond, Strom, 281–82, 284–85, 288, 616
Time, xviii, 42, 45, 54–55, 96, 101, 180, 191–92, 253, 375, 451, 639
Time for Decision, The (Welles), 213
Titanic (ship), 4
Tobias, Andrew, 396–97
Toklas, Alice B., 649
Tolson, Clyde, xvii, 35–37, 75, 150, 261, 648
Toole, John Kennedy, 379
Top Gun (film), 533
Tower John, 485
Townsend, Mathilde, 14
Tragedy of Woodrow Wilson, The (Bullitt), 19
Transportation Department, 569
Treasury Department, 5, 193, 241
Tree, Marietta Peabody, 259, 284
Trillin, Calvin, 185
Trilling, Lionel, 369
Trimble, Jimmie, 250
TRIM magazine, 237
Trotta, Liz, 527–28, 531, 630–31
Truman, Harry, xviii, 7, 92–93, 97, 121, 124, 127, 131, 137, 157, 165–66, 179, 219, 240, 281, 317, 349, 387, 599, 632
Truman, Margaret, xviii, 165, 167
Truman Doctrine, 317
Truth About Gays Political Action Committee (TAG-PAC), 552
Tuchman, Barbara, 31
Tucker, Nancy, xix, 388–89, 417, 572–73
Tuttle, Holmes, 356, 578
Tydings, Millard, 131, 135, 187
Tylenol scare, 556
Tyler, Patrick, 507, 512

U-2 spy plane, 278
Udall, Morris, 455–56
Udall, Stewart, 210
Ukraine, 97
Ullman, Robert, 66–68
Ulrich, Otto, 238, 272, 347
Ulysses (Joyce), 27, 57
Union Army, 62
Union of World Federalists, 139
United Nations, 92, 96; Charter, 96; General Assembly, 352
United Press International (UPI), 51, 292, 320, 346, 427
U.S.A. Confidential (Lait and Mortimer), 147
U.S. Army, 131, 281, 192–200; Map Service, 228, 441. *See also* Army-McCarthy Hearings

U.S. Commission of Fine Arts, xix, 4
U.S. Congress, 4, 7, 15, 108, 119, 132, 143, 145,
  151, 158, 166–68, 185, 210, 239, 252, 265,
  279, 298, 303, 344, 381, 411, 472, 481–86,
  502–4, 512–14, 539–40, 546–50, 565–66,
  595–97, 647
U.S. Constitution, 232, 266, 465
U.S. District Court for the District of Columbia,
  231
U.S. House of Representatives, 130, 138, 166,
  245, 274, 303, 315, 321, 344, 350, 412, 443,
  470, 491–92, 494, 540–42, 546, 565–66, 607,
  634, 645; Clerk's Office, 543; Committee
  on Standards of Official Conduct (Ethics),
  547, 550–51, 636; Doorkeeper's Office, 543;
  Postmaster, 552
U.S. Information Agency, 182, 478
U.S. Institute of Peace, 523
U.S. Marine Corps, 451, 454, 512–14, 530
U.S. Marshals, 238
U.S. Navy, 37, 140, 159
U.S. Park Police, 108, 455
U.S. Senate, 19, 21, 37, 45–47, 49, 53–57, 129,
  135, 137, 141, 174–75, 186–87, 245, 274,
  282, 284, 297, 303, 321, 344, 350, 517,
  606; Appropriations Committee, 124, 171;
  Appropriations subcommittee, 120, 122;
  Armed Services Committee, 352; District of
  Columbia Committee, 187; Expenditures in
  the Executive Departments Investigations
  Subcommittee, 129, 131; Foreign Relations
  Committee, 172; Government Operations
  Committee, 179; Internal Security
  Subcommittee, 278, 280–81, 340; Naval
  Affairs Committee, 46, 49, 55; Permanent
  Subcommittee on Investigations, xviii, 189–
  209; Select Committee on Intelligence, 479;
  Special (Kefauver) Committee to Investigate
  Organized Crime in Interstate Commerce,
  86. See also Army-McCarthy Hearings
U.S. Supreme Court, 46, 82, 88, 96, 126, 237,
  239, 256, 264–65, 269, 271, 287, 317, 344,
  349, 465, 557, 646
U.S. Travel Service, 248
University of California: Berkeley, 66; Los
  Angeles, 382
University of Kansas School of Medicine,
  125
University of Miami, 215
University of Michigan, 287
University of Southern California, 402, 436
University of Texas, 305, 520
University of Washington, 493
University of Wisconsin, Conservative Club, 375
Unruh, Jesse, 354, 495

Valenti, Jack, 315, 319, 337, 522
Van Court, Art, 354, 357
Vandenberg, Arthur, Jr., xviii, 158–60, 178,
  215–17, 315, 324, 398
Vandenberg, Arthur, Sr., 82, 158–60
Vandenberg, Hazel, 82
Van Doren, Mark, 97, 101
Vanity Fair, 572, 644
Variety, 274–75, 569
Vatican Council, Second, 370
venereal disease, 556
"Venona" decrypts, 117
Verdi, Giuseppe, Un ballo in maschera, 29
Versailles, Treaty of (1919), 8, 19, 20, 64
VerStandig, Helen, 427
Vidal, Gore, xix, 46, 106, 243, 249–54, 258,
  260–61, 313–15, 369–72, 377–78, 384, 397
Vidal, Gore, Sr., 46
Vienna, 58–60
Vietnam War, 370, 390–91, 410, 427, 435, 452,
  496, 528, 532, 539
Viguerie, Richard, 557
Village Voice, 503–4
Vincenz, Lilli, xix, 266–67, 346, 388–89
Virginia Highway Department, 210
Vital Center, The (Schlesinger), 118
Voice of America, 151, 186, 192

Waldeck, Countess R. G., 154–55
Waldron, Robert, xix, 297–312, 329–41, 348,
  398, 647–48, 651
walkers, 5, 80, 166–67, 254–55, 302, 524, 579
Wallace, George, 287
Wallace, Henry, 15, 124, 156
Wall Street Journal, 322, 410, 556, 572, 574
Walsh, David Ignatius, xvii, 45–49, 53–57,
  63–64, 81, 89, 132, 187, 562, 639, 651
Walsh, Joseph C., 182
Walter, Francis, 241–42
Walter Reed Army Institute of Research, 617
Walter Reed Army Medical Center, 267,
  324
Walton, William, xix, 253–55, 260, 289, 302
Wanniski, Jude, 494–95, 512
War Department, 18, 82
Ware, Harold, 96
Ware Group, 96–98
Warhol, Andy, 526
War of Independence, 2–3
Warren, Earl, 164, 289–90
Warren, Robert Penn, 161
Warren, Virginia, 164
Warren Commission Report, 290
Washburne, Elihu, 31
Washington, George, 3, 18

Washington, DC: Board of Education, 462;
City Council, 442, 462; Department of
Human Services, 591; Delegate election of
1971, 411–14; governed by Congress, 108;
Superior Court, 482
Washington Afro-American, 346
Washington Better Business Bureau, 621
Washington Blade (formerly *Gay Blade*), xx, 513,
542, 544, 547, 549–50, 552, 562, 572–73,
589, 622, 646
Washington City Paper, 629
Washington Confidential (Lait and Mortimer),
146–48, 152, 153, 214, 540
Washington Daily News, 66, 318
Washington Evening Star, 113, 151, 226–27, 254,
300, 316, 317, 318, 346, 356, 359, 373, 389,
437, 442–43, 463, 468
Washington Goes to War (Brinkley), 82
Washington Herald, 32
Washingtonian, 482
Washington Merry-Go-Round (Pearson
column), xvii, 17, 357, 387
Washington Monument, *v*, 5
Washington Post, xix, 5, 80, 97, 108–9, 112, 130,
174, 197, 213, 218, 254, 282–83, 313–15,
326, 342–43, 356–57, 401, 406, 408–9, 414,
423, 426, 429, 433–34, 443–44, 455–56,
462–63, 468, 480, 502, 504, 507–12, 516–17,
522, 525, 529, 535, 544, 548, 550, 555, 557,
568, 576, 578, 581, 583–85, 588–90, 592–93,
605, 608–13, 615, 619, 630–31, 647
Washington Redskins, 442, 581
"Washington Sex Story, The" (Lerner), 131–32,
207
Washington Times, 584–86, 591, 611, 626–33,
635–36
Washington Times-Herald, xvii, 17, 41, 187, 205,
254
Washington Weekly, 553
Watergate scandal, 4, 116, 405, 426, 435–38, 460,
496, 508, 539, 544, 591
Watson, Edwin M., 32, 38, 41
Waugh, Evelyn, 489, 534, 587
Webber, Mildred, 614
Wechsler, James, 114
Weimar Republic, 51
Weir, Robin, 525, 526–27, 575
Welander, Robert O., 392
Welch, Joseph, 199–201, 206
Welker, Herman, 186–88, 205, 208
Welles, Benjamin, 41, 280
Welles, Orson, 636
Welles, Sumner, xvii, 13–18, 20, 28–32, 38–42,
46, 71, 77–81, 87–92, 213–15, 258, 279–80,
320, 357, 376, 398, 517, 571, 651

Welles Declaration, 14
Wellington, Madame, 647
Wellman, Walter, 540, 541
Welsh, Edward, 309
West German intelligence, 547
West Germany, 139
West Hollywood City Council, 616
West, Rebecca, 152
Westring, Dana, 647
Weyrich, Paul, 557, 560–61, 585–86, 633
Wheeler, Burton K., 16–17
When the Kissing Had to Stop (Fitzgibbon), 376
Where's the Rest of Me? (Reagan), 362
Wherry, Kenneth, xviii, 125–27, 129, 131, 137,
145, 219–20
Whipple, Evangeline Simpson, 4
White, Edmund, 264–65
White, G. Edward, 117
White, Jean M., 343
White, L. K., 212
White, Nancy, 254
White, Teddy, 245–46, 324
White Horse Inn, 198
White House Communications Office, 523
White House Correspondents' Association
Dinner, 275, 592
White House Special Investigations Unit
(Plumbers), 390–93, 435–37, 509
White House Years (Kissinger), 422
Whitman, Walt, 3, 11, 47, 654
Whitman-Walker Clinic, *v*, 572, 573, 589, 646
Whittier College, 396
"Why Has Washington Gone Crazy?" (Alsop),
219
Wieland, William E., xix, 278–81
Wiggins, J. Russell, 318, 328
Wilde, Oscar, 371, 400, 588, 623, 649
Wiley, Bill, 302
Wiley, John C., 63–64
Wiley, Mary Margaret, 302, 315, 334–35
Wilkins, Roy, 284–85
Williams, Leroy, xxi, 541–51, 565
Williams, Pete, xxi, 639
Williams, Tennessee, 71, 220, 251, 253
Wills, Garry, 424
Wilson, Edith, 20
Wilson, Woodrow, 18–20, 31, 79, 116
Winchell, Walter, 49–50, 55
Windsor, Duchess of, 25, 192
Windsor, Duke of, 192
Winnebago Indian Reservation, 225
Wisner, Frank, 135, 137, 140
Wisner, Graham, 137
Wisner, Polly, 137
Witeck, Bob, 423, 444

Witness (Chambers), 114–15
Wizard of Oz (film), 534
Wolfe, Tom, 426
Womack, Herman Lynn, xix, 235–39, 269–73, 348, 412
Women's Army Corps (WAC), 81, 135, 267
women's liberation, 427, 653
Woods, Rose Mary, 382, 427, 433
Woodward, Bob, 426, 507, 511, 576, 592–93
Woodward, Joanne, 414
Woodward, Robert F., 181–82
Woollcott, Alexander, 218
World Affairs Council, 449
World of Yesterday, The (Zweig), 51
World War I, 18, 31, 50, 53, 59–60, 62, 107, 123, 219
World War II, 6, 17, 31, 41–42, 44, 46, 61–68, 71, 81–82, 91, 107, 125, 129, 136, 158, 180, 219, 228, 372
Wright, Jim, 633–34
Wyman, Jane, 560
Wyoming, 186

Yaffe, Henry, 389
Yale University, 22–23, 63, 66, 121, 139, 174, 180, 185, 249, 360, 404–5, 558, 579, 607
Yalta Conference, 96, 121, 168, 175
Yarr, Michael, 415

YMCA, *v*, 147, 313–14, 316, 318, 322–26, 332, 516
Yom Kippur War, 425
York, Michael, 428
Young, David, 392
Young, Perry Deane, 562–63
Young, Ruth, 131
Young Americans for Freedom (YAF), 375–77, 466, 470, 482–83, 493, 497, 500, 511, 520, 558
Young Communist League, 282
Young Man from the Provinces (Helms), 256
Young Republicans, 415, 520
Young Socialist Alliance, 437
Youth for Goldwater for Vice President, 375
Youth International Party "Yippies," 420

Zeffirelli, Franco, 75
Zeligs, Dr. Meyer A., 116–17
Zeller, Duke, 431
Zephyr Bar and Restaurant, 416
Ziegler, Ron, 435
Zipkin, Jerry, 525–26, 579
Zuschlag, Alan, 526, 532–35
Zweig, Stefan, 51, 58
Zyklon B gas, 135

About the Author

James Kirchick has written about human rights, politics, and culture from around the world. A columnist for *Tablet* magazine, a contributing writer to *Air Mail*, and a nonresident senior fellow at the Atlantic Council, he is the author of *The End of Europe: Dictators, Demagogues, and the Coming Dark Age*. Kirchick's work has appeared in the *New York Times*, the *Washington Post*, the *Wall Street Journal*, the *Atlantic*, the *New York Review of Books*, and the *Times Literary Supplement*, among other publications. Previously, Kirchick served as a visiting fellow at the Center on the United States and Europe at the Brookings Institution, was writer-at-large for Radio Free Europe/Radio Liberty based in Prague, a fellow of the Robert Bosch Foundation in Berlin, and an editor at the *New Republic*. A graduate of Yale with degrees in history and political science, he resides in Washington, DC.